JIMMY SWAGGART
BIBLE
COMMENTARY

JIMMY SWAGGART BIBLE COMMENTARY

Genesis through II Chronicles

Volume One

**WORLD
EVANGELISM
PRESS**

TABLE OF CONTENTS

—■—

INTRODUCTION

—■—

THE BIBLE IS THE ONLY BODY OF REVEALED TRUTH IN THE WORLD TODAY.

I realize that the caption *"The Bible Is The Only Body of Revealed Truth In The World Today"* is a startling statement! Actually, it is so startling that one has to stop and contemplate what is being said.

The Bible is the revealed Word of God. Simon Peter said this about it:

> *"For the prophecy came not in old time by the will of man: but holy men of God spake as they were moved by the Holy Ghost."* (II Pet. 1:21)

The book of Job is probably the oldest book in the Bible, possibly having been authored by Job himself and compiled by Moses who also wrote the Pentateuch (Genesis, Exodus, Leviticus, Numbers, and Deuteronomy). He may have written Genesis while he was on the *"backside of the desert"* and before leading the children of Israel out of Egyptian bondage. Exodus and Leviticus were written as God gave the Law. Numbers was written during the travels in the wilderness, with Deuteronomy being written shortly before his death. At that time that was the "Bible." It was the only Body of Revealed Truth in the world. Beginning with Moses and spanning a time period of some 900 years, the balance of the Old Testament was written (all by Jewish authors), culminating with Malachi.

During Jesus' day the Old Testament, beginning with Genesis and concluding with Malachi, was the "Bible" that He used. When the prophecy concerning the Messiah was given in the 119th Psalm, it was from Genesis through Malachi of which it was prophetically speaking:

> *"Oh how love I thy law! it is my meditation all the day.*
> *"Thou through thy commandments hast made me wiser than mine enemies: for they are ever with me.*

> *"I have more understanding than all my teachers: for thy testimonies are my meditation.*
> *"I understand more than the ancients, because I keep thy precepts.*
> *"I have refrained my feet from every evil way, that I might keep thy word.*
> *"I have not departed from thy judgments: for thou hast taught me.*
> *"How sweet are thy words unto my taste! yea, sweeter than honey to my mouth!*
> *"Through thy precepts I get understanding: therefore I hate every false way."* (Psa. 119:97-104)

These passages from the 119th Psalm proclaim through prophecy that the Lord Jesus Christ, even as a child and a teenager, would meditate constantly in the Word of God (St. Luke 2:49). If one will notice, various words such as *"law, commandments, testimonies, precepts, word, and judgments"* are used. Today, we use the word "Bible," meaning a compilation of letters, epistles, and books.

Beginning in the 1st Century A.D. as the Holy Spirit moved upon them, holy men began to write what we refer to as the New Testament. These men were Matthew, Mark, Luke, John, Paul, James, Simon Peter, and Jude. All were Jews.

The Jewish people who sprang from the loins of Abraham were called by God for three purposes:
- To give the world the Word of God.
- To bring the Messiah into the world.
- To evangelize the world.

The last book of the Canon of Scripture was written by the Apostle John on the isle of Patmos about A.D. 96. The very first words given to Moses a little over 1600 years earlier were,

> *"In the beginning God created the heaven and the earth."* (Gen 1:12)

v

The last words as they were given to the Apostle John some 1600 years later were,

> *"The grace of our Lord Jesus Christ be with you all. Amen."*   (Rev. 22:21)

It begins with God. It ends with God's gift to hurting humanity: *"The grace of our Lord Jesus Christ."*

As we have stated, the Bible is the only Body of Revealed Truth that mankind has ever known. All else is darkness.

A LOVE FOR THE WORD OF GOD

Understanding the tremendous statement that has been made ("The Bible is the only Body of Revealed Truth"), then it should be incumbent upon every individual to master its contents. It should be read daily; it should be meditated on constantly.

When Moses handed to Joshua the very first copy of the written Word of God, then consisting solely of the Pentateuch and possibly the book of Job, Joshua was told,

> *"This book of the law shall not depart out of thy mouth; but thou shalt meditate therein day and night, that thou mayest observe to do according to all that is written therein: for then thou shalt make thy way prosperous, and then thou shalt have good success."*   (Josh. 1:8)

If we want prosperity and good success in the Lord, then we should obey Moses' command to Joshua to *"meditate therein day and night."*

Personally, I love the Bible more than I have the vocabulary to express. I started reading it when I was 8 years old. At that tender age, I asked the Lord to help me to understand it. Realizing that no human being has even remotely begun to plumb its depths, still, I thank the Lord so much for the insight that He has given me. The Word has never failed me. It is truly *". . . a lamp unto my feet, and a light unto my path"* (Psa. 119:105).

My personal Bible study is constant and never ending. I always read the Bible systematically, beginning with the book of Genesis and going straight through the book of Revelation. It takes from four to eight weeks to do so – then I begin all over again. It never grows old. Time and time again, the Lord will illuminate a passage that will literally *"burn"* within my heart, providing strength, direction, and intelligence. It is my life.

Every Bible should be a worn-out book in the hands of every Christian. We should pore over its pages, perusing them constantly; we should memorize its texts, always asking the Lord to give us insight into its depths. I read it just as much for my own personal strength and enlightenment as I do for its instruction and guidance, yet the Bible is never boring; I never tire of it.

WHY I WROTE THIS BIBLE COMMENTARY

In my library at home I have any number of Commentaries. A few provide some help, but most provide none at all. I found in my own personal study that most Commentaries provide such a volume of information that it makes it very difficult to ferret out what is needed. I don't for a moment intend to demean any effort by anyone else endeavoring to help the student learn more about the Word of God. But in this Commentary I have attempted to condense the meat of the text and to put the help at your fingertips, not requiring volumes of reading to search out what is desired. I pray that, at least in some small measure, I have succeeded.

THE STYLE IN WHICH IT IS WRITTEN

I have attempted to do several things which I believe make this Commentary unique:

• These volumes are written with the lover of the Bible in mind, whether minister or layman. Consequently, regardless of educational background, the information provided will be instant and useful – without having to read volumes of material.

• I have not attempted to write a commentary on every Scripture in each chapter. Rather, I have taken the salient verses which contain the meat of each chapter and have directed the commentary toward these Scriptures given by the Holy Spirit. In this fashion, each chapter is covered using the salient Scriptures.

• Where applicable and obtainable, I have given the historical and cultural background of scriptural settings that more clearly bring to life the person, place, or object in question. Understanding this helps us to better understand what the Holy Spirit has for us.

• The strong point of this Commentary is the effort to draw out the *types, allegories, symbolism,* and *portrayals* given by the Holy Spirit. Few Commentaries do this. Whether you're preparing a message, a Bible study, or just reading for your own scriptural study, I believe this will be invaluable, giving you an insight into the Scriptures that, prayerfully, opens up what the Holy Spirit is telling us.

• Most of the passages in the Word of God which have proven to be somewhat difficult for some Bible students hopefully have been made simple to understand. The difficulty with these passages seems to be in the translation. Referring to the Hebrew or the Greek will often clear them up. Therefore, the works of some of the brightest Hebrew and Greek scholars have been used as reference sources while writing this Commentary.

I believe this is a Commentary that you will use constantly. It could very well find a prominent place beside your Bible to be used over and over again. Anything that helps one understand the Word of God a little better is literally worth its weight in gold. That's what this Commentary is all about. The statement of its value can be reduced to this:

"I believe the **Jimmy Swaggart Bible Commentary** *will help you understand the Word of God better."*

THE
BOOK OF GENESIS

The first 34 verses of Genesis (down through verse 3 of chapter 2) is a composite of the entirety of the plan of God for the human race.

The 1st verse of the 1st chapter reveals God as Creator of the heavens and the earth at some unknown period in the past.

The 2nd verse points to a tremendous convulsion that affected the earth.

As one observes the remainder of chapter 1, one sees the renewing power of the Holy Spirit in bringing light, salvation, and regeneration out of chaos.

Verse 3 of chapter 2 ends with the Sabbath, which speaks of *"rest."*

Likewise, when man fell, chaos and catastrophe is the best way for this horror to be described.

At salvation, the Holy Spirit goes about His work to renew and restore that which was lost in the fall. As a chaotic world could not pull itself out of its ruin, as well, man cannot save himself. As the Holy Spirit is the agent in the re-creation, so is the Holy Spirit the agent in the re-creation and restoration of man.

After the great work of re-creation was carried out on this planet called earth, the Bible says, *"And God saw every thing that he had made, and, behold it was very good"* (Gen. 1:31). Likewise, the great plan of redemption is beheld as *"very good"* (Gal. 1:4-5).

When God finished His great work, He rested (Gen. 2:3). Likewise, when man enters into Christ, he rests from his own labors (Heb. 4:5).

One day very soon, the great millennial reign will begin with Christ's appearance (the Second Advent), of which the 3rd (ch.2) verse is a type.

So as the first 34 verses of the book of Genesis portray the re-creation of planet earth, it as well portrays the re-creation of man (II Cor. 5:17).

CHAPTER 1

"In the beginning God," is the way the Bible begins. God must be the beginning of our endeavors, if we are to have a successful conclusion.

God does not explain Himself at the outset of His Word. And why? The reason is that man cannot understand God through his intellect; he can only understand God by revelation. The revelation comes from God the Father, through His Word (St. John 1:1), through His Spirit (St. Luke 2:26), and through His Son, Jesus Christ (St. Luke 10:22).

When God created the heavens and the earth, no one knows. Many hold to the young-earth theory, that the earth is less than 10,000 years old. However, if science can prove that planet Earth is billions of years old, etc., there is no Scripture to dispute such. The Lord doesn't say when; He just says *"the beginning."*

When God created the heavens and the earth, it was *not* originally created *"without form and void."* It became that way after some type of convulsion, which some Bible scholars believe was the time of Lucifer's rebellion. How long the earth remained in this chaotic state, is not said. The account that is given of the re-creation of the earth was not the creation that took place in the beginning.

The moving of the Spirit of God is the

1

beginning of life. He must move in our lives, our churches, and our efforts for the cause of Christ. Otherwise, nothing is done.

"And God said," is all that is required, and it is done. The days and nights that God speaks of were literal 24-hour days, because they speak of the *"evening and the morning."*

The words, *"after his kind,"* totally refute the theory of evolution. Evolution speaks of the "missing link." Actually, the entire chain is missing. In all man's selection and cultivation, he can work only within the limits of the species. No change into new species has been produced either by natural or artificial selection. The iron law of sterility stands guard at the far frontiers of the species, and everything continues to reproduce *"after his kind."*

The words *"made"* and *"create"* are two different words altogether. The word *"made"* does not speak of creation. These great lights (the sun, moon, and stars) were created in the beginning before the earth was. But during the chaos between verses 1 and 2, they were forbidden to give light on earth until judgment had been completed. They were then brought back to their desired position – hence *"made."*

The word *"create"* speaks of bringing into existence (vs. 21).

So, some things were restored, and some things were created anew.

The words *"let us"* in verse 26 demand a Divine Trinity. The word for *"our image"* in the Hebrew is "tselem," and it means "resemblance." Its usage could also refer to outward form as well. However, it does not necessarily refer to attributes. The word *"likeness"* in the Hebrew is "demuwth," and means resemblance, model, and shape. It, as well, could refer to the outward form. The word *"dominion"* refers even to the sun, moon, and stars (Psa. 8). In the final restoration, man will again have such rulership (I Cor. 15:24-28; Eph. 1:18; Heb. 2:7-9).

In the creative act of God, which brought the beast and man into being, their bodies were formed, but their life was created. Man's creation *alone* was not merely accomplished by a divine fiat, but was also the subject of a divine counsel (verses 26-28). So, as had been decreed by divine counsel, God created man in His own image. Man was a work of God, not of mole-

cules and monkeys.

In verse 28, the word *"replenish"* could prove a social system before Adam. Some Bible scholars feel that this social system (prior to Adam) was ruled by Lucifer before his fall (Isaiah 14:12-15; Ezek. 28) (verse 29). Man was given grain, fruits and other higher products to eat. Animals were also created to be eaten by him (I Tim. 4:3-5; I Cor. 6:13) (verse 30). Animals were not created to eat each other, and will not do so in the Millennium, and the New Earth (Isaiah 11:6-9).

CHAPTER 2

The heavens and the earth being finished, does *not* refer to the original creation. The work that is being spoken of refers to the 6 days of chapters 1 and 2, to regulate the solar system in connection with the restored earth, and to make it habitable again.

Verse 2 ascribes everything to God, hence no room for evolution, without a flat denial of the divine revelation.

Verse 3 gives the third of three blessings found in Genesis chapters 1 and 2.

1. Upon the fish and fouls (1:22).
2. Upon man and animals (1:28).
3. Upon the 7th day (2:3, Exodus 20:11).

The word *"sanctified"* means separation from a profane to a sacred purpose.

In the 8th verse, we are told of the Garden of Eden. The first Adam was given a perfect environment, and failed. The second Adam was given a hostile environment, and succeeded (St. Matt. 4).

The 9th verse tells us of *"the Tree of Life,"* which is a type of Christ, and *"the Tree of Knowledge of Good and Evil,"* which is the source of all that is destructive. Notice, this tree is not only a tree of evil, but of good. All of the so-called good that stems from this tree, will tend toward destruction. Hence, all the *"good"* in the world that does not come from God, comes from the *"Tree of Knowledge of Good and Evil."* Man is so easily deceived by the *"good."*

Verses 10 through 14 describe the river that

went out of the Garden of Eden, branching into four heads. Its location was somewhere in modern-day Iraq (Hiddekel-Tigres, and Euphrates), possibly in the general locality where ancient Babylon was built.

In verse 17, Adam was told he would die if he ate of the *"Tree of Knowledge of Good and Evil."* The type of death that was being spoken of was "spiritual death," which was separation from God. The moment that Adam failed, he spiritually died *("surely die.")*

Verse 18 proclaims the Lord God saying, *"It is not good that the man should be alone."* This statement applies to a wife, but, as well, to the help that others give us in this journey for the Lord.

The 19th verse reveals a level of intelligence on the part of Adam that has never been equaled in human history. The names that Adam gave the creatures encompassed everything that could be known about the particular animal, or creature of every type. This was Adam's intelligence before the fall. It was super intelligence. Actually, man has never been viewed or observed as God originally made him. We only see at the present time the product of the fall. Evolution claims progression. The Bible portrays a regression regarding man. One cannot believe the Bible and evolution at the same time. They are totally antagonistic to each other.

As is recorded in verses 21 and 22, when God made woman, He took her from Adam's side. He did not take woman from man's head so that man would lord it over her; neither did He take her from man's feet, that woman would be walked on; but from man's side that she would be equal, from under his arm to be protected by him, and from near his heart to be loved by him. The word *"made"* in Hebrew is "banah," which means "skillfully formed." In the 23rd verse, the word *"woman"* in Hebrew is "ish shah." It means "she-man."

The 25th verse speaks of both Adam and Eve being naked, which means "without clothing." However, some Bible scholars believe that before the fall they both lived in an aura of light.

CHAPTER 3

In chapter 3, we are given the record of man's fall. Satan's method of temptation has never been changed from that day to this. Satan's first effort is *"the pride of life"* – *"ye shall be as gods"* (verse 5). The second temptation is the *"lust of the eye"* – *"and when the woman saw. . . ."* If Satan can tempt man into committing the sin of *"the pride of life,"* man thereafter is by and large helpless regarding his resistance of *the lust of the eye,* and *the lust of the flesh.* The last step in this sinful regression is *"the lust of the flesh."* The Scripture records it as *"she took"* (verse 6). This is the pattern of temptation used then; it is the pattern of temptation used now (I John 2:16).

In the first verse, Satan uses the body of the serpent (snake). Satan did not transform himself into a snake, because he has no power to do so. He is an angel (fallen) and always will be. A literal serpent is involved as a tool of Satan, otherwise it would be unjust of God to curse it. Satan's method was to question God's Word, *"hath God said?"* There was nothing said at first by Satan to awaken suspicion or to shock the moral sense: Merely a sly insinuation calculated to excite a natural curiosity. Then in verses 4 and 5, we have a direct lie, combined, however, with just enough truth to give it plausibility.

In verse 4, the first direct lie is given, *"You shall not surely die."* Satan has been lying ever since. The entirety of the fabric of his kingdom of darkness is based on a lie.

In the 5th verse, God only knows evil by His omniscience (all knowing). He does not know it by experience.

In the 7th verse, when it said *"they knew,"* it means by experience. They lost God-consciousness and gained the power to do only evil. Thus, becoming like God, they became unlike Him, in that He has the power to do only good. They sewed fig leaves together to cover their nakedness. Sinners clothe themselves with morality, sacraments, and religious ceremonies; they are as worthless as Adam's apron of fig leaves. Every false way of salvation is *"fig leaves."*

Verse 8 implies that God daily walked with Adam and Eve in the Garden, in the cool of the day. The 8th verse portrays God seeking Adam and Eve. God has been seeking sinners ever since. Whenever the sinner is saved, he does not as much find the Lord, as the Lord finds him. Sin and guilt cannot stand the presence of God. Consequently, it seeks to "hide." With more of the presence of God in our churches, fewer Christians will have sin in their lives.

In the 9th verse, God calls. He has been calling man ever since.

The first word uttered by man as recorded in the 10th verse says, *"I was afraid."* Fear, incidentally, has taken its deadly toll from the very beginning. The word *"naked"* refers to "naked to the judgment of God." Sin always demands judgment.

The 11th verse speaks of the command. Incidentally, they are not suggestions.

The 12th verse portrays a total lack of repentance. The man blamed the woman (verse 12); the woman blamed the serpent (verse 13). The first requirement of true godly repentance is to take the blame and put it where it rightly belongs, on ourselves. God is always justified; man is always guilty.

The 14th verse indicates that the serpent originally walked upright before the fall. There is some indication as well that the serpent was the most intelligent of all of the animal or reptile creation. There is even some indication that the serpent could speak. Its curse will remain forever.

The 15th verse records the first great promise of the redemption of man. Satan has hated woman from the very beginning, because she would be the one who would bring the Messiah, the Redeemer into the world. *"Thy seed"* refers to the progeny of Adam. *"Her seed'* refers to the birth of the Son of God. The virgin birth is one of the most essential doctrines of the whole plan of God. Without faith in it, and in the death, burial, and resurrection of Jesus Christ, one cannot be saved (I Cor. 15:1-8). At Calvary, Christ would bruise the head of Satan, thereby destroying the federal head of evil. In turn, Christ would be bruised at Calvary.

There are seven promises of the coming Redeemer in the Old Testament, four in Genesis and three in the remaing books.

1. The Redeemer should be of the *human* race (Gen. 3:15).

2. Of a section of that race. *Shem* (Gen. 9:26).

3. Of a nation belonging to that section, the *Hebrew* (Gen. 12:3).

4. Of a tribe in that nation, *Judah* (Gen. 49:10).

5. Of a family in that tribe, *David* (II Sam. 7:16).

6. Of a member of that family, a woman, the *Virgin* (Isa. 7:14).

7. And lastly, in a village belonging to that woman, *Bethlehem* (Micah verse 2).

In verse 16, the curse upon woman was not in having children, for this was commanded before the fall (Gen. 1:26-28). But it was multiplied sorrow in conception. When the curse is removed in the new earth, there will be no pain in child-birth for the coming generations (Rev. 21:3-7). As well, woman lost her equality with man; now man is the head of the woman (I Cor. 11:3-12; Eph. 5:22). Modern feminism attempts to abrogate the Word of God by claiming woman's independence of man and her superiority. Modern feminism is thereby unscriptural and ungodly.

In the 17th verse, Adam hearkened unto his wife instead of God. Consequently, the earth in which he lived would now be cursed, making it very difficult for him. The curse would include the rational creation, as well as the animals, the ground, and all it produces (Rom. 8:19-23; Rev. 21:4). If Eve only had sinned, the sin could have been repented of without the earth and all that is therein experiencing the fall. Eve alone would have been cursed, because the seed is in the man. If Eve had not sinned and lived true to God, she could have had children and they would have been accounted sinless. For it was reckoned that the sin passed to others by the *father,* not the mother (Exod. 20:5; Ezek. 18:2-4; Rom. 5:12-21).

The first animal sacrifice is recorded in the 21st verse. The Lord did away with Adam's *"fig leaves"* and made him a *"coat of skins and clothed them."* The clothing was made from the animals that God had taught Adam to offer as sacrifice in looking forward to the coming Redeemer (Heb. 9:22).

In the 24th verse, man is expelled from the garden, lest by eating of the Tree of Life he should perpetuate his misery. But God's love for him, though fallen and guilty, is so strong that He accompanies him into exile, making His dwelling place with him at the east of the garden between the cherubim; a sword made of flame forbids access to the Tree of Life.

Incidentally, in verse 18, the word *"thistles"* may as well include noxious insects.

CHAPTER 4

Eve's firstborn was Cain. She honestly thought that Cain was the redeemer that God had promised in Gensis 3:15. She used the word, *"a man from the Lord"* with the title *"Lord"* meaning *"Covenant God."* When she listened to Satan, instead of receiving light, she received darkness.

The 2nd verse tells of the birth of Abel. His name means "that is vanity." By now she has become disillusioned.

In verses 3 and 4, we are told of the sacrifices offered by Cain and Abel. This must be understood: There is no difference between the brothers, but an eternal difference between their sacrifices. They were both corrupt branches of a decayed tree. Both were born outside Eden, both were guilty, both were sinners with no moral difference, and both were sentenced to death.

We know that God had already revealed a way of approach to them. The words *"by faith"* in Hebrews 11:4 teach us that. Abel accepted God's way; Cain rejected it. Abel's offering spoke of repentance, of faith, and of the precious blood of Christ, the Lamb of God without blemish. Cain's offering tells of pride, unbelief, and self-righteousness.

Abel's offering was beautiful to God's eye, but repulsive to man. Cain's offering was beautiful to man's eye, but was repulsive to God.

These same two altars exist today all over the world. There are very few gathered around Christ's altar. Around Cain's altar, there are many. God accepts the slain Lamb and rejects the offered fruit – and it must be hurriedly

stated that with the offering being rejected, so of necessity is the offerer.

In the 4th verse, it says, *"And the Lord had respect unto Abel and to his offering."* In the Hebrew, it tells us that in the acceptance of Abel's offering, God sent fire from heaven and consumed the sacrifice.

In verses 6 and 7, we find that God loves Cain and wishes to bless him also. The words, *"Sin lieth at the door,"* refer to a tabernacle with a sin offering (lamb) right outside the door. All Cain had to do was to get the acceptable sacrifice and offer it. Regrettably, Cain did not do that.

As well, it seems that the Lord with the words, *"And unto thee shall be his desire, and thou shalt rule over him,"* was telling Cain that if he would be obedient, dominion over the earth would be given to him, and his brother Abel would submit to his leadership . . . because of Cain being the firstborn.

However, the 8th verse says that Cain rejected God's offer and killed his brother. He was too "cultured" to offer up a slain lamb, but not too "cultured" to kill his brother. Adam sinned against God, and his son, Cain, sinned against man. In these two sins, we see all of its deadly forms – and that on the first page of human history.

God's way of salvation fills the heart with love. Man's way of salvation, which constitutes religion, fills man's heart with hate. "Religion" has ever been the greatest cause of bloodshed.

In the 10th verse, God said, *"The voice of thy brother's blood crieth unto me from the ground."* Could this refer to Abel's posterity, which was cut off forever by his death? In murder, one not only sins against God and the man he kills, but also against the murdered man's posterity for eternal generations.

The 11th verse tells us that Cain rejected God's offer. So, no longer was fellowship at the tabernacle of God now possible. So, Cain becomes a wanderer. Without God, man continuously wanders. Nothing ever satisfies, so he wanders from one place to the next. Still, God loves him and reaches out to him. He promises to protect Cain (15th verse).

How great is the love of God that would continue to reach out to this murderer? How great is the love of God to all of us?

No, the "mark upon Cain" recorded in the 15th verse had nothing to do with Cain being changed from white to black. The black race did not begin with Cain; all of his line perished in the flood. All races as we know them now began after Noah (Gen. 10:1-32).

The 16th verse says that Cain went out from the presence of the Lord (left the tabernacle). Many feel thay can leave God's presence and thereby escape the consequences. The answer is not running *from* God, but running *to* God.

Incidentally, by now, Adam had been on earth about 130 years. At a very moderate rate of increase, there could have been several hundreds of thousands of people on the earth. Cain himself built a city which required many people. Every son of man had sons and daughters and started branches of the race (verses 17-18).

The 19th verse records Lamech, who was the 7th from Adam in Cain's line. He became the first polygamist, and the second murderer (verse 23).

The 23rd verse records the first poem or song.

He reasoned that if Cain could be protected by God, insomuch as he was a greater sinner, then he (Lamech) would be protected even more. Consequently, man's first poem in human history glorifies immorality and murder, and denies coming wrath. Lamech, in effect, says that God would be to blame if anything happened to him. Men have been blaming God ever since and denying the coming future punishment.

The 25th verse records the birth of Seth. Ironically enough, Eve, lacking faith, no longer believed in the promises of God. She no longer used the covenant name "Lord," but now addresses Him as *"God,"* which denied the covenant. She used the word *"another seed,"* meaning that she did not believe the word *"her seed"* (Gen. 3:15). Her lack of faith destroyed her, but it did not hinder God. In fact, Seth was the very one that she was looking for, for he would be in the lineage of the coming Messiah (St. Luke 3:38). Man loses faith quickly, but God is always true to His Word.

In the 26th verse, the words *"then began men to call upon the name of the Lord,"* seems to be a statement of contempt. As followers of the Lord at Antioch were contemptuously called

by the name of Christ (Christians), likewise, contempt was heaped upon anyone who spoke favorably of the covenant of the Lord to bring a redeemer into the world – with the title *"Lord"* meaning *"Covenant God."*

CHAPTER 5

Verse 1 opens with the words, *"This is the book of the generations of Adam."* Why does it use the words in exactly this manner? St. Matthew 1:1 gives the answer, *"The book of the generation of Jesus Christ."* Christ was the last Adam.

In this chapter, we have the family history of the first man Adam, showing the line through whom the second man Adam, the seed of the woman, should come into the world.

Verse 1 says that Adam was created in the likeness of God. Verse 3 says that men now, due to the fall, are begotten in Adam's likeness. When a baby is born into the world, it is born a son of Adam. To be a son of God, one must be born again (St. John 3:3).

Due to the fall, the heavenly race ends in death. No matter how long a member of this family lived, yet, three words attend his name, *"And he died."*

Verse 21 states that at 65 years of age, Enoch had an experience with God, and entered into divine fellowship. Three statements are made in the Bible respecting Enoch: *"He walked with God"* (Gen. 5); *"he witnessed for God"* (Jude); *"he pleased God"* (Heb. 11). Prior to the fall, God walked with man; after the fall, man walked with God – at least one did.

The 22nd verse says that Enoch lived for God some 300 years. He did not live a life of isolation, though he did live a life of separation. What a testimony of the power of God to keep one from this evil world.

The 24th verse says that *"God took him,"* that is, he translated him without dying as in the case of Elijah (Heb. 11:5). Enoch's is one of the briefest and most outstanding biographies – one sentence revealing the history of 365 years, 300 of which were in a believing, humble, holy walk with God. What a testimony!

The name *"Methuselah"* means, *"it* (the deluge) *shall be sent, when he is dead."* A short time after Methuselah's death, the flood destroyed the world of the ungodly. No doubt Methuselah heard his father, Enoch, speak of this coming flood.

The Lamech mentioned in the 28th verse is not the same Lamech that was mentioned in the 4th chapter.

The first Lamech sang of lust and vileness. Lamech, Noah's father, sang of comfort and peace. He called his child *"Noah,"* which means rest, comfort, and consolation. There is a possibility that Lamech was a true believer of the living God, teaching Noah of the ways of God.

The 32nd verse says that Noah was 500 years old. It also says that Noah begat Shem, Ham, and Japheth. The Scripture also says that Noah was 600 years old when the flood came (Gen. 7:6). It also says that his son, Shem, was only 100 years old two years after the flood. So, Noah could not have been 120 years building the ark. Actually, the 120 years refers to Adam and not to Noah.

CHAPTER 6

In the 6th chapter of Genesis, we have one of the most powerful witnesses of evil, and of redemption found in the entirety of the Word of God. In the 2nd verse, the statement is used, *"Daughters of men."* In the Hebrew, the word "men" is singular, meaning "daughters of the man Adam." So it seems that the terrible corruption of the human race by fallen angels cohabiting with women began with Adam's daughters and spread to the entirety of the human race.

The 3rd verse does not pertain to Noah having 120 years to warn men, but to Adam. In the Hebrew, the word *"man"* actually says "the man Adam." The meaning is, *"For that he* (Adam) *is also flesh* (as all other men are): *Yet his* (Adam's) *days shall be an hundred and twenty years."* The fact is, the 3rd verse reveals that Adam had corrupted his way upon earth as all other flesh had done, and that God, in His

mercy, gave him 120 more years in which to repent and conform his life to the will of his creator. Whether Adam did this or not, is not known.

The 4th verse records one of the most controversial passages found in the entirety of the Word of God. The word *"giants"* refers to beings of abnormal size in body. That these types of individuals lived on earth is one of the most clearly stated truths in Scripture. The Hebrew "nephilim" for giant means clearly they were larger in size than ordinary. In Numbers 13:33 it says, *"The men of Israel were as grasshoppers in size compared to them."* They were called by several different names, the Anakims (Deut. 1:28), the Emims (Deut. 2:10-11), the Zamzummims (Deut. 2: 19-21).

A valley of the giants is mentioned in Joshua 15:8; 18:16. Who were these individuals?

These sons of God, as are given in the 4th verse, are fallen angels. They came down and cohabited with women, producing the giants.

The expression *"sons of God"* is found only five times in the Old Testament, and every time it is used of angels (Gen 6:1-4; Job 1:6; Job 2:1; Job 38:7). In Daniel 3:25-28, an angel is called the Son of God.

Josephus, the great Jewish historian, said, "Many angels of God accompanied with women, begat sons that proved unjust and despisers of all that were good." Again he says, "There was the race of giants, who had bodies so large and countenances so entirely different from men, that they were surprising to the sight and terrible to the hearing. The bones of these men are still shown to this very day (Ant. Book 5 ch.2).

Both testaments of the Bible teach that some angels committed sex sins and lived contrary to nature.

Some teach that angels are sexless, derived from Matthew 22:30. However, this passage does not say they are. It states that *"in the resurrection they neither married, nor are given in marriage, but are as angels of God in heaven."* The purpose of this verse is to show that men and women who have part in the resurrection do not marry, nor do they need to in order to keep their kind in existence. In the resurrected state, they live forever, but not as sexless beings. Paul said that everyone will have *his own body* in the resurrection (I Cor. 15:35-38). If one is a male, he will continue as such with all his bodily parts. If one is female in this life, she will be resurrected as such, even though her body is changed from mortality to immortality, and is called a spiritual body (I Cor. 15:35-54).

Jude said (Jude 6) that some angels, *"kept not their first state, but left their own habitation."*

There are actually two classes of fallen angels, those presently loose with Satan, who will be cast down to earth during the future tribulation (Rev. 12:7-12), and those who are now bound in hell for committing what the Bible calls fornication (II Peter 2:4; Jude 6-7). Had these *"sons of God"* (fallen angels) not committed the additional sin of fornication, they would still be loose with the others, to help Satan in his present efforts to destroy mankind. Their present confinement proves they committed a sin besides that of original rebellion with Satan. That it was sex sin, is clear from II Peter 2:4 and Jude 6-7, which in fact identifies this class of fallen angels as *"the sons of God"* of Genesis 6:1-4.

It was the purpose of Satan and his fallen angels to corrupt the human race and thereby do away with pure Adamite stock through whom the seed of the woman should come. If successful, they would avert their own doom and make it possible for Satan and his kingdom to maintain control of planet earth indefinitely. The Lord said to Adam and Eve that the seed of the woman should defeat Satan and restore man's dominion. That seed was to be the Lord Jesus Christ (Gen. 3:15). The only way for Satan to avoid this predicted defeat, was to corrupt the purity of the human race so that the coming of the seed of the woman into the world (Jesus Christ) would be made impossible. This he tried to accomplish by sending some of his fallen angels to marry the daughters of men, as in Genesis 6:1-4, and producing the giant nations through them.

There are two such eruptions of fallen angels taught in Gensis 6:4. There were giants in the earth *"in those days"* (before the flood); and *"also after that"* (after the flood).

Satan almost succeeded in his plan during the first eruption, for the Bible says, *"All flesh hath corrupted his way upon the earth."* Of all the multitudes of human beings on planet Earth at this time, Noah and his sons were the only ones that were pure in their genealogy and in their walk with God. The main object of the flood was to do away with all satanic corruption, destroy the giants, and preserve pure human stock so as to make good the guarantee of the coming of the seed of the woman, as in the plan of God.

Satan made a second effort to destroy the human race by this deadly mixture after the flood. He came within "eight souls" of doing it *before* the flood, so he would try it again *after* the flood.

Once again, this ungodly union of the sons of God (fallen angels) and the daughters of men produced giants, and races of them occupied the land of promise where the seed (Jesus Christ) should be born.

This explains why God commanded Israel at times to kill everyone even to the last man, woman, and child.

This again explains why he destroyed all the men, women, and children, besides Noah and his family, at the time of the flood. It also answers the skeptics' questions regarding why the children were taken away with the adults in the flood. God had to do away with this corruption entirely in order to fulfill His eternal plan and give the world its promised redeemer.

The Redeemer, the Lord Jesus Christ, has now come, so Satan is reserving his forces for a last stand at the Second Coming of Christ, at the Battle of Armageddon.

The 6th verse says that the sin of man *"grieved Him* (God) *at His heart."* This reveals the tender love of God. A heart of stone cannot be grieved, only a heart that loves. But only one man is found amid the millions of mankind to respond to that love; it was Noah.

However, it must be understood that Noah's salvation was not because of any moral excellence discovered by God in him. But his salvation was totally "by the grace of God."

The 9th verse says that Noah was a godly man, as well as uncorrupted in his generations. (In other words, none of the daughters of his family, all the way back to Adam, had corrupted themselves with the fallen angels.)

Enoch walked with God, so Noah walked with God as well.

The 11th, 12th, and 13th verses say that *"all flesh hath corrupted his way upon the earth"* (except Noah and his family).

All stands now in contrast with Eden. Eden was a realm of life, with the tree of death in its midst. Now, the world was a realm of death, with the "tree of life" (Christ) in the midst. For of a smitten tree was the ark made. There was death in the tree, but life in the ark. In the Garden of Eden, God said, "Away from the tree of the knowledge of good and evil." Satan said, "Hasten to it." God now says, "Hasten to the ark and live!" Satan says, "Keep away from it!" Conscience drove Adam from God; revelation draws Noah to God.

Verses 14, 15, and 16 give the dimensions of the ark. Using 18 inches to the cubit, the ark was 450 feet long (a football field and a half long), 75 feet wide, and about 45 feet high. Up to the 1800's, there was no other ship in the history of the world as large as the ark. The ark was easily big enough for all it was to hold.

In the 20th verse, even after some 1600 years, the law of reproduction is still in force *(after their kind)*. God's law of reproduction *(after His kind)* has never been broken and never will be broken.

CHAPTER 7

Noah believed the Lord and was actually terror-stricken. The epistle to the Hebrews states that Noah prepared the ark because he believed the divine warning (Hebrews 11:7). Quite possibly, Enoch was given this revelation from God, and before his translation related it to Noah. Then Noah was called by God to build the ark.

Verse 5 says that Noah did all that the Lord commanded him.

Verse 7 says that *"Noah went in."* The Holy Spirit has been trying to get people to come into the ark (Christ) from the very beginning.

The 10th verse says the waters of the flood were upon the earth. Those who dwelt upon the tops of the loftiest mountains perished

equally with those who lived in the deepest valleys. Many who live upon the mountains of morality think themselves secure from the judgment of fire that is now coming and pity the certain fate of those who live in the depths of vice. But all that are without Christ, moral or otherwise, will likewise perish.

The 11th verse says in Noah's 600th year that the flood came. It insinuates in Genesis 5:32 that God spoke to Noah about the coming deluge when Noah was 500 years old. Quite possibly, Noah had a hundred years to build the ark and to warn men.

The 13th verse says that Noah and his family entered the ark. This illustrates the Scripture terms "lost" and "saved." Standing outside the door of the ark, Noah was lost, that is, exposed to the coming judgment and sure to perish. Standing inside the door, he was saved, that is, sheltered from the coming doom. To pass from the one condition to the other, he had but to take one step – a step into the ark – and he was in immediate safety.

Noah was saved through the baptism of the ark. The ark was sinless, Noah was sinful. The ark suffered the fierceness of divine anger – a baptism into death – but not one wave of that judgment reached Noah. He was absolutely safe. Noah could not perish because the ark could not perish. The ark could not perish because Jehovah was in the ark (the ark was a type of Christ).

In the 1st verse, God did not say, "Go into the ark," but *"Come into the ark."* So, God was in the ark with Noah and his family.

The 24th verse says that *"the waters prevailed."* Even though some segments of Christianity proclaim the lie of "dominion teaching," nevertheless, God is *not* saving the society; He is saving men out of the society. Society is doomed; it cannot be reconciled to God. The only thing the church can ever hope to be to society is "salt" and "light." The world will not gradually get better and better as dominion teaching proclaims, but actually worse and worse (Rev. 4-19). As the waters of judgment prevailed then, the waters of judgment will prevail in the near future. *"The great day of his wrath is come, and who shall be able to stand?"* (Rev. 6:17).

NOTES

CHAPTER 8

The 1st verse said that God remembered Noah. God never forgets our labor of love. Jesus borrowed the disciples' boat, using it for a pulpit to preach to the crowd on the shore. When concluded, He repaid that favor with a great catch of fish. The 1st verse also says that, *"God made a wind to pass over the earth."* God is a miracle-working God. The church needs to believe that God works miracles even today. He is not just a God of yesterday, but as well of today, and shall be forever.

In the 16th verse, God said to Noah, *"Go forth of the ark,"* not "come forth." God was the first One in the ark (7:1) and the last One to leave the ark. Noah and God had dwelt together in the ark for a full year.

The 20th verse says that Noah built an altar. He worshiped not the ark, but God. The ark was the instrument of his salvation, which was a type of Christ, as the cross was an instrument of salvation for the Apostle Paul. However, the Apostle Paul did not worship the cross, as multitudes do today, but worshiped Him Who died upon it. As long as Noah built altars, the Lord smelled a sweet savour (verse 21), and He blessed Noah (9:2). However, when Noah planted his vineyard (9:20), he then was drunk and uncovered. The moment that man ceases to build his altar (look to Calvary), he fails. The only savour that has a sweet smell to God is that which comes from the whole burnt offerings on the altar. This whole burnt offering was very similar to the one that was offered by Abel. The offerings represented two things.

A. That the offerer would give his all to the Lord.

B. That the Lord would give His all to the offerer.

The altar stood for Calvary. It is a sweet smell to the Lord whenever our all is given to Him on the altar of sacrifice. Nothing else moves Him. Paul said, *"Christ and Him crucified"* (I Cor. 2:2). Hallelujah!

CHAPTER 9

The 9th chapter of Genesis begins with blessing and ends with death. However, we know that Noah made things right with God, simply because of the words concerning Noah's righteousness that were given to Ezekiel over a thousand years later (Ezek. 14:14). Once again, the word *"replenish"* is used. It means to refill (not just fill) the earth. The same word was used with Adam (1:28). As the word *"replenish"* concerning Noah meant that there were people here before Noah, likewise, there seems to have been some type of civilization on planet Earth before Adam. It is possible that at that time it could have been ruled by Lucifer (before Lucifer's fall).

In the 4th verse, the Noahic Covenant demands that no blood be eaten. Before the flood, God gave man a vegetable diet. However, He retained the tree of the knowledge of good and evil to attest His own supreme lordship, and to remind Adam of the conditions of his tenure. Now, with animal food permitted and added to the vegetable diet, he likewise retains a portion – the blood. This testifies that He alone is the giver of all life (Lev. 3:17).

In the 6th verse, God demanded the death penalty for murder. That command, even under the New Covenant, is still in force (Rom. 13:1-7).

The command by God in the 7th verse as well, continues in that man is to be fruitful and multiply. That command also has not been lifted. The problem of planet Earth is not over-population; the problem is sin. It has been estimated that the planet, even under present conditions, could easily feed approximately 100 billion people. Food could be grown abundantly on earth were it not for ungodly philosophies, superstition, demon worship, and lack of adherence to the Word of God. Someone has said if you have *"much Bible,"* you have much freedom; if you have *"some Bible,"* you have some freedom; if you have *"no Bible,"* you have no freedom.

The 11th verse tells us that the flood was universal, not localized as some claim.

The 12th verse uses the word *"perpetual generations."* This means exactly what it says, that children will continue to be born even in the millennial reign and even in the perfect age that is to come. It means exactly what it says, *forever.*

The 18th verse tells us that all the colors and types of men came into existence after the flood. Up to the flood, all men were white, for there was only one family line – that of Noah, who was white and in the line of Christ. So, the entirety of the human race as we know it today stems from Shem, Ham, and Japheth.

Verse 19 says, *"Of them was the whole earth overspread."*

The 20th and 21st verses record the first vineyard planted and the first case of drunkenness. (No doubt both had been in existence almost from the beginning.) Noah failed. Regrettably, man fails in every position in which he is put by God. However, the great grace of God has provided a way of redemption.

The 22nd verse records a grievous sin. It seems that Canaan was confederate with his father Ham, and they did more than view the nakedness of Ham's drunken father. There may have even been a homosexual act committed by Canaan and allowed by Ham.

The 23rd verse records Shem and Japheth covering the nakedness of their father. Peter said that *"love covers the multitude of sins"* (I Pet. 4:8). If there is no love, we will be quick to "uncover." If there is love, we will be quick to "cover."

The 24th verse, as well, lends credence to the fact that more was done to Noah by Ham and Canaan than just to observe.

Verses 25, 26, and 27, even though brief, outline the future of all the peoples of planet Earth. Canaan was cursed (hence, probably being the one who carried out the act on his grandfather Noah). Canaan's descendants settled in the Middle East, as we know today as Israel, as well as North Africa. They, by and large, consisted of seven powerful tribes that inhabited the Promised Land and were dispelled by the sons of Israel. Shem was blessed, and in this short prophecy we have the promise of Christ who was to come through Shem. Through Shem came the Jewish as well as the Arab people. However, the Arab people,

through Ishmael, were not the promised seed and, thereby, did not receive this blessing of the Lord God. The Messiah was not promised through Ishmael, but through Isaac.

As well, Japheth was blessed. Japheth's descendants populated Europe, as well as England, and ultimately America. Truly, Japheth has been enlarged, and the great blessing of prosperity that was to come to Shem was diverted to Japheth – and because Shem (the Jew) rejected Christ, Japheth now dwells in the tents of prosperity that were originally meant for Shem. It is amazing how this short prophecy, given by Noah some 4400 years ago, forecasts the direction of the human race. It has been fulfilled to the letter.

At this point would be a good place to insert the dispensational plan of God for the human race between the two eternities – the eternal past and the eternal future. It has been said that if the Bible student understands dispensationalism, he understands the Word of God.

1. THE DISPENSATION OF INNOCENCE (Gen. 2:15 – 3:21)

It is given this name by Bible scholars because man was tested and put on probation while in innocence. No one knows exactly how long it lasted. It probably lasted less than a week.

2. THE DISPENSATION OF CONSCIENCE (Gen. 3:22 – 8:14)

It was given this name because man was to be tested to see if he would obey his own conscience regarding right and wrong (Rom. 2:12-16). At this time there were no written laws. Its length was about 1600 years. It lasted from Adam's day to the 600th year of Noah (the flood).

3. THE DISPENSATION OF HUMAN GOVERNMENT (Gen. 8:15 – 11:32)

It was given this name because human laws in human government were instituted to regulate man's life after a long age of freedom of conscience. God now gave Noah certain laws to govern the race by, and man was held responsible for self-government. Some of these laws have formed the basis of human laws in all ages since. Human governments are part of the moral government of God and are needed for the preservation of human society on earth. Without law enforcement and punishment, no government could long endure. The chief aim of moral and civil government should be to the highest good of all. It is the duty of all people to help establish, maintain, support, and take part in human government for the preservation of society. Its length was approximately 400 years. It lasted from Noah's flood to the call of Abraham when he was 75 years old.

4. THE DISPENSATION OF PROMISE (Gen. 12:1 – Ex. 12:37)

It was given this name because of the promises and covenants made with Abraham and his seed. In this period, God began to predict and emphasize the coming of the seed of the woman (Jesus) to be through a particular branch of the race. There had been prophecies given before, but now Abraham's seed was designated by the special line through whom Christ should come. It lasted a little over 400 years as well – from Abraham's call at 75 years of age to the exodus from Egypt.

5. DISPENSATION OF LAW (Ex. 12:38 – St. Matt. 2:23)

It was given this name because of the law that was given to Moses, which became part of the rule of faith and practice during the period between Moses and Christ. Its length was about 1600 years. It lasted from the exodus from Egypt to the preaching of the kingdom of heaven by John the Baptist.

6. DISPENSATION OF GRACE (St. Matt. 3:1 – Rev. 19:10)

It was given this name because of the fullness of grace brought by Jesus Christ. Men had grace in all previous ages, but not in fullness. Its length has been nearly 2000 years thus far. It continues on even at this present hour. It started with the preaching of the kingdom of heaven by John, and it will end at the Second Advent (Coming) of Jesus Christ.

7. THE DISPENSATION OF DIVINE GOVERNMENT, OR THE MILLENNIUM (Rev. 19:11 – 20:15)

It is given this name because it will be a divine government. Jesus Christ will rule personally from Jerusalem, and that over all human governments. This 1000 years of theocracy of God's rule on earth is also called the millennium, meaning 1000 years. It will last from the Second Coming of Christ during the Battle of Armageddon to the Second Resurrec-

tion and the Great White Throne Judgment, which will usher in the renovation of the heavens and the earth and the beginning of the new heavens and new earth. Thus will conclude the dispensations of man.

8. THE DISPENSATION OF FAITHFUL ANGELS AND THE REDEEMED (Rev. 21-22)

Actually, this dispensation will never end. It will be eternal. Faithful angels (those that did not fall with Lucifer in the past) and resurrected saints will help God administer the affairs of the universe(s) from the earth which will be the eternal headquarters of God's government. This is what we call *"the new heaven and the new earth."* It also could be called the eternal future, the eternal perfect state, or the eternal sinless career of planet Earth. For it is to be an age of eternal ages, like an endless chain with endless links. It will last forever, world without end – eternal life. Hallelujah!

CHAPTER 10

Verse 1 gives God's intended order: *"Shem, Ham, and Japheth."*

However, the 2nd verse does not start with Shem as was the original order, but instead starts with Japheth. Why? Japheth means enlargement; consequently, because Shem forfeited his enlargement due to his rejection of the Lord Jesus Christ, Japheth's sons now practically govern the world. Ham's sons are degraded and oppressed. Shem means in the Hebrew, "Name of Renown." Out of Shem sprang Jesus, *"the Plant of Renown"* (Ezek. 34:29).

The pattern developed by the Holy Spirit from verse 1 to verse 2 (God's divine order being set aside because of failure) is an example of the Holy Spirit recording facts out of chronological order so He can make prominent a spiritual lesson.

The 8th verse mentions Nimrod. He is the central figure of this chapter. As well, the central city is Babylon, which he built. Nimrod and his city foreshadow the coming Antichrist and his city, which will as well be Babylon. Nimrod, incidentally, was a son of Ham, and not of Shem. As well, he quite possibly built the Tower of Babel. He was practically the king of the whole earth of that day.

The 9th verse records him as a *"mighty hunter."* This has nothing to do with hunting animals, but it does mean to make slaves of men. He did this *"before the Lord,"* in defiance of the Lord.

The 10th verse talks about the *"beginning of his kingdom."* It speaks of the beginning of empires among men and not necessarily divine institutions guaranteeing law and order among men. The achievements of these lawless tyrants taught men to revolt against divine laws and duly constituted authority. There were eight cities constituting the first two empires – Babylon and Assyria.

The 25th verse records a most interesting statement, *"For in his days was the earth divided."* This explains the word *"Peleg."* In his days, the earth was divided into continents and islands. Before this time (about 200 years before Abraham), it seems that the land mass of the earth was all in one section. Even though the information is extremely skimpy, it seems that a great upheaval took place at about this time and divided the continents. If one will look at a world map, one can see that the East coast of South America pretty well fits the coast of West Africa. This would well explain how individuals of over 4000 years ago came to be on islands, continents, etc. They were there before the land mass separated, and of course continued thereafter.

From the 32nd verse, we may conclude that the descendants of Japheth settled in the north, west, and east of Europe as well as Asia, that Ham's settled in Africa, and, ultimately, that Shem's settled in countries surrounding Palestine.

CHAPTER 11

Verse 1 speaks of *"one language and one speech."* What language was this? There is some small evidence that Hebrew was the original language of the whole earth. It is impressive that it was the language that God

NOTES

used to give His revelation of the Old Testament to man; likewise, it was the one Christ used when speaking to Paul concerning the New Covenant, although the Apostle knew Greek well (Acts 21:40; 22:2; 26:14).

The 2nd verse records the first planned rebellion against God. According to tradition, Nimrod headed this rebellion. It was *"in the land of Shinar"* (Babylon). Some scholars feel that this is the same area where the original Garden of Eden was located. It is ironic; it started here, and it will end here. The book of Revelation records the Antichrist making his debut from a rebuilt Babylon (Isa. 14:4). The events that have transpired in the Middle East in the recent past are the beginning of the end. God has His Prince (the Lord Jesus Christ) and His city (Jerusalem). Satan has his prince (Nimrod and later the Antichrist) as well as his city (Babylon). These opposing princes with their cities occupy most of the pages of the Bible – the closing pages of the Book revealing the triumph of Emmanuel and Jerusalem over Antichrist and Babylon. Satan's first emissary raised up after the flood to thwart the plan of God was Nimrod. The weapon he placed in Nimrod's hand was idolatry.

In the 4th verse, the words *"may reach unto heaven"* could probably be better translated "whose top was dedicated unto the heavens." There are actually no words in the Hebrew for "may reach." The top of the tower was to be dedicated to the Zodiac. The Zodiac's signs would be portrayed on the top as visible objects of worship. Up to this time, the whole race had only one language and one form of religion (evil). When God confounded their language, they began to disagree on religion and on other matters, branching off into sects and parties. A Babylonian description of the Tower of Babel, discovered in 1876, indicates there was a grand court 900 by 1156 feet and a smaller one 450 by 1056 feet, inside of which was a platform with walls about it, having four gates on each side.

In the center stood the tower with many small shrines at the base dedicated to various gods. The tower itself was about 300 feet high, with decreased width in stages from the lowest to the highest point. Each was square.

There is evidence that the tower was

finished, for the work was stopped on the city only. One ancient Babylonian tablet reads, *"The building of this illustrious tower offended the gods. In a night, they threw down what they had built. They scattered them abroad and made strange their speech. Their progress was impeded. They wept hot tears for Babylon."*

The 6th verse says that the ability of man to circumvent the will of God, bringing into existence powerful strategies to further their rebellion, has forced God oftentimes in human history to step in and confound their efforts. So, the Lord stepped in and confounded the efforts of man at the Tower of Babel.

The 9th verse calls it *"Babel,"* which means confusion. Man's efforts have always led to confusion and, thereby, to darkness. God's direction always leads to light.

The 10th verse records the beginning of the fulfillment of Noah's prophecies. It begins with Shem. From Shem would eventually come Abram and, ultimately, the Lord Jesus Christ. The early verses of the 11th chapter record man's efforts to establish himself in the earth and to make for himself a name.

Beginning with the 10th verse down through the 32nd verse, it shows God calling a man out of the earth – Abram – and giving him a name. Man said, *"Let us make us a name."* God said to Abraham, *"I will make thee a name."*

The 28th verse lets us know that Abram originally was an idolator (Josh. 24:2). He, as we, could lay no moral claim on God, because he was *"a Syrian ready to perish"* (Deut. 26:5).

CHAPTER 12

Verse 1 says, *"The Lord had said,"* referring to a past-tense action. From Acts 7:2, we learn that God first called Abram before he went to Haran. From Joshua 24:2, we learn that Terah and his family were idolators previous to this call. It was Terah that took Abram and others to go into Canaan. Terah seems to have become converted to Abram's God and desired to flee idolatry and persecution from his neighbors. In this case, Abram was not as disobedient as

NOTES

he is generally pictured. In this first verse, God repeats His call to Abram, which was first given in Ur of the Chaldees (Acts 7:3).

From verse 2, we learn of the great blessing that God gave to Abram. From Abram came the Jewish nation. It gave the world "the Word of God" and, above all, "the Messiah, the Son of the Living God."

In verse 3, there is a blessing and a curse. God will bless those that bless Israel and curse those that curse Israel. Truly, all the families of the earth have been blessed in the coming of the Lord Jesus Christ as the Saviour of mankind. What a blessing, the greatest that has ever been given to any one human being!

The 4th verse says that *"Abram departed."* This was his first surrender. There were to be five in all.

1. His native land.
2. The veil of Jordan.
3. The riches of Sodom.
4. Ishmael.
5. Isaac.

Each painful surrender was followed by increased spiritual wealth. Abram's experience as he departed out of Haran to go into the promised land is a picture of the Christian experience. The sinner believes (leaves Haran – the world) and is saved. Into the "land of Canaan" he comes. This is the first step in the life of faith.

The 6th verse says, *"The Canaanite was in the land."* This is the promised land, and, yet, the hostile Canaanite is there. This was faith's first trial. If it was God's land, how could the Canaanite be in God's land? So, in this present day, the young believer believes that after his conversion he will find nothing in his nature hostile to Christ, but is distressed and perplexed very soon to painfully learn that, alas, the Canaanite is in the land and that he is now commencing a life-long battle with what the New Testament calls "the flesh." However, if the Canaanite is in the land, so also is the Lord.

The 7th verse says that *"the Lord appeared unto Abram."* Notice, the Holy Spirit said that the Lord appeared immediately after the recognition of the Canaanite in the land. Incidentally, the promised land was originally named after Canaan, the son of Ham. Abram was *in* the land, but not *of* it. We, as Christians, are *in* this world but not *of* it. Abram built an altar; he was ever an altar builder. The altar was a type of the crucifixion of Christ. It is also a type of the crucifixion of self. God said, *"Unto thy seed will I give this land."* Satan has contested that promise every foot of the way. It is being contested even unto today. But, ultimately, the promise of God shall prevail.

The 8th verse says that Abram moved to a mountain on the east of Beth-el. He had Beth-el on the west and Hai on the east, and there built an altar. This passage tells us something.

Beth-el means "the house of God." Hai means "garbage dump." In this passage, we have a slight glimmer of the direction of the gospel for coming generations. Beth-el was the house of God; Hai represented the world. The gospel eventually went west to Europe, hence, to England and, ultimately, to America. It has to this day made scant inroads to the east. Abram called upon the name of the Lord (Covenant God). He was the only man in the world of that day that was calling on the Lord. As well, narrow is the way, and few there be that find it.

The 10th verse tells us of a famine in the promised land. It was no doubt a mystery to Abram then, as well as to us now, that there could be the Canaanite and a famine in God's chosen land. How could these things be? Why do we have the flesh in the midst of our Christian experience? God always tests faith. Soon after we enter upon the path of faith comes the test, that is a famine. The temptation is always to go to Egypt. As Abram failed, most of us fail as well. However, we will see in this great test of faith that oftentimes the real definition of faith is in the failures rather than the victories. Faith has its failures exactly as doubt does. The difference in faith and doubt is this: doubt quits; faith never quits. It may fall on its face, but it will get up, dust itself off and proceed forward toward the goal outlined by the Holy Spirit.

Even though Abram little understood, still, Satan is the author of this plan to defeat God. Through Abram's failure, he will come near to doing so. Oftentimes we, as Christians, little see or understand the big picture.

The 13th verse says that Abram, in Egypt, presented a repulsive picture of cowardice. To save himself, he denied his wife and placed her in the home of another man to be his wife.

Selfishness is the opposite of Christlikeness.

The 15th verse says that Sarai was taken into Pharaoh's house. Satan's plan in causing the famine was to cause Abram to flee the promised land to Egypt. Satan would induce Pharaoh to take Sarai into his harem. Out of the harem would be selected the most beautiful women in order to produce a possible heir to the throne of Egypt. Satan's plan was subtle, but potent. Satan, knowing that God had intended for Sarai to bring the promised seed (Isaac) into the world and ultimately the Saviour (the Lord Jesus Christ), would produce not a "man of God," but a "man of the world," with Pharaoh as his father. He came very close to succeeding.

The 17th verse says the Lord intervened and plagued Pharaoh. How many times has the Lord intervened to save us from the clutches of Satan? It was certainly through no moral excellence of Abram that he was saved from this terrible dilemma. It was grace that protected Abram. Likewise, no moral greatness has saved any of us, but the grace of God. In the land of promise, Abram was a blessing; in Egypt, he was a plague. Likewise, in the Christian walk, the child of God is "salt" and "light." In a backslidden condition, he is only a plague to the world.

In verses 18 through 20, Pharaoh keeps asking "Why?" The question, "Why?" has ever been asked. The answer is the weak, failing, flawed flesh of stumbling, trembling humanity.

CHAPTER 13

In Genesis 12:10, it says that Abram went *"down"* into Egypt; 13:1 says that Abram went *"up"* out of Egypt. Whenever the Christian reverts to the world, he truly goes "down" spiritually. When he comes back out of Egypt (the world) toward God, he truly goes "up" spiritually. Lot would come up with Abram out of Egypt; however, Egypt would take its toll on Lot. When he had a choice, it would be toward Sodom and Gomorrah, which was *"like the land of Egypt"* (verse 10). Something is always lost with our excursions away from God and into the world.

The 2nd verse records Abram being very rich. However, all of his money and worldly goods could not bring back the peace of mind that he had lost in Egypt. That could only come by the altar (Calvary).

So, the 3rd verse says that he goes back to the place of *"the beginning."* Many Christians desperately need to go back and do their *"first works"* over again.

The 4th verse says, *"unto the place of the altar."* That is the only place for the Christian; no other place will do. – There, doubtless with tears and shame, he called by sacrifice on the name of the Lord. His backslidings were forgiven; his soul was restored. He resumed his true life as a pilgrim and a worshiper with his tent and his altar, neither of which he had in Egypt, for he built no altar in Egypt.

Egypt had taken its toll on Lot, so the 7th verse says, *"There was strife."* The Holy Spirit brings out the fact of the Canaanite and the Perizzite, all heathen, that observed this strife. How so much the world looks on and observes the strife in Christendom. How so much it hinders the testimony.

The 8th verse tells us that the plea of the Holy Spirit is *"Let there be no strife."* And the reason? *"For we are brethren."* And, yet, regrettably, strife is probably one of the cardinal sins of the church.

The separation demanded in the 9th verse had already been demanded by God in 12:1. Abram was not only to get out of his country (Ur of the Chaldees), but as well from *"thy kindred."* Now, this command is finally to be obeyed.

The 10th verse says that Lot, seeing with the *"eyes of carnality,"* selects that which resembles Egypt. He receives only a few acres. How so much the church does the same. Abram looks with the *"eyes of faith,"* and he receives everything.

There were six steps in Lot's downfall. First, he *"strove"* (13:7); second, he *"beheld"* (13:10); third, he *"chose"* (13:11); fourth, he *"pitched toward Sodom"* (13:12); fifth, he *"dwelt in Sodom"* (14:12); and last, he *"sat in the gates of Sodom"* (19:1). This records the downward steps of any child of God who trades the "faith

NOTES

walk" for the "sight walk."

The 13th verse tells us that the Lord was very displeased with Lot's choice. It says, *"The men of Sodom were wicked and sinners before the Lord exceedingly."* The Holy Spirit is telling righteous Lot that he will compromise his righteous testimony. The Lord was pleased with the separation, but not with its direction.

Beginning with the 14th verse and after the command of God to separate from his kindred was obeyed, God gives Abram a tremendous promise.

1. *He promises to give to Abram and his seed the whole of the promised land.* Strangely enough, Abram never really personally owned any of it except for his burial place. However, God will keep that promise. One day in the millennial reign, Abram will, in essence, "own it all." At this particular time, powerful forces are striving to take part, if not all, of the land from Israel. However, they will not succeed. For God said, *"To thy seed forever."*

2. *An innumerable people.* Actually, that promise given in the 16th verse has not yet been fulfilled. There is a total of approximately 10 million Jews in the world today, with only about four million being in Israel. (There are over 100 million Arabs.) As well, this promise will be ultimately fulfilled in the millennial reign and thereafter.

Once again, it is much better to let God choose than for the Christian to choose. Lot lifts up his eyes in *self-will* and obtains a few acres; Abram lifts up his eyes in self-denial and is given the whole land.

The 18th verse records that Abram, evidently moved upon by the Holy Spirit, moved his tent (a pilgrim) and dwelt in Hebron. The Bible says, *"And built there an altar unto the Lord."* Abram was a pilgrim and an altar builder. The Christian, likewise, is a pilgrim and an altar builder (Calvary). The moment we, as Christians, try to set our affections on the things of this world (cease to be a pilgrim), we lose our way exactly as Lot lost his way. That which we try to hold to, we lose. That which we give away, we keep. Such is the way of the pilgrim and the altar builder (Christ and Him crucified).

CHAPTER 14

The "Amraphel" of verse 1 is probably Hammurabi, King of Babylon, who was a celebrated warrior, builder, and law giver of the famous Babylonian code of laws for regulating courts of justice and daily life of his subjects.

The 2nd verse records the first war on record. No doubt many were fought before this. There was a war between the opposing forces of the world. Righteous Lot, having abdicated his pilgrim walk with God, is caught by demon forces. The end result of the wayward Christian can only be the same as wayward Lot.

Verses 5 through 7 record that the giants (offspring of the sons of God and the daughters of men) now inhabit the promised land. They are the *"Rephaims,"* the *"Zuzims,"* and the *"Emims."* Two opposing evil forces fight each other. They are trying to "save the society." Regrettably, the church spends most of its time and energy trying to "save the society," when, in fact, the society is doomed (II Tim. 3:1). Instead, God has called us to save men *"out of society."*

As a result of Lot's compromise, the 12th verse records that Lot was *"taken."* The Holy Spirit records that he is Abram's brother's son. It says he *"dwelt in Sodom."* Lot could deliver neither Sodom nor himself. Abram could deliver both. The only way to help and bless the world is to live apart from it in fellowship with God. But genuine separation from the world can only result from true fellowship with God. Isolation is not separation. Isolation chills; separation warms. Isolation makes self the center; separation makes Christ the center. Isolation produces indifference to the need of others; separation fills the heart with love and interest for the needy and perishing. As soon, then, as Abram hears of the captivity of his relative, he immediately sets out to save him. Such is the energy of love. Abram's was the faith that not only overcomes the world, but that works by love. Such is the nature of divine faith; it purifies the heart; it rescues the perishing.

Verses 13 through 16 record the perfect "type" of restoration (Gal. 6:1). Lot had been

NOTES

taken by the enemy. When Abram heard that his brother was taken captive (verse 14), he did what was necessary to rescue him.

The 16th verse says he brought back all the goods as well as Lot and all that were with him. What a lesson for the church. Love does not gloat over the fall of a fellow brother. Neither does it remember the past *"strife"* (13:7). They that are spiritual are commanded by the Holy Spirit to restore the one that is fallen, remembering that they, as well, may need restoration tomorrow.

The 17th verse records that a time of great danger (temptation) came to Abram immediately after a great victory. There is no time so dangerous to the Christian as the morrow after a great spiritual victory. Actually, Abram won two victories, one over the King of Elam and the other over the King of Sodom. The victory over the King of Sodom was far greater than the victory over the King of Elam. Abram pursued the King of Elam to rescue Lot, but the King of Sodom now pursues Abram.

At this intersection of the 18th verse, the Holy Spirit records the intervention of Melchizedek, King of Salem (Jerusalem), who was a type of Christ. Melchizedek, recognizing the danger which threatens Abram, steps between him and the oncoming temptation and makes a fresh revelation of God to his soul. At times, Abram failed. At this time, praise God, he did not. It should be noted that no man-made priest has power to step between man and God. However, the Melchizedek priest, who was a type of Christ, alone could do this. Today, Jesus Christ is our great High Priest. As well, all saints are recognized as priests of God. God recognizes no other priest, appointed by man, who serves as a mediator between man and God.

Who was Melchizedek? Some Bible scholars have suggested that possibly Melchizedek was Shem. We know that he was alive at this time and actually lived 60 years longer. He died when Abram was 150 years of age.

The 20th verse records the first example of paying tithe. However, it seems that the tithe paying may have started with Abel. The Scripture says that Abel brought to the Lord *"the firstlings of his flock"* (Gen. 4:4), with the word *"firstlings"* referring to the *"tithe,"* or tenth.

Salem (or Jerusalem) where Melchizedek (possibly Shem) dwelt, is mentioned 807 times in Scripture. Earthly Jerusalem has undergone 30 sieges, of which 12 are recorded in Scripture. It was the capital of Israel from David's time until Nebuchadnezzar (II Sam. 5 – II Chron. 36) and became the capital of restored Israel in the days of Ezra and Nehemiah (Ezra 1:2; Neh. 13:20). It was totally destroyed in A.D. 70 when Israel was scattered among the nations the second time (St. Luke 21:20-24). It will become the capital of the new, modern Israel before the days of Antichrist when he will conquer Israel and make Jerusalem his capital for the last three and one-half years of this age (Rev. 11:1-2). It is God's chosen place for the capital of His earthly kingdom under the Messiah (II Chron. 6:6; Isa. 2:1-4; Jer. 17:25; Joel 3:20; Zech. 14:1-21). Jerusalem will be the center of the Battle of Armageddon (Zech. 14; Rev. 19). As well, present-day Jerusalem will ultimately be replaced by the New Jerusalem that will come down from God out of heaven (Rev. 21, 22).

The 23rd verse records that Abram would not even take a thread or a shoelace from the King of Sodom. What a lesson for modern-day Christendom. The Apostle Paul says, *"Come out from among them."*

CHAPTER 15

It is not clear how much time has passed from the military victory won in the 14th chapter to the *"after these things"* in verse 1. This we do know: Abram had come to the place of fear. It seems the fear was regarding the promise God had given him in 12:1. Both he and Sarai had passed the age of child-bearing. In his mind, he cannot understand how God can bring this promise to pass. God promises Abram two things: to be a *"shield"* unto him (a shield from the powers of darkness) and the *"guarantor"* of his *"exceeding great reward."* Unfortunately, the Holy Spirit must reinforce the promises that He gives to us. Weak flesh must be constantly reinforced.

In the 2nd verse, Abram feels that the stew-

ard of his house, "Eliezer," will be the heir.

As in verse 1, verse 4 as well reinforces to Abram God's previous covenant with him by using the name "Lord," which means "Covenant God." Emphatically, he is told that Eliezer would *not* be the heir, but that the heir would come forth from Abram himself. So, with this promise, Abram now knows that he will father the child. However, nothing is said about Sarai. So the 16th chapter will record Sarai's effort's to "help God."

The 5th verse records the promise of God to Abram by instituting another "look." Four times the Lord told Abram to look: "over the earth" (13:14); "toward heaven" (15:5); "at Jehovah" (18:2); "at a substitute" (22:13).

The 6th verse records that Abram believed God. The Lord directed Abram's look away from his own dead body (too old to bear children) and to look toward the stars, believing what God said. He believed God, and the Lord declared him a righteous man (Rom. 4; Gal. 3). Why did God declare him righteous in regard to this simple obedience?

Because through Abram's heir (the coming Isaac) would directly come the Saviour of all mankind, the Lord Jesus Christ. So, Abram was saying, in effect, "I don't understand it all, but I believe it."

The faith that is required of the sinner now is identical to the faith that was required of Abram. The sinner little understands what God demands, but the moment he believes God's testimony about His beloved Son, he is not only declared righteous, but he is made a son and an heir. This is the foundation of the faith (St. John 3:16).

Verses 1 through 6 record the *"sonship"* of salvation. Verses 7 and 8 will record the *"heirship."* In fact, Abram owned none of the promised land at the time of his death. At the time of the Christian's death, likewise, he has not yet inherited that which is promised. His soul and spirit will instantly go to be with the Lord Jesus Christ, with his body awaiting the first resurrection of eternal life. At that time the heirship will then be complete.

The 9th verse records five living creatures to be sacrificed to establish the Covenant. Five is the number of grace. As well, Jesus is given five names in Isaiah 9:6. There is a five-fold calling of ministry to the Church (Eph. 4:11). Also, there were five support posts at the front of Moses' tabernacle. Furthermore, there were five great offerings in the Levitical Law. The terrible blood-letting of these sacrifices was a picture of the coming horror of Calvary. Our salvation was not purchased cheaply.

The 10th verse records the division of the heifer, goat, and ram, telling us that sin is not just a surface problem; it is a problem that goes to the very core of man's being. As well, Jesus suffered five major wounds at the crucifixion – the thorns, the plucking of his beard, lashing of the whip, thrusting of the spear, and the driving of the nails.

The fowls of the 11th verse represent the demon forces of hell that sought to hinder the crucifixion. (Psa. 22).

The deep sleep and horror of great darkness recorded in the 12th verse speak of the suffering of the heirs of promise that comes to every believer, *"If we suffer with him, we shall reign with him"* (II Tim. 2:12).

Verses 13 through 16 predict that Abram's seed would be sojourners for 400 years more, that Egypt would be punished for enslaving Israel, that Israel would become rich, that Abram would live long, and that his seed would come out of Egypt in the fourth generation to defeat the Amorites. All of the prophecy was fulfilled in the exodus and settlement of Canaan under Moses and Joshua (Ex. 7:1; 14:28). The actual sojourn of Abram's seed in Egypt was only 215 years. The 400 years of Genesis 15:13 and Acts 7:6 date back to the time when Isaac was weaned and confirmed as the seed, and Ishmael was cast out.

Other Scriptures speak of the entire period being 430 years (Ex. 12:40; Gal. 3:14-17). The entire 430 years reckons from Abram's call (Gen. 12:1-4) to the exodus from Egypt (Ex. 12:40).

The 17th verse records the smoking furnace and the burning lamp. The furnace of fire that passed between the parted sacrifices expressed the burning trials that the sons of the Kingdom must suffer at the hands of Satan and men. However, the lamp of fire symbolizes the perpetual presence and sustaining grace of the Spirit of God in these trials.

In the 18th verse, the Lord says, *"I have*

given thee this land." Previously, He had said, *"I will give thee this land."* Promises based upon the precious Blood of Christ are so absolutely sure that faith can claim them as already possessed. Hence, the believer in the Lord Jesus Christ is neither ashamed nor afraid to say, "I am saved."

Verses 19 through 21 record the various peoples that occupied the promised land. They were types of hindrances to our Christian walk, such as "jealousy, envy, malice, pride, etc." As victory was promised over these "enemies," likewise, victory is promised to the Christian as well.

CHAPTER 16

In Genesis 15:4, the Lord had told Abram that Isaac would be born from Abram's seed. The 6th verse says that *"he believed in the Lord."* However, his faith was not perfect. Evidently, he thought this promise did not include Sarai. So, now the both of them will proceed to "help" God. How much we get into trouble when we use the flesh to "help" the Spirit.

The 2nd verse records Sarai's faithlessness. From the term she uses, *"The Lord hath restrained me from bearing,"* it seems that Sarai, very well aware of God's promise to Abram, resented the supposed fact that she was not included; at least that was her thought. Now, her faith breaks down completely, and she concocts a scheme to "help the Lord." How much trouble are we in today because of our "helping the Lord"? Most of the problems of the Church world are found in this 2nd verse. We assume we know what God has said, when in reality, we don't.

The 3rd verse records that ten years have passed with Abram in the land of Canaan and still no heir. So, the "flesh" can neither believe nor wait for a divine promise. The path of faith is full of dignity; the path of unbelief full of degradation. Abram joins in with Sarai's unbelief despite the fact that chapter 15 verse 6 records the greatest statement of faith to that date ever uttered. But now he wavers. So is the pilgrim journey. Sadly, it is checkered with victory and defeat. So now, Abram, finding that God has failed to give him a son and tired of waiting, no longer sets his hope upon God, but upon an Egyptian slave girl. The natural heart will trust anything rather than God. This clever plan, they think, will bring to pass the divine promise; the result is misery. He succeeds in his plan, as so often we do. Ishmael is born, but better were it for Abram and the world had he never been born. It is disastrous when the self-willed plans of the Christian succeed.

The Epistle to the Galatians declares that Sarai and Hagar represent the two principles of law and grace. Hagar represents a false salvation by works; Sarai, the true salvation by faith (despite Sarai's failure). These principles are diametrically opposed to one another. Ishmael is born as the result of man's planning and energy. Isaac is born as the result of God's planning and energy. In the birth of Ishmael, God did nothing. In the birth of Isaac, God did it all. So it is today; salvation by works depends entirely on man's capacity to produce them; salvation by faith upon God's ability to perform them. Under the covenant of works, God stands still in order to see what man can do (which is nothing). Under the covenant of grace, man stands still to see what God has done. The two covenants are opposed; it must be either Hagar or Sarai. If it is Hagar, God will have nothing to do with it; if it is Sarai, man will have nothing to do with it.

At the time of this test of faith, Abram was 86 years old, some 14 years before Isaac was born.

The 4th verse tells us how the flesh despises the Spirit. The 5th and 6th verses record the conflict that always ensues as a result of a work of the flesh.

Despite Hagar's hatred of Sarai, grace, in respect to the angel of the Lord, found her by a fountain of water in the wilderness.

The 8th verse records the angel of the Lord asking Hagar, *"Whence camest thou?"*

God not only raises questions, but offers a solution for them. He always asks men to do the best thing, though it may be the hardest to do. Hagar did submit, but was cast out of Abram's home when Ishmael was about 19 years old (17:24-25). This is the event referred to in the allegory of Galatians 4:21-31, which

proves that the law of Moses has been abolished, that the old covenant has been cast out, and that the new covenant has now taken the place of the old.

The 10th verse has been fulfilled exceedingly so. Today, there are over 100 million Arabs, all descendants of Ishmael.

The 12th verse depicts the nature of Ishmael and his descendants to this day.

At this juncture, Hagar, and later Ishmael, could have known the great blessings of God. But, instead, this "work of the flesh" refused to submit totally as God demanded (vs. 9). This refusal to obey has resulted in a false way of salvation by route of a false prophet (Mohammed) and a false Bible (the Koran).

CHAPTER 17

The last verse of chapter 16 closes with the Holy Spirit telling us that Abram was 86 years old. It opens with the 1st verse of chapter 17 by informing us that Abram was 99 – a difference of 13 years. What happened during those 13 years? This 13 years of silence just may have been Abram's hardest test. God did not speak; there was no direction. Had the sin with Hagar written "finish" between God and Abram? The answer is a resounding "no." The first thing that God tells Abram is, *"I am the Almighty God."* The Hebrew is "El Shaddai." El signifies "the Strong One" and Shaddai," the Breasted One." This pictures God as the Strong-Nourisher, Strength-Giver, Satisfier, and All-Bountiful, the Supplier of the needs of His people. Its first occurrence here reveals God as the Fruitful One who was to multiply Abram abundantly; the Life-Giver who was to restore life to Abram and Sarai who were as good as dead as far as offspring were concerned. Through Him, they were to have future offspring as the dust, as the stars, and as the sand in number.

Then God demands that Abram be *perfect.* The word *"perfect"* here means "guileless." That is, God says, "be simple, leave all to Me, let Me plan for you, I am Almighty. No longer scheme to beget an Ishmael, but trust Me to give an Isaac." This is the meaning of *"perfect"* in this passage.

The 4th verse records that the great promise of 12:1-4 is enlarged.

The 5th verse records the name change from Abram to Abraham. Abram meant "exalted father," whereas Abraham means "father of a multitude." God changed his name from exhaltation to humility. Incidentally, Abraham's name change was a part of the covenant.

The 6th verse speaks of kings that would come from Abraham. One of those kings, which would be "the King," would be the Lord Jesus Christ. What an honor!

The 7th verse says that the covenant would be everlasting.

The 8th verse tells us that the land of Canaan would be a part of that "everlasting possession." From that time, Satan has tried to abrogate that covenant. The contest continues even unto today regarding the West Bank of Israel. It will be intensified in the not-too-distant future when the Antichrist signs his seven-year nonaggression pact with Israel. Then, in the middle of the seven-year tribulation period, he will break his covenant and attack Israel, transferring his headquarters from rebuilt Babylon to Jerusalem. Israel, by and large, has become faithless regarding the *"everlasting possession."* Jesus, she would not accept; *"another,"* she would (St. John 5:43). She will find that God keeps His covenants. She will also find that Satan does not keep his.

Verses 9 through 14 give the external sign of the covenant. The sign will be circumcision, which would be a sign of separation. Three classes were to be circumcised:

A. All male children of Israelites,

B. All male servants and children,

C. All males of foreigners in Israel.

The little boy babies were to be circumcised on the eighth day.

The words *"cut off"* in the 14th verse meant "cut off by death." The manner of death is not stated. One was simply under the sentence of death if he willfully neglected the sign of the covenant. It is evident that the letter of the law was not carried out, for children were not circumcised in the wilderness (Joshua 5:2-10).

The 15th verse records the change of Sarai's

NOTES

name to Sarah. Sarai means "princess." Sarah means "queen of princesses."

Whereas, the 15th chapter (vs. 4) records the great promise to Abraham, now the promise includes Sarah. Why did the Lord separate these two promises by a time span of at least 13 years and possibly more? Of course, it would be impossible to go into the mind of God to determine every reason. However, this we do know. It was a test of faith for both Abraham and Sarah. So much that happens to us in this life's journey is, in fact, a test of faith.

The laughter of Abraham recorded in the 17th verse was not the laughter of unbelief, but of faith. Romans chapter 4 bears that out. It was the joyful laughter of a worshiper when Abraham fell upon his face. The Lord Jesus Himself in St. John 8:56 no doubt pointed to this occasion when He said that Abraham rejoiced to see His day and was glad. The latter part of the 17th verse is only an exclamation of faith. It was not a question of unbelief.

Likewise, the exclamation of Abraham concerning Ishmael was one of faith as well. He was not praying that Ishmael would be the child of promise, but it was a cry of faith that Ishmael might receive some measure of divine blessing.

In the 19th verse, God tells Abraham what the name of this promised child will be, Isaac. His name means "laughter." It would seem from the context that the name was given in derision because of Abraham and Sarah's laughter. However, as we have stated, this was not the case at all. The laughter of this miracle child would be the laughter of pure joy that accompanies a converted soul. Jesus said it in St. John 10:10, *"I am come that they might have life and that they might have it more abundantly."* The *"everlasting covenant"* would culminate in the Lord Jesus Christ, the Son of the Living God. His life-giving properties would be eternal.

The 20th verse records God's answer concerning Ishmael. He would have 12 sons (princes). From him would spring the great Arab people.

The 21st verse records the emphatic claim of God concerning Isaac. The covenant would be with Isaac, not Ishmael. Satan has fought that covenant ever since. Because of this covenant, the world has enjoyed great blessing. Even though Israel rebelled against God and rejected the Lord Jesus Christ, still, her contribution to society has been phenomenal. Israel is the fountain-head of the Word of God given to holy men of old. From it springs the only light that mankind knows. And, if possible, even above that, Israel was the womb of the Messiah, the Lord Jesus Christ. Truly, as God promised Abraham in the beginning (chapter 12), he would be a "blessing" to the whole of the human family. As well, so much of the great strides in the advancement of medicine, engineering, and scientific achievements has come from the Jewish mind — because of the covenant established with Abraham, Isaac, and Jacob. Even though the world little knows it or realizes it, a debt of gratitude is ever owed by the Gentiles to the Jewish people.

Verses 23 through 27 record the instant obedience of Abraham regarding the command of circumcision.

Circumcision is a compound Latin word meaning to "cut around," removing the foreskin.

The epistles to the Romans, the Galatians, and the Colossians teach that Christians are to be circumcised in the heart at the cross of Christ, baptized into the death of Christ, and raised in the Resurrection of Christ.

Circumcision was to be a physical sign to the children of Israel that they were people of God and not of the world. As stated, it was a sign of separation.

It seems from Abraham's day to Moses that the practice somewhat waned. When the Law was given to Moses at Mount Sinai, circumcision would be a strong part of the Mosaic ritual.

It holds no command in the New Testament and is not a part of the New Covenant. However, from a health point of view, it is no doubt an excellent practice. The little boy baby should be circumcised when he is 8 days old, that particular day being specified as being physically the best because of the body chemistry of the new-born child.

NOTES

CHAPTER 18

The 1st verse appears to be a preincarnate appearance of Christ. With Him were two angels.

From verses 3, 4, and 5, it would seem that Abraham knew that one of these three individuals, addressed as *"three men,"* was the Lord. The seeming familiarity stems only from the fellowship and experience of the past nearly 25 years.

Verses 6 through 8 pertain to the meal that Abraham prepared for the Lord and the two angels. It seems incongruous to some that God and angels would eat. However, God and angels eat even in heaven, so why not on earth? (Psa. 78:25; St. Luke 22:16,18; Acts 10:41; Heb. 13:2; Exod. 24:11). These passages mean exactly what they say. One of the great promises of Christ to His disciples, to be fulfilled after their bodies have been resurrected and glorified, pertains to eating. St. Luke 22:30 says, *"That ye may eat and drink at my table in my kingdom."*

After the nearly 25 years of promise, now the time for the birth of Isaac is given. The promise had been given, even the name of the child had been given by God (17:19), and now the date the child will be born is given.

The 11th verse says that both Abraham and Sarah were past the age of child-bearing. Why did God wait so long? There were no doubt many reasons. Faith had to be tested. However, the main reason is that the flesh had to die completely before the Spirit could gain ascendancy. The Scripture uses these terms, *"old and well-stricken in age; and it ceased to be with Sarah after the manner of women."* The greatest hindrance to the child of God is the flesh. If we walk after the flesh, we shall die (Rom. 8). If we walk after the Spirit, we shall live. During the last 24 years, so much had been attempted in the flesh. Now, when there is absolutely no possibility of the flesh bringing forth anything else, God steps in and gives the date. It is now none of the flesh and all of the Spirit. When one looks at verse 11, one is looking at the place and position that the Holy Spirit is attempting to bring the child of God.

Past the place of personal effort, God brings us until the flesh is *"well-stricken"* and *"ceases to be."* This was the battle that Abraham and Sarah fought; this is the battle that every child of God fights.

The laughter that was recorded in 17:17 was the laughter of faith. The laughter that is recorded here in verse 12 is the laughter of unbelief. Thinks Sarah, "It is impossible." Thinks Sarah right; it was impossible, but not with God. The problem of the church is twofold: the flesh and unbelief.

The answer to the flesh, as well as unbelief, is the question asked by the Lord, *"Is any thing too hard for the Lord?"* Even though it was a question, it was asked in the realm of a statement. Let the Church understand, "There is nothing too hard for the Lord."

The 16th verse says that the attention is now diverted from Sarah to Sodom. God rules in the affairs of men. Even though Sodom and Gomorrah are the only two cities that have been destroyed in the manner recorded (brimstone and fire), still, God has measured many cities and even countries for destruction. Because of the evil perpetuated by the Nazis in World War II, God measured their cities for destruction. It was summarily carried out. The same could be said for cities in Japan, as well as much of Europe. The manner in which it was carried out may have been different, but the author of destruction was God. A cruel act? No. It was the same as a medical doctor performing surgery on a patient removing a cancer. If the cancer is not removed, it will destroy the patient. Therefore, God performs major surgery on people, cities, and nations – and that from the very beginning of time.

In Genesis chapters 18 and 19, we are given a behind-the-scene observation into the manner of God's approach.

The 17th verse records that at times God will inform His prophets of His future plans. Abraham was a prophet (Gen. 20:7).

The "knowing of Abraham" given in the 19th verse is the result of the "test of faith." God commands the same of us today, that we command our children and household after the ways of God. Can He say of us as He said of Abraham, *"for I know him"*? No wonder

Abraham was called *"the friend of God."*

The 20th verse tells us that there is a difference in sin. All sin is grievous in God's eyes; however, some sin is worse than other sin (St. John 19:11). Some have felt that the sin of sodomy is at least one of the most grievous sins that a person could commit. This we do know. It is the only sin that God has taken such a hand that He would blot two cities off the face of the earth until there is no trace left. Even for the sin of sodomy, if a person will repent, God will forgive, cleanse, and justify (I Cor. 6:11). However, it must be understood that God does not save a person *in* sodomy, or drunkenness, or adultery, etc., but *from* these particular sins. It is not possible for an individual to remain in these sins and at the same time be saved (Gal. 5:19-21).

The 21st verse tells us that God is a God of judgment as well as of mercy and grace. However, His judgment is always tempered with mercy. He will search and seek to find a way to keep from destroying these cities. Every act of God is redemptive. It is never punitive. Even with grievous wickedness such as that which characterized Sodom and Gomorrah, God would search for a way to avoid judgment. Even when that way could not be found, the act of God in carrying out judgment against these twin cities was, in fact, an act of mercy for the rest of civilization. If this cancer had been allowed to continue, it would have been a terribly destructive force on humanity.

The 22nd verse says that the two angels went on toward Sodom, but the Lord lingered back with Abraham.

The 23rd verse records the power of righteous intercession. Abraham pressed the issue, asking that the cities not be destroyed if 50 righteous could be found. He presses his point even down to ten. The Holy Spirit was pleased with the type of intercession that Abraham offered. We know this because of the positive position in which Abraham's intercession was placed. With intercession of this nature, much could be changed in this world.

The 32nd verse tells us of the premium that God places on the righteous that are found in any area, when we realize that the grievously wicked cities of Sodom and Gomorrah would have been spared if there had only been *ten* righteous people in the city. Jesus called us *"salt"* and *"light"* (St. Matt. 5:13-14).

Even though the 32nd verse does not give us total details concerning all of the communing of the Lord with Abraham, still, we know that Abraham's intercession saved Lot. It seems that because of his intercession, the Lord would pull Lot and his family (if they would come) out of the city. Truly, His mercy endureth forever.

CHAPTER 19

The principle of evil, which the Bible calls "sin" and which has wrought such ruin in human nature, painfully appears in this chapter. The portrayal of Sodom in the 19th chapter is quite a contrast to the portrayal of Abraham in chapter 18. If the Christian looks at chapters 18 and 19, he receives a panoramic view of, first of all, the burden of the child of God (chapter 18) to rescue the perishing and care for the dying. As he looks at chapter 19, he sees the horror of a world that has forgotten God days without number and the judgment of God upon its sin and ungodliness.

The 1st verse records two angels visiting Sodom at evening. I wonder how many angels have visited cities since that day. Some have come for glory (St. Luke 2:8-9), and some have come for judgment.

Lot is not mentioned by the Holy Spirit from the time he chose the plain in 13:10-13 until now. Here he is seen in the gate of Sodom, quite possibly representing a position of high office. (The events of the great victory by Abraham, as recorded in chapter 14, probably placed Lot in a very exalted position in the eyes of the King of Sodom.) Even though in Lot's and Sodom's eyes he had come "up" in the world, still, the Holy Spirit took no notice of it. Actually, in the eyes of God, Lot, even though retaining his righteous outlook (II Peter 2:7-9), still suffered terrible spiritual deterioration.

The 18th chapter records no reluctance whatsoever on the part of the Lord and two angels to have fellowship with Abraham. However, there seems to be great reluctance on

NOTES

the part of the angels to abide with Lot. What a lesson in contrasts. Is our conduct such that the angels would desire to be with us, or would they rather desire to shun us?

Verses 4 and 5 record the fact that the evil of Sodom had become so great that any visitor was prey. The words *"that we may know them,"* speak of the homosexual act.

Homosexuality, as drunkenness, adultery, stealing, etc., is not a sickness, disease, or hereditary condition. In other words, no homosexual is born a homosexual. Homosexuality is a perversion, a sin. No homosexual, as no drunkard, adulterer, etc. that continues in this sin can be saved. God does not save *in* sin, He saves *from* sin.

James said that no man could blame his temptation on God (James 1:13) – in other words, that he was born that way. Perversion and sin occur when the individual, even as a child, is tempted, drawn away of his own lust, and enticed. Homosexuality is an acquired perversion. Sodomy in the Bible is absolutely forbidden (Exod. 22:19; Lev. 18:22; 20:13; Deut. 23:17; I Cor. 6:9-10; I Tim. 1:10; Isa. 1:19; 3:9; Judg. 19:22; Rom. 1:18-32). However, there is forgiveness, cleansing, and mercy for the homosexual, as well as the drunk, drug-addict, adulterer, etc., if they will only turn to Christ (St. John 3:16).

The 7th verse says that Lot calls the Sodomites, *"brethren."* Compromise is the road to destruction, yet it is the sin of the church. How many do we call *"brethren"* that are, in reality, in the same posture as the Sodomites?

The 8th verse hints that Lot may not have known at this time that the two men were angels. However, whatever conversation he has had with them lets him know that they are godly. Whatever knowledge he has, he is willing to sacrifice his two daughters. How many Christians today are sacrificing their children because of their having lived too close to the world?

The 13th chapter says that Lot moved his tent toward Sodom. Now, Sodom moves toward his tent.

The 9th verse lends some credence to the fact that Lot had gained prominence (sat in the gate). As long as he judged in their favor, there was little problem. But now his judgment is against them, and they *"pressed sore upon the man."* Sin, regrettably, will break down the door.

Verses 10 and 11 record an act of intervention by God. How many wayward Christians or wayward sons and daughters, for that matter, have been pulled into the safety of the house by angels because of an intercessor such as Abraham? How many of us today are saved by the Blood of Jesus because the Lord personally intervened and "blinded" those that would destroy us?

In the 12th verse, the appeal is given to save the entire family. But such was the testimony that none would be saved. We are given no information concerning Lot's sons. Evidently, they were homosexuals as well as most of the other men in the city. That his sons-in-law chose to remain is clear. It seems that they were only espoused to his two daughters and had not yet entered into marriage relationship with them. If they, in fact, had entered into the final marriage contract, then they perhaps lived with Lot's daughters in name only. This is done among Sodomites, as is stated in Romans 1:27, which says, *"The men, leaving the natural use of the woman, burned in their lust one toward another; men with men."*

The 13th verse says, *"We will destroy this place."* This world is headed toward destruction. It is called *"the Great Tribulation"* (St. Matt. 24:21). Simon Peter pictures the destruction of Sodom and Gomorrah as of the coming judgment (II Pet. 2:4-6). He pictures just Lot as being delivered, as by the Rapture, from these wicked cities (II Pet. 2:7-9). As the angels at Sodom prepare to destroy these two cities, as well, the angels of the book of Revelation are preparing to destroy planet Earth. As near as the destruction was in verse 13, so near is the destruction now. As the angels were telling Lot and all with him, *"Bring them out of this place,"* likewise, the Holy Spirit is saying the same to the Church today.

Verse 14 records the scoffing of Lot's sons-in-law, much the same way the scoffers of II Peter 3:3-4 are predicted to receive teaching about Christ's coming in the last days.

In the 15th verse, the angels hastened Lot. Likewise, the Holy Spirit is hastening us today.

The 16th verse proclaims the mercy of God.

Still, He lingers. The attraction of the world has a powerful pull, even in the face of certain destruction. The prayer of Abraham is being answered.

The 17th verse denotes the place of escape, which was to be the mountain. He (Lot) seems to prefer his own place of safety to that proposed by the angels. All of this illustrates the deep unbelief of his heart. Living in Sodom had given him a distaste for the mountain proposed by the angels, so he pleads for permission to settle down in Zoar. He would not heed the angel's demand and would, thereby, reap the results of his folly.

The 20th verse records the amazement of an individual that would think a "little sin" is satisfactory. (Zoar was slated for destruction as well as Sodom and Gomorrah.)

The 21st verse tells us that the angels accepted Lot's demand. However, he received leanness of soul (Psa. 106:15).

Verse 22 gives us an example of man hindering and delaying the work of God. The incapacity of God is not from lack of power, but of will. The purpose of mercy *must* precede that of judgment. Likewise, God cannot send judgment upon this world until the Church is taken out in the Rapture (II Thess. 6-8).

Verses 23 through 25 describe Jehovah raining burning brimstone from Jehovah out of heaven. (Incidentally, the two Jehovahs tend toward the Trinity.) Jesus mentioned the judgment of these cities in St. Matthew 10:15.

Lot's wife, in the 26th verse, was so attached to the world that she disobeyed the angel's command and *"looked back."* The "looking back" describes a longing for the sin of Sodom.

Verses 27 through 29 once again denote the fact that it was Abraham's intercession that rescued Lot. How many of us are safe today because an Abraham interceded for us?

The evil of Sodom had so ingratiated itself in the natures of Lot's daughters that they continued to pursue its disastrous conclusion. Drunkenness and incest are the result of the *"pitching of his tent toward Sodom."* The result of this incest is two children, with the first named "Moab," who was the father of the Moabites; the second was called "Benammi," who was the father of the children of Ammon. They were both begotten in shame; they both had a shameful history. Both were cursed (Deut. 23:3; Neh. 13:1; Isa. 11:14; Zeph. 2).

CHAPTER 20

The 20th chapter records the few months prior to the birth of Isaac. The "miracle child" is now in Sarah's womb. And, regrettably, again, even after the great promises of God, Abraham will once again fail. Sin is just as hateful (or even more so) in a man of God as in a man of the world – and his guilt is greater. At this stage, there is no way for us to know exactly how much information Abraham personally had about Lot. But knowing Abraham's heart, by this time he was probably well informed of the terrible failure of his kindred. He must have been shocked at their unbelief, but now he will fail himself. How so much the Church enjoys the pointing of fingers at those that it considers failures, when, in reality, that is a failure itself. It is easy for us to observe Lot and to carefully note his failure, but it is more difficult to understand Abraham's failure. The truth is, all of us are failures.

Kadesh and Shur are not in Egypt but are definitely toward Egypt (toward the south country). The sin and misery that resulted years before from journeying *"toward the south country"* should have taught him never again to move in that direction. But man, as such, never learns nor can learn spiritual lessons. Progress from God does not come from "education"; it comes from "revelation." Abraham once more forsakes the path of faith, and, in denying his wife, sinks to a depth of moral degradation that is contemptible in the extreme. His fall on this occasion was deeper than on the prior one, for he now had the divine promise that within that very year Sarah should become the mother of a miracle child. His sin was even more contemptible than the sin of Lot.

As an aside, the 2nd verse relates to us the miracle of rejuvenation that had already begun regarding Sarah. Evidently, the touch of God

upon her physical body in regard to the coming birth of Isaac, must have renewed her youthfulness and her beauty as well. At any rate, Abimelech, as Pharoah, desired her ("Abimelech" was a title such as "Pharaoh"). In the words *"she is my sister"* there is in the confession of Abraham to Abimelech this painful feature revealed in his character. He starts upon this course with a falsehood and compels his wife to be the degraded sharer of the lie. Regrettably, these facts revealed by unsparing truth make it plain that Abraham by natural disposition and character was cowardly and false. He was only noble when energized by faith. Sad as all of this is, there is encouragement in it for the weakest, for it teaches that the most abject and contemptible man may become noble and strong if, by faith, he surrenders his broken humanity to Him who can subdue all things unto Himself.

This was Satan's second effort to bring about the birth of the Messiah by the intervention of a heathen father, and that, therefore, he would and could incite Abimelech to this action.

So successful was Satan and his planning that but for the special intervention of God, there would have been a catastrophy. Sarah is delivered through a dream. (Twenty such are recorded in the Scriptures.)

The 3rd verse tells us something beautiful. God, in His amazing grace, is not ashamed to be called the God of a poor, feeble, imperfect, and stumbling man. If, despite the weakness, faith and love reside in the heart, God will always honor it. This is a lesson that self-righteousness seems to never learn. True, the patriarch, by his own faithlessness, had deeply degraded himself, so he is to be justly rebuked by the heathen prince. Yet God, in His faithfulness, clothes Abraham with dignity, and honors him in the presence of Abimelech. Oh, how great is the grace of our loving Lord.

The 7th verse tells us that despite Abraham's failure, his calling as a prophet has not been diminished, but has even by God been proclaimed, *"for he is a prophet."* The power that resides in this prophet (despite his failure) to pray for others that life may be restored has not waned. In the 7th verse we have as well the words of David, *"touch not the Lord's anointed."* How so quickly men are prone to lay their hands on that which is God's. How so quickly they set themselves up as the judge, but to their ruin.

Verse 14 records that Abimelech obeyed God. However, it must be noted that natural goodness and integrity, as in the case of Abimelech, do not necessarily make a man a child of God. And, on the other hand, a temporary moral lapse through fear does not unmake the believer a member of the household of faith.

The 16th verse records a rebuke given by Abimelech to Sarah. He said, *"I have given thy brother. . . ."* She is reproved by the irony; she is a type of Israel as Isaac would be a type of Christ (Gal. 3). And the Gentile, as typified by Abimelech, returns her to her true position with the cutting reproof that she at least ought to have known and maintained her relationship to the Lord. Today, the Gentile Church, with Abimelech being a type, is a cutting reproof to present-day Israel.

Verses 17 and 18 give a solemn lesson regarding all of Christendom. Because of Abraham's abandonment of the path of faith, and for as long as he failed to walk in that path, there were no children born to Abimelech and to his household. This physical fact illustrates a spiritual reality in Christian experience. It is not unreasonable to learn from all this that the birth of spiritual children in the gospel is hindered or delayed by the inconsistent conduct of those that are "Christian."

CHAPTER 21

The moment that God makes visible His plan, Satan begins his hindrance. But despite all of Satan's efforts, Isaac, the progenitor and type of the Messiah is born. The preceding chapters portray the tremendous opposition by the evil one. Any call of God will attract fierce satanic opposition. If there is no opposition by Satan, there is no call of God. Regrettably, the Church welcomes with open arms that which is little contested by Satan and totally rejects that which is greatly opposed by the evil one.

Sadder still, they fail to see that a "great call" such as Abraham's attracts "great opposition." There is no record in the Bible of a great call of God that did not attract powerful opposition by the powers of darkness.

The 2nd verse records a "set time" of which God had spoken to Abraham. God's timing is a part of His will.

The forceful repetition of Sarah's name in the first three verses is emphatic with the Holy Spirit impressing the fact that Sarah was in very truth the mother of this miraculous child. The Holy Spirit desires the reader to know and understand that the "works of the flesh" did not and could not succeed but that the Holy Spirit was able to bring forth the miraculous.

The 6th verse proclaims the joy of Sarah and, as well, the joy of all of those that would accept Jesus Christ as their personal Saviour and *"will laugh with me."*

The 8th verse tells us of the great celebration of the "miracle child." He was about five years old when weaned. At this time, Hagar knew that the divine promise had been fulfilled, and it was not Ishmael.

The 9th verse proclaims the hatred of Ishmael for Isaac. Galatians 4:29, using the word *"persecuted,"* tells us of the hatred of Ishmael and Hagar for Isaac (the word *"persecute"* in the Hebrew could mean "murder").

The effect of the birth of Isaac was to make manifest the character of Ishmael. Ishmael was about 20 years old at this time. Encouraged by his mother, he sought to murder Isaac. Because of that, he and his mother were justly expelled. Thus the birth of Isaac, which filled Sarah's heart with mirth, filled Hagar's with murder.

Isaac and Ishmael symbolized the new and the old nature in the believer. Sarah and Hagar typified the two covenants of works and grace, of bondage and liberty (Gal. 4). The birth of the new nature demands the expulsion of the old. The reader must understand that it is impossible to improve the old nature. The Holy Spirit says in Romans 8 that *"it is enmity against God, that it is not subject to the law of God, neither indeed can be."* If, therefore, it cannot be subject to the law of God, how can it be improved? How foolish, therefore, appears the doctrine of moral evolution! The divine way of holiness is to *"put off the old man"* just as Abraham "put off" Ishmael. Man's way of holiness is to improve the "old man," that is, to improve Ishmael. The effort is both foolish and hopeless. Yet, the casting out of Ishmael was *"very grievous in Abraham's sight,"* because it always ensues a struggle to cast out this element of bondage, that is, salvation by works. For legalism is dear to the heart. Ishmael was the fruit, and, to Abraham, the fair fruit of his own energy and planning. But the Epistle to the Galatians states that Hagar, the bond-woman, represents the covenant of the law and that her son represents all who are of *"works of the law,"* that is, of all who seek righteousness on the principle of works of righteousness. However, the bond-woman cannot bring forth a free man! The Son alone makes free, and He makes free indeed. Sarah, the free-woman, symbolizes the covenant of grace and liberty. "So, then, we are not children of the bond-woman, but of the free."

In verses 1 through 8, Sarah is a type of obedient Israel. In verses 17 through 21, Hagar is a type of disobedient Israel. Because of her rejection of the miracle child, the Lord Jesus Christ, she has been *"cast out."* The 17th verse says that even in Israel's dispossessed state that *"God will open her eyes"* (Zech. 12).

The mighty words, *"In Isaac shall thy seed be called"* (vs. 12), are explained in Galatians 3:16 as referring to Christ. The birth of Isaac marks a distinct advance in the spiritual experience of Abraham. From this moment onward, all is strength and victory. He casts out the bond-woman and her son; he no longer fears the prince of this world (Abimelech), but reproves him. Now that the heir is come, Christ in type, he knows himself to be the possessor of heavenly as well as earthly promises. The heathen prince as well confesses that God is with Abraham (vs. 22). The well of the oath is witness to Abraham's title in the earth and to Abimelech's confession of the fact. Accordingly, Abraham takes possession of the land, plants a tree (Calvary), and worships Jehovah as the everlasting God. For the God that gave Isaac must be, in truth, the everlasting God.

So, Abraham now dwells where the power of the world had once been. Abimelech, as well

as Ishmael, withdraws from his land (vs. 32).

All of this is a pledge of what Israel shall have in the Millennium and of her glory and dominion that will be hers in Christ, and with Christ, as the everlasting God.

CHAPTER 22

The word *"tempt"* in the 1st verse in the Hebrew is "nacah" which means to test or to prove. It would have been better translated in that fashion. It has no indication whatsoever of inducement to sin. That which will transpire in the 22nd chapter is at least one of the most powerful "testings" that God ever required of any human being. This chapter is one of the most glorious in the entirety of the Bible. It is a portrayal of the death and resurrection of the Lord Jesus Christ. How beautiful are the words, *"God did test Abraham."* There is no verse which says, "God did test Lot." It is a high honor to be tested by God. There are various kinds of tests. Some tests come from circumstances, some from the hand of Satan. But the highest character test and its full dignity, is that which comes from God Himself. The words *"Behold, here I am,"* speak of a place of consecration that not many Christians have attained.

The 2nd verse gives the great command, *"Thine only son Isaac."* And then it says, *"Offer him."* That which God asks of Abraham was beyond human comprehension. It had taken some 25 years for this "son of promise" to be born. (Incidentally, Isaac was probably in his mid or late teens.) In this verse, the word *"love"* is used for the first time in the Bible. It will be used much thereafter, for God is love. What made this test so stupendous was the fact that God was demanding of him that he offer up human sacrifice, which was common with the surrounding peoples. As well, it was abhorrent with God. This was a test beyond human comprehension. Not only was God demanding that Abraham offer up his son, which would be a type of God giving His Son, Jesus Christ, but what God was asking Abraham to do was actually opposed by the very law of God. From the very beginning, God had demanded a clean animal (lamb, bullock, ram, etc.), but never a human sacrifice. How could Abraham be sure that this was not an "angel of light" and thereby a trick of Satan? The answer to that is "relationship." Abraham's relationship with God was such that he "knew" the voice of God. The Holy Spirit says in Hebrews 11 that the patriarch fully believed that God would raise him up from the dead.

The land of Moriah means all the mountains of Jerusalem – Calvary, Zion, Olives, Moriah, and others. It is claimed that the spot over which Abraham was to offer Isaac was the spot over which Solomon built his temple and that the Holy of Holies resided over its exact place. Incidentally, the Dome of the Rock, one of the most sacred places in Islam, now occupies this particular spot in Jerusalem.

The 3rd verse exemplifies Abraham's complete obedience; the early rising, saddling, cleaving the wood, and going three days journey to slay his only son of promise, proves his deliberate and complete obedience. The prophet would later say (I Sam. 15:22) that obedience is better than sacrifice. God would honor Abraham's obedience and would thereby allow the sacrifice to be in type only. In other words, God had no interest in the sacrifice, except in type. He *was* interested in the obedience.

The 4th verse speaks of the third day of travel. What must have gone on in Abraham's mind in this some 72 hours. The pain and the anguish can only be guessed at. When he lifted up his eyes and God said, "This is the place," what must his thoughts have been? Within himself, Abraham could not have done such a thing. He could only have done so by the strength of the Lord. Likewise, if we walk after the flesh, we shall die. But if we shall walk after the Spirit, we shall live (Rom. 8).

The 5th verse says there were several that were traveling in Abraham's party. The young men are told to remain while he and Isaac go yonder and worship. This is the epitome of consecration. Abraham would label this act that God had demanded of him, which was so horrible to the flesh, as worship. Has our relationship with God reached a place to where the tests that come our way, no matter how severe,

NOTES

can be labeled "worship?" When, and if, we reach this place, we have truly known true relationship with God. Notice the faith that is paramount, *"and come again to you."* He was fully committed to going through with this sacrifice. But, as we have stated, he believed that God would raise Isaac from the dead.

The 6th verse says the *"wood of the burnt offering laid upon Isaac his son."* The wood is a type of Calvary; the burnt offering is a type of the offering up of the Lord Jesus Christ as He would be placed upon that wood. The *"fire in his hand"* speaks of the judgment of God that should have fallen on us but, instead, fell upon God's Son. The *"knife"* speaks of the terrible wounds that were suffered by the Lord, *"Yet it pleased the Lord to bruise him"* (Isa. 53:10). The words, *"And they went both of them together,"* speak of the beautiful picture of the father and the son in the antitype (II Cor. 5:19).

The 7th verse records the great question, *"But where is the lamb for a burnt offering?"* This speaks of Gethsemane, *"And when he was at the place, saying, Father, if thou be willing, remove this cup from me"* (St. Luke 22:40, 42).

The 8th verse proclaims the great promise that God had given originally in the Garden of Eden, *"God will provide himself a Lamb"* (Gen. 3:15). The words, *"So they went both of them together,"* is a striking type of him that said, *"I delight to do thy will, oh my God"* (Psa. 40:8). It also speaks of Jesus' surrender in Gethsemane, *"Not my will, but thine, be done"* (St. Luke 22:42).

The 9th verse, as well, says, *"And they came to the place,"* and once again speaks of Gethsemane (St. Luke 22:40). The words *"which God had told him of"* were that which was ever before Christ. The *"altar"* was a type of Calvary. The *"wood"* was a type of the cross. *"Isaac"* was a type of Jesus Christ, laid on the altar "upon the wood."

The 10th verse records the "type"; however, the "antitype" some 1800 years later would carry it through to its horrible completion, *"It is finished"* (John 19:30).

The 11th verse records the revelation of God *"out of heaven."* All revelation is "out of heaven." Paul saw a *"light from heaven"* (Acts 9:3). John heard a voice that *"came from heaven"* (St. Luke 3:22). The same one who said, "Abraham, Abraham," was the same mighty God who said, "Martha, Martha"; "Simon, Simon"; "Saul, Saul."

There are two interpretations to the words of the 12th verse, *"For now I know."* The first interpretation is:

God is omniscient (all knowing) and only does such things, not that He might know, but that we might know. However, there is a second interpretation:

Here, God confirmed what He thought about Abraham, as stated in Genesis 18:19. As a free moral agent, Abraham could have disappointed the Lord, but testing him made it possible to say, *"Now I know."* God limits His own attributes to conform to His plan for free moral agents. This makes Him no less omniscient, but makes it possible for Him to respect the sovereign will of man. Thus, God does not plan man's choices or acts but holds him responsible for them should he choose and act contrary to the best good of all.

Verses 13 and 14 give us clearly the "doctrine of substitution." As the ram became a substitute for Isaac to spare his life, so Christ became a substitute for all men, dying in their place so that they might go free from eternal death in hell should they desire to accept Him as their sacrifice (Isa. 53; St. John 3:16). All the animal sacrifices of the Old Testament portrayed Christ paying the penalty in our stead. That the experience of Abraham with Isaac and the ram pre-figured the works of Christ is clear from Hebrews 11:17-19. The title *"Jehovah-Jireh"* means "the Lord will provide." The question should be asked, "Provide what?" A new car? A new home? Nice clothes? Certainly the Lord will answer prayer and provide all of these things that we need. However, we border blasphemy when we lower the meaning of *"Jehovah-Jireh"* to "things." Jesus said *"a man's life consisteth not in the abundance of the* things *which he possesseth"* (St. Luke 12:15). The great need of man is not things, but a Saviour.

The 15th verse records the *"angel of the Lord,"* which is actually Jehovah Himself.

Once again, we must emphasize that the doctrine of substitution and identification is the foundation of the Christian faith (Rom. 6:3-5). Christ became my substitute at Calvary;

NOTES

I identify with that.

He became my substitute in His burial; I identify with that (the old man buried). He became my substitute in the resurrection; I identify with that. He became my substitute in the ascension; I identify with that as well. This is what the *"whosoever believeth in Him"* of St. John 3:16 means.

Verses 15 through 18 record "the Abrahamic Covenant" enlarged. The 17th verse says that Abraham passed the test and was blessed accordingly. The "seed" of verse 17 in its ultimate conclusion refers to Christ, *"the gates of his enemies"* – *"the gates of hell shall not prevail"* (St. Matt. 16:18).

The nations of the earth of verse 18 can only be blessed as the Great Commission of the gospel of Jesus Christ is carried out. The seed (Christ) can only be a blessing if they know about Him. It is our responsibility that they know.

The 19th verse records the returning of Abraham and Isaac. What a celebration!

The 20th verse records the introduction to the story of Rebekah, which will commence in Genesis 24. Nahor did not start for Canaan with Terah and Abraham, but settled in Haran while Abraham was still there. Nahor had 12 sons, as did Ishmael and Jacob.

CHAPTER 23

The 1st verse records the only woman in the Bible whose age, death, and burial are recorded. This is significant, partly, no doubt, because she is the mother of the Hebrew nation and partly because the promised heir having come, then the vessel of the promise, Sarah – the first covenant necessarily passes away.

The 2nd verse gives the ancient name of Hebron, meaning "stronghold of Arba," because of being built by Anak and the sons of Arba of the race of giants (Josh. 14:15; Num. 13:22). Many years from this particular time, it would be given to Caleb (Judg. 1:10). David's first reign was there (II Sam. 2:5). Absalom started his rebellion there (II Sam. 2:5). It became the burial place of Abraham, Isaac, and

Jacob (Gen. 23:1-20; 33:18-20). Sarah lived 37 years after Isaac was born.

In the 4th verse Abraham signifies that he is a pilgrim, *"A stranger and a sojourner with you."* I wonder if the sons of Heth knew who this *"stranger"* was? Likewise, the child of God, to this world system, is a stranger and a sojourner. Abraham did not have this land as of yet, even though God had promised it to him. Ultimately, his children would own it all. And then one day in the great millennial reign, he, as well, will take possession of it in the name of Christ. We, as Christians, likewise, are sojourners in this present world. We have been told that the *"meek shall inherit the earth."* We do not yet have it, but one day in the millennial reign we shall. As well, Abraham, by faith, looked forward to a resurrection. In the tomb of Hebron, Sarah's body, along with Abraham's, Isaac's, and Jacob's, etc., have long since turned to dust, with their souls and spirits present with the Lord Jesus Christ. However, at the first resurrection, God will give the soul and spirit a glorified body, and that for every saint.

The 9th verse says it was the *"cave of Machpelah."* The Hebrew words mean "double." It still exists inside a massive wall which must have been built before the Christian era. It is one of the holiest shrines of the Moslem world. Neither Jew nor Christian is permitted to enter it.

The 15th and 16th verses say that Abraham paid "400 shekels of silver" for the land. In today's inflated dollar that would be worth approximately $2500. The sons of Heth offered him the choicest of their sepulchers, but in death as in life the man of faith would be a pilgrim, would have no fellowship with the children of darkness, would not be indebted to them even for a grave, and, accordingly, insisted on this purchase. They had no idea that Abraham was looking forward to the possession of the whole land and because he did so look forward, the possession of a grave was by no means a small matter to him. Hebrews 11 states, *"These all died, not having received the promise."* But in dying, as in living, they found the promises real and satisfying. His purchase of this tomb was not only a proof of his love for Sarah, but his testimony to his belief that she would rise again and with him possess the whole land.

CHAPTER 24

The 1st verse states, in effect, that Abraham was 140 years old at this time. As well, it says that *"the Lord had blessed Abraham in all things."* Once again we should emphasize that after the birth of Isaac there was no more failure on the part of Abraham. By and large, Abraham's mission and call from God had been fulfilled. Satan's intense pressure would now slacken, at least to a degree. The story in this chapter is in a small way a type of the Holy Spirit (Eliezer) seeking a bride (Rebekah – the Church) for Isaac (a type of Christ). Naturally, all types ultimately break down. However, this chapter will at least serve as a picture of the Church being brought to Christ.

The *"eldest servant"* referred to in verse 2 doesn't necessarily mean the oldest in age, but, in effect, means the "head servant." This was Eliezer. The *"putting the hand under the thigh,"* which represented the organs of generation, was most sacred according to ancient Jewish expositors. The act, according to the custom, was a sign of subjection. God touched Jacob's thigh when He changed his name as a sign of blessing.

The 3rd verse records the horror that Abraham, Isaac, and Jacob all had of intermarriage with Canaanites. The reason was the giant races whom the devil was then using in an effort to do away with pure Adamic stock so that the seed of the woman (Jesus) could not come into this world.

The 4th verse is somewhat symbolic of the Holy Spirit Who was sent from heaven to secure a bride for Christ.

In effect, and for the second time (vs. 6), in verse 8 Abraham told Eliezer not to come back empty-handed, *"He shall send his angel before thee."*

The 10th verse says that *"all the goods of his master were in his hand,"* symbolizing the power of the Holy Spirit (Acts 1:8).

Verses 12 through 14 is a beautiful example of being specific in prayer. It is a prayer of faith straight to the point, petitioning the covenant God *("Oh, Lord God")* for exactly that which is needed. God always responds to a prayer of faith.

The 15th verse speaks of Rebekah, whose name means "captivating," and Bethuel, whose name means "separated unto God," thus implying that Nahor knew Abraham's God, else he would not have named his child Bethuel. Incidentally, the pitcher upon Rebekah's shoulder could portray the Church taking the water of life (Jesus Christ) to a lost and dying world.

The 16th verse says the damsel was *"fair to look upon,"* and, likewise, the Church is "a glorious Church." As well, she was a *"virgin,"* *"Come out from among them and be ye separate, and touch not the unclean thing."*

In the 17th verse Eliezer refers to himself as *"the servant."* He was ever there by his Father Abraham to perform a mission for Abraham's son Isaac. Likewise, the Holy Spirit *"testifies of Christ"* (St. John 15:26).

The 22nd verse, in effect, says that Eliezer gave Rebekah *"gifts."* Likewise, the Holy Spirit gives gifts (I Cor. 12).

The 23rd verse asks the question, *"Is there room in thy father's house for us to lodge?"* The Holy Spirit is asking the Church today, "Is there room for Us (the Father, Son, and Holy Ghost) to lodge?"

The 25th verse gloriously proclaims her positive answer, *"There is room."* How great and wonderful the Church would be if it would only give the Holy Spirit "room."

The 31st verse says that if we make room for Eliezer (the Holy Spirit), we must make room as well "for the camels." There are many people that want certain things from the Holy Spirit, but other things they would rather "leave off." Some want the Holy Spirit, but they do not desire the "tongues." Others do not want the "manifestations" or the "demonstrations"; however, the camels go with Eliezer.

As in the 32nd verse, many people want the Holy Spirit, but they do not like *"ungirding the camels"* or *"giving straw and provendor for the camels."* However, if you are willing to do what Jesus said, and that is to "wash feet" (be a servant), then the acceptance of the camels will be no problem.

The 33rd verse records the business of Eliezer. Likewise, the Holy Spirit says, "I will not eat with the saints at the marriage supper of

the lamb until I have told mine errand."

Once again, the 34th verse characterizes Eliezer's meekness *"as a dove,"* "I am Abraham's servant."

The 36th verse says, *"And unto him hath he given all that he hath,"* speaking of Isaac. God the Father has given everything to His Son Jesus Christ (Rom. 8:17).

Verses 35 through 49 characterize the mission of Eliezer. Likewise, chapters 14 through 17 of St. John characterize the mission of the Holy Spirit.

The 53rd verse records Eliezer giving precious things to Rebekah's mother and brother. Likewise, the Church has *"precious things"* to give to the world.

The 56th verse proclaims *"hinder me not"* and *"send me away that I may go to my master,"* telling us that nothing must hinder the Holy Spirit and His work. As well, He will soon take the Church home to Isaac (Christ).

The 58th verse has a beautiful statement by Rebekah, *"I will go."* The question was asked if she would go with Eliezer (a type of the Holy Spirit), but, in effect, she was being asked would she go with Isaac (a type of Christ). She answered, *"I will go."* "Happy day, Happy day, When Jesus washed my sins away!"

The 61st verse says, *"The servant took Rebekah, and went his way."* Very soon the trump of God is going to sound and . . . (I Thess. 4:16-17).

In the 61st verse, it says that Rebekah *"saw Isaac."* One day we will "see Him face to face, and to tell the story, saved by grace."

The 67th and final verse of the 24th chapter says that *"he loved her."* Jesus loves the Church and gave His life for it.

CHAPTER 25

At the outset of the 25th chapter, by inference, we know that Sarah is dead, signifying that the Jewish covenant of works and exclusive salvation have as well passed away. Keturah, the Gentile, now appears with her sons. Thus is the future pictured. As Isaac, who in type was slain and raised to life again

(Christ) takes to himself a bride, likewise, Rebekah (Israel), in a future happy day, will be brought back to Christ (Zech. 13).

Of all the sons of Abraham's second family that are mentioned, Midian was the most prominent. He and his people are mentioned 67 times by name. He was defeated by Esau (Gen. 36:35). Moses fled to his land and married a woman of Midian (Ex. 2:15-16). Midianites became a snare to Israel (Num. 25:1-15), for which God commanded Israel to war with them (Josh. 13:21). Midian was the nation defeated by Gideon with such great destruction that its downfall is referred to in the Bible as *"the day of Midian"* (Isa. 9:4; Psa. 83:9).

Abraham's Gentile sons are a type of the Gentile Church, which has raised up children to Abraham and will receive their inheritance.

The 5th verse records Abraham giving all to Isaac, who was a type of Christ. Insomuch, by the fact of our accepting Christ as our personal Saviour, we now become joint-heirs with Christ (Rom. 8:17). Even though Abraham *"gave all,"* still, Isaac did not receive all, and will not until the second coming. Likewise, we as Christians have been "given all" (joint heirs), but will not receive all until the Second Coming.

Verses 7 and 8 record the lifespan and death of Abraham. Without a doubt, he was one of the godliest men that ever lived. Jacob was 15 years of age when Abraham died. Abraham was born only two years after the death of Noah, and was 150 years of age when Shem (Noah's son) died. He was, therefore, in a position to receive from many witnesses the facts affecting the antediluvian world. He was born of the Spirit at about 75 years of age and departed to be with Christ at 175. He was, therefore, a sojourner for 100 years.

Verse 9 says that Isaac and Ishmael stood side by side at their father's grave. Likewise, "Isaac" (Israel) and "Ishmael" (the Gentile Church) will stand side by side in the millennial reign of Christ.

The 11th verse says that *"Isaac dwelt by the well La-hai-roi,"* with this word meaning "having lived after having seen." Those that follow Isaac (a type of Christ) will have eternal life after having seen the narrow way of Christ.

The 21st verse says that Satan once again

NOTES

endeavors to stop the triune of "Abraham, Isaac, and Jacob." Rebekah was barren, having been so for nearly 20 years. Once again the Lord intervenes and Rebekah conceives. She will have twins. The two that are in her womb will be types of the "two natures" (The Christ nature and the sin nature) that struggle within the believer for supremacy.

The 22nd verse says that she asked the question, *"If it be so, why am I thus?"* It may be paraphrased thus: "If in answer to prayer God is about to give me the joy of being a mother, why am I so physically oppressed that I am in danger of death?" God had answered the prayer of Isaac and her, yet this answer to prayer is accompanied by such mysterious suffering. Why? Many Christians have had in their spiritual life, in union with answered prayer, spiritual sorrows which Rebekah's experience illustrates. And, further still, two energies, the one believing and the other unbelieving, struggled within her like the two natures within the believer. The younger would be the stronger. So, the two boys may represent the two natures in the Christian. The divine nature is the younger, but it is to have the victory. Praise God!

Her inquiry of the Lord as to the reason for this great struggle is given in far-reaching detail.

The 23rd verse says that it concerned the struggle between Jacob and Esau and was particularly fulfilled in their descendants many times. It will be completely fulfilled in the Millennium and the New Earth when Israel under their Messiah will be the head of all nations (Isa. 2:2-4; 9:6-7).

The 26th verse records the *"struggle"* that Jacob would have all his life. His *"hand on Esau's heel"* is a graphic account of the struggle between the Spirit (Jacob) and the flesh (Esau). He was called *"Jacob"* (Hebrew Yaaqob). The word means "heel-catcher, supplanter, cheater, defrauder, deceiver" – and yet he was one of the greatest men of God that ever lived. Jacob more perfectly portrayed the Christian struggle than any other of the Old Testament Bible greats. In Romans, Paul wrote of the Lord, *"Jacob have I loved, but Esau have I hated"* (Rom. 9:13; Mal. 1:1-3). *"Because God loved one and hated the other, is he unrighteous?"* Paul asked. He answers it with a

"God forbid." There is no unrighteousness with God, for He sees the dispositions of two boys and chooses on the basis of what He can foresee in each one. He had to make the choice of Jacob over Esau due to the dispositions and lives of the boys. Jacob, even though beginning with the handicaps mentioned, will, by the Holy Spirit, become the example of that which God loves.

The 28th verse says that *"Isaac loved Esau."* His love for Esau spoke of a negative spiritual condition in Isaac's life – a condition, incidentally, that would portend great spiritual difficulties.

The 31st verse records Jacob's desire for the birthright. It is an example of the flesh trying to obtain the things of the Spirit, which cannot be done. Jacob's desire for the birthright was implanted by God. Esau's hatred of the birthright, as recorded in the 32nd verse, shows that he had little desire for spiritual things.

The birthright was to go to the firstborn. It included the bulk of the family inheritance. Upon the passing of the father, the firstborn would become the ruling head of the whole tribe. He would, as well, obtain the father's blessings. He would be the spiritual leader and priest of the family or tribe. He would be a special party to the Abrahamic Covenant as well as the "father" of the Messiah (Gen. 12:3; 21:12; 22:17; Rom. 9:7; Gal. 3:16).

Jacob, deplorable as was his character, valued divine and eternal blessing. As he placed himself in God's hands, the prophecy made to his mother before he was born would have been fulfilled to him, and without the degradation and suffering which his own scheming ultimately brought upon him.

In the 34th verse, with deep pathos, sorrow, and with indignation, the Holy Spirit adds, *"Thus Esau despised his birthright!"*

CHAPTER 26

As Satan had caused Abraham to fail, now he will use the same tactics on Isaac. Satan really never changes his methods; he doesn't have to, they work well. Regrettably, it is not

difficult for Satan to break down the faith of a believer. Fear, being one of his chief weapons, proves tremendously successful. Isaac, it seems, is on his way to Egypt exactly as his father Abraham had done. He makes it as far as the land of the Philistines. It is disastrous to the spiritual life of the Christian to go down into "Egypt." It is dangerous as well to go down into "Gerar," for it is a half-way house to Egypt. Isaac would be blessed by the Lord in "Gerar", but, as well, would suffer spiritually by continually contending with the Philistines.

The 4th verse says that the Lord reaffirms the great promise to Isaac that He had given to Abraham, *"In thy seed shall all the nations of the earth be blessed."* Once again, that "seed" would be Christ.

The 5th verse is a beautiful portrayal of the New Testament doctrine of "justification." The Lord does not mention Abraham's failures, only his victories. Abraham's "justification by faith" (Gen. 15:6) laid the foundation for the greatest work of God ever recorded in the human heart – the death and resurrection of our Lord Jesus Christ. The Holy Spirit in the 6th verse says that *"Isaac dwelt in Gerar."* And in this "half-way house" to Egypt, he lies about his wife Rebekah, as his father Abraham had done about his wife Sarah. Beautifully enough, the Holy Spirit saw fit to put the lovely 5th verse extolling the "justification of Abraham" in the midst of spiritual declension and failure.

The 12th verse records the blessing of the Lord upon Isaac.

The 14th verse says that the *"Philistines envied him."* In a small measure, the Lord would desire that the world see the blessings of God upon our lives, which makes us "Christ-like," and, thereby, desirable.

The 15th verse speaks of wells that had been "stopped," filled with earth. The "well of water springing up unto everlasting life" is the hallmark of the child of God. Satan, through the world, attempts to "stop" these wells of eternal life.

The 18th verse says that *"Isaac digged again the wells of water."* He also called them by the same names. Each generation has to redig the wells that the previous generation dug. God has no grandchildren. The experience my father had was great for him, but it will not do for me. I must have my own experience with God. The death of the church is when the wells are not *"digged again."*

If we dig, we will find the well of "springing water" as recorded in the 19th verse (living water).

The 20th verse says this well was called *"Esek"*; it means "contention or strife." Our walk with God will be met with great contention and strife. The battle between the flesh and the spirit is unending.

The 21st verse records another well, *"Sitnah,"* meaning "opposition and accusation." What a description. Satan opposes greatly our every footstep toward victory. Truly, he is as well "the accuser of the brethren."

Verse 22 speaks of another well called *"Rehoboth"* meaning "room." God will make room for us in His great vineyard ultimately.

Once again, in the 24th verse it says, *"And the Lord appeared unto him."* He says to him as He had said to Abraham, *"Fear not."* The fear was with Isaac as it had been with Abraham. In this struggle to carry out the great work of God, how often fear plagues us. And so the Lord says, *"Fear not."*

The 25th verse says he *"builded an altar there."* He did five things:

1. Built an altar.
2. There.
3. Called upon the name of the Lord.
4. Pitched his tent there.
5. Digged a well.

If "there" is a problem, build an altar (Calvary), call upon the name of the Lord and He will answer you. Pitch your tent there; don't let Satan run you off. And dig the well that God has told you to dig.

Whenever Isaac did these things, his enemies saw, as is recorded in the 28th verse, *"that the Lord was with thee."*

Verses 32 and 33 speak of victory – great victory, "We have found water." *"If you drink of the water that I give you, you shall never thirst. It shall be in you a well of water."* The word *"Shebah"* means seven. It is referring to the seven lambs that were offered by Abraham in the 21st chapter, with *"Beersheba"* meaning "the well of the seven." Seven speaks of perfection and completion. It is God's number.

Verses 34 and 35 record Esau's profanity in

selling his birthright, which was quickly followed by his double marriage with the Hittite. So, it is ever, the heart that despises heavenly things very quickly becomes doubly yoked to this present evil world.

CHAPTER 27

The history of Jacob underlines the love of God, the grace of God, and the depravity of man. Many have the tendency to believe that God selects particular individuals because of their noble qualities. However, that is not the case at all. God looks at every person's heart, knowing that at the outset it is depraved. However, through foreknowledge, He knows how that heart will respond to His love and to His grace. When God chooses individuals for leadership, it is because He knows that ultimately they will respond favorably. Even then, it is a slow process which can best be characterized by John Newton's beautiful song, "Amazing Grace."

"Thro' many dangers, toils and snares,
"I have already come.
"'Tis grace hath bro't me safe thus far,
"And grace will lead me home."

It would seem that Jacob was the most unlovely member of his family, yet grace chose him to be the Head of all the nations of the earth. Grace banishes all human pretensions and asserts God's right to act as He will. Grace heaps everything upon those who deserve nothing. Why did God love Jacob? The only answer that could be given is that God chose him, not because of what he was, but because of what Jacob would allow the Lord to make of him. Perhaps Jacob is the greatest example of the Christian's struggle to be what God wants him to be. The hurt, the drama, the pain, the sin, the mercy and forgiveness are all there.

In Psalm 46:11, we have perhaps one of the most beautiful descriptions of Who God really is.

The title, *"Lord of Hosts,"* presents Him as the God of countless hosts of sinless angels. The other title, *"God of Jacob,"* proclaims Him the God of one stumbling, sinning, scheming, planning, and broken man! These two divine titles link Almighty power with infinite grace.

Jacob's example shows us what the natural will is so slow to learn, that planning for self instead of resting in the hand of God brings sorrow. Hence Jacob's miserable testimony to Pharaoh, *"Few and evil have been the years of my life"* (47:9).

And yet, for all of his weaknesses, Jacob became a mighty man of God and will go down in eternal history under the title, *"The God of Abraham, Isaac, and Jacob."*

Isaac pictures the elect nation of Israel living within the promised land and waiting for its possession. Jacob is a type of the elect people (Israel), heir of the promises, wandering among the Gentiles because of his own misconduct, an outcast, and, yet, watched over by God.

Verses 1 through 4 picture Isaac in a backslidden condition, denying the prophecy (25:23) and the promise of God. Despite Esau despising his birthright, Isaac would *"bless thee before I die."* How determined man is to have his own way versus God's way. We are so prone to judge by appearance, and, thereby, fail to make righteous judgment. God had chosen Jacob; Isaac knew that. In his rebellion he would lay aside the choice of God and make his own choice. How so much like the modern-day Church. If Esau were ready to sell the birthright for a mess of pottage, his father was prepared to sell it for a dish of venison. What a sad picture; a man of God stumbling in his own way, instead of walking in God's way! Incidentally, Isaac was now about 138 years old. However, he would not die now as he had thought; he would actually live some 42 years after this time.

Verses 5 through 29 record the plot to get the birthright. The desire for the birthright was God-given. Rebekah, ever mindful of the promise of God when the boys were born, schemes to make the prophecy come to pass. Her efforts will result only in hate, separation, and loneliness. When we take situations out of the hands of God and place them into our own hands, or the hands of other men, we have then incurred upon ourselves the results of our folly. Her reasoning was:

God had promised it (25:23); Jacob wanted

it (25:31); Esau despised it (25:34). The end never justifies the means. Verses 5 through 29 present a despicable picture of the modern-day Church. Church politics, rife in hierarchical scheming, would so often fit neatly into the terrible deception of Rebekah and Jacob.

Verse 33 says *"Isaac trembled very exceedingly."* His fear had to do with the promise of God. He had almost abrogated it, and would have if left to his own devices. What a sorry state of God's chosen people.

Verses 34 through 38 record that Esau thought he could have the blessing without the birthright. He despised the birthright. However, he still wants the blessing.

How so much like the Church of today. We want the blessing without the reproach. Everyone wants blessing just as Esau did, but precious few want the birthright with all that goes with it – the enmity of the world, persecution, and even hate.

The 41st verse says, *"Esau hated Jacob."* The flesh always hates the Spirit. At this stage, it's very difficult to equate Jacob with the Spirit, as it is very difficult to equate most of God's children with the Spirit. However, we should look at Christians as God looks at them, not as they are, but as He will make them – if they will only humble themselves.

The *"few days"* of the 44th verse turned into 20 years. Actually, Rebekah would never see her son Jacob again – at least on this side of glory.

CHAPTER 28

Verses 1 and 2 portray Isaac now attempting to obey God in giving Jacob the birthright. He has *"trembled very exceedingly"* (27:33), realizing his terrible failure and is now trying to rectify it. Once again, what a picture of Christendom. We fail and then we attempt to rectify our failure. Verses 1 and 2 show repentance on the part of Isaac. Repentance always brings obedience. God always accepts it.

In verse 3, he mentions *"God Almighty,"* which spoke of the promise to Abraham (17:1), which meant in the Hebrew "El Shaddai," meaning the "Strong One," the "Breasted

NOTES

One," the "Strong Nourisher," "Strength Giver," "Satisfier," and "All-Bountiful." No doubt the meaning of "El Shaddai" had been handed down by Abraham to Isaac. Now he assures Jacob of the same promise. Hallelujah!

The 4th verse mentions *"the blessing of Abraham."* What is the *"blessing of Abraham"*? It is justification by faith (Gen. 15:6). Praise God, *"the blessing of Abraham,"* has come all the way to this present generation.

Verses 6 through 9 record Esau's attempt to please his mother and father by taking wives of the daughters of Ishmael. Thus are the ways of the flesh; it always concocts its scheme to please God, but it does not please God, because the flesh cannot please God.

Verses 10 through 19 record Jacob's vision. The 11th verse mentions *"a certain place."* This is the place that God had been attempting to bring us. Oftentimes, our foolishness in resorting to works of the flesh rather has the opposite effect of Satan's intentions. He intends to destroy us, but, as Paul said (II Cor. 12:9), the infirmities drive us to our knees and thus to Christ. When Jacob leaves his home, he is a broken man, fleeing for his life, attempting to secure the things of God by the means of the flesh. The discouragement must have been great. Jacob merits nothing, but, instead, God will promise him everything. Such is grace!

The vision recorded in verse 12 was God's way of telling Jacob that he was the object of heaven's love and care and that the angels of God were busily employed, coming and going from heaven to earth in ministering to him. For the first time in Jacob's life, heaven and earth would be united. This is the only cure for the soul; there is no other. If the child of God would have his eyes "opened," he no doubt would experience similar observation regarding God's love, protection, and care of even the most lowly and humble child of God.

Once again (vs. 13) God restates the promise that had been given to Abraham and Isaac. It is now given to Jacob. That beautiful statement in verse 14 reverberates in Jacob's heart, *"And in thee and thy seed [Jesus] shall all the families of the earth be blessed."*

And then in the 15th verse the Lord says something that is the dearest word that could ever be spoken to the human heart, *"I am with*

thee, and will keep thee in all places whither thou goest." And then He assures him, *"For I will not leave thee, until I have done that which I have spoken to thee of."*

Verse 16 says these beautiful words, *"Surely the Lord is in this place."* The song says, "Anywhere is home, if Christ my Lord is there."

The 17th verse records the words, *"The gate of heaven."* The religions of the world try to reach, through their own efforts, in their works of the flesh, this vaulted place. They ever fail, as fail they must. We can only reach that gate in one way, and that is by the ladder, and the ladder is Jesus Christ (St. John 1:51).

The stone that is mentioned in verse 18 was set up for a monument and anointed to consecrate it to God as an altar. About 30 years later, Jacob would repeat his solemn vow in the same place (35:14). There is an unfounded tradition that the stone Jacob set up was afterwards brought to Jerusalem, later taken to Spain, then to Ireland, and finally to Scotland. On what is supposed to be that very stone, the kings of Scotland sat and were crowned. Edward I had it brought to Westminster and placed under the chair on which kings of England were to be crowned. It is there even today.

In the tradition of Abraham (vs. 22), Jacob promises to the Lord "the tenth." Jacob, a little later, will learn better and give Him all.

CHAPTER 29

The journey recorded in verse 1 would involve much sorrow. It would last for some 20 years. In this 20 years, all the sons of Jacob with the exception of Benjamin would be born to him, Rachel, and Leah. Jacob had practiced deception, now deception would be practiced on him. What we sow, we reap. Incidentally, Jacob was in his mid 70's at this time.

The 6th verse records the first mention of Rachel. She will be God's elect, and that despite her weaknesses of the flesh. To her Joseph would be born, who would be a type of Christ.

From verses 15 to 30 it seems somewhat that Jacob worked 7 years before Leah and

Rachel were given to him, but this could not be if we are to have harmony regarding all the facts in Scripture. Actually, he received his wives immediately. In other words, the contract was signed that Jacob would work a certain number of years for each wife. He received them immediately, and then worked the appointed 14 years.

The 31st verse mentions specifically that, *"The Lord saw that Leah was hated."* Evidently Jacob and Rachel did not conduct themselves toward Leah as they should. The Lord saw it, and retribution was swift. Because of their conduct toward Leah, God blessed Leah and caused Rachel to be barren. God is mindful of our every action.

Beginning with verse 32, Reuben is born to Leah. He will be Jacob's firstborn. Beautifully enough, in the birth of Leah's sons, in their names we have the perfect plan of salvation. Reuben means *"behold a son."* In God's plan, it signifies that a son is born to a family.

Verse 33 speaks of the birth of Simeon, meaning *"hearing."* When the son is old enough, he hears the Gospel.

The 34th verse records the birth of Levi, which means *"joined."* The son is born, he hears the Gospel and is joined to the Lord Jesus Christ.

Verse 35 tells us of the birth of Judah, which means *"praise."* The son is born, he hears the Gospel, he is joined to Jesus Christ, and he praises the Lord.

Verse 18 of chapter 30 records the birth of Issachar to Leah. His name means *"reward."* After the Christian starts to praise the Lord, reward always comes.

The 20th verse of chapter 30 records the birth of Leah's last son, Zebulun, which means *"dwelling."* Here, the plan is fulfilled. A son is born, he hears the Gospel, he is joined to Jesus Christ, he praises the Lord, he receives reward from God, and ultimately he will dwell in the house of the Lord forever.

CHAPTER 30

In verse 1, we are told that *"Rachel bare*

Jacob no children." Her hatred of Leah had resulted in her womb being barren. The reader may have difficulty in understanding why the bearing of children was so important.

First of all, these children must be born to Jacob or else there will be no nation of Israel. Consequently, there will be no Bible, and no Messiah. Therefore, the craving for children by both Rachel and Leah was given by God, and yet Rachel is barren. The words *"give me children, or else I die,"* came from the very depths of Rachel's soul. Her barrenness was because of her sin, and yet the call remained. Of course it did. God's gifts and His calling are without repentance. Several years had passed and still no children. Several years more will pass before Joseph is born. She is God's chosen, but yet she is sinful and, consequently, barren. Why does not God answer her petition at the moment of her request? Why doesn't God answer our petitions at the moment of our requests? The following passages will give the answer.

The 3rd verse records that Rachel would follow in the footsteps of Sarah. As Sarah used Hagar to bring about the plan of God (which it did not), Rachel would do the same. She would use her maid, Bilhah. Bilhah will have two sons, Dan and Naphtali. Dan means "judging," with Naphtali meaning "wrestling."

Now verses 9 through 13 record Leah following suit and using her maid Zilpah. Two sons will be born to this union of Zilpah and Jacob: Gad, meaning "a troop," with Asher meaning "happiness."

It should quickly be added here that the meaning of the names of these sons would be fulfilled in its entirety down through the centuries. Evidently, the Holy Spirit guided both Leah and Rachel when they named these boys.

Verses 14 through 16 record at least one of the reasons that God did not answer Rachel's petition in verse 1. Rachel will resort to superstitious witchcraft. Her womb will remain closed. Incidentally, mandrakes were a lettuce-like plant of dark green color, with purple flowers, and fruit about the size of a small apple. It was much used in so-called love potions. It was believed that conception was insured by eating it.

The 22nd verse tells us that Rachel cried to

God. She finally left behind the hatred of Leah, the envy of Leah (vs. 1), and the superstition of Reuben's mandrakes. She finally resorts only to God. The Bible said, *"God hearkened to her, and opened her womb."* All works of the flesh are doomed to failure. Only that which is ordained by the Spirit can succeed.

The 24th verse says that she called the name of her newborn son, Joseph. Incidentaily, in the culture of these ancient people, the woman named the child. Joseph's name meant "adding." Then Rachel prophesied, *"The Lord shall add to me another son."*

Some have said that the birth of these sons to Jacob portrays a perfect pattern of the Church from the Day of Pentecost until the rapture. It has been said that Joseph was a type of the great Pentecostal outpouring at the turn of the century. However, God has said, *"Add to me another,"* looking forward to the birth of Benjamin, meaning *"the son of my strong right arm."* The Lord is not coming back after a weak Church, but a strong Church ("Tis a glorious Church"). Joseph was born about 6 years before going back to the land of promise.

The 30th verse records the blessing of God, not only upon the principal (Joseph), but, as well, on all that are associated with him. Too often the Church rallies around that which God has not sent. Jacob is not exactly the most beautiful example that one would like, and there is a reason for it. Jacob's call will also attract tremendous satanic opposition. Satan little opposes that which is not called of God. He strongly opposes that which is called of God. Why does God allow this? The reasons are obvious. The ones called are never at the outset qualified for the task. They must "grow in grace." The allowed opposition by Satan drives the called ones to their knees. Ultimately, Jacob, the schemer, will become Israel, the prince of God.

Laban, a type of the worldly Church, will change Jacob's wages some ten times. But Laban will little regard that he has experienced blessing since Jacob came. Laban was blessed by Jacob's presence; he little recognized it. How much more Laban could have been blessed if he had recognized God's call upon Jacob.

NOTES

CHAPTER 31

The 1st verse tells us that Laban's sons, as well as Laban (vs. 2), little recognized Jacob as the source of their blessing. Likewise, the world, and even the Church never realize that the source of their blessing has nothing to do with hierarchy or religious political in-fighting, but, in fact, resides in the ones on whom God has laid His hand. How blessed Laban was, and he did not know it.

The 3rd verse says that Laban's time of unappreciated blessing is over. God will tell Jacob, *"Return into the land of thy fathers."* At Bethel, Jacob was to learn Who God was; at Haran, who man was. And what a difference! At Bethel, God enriched him; at Haran, man robbed him!

The 7th verse proclaims God's cherished protection.

The 10th verse says that God told Jacob how to obtain wealth by giving him a dream.

The 19th verse says that Rachel had now gone back to her superstition *"images."* How soon man departs from the Spirit of God to resort to the flesh.

It is the Euphrates River which is spoken of in verse 21.

The 24th verse says that *"God came to Laban in a dream by night."* In effect, He told him, *"Take heed how you speak to Jacob."* "Touch not the Lord's anointed." God never in any fashion condones sin in His anointed, but neither does He condone harm intended by others.

Verses 30 through 35 record Laban searching for his "gods" (images). God has appeared to him in a dream by night (vs. 24), but Laban will continue to consult his idols. How so far fallen are the fallen. Man would rather consult dumb idols than the living God. Today, the modern Church would rather resort to humanistic psychology than trust the living God. How so very foolish we are!

CHAPTER 32

Verses 1 and 2 promise Jacob God's divine protection. The Bible says, *"Jacob saw them."* The word "Mahanaim" means "two camps." These hosts of heaven met Jacob to assure him of the promised protection as he entered Canaan. They became visible as two hosts, one on each side of Jacob's company.

The sin of 20 years before between Jacob and Esau had lain dormant, but now "finds Jacob out." It always does. Esau, coming with 400 men, had plans other than fellowship, to be sure.

The 7th verse proclaims Jacob's fear and distress. Why, especially when he has seen two hosts of angels surrounding his family? Despite the powerful presentations of the Holy Spirit, the heart of man (even God's choice) is so given to fear.

Verses 9 through 12 record a different Jacob than the Jacob of some 20 years before. His prayer is actually very similar to what we call "The Lord's Prayer." He first addresses God as a "Covenant God," and then the God of promise, *"I will deal well with thee."*

Verse 10 says, *"I am not worthy,"* which is the first time Jacob confessed his unworthiness of God's blessings. He was finally brought to the point of surrender to God and to help-lessness without Him.

Then he cries, *"Deliver me"* (vs. 11). There is no deliverer but God. How long will it take the Church to understand that?

Even though Jacob did pray, and he prayed correctly, however, he first planned and then prayed. He should have prayed and then planned. It is very difficult for men to cease depending on the flesh.

Even after Jacob has greatly supplicated the Lord, verses 13 through 23 record his continued scheming to ameliorate the 20-year-old problem of Esau. The Holy Spirit devoted this much attention to Jacob's plans for a reason. We would then find that Jacob's scheming and planning were to no avail. You see, Jacob's problem was not Esau; Jacob's problem was Jacob. Likewise, your problem is not all the

NOTES

many things in which you think, if corrected, will bring blessing and satisfaction. Your prob-lem is you. My problem is me. God doesn't change circumstances nearly as much as He changes people. Verses 24 through 32 will rec-ord this change. Man continues to think that his problem is environment, money, educa-tion, etc. The world keeps treating the symp-toms. What the world needs is Jesus, because only Jesus can change the heart.

Verse 24 says, *"Jacob was left alone."* Jacob had finally run out of options; he finally had to face himself. He now "wrestled a man." That Man was God. Jacob had thought his "wres-tlings" all these many years were with Esau or a disobedient Isaac,or surely it was Laban? But, no, it was none of them. It was God that Jacob had been wrestling with all along. The flesh must be totally defeated; only God can do that.

Even then the 25th verse says that Jacob did not yield easily; the flesh never does. It cannot be controlled, educated, or spiritualized. It must be crippled *"out of joint."*

The 26th verse tells us of the command of God, *"Let me go."* But Jacob will not. In all of his wrestlings, through all the years, he knows this "wrestling" can change him. You can hear that cry in Jacob as he says, *"I will not let thee go, except thou bless me."* This must be the cry of every child of God. It is the cry of despera-tion, of a broken heart.

And then God asks, *"What is thy name?"* Jacob knew what the Lord was asking, and he answered Him thusly. *"Jacob",* was the reply. God was asking, "What are you?" And Jacob was answering, finally so, "I am a schemer, a deceiver." God cannot change us until we first admit what we are. In Isaiah 41, God would say, *"Thou worm Jacob."*

And then, the great miraculous change, *"Israel,"* "a prince with God." It means "power with God and with men." How wonderful it must have been for Jacob to hear the words, "No more Jacob, but Israel"; no more schem-ing, no more deceiving.

The 29th verse says that Jacob asked for God's "covenant name." God would not give him a covenant name, but, instead, showed him His face, which is much better.

The 30th verse says, *"Jacob called the name of the place Peniel."* Peniel means "the face of

God." Jacob said it: *"I have seen God face to face."* The cry of the human heart is to see the face of its Creator; that has been given to us in the face of Jesus Christ.

The 31st verse forever records *"the halted thigh"* meaning "the limp." The flesh was forever crippled; the limp would forever be a reminder that the flesh was dead and the Spirit was alive. The writer of the book of Hebrews tells of the dying Jacob blessing both the sons of Joseph, and worshiping. And then it says, *"leaning upon the top of his staff."* Jacob would remain a cripple the rest of his life. And strangely enough, God would say of him, "You win," *"hast prevailed"* (vs. 28). With God, we win by losing. With the world, we lose by winning.

CHAPTER 33

Verses 1 through 4 proclaim the meeting of Jacob with Esau. The Jacob that meets him is no longer the Jacob that Esau once knew. He is a different man now, albeit the two natures of the flesh and the Spirit struggle with him. However, now *"the elder will serve the younger"* (25:23). The schemer that Esau came to meet no longer existed. So, the gifts that Jacob would give are now unneeded. Likewise, the 400-man army is no longer needed. The cause of wars is an evil heart. The cause of peace is a regenerated heart.

Verse 14 says that Jacob intended to *"come unto my Lord unto Seir"* (Petra). However, history records that Jacob never went to Seir. Likewise, the child of God has no place or business in the home of Esau.

Through the balance of the life of Jacob, as is recorded in the book of Genesis, the Holy Spirit will address Jacob thusly, or by the name of "Israel," all according to the supremacy of the flesh or the Spirit. Gradually, as we go from chapter to chapter, we will see less Jacob and more Israel. And so it is with the child of God.

The 17th verse says that *"Jacob journeyed to Succoth."* Once again Jacob fails God. He is in the wrong place, and evil will ensue. The Bible did not say, "The God of Succoth," but it said, *"I am the God of Bethel."*

Jacob builds a house. This is the first mention of a "house" in connection with the patriarchs. The life of pilgrimage is only easy to him who keeps his eye upon the promises.

Verse 18 says that once again he moved to "Shalem." Here, he bought a field and *"spread and pitched his tent."* And that, *"before the city."*

The 20th verse says he built *"an altar."* However, the divinely chosen place for the altar was Bethel and not Shechem. Our folly increases when we try to sanctify a work of the flesh.

CHAPTER 34

Jacob's sin now compounds itself. The *"daughters of the land"* are appealing to Dinah. Satan will try to corrupt the "daughter of Israel" and, thereby, hinder the coming of the Messiah. Dinah was about 15 years old at this time. Josephus, the Jewish historian, says she went to one of the festivals at Shechem.

And now, so says the 5th verse, Dinah is *"defiled."* If we pitch our tent before the city (33:18), sooner or later our children will be defiled. Too many Christians enjoy living as citizens in Shechem when they ought to be pilgrims at Bethel.

Verses 6 through 12 record the proposal by *Hamor* for even closer fellowship. Compromise is ever one of Satan's chief weapons. Satan says, "Come in." God says, "Come out."

Verses 13 through 29 record a pitiful example of God's chosen. Simeon and Levi will be the ringleaders. Because of their violence and cruelty, they will forfeit a possession in the promised land. What a sorry example of the Church. How so often it resorts to the ways of the world. A child of God out of the will of God brings no blessing to those around him, only a curse. A child of God can only be a blessing when he is "salt" and "light."

Verses 30 and 31 record Jacob blaming Simeon and Levi for his own sin. Jacob should have gone to Bethel, but, instead, he went to Succoth and to Shechem. The reaping always follows the sowing.

CHAPTER 35

God speaks to Jacob and tells him, *"Go up to Beth-el"* (Bethel meaning "the house of God"). God always tells us to come back to His house. He said, *"dwell there."* In Shechem, Jacob was out of the will of God. At Bethel, he is in the will of God. He built an altar at Shechem, but God would not recognize it, because Calvary can never be a part of the world. It is for the world but not of the world. The only "altar" that God will recognize is that which is built in His place. When Esau was chasing Jacob, he went to Bethel. Now that the *"inhabitants of the land"* look like they will chase him, he goes back to Bethel. The only place for the child of God is the house of God.

The 2nd verse speaks of revival. How awful that *"idolatry"* has become a part of Jacob's family. How much it is a part of present-day Christendom. And then, *"be clean."* How often God tells us to "clean up" both morally and spiritually, and then *"change your garments."* The garments of Jacob's family had become the garments of Shechem. Now they are to be changed to the garments of the pilgrim. The 2nd verse shows that Jacob realized that things were not well spiritually. If every Christian would take spiritual inventory, no doubt many would find themselves in the same position as Jacob. If they did the right thing, they would put away the "idols," "clean up," and "put away the garb of the world."

The 3rd verse records Jacob going to *"Beth-el,"* the house of God. There is a great spiritual lesson to be learned here. Genesis 13 records Abraham, after his sojourn in Egypt, going back to "Beth-el." It says, *"Unto the place of the altar, which he had made there at the first."* Jeremiah, likewise, said, *"Ask for the old paths"* (Jer. 6:16). In Revelation 2:5, Jesus told the pastor of the church of Ephesus, *"Do the first works."* So, it is back to the altar, back to where God spoke at the beginning. God really never leaves us; we leave Him. In Jacob's day, it was geographical as well as spiritual. Today, it is spiritual only, but the implication is the same.

In verse 4 we have Jacob "doing right" and

NOTES

Jacob "doing wrong." He did right in absolving himself of these "strange gods," etc. However, the wrong was in burying them instead of burning them. They should have been burned. Incidentally, the *"earrings"* were a part of idol worship. They were not regular earrings as we think of such.

Once again, the protection that Jacob had seen in 32:1 is now evident.

The 7th verse says that Jacob *"built an altar."* Once again, this is a type of Calvary. Under the guidance of the Holy Spirit, he calls the place *"El Beth-el."* It means, "the God of the house of God." In 28:19, he called the place *"Beth-el"* which means" the house of God." Why did he change the name?

Genesis 28:22 says that Jacob, immediately after his *"Beth-el"* experience, promised God to *"surely give the tenth unto thee."* In other words, at that particular time (his first visit to Beth-el), Jacob's interest was more on what God could do for him instead of who God was. Now, many years later, little by little, his desire is not that much after the things of God, but after God. Hence, *"El Beth-el,"* "the God of the house of God."

The 8th verse records Jacob's grief at the death of his mother's nurse. No doubt, Jacob had spent many hours speaking to Deborah about his mother concerning the 20 missing years. So there he weeps, *"Allon-bachuth,"* meaning "the oak of weeping."

The 9th verse records God once again appearing to Jacob. When we come back to God's way, God then comes our way.

The 10th verse records a beautiful moment. God reaffirms His promise to Jacob, "You are no longer a deceiver, but a prince of God."

Throughout the chapter, the patriarch is called Jacob (except verses 21 and 22). How strange this contradiction appears to human wisdom! Jacob is his name of weakness, Israel of strength, and, yet, is he only named Israel in connection with wandering and dishonor? So it is at all times! Bitter earthly sorrows may often closely follow sweet spiritual experiences.

Verse 11 records the great promise of God, *"I am God Almighty,"* meaning "All-Bountiful" or "All-Sufficient One." It was that same word that God had given to Abraham (Gen. 17:1). God will be the same to this generation as He was to the previous generations. If we will meet His conditions (which is humility), He will give us the same as He gave them.

The 14th verse records the first *"drink offering"* in Scripture. When God first revealed Himself to Jacob at this spot, Jacob poured oil upon the pillar; now he pours both oil and wine. The oil symbolized the Spirit; the wine symbolizes joy. It has taken a long time for the joy to be coupled with the Spirit. The stone, as a memorial, was a type of "the Rock of Ages," the Lord Jesus Christ.

Verses 16 through 19 record the birth of Benjamin. Rachel, as a type of the Church, travails and is in hard labor. There will be no children born to the Church unless there is *"travail and hard labor."* We have tried to substitute other methods. We have been somewhat successful in quantity but very little in quality.

The 18th verse says that in her dying she would call the child "Benoni," meaning "child of my sorrow." (It was the custom for Hebrew women to name the child.) However, faith steps in with respect to Jacob and changes that name to "Benjamin," which means "man at God's right hand." This is a perfect type of the Lord Jesus Christ. He was, first of all, *"a Man of sorrows."* And now He is *"the Man at the Father's right hand."*

Strangely enough, in the 21st verse the Holy Spirit refers to Jacob as *"Israel."* It's a time of great sorrow for Jacob, especially since he has lost Rachel. The little crying baby will ever be a reminder of her. The world at this time would have looked at him as a weakened failure, but, instead, God calls him *"Israel, the Prince of God."* Oh, if the Church could only look at situations as God looks at them!

In the midst of Israel's sorrow, Reuben, the firstborn, commits a grievous sin by committing adultery with his father's concubine – and, yet, God calls Jacob *"Israel."*

Verses 27 through 29 record the death of Isaac. It is time for the great patriarch to go. The Holy Spirit records three things about his passing:

A. *"He gave up the ghost."*

B. *"And died."*

C. *"And was gathered to his people,"* the Holy Spirit signifying his work was complete,

his mission was finished, *"the God of Abraham, Isaac, and Jacob."*

CHAPTER 36

Chapter 36 records the generations (or sons) of Esau.

Esau and his sons were born in Canaan, the land of promise. The spiritual opportunity that lay before them was unexcelled. But yet, the 6th verse says, *"And went into the country from the face of his brother Jacob."* He actually went to Seir (Petra).

All of Jacob's sons were born outside of the promised land (except Benjamin), but yet came into it. What a contrast with Esau's sons. Regrettably, as is obvious, all (both Jacob's and Esau's sons) were evil. However, Esau and his sons would not allow the God of his fathers to change their evil to righteousness. Jacob and his sons did the very opposite. They brought their evil to the Cross.

Verse 12 speaks of "Amalek." This was Esau's grandson. Amalek, in the Bible, is a type of the flesh. It is recorded in Exodus 17:8, *"Then came Amalek."* They attacked the weak and faint people at the hindmost part of the camp to plunder and take a spoil. Amalek was not a product of Jacob (the Spirit); he was a product of Esau (the flesh); hence, would ever oppose the people of God.

In following the verses of chapter 36, we see that Esau and his sons were men of the world who have their portion in this life (Psa. 17:14). They established themselves in power with their kings and their dukes and their riches and their possessions, while the heirs of Promise, that is, Jacob and his sons, are still pilgrims and strangers. This furnishes a prophetic picture. The child of God is ever reminded that, "This world is not my home, I'm just a passing through." However, the conclusion of the final conflict will not be that the evil inherit the earth, but that *"the meek inherit the earth."*

CHAPTER 37

Nearly 25 chapters in the book of Genesis are devoted somewhat to the life of Jacob. His life, more so than any other Bible great, typifies the struggle of the child of God. Whenever a Christian looks at Jacob, he is looking at himself. Now begins the story of Joseph. In Joseph, we will see one of the most beautiful types of Christ found in the entirety of the Word of God. We will also see the future of Israel and their coming back to the Lord. It is all laid out in beautiful prophetic detail.

Verse 2 says at the time of this history Joseph was 17 years old. Jacob was about 107 years old. Reuben, the oldest son, was about 29 years old, with Benjamin, the youngest, being perhaps 7 or 8. All the brothers who sold Joseph to the Ishmaelites were from 18 to 29 years old.

In the 3rd verse, the love that *"Israel"* showed for Joseph more so than all his other children was orchestrated by the Holy Spirit. At this juncture, the Holy Spirit calls Jacob *"Israel,"* meaning that the Lord desired that Joseph would have the birthright over Reuben the firstborn. Actually, Joseph was no more the *"son of Jacob's old age,"* than Benjamin, etc. Hence, this phrase must refer to a son especially devoted to the care of Jacob in his old age. The *"coat of colors"* was a mark of honor and rank and worn only by the chief and heir. Joseph inherited the birthright (I Chron. 5:1-2). The garment was of many colors, not pieces, marking it as a priestly and royal garment. Whoever wore this coat was the one to whom the birthright was given.

Consequently, the hatred that his brothers had for Joseph was, at least in part, because of the Holy Spirit's choice of Joseph as the receiver of the birthright. Joseph was a type of Christ, with his father loving him more than anyone else. Consequently, as Joseph's brethren hated him, Israel would hate Christ and could not *"speak peaceably unto him."*

The dreams of verses 5 through 11 are a type of the prophecies foretelling the reigning power of the coming Lord Jesus Christ.

NOTES

The 8th verse says that Joseph's brethren hated him, *"yet the more for his dreams, and his words."* Israel, likewise, would hate the Lord Jesus Christ because of the prophecies and His words. These dreams are not only a portent of Joseph's brethren bowing down to him, but, as well, a picture of the coming day when Israel will bow to the Lord Jesus Christ.

The 2nd verse sets Joseph forth as a shepherd. Verses 12 through 17 further emphasize that fact. Likewise, the Lord Jesus Christ is the *"Good Shepherd."* As Joseph was sent by Jacob to the brethren and the flock at Dothan, likewise, the Lord Jesus Christ was sent to Israel. The words of Joseph, *"Here am I,"* portray the prophecy, *"Here am I oh God to do thy will."*

Verses 18 through 22 portray the parable of the "householder" that Jesus told to the elders (St. Matt. 21:33-43).

Verses 23 through 28 record the rejection of Joseph. Verse 23 says they *"stripped Joseph of his coat."* Likewise, they cast lots for Jesus' robe.

The *"pit"* described in verse 24 was a type of the tomb that Jesus was put in.

The 25th verse says they *"sat down to eat bread: and they lifted up their eyes and looked."* Likewise, Matthew said concerning the crucifixion of Christ, *"and sitting down they watched Him there"* (St. Matt. 27:36).

The 27th verse speaks of Joseph being sold *"to the Ishmaelites"* (Gentiles). Likewise, Matthew said, *"When they had bound him, they led him away, and delivered him to Pontius Pilate, the Governor"* (St. Matt. 27:2).

The 28th verse speaks of Joseph being sold for 20 pieces of silver. Likewise, Jesus was sold for *"30 pieces of silver"* (St. Matt. 26:15).

Verses 29 through 36 portray the resurrection as well as Israel's deception.

The 29th verse speaks of Reuben looking into the pit and *"behold, Joseph was not in the pit."* St. Matthew 28:6 says concerning the resurrection, *"He is not here, for he is risen."*

Verse 30 records Reuben saying, *"The child is not."* Luke records these words, *"And then entered in, and found not the body of the Lord Jesus"* (St. Luke 24:3).

The 31st verse says they took Joseph's coat and dipped it in blood. Likewise, Matthew said, *"His blood be on us, and on our children"* (St. Matt. 27:25).

The 32nd verse says the coat was given to Jacob and the question asked, *"Know now whether it be thy son's coat or no."* Matthew said, *"And they crucified him, and parted his garments"* (St. Matt. 27:35).

The 34th verse says that *"Jacob rent his clothes, and put sackcloth upon his loins, and mourned."* Mark said, *"They mourned and wept"* (St. Mark 16:10).

The 36th verse says that Joseph was *"sold into Egypt."* As the story will tell, Joseph will become the second most powerful man in Egypt. As well, Jesus Christ would rise from the dead and become the Head of the Church, which is, by and large, made up of Gentiles.

CHAPTER 38

Chronologically, chapter 38 should follow chapter 33, for 33 years after Jacob left Haran, he went into Egypt. By that time, Judah's son's widow had given birth to twins, and they were old enough that one of them had married and become the father of twins.

This story is given as a necessary link in the genealogy of Christ and is inserted here so that the history of Joseph, which immediately follows, may not be interrupted.

The 1st verse speaks of Adullam, which was the ancient capital of the Canaanites or giants who occupied the southern part of Canaan.

The 2nd verse says that *"Judah saw there a daughter of a certain Canaanite."* Judah certainly knew that marriage to Canaanites was forbidden. At this time, he did not realize that he would be the one through whom the *"Lion of the tribe of Judah"* would come. How so much we forfeit in our faithlessness.

The 3rd verse says that *"she conceived, and bare a son."* The baby's name was Er. He was the firstborn of Judah and seemed to have been the chosen one in Judah's family through whom the Messiah was intended to come. For even after his death, Tamar, his widow, bore a son to Judah whose name (Pharez or Phares) appears with hers (Thamar) in the line of Christ (St. Matt. 1:3). No doubt the wickedness of Er included despising his privilege to bring forth

one in the lineage of Christ.

In the 6th verse, it says that *"Judah took a wife for Er his first-born, whose name was Tamar."* Who she was is not known, except that she was evidently a Canaanite. Amazingly, she was in the line of Christ.

Verses 8 through 10 record the sin of Onan. It seems he resented a child of his being born to carry on Er's name instead of his own. Both were wicked men. Sin had likely made them bitter enemies; hence, Onan wanted his brother's name to be blotted out of the earth. The firstborn in such cases did carry on the dead man's name and not his own father's (Deut. 25:6-10). Furthermore, perhaps the devil had stirred up hatred in Onan concerning the Seed of the woman who seems to have been intended to come through Er's offspring. This deep-seated anger could have caused him to behave as in verse 9 to prevent such offspring from coming in his brother's name.

At any rate, what he did *"displeased the Lord,"* and the Lord *"slew him also."*

Verses 11 and 12 record Judah's plan. His two sons were now dead, having been slain by the Lord. Still, the law had not been fulfilled, so he promised Tamar his third son when he should be old enough. This would not have been long, possibly one or two years, as the three sons had been born in quick succession. The fact is, he may have been old enough for marriage at the time, but Judah hesitated to give him to her lest he die as the other sons had done. This was Judah's wrong, and it caused Tamar to carry out the plan of having a child by Judah himself, whose own wife was now dead.

Verses 13 through 18 have no meaning of Tamar being a harlot. Actually, she was imitating the temple prostitutes who were consecrated to the abominable worship of Astarte.

Verses 19 through 24 record that Judah was very quick to condemn Tamar. So it is, being very easy to condemn others while justifying ourselves. This sin started in the Garden of Eden with Adam and Eve. For his sin, Adam blamed Eve; for her sin, Eve blamed the serpent, and now Judah blames Tamar.

Verses 25 and 26 at least record Judah's acknowledgment of his sin as well as Tamar's.

Verses 27 through 30 record the birth of the twins, resulting from the union of Tamar and Judah. One of the twins was named *"Pharez."* He was in the direct line from Adam to Christ (St. Matt 1:3). This is basically why this parenthetical chapter is inserted here. It shows that the Messiah came of Judah and Pharez.

Other than the information just given, the chapter holds several meanings.

The chapter is introduced here as an actual picture of the sin, darkness, corruption, and self-will of Joseph's brethren during the whole period of his absence from them and as the certain fruit of their rejection of him.

As well, it is a fore-picture of the moral condition of the Jews today as the result of their rejection of the Messiah.

And, most of all, this chapter shows how truly Christ made Himself of no reputation, and being born a member of the tribe of Judah, humbled Himself. For in that genealogy, the names Tamar and Bathsheba appear.

Why did Christ have to come by such lineage?

He said it Himself so succinctly, *"I did not come to call the righteous, but sinners to repentance."* Christ came for a fallen, depraved, perverted human race. However, it must ever be noted that He in no wise inherited from any of his ancestors the slightest taint of sin, for He was conceived of the Holy Spirit, and though born of a woman from such wicked, sinful lineage, was wholly free from moral corruption.

The 38th chapter of Genesis is a portrayal of the human race, of which we are a part, that Jesus came to redeem.

CHAPTER 39

Now we pick up the story of Joseph, the most glorious type of Christ. It is not recorded anywhere in Joseph's history that he sinned, and that was because he was a type of Christ. However, we do know that he sinned, because the Scripture says *"all have sinned."* From the life of Joseph, we will learn many things, not only about ourselves, but about God and His leadership. We will learn dependence, trust,

and faith. We will, as well, learn that God's ways are not man's ways. However, if we yield totally to Him, He will take that which seems to be certain destruction and turn it into certain blessing.

In verse 1, it seems strange that Potiphar would be called *"an Egyptian."* However, at this particular time (throughout Joseph's life) an Eastern race had conquered and now governed the country of Egypt. So, actually, the Pharaoh would not have been an Egyptian. However, certain government officials such as Potiphar were. What were Joseph's thoughts when he was being sold by the Ishmaelites to Potiphar, the captain of the guard (the chief law-enforcement officer in Egypt)?

In verses 2 through 5 we are told five times by the Holy Spirit that Divine blessing accompanied Joseph. As well, five is the number of grace, which explains God's dealings with Joseph.

The 6th verse says *"Joseph was a goodly person, and well favored."* In the Hebrew, this means that Joseph was very handsome. Actually, the beauty of Joseph was celebrated all over the East. Persian poets of the 12th chapter of the Koran speak of his beauty as perfect. Old traditions say that Zuleekah, Potiphar's wife, was at first the most virtuous of women, but when she saw him she was so affected that she lost all self-control and became a slave to her passion. On one occasion, she supposedly made a dinner inviting 40 of the most beautiful women in Egypt who, when they saw Joseph, were so moved with admiration that they exclaimed with one accord that he must be an angel.

The 8th verse says that *"he refused"* the woman's advances. His character stands out as one of the purest in all history. He allowed no temptation to affect his high morality, no calamity to shake his implicit faith in God, no adversity to depress him, and no power or position to make him proud and haughty.

The 12th verse says, *"She caught him by his garment."* This is the second occasion that the Sacred History speaks of Joseph's garment. His brothers took the first one; Potiphar's wife the other. The brothers try to hide their sin with the first garment. She tried to hide hers with this garment.

Verses 19 and 20 record that Joseph's status changed in a moment's time. He went from the palace to prison. In the eyes of man, this may have seemed very cruel, and no doubt was. However, Potiphar just may have done Joseph the greatest favor of all by removing him from the presence of his wife.

The 21st verse proclaims in the midst of adversity, *"But the Lord was with Joseph."* It would seem strange to some that this would be said, especially in view of the fact that the Lord did not save Joseph from prison. And to be sure, the prison was not pleasant. Psalm 105 says, *"Whose feet they hurt with fetters: He was laid in iron; until the time that his word came: The word of the Lord tried him."* Faith must ever be tested. And even in prison, the Sacred Text records, *"And that which he did, the Lord made it to prosper."* There is blessing even in the midst of the test.

CHAPTER 40

Several things open up to us in the 40th chapter.

1. There is no record that Joseph ever murmured or complained.

2. God's manner of speaking to individuals, both godly and ungodly, through dreams.

3. The closeness of Joseph to God, insomuch that God could speak to him even in prison.

The 4th verse says concerning Joseph and the prisoners, *"He served them."* What a beautiful type of the Lord Jesus Christ, who so faithfully served the entirety of the human race who were none other than prisoners. As Joseph was put in prison, in effect, Christ was put in the "prison of this world."

Verses 9 through 19 tell of the dreams of the chief butler and the chief baker. It also tells of Joseph's interpretation of these dreams. In these interpretations, he preached faithfully the Word of the Lord, whether it announced grace or wrath – and so did the Lord Jesus Christ.

Verses 14 and 15 record that Joseph never accused his brethren. He merely said, *"I was*

NOTES

stolen away out of the land of the Hebrews." Likewise, Jesus did not come to condemn, but to save.

Verse 23 proclaims that the chief butler did not remember Joseph *"but forgat him."*

As well, this was in the will of God. God's timing is a part of His will. If Joseph had been released at this time, he would have only been an unemployed slave, whereas God had much better in store for him.

CHAPTER 41

Chapter 41 is a remarkable chapter. The dreams of Pharaoh interpreted by Joseph not only marked out the future of Jacob and his family, but, as well, even in more graphic detail, marked out the future of the nation of Israel. Possibly upon this world will be seven years of great harvest of souls, immediately followed by seven years of tribulation *"that has never been before, and shall never be again"* (St. Matt. 24:21).

The 1st verse records Pharaoh's dream. How so often God has spoken through dreams. It was the dream of seven fat cattle and seven lean cattle. The dream was doubled, proclaiming its certainty. Seven fat ears of corn versus seven thin ears of corn.

The *"east wind"* from the 16th verse localizes the Great Tribulation period that is coming, which will affect the entire earth but will have its beginnings in the Middle East.

The 8th verse says, *"None could interpret them unto Pharoah."* Likewise, the pundits of this world little know or understand the happenings of the near future. They are *"spiritually discerned."*

The 14th verse says, *"Pharaoh sent and called Joseph."* Pharaoh, a type of the Gentile Church, has "called Christ" after his "brethren" have hated and rejected him.

As the 16th verse tells of Joseph answering Pharaoh saying, *"It is not in me: God shall give . . . ,"* likewise, Christ said, *"My meat is to do the will of him that sent me, and to finish his work"* (St. John 4:34).

As verses 17 through 24 portray the relating

of the dreams to Joseph by Pharaoh, as well, the book of Revelation given by Jesus Christ to St. John has been, by and large, interpreted by the Gentile Church.

The 25th verse says, *"What he is about to do."* The book of Revelation says, *"To show unto his servants things which must shortly come to pass"* (Rev. 1:1).

The 32nd verse uses almost the exact words as Revelation 1, *"Things which must shortly come to pass."*

Verse 38 proclaims Joseph as *"a man in whom the Spirit of God is."* Matthew said, *"And he saw the Spirit of God descending like a dove and lighting upon him"* (St. Matt. 3:16).

The 39th verse says, *"There is none so discrete and wise as thou art."* Matthew said, *"What manner of man is this"* (St. Matt. 8:27).

The 45th verse says that Pharaoh called Joseph's name, *"Zaphnath-pa-a-neah,"* means *"Saviour of the World."* John said, *"Behold the Lamb of God, which taketh away the sin of the world"* (St. John 1:29).

The 46th verse says, *"Joseph was thirty years old when he stood before Pharaoh King of Egypt."* Luke said, *"He began to be about thirty years of age"* (St. Luke 3:23).

The 49th verse says, *"Joseph gathered corn as the sand of the sea . . . without number."* Peter said, *"And it shall come to pass in the last days, saith God, I will pour out of my Spirit upon all flesh"* (Acts 2:17). As stated, the seven years of plenty represent the tremendous harvest of souls that is even now on the eve of being fulfilled.

Verses 50 through 52 tell of Joseph's two sons born to him; they also portray Joseph's great spiritual victories. The firstborn was *"Manasseh,"* meaning "God has made me forget." Paul said, *"Forgetting those things which are behind."* Joseph "forgot" the wrongs that had been done him by his brethren. We, as well, must forget. The second child was named *"Ephraim."* This means "fruitful." Because Joseph, by the help of God, was able to "forget," likewise, God made him *"fruitful."*

The *"all lands"* of the 54th verse proclaims the tribulation of the last days affecting the entire earth. The book of Revelation says, *"And deceiveth them that dwell on the earth"* (Rev. 13:14).

NOTES

CHAPTER 42

In God's way, the great story now begins to unfold. The famine is now sore in the land, and Jacob will send his sons to Egypt to buy food. Likewise, in the Great Tribulation period Israel, as is recorded in verse 5, will no doubt lean heavily on America or other Gentile countries for help and sustenance, for this entire story is not only a picture of the happenings of so long ago, but, as well, is a portrayal of what will happen to Israel at the end time.

The 6th verse says that *"Joseph was the governor over the land."* Joseph's brethren will *"bow down themselves before him."* Likewise, as Israel seeks the help of Gentile nations, now, as then, she is, in effect, bowing down to the Lord Jesus Christ. As Joseph, the type of Christ, was ruler over Egypt, likewise, the Lord Jesus Christ has been the source of blessings in America. The reason America has been able to somewhat sustain Israel with loans, grants, and outright gifts is because of the blessings of the Lord Jesus Christ on this land. When Israel accepts this help, whether she realizes it or not, she is bowing to the Lord Jesus Christ.

The 7th verse says that Joseph *"spake roughly unto them."* In the Great Tribulation period, the Lord Jesus Christ will deal "roughly" with Israel. It will be called the time of *"Jacob's trouble."*

The 8th verse says that *"Joseph knew his brethren, but they knew him not."* Of course the Lord Jesus Christ knows Israel, but, sadly, *"they know not Him."* Joseph's dealings with his brothers is a picture of the future action of the Lord Jesus Christ in bringing Israel to recognize her sin in rejecting Him and the consequent enormity of that sin against God. Had Joseph only been concerned about his own dignity, he would have revealed himself at once to his brothers. Likewise, Christ could easily reveal Himself to Israel immediately. However, as such revelation would have produced only confusion among Joseph's brethren, likewise, such revelation would only produce confusion with Israel. There has to be biblical repentance before there can be glorious revelation.

The 17th verse says, *"Into ward three days."* Likewise, Israel will be under tremendous pressure by the Antichrist for a little over three years.

The 21st verse speaks of the remorse of Joseph's brothers. The sin was approximately 20 years old, but it still lay heavily upon their consciences. I cannot help but believe that during the Great Tribulation period, when Israel is threatened with extermination, that the Lord Jesus Christ will loom large before them, and they will remember what happened 2000 years ago.

The 25th verse says that he gave them, *"provision for the way."* The Scripture says this concerning Israel during the Great Tribulation period, *"Where she hath a place prepared of God, that they should feed her there twelve hundred and sixty days"* (Rev. 12:6).

The 38th verse speaks of Jacob's great sorrow. The Great Tribulation period is called, *"The time of Jacob's trouble"* (Jer. 30:7).

CHAPTER 43

The 1st verse says, *"The famine was sore in the land."* Likewise, the Great Tribulation period will be "sore in the land of Israel."

In verses 8 and 11 the Holy Spirit uses the chosen word *"Israel,"* speaking of Jacob as a "Prince with God." However, it is noteworthy to look at the circumstances under which the Holy Spirit called him "Israel." It was a time of total helplessness on Jacob's part. He feels everything he has is being taken away from him. Now, they are asking for Benjamin, and yet the Holy Spirit, at this given time, calls him *"Israel."* The world, at this time, would have called Jacob "weak," but God called him "strong." Most of the time when we think we are so strong in the Lord, actually we are "weak." And when we think we are so "weak," we are, in fact, "strong."

The 14th verse speaks of *"God Almighty."* Jacob, in his instructions to his sons, invokes that all-powerful name. It means "El-Shaddai," the "All-Bountiful" or "Supplier of all needs." In effect, Jacob is saying, "I don't understand what's happening, but I believe God."

As the 17th verse speaks of the men being brought into Joseph's house, likewise, Israel will ultimately be brought into Jesus' house. Verse 30 speaks of Joseph's sorrow. How much sorrow has Israel's rebellion caused the Lord Jesus Christ?

The 34th verse speaks of Benjamin receiving *"five times so much as any of theirs."* Benjamin is a type of the Jewish generation that will be alive at the Second Coming of Christ. That which Israel will receive then will be far more than any generation before them, even five times as much.

CHAPTER 44

The 44th chapter of Genesis contains one of the most impassioned pleas ever made by one man to another. Judah will make this plea unto Joseph. The distress of Judah and the others shows that they were no longer in heart the men of 20 years back. Zechariah 9:13 says, *"When I have bent Judah for me."* In that day Judah will repent.

Zechariah, as well, said, *"In that day there shall be a great mourning"* (Zech. 12:11).

Once again, the 18th verse says, *"Then Judah came near unto him."* Finally, at the Second Coming, Judah will "come near unto Him."

CHAPTER 45

The 1st verse says, *"Joseph made himself known unto his brethren."* Zechariah said this, *"And they shall look upon me whom they have pierced"* (Zech. 12:10). As well, he said this, *"And one shall say unto him, what are these wounds in thine hands?"* (Zech. 13:6).

In the 3rd verse it says, *"I am Joseph."* Revelation to the brethren was made. What will Israel's reaction be whenever Christ says, "I am Jesus"?

Verse 13 speaks of Joseph telling his brethren to tell Jacob of *"all my glory in*

Egypt." Isaiah said this, *"And they shall declare my glory among the Gentiles"* (Isa. 66:19).

In the 26th verse, one of the most poignant, heart-touching scenes is recorded, *"Joseph is yet alive."* Zechariah said this, *"And the Lord shall be king over the earth: In that day shall there be one Lord, and his name one"* (Zech. 14:9). As Jacob's *"heart fainted,"* likewise, the hearts of Israel will faint when they realize, "Jesus is alive."

The 28th verse records Israel saying, *"I will go and see him.* Zechariah prophesied these words, *"Shall even go up from year to year to worship the king, the Lord of hosts"* (Zech. 14:16).

Hallelujah!

CHAPTER 46

This is a beautiful chapter evidencing Holy Spirit leading, faith, and relationship, with some fear.

The Holy Spirit begins His account of Jacob's journey into Egypt by using the name that God had given him, *"Israel."* Whenever faith reigns, God uses the name *"Israel."* When doubt prevails, the Holy Spirit resorts to *"Jacob."* What a lesson for all of us. When he does not believe, he faints and is called *"Jacob."* When he does believe, takes courage and boldly steps out, he is called *"Israel."* When he was offering sacrifices, which were a type of Calvary, and, thereby, believing, God addressed him as *"Israel."*

The 2nd verse says that, *"God spake unto Israel."* And, yet, when He spoke to him personally, He said, *"Jacob, Jacob."* Why the seeming contradiction?

Actually, there is no contradiction. When you look at the 2nd verse, you are looking at both types of sanctification. The type of sanctification that God gives to us, which refers to our position in Christ, never changes. Hence he would be called *"Israel"* (but you are sanctified – I Cor. 6:11). The address by God, saying, *"Jacob, Jacob,"* spoke of Jacob's condition, *"sanctify wholly"* (I Thess. 5:23). There is a positional sanctification given to us freely by

Jesus Christ. We did not earn it or merit it; it is a work of grace, hence Jacob being called *"Israel."* As well, there is a conditional sanctification, hence God saying, *"Jacob, Jacob."* The Holy Spirit's every endeavor is to bring our condition up to our position.

The 3rd verse speaks of *"fear."* Evidently, Jacob, knowing that God had been sorely displeased with Abraham's sojourn into Egypt, and that He had forbidden Isaac to go, feared to go himself. This one word of salutation by the Heavenly Father, *"Fear not to go down into Egypt,"* tells us much about a changed Jacob. No longer does he plan and scheme; now he waits on the Lord. That is the place the Holy Spirit is attempting to bring us as well.

Then in the 4th verse the great promise is given, *"I will go down with thee into Egypt."* There need be no fear if the Lord is with us. And then comes the second promise, *"I will also surely bring thee up again."* That He did with a high and mighty hand, with the children of Israel being led out of Egyptian bondage. The third promise states, *"For I will there make of thee a great nation."* They would go in just a few souls; they would come out millions strong.

The 4th verse says that the man he thought he would never see again would, instead, stand beside him when he died. How faithful is our God.

The 5th verse once again portrays God saying, *"Israel."* If the world had to pass judgment on Jacob's sojourn at this time, he would be looked at in weakness. But God looks at him in strength because of his obedience.

In the 8th verse, God once again says, *"Israel,"* and this is because of what He will do with, and make, of this people. Through them, the Messiah will come; hence, "the children of Israel."

In the 28th verse, it says, *"And he sent Judah before him unto Joseph."* Judah had natural traits that made him an outstanding leader of men and one to be trusted. In prophecy, he was destined to have the chief place among the brethren. His was to be the ruling tribe through whom the Messiah would come and rule all nations forever (49:10). In history, Judah had the ruling part in Israel from David to the Babylonian captivity, a period of 473 years. This tribe, along with Benjamin and multitudes from all the other tribes, continued as a nation for 133 years longer than the apostate northern kingdom of Israel. Judah was the leader in the return from captivity until the Messiah came the first time. Judah will be the leading tribe under the Messiah in the Millennium and forever.

In the 29th verse the Holy Spirit calls him *"Israel"* as he meets Joseph for the first time in over 20 years. The Holy Spirit refers to him as *"Israel"* because of the future meeting that will take place whenever Israel and the Lord Jesus Christ meet at the Second Coming after such a long estrangement.

Once again, in the 30th verse the Holy Spirit refers to him as *"Israel,"* because his mission is, by and large, now complete. Actually, he will live some 17 more years, and it will be in great victory.

CHAPTER 47

The 1st verse speaks of Joseph telling Pharaoh of his father and his brethren. He never at any time mentions to Pharaoh the perfidy of his brethren. As far as we know, no one in Egypt knew anything about the horror of their past deed; such is true forgiveness. It not only forgives sin, but it forgets as well.

The 3rd verse says the brothers of Joseph claimed as their occupation, shepherds. A shepherd was an abomination to Egyptians. However, Pharaoh was not an Egyptian. He was actually of another country that had defeated Egypt in battle. History would record him as a "shepherd king."

The 7th verse proclaims Jacob being brought before Pharaoh, the mightiest monarch on the face of the earth. Jacob will bless the mighty Pharaoh, *"the less is blessed of the better."* I wonder what the thoughts of Pharaoh were as he looked at this aged patriarch? The least and most faltering of God's children is superior to the mightiest monarch, and is conscious of the superiority *"of whom the world was not worthy."*

In the 9th verse Jacob calls his years of

following the Lord *"a pilgrimage."* Such is with the Child of God. At this time he was 130 years old. Reuben would have been about 51; Simeon 50; Levi 49; Judah 48; Dan 46; Naphtali 45; Gad 44; Asher 43; Issachar 42; Zebulun 41; Dinah 40; Joseph 39; and Benjamin about 30.

Jacob considered his life as blessed as the lives of Abraham and Isaac, who were pilgrims wandering in a strange land, with a view of another home (Acts 7:3-7). Two hundred and fifteen years had gone by since God had called Abraham. This was the halfway mark of the 430 years of the whole sojourn of the chosen race (Ex. 12:42; Gal. 3:17). These 215 years were made up of the 25 before Isaac was born, 60 before Jacob was born, and the 130 years Jacob had lived up to this time of going into Egypt. Recorded as happening during this first 215 years, we have the story of Abraham from his call at the age of 75 years to his death, a period of 100 years (total 175 years); the story of Isaac from his birth to his death in the 120th year of Jacob's life, a period of 180 years; the story of Jacob's life before going into Egypt, a period of 130 years, and the story of Joseph and his brethren the last 22 years. The lives of Abraham, Isaac, Jacob, and Joseph overlapped in this period. The last 215 years of the 430 were from Jacob's entrance into Egypt to the 80th year of Moses. Israel left Egypt the same day in the 430th year after God called Abraham to leave for Canaan (Ex. 12:40-41).

The 27th verse records the Holy Spirit saying *"Israel."* His doing so spoke of the will of God.

Once again the 29th verse says, *"Israel."* This pertains to the promise concerning the land of Israel. He would want his bones to be placed where his heart was, and so it would be. By faith Joseph saw that which God had intended. Regretfully, it has not been totally realized even yet, and that is because of sin. However, in the Millennial Reign Jacob will finally see the promise brought to total fulfillment.

CHAPTER 48

Hebrews 11:21 throws much light on the

beautiful 48th chapter of Genesis. In chapters 48 and 49, Jacob shines as never before. And if it will be noted, the Holy Spirit refers to him again and again as *"Israel."* This is the great faith action of his life. Feeble and dying, and having nothing except the staff on which he leaned and worshiped, he yet bestowed vast and unseen possessions on his grandsons.

In verses 3 and 4 Jacob reiterates the great appearance of the Lord. He calls him *"God Almighty"* (the Great Provider). He then tells how God gave him the gift of the land of Canaan.

In verse 5 he makes the two sons of Joseph, Ephraim and Manasseh, his own. What an honor.

In verse 7 he mentions his beloved Rachel. He buried her in Bethlehem. Her burial would be the seed of a birth – a birth that would change the history of mankind – the Lord Jesus Christ.

Even though Jacob was blind, the 10th verse portrays the Holy Spirit referring to him as *"Israel,"* because he could "see" by faith.

The 11th verse once again names him *"Israel,"* because of his great faith in God. Satan had told him, "You will never see Joseph again." And now the Holy Spirit says, "You have not only seen Joesph, but his sons as well."

The 13th verse says that Ephraim and Manasseh stand before Jacob.

Then he claims them as a part of the great nation God has promised him. They become the heads of two of the 12 tribes of Israel. One took the place of Joseph and the other the place of Levi, whose tribe became the priestly line and was not reckoned as one of the 12 tribes during the organization of the nation.

Verses 14 through 19 portray Israel (Jacob) blessing the two sons of Joseph. Jacob's faith overcame Joseph's will. The younger brother, Ephraim, will become a name synonymous with Israel and will truly be the greater.

Once again, in the 21st verse, the Holy Spirit refers to this patriarch as *"Israel."* Prophecy is here connected with the will of the Holy Spirit. If you will notice, Jacob never really shines until faith takes hold. Likewise, God is never honored until we believe Him.

The 22nd verse says that Joseph will inherit the birthright as the firstborn instead of it

NOTES

being given to Reuben, who was actually the firstborn, but who was disinherited because of his sin. Esau sold his birthright, and Reuben forfeited his. Jacob therefore could bestow it on whom he pleased. Joseph had a double claim; he merited the birthright, and, also, he was the firstborn of Rachel who was Jacob's true wife.

It was on this occasion that Jacob worshiped leaning on the top of his staff.

The anxiety of Jacob's faith throbs in this chapter. He fears the influence of Egypt upon his sons. His nature led him all of his life to grasp at wealth and position, but now faith shines brightly, and he earnestly points Joseph and his sons to the true riches promised by God. They were in great danger respecting Egypt. Joseph was viceroy, and brilliant prospects in Egypt were within his reach for his children. The aged patriarch urges Joseph not to make his home in Egypt, but to set his heart in Canaan.

CHAPTER 49

In verses 1 and 2 the Holy Spirit impresses the use of both names, *"Jacob"* and *"Israel."* As the 12 sons gather in his presence, he is referred to as *"Jacob."* However, when it refers to the prophecies that will be given, *"hearken unto Israel your father,"* he is referred to by his princely name, *"Israel."* The *"last days"* of verse 1 are mentioned some 33 times in Scripture. It refers here to days before both the First and Second Advents of the Messiah (the First and Second Comings).

The prophecies begin with the firstborn, *"Reuben,"* in the 3rd verse. Even though the future predictions of these tribes were very limited in detail, it is amazing at the words chosen by the Holy Spirit as to how exact they were in their future pronouncements. Some scholars have felt that the prophecies for the tribes actually gave not only the personality and spiritual direction of the tribes, but, as well, gave prophetic direction from the day that Jacob gave them to the eternal future. It is said that Reuben, Simeon, and Levi contain the moral history of Israel up to the birth of Christ.

In the more immediate future, Simeon and Levi (vs. 5) were truly divided (vs. 7) and scattered in Israel because of the slaughter at Shechem. Actually, Simeon, when the land would be parceled out at the command of Joshua upon the arrival across the Jordan, would receive no inheritance but, in fact, would have their part in the inheritance of Judah. As well, Levi would have no inheritance at all but would have their curse turned into a blessing as they became the priestly tribe of Israel. The priestly tribe of Levi held great power when Jesus was born. The high priest led the charge against Christ and was truly an *"instrument of cruelty."*

The 7th verse says, *"Cursed be their anger."* Truly, they were cursed. The high priest, Caiaphas, committed suicide, and eventually the whole of the priestly system was slaughtered when Titus laid siege to Jerusalem in A.D. 70.

Verses 8 through 12 speak of *"Judah."* This is the first prophecy that proclaims the Messiah coming from the tribe of Judah. In the 10th verse, the Messiah is called *"Shiloh."* Judah is called *"God's law-giver."* The word *"sceptre"* in the 10th verse means the sceptre of government and rule that shall not depart from Judah. When Jesus was born, the *"sceptre"* departed from Judah and was given to *"Shiloh."* The latter part of the 10th verse, *"And unto him shall the gathering of the people be,"* refers to Christ's Second Advent when Israel will be gathered from the four corners of the earth.

As the 9th verse speaks of *"the lion of the tribe of Judah,"* the 11th verse speaks of Jesus coming back in the midst of the Battle of Armegeddon, defeating the Antichrist, and overthrowing the powers of darkness, *"His garments in wine and his clothes in the blood of grapes."*

Verses 13 through 15 speak of *"Zebulun"* and *"Issachar,"* that pertain to the subjugation and dispersion of the Jews among the Gentiles.

Verse 17 speaks of *"Dan."* It says, *"Dan shall be a serpent by the way, an adder in the path."* Many feel that Dan speaks of the appearance and kingdom of the Antichrist, and believe the Antichrist could be a member of this tribe.

The 18th verse saying, *"I have waited for thy salvation, oh Lord,"* speaks of the Great Tribulation period ending with the Antichrist being defeated and Jesus Christ coming back.

The 19th verse tells us of *"Gad,"* speaking of the difficulties of Israel and the Great Tribulation period, and of the great victory that will come at the advent of the Lord, *"But he shall overcome at the last."*

Verses 20 through 26 speak of *"Asher,"* *"Napthali,"* and *"Joseph."* This speaks of Israel's glory in the millennial reign. The *"bread shall be fat"; "he shall yield royal dainties."* As well, Israel will *"give goodly words."* In the millennial reign, how *"fruitful"* Joseph will be. The *"shepherd, the stone of Israel,"* the Lord Jesus Christ, will rule and reign in Israel. Truly, it will be a time of *"bless thee with blessings."*

The 26th verse says the *"crown shall be on Joseph,"* who is a type of Christ. Jesus Christ will rule and reign.

The 27th verse speaks of *"Benjamin."* His prophecy is given last. It concerns the conclusion of the millennial reign when Satan will be loosed for a season. However, the Lord shall make short shrift of Satan's efforts at that time, *"In the morning he shall devour the prey, and at night he shall divide the spoil."*

Verses 28 through 33 conclude the great prophecies given by Jacob to his sons. He charges them to bury him in the land of Canaan. He would not that even his bones should remain in Egypt. He had seen much in Egypt; no doubt luxury had come his way, especially since his son practically sat upon the throne. However, at the last, Jacob did not see Egypt, but Canaan's fair and happy land. His faith was not wrecked; his fortune and his hopes were not in Egypt. They were in Canaan. He says to his sons, *"Bury me with my fathers in the land of Canaan."* The last part of verse 33 says, *"And was gathered unto his people."* What an example of the power of Christ, as Paul wrote, *"That his power may rest upon me"* (II Cor. 12:9).

CHAPTER 50

Verse 1 is a picture of Christ weeping over Israel. Jacob was dead physically and alive spiritually. Israel was alive physically and dead spiritually.

The 2nd verse mentions the first case of *"embalming."* The process was tedious and expensive, requiring the brain and intestines to be removed and the head and body filled with costly spices. After being steeped in natron for 70 days, the body was then washed, wrapped in bandages of linen, covered with gum, and placed in a wooden case.

The 3rd verse speaks of the Egyptians mourning him for *"70 days."* During this time, Joseph did not shave and, therefore, could not enter the royal presence.

The 5th verse once again alludes to the fact of Jacob's heart being in *"the land of Canaan."* The heart of every Christian must be thusly.

The 9th verse speaks of *"chariots and horsemen,"* as well as *"a very great company."* The grandeur of Jacob's funeral procession speaks of the burial of Christ in the tomb of the rich (St. John 19:41). It is amazing to think of this great patriarch, a pilgrim all of his life, being carried to his final resting place by the grandeur of mighty Egypt. It is one of the few times in history that the world recognized the greatness that was among them.

The 10th verse mentions *"beyond Jordan."* This does not mean on the east of Jordan, for Hebron is south of Jerusalem and the Jordan is farther on. The phrase, *"beyond Jordan,"* must be understood from the standpoint of where the writer was at the time of writing Genesis. Here, it must signify west of Jordan, for that was the true location. Thus, we must believe that Moses was on the east of Jordan when he wrote this.

The 13th verse mentions *"the field of Machpelah."* This was to be his burial place. There, Abraham and Isaac are buried as well. The tomb of Machpelah is an example of that which we take with us at death. Abraham and Isaac, both pilgrims, were buried at Machpelah. Jacob, a pilgrim as well, but yet with all the glory and riches of Egypt, was there laid to rest. However, none of them took anything with them *"but their faith."*

The 15th verse records that Joseph's brethren never did quite understand who their brother was or what he was. Now that their father Jacob was dead, they expected evil of Joseph. They did not, and even perhaps could not understand that Joseph, being a type of

NOTES

Christ, would deal with them not with judgment, but with mercy and grace. How beautiful it would be if the Church would learn the simple and yet beautiful act of Joseph as well.

The 18th verse records the last of five times the brethren fulfilled the dreams of Joseph (37:5-11). One day in its great fulfillment in the latter days, Israel will fall down at the feet of the Lord Jesus Christ, of whom Joseph was a type.

The 20th verse holds one of the greatest promises found in the entirety of the Word of God. God can take the evil that is planned against the child of God, if the child of God will trust and believe, and turn it to good. As well, nothing can happen to a Christian but that God either causes it or allows it. No, God did not cause Joseph's brethren to commit their foul deeds, but He did permit it. And, as well, grace turned the terrible ugliness to glorious beauty. Once again, how beautiful it would be if the Church could grasp and understand this.

Verses 22 and 23 say that Joseph was 110 years old when he died. He lived in Egypt 93 years, and his father's descendants lived there 215 years. This man that was sold as a slave into Egypt became a viceroy of the most powerful and richest nation on the face of the earth. He saw his great-great-grandchildren and held them upon his knees.

Verses 24 through 26 record Joseph's death. Hebrews 11:22 draws attention to the double testimony of Joseph's faith when dying.

1. God would surely redeem the children of Israel out of Egypt.

2. And they were to carry his bones out with them when leaving.

Joseph knew and believed what God had said to Abraham, to Isaac, and to Jacob regarding the gift of the land of Canaan.

The book of Genesis starts with life and ends with death. It starts with creation and ends with a coffin. The book of Genesis begins with a living God and ends with a dead man.

THE
BOOK OF EXODUS

◼

The 1st verse of Exodus begins with the word *"now,"* and connects this book to the preceding one – Genesis and records the fulfillment of Genesis 15:13-16 – 46:3-4. Both Leviticus and Numbers begin the same way, proving that the Pentateuch was originally one book. The book of Genesis was the story of the fall of man. The book of Exodus is the story of the redemption of man. Hence, the work of redemption by Christ is called His "Exodus" (deceased, going out of the world, St. Luke 9:31).

The Hebrew title for the book is "These are the names." (The Greek title is Exodus.) This book teaches that redemption can only be effected by blood. It opens with Israel as a helpless slave in the power of the enemy, and doomed by him to destruction. In Exodus, Egypt is a type of the world with all of its evil systems and, as well, ruled by the prince of darkness, Satan. The book closes with Israel redeemed, enriched, and free. The method of deliverance was the death of the Paschal Lamb. In this great plan of redemption, the book of Exodus teaches us that without blood there is no salvation.

The book starts with names, hence salvation is a personal matter.

◼

CHAPTER 1

Verse 8 records a *"new king over Egypt."* This was a fresh or new dynasty. The founder was the Assyrian of Isaiah 52:4, who conquered Egypt, and was perhaps Rameses II, whose son Menaptah would be the Pharaoh of the exodus.

Joseph died 144 years before Israel left Egypt, or 64 years before Moses was born. The king who started enslaving Israel reigned during the last part of this 64 years, for when Moses was born his policy was in force. It would be this king's daughter that brought up Moses. His son could have been reigning when Moses came back from the desert to deliver Israel.

Verses 9 through 11 portray the plans of an evil king to destroy God's people. These plans were keen and far-reaching, at least as long as God was left out. But the entrance of God into these plans turned their wisdom to folly. All schemes which ignore God illustrate the same.

Verse 11 talks about the treasure cities of *"Pithom and Raamses."* The ruins of these great treasure cities still exist today.

Verse 12 speaks of persecution. However, it should be noted that persecution has always caused the Church to grow (Acts 2:13; 4:1-37; 5:1-42).

Verses 15 through 22 portray the two leading Hebrew midwives, Shiphrah and Puah. It is ironic that the names of the mighty Pharaohs of that day are all but lost to history, whereas, the names of these two women who obeyed God are recognized by multiple millions in every generation.

The 19th verse should not be thought of as an untruth; actually, the answer was literally true, for both men and women in Israel were forced to do hard labor in the fields (vs. 14). And while it was hard for Egyptian women (who were delicate, soft, and unused to labor) to give birth to children, it was easier for Hebrew women who were strong and healthy. Perhaps many did not even need to have the service of a midwife.

Verse 21 speaks of God's blessings upon these midwives by enlarging their families and protecting them from death by Pharaoh.

CHAPTER 2

Verses 1 and 2 record the beginning of the deliverance of the children of Israel. The woman was Jochebed, and this was her second son and third child. Moses was the seventh from Abraham, the line being: Abraham, Isaac, Jacob, Levi, Kohath, Amram, and Moses. Abraham was the seventh from Heber, the line being: Heber, Peleg, Reu, Serug, Nahor, Terah, and Abraham. Enoch was the seventh from Adam, the line being: Adam, Seth, Enos, Cainan, Mahaleel, Jared, and Enoch. The Hebrew word for *"goodly"* is "towb," meaning beautiful, well-formed, and exceeding fare. This very fact would cause Pharaoh's daughter to desire him. The simple statement, *"She hid him three months,*signifies a great God-given faith on the part of the child's mother. From her actions there is every indication that the Lord had dealt strongly with her heart concerning this child, hence every effort must be made to save him.

The making of the ark in verse 3 was no doubt an act of faith. The little ark was made water-tight with pitch. As well, it was an ark daubed with pitch in which Noah was saved.

The 4th verse records his sister who *"stood afar off, to wit what would be done to him."*As well, God stood near. The Ark, no doubt, was made by divine command. The child laid in it was by divine command as well.

The 5th verse says, *"The daughter of Pharaoh came down to wash herself at the river."* The Holy Spirit orchestrated the timing of the daughter of Pharaoh.

The 6th verse says, *"the babe wept."* Somebody said that God floated His navy on the tears on a baby's cheeks. In this act lay the defeat of Satan, the preservation of a nation, the fulfillment of prophecy, and the furtherance of God's plan concerning the coming of the seed of the woman (Gen. 3:15).

Verse 9 speaks of the child being nursed by

his own mother, all paid for by Pharaoh but designed by God. Pharaoh's daughter knew what was happening, but she did not know what was going on. What was going on was powerful. God worked it out so that Moses' own mother brought up the same child who was to defeat Pharaoh in Egypt, and she received pay for it.

Verse 10 speaks of the weaning of the child. He was probably about 4 or 5 years old. Whatever name, if any, that Jochebed gave him is not known. Actually, an Egyptian princess will name him *"Moses."* The word means "drawn out." Moses became the great law-giver and leader of Israel. His name is mentioned 813 times in Scripture. He was one of the greatest men of God who ever lived. The 10th verse says, *"He became her son."* Moses was now to begin his education as the son of Pharaoh's daughter. He was *"learned in all the wisdom of the Egyptians and became mighty in words and deeds"* (Acts 7:22). Josephus says he was put in command of the Egyptian war against the Ethiopians and conquered them completely.

In verses 11 through 14 we have the account of Moses' efforts *"in the flesh"* of siding with the children of Israel. From the language of Hebrews 11:24, it is clear that there was a time when Moses had the choice of accepting or refusing the throne of Egypt. He refused and cast in his lot with the hated and oppressed Hebrews.

Verse 15 records that *"Pharaoh sought to slay Moses."* It would seem from the terminology that Pharaoh was aware of Moses' inner struggle. Now the die was cast; there would be no turning back. Moses' beginning as the deliverer of Israel is very inauspicious. To begin the great call of God by committing manslaughter is not exactly the road to consecration, but so ordained is the flesh. The flesh must "do something," and it always does wrong.

Moses went to *"the land of Midian"*; it included the Eastern coast of the Red Sea to the borders of Moab, taking in all the Arabian Peninsula. Midian was the fourth son of Abraham and Keturah (Gen. 25:1-7). The *"well"* that is mentioned in verse 15 is *"the well of Jethro,"* called *"Reuel,"* *"Raguel,"* *"Jethro,"* or *"Hobab."* No doubt, this man was a believer of the true God, and served as *"the priest of Mid-*

ian" (vs. 16).

Jethro was chief of a large tribe and exercised the rite of priestly functions for his people, as did Melchizedek (Gen. 14) and Job (Job 1). What Moses learned from Jethro is not stated, but they had common knowledge of their ancestors and many traditions of the family of Abraham, from whom both had descended – one through Isaac and Jacob, and the other through Midian (Gen. 25:1-7). It is supposed that during this 40-year period Moses wrote the books of Genesis and Job.

Verse 22 records Moses as *"a stranger in a land."* As Joseph was a type of Christ, so is Moses a type of Christ. Joseph's person was rejected by his brethren. Moses' mission was rejected by his brethren (vs. 14).

Verses 23 through 25 portray the misery and bondage of Israel. It is not clear here how much the Israelites were conscious of God or whether they had almost forgotten Him. It was God who took the initiative in their deliverance in view of His covenants and promises to their fathers. As well, it is God who takes the initiative in our salvation. Many people proclaim, "I found the Lord," when in reality, "the Lord found them." Perhaps a few in Israel knew God, but as a whole the enslaved nation was in apostasy and rebellion. So, God did not chose to deliver them on their merit; He did it because of His grace, His love, and His promises. Likewise, God does not save us because we merit salvation, but He does so because He loves us, and because He has promised redemption.

—■—

CHAPTER 3

The 1st verse of chapter 3 tells us so very much about the ways of God. What God would do with Moses was not learned in the palaces of Egypt but was learned at *"the backside of the desert."* Forty years of the desert was needed to humble the strength of the "flesh: and to destroy its hope. The possible King of Egypt was now an obscure shepherd. The *"backside of the desert"* is not exactly where most people would aspire to be. However, it was here that –

NOTES

1. "The angel of the Lord appeared unto him."

2. "The bush burned with fire, and the bush was not consumed."

3. "God called unto him out of the midst of the bush."

4. "The place whereon thou standest is holy ground."

5. "I will send thee unto Pharaoh" – the Great Commission.

The 2nd verse speaks of *"the angel of the Lord."* However, actually, this is God Himself. The bush burning with fire and not consumed is a type of the Spirit upon us. Whatever we try to do with "the flesh" will consume us. However, the Spirit can burn brightly, and we will not be consumed.

As well, the flame of fire in the bush was an emblem of the deity of Christ, as the lowly bush was an emblem of the humanity of Christ.

The 4th verse says that *"God called unto him out of the midst of the bush, and said, Moses, Moses."* This was the same one who said, *"Martha, Martha,"* and *"Simon, Simon,"* and also, *"Samuel, Samuel."*

The pulling off of the shoes in verse 5 was a demand of reverence for the place where God was; *"holy ground."* As well, it was another sign to Moses that the "flesh" could not be used. The ground would be barren and rocky, and therefore little headway made with barren feet. Hence, the total trust in "I am." Also, shoes denoted ownership. Slaves did not wear shoes because they owned nothing. In effect, God was telling Moses, "You will forfeit all claims to personal ambition, and will become a slave of Jesus Christ."

The 6th verse says, *"For he was afraid to look upon God."* Man's fear is brought about by man's sinfulness, *"For all have sinned."*

The 7th verse says, I have surely *"seen". . ."heard". . ."know."* God sees, God hears, and God knows. What does He see? He sees the affliction of His people. What does He hear? He hears their cry for help. What does He know? He knows their sorrows.

The 8th verse proclaims one of the greatest promises ever given to mankind, *"I am come down to deliver them out of the hand of the Egyptians."* Whenever the individual accepts Christ, he is "delivered out of the hand of

Egypt," which is a type of the world. However, that is only the first step. The second step is that he *"brings us up unto a good land and large, unto a land flowing with milk and honey."* But regrettably, as the Canaanite was in the land during the days af Abraham, the *"Canaanite"* is still in the land along with the *"Hittites," "Amorites," "Perizzites," "Hivites,"* and the *"Jebusites,"* which are types of uncontrollable temper, jealousy, envy, malice, greed, pride, and self-will. These opposing forces of Satan will seek to hinder the child of God from possessing this *"good land."*

The 9th verse speaks of *"the oppression wherewith the Egyptians oppressed them."* Oppression comes from Satan. It is lethal, and its deliverance can only be effected by the power of God. The world of psychology, psychotherapy, drugs, etc., can only worsen the oppressed. There is no help from these sources. Egypt cannot deliver Egypt.

The 10th verse says that God spoke to Moses, *"that thou mayest bring forth my people the children of Israel out of Egypt."* That call had no doubt been there 40 years earlier, but Moses was not ready. Now Moses is ready. There was little difficulty in getting Moses out of Egypt, but it took 40 years to get Egypt out of Moses.

The 11th verse says that the self-confidence that Moses had in 2:12 is no more. The words *"Who am I?"* characterize this.

The mountain that was spoken of in the 12th verse was Mt. Sinai. In effect, God was telling him, "Moses, as you stand here on this spot having looked at this burning bush upon this mountain, this area will be filled with people who have been delivered from Egypt." In effect, the Lord was saying to Moses, "Have faith."

The request for the Name in verse 13 that is given in verse 14, *"I am that I am,"* seems at first glance somewhat strange. However, in effect, God is giving Moses carte blanche. In effect, God is saying, "I am whatever you need." Do you need power? "I am power." Do you need resources? "I am resources." Do you need wisdom? "I am wisdom." The Hebrew name for the title, *"I am that I am,"* is "Eheyeh asher Eheyeh," meaning *"I am that I am, I am the Self-existent One: the Eternal, the One who*

always has been and always will be, the Ever-present and Living One." It is equivalent to "Jehovah the Eternal."

In the 15th verse he says, *"This is my name forever."* And then further says, *"Unto all generations."* Therefore, the great promise that God gave to Moses has been given to us as well.

The 16th verse tells us that there was a regular government of sort in the Israel of bondage: *"the elders of Israel."* Moses was to tell them that God had *"appeared unto me."* Regrettably, this is not always believed by the hearer.

The 18th verse says the directions that were given to Moses regarding Pharaoh were that the *"elders of Israel"* were to stand by him when he made the demands of Pharaoh concerning letting Israel go.

Through foreknowledge, as is recorded in the 19th verse, God knew that Pharaoh would not allow the children of Israel to leave.

Consequently, as is portrayed in the 20th verse, He would use Pharaoh's obstinate heart to serve as a warning of the power and glory of God to all the surrounding nations. God can take whatever is done and turn it to His good if His people will only believe Him.

Verses 20 through 22 tell us that God planned that His people should receive proper wages for all their hard labor before leaving Egypt.

The word *"borrow"* in the 22nd verse does not mean to borrow in the sense that we use the term. It means "to ask" or even to "demand." The implication is that the Egyptians had stripped from the Israelites their jewels, clothing, and other riches which they had when they came into Egypt. Now, Israel would not only receive back what had been taken from them, but also what they had earned by their hard labor.

CHAPTER 4

Verse 1 signals the beginnings of faithlessness in Moses. However, the Lord was patient with him as He is with us. The Christian will find that the most difficult thing to do is to simply "believe God." And, yet, the greatest thing a child of God can do for the Lord is to simply "believe Him." The hesitating and timid Moses of Mount Horeb was the same courageous and self-reliant Moses who smote the Egyptian dead! His strength then unfitted him as a divine instrument, and now his weakness unfitted him. God cannot use our strength, neither can He use our weakness – unless we allow the power of Christ to rest upon our weakness (II Cor. 12:9). The weakness, as was evidenced in Moses, would bud into unbelief and blossom into rebellion. But how tenderly God dealt with him! The burning bush proclaimed God's holiness. The words of God proclaimed His grace.

Verses 2 and 3 record a tremendous lesson given by the Lord to Moses, the rod in his hand, *"and he cast it on the ground, and it became a serpent."* What lesson was the Lord teaching Moses? The Christian could well understand the rod turning into a dove, etc. But why a serpent? God was showing Moses that in the deliverance of Israel, his opposition would not merely be man, but by Satan working through man. The minister of the gospel is little equipped if all he has is a doctorate in theological education. The powers of darkness that he will meet will respond little to higher learning or any other accoutrement of man. Well, we must *"study to show ourselves approved."* But if we do not have "the Spirit," the "study" will little suffice. Egypt was controlled by the demon powers of hell. Idol worship was the foundation of her religion. The Scripture says, *"And Moses fled from before it."* The confrontation of the powers of darkness cause most Christians to "flee before it." Actually, the number of churches in the land are miniscule that will *"walk after the Spirit"* and *"cast out devils."*

The 4th verse proclaims the command of the Lord, *"Put forth thine hand and take it by the tail."* Why not the head? The Lord Himself would *"bruise his head."* By faith in the mind of God, it was already done. So, Moses would take the serpent by the tail, signifying the future defeat of the federal enemy of God, Satan himself.

The next sign, as is recorded in verse 6, was the *"leprous hand."* The Lord was showing

Moses that the hand that grasps the tail of the serpent, *"and it became a rod in his hand,"* had nothing to do with the defeat of Satan. *"Thine hand into thy bosom,"* portrayed the depraved heart of man, as well as the sinful hand. So, no credit must be taken whatsoever for that which is done *"in the name of Jesus."* The Lord was wanting Moses to know and understand that the *"leprous hand"* was representative of what Moses, within himself, actually was.

Then the 7th verse says the Lord told him, *"Put thine hand into thy bosom again."* This he did and withdrew it, and it was whole. Only the Lord can do that. Actually, the *"leprous hand"* is a type of the born again experience. God is the only One who can change a human heart and thereby a human life.

The 8th verse presents the possible skepticism of the people. The Church has ever been ready to believe the world, but, sadly, has little confidence in God. And now the last sign will be presented.

The 9th verse says, *"Take the water of the river, and pour it upon the dry land and it shall become blood."* Three signs were given to Moses: the serpent, the leprous hand, and the poured-out blood. In these three signs we have the whole of salvation. Our antagonist is *"that old serpent the devil."* Man is depraved and cannot save himself, only *"the blood of Jesus Christ cleanseth from all sin."*

Verses 10, 11, and 12 portray the call of God upon man, *"I am not eloquent."* And even if we were, it would not save anyone.

And then the Lord says in verse 12, *"I will be with thy mouth."* God, give us preachers where the Lord is *"with thy mouth."*

The 13th verse, in effect, says that Moses registered unbelief.

The 14th verse says, *"And the anger of the Lord was kindled against Moses."* Unbelief angers God. It is ironical; promised the companionship of God, Moses refuses to go. But he willingly volunteers if accompanied by his brother Aaron, a feeble, fellow-creature. He would feel safer leaning on the arm of Aaron than on the arm of God. Such is the human heart. And, yet, Aaron was no real help to him, but the contrary.

This is the first mention of Aaron whose name appears 406 times in Scripture. He, the brother of Moses, was the first high priest of Israel.

The 15th verse, *"put words in his mouth,"* clearly defines inspiration. It is simply God putting words in the mouths of prophets and being with them in all they say. This indicates that prophets were spokesmen for God and were qualified only by His Spirit, having been placed in the prophetic office by Him.

Verses 18 and 19 portray Moses requesting of Jethro his father-in-law that he be allowed to leave.

The Midian of the 19th verse was not the Midian of the Dead Sea region but of the Eastern shore of the Gulf of Akaba. The town of Madyan stands there at this time, and the Moslems of the town welcome pilgrims on the way to Mecca shouting, "come into the city of the father-in-law of Moses."

In the 21st verse God said, *"But I will harden his heart,"* speaking of Pharaoh. This word, which will be repeated several times, in no way means that God will tamper with Pharaoh's will. By foreknowledge, God looked at Pharaoh's heart, knowing what Pharaoh would do. God would simply supply the opportunity. Actually, God gave Pharaoh the occasion to resist Him and harden his own heart, which he did. In the same way, the Gospel saves or damns today, softens or hardens, and makes alive or kills all who hear it (Rom. 2:4-11; II Cor. 2:15,16). The sun hardens clay and softens wax; so it is with truth. The result is not in the sun (or in God) but in the materials.

In the 23rd verse, the Lord said, *"Let my son go."* Here, God calls the nation of Israel His son and firstborn, as contrasted with the firstborn of Egypt. Pharaoh would understand this terminology fully, for he, himself, was called "Son of Ra," or "Beloved of his god." God was telling Pharaoh that He loved Israel as Pharaoh loved his firstborn.

Israel could not serve God in Egypt, for part of their sacrifices were cattle, which were most sacred to the Egyptians. At the outset God told Pharaoh, *"I will slay thy son, even thy firstborn."* So, Pharaoh was not without warning. At any time along the way he could have repented, and his firstborn would have been spared, as well as the destruction of Egypt. It was the mercy of God in speaking to Pharaoh

NOTES

thusly. The choice of what happened was Pharaoh's and not God's. The Israelites belonged to God, and He had the right to take them out.

Verses 24 through 26 portray the justness of a just God. Moses would learn that God would judge him before He judged Pharaoh, and that rebellion in the one was the same as rebellion in the other. Moses must learn that disobedience and rebellion in him, in any form, was just as hateful as in Pharaoh. God must judge sin wherever sin is found. Moses, because of his wife Zipporah, had not circumcised the little boy, Eliezer. It seems that she had no confidence in the precious Blood of Jesus Christ. These passages throw a great light upon the inner life of Moses. It may be assumed from what is related that he yielded to the wishes of his wife in this matter, though he knew he was disobeying God. The particulars are not fully given because the Holy Spirit did not think it necessary. But, evidently, in order to save the child's life and urged to it by Moses, she circumcised the child herself, and then with anger and passion declared that her husband's religion was a religion of blood. And so it is. Obedience brought life, as it always does. God allowed the boy to live. Circumcision was a sign of separation from the world unto God. Christians, under the New Covenant, are circumcised in the death of Jesus Christ; that is, they "die" as to their old nature – in other words, a spiritual circumcision.

Verses 27 and 28 record the Lord telling Aaron, *"Go into the wilderness to meet Moses."* Aaron met Moses at Mount Sinai, perhaps at the time he received the revelation of the burning bush, etc. The brothers had been separated for some 40 years.

Verses 29 through 31 record the first spiritual revival of the children of Israel since they had been in Egyptian bondage. The Bible says, *"And the people believed"*; Then, *"they bowed their heads and worshiped."* This is a perfect description of every moving of the Holy Spirit. God will *"do signs,"* and then, if the people believe, the Spirit of God will fall and result in the worship of the Lord.

CHAPTER 5

For a few moments, regarding verses 1 and 2, I want the reader to imagine the scene that must have presented itself as Moses and Aaron stood before Pharaoh, the two prophets of God standing there in their simple shepherd's garb. And yet, Moses is very familiar with this palace because it is probably the one he was raised in. The throne on which Pharaoh is seated could have been his. But if so, what a step down it would have been. When he looks at Pharaoh, the scene that meets his eyes is graphic. On Pharaoh's head would have been the replica of a coiled cobra made of gold. The cobra's head with two rubies for its eyes would have protruded like a hood over Pharaoh's head. The cobra was one of the gods of Egypt. Now, no doubt, Moses begins to understand a little more why the rod was turned into a serpent.

In verse 2 Pharaoh said, *"Who is the Lord?"* How many millions have uttered those words, and how many millions have learned the hard way?

The 3rd verse mentions *"sacrifice."* Sacrifice was necessary for the redemption of man and the restoration of his dominion. The entirety of the Bible centers around the sacrifice of Christ, which all animal sacrifice typified (Heb. 9:22).

Verses 4 through 18 describe the increased burdens of Israel. The bricks they were to make were made up of chopped straw and clay dried in the sun. This straw preserved the original color. Egyptian bricks were about 20 inches long, 8 inches wide, and 7 inches thick. The new task was to go over the fields and gather the stubble which would replace the straw that had been previously furnished in plentiful lots. With this additional work, they were to make the same number of bricks as before. This assignment was made to punish the people for demanding to leave Egypt so they could sacrifice to God.

Oftentimes, the setting to carry out the will of God will result in Satan's anger and opposition being increased. Foolishly, some Christians believe that if it's the will of God,

NOTES

there will be no difficulties. Actually, the reverse is true. The carrying out of the will of God can bring great opposition from Satan.

Verse 14 says, *"The officers of the children of Israel were beaten."* The ordinary punishment in Egypt for common offenses required a person to lie on his stomach with his legs and feet upward. The executioner then struck many blows on the soles of the feet. This made it almost impossible to walk for weeks and for some, perhaps for life.

Of course, the question is asked, "Why does God allow Satan this type of persecution?" God permits the bitter experience of Satan's power in order to exercise and strengthen faith. It is good for man to learn painfully the nature of sin's dominion and man's absolute helplessness in the grip of that monarch.

The first move of Israel toward deliverance plunged her into deeper misery so that the people would have preferred being left quietly in their slavery. This is oftentimes the spiritual experience of awakened sinners.

Verses 19, 20, and 21 portray the Israelites blaming Moses and Aaron for their plight and calling God to witness the truth of their accusation. Spiritual birth, due to Satan's grip on the human heart, is not painless. But the people were blaming the wrong party. It was Satan working through Pharaoh who caused their terrible discomfort. How easy it is to blame Moses and Aaron. The plight of so many Christians is that they do not understand nor see the real cause of their circumstances. Verses 22 and 23, regrettably, present Moses in no better light that the faithless children of Israel. The people laid the blame of their plight on Moses and Aaron; Moses laid the blame on Jehovah. The people refused to hold their tongue and be patient until they saw what God would do, and Moses, after all his training in the wilderness, his call, and the miracles, was just as quick to lose patience and complain.

Little has changed through the centuries. As today we have fast-food, likewise, we have fast-faith. As one of today's fast-food emporiums advertises its McRibb's, etc., so the church advertises its "McFaith." Whatever is to be done, God must do it immediately. What will it take for the Church to learn that God doesn't work according to our timetable, but we work according to His.

Chapter 4 concluded with the people worshiping the Lord; Chapter 5 concludes with the same people formerly worshiping now filled with unbelieving bitterness. The glad tidings of salvation is one thing; the struggle against the power that keeps the souls in bondage is another. Satan will not let his captives go free easily.

CHAPTER 6

In verse 1 God responds to Israel's and Moses' complaints with love, pity, and grace. He encourages them by telling them what He was, and what He will do. Five times in this chapter He declares that He is *"Jehovah,"* and seven times He utters the great words, *"I will."* Three times He declares, *"I have."*

The 3rd verse gives a further revelation of God to Moses. God testified here that He had personally appeared to Abraham, Isaac, and Jacob by the name of *"God Almighty"* (El Shaddai), the All-Sufficient One. He made many promises to them. He used this name instead of *"Jehovah,"* which means the Self-Existing or Eternal One who keeps covenants and fulfills promises. While it is true that the name *"Jehovah"* was used from the very beginning, nevertheless, the full meaning of it was not made known to man until it was time to fulfill the promises and covenants with Israel as a nation.

God had made known to the three men His name "El Shaddai" or "All-Sufficient One" by His continual provision and protection of them. But the full import of *"Jehovah"* was made known only to their descendants in the deliverance from Egypt and the settlement in Canaan as promised Abraham and Jacob.

The fact that God speaks of His covenant with them in verses 3-4 proves that *"Almighty God"* is His name in the making of the covenant and its many provisions, but *"Jehovah"* is His name, used in the fulfillment of the covenants and promises to their descendants.

The covenant provision mentioned here is the giving of the land of Canaan to the descen-

NOTES

dants. The three patriarchs were merely pilgrims in Canaan and did not inherit any part of it as long as they lived (Heb. 11:9). Stephen confirmed this truth when he said *"And He gave him none inheritance in it"* (Acts 7:4-7).

The 6th verse gives a picture portrayal of the great redemption afforded to the believer.
"I am the Lord."
"I will bring you out from under the burdens of the Egyptians."
"I will rid you out of their bondage."
"And I will redeem you with a stretched-out arm, and with great judgments."
Verse 9 says, *"But they hearkened not."* Such is the unbelief of the natural heart once pressure is applied. Lest we criticize them, how many of us have done any better?

Verse 12 portrays a discouraged Moses, *"Behold, the children of Israel hath not hearkened, how then shall Pharaoh hear me."*

Verse 13 declares that God answered the complaints of Israel and the discouragement of Moses with *"a charge."* In other words, "God drew a line." Egypt would let Israel go, or Egypt would be destroyed.

Verses 14 through 27 record the names of slaves. Pharaoh has declared that he would not let them go, but God has numbered those that belong to Himself. He calls them *"my people"* even though they are still in the power of the enemy. To make this grace more amazing, the three tribes of *"Reuben," "Simeon,"* and *"Levi"* are chosen as representing the whole nation. They were the three that had some of the worse curses levied upon them. When we behold the 6th chapter, we are beholding amazing grace. How many people today has God numbered *"my people,"* when in reality they are still unsaved and not yet born again? However, known in the hallowed halls of heaven, they shall be delivered. That, as well, could include your son, daughter, mother, dad, and loved one. Hallelujah!

Verses 29 through 30 portray the commission of God to Moses renewed, but closes once again with Moses in unbelief.

Finally, despite an unbelieving Moses, God's power will now be shown. Someone has said, "The mills of God grind slowly, yet they grind exceedingly fine." It seemed that God would never fulfill His covenant and promises to Abraham, Isaac, and Jacob, or even those promises to Moses in his generation. He and all Israel became fully discouraged, but God on a certain day began to work, and in a period of a few weeks his mills had ground Egypt to utter helplessness and ruin.

CHAPTER 7

Verses 1 through 5 speak of *"great judgments"* that would come upon Egypt. God's will is not always carried out, but God's plan is always carried out. Nations that defy Him are "judged." Egypt, at this time, is the mightiest nation on the face of the earth. In about six weeks time it will be totally destroyed.

Verses 6 and 7 record the ages of both Moses and Aaron, 80 and 83 respectively. Why did the Holy Spirit give us this information? In part, that we may understand that it is no simple matter to be "used of God."

Verses 8 and 9 portray the beginning of miracles. Each miracle was designed by God to embarrass and show the utter helplessness of Egypt's gods against the God of Israel. When Moses and Aaron stand before Pharaoh and speak of their God, Pharaoh will demand of them, *"Show a miracle for you."* Now, as in the wilderness, they will throw down the rod *"before Pharaoh, and it shall become a serpent."* Pharaoh, before his eyes, will see a mere rod change into one of the helpless gods of Egypt.

Verses 10 through 13 portray demon-possessed sorcerers and magicians of Egypt attempting to imitate the miracle of Moses. Likewise, their rods become serpents. Some have said that these demon-possessed sorcerers and magicians were able through the powers of darkness to take a live snake, put it under a spell, and cause it to be as rigid as rod. When it was thrown on the floor, the spell would be broken and the serpent would take on its true nature. However, *"Aaron's rod swallowed up their rods,"* proving that God's power is greater than Satan's.

These magicians were able to perform three miracles: turning rods to serpents, turn-

NOTES

ing water to blood, and bringing up frogs. However, they could not protect themselves from the plagues. Satan, though he can perform some miracles, is limited in his power. In the future he will call fire down from heaven, and do various kinds of miracles to deceive men (Rev. 13:2; 16:13-16; 19:20).

Verses 14 through 25 record the first plague upon Egypt. It was the turning of the River Nile and all of its tributaries into blood. (The River Nile was worshiped by Egyptians under various names and symbols. It was called the "father of life" and the "father of the gods.") Thus, this miracle was a blow to the gods of Egypt. The Egyptians abhorred blood, and their horror must have been extreme when they saw their sacred river and all other water in their country turn to blood.

Verse 15 suggests that this plague took place at the moment that Pharaoh arrived on the bank of the river in order to worship it.

Verses 22 through 25 portray Pharaoh becoming harder before God, *"Neither did he set his heart to this also."* Man is not saved or lost through intellect; he is saved or lost either through the acceptance or rejection by his heart. Preachers make a mistake when they appeal to the intellect. The Holy Spirit appeals to the heart.

Going back to verses 9 and 10; why did Moses' rod turn into a serpent? Why not a dove? That, we could understand, but a serpent?

It was turned into a serpent because *"He that knew no sin would become sin, that we might be made the righteousness of God in him."* (II Cor. 5:21)

For the serpent of Moses and Aaron would *"swallow up their serpents."*

CHAPTER 8

Verse 1 portrays the demand by God to Satan, *"Let my people go, that they may serve me."* This is the only power that Satan recognizes. The Church helplessly flounders when it uses the *"ways of Egypt"* to deliver men from Egypt. It simply cannot be done. Only God can deliver.

Verse 2 proclaims the judgment of *"frogs."* This plague was directed against the frog-god that was an object of worship in Egypt. Very soon they would have plenty of frogs to worship.

Verse 3 says that in every conceivable place there were frogs, in the bed, on the floor, on the stoves, and even in the bowls where they made their bread; there were frogs everywhere. In a matter of hours, the people would be "sick to death" of their frog-god. However, I wonder if our "enlightened" age is any better.

Ironically enough, as if the land of Egypt didn't have enough frogs, *"the magicians did so with their enchantments, and brought up frogs upon the land of Egypt."* I am certain the people really appreciated that.

The 8th verse portrays Pharaoh seemingly willing to let the people go.

In the 9th verse Moses uses the word *"glory over me,"* which means "the honor is yours to tell me when you want the frogs removed."

Strangely enough, in answer to Moses' question as to when the frogs would be removed, the 10th verse says, *"And he said, tomorrow."*

Why tomorrow? One more night with the frogs. Why didn't he say, "Now!"? Millions are dealt with by the Holy Spirit, and when pressed, their answer is "tomorrow." One more night with the frogs.

Verses 16 and 17 record the third plague when the dust of the land became *"lice."* This was a creation of billions of lice out of the dust. Beside this insect, many other kinds were also included (Ps. 78:45). This plague showed the utter helplessness of the insect-god to protect Egypt.

Now, the 18th verse says that *"there were lice upon man, and upon beast."*

Despite the magicians telling Pharaoh, *"This is the finger of God,"* the 19th verse says, *"And Pharaoh's heart was hardened."* Man's ability to resist God is remarkable.

Verses 20 through 24 portray the fourth plague of *"flies."* This plague was a severe blow to the idolatrous worship of Egypt and designed to manifest the helplessness of Beelzebub, the god of flies, who was supposed to have power to prevent flies. Cleanliness was necessary in such worship, and the putrid con-

NOTES

ditions brought about by unclean flies would be a great hindrance to the idolaters. The plague, once again, proved that the God of Israel was more powerful than any other god.

Verses 25 through 32 portray two of the compromises that Pharaoh suggested to Moses. They are as follows:

1. *"Sacrifice in the land"* (vs. 25).

2. *"Only you shall not go very far away"* (vs. 28).

Satan's efforts always are directed to prevent a definite breach between the Church and the world. Compromise, which Satan tried at least four times with Moses, is still the bane of the church. The Word says, *"Come out from among them."* However, Satan says, "You can be of the world and still worship God." If that does not succeed, he will say, "Don't go very far away." In other words, "Don't be fanatical about it. A little religion is all right, but too much is not necessary." And then the third compromise was directed to the men. They could go, but their families must be left behind:

3. *"Let your men go only"* (10:11).

The Lord wants "the entire family," and then "leave your flocks behind." In other words, "You can involve yourself, but your possessions belong to me":

4. *"Go, but leave your flocks behind"* (10:24).

All of it presents a compromise designed to keep the Christian from doing the whole will of God.

CHAPTER 9

The 9th chapter of Exodus portrays the plagues of God deepening in their intensity. When they are concluded, mighty Egypt will be little more than wreckage.

Verse 1 says that the Lord God of heaven was not ashamed to call Himself *"the Lord God of the Hebrews,"* individuals that were slaves. He calls them *"my people."*

The 3rd verse proclaims this plague as *"a very grievous murrain."* Whatever the plague was, it was very grievous and brought death. This was also directed against the gods of Egypt who were supposed to be manifested in the various animal forms, all of which were considered sacred. It proved once again that the God of Israel was greater than the gods of Egypt who were powerless to protect themselves. God would even differentiate between the *"cattle of Israel"* and the *"cattle of Egypt."* That which belongs to God's people is special in God's eyes.

The 6th verse says that *"the cattle of Egypt died,"* and then it says, *"but the cattle of the children of Israel died not one."*

Verses 8 through 12 portray far more than meets the eye. *"The furnace"* that is spoken of in verse 8 means the place of human sacrifices. Sacrificial human offerings were made in the fire to propitiate the god Typhon, the evil principal, in the hope of averting plagues. Moses used those very ashes to produce another plague instead of averting one.

Verse 10 portrays *"the ashes of the furnace sprinkled toward heaven."*

The 11th verse says that *"the magicians could not stand before Moses because of the boils."* These boils were a most severe inflamation causing one to have fever with the afflicted part of the flesh burning and swelling.

Verses 13 through 26 portray the plague of *"thunder and hail,"* along with *"the fire that ran along upon the ground."* This plague was directed against Isis and Osiris, the gods of light, health, fertility, arts, and agriculture. The water, fire, earth, and air were all objects of Egyptian idolatry. God showed Pharaoh and his people that He was the Supreme One over these elements, and that instead of helping the Egyptians, they, under his will and command, were instruments of destruction.

The plague consisted of a series of thunder peals, with large hailstones falling, and continuous fire that ran along the ground devouring everything in its path.

The 16th verse says, *"And in every deed for this cause have I raised thee up, for to shew in thee my power."*

This has been translated several ways: I have raised you to the throne, to show you my power . . . . I have let you remain for the purpose of showing you my power. Paul quoted it: *"I have raised you up, that I might shew my power in you"* (Rom. 9:14-21).

There is no statement here that God, from

NOTES

all eternity, chose Pharaoh to resist Him. The idea is that since he was the type of man to be stubborn and rebellious even to the point of self-destruction, since he was one who would not listen to God, and since he was the kind who would voluntarily choose to resist the Almighty, He could use Pharaoh to make His power, love, patience, and longsuffering known to all men. We can believe that God influenced human affairs so that such a person would be on the throne of Egypt at the time one was needed in the fulfillment of His plan, but we cannot believe that Pharaoh would not have been permitted to repent and become submissive had he chosen to cease being rebellious. It was purely a personal choice with him, as it is with everyone else in the acceptance or rejection of the gospel (Mark 16:16; St. John 3:16; II Cor. 2:15-16). He gave him free and complete choice on numerous occassions to break and submit to His will. Since he would not, then all God could do was to send enough judgments to make the king willing to let Israel go.

CHAPTER 10

Verses 1 through 9 present the great question that God ever asks the human family, *"How long wilt thou refuse to humble thyself before me?"* Humility is the position to which the Holy Spirit endeavors to bring us. Pride, the capital sin of mankind, is the opposite of humility. The statement, *"the Lord God of the Hebrews,"* literally means "the Eternal, Self-existing, Covenant-keeping One, the Supporter, Defender, Protector, and Creator of the Hebrews."

The 4th verse says, *"Tomorrow will I bring the locust into thy coast."* This plague was directed against the god Serapis who was supposed to protect the land from locusts. The creatures came at the command of God and went when He said for them to go, proving another time that He was the God of gods, and that the gods of Egypt were false and powerless.

The 7th verse proclaims for the first time that Pharaoh's officers intervened and requested Pharaoh yield. Their statement is, *"Knowest thou not yet that Egypt is destroyed?"* Great is the power of God.

In the 16th verse, Pharaoh admits, *"I have sinned against the Lord your God, and against you."*

The 17th verse proclaims his asking, *"Forgive."*

This was the first time Pharaoh asked forgiveness for his stubbornness and sin against Israel. It was not the kind of repentance that works salvation and needs not to be repented of (II Cor. 7:10) but was a shallow-mouth-confession and acknowledgment that he was in the wrong without a real change of heart which would cause him to forsake sin (Prov. 28:13). All Pharaoh wanted was relief from his suffering and the opportunity to escape from the death he knew was coming.

The 21st verse records the most powerful plague of all, *"even darkness which may be felt."*

This plague was directed against the sun god, who was supposed to protect from any curse of the sun and bring natural blessings of light, warmth, and fruitfulness. It must have been a horrifying thing to experience such thick darkness throughout the region occupied by the Egyptians, and a beautiful sight to behold the light which was preserved only in the land of Goshen (vs. 23).

The 4th and final compromise was suggested by Pharaoh to Moses in verse 24, *"Only let your flocks and your herds be stayed."*

Moses' answer as recorded in verse 26 is powerful, *"There shall not be an hoof left behind."* That's exactly the answer God demands of every Christian.

CHAPTER 11

The tenth and last plague, *"one plague more,"* would touch the dearest of all in Egypt, the firstborn, and that from Pharaoh down. It would be of both man and beast. Egypt, by now, was wreckage. What had formerly been the most powerful nation on the face of the earth was now virtually destroyed. To understand

NOTES

God is to know that the plagues were not the vengeful wrath of a despotic ruler, but were actually the mercy of God. The children of Israel belonged to God; they did not belong to Pharaoh. They had been treated like slaves, and, in fact, were slaves for over two centuries. God had the right to demand their release. At any time Pharaoh could have relented and repented; however, his stubborn obstinate heart would not allow such to be done. God so oftentimes deals with individuals in the same manner that they may come to Him and be saved, for He speaks with mercy. If not, he speaks with judgment. If the obstinacy continues, He increases the pressure. Some relent and are saved; some reject and are eternally lost.

The announcement as recorded in verse 2 that Moses was to give to Israel, *"Speak now in the ears of the people,"* was the signal that it was time to go.

The *"favor"* that is mentioned in verse 3 came only after Egypt was destroyed. By now, Egypt was ready to relent in regards to any request that Israel made.

Verses 4, 5, and 6 tell what the tenth and last plague will be. It will happen at *"midnight"* and *"all the firstborn in the land of Egypt shall die."* (This was always the firstborn of the males; however, if there were no males in the family, the oldest daughter would serve in that capacity.) It should be noted that in most families there was a male for the simple reason that the family name could not continue unless there was a male born into the family. Therefore, most continued having children until a boy was born. In the 1700's massive graves were opened in Egypt by archaeological excavations. These contained the bodies of multiple thousands of males. The ages were from little infants up to adults. Tests showed they all died and were embalmed at approximately the same time. Even though there was no concrete proof that the burial of all these males at the same time pertained to the tenth and last plague, still, it was ascertained that they were buried at approximately the same time of the exodus from Egypt, and could very well have been the bodies of those, the firstborn, stricken by the death angel.

The *"cry"* that was registered in Egypt, as

outlined in the 6th verse, must not be blamed on a loving and compassionate God, but on the stubbornness of a hard-hearted people.

The 7th verse plainly tells us that there is a difference between the Egyptians and Israel, and it's a difference that God has placed there. Egypt is a type of the world; Israel is a type of the Christ-filled life. If the individual is truly born again, there is a difference.

The 8th verse does not actually state that Moses once again stood before Pharaoh, but actually messengers from Pharaoh spoke to Moses, not Pharaoh personally. The word was given in the 8th verse that the servants of Pharaoh would bow down to Israel saying, *"Get thee out, and all the people that follow thee."* Nations that place themselves in the path of God, with obstinate desire to circumvent His plan, are always destroyed. Men thought it would take 100 years for the Berlin Wall to come down; it came down in hours. Others thought the Iron Curtain would never crumble; it crumbled in days. At this moment, the nations of the world are being jockeyed into position for the Great Tribulation period and the rise of the Antichrist. The Bible is God's Word. As He spoke to Pharaoh through Moses and carried out exactly what He said He would do, as well, He will do exactly what He says He will do in these last days.

CHAPTER 12

The 12th chapter of Exodus is a perfect picture of Christ, the true Paschal Lamb. The Passover was to forever serve as the "type" of Christ, and it had been kept for nearly 1600 years. Actually, Christ died at 3 o'clock in the afternoon at the exact time the Passover lamb was being offered. The blood of bulls and goats could never take away sin; so, the people were saved not by what the sacrifice was but by what it represented. It represented the coming Redeemer, the Lord Jesus Christ. Consequently, every person before Calvary was saved by looking forward to Calvary. We are now saved by looking backward to Calvary. Every human being that has ever been saved has been

NOTES

saved by the precious shed Blood of the Lord Jesus Christ. There has never been any other way, and there will never be any other way.

Verse 1 says, *"The Lord spake unto Moses and Aaron."* The Lord had spoken much to these two individuals, but the words that will be spoken now would be the greatest to date He had ever spoken – a type of the First Coming of Christ.

Verse 2 speaks of *"the beginning."* Actually, Israel's sacred year would now begin with the month Abib (later called Nisan). This corresponded somewhat with our month of April. As an individual comes to the Lord Jesus Christ, it is actually *"the beginning."*

The 3rd verse speaks of *"a lamb for an house."* With Abel it was a lamb for a person. With Israel in Egypt it was a lamb for a house, then a lamb for a nation. When Jesus came it was, *"Behold the Lamb of God which taketh away the sin of the world."*

The 5th verse says, *"without blemish."* It was to represent Christ, being inspected minutely for four days (from the 10th to the 14th of the month). Even after it was killed, the flesh would be laid open at the backbone and inspected minutely for even a slight discoloration. If so, it would be laid aside and another lamb selected. It was to be *"a male,"* as would be obvious for Christ.

The 6th verse says, *"Kill it in the evening,"* which stood for the evening sacrifice at 3 p.m. and was the exact time that Jesus died.

The 7th verse says, *"Take of the blood."* *"Without the shedding of innocent blood, there is no remission of sins."* This represented the shed Blood of Christ. At this time, it would be put on the side post and the upper post of the house. Later, it would be applied to the Mercy Seat on the great Day of Atonement. Now, by faith, it is applied to our hearts (St. John 3:16).

The 8th verse said, *"Eat the flesh."* Jesus said, *"Unless you eat my flesh and drink my blood"* (St. John 6). The *"roast with fire"* speaks of the judgment of God that should have come upon us but came upon Christ instead. The *"unleavened bread"* speaks of His sinless body. Leaven is a form of rot or sin. Christ *"knew no sin."* The *"bitter herbs"* were to remind Israel of their bitter slavery in Egypt from which God was now ready to deliver them.

The 9th verse says, *"Eat not of it raw,"* which has two meanings. First of all, the Egyptians ate raw flesh in honor of Osiris. Thus, God was seeking in every conceivable way to make Israel free from all idolatrous practices. Second, and most of all, the flesh *"roast with fire,"* spoke of the finished work of Christ in taking the judgment intended for us upon Himself. The lamb was to be roasted with fire, including the head, heart, liver, kidneys, but not the intestinal canal, which spoke of Christ giving His all.

The 10th verse says, *"Let nothing of it remain,"* meaning that we should eat all of Christ, or none of Christ. The bane of the Church is that they eat a "little of Christ, and a little of the world."

The 11th verse says they were to eat with *"your loins girded,"* meaning ready to go, and *"shoes on your feet,"* ready to travel, and *"staff in your hand,"* ready now and *"eat it in haste,"* go at any moment, which is a picture of the coming Rapture of the Church. It is now called *"the Lord's Passover."* The difference in future Passovers after arriving in the Promised Land was that they ate "resting." This Passover would typify the present deliverance; all future Passovers would typify a past deliverance.

The 12th verse says, *"Will smite all the firstborn in the land of Egypt."* It must ever be understood that the children of Israel, in respect to personal holiness, were no different than the Egyptians. The difference would be *"the Blood."*

The 13th verse says, *"The blood shall be to you for a token."* There is no other token. And then the words, *"And when I see the blood, I will pass over you,"* are the greatest words that were ever uttered. The shed Blood of Jesus Christ is the only panacea for the *"plague"* of sin that destroys the human race.

When God saw the Blood applied and all conditions met, He gave security to that home. Doubt by the occupants of the house might destroy the peace but not the security, because it was founded on God's Word. But faith and a security without the Blood being applied would not have brought any security regardless of personal feelings in the matter. So it is in the Gospel program, that all conditions

NOTES

be met, repentance must be sincere and accompanied by a turning away from sin before there is security in Christ. No one is secure in Him while living in sin and when the terms of repentance and living free from sin are not being met (Heb. 3:6; II Pet. 2:20-22, etc.).

The 14th verse said, *"for a memorial."* And then it said, *"Ye shall keep it a feast by ordinance forever."* The word "memorial" means as long as one continues as a people in obedience to God. The Passover and certain other memorials are eternal and will be observed eternally in the eternal reign of Christ (Ez. 45:17; 46:14). Actually, the *"Lord's Supper"* of Christianity is an outgrowth of *"the Passover."*

The 15th verse speaks of *"the Feast of Unleavened Bread."* This is the first mention of such, a distinct feast from the Passover. It began with the Passover and continued seven days, the first and seventh days being holy convocations.

The 19th verse says that for *"seven days,"* speaking of God's perfection, that *"no leaven found in your houses."* All leavened or fermented bread was to be put out of all houses during the Feast of Unleavened Bread. Leaven is a symbol of evil (I Cor. 5:6-8; Gal. 5:9) and false doctrines (Matt. 13:33; 16:6-12; Mark 8:15).

As well, the death penalty was passed upon all who ate leavened bread during the Feast of Unleavened Bread, which was a type of the spotless, sinless, pure, unadulterated life of the Lord Jesus Christ.

The 21st verse says, *"and killed the Passover."* The Passover and the Feast of Unleavened Bread began at the same time, the 15th day of Abib or Nisan, which would be sometime after sundown on the 14th. The Passover Lamb was killed and prepared before sundown so that both observances could be carried out together, beginning on the 15th.

The 22nd verse said, *"take a bunch of hyssop."* It was a small bushy plant about one and a half feet high, aromatic, leafy, and with pungent taste. It grew abundantly in that part of the world. It spoke of frail humanity. They were to *"dip it in the blood"* and *"strike the lintel and the two sideposts with the blood."* The blood in the basin was of no effect. It had to be applied to the doorpost. Likewise, the Blood that Jesus shed for us is of no effect unless it is applied by faith to our hearts.

The 23rd verse says, *"And when he sees the blood,"* not our good works, our church membership, our social contacts, or our wealth, but "the Blood," and the Blood of Christ at that. That is the only thing that will keep back *"the destroyer."* This is the old gospel story. It has not changed; it will never change.

The 24th verse says *"forever."*

The 29th verse proclaims, *"At midnight the Lord smote all."* This is a picture of the Great White Throne Judgment that is one day coming.

The 30th verse says, *"There was a great cry in Egypt."* No people of antiquity were any more emotional in mourning than the Egyptians. They whipped, beat, tore themselves, and howled and screamed in excessive grief. What a manifestation there must have been when the whole nation turned to mourning over the firstborn!

Now, the 31st verse says of Pharaoh pertaining to the children of Israel, *"Go."* It could have been said at the beginning and would have avoided all the suffering that Egypt had to go through.

The 37th verse says, *"About six hundred thousand on foot that were men, beside children."* Actually, this meant 600,000 men of war, without reckoning the priestly tribe of Levi. Besides these, there were wives, children, older men and women, and a multitude of mixed people who were the descendants of the servants of Abraham, Isaac, and Jacob. It is estimated that from 3 to 6 million people made the exodus from Egypt at this time.

Verses 40 through 42 say, *"The sojourning of the children of Israel."* And then it says, *"Was four hundred and thirty years."* The whole of the sojourn was from the 75th year of Abraham's life when he entered Canaan, to this day of exodus. The entire sojourn took place in Mesopotamia, Syria, Canaan, Philistia, and Egypt. The actual sojourn in Egypt was only 215 years, one-half of the 430 of the whole period. This is the whole length of the dispensation of promise – from Abraham to Moses.

The words in the 41st verse, *"Even the selfsame day,"* indicate that Abraham began his sojourn on the 15 day of Nisan or April, exactly 430 years before the exodus.

CHAPTER 13

Verses 1 and 2 proclaim the Lord telling Moses, *"Sanctify unto me all the firstborn."* The Hebrew word means "to set apart" from a profane to a sacred purpose. It has no reference to cleansing from sin or removal of what is commonly called "the old man." In this passage it refers to the setting apart of the firstborn of both man and beast for holy uses. Even beasts who are not involved in sin can be sanctified to God in this sense, as well as man.

Verse 3, as well as the remainder of the chapter, demands that Israel *"remember this day."* Likewise, every child of God should understand that the greatest day of his or her life is the moment they gave their heart and life to Jesus Christ, *"Remember this day."*

Immediately after Israel was redeemed out of Egypt, instructions were given respecting the annual observances of the Passover. That is to say, Israel was to perpetually confess to the world that her salvation out of Egypt, and her settlement in Canaan was wholly due to the preciousness of the blood of the Paschal Lamb. Likewise, every Christian today should give a like testimony.

The 9th verse says, *"With a strong hand hath the Lord brought thee out of Egypt."* Likewise, with a "strong hand" has the Lord brought us out of the powers of darkness and set us free from the terrible bondage of sin.

The *"token"* of verse 16 actually refers to the Word of God.

Verses 17 and 18 explain why God led the nation of Israel around the long way, through the wilderness and Red Sea, instead of taking them through the land of the Philistines. He knew that Pharaoh would try to stop them, and the Philistines would also help out in this. With war on every hand so soon there would be the possibility of Israel wanting to return to Egypt immediately. The long slavery of Israel had weakened their will to resist to such an extent that God saw it was better to enable them to escape a military campaign at the very outset of leaving Egypt. This weakening of the will may also explain why the people were degraded enough in mind and soul to commit the ungodly and rebellious deeds they did against God and Moses in the wilderness experiences. Thus, God led the nation around the land of Philistia by taking them across the Red Sea, and they entered the Sinai Peninsula south of the Philistine country.

The root of the Mediterranean Sea coast toward Gaza and Philistia was nearer, but God led them into the wilderness of the Red Sea area southward to Pi-hahiroth on the shore of the Red Sea, about 100 miles south of Rameses. How long it took for the journey is not stated, but Pharaoh concluded they had missed the way out of Egypt and were hemmed in by the wilderness. The valley the Israelites were in terminated at the sea, and on the north and south there were mountains cutting off their escape. Pharaoh came into the valley from the rear and that cut them off entirely from any way of escape.

The actual place of passage through the Red Sea is supposed to have been 12 miles wide from the border of Egypt to the wilderness of Shur.

The 19th verse tells us that Moses *"took the bones of Joseph with him."* The passage suggests as well that the bodies of "the fathers" were also taken from Egypt.

Verses 21 and 22 record the beautiful presence of the *"pillar of cloud by day"* and the *"pillar of fire by night."*

Going back to the 13th verse it says, *"And every firstling of an ass thou shalt redeem with a lamb."* This is humbling to human pride. The ass was an unclean animal, and its broken neck fitly pictured the true moral condition of the most highly cultivated man, but the death of the lamb obtained redemption. Only thus can sinners be saved.

CHAPTER 14

Verses 1 and 2 speak to the children of Israel that they should *"encamp by the sea."* Israel had left Rameses (present-day Cairo) and had

journeyed to Succoth. Then they went to Etham, which was a fortress of Egypt where the sun-god was worshiped. Then they went to Pi-hahiroth, a place on the Red Sea near Migdol, a fortress that served to defend Egypt from Asia, and close to Baal-Zephon, a sacred place to Typhon, the evil demon of Egyptian mythology. God would perform His greatest miracle in the very shadow of one of Egypt's chief gods.

Verses 3 through 9 once more speak of Pharaoh's dedication to destruction. Pharaoh would lead his mighty army to destroy the children of Israel. In his mind the children of Israel were hemmed in. It was a perfect military ambush – but for God. His (Pharaoh's) army consisted of 600 chosen chariots comprising the king's guard, the pride of Egypt. And then there were all the rest of the chariots of Egypt as the main body of the army, including chariot drivers and combatants in each chariot. Josephus says that Pharaoh had 50,000 horsemen and 200,000 footmen, as well as all the chariots.

Verses 10 through 12 record the complaints of Israel. The fear, unbelief, and anger of the very people who had witnessed God's wonders in the land of Egypt would appear incredible, but that each Bible student finds these evils in his own heart, and learns by sad experience that great depression of mind usually follows exceptional spiritual triumphs.

So it was with Israel at the Red Sea. Unbelief cried out: "The wilderness will become our grave"; but the result was that the "sea became Pharaoh's grave."

Verses 13 through 18 portray the action of faith. The message ever is, *"Fear not."* And then Paul said, *"God has not given us the spirit of fear."* The words *"stand still"* refer to a total lack of dependence on the flesh. There are five "stand stills" in the Bible.

1. *"Stand still and see the salvation of the Lord."* (Gen. 14:13)

2. *"Stand still and hear what Jehovah will command concerning you."* (Num. 9:8)

3. *"Stand still awhile that I may shew you the word of God."* (I Sam. 9:27)

4. *"Stand still and see the salvation of the Lord with you."* (II Chron. 20:17)

5. *"Stand still and consider the wondrous*

works of God." (Job 37:14)

If we allow all fear to be rooted out and *"stand still,"* the enemy we have seen, *"Ye shall see them again no more forever."*

In the 15th verse God demands that Israel cease their complaining to Him. In other words, *"go forward."* Faith is ever forward. The *"stand still"* is strickly a command to the efforts of the flesh, that faith may *"go forward."*

The *"angel of God"* spoken of in the 19th verse was actually a preincarnate appearance of the Lord Jesus Christ. The cloud that stood between the encampment of Israel and the Egyptians was darkness to the Egyptians and light to Israel. So is the Word of God. It is darkness to the world and light to the child of God.

The *"strong east wind"* that God used to push back a path through the sea was a divine miracle, not something accomplished by the mere forces of nature itself. Not only was this done suddenly by divine power, but it was likewise undone suddenly by the same power. A wind blowing strong enough to make a path through the sea 12 miles across and hold the waters up like a wall 75 to 100 feet high would have been strong enough to blow all the Israelites and Egyptians away as well had God not directed it. The *"wall"* on either side of the children of Israel was actually a wall of water straight up to nearly 100 feet high. The bottom of the Red Sea was actually made dry.

Verses 23 through 25 say that the Lord personally intervened and *"troubled the host of the Egyptians."* It also said, *"And took off their chariot wheels."* Hebrews 11 suggests that Israel had to keep believing while passing through the sea that the waters would not overwhelm them. The Egyptians did not have to exercise any faith, for they saw the open road before them, yet they were drowned. The way of faith is life to the redeemed but death to the rebellious.

Verses 26 through 31 record the promise of God, *"Ye shall see them no more forever."*

CHAPTER 15

The song of Moses that is recorded from

verse 1 through 19 was composed by Moses and sung by him and all Israel on the occasion of the destruction of the Egyptians in the Red Sea. It was the real beginning of Hebrew poetry. The song is in three parts distinctly marked. The first part is verses 1 through 5; the second part is verses 6 through 10; and the third part is verses 11 through 19. Each part begins with praise to God and increases in length and varied imagery until the triumph and ending which shows Jehovah reigning forever and ever, having triumphed over all His enemies. This song of victory over Pharaoh is mentioned as being as important as the future triumph song over the Antichrist (Rev. 15:2-4; Isa. 14:4-17).

This is the first song of Israel on record. They certainly did not sing much in Egypt. Their stay there the last 80 or more years was one of groaning and sighing.

It was evident that only God could do what had been done the past 24 hours. Due praise was given Him as the Author of salvation from destruction by the Egyptians.

The Red Sea pictures death to sin – the Jordan, death to self. The one separates from Egypt; the other from the wilderness.

It is ironical that Moses began and ended his wilderness life with a song (Deut. 32).

Verses 20 and 21 seem to imply there were two companies of singers – one formed of men, led by Moses; the other of women, led by Miriam. She and her choir *"answered them."* Miriam is the first prophetess mentioned in the Bible.

This is the first of ten songs of praise recorded in the Bible. The last song of praise is in Revelation 15:3.

"Self" is absent from this song; it is all about Jehovah and His power to save.

The first song in the Bible was sung on a shore heaped with dead men – an appalling scene of Divine wrath – and the last song in the Bible will be sung in a scene of yet greater wrath and destruction (Rev. 19). These are inspired records of God's ways on earth and His action toward sin, anger, and the self-righteous heart.

Verse 22 records the first "test of faith" after the tremendous victory of the Red Sea, *"and found no water."* God tests faith in order to strengthen and enrich it.

Verses 23 and 24 record an extra "test of faith." When they finally found water, it was "bitter." The people murmured. This was sin and would result in terrible anger by God directed at them. But, yet, when God tests faith, it seems our response as well is little better.

The 25th verse portrays a beautiful picture of Calvary as the only answer for the ills of man, *"And the Lord shewed him a tree."* The Lord has shown the world *"a tree"* (Calvary). However, the tree must be *"cast into the waters."* Regrettably, most in the world have no confidence in *"the tree."* Even the church has little confidence in *"the tree."* The bitter waters can be made sweet only if the tree is cast into the waters. The Bible said, *"There he proved them."* When God proves us, I wonder if our performance is any better?

Verse 26 records a tremendous promise, *"I will put none of these diseases upon thee."* And then He said, *"For I am Jehovah-Ropheka that healeth thee."* However, for this to be brought about, there were four conditions.

1. *"Diligently hear God's voice."*
2. *"Live righteous lives in His sight."*
3. *"Give ear to His commandments."*
4. *"Keep all His statutes."*

The 27th verse records a great blessing, *"Twelve wells of water"* along with *"seventy palm trees."*

CHAPTER 16

Chapters 14 through 17 of Exodus portray the progress of the child of God.

1. The deliverence of the children of Israel from Egypt (ch. 14) – a type of the sinner being delivered from the clutches and bondage of sin, with Egypt as a type of the world.

2. The giving of the manna (ch. 16) which is a type of Christ. The Christian now, after being delivered from the world (Egypt), has a daily allotment of bread from heaven (Christ).

3. The Sabbath (ch. 16). When the individual is delivered from Egypt, receiving Christ as his Saviour, then comes a "sabbath" which

means "rest" from our personal efforts to save ourselves. We rest from our own works.

4. The water out of the rock (ch. 17) which is a type of the Holy Spirit. The person comes out of Egypt (salvation), receives the bread from heaven (Christ), enjoys a "rest" from his own labors and then is baptized in the Holy Spirit, with the water out of the rock being a type of Christ baptizing in the Holy Spirit (St. John 7).

5. *"Then comes Amalek"* which is a type of the flesh with which the Christian has to war constantly.

The 1st verse tells us that the children of Israel had been on the road exactly one month, having left Egypt the 15th of the first month. This indicates that they moved slowly and stopped perhaps several days at a time. About one more month would bring them to Sinai.

Verses 2 and 3 once again proclaim that the *"children of Israel murmured."* It does not take very much to cause the average person or congregation to murmur. The slightest temporary lack of water, food, clothing, money, or convenience will test the metal of every man. Regrettably, the best will finally complain if the pressure increases beyond normal.

The murmurings of verses 6 through 8 proclaim that God hears and sees all the acts of man and will hold each person responsible as to right and wrong in every detail (I Cor. 3:11-15).

Verses 9 through 12 record God promising more miracles to prove that He was the One who had brought them out of Egypt, and that He was still with them, leading them into Canaan. Past miracles are convincing. But unless there are fresh evidences of God, the natural man will soon forget and lapse into unbelief again. God now planned to give Israel daily miracles. Quails were to be given in the evening, and bread was to be rained from heaven in the morning – enough to supply millions of people. It seems that the quails were to be a temporary provision while the bread was to continue indefinitely.

Verses 13 through 20 record the miracle of the quails and the manna. The manna prefigured the descent of the true bread of which if a man eat, he shall live forever (St. John 6:51). In Egypt, Israel had slave food; in the desert, angels food. The test quickly revealed that the natural man had little appetite for heavenly things, for the people soon called it *"light food."*

The manna was so precious that it could not bear contact with the earth. It fell upon the dew and had to be gathered before the sun came up. Yesterday's manna did not do for today, nor today's for tomorrow. Thus, must the Christian feed upon Christ every day as He reveals Himself in the Scriptures.

Israel in the desert presented a striking picture! Egypt was behind them, Canaan was before them, the wilderness was around them, and the manna was above them.

Every time they looked back toward Egypt they murmured; when looking forward toward the wilderness, they saw the glory of the Lord. The manna was a type of Christ as well as the Word of God.

Verse 23 proclaims the *"Holy Sabbath,"* which was *"the rest."* The day of rest suddenly reappears after a silence of more than 2000 years. Redemption being accomplished (deliverance) from Egypt, the Sabbath is given to Israel. But, sadly, man has little heart for God's rest. Man's nature is bad. He can neither rest with nor work for God. If God makes a rest for him, he will not keep it, and if God tells him to work, he will not do it. In this chapter Israel will refuse the Sabbath as a gift and in the book of Numbers disobey it as a law.

The 31st verse proclaims once again the name of the miracle bread from heaven, *"manna."* In the Hebrew it means, "What is it?" They had no name for it because there had never been anything like it on earth previously. Actually, it was angels' food and was sent from heaven (Psa. 78:25). As the people would reject the manna, likewise, they would reject Christ.

CHAPTER 17

Once again faith must be tested. They are taken by the *"commandment of the Lord"* to *"Rephidim."*

It would seem somewhat strange that God

NOTES

Who professed to love them should lead Israel into a desert both foodless and waterless. However, it was love that led them there that they might learn the desperate unbelief of their own hearts. The child of God does not really know what he is until tested. And neither can the child of God know Who God is until tested. In this situation Israel without God would have nothing, but with God they would have everything.

In verse 3 once again *"Egypt"* is thrown up to God. The child of God in the time of test is tempted strongly to think his life with Satan was of greater profit then his life now is with God. It is one of Satan's favorite ploys. It angers God greatly. All sin is deplored and hated by God. However, the Church, by and large, focuses on certain sins and ignores many sins that God hates.

Verses 5 through 7 record one of the greatest miracles yet, plus one of the greatest "types" found in the entire Word of God.

The water from the smitten Rock foretold the living water, the Holy Spirit, to be sent forth by the smitten Saviour. The Holy Spirit is the fruit of Christ's great sacrifice (I Cor. 10:4). The Rock was smitten by the very same rod of judgment that smote the land of Egypt. As the Rock was smitten, Christ would be smitten as well. It was the judgment of God upon Him rather than on us who rightfully deserved it. But as out of the smitten Rock water gushes forth, likewise out of the smitten Christ eternal life gushes forth. At Rephidim travelers have described what is believed to be the rock smitten by Moses. It is said to be a vast block of granite, 15 feet long, 10 feet broad, and 12 feet high. It has holes and channels which could have been formed only by the bursting and running out of water. The rock Moses smote supplied water for perhaps 3 to 6 million people and their stock. The Psalmist said, *"He brought streams also out of the Rock, and caused waters to run down like rivers."* There was no lack. It was not a trickling stream, but, rather instead, a flowing river plenty enough for all.

The 8th verse records the coming of the "flesh." It says, *"Then came Amalek,"* a type of the flesh. They *"fought with Israel"* and it was at *"Rephidim."* The reception of the Holy Spirit immediately causes war. Up to this point God had fought for them. But now, as is recorded in the 9th verse, the Scripture says, *"Go out, fight with Amalek:"* There is an immense difference between justification and sanctification. The one is Christ fighting for us; the other, the Holy Spirit fighting in us. The entrance of the new nature provided by the Holy Spirit is the beginning of warfare with the old. Amalek pictures the old carnal nature. He was the grandson of Esau, who before and after birth tried to murder Jacob, and who preferred the mess of pottage to the birthright. This carnal nature wars against the Spirit, *"It is not subject to the law of God neither indeed can be,"* and God has decreed war against it forever.

God did not destroy Amalek, but determined to have war with him from generation to generation. Amalek would dwell in the land but not reign in it. Romans 6 says, *"Let not sin therefore reign in your mortal bodies."* The command would be meaningless if sin were not existent in the Christian. Sin dwells in a believer (the sin nature), but must not reign. Sin dwells and reigns in an unbeliever.

In verses 8 through 16 we have the Spirit-directed formula for victory over the flesh. There is no other.

The *"rod of God"* outlined in the 9th verse, was a sign from God of Israel's greatest opposition – the serpent, Satan.

The *"top of the hill"* in verse 10 is a type of Calvary. Every victory comes through Calvary.

The 11th verse says, *"When Moses held up his hand."* This was a sign of surrender to God, of total dependence on the Holy Spirit, and none on the flesh. When he would let down his hand, *"Amalek prevailed."* Total dependence on God, victory. Total dependence on the flesh, defeat.

The 12th verse says, *"Moses' hands were heavy."* The struggle of total dependence upon God is never an easy struggle, and at times "falls." The *"stone"* that was *"put under him"* is a type of Christ. The Scripture says, *"He sat thereon."* Our own efforts soon result in spiritual exhaustion. But once we are in God's way, the victory is ours. *"Aaron and Hur stayed up his hands"* is a type of our need for others in the Body of Christ. Jesus requested the trio to *"watch with Him one hour."* When Moses tried

the task alone, he failed. And when he failed, as fail he must, Amalek prevailed. But once he has the help of *"a stone"* and *"Aaron and Hur,"* then *"his hands were steady."* But how hard it is for us to learn this.

Incidentally, Hur was the son of Caleb of Judah (I Chron. 2:19-20). He was closely associated with Moses and Aaron. Josephus said that he was the brother-in-law of Moses and Aaron, having married Miriam.

Verse 14 records the birth of the Bible as a written book. In the same breath of the command to write *"the Book"* is the promise to *"utterly put out the remembrance of Amalek from under heaven."* Amalek, being a type of the flesh, which is the Christian's greatest enemy, was sworn to defeat. In the physical sense there are no people on earth today called Amalekites. As well, in the spiritual sense, the flesh will be utterly defeated at the First Resurrection. It will happen.

Verse 15 portrays *"Jehovah-Nissi,"* meaning "the Lord our banner."

Once again, it is remarkable that the first mention of the Bible should be in connection with the hostility of the natural man (Amalek) to the spiritual man (Israel). War has ever since accompanied the Book. Satan has ever fought it. No book has been so hated and so loved.

CHAPTER 18

Chapter 18 is parenthetical. It actually occurred between verses 10 and 11 of Numbers 10.

Verses 1 and 2 are the divine comment on what happened after the event of 4:24-26. Moses simply sent his wife back home for some unknown reason. Whether at the advice of Aaron or to protect the family from what they would face in Egypt, or if he thought his wife would be a hindrance to his present work, we do not know. We know only that he sent her home. Perhaps he had an understanding with her that when Israel was delivered, he would reunite with the family at this place.

In some ways the events narrated in chapter 18 give a prophetic picture of the coming millennial kingdom.

Verses 9 through 12 portray Jethro, a Gentile, united with Israel, *"And all the elders of Israel, to eat bread with Moses' father-in-law before God"* (vs. 12).

It is striking as portrayed in the 19th verse that Jethro the Gentile says, *"I will give thee counsel,"* referring to Moses who represented Israel. In the millennial reign the Church will definitely give Israel counsel.

The *"rulers"* in the 21st verse are but pictures of that which will be common in the millennial reign. They will be *"able men, such as fear God, men of truth, hating covetousness."*

The 26th verse says, *"the hard causes they brought unto Moses."* Moses was a type of Christ. And the Scripture says, *"The government shall be upon his shoulders,"* meaning Christ.

CHAPTER 19

Chapter 19 portrays *"Israel camped before the mount of Sinai."* The words *"in the third month"* mean *"on the first day of the third month."* This would make the day of the giving of the Law the 50th (or Pentecost) after Israel left Egypt on the 15th day of the first month. The Day of Pentecost was after seven Sabbaths (49 days) were completed, or the 50th day after the Sabbath after the Passover. Thus, beginning with the 16th day of the first month and counting 50 days would mean the Law was given on Pentecost.

The 3rd verse says, *"Moses went up unto God."* Moses had eight ascents and eight descents.

The 4th verse describes Israel's salvation as *"on eagle's wings."* The Lord then used the term *"brought you unto myself,"* speaking of a salvation wholly of God.

The 5th verse proclaims Israel being called *"a peculiar treasure,"* and then more specifically *"unto me."* Now, in Christ, spiritual Israel is a part of this *"peculiar treasure."*

The *"kingdom of priests and an holy nation"* were to serve as a light of salvation to a

lost world.

In verses 7 and 8, as a result of the flesh, the people foolishly answer regarding the commands of God, *"All that the Lord hath spoken we will do."* Had they known their own hearts, they would have replied that such a condition was impossible to them, and they would have cast themselves upon God that He should give them new hearts capable of such obedience. Man has ever proclaimed his ability to obey God and has ever portrayed his constant failure.

Verses 9 through 25 portray the coming of the Lord down upon Mount Sinai (vs. 20). This was done on the Day of Pentecost, foreshadowing another coming on another Day of Pentecost some 1600 years later. The preparations to meet God are the same preparations to be baptized in the Holy Spirit. The sanctification and washing of verse 10 is a prelude to the human heart preparing for the incoming of the Holy Spirit.

The *"fire"* of verse 18 was symbolic of the *"fire"* that would set upon the heads of those baptized in Acts 2.

The *"voice of the trumpet sounded long"* in verse 19; whereas, the sound of the mighty rushing wind in Acts 2 signaled the coming of the Holy Spirit.

Verse 20 says, *"And the Lord came down."* Acts 2 portrays the Holy Spirit coming down.

The 25th verse says, *"And spake unto them."* Likewise, Peter on the Day of Pentecost said, *"Hearken to my words."*

CHAPTER 20

The Ten Commandments given by God to Moses on Mount Sinai are the foundation of all law for the entire world. Every system of law in every nation of the world, irrespective of religious preference, has at least in part the "Ten Commandments" as its basis of foundation. The Ten Commandments, therefore, were of universal application. Their function was to make man conscious that he was a sinner, that he could not save himself, and that he desperately needed a Saviour (Rom. 7:7). The Commandments were like a mirror let down from heaven in which man could see his own vileness.

Jesus in St. Matthew 22 divided the Ten Commandments into two groups. The first five direct our attention toward God and our responsibility to Him. The second five enjoin us to love others as the first five commanded that we love God. The Lord encapsuled all ten in the words, *"Love the Lord thy God with all thy heart . . . and thy neighbor as thyself."*

Verse 1 says that God spake the Ten Commandments, and then Israel begged that His voice be heard no more lest they die (Deut. 5:22-29). God then stopped speaking with an audible voice in the presence of the whole nation and spoke to Moses, giving the rest of the commands which Israel should obey. Moses wrote the Ten Commandments and many others in a book which he ratified by the blood of animals (24:3-8).

In verse 5 it says, *"The iniquity of the fathers."* Never does it say the iniquity of the mothers, for the following reason: Adam, not Eve, was the fountainhead, the source, the moral, spiritual, and legal head and representative of the whole race. Actually, all were in Adam's loins before the fall and before he committed sin. When he sinned, he acted in essence for the entire race, and as their source he was responsible for sin being passed upon all men. When he acted he did so not as a private person, but for the race that was to come from him, to share his blessings if he obeyed or his curses if he sinned (Gen. 2:17; Rom. 5:12-21). Scripture recognizes the woman as the means of reproduction of man without sinful responsibility as far as passing sin from parent to offspring is concerned. This is how Jesus could be born of a woman, a virgin, and still not be sinful flesh.

In the 7th verse, *"Thou shalt not take the name of the Lord thy God in vain"* is a commandment against all false swearing, blasphemy, and all profane, vain, trivial, light, and irreverent use of God's name in ordinary life. It also refers to using God's name in false religions, witchcraft, conjuring - any abuse of the sacred and holy name whatsoever. The right use of His name is confined to that which is sacred - prayer, praise, prophecy, teaching,

NOTES

worship, and communion with God and saints.

The commandment of Sabbath-keeping of the 10th verse is the only commandment that was not carried over into the New Testament. Actually, it is not in the New Covenant at all, and so, since the Old or Mosaic Covenant has been abolished, it is not in force anymore whatsoever. Christians are now free to observe any day of rest of their choice. (Actually, the Sabbath was a day of rest and not necessarily a day of worship.)

In the 12th verse concerning *"honor thy father and thy mother"* is the first commandment of the ten giving promise. It implies a longer life, proving there is no set time to die and suggesting that man, more or less, determines his own length of life (whether long or short) and destiny.

The 13th verse, *"Thou shalt not kill,"* does not prohibit killing as punishment for crimes or killing in war, which God Himself commanded these same people to do, but it does prohibit killing for malice and premeditated,willful destruction of man who was made in the image of God.

The 14th verse, *"Thou shalt not commit adultery,"* prohibits all unlawful sexual relationship and upholds the sacredness and divine appointment of marriage for the propagation and multiplication of the human race.

The 15th verse, *"Thou shalt not steal,"* prohibits secret and open removal of the property of another, any injury done to it, and carelessness about that which belongs to a neighbor.

The 16th verse, *"Thou shalt not bear false witness,"* prohibits false testimonies in courts of justice, and lying about the acts, word, and property of a neighbor.

The 17th verse portrays the last of the Ten Commandments, *"Thou shalt not covet,"* which prohibits the inward desire of the heart from longing for, scheming, and putting forth any effort to acquire anything that belongs to another.

Verses 18 through 21 seem to portray that at the end of each commandment there was lightning and a long, loud, deafening peal of thunder to impress Israel with the sacredness of the Divine Majesty and the holiness of Jehovah and His law. The people became terror-stricken and fled from the mount, whereas, before they were pressing so close toward it that Moses had to go down and warn them not to break through in their gazing. The sight and sound were so terrible that even Moses who was with God said, *"I exceedingly fear and quake"* (Heb. 12:18-21). The holiness of God is the reason that a mediator was demanded.

In respect to the 4th verse and *"Thou shalt not make unto thee any graven image,"* regardless of many commands in both Testaments against idolatry, the love of images and their worship are indulged in by millions today, even in so-called Christian lands. And it must be ever remembered that those who break God's laws are destined to God's wrath. Idolatry was God's big problem with Israel. No Bible writer ever mentioned images in worship to God in the Tabernacle or Temple rituals, except when Israel was backslidden and served idol gods. Images are the work of man (Isa. 2:8; Jer. 10:1-9). Being mere imitations of creatures and made of dead material, it is folly to make them part of one's worship.

In the Early Church the first Christians were not adverse to art, but they had no images of Christ. From A.D. 100-400, Christian leaders rebuked various individuals for seeking to introduce images of Christ and saints into their worship. The 36th Canon of the Synod of Elvira prohibited images as a hindrance to the spiritual worship of God. Eusebius, father of church history, opposed them as well.

Ambrose, Jerome, and Augustine all mentioned pictures made of apostles and Christ in the worship of images as beginning in their day. The use and adoration of images were popular in the East, being increased by pagan concepts and customs in worship. The theory that images represent the invisible persons became very prominent in some circles.

Images began to be used as sponsors, and reverence began to be paid them. Opposition to image worship then became acute for some time, the conflict being between the emperors and many of the bishops. Emperors often condemned images as heresy and idolatry, and religious relics were destroyed and thrown into the sea. In A.D. 766 Constantine sought to impose an oath against image worship, but the Lateran Synod sanctioned images in 769.

Tarasius, an advocate of images, was made patriarch of the East in 784, and in 787 the Synod of Nicea ascribed reverence to images and worship to God through them. The same decision was reached in the West at the Synod of Frankfort, A.D. 794, and images were again sanctioned at Paris in 825. Emperors in the East continued their opposition, and advocates of images were exiled for some time.

After A.D. 850 the cult of image worship in churches began to grow due to arguments for images and stories of miracles performed through them. Blessings were claimed for the images themselves. And finally, in 1188, it was declared that denial of images was a denial of God. In 1225 it was said that Christ was not Christ unless He was graven. The 25th session of the Council of Trent (1551) of the Catholic Church justified the worship of images. Thus, from the beginning until now, the controversy has raged, and image worship has been accepted by many as authorized of God.

The fact remains, though, that the Bible is opposed to all use of images in worship.

In verse 21 the Bible says, *"The people stood afar off."* And now in verses 22 through 26, God devises a way for man to approach Him; it is by the way of the altar.

In verse 24 it speaks of *"an altar of earth."* The altar pictures the Lord Jesus Christ, and, of course, is a type of Calvary. The earth, as this altar was to be made, was a picture of the humanity of Christ. If the altar were to be made out of stone, this would picture His deity. If so, it must not be of *"hewnstone,"* because hewnstone signified the works of man. The altar of stone made in this fashion typified that man is not saved by human works; salvation is not of works (Eph. 2:8- 9). The Blood that would be shed on that stone from the whole burnt offerings and peace offerings would typify the priceless life-blood of Christ sacrificed to put away sin and bring the sinner back to God.

No tool was to embellish the altar; it was perfect in its beauty to the eye of God, and such was Jesus. We may as well seek to paint the lily or adorn the rose as for man to attempt to add to the beauty of Him Who is altogether lovely. The altar, as well, was to stand on a level with the people. Such was the Christ; He was accessible to all. There were to be no steps up to the altar. When man exalts himself above God, he only exposes his own moral nakedness.

Heathen worshipers who imitated the rites of the true God made their altars very high, partly through pride and partly in the belief that their gods might hear them better. "High places" are mentioned 77 times in Scripture, and are always sinful.

CHAPTERS 21, 22, & 23

The legislation involved in these three chapters points to a loving God charting a moral course for a corrupt people. This legislation was called *"judgments."* Almost every conduct concerning life and limb was given by God to these former slaves. There were laws in the world hundreds of years before the giving of the law by God to Moses, but they all were man-made. These laws were God-made. Many of the laws were civil, many were moral; all were from God.

For instance, the law of 21:23, *"life for life,"* not only reduced the need for jails, but reduced crime to a minimum. If such laws of God were enforced today, crime would be diminished greatly and fast. But so long as there is little real fear of punishment, crime rates will be increased. This "law" set a pattern for life for God's chosen people. It was a law of love that even took into consideration the tooth of a little slave girl and enacted that she should be set free if so slightly injured (21:27).

However, the law could not save. It was never meant to save; it was only to be a mirror to show Israel how corrupt that man really was. It was basically designed by God for two reasons:

A. To form a system and basis of government for people that were to represent God.

B. As a schoolmaster to bring men to Christ, showing them that they were helpless to obey its commands, and thusly to seek the help of a Saviour Who would be the Lord Jesus Christ.

Regrettably, Israel turned God's law into idolatry. They went about trying to establish their own righteousness. God gave the law and

NOTES

demanded that man keep it. There were severe penalties for not keeping it. And yet, God, knowing that man would not and, in fact, could not keep it because of his depraved condition, provided sacrifices to atone for man's sin and failure. Sacrifices, in effect, could not take away sin but would point toward One Who was to come, the Lord Jesus Christ Who would, in fact, take away sin. Such laws had to be made to protect men from the appalling evil which prompted them to oppress one another.

Verses 14 through 16 of chapter 23 proclaim three yearly feasts of Jehovah to be kept by all the men.

First, there was the *"Feast of Unleavened Bread,"* which included the feasts of the Passover and Firstfruits, the Passover being a type of Christ's death at Calvary, and Firstfruits being a picture of His resurrection.

The second feast was the *"Feast of Pentecost."* This was a type of the mighty Baptism in the Holy Spirit, and, in fact, the Holy Spirit came on the Day of Pentecost.

The third feast was the *"Feast of Tabernacles,"* which symbolized the millennial reign. There were seven feasts in all.

1. Passover - typifying the death of Christ at Calvary.

2. Unleavened bread - typifying the sinless body of Christ buried on our behalf.

3. Firstfruits - typifying the resurrection of Christ.

4. Pentecost - typifying the outpouring and infilling of the Holy Spirit.

The above four feasts were held in the spring of the year, with three being conducted the first week beginning with Passover, and then seven weeks after Passover on the 50th day, Pentecost (meaning 50th).

5. Trumpets - signifying the Rapture and not yet fulfilled.

6. Atonement - the cleansing of Israel as a nation with the new temple described by Ezekiel being built in a newly-built Jerusalem - unfulfilled.

7. Tabernacles - a type of the millennial reign (Millenium)- unfulfilled.

The last three feasts were conducted in the fall of the year. Therefore, the men of Israel obedient to God's commands could attend the first three feasts beginning with Passover, which would last about a week. Then some seven weeks later, they could attend the Feast of Pentecost. And then in the fall of the year, they could assemble again, attending the last three feasts which would last somewhat over a week. The eighth day of the feast that is described in St. John 7, where Jesus attended and cried the words, *"If any man thirst,"* was on the last day of the Feast of Tabernacles.

CHAPTER 24

Nadab and Abihu were the two oldest sons of Aaron who were slain by God for being inebriated (drunk) and then offering strange fire in the Tabernacle (Lev. 10). The *"seventy"* were the ones that God chose to put His Spirit upon (Num. 11:16-25). The 24th chapter portrays the sealing of the Mosaic Covenant.

Verses 3 and 4 portray Israel once again saying, *"All the words which the Lord hath said will we do."* Man is ever ready to proclaim his willingness and capability, but, as always, fails. Israel, as we, would have been far better off to have said, "Oh Lord, we are unable to obey Your words; please allow Your strength to rest upon our weakness." The *"twelve"* pillars are explained here as representing the 12 tribes of Israel. With the altar standing for access to God, both God and Israel were thus represented as making a covenant together. God proposed the covenant, promising curses for breaking it and blessings for keeping it. The covenant was ratified by the blood of animals, which signified that disobedience caused life to be forfeited and showed faith in the coming Redeemer. The 12 pillars were of uncut stones, signifying that salvation is wholly of God and none of man. If the stones had been cut, designed, and polished, it would have portrayed a design by man. All religion is an altar of stones cut and designed by men in an effort to reach God. None will, for God will not accept that which is not His and His alone.

Verses 5 through 8 portray half the blood being poured on the altar, pledging God to keep the covenant; the other half was sprinkled upon the people, so pledging them.

NOTES

The 5th verse mentions *"burnt offerings"* as well as *"peace offerings."* The law regarding offerings had not yet been given, as in Leviticus 1-7. However, man knew what type of offerings to sacrifice from the time of Adam (Gen. 4:3-7, 13:4, 22:13, 31:54).

Verses 9 through 11 twice say, *"They saw the God of Israel"* and *"They saw God."* This does not contradict St. John 1:18 where it says, *"No man hath seen God,"* with the word *"seen"* meaning "comprehended." In other words, no man has fully seen or fully comprehended God at any time. However, verses 9 and 11 mean exactly what they say, *"They saw God,"* which was a preincarnate appearance of the Lord Jesus Christ *(the glory I had with thee before the world was).*

In some way *"Mount Sinai"* of verses 12 through 18 represents and pictures the temple. The foot of the mountain with its great altar of burnt offerings, and the multitude formed the outer court. Higher up the mountain the nobles worshiped in the inner court, and on the summit were Moses and the Holiest of All. The *"sapphire stone"* of verse 10 expressed the purity of God.

Verse 16 says that Moses stayed in the cloud *"six days"* before God *"called unto Moses."* Six is the number of man, meaning imperfection and incompletion. *"The seventh day"* represents God's complete and perfect number, meaning completion, fulfillment, and totality. Moses was saturated by the presence of God some six days before called into the presence of God.

Incidentally, the words *"and did eat and drink"* of verse 11 speak of the "Fellowship of Access." Acts 10:41 speaks of the "Fellowship of Testimony." Luke 22:30 speaks of the "Fellowship of Glory."

It was grace that furnished the table of Exodus 24:11, for the elders did not bring their meal up the mountain with them. They were made nigh by the blood of Christ (Eph. 2). Only those who continue with Him in His rejection will feast on thrones with Him in His glory.

CHAPTER 25

Beginning with chapter 25, we have the commands of the Lord to make the Tabernacle and furniture. The materials, the furniture, the vessels, and everything within and without the Tabernacle symbolized the person, atoning work, the ministries, the glories, and the perfections of Christ as Jehovah's Perfect Servant, and as the Saviour and High Priest of His people.

Access to God is the lesson the Tabernacle and its furniture teaches. The Tabernacle, therefore, is a manifestation of the glory of the grace of the Lord Jesus Christ, and of His relationship with sinners who draw nigh unto Him.

All of the specifications for the Tabernacle and its furniture were given by God to Moses. Moses was not given just a plan but, in fact, a literal model to go by. So, it was all of God and none of man, as salvation is all of God and none of man.

Every design of the Tabernacle, the furniture and all that pertained to it, were actually representations of the heavenly. All were symbolic but pointed to the real in heaven.

The 2nd verse said, *"Every man that giveth it willingly with his heart."* The people had to give willingly or not at all. Likewise, salvation is *"Whosoever will."* God forces no one to be saved; His salvation must be accepted willingly.

The 3rd verse speaks of *"Gold, silver, and brass (copper)."* Gold was symbolic of deity, silver of redemption, and copper of humanity.

Verse 4 speaks of *"blue,"* meaning the heavenly, *"purple,"* which represents His kingship. *"Scarlet"* represents the blood that He would shed for the salvation of humanity. The *"fine linen"* stands for His righteousness. The *"goat's hair"* came from the beautiful Asian goats which had long beautiful hair almost as fine as silk and valued as much as wool from the sheep. It represents His prophetic office.

In the 5th verse the *"ram's skins"* represented His becoming a sacrificial offering. They were *"dyed red,"* representing His shed blood. The *"badger's skins"* was the last

NOTES

covering on the Tabernacle. It is that, looking from the outside, that the world saw. It was not very attractive. Likewise, Christ's life as a peasant was not very attractive. The *"shittim wood"* came from the acacia tree, which produced a beautiful and durable wood sometimes called indestructible wood; in other words, it would not rot. It was representative of His perfect, sinless, spotless body.

The 6th verse speaks of *"oil for the light."* This was representative of the Holy Spirit. The *"spices for sweet incense"* spoke of His prayerful and constant intercession on behalf of the child of God.

The *"precious stones"* of the 7th verse that would ultimately go in the ephod and the breastplate were all symbolic of God's grace and glory toward the children of Israel.

The 8th verse says, *"Make me a sanctuary that I may dwell among them."* Here, God, condescending to dwell in Israel, commanded that a special dwelling be erected for Him where His presence could be manifest daily to them and from which He would commune with them through Moses and the High Priests in generations to come. Every part of the Tabernacle was typical of the nature of God: the coming redemption, the sinfulness of man, the means of pardon through grace, and the full reconciliation of man to God. God has always wanted to *"dwell"* with man.

"The pattern" of the 9th verse is totally of God and none of man. Man has always tried to introduce his own pattern. God will never accept any of man's patterns; He will only accept His own *"pattern"* Who is Jesus Christ. We Christians are very quick to speak of God blessing us, and we should, but, actually, God does not bless sinful man. He blesses only the Lord Jesus Christ Who is in redeemed man.

Verses 10 through 16 give the directions and description of the *"Ark of the Covenant."* The *"Ark"* represented the throne of God; likewise, salvation begins with God and not man. According to our study, we believe the cubit represents 18 inches.

The *"pure gold"* of the 11th verse was symbolic of deity. The *"crown,"* symbolic of Christ the King, was round about the Ark whose overlay of *"shittim wood,"* was symbolic of His perfect humanity.

The *"Staves"* of the 13th verse represented the fact that the Ark was constantly on the move because God's dwelling place was only symbolic. Even though redeemed man in Christianity enjoys the privilege of Christ dwelling within him by the power and the agency of the Holy Spirit, still, this Tabernacle groans for redemption and the coming of the Lord. The Temple that Solomon would build would be symbolic of Christ's actual dwelling place on earth and speaks of the Millennium.

"The testimony" of verse 16 was the Ten Commandments.

Verses 17 through 23 speak of the *"mercy seat."* It was *"pure gold."* The solid gold mercy seat was the covering of the Ark which held the Ten Commandments. This signified that mercy and grace overshadowed law, that judgment and death were the penalty for sin, and that justice and mercy could be reconciled through grace and faith in the blood.

The *"two cherubims of gold"* represent the holiness of God. Man has never yet been able to comprehend or understand the thrice holy God. These two cherubims represented the cherubims of the 4th chapter of Revelation. The cherubims, patterned after heavenly spirit beings, were a further symbol of the Divine Presence. Between them was the mercy seat, the visible symbol of the presence of God from Whom came the mercies and curses of the Law. Their wings stretching over the mercy seat and their faces looking toward it symbolize the eternal watchfulness and ministry of angels to the redeemed and their cooperation with God in the plan of redemption as typified by the Tabernacle and offerings of the Law of Moses.

The 20th verse says, *"Toward the mercy seat shall the faces of the cherubims be,"* meaning that the cherubims, who in heaven cry "holy, holy, holy," continuously look down on the mercy seat under which is the Law – the Law, we might add, that was broken.

So, blood would be applied to the mercy seat, which would shield the gaze of the cherubims on the broken Law (vs. 21).

Verses 23 through 30 portray the instructions given for the making of the *"table of shewbread."* As well, the *"table"* was made of gold. Actually, all the shittim wood of the Tabernacle was covered with gold. The only two

items that were not originally of wood (to be covered with gold) were the candlestick and mercy seat. The gold typifies God's real and eternal dwelling place - the Holy City, the New Jerusalem which is made of pure gold (Rev. 21:18, 21), as well as the Deity of Christ. Furthermore, in the Word of God gold symbolized seven things: *"God's Word"* (Psa. 19:10), *"Wisdom"* (Prov. 3:13-14), *"Knowledge"* (Prov. 8:10), *"Truth"* (Prov. 8:19), *"Good Name and Loving Favor"* (Prov. 22:1), *"Trials"* (Zech. 13:9; I Pet. 1:7), and *"Words"* (I Cor. 3:12).

The 25th verse speaks of *"a golden crown to the border."* Three items of furniture had crowns which typify the kingly glory of the Lord Jesus Christ: *"The Ark"* and the *"Table of Shewbread,"* as well as the *"Altar of Incense."*

The 30th verse says, *"The table of shewbread,"* meaning "bread of face"because it was to lie continually before Jehovah as a thanksgiving offering presented by the 12 tribes. The bread was not for Jehovah to eat, but was for the priests as a symbol of spiritual food. It was at the end of the week when the bread was changed that the priests could use it for food for themselves and their families. The loaves were large but would not feed all the priests, so, evidently, they were eaten only by the officiating ones in their turn.

Verses 31 through 40 give the instructions for the making of a *"candlestick of pure gold."* The candlestick did not begin with shittim wood but was made entirely out of *"pure gold."* Actually, this beautiful work was all of one piece, *"shall be of the same."*

The 32nd verse says, *"Six branches shall come out of the sides of it."* This would refer to three to a side which symbolized the Church made up of humanity with the number six being the number of man. However, it must be noted that the branches were not welded or fastened to the main branch, but were actually a part of the branch, showing the oneness of the child of God with the Lord Jesus Christ.

The *"bowls"* on each one of the branches *"made like unto almonds,"* actually were lamps, with the almonds symbolizing life. The "knot" of verse 33 speaks of spiritual growth, with the *"flower"* speaking of purity. So, the child of God is to be pure, enjoying spiritual growth, which will symbolize Christ.

The 37th verse speaks of *"seven lamps"* with the three on each side accounting for six and symbolizing the Body of Christ, which when added to the main branch in the center symbolizes Christ Himself and portrays perfection, hence the number *"seven."* When the Church functions properly in Christ, it provides a perfect illumination for a darkened world. The Word says, *"That they may give light over against it,"* speaking of the *"table of shewbread"* along with the *"altar of worship."* There could be no understanding of Christ of Whom the bread was a symbol or worship without the illumination of the golden lamp stand. Likewise, in Christendom, if we are not properly in Christ, there can be no illumination to really know Christ or to worship Him.

The *"tongs"* and *"snuff dishes"* represent the cleaning of the wicks of the lamps. The wick had to be trimmed every morning and every evening. Likewise, the Lord *"chastises those He loves."*

Verse 40 says, *"Make them after their pattern."* The pattern was not to be deviated from. Unfortunately, man has, consistently, inserted his own patterns which give no light.

CHAPTER 26

Verse 1 says, *"Thou shalt make the tabernacle."* The top or roof of the Tabernacle actually had four coverings. The innermost covering, or the covering that was seen by the priests who entered into the holy place, was *"fine linen"* (white) which represents the righteousness of Christ. The covering that was immediately above was the *"goat's hair,"* which represents Christ in His prophetic office. And third, next to the outside covering, were *"ram's skins dyed red,"* which represent Christ's sacrificial and, thereby, high priestly function. The outside covering, or that which was seen by the bystander, was of *"badger skins,"* which portrays very little beauty, and is a type of Christ's peasant humility *(meek and lowly in heart)*. Actually, everything in the Tabernacle represents Christ. Of that which has colors, the meaning is: *"fine twined linen* (white), righ-

teousness of Christ; *"blue,"* our salvation is of heavenly origin; *"purple,"* Christ's royal kingship; *"scarlet,"* His blood shed for the sins of man. The *"cherubims"* portrayed in the 1st verse are heavenly creatures representative of God's presence and have certain divine duties to perform:

1. They guarded the Tree of Life in Eden when man was driven out (Gen. 3:24).

2. They are one means of God in travel (II Sam. 22:11; Psa. 18:10).

3. They take God's throne (at least His traveling throne) from place to place (Ezek. 1; 10:1-20; 11:22). Since the mercy seat represents the presence of God, and cherubims actually dwell in His presence in heaven, it was only proper that they be represented on the linen curtains to further impress men with the fact of Divine Presence. (Ordinary angels are called cherubs - Ezek. 28:11-17.)

The 2nd verse says the length of each curtain was 42 feet long. They were 6 feet wide.

The 6th verse says, *"fifty taches of gold,"* with gold always in the Tabernacle representing the deity of Christ. Even though there were many parts to the Tabernacle, there was still "one tabernacle." Christ has many functions; He is Priest, Prophet, and King. As well, He is 100 percent man and 100 percent God. But, yet, He is one Lord.

Verses 15 through 25 speak of the 50 boards which were made of *"shittim wood."* They would be overlaid with gold. Once again, they typify with the wood Christ's humanity, and with the gold, the deity of Christ.

The 19th verse speaks of *"sockets of silver."* The boards overlaid with gold were fastened into redemption's silver and crowned with the same. The crown was visible, the foundation not. The redemptive work of Christ reaches from the depths of the sinner's need to the heights of God's glory.

Verses 26 and 27 speak of the *"bars"* made of *"shittim wood."* There were five bars on each side and five bars on the end, running length wise. They held the boards together. Perhaps every board, not just part of them, was fastened to the bars with rings of gold. The middle bars on the sides and end reached the whole length of the walls. The length of the other four bars on each wall is not given. The bars, as well as the posts in the front of which we will discuss later, stood for the fivefold ministry: *"apostles, prophets, evangelists, pastors, and teachers"* (Eph. 4:11). If we start at the top bar and symbolize it as the apostle with the second bar symbolizing the prophet, then the 3rd and longest bar would symbolize the evangelist. It is the longest bar, having the greatest reach. Of necessity the evangelist reaches further with the Gospel due to his calling. It in no way means that he is of greater importance than the apostle or the prophet. To be frank, the calling of the apostle, which would entail all of the callings embodied in the one, would no doubt be construed as at least the most powerful. In God's callings one does not take preeminence over the other. Whatever is needed for the time and place is the most important at that particular moment. All the bars were attached to the boards, with the boards being a type of Christ. As stated, the bars were made of shittim wood which denoted Christ's humanity. They were then overlaid with gold. The bars were attached to the boards, denoting their reason for being.

Verses 31 and 32 speak of the *"veil."* It separated the holy place, which contained the *"table of shewbread,"* the *"golden lamp stand,"* and the *"altar of worship,"* from the most holy place which contained the *"Ark of the Covenant"* with the *"mercy seat"* and *"cherubims."* None of the priests could go past the veil except the Great High Priest and that once a year on the Great Day of Atonement. Since Christ died and shed His precious life's blood, paying the price for man's sins, the veil has been taken away. Now, through the precious blood of Jesus Christ, any child of God can approach the Lord at any time. Once again, the four colors of *"blue, purple, scarlet, and white"* (twined linen) decorated the veil.

Verses 36 and 37 tell us of *"the door."* Of course, this ,as well, is a type of Christ, and its colors were *"blue, purple, scarlet, and white."*

Verse 37 says at the front of the Tabernacle were *"five pillars."* As well, some have said this denotes the fivefold calling of *"apostles, prophets, evangelists, pastors, and teachers."* They were made of *"shittim wood,"* denoting Christ's humanity and overlaid with *"gold,"* showing deity. The five posts were embedded in *"brass"*

at the bottom, denoting humanity.

CHAPTER 27

Verses 1 through 8 portray the great brazen altar. It represents Jesus and Calvary. Once again, it, as well, was made of *"shittim wood,"* signifying Christ's humanity. It was overlaid with brass, portraying the judgment of God upon sin. Using 18 inches to the cubit, the altar was 7½ feet long and 7½ feet wide.

The 2nd verse says, *"The horns of it upon the four corners thereof."* These horns pointed outward to all points of the compass, signifying God's plan of salvation for the entire world. It sat in front of the entrance to the Tabernacle, showing that the crucified Lamb of God is the one and only way to God. As well, it was borne by *"staves,"* accompanying the people in their pilgrim way to Canaan, so teaching the lesson that there never comes a period in the Christian life where the atoning Blood of Christ can be dispensed with.

Verses 9 through 15 portray the *"outer court."* Using 18 inches to the cubit, it was 150 feet long and 75 feet wide. The curtain was of *"fine twined linen"* and surrounded the enclosure. The pillars holding the curtain were socketed in *"brass."* Brass stakes were driven in the ground close by the pillars with silver rods running between the pillars and the brass stakes to hold up the posts and the curtains.

The worshiper would approach the Tabernacle and see the beautiful white curtains of the court enriched with brass and silver. This again was a portrayal of the Lord Jesus Christ Whose life was sinless. As well, it was adorned with Divine beauties.

Verses 16 and 17 speak of *"the gate."* It was 30 feet wide. It was different from the curtains of the outer court, having the colors of *"blue, purple, scarlet, and white."* It is interesting as to how wide the gate was. It took almost half of the entire front and was symbolic of the great *"whosoever will, let him come."*

Verse 18 says that the fence of the outer court was 7½ feet high. It was tall enough that the inquisitive need not approach. The one gate at the front symbolized the one Redeemer, the Lord Jesus Christ.

Verses 20 and 21 portray the *"pure oil olive,"* which is a type of the Holy Spirit. It was made by olives being bruised in a mortar or mill without the application of heat, *"beaten for the light."* Likewise, He was *"bruised for our iniquities."* It was to *"burn always."* As well, the child of God is to let his light shine constantly, which can only be done by the power of the Holy Spirit.

CHAPTER 28

Verse 1 portrays Aaron being chosen by God as the great High Priest, with his four sons chosen to the priesthood as well. Verse 2 speaks of the *"holy garments for glory and for beauty."* All the garments designed by God for the priests were beautiful, but the garments for Aaron, the great High Priest, were beautiful beyond compare. They were so because Aaron was a type of Christ.

The 3rd verse mentions *"the Spirit of wisdom."* The Holy Spirit is here shown as giving *"wisdom"* as to the making of the garments. Likewise, the Holy Spirit will help us in all righteous things we do, even our secular employment.

Verse 5 tells us that *"gold"* was added to the *"blue, purple, scarlet, and fine linen* (white)." Actually, the gold was made into fine wire which could be woven with the linen threads of blue, purple, scarlet, and white to make the pomegranate patterns of the hem-line of the ephod. Along with the other colors symbolizing Christ, the gold thread was added to symbolize His deity.

Verse 6 speaks of the *"ephod."* As well, it was *"gold"* (for deity), *"blue"* (heavenly), *"purple"* (royalty), *"scarlet"* (shed blood), and the *"fine twined linen"* (righteousness) with *"cunning work."* The High Priest was a type of the Lord Jesus Christ. He served as the mediator between God and the people, a type of that Who would be *the* mediator, the Lord Jesus Christ. The *"cunning work"* spoke of the perfection of Christ.

The ephod was a shoulder-piece vestment worn over the shoulders and hanging down both front and back to the hips, being held together at the shoulders by two shoulder-pieces. The ephod was the special garment of the High Priest to which the breastplate of judgment was attached. Below the arms and above the hips, the two pieces were held together or kept in place by the curious girdle of the ephod. On the two shoulder-pieces were two onyx stones with the names of the 12 tribes engraved on them. The stones were set in gold encasements and fastened to the shoulder-pieces. The breastplate was put on the breast over the ephod. It had 12 stones on which were engraved the names of the 12 tribes of Israel, and was fastened to the shoulder-pieces of the ephod by gold chains. Aaron symbolized Christ in the mystery of His divine manhood, bearing His people on His shoulders, the place of strength, and bound upon His heart, the place of love. On the shoulders the names were according to their birth (vs. 21). The *"curious girdle"* of the 8th verse, like the ephod, was to be made of *gold, blue, purple, scarlet, and white.* It held the front and back pieces of the ephod together above the hips and below the breastplate.

Verses 15 through 29 speak of the *"breastplate of judgment."*

The 30th verse speaks of the *"Urim and the Thummim."* The first word means "light" and the second word means "perfections." It seems that whatever they were was something material, separate from the breastplate pouch and the stones in the breastplate. They were the means of obtaining an answer from God, when needed, regarding any problem which concerned Israel. From this time until the time of David, there are references to them being used (Josh. 7:14-18; 18:4-10; Judges 1:1-2; I Sam. 10:20-22; I Sam. 22:10-15; II Sam. 2:1; I Chr. 14:10). However, after the days of David there is no instance of their use, although after the Babylonian captivity, the question of who had the right of the priesthood to use the Urim and Thummim was discussed. They were probably two precious stones which were at times drawn from the bag to give God's judgment or message. Some claim that one stone had a "yes" and the other a "no" on it, so that whichever one the High Priest took out would give a direct answer, either affirmative or negative.

Verses 31 through 35 speak of the *"robe of the ephod."* It was all of blue and on its hem were bells of gold and pomegranates of blue, purple, and scarlet. This symbolizes Christ as our great High Priest in heaven (Heb. 8:4). It is said that when the great High Priest on the great Day of Atonement went into the Holy of holies, before entering he would have to pull off the beautiful robe of the ephod, signifying that when Christ died on Calvary and offered His precious blood, it was not done with the garments of *"glory and beauty,"* but with His glorious body which was sinless, typified by the linen (white) vest and breeches.

The thousands of Israel would await outside the Tabernacle to see if God accepted the offering of sacrifices offered by the great High Priest. If the Lord did not accept it, the great High Priest would be stricken dead. (There is no record of any being stricken.)

The way they could tell if the offering was accepted was that when he came back into the holy place, he would once again put on the garments of glory and beauty which included the *"robe of the ephod."* And when he did so, the *"bells of gold"* would begin to ring. The other priests would hear it and would give the great message of joy to Israel.

Our great High Priest, the Lord Jesus Christ, has gone into the Holy of holies where He has placed His precious blood on the mercy seat. The way we know it has been accepted is because He has sent back the Holy Spirit with the fruit of the Spirit (pomegranates) and the joy of the Lord (the ringing of the bells). Israel knew that when the bells started to ring the great High Priest was soon to come out of the holy place. Every time we see a demonstration of the Holy Spirit, we know that our great High Priest, the Lord Jesus Christ, is about to come back.

Verses 36 through 38 portray the *"mitre,"* which was the holy crown. It first had a *"plate of pure gold,"* which means the headship of Christ, with the words written on it, *"Holiness to the Lord."* The *"blue lace"* on the holy crown stipulated that the headship of Christ was from heaven. In the Millennium the words *"Holiness unto the Lord"* will appear on the bells of the

horses (Zech. 14). Even though Israel was imperfect, as she was thus represented by Aaron and his crown, she was to represent holiness.

The words are used, *"upon his heart before the Lord continually"* (vs. 30) and *"upon his forehead before the Lord continually"* (vs. 38). These statements united together reveal the untiring activity of the heart and mind of the Greater-than-Aaron on behalf of His people.

CHAPTER 29

The 29th chapter of Exodus pertains to the consecration of the priests. Their consecration would begin with sacrifice, *"bullock, two rams without blemish."* The very life of Jesus Christ was a sacrifice. Consequently, the priests, who were types of Christ, would begin their consecration with sacrifice.

The 2nd verse would speak of *"unleavened bread"* and, as well, *"tempered with oil."* This would typify Christ's sinless life and His being filled with the Holy Ghost beyond measure.

The 4th verse says, *"shalt wash them with water."* The washing portrayed a death of sin and self.

Verses 5 through 7 say, *"Pour it upon his head, and anoint him."* Likewise, at the beginning of Christ's public ministry He was anointed with the Holy Ghost, *"The Spirit of the Lord is upon me because he hath anointed me"* (St. Luke 4:18).

Verses 10 through 14 portray the *"sin offering."* Even though Aaron was a type of Christ, still, he was a sinner and had to offer sacrifice for his own sins. Christ offered Himself for the world's sins.

In verse 12 they took the *"blood of the bullock, and put it upon the horns of the altar."* The horns pointing in all directions of the compass signify that all men everywhere must come by the shed Blood of the Lamb. Then they did *"pour all the blood beside the bottom of the altar."* This spoke of Jesus shedding His blood at Calvary.

The 13th verse speaks of the *"fat"* and the *"caul,"* as well as the *"two kidneys,"* and then it said, *"and burned them upon the altar."* These items spoke of the prosperity of Israel. They were to forever remember that it came through Calvary.

The 14th verse speaks of the *"flesh"* as well as the *"skin"* and *"dung."* It says, *"Shalt thou burn with fire without the camp."* The flesh of the sin-offering was destroyed outside the camp as a type of Christ paying the penalty for sin outside the camp (Heb. 13:11-13).

Verses 15 through 18 portray the *"whole burnt offering."* The whole burnt offering signified that God would give His all for Israel, and Israel must give their all for God. Even in a more direct sense, Jesus Christ would give His all. This is the reason it was *"a sweet savour"* unto the Lord.

Verses 19 through 21 portray the consecration offering of the priests. The 19th verse saying, *"Put their hands upon the head of the ram,"* signifies they were sinners, and they were transferring their transgressions to this innocent victim. The portrayal in the levitical offerings of substitution and identification is the very heart of the Gospel. Jesus Christ became our substitute, and we identify with Him and are, thereby, saved.

The 20th verse spoke of blood being applied to the *"tip of the right ear of Aaron and his sons,"* and *"upon the thumb of their right hand, and upon the great toe of their right foot."* This spoke three things.

A. The ear - hear only that which is of God.

B. Thumb - grasp only that which is of God.

C. Toe - go only in God's direction.

The 21st verse said, *"Take of the blood, and of the anointing oil, and sprinkle it upon Aaron and his sons."* The blood and oil were sprinkled upon both Aaron and his sons, as well as upon their garments. They had to be washed before and after such ritual. The blood on their bodies and garments served to make the awfulness of sin and its penalty more vivid. It was a visible evidence that life had been taken away and God's law vindicated. Every sacrifice testified of the death of an innocent substitute, the sinfulness of the offerer, the surrender of the guilty to God and His service, and deep humility and gratefulness to the victim which became the substitute. Verses 22 through 28 portray the wave and heave offerings. The bread

NOTES

of different kinds was intended to show gratefulness for God's blessings of abundant supply for daily needs. All the parts of the ram and the different breads were waved and heaved before God to acknowledge Him. This is the motive of all true worship.

Verses 29 through 37 portray the final consecration rites.

The 37th verse says, *"Seven days thou shalt make an atonement."* These seven days were after the Tabernacle was set up at the time the priests were set apart and when they began their ministry. They remained inside the Tabernacle day and night during the seven days. This, in a way, typifies the 40 days and nights of Christ's temptation.

Verses 38 through 42 speak of the daily burnt offerings. Verse 39 speaks of *"one lamb"* in the morning and the *"other lamb"* at evening. The time of the offering of the morning lamb was 9 a.m. and the evening lamb at 3 p.m. Jesus died at 3 p.m. on the Cross of Calvary, signifying the offering of the evening sacrifice.

Once again the 41st verse would call it *"a sweet savour"* only because it would typify the death of Christ to redeem fallen humanity.

Verses 43 through 46 portray the promise of God's glory and presence among His people. If the sacrifices and obligations of the priests were carried out exactly as commanded, God said, *"I will meet with the children of Israel."*

And then in the 45th verse He said, *"And I will dwell among the children of Israel, and will be their God."* God will not meet with us or dwell with us unless we go by the route of the slain Lamb. Only that is a *"sweet savour";* only that will He honor and recognize. The world's religions through various means have ever tried to coax God to meet with them and dwell with them. They have done so with a bloodless sacrifice. They have always failed as fail they must. Christ and Him crucified is the message of the true Church.

CHAPTER 30

Verses 1 through 10 proclaim the command to make the altar of incense.

Verse 2 says the altar was small, being only 18 inches wide, 18 inches long, and 3 feet high. As well, of course, it was *"foursquare,"* showing that all worship all over the world respecting Christ would always be identical. If it is the Lord, the worship is the same, *"in Spirit and in Truth."* There were *"horns"* at each corner. It, as well, was made of *"shittim wood"* and was overlaid with *"pure gold."* This so beautifully speaks of Christ's humanity (the wood) and His deity (the gold). There was a *"crown of gold around about,"* it says in the 3rd verse, signifying that Jesus Christ is King and worthy of all worship.

Verses 7 and 8 say that Aaron would *"burn sweet incense"* every morning and evening. Constantly, the Lord is making intercession for us, and, constantly, we should praise His name, morning and evening.

Verse 9 speaks of *"strange incense."* This would be any kind of incense that was not like that commanded to be burned on this altar. In many passages in the Old Testament we read of incense being offered before God in a censer - a bowl-shaped vessel. Burning incense was one of the most prominent rituals in Divine worship which foreshadowed things to come. The heathen copied from this, and many references speak of burning incense to idols. Only the priests were to offer incense. Smoke of sacrifices and prayers are considered incense (Psa. 66:15; Rev. 5:8). Incense, as well, is offered in heaven (Rev. 8:3-4). Sadly, millions today offer *"strange incense"* before God which will not be accepted. Once again the only worship that God will accept is that which is in *"Spirit and in Truth"* (St. John 4:24).

Even though incense was offered twice daily, the blood applied to the horns was only *"once in a year."* This was on the great Day of Atonement, signifying as well that our worship is made possible by His shed blood. The word *"atonement"* means "to cover." Not only were the sins covered, but the sinner was covered as well. However, the blood of bulls and goats could only cover sin, not take it away. Thank God, since Calvary, Jesus Christ *"takes away"* our sin (St. John 1:29).

Verses 11 through 16 portray the ransom or redemption money. It said, *"every man a ransom for his soul unto the Lord."* The whole of

Israel must be ransomed. This spoke of the men which answered for the entire household. The money was a special tax of registration in Israel as a memorial or reminder of God's provision of redemption and of their obligation under the terms of the Mosaic Covenant. God promised freedom from plagues when the men were numbered.

The 13th verse says, *"half a shekel."* It was no doubt silver. Hence, silver, in all of the Tabernacle furniture and fittings means redemption.

The 15th verse said the *"rich"* and the *"poor"* would give the same. This placed every man in Israel on an equal footing in relation to God and obligation to the law. Likewise, it said that all had to be redeemed the same way. However, it should be noted that the money did not actually redeem the soul. Not even the blood of bulls and other animals did this (Heb. 10:4; I Pet. 1:18-23), but rather faith in the Blood of the coming Redeemer of which the blood of sacrifices was a type. The same amount was to be paid, stating that in matters of atonement there is no difference among men. All must come the same way.

Verses 17 through 21 speak of the *"laver of brass."* It is a type of the Word of God. Its surface was burnished brightly that the priests might see their reflection, not only in the water but in the container as well. Likewise, the child of God sees himself in the Word of God.

Verses 19 through 21 say that the priests, including the High Priest, must wash their *"hands"* as well as their *"feet"* before going into the *"tabernacle of the congregation"* or to offer burnt offerings on the brazen altar. They did it, the 21st verse says, *"that they die not."*

This represents the believer's constant need of renewal, replenishing, and refreshing. Despite our efforts to live a sanctified life, still, because we are in this present world and constantly struggling with the flesh, we become contaminated. Therefore, there has to be the constant washing of the water of the Word that we *"die not."*

Verses 22 through 33 speak of the holy anointing oil. They were told exactly how to prepare it.

The 23rd verse says, *"myrrh."* It was a gum which came from the stem of a low, thorny, rugged tree. It tells of the difficulties of a Christian life. *"Cinnamon"* came from the inner-rind of a tree, meaning the very heart of the tree with it crushed. This speaks of the broken heart. And then it says, *"Sweet calamus."* This was a fragrant cane whose root is highly prized as a spice. It speaks of the very depths of one's being, and then of *"oil olive,"* which of course means the crushed life. Even the weight of each spice was to be exact, showing that God only demands so much of each. Then there was *"cassia,"* which came from the aromatic bark of a shrub. This speaks of all externals being stripped away.

The 25th verse says when it was all put together it was *"an oil of holy ointment."* It even says, *"after the art of the apothecary,"* speaking of minute attention being given to the kind and the weight. The anointing of the Holy Spirit that we must have to minister in this world does not come easily. No wonder Paul said, *"I will glory in my infirmities, that the power of Christ may rest upon me"* (II Cor. 12:9). Regretfully, too many preachers desire the anointing of the Holy Spirit without the broken life, broken heart, and stripped life of consecration.

The 32nd verse said, *"After the composition of it,"* there shall be no other. It was not to be used at random, but only as God commanded. It would never be upon *"a stranger"* (vs. 33).

Verses 34 through 38 tells us of the holy incense. There were four spices, *"stacte,"* which was a type of gum that came from a tree that had been cut. Likewise, the Child of God will bleed. And *"onycha"* which comes from a shell found on the shores of the Red Sea and the Indian Ocean and signifies our baptism of death to the world. And then there was *"galbanum,"* which was the juice of a shrub, and once again spoke of being crushed. And then, *"pure frankincense,"* that seems to be the most important of the aromatic gums and is regarded by itself as a precious perfume. It was one of the gifts of the wise men to Jesus (Matt. 2:11). It comes from a tree that grows abundantly in India. The word "pure" used here refers to the free-flowing and liberal giving forth of its odors.

The 36th verse says it was to be *"beaten very small."* Likewise, that which seems to be so

insignificant to the world is so holy to God.

In this 30th chapter we are given a symbolic portrayal of the "brokenness" that God demands for our lives to be anointed and for our worship to be accepted.

CHAPTER 31

Verses 1 through 6 portray those who God called to do His work. Not only did He tell what should be done and how it should be done, as well as the materials of which it should be made, but He calls special men to do it and gives them *"the Spirit of God"* to accomplish the task. God's ministry in the five-fold callings (Eph. 4:11) is no less God-called, God-directed, and God-led. Unfortunately, man has inserted much into the spiritual order that God did not ordain. Bezaleel and his companions did not appoint themselves to this ministry. It was said of them concerning the Lord and their call, *"I have called," "I have filled," "I have given," "I have put," "I have commanded."* Men do not call or ordain men to preach. God calls and ordains. Men are commanded to recognize what God has ordained, but recognition is all that man can give. And even if man fails in giving recognition, that failure in no way diminishes the call.

In verses 7 through 11 the Holy Spirit is extremely explicit concerning the exact items of furniture, articles, garments, anointing oil, sweet incense, etc. Even the Tabernacle was included. Likewise, the Holy Spirit is that explicit regarding the call of God that is placed upon peoples' hearts and lives. I think it would go without saying that Bezaleel and Aholiab were extremely proficient in that which God by His Spirit called them to do. However, if they had gone into other areas of service, it would have been without the help of the Spirit of God. How incumbent it is upon the minister of the Gospel, as well as every Christian to ascertain the mind of God regarding the call of his or her life - and there is a call of God on the life of every single Christian. Unfortunately, too many do what they want to do instead of what the Holy Spirit wants them to do.

Verses 12 through 17 portray the weekly Sabbath as a sign of the Mosaic Covenant. This was a sign between the Lord and Israel, not between the Lord and the Church. However, it was a type of that which would be given to the Body of Christ. That which distinguished God's people was participation in God's rest. Now, under the New Covenant, the Sabbath no longer holds that distinction, as it was not even included in the New Covenant. Now, Christ is God's rest (Heb. 4). The honor or dishonor done to the Sabbath was the test under Law; the honor or dishonor done to Christ, the test under grace. Death was the penalty of dishonoring the Sabbath. Spiritual death is the penalty for dishonoring Christ. The building of the Tabernacle, plus the fashioning of all the articles and the furniture, was definitely important; however, the significance of these things was not to interfere with God's rest. As well, there is much to be done under the New Covenant. But at the same time, the doing of it is to never be a work of the flesh, but it is always to be a work of the Spirit. This can only be done if Christ is our rest.

The 18th verse speaks of Moses coming down from the mount at the end of 40 days of fasting on Sinai. In these 40 days he had received all the revelation concerning the Tabernacle, the priesthood, garments, and services. As well, this would include the anointing oil and the incense. Also, he was given instructions about the Sabbath. The Scripture uses the words *"finger of God."* This should be taken literally.

CHAPTER 32

Israel could not go for very long without strong spiritual leadership. Soon they would cry, *"Make us gods."* Moses was on the mountaintop pleading for Israel. Israel was at the base of the mountain insulting Moses. It has little changed. Aaron will acquiesce to the demands of the people as too much of the spiritual leadership does today.

Verses 2 and 3 proclaim the giving of the *"golden earrings."* Strangely enough, the next

time they would do such would be to make the Tabernacle. This is a perfect picture of religious man who is very quick to go from the ridiculous to the sublime and then back again. Tragically, unless we hover close to Christ, none of us are very far from the *"golden calf."*

Verse 4 says that Aaron *"made it a molten calf."* Everything was done by Aaron under the cover of "religion." The design of Satan is not to abolish God but to represent Him by something visible. So Israel would make a god that they could see. So it is today. Christendom prefers a human priest and a little piece of bread that may be seen and handled to the Divine Priest Who has passed into the heavens. The calf was the great god of the Egyptians. It was carried in the vanguard of their possessions. Sacrifices were offered to it, and lascivious dances executed in its honor. It was worshiped as the generator of life.

Actually, this idol was a facsimile of the chief Egyptian god, a young bull called Apis, which was worshiped at Memphis near the land of Goshen. Israel, sadly, worshiped idols in Egypt as well (Joshua 24:14).

Verse 6 says the people *"offered burnt offerings"* and brought *"peace offerings."* They had incorporated the worship of God with the worship of Satan. In this passage the word *"play"* is used of fornication as in many other passages of the Word of God. This refers to the immoral practices that were associated with idolatry in most lands of that day.

All idol gods had their consecrated women who were devoted to immoral practices. This is how the corrupt priesthood of idol gods made their living, and such is still being carried on in many pagan countries. That the children of Israel may have gone to the depths in idolatrous practices is suggested by the statement, *"have corrupted themselves."*

Actually, all Israel had sunk so low in sin and moral depravity during these days of the absence of Moses that God was literally ready to destroy the whole nation. He promised to do so and raise up another nation of the seed of Moses if he would be willing for this, but Moses interceded for the nation until God spared the people from such fate. If Moses had accepted this, the program of God for Israel to occupy Canaan would have been postponed indefinitely, and the literal fulfillment of many prophecies would have been delayed. God hates idolatry and immorality and is determined to rid them from the earth.

The words, *"these be thy gods, oh Israel,"* is the same word used for Almighty God Who actually did bring them out of Egypt. Now the people were equating a golden calf with God.

The word *"repent"* in verse 12 has no connotation of meaning that God had sinned. It simply meant that God would "turn."

The 14th verse says, *"The Lord repented,"* meaning that He turned from the direction that He had intended to go regarding the destruction of these people. As Moses pleads with God, he has not yet come down from the mountain to actually see the depths to which Israel had fallen.

Verses 15 through 18 are very quick to point out, *"The two tables of the testimony"* that were with Moses. This moment portrays the greatest hour to date in human history. God is ready, but the people are not. They, instead, have forsaken *"the writing of God,"* which was God's Word for a work of their own hands. The world today has done the same thing: no Bible, no freedom - a little Bible, a little freedom - much Bible, much freedom. Regrettably, the majority of the Church has forsaken *"the writing of God."*

Verse 19 proclaims Moses' reaction when *"he saw the calf, and the dancing."* Concerning *"the writing of God,"* he *"break them"* because the people, in spirit, had already broken them.

Verses 21 through 24 record Aaron's excuse. He blames his actions on the people. Bible repentance demands that God be justified and we be condemned. God demands that we accept the blame for our failure. That is the only kind of repentance that He will honor.

The 25th verse says, *"The people were naked."* Quite possibly they had removed their clothing. However, the greater meaning was that Israel was exposed to the judgments of God and the vengeance of their enemies without God's protection. In other words, they were naked to the judgment of God and to the anger of their enemies. How much the Church needs to learn that sin removes the "covering" God has over us!

In the 26th verse the *"sons of Levi"* gained

NOTES

the priesthood and also erased the terrible failure of their father Levi in the massacre at Shechem, *"Gathered themselves together unto him."*

The command to *"slay"* recorded in the 27th verse included those who continued in stubbornness and rebellion against God and Moses. *"Three thousand men"* were killed.

The words, *"Consecrated yourselves today to the Lord,"* mean "be installed as priests to the Eternal this day." The words, *"May bestow upon you a blessing this day,"* was the granting of the priesthood to the tribe of Levi.

The 30th verse says, *"Peradventure I shall make an atonement for your sin."* Moses would fail as Moses must, because no man can atone for sin. There is no atonement without blood sacrifice, and the only blood sacrifice that God will accept is that of Christ Himself. Moses even offered himself as an atonement, portrayed in verse 32. But Moses was a sinner and could not be accepted as such.

For the first time *"The Book"* is mentioned in which all the names of the righteous are written. It is referred to throughout Scripture under various terms, being called, *"thy Book"* and *"My Book"* (Ex. 32:32-33); *"The Book of the Living"* (Psa. 69:28); *"The Book"* (Dan. 12:1); *"The Book of Life"* (Phil. 4:3); and *"The Lamb's Book of Life"* (Rev. 21:27).

Because the term *"Book of Life"* does not appear in all of these passages, it does not mean that the reference in any one instance is to something else, just as we have several names for the Bible, *"the Holy Scriptures"* (Rom. 1:2); *"the Oracles of God"* (Rom. 3:2); *"the Law and the Prophets"* (Luke 24:25-44); *"the Word of God"* (Mark 7:13); and other names. So we also have several names for the Book of Life. Scripture teaches plainly that God blots the name of the rebellious out of His Book. The Psalmist predicted it to happen in the case of Judas (Psa. 69:20-28). Christ warned of it regarding all who would not overcome sin (Rev. 3:5).

In verses 33 through 35 the answer is given, *"Him will I blot out of my book,"* referring to the individuals who had sinned and would not repent.

CHAPTER 33

In the 1st verse we are given a chilling account of the mind of God. The Lord basically disowns Israel. With His omniscience (foreknowledge), He knows they will ultimately have to be destroyed - and that they were. Only the children below 20 years of age would go into the Promised Land. Sometimes we wonder at the severity of God's dealings with certain individuals. The answer is simple. God, through foreknowledge, knows that they will continue to rebel and will refuse to repent. He also knows those who will humble themselves before Him, and treats them accordingly - even before the fact. His disavowal of Israel is shown in the words, *"which Thou hast brought up out of the land of Egypt."* He then uses the words, *"I swear . . ."* meaning if He had not made promises to Abraham, Isaac, and Jacob, He would have no respect at all unto *"thy seed."*

Due to their rebellion that God knew would continue, He is now refusing to go with Israel Himself, but *"will send an angel before thee."*

The 3rd verse says that God cannot abide continued sin and rebellion. Therefore, He said, *"For I will not go up in the midst of thee."*

The *"ornaments"* of verses 4 through 6 say, "grace clothes naked sinners, but a sinner decked in ornaments must be stripped."

The *"tabernacle"* of verse 7 was not the Tabernacle that Moses had been given instructions to build. That Tabernacle that would be "the Tabernacle" was not yet built. Evidently, this was a tabernacle of meeting that Moses had built himself. It was moved nearly a mile outside the camp.

In verses 10 through 17 several things are portrayed to us.

1. The people did not know what God would do.

2. The "cloudy pillar," representing the presence of God, had departed from the people and now "stood at the door of the tabernacle." Verse 10 says, *"All the people rose up and worshipped."* However, a few hours before they had worshiped a golden calf. Regrettably, their wor-

NOTES

ship meant little. Man was created to worship God. If he does not worship God, he will worship idols. Regrettably, much of the Church alternates between idols and God. Worship without God is no worship at all, and God was not there.

The 11th verse says, *"face to face."* Man has seen God face to face out of His glory but never in His glory. God's face cannot be seen in His usual glory, and the light that He dwells in no man has seen nor can see (I Tim. 6:16). Moses *"turned again into the camp."* But *"Joshua departed not out of the tabernacle."* It is never very pleasant having to deal with sin and sinners. Moses, with a love for the people, continues to intercede for them with God.

Verses 12 through 17 say that Moses *"found grace."* Therefore, Moses seizes upon the word *"grace"* and with wonderful, spiritual intelligence pleads that God should continue to accompany them because they were a stiffnecked people.

Verse 13 says, *"Shew me now thy way."* Here, Moses was pleading with God to show him the way He intended to help him lead Israel into Canaan, since God had seemingly resigned the direct oversight of the journey. Also, Moses was asking God to take Israel back, forgive them, return to their camp, and proceed to lead them by His presence, as He had done before. The fact that Israel was a stiffnecked people is urged as an argument, for it was just such a people that grace and only grace could bless.

Verse 14 says, *"My presence shall go with thee."* In the 15th verse Moses says, *"If thy presence go not now with me, carry us not up hence."* What a statement! The Church, by and large, tries to go without God's presence or else mistakes something else for God's presence.

Verse 16 says, *"So shall we be separated, I and thy people, from all the people that are upon the face of the earth."* It has ever been, and it ever shall be. God's people are different. The idea of God's people saving this wicked society is foolishness indeed. It is not our business to save the society, it is our business to save men out of the society. Society is doomed.

Even though God will acquiesce to Moses' request, still, it will only be grace that does so, because God through omniscience knows that this people, this stiff-necked people, will ultimately rebel to their doom.

Verses 18 through 23 beautifully portray a greater revelation of God than ever. Wonderfully enough, great revelation often follows great failure, but only to those who would humble themselves. Several things were done in this revelation.

1. God would show Moses His *"goodness"* instead of His wrath.

2. Moses would have the name of the Lord *"proclaimed"* to him, meaning that it was God and none other.

3. God will reserve the right to show grace and mercy to whom He desires. Even though He has acquiesced to Moses' request, still, the recipients of grace and mercy are decided by God and not by others.

4. The *"rock"* of verse 21 was the Lord Jesus Christ. Our only reference to God is by His Son Christ Jesus.

5. The *"clift of the rock"* is the precious shed blood of Jesus Christ that *"will cover thee."* (Some have thought that this "clift" was the same place that Elijah went to during a time of acute discouragement.)

—■—

CHAPTER 34

In verse 1 the Lord reminds Moses that he broke the first tables, *"which thou brakest"* but does not reprimand him. The repetition of the giving of the Ten Commandments the second time underlines God's love and patience with us. Many times He has to do the work all over again within our lives. This will be Moses' eighth and final ascent up Sinai. The first two stones on which the Ten Commandments were given were the work of God. Now, Moses will hew out stones himself like the ones that he had destroyed and come upon the mount where God would write again what He had previously written on the first stones. The 4th verse says that *"Moses went up."* And the 5th verse says, *"The Lord descended."* Verses 5 through 7 proclaim in the Hebrew ten different names and attributes of God proclaimed by Himself. They are as follows, and will begin

with the Hebrew word.

1. *"Yehovah,"* meaning Jehovah.

2. *"El Yehovah,"* meaning Strong Jehovah.

3. *"Rachum,"* meaning merciful, full of tenderness and compassion.

4. *"Channum,"* meaning gracious.

5. *"Arek-aph,"* meaning long-suffering, not easily angered or irritated.

6. *"Rab-checed,"* meaning abundant and sufficient in goodness, kindness, and love.

7. *"Emeth,"* meaning truth, trustworthiness, and faithfulness.

8. *"Natsar checed,"* meaning guarding or protecting kindness and mercy.

9. *"Nasa avon pesha chattaah,"* meaning lifting up and carrying away moral evil and perversity, moral and religious revolt, and all offenses.

10. *"Paqad avon,"* meaning overseeing punishment for moral evil.

All of these words combine to give the real meaning of the word Jehovah, thus, He is all things to all men. God exercises all the above qualities in His many dealings with man - manifesting strength, mercy, tenderness, compassion, graciousness, longsuffering, goodness, kindness, love, faithfulness, trustworthiness, and moral cleansing, as well as administering punishments whenever they are needed.

Verse 8 says, *"And worshipped."* Little wonder that Moses worshiped, and so should we !As is noticed, when the Lord *"proclaimed the name of the Lord,"* it was all of mercy and grace. Praise the Lord!

In verse 9 Moses pleads for mercy for the people, admitting that they were *"a stiff-necked people."* Even though Moses repented for them, they did not repent for themselves. The Lord has just given Moses His answer. He is merciful and gracious, and if the people will only admit their sin and truly repent and follow the Lord, mercy and grace will be extended to them. But, of course, God knows they will not do that. Ultimately, they will go to their destruction.

Verses 10 and 11 proclaim a work that will be miraculous and astounding. As well, He will do the very same thing in our lives if we will only allow Him. The *"Amorite"* and the *"Canaanite"* are types of works of the flesh within our own lives. If we will only believe in this great God of miracles, He has said, *"Behold, I drive out before thee . . ."*

Verses 12 through 16 demand separation. That separation is no less demanded today.

In verse 13 for the first time the *"groves"* are mentioned. In the Hebrew the word is "Asherah." It means a pillar or image of wood. It was set up with the image of Baal and worshiped by libidinous rites and lascivious practices. The pillar was set upright or erect in the ground like a totem pole. It was either a living tree with the top cut off and the trunk fashioned into a certain shape, or a log fashioned into an idol and set erect in the ground. That they were not groves of trees is clear from II Kings 17:10, where they are forbidden to be set up under any green tree.

Originally, the idol was worshiped as a symbol of the Tree of Life but later perverted to mean the origin of life and pictured with the male organs of procreation (Ezek. 16:17). Such symbols (the Phallic) became the objects of worship and involved all forms of impurity, perversion, and licentiousness by crowds of devotees involved in demonized and obscene orgies. This worship centered in the Canaanite nations and then spread into others. Relics of it are found among all heathen peoples. The first mention of the idol in the Bible stamps it as a special object of God's hatred, and it was at this idol that God revealed His name as *"Jealous."*

It led to the destruction of all Canaanite nations and, with other things, caused Israel to be banished among other nations.

The 23rd verse says that *"Thrice in the year shall your men children appear before the Lord God."*

Israel could gather three times in a year and attend all the seven yearly feasts of Jehovah. The first gathering would take in the *"Passover,"* *"Feast of Firstfruits,"* and *"Feast of Unleavened Bread,"* covering eight days (in the spring).

The second gathering would take in the *"Feast of Pentecost,"* which would be the 50th day after the Passover.

The third gathering would take in the last three feasts, the *"Feast of Trumpets,"* the *"Feast of the Great Day of Atonement,"* and *"the Feast of Tabernacles."* This would cover

NOTES

about 21 days and would begin on about October 1.

The 29th verse says, *"The skin of his face shone while he talked with him."*

This indicated that the glory of God in Moses' face was like rays or darts of lightning shooting forth. He had been in the presence of God so long in the mountain that his own eyes did not recognize the shining rays from his face. Like one blinded by the sun who cannot see a candlelight, Moses was not aware that his face shone. The Vulgate reads: "He did not know that his face was horned" (encased in light). Because of this, some painters have represented Moses with two horns. Others have promoted the idea by painting halos or luminous circles around the heads of saints supposed to have had special contact with God. This not only prevails in part of the Christian world, but also among Moslems, Hindus, and Chinese, who evidently got the idea from stories of the many manifestations of the glory of God in Old Testament days.

———◼———

CHAPTERS 35 ‒ 40

These chapters portray a minute repetition of the materials used in the construction of the Tabernacle, the vessels, and furniture of that place of worship. As well, the Lord must repeat His word to us, seemingly over and over.

The 35th chapter opens with the *"Sabbath."* This was a type of God's rest which the people were to enjoy as well. The 40th chapter closes with the command to set up the Tabernacle, which was God's resting place. So, it opens with rest, and it closes with rest. He invites man into His own rest and then comes and dwells with him (Heb. 4). Even when building the Tabernacle, the Sabbath rest was to be observed. Likewise, in the great work for God, we must never forget that our personal communion with Christ is demanded. The Sabbath was ever a sign to Israel of God's rest, meaning that man would one day enter into Christ's rest.

Verses 42 and 43 of the 39th chapter say, *"According to all that the Lord commanded Moses"* and then it said, *"As the Lord had com-*

manded." Nothing was left to man's ingenuity or taste. Regrettably, too many religious organizations go beyond the Word of God.

The 34th verse of the 40th chapter says, *"Then a cloud covered the tent of the congregation, and the glory of the Lord filled the tabernacle."* This is the culmination of all of our living for God. If the *"cloud"* of the anointing is not there and the *"glory"* is lacking as well, all else is futile. However, none of this could happen until *"the anointing oil"* of chapter 40 was applied (vs. 9). And then in the 29th verse the *"burnt offering and the meat offering"* were offered. The blood, of course, was poured out at the base of the altar.

So, before the *"cloud"* and the *"glory"* filled the place, there had to be the shedding of the blood of the sacrifice and the oil of the anointing. We desire the *"cloud"* and the *"burnt offering."*

Verse 35 says, *"Moses was not able to enter into the tent of the congregation, because the cloud abode thereon."* Today, we are too able to go where we desire. Could it be because the *"cloud"* is not there?

Israel soon learned, as is recorded in verses 36 through 38, that they must follow the cloud, *"went onward in all their journeys."* The *"cloud of the Lord by day"* and the *"fire by night"* was visible to everyone. God help us, even though we may be criticized, ridiculed, and even ostracized, may we still see the *"cloud"* and the *"glory."* If we lose all else and retain the *"cloud"* and *"glory,"* then we've really lost nothing. If we gain all else and lose the *"cloud"* and *"glory,"* then we have lost everything.

NOTES

THE
BOOK OF LEVITICUS

—■—

The first word in the book of Leviticus is *"and,"* thereby, connecting it with the book of Exodus. In fact, all five books of Moses (the Pentateuch) make one law. Leviticus is the only book of the five books of the Pentateuch written by Moses in which no other Hebrew word besides Jehovah is used for the name or title "Lord."

There were five great offerings: the *"burnt offering,"* the *"meat* (food) *offering,"* the *"peace offering,"* the *"trespass offering,"* and the *"sin offering."* It took these five offerings to adequately portray the one great offering of the Lord Jesus Christ at Calvary's Cross.

—■—

CHAPTER 1

The 1st verse says, *"The Lord called unto Moses."* This was for the first time done so out of the "Tabernacle," where God dwelt between the Mercy Seat and the Cherubim.

The word *"if"* of the 2nd verse speaks of a willing heart on the part of the person bringing the offering. Everything was to be from choice not compulsion. No man was forced by God to obey the Law, but if he did not obey he would die. No man is forced by grace to serve God, and, of course, many do not, but if he does not he will suffer eternal hell. Obedience and conformity to God have always been and always will be the condition of salvation and eternal life. All worship of God and seeking means of reconciliation to God are, and always have been on a freewill basis. Even where certain things were commanded by God, the individual was not forced to obey. The offering that would be

brought would be a type of the coming Redeemer.

The 3rd verse says, *"a male,"* which would typify Christ. And then, *"without blemish,"* which would as well typify the perfect spotless sacrifice of the sinless Christ. Once again the Scripture portrays *"his own voluntary will."* The sacrifice was to be brought to the *"door of the tabernacle."* Jesus Christ is the Door. And then it says, *"before the Lord."* Our sin is committed before the Lord, and, thereby, the sacrifice of atonement will be before the Lord as well.

The 4th verse says, *"Put his hand upon the head of the burnt offering."* First, the sinner himself and not someone else did this. And why? The act stated that the person recognized his guilt and was now transferring it by the commandment of the Lord to the innocent victim. Hence, when Christ would become our substitute and we would identify with Him, we would, thereby, be saved (St. John 3:16). This *"shall be accepted for him."* Nothing else would be accepted. The individual cannot make up his own rules. Sadly, millions today try to reach God in a manner that He will not accept. The words *"atonement for him"* mean "to cover." And it meant to cover not only the sin of the person, but the person as well.

The 5th verse says, *"The sinner had to kill the bullock."* It was his sin that had caused this; therefore, he would have to do the killing. Likewise, it was our sin that nailed Christ to the Cross. The blood would be caught in a basin by the priests. It would typify the shed blood of Jesus Christ. And it says, *"sprinkle the blood round about upon the altar,"* once again portraying that Jesus Christ shed His blood on Calvary's Cross, which would cover and take away the sin of everyone who would come.

The 6th verse says, *"He shall flay the burnt offering, and cut it into his pieces."* This speaks of the horror of sin that goes to the very core of the individual. Sin is not an external matter only; hence, it cannot be cured or handled by external measures.

The *"fire upon the altar"* of verse 7, speaks of the judgment of God that should have come upon us but instead came upon Christ. The *"wood in order upon the fire,"* speaks of Calvary's Cross that would receive the punishment. The whole burnt offering signified that Christ gave His all. Likewise, the 8th verse portrays even *"the parts"* laid *"upon the altar."* As well, we have to accept all of Christ and not just part of Him. Many are fond of accepting part, but most do not desire to accept the whole. Christ is either accepted totally or not accepted at all.

The 9th verse says, *"a sweet savour unto the Lord."* How could something as ghastly as this be a *"sweet savour"*? To the carnal mind, it could not, but it was *"a sweet savour unto the Lord"* simply because it represented the salvation of mankind. That which delights God seldom delights the world or even the Church.

Verses 14 through 17 portray the consideration of God concerning even the poorest of the poor. Some could not afford a lamb or a goat; therefore, they could bring a *"turtle dove"* or a *"young pigeon."* These were very inexpensive and the Lord would accept such according to the ability of the individual. If the birds were brought, it seems that the priests did all the work. But with the large animals, the sacrificer helped.

CHAPTER 2

The *"meat offering"* of the 1st verse actually should have been translated *"food offering,"* which meant no flesh of animals. This offering was made of three basic parts. *"Fine flour"* represents the spotless, stainless, sinless life of the Lord Jesus Christ. The statement, *"And he shall pour oil upon it,"* refers to the Holy Spirit being given to Christ without measure.

"Frankincense" was a beautiful fragrance but bitter. Yet, when mixed with other ingredients, such as the *"fine flour"* and the *"oil,"* it would lose much of its bitterness. It spoke of His humiliation.

This offering, as mentioned in verses 2 and 3, was pointed in two directions. Part of it was to be put *"upon the altar,"* which typified Christ going to Calvary. The *"offering made by fire"* would typify the judgment of God upon Christ's spotless, sinless life.

The rest, as spoken of in the 3rd verse, was to be eaten by *"Aaron and his sons."* This spoke of Christ in the Garden of Gethsemane *"drinking of the cup."* It was called *"most holy"* because it represented three things:

A. The spotless, sinless life of the Lord Jesus Christ.

B. His life totally directed to the will of the Father.

C. It would be a *"sweet savour unto the Lord."*

The 11th verse says, *"No meat offering with leaven."* Leaven was a type of rot or fermentation. It was disallowed because in Christ there was no sin *"nor any honey."* Honey represented the good life. Christ came as a Peasant. Even though He was a King, a Prophet, and the Great High Priest, still, He exercised in His sojourn on earth none of these offices but only the life of a Peasant.

The 13th verse says, *"Thy meat offering shalt thou season with salt."* And then it says, *"With all thine offerings thou shalt offer salt."* The salt represented the incorruptible, preservative, and faithful Word of God.

The *"meat offering"* (food offering) signifies a gift from one who is an inferior to a superior. In the Law, it was generally used to denote grain, vegetable, and fruit offerings as distinguished from animal offerings. It could also be called a *"thanksgiving offering."* This offering, the *"minchah,"* was more simple than animal sacrifices, being merely something given to God which was of value to man as a means of living – the fruit of man's labor. It is supposed that it expressed a confession that all good works are a blessing of God. The *"meat (or food) offering"* was much of the time offered with the *"burnt offering."*

CHAPTER 3

Chapter 3 portrays the *"peace offering."* The peace offerings were sacrifices distinct in purpose from the burnt and sin offerings. In the latter, sin and atonement for sin were the chief things symbolized; whereas, in the peace offerings fellowship with God as the result of atonement was the chief point. Portions of the peace offerings were to be eaten by the offerer (7:15), signifying the enjoyment of fellowship with God as a pardoned and reconciled sinner. In effect, they were somewhat a "thank" offering because the offerer was at peace with God and thankful for it.

The *"burnt offering"* pictures Christ dying; *"the meal or food offering"* pictures Christ living. The *"peace offering"* presents Him as making peace by the blood of His cross and so establishing for man communion with God.

The 1st verse requires *"a male or female,"* stipulating that all, both man and woman, can have fellowship and peace with God. *"Without blemish,"* once again, represented Christ's spotless life.

The 2nd verse portrays, *"Lay his hand upon the head of his offering."* Once again, the beautiful doctrine of substitution and identification is paramount. The animal became the substitute in the sinner's place, and by the laying of his hand on the head of his offering, he identified with that substitute. That is the heart of the gospel. Christ becomes our substitute and we identify with Him. And then, *"Kill it at the door of the tabernacle."* A sacrifice that wasn't killed was no sacrifice at all. And then it said, *"Sprinkle the blood upon the altar round about."* Christ would have to die; His blood would have to be poured out in order for man to have peace with God.

Verses 3 through 6 portray a difference in the *"peace offering"* from the previous offerings. *"The fat,"* as well as *"the two kidneys,"* along with *"the caul . . . shall burn it on the altar upon the burnt sacrifice."* These items symbolized prosperity in two ways.

A. Israel's prosperity, and their recognition that it came from God.

NOTES

B. Jesus Christ, *"And from his innermost being would flow rivers of living water"* (St. John 7), signifying Israel's true prosperity.

All this, according to the 16th verse, would represent *"a sweet savour."* It is difficult for the carnal mind to understand how something of this nature, which would seem gruesome, could be *"a sweet savour"* unto the Lord. However, God, knowing what it represented, which was the salvation of mankind that would give man peace with God, called it *"a sweet savour."* The words *"all the fat is the Lord's,"* tell us as well that prosperity comes from the Lord, and that the *"fat"* as it is presented here is a picture of God's and man's true prosperity, Jesus Christ.

The 17th verse says, *"Eat neither fat nor blood,"* meaning that Israel was always to know that her prosperity came from God, and the fat represented this. Their not eating of it signified to all that they were aware of such. The *"blood"* represents life, and more specifically, the life's blood that Christ would pour out on Calvary's Cross.

CHAPTER 4

Chapter 4 represents the *"sin offering."* The words in the 2nd verse, *"through ignorance,"* signify that a person irrespective of his knowledge of the Word of God, cannot really know what sin actually is. The Church, in its foolishness paints some sins as heinous with others even more heinous being ignored altogether. Man has a tendency to speak lightly of his own sin irregardless of its dreadfulness. So, even the strongest child of God little knows how terrible that sin really is. This is humbling and comforting. It reveals that the efficacy of Christ's atonement for sin is not to be measured by man's consciousness of sin but by God's measurement of it. To believe this fact fills the heart with Divine peace. *"Sin is transgression of the law"* (I John. 3:4), so breaking any single one of the commandments was sin and incurred the penalty of the broken Law. This applied to all men, priests or laymen. Sin is sin regardless of who commits it, or when it

NOTES

is committed. So, according to Scripture, God deals with all who sin on the same basis. The *"young bullock"* of verse 3 signifies Christ as a young man and without sin, dying in man's place. In other words, He *"without blemish unto the Lord"* became *"a sin offering."* In the *"burnt offering,"* the sinlessness of the victim was transferred to the worshiper. In the *"sin offering,"* the sinfulness of the sinner is transferred to the victim. The words, *"And sprinkle of the blood seven times before the Lord, before the veil of the sanctuary,"* portray restored relationship. Sin, immediately and automatically, destroys and breaks relationship with God. It speaks of Christ's constant intercessory work. The 5th verse says, *"And the priest that is anointed shall take."* Christ was anointed above all His fellows. He alone can take the blood to the altar of worship and sprinkle it before the Lord, thereby restoring fellowship. The *"seven times"* speaks of a complete restoration; of a complete redemption; of a complete relationship. The 7th verse says, *"Some of the blood upon the horns of the altar of sweet incense before the Lord"* (altar of worship). The words, *"before the Lord,"* speaks of the Lord Who dwelt between the Mercy Seat and the Cherubim, which was separated only by *"the veil of the sanctuary"* (vs. 6). The *"blood upon the horns of the altar"* speaks of restored worship. All four horns speak of a complete restoration to worship. To *"pour all of the blood of the bullock at the bottom of the altar of the burnt offering"* was the proper place for all sacrifices or offerings to be poured out, signifying deep humility and surrender of life on the part of the offerer. In other words Jesus was saying, "When I died on Calvary, not only did I die for your salvation, but also for complete restoration of relationship during the Christian life when sin is committed." Verse 10 says that some portions of the *"sin offerings"* and *"peace offerings"* were to be burned on the brazen altar, showing that the offerer was pleading for forgiveness and wanting peace with God. Verses 13 through 21, in effect, say that when it becomes known that sin has been committed, responsibility for getting rid of it is clear. Then immediate action must be taken regarding it. God, being just, passes over sin until it is made known by the conscience, the

Word, and the Holy Spirit. Then He holds sinners responsible and will judge and punish them if sin is permitted to continue (St. John 16:7-11; Rom. 2:12-16). There were two kinds of sin referred to in the Law, *"sins of ignorance"* and *"presumptuous sins."* Sins of ignorance were acts done through ignorance of what the Law required, as well as those known to be wrong but were done accidentally (Deut. 19:4). Presumptuous sins were sins that were committed willfully, knowingly, and stubbornly (Heb. 10:26-31).

———◼———

CHAPTER 5

Chapter 5 portrays the *"trespass offering"* (vs. 6). *"Trespass offerings"* were sin offerings of distinct types to make atonement for the trespasses named in the sins.

The words in the 7th verse, *"And if he be not able to bring a lamb,"* then go on to say that he can bring *"two turtledoves, or two young pigeons."* God always makes it possible for anyone to meet His terms of reconciliation. This is why He permitted different kinds of offerings for the rich, poor, and the very poor — from rams to turtledoves, and pigeons to a handful of flour.

The 17th verse speaks of the different types of sins. These are sins that are committed through error, negligence, or ignorance. When the transgressor came to know of his fault, then he was bound to make compensation and present the offering specified for that particular sin. The word denotes both the offense and the offering required for it. In every offense, there is guilt and penalty incurred, and where these are there must be atonement. Consequently, the first pigeon or turtledove was a *"sin offering"* which required the shedding of blood, and the second one was a *"burnt offering"* symbolizing satisfaction to God by perfect obedience to Him in making atonement. Both symbolized the perfect obedience of Christ as man's substitute.

In the 5th verse it says, *"With thy estimation by shekels of silver, after the shekel of the sanctuary, for a trespass offering."* And then says, *"And shall add the fifth part thereto"* (vs. 16). Christ, as the *"trespass offering,"* not only restored to God that which was taken away, but he added the one-fifth thereto. In redemption, He brought greater glory to God than the glory lost in creation.

The expressions, *"through ignorance"* (vs. 15) and *"wist it not"* (vss. 17-18), dispose of the popular fallacy that sincerity secures salvation.

Incidentally, the silver paid had nothing to do with atonement, but the cost of the damage done was paid back in silver plus 20 percent interest. The actual atonement was made by the ram. However, silver, in effect, due to the payment of such in the trespass offering, is a type of redemption, but it never specifies that salvation can be purchased. Redemption by Christ makes even the lowest of sinners to be without blemish before God (Eph. 5:27). All the redeemed one day will be presented to God without blame (I Thess. 3:13; Jude 24).

The words, *"He hath certainly trespassed against the Lord"* in the 19th verse, settle the question of guilt on the part of the one breaking the Law, whether he was conscious of his sin or not when the wrong was committed. He was just as much a law-breaker before knowing as afterward. Thus, ignorance is no excuse for breaking the Law or being freed from responsibility after it is broken. The need is constant for the ever cleansing of the precious Blood of Jesus Christ in the life of the believer. There is so much we do in the eyes of God that is not pleasing to Him which He actually classes as sin, and, thereby, must be constantly washed. It may be an attitude, a spirit, a thought, or direction that is not pleasing to Him, and in God's eyes we have *"certainly trespassed against the Lord."* But, thank God, the Blood of Jesus Christ in the life of the believer cleanses (constantly cleanses) all sin, even that which we are not aware of at the time committed.

CHAPTER 6

The words, *"against the Lord,"* in verse 2 reaffirm what so often appears in the Bible, that to sin against a neighbor is to sin against

God. He makes human sorrows His own.

The 5th verse says, *"He shall even restore it in the principal and shall add the fifth part."* This means that whatever was taken by fraudulent means would be restored plus 20 percent interest. There is very little evidence of jails in those days. The person was made to restore what he had taken fraudulently with the 20 percent penalty, and if it was a capital crime, he paid with his life. The corrupt, unprofitable, debilitating penal system of modern times can hardly say that it has improved upon God's methods.

The *"law of the burnt offering"* in verse 9 states that it was to be *"burning upon the altar all night unto the morning."* In the morning, dressed in clean linen garments, the priest was to gather its ashes and place them beside the altar, and then in his garments of beauty, bring them with befitting glory unto a clean place. This speaks of the Millennium which shall one day come. Through this *"all night"* burning, the fragrance of Christ's offering up of Himself to God ascends continually. The words, *"unto morning,"* of verse 9 speak of a completed sacrifice when Jesus Christ will come back crowned King of kings and Lord of lords.

The 13th verse says, *"The fire shall ever be burning upon the altar; it shall never go out."* The fire that consumed the burnt offering originally came from heaven (9:24) and was maintained perpetually burning by the unwearied ministry of the priest. It testified on the one hand to the unceasing delight of God in the sacrifice of Christ, and on the other hand to His unceasing hatred of sin. False teachers today put out this fire by denying the doctrines of the atonement and of the judgment to come.

The *"law of the meat offering"* in verses 14-18 was the *"sin offering"* and the *"trespass offering,"* and each was considered *"most holy."* Thus, the Holy Spirit testifies to the sinlessness of Christ as man and the moment in which He was *"made sin"* upon the cross.

Verse 18 says, *"Concerning the offerings of the Lord made by fire: everyone that touches them shall be holy."* This symbolized that whoever touched Christ could be made whole.

Verses 19 through 23 portray *"the offering of Aaron and of his sons."* This pointed to two things.

A. That Aaron was a sinner as well and had to shelter himself, in type, behind a sinless Saviour.

B. That Aaron was a type of Christ who would be the perfect sacrifice.

Verses 24 through 30 speak of the *"law of the sin offering."*

Verse 26 explains what was done with the flesh of the sacrifices of rulers and others. The fat was wholly burned, and the flesh eaten by the priests. Eating of it signified acceptance of the offerer by the Lord and the reestablishment of communion between them.

Verse 28 speaks of *"the earthen vessel wherein it is sodden shall be broken."* And then it said, *"In a brazen pot, it shall be both scoured, and rinsed in water."* So desperate a malady is sin that anything that came in contact with the *"sin offering"* had to be washed, broken, and scoured.

The *"sin offering,"* whose blood was brought into the sanctuary (vs. 30), symbolizes Christ bearing before God the sin of the whole world. The *"sin offering,"* whose blood was not so brought in but whose flesh was eaten by the priests, presents Christ as making His own the sins of the individual sinner who believes upon Him.

CHAPTER 7

As we have stated, it took five levitical offerings: *"burnt offering," "meal offering," "peace offering,"* the *"sin offering,"* and the *"trespass offering"* to adequately portray the one sacrificial offering of Christ at Calvary. Each one of the levitical offerings gives satisfaction to the demand of God. The instructions of the offerings were twofold – the person bringing the offering (the sinner) and the priest. The by far greater responsibility lay with the priest, hence, the multitudinous instructions. As well, the glory of our salvation does not lie with us, the sinner; it lies with the Lord Jesus Christ. About all the person could do was to bring his offering and to believe the instructions he was given concerning the atonement. Likewise, at this time, all the sinner can do is

present himself before the Lord and believe (St. John 3:16). All the work is done by our Great High Priest.

First, *"the trespass offering is most holy."* Why is it most holy? Simply because it represents the Lord Jesus Christ.

According to verses 2 through 5, the priest was given careful instruction regarding the *"kidney,"* the *"caul,"* and the *"fat."* This represented prosperity and that the Lord was the author of the same.

The 8th verse says, *"The priest shall have to himself the skin of the burnt offering."* It is believed by some that the right of the officiating priest to get the skin goes back to Adam who was clothed with the first skin of sacrifices (Gen. 3:21).

Verses 11 through 21 portray the *"law of the sacrifice of peace offerings."*

The 12th verse tells us that the *"peace offerings"* were at times offered as *"a thanksgiving."*

Strangely enough, in the 13th verse he is instructed to offer *"leavened bread with the sacrifice."* Leaven, commonly used at social feasts, was permitted in the *"thank offering"* because this was the spontaneous expression of devotion from lives that were not entirely rid of sin and evil in every case. In other words, no life was perfect. And the eating of the *"leavened bread"* was a constant reminder that the offerer was a poor weak sinner, and that all of the Grace was in the Lord Jesus Christ. There were some offerings of thanksgiving that were given with *"unleavened cakes,"* which signify the perfect unblemished, sinless body of the Lord Jesus Christ.

The 15th verse indicates that the offerer could have a feast with his friends, which would symbolize the blessings of the Lord. However, all was to be eaten on that particular day or the next day. If any was left after that, *"on the third day it shall be burnt with fire."* All of this symbolized the continued need of the blessings of God.

The 19th verse speaks of *"touching any unclean thing."* The principle of touching any unclean thing which made one unclean also applied to touching any holy thing which made one clean or holy. It typifies two things: first of all, the touching of Satan (his works) which made one unholy, and touching Christ, which made one holy.

Verses 22 through 27 portray the law against eating *"fat"* and *"blood."* The *"fat"* portrayed the prosperity that God gives to his children, which at times was *"burned on the altar."* The *"blood"* typified life, and more importantly that which Christ would give for the sins of man. As far back as Genesis 9:24, the blood of the life of the flesh was forbidden. This command became a part of the Law of Moses. Actually, this same Law was also made a part of the New Testament (Acts 15:19-20, 29). Nothing is said about *"fat"* in the New Testament.

Verses 28-38 portray the priest's portion.

Several commands were given to the people concerning the priest's portion.

1. The one who offers *"peace offerings"* shall give a portion of it to the Lord for the priest (vs. 29 with vs. 14). This symbolizes two things: first of all, that the minister of the Gospel should live of the Gospel; and, second, the eating of the offering by the priest as well as the offerer, symbolizes partaking of Christ.

2. The offerer shall bring the offering made by fire, the *"fat"* to burn and the *"breast"* for the *"priest's portion"* (vs 30-31).

3. The *"right shoulder"* shall be given to the priest offering the *"blood"* of atonement and burning the *"fat."* The *"shoulder"* and the *"breast"* in point two signify the strength and the love of the Lord Jesus Christ given to His people.

4. The *"wave offering"* derived its name from the fact that whatever was offered was waved toward the brazen altar, symbolizing it was offered to the Lord, and away from the altar symbolizing that it was returned to the priest for their services. Once again it signified a thank offering to the Lord.

The 32nd verse speaks of the *"heave offering."* The *"heave offering"* was a little bit different than the *"wave offering"* in that the *"heave offering"* was lifted up and down several times, up as a symbol of offering it to God Who is above, and down again as a symbol of offering it to God's servants on earth.

The laws of sacrifices given in verses 37 and 38 and all other laws and commands, were given mainly on Sinai and made the one Law of God and of Moses for Israel. The Lord commanded the laws of sacrifices and offerings, the

judgments, statutes, and ordinances, as well as the Ten Commandments. Therefore, all of the other sacrifices and offerings are commandments just as much as the Ten. Nine of the Ten Commandments were carried over into the New Testament (the New Covenant) with the commandment of keeping the Sabbath eliminated. As well, all of the other laws given were fulfilled by Christ, and, thereby, done away with, with the exception of the eating of the blood. (Acts 15).

CHAPTER 8

This chapter pertains to the consecration of the priests.

Verse 2 says, *"Take Aaron and his sons with him."* Even though Aaron was the Great High Priest, he and his sons who were priests as well had to undergo the same sacrificial offerings as the worst sinner in Israel. All of this was a reminder that even though Aaron was called, anointed, and directed by God, still, he was flawed flesh and needing a Redeemer. The *"anointing oil"* was a type of the Holy Spirit. Jesus, our Great High Priest, was *"anointed with the oil of gladness above His fellows."* The *"bullock for the sin offering"* and *"two rams"* as well as the *"unleavened* bread" stood for sacrifice and cleansing, with the "unleavened *bread"* standing for the perfection demanded by God that could never be obtained except by sacrifice.

Verse 3 says, *"Unto the door of the tabernacle."* All of Israel gathered to see the consecration rites of Aaron and his sons. By this they were to understand that Aaron, even though the Great High Priest, was still a poor mortal, exactly as they were.

The 4th verse states, *"As the Lord commanded him."* Note that these were not suggestions; they were commands. Moses must carry it out to the letter. Regrettably, so many attempt to bring about their own salvation, leaving the commands of the Lord to *"believe on the Lord Jesus Christ and thou shalt be saved."*

The 6th verse, *"And wash them with water,"*

speaks of the *"washing of water by the Word."* All of this is a type of Christ.

The 7th verse speaks of *"the coat"* which speaks of Christ's deity. And then it says, *"girded with him a girdle."* This was His service to humanity. John said this, *"And took a towel, and girded himself"* (St. John 13:4). The *"robe"* speaks of his righteousness. The *"ephod"* was that which had the names of the children of Israel on each side (six to a side) on each shoulder. The Lord would carry His people on His shoulders.

The *"breastplate"* of the 8th verse contained the 12 precious stones listing the names of the 12 tribes of Israel. It was over the heart of the Great High Priest. In a pouch under the breastplate were the *"Urim and the Thummim."* The two words meant "lights and perfection." No one really knows what they were, whether God made them or Moses did by God's direction. Some think they were two stones with the word "yes" on one and the word "no" on the other.

The *"mitre"* of the 9th verse speaks of authority. Jesus is the *"Head"* of the Church.

Verse 12 says, *"And he poured of the anointing oil upon Aaron's head."* If one will notice in the 30th verse that even though Aaron was dressed in the garments of glory and beauty of the High Priest, still, Moses sprinkled the oil and the blood upon *"Aaron and upon his garments, and upon his sons."* To the carnal and natural mind this would seem to be ludicrous to have the *"anointing oil"* and *"the blood"* sprinkled all over these beautiful garments. However, with the spiritual mind we realize what gives the power is the Blood and the Holy Spirit.

The 14th verse says that even though Aaron was anointed by God, still, he was a sinner and, thereby, *"Laid their hands upon the head of the bullock for the sin offering."* At this time they would confess their sins as well. This signifies that their sins were transferred to the animal who became their substitute for sin.

The 15th verse says, *"And he slew it,"* typifying the death of Christ and *"poured the blood at the bottom of the altar,"* typifying the blood of Jesus that would be shed at Calvary. The word *"reconciliation"* is given here for the first time. Reconciliation applies to the doing

NOTES

away of an enmity, the bridging over of a quarrel. It implies that the parties being reconciled were formerly hostile to one another. The Bible tells us bluntly that sinners are *"enemies of God"* (Rom. 5:10; Col. 1:21). We should not minimize the seriousness of these and similar passages. An enemy is not someone who comes a little short of being a friend; he is in the other camp and is altogether opposed. The New Testament, as well as the Old, pictures God in vigorous opposition to everything that is evil.

Somehow, the root cause of the enmity must be dealt with. Christ died to put away our sin. In this way He dealt with the enmity between God and man. He put it out of the way. He made the way wide open for men to come back to God. This is *"reconciliation."*

It is interesting to notice that no Bible passage speaks of Christ as reconciling God to man. Always, the stress is on man's being reconciled to God. It is man's sin which has caused the enmity. It is man's sin that has had to be dealt with.

That which set up the barrier between God and man was the demand of God's holiness for uprightness in man. Man, left to himself, is content to let bygones be bygones. He is not particularly worried by his sin. Certainly, he feels little or no hostility to God on account of his sin. The barrier arises because God demands holiness in man.

This enmity in no way impacts or changes God's love. The Bible is very clear that God's love to man never varies no matter what man may do. Indeed, the whole atoning work of Christ stems from God's great love. It was *"while we were yet sinners"* that *"Christ died for us"* (Rom. 5:8). However, God's love in no way overlooks our sin. His love alone could never do away with sin. The price had to be paid for sin for the enmity to be taken away. It was paid by the death of Christ at Calvary.

The *"fat,"* the *"liver",* and the *"kidneys"* were *"burned upon the altar."* This represented the prosperity of Israel and that it came from God.

The words in the 17th verse, *"without the camp,"* signify that the Lord paid for redemption of man *"without the camp."*

Verses 22 through 26 portray *"the consecration ram."* The blood was to be applied *"upon the tip of Aaron's right ear,"* and upon the *"thumb of his right hand,"* and upon the *"great toe of his right foot."* This speaks of hearing only that which was of God, holding only that which was of God, and walking totally in God's direction.

Many special offerings are mentioned in the sacrifices, nearly all being male sacrifices, implying by figure and type the responsibility of Adam, not Eve, as the agent of God and emphasizing the iniquity of fathers, not mothers. It symbolizes the Redeemer Who came as a man (I Tim. 2:4-5). Female offerings of animals that were permitted simply implied that the woman had a part in the transgression of man and was also provided for in redemption. Females were used only in *"peace offerings"* (Lev. 3) and in minor *"sin offerings"* of a personal nature, never in the whole *"burnt offerings"* or any that definitely symbolized Christ as the sin-bearer of all men.

The *"wave offering"* of verses 26 through 29 simply means that they waved the whole burnt offering back and forth before burning it. This symbolized that the instructions had come from heaven and that salvation was of the Lord.

Once again in the 30th verse, the *"sprinkling of the blood"* and *"anointing of oil"* together on the bodies and garments of the priests were fitting conclusions to their consecration and the entire rite of such sanctification. Blood had been applied before this to the bodies and to the altar. Even Aaron had been anointed as High Priest, so the new part of the ritual did not cleanse from sin, sanctify, or bless in any particular way, except to show the necessity of continued trust in the Blood and the need of continued anointing with the Spirit.

The outward ritual of anointing with oil signified the choice of God, the calling of God, and the enduement of power for the particular work one was called to do. Priests, prophets, and kings were anointed, and if they carried out their calling, they had the backing of God. If they sinned and failed, they received the curse of God until they repented and came back to the original calling and fulfilled it. If they never came back, the curse of God remained upon them forever.

Verses 33 through 36 proclaim the *"seven*

NOTES

days" as separation.

The rites of consecration were to last *"seven days,"* during which time the priests were not to leave the Tabernacle day or night. They were to go through the same rituals and offer the same sacrifices daily for the *"seven days."* They ate of the sacrifices and the bread and slept inside the court, perhaps on the ground on skins.

This *"seven days"* symbolizes their total and complete consecration. God never demands less.

CHAPTER 9

The 9th chapter of Leviticus is a portrayal of the ministry of the priests. As well, it forepictures the coming millennial reign when Christ will come from His heavenly sanctuary, and then the glory of the Lord will fill the whole earth. This chapter, in type, is a picture of that glorious time that is soon to come.

Now Aaron and his sons, fully robed and anointed by both oil and blood, were ready for their priestly duties. The great perfect plan of salvation yet to come will be foreshadowed by the events of this chapter. Israel was told (in the 4th verse) that *"today the Lord will appear unto you."* The anticipation was high. God would do mighty things. However, God could not appear until the proper offerings were offered, *"sin offering"* and *"whole burnt offerings."* These two offerings were on behalf of Aaron and his sons. Even though they were called of God and robed in beautiful garments and stood as leaders of the people, they were poor, frail, flawed, sinful mortals, and, thereby, must have the same sacrifice as the worst sinner in Israel.

Verses 3 and 4 proclaim six offerings for the people. As all of this was going on, the people did not realize what was happening. Likewise, we, as Christians, little realize the tremendous intercessory work that is being carried on by our Great High Priest, the Lord Jesus Christ, at this very moment.

The 5th verse records the numerous people of Israel drawing near to the Tabernacle. This would have been an awesome sight with the cloud hovering heavily over the Holy of Holies, and, if by night, the fire playing above the Tabernacle. The people were told, *"And the glory of the Lord shall appear unto you."* The Church desires the glory (at least some do), but few desire to go God's way to receive the glory.

Once again (7th verse) the Great High Priest, Aaron, had to *"make an atonement for thyself,"* and then *"make an atonement for them"*, the people. The word *"atonement"* means "to cover" not only the sins but the people themselves.

That which was burnt with fire *"without the camp"* (vs. 11), symbolizes complete expiation (to do away with the guilt incurred). The whole curse fell upon the substitute. An atonement was not completed until the whole sacrifice was consumed.

The *"burnt offering"* portrayed in the 12th verse, was for Aaron. The *"burnt offering"* was for general guilt and original sin. It symbolizes Jesus Christ as the one all-sufficient offering for sin.

The 15th verse portrays Aaron offering the *"sin offering"* for Israel's atonement. The *"burnt offering"* typifies complete surrender. The *"meat offering"* was to render thanks, and the *"peace offering"* was for the people to have communion with God. All of this is portrayed through verse 21.

Verses 22 and 23 proclaim the blessing of the people. The lifting up of hands became a custom of priests in blessing the people when completing their duties for them in the rituals. What the priests said to them on this occasion is not stated, but it could have been what was established for priests in Numbers 6:24-26. One of the Jewish Targums reads, *"May your offerings be accepted, and may the Lord dwell among you and forgive you of your sins."*

After they *"blessed the people,"* the Bible said, *"And the glory of the Lord appeared unto all the people."* How did this happen?

The 24th verse tells us, *"And there came a fire out from before the Lord."*

This fire did not come directly from heaven but rather came from God who dwelt between the Mercy Seat and the Cherubim. A literal tongue of flame came from the Holy of Holies through the veil without burning it and struck the brazen altar and consumed the *"burnt*

offering and the fat." It was visible to all of Israel. The Bible said, *"When all the people saw, they shouted, and fell on their faces."* Likewise, on the Day of Pentecost, *"tongues of fire sat upon their heads."* Likewise, we are baptized with the *"Holy Ghost and fire."*

An old Jewish tradition maintains that the fire of the brazen altar was first kindled by this fire from the Lord, and that it was kept alive on the altar until the dedication of the Temple of Solomon, when it fell from God again. However, it seems from Leviticus 8:16; 9:10, that fire had already been kindled on the altar. If so, then the fire from God only manifested His Divine presence and acceptance in burning up the sacrifices.

CHAPTER 10

Chapter 10 portrays the judgment of God upon the sinner instead of the sacrifice. And why? It was because of *"strange fire";* the same *"strange fire"* that is so abundant in false doctrines, false sacrifices, and false prophets even in this day and age. Both *"Nadab"* and *"Abihu"* were *"sons of Aaron."* They took their *"censers"* and *"put fire therein."* They as well put *"incense thereon."* However, the fire was *"strange fire."* And what did that mean?

It meant that it was fire that did not come from the brazen altar, which was a type of Jesus Christ. It, therefore, had no connection with the atonement. It was the sin of Cain. It is the sin largely committed today, as well. Jesus said, *"I am the Way, the Truth, and the Life, no man cometh unto the Father but by Me."* Acceptable worship can only be in the energy of the Holy Spirit, in the truth of the shed Blood, and in obedience to the inspired Word. The fire of the Holy Spirit associates itself alone with the Blood of the crucified Saviour; all other fire is *"strange fire."*

The 2nd verse states, *"And there went out fire from the Lord and devoured them, and they died before the Lord."* It was the same fire that came from the same Lord between the same Mercy Seat and Cherubim. However, instead of consuming the sacrifice, it consumed these priests. And why?

They took *"fire"* from their own cook pot or from some other ignition. Why would they have done such in direct violation of the commands of God?

It seems from verse 9 that they were drunk with wine and strong drink. They took the things of God lightly. It is the sin of the Church today; *"strange fire"* is offered and the same death applies – spiritual death. The Church today is rife with spiritual death because of the *"strange fire."* How many preachers still preach *"Christ and Him crucified?"* How many Bible colleges and seminaries still teach *"Christ and Him crucified?"* How many today are offering a "prosperity gospel," a "possibility gospel," a "self-esteem gospel," a "psychological gospel," all *"strange fire,"* all bringing spiritual death.

Strangely, the fire that *"devoured them"* did not burn their priestly garments (vs. 5).

Verse 3 says, *"I will be sanctified in them that come nigh me,"* and then *"Before all the people I will be glorified,"* a lesson of warning for all. God says what He means, and means what He says. Carnal men would read these words in Leviticus 10 and think of God as cruel. However, God would have been cruel not to have done such. The brazen altar, a type of Christ from which the fire must come, cannot be replaced. There is no other way of salvation; all else is sinking sand.

Verses 6 and 7 tell us that Israel, as well as the priests, stood very close to judgment, *"lest ye die."* Verse 6 says there was to be no recognition of what had happened by the other priests; they were to continue their duties. Instead, *"the whole house of Israel bewail the burning which the Lord hath kindled."* And why was this?

The priests were to continue their duties because all would need continued sacrifice. The people would *"bewail"* because they were in no better condition than Nadab and Abihu who had been killed.

Verse 12 says that Moses commanded Aaron to *"take the meat offering that remaineth of the offering of the Lord made by fire, and eat it without leaven beside the altar."* In doing so, Aaron, the Great High Priest, would make the sins of the people his own. His other two sons,

"Eleazar and Ithamar," would help him.

However, the 16th verse says that Aaron, along with his two remaining sons, burnt the *"sin offering instead."* Moses grew angry because of the disobedience.

The 19th verse asks, *"Should it have been accepted in the sight of the Lord?"* In other words, Aaron was saying, "God's judgment has come upon two of my sons already, and I was very fearful that if we had eaten the sacrifice as commanded on behalf of the congregation of Israel, that it would not have been accepted by God, and we too would have been smitten." Aaron realized that he and his two remaining sons were skirting the very edge of death themselves. The Lord had said as much in verse 10, *"That you may put difference between holy and unholy, and between unclean and clean."* Our confidence must ever be in the slain Lamb and not in the *"strange fire"* of our own making. God help us!

CHAPTER 11

The binding dietary laws of the 11th chapter were not carried over into the New Testament. Actually, they were refuted, as is described in Acts 10.

Why was God this specific under the Old Covenant concerning the things that Israel should or should not eat? The main purpose was this: Israel was elected to be a peculiar treasure to God; therefore, she was to cleanse herself from all filthiness of the flesh and spirit and to be holy, for God was holy. In other words, they were His people. Actually, Israel was raised up for three great tasks.

1. Israel was to give the Word of God to the world.

2. Israel was to be the womb of the Messiah.

3. Israel was to evangelize the world.

With great difficulty Israel carried out the first two. She failed in the third.

It must ever be understood that none of these laws caused Israel to be righteous. They contained no saving grace. They were strictly for two purposes:

1. That Israel might be set apart from the

rest of the heathen world.

2. That Israel would be a peculiar people, a holy treasure unto God.

In this 11th chapter the God of Israel entered with amazing detail into the daily food and sustenance of His people in order to teach them to make a difference between the unclean and the clean. Love was the basis of this legislation. The same command, even in exact detail, is given to the Christian today, *"Come out from among them and be ye separate."* And yet, the child of God must be very careful that He does not concern himself with legalism – meaning works of the flesh concerning the making of rules, laws, works, or legislation, which, if we keep, somehow adds to our salvation. Man is not saved by works (legalism); he is saved by faith, and faith alone. The moment we insert works (legalism) into our faith, at that moment our faith is negated and becomes of no value. While it is certainly true that true faith will produce good works, at the same time good works will not produce faith (James 2:20). It is the same as offering *"strange fire."* It comes from one's own cook pot instead of the designated brazen altar which typified Calvary. God accepts no sacrifice other than that of His Son. He blesses the labor of no one's hands except His Son's. How long will it take for us to learn?

There is something in man which stems from the fall that thinks we can somehow contribute something toward our salvation. Therefore, we try, and we try, and we try. However, salvation is not in doing but in trusting what has already been done.

CHAPTER 12

Verses 1 through 5 portray certain things that should be done by a woman after the birth of a baby boy and a little baby girl. If it were a little boy who was born, she would be *"unclean seven days,"* and for 33 days, making a total of 40 days she could not *"come into the sanctuary."* If it were a little girl, she could not *"come into the sanctuary"* for 80 days.

For what reason is this? The birth of a child recalled the sin and disobedience of the woman

in the Garden of Eden, and that woman was the instrument of rebellion. This was an ever reminder to Israel of the terrible consequences of the fall. These laws constantly stated that man was defiled and needed cleansing. And yet, it pointed the way toward the coming Redeemer.

Verses 6 through 8 say that at the end of the appointed time (40 days for a little son, 80 days for a little daughter), she would carry out a ritual for her purifying. She should bring a *"lamb of the first year for a burnt offering."* However, if she were too poor to bring such, she could substitute *"a young pigeon or a turtledove."*

The extreme poverty of the Lord's earthly parents was evidenced by their bringing two pigeons, the one for a *"sin offering,"* the other for a *"burnt offering"* (St. Luke 2:24).

Tender love and amazing grace shine forth in this chapter; amazing grace, for He, the Lord of Glory, condescended to be made of so poor a woman; tender love, for He commanded that women during the time of their greatest weakness should be protected.

The Virgin Mary knew she was a sinner and needed the cleansing of atoning blood, for she brought the two pigeons here as the Law commanded.

CHAPTER 13

Leviticus 13 portrays the discovery of leprosy. Leviticus 14 portrays the cleansing of leprosy.

Leprosy in Old Testament times vividly illustrated sin. It was ordained by God as such. Leprosy is infectious but not contagious. In other words, it is dangerous only if the person touches the leper, hence infectious. It is loathsome, incurable, and fatal. It is a perfect picture of sin. God intended for leprosy and all its loathsome horror to be a constant picture of what sin does to the human being. As leprosy will eat away at the body, sin will eat away at the soul.

Leprosy will attack the body to such an extent that the body members will ultimately fall off. Fingers will literally come apart from the hands, toes from the feet. It is especially horrible on the face, with the ears ultimately falling off, the nose finally separating from the face, and even the lips being eaten away. In its last stages, the body finally just falls to pieces. Jesus healed many lepers during His earthly ministry. There were precious few healed in Old Testament times.

Every Israelite understood what leprosy represented, and in their minds they finally came to the place to believe that leprosy was judgment of God upon the individual, and, consequently, the person could not be saved. This was incorrect, but not in the minds of most Israelites.

The minute directions given in the chapter, and the care and patience enjoined upon the priests, show how God distinguishes between sin and infirmity. Man might have a form of skin disease in appearance like leprosy, but the priests were skilled to pronounce it other than leprosy. Our Heavenly High Priest is a Priest for infirmity as well as for sin; however, there is a great difference in the two.

Actually, the legislation of this chapter reveals how tenderly, faithfully, and patiently Jesus acts toward the sinner.

Verses 45 and 46 pronounce four different signs of the leper. They are perfect examples of what sin does to the sinner.

1. *"His clothes shall be rent."* This speaks of the outer garment which had to be ripped down the back from collar to hem. It had a spiritual meaning. It meant that man's righteousness was insufficient for acceptance by God. The leper's torn garment said, "I am undone, useless, and I am separated from God. Furthermore, all of my good works can never bridge the gap."

2. *"His head bare."* This signifies that the sinner had and has no protection against the anger of God. In those days, as now, all Jews wore a covering on their head as a sign to the world that God was their protection and their covering. Today, male Christians when worshiping do not wear any type of covering on the head, signifying that Christ is their covering. He needs no symbolism because He is ever present in our heart in the power of the Holy Spirit. The *"head bare"* meant that there was

NOTES

no covenant between God and the individual. He was a sinner and, thereby, a declared enmity against God.

3. *"And he shall put a covering upon his upper lip, and shall cry, Unclean, unclean."* The moment an individual came within 100 feet, the leper would cry, *"Unclean, unclean."* They must not come closer. If the leper did not shout out these words, he could be stoned to death. In reality, the terrible problem has not changed. Today, when asked, "Are you saved?", and the individual says, "I am a member of a _____ church, they are in effect crying, "Unclean, unclean." If there is any answer other than, *"I am saved by faith in the Lord Jesus Christ and accept the price He paid at Calvary and the Resurrection,"* then the individual is shouting to the whole world, *"Unclean, unclean."* Most of the world today when speaking of their religious affiliation is, without knowing it, shouting, *"Unclean, unclean."*

4. *"He shall dwell alone."* There is a terrible loneliness to sin. Even in the midst of a crowd, the loneliness seems to increase rather than to decrease. Man was created by God to serve God. There is a void in man's heart that all the money, power, prestige, and education can never fill. The soul of man is so big that only God can fill it. Without God, man is *"alone"* and, oh, so lonely.

Thank God, there is a cure for sin, and that cure is the Lord Jesus Christ. St. Mark chapter 1 beautifully illustrates the cry of the leper, *"If thou wilt, thou canst make me clean."* The answer of the Lord Jesus Christ will ever reverberate across the annals of history, *"I will."*

He further cries, *"Whosoever will let him come and take of the water of life freely."* The leper can be cleansed; the sinner can be saved; sin can turn to salvation; death can turn to life; sickness can turn to health; hell can turn to heaven, but only by the Lord Jesus Christ. There is no other Saviour. Man cannot reach God through Buddha, Mohammed, Confucius, or through any other way or method. Jesus said, *"I am the way."* There is no other way.

CHAPTER 14

The 14th chapter portrays a beautiful example and symbol of Christ's atoning work at Calvary and His Resurrection. We are shown in this chapter how the leper is cleansed and the sinner saved. If we properly understand, it portrays Christ gloriously so. As well, it will help us to see ourselves for who and what we really are and Christ for who and what He really is.

The 2nd verse says, *"He shall be brought unto the priest."*

Then the 3rd verse says, *"And the priests shall go forth out of the camp."* There is no contradiction. The leper was to be brought to a designated place outside the camp, and the priests would go forth to meet the leper. It is our responsibility as Christians to bring the precious unsaved souls to their appointment with their Creator. That's the reason that Jesus told us, *"Go ye into all the world and preach the Gospel"* (Mark 16).

As the priests went forth outside the camp looking for the leper, likewise, Christ has come all the way from the portals of glory to look for the sinner. The loathsome condition of the leper is a perfect description of the loathsome condition of the sinner.

The 4th verse begins the beautiful ceremonial cleansing of the leper which portrays Christ in His beautiful Calvary work, *"Two birds alive."* One would represent Christ Who died; the other would represent the resurrected Christ. The *"cedar wood"* represented the Cross of Calvary. The *"scarlet"* represented the blood shed. *"Hyssop"* was a type of grass that grew in the crevices of rocks. It was used in Egypt to splatter the blood on the doorposts. It was a type of Christ's humanity.

The 5th verse says, *"One of the birds be killed."* This was the one that represented Christ on Calvary. The *"earthen vessel"* signifies Christ's perfect humanity. The *"running water"* is symbolic of the Holy Spirit Who forever attended and filled Christ without measure.

In the 6th verse the *"living bird"* represents the resurrected Christ. The *"scarlet"* was red

NOTES

thread, symbolizing the blood of Christ used to tie the bird to the *"cedar wood,"* representing the Cross of Calvary. The *"scarlet"* represented the blood that covered the Cross. The priest would then take the *"living bird"* bound to the *"cedar wood"* and dip its tail feathers in the bloody water from the bird that had been killed. The living and dead birds typify the death and Resurrection of Christ through which sin, sickness, and the entire curse would be removed from mankind. They also picture the leper freed from sin, sickness, and suffering to go free and walk in newness of life and perfect deliverance from his curse, enjoying salvation and health, fellowship with his own kind, and communion with the Lord.

The 7th verse says that the priest would take the *"living bird"* tied to the *"cedar wood,"* dip it in water, and sprinkle the leper *"seven times."* This symbolized completeness and perfection of the remedy and foreshadowed the removal of all sin, sickness, pain, and suffering through Jesus Christ. Then the *"living bird"* would be let loose into the open field, symbolizing the Resurrection of Christ, as well as the resurrection of the sinner. When Christ died, He became our substitute, and we identify with Him. When He was buried, He became our substitute, and we identify with Him. When He was resurrected, He became our substitute, and we identify with Him.

On the 8th day according to the 10th verse, after the ceremonial cleansing, several sacrifices would be offered. There was to be a *"meal offering,"* a *"trespass offering,"* as well as a *"sin offering"* and a *"burnt offering."*

According to the 4th verse, the priest would take some of the blood of the *"trespass offering"* and put it upon the *"tip of the right ear"* of him who was to be cleansed." This signifies that from here on he would hear only God. And then, *"Upon the thumb of his right hand,"* for henceforth he would grasp only that which belonged to the Lord. By placing blood upon the *"great toe of his right foot,"* he signifies that his direction would change.

The 16th verse says, *"And shall sprinkle of the oil with his finger seven times before the Lord."* This speaks of the completed work of the Holy Spirit. The oil was to be applied in the same places that the blood had been applied.

Not only was he now cleansed in order that he be accepted by God, but at the same time he was anointed by the Holy Spirit to do that which God wanted him to do. Even though we are cleansed by the blood, we still must have the power of the Holy Spirit to help us live as we ought to live.

The 18th verse says, *"Shall pour upon the head of him that is to be cleansed."* This signifies the help and power of the Holy Spirit Who helps people to completely change their thinking from that of rebellion to obedience.

The 14th chapter closes with the words, *"This is the law of leprosy."* As stated, it is a beautiful picture of the tremendous price paid by the Lord Jesus Christ for the cleansing, salvation, and direction of the poor lost sinner. Hallelujah!

Going back to verse 7, the Scripture says, *"And shall pronounce him clean."* This speaks of justification. That's why the Lord told Simon Peter, *"What I have cleansed call not thou common."* The priest was a type of Christ who pronounced the leper clean. Likewise, it is Christ Who pronounces us clean. When He does pronounce us clean, how dare anyone else pronounce us other than that which Christ has pronounced, *"Clean."*

CHAPTER 15

There are several issues divulged to us in the 15th chapter of Leviticus. They are as follows:

1. *The holiness of God and His dwellingplace.* Over and over again, the word *"unclean"* or *"uncleanliness"* is used. Even though these directions concerned physical cleanliness, still they are a shadow and type of the spiritual cleanliness that God demands. Fallen man little knows or understands spiritual cleanliness. That which man signifies "clean," God signifies "unclean." Man little recognizes God's spiritual cleanliness. Sadly, the Church follows suit. Man thinks that good works signify spiritual cleanliness. A far greater percentage of the Church believes the same. God's order of spiritual cleanliness can

only be brought about by the precious shed blood of Jesus Christ being applied to the sins of man. God is a holy God, and where He dwells He demands cleanliness. That's the reason He tells us, *"Present your bodies a living sacrifice holy and acceptable unto God, which is your reasonable service"* (Rom. 12:1). The spiritual cleanliness that God demands cannot be brought about by a *"work of the flesh."* It can only be brought about by a *"work of the Spirit"* (Rom. 8).

2. *The loving and minute interest that God takes in the habits and daily life of His children.* Nothing is too small or too private for Him. Your clothing and your health concern Him deeply. Amazingly enough, vaunted medical science stopped losing most of its patients on the operating table when they read Leviticus 15:13, *"And bathed his flesh in running water, and shall be clean."* The *"running water"* was the key. Before a medical doctor saw this passage in Leviticus and applied it to the operating procedure, most of the patients died. The doctors would wash their hands and their instruments in the same water, or wash not at all, thereby transferring disease, germs, and corruption to the patient at hand. Finally, a medical doctor saw this passage in Leviticus and started incorporating the simple command in his operational procedures. He demanded that hands and instruments be constantly washed in running water. Wondrously enough, his success rate leaped dramatically. Finally, the rest of the medical profession followed suit. The answer was in the Word of God all the time, just as the answer to every other problem that man has is found somewhere in the Word of God.

3. *The corruption of fallen nature.* Just about everything that man does conveys pollution. Whether it is walking, waking, sleeping, sitting, standing, or lying down, its every touch conveys pollution. What a painful lesson for proud humanity. Man's greatest sin is that he does not know how lost he is, and, conversely, the saved man does not know how saved he is.

4. *The cleansing power of the shed Blood of the Lord Jesus Christ and the sanctifying virtue of the Word of God is the only way of cleansing and holiness.* As this chapter is inspected, we find that almost everything that man touches, he defiles - even that which is

unavoidable. There was provision made for restoration to communion with God with a *"sin offering,"* a *"burnt offering,"* and *"washing with water"* (vs. 15).

Justification assures of salvation from the guilt of sin (Romans). Sanctification effects separation from the guilt of sin (Hebrews).

CHAPTER 16

Chapter 16 describes the Great Day of Atonement. It occurred only once a year. There was no other day like it. It dealt with the sins of the whole nation for 12 months. It foreshadows the Lamb of God taking away the sin of the world. Abel's lamb redeemed one man; the Paschal Lamb, one family; the Day of Atonement lamb, one nation; the Lamb of Calvary, the whole world!

The *"holy place"* of verse 2 refers to the Holy of Holies. The Tabernacle was divided into two compartments. The first part, as one came through the door, contained the *"table of shewbread"* on the right, with the *"golden lamp stand"* on the left. Immediately in front before the veil was the *"golden altar of worship."* Immediately behind the veil was the *"holy place"* which is referred to as the *"Holy of Holies."* God dwelt in this place between the Mercy Seat and the Cherubim. This was where God promised to appear and commune with Israel. The cloud veiled His holy form. No priest could enter into this place at all with the exception of the Great High Priest, and then only once a year with blood.

The 3rd verse portrays the offering of a *"young bullock for a sin offering,"* and a *"ram for a burnt offering."* These offerings were not for Israel; they were for Aaron himself. He was ever reminded that even though he was the Great High Priest chosen of God to stand between God and Israel, he was still but a sinner and, thereby, had to offer up sacrifice the same as the lowest and most ungodly in Israel.

The Great High Priest had garments designed by God that were more beautiful than any of the other priests. They were called

NOTES

"garments of glory and beauty." However, when he entered the *"Holy of Holies,"* he could not wear these garments of *"glory and beauty,"* the reason being that the Lord Jesus Christ did not redeem us by His deity but through the incarnation of God becoming man. Therefore, the *"linen"* would be the proper attire; it represented the righteousness of Christ.

The 5th verse says that the offerings for Israel would be carried out immediately following his own and would be *"two kids of the goats for a sin offering, and one ram for a burnt offering."* These would be offered after the sacrifices had been offered for himself. Incidentally, this Great Day of Atonement was on the 10th day of the 7th month, which would correspond somewhat with our October. Verses 7 through 10 portray the *"scapegoat."* According to tradition, the two goats were to be the same in size, color, and value, and as nearly alike as possible. Both were presented to the Lord by the High Priest, and then the lots were cast to determine which one should die and which should live. The one that would live (sent into the wilderness) was called the *"goat of departure."*

The two goats represented and completed one atonement for sin. The goat which died typified the death of Christ, and the one which lived typified His resurrection. The two goats represented the same idea as the two birds, (for leprosy) one of which was killed and the other turned loose in the open fields (14:4-8). When the goat was led into the wilderness, atonement was complete; the sins transferred figuratively on the goat were already atoned for, and the blood was sprinkled before the Lord. No other sacrifice could be allowed for sin after this on the Day of Atonement, (at least for the nation as a whole) signifying that when Christ died and entered into heaven, there was no more sacrifice for sin. The words *"and offer him for a sin offering"* (vs. 9) typify Christ Who became sin for us though He knew no sin (II Cor. 5:21).

The words in the 10th verse, *"to make an atonement with him, and to let him go for a scapegoat into the wilderness,"* were the completion of the atonement in that He took sin away, typifying the removal of sin by the Resurrection of Jesus Christ. The words *"the wilder-*

ness" simply mean the wilderness regarding the trek through that barren waste land. However, after the Temple was built in Jerusalem, it simply means to a place uninhabited. Thus, there was no particular place called "Azazel" as some erroneously teach, where the goats were taken year after year to be turned loose.

The *"coals of fire from off the altar before the Lord"* in verse 12 was the only fire acceptable, which was from the brazen altar where atonement had been made. Only this could be used for burning incense on the golden altar and in censers. All other fire was *"strange fire"* and would bring death. The fires, incidentally, burned continuously 24 hours a day, 7 days a week on the brazen altar. The *"sweet incense"* was a symbol of prayer ascending up before Jehovah. It was poured on the fire which consisted of coals from the brazen altar.

In the 13th verse, *"shall put the incense upon the fire before the Lord,"* means that the censer was perhaps placed on the Mercy Seat, which was the lid of the Ark; this permitted the cloud and fragrance of the incense to cover it while the High Priest went out for the blood of the sin offering to put on the Mercy Seat and sprinkle before it seven times. This particular sprinkling was done for himself and his house. After making atonement for himself and his family, the High Priest went through the same ritual for the people (vs. 15).

The 16th verse says, *"The uncleanliness of the children of Israel, and because of their transgressions in all their sins."* This explains why atonement for the most holy place was made, and the same should be understood in connection with the High Priest and his house. They also had uncleanliness and transgressions for which blood atonement had to be made. God looks on ministers and laymen alike where guilt is concerned; any sin committed by one class is as black as that of the other, and it takes the same blood atonement for both (Heb. 5:1-4; 9:22).

The 16th verse says, *"And he shall make an atonement for the holy place,"* which means that the High Priest was commanded to sprinkle the blood on the golden altar in the *"holy place"* as he had done with the *"mercy seat"* in the *"most holy place."* The blood was to be

NOTES

applied to the golden altar as to the Ark inside the veil.

The 17th verse says, *"And there shall be no man,"* meaning that no man was allowed in the Tabernacle while the High Priest was making atonement for the *"most holy place,"* the *"holy place,"* and the *"outer court."* This nullifies all the arguments and practices of pretentious priesthoods that make claims of direct representation as mediators between God and the people, while Christ is in the heavenly Tabernacle, as now, carrying on His priestly work (Heb. 4:14-16; 5:1-14). Christ is the only mediator between God and man (I Tim. 2:4-6; Heb. 9:24). No man can sacrifice Christ anew, for He has been sacrificed *"once for all"* (Heb. 7:27; 9:26-28; I Pet. 3:18), and His flesh cannot be mystically made into bread or wafers which are the creation of man.

Verses 20 through 22 proclaim the scapegoat who was sent away.

The 21st verse says, *"And Aaron shall lay both his hands upon the head of the live goat and confess."* This is the only occasion where both hands are definitely referred to in the atonement ritual.

The *"by the hand of a fit man into the wilderness"* simply means a qualified man chosen for the time and occasion. Tradition says that he was chosen for this work a year in advance.

The two goats completed the one type of Christ in His work of death and resurrection. One alone could not do this because being killed would make it impossible for an animal to represent the Resurrection as when it was taken into the wilderness. If Christ had died and remained dead, His atoning work would have been in vain. It was the Resurrection that made it effective. The scapegoat being sent off represented Christ in resurrection, *"having removed our sins as far as the east is from the west, and remembering them against us no more"* (Psa. 103:12; Heb. 10:17).

The 24th verse says, *"Offer his burnt offering."* The burnt offerings completed the extra ones on the Great Day of Atonement mentioned in this chapter. The regular daily sacrifices were also made but are not listed here. This washing of Aaron took place after the goat had been sent into the open country outside the camp, it being necessary at this time because of his transferring the sins of Israel with his hands upon its head. This very act of contacting sin, even in a symbolic way, caused the High Priest to be so unclean that washing and more sacrificing were required. This teaches us that any contact with sin makes one unclean and sinful, and if he transgresses after confession and cleansing, he must put away sin and be cleansed in like manner as at the first time.

Verse 27 says, *"Shall one carry forth without the camp."* This typifies Christ as a *"sin offering,"* dying outside the camp.

The 29th verse says, *"And this shall be a statute forever unto you."* It was observed more or less until the Babylonian captivity and afterward in the restoration until the destruction of Jerusalem in A.D. 70. When Israel failed God and had to be judged, God was no longer obligated to fulfill His covenant with them.

The Great Day of Atonement is the most beautiful example of the sacrificial atoning work of Calvary and the Resurrection. Its type will be fulfilled at the beginning of the Millennium when Jesus Christ comes back and cleanses Israel after their return to Him. But more importantly it is a type of our glorious salvation given to us more perfectly by the Lord Jesus Christ.

—■—

CHAPTER 17

In the 17th chapter Israel was told of one place of sacrifice and, thereby, one God to worship.

The first nine verses will determine the one and only place where sacrifice could be offered. It would be the door of the Tabernacle. The 4th verse even says that if such were not done *"that man shall be cut off from among his people,"* in other words, executed.

The 7th verse says, *"And they shall no more offer their sacrifices unto devils."* This shows that all pagan sacrifices wherever they may be offered are, in fact, worship to devils and not to God. No matter what type of worship that men may engage in, and no matter how much they

may claim it is to God, if it, in fact, is not by the power of the Holy Spirit through the shed blood of Jesus Christ, it is not to God but to devils. So, most of the worship that is going on in the world today is to Satan. The Lord said this of Israel even at this time, *"After whom they have gone a whoring."* This affirms that Israel by this time (before leaving Sinai and during the first year after the exodus) had already gone whoring in some measure after idols and gods of other nations. This was the sin so detested by God and for which the nation not only met defeat many times, but went into Babylonian and Assyrian captivities (II Kings 17:25).

In verses 10 through 14 we have the law against eating blood, as well as an explanation showing how serious the sin is, *"For the life of the flesh is in the blood"* (vs. 11). And then He said, *"For it is the blood that maketh an atonement for the soul."*

When man fell, Satan, thereby, owned man. In effect, he owned the life of man, and the life was in the blood. Consequently, no human being could ever be sacrificed and, thereby, pay the penalty because every human being's blood was tainted by sin. Therefore, God would become man (the Lord Jesus Christ) whose blood would be pure, and could, thereby, be offered up in sacrifice which would pay all of the penalty. Therefore, God placed the death penalty on anyone who would dare eat blood, *"Whosoever eateth it shall be cut off."*

—■—

CHAPTERS 18-20

The first five verses of the 18th chapter proclaim the holiness of God and, thereby, demand holiness of God's people. The warning was, *"After the doings of the land of Egypt, wherein ye dwelt, shall ye not do"* (vs. 3). As the *"doings"* of Egypt was the bane of Israel, the world is likewise the bane of the Christian.

There was to Israel, in exact detail, direction and specification as to the totality of their actions. Every possible situation was addressed. When we look at these three chapters, once again we see the total degradation of man. God said this in the 25th verse, *"And the land itself vomiteth out her inhabitants."* The situation could become so evil then or evil now that the same will happen. The land will *"vomit out her inhabitants."*

Verses 9 and 10 of chapter 19 reveal God's welfare program for Israel, *"Thou shalt not wholly reap the corners of thy field, neither shalt thou gather the gleanings of thy harvest."* And then He said, *"Thou shalt leave them for the poor and the stranger."* However, it must be noted, this food that was left was not delivered to the *"poor and the stranger."* They had to exert themselves by going into the fields or the vineyard to glean such.

The 13th verse states that the *"wages"* should be paid at the end of each day. What a careful thought for the most humble member of society.

Verses 35 through 37 demand *"just balances, just weights"* - in other words, honesty.

In the 20th chapter verse 6, we have the death penalty stated for those going after witches and wizards or having traffic with demon spirits. I wonder how well that would stand up today with those even in the Church, who seek after horoscopes, mediums, or psychology.

In verse 15 it says, *"And if a man lie with a beast, he shall surely be put to death."* He then said that if such would happen, *"and you shall slay the beast."* Why did God demand this?

Bestiality (sexual relationship with a beast) has been practiced in pagan nations by both men and women. For this and other sins the Canaanites were destroyed. The Bible speaks of a man's relationship with a woman as making them one flesh, even in harlotry (I Cor. 6:15-18). On these grounds, bestiality would lower the image of God to becoming one flesh with the beast; hence, it insults the Creator more than some other sins. It was God's plan for man to be higher in morals and principles than to cohabit with senseless dumb animals. Just as murder is a serious crime against God because it takes the life of one created in His image (Gen. 9:6), so bestiality is a depraved crime against Him because it lowers one of His likeness to the level of a beast. For this sin both the man and the beast were to be killed. Though the beast had no moral responsibility,

NOTES

it had to be destroyed. Actually, the disease of syphilis came about as the result of men cohabiting with sheep - hence the reason that the animal should be destroyed as well.

CHAPTERS 21 & 22

Chapter 21, along with part of chapter 22, gives commands concerning the priests and what would disqualify them. All the priests in the society of Israel were to be types of Christ. Therefore, they had to basically *be "without blemish"* as Christ was *"without blemish."*

Chapter 22 verses 17-33 proclaim that the offerings as well should be *"without blemish."* God demanded the unblemished priest and an unblemished sacrifice simply because both represented the umblemished Christ.

In chapter 22 verses 26 and 28, we are given instructions concerning the sacrifice of certain animals. Even though it may seem to be the same instruction, we should not allow its lesson to be lost on us. This is what it teaches us.

In the life of separation unto God there must be holiness but not hardness. So often the Church mistakes hardness for holiness. So often those who would be holy produce hardness. True holiness is always meek and humble. The very idea of such being the other is anathema to the Lord.

CHAPTER 23

The 23rd chapter lists the seven great feasts of Jehovah, *"These are the feasts of the Lord."* Regrettably, when Jesus came these feasts had ceased to be *"Feasts of Jehovah"* and had become *"Feasts of the Jews"* (St. John 2:13).

The weekly Sabbaths of verses 1 through 3 proclaim *"the Sabbath rest."* It was a prophecy and a promise of the rest in Christ that remains to the people of God (Heb. 3 and 4).

Verses 4 and 5 proclaim the *"Feast of the Unleavened Bread."* This represents Christ's spotless, sinless body that was buried for humanity. The *"Feast of Unleavened Bread"* was on the 15th of the month through the 21st.

Verses 9 through 14 portray the *"Feast of Firstfruits."* This feast was conducted on about the 17th of the month, three days after the Passover, and typifies the Resurrection of Christ.

Verses 15 through 21 proclaim the *"Feast of Pentecost."* This would be 50 days after the Passover. This feast typifies the great outpouring of the Holy Spirit, *"And when the day of Pentecost was fully come."*

Verses 23 through 25 proclaim the *"Feast of Trumpets."* This was conducted in the seventh month and corresponded to some extent with our month of October. The previous feasts in type have been fulfilled. The Feast of Trumpets, Atonement, and Tabernacles have not yet been fulfilled. The *"Feast of Trumpets"* is a type of the coming Rapture of the Church.

Verses 26 through 32 proclaim the *"Feast of the Great Day of Atonement."* This was the Great Day of Atonement when Aaron the High Priest was to go into the most holy place to make atonement for all Israel, including himself and his family. The Lord Jesus Christ at the Second Coming will fulfill this type when He cleanses Israel in the newly-built Temple in Jerusalem at the beginning of the millennial reign.

Verses 33 through 44 portray the *"Feast of Tabernacles."* It would begin on about the 15th of our October and would last eight days. In St. John chapter 7, this is referred to when it says, *"On the last day, that great day of the feast."* It was on this day 16 centuries later that Jesus promised the Holy Spirit in fullness. This type portrays the coming 1000 year millennial reign. During this eight days, some 199 animals would be offered up in sacrifice. During the Millennium, these sacrifices will be reinstituted. They will be done so as a memorial (Zech. 14:16-21).

CHAPTER 24

Verses 1 through 4 portray the oil for the

NOTES

perpetual light.

The 2nd verse says it was a *"Command."* The golden lampstand was a portrayal of the Lord Jesus Christ Who is the light of the world. The golden lampstand sat to the immediate left as the priest walked in the door. It was the only light in the holy place. Likewise, Jesus is the only light in the world. There is no other light, *"They that sat in darkness saw great light"* (St. Matt. 4:16). Buddha is not a light; Karl Marx is not a light; Muhammad is not a light; Confucius is not a light. There is no light but Jesus Christ. The *"oil olive"* was a type of the Holy Spirit, *"How God anointed Jesus of Nazareth."* The Scripture said, *"To cause the lamps to burn continually."* The command was that the lamps should never go out. Likewise, the light of the Lord Jesus Christ that is in the child of God must *"burn continually."*

Verses 5 through 9 portray the *"shewbread"* (the bread of the face, because it sat before the face of God).

The 6th verse says, *"Six on a row, upon the pure table before the Lord."* Evidently the 12 cakes were stacked one upon the other, six in a stack, with a gold dish of frankincense at the top. Some say the cakes were square not round. The burning of the frankincense at the top of the stacks made the shewbread an offering by fire unto Jehovah, as mentioned in verse 7 of this chapter. Actually, the loaves were not burned in the fire for they were to be eaten by priests in the holy place as the most holy of the offerings (vs. 9). They simply became *"a memorial, even an offering made by fire"* through the bowls of burning frankincense on top of each stack.

Note that the stacks of shewbread were to be upon the *"pure table";* this was the table covered with pure gold that stood before the Lord. Also, pure frankincense was to be burned upon the pure table. This signifies that all things connected with Jehovah and His worship were to be pure, thus typifying the purity of life and conduct of the worshipers who came before him.

The 8th verse says that the shewbread was to be changed every Sabbath, and loaves that had been removed were to be eaten by the priests in the holy place. This was the most holy of all offerings made by fire. Not only was the light of the lamps to be burning continually, but the shewbread also was to be set continually before the Lord.

Verses 10 through 16 record the first jail (ward) in Israel.

The 12th verse portrays the careful question of the children of Israel, *"That the mind of the Lord might be showed them."* They were to do nothing according to their own dictates but only that which the Lord desired.

There seemed to be very few jails in Israel, and they were only with the intention that the Law be carried out. An individual if guilty of certain things was to repay what had been taken, stolen, or defrauded with 20 percent interest. If the crime was in the nature of the death penalty as this one was, it was to be carried out, *"Shall be put to death"* (vs. 16).

The Law as portrayed in verses 17 through 22 was to serve the *"stranger"* (Gentile) as well as *"one of your own country."* There was to be no partiality.

CHAPTER 25

The 25th chapter proclaims God's laws concerning the land, property built by man, the year of jubilee, and of slaves.

The year of jubilee was the most unique, innovative, and original economic plan ever given to humanity. Governor Huey Long of the State of Louisiana during the 1920's tried to model his economic program on God's *"year of jubilee."* He claimed that it was the most equal distribution of wealth of any plan ever devised, and so it was. The doctrine of this chapter is that the people of Israel and the land of Israel belonged to Jehovah, and that He, the Redeemer, had redeemed them both at the expense of His own precious blood.

Verses 1 through 4 proclaim by God that every *"seventh year shall be a sabbath of rest unto the land, a sabbath for the Lord."* It took faith for the children of Israel to believe God for the seventh and sabbath year. They would have to trust God to give them such a bountiful harvest on the sixth year that it would be more than enough to take care of the seventh. God

NOTES

promised that He would do just that.

Verses 5 through 7 proclaim that they were not to plant at all in this seventh year, but all the crops that grew of their own accord could be gathered by the owners, the servants, strangers in the midst, or even their stock.

Verses 8 through 10 proclaim the year of jubilee. It was the 50th year. Consequently, at this time there would be two years that no crops would be sown. At the end of the seventh and Sabbatical year (the 49th year), the ground was to lie fallow and then the 50th year as well, thus, making two years in a row which were to be held sacred.

On the *"great day of atonement"* (vs. 9), *"the trumpet of the jubilee was to sound."* It was to be *"throughout all your land."*

The 11th verse calls it "a jubilee", and in the 13th verse, *"You shall return every man unto his possession."*

The principles that these laws expressed are singular to the Bible. Private property or land was forbidden - it belonged to the Lord, *"For the land is mine"* (vs. 23). Usury upon money, or a percentage upon goods was not permitted in respect to loans to needy neighbors. All the food produced by the earth in the sabbatic and jubilee years was common property to be eaten but not to be stored. Land or its fruits might be mortgaged, but the mortgage became void at the jubilee, and at any time prior to the jubilee, either might be redeemed at the option of the borrower. A distinction was made by property created by man's industry (as for instance a house in a walled city) and property created by God, such as land. The house could be sold in perpetuity and, consequently, bequeathed by will. Land could never be treated as such. A house in a village was deemed to be an agricultural asset and could not, therefore, become personal property. The jubilee voided all contracts and released all slaves.

As stated, the *"trump of jubilee"* which proclaimed liberty to all was to be sounded on the *"great day of atonement."* The cancellation of all debts and the liberation of all slaves was effected by the death of the atoning lamb. Thus, was foreshadowed the worldwide redemption purchased by the spotless Lamb of God.

In Luke 4 when Jesus said, *"The Spirit of the Lord is upon me ...."* and then when He closed the dialogue by saying, *"to preach the acceptable year of the Lord,"* this typified the year of jubilee when liberty was proclaimed to all people. When the atonement of Christ is fully embraced, the sick, sinful, helpless, and needy are restored to health, holiness, power, and prosperity, as well as full dominion over Satan and membership and communion in God's family.

Whenever the jubilee trump sounded, all mortgages were cancelled, all servants released, and all bondages of men annulled. Debts were forgiven, and lands reverted to the original owners. The new start in business at the end of jubilee was based upon another year of release 50 years in the future, and, thereby, increased or diminished the value of a sale or mortgage. Likewise, as the Christian realizes the nearness or remoteness of the Coming of the Lord, so he places a low or a high value on earthly things.

CHAPTER 26

The 26th chapter gives the conditions of blessings in the land.

The promised blessings were phenomenal: (Vs. 4) *"Rain in due seasons,"* (Vs. 5) *"Your threshing shall reach unto the vintage,"* (Vs. 6) *"I will give peace in the land,"* (Vs. 7) *"You shall chase your enemies."* If certain things are done, *"I will set my tabernacle among you"* (vs. 11). And then He further said (vs. 12), *"And I will walk among you and will be your God, and ye shall be my people."*

The 13th verse ever reminds us of what He has done for us in our great deliverance, *"brought you forth out of the land of Egypt"* (a type of the world). And then He says, *"should not be their bondmen"* (slaves); *"broken the bands of your yoke"* (set us free); *"made you go upright."* This is a perfect description of redemption. Man does not and, in fact, cannot walk upright spiritually until the Lord sets him free. Sadly, most of the world today is in terrible bondage. Man has constantly thought that

NOTES

money and power would cause him to be *"upright."* This always fails as fail it must. The only one who can put man upright is Jesus.

Verses 14 through 39 describe the curses that would be upon the children of Israel if they did not obey God's laws and statutes. God means exactly what He says. For instance:

The 34th verse says, *"Then shall the land enjoy her sabbaths."* After David and Solomon, Israel largely forgot the commandments of the Lord. Among those commandments was the seventh year when crops were not to be sown or harvested. Then Nebuchadnezzar destroyed Jerusalem, and Israel was taken captive into Babylon. Their time of confinement was about 70 years, which accounted for all the "seventh" years that had been ignored. Once again we state, "God means what He says."

From verse 40 through 46 the door of mercy is opened to the backslider, *"If they shall confess their iniquity,"* then, *"If then their uncircumcised hearts be humbled."*

The 45th verse says that God will *"remember the covenant of their ancestors"* only if they do what He has told them to do, and that is to repent.

It must be remembered that God cannot and will not fulfill His covenants with men while they are in rebellion. They must come to repentance and obedience and meet the terms of God's covenants and promises before the benefits can be enjoyed. The theory of unconditional covenants and promises and of eternal life while living in sin is an idle fancy. No man has the blessing and curse of God on him at the same time - life for obedience and death for sin at the same time. No man can be saved and unsaved, converted and unconverted at the same time. The only way one can serve two masters is to serve one at a time, not both of them together. When sin is committed, it brings forth death, not life (Gen. 2:17; Ex. 32:32-33; Ezek. 18:4; Matt. 6:24; Rom. 6:16-23; I Cor. 6:9-11; Gal. 5:19-21).

The 44th verse says, *"I will not cast them away,"* simply meaning that God has not utterly cast away His people whom He foreknew; He will yet bring them back to repentance and make a great nation out of them (Isa. 11:10-12; Zech. 12:10-13; Rom. 11:1-2).

CHAPTER 27

The theme of Leviticus has been worship. The land called *"Israel, the Promised Land"* was God's land. It was Immanuel's land. Jesus Christ is the true Priest of Israel. Sadly, Israel valued Him at 30 pieces of silver, but He valued Israel and the land at the price of His own blood. Verses 1 through 13 concern vows to God. The vows were voluntary, and most vows were made in cases of illness and danger or under emotional impulse, either in thanksgiving for blessings received or pleading for things desired of God. A man might dedicate himself, his wife, his children, or his servants. The Law simply ordained that a religious tax according to the age and sex be paid for special vows. The money went to the priest.

No man was forced to make a vow, but he was under obligation to pay one after making it (Num. 30:2). According to Psalms 15:4, one of the characteristics of a righteous man is that he keeps his word. A person should not use vows to obtain an answer to prayer or to bring about some desire. Faith is the ingredient that will produce answers to prayer and not unnecessary vows before God. For instance, Jephthah made a rash vow in his anxious hours of striving for a victory over his enemies and had reason to regret it (Judg. 11:29-30). He would have defeated his enemies anyway, for God would have given him victory.

If an individual rashly makes a vow before God and then finds that it's impossible to keep, the individual should repent before God of making the vow and ask His forgiveness, then lay it aside. However, if it's possible to keep it, it should be kept.

Verses 26 through 33 proclaim three things that belong to God eternally:

1. Firstborn of man and beasts (vs. 26).
2. All devoted things (vs. 28-29).
3. All tithes of all people (vs. 30-33).

Why did God demand this? The first two were a part of the Mosaic Law, and were not carried over into the New Testament.

The firstborn of man and beast, as well as the 10 percent of one's income (the tithe),

pointed toward the firstborn who was to come, namely the Lord Jesus Christ. Jesus was the firstborn of His mother (Matt. 1:25). As such, Jesus was taken to the Temple by Mary and Joseph to be offered to God (Luke 2:22-24). Since Luke omits mention of a price being paid to redeem the child, he may have intended the incident to be regarded as the dedication of the firstborn to the service of God. Jesus is also the firstborn of His Heavenly Father. He is the firstborn of all creation, not in the sense that He Himself is a created being, but, rather, that as God's Son (in the incarnation), He was His agent in creation, and, hence, has authority over all created things (Col. 1:15-17). Similarly, He is the firstborn in the new creation by being raised first from the dead, and is thus Lord over the Church (Col. 1:18; Rev. 1:5). He is the firstborn in a whole family of children of God who are destined to bear His image.

Finally, God's people, both living and dead, can be described as the firstborn who are enrolled in heaven, since they share the privileges of the Son.

THE
BOOK OF NUMBERS

◼

The divine title for this book in the Hebrew is *"In the Wilderness."* Its subject, therefore, is pilgrimage and warfare. It begins with *"And"* indicating that it is only a part of the Law of Moses, which was originally in five sections, rather than in five books.

The theme of Leviticus is worship; that of Numbers is warfare. We must be warriors as well as worshipers.

◼

CHAPTER 1

Verses 2 through 19 portray to us two things:

A. That God would now set His "Church" in order;

B. That He did so in the wilderness.

God has brought Israel to this place so that they would be wholly dependent upon Him for food, clothing, health, protection, and, actually, for all things. Israel was to learn what God could be to the heart that trusts Him. These lessons could not be learned either in Egypt or Canaan. They could only be learned in the wilderness. We as Christians oftentimes chaff at the *"wilderness"* experiences. Much of the so-called Gospel of the last few years has tried to abrogate this part of God's training ground. As a result, we have bred a generation of spiritual pygmies. Admittedly, most of Israel's experience in the wilderness was of their own doing and because of their own failure. Of that we do not particularly speak at this time. However, God definitely intended for Israel to go through a wilderness experience. His intention was that it was thoroughly instructed but yet

short lived. But, due to her failure, it was extended to 40 years.

The 3rd verse says, *"From twenty years old and upward, all that are able to go forth to war in Israel."* The organization of each tribe was to be for the purpose of warfare. The Lord Himself in verse 1 had given the instructions for this organization. Regrettably, there is very little understanding today of what the Church is all about. We have been taught mainly that we are only to receive blessings. However, the real purpose of the Church is, *"all that are able to go forth to war."* Paul told Timothy, *"War a good warfare."* He also said, *"We wrestle not against flesh and blood"* (Eph. 6:12). The only opposition in this world against the powers of darkness is the Lord Jesus Christ by the power of the Holy Spirit ensconced in the Church. Our mission is *"war"*; our calling is *"war"* against the powers of darkness. The world lies in darkness, and the only light is the Lord Jesus Christ. There is no other. The entirety of the effort is spiritual warfare and, hence, 14 times in this chapter occur the words, *"all that were able to go forth to war."* Fellowship with God means warfare with the world.

It is a sobering thought when we realize that of the 603,550 people, only two made it to the Promised Land. They perished because of unbelief. As is recorded in Exodus 32, even though God gave them grace for their terrible sin of the golden calf, God knew their rebellious hearts would continue in the same direction of unbelief, and so they did.

The book of Numbers records events from this day in question to the death of Aaron, a period of over 38 years. It would be, by and large, 38 years of unbelief. For our own spiritual edification we need to look at these names and numbers very closely. They did not make it; because of unbelief, they perished.

In the 12 tribes Ephraim took the place of Joseph, and Manasseh took the place of Levi in the 12-tribe arrangement of Israel. The tribe of Levi was not counted, being chosen as the ministers of the other tribes and without any definite allotment of land among the other 12 tribes.

CHAPTER 2

The 2nd chapter has to do with God's order which authorizes God's blessings. All was laid out by the Lord. No individual chose his own position; God chose it for him. Likewise, the Church does not call men to be apostles, prophets, evangelists, pastors, or teachers; God calls them, *"And the Lord spake unto Moses and unto Aaron, saying . . . ."* The problem with the Church is that it tries to incorporate the ways of the world, then asks for the blessings of the Holy Spirit upon such. God will have none of it. If God's order is abrogated, God's blessing will be withheld. As God had a place for every single Israelite, God has a place for every single child of God. We are to find that place, get in that place, and let God bless us in that place.

The 2nd verse says, *"By his own standard, with the ensign of their father's house."* Tradition says that each standard (flag) was of the color of the stone on the breastplate of the high priest that bore its name. Likewise, tradition says that on each standard, one of the 12 constellations was depicted as its sign. The position of the standard and of the entirety of the tribe was determined by the position of the Tabernacle. Everything focused around the Tabernacle. The Tabernacle was the center, the core, and the heart of all of Israel, because it was there that God dwelt. God has always sought a dwelling place among His people. Now He no longer occupies a Tabernacle or a Temple made by hands. He, in fact, occupies the Temple of our hearts (I Cor. 3:16). Likewise, everything must revolve around the moving and the flow of the Holy Spirit. We are the

NOTES

Tabernacle; He occupies us. We look to Him, not the Pope in Rome, not some denominational headquarters, not some presbytery of men, but to Him. We seek the goodwill, counsel, and advice of our brethren. We want it; we desire it. However, we will not move until there is a *"thus saith the Lord."*

When God's instructions were followed to the letter, there was order. God is never the author of confusion but always of order. One of the reasons we have so little success in spiritual warfare is because there is so little order. Yes, we have man's order, but we do not have God's order, and man's order is no order at all.

When marching, Judah went first. The 9th verse says, *"In the camp of Judah."* And then it said, *"These shall first set forth."* Therefore, Israel was led by praise, for Judah means praise.

As they marched, Dan *"shall go hindmost with their standards"* (vs. 31). Dan means *"judgment."* Therefore, Israel was led by *"praise"* and pronounced *"judgment"* on all those who would try to attack her from the rear. In the middle was the Tabernacle which speaks of *"communion."* The praise of Judah came from the Tabernacle. The power of the judgment of Dan, likewise, came from the Tabernacle.

The 17th verse says, *"Every man in his place by their standards."* If every Christian is in his place according to the Tabernacle (the Spirit of God), it will be a mighty army.

The last verse (34) says that they marched when the Lord said march, and they camped when the Lord said camp.

As we have surveyed this chapter, we have learned about God's order. We have learned that *"praise"* must lead the way. And if *"praise"* rightly leads the way, drawing sustenance from the *"communion"* that is in the center which comes from the Tabernacle and nourishes all, then divine judgment will protect the rear guard against all of the powers of darkness that would seek to hinder the Church of the Living God.

CHAPTER 3

Chapter 3 presents the numbering and the service of the Levites.

It was grace that entrusted the Levites with the Tabernacle and its vessels when on the march. This is even more beautiful when one considers that Levi along with Simeon was cursed by God (judgment) because of their terrible sin of killing the Shechemites. Jacob, on his death bed, said, *"Cursed be their anger."* He further said, *"I will divide them in Jacob and scatter them in Israel"* (Gen. 49:7).

So, in the 6th verse when the Lord says, *"Bring the tribe of Levi near, and present them before Aaron the priest, that they may minister unto him,"* it presents itself as a beautiful work of grace.

This is hard, if not impossible, for the natural man to conceive or comprehend. Man constantly tries to earn his way with God, and God will have none of it. That God would use Levi at all, especially due to his past, would be especially obnoxious to the world and even to the Church. However, mercy is the nature of grace. No, God does not extend grace to one who continues in rebellion, except to try to bring him to a place of repentance. And then, if there is repentance, grace will cover and wash the past and God will use the individual mightily. That is the nature of God; that is the nature of grace.

The 8th verse says, *"And they shall keep all the instruments of the Tabernacle of the congregation."* It should be readily understood that there was far greater dignity in carrying the least pin of the Tabernacle than to wield the mighty sceptre of Egypt. From this we should learn that any service in the work of God, no matter how seemingly small, is of eternal consequence and, thereby, of far greater import than anything the world might have to offer.

The *"firstborn"* of verses 11 through 13 who were owned and *"hallowed"* by God of *"both man and beast"* were types of *"the firstborn"* Who was to come, the Lord Jesus Christ, *"the firstborn of many brethren."*

Verses 14 through 26 give us the work of the

"Gershonites." They were in charge of the tapestry of the Tabernacle, which included four coverings: linen, goat's hair, ram skins, and badger skins. They were also in charge of the hanging of the outer court, the walled curtains, the door curtains of the outer court, and the cords. The Holy Spirit outlined their duties down to the minute detail. Therefore, the *"Gershonites"* had absolutely no doubt as to their task. Likewise, the Holy Spirit has designed for each and every Christian his duties down to the most minute detail. Unfortunately, most of us are so taken up with our own pursuits that we know little of His perfect plan for our life, much less the carrying out of the same.

Verses 27 through 32 give us the work of the *"Kohathites."* They were in charge of the Tabernacle contents, which included the *"ark of the covenant"* and the *"table of shewbread,"* along with the *"candlestick,"* the *"brazen and golden altars,"* and, with, no doubt, the *"brazen laver."* They were also in charge of the *"vessels of the sanctuary,"* along with the *"hanging, and inner veil."*

It would seem that the *"Kohathites"* were the most important. However, God did not look at it this way. All had to carry out their work for the work of God to be complete. If the slighest individual let down in their task, the whole Tabernacle was affected.

From verses 33 through 38, we are given the work of the *"Merarites."* They were in charge of the *"boards of the tabernacle,"* plus the *"bars that hold the boards,"* as well as the *"pillars of the tabernacle,"* and the *foundation sockets."* What is the task that God has given you to perform? Is it to take care of the *"sockets"* under the foundation, or to attend the *"ark of the covenant?"* One is just as important as the other, for they all represent Christ. Repeatedly the Lord in His earthly ministry sought to impress upon His disciples the ministry of servants. Regrettably, how little we have learned this.

These three, *"the Gershonites, the Kohathites, and the Merarites,"* were many years before the sons of Levi. Now their descendents will carry on this great work.

CHAPTER 4

The 4th chapter portrays the work of the priests along with the other various groups who served in the tearing down, moving, and setting up again of the Tabernacle. God gave explicit instructions concerning the same. They were to be followed to the letter. Even though this was under Law, still, under Grace the instructions in minute directions of the Holy Spirit are just as binding. If we would seek the face of God as Moses sought the face of God in order that we might have direction, surely the results of the Ministry would be far more prolific. Let's look at some of the things that God demanded:

"The covering." Each piece was to be handled according to instructions. The disposition of these coverings, which were different in some cases, that hid the Ark, the table, the lampstand, the altar of incense, the vessels of ministry, and the brazen altar, told of the sufferings of Christ and the glories that should follow. For instance, over the *"ark of the covenant,"* the *"veil"* that separated the holy place from the most holy place was to cover the *"ark."* The veil had cherubims embroidered on it proclaiming the holiness of God. Next would go *"the covering of badger skins."* This signifies Christ's humanity. And then finally, *"And shall spread over it a cloth wholly of blue."* This speaks of salvation as being from a heavenly source. The *"table of shewbread"* would have a *"cloth of blue"* placed over it, signifying that Jesus Christ was heaven's gift, and then over that, *"a cloth of scarlet,"* signifying that heaven's gift would shed His blood for a dying humanity, and would *"cover the same with a cover of badger skins."* This typifies the incarnation and His humanity.

On the *"golden altar"* would be *"spread a cloth of blue,"* signifying that worship ascends to the heavenlies. It was then covered with *"badger skins,"* once again signifying the incarnation and Christ's humanity opening up the way to heaven's gate by way of worship.

The *"ashes from the altar,"* signifying the judgment of God that had been satisfied, were

spread over with *"a purple cloth."* This signifies that a king would die for humanity; of course, that King was Christ Jesus.

Once again the *"badger skins"* went over it, signifying His incarnation and humanity.

There is a possibility that some of the larger items were put on wagons, but basically, some pieces of the Tabernacle furniture were carried by men, *"shall come to bear it"* (vs. 15).

It should be noticed that most of the articles of furniture were finally covered by *"badger skins,"* signifying that outwardly *"there is no beauty that men should desire Him"* (Isa. 53:2).

"But they should not touch any holy thing lest they die" (vs. 15). The priests alone were to handle, cover, wrap, and otherwise prepare each item for travel, then unpack and set all pieces back in order for service when the Tabernacle was set up again. Even though the priests were Levites, still, no ordinary Levite (one not in the priesthood) was permitted to touch any of the holy things, lest he die. He could only carry them after they were wrapped and ready for travel. It was a death penalty for others to do this work.

Verse 16 tells us that Aaron, the High Priest, had *"the oversight of all the tabernacle, and of all that therein is."* Aaron was a type of Christ and, thereby, had the oversight. Christ is the Head of the Church (Col. 1:18). Unfortunately, most of the church world treats Him as a passive head instead of an active head. Thereby, men are appointed by other men and given the headship of the Body. This, of course, is prevalent in the Catholic church with the Pope, and their hierarchy as its head. But, sadly, it is also prevalent in the Protestant world. Make no mistake about it, Christ is the Head, and He is an active Head. Anyone who attempts to usurp authority over Him will suffer spiritual death.

Verses 21 through the balance of the chapter give the work of the *"Gershonites and the Merarites,"* including the *"Kohathites."* These Levites performed all the work of the Tabernacle. Their duties were spelled out minutely. As well, the Lord has given every single person who names the name of Christ a special task in the kingdom of God. If one of these Levites fell down at their task, all the others suffered. Likewise, if one single Christian falls down in his task, all suffer. Paul, in Romans 12, graphically outlined the various duties, specifics, gifts, and ministry that is given to every single child of God.

Verses 34 through 49 give us the exact numbers of these individuals. That's how important they were to God. Also, every single child of God is numbered by the Lord and expected to carry out the task that is assigned to him. In Elijah's day the Lord knew exactly how many had not bowed the knee to Baal. He knew exactly how many were to attend the Tabernacle. At this time, He knows exactly how many name the name of Christ and are fulfilling their task.

CHAPTER 5

Chapter 5 is basically divided into two parts:

Verses 1 through 10 pertain to religious and social laws;

Verses 11 through 31 pertain to the law of jealousy.

In regard to the religious and social laws, these were given by a loving God for the benefit of a contaminated people. Many today blanch at God's Laws (His Word), but only because they refuse to admit that they are contaminated and that God is everlasting and over all.

Verse 4, *"Put them out without the camp,"* is the first reference to carrying out the commands regarding segregation of persons with contagious diseases – hospitalizing them or putting them under quarantine. They, no doubt, were treated humanely in a prepared place outside the camp.

Verses 5 through 8 basically speak of the sin of stealing. No jail for such a crime was mentioned. Actually, the culprits were to *"confess their sin,"* return the item they had stolen or the equivalent thereof in money, *"with the principal thereof,"* and then, *"add unto it the fifth part."* They were to *"give it unto him against whom he had trespassed."* If he were dead, they were to give it to *"kinsmen."* If *"no kinsman"* were allowed, they were to give it *"unto the Lord."* If such was done today we

NOTES

would, no doubt, have less stealing.

The law of jealousy, as outlined in verses 11 through 31, was, in effect, a loving provision made by God for the protection of helpless women. The *"spirit of jealousy,"* as outlined in verse 14, is the work of a supernatural diabolic influence, or a passion stirred up by the imagination. The purpose of the trial was to determine the truth and justify the woman if her husband were merely jealous, or prove her worthy of punishment if she were guilty. In these passages no provision is made for a jealous wife.

This *"law of jealousy"* would seem strange to the modern mind. However, one must remember that it was designed by God, with minute instructions given by God, and as we have stated, all of this to protect helpless women. At that time, women had very little status. Due to Eve being the instigator of the fall in the Garden of Eden, it seems that the status of women was diminished somewhat. This *"law of jealousy"* is God's designated protection of women, which would be ultimately completed at Calvary.

As is described in verse 15, the *"offering of jealousy"* consisted first of all of *"barley meal,"* which is a type of the Word of God.

The *"holy water"* of verse 17 was water from the brazen laver which had been sanctified to holy use only. The *"earthen vessel"* was a type of Christ and His incarnation. The *"dust"* from the *"floor of the tabernacle"* was symbolic of vileness and misery, and a state of condemnation. The dust was *"put into the water."* The woman was then made to drink *"this bitter water."* The bitter water, if the woman were guilty, would cause tremendous physical infirmities, if not death. If not guilty, there would be no ill effect. No doubt, the Holy Spirit superintended this.

In a way, this is a type of the whole of humanity; the difference being that all are guilty. However, instead of us having to drink the cup, Jesus drank the cup in our place (St. Luke 22:42). He tasted death for every man.

CHAPTER 6

Chapter 6 portrays the voluntary Nazarite vows.

Nearly always the term *"Nazarite"* is thought of as referring to men, but according to this, a woman could also take the Nazarite vow (vs. 2) and separate herself unto God and His service.

From the Nazarite idea came the Rachabites (Jer. 35), the Essenes, Anchorites, hermits, monks, and other monastic orders. To say that Christ was a Nazarite is unscriptural, for He drank of the fruit of the vine and touched the dead, which Nazarites were forbidden to do (Matt: 9:25; 11:19; 26:29; Mark 14:25). Whether He cut His hair or not is not stated. But we know that His consecration was more complete and genuine than that of a Nazarite, because He was sanctified when He was sent into the world (St. John 10:36) and depended on the Holy Spirit's anointing to distinguish Him as separated unto God, rather than the outward show of abstinence from grapes and refusal to cut His hair or touch the dead.

Incidentally, the word *"Nazarene"* of Matthew 2:23 had no connection with "Nazarite", for it simply means an inhabitant of Nazareth, a place whose name bore reproach (St. John 1:46). The word *"Nazarene,"* as used in Acts 24:5, means a follower of Jesus of Nazareth.

Separation is the keynote of this chapter. Both, chapters 6 and 7, should idealize the Spirit-filled life.

Verse 3 said, *"He shall separate himself from wine and strong drink."* Wine, being the source of earthly joy, was to be rejected by the Nazarite. The *"joy of the Lord is his strength."*

Verse 5 says, *"Shall no razor come upon His head."* The Nazarite vow could be for a short period of time or for life. But, whatever time it was, his hair could not be cut. In the New Testament (I Cor. 11) long hair is a shame to a man. The meekness and gentleness of Christ composes the Christian's crown, but to the natural man that type of meekness has the appearance of effeminacy and is regarded with contempt. The long hair symbolizes weakness.

NOTES

Thus the Nazarite was and is an enigma to the children of this world. To be joyful, he withdrew from joy (wine). To be strong, he became weak (long hair).

The 6th verse says, *"He shall come at no dead body."* Natural affection was not to have the first claim in the life of separation to God or even to interrupt it. Natural affection does have *"its"* place, but it is not to have *"His"* place. If the Nazarite touched a dead body the 9th verse says, *"Then he shall shave his head."* In other words, he would have to start all over again by offering up four different sacrifices (vss. 14 and 15). His life of separation would have to be resumed afresh. By the offering up of sacrifices, which admitted that he was a sinner, he could not boast of his past consecration.

The 18th verse says, *"and shall take the hair of the head of his separation, and put it in the fire which is under the sacrifice of the peace offerings."* The long hair which he was forced to cut might tempt him to keep it as a proud memorial of his consecration. He must throw it into the fire to be burned. What a lesson for us today.

Verses 22 through 27 immediately follow the *"law of the Nazarite,"* and pertain to the blessings of the Lord, *"The Lord bless thee, and keep thee."* Even though all the separation was done by the Nazarite, he must ever understand that the separation itself contained no blessing. The blessing came from the Lord.

The 25th verse says, *"The Lord make his face shine upon thee."* What a beautiful thing to have *"His face shine upon thee."* However, once again we must understand that all of the separation and the "thou shalt nots" of the preceding verses do not make His face shine upon us. It is done solely by grace, *"And be gracious unto thee."* How very many times we think that the blessings come because of our separation, consecration, or dedication. However, it must forever be understood that God cannot bless sinful man, irrespective of his dedication or consecration, but, rather, He blesses Christ within us and Christ alone.

CHAPTER 7

Chapter 7 concerns itself with the dedication of the altar and the gifts of the 12 tribes of Israel. What lesson does this 7th chapter teach us?

The 3rd verse says, *"And they brought their offering before the Lord."* If one will notice, he will see that the 12 offerings of the princes were exactly alike. They were actually gifts from the tribes, not from the princes personally. This indicated that all the tribes of Israel were equally indebted to God for blessings, so all should testify of their obligation to Him and share alike in expressing thanksgiving. The vessels were all sacrificial ones; the animals were all clean beasts fit for sacrifice. Everything was intended to show the gratitude and worship of the nation. Such equality excluded all jealousy and competition with one another to see who could give the best or most costly things to God. Thus, the sin of emulation was curtailed (Gal. 5:20).

As well, it should be noticed that the tribes came in order of their encampment around the Tabernacle.

If man would have been authoring the account of these offerings, he would probably have compressed such into just one verse – for they were all identical. But to God, they were so precious that they are minutely detailed and repeated. So, the offerings of little Benjamin and his gifts are given as much importance as great Judah and his offerings.

Likewise, each gift contained silver and gold. However, the greater part of the offering was always the clean animals that were offered for sacrifice. At this present time, it seems that we have reversed the order. We have increased the silver and the gold and decreased Calvary of which the animal sacrifices were a symbol. Peter, with John, said, *"Silver and gold have I none; but such as I have give I thee."* The Church may have silver and gold, but most of all it must have, *"such as I have,"* which was Calvary.

Verse 89 says, *"Then he heard the one speaking unto him from off the mercy seat."* It

NOTES

was the same voice that had spoken from the flame of the burning bush. It was also the same voice that said, *"Learn of me"* (Matt. 11:29). May we earnestly hear that voice today, whether it be through the Word of God by inspiration, by the preached Word, or by the sweet, small voice of the Holy Spirit to our spirit. However God speaks, it will never take away, add to, or abrogate the Word of God. It will always coincide with God's Word.

CHAPTER 8

Chapter 8 pertains to the consecration of the Levites. The Holy Spirit begins this consecration by a portrayal of the golden lamp stand and the light that it gave. It was a symbol of what the Levites were to be.

Verses 1 through 4 portray the first lighting of the lamps which were to burn perpetually as a symbol of the Divine presence. The *"seven lamps"* on the one lamp stand spoke of perfection. The *"candlestick"* was a type of Christ. There is no light in the entirety of the world but Christ; all else is false. The 4th verse says, *"And this work of the candlestick was of beaten gold,"* in other words, pure gold. First of all, the lamp with its branches totalling seven lamps was all of one piece. The center branch portrays Christ. The three branches on either side portray the Church. It seems the branches were not welded or fastened onto the main stem, but instead, the entirety of the work was one piece. The Scripture says, *"according to the pattern which the Lord had showed Moses."* The *"pattern"* for the light was designed by the Lord. The greatest sin of the Church is instituting its own pattern, in other words, that which is not the Word of God. Jesus likened Himself and the Church to the portrayal of the golden lamp stand by saying, *"At that day you shall know that I am in my Father, and you in me, and I in you"* (St. John 14:20).

In verse 7 the *"water of purifying"* was probably taken from the laver and prepared according to the law of the red heifer (Num. 19:1-22). The literal meaning is, *"water of the sin offering,"* as it was made by sprinkling the ashes of a red heifer into the water which was then sprinkled on the people.

In verse 8 two *"young bullocks"* were offered as an atonement, along with the *"meat (meal) offering."* No peace offering was offered because the subject was not worship but cleansing from sin. The atonement was for the Levites and not for Israel as a whole. This atonement preshadowed Calvary.

Verses 9 through 14 portray the following: *"The children of Israel shall put their hands upon the Levites."* Both the Levites and all Israel were gathered together at the Tabernacle for this solemn consecration. Through chosen representatives, no doubt, all Israel was commanded to lay hands upon the Levites. This was to signify that Israel freely and completely gave them to Jehovah as His servants and freed them from all secular work in order that they might devote themselves wholly to the spiritual, physical, and educational needs of the nation. This was a formal dedication of the Levites by prayer and laying on the hands of Aaron and the people. The congregation, by the laying of their hands on the Levites, portrayed as a symbol the imparting of their blessings upon them and assured them of their support and cooperation. In turn, the Levites laid their hands upon the bullocks as a sign of imparting their sins to the animals being offered to make atonement for their sins.

The Scripture says in the 19th verse, *"And to make an atonement for the children of Israel: That there be no plague among the children of Israel."* The Levites were to carry on the work of the Tabernacle, performing the services needed to keep Israel free from sin, condemnation, sickness, and hell. All atonement for Israel was made to this end, that God might be in their midst. The priests were to make proper atonement for the nation as a whole and for the sins of each individual. Sin was to be kept in check so that no plague would be among them. Sickness and plagues were connected with sin and rebellion. God had promised to take away sickness upon obedience (Ex. 25) and to keep Israel in perfect health upon continued obedience (Ex. 15:26; Lev. 26; Deut. 28). He actually healed everyone so that there was not a feeble one in all their tribes (Psa. 105:37; 107:20). The means of heal-

ing and health were made a part of the Mosaic Covenant.

It should be noticed from the 19th verse that freedom from plagues is connected with atonement. Certain plagues were stayed when atonement was made (II Sam. 24:18-25). Others were stayed in answer to prayer (Num. 11:2).

Verse 21 says, *"And the Levites were purified and they washed their clothes."* If the Levites had gone into the Tabernacle to serve and minister without proper consecration and before they were completely set apart and accepted by God, they would have been destroyed, as were Nadab and Abihu. Likewise, today sin will destroy all that come before the Lord, even those who are called into His work. Even under the great Covenant of Grace, God can condone sin no more now than He could then. As it destroyed then, it will destroy now. As it killed then, it will kill now.

———■———

CHAPTER 9

Numbers 9 is broken up into two parts. Verses 1 through 14 pertain to the second Passover. Verses 15 through 23 concern the guiding presence of the Lord. The guiding presence would be there only if there was redemption by blood as evidenced in the Passover. The Lord can only give us His guidance and His presence if we are totally trusting in the blood. The shed Blood of Christ alone saves and cleanses. It alone avails; God honors it alone. Regrettably and sadly, the modern Church little believes, preaches, or proclaims the Blood. Consequently, there is no guiding presence of the Lord.

No man was allowed to keep the Passover when out of the land or away from where the Tabernacle or Temple was located. Paul and others traveled from all parts of the Roman Empire to keep the various feasts at Jerusalem (Acts 2:1-14; 20:16; I Cor. 16:8). As well, there was to be but one place of sacrifice (Deut. 12:3-26). The reason for this was because it was God's dwelling place, between the Mercy Seat and the Cherubim in the Tabernacle or the Temple. Now, due to Christ's atoning work at

Calvary and the Resurrection, the Lord dwells within our hearts. Therefore, the Passover, which pointed to a finished work that was yet to come, has been discontinued because the work has been finished. Now, the child of God partakes of the Lord's Supper which is an outgrowth of the Passover. It can be taken anywhere or at any time, simply because wherever the child of God takes it is where the Lord abides (I Cor. 3:16).

Verse 15 says, *"The cloud covered the tabernacle."* This was during the day and at night. *"There was upon the tabernacle as it were the appearance of fire."* What a sight that must have been; the constant abiding presence of God by day and by night. Jesus said, *"Lo, I am with you always."* They were told when to journey, *"That the children of Israel journeyed,"* and they were told when to stop, *"There the children of Israel pitched their tents."* These verses give us a loving picture of true liberty because of absolute dependence. God protected them by day and by night. He planned for them, He chose their camping ground, He decided when they were to march, and when they were to rest. According to the Word of the Lord, they journeyed, and according to the Word of the Lord, they abode in their tents. The Lord led them so beautifully. If He did so much under the Old Covenant, will He not do even more under a New Covenant based on better promises?

—■—

CHAPTER 10

Numbers 10 is basically divided into three sections: the blowing of the trumpets, the order of the march, and the invitation extended.

At this time there were only two sons of Aaron who were priests, so, only two trumpets were made. In the time of Joshua there were seven trumpets which were made of rams' horns and used for special purposes (Josh. 6:4). In the time of Solomon there were 120 priests with trumpets (II Chron. 5:12).

The long blowing on both trumpets called the whole assembly together. A long blowing

on one alone called only the princes together. An alarm was in short, sharp tones instead of a continuous note, unless there was a long one at the end. The first alarm caused the camps in the east to move; the second caused those on the south to move; the third and fourth caused those on the north and west to move. These last two camps were not mentioned here, but the Septuagint reads, *"And when you blow the third alarm, the camps on the west shall begin their march; and when you blow the fourth alarm, the camps on the north shall begin their march."* Here we have the greatest order and discipline for the Israelite camps. No military march of others could be better regulated, and, no doubt, no other great organization was better trained to respond quickly to their duties. This is understandable, for Moses was once a great military man in Egypt.

The 3rd verse says, *"At the door of the tabernacle of the congregation,"* meaning that when the trumpets blew it was for the purpose of gathering the representatives of each tribe to the Tabernacle. The blowing of the horns in whatever perspective, whether for the sound of alarm or otherwise, was a type of Holy Ghost filled preachers of the Gospel proclaiming the Word of God. God help all preachers to blow a "certain sound."

If they did so, verse 9 says, *"And you shall be remembered before the Lord your God."* Those that blew the trumpets were basically responsible for the safety, the welfare, and the protection of God's people. Likewise, they that preach this great Gospel of Jesus Christ are responsible for the spiritual welfare of all those who sit under them. God give us preachers who will blow the trumpet loudly!

It seems the words, *"The cloud was taken up from off the tabernacle,"* mean that the cloud that hovered over the Tabernacle moved to the front of the column to lead the children of Israel. That was the sign that the Tabernacle was to be torn down and prepared for moving. The actual structure of the Tabernacle was borne by the Gershonites and Merarites immediately after the camp of Judah, which consisted of Judah, Issachar and Zebulun with Judah leading. They could perhaps have the Tabernacle set up by the time the Kohathites arrived with the sacred vessels and furniture. The

Kohathites were the marchers in the middle of the 12 tribes. The following is the order of march:

1. Judah – They led the way.
2. Issachar.
3. Zebulun.

(These were followed by Gershonites and Merarites with the Tabernacle.)

4. Reuben.
5. Simeon.
6. Gad.

(Then came the Kohathites with the sanctuary.)

And then after them:

7. Ephraim.
8. Manasseh.
9. Benjamin.
10. Asher.
11. Naphatali.
12. Dan.

It is said of Dan, *"Which was the rereward of all the camps throughout their host"* (vs. 25). So this was the line of march and it was orchestrated by the Holy Spirit. Actually, the blowing of the trumpets did two things. First of all, it called the people to the Tabernacle, and second, it set them in motion for Canaan.

That is the task of the preacher of the Gospel. We are first to call the people to the Lord (the Tabernacle) and, second, to set them in motion toward glory land. Hallelujah!

The 29th verse records the great invitation that was given to "Hobab" (Jethro). The invitation was, *"Come thou with us, and we will do thee good."* These are the words of the Holy Spirit through Moses. They were not only given to Jethro but also to the whole of mankind. God helps us to carry out the Great Commission of Jesus Christ to take this Gospel to a lost and dying world. What is the good that He has promised? *"I am come that they might have life and that they might have it more abundantly"* (St. John 10:10). Sadly, Jethro foolishly refused. I wonder if his refusal had anything to do with the constant harping and complaining of Israel as is recorded in chapter 11. I wonder how much bickering, fighting, strife, turmoil, complaining and murmuring in the Church today causes millions to say, as Jethro said in verse 30, *"I will not go"*?

In verse 33 the words, *"To search out a*

resting place for them," speaks of loving, tender care by the Holy Spirit for Israel. The activity of Israel centered around the Ark. Our activity today must center around the Word of God, Who is Jesus Christ. Verse 34 says, *"And the cloud of the Lord was upon them by day."* God help us that the *"cloud of the Lord"* will be upon us!

In verse 35 the words, *"Rise up, Lord, and let thine enemies be scattered,"* are a petition of protection and praise. And then, *"Return, oh Lord, unto the many thousands of Israel."* Whether the Ark was moving or whether it was stationary, it was to be saturated with praise. Today, with the greater Covenant, our very lives should be filled with songs of praise.

CHAPTER 11

Chapter 10 closes with a beautiful exclamation of the tender love of the Lord going out before Israel to search out a resting place for them. But then, tragically, chapter 11 opens with the murmurs of the people complaining of the fatigue of the journey and the discomfort of the resting place. Murmuring means unbelief, so the result was death.

Verse 1 says, *"And when the people complained, it displeased the Lord: And the Lord heard it."* God hears every complaint. It only needed the test of the wilderness to make visible the incurable belief and ignorance of their hearts. Their murmuring amounted to open rebellion, so the Lord sent fire among the worst ones and consumed them in all the uttermost parts of the camp. Most likely, the fire came out from the holy place and sought out the worst offenders by the direction of the Lord. Murmuring and complaining will bring the fire of God's judgment, causing spiritual death today just as it did then.

The 4th verse says, *"And the mixed multitude that was among them fell a lusting."* These would be the descendants of the original servants of Abraham, Isaac, and Jacob, besides a few Egyptians who had married Israelites (Lev. 24:10) and the Kenites who also went with Israel. The "mixed multitude" given here proves that the children of Israel were not the same as the mixed multitude and had not integrated with other people. Very rarely would an Israelite marry one of another nation. Judah did (Gen. 38); and Moses (Ex. 2-3; Num. 12); and Boaz (Ruth 4). Here and there it happened, but this was contrary to God's will in general and to the Law in particular. This *"mixed multitude"* easily remembered the so-called good things in Egypt but did not remember the slave master's lash. They then proceeded to criticize the *"manna"* which God had given them. How successful Satan is in glamorizing his bondage and denigrating God's blessing. How quick we are to believe it.

Verses 10 through 15 find Moses joining the people in complaining, *"Wherefore hast thou afflicted thy servant?"* Regrettably, if the pressure is applied enough, the very strongest among us will begin to complain. Moses, under pressure, begins to accuse God of causing him all this trouble. He considered it an affliction to be under such a load and felt he was not favored of God when he was given the responsibility of taking Israel out of Egypt. He was in such despair that he requested to die, *"And if thou deal thus with me, kill me, I pray thee, out of hand."* This occasion was a test of faith not only for all the people, but for Moses as well. Regrettably, all failed.

In verse 16 the Lord says, *"Gather unto me seventy men of the elders of Israel."* Just when and by whom the 70 elders were chosen, appointed, or elected is not known, but they existed about a year before this mention of them (Ex. 24:1-11). Here, they were commissioned and anointed with the Holy Spirit to take part in the responsibility of Moses as head of the nation. Jewish tradition says that this was the beginning of the Sanhedrin. Just where the 70 came from as to tribes is not known, but if six had been taken from each of the 12 tribes, there would have been 72 men. One thing is clear, and that is they were the elders of Israel.

"Why came we forth out of Egypt?" was the insult hurled at God in verse 20. Whenever we murmur and complain, we actually praise the devil. By our complaining we are claiming that God is not able. *"Because that you have despised the Lord which is among you"* is what

God said of them. It doesn't matter where you put man, he sins. Placed in Eden, he sins. Placed on the renewed earth after the flood, he sins. Placed in the miracle-filled wilderness, he sins. Placed in the land of milk and honey, he sins. Placed in a New Covenant at Pentecost, he sins.

Moses had seen more miracles than any human being who had ever lived. And, yet, in response to where the diet of meat will come from, he asks, *"Shall the flocks and the herds be slain for them, or shall all the fish of the sea be gathered together for them?"* (vs. 22). Unbelief blinds us to miracles of the present, and, thereby, causes us to forget the miracles of the past. Moses looks at a barren wilderness and cannot figure out how God will supply enough meat to feed the whole nation of Israel. The Lord's answer was, *"Is the Lord's hand waxed short?"*

Verse 25 says, *"When the Spirit rested upon them, they prophesied, and did not cease."* The *"seventy men of the elders"* began to prophesy as the Lord took of the Spirit that was upon Moses and gave it unto them. In the Hebrew their prophecy was not foretelling but was forth-telling. The inference in the Hebrew is that they began to proclaim the great miracles God had brought about in the past, which were so numerous, they never repeated themselves one time. This was God's answer to unbelief. It should be a lesson to us. The songwriter wasn't far off when he said, "Count your blessings and name them one by one."

Two things should be said concerning this tremendous episode.

First of all, here is an example of a man having a great anointing of the Holy Spirit and a part of this power being taken from him by the Lord to be divided and used to anoint 70 others. This meant that if Moses did not want to do all the work God had called him to do, he did not need all the Spirit-anointing enabling him to do this work. So, the help that Moses was given, in effect, little helped Moses.

Second, it is noticeable that any degree, measure, or gift of the Holy Spirit, if, and when one receives it, makes him able to do immediately whatever the Spirit anoints him to do (I Cor. 12:1-11).

In verses 26 through 30 it seems that two of

the elders continued to prophesy even after leaving the Tabernacle and going back into the camp. Joshua felt that they might be out of order, but Moses says, *"Would God that all the Lord's people were prophets, and that the Lord would put His Spirit upon them!"*

The lesson was not lost on Moses. In effect, the Lord was telling him, *"Moses, if you do not desire to do what I have called you to do, I will then choose someone else, place my Spirit upon him, and he will do it."*

Verses 31 through 35 says out of their unbelief the people demanded. Their demand was met, but it brought death, *"And the Lord smote the people with a very great plague."* Too many times we ask for things from God out of unbelief and out of lusts. At times they are granted but are to our destruction. It is so much better to say, *"Not my will but thy will be done."*

CHAPTER 12

Verses 1 through 3 portray the complaints against Moses by Miriam and Aaron. Miriam seems to have been the ring-leader. It was because of Moses' wife, Zipporah. She was an Ethiopian and, thereby, a Gentile. There must have been a feeling of great bitterness and jealousy toward Zipporah for Miriam to have stooped so low as to take a stand against her own brother, Moses. As far as we know from the record, her sister-in-law, Zipporah, showed no malice toward her. It seems that Genesis 24:3 forbade any marriage by Israelites to Gentiles. Miriam evidently felt that she had just grounds for condemning Moses. However, jealousy instigated her actions. Whatever her motives were, it seemed that she objected on the grounds that Zipporah was Gentile. Next, she questions Moses' leadership.

It is very noteworthy that the 3rd verse records this statement, *"Now the man Moses was very meek."* These words are inserted here to explain how Moses did not take steps to defend or vindicate himself, and furthermore show why God so promptly intervened. It should be noted that the Holy Spirit records

the good points about men whenever it is wise to do so, as well as their faults. In chapter 11 Moses murmured, and the Holy Spirit recorded it. Now it records his meekness. Was Moses wrong for marrying this Ethiopian woman? (This had been done some years before.)

These passages do not prove Moses wrong. They rather say this, *"Who is faithful in mine house"* (vs. 7). The Lord then further says this, *"Wherefore then were you not afraid to speak against my servant Moses?"*

Moses did not defend himself, as is described in verse 3. His defense was left up to God, and retribution was swift. It is a serious thing to speak against a servant of God. No one is to condone sin, but at the same time, no one is to take it upon themselves to order the chastisement. That prerogative belongs to God and God alone (Rom. 12:19). To take it upon oneself to judge the servant of the Lord is to conclude, *"The anger of the Lord was kindled against them."*

What God's thoughts were concerning this fault-finding is boldly proclaimed, *"Miriam became leprous"* (vs. 10).

Verses 11 and 12 tell us what repentance will do. Aaron freely admitted, *"We have done foolishly, and wherein we have sinned."* Consequently, the anger of God that was *"kindled against them"* (vs. 9) was stayed regarding Aaron because of his repentance.

Moses not only manifested a spirit of meekness in the face of bitter opposition to himself but also mercy and forgiveness. This is the duty of every child of God, but, regrettably, is manifested so little.

The *"seven days"* of verse 14 portrays the present Israel of today, *"shut out from the camp."* The entirety of Israel's march was shut down for *"seven days"* until *"Miriam was brought in again."*

We should take note from this chapter that God is angered very swiftly when individuals take it upon themselves to confront the man (or woman) of God. Whether Moses was right or wrong in regard to the Ethiopian woman was between God and Moses; it was not between Miriam and Moses. Miriam and Aaron made it their business. They would ruefully regret it. Too many in the Church think lightly of laying their hands suddenly on that which is of God. Even though today we are living under a New Covenant, still, the death God brought then, He will bring now.

CHAPTER 13

Verse 1 says, *"The Lord spake unto Moses, saying";* however, Deuteronomy 1:19-22 tells us that this command was given by the Lord only at the demand of the people. The people did it in unbelief. The Lord allowed them to have their way. They asked for quails, and they got quails. They would later ask for a king, and they would receive a king. Here, they demand for spies to be sent out, and it is granted unto them. Had they allowed the Lord to plan for them, how different would have been their history. Deuteronomy 8:7-9 declares that God had already spied out the land for them. Had they believed Him, they would have never made this request.

Verses 4 through 16 give the names of the unbelievers as well as the believers. Such is kept of all who name the name of the Lord.

Verse 20 says, *"Now the time was the time of the firstripe grapes."* Grapes ripen in southern Palestine in July and August. So, it was about the first part of July when the spies entered Canaan.

Verse 22 says, *"Now Hebron was built seven years before Zoan in Egypt."* As Zoan was the Tanis of heathen historians and the capital of lower Egypt, thus Hebron was of greater antiquity than the proud city of which the Egyptians boasted the highest antiquity.

Verse 25 says, *"Searching of the land after forty days."* Because of doubt and unbelief, this 40 days was to cost them 40 years.

Verses 26 through 33 tell us that faith sees only what God can do. Unbelief sees the *"walled cities,"* the *"giants,"* the *"land that eateth up the inhabitants,"* and sees themselves as *"grasshoppers."* Faith sees God; unbelief sees the problems. With faith, God gets bigger and bigger; with unbelief, the problems get bigger and bigger. The language of unbelief is, *"We saw," "We are not able," "We are not as strong as*

they." Caleb and Joshua walked by faith, saw by faith, and acted by faith. The language of faith is always optimistic – *"We are well able"; "The Lord will bring us into the land"; "The Lord will give the land to us"; "The giants are bread for us"; "The giants are defenseless"; "The Lord is with us"; "We will not fear."* The majority report says, *"We be not able."* The minority report says, *"Let us go up at once and possess it; for we are well able to overcome it"* (vs. 30).

The *"giants"* of verse 33 were the *"sons of Anak"* who was also the son of a giant. This proves that giants reproduced giants. All Anakims were giants (Deut. 2:11). Josephus speaks of giants whose bodies were so large and their countenances so entirely different from other men that they were surprising to the sight and terrible to the hearing. He declares that their bones were still exhibited in his day, which was in the time of Christ.

CHAPTER 14

Verses 1 through 4 record the doubt and the unbelief of the children of Israel. This unbelief stopped the entire plan of God at this time for the whole of planet Earth. Think about it! All of heaven was ready for Israel to enter the Promised Land. God had already prepared the way, but doubt and unbelief stopped it cold. How much does doubt and unbelief stop the will of God even today? How many times has heaven prepared for a certain thing to take place, but God could not get anyone to believe Him? God is ready; the angels are ready; all of heaven is ready; Moses is ready; Joshua and Caleb are ready, but Israel in verse 2, *"murmured against Moses and against Aaron."* Murmuring always registers unbelief.

The 4th verse says they will dislodge God's leadership and install *"a captain"* of their own making. Any leadership that is man-chosen will always lead the people to Egypt.

Verse 5 says, *"Then Moses and Aaron fell on their faces."* Moses took no steps but those that God directed. He did not try to defend himself; he allowed the Lord to defend him.

Verses 6 through 9 proclaim the appeal of

Joshua and Caleb. Their appeal was, *"And the Lord is with us: Fear them not."* Their faith would purchase them a ticket into the Promised Land. However, their faith could not do away with the doubt and unbelief of the balance of Israel.

Verse 10 says that unbelief always tries to kill faith, *"But all the congregation bade stone them with stones."* The truth is not popular. If God had not undertaken, the people would have killed Moses and Aaron, along with Joshua and Caleb, and started back to Egypt.

Verses 11 and 12 record the anger of God at the unbelief. Nothing angers God like unbelief. *"And how long will it be ere they believe me."*

Verses 13 through 20 record the intercession of Moses and the mercy of God. The Lord answered the prayer of Moses only in the sense of the time of their destruction, *"And the Lord said, I have pardoned according to thy word"* (vs. 20). God could not pardon the sin of people who did not want it pardoned and would not repent. The cry of a parent for a wayward child can only be answered by God to the extent that God will continue His mercy regarding the length of His patience and compassion. However, God cannot forgive and pardon the sin of an individual who will not repent of that sin.

Verse 21 is spoken of in the future tense. God is saying, *"Irrespective of the doubt and the unbelief of those who carry my name, ultimately, all the earth shall be filled with the glory of the Lord."* It will happen in the Millennium and forever thereafter.

Verses 22 through 25 record the *"glory"* and *"miracles"* which should have built faith. However, these things, as wonderful as they are, have built little faith through the ages. Faith doesn't come by *"glory"* or *"miracles"*; it comes by hearing, and hearing by the Word of God. If men will not believe the Word of God, they will not believe the miracles of God.

The 25th verse says that "the unbelief and doubt imprisoned God's people in the wilderness." *"Tomorrow turn you, and get you into the wilderness."* Tomorrow could have been preparation for the Promised Land, but instead it was for the wilderness.

Verses 26 through 35 record God's pronouncements. The 28th verse says, *"As you*

have spoken in my ears, so will I do to you." God said, *"Shall fall in this wilderness,"* so they would eventually fall. The *"little ones"* who they said God could not take care of, *"them will I bring in."*

In the 34th verse He says, *"You shall know my breach of promise."* This means: My withdrawal from My original intentions of taking you into the land. In reality, you are the ones that have broken your promises and have so rebelled that you forced Me to turn from you and punish you. Many have tried to conclude that God's promises are not conditional. In other words, they can sin with impunity and still make heaven their eternal home. These passages refute that.

Verses 36 and 37 say, *"By bringing up a slander upon the land."* The land that God called *"a land of milk and honey"* was called by *"those men"* an *"evil report."* They died by *"the plague."* What kind of plague they died of is not stated. A special stroke or plague was permitted by God to punish them for the great evil of causing the whole congregation of Israel to rebel and be killed in the wilderness, and, the program of God to be delayed for 40 years. Think of ten men causing all this because of their fear and cowardice! This tells us that doubt and unbelief are contagious. God's actions are limited to our faith or to our unbelief.

Verse 38 records the faith of Joshua and Caleb because the Word of God always records the faith of God's people.

Their words, *"We have sinned,"* in verse 40, were not honest and sincere. Their hearts were still in Egypt; they only paid lipservice to God. The 43rd verse says, *"Because you are turned away from the Lord."* They tried to change their actions at the last minute; however, God knew their heart had not changed. There is much lip-service repentance today also, but very little heart-changing repentance.

CHAPTER 15

Chapter 14 pronounced great judgment among all the unbelievers in Israel. (Everyone except Joshua and Caleb. It also seems that the priests and the Levites were not included in this judgment.) However, it must be noted that God's plan for the younger generation of Israel to come into the Promised Land was still in force. So, His turning them away from the land did not do away with his plan, it only postponed it for 38 years. And during the next 19 chapters, we have the record of Israel's wandering in the wilderness during the 38 year period of the curse. The message of the 15th chapter about going into the Promised Land was spoken to encourage the younger generation to believe that they would enter it. The ordinances given here were addressed to all Israel for them to obey when they came into the land. So, we have to understand that the instructions given in Numbers 15 are given at the close of this 38 year period (40 years counting the first two years before their failure). During this time, it is likely that not many sacrifices were offered by reason of the scarcity of animals, wheat, wine, and other things essential to offerings. The commands to make such offerings were given in view of entrance into the land where the supplies would be in abundance.

Verses 13 through 16 proclaim, *"One law and one manner shall be for you, and for the stranger."* God's salvation plan was the same for all; it did not differ or vary. Likewise, God's salvation plan is the same for all today, the rich, the poor, the great, or the small; all must come the same way. The Scripture uses the term, *"One manner for you"* and then the same for *"the stranger."* When Jesus died on Calvary, He died not only for Israel, but for the rest of the world as well, *"For God so loved the world"* (St. John 3:16).

Verses 22 through 31 pertain to sins of ignorance and willful sins. God made it clear that there was difference between the sins of ignorance and presumptuous sins. Admittedly, both were sins. However, atonement could be made for the sin of ignorance. This sin was an act of breaking the Law without knowing that the Law was being violated. When it was called to the attention of the law-breaker, then the proper sacrifices would be offered, atonement would be made, and the sin would be forgiven, *"And if any soul sin through ignorance, then he shall bring a she-goat of the first year for a sin*

NOTES

offering" (vs. 27). And then it says, *"The priests shall make an atonement for the soul."* And as well it says, *"It shall be forgiven him"* (vs. 28).

However, a presumptuous sin is different, *"But the soul that doeth aught presumptuously that soul shall be cut off"* (vs. 30). And that went for the stranger as well. What was a presumptuous sin? It was a sin of willful disobedience, a sin of rebellion. In other words, it was not the case of tremendous temptation by the powers of darkness or flesh. It simply means that a person with cold calculation says in his heart, "I will do what I desire to do regardless of what God says." There is no forgiveness for that type of sin, because there is no true repentance for that type of sin. The Scripture uses the term, *"Because he hath despised the Word of the Lord"* (vs. 31).

Then in verses 32-36 an example of presumptuous sin is given, *"They found a man that gathered sticks upon the Sabbath day."* This man knew better, but in open defiance he willfully disobeyed God exclaiming that he would do what he desired to do. The penalty was death, *"All the congregation shall stone him."*

The situation really has not changed from the Old Covenant to the New. There are many sins of ignorance that the child of God commits. Ultimately the Holy Spirit will call it to our attention. It is then to be repented of and will then be forgiven and put behind us. Also, there are many sins committed by Christians as a result of the powers of darkness, with the individual under great pressure (St. Luke 22:31-34). However, it must be understood that even though this sin is committed as the result of powerful temptation by the powers of darkness, still it is sin and must be confessed, repented of, and washed by the Blood of Christ. However, presumptuous sins that speak of rebellion in the heart against God and determine to have one's own way irrespective of the Word of God, have no forgiveness simply because forgiveness is not desired (Heb. 6:4-6 and Heb. 10:26-31).

The passage in Hebrews 6 means that the individual judges Christ as an imposter. They no longer believe in Him or His atonement. Since such faith is the only thing that could renew them again to repentance, it then becomes impossible for them to be renewed, simply because they no longer believe.

The passage in Hebrews 10 speaks of *"willful sin."* These are individuals who once knew the Lord just as the individuals described in Hebrews 6 once knew the Lord. They now count the Blood of Christ a common thing, esteeming it of no value as an atonement. There is no forgiveness for this type of sin simply because the individual will not believe in that which is the only atonement for sin, the Blood of Christ. These are perfect descriptions even under the New Covenant of *"willful sin."* We would do well to heed it.

Verses 37 through 41 speak of the Word of the Lord. The Word says, *"fringes in the borders of their garments."* It was to be a *"ribband of blue,"* and it was for the purpose of *"remembering all the commandments of the Lord, and to do them."* The Holy Spirit is saying, *"The Word of God is not to be trifled with."* If we lay it aside, there is no other salvation, so allow this *"ribband of blue on the border of your garments"* to be a constant reminder. Under the Old Covenant the children of Israel individually did not have copies of the Law, so they had to be reminded. Today, the Word of God is our *"ribband of blue."*

———■———

CHAPTER 16

More and more we see why this generation was doomed. I'm sure the question is asked, "Was everyone of that generation (20 years old and older) eternally lost?" No, I'm sure they were not. Some of them no doubt repented even though they were not allowed to go into the Promised Land. Still, they made heaven their eternal home. Even Moses did not go into the Promised Land because of the sin he committed of striking the rock the second time instead of speaking to it. However, we know that Moses repented and is now with the Lord. As well, this wrongful act committed did not take away from his being one of the greatest men of God who ever lived. At the same time, I think that when the eternal record is shown it will show that precious few of these people

NOTES

were saved. Most continued in their rebellion and, consequently, died lost. This chapter is but another example of this rebellion.

It seems that Korah was first cousin to Moses and Aaron (I Chron. 6:2-3). He was encamped close to Reuben and, hence, their association in this rebellion. The Reubenites were perhaps discontented because the birthright had been taken away from them, and they had not been given what they considered their proper place among the tribes. Korah's objective was not to abolish the distinction between the Levites and the people, but to win the priesthood for himself and his kinsmen. This design was hidden under the pretext that all the people were holy and should be equal.

God chose Aaron to be the high priest. Korah *"gainsayed"* that, likewise, the princes of Reuben attacked the leadership given to Moses by God. Satan has always questioned God's leadership and in the world of religion has always endeavored to insert his own. He has by and large been successful. God's leadership under the New Covenant is centered in *"apostles, prophets, evangelists, pastors, and teachers"* (Eph. 4:11). All other designations or titles such as overseers, superintendents, bishops, presidents, popes, and cardinals are man-made. It is not wrong to have and hold some of these, providing that the bearer realizes they are man-made and, thereby, administrative only, holding no spiritual authority whatsoever. The tragedy is that most do think that some type of God-given authority goes with these unscriptural titles. It does not. Actually, there is absolutely no such thing as a hierarchy in the Early Church. Such did not come into the picture until spiritual declension came. (The offices of bishop, presbyter, pastor, elder, and shepherd all refer to one position, that of pastor. There is no such thing as the office of "bishop" with some type of spiritual authority concerning a region or group of churches. It simply means the pastor of one church.)

Verses 4 through 11 give the real cause of the rebellion.

Verse 4 says, *"And when Moses heard it, he fell upon his face,"* that is, he stepped aside so that the rebels should stand face to face with God. Anyone who is attacked by other so-called

Christians should act similarly. Moses did not attempt to defend himself and Aaron. He left all to the judgment of God. That judgment was terrible.

Verses 15 through 18 seem to insinuate that the anger against Moses was that he was enriching himself, *"I have not taken one ass from them."* It seems to have changed little if any today.

Verses 19 through 27 seemingly say that the majority of Israel sided with the rebellion of Korah. The 19th verse says, *"And the glory of the Lord appeared."* The glory of the Lord can be life giving or it can be death dealing. To the lame man at the gate called Beautiful in the book of Acts, it brought life. To Ananias and Sapphira as recorded in the book of Acts, it brought death. Once again, God desires to destroy them and rightly so, *"that I may consume them in a moment."* The only difference was in their being consumed in a moment or throughout the 40 years.

Verses 28 through 35 record this judgment. In answer to Moses' prayer the wives and only those sons and children who joined in the rebellion perished. The sons of Korah who did not rebel, did not die with their father (Num. 26:11). Actually, some of the descendants of Korah wrote some of the Psalms. How wondrous is the grace of God. The 30th verse says, *"These men have provoked the Lord."* Provoking God has been a great sin in all generations. Israel's history shows that they repeatedly provoked Him to anger. The 32nd verse says, *"The earth opened her mouth and swallowed them up."* This no doubt was an earthquake timed by the Lord to happen the moment Moses finished prophesying. It seems that the earth opened from the surface to the center where hell is located. These individuals *"went down alive into the pit."* The 35th verse says, *"There came a fire from the Lord and consumed the two hundred and fifty men that offered incense."* These who were so bold as to intrude into the office of the priest who was called of God, were immediately consumed as fire came out from the Lord Who dwelt between the Mercy Seat and the Cherubim. This must have been a striking sight for the fire-like lightning bolts to come out from the Tabernacle and especially to kill only these 250

NOTES

men. This was the third fire that was sent from the Lord to destroy rebels. It seems the fire they offered was *"strange fire"* as well.

Verses 41 through 50 portray only more rebellion, *"all the congregation of the children of Israel murmured against Moses and against Aaron."* The only thing that can change an evil heart is repentance. Mercy should change it, but it doesn't. Judgment should change it as well, but it doesn't either. The 16th chapter shows us what man is and what God is. At any time these people could have repented and averted the judgment, but they would not repent.

Verses 44 through 50 are a perfect portrayal of the condition of this world. It says, *"The plague has begun."* As the plague had begun then, it is rampant now all over the world. That plague is sin. There is only one answer and that is *"fire from off the altar."* The altar represents Calvary; the fire represents God's judgment upon His son Jesus Christ instead of where it rightfully belongs, namely upon you and me. Moses told Aaron, *"Take a censer, and put fire therein from off the altar and put on incense."* Aaron represents today's preacher of the Gospel. The *"altar"* represents Calvary. The *"fire"* represents judgment but at the same time salvation. The *"incense"* represents the intercessory prayer of God's people. The words *"go quickly into the congregation"* are the words of our Lord and Saviour, *"Go ye into all the world and preach the Gospel."*

As Aaron *"stood between the dead and the living,"* the preacher of the true Gospel of Jesus Christ, likewise, stands *"between the dead and living."* The situation today is not only as alarming as it was then; it is even more so. The only thing that stopped the plague was Aaron going with a fire from the *"altar."* That is the only thing that will save men today. That's the reason Paul said, *"I determined to know nothing among you save Christ and Him crucified."* Nearly 15,000 people died in a few minutes time. In today's world the plague of sin is killing millions, and the only answer is the Gospel.

CHAPTER 17

"Write thou every man's name upon his rod" are the words of the second verse. Consequently, each rod of the 12 bore a mighty name. Through the night, no doubt, while these rods lay hidden within the Tabernacle, the sons of Israel might have expressed confidence in their name. As well today, men by the millions express confidence in a denomination, a doctrine, a Pope, or a man. However, it must clearly be noted that in the morning all the rods were found to be dead sticks, notwithstanding the names they bore, except the rod of Aaron. It alone was living, beautiful, and accepted.

The 5th verse says, *"That the man's rod, whom I shall choose, shall blossom."* This was Aaron's rod, and it is a type of Christ. Hebrews 9 recalls that it and the manna accompanied Israel and the Tabernacle through the wilderness. Some even think that it was the rod that Moses was told to take and hold in his hand and to *"speak to the rock"* (Num 20:8). This living rod is Jesus. Those who trust Him and Him alone will be safely brought through the wilderness of this world to heaven.

The budded rod taught the lesson that certain death awaited those who presumed to approach God in their own person, but certain life was for those who drew near through the accepted person and precious Blood of the Great High Priest, the Lord Jesus Christ. Sadly, man understands neither holiness nor grace, *"Behold, we die, we perish, we all perish"* (vs. 12). In Chapter 16 the people claimed the right to enter the Tabernacle because they said that all the congregation was holy. In verse 13 of Chapter 17 they cried out for the suppression of the Tabernacle because it was an agent of death to them! The flesh presumes when it ought to retire and distrusts when it ought to confide.

CHAPTER 18

Verse 1 says, *"Aaron, thou and thy sons and*

thy father's house with thee shall bear the iniquity of the sanctuary." God's gracious answer to this pride and folly was, in type, to reveal still more of the glory and power of the High-Priesthood of Christ. In response to the cry of alarm, *"Shall we be consumed with dying?"* God answered, *"Aaron shall bear the iniquity of the sanctuary that there be no more wrath upon the children of Israel."* Thus they found security in the very priest whom they despised and rejected.

The first 19 verses of Chapter 18 concerned the priesthood. The remainder of the chapter concerns the ministry of the priesthood.

Aaron and his sons were to make the sins of the people so truly their own that they were to eat the sin-offerings, as already commanded in Leviticus.

The 19th verse speaks of the *"covenant of salt."* Salt, being scarce and precious and used in every sacrifice (Lev. 2:13) as well as to preserve meat, became the symbol of incorruptibility of God's Covenant and the perpetuity of man's obligation to him. The term, *"a covenant of salt,"* refers to the solemnizing of any general Covenant.

Verses 20 through the remainder of the chapter concern ministry and make it clear that God was to be the inheritance of the priests and Levites, and that they were to have no part in the inheritance of Canaan. The things dedicated to God, those that He reserved from the offerings of Israel and the tithes, were to be for the support of the ministry, and in this sense God was their inheritance.

In verse 32 the words are used, *"the best of it."* Israel was supposed to give from the best of their crops and animals and honor God with the firstfruits of all their increase as a token of appreciation for His many blessings in making such things possible.

CHAPTER 19

It should be noted first of all that the law of the red heifer was given by the Lord and not by the priest. *"This is the ordinance of the law which the Lord hath commanded."*

The *"red heifer"* of verse 2 is a type of Christ. The *"red"* signifies the blood that He would shed. The *"without spot"* typifies that He is spotless externally and *"without blemish"* internally. The words, *"and upon which never came yoke,"* signifies that He is never in bondage to any sin, and the Law has no claim upon Him as a debtor.

The 3rd verse says, *"May bring her forth without the camp."* So was Christ led of the Spirit to Calvary, where He offered Himself up. As well, He was offered up *"without the gate."* The words, *"One shall slay her before his face,"* speak of those who crucified Christ in the face of God.

Verse 4 says when the blood was shed that *"Eleazar the priest shall sprinkle of her blood directly before the tabernacle of the congregation seven times."* The *"seven times"* speaks of perfection, totality, and completeness. Jesus Christ offered up His own Blood on the Mercy Seat of Heaven of which this is a type.

The order to *"burn the heifer"* in verse 5 signifies that Christ gave His all for our redemption. He literally suffered, in effect, the pain of Hell in our stead.

The *"cedar wood"* of verse 6 typifies Calvary's cross. The *"hyssop"* typifies Christ as a peasant, *"He had no beauty that we should desire Him"* (Isa. 53). The *"scarlet"* typifies His shed Blood.

The *"ashes of the heifer"* in the 9th verse were used in the *"water of separation."* They were called this because they were used in the ceremonial cleansing of defiled persons wanting to separate themselves from uncleanness.

The 11th verse speaks of being *"unclean."* Actually, there were ten things that could render one unclean. If found unclean, one would have to go through the *"water of separation for a purification of sin."* Out of these ten things that could cause uncleanness, seven times out of ten it refers to the touching of a dead body, a bone of a dead body, or a grave. Death came upon man as a result of the fall. Death was never intended by God. It is the result of sin. It will one day be cast down and abolished.

All members of a household where a person died were to use the water of separation, for all became defiled and needed to be purified (vs.

NOTES

14). In such a vast population there would be a daily need for this water, which suggests that many red heifers may have been killed from time to time. Some Jewish writers say the ashes were made yearly, and the sprinkling ingredients were added and distributed to all cities and towns of Israel at that time. But the language of verses 9 and 17 seems to indicate that the mixture of running water and ashes was made fresh when needed. The main purpose of the rite, no doubt, was to prevent the Israelites from imitating the superstitious customs of the Egyptians who kept their dead around them in mummified form. This law encouraged a speedy burial for all, the maintaining of graveyards at a distance from the dwelling places, and helped prevent the spread of disease in the camp. Fields had to be cleaned up of persons slain in battle, whether Israelites or others – strangers and foreigners.

The uncleanness would last for seven days in the case of one being defiled by the dead, but only one day in the case of being defiled in connection with the sacrifice of the red heifer.

The 18th verse seems to say that any *"clean person,"* not necessarily a priest, could apply the water of separation.

The 20th verse tells us how important that God considered even this ceremonial cleansing, *"that souls shall be cut off from among the congregation."* So, how much more would one be cut off if he did not give evidence of a real cleansing from sin of which the outward ceremonial cleansing was only a figure.

How foolish we are when we think God can condone unconfessed sin in the life of a Christian. Just as the Israelite was not automatically cleansed just because he was an Israelite but, instead, had to go through this ceremonial cleansing, likewise, the child of God is not automatically cleansed when he sins just because he is a child of God. He must properly confess and forsake the sin. *"If we confess our sins, He is faithful and just to forgive us our sins"* (I John 1:9).

CHAPTER 20

The *"first month"* of verse 1 was the first month of the 40th year after Israel had come out of Egypt. There is a blank of nearly 38 years between the occurrences of Chapter 20 and the mission of the spies in Chapters 13 and 14. Tragically enough, it is the *"new"* generation that is now chiding with Moses. So, those who will go into the Promised Land will be no better than the ones who died in the wilderness. When will the Church ever learn that all of our righteousness is self-righteousness and that the only righteousness that God will recognize is imputed righteousness given freely to us by the Lord Jesus Christ; righteousness, I might quickly add, that we did not earn or merit and, in fact, we could not earn or merit.

The 5th verse says they called where they were *"this evil place."* As usual, man's complaints are senseless. If the nation had obeyed God in the first place, they would have already been through the wilderness and out of it now for 38 years. (It seems that God only intended for the wilderness experience to last for approximately two years.) They themselves were responsible for their being in such an evil place. So, the situation in which they now find themselves is of their own doing.

We who are Christians, when we find ourselves in *"this evil place,"* must never complain. We are either there through no fault of our own with God, thereby, using the situation to bring about some good things that are just ahead, or else He is doing it for our own good. (Joseph, for instance – Psa. 105:18) Or else we are in *"this evil place"* because of our own sin and failure. In either case God will not tolerate our complaints and unbelief. In any case we must praise Him. In the first place, we should praise Him because some good things will ultimately happen to us, and in the second place, that the situation is no worse than it is.

In the 7th verse *"the Lord spake."* In the 8th verse He commands Moses *"speak ye unto the rock before their eyes."* To *"speak to the rock"* was all that was required of Moses, and it would have been very effective in proving to

NOTES

Israel the intended truth of benefits to be received from the Messiah who the rock typifies (I Cor. 10:4). The rock had already been smitten once, typifying the crucifixion of Christ, which was to be once and only once for all men (Rom. 10; Heb. 9:25-28). Merely speaking to the rock at this time would have brought the same benefits as smiting it before. The same is now true regarding Christ – all that one is required to do is to ask and receive (Matt. 7:7-11; 21, 22; Mark. 11:22-24).

The 10th verse records that, tragically, Moses spoke to Israel instead of the rock. How so often we do the same. We speak to our problem or to those who cannot help us instead of the One Who can help us, Jesus Christ. *"Must we fetch you water out of this rock?"* This word called attention to *"we"* – Moses and Aaron – as the source of supply, not Jehovah. Thus, Moses did not sanctify God (set Him apart as sacred and revered) before all the people.

The 11th verse says, *"He smote the rock twice."* The chief reason for this being such a serious sin against Jehovah, and one that displeased Him greatly was that the rock was the spiritual rock of Israel, identified with the Messiah, and smiting typified His crucifixion. To smite the rock twice meant crucifying Christ afresh. Thus, God punished for transgression in type, the same as He will punish for reality, though not as severely as He will punish one who actually crucifies to himself the Son of God and puts Him to an open shame (Heb. 6:4-9; 10:26-29). The Scripture says that despite the sin, *"the water came out abundantly."* It came out as it did when the rock was first smitten (Ex. 17:6), typifying that the benefits of the crucifixion are abundant to all men, even hardened rebels. Regrettably, the stumblings of the Church, which would include us all, so oftentimes fail to sanctify the Lord before the people. So often we present an imperfect picture of Calvary, both in our presentation and our example. However, the water still flows and, *"Whosoever will may come and drink of the water of life freely."* Hallelujah!

The 12th verse says, *"Because ye believed me not."* Unbelief is the basic foundational problem of all failure. Moses spent the most of 120 years either in preparation or the actual work of getting the children of Israel out of bondage and bringing them to the Promised Land. And now at the last moment, he was not permitted to see the work completed. This does not mean that he was lost or cut off from heaven, but only that he was denied the fulfillment of his life-long desire because of disobedience. This experience should be an everlasting lesson to all of us. God does not play favorites. He cannot brook disobedience, unbelief, or sin in any manner. The only reason that any of us are saved at present is because of the righteousness of Christ. There are no good Christians; there is actually only a good Christ, *"there is none good but God"* (St. Luke 18:19).

Verses 14 through 21 portray the request of Israel to *"pass through thy country."* The 21st verse says, *"Thus Edom refused."* The Edomites were the descendants of Esau. They had been multiplying for the many years Israel had been in Egypt. Even when Jacob came from Haran, Esau already had hundreds of soldiers (Gen. 32:6). Now the whole nation mobilized to oppose the passage of Jacob's descendants to their land. Even though Israel was refused passage, still, God instructed Israel not to fight with them (Deut. 2:4-9).

This exchange between Israel and Edom shows the gentleness of the one and the hatred of the other. Just as God would not let Esau injure Jacob, so now He forbade Jacob to injure Esau.

Verses 23 through 29 portray the death of Aaron. (Miriam preceded him by about four months.) Both will die in this 40th year. Aaron will die and not be allowed into the Promised Land because of his part with Moses in the sin of failing to speak to the rock. However, as Moses, Aaron did not lose his soul and was not denied access to heaven. He is there now, having been liberated by Christ out of paradise, awaiting the Resurrection morn' when his soul and spirit will be reunited with a glorified body. Moses awaits there as well.

CHAPTER 21

The 1st verse says, *"King Arad the*

NOTES

Canaanite." It should read, *"The Canaanite, King of Arad,"* as Arad was a city in the southern part of Canaan about 20 miles south of Hebron. The Word says, *"He fought against Israel."* This Canaanite king is a type of Satan. The Bible says, *"And took some of them prisoners."* Satan desires to take God's people *"prisoner."*

The 2nd verse says, *"Vowed a vow unto the Lord,"* and then, *"If thou will indeed deliver."* Only God can deliver. Their first effort was by the flesh. It failed, as it had to. Their second effort was by the Spirit. It succeeded, as succeed it must. The entire passage speaks of disobedience at the outset, with obedience that followed, *"The Lord hearkened to the voice of Israel."* God will not hearken until we obey.

The 4th verse says that immediately after their victory over the Canaanite, *"The soul of the people was much discouraged because of the way."* Once again faith is to be tested; once again they will fail.

The 5th verse says, *"And the people spake against God, and against Moses."* They then blamed God for bringing them out of Egypt. They criticized the manna, once again registering unbelief. The complaints of Israel through the entirety of the 40 years rings as a drum beat in our ears. We want to say, "Not again!" Still, the question must be asked, "Do we conduct ourselves any better in this present age?"

The 6th verse says, *"And the Lord sent fiery serpents among the people."* There is some indication that through the 40 years of wandering that God had sent angels ahead to clear the area of these *"fiery serpents."* Now that the people were showing no gratitude for God's sustaining hand, He would, at least briefly, remove the angels, allowing them to face the *"fiery serpents"* alone. The Bible says, *"Much people of Israel died."* These *"fiery serpents"* were types of demon spirits that sought to destroy the people of God, as they seek to destroy the people of God today. We may at times think our situation is precarious and that God is not too well attending us; however, if we could look into the spirit world and see how well He actually is attending us by holding back the powers of darkness, we would be more thankful for His guiding hand that we presently have. The 21st chapter of Numbers should be a lesson to us.

Some have called the repentance of the 7th verse incomplete, perhaps so. But God so longs for repentance that even the most feeble effort on the part of the wayward child will open the ears of heaven.

Verses 8 and 9 are the passages that Jesus used to help Nicodemus understand the way of salvation. The fiery or brazen serpent that was placed on a pole was clearly a type of Christ bearing the sins and sicknesses of all men (Matt. 8:17; I Pet. 2:24).

1. The serpent itself was a symbol of sin, and Christ was made sin for us that we might be made free from sin (II Cor. 5:21).

2. The serpent was lifted up on a pole, and Christ was lifted up on a Cross (St. John 3:14-15).

3. The sick of Israel received healing by looking on the brazen serpent; others have received healing by looking to Christ (Matt. 8:1; I Pet. 2:24).

4. As the Israelites who looked on the serpent continued to live, so those who truly look to Christ will live eternally (St. John 3:14-15).

5. God provided no other remedy for the Israelites at this time; so Christ is the only remedy for those who wish salvation (St. John 3:14-16; Acts 3:16; Rom. 10:9-10).

6. As the Israelites had to have faith in the brazen serpent as the remedy for their sin and sickness, so men today must have faith in Christ (Eph. 2:8-9).

7. As God's power was the invisible force in the brazen serpent remedy, so it is with salvation through Christ (Matt. 1:21; Rom. 1:16).

8. As the serpent on the pole brought peace and reconciliation with God, so Christ on the Cross brings peace and reconciliation with Him (Col. 1:20-21).

9. As confession of sin and prayer were necessary for Israel to receive the benefits of the brazen serpent remedy, so they are necessary to obtain the benefits of Christ and the Cross (St. John 3:14-16; I John 1:9).

Verses 10 through 20 record Israel's song and the great miracle of the well.

Verse 14 mentions *"the book of the wars of the Lord."* What this book refers to is not known, for nothing more is said about it. However, the child of God, even from this brief

NOTES

mention, should always understand as Paul told Timothy, *"War a good warfare"* (I Tim. 1:18). This is truly a war that we are in. The stakes are beyond comprehension. The end results will be victory if we depend on the Lord.

Verse 16 says that once again the people asked for water, and once again God says, *"I will give them water."*

The 17th verse says that God's first requirement for the miracle was that *"Israel sing this song."* The words were, *"Spring up, oh well,"* and that in a barren wasteland where no water was. Should this be a lesson to us? If you have a problem, *"Sing ye unto it."*

The 18th verse says, *"The princes digged the well."* As verse 17 is faith in worship, verse 18 is faith in action. Many join their faith in worship but never proceed to take their faith into action. This is the faith plus the works that James spoke of. There was a miraculous supply of water.

Verses 21 through 32 speak of victory in the Spirit.

The 24th verse says, *"Israel smote him with the edge of the sword, and possessed his land."* Every inch of victory won by the child of God can only be accomplished by *"walking after the Spirit."* (Rom. 8)

The 29th verse says that Israel taunted the national deity of the Moabites, *"Thou art undone, oh people of Chemosh."* Israel had defeated the Moabites and had taken their land. This is the language of the faith-filled victorious child of God. It is not meant for Satan to taunt us; it is meant that we taunt Satan.

The 30th verse says, *"Heshbon is perished."* This refers to the conquering of Sihon by Israel. This defeat of such a prominent and powerful military king of the Amorites was often mentioned as a warning to those who would rise up against Jehovah and His people. The testimonies of God's people are forever to be victorious, irrespective of the concentrated efforts of the powers of darkness.

The 31st verse says, *"Thus Israel dwelt in the land of the Amorites."* Sadly, the Amorites dwell on too much of the land that belongs to the child of God. God help us to not only push out the enemies of the Lord from the spiritual land that God has promised us but, also, to *"dwell in the land."*

The 34th verse says, *"Fear him not."* This was speaking of *"Og,"* the giant king of Bashan. He ruled over some 60 cities. His defeat took place after that of Sihon at Edrei. Og and his people were utterly destroyed. He is described as the last of one branch of the giant races after the flood, the Rephaim, and as having a bedstead of iron a little over 12 feet long and a little over six feet wide. This great victory over Og is often referred to in Israelite history. The song says:

"We are able to go up and take the country,"
"And possess the land from Jordan to the sea."
"Though the giants may be there our way to hinder,"
"God has given us the victory."
Hallelujah!

The 35th verse says, *"And they possessed his land."* With God all things are possible. With God we can possess the land; without God we possess no land and never will.

CHAPTER 22

Numbers 22, 23, and 24 are some of the most startling chapters in the entirety of the Word of God. Here, we find the failure of a prophet but yet the blessing of Israel. The Holy Spirit in Jude and II Peter says that Balaam loved money. He loved it so much that he was willing to attempt to curse what God had blessed. Israel would here find herself opposed not only by the world but, also, by a prophet of God. For in the beginning, Balaam was a true prophet of God. The 1st verse says, *"And pitched in the plains of Moab on this side of Jordan by Jericho."* This was after the defeat of Sihon, King of the Amorites. Israel now possessed all the land north of the River Arnon – the northern border of Moab. Israel camped east of Jordan opposite Jericho, ready to enter the land of Canaan itself (Josh. 2:1). The book of Deuteronomy was spoken and written here, between the conquests of Sihon and Og and the conquest of Jericho in Joshua 2:1. While here, the experience of Balaam took place, as well as all of the events of Deuteronomy.

The 2nd verse says, *"And Balak the son of Zippor saw all that Israel had done."* Balak was sore afraid of Israel after seeing others so easily destroyed by them, so he schemed to get the nation cursed by Balaam, hoping then that they could be defeated. Although the plan failed, Balak learned the secret of how Israel might surely be defeated – by causing them to commit sin so that God, Himself, would curse them.

The 4th verse says, *"And Moab said unto the elders of Midian."* Moab, Midian, Balak, and Balaam are prominent in the next four chapters. Moab was a son of Lot (Gen. 19:37), and Midian was the son of Abraham (Gen. 25:2). Balak was a Moabite, and Balaam was an Edomite, a descendant of Esau, a son of Isaac. In effect, Israel would have her "relatives" opposing her.

The 5th verse says, *"He sent messengers therefore unto Balaam."* The story of Balaam is one of the most interesting in all of Scripture. He is a subject of controversy. Many think he was a mere soothsayer used by God temporarily, but the opposite is true. He was a genuine prophet of God until he finally betrayed Israel for a reward. It is evident that he became a soothsayer after Jehovah left him because of his sin and refused to help him by the power of the Holy Spirit.

The 7th verse says, *"The elders of Midian departed with the rewards of divination."* This refers to money which procures divination, or as interpreted in II Peter 2:15, *"The wages of unrighteousness."* Pagans knew only of enchantments, magic, and witchcraft and, therefore, thought this was how Balaam made predictions. However, such does not prove this was Balaam's method when prophesying regarding Israel. Scripture teaches that he made his predictions by God as did other prophets of the Lord.

The 8th verse says, *"As the Lord shall speak unto me."* Balaam had absolute faith that Jehovah would answer him that night, and this alone proves that he knew God and how to get answers from Him when he inquired and was in the habit of making contact with Him.

The 9th verse says, *"God came unto Balaam."* Notice how quickly God came to Balaam in all of his efforts to contact Him.

The 12th verse records the present and eternal destiny of those who follow Christ, *"For they are blessed."*

The 20th verse proclaims, *"God came unto Balaam at night* and said, *"Go with them."* The Lord had repeatedly told him not to go, *"Thou shalt not go"* (vs. 12). Is there a contradiction recorded here? No, God works on the basis of what is, not on the basis of what should be. He knew that Balaam was determined to go. The lure of the ever-increasing reward was *too great, "the wages of unrighteousness."* God will not force a man's will. If the man wills to sin, God will allow it. However, in this case He would turn Balaam's effort to curse into a blessing.

The 22nd verse says, *"And God's anger was kindled because he went."* It is amazing at the lengths God will go to to keep a man from going to hell. He will send angels, *"The angel of the Lord stood in the way."* The 28th verse says He would even cause the ass (mule) to speak, *"And the Lord opened the mouth of the ass and she said unto Balaam."* This miracle must be taken literally as interpreted by Peter, *"The dumb ass speaking with man's voice"* (II Pet. 2:16). This happening has been a puzzle to believers and the subject of ridicule and reproach with infidels, but there is no reason for this unless the Christian admits, and the infidel asserts, that God is limited in power. The believer will not and the infidel dare not, unless they are willing to face Him in judgment.

The 32nd verse records the angel of the Lord saying, *"Because thy way is perverse before me."*

The 34th verse says, *"I have sinned."* Pharaoh, Balaam, Achan, Saul, David, and Judas, said respectively, *"I have sinned."* But only David said this sincerely.

Verse 41 says, *"That Balak took Balaam, and brought him up into the high places of Baal."* Now the former prophet of God finds himself in alignment with Baal. Man must learn; we must serve Jehovah, or we must serve Baal; there is no in-between. Israel served God; Moab served Baal. Balaam could make either choice that he desired. He could serve the God of Israel, or he could serve Baal of Moab. He could not serve both, which is what he tried to do, and which is

NOTES

what the majority of Christendom tries to do.

CHAPTER 23

In verses 1 through 3 we see a perfect picture of the religion of the world which opposes God's only way of salvation, thru Jesus Christ. The Lord had one altar. Balaam will build "seven altars." When man intrudes his own way, which is death, he thinks more is better. So, one altar for sacrifice is not enough; there must be seven.

Verses 4 and 5 show us a God of grace and mercy. Balaam has long since made up his mind to seek the *"wages of unrighteousness,"* still, God will appeal to him by using him.

Verses 6 through 10 record Balaam's first prophecy. It is not witchcraft; it is from the Lord, *"And the Lord put a word in Balaam's mouth"* (vs. 5).

In the 8th verse he says, *"How shall I curse, whom God hath not cursed?"* In fact, it cannot be done. However, the eternal failure of all efforts does not discontinue the trying. It is sad indeed when a man once used of God seeks to hinder that which God has laid His hand on.

The 9th verse records the first prophecy, *"Lo, the people shall dwell alone, and shall not be reckoned among the nations."* This prophetic future of Israel has been fulfilled from that time until now. They have never lost their identity as a people and have never intermarried with other races, except for a very few. They have maintained their own customs, traditions, and religion, segregated from the peoples among whom they have dwelt and will continue to do so. The words, *"dwelling alone,"* literally mean living in peace and security away from the strife, sins, and religions of the mingled peoples of the earth. And this they did until they turned their back upon God. The words, *"not be reckoned among the nations,"* literally mean that they would remain a distinct people from all others, and that God would not deal with them on the basis of being one with the Gentiles. They will always be a separate class of people (I Cor. 10:32) and a distinct nation.

The 16th verse says, *"And the Lord met Balaam and put a word in his mouth."* Some of the most profound prophecies that ever came from the lips of man came from Balaam. Sadly, he still lost his way with God.

Verses 17 through 24 portray Balaam's second prophecy. This prophecy is one of the greatest and most comprehensive promises and revelations of God in Scripture. Truly, God is not a man but a Spirit-being, as taught by the Lord Jesus Christ (St. John 4:24).

Verse 19 simply says that, *"God is a not a man."* Consequently, He will not lie. Similarly, He does not sin that He has to repent. He will not go back on His word, *"or hath he spoken, and shall he not make it good?"*

The 20th verse says, *"And I cannot reverse it."* When God blesses a man, a people, or a nation, nothing can reverse that blessing except the individual(s) turning their back on God. Satan, with all of his power, cannot reverse it. The child of God who is following Jesus should boldly proclaim, *"I am blessed, and nothing can reverse it."*

Verse 21 proclaims the great doctrine of justification, *"He hath not beheld iniquity in Jacob, nor hath he seen perverseness in Israel."* What a statement!

We have just covered several chapters of Israel's failures, and, yet, God says He has not *"beheld iniquity,"* and then says, *"neither hath he seen."* What does this mean? It means justification! Justification is a legal process which, as stated by God, declares one *"not guilty."* Justification is the foundation of the Christian faith. The declaration of *"not guilty"* is based not upon the salvation merit of the person in question, but, instead, upon that person's faith in the Lord Jesus Christ Who became man's substitute. And, thereby, man by identifying with Him attains a perfect salvation, which in no way he could attain on his own. God justifies not on the merit of the sinner but, rather, on the merit of the sacrifice Who is Jesus Christ. However, it must be ever understood that a declaration of *"not guilty"* does not give the affected one license to continue in rebellion and sin. Justification declares the veracity of the finished work of Christ applied to the heart and life of the believer, but it never gives freedom to commit sin. Thereby, even though God

had justified all of Israel, still, those who persisted in rebellion would by their own actions remove themselves from justification, and, thereby, by their willful action cause themselves to be eternally lost. Howbeit, the actions of rebels or even most who would defile and abrogate the justification process, still, could never abrogate God's Law of justification. So, God could say of those who met His requirements, *"Neither hath he seen perverseness in Israel."* The *"shout of a king"* is the status to which justification brings the child of God.

Verse 22 portrays the *"strength"* of the child of God. The name, *"unicorn,"* means rhinoceros. The rhino is the strongest animal on the face of the earth. Whenever the child of God knows his place and position in Christ, then Satan sees him as an adversary of this power.

Verse 23 speaks of witchcraft that is practiced by evil workers against the child of God. The Holy Spirit simply says, *"No enchantment"* will work. And neither will any *"divination."*

The 24th verse says that Israel, as being compared to a rhino, is also compared to a great and full grown lion. The words, *"He shall not lie down until he eat of the prey, and drink the blood of the slain,"* predicts Israel as becoming victorious over the nations of Canaan and becoming settled in the land. It, as well, predicts that every child of God under the New Covenant shall totally overcome his adversaries.

Verses 25 through 30 portray continued effort and the first glimmer of the subterfuge that will cause Israel many problems. The 28th verse says, *"Unto the top of Peor."* This was a lofty summit of the Moab mountain range where the famous Baal-peor had its chief temple and where obscene and immoral rites were carried on. This is what became the snare to Israel in Numbers 25:1-9.

CHAPTER 24

The opening verse says, *"And when Balaam saw that it pleased the Lord to bless Israel."*

This passage aggressively portrays God being very pleased with those who would bless that which He has anointed. Few people realize this, obey it, and are subsequently blessed. Sadly, most, even in the Church, try to curse God's anointed instead of bless.

Verse 2 says, *"And the Spirit of God came upon him."* God's Spirit came upon him in the same sense as upon other prophets, which proves that Balaam was a true prophet of God before he went into error.

Verse 3 says, *"Whose eyes are opened,"* meaning that God had opened Balaam's eyes. And, yet, despite all this, he will still reach out for the *"wages of unrighteousness"* until he is destroyed.

Verses 5 through 9 portray the third prophecy.

The *"tents"* of Israel would refer to God's people, and the *"tabernacles"* would refer to God's dwelling place.

Verse 6 portrays God's people as *"valleys"* and *"gardens by the river's side."* The *"trees of lign aloes"* were trees that grew in central Asia. The wood was very fragrant and much prized by the ancients. It also says, *"Which the Lord hath planted."* The *"cedar trees aside the waters"* speak of the image of majestic beauty and strength.

The 7th verse portrays the Messiah and His coming kingdom on earth (Isa. 9:6-7). The word *"He* (speaking of the Messiah) *shall pour water out of His buckets"* speaks of abundance, fruitfulness, and plenty. The words *"His seed"* refer to Christ, with the words, *"many waters",* referring to the many nations of the world, meaning that multiple millions will come to Christ of every tongue, tribe, and nation. *"His king"* is the Lord Jesus Christ. Agag was the title of all the kings of Amalek, meaning high, as Pharaoh was the title of Egyptian kings. With Egypt having been destroyed by the Lord about 40 years earlier, the Amalekites were the most powerful nation in the world at that time. So it was fitting that the prophet should speak of Israel's future king, the Messiah, as being higher than Agag. The words, *"His kingdom shall be exalted"* speak of the Messiah's kingdom being exalted over all nations at the Second Advent (Isa. 2:1-4; Dan. 2:44-45; Zech. 14; Rev. 20:1-10).

NOTES

The 8th verse once again pictures Israel with the *"strength of a rhino."* Under David this prophecy was partially fulfilled, and under the Messiah in the Millennium will be totally fulfilled.

Once again in the 9th verse, the prophecy says, *"Blessed is he that blesseth thee, and cursed is he that curseth thee."* This is carried over from Genesis 12:3, and still holds true today. Part of America's blessing in the world is her blessing of Israel. Likewise, part of the curse of others nations is the curse of opposing Israel.

The 14th verse says, *"In the latter days."* This speaks of the end time, which, as of yet, has not come to pass but will shortly.

In the 17th verse, the *"star out of Jacob"* is the Lord Jesus Christ, as is the *"sceptre out of Israel."* Jacob had prophesied these words concerning Judah, as well, shortly before his death. This is Balaam's fourth prophecy. The words, *"I shall see Him, but not now,"* in the literal translation is, *"I shall have a full view of Him, but the time is far distant."* That is, the person I am prophesying about does not now exist among these Israelites, nor shall He appear in this generation. The *"corners of Moab,"* along with *"Edom"* and *"Seir,"* refer to Israel's enemies who shall ultimately be defeated and destroyed. *"Sheth"* of the 17th verse refers to *"Seth."* This refers to all of mankind, for all descended from Seth through Noah. The Messiah will reign until all enemies are put under His feet – those of the human race and otherwise (I Cor. 15:24-28).

The 20th verse portrays the fifth prophecy. It speaks of *"Amalek"* and says, *"But his latter end shall be that he perish forever."* Amalek is a type of the flesh. It has always opposed the Spirit. It will one day be totally defeated. In history Amalek was a descendant of Esau, brother of Jacob. The Amalekites were the first to fight against Israel when coming out of Egypt, and they were considered to be the first of the nations.

Verses 21 and 22 contain the sixth prophecy. It says, *"The Kenite shall be wasted."* This would refer to Israel's victories over these people who were near the border of Israel. The victory would remain until *"Asshur shall carry thee away captive."* The captivity Balaam refers to here is that of the ten tribes and their allies and later the remaining Jews who were taken to Babylon, which ruled Assyria.

Verses 23 through 25 record Balaam's seventh and final prophecy. He says, *"Who shall live when God doeth this?"* This prophecy was to be fulfilled in the distant future; no person of that generation would still be living when it took place. Actually, the fulfillment will be when multitudes will be killed off during the Tribulation and Battle of Armageddon. The words *"Chittim," "Asshur,"* and *"Eber"* refer to the following. *"Chittim"* pertains to the Island of Cyprus west of Palestine. This refers to the Romans who ruled the island in the days of Antiochus Epiphanes, but here, refers to the Greeks and Syrians who will be under the Antichrist in the day of the final fulfillment of this prophecy. Both the Assyrians and Hebrews will be afflicted by the Antichrist, and then he (the Antichrist) will be defeated to perish forever. The Grecian Empire will be revived by the Antichrist who will take over Assyria, Palestine, and many other lands, then fight against Jesus Christ at Armageddon, and at last be cast into the Lake of Fire forever.

CHAPTER 25

The three previous chapters record the greatest and most glowing prophecies ever given concerning Israel. Yet, of these same people, chapter 25 records the basest of sin. Why?

Within Israel there was what one might call two Israels; spiritual Israel who belonged to God, and harlot Israel who belonged to Satan. Some of both made up each tribe. Hosea described it graphically in his book. Likewise, today in the Church there are what might be called two churches, the spiritual Church who belongs to the Lord, and the harlot church who belongs to Satan. In every denomination (basically) you can find some of both. Even in individual churches you can find some of each. When God spoke of Israel in the preceding chapters in such glowing terms, He was speaking of those who were His. The Scripture says,

"The Lord knoweth them that are his" (II Tim. 2:19). Similarly, the Lord told Elijah that He had 7000 in Israel who had not bowed the knee to Baal. So, in this chapter we will see some who belong to the Lord and some who do not.

Verse 1 says, *"And the people began to commit whoredom with the daughters of Moab."* The judgment of this chapter was brought about by the cunning of Balaam (Num. 31:16). Likewise, the deadly subtlety of Balaam's teaching is evidenced by his being mentioned ten times in the Bible outside of these chapters. Balaam advised Balak to entice Israel instead of trying to get God to curse Israel, which God would not do. So, Israel would curse themselves.

Verse 2 says, *"And they called the people unto the sacrifices of their gods."* At these *"sacrifices"* the prostitutes of Moab and Midian, who were set apart as the most beautiful women of these nations, were used to tempt and seduce the men of Israel to commit the sins of idolatry, fornication, and adultery. It says, *"The people did eat, and bowed down to their gods."* Not all of them did so, but many did, and the number was growing. According to other passages and I Corinthians 10:8, there were some 1000 chief men as well as some 23,000 others who entered into this terrible sin.

In the 3rd verse it says, *"And Israel joined himself unto Baal-peor."* Baal was the name of the idol god of Moab, and Peor was the name of the place where the idol was worshiped. The passage says, *"And the anger of the Lord was kindled against Israel."* God is always angry at sin.

Verse 4 says, *"Take all the heads of the people, and hang them up before the Lord."* This may seem harsh; however, it was actually merciful. These were individuals who brazenly broke the Law and encouraged others in Israel to sin as well.

The 6th verse says, *"One of the children of Israel came and brought unto his brethren a Midianitish woman in the sight of Moses."* This man was a prince of Israel, and the woman was a princess of Midian which indicates that this was no chance meeting but rather the result of a deliberate plan on the part of Midian and Moab. They concentrated their efforts on the leaders, getting 1000 of them to sin, and then many others followed. The plot would have caused most of Israel to sin if the rebels had not been stopped.

The *"weeping before the door of the tabernacle"* was the result of the plague that evidently had already started.

The 7th verse says, *"Phinehas, the grandson of Aaron, thrust both of them through"* (vs. 8). Sin repented of will always be met by God with mercy. Sin coupled with rebellion will always be met by judgment.

Concerning Phinehas, the 13th verse says of him, *"Even the covenant of an everlasting priesthood."* Actually, he became the third High Priest. As well, God gave him an everlasting priesthood because of his zeal for righteousness in slaying these rebels. He will be an everlasting priest like all redeemed who are made kings and priests to reign on the earth (Rev. 1:5; 20:6).

Verses 14 and 15 show that over 1000 leaders in Israel went into depravity and were fully converted to Baal. In other words, they said, *"Jehovah is no longer our God, but Baal."*

In the 18th verse it says, *"For they vex you with their wiles."* These were the words of the Lord concerning the Midianites. Satan's *"wiles"* did not die with the Midianites. Satan still uses this method with great success.

Hence, in the 17th verse the Lord would say, *"Vex the Midianites, and smite them."* Every lustful, unclean, adulterous, lascivious act in the life of the Christian must be smitten. The command is pure and simple, *"smite them."*

◼

CHAPTER 26

Verses 1 through 4 proclaim the command of the Lord, *"That the Lord spake unto Moses,"* concerning the new generation being numbered. This is the group that was under 20 years of age some 38 years earlier when God pronounced judgment on their parents. Spiritually, they are no better than their parents. Of course, the question begs to be asked, "Why didn't God destroy them as well?" The judg-

ment of Numbers 14 on those who would not go into the land was only on those who would not believe God. Regrettably, the whole of Israel (minus the priests and Levites) who were 20 years old and above were unbelievers and were refused admittance into the Promised Land. Joshua and Caleb were believers and, therefore, were given entrance.

As well, in the new generation those who sinned and refused to believe as in Numbers 25 experienced judgment and were slain by the Lord. God's dealings with humanity are always equal. The only unequal dealings are men among men (Ezek. 18:25).

Verses 9 and 10 once again emphasize the hatred of God for the rebellion of Korah and company, confirming the fact that Korah was swallowed by the earth with Dathan and Abiram instead of being burned with the 250 princes. The children of Korah did not die in the judgment with the rebels, not being in the rebellion with their father. There were ten Psalms made for the sons of Korah. (It seems they were the writers.) This shows the beautiful grace of God.

The 12th verse says, *"The sons of Simeon."* This tribe suffered the largest decrease of any of the tribes between the two numberings. To this tribe belonged Zimri, who was chief leader among those who sinned in the matter of fornication and worship of Baal. He took the Midianite woman into his tent in the presence of weeping Israelites and was killed by Phinehas. As chief of his tribe, it could be that more Simeonites followed him than members of other tribes, and perhaps more Simeonites were killed in this judgment.

Once again it must be remembered that these tribes were numbered for the express purpose, *"that are able to go to war in Israel."* Always remember that the mission of the Church is war against the powers of darkness. Paul told Timothy, *"War a good warfare."* It is our business to bring the light of the Gospel of Jesus Christ into that darkness. Sadly, the majority of the Church wars are in that which is of little consequence. We have not been called by God to save the society; we have been called by God to save men out of the society. To be frank with you, society is doomed; it cannot be salvaged. The mission of the Church in this war is to take the Gospel of Jesus Christ to a lost and dying world. Nothing else counts. All else is of little significance. What is the Gospel? The Gospel is *"Jesus Christ and Him crucified."* Once again the 65th verse extols the faith of Caleb and Joshua, *"save Caleb the son of Jephunneh and Joshua the son of Nun."* The greatest thing that a human being can do is to simply *"believe God."*

—■—

CHAPTER 27

Verse 1 says, *"Then came the daughters of Zelophehad."*

Verses 1 through 11 give us one of the most beautiful stories of faith found in the entirety of the Word of God. So often in the book of Numbers we read of the unbelief of Israel. However, Numbers 27 is a striking contrast.

The 2nd verse says, *"And they stood before Moses, by the door of the tabernacle."* They had come to make petition. The astounding thing was that there was no provision for their petition in the Law.

The 4th verse says that their petition was, *"Give unto us therefore a possession among the brethren of our father."*

The Law said that the possession was to go only to the sons. Actually, this is the first example in Scripture of women pleading for their rights before the judges and leaders of a nation. Their case concerned inheritances. As stated, no provision had been made for daughters. There were five daughters of Zelophehad of the tribe of Manasseh. I want you to notice the example of their faith.

1. They brought their case before the highest tribunal in the land, Moses himself. Eleazar, the high priest, and the princes of the congregation were included. Under the Law of God, Moses was their intercessor. The modern Church should understand the faith of the daughters of Zelophehad. Today, under the New Covenant we can go directly to the Father in the name of Jesus Christ. Why go to the Virgin Mary when there is no answer from her? Why go to mere men such as psychologists when there is no answer whatsoever? Why not go

NOTES

directly to God the Father in the name of Jesus (St. John 16:23)?

2. They did not justify the sin of their father, *"but died in his own sin"* (vs. 3). They were pleading grace, not justice. The moment we as Christians start to plead justice before God, in other words that we deserve something, we have just lost the case. Whenever we plead grace as the daughters of Zelophehad did, the answer will be forthcoming. God will operate on no other premise.

3. Even though there was no provision for them in the Law, they petitioned anyway. Others will tell you that you cannot have it. They will say, "The days of miracles are over." The list is endless. Don't listen to the doubt and the unbelief. No doubt many told these five young women that they were wasting their time, but they did not listen to man. They had faith, and they believed God.

4. Their petition was direct, *"Give unto us therefore a possession among the brethren of our father."* They stated exactly what they wanted. Faith always does. Jesus said, *"Ask and ye shall receive."* James said, *"We have not because we ask not."* They asked, and exactly as the Bible said, they were given.

Verse 6 beautifully portrays, *"And the Lord spake unto Moses, saying."* God answered as He always will. He responds to faith; He will not respond to doubt. Jesus illustrated this beautifully in the book of Luke, *"Yet because of his importunity he will rise and give him as many as he needed"* (St. Luke 11:8).

The 7th verse boldly proclaims, *"Thou shalt surely give them a possession of an inheritance among their father's brethren."* What a victory!

Verses 6 through 11 tell us that because of the faith of these five women, the Bible was rewritten. God loves faith! I think by now it should be obvious.

The *"Mount Abarim"* of the 12th verse was a mountain range westward from Heshbon. From its summit, Moses could see the wastes of the Dead Sea and the valley of Jordan. The particular mountain of this range which he climbed was Nebo, also called Pisgah.

Verses 15 through 23 will record the transfer of leadership from Moses to Joshua.

The 16th verse says, *"Set a man over the*

congregation." God has "a set man" over every congregation. Unfortunately, man has tried to usurp authority over God and insert his own *"set man."*

Israel's government was a theocracy, a God-ruled system. God was their invisible King Who chose certain men to lead His people. There were no political parties, campaigns, or elections of popular men. As long as Israel continued under this form of government, depending on God and living right, they had victory and miraculous experiences, but when they demanded a king so as to be like other nations, they came to an end like others who forgot God. When they come back to God in the latter days, the theocracy will be restored to remain forever (Zech. 14; Rev. 11:15).

In the 17th verse Moses says, *"That the congregation of the Lord be not as sheep which have no shepherd."* Moses prayed for a leader who, like a shepherd going before the sheep and leading them in and out to pasture, would care for Israel. There is a world of difference in the sheep and the shepherd. That bridge cannot be crossed by man. The shepherd leads; the sheep are led.

The 18th verse records God's choice, *"Take thee Joshua the son of Nun, a man in whom is the Spirit, and lay thine hand upon him."* Unfortunately, man has laid his hand on those so often whom God did not choose. The one in whom is no Spirit is the bane of the Church. The one *"in whom is the Spirit,"* is the salvation of the Church (Eph. 4:11).

The 23rd verse says, *"And he laid his hands upon him."* Giving charge was a solemn rite, and so it should be today when the ordination by God of men to the ministry is recognized by other men. This verse says as well, *"And gave him a charge."* What is that charge? Volumes could be written, but perhaps it would be better summed up in two words that Jesus gave to His disciples, *"Follow me."*

CHAPTERS 28 & 29

The doctrine of these offerings and those of Leviticus and Exodus is the same. They would

NOTES

pertain to life and righteousness through an atoning Saviour. It was as beautiful to Moses at the conclusion of the 40 years as it was in the beginning.

The *"sweet savour"* of verse 2 could only be understood in the light of the redemption that the sacrifices represented. That which is sweet savour to the world has absolutely no appeal to God. Regrettably, that which is a *"sweet savour"* to the Lord has no appeal to the world.

The 4th verse constitutes the Law of daily sacrifice. It was to be done seven days a week with some addition on the Sabbath. The *"one lamb thou shalt offer in the morning"* and *"at even"* was at 9 a.m. and 3 p.m. Jesus died at the offering of the evening sacrifice at 3 p.m. All the lambs were to be *"without spot,"* which represents Christ. Each day these were to be a *"continual burnt offering,"* with the word *"continual"* specifying that the one sacrifice of Christ would be continual for all time, for all people who would believe. The *"meat offering"* (meal) was to be offered along with the burnt offering. It was basically a thanks offering.

Verses 9 and 10 of chapter 28 portray the *"Sabbath day"* sacrifices that were to be doubled, in other words two lambs in the morning and two lambs in the evening, plus the doubling of the *"meat offering."*

Verses 11 through 15 portray the sacrifices that were to be offered at the beginning of each month, in other words the first day.

Beginning with the 16th verse of chapter 28 through chapter 29, we are given the various feast days through the year. These feast days are described in detail in the commentarial notes from Leviticus chapter 23.

CHAPTER 30

Chapter 30 contains the Law of vows. Verse 1 says, *"This is the thing which the Lord hath commanded."* Therefore, we realize how serious this matter, the Law of vows, is in the sight of God.

Verse 2 says, *"If a man vow a vow unto the Lord. If a man makes a vow to Jehovah and binds his soul by an oath, he shall not break word, but shall perform all that comes from his mouth."* (There is an exception to this on which we will comment at the end of this chapter.)

Verse 3 says, *"If a woman also vow a vow unto the Lord."* If an unmarried woman makes a vow to Jehovah, binding herself by an oath, it shall stand, and she shall perform it unless her father refuses to permit it to stand in the day that he hears of it. If he objects to her vow in that day, then it shall not stand, and the Lord will forgive her because her father objected.

Verse 6 says, *"And if she had at all an husband when she vowed."* This means that if a married woman makes a vow to Jehovah and binds herself with an oath, it shall stand and she shall perform it unless her husband objects to it in the day that he hears of it. If he objects to it in that day, then it shall not stand, and the Lord will forgive her because her husband objected.

Verse 9 says, *"But every vow of a widow, and of her that is divorced."* This means that if a divorced woman or a widow makes a vow and binds her soul with an oath to Jehovah, it shall stand.

If the vow of a divorced woman or a widow was made while she had a husband, it shall stand unless her husband objected to it the day he heard of it. If her husband objected that day, it shall not stand, and the Lord will forgive her because her husband objected.

Verse 14 says, *"But if her husband altogether hold his peace."* This means that every vow and binding oath that a married woman makes, may be established by her husband or made void by her husband. If he holds his peace day after day then he establishes her vow, but if he objects the day he hears about it, it shall not stand.

Verse 15 says, *"Then he shall bear her iniquity."* This means that if a husband hears a wife's vow or her oath and does not object to it the day he hears about it, then later makes it void by objecting to her fulfilling it, he shall bear her iniquity for causing her to break it.

Going back to verse 13, it says, *"Her husband may make it void."* Here, God recognized the authority and rights of the husband of the married woman. He did this to emphasize the proper lordship of the man over the woman

NOTES

and to keep peace in the home (I Cor. 11:3; I Pet. 3:6). Jehovah simply left such matters to the family unit, thus revealing Himself as a just and righteous God, always consecrated to the unity of the home. It may be said at this point that Christianity is not a religion of breaking up homes but of keeping them together. To this end, the Holy Spirit gave the laws concerning marriage and divorce (St. Matt. 19; I Cor. 7).

Returning to verse 14, it says, *"But if her husband altogether hold his peace."* This means that if the husband did not object *on the day* that he heard of the vow of his wife, he then had to let it stand. He could not go beyond that one day to think the matter over, and he could not permit his wife to begin paying her vow, then decide that he did not want her to continue. If he caused her to break her vow after the first day he heard of it, then he was to pay the penalty of the broken vow which she would have had to pay if she, herself, had broken it. Only daughters and wives could be freed from vows if objected to by fathers and husbands.

No provision was stated for annulling vows of boys and young men, but it is supposed that they were held responsible to Jehovah for their vows unless objected to by those having authority over them with power to permit or not to permit them to fulfill vows. Parents were to determine the case of their children and husbands the cases of their wives. Rabbis say that under the age of 12, boys were subject to the sole authority of their parents and, consequently, had no power to make vows.

Vows were supposed to be lawful and if made concerning right things, to be considered binding. Making a rash vow to do evil did not make it right or an act of righteousness. Instead of being kept, rash vows were to be repented of and proper atonement made for such sin. The performance of unlawful vows constituted unlawful acts. The whole chapter teaches that making vows is a serious matter. Scripture does not require the making of vows; it only gives commands concerning them if they are made. Care should be taken in the making of a vow, for it is better not to make one than to make it and break it. Lawful ones should be kept even if a person swears to his own hurt (Psa. 15:4).

Likewise, in the 14th verse it says, *"Are all*

her bonds." Bonds seem to be different from vows. The vow is positive, and the bond negative and restrictive. By a vow, a man might dedicate himself or some of his possessions to God or vow to accomplish some work for Him. By a bond he might cut himself off from some privilege. A vow involved an obligation to do, and a bond involved an obligation to forbear doing.

As stated, the Law said there was no relief for a man if he made a vow (unless it was an unlawful vow). Hence, when the Man Christ Jesus said, *"I will pay my vows unto Jehovah,"* and *"I delight to do thy will, O my God,"* there was no release for him. The bitter cup of Gethsemane had to be drained.

As well, there was release for a woman, but she could not effect it herself; only one that was related to her and that loved her could do so. Such was Israel. She vowed at Sinai to perform all that Jehovah commanded. Her Divine Bridegroom and Husband permitted the vow, but she, having failed to keep it, came, therefore, under sentence of death. To redeem her from this doom, her Husband, in grace, took it upon Himself and so delivered her from her vow. She could not deliver herself. Her husband, in effect, was the Lord Jesus Christ.

In all of these statutes and commandments, Christ is found throughout; His sufficiency is revealed, and man's sinfulness and inability to save himself declared.

CHAPTER 31

Verse 1 says, *"And the Lord spake."* The Church too often hears the voice of man; may the Lord help us to hear His voice. All else is sinking sand.

Verse 2 says, *"Avenge the children of Israel of the Midianites."* God is the only One to do the avenging, *"Vengeance is mine; I will repay, saith the Lord"* (Rom. 12:19). God means exactly what He says. The vengeance is His; it belongs to no one else.

The 3rd verse says, *"Arm some of yourselves unto the war."* Israel was to be Jehovah's instrument of vengeance upon Midian. However,

under the New Covenant of Grace, the child of God is never to be the instrument of vengeance, *"Dearly beloved, avenge not yourselves"* (Rom. 12:19). The Midianites were the ones who had caused Israel to sin (Num. 25). Even though Israel would be chosen as the instrument of vengeance, still, strict restrictions would be placed upon her.

The 6th verse says, *"And Phinehas the son of Eleazar the priest, to the war, with the holy instruments."* The insertion of Phinehas with the holy trumpets signifies that the battle carried far greater spiritual connotations than usual. The implication was that Israel, even though the instrument of vengeance in God's hand, was not entirely without fault herself – hence, the insertion of Phinehas and the holy trumpets. This should be a lesson to those of us who are used of the Lord. When we proclaim, *"Thus saith the Lord,"* we must always remember that we are sullied, as well, and stand only in the Grace of God.

Verse 7 says, *"And they warred against the Midianites as the Lord commanded Moses."* The war that the Church engages in is too often not the war that *"the Lord commanded."*

The 8th verse says, *"Balaam also the son of Beor they slew with a sword."* Balaam did not die the death of the righteous but perished fighting against the people of God despite all the efforts of God to save him.

Verses 9 through 13 speak of Israel's partial obedience. The 13th verse says, *"Went forth to meet them without the camp."* The captives and the spoils were not to be brought into the camp before being inspected to determine what was permissible to keep and what was to be destroyed. The camp had to be kept clean of all defilement at all times.

Verses 14 through 16 portray Israel's sin. Verse 14 says, *"And Moses was wroth with the officers of the hosts."* It seems that Moses was only slightly angry concerning accusations against his person. However, his anger would burn red hot concerning sin against God. As the leader he knew what the implications were. They included (vs. 16) *"a plague among the congregation of the Lord."* What the plague was, we are not told.

Verse 16 says, *"Through the counsel of Balaam, to commit trespass against the Lord."*

This was why they were commanded to be destroyed. It was not that God did not love certain nations; it was because of their sinful depravities and their war against Him and His program of ridding the earth of sin and rebellion. It was the same as a doctor excising cancer from a patient.

The words, *"Kill every male among the little ones,"* was done to avoid further and future trouble from these children who would grow up to take vengeance if possible. Examples of what might have happened can be seen in Hadad and others after the males were nearly all destroyed (I Kings 11:14- 40). In the eyes of God this was the same as people who were contaminated with a contagious and killing disease being exterminated to save those who were healthy. These Midianites could have blessed Israel. Time and time again God requested they do so. Had they done so and accepted Israel's God, they would have not only been spared, but blessed as well. Sadly, they chose to rebel; therefore, these steps had to be taken.

The cleansing of verses 19 through 24 speaks of the seven days of ceremonial cleansing. This was done because the soldiers had touched dead men. This had to do with the Law of the red heifer. All of these Laws may seem to be cumbersome and somewhat unnecessary to the spiritual mind. However, they were given as acts of grace and mercy. Sin is a horrid business. Its tentacles reach much further than we realize. This very world is contaminated; therefore, we need constant washings by the water of the Word.

Verses 25 through 47 give us the Law of dividing the spoil.

Verse 27 says, *"Divide the prey into two parts."* This means that the spoil was to be divided between the combatants and the non-combatants, which rewards the desire to battle for His name as though the desire became fact. David would do the same regarding his spoil.

Verses 48 and 49 give the report of the casualties, *"And there lacketh not one man of us."* The officers of the army reported that they did not lose a single man in the war with Midian, which in itself was a miracle and showed a direct intervention of heaven.

Verses 50 through 54 record the thanksgiv-

ing offering brought to the Lord for His protection, *"We have therefore brought an oblation for the Lord."* This offering brought by the captains was partly out of gratitude for the preservation of their lives in battle and partly to express remorse for having disobeyed the Lord in not exterminating all the people who had caused Israel to sin.

Incidentally, back to the 35th verse, it speaks of 32,000 women (virgins) who were taken captive. These 32,000 females were not reserved for any immoral purposes whatsoever but for domestic service. The Law permitted a Hebrew to marry a captive woman but only on the condition of strictly observing the legislation made in her favor that was designed to make immorality and slavery impossible. She could at any moment become a member of the family of Israel and claim her freedom after seven years.

CHAPTER 32

The 32nd chapter portrays the settlement of Reuben and Gad east of Jordan.

The 1st verse says, *"And when they saw the land of Jazer, and the land of Gilead."* The land east of Jordan had now been conquered and was ready for settlement. The tribes of Reuben and Gad, being the chief cattlemen of Israel, requested this as their inheritance. Moses objected to their settling here on the grounds that they were needed to help conquer Canaan. They then promised to help if they would be granted the land they desired.

Jazer in particular was a place of grazing for cattle, and this made the cattlemen desire it without waiting to see what was on the other side of Jordan.

It would seem from Moses' objection to their settlement on the east of Jordan, that the first intention was to settle in Canaan only, but this was out of line with the promises to Abraham (Gen. 15:18-21).

No doubt, they would have gone on to Canaan if Sihon had permitted Israel to pass through his land, but he would not, so a war had to be fought with him. When he was destroyed, naturally the Israelites took over the land. Also, when they had to fight with Og, King of Bashan, they took over his land as well. The original Promised Land was from the Euphrates to the river of Egypt. In the Millennium, the land will be divided into 13 sections, from Hamath on the north to the river and the great sea (Ezek. 48). This means that all the Arabian Peninsula to the Red Sea will be the land of Israel. In fact, Israel will be the head of the nations and, no doubt, will take as much land as needed, even beyond the original Promised Land, for normal expansion and worldwide activity for the kingdom of the Messiah Who will reign from sea to sea and to the ends of the earth (Isa. 9:6-7; Dan. 7:13-14; Zech. 14:9; Rev. 11:15; 22:4-5).

Verses 6 through 15 record the objections of Moses to settling east of Jordan.

It seems that Moses thought the Reubenites and Gadites wanted to settle at once and not help the other tribes conquer Canaan. He perhaps feared another rebellion like the one at Kadesh-Barnea some 38 years before. But the tribesmen of Reuben and Gad assured him that they fully intended helping the others conquer Canaan, and, so they were granted their request.

It should be noted that there is no record regarding this request that Moses ever took this to the Lord. It seems he made the decision on his own. Quite possibly he remembered the promises that God had made to Abraham and, thereby, did not contest the request regarding its locality.

Verses 16 through 19 portray the objections of Moses overcome by giving the promises of Reuben and Gad. The proposition to Moses was that they would build sheepfolds and pens for the stock and cities for their wives and children after which they would go armed to help the other tribes conquer Canaan. This was acceptable with Moses.

Verses 20 through 24 record the conditions of the grant. The 20th verse says, *"If you will do this thing, if you will go armed before the Lord to war."* This is a picture of what the Church ought to be. Even though the enemies in the area that Reuben and Gad desired to occupy had been defeated, still they were required to help subdue the balance of Canaan-land. All of

the Church is responsible for World Evangelism. Regrettably, the amount given per day from those who claim to be born again to evangelize the world is less than one penny per person. Therefore, most of the Church is saying to a tiny few, "Bear the load yourself."

The 23rd verse calls this sin, *"But if you will not do so, behold, you have sinned against the Lord: And be sure your sin will find you out."*

Verses 25 through 27 record the promise of Reuben and Gad, *"Thy servants will do as my Lord commandeth."* Would to the Lord that the entirety of the Church would obey thusly regarding World Evangelism.

Moses approved of the plan of the Reubenites and Gadites to inherit the land east of Jordan upon the condition that they would go armed with their brethren and stay with them until they had conquered their enemies and become settled in the land. According to Joshua 4:12-13, only 40,000 of the Reubenites, Gadites, and one-half of the tribe of Manasseh, who eventually occupied the land east of Jordan, went to war. According to the second numbering of the list, some 40,000 went to war, leaving some 70,000 to guard the families and flocks against neighboring tribes while Canaan was being subdued.

Verse 33 says, *"Unto half the tribe of Manasseh."* Instead of the whole section east of Jordan being given exclusively to the Reubenites and Gadites, a portion was given by Moses to one-half the tribe of Manasseh as an inheritance. No explanation is given here for this tribe being divided to receive its inheritance, but it can be relied upon that God planned it Himself, for all the inheritances were given by lot with the Urim and Thummim.

The 39th verse says, *"And dispossessed the Amorite which was in it."* The spiritual inheritance that God gives us is not free of the Amorite (the flesh). Therefore, it is up to us by the power of the Holy Spirit to *"dispossess"* this hindrance to our spiritual progress. It must ever be remembered, we will dislodge the Amorite or the Amorite will dislodge us. There is no middle ground; there can be no compromise.

CHAPTER 33

Chapter 33 is a summary of the journeys of Israel from Rameses to the plains of Moab.

There are variations in the list of places where Israel camped, as mentioned in the books of Exodus, Numbers, and Deuteronomy, but there are no contradictions. With the vast nation of over 3 million people, very few stations would be large enough for all to encamp. The stations of Exodus refer to the halting places of Moses, the chief men, and as many of the people as were associated with them. While the list in this chapter embraces over and above these, the intermediate and adjoining stations of the whole encampments, here we have mainly those places where prolonged encampments were made, from which the people disbursed their flocks and herds to pasture in the surrounding lands. What we have in this list are the marches from one place to another on going out of Egypt, not necessarily every station of breaking-up of camp and then a march. We have Israel's places of departure according to their marches to more permanent places, not every temporary station of encampment.

Verse 2 says, *"And Moses wrote their goings out according to their journeys by the commandment of the Lord."*

The same love that led Israel through the great and terrible wilderness for 40 years so that they lacked nothing, commanded Moses to minutely record their wanderings. This shows that their Divine Shepherd accompanied them every step of the way from Egypt to Canaan. In all of their afflictions He was afflicted. He cherished them as a nurse would cherish her children. He suffered not their garments to wax old, nor their feet to swell (Neh. 9). When one peruses this chapter, one realizes that the Lord never lost sight of them for a single day.

As one goes down the list looking at the different places, it is impossible not to be affected by the memories which gather around particular names – names like Rameses, Pihahiroth, the Red Sea, Marah, Elim, Rephidim, and others. There were victories and there were defeats, but not one time did He ever leave them.

NOTES

As one looks at this chapter, one realizes that God's unchanging love is watching over us with every day's journey, and there is not a difficulty or sorrow in that journey unnoticed by God's love. What a comfort; what a joy; what a vested confidence.

Actually, Israel was not constantly on the move during the 40 years of wandering. They, no doubt, stayed literal years in certain places, camping at all of the 17 places during the 40-year period.

In the 49th verse it says, *"And they pitched by Jordan."* The long march is finally over. There have been defeats; there have been many victories. In all of it God was so very real to them. Now they are ready to go into the promised land.

The 51st verse says, *"Speak unto the children of Israel, and say unto them."* There were four commands that were given regarding the laws of conquest. They are as follows:

1. When you come into Canaan, you shall drive out all the inhabitants of the land from before you, destroy all their pictures, molten images, and pluck down all their high places. The pictures here refer to carved and embroidery work having designs of idols. The molten images were metallic idols supposed to have supernatural power and virtues.

2. You shall dispossess the inhabitants of the land and dwell therein, for I have given you the land to possess it.

3. You shall divide the land by lot for an inheritance among your families according to the size of the family they shall inherit.

4. Every man's inheritance shall be in the place where his lot falls according to the tribes he shall inherit it.

Verse 55 says, *"But if you will not drive out the inhabitants of the land from before you."* Not only did the nations whom Israel failed to drive out become a constant source of trouble, but the nation of Israel itself was eventually driven out – and for the same reason these former peoples were rejected by God. The sins of idolatry, adultery, rebellion, and total moral depravity caused Israel also to be judged. After the rejection of the Lord Jesus Christ, Israel was completely destroyed as a nation, and the people have remained in dispersion now for over 1900 years with 1948 marking the beginning of the end of this long judgment.

CHAPTER 34

God's plan for Israel was basically tri-fold They were to produce three things:

1. The Messiah.
2. The Word of God.
3. Evangelization of the world.

Through great struggle they gave the world the Messiah and the Word of God. They failed regarding World Evangelism. That task is now being attempted by the Church.

To do this, God would have three things:

1. A people called Israelites.
2. A land called Israel.
3. A city called Jerusalem.

In the 34th chapter the Lord will give the borders of the Promised Land. The Hand of Grace that delivered the children of Israel from Egyptian bondage, that opened a path through the Red Sea, that performed great miracles in the wilderness, would now fix the boundaries of their habitation. It was only a very real and tender love that could occupy itself with such details. These people were Jehovah's people, this land, Emmanuel's land. Therefore, nothing is small or insignificant.

Regrettably, it would be hundreds of years before they would take full possession of the land under David's reign. Not long after David, spiritual declension would set in, and ultimately they would lose the entirety of that which God had given them.

A brighter day, however, is to dawn when Israel, redeemed and blessed under the New Covenant, will be brought by the Divine Joshua into Jehovah's pleasant land and established there in righteousness forever (Ezek. 47).

The 13th verse says, *"This is the land which you shall inherit by lot."*

The borders of the land of Canaan were for the purpose of having definite bounds so as to divide the land for each particular tribe. Actually, this was not all the Promised Land, for the entire extent of it was from the Mediterranean

on the west to the Euphrates on the east, and from Hamath on the north to the Indian Ocean on the south, including all the Arabian Peninsula. It was never fully inhabited, even under David. However, it will no doubt be totally occupied during the millennial reign and possibly even expanded.

Generally speaking, the tribes as listed here received their inheritance from south to north. As stated, the division of these tribes was not by committee. The Scripture says, *"Which you shall inherit by lot."* The word *"lot"* probably meant by the Urim and the Thummim which was held by the High Priest. The beautiful way in which the Holy Spirit placed the tribes goes back all the way to the birth of their founding fathers.

For example, the tribes of *"Judah"* and *"Simeon,"* sons of Leah, dwelled by each other. Those of *"Benjamin,"* the son of Rachel, and *"Dan,"* the son of Rachel's maid, were by each other. Tribes of *"Manasseh"* and *"Ephraim,"* sons of Joseph, were side by side. Those of *"Zebulun"* and *"Issachar,"* sons of Leah, were together. Tribes of *"Asher,"* the son of Leah's maid, and *"Naphtali,"* the son of Rachel's maid, were together. Those of *"Reuben,"* the son of Leah, and *"Gad,"* the son of Leah's maid, were together on the east of Jordan. Thus, in Divine Wisdom, God divided the land to the tribes.

What a mighty God we serve!

CHAPTER 35

The 35th chapter concerns the cities of the Levites and the cities of refuge.

Verses 1 through 8 speak of the cities of the Levites. There were 48 total scattered all over Israel. Thus, the prediction of Genesis 49:7 was fulfilled, *"And scatter them in Israel."* It was a curse because of Levi's sin. It was fulfilled and, at the same time, turned into honor and blessing, no doubt, at least in part because of Levi's faithfulness as is recorded in Exodus 32:26, *"Who is on the Lord's side? Let him come unto me. And all the sons of Levi gathered themselves together unto him."* Thus is the Grace of our Lord Jesus Christ. He takes our wrong, places it into His right, and makes everything right.

Verses 9 through 15 portray the *"cities of refuge."* There were six in number. It says in verse 11, *"That the slayer may flee thither."* Three of these cities were west of Jordan and three were east of Jordan (they were part of the 48 cities of the Levites).

In the *"city of refuge"* the man-slayer found safety, and when the High Priest died, he would find liberty. The avenger of blood symbolizes the Law. It demanded the death of the man-slayer. When the High Priest died (of old age), this satisfied the claim and liberated the man-slayer. Likewise, Christ's death, not His life, rent the veil, and frees the sinner from the curse of the Law. Upon the death of the High Priest, the man-slayer was then at liberty to return to his possession. Likewise, when Israel shall look upon Him whom they have pierced, it will then be revealed to them that His death restores them to the land and the family of God.

Thus, a *"city of refuge"* stood almost at every man's door, but to enjoy its safety, the man-slayer had to flee there. Any man who ignored this Law would perish.

Verses 30 through 34 say, *"Whoso killeth any person. . . . the murderer shall be put to death."* Therefore, no murderer could find refuge in any of the *"cities of refuge,"* nor liberty in the death of the High Priest. Sinners who flee to Jesus prove that they are not willingly guilty of His blood, and they, therefore, find in Him both safety and liberty. But sinners who refuse thus to seek mercy in Him, demonstrate by their refusal that they are verily guilty of His death, and for these individuals there is no salvation.

The Holy Spirit writes of these *"cities of refuge"* in Exodus 21, Numbers 35, Deuteronomy 4 and 19, and Joshua 20.

Verse 33 says, *"For blood it defileth the land."* It means that blood unlawfully shed defiles the land.

In verse 30 it says, *"The murderer shall be put to death."* This law was given in Genesis 9:6. It was continued under the New Covenant in Romans 13:1-7.

Therefore, God's command that murderers be executed began near the dawn of time, con-

NOTES

tinued under the Law and, as well, into the age of Grace, which covers us at this present time.

CHAPTER 36

Chapter 36 gives us the Law of inheritances. Once again it refers back to chapter 27 concerning the daughters of Zelophehad.

It is very easy to pass over Numbers 27 and, thereby 36, and miss the beautiful portrayal of faith and obedience. In Numbers 27 we see a powerful faith in action that literally rewrote a part of the Bible – and that on behalf of the daughters of Zelophehad.

Verses 5 through 9 proclaim the obedience that must follow the tremendous victory of faith. There was discussion over who these girls could marry. The 5th verse says, *"According to the Word of the Lord."*

Verse 6 says, *"Only to the family of the tribe of their father shall they marry."* Faith had won them a tremendous victory, and now the Lord requires obedience. However, the requirement was not grievous at all. They were to marry their first, second, or third cousins which was permissible in those days.

Verses 10 through 12 tell us of the willful obedience of the *"daughters of Zelophehad."*

Verse 11 once again gives their names. The Holy Spirit, rejoicing in their faith and obedience, heralds them for eternal glory.

Verse 13 says, *"These are the commandments and the judgments."* These commandments complete the Law of Moses as recorded in the book of Numbers. Others follow in the book of Deuteronomy.

THE
BOOK OF DEUTERONOMY

The Hebrew for the name "Deuteronomy" is "Words," speaking of the words of Moses.

CHAPTER 1

From verse 1, it would seem that the location of Moses' speech-making was near the Red Sea and way down in the wilderness of the Sinai Peninsula; but this is not the case. For in verses 4 and 5, we have the time and place, *"on this side of Jordan in the plains of Moab after the defeat of Sihon and Og."* This does not contradict verse 1, which, according to the Septuagint should be translated, *"These are the words which Moses spoke to all Israel, on the bank of the Jordan, west of the wilderness which reaches to the Red Sea."*

In verse 8 it says, *"Go in and possess the land."* Exodus and Deuteronomy illustrate the two great steps of the Christian life. Exodus speaks of being brought *"out of."* Deuteronomy speaks of being brought *"into"* – out of the house of bondage into the land of corn and wine.

This second step demands a far greater energy of faith than the first. To enjoy salvation by faith is a vital and great experience, but to claim and consciously possess all spiritual blessings in the heavenlies demands a deeper and richer faith. However, in both experiences there must be the obedience of faith as well.

Verse 22 says, *"We will send men before us and they shall search us out the land."* This reveals the fact that Moses, instead of sending spies, would have gone up immediately to occupy Canaan from the south. The people were the ones who suggested sending the spies. In fact, God had already spied out the land for the people with all of heaven ready to occupy the Promised Land. So, the very act of the people desiring to send spies into the land was an act of unbelief. Moses made inquiry of God who then told him to go ahead and send the spies (Num. 13:1-2).

The 26th verse says, *"Notwithstanding you would not go up, but rebelled."* This was, without doubt, Israel's biggest blunder. If the nation would have obeyed Moses as he commanded in verses 20 and 21, and not demanded that spies be sent to see if the land were as God had described it to them, they would have been blessed immeasurably. The following blessings were forfeited.

1. Settlement in Canaan 38 years earlier.

2. The old generation would not have been condemned to die.

3. Freedom from 38 years of hardships, plagues, and other curses.

4. Their own bravery would have been confirmed and God-honored.

5. They would not have suffered disgrace and defeat by their enemies.

6. Korah and company very likely would not have rebelled, and peace would have continued.

7. The people would have had better living conditions, food and raiment 38 years sooner.

The 28th verse says, *"Our brethren have discouraged our heart."* It is remarkable how easily brethren can discourage one another with a few words. There really was no danger at all, for God was with them, as he was 38 years later. The words, *"greater and taller than we,"* referred to actual giants who were from nine to twelve feet tall.

The 32nd verse says, *"Yet in this thing you did not believe the Lord your God."* All the miracles Israel had seen did not cure them of unbelief, nor will miracles today accomplish anymore. The disciples saw more miracles than the nation did coming out of Egypt; yet, they were full of unbelief and hardness of heart regarding the resurrection miracle, even after Christ's many infallible proofs concerning it (St. Mark 16:14; St. Luke 24:25). If one will not believe the Word of God, he will not believe though one should rise from the dead (St. Luke 16:30-31). The Israelites had several daily miracles in their midst – the manna (Ex. 16), the pillar of fire by night and the cloud by day, besides other miracles when needed, and, yet, they could not seem to have complete trust in God.

Verse 33 says, *"Who went in the way before you, to search you out a place to pitch your tents."* The love that the Lord gave Israel by searching out every resting place for their camp is a delightful blessing for every child of God today just to know that the Heavenly Father watches over us daily.

In verse 38 it says, *"Encourage him,"* speaking of Joshua. It would seem that men with such great power as Moses, Joshua, and others, would not need encouragement, but they do. The possibility of failure is present regardless of the amount of authority and responsibility.

Verse 39 says, *"Moreover your little ones, which you said should be prey,"* shows us that the very things we fear are sometimes what God uses to show His power and to teach us lessons.

The 43rd verse says, *"So I spake unto you; and you would not hear, but rebelled."* This shows the stubbornness and presumption of the old generation. God definitely commanded them not to go up, and faithfully warned them of the consequences – defeat, but they went contrary to His orders and were defeated as predicted. They rebelled when God told them to go up, then rebelled again when He told them not to go up.

Verse 45 says, *"And you returned and wept before the Lord."* Weeping before God does not always mean the persons are brought to obedience. Sometimes the weeping, as here, is

over defeat and not their consecration to obey God. Already, God had given them up to die in the wilderness because of repeated acts of rebellion. He had endured enough with them and was now holding to His decision of doing away with the old generation. Their weeping did not constitute repentance, was not sincere, and was not from the heart.

CHAPTER 2

Verse 1 says, *"And we compassed Mount Seir many days."* The entirety of chapter 2 concerns wanderings, representing 38 wasted years. The impotent man at the pool of Bethesda in St. John 5 pictured the nation of Israel in its 38 years of impotent existence because of unbelief. As Jesus lifted up the man, putting him on his feet, and thereby in victory, so did Jesus, the true Joshua, bring Israel over the Jordan into the goodly land. It is doubtful that the children of Israel really understood the grace and the glory that was afforded them at that time by the Lord Jesus Christ. Also, the Pharisees and Scribes of Jesus' day were blind as well. Sadly, the situation for the Pharisees and Scribes of the present time have changed very little.

Regarding verse 1, regrettably, Israel's picture in the wilderness is too similar to our own present experiences. We stay in the land of defeat too long. It seems the battle is intentioned by the Holy Spirit. However, the unbelief and spiritual quagmire which is the result is our own doing.

Verse 5 says, *"Because I have given Mount Seir unto Esau for a possession."* It seems that the children of Esau, (Edom) along with the Moabites and with the children of Ammon, were protected by God from harm even though they were enemies of God. This shows the wonderful character of our Lord – to remember and bless relatives of his friend, Abraham. He spared Lot from destruction in Sodom because of Abraham (Gen. 19:29), and now, after 400 years or more, He still remembered his friend and was protecting his descendants. God, likewise, remembered the son of Isaac, Esau, for the same reason; he was a relative of

Abraham and Isaac.

In verse 10 it says, *"The Emims dwelt therein in times past, a people great, and many, and tall, as the Anakims."*

The 11th verse says, *"Which also were accounted giants."*

In this chapter, several branches of giants are mentioned - Anakims, Emins (terrible ones), Giants (Rephaim), Horims, Zamzummims (loved ones), and Avims.

These giant races came from the sons of God and daughters of men.

This was only about 900 years after the flood of Noah, so the dwelling of the giants in Edom, Moab, and Ammon in old times, had to be during this period for them to be dispossessed by the Ammonites. The giants mentioned in this chapter came from the second eruption of angels among men for the purpose of occupying the Promised Land in advance of Abraham in an effort to keep the Messiah from coming into the world. Like those of the first eruption (before the flood), these giant races since the flood came from fallen angels and daughters of men.

In the 24th verse it says, *"Begins to possess it,"* which speaks of the actual beginning of Israel to possess the land promised to Abraham some 470 years before. From here on Israel expanded her conquests until in the prosperous reigns of David and Solomon, the nation ruled over all surrounding lands, even to the River Euphrates, dominating the Syrians, Moabites, Edomites, Ammonites, Philistines, and many other peoples.

Verse 33 says, *"And the Lord our God delivered him before us."* Each one of these powerful nations was stronger than Israel. So the Lord had to deliver Israel. Likewise, the powers of Satan arrayed against the child of God are stronger than we. Consequently, as the Lord delivered Israel so long ago, the Lord is the only One that can deliver us today. Regretfully, most of the church world opting for the psychological way, believes little in the God that delivers. Therefore, the bondage continues.

Verse 37 says, *"Only unto the land of the children of Ammon thou camest not, nor unto any place of the River Jabbok."* Ammon was located west and a little north of the kingdom of Sihon, and somewhat south and west of the

NOTES

kingdom of Og, near the River Jabbok which separated Sihon and Og. It was on this river bank that Jacob wrestled with Jehovah (Gen. 32:22-32). The Ammonite territory was exempt from this present conquest, as well as were Moab and Edom.

CHAPTER 3

Verse 1 says, *"Og the King of Bashan came out against us."* Og was a giant, one of the Rephaim, a man who had a bedstead about 15 feet long and about 6 feet wide. Some tribes were made up of many giants; but it appears that the Rephaim branch was about exterminated.

Verse 2 says, *"And the Lord said unto me, Fear him not."* This giant, no doubt, represented a formidable opposition. Within Israel's own power they could not have hoped to win the victory. But with the Lord, giants would fall. God evidently gave Israel a supernatural wisdom, intelligence, and battle prowess. In other words, He gave them whatever they needed to defeat the enemy, irrespective of the strength of the enemy. Likewise, the Lord gives us whatever we need to defeat the enemy, *"We overcome by the blood of the lamb and by the word of our testimony."* (Rev. 12:11)

Verse 6 says, *"And we utterly destroyed them."* This is the only type of victory that God will recognize. Too often we destroy the things of the world that are ugly, but fail to destroy that which seems to be attractive and enticing. Here, for a change, Israel utterly destroyed all.

Verse 23 says, *"And I besought the Lord at that time, saying."* This was Moses' last plea to be allowed to go over into the land, and for God not to deny him because of the one sin of smiting the rock twice. He wanted so much to enter the land, but God said, *"Let it suffice thee; speak no more unto me of this matter"* (vs. 26). It may seem that Moses' punishment was too severe, but when we consider that the smiting of the rock the second time broke the all-important type set before Israel, as well as the whole world, to portray the truth of Christ being crucified once and only once for sin, and when we realize that the second smiting pictured crucifying Him afresh and putting Him to open shame, then we know that what Moses reaped was just and right.

God considered it necessary to do this. The sin of Moses involved the greatest truth of the ages, so it could not be looked upon by God as a trifling matter, regardless of how much He loved Moses and would like to give him permission to enter the Promised Land.

When the final chapter is written, God will see to it that Moses did not really miss very much after all, and, at the same time, will ultimately reign supreme in the Promised Land, and that during the millennial reign, and, thereby, forever.

Verse 28 says, *"But charge Joshua, and encourage him, and strengthen him."* Oftentimes, the Church of today treats its modern Joshuas in the opposite manner of that commanded here. The modern Joshua is too often hated by fellow ministers and idolized by the laity. Both are wrong. First of all, if the ministry truly understood the terrible responsibility that God places on a modern Joshua, they would pray for him, encourage him, and strengthen him, and as well, thank God that the Lord called this certain individual and not them.

Likewise, the laity little encourages or strengthens modern Joshuas. They rather idolize them, thinking they are types of spiritual giants far above the fray, and, thereby, not subject to that which is *"common to man."* If they disappoint them, which sooner or later happens, the laity too often turn on them with viciousness.

CHAPTER 4

In this 4th chapter, there are nine commands of obedience given by God to Israel. They are as follows:

1. *"Hearken,"* which means to hear intelligently; to be obedient; regard, publish and show forth; in other words pay careful attention to the statutes and judgments (vs. 1).

2. *"You shall not add to the word which I*

command you, neither shall you take anything from it, that you may keep the commandments of Jehovah" (vs. 2). Sadly, adding to and taking away is the bane of the modern church.

3. *"Keep and do the statutes of Jehovah, for this is your wisdom and understanding in the sight of all nations"* (vss. 5-6).

4. *"Only take heed to yourself, and keep your soul diligently, lest you forget what you have seen and your heart depart from them"* (vs. 9).

5. *"Teach these things to your sons and coming generations, that they may learn to fear me all their days"* (vss. 9 and 10).

6. *"Take good heed to yourselves, lest you corrupt yourselves by making graven images, and lest you worship the heavenly bodies like the heathen"* (vss. 15-20).

7. *"Take heed to yourselves lest you forget the covenant of Jehovah and make false gods and be consumed by the jealousy of God"* (vss. 23 and 24).

8. *"Know this day and consider in your heart that Jehovah is God"* (vs. 39).

9. *"Keep His statutes and commandments, that it may be well with you and that you may live long lives"* (vs. 40).

Verse 6 says, *"This is your wisdom and your understanding in the sight of the nations."* The outstanding example of Israel among the nations in revealing a contrast between Jehovah and idols and the great blessings of serving God, was not manifest in outward show, but in simple obedience to Jehovah. Physically, mentally, spiritually, supernaturally, militarily, materially, and governmentally – in every phase of human life and success, Israel was so far above the other nations – and that even in the wilderness. Ultimately, under David and Solomon, Israel would become the most powerful nation in the world of that day.

Verse 9 says, *"But teach them thy sons, and thy son's sons."* It was the duty of every parent in Israel to teach and instill in the heart of every child the wisdom and knowledge of God as stated in the Scriptures (II Tim. 2:14; 3:15-17). If this were done today in America and Canada, or any country in the world for that matter, racial hatred would end, the runaway crime rate would end, cities would become pleasant places instead of animal-crawling jungles. But regretfully, there is no room in the public school system in America nor in its jurisprudence system for God. So, we have anarchy, crime, murder, theft, adultery, and drugs instead.

In verse 10 it says, *"That they may learn to fear me all the days that they shall live upon the earth, and that they may teach their children."* Actually, this is the primary purpose of hearing the Word of God in all ages (Rom. 10:17; II Tim. 2:15).

Verse 13 says, *"Even ten commandments."* Here, God's covenant with Israel is called the Ten Commandments, because they give a gist of the whole law and summarize the principles thereof. Actually, the Old Covenant of Sinai was abolished, done away, and completely annulled with the death of Christ at Calvary. However, under the New Covenant of Grace as was given to the Apostle Paul, nine of the Ten Commandments became a part of the New Covenant. The fourth commandment, to remember the Sabbath, was omitted altogether, and is not binding on Christians.

The 15th verse, *"For you saw no manner of similitude on the day that the Lord spake unto in Horeb."* This command was to take heed not to attempt to make any idol or image of anything they thought God would look like, though they saw no actual form when they heard His voice. This suggests the reason God did not show Himself to the people in general – lest the ones who were weak and bent on idolatry would begin to make graven images like unto what they had seen Him to be. This does not teach that God has no form, image, or likeness bodily, nor does it mean that He did not show Himself in a real, visible, tangible, and bodily form to anyone, for this He did. He showed Himself to 74 elders of Israel at one time, and they ate and drank with Him" (Ex. 24:9-11). He showed Himself to Moses and others many times in visible, bodily form. He promised to show His similitude to Moses and speak face to face with him. Whatever similitude He did *not* show to all Israel, He *did* show to Moses, for the same English word is translated from the same Hebrew word in both statements and means the same thing. Actually, God has a Spirit body.

NOTES

In verse 20 it says, *"Brought you forth out of the iron furnace."* This emphasizes the terrible sufferings of the people under bondage to Egypt. It also in type emphasizes the terrible suffering of any unsaved person under the domain of Satan.

Verse 26 says, *"That you shall soon utterly perish from off the land."* Moses made seven major predictions concerning Israel. The following is what he said:

1. Remain in the land many generations (vs. 25). They did stay in the land for about 35 generations after this prophecy; then in A.D. 70 the Romans destroyed the nation, scattering Israel among all other nations (Matt. 23:37).

2. Remain in the land a long time (vs. 25). They did for about 1600 years before final dispersion, excluding the 70 years of captivity to Babylon (Jer. 25:11-12).

3. Corrupt yourselves in the land (vs. 25). Israel began doing this soon after the death of Joshua and the elders who outlived him who had seen the works of God (Josh. 24:31; Judg. 2:7-23). They lived more or less in corruption and sin until they had to go into captivity, as revealed in the books of Judges, Samuel, Kings and Chronicles. They continued in rebellion until they rejected the Messiah and were totally destroyed as a nation in A.D. 70. The corruption was in the forms of all kinds of idolatry, moral sins, rebellions, and finally in the rejection of Christ and the apostles (St. Matt. 23; St. Luke 21:20-24).

4. *"You will utterly perish from the land"* (vs. 26). This was literally fulfilled in 749 and 616 B.C. when Jerusalem was destroyed and all the people except a few who were taken to Babylon (II Kings 17 and 25). It happened again in A.D. 70, and since then until 1948, not many Jews have lived in the land (St. Luke 21:20-24).

5. *"The Lord shall scatter you among the nations and you shall be left few in number among the heathen"* (vs. 27). This has been literally fulfilled and continues in fulfillment.

6. *"You will serve other gods among the heathen"* (vs. 28). This also was literally fulfilled (Isa. 2:18-20; Zech. 10:2; 13:2).

7. *"When you are in tribulation in the last days and you seek the Lord, you will find Him and obey Him"* (vs. 29-31). This will be fulfilled at the Second Coming of Christ.

Incidentally, this repeated lapsing of Israel into idolatry destroys the theory that Jehovah was a creation of the religious emotions of the Israelites; for history proves that nations cleave to the gods that they invent, whereas Jehovah and Israel were perpetually at war.

CHAPTER 5

The 2nd verse says, *"The Lord our God made a covenant with us in Horeb."* The word *"made"* means to cut. It means to make a contract, an alliance, or a bargain by cutting a sacrifice in pieces and passing between them, thus binding the parties of the contract together by blood and by death. It is used of making covenants.

In the 3rd verse it says, *"The Lord made not this covenant with our fathers."* Moses made it very clear that God made (cut) a covenant with them at Sinai, that He did not make this covenant with their fathers (Abraham, Isaac, and Jacob), but *"with us, even us, who are all of us here alive this day."* In view of this simple statement, we can say with authority that Adam, Abraham, Isaac, and Jacob did not have the Ten Commandments and that Sabbath-keeping therefore was not commanded from Adam's time on, as some teach. The evident facts are that neither Adam nor any other man was commanded to keep any special Sabbath for over 2500 years, and, as well, the Sabbath is not a part of the New Covenant.

Verse 12 says, *"Keep the Sabbath day to sanctify it."* The 15th verse says, *"And remember that thou was a servant in the land of Egypt."* What was it they were supposed to remember? It was not simply a Sabbath or day of rest, but *why* a Sabbath or day of rest was commanded. It was solely because they had been slaves in the land of Egypt without rest on any particular day, and God brought them out with a strong hand. Therefore, because of this reason Jehovah commanded them to keep a Sabbath day. Thus, it was to commemorate Israel's deliverance from Egyptian bondage, and not because God rested on the seventh day, as in Gen. 2:3-4. Even the command in Exodus

NOTES

20:8 was not to remember the one Sabbath on which God rested; but to remember the Sabbath that was commanded Israel in Exodus 16:22-26, where we have the first commandment for any man ever to keep a Sabbath day. This was over 2500 years after God's Sabbath. Israel could never remember the Sabbath God rested on, for they have nothing to do with His Sabbath. Thus, we are to understand that the word *"remember"* in Exodus 20:8 refers to Exodus 16:22-23, and the word *"remember"* in Deuteronomy 5:15 refers to their slavery and deliverance from Egypt, as in Exodus 1:1 and 14:31. Actually, this commandment, *"Remember the Sabbath,"* is the only commandment that has no moral connotation, and for the reasons given. Consequently, it was not included in the New Covenant.

Verse 22 says, *"These words the Lord spake."* This is speaking of the Ten Commandments, and that God spoke them with an audible voice to all Israel. An estimated 3 to 5 million people heard Him at one time out of the midst of the fire, cloud, and thick darkness of Sinai. The Ten Commandments were all that these estimated millions of people heard from the voice of God, for He added no more by an audible voice. Those that He added were through Moses.

Verse 25 says, *"For this great fire will consume us: If we hear the voice of the Lord our God anymore."* These verses (23-33) contain a much fuller narrative of the events briefly described in Exodus 20:18-21. Because of the entreaty of the elders of Israel, Moses took on him the responsibility of being the channel of communication between God and Israel. God approved the request of the people (vs. 28), because it showed their feeling of unworthiness to enter into direct communication with Him. The terrors of the occasion had done their work, and the whole nation was conscious of sinfulness and unworthiness to approach God.

CHAPTER 6

Verse 2 says, *"That thou mightest fear the*

Lord thy God." This kind of fear is not the dread of a vengeful being standing over man to punish for the least infraction of his law; it has more to do with the respect and reverence of God as Father and Benefactor. Men must learn to respect God as the Law-giver and Judge, keeping in mind the justice of God as well as His mercy and longsuffering. No man can walk with Him conscientiously or safely who has lost the fear of God. The 2nd verse also says, *"And thy son, and thy sons' son."* In all generations, whoever fears God will endeavor to bring his children up in the way of righteousness, that they also may fear Him and live clean and holy before Him in word and deed (II Cor. 7:1; Eph. 6:4).

The Lord Jesus Christ in Matthew 22:35-40, pointed to verses 4 and 5 of this chapter as being the first and great commandment of the law. Incidentally, the word *"one"* could have two meanings, with the first meaning *"single"* and the second meaning "a compound unity." It is the second that is used in verse 4, so this verse implies the Trinity.

In the 13th verse the words, *"and shalt swear by his name,"* mean to worship God.

Verse 15 says, *"Lest the anger of the Lord thy God be kindled against thee."* With all the promises and benefits of the Bible and all the present contracts in force between God and man, there are, without exception, certain conditions and warnings given. God has always promised to curse the same people for disobedience whom He has promised to bless for obedience. God is no respecter of persons and there are no unconditional covenants, promises, or blessings.

Verses 20 through 23 proclaim to us that Israel was never to forget two great facts in her past history, and was never to be ashamed to point them out, slavery and salvation.

Verse 25 says, *"And it shall be our righteousness if . . ."* The sad fact is no one ever kept *"all these commandments."* No one, that is, except the Lord Jesus Christ. Man did not keep them and, in fact, could not keep them. However, the Lord Jesus Christ did. With my acceptance of Him as my own personal Saviour, God now looks at me as law-keeper instead of a law-breaker. Jesus did for me what I could not do for myself.

NOTES

Incidentally, the 16th verse was quoted by the Lord to Satan in the temptation in the wilderness.

CHAPTER 7

Verse 1 says, *"And hath cast out many nations before thee."* Israel was God's sword for the destruction of the seven nations of Canaan. God Himself could have destroyed them, as He destroyed the Antidiluvians and the people of Sodom and Gomorrah. However, instead, He employed Israel as His instrument of wrath in this just judgment. He did it this way so as to write upon Israel's heart a horror of idolatry and of the unspeakable wickedness which it sanctioned and sanctified. One archaeologist stated, "The God of the Old Testament that ordered the extermination of these people did the world and future generations an untold service." Of course he was speaking of their terrible wickedness (vss. 1-5).

When executing the divine wrath upon these corrupt nations, they were not to assume themselves morally superior to them, but to remember that they owed everything to the electing love of God - God chose to love them because of a sufficient reason which He discovered in Himself, but not in them (vss. 6-11).

God demanded total segregation from these seven wicked nations. The following are the reasons:

1. They will turn away your children from following me (vs. 4).

2. They will cause them to become idol worshipers, so that I will have to destroy them.

3. You are a holy people unto me (vs. 6).

4. I have chosen you to be a special people unto me above all others on the face of the earth.

God gave many such warnings to Israel before their backslidings to assure them that He was a God of justice and judgment, as well as one of mercy and forgiveness (vs. 4). He plainly outlined His will for them, promising rewards for obedience and specific curses for disobedience. God was therefore under as much obligation to curse them as to bless them. It is contrary to Bible truth to say that His love, mercy, and grace obligate Him to bless only and not to curse for disobedience. Grace covers sins only if they are properly confessed and put away.

Verse 15 says, *"And will put none of the evil diseases of Egypt, which thou knowest, upon thee."* All sicknesses and diseases are but progressive forms of death and are the wages of sin, whether of the principle or of original sin. They are called evil here because they come from evil, sin, and the fall of man, and are propagated by satanic powers (St. Luke 13:16; Acts 10:38).

Verse 16 says concerning the seven wicked nations, *"No pity upon them."* No pity was to be shown because of the depravity of the people, and the fact that Israel would be led into sin and eternal hell through them if permitted to integrate in any degree.

Verse 26 says, *"A cursed thing."* A cursed thing was anything devoted to destruction. The Church wastes its time trying to salvage that which God has cursed. For instance, He has cursed this world's system; it cannot be salvaged or made holy. Ultimately, it will be totally destroyed. As well, society cannot be redeemed; it is cursed. Therefore, we do not try to save society, but conversely save men out of society. Society is ultimately doomed.

—■—

CHAPTER 8

"All the commandments" of verse 1 speaks of the Law. The Law was a strange vehicle. It was given by God and thereby holy. It had a curse to it, but no salvation. In other words, when God gave the Law, He did not give any power to men in order that they may keep the Law. And why didn't He? He didn't, because no power can be given by Law. It must come from a person and that person must be Jesus Christ. The sad thing is, they could not keep the Law. So, if they could not keep the Law, was God not cruel in demanding that they keep the Law? Definitely not. A holy God can only demand a holy life.

Even though there was no salvation in

keeping the Law, and neither was there any power given by God to help them obey the Law, still God made a way through the slain Lamb for mercy, compassion, and forgiveness. The Law was never intended to save, and in fact could not save. It was intended by God to show man how utterly helpless he was in trying to keep this simple code of ethics. Man was (and is) depraved, fallen, and thereby helpless. However, man does not really seem to know how depraved, fallen, and helpless he really is. The Law was intended to show him this depravity. Did it succeed? With some few it did, with most it didn't. Israel gradually made a god out of the Law. They became utterly pharisaical in their self-righteousness, and would ultimately kill the Lord of glory when He came. And they would do it in the name of the Lord.

Salvation has never been in commandments, rules, laws, bylaws, stipulations or works of any nature. Salvation is in a Man, and that Man is Christ Jesus. Every Jewish believer from the time of Abraham who was saved was not saved as a result of law-keeping, neither were they saved as a result of the sacrifices (for the blood of bulls and goats cannot take away sin). But they were saved by having faith in what the sacrifices represented, namely a Redeemer that was ultimately to come. The prophets proclaimed his coming even from the time of Adam and Eve (Gen. 3:15). The Lord told Abraham that through Him (the seed) would be the blessing of all of mankind (Gen. 12:3).

Jacob, on his dying bed, prophesied that this Redeemer would come from the tribe of Judah (Gen. 49). Isaiah said He would be born of a virgin. Micah said He would be born in Bethlehem. Daniel came close to pinpointing the year that He would come. So, there was no excuse for Israel.

When Jesus Christ came, born under the Law, He fulfilled the Law in every respect. He never failed in one tiny point. Now (as then), everyone who trusts our substitute, the Lord Jesus Christ, and identifies with Him receives by adoption the benefits that He purchased for us. The first and foremost of these great benefits is redemption. However, in redemption's great plan there are many other benefits as well. One of those is as follows:

When we identify with our substitute, the Lord Jesus Christ, by faith; inasmuch as He kept the Law in all of its totality, God looks at us now not as law-breakers, but law-keepers. Jesus took the curse of the Law upon Himself, which rightfully should have come upon us.

So, God gave mankind a code of law that would order his life and steps, and demanded that he keep it. At the same time, He knew he wouldn't and in fact couldn't. So, God would provide a substitute, the Lord Jesus Christ, Who would keep the Law and, thereby, redeem all those who would trust in Him.

Verse 3 says, *"Suffered thee to hunger, and fed thee with manna."* An explanation is given here showing why Israel was permitted to be tested with hunger and then supplied with the manna - that God might teach them that man does not live by material food alone, but also on spiritual food by the Word of God.

The latter part of the 3rd verse was quoted by Christ in His great victory over Satan (St. Matt. 4:4; St. Luke 4:4).

The 4th verse in few words reports one of the greatest miracles ever recorded, especially when one considers how fast clothes wear out. This does not mean that clothes grew larger or smaller (for infants when needed), but that the various sizes and kinds of garments for the families lasted throughout the 40 years.

Verses 7 through 9 portray the *"good land."* This is a type of the inheritance that the Lord has given unto us through Jesus Christ. The *"brooks"* and *"water,"* as well as *"fountains"* and *"depths that spring out,"* refer to the living water that comes to us at salvation.

The *"wheat"* and *"barley,"* as well as *"vines, and fig trees, and pomegranates"* refer to the Word of God that the child of God now has. The *"olive oil and honey"* refer to the Holy Spirit, the power and the joy.

The 9th verse says, *"Thou shalt not lack anything in it."* God's salvation is a "whole salvation."

Incidentally, the word *"brass"* throughout the Old Testament should have been translated copper. Brass is copper that is added with zinc and other materials. There is no evidence that the metallurgy of that nature existed then. As well, men do not dig brass out of hills, they dig copper.

NOTES

The 12th verse says, *"Lest when thou hast eaten and art full."* How accurately God knew Israel in speaking prophetically of their natural inclination to forget Him in times of prosperity and success. The same trait is found in all nations with few exceptions. Seemingly, only a few individuals have guarded themselves against this temptation. Man is so depraved that he wants to take credit to himself for success and prosperity, when the truth is that God is the One with the power of wealth, as stated to Israel in verses 17 and 18. It is the highest will of God that all men prosper, especially His own children, who should give Him the glory for the same. To this end He has made abundant provision and given exceeding great and precious promises that we might have *"all things that pertain to life and godliness"* (II Pet. 1:3-4). The believer in Christ can ask what he will and it shall be done in the will of God (St. Matt. 17:20; St. Mark 11:22-24; St. John 15:7). There is no limitation to the one who is unselfish, uncovetous, and consecrated to the best good of all. It is only when one becomes selfish and seeks prosperity at the expense of others that he disqualifies himself in claiming the fulfillment of all the promises of God.

The 16th verse says, *"Who fed thee in the wilderness."* The daily supply of food, fuel, and water for Israel's estimated 3 to 5 million people would be tremendous. Yet, the supply was provided from natural and heavenly sources for the 15,065 days of the 41 years and 3 months of their journey from Egypt to Canaan.

The 18th verse says, *"It is he that giveth thee power to get wealth."* God gives power to get wealth, so it is not sinful in itself. It is the misuse of wealth, its use contrary to the law and will of God that constitutes sin.

The 19th verse says, *"If thou do at all forget the Lord thy God."* God promised to destroy Israel for certain sins - the same sins for which He caused them to destroy the wicked nations of Canaan. This points to the fact that God is no respecter of persons and that no individual or nation that backslides and lives in sin after serving Him can hope to escape His righteous judgment. Israel, as a nation, knew God and had many experiences of grace and power not enjoyed by any others; yet God said they would be destroyed because they did not continue in obedience, and they were ultimately destroyed.

CHAPTER 9

In chapter 9 Israel is made to know by Moses that it was not because of their righteousness that they are being given the land of promise. The Lord has ever reminded His people, including the modern-day church, that whatever blessings come to us are never because of any righteousness on our part, but, instead, because of righteousness on His part. Sadly, how little we learn this.

The 1st verse says, *"Hear oh Israel."* This could well be given to the present-day Church. Six commands are given in this chapter - commands for obedience:

1. *Hear* - You are to pass over Jordan and possess nations greater than you (vs. 1).

2. *Understand* - that I will go before you like a consuming fire to destroy them before you (vs. 3).

3. *You shall* - drive them out and destroy them quickly.

4. *Speak not* - in your heart, after I have cast them out before you, that it was for your righteousness that the Lord caused you to inherit the land; it was because of the wickedness of those nations (vs. 4-5).

5. *Understand* - that the Lord does not give you this land because of your own righteousness, for you are a stiff-necked people (vs. 6).

6. *Remember* - Forget not, how you provoked Me to wrath in the wilderness from the exodus until now and have been rebellious against Me (vs. 7).

Verse 1, as well says, *"Nations greater and mightier than thyself."* The Lord gave a threefold description of Israel's enemies.

1. Nations greater and mightier than you.

2. Cities great and walled up to heaven.

3. A people great and tall.

God Himself recognized that the giants facing Israel were greater, mightier, and taller, and had cities walled up to heaven, as it were. They were the giants from the second eruption of fallen angels and the daughters of men, after

NOTES

the flood of Noah.

The 2nd verse uses the words *"children of the Anakims."* These were the descendants of Anak, one of the most powerful of the giants.

Not only did God tell Israel the truth concerning their enemies and how it would be impossible to overcome them without His help, but He assured them of His going before them like a consuming fire to devour these giant races.

The 4th verse says, *"Speak not thou in thine heart."* This is the equivalent of saying: When the Lord enables you to get complete mastery of your enemies, do not take the credit to yourselves; you must recognize that you were powerless in yourselves, and that it was only through the help of God that you overcame them; furthermore, that it was not for any righteousness of your own that God gave you victory over your enemies, but, rather, because of the wickedness of those nations and the promise of God to give their land to Abraham, Isaac, and Jacob.

This clearly illustrates the doctrine of salvation by Grace through faith and that not of self. God makes it distinctly clear that Israel was not righteous in themselves, but they were a stiff-necked and rebellious people. In the following passages Moses gave many instances of their rebellions to prove that it was not because of their goodness that God helped them.

It is readily obvious in the Christian's journey that the enemies facing him are far more powerful than he could ever hope to be within himself. And furthermore, within his own abilities it is impossible to overcome the powers of darkness. It can only be done through the Lord Jesus Christ. Regretfully, the church world as a whole has opted for man's ways. It little knows nor understands, or even desires that which comes from God.

The 20th verse says, *"And the Lord was very angry with Aaron."* Modern religious thought, recognizing good in all religions, would have applauded Aaron's conduct in the matter of the golden calf as wise, gentle, large-minded, and sympathetic, and Moses' action as narrow, ill-tempered, and disastrous. But God's judgment was otherwise, for He would have killed Aaron had not Moses interceded for him. The Apostle

Paul's language and conduct in the epistle to the Galatians would similarly receive the approbation of God and the condemnation of man.

The 23rd verse says, *"Go up and possess the land."* Moses made it clear here that he did not originally intend to send the 12 spies; he had commanded Israel to go up immediately from Kadesh-Barnea to possess the land. Instead, the elders came pleading with him to send spies to see if the land was as God had described it so they would know whether they could overcome the people in it. Thus, Israel rebelled against the commandment of God, questioned His revelation regarding the land, and did not really believe that He would enable them to conquer the giants and other inhabitants of Canaan.

—◼—

CHAPTER 10

Verse 1 says, *"At that time the Lord said unto me."* This refers to the second 40-day fast. The Scripture said, *"Hew thee two tables of stone like unto the first."* Who hewed the first tables of stone is not stated. It is only said that God would give them (on which He had written the Ten Commandments) to Moses (Ex. 24:12). Then He said, *"Make thee an ark of wood."* This is no doubt the same Ark mentioned in Exodus 25:10-22. Moses had received the instructions on how to build the tabernacle and its furniture during the first 40 days, so it could be that the workers of the tabernacle built it for him before or during his stay on the mount the second 40 days. It seems from verses 3, 5, and Exodus 34:4, that just the stones were taken up on the mount in Moses' hands and were brought back down and put into the Ark which had remained in the camp.

Verse 2 says, *"And I will write on the tables of the words."* God promised to write the Ten Commandments again on stone as He had written them before (Ex. 24:12). From Exodus 34:27-28, it might seem that Moses wrote on the new stones, but upon close examination and from the above passages, it is clear that the pronoun refers to Jehovah and not to Moses.

NOTES

What could be referred to in Exodus 34:27 is a command from Moses also to write the Ten Commandments as a separate record. The fact is that Moses did write them two times (Ex. 20; Deut. 5). Besides this, he wrote parts of them in other places of his writings. Moses, himself, testified that God wrote on the second tables and gave them to him.

Verse 5 says, *"Put the tables in the ark which I have made."* This confirms the fact that the Ark remained in the camp, and that when Moses came down with the tables of stone that he put them in the Ark, and there they were as the Lord commanded. It also confirms the fact that this Ark was the permanent one which continued to hold the tables.

Verse 8 says, *"At that time the Lord separated the tribe of Levi, to bear the Ark of the covenant of the Lord."* This was at the terrible sin of the golden calf (Ex. 32). The Levites quickly responded to the call of Moses to be on the Lord's side and slay all, even closest relatives, who continued to rebel and refused to come back on God's side. Three thousand held out in rebellion and were slain. That day the Levites won the priesthood.

Verses 12 through 13 record 5 commands.

1. Fear the Lord your God.

2. Walk in all His ways.

3. Love Him with all your heart and with all your soul.

4. Serve Him with all your heart and with all your soul.

5. Keep His commandments and statutes.

The 16th verse says, *"Circumcise therefore the foreskin of your heart."* Circumcision of the heart - opening it to God by removing all reservations, coverings, secrets, and unbelief - is a command. God promises to help man in this matter (Lev. 26:41; Acts 7:51), providing man will humble himself and permit Him to.

The doctrine of circumcision is mentioned in only eleven passages of the Old Testament and in only four after this one. It is mentioned only two times outside the Pentateuch (in the Old Testament), and referred to in 27 passages of the New Testament, mostly to expose the lack of merit of literal circumcision as a means of salvation.

Verse 17 says, *"For the Lord your God is God of gods."* In the Hebrew the literal meaning is, "Jehovah your Elohim is Elohim of Elohim, Adonai of Adonim, the great El, a Gibbor, and Y are." Literally, the Eternal, your Creator, is the Creator of creators, the Sovereign of sovereigns, the Strong One, the Mighty One, the Fearful One who champions the cause of the fatherless and widows without respect to persons.

CHAPTER 11

Verse 1 says, *"Love the Lord thy God, and keep his charge."* Actually, there are seven commands in this chapter. They are as follows:

1. Love the Lord your God (vs. 1).

2. Keep His charge, His statutes, His judgments, and His commandments always (vs. 1).

3. Take heed to yourselves, that your heart be not deceived to turn aside to serve other gods and worship them (vs. 16).

4. Lay up those words in your hearts, and bind them for a sign upon your hand and frontlets between your eyes (vs. 18).

5. Teach them to your children, speaking of them when you sit in the house, walk by the way, lie down, and rise up (vs. 19).

6. Write them upon the door-post of your house, and upon your gates (vs. 20).

7. Observe to do all the statutes and judgments which I set before you this day (vs. 32).

Verse 2 says, *"And know ye this day:"* As well, there were ten things Israel was to remember. They are as follows:

1. The chastisement of Jehovah (vs. 2).

2. The greatness of Jehovah.

3. The mighty hand of Jehovah.

4. The stretched-out arm of Jehovah.

5. The miracles of Jehovah (vs. 3).

6. The acts of Jehovah in Egypt.

7. His judgment upon the arm of Egypt, their horses and chariots (vs. 4).

8. His miracle in melting the Red Sea to destroy the Egyptians.

9. His miracles in the wilderness (vs. 5).

10. The miracle of the earth swallowing Dathan and Abiram and all their households (vs. 6).

The 8th verse says, *"That ye may be strong."* Beautifully enough, there are 12 bless-

NOTES

ings promised if the commands of the Lord are obeyed. They are as follows:

1. Power to be strong (vs. 8).

2. Success in possessing the land.

3. Length of days in the land (vs. 9).

4. A better land than that of Egypt (vss. 10-12).

5. Rains in due season (vs. 14).

6. Abundant crops (vss. 14-15).

7. Days of heaven on earth (vs. 21).

8. Complete mastery of enemies (vss. 22-25).

9. Success in all places (vs. 24).

10. No man able to defeat you (vs. 25).

11. Fear in the hearts of enemies.

12. Blessings of all kinds (vs. 27). Hallelujah!

Verse 10 says, *"And wateredst it with thy foot."* Scarcely ever any water fell in Egypt. Irrigation was carried on by hard labor, digging trenches, and turning wheels by treading so that water would be brought up from the river in buckets and poured into the trenches. In Israel, there was plenty of rainfall for the crops.

The 13th verse says, *"And it shall come to pass."* What will come to pass? A blessing if the commandments are obeyed, a curse if they are ignored. However, it must always be noted that God is never defeated. Ultimately, the curse will be totally eradicated from Israel, and she will be restored once again to her place of glory and power under the Messiah.

Verse 13 also says, *"If you shall hearken diligently unto my commandments."* This is what is commonly referred to as the Palestinian Covenant. There were 15 conditions to it. It is as follows:

1. If you hearken diligently to my commandments (vs. 13).

2. Love Jehovah your God (vss. 13, 22).

3. Serve Him with all your heart and with all your soul.

4. Take heed to your heart not to be deceived (vs. 16)

5. Do not turn aside to serve other gods and worship them.

6. Lay up My Words in your heart and in your soul (vs. 18).

7. Bind them for a sign upon your hands and frontlets between your eyes.

8. Teach them to your children when you

sit in your house, walk by the way, lie down, and rise up (vs. 19).

9. Write them on the door-post of your house and upon your gates (vs. 20).

10. Diligently keep and do all my commandments which I command you (vs. 22).

11. Walk in all His ways.

12. Cleave to Him.

13. I set before you a blessing and a curse – a blessing if you obey the commandments; a curse, if you will not obey, and if you turn away from them to go after other gods (vss. 26-28).

14. In the land you shall write the blessing on Mount Gerizim, and the curse on Mount Ebal (vss. 29-30).

15. You shall observe to do all the statutes and judgments which I set before you this day (vs. 32).

Verse 14 says, *"That I may give you."* Fourteen blessings were promised in the Palestinian Covenant. They are as follows:

1. Rain in due season upon the land, the former rain and the latter rain (vs. 14). The early rain fell in October to moisten the parched soil and prepare it for sowing. The latter rain fell in March to bring the crops to maturity.

2. Abundant crops of corn, wine, and oil.

3. Good pastures for stock that you may be prosperous and full (vs. 15).

4. Your days multiplied (vs. 21).

5. The days of your children multiplied in the land.

6. Blessings of the days of heaven upon earth.

7. Complete victory over all the nations of the promised land (vs. 23).

8. You shall possess all their lands and property.

9. Everywhere you walk shall be yours, from the wilderness on the south to Lebanon on the north, and from the River Euphrates on the east, to the Mediterranean on the west (vs. 24).

10. No man shall be able to defeat you or stand before you as long as you keep My covenant (vs. 25).

11. God will put a fear of you upon all the inhabitants around about.

12. A blessing if you obey the covenant (vs. 27).

NOTES

13. A constant reminder of God's covenant (vss. 29-30).

14. Success in the conquest and possession of the land to dwell therein (vs. 31).

Verse 17 says, *"And the Lord's wrath be kindled against you."* This speaks of the five curses of the Palestinian Covenant. They are as follows:

1. The Lord's wrath kindled against you.

2. No rain from heaven.

3. Crop failures.

4. To perish quickly from off the good land given you by Jehovah.

5. A curse if you disobey My covenant or if you go after other gods and worship them (vss. 26-28).

Verse 18 says, *"And bind them for a sign upon your hand, that they may be as frontlets between your eyes."* Whether these commands concerning the binding of portions of the law on the hand and forehead were intended to be taken literally or figuratively has been a matter of dispute among commentators. The Jews have for ages attached to them a literal meaning. The passages they selected were Exodus 13:1-10, 11-16, and Deuteronomy 6:4-9; 11:13-21. Two kinds of phylacteries were used. The one for the arm was a strip of parchment on which these texts were written. It was enclosed in a small square case made of parchment or calf-skin, and fastened with a long narrow leather strap to the inside of the arm, between the elbow and the shoulder. When the arm touched the body, the law would thus be near the heart. The strap was carefully wound around the arm and fingers so that the ends came out by the tip of the middle finger. Sadducees wore phylacteries on the palm of the hand instead of the arm. The case for the forehead was divided into four cells with a parchment in each. It was fastened with leather straps to the forehead between the eyes and near the roots of the hair. Phylacteries were worn by men only. The common people wore them during prayer only; but the Pharisees wore them continually and even enlarged them to call attention to their piety. They became badges of vanity and hypocrisy, sometimes being worn as amulets. The show of them was rebuked by Christ (St. Matt. 23:5).

Verse 19 says, *"And you shall teach them*

your children." Parents were to teach their children the Word of God in all places and at all times so that it might become instilled within their hearts.

Verse 21 says, *"That your days may be multiplied."* This is another passage proving that God has no set time for men to die; He planned that they should live long lives through obedience to Him (Psa. 91; I Pet. 3:10-11). The Lord used the term, *"Days of heaven upon the earth."* God made this statement by inspiration through Moses, and we have here His confirmation that heaven is a real, material planet like the earth – not an invisible, intangible place or some spiritual state into which men go.

In verse 24 it says, *"Shall your coast be."* This verse gives the general boundaries of the promised land. It took in the Sinai Peninsula on the south, extended to Lebanon on the north, and from the Euphrates on the east, to the Mediterranean on the west (Gen. 15:18-21; Ezek. 48).

Verse 27 says, *"If you obey."* All blessings and curses of Scripture are based upon obedience and disobedience to the will of God as revealed therein. If all free moral agents had obeyed God from their creation until now, there would have been no sin, and no curse of any kind in the entire universe. All God's covenants are based upon this principle of right and wrong, sin and righteousness. There is no such thing in Scripture as the government of God or man without strict obedience to law as the basis of assurance of continued grace or favor with those in charge of the government. In the event of sins against both God and man, there must be punishment to assure continued respect for government and those who govern. It would be a great incentive to rebels if they knew there would be no punishment for rebellion. No government could endure for very long where there was leniency or respect of persons with those who plot and practice the overthrow of good government. If laws and penalties are revealed to subjects of government and they ignore, reject, and willfully disobey them; if the government is loose and the rulers too weak to punish rebellion; or, if rulers are too lenient, merciful and forebearing to execute the laws and mete out judgment to

sustain good government, rebels will ultimately take over.

God is not such a ruler, nor does He carry on a weak government; He upholds law and order and metes out punishment and reward as required, thus qualifying Himself as being capable of His sovereignty and moral responsibility. Whether the subjects are holy angels or men, God must demand obedience to all His laws, and He is under obligation to punish as His law prescribes, or bless as He has promised whenever disobedience or obedience is rendered. For God to be lenient in just one case and fail to execute punishment upon the sinner would break down respect for Him in the hearts of all others who are assured of justice should they sin. There can be no respect of person with Him (Rom. 2:11; James 2:9-10). However, it must always be understood that if God's laws are broken, it is God that does the punishing and not man. God's punishment is always redemptive. Sadly, man's punishment is always destructive.

Verse 29 says, *"Thou shalt put the blessing upon Mount Gerizim, and the curse upon Mount Ebal."* Mount Gerizim, located south and Mount Ebal north of Shechem (Josh. 8:33-34) extend east to west almost parallel with the beautiful valley of Shechem. They are about 2,700 to 2,800 feet high, about 600 feet apart, 3 miles long and somewhat in a semicircle. Mount Ebal is the more barren. Gerizim to the south is more beautiful and fertile, so that the two mountains by nature could be emblems of blessing and cursing.

CHAPTER 12

Verse 1 says, *"These are the statutes and judgments."* In this section of laws, we have old laws repeated with new details. This is understandable since the Sinaitic legislation was now nearly 40 years old, and had been given under different conditions and circumstances. The original laws were not set aside or in any way abrogated; on the contrary they were recognized as the basis of all new instructions. Actually, the keynote of this chapter and most that follow are Jehovah and the land. Conditions are specified under which God and Israel could dwell in fellowship in that land. Over and over again blessings are promised for obedience. As well, over and over again judgment would come upon disobedience.

The commandments basically claimed that as a people they belonged to Him. They were to give up every other relationship in order to be only His. They were to utterly destroy everything having even a remote connection with idolatry, and they were to have but one place of worship, and that place He Himself would choose.

Verse 5 says, *"But unto the place which the Lord your God shall choose."* This place, and this place only which would ultimately be named was where the people were to sacrifice. This one center for national worship foreshadowed Calvary to which, in Spirit, all must go in order to meet God and worship Him.

Verse 15 says, *"Notwithstanding thou mayest kill and eat flesh in all thy gates.* This verse, with verses 20-22, permits the killing and eating of all animals, such as were used for sacrifices, at all places and times, not merely at the time and place of sacrifice. Israel could eat freely of the clean animals, even those besides sacrifices - animals, such as the roebuck, hart, and others listed in Leviticus 11 and Deuteronomy 14. Because such as the ox, heifer, ram, sheep, goat, pigeon, and turtledove were specified as suitable for sacrifice, did not mean they were to be excluded from table food. Only the blood was forbidden to be eaten because of its unhealthful effects, and furthermore, it was reserved to be an atonement for the soul (Lev. 17:11). The straight injunction of bringing everything to be killed to the tabernacle could only apply to sacrifices. It is clear here that whatever was killed at home for table use was legal, and the ceremonial injunctions did not apply in such cases anymore than they applied to the hart, roebuck, and other clean animals not permitted as sacrifices.

Verse 19 says, *"Take heed to thyself."* There are three "take heeds" in this chapter.

1. Take heed to yourself that you offer sacrifices only in the one place chosen by Jehovah (vss. 13-14). Once again, this typifies Calvary as the only way of salvation.

2. Take heed to yourself that you do not forsake the Levite as long as you live (vs. 19). As well, this "type's" the fivefold ministry gifts (Eph. 4:11).

3. Take heed to yourself that you be not snared into following the nations which you are to dispossess (vs. 30). This portrays Paul's teaching, *"Come out from among them and be ye separate"* (II Cor. 6:14-18).

Verse 25 says, *"Thou shalt not eat it."* The blessing of having everything go well for coming generations is again dependent upon obedience to God regardless of the kind of command to be obeyed. Merely refraining from eating blood will not make one prosperous, but obedience to God will (vs. 25).

CHAPTER 13

Seduction to idolatry is the subject of this chapter. Every trace of idol worship was to be utterly destroyed, for what men do not see does not tempt them as powerfully as what they do see.

Verse 1 says, *"If there arise among you."* There are three great "ifs" of chapter 13. They are as follows:

1. If any prophet, dreamer, or teacher performs a sign or a wonder, or predicts anything that comes to pass, seeking to lead you away from Jehovah, you shall not follow him. You shall cleave to God and destroy that false religious leader (vss. 1-5).

2. If any man, even your closest relative or friend, secretly entices you to serve gods other than Jehovah, you shall not consent to leave Jehovah but shall kill that rebel (vss. 6-11).

3. If the inhabitants of any city forsake Jehovah, or seek to lead you away from Him to serve other gods, you shall completely destroy that city with all its inhabitants (vss. 12-18).

Verse 1 continues to say, *"A prophet."* In this passage it refers to a false prophet. Even though he might predict something which would come to pass and be supported by a supernatural sign or wonder (vs. 1), such miraculous power in a false prophet would be the power of Satan (St. Matt 24:24; II Thess.

2:8-12; Rev. 13:1-18). The real test of truth is not a sign, wonder, or prediction coming to pass; it is the truth itself - the Word of God as plainly written (Isa. 8:20; 55;11; St. John 8:32-36; II Tim. 3:15-17; Rev. 22:18-19). Anything contrary to what is plainly stated in Scripture is false regardless of its seeming inspiration. God allows signs and wonders to prove men, temptations to test one's love for Him, and heresies to make truth manifest (I Cor. 11:18-19; II John 7-11). There would be no way of manifesting light if we had no darkness.

The great deception of the last days will be this very factor, false prophets producing signs, wonders, and miracles, and deceiving, if it were possible, even the very elect. The False Prophet under the Antichrist will be greatly instrumental in bringing in the one world church, which is actually already beginning, and which will take the world to the very brink of total destruction. The general Christian public hardly knows or understands the Word of God so they have great difficulty in discerning the false from the real.

The 3rd verse says, *"For the Lord your God proveth you."* There are basically two purposes of God in permitting false religions and satanic powers to operate:

1. To prove men (Ex. 16:4).

2. To know whether men will love God with all their heart and soul (I Cor. 11:18-19; II John 7:11).

The 8th verse says, *"Thou shalt not consent unto him."* Apostates turn people from God which causes their damnation and is the highest crime possible against the Lord and others. This is why Jesus pronounced woe upon certain ones in His day (St. Matt. 23:13). On the other hand, *"greater love can no man have than to lay down his life for his brethren to save them from eternal hell"* (St. John 15:13; Rom. 9:3).

The 10th verse says, *"Which brought thee out of the land of Egypt."* This was such a mighty act of God that it is referred to some 52 times in the Pentateuch alone. The deliverance from Egypt is a type of our salvation from sin, Satan, and the world. As the Holy Spirit constantly referred to Israel's deliverance, as well, we should constantly refer to the great miracle of redemption that brought us to the Lord

NOTES

Jesus Christ.

The 11th verse says, *"And all Israel shall hear, and fear."* This is the purpose of all public executions. If men today were executed for capital crimes without failure, there would be very little crime among men; but with enumerable ways of obtaining leniency, reprieves, and endless delays, besides governmental corruption and unqualified judges, the justice required by God's law is not always carried out.

CHAPTER 14

Verse 1 says, *"Ye are the children of the Lord your God."* Israel was called "the children of the Lord." Consequently, their entire life and walk was regulated by this principle. They were to be a set apart people. They were different from anyone on the face of the earth simply because the Lord was their God. In this one verse, two of the commands are given concerning this difference.

1. Do not cut your flesh or hair in honor of worship to any god. It was the custom among Canaanite nations to cut the flesh to manifest sincerity in worship and earnestness in prayer to idol gods, as in I Kings 18:28. More often this was done for the dead (Lev. 19:28; 21:5). This was considered meritorious and helped in washing away sins.

2. Do not make any baldness between your eyes for the dead. It was a custom in certain nations to cut the hair off and consecrate it to the gods; in others the practice was to cut the hair a certain way in mourning for the dead. Israel was forbidden such marring of the body or cutting of the hair for two reasons:

a. You are holy people to Jehovah your Elohim.

b. God has chosen you to be a peculiar people unto Himself, entirely different from the heathen and their superstitious practices.

Verse 3 says, *"Thou shalt not eat any abominable thing."* As well, their diet was to be different.

Verse 22 says, *"Thou shalt truly tithe all the increase of thy seed."*

Actually, there were three tithes required of

Israel.

1. The first tithe was for Levites (Lev. 27; Num. 18). This was a tithe that was to be paid constantly.

2. There was a second tithe required of the Lord for the individual himself and his household to cover expenses at the national feast so there would be no excuse for not going (Deut. 14:25).

3. There was a third tithe that was actually a charity tithe to relieve suffering of poor neighbors. This tithe was to be given only every third year, so it was not a burden in any degree; actually, it was a part of God's welfare plan. God more than made up for it in His blessings of prosperity on the crops and stock of the whole nation. Spread out over the three-year period, the yearly tax for the poor would amount to 3⅓ percent of the nation's increase (vss. 28-29). This tithe was not to be taken to the place of worship, as the other two tithes, but distributed locally as needed throughout the three years it covered.

So, 23⅓ percent was required by the Lord of His people - 10 percent to provide for the priesthood (Levites, etc.), 10 percent to cover the person's own expenses in attending the feast, and then 3⅓ each year for the poor.

I am concerned that in today's great Covenant of Grace, too often we do not even give as much to God as was given under the Law. I think the Bible definitely teaches the tithe (10 percent) as a foundation of our giving. But I feel if we are only 10 percent Christians, we are not exactly what God wants us to be. God does not own 10 percent of our income; He owns it all. Therefore, we should give to Him as He has blessed us. He will abundantly bless those that do such.

CHAPTER 15

Verse 1 says, *"At the end of every seven years thou shalt make a release."* Actually, there were four commands given regarding this sabbatical year. They are as follows:

1. Every seventh year you shall make a release of all payments of debts and all service

NOTES

of servants (vs. 1).

2. Every creditor that lends ought to his neighbor shall release him of all payments that year (vs. 2).

3. He shall not require payment in full or in part from his neighbor during the sabbatical year.

4. Of a foreigner you may require payment during the sabbatical year (vs. 3). This law was made solely for the poor, for in verse 4 it is stated that there will be no need of such law when the poor have ceased to be in the land. It was a release of all payments of debts for a whole year to give the poor man relief and cause the land and servants to rest.

Verse 2 says, *"The Lord's release."* It is called this because:

1. The Lord wanted release from all debts, so as to relieve the poor a whole year (vss. 1-4).

2. He wanted Israel to learn mercy, and have compassion on the poor and needy (vss. 7-11).

3. He wanted to create a brotherly relationship among all His people, one that would be an outstanding example to the heathen around about (vss. 7-15).

4. He wanted a set time every seven years for the release of slaves (vss. 12-18).

5. He blessed men with abundant crops during the six years between the sabbatical years so as to relieve men of suffering of want during a year of rest (vs. 4; Ex. 23:10-11; Lev. 25:2-4).

6. He wanted the land to rest a whole year (Ex. 23:10-11; Lev. 25:3-4).

7. He wanted the poor to have the crops that grew during the seventh year (Ex. 23:10-11; Lev. 25:5-7).

8. He wanted the servants and stock to have a year of rest from hard labor (Ex. 23:10-11; Lev. 25:5-6).

Foreigners who were not of the nation of Israel, and, therefore, not under any obligation to keep the Law of Israel, did not enjoy the debt release or other blessings of the law of Moses. This would encourage men to become converts to God and His ways of life.

Verse 7 says, *"If there be among you a poor man."* Actually, there would have been no poor people in Israel if all had obeyed the covenant and lived in harmony with God and His laws of prosperity. However, knowing that some would fail to be diligent in business, not consulting Him in matters concerning the spiritual and material life, He made this provision - that if one failed to make good in his inheritance, his brethren should help him and give relief in his distress (vss. 7-11).

Verse 7 also says, *"Nor shut thine hand from thy poor brother:"* Actually, there were five commands regarding the relief of a poor brother:

1. If a brother becomes poor, do not harden your heart or shut your hand against him (vs. 7).

2. You shall open your hand wide to him and lend him as much as he needs (vs. 8).

3. Beware that you do not scheme against your brother or evade your responsibility of helping him because it is near the sabbatic year of release from paying debts (vs. 9).

4. You shall surely give to him; and do not be grieved in your heart when you do so, for the blessing of God depends upon your doing right according to the Law (vs. 10).

5. You shall ever be ready to help the poor and needy, for they will always be in your land (vs. 11).

To harden the heart and shut up the bowels of compassion against a man in need was one of the surest ways of receiving the curse of God and cutting off His blessings of material prosperity; for it was because of the kindness, compassion, and right-doing toward all men, especially the poor, that guaranteed the continued blessings of God.

Verse 9 says, *"A thought in thy wicked heart."* A wicked thought in this case would be to reason that the sabbatic year was near; thus, if a loan was made, no payment would be possible during the year of release from debt. To withhold from the needy for this reason and making it appear that one had nothing to lend was wicked.

Verse 10 says, *"Thine heart shall not be grieved when thou givest unto him:"* This is the divine principle of giving - give and do it cheerfully and wholeheartedly. If one does this, he has a reward; but if one gives to earn merit with God or to make a show, he already has his reward.

Verse 16 says, *"I will not go away from*

thee." All perpetual servants of Hebrew stock became such only by personal choice; otherwise, they were to be free at the end of six years of service (vs. 17). The word *"forever"* is absolute and unlimited in time where no limit exists, as with eternal things; but it is limited where such a limit is implied or declared, as here.

The 19th verse says, *"Shalt sanctify unto the Lord thy God."* In this case, it is speaking of animals, and the word "sanctify" means a "setting apart" for divine use, not a cleansing from sin or the removal of what is termed "the old man."

CHAPTER 16

Chapter 16 portrays the three great annual feasts of all Israel. They were as follows:

1. The Feast of Unleavened Bread, which included the Feast of Passover and Firstfruits.

2. The Feast of Pentecost or Feast of Weeks, which was held 50 days after the Passover Feast.

3. The Feast of Tabernacles, which was near enough to the time of the Feast of Trumpets and the Great Day of Atonement that these three could be attended in a 22 day period.

There were three commands regarding these feasts:

1. All males shall appear before the Lord and hold feasts in the place where the Lord shall choose to put His name (vs. 16).

2. They shall not appear before Me empty, but shall bring free-will offerings for the feast (vss. 10, 15-16).

3. Every man shall give his free-will offering as he is able, and as the Lord has prospered him (vs. 17).

As to these feasts, God surrounded Himself with joy. He invited His people to share that joy, and He urged them to bring the stranger and the needy into that joy. Christ, in His fullness, was pictured in these glad feasts.

There was a distinct joy in all of the feasts; however, the joy of Pentecost was different from the joy of Tabernacles.

The 12th verse says, *"And thou shalt*

NOTES

remember that thou wast a bondman in Egypt." This feast was associated with redemption from Egypt, and this joy was to be joined with watchfulness. However, the Feast of Tabernacles was to be a joy without care, *"And thou shalt rejoice in thy feast"* (vs. 14). For this feast foreshadowed the coming millennial reign of Christ.

CHAPTER, 17

Verse 1 says, *"Thou shalt not sacrifice wherein is blemish."* The animal that was sacrificed was to be a type of Christ. Therefore, to offer one with blemish, *"is an abomination unto the Lord thy God."*

Verse 3 says, *"Either the sun, or moon, or any of the host of heaven."* And then in the 4th verse it says, *"Such abomination is."* It is an abomination to God for His people to worship the sun, moon, stars, and other works of His hands, even though they were perfect. It was a greater abomination for them to worship things made with human hands which are imperfect.

Verse 6 says, *"At the mouth of two witnesses, or three witnesses."* If individuals flagrantly disobey the laws of God and there were two or three witnesses to that effect, he shall *"be put to death."* Verses 6 and 7 are the two verses used by the Sanhedrin to put Jesus to death. The only thing different was that they could not agree as to what He had done. Actually, He had done nothing wrong, but everything he had done was right. It is ironic; men kill the Lord in the name of the Lord and try to use the Word of God to substantiate their foul deed.

Verses 8 through 13 say that matters of controversy were not to be decided independently of God, but, on the contrary, in direct connection with Him. If all Christian people would be careful to bring God in upon the scene of their bickering, how swift and satisfactory would be the settlement!

Should Israel desire a king, he was to obey the instructions of verses 14-20.

1. He was to write a copy of the Bible with his own hand. (vs. 18).

2. He was to read it every day (vs. 19).

3. He was to obey it (vs. 19).

4. He was not to deviate from it in any particular (vs. 20).

5. He was not to multiply horses, lest doing so should excite a desire on the part of the people to return to Egypt (vs. 16).

6. He was not to be a polygamist because that would lead to idolatry (vs. 17).

7. He was not to heap up gold, for the love of money is the root of all evil (vs. 17).

CHAPTER 18

The 18th chapter is a chapter of commands. As well, the 13th verse will say, *"Thou shalt be perfect with the Lord thy God."* Perfection here simply means to refrain from all these pagan practices (vss. 9-14).

In the 16th chapter God appointed judges. In the 17th chapter, He said that one day kings would come. In the 18th chapter He speaks to the priests. Regrettably, all would fail in keeping the nation in touch with God. However, in verses 15 through 19, it is said, *"The Lord thy God will raise up unto thee a Prophet from the midst of thee"* (vs. 15). In this Prophet Who would be the Lord Jesus Christ, there would be no failure. Praise the Lord!

The One that was to come, even though meek as a lamb, would still have the power of the great fire that was on Mount Sinai. It was so awful with the entire mountain burning that the people would say, *"Neither let me see this great fire anymore, that I die not"* (vs. 16).

Concerning false prophets and false prophecies, the 21st verse says, *"How shall we know the word which the Lord hath not spoken?"* All prophecy is not of God, nor by the name and inspiration of God. Prophecy that is supposed to be in His name may not be of Him. A mere claim is no proof. If the prophecy comes to pass, it is generally accepted as from God (vs. 22). However, this test is not absolute, for in chapter 13:1-3 God even states that He may allow a sign or wonder (spoken by a false prophet) to come to pass to prove His people and see if they will act contrary to His own Word. Therefore, the real test is not only to see whether a prophecy comes to pass or not, but also to see if it is in harmony with the Word of God. This is the final and complete test. Anything contrary to the Word is false, for God will never contradict Himself. Actually, there are three sources of prophecy. They are as follows:

1. God through the Holy Spirit (Acts 3:21; II Tim. 3:15-17; II Pet. 1:21).

2. Satan through demonic inspiration (Gen. 3:4-5; I Sam. 28; II Thess. 2:8-12).

3. Man's own personal spirit (Ezek. 13:1-23; I Cor. 14:29-33).

Men are to fear God and His true prophets but not false prophets who can be known by their teachings and fruit (St. Matt. 7:16).

CHAPTER 19

For notes on the cities of refuge, refer back to Numbers 35.

Verse 14 says, *"Thou shalt not remove thy neighbor's landmark."* The landmark that is spoken of here is the landmark that was originally set in the inheritance when the land was divided. Those who removed them were classed as wicked and cursed by the Law (27:17). In Israel, by and large, the fields were not marked by fences, but boundaries were indicated by heaps of small stones, by a ridge, by posts or single large rocks set up at certain distances. It was easy for a dishonest man to remove landmarks little by little each year and so, gain some ground from his neighbor. Not only did the Mosaic Law condemn this, but other nations, especially the Romans, had strict laws against removal of landmarks as well. Some landmarks even had curses written on them for those who would remove them.

Under the Law of Moses the 21st verse says, *"But life shall go for life, eye for eye."* But Jesus Who fulfilled the Law instructed in Matthew 5 that we should offer forgiveness to the aggressor upon the confession of his fault. In other words, we are instructed to conduct ourselves under the New Covenant exactly as God conducts Himself toward us, in that He for-

NOTES

gives all manner of sin provided it is repented of.

CHAPTER 20

Chapter 20 concerns war. It is a literal type of our spiritual warfare. The commands given therein for the warfare of Israel would apply as well to our warfare in the spiritual.

Verse 1 says, *"Which brought thee up out of the land of Egypt."* Almost all the time, Israel's enemies were more numerous and greater, just as the demonic powers that come against us are more numerous and greater. Yet, the great miracles that God performed in bringing His children out of Egypt, typifying our salvation experience in being brought out from the domain of Satan, will be used in all of its mighty power to give us victory in each conflict. The only way we can fail is to lean on the arm of flesh instead of the arm of the Lord.

In verse 3 we are told, *"Let not your hearts faint, fear not."* Twice, in four verses, Israel is told not to be afraid of their enemies, and twice they are assured that God will fight for them to give them victory. God always did give victory when Israel lived in obedience and trusted in Him, but when Israel sinned all the assurance of all the priests could not guarantee them the blessing of God. If we follow the Lord, likewise, we need not fear.

In the 12th verse it says, *"Then thou shalt besiege it:"* The Mosaic Law was distinctly opposed to wars of aggression and foreign conquest – any that were not necessary to occupy the Promised Land and keep it safe from enemies. This passage simply outlines the accepted procedure in cases of war beyond the borders.

Verse 13 says, *"And when the Lord thy God hath delivered it into thine hands."* The Lord was always to be considered the Commander-in-chief of the armies of Israel. He was their King, Captain and Guide in times of war and peace. In His hand were the blessings and curses, the prosperity and poverty, the health and sickness, the victories and defeats, and the life and death of all Israel. They were to look to

Him and depend upon Him for the blessings of life, which they always received when they obeyed (Ex. 15:26; Lev. 26; Deut. 28). Likewise, we Christians should only realize that Jesus Christ has already defeated the powers of darkness, and that, consequently, every single demon spirit that comes against us has, in fact, already been defeated. Consequently, the Christian should not really say *"no"* to sin, but actually should say *"yes"* to the Lord Jesus Christ. When the Christian says "no" to sin, in effect, he is trying to fight the battle himself. When he says "yes" to the Lord Jesus Christ, he is recognizing Christ as his Commander-in-chief and, consequently, is assured of victory.

CHAPTER 21

The 1st verse says, *"If one be found slain."*
Then the 2nd verse says, *"Then thy elders and thy judges shall come forth."* Verses 1 through 9 give the law of inquest. The ceremonies here ordained to be observed upon the discovery of a slain man in the open field, were to teach and impress upon Israel several things:

1. The sacredness of a human being who is created in the very image and likeness of God (Gen. 1:26-28).

2. The awfulness of murder - cutting off a human life from further service to God or man and from making any preparation for eternity. This is a horrible crime.

3. The justice and civilized enlightenment of the new laws of God to men, in contrast to the laws of pagans.

4. The fear and vengeance of God for such unthinkable crimes.

5. The results of such crimes should they go lightly punished or unpunished.

6. The pollution the people of God would endure if innocent blood were shed and all efforts to erase the guilt passed up.

According to Jewish writers, the Sanhedrin took charge of such cases by sending out a deputation to examine the neighborhood. After receiving a report as to which was the nearest city to the place where the slain man was

NOTES

found, they issued an order by their supreme authority to the elders or magistrates of that city to provide the heifer at public expense for the required ceremony. The many ceremonial acts necessary to carry out this law made the horror of murder very impressive to the public.

Verses 10 through 14 give the law of taking captives for wives and of divorcing them.

Verse 12 says, *"And she shall shave her head, and pare her nails."* In the East, shaving the head was a sign of renouncing one's religion and becoming a proselyte of another. In this case, it signified that the captive woman had put away her religion and nationality to become an adopted Israelite.

Verse 14 speaks of the divorce law and says, *"If thou have no delight in her, then thou shalt let her go whither she will."* Instead of being unfair, the law of this passage was a great improvement over the laws of other nations at that time. Among all ancient peoples, the custom of war was that captives should become slaves to the victor who had the sole control and right to those captured. According to Israel's law, if a master became desirous of marrying a beautiful woman who by right of spoils of war had become a slave, he was required to wait a month before completing the marriage. This gave the woman time to go through certain rites, calm her perturbed feelings, and become reconciled to her new condition in life. It also gave the master time to test his affections concerning her. If he became indifferent toward her during this period, he was not to lord it over her, sell her as a slave, or retain her in some subordinate position in the household. The slave woman was to go free wherever she willed to go with the provision the master made for her. There is no indication that he may have had relationship with her. Proposing to make her his wife and then rejecting her at the end of the month was humiliating enough that she go free to make her own way in life. In marriage, she would have had an exalted position.

Verses 15 through 17 give the law concerning no respect of persons in the home. The 16th verse says, *"Then it shall be, when he maketh his sons to inherit."* The command is this, if a man has two wives, one loved and the other hated, he shall not put the firstborn of the loved before the firstborn of a hated wife in giving his inheritance to his sons. To hate in this instance means to prefer one above another in the same sense that Jacob preferred Rachel to Leah (Gen. 29:31) and God preferred Jacob to Esau (Mal. 1:2-3; Rom. 9:13). This is also the meaning in the New Testament where disciples are required to hate parents and others (St. Luke 14:26).

Verses 18 through 21 portray the law of death for rebellious sons.

From the passages it seems that every effort is made to reach the individual, *"when they have chastened him"* (vs. 18), but continues to remain *"stubborn and rebellious"* (vs. 20). This was done *"to put evil away from among you,"* and that *"all Israel shall hear, and fear."* Realizing this is an Old Testament law, still, if this law were carried out presently, much of the problems in America and Canada would be handled.

Verse 23 says, *"His body shall not remain all night upon the tree."* This is the verse that the hard-hearted priest quoted to Pilate at the crucifixion of Christ. Religion is a hideous business; it is without doubt Satan's greatest effort.

To sum up the confession of verses 7 and 8, *"Our hands have not shed this blood, be merciful, oh Lord unto thy people Israel,"* will be that of Israel in the latter days when in the light of Calvary (vss. 4-6) they will clear themselves of the murder of the Messiah.

Meanwhile, the unbelieving members of the nation will suffer the doom of the stubborn and rebellious son that we have just mentioned (vss. 18-21).

CHAPTER 22

The laws that are given in the 22nd chapter are an enlargement upon some that have already been given, and many are new laws. All of this shows God's total intended care of His people. Among the nations of the world, the laws that God gave to Israel were millennia ahead of the laws of pagan countries. God's attention was even directed toward a helpless animal that had fallen down, *"Thou shalt*

NOTES

surely help him to lift them up again" (vs. 4). Such detail, care, and concern was unheard of in pagan countries. Israel was to be a light, an example to the whole world; sadly, they failed. Today we in Christendom are supposed to be the light of the world; sadly, we fail as well.

Verse 5 says, *"The woman shall not wear that which pertaineth unto a man, neither shall a man put on a woman's garment."* Men and women were not to wear the garments of each other or anything that would violate the distinction of their sex. The dress of the sexes in those days was more alike than in our day, and there was more need for regulation. The law was perhaps made not only to preserve decency and the clear distinction between males and females, but also because pagans were in the habit of erasing such distinction in idolatrous worship. Men wore the colored dress of women when they presented themselves before the star of Venus, and women wore men's armour when presenting themselves before the star of Mars. Idols were frequently represented with the features of one sex and the dress of the other; and their worshipers endeavored to be like them.

Even today when idol worship is not involved, it is an outrage of decency and nature for men and women to seek to erase the distinction of their own sex. Imitating each other fosters softness and effeminacy in the man and impudence and boldness in the woman. It breeds levity and hypocrisy in both and opens the door to many evils which are abominations to God and a disgrace to man. The passage does not refer to clothing only, but to anything peculiar to each sex that clearly and unmistakably distinguishes one from the other. Where modern machinery requires women to change from skirts to slacks for their own safety, etc., they can still meet their needs without turning strictly to man's apparel.

Verse 6 says, *"If a bird's nest chance to be before thee in the way."* Verses 6 and 7 show the normal, humane spirit of the Mosaic Law in regulating the tendency of fallen man to wanton destruction of any created thing. It encourages the kind and compassionate element of his being, the tenderness of man - the responsible ruler of creation - toward the smallest parts of creation. To cause any species of birds to be extinct would have worked against the betterment of man; without their help the poisonous snakes, scorpions, swarms of insects, flies, locusts, mice, and other creatures could have multiplied so fast as to cause man to suffer, and perhaps be driven from the land.

Today's modern environmental movement, by and large, is not of God because oftentimes it is based on unfair legislation, or the demand for some that abrogates God's laws of man's dominion. However, at the same time, wanton destruction with little regard for the environment or the various species is ungodly, as I think is adequately portrayed in verses 6 and 7. While it is true that many species of animals become extinct through the normal workings of nature, still, man should do what is proper and reasonable to preserve the species. We are now finding to our dismay that the wanton destruction of plant life is at the same time eradicating valuable chemicals in certain plants that can bring healing for various diseases. So, modern science is now beginning to understand why God gave laws concerning even *"a bird's nest"* (vs. 6).

Verse 8 concerns the law of accident prevention. It says, *"Then thou shalt make a battlement for thy roof."* Roofs in the East were generally flat, and a banister was needed to keep people from falling off day and night. Because of the climate, in the warmer months many ate meals on the roof as well as slept there in the open air. The battlement was a wall about three feet high on all sides of the flat roof. It was commanded by God to be there, showing His concern for even the smallest detail.

When God makes laws, they are fair and equitable. Regrettably, when man makes laws without the wisdom of God and ignores God's Word, these may become unfair and ridiculous. For instance, it is against the law in the United States to transport a lobster in the third trimester of its pregnancy, but it is not against the law to abort an unborn human being. God help us.

Verses 9 through 11 give the laws of segregation. Three commands in these verses express three principles antagonistic to modern religious thought and action.

1. Divers seeds - mixed teaching.

2. Ox and ass - mixed service.

3. Woolen and linen - mixed conduct.

Mixed teaching, like mixed seeds, produces sterility. At creation (Gen. 1) there was no mixture, and, hence, fertility. Every seed was *"after his kind"* and was pronounced by God to be *"good."* The seed that Christian workers and ministers are to sow must be the unmixed Word of God. His Word is not to be mixed with man's philosophy. Christ, the true Minister, said, *"I have given them thy word"; "I have not spoken from myself."*

The ox was "clean," the ass "unclean." Together they formed an unequal yoke. When Christian people join with the unconverted in Christian work, marriage, or business, it is an unequal yoke and can never have Divine approval.

Clothing in Scripture concerns conduct. White linen represents the righteous acts of the saints (Rev. 19). Christian action is to be unmixed; it is to be absolutely clean and sincere.

CHAPTER 23

Verse 1 says, *"He that is wounded in the stones."* It was a very ancient practice among many pagan nations for the priests of heathen deities to be eunuchs and for parents to mutilate their children with the view of training them for such priesthood or for services to kings and great men. Here, God forbade such mutilation of the children of Israel. As no animal was fit for sacrifice if not perfect, so no man was qualified to enter the congregation of the Lord if mutilated. This was God's method of preventing castration of male children in Israel. Actually, there were five classes that could not enter the congregation of the Lord.

1. Men wounded in their stones (testicles) - castrated (vs. 1).

2. Men with private parts cut off.

3. Bastards (vs. 2).

4. Ammonites (vs. 3).

5. Moabites.

The *"congregation of the Lord"* (vs. 2) means the assembly of Israel. It is no reference to heaven or of being converted in the New Testament sense of salvation. Persons in all these groups could have been redeemed by turning to God and meeting His demands just like others. God has never turned down a penitent sinner of these classes or any other. He loves the whole world and will save all who turn to Him with all their hearts, repent, and call upon His name. The passage does not mean that such persons were not allowed to mingle with Israelites or live in the nation of Israel. It could only mean that such could not hold public office as an elder, magistrate, judge, priest, or other official in Israel.

The reason is clear: No man with a personal defect that would render him contemptible to others should bear rule over others (Old Testament). No bastard or foreigner, as an Ammonite or a Moabite could rule or enjoy full privileges as true Israelites. Precaution was taken lest friendship and marriage with strangers and foreigners would lead Israel into idolatry. One could even enjoy the smallest privileges as a citizen of Israel by being converted to the Jewish faith, but he would be limited and not be able to rule.

The Ammonites and Moabites were the result of incest (Gen. 19:30-38). This law against them was given for two reasons explained in verse 4. It either applied to males only, or there were exceptions. Ruth, the Moabitess, was an exception (Ruth 1:4; 4:13; St. Matt. 1:5). The law applied only to these two classes of people, for in verse 7 others are dealt with on a different basis.

Verse 6 says, *"Thou shalt not seek their peace nor their prosperity all thy days forever."* It may seem that this is contrary to the law of love in Leviticus 19:18,34, but because of avowed enemies who sought the destruction of Israel through whom the Messiah was to come, the Word of God was given and through whom God planned to bless and rule the world, such a command was necessary. Israel needed to be brought to the point of destroying the nations of Canaan that were already appointed to total destruction because of their wickedness, so that God's plan could be realized.

Verse 18 says, *"Thou shalt not bring the hire of a whore, or the price of a dog, into the house of the Lord."* This does not refer to

selling an ordinary dog - a common domestic animal, but to using for sacred purposes any money received by a sodomite (homosexual) for immoral services. Such money was filthy and sinful, and not to be used in connection with God or worship of any kind. In religious rites among idolatrous nations, both male and female prostitutes were a common part of the worship, especially that of Ashtoreth or Astarte (Mic. 1:7).

CHAPTER 24

The minute regulations of these chapters show how God became involved in the most intimate concerns of His people. To those who loved Him, this was a deep joy, but to those who did not love Him, an intolerable and irritating intrusion. But it was a love both deep and tender that interested itself in soldiers, escaped slaves, physical emotions, divorce, the poor, the pay of the day – the labourer.

The spirit of all these ordinances is very touching, as it shows the goodness and pity of God Who deigns to take knowledge of all these things and to teach His people delicacy, propriety, consideration for others, sensitiveness – in a word, Christ-likeness.

Verse 1 says, *"And it come to pass that she find no favour in his eyes."*

It appears, regarding divorce, that only the man had authority. Perhaps this was true in early times, but later, especially in Christian times, a woman had the right under circumstances as well.

In Israel, the right to divorce was also a right to remarry; a legal divorce was the absolute end of marriage. In Matthew 19 Jesus did not change the meaning of divorce. The question then was: For what reason may one lawfully seek a divorce?

Jesus said Moses wrote the law on divorce because of hardness of the heart of the people, and except for fornication, one must not divorce his wife (St. Matt. 5:31). If one so puts away his wife, he causes her to commit adultery; and by so dissolving a marriage, one who marries her that is put away commits adultery.

All hardness-of-heart divorces for any and every cause are wrong, and only those for a scriptural reason give the right to remarriage. The man and woman who get a divorce without scriptural grounds sin by forcing each other to marry someone he or she has no right to. In Paul's writings we find one more scriptural reason for divorce – willful desertion because of Christ and the Gospel (I Cor. 7:12-15).

However, if fornication is committed by one party, it does not mean that the partner must seek a divorce, but it means only that the partner can scripturally seek a divorce.

The word "fornication" means homosexuality, repeated adultery with many partners, and participation in heathenistic religious practices involving male and female prostitutes to heathenistic gods. Fornication and adultery are two different words. All fornication is adultery; however, all adultery is not fornication.

Verse 4 says, *"Her former husband, which sent her away, may not take her again to be his wife."* This is in contrast to some modern teaching that a second marriage which may have come about while the couple was yet in sin, should be broken up at the time of their becoming Christians so that one or both might return to former companions. Such a theory is not supported in either Testament. The nearest instructions we have are those in I Corinthians 7:10-16 where a Christian woman who leaves her husband without getting a divorce is required to remain unmarried or be reconciled to him.

Also, verse 4 says, *"After that she is defiled."* A woman divorced and remarried was considered defiled as far as her former companion was concerned but not as far as the new husband was concerned, or God's Law would not have tolerated her marriage to him. The word *"defiled"* as used here refers to that which is illegal. The word is used in various ways. Dinah was defiled by the Prince of Shechem (Gen. 34); a woman committing adultery is spoken of as defiled (Num. 5:13-14). A person was defiled if he touched a dead body (Num. 6 and 9); and sowing different seeds in a vineyard defiled the fruit (Deut. 22:9).

Verse 11 says, *"Thou shalt stand abroad."* This command – not to go into a man's house

NOTES

for his pledge (money owed) – was designed to curb greediness and protect the poor man from the money lender. A lender could not enter a well-respected house but stood outside and called the owner to come out and meet him. Without this law he might intrude rudely into the rights of the poor and unfortunate, and by showing himself so anxious that he must go into a man's house to get the pledge of a loan, he would prove himself inhuman, greedy, and lustful for material gain. One purpose of the law was to prevent the lender from selecting the pledge himself, thus leaving the choice up to the poor man. He could bring out what he pleased if equal in value to the money borrowed.

CHAPTER 25

Verses 1 through 3 give the law of punishment by scourging.

Due punishment was not to be inhuman. The condemned was not to receive more than 40 stripes. To assure obedience to this law, the Jews cut the stripes down to 39 and gave them all in three strokes, using a scourge of 13 cords.

The Apostle Paul five times received these 40 stripes save one (II Cor. 11:24), but unjustly, we might add.

Verse 4 says, *"Thou shalt not muzzle the ox when he treadeth out the corn."* The Apostle Paul quoted this in I Corinthians 9:7-14 giving instructions concerning care for ministers of the Gospel. However, in other kinds of labor the oxen were often muzzled.

Verses 5 through 10 give the law of perpetual families. There were five commands:

1. If a married brother dies childless, the living brother shall go into his brother's wife and raise up seed to him.

2. The firstborn from such a union shall succeed in the name of the dead brother that his name not be blotted out of Israel (vs. 6).

3. If a man refuses to raise up seed to his brother, then his brother's wife shall take her case before the elders of his city for justice (vs. 7).

4. The elders shall call the man and inquire

of him concerning his reason for not raising up seed to his brother (vs. 8).

5. If he persists in not fulfilling his obligation according to the law, then the brothers' wives shall come to him in the presence of the elders, loose his shoe from off his foot, spit in his face, and say that such disgrace rightly belongs to the man who will not build up his brother's house. His name in Israel shall be called *"the house of him that hath his shoe loosed"* (vss. 9-10).

The primary reason for this command was the coming of the Messiah through one of the families of Israel. And, as well, that each family was a descendant of Abraham, Isaac, and Jacob.

Verse 11 says, *"And taketh him by the secrets:"* The 12th verse says that the hand of one seeking to injure the productive organs of a man should be cut off. This shows how serious it was for one to be denied the power of reproduction, suggesting that God was not in sympathy with the making of eunuchs which was so common at that time.

Verses 13 through 16 give the laws of *"just weights."* Over and over again in the Bible we are told how God rewards honesty and detests dishonesty. Perfect and just weights and measures meant they were true weights and measures according to what was legal and right, and that the same ones were both used to buy and sell (vs. 15).

Verses 17 through 19 give us the law of vengeance on Amalek. Amalek was to be utterly destroyed; not so the Egyptian. The Egyptian pictures man, as such; the Amalekite, man as the willing agent of evil. The Christian's attitude toward ordinary men of the world is necessarily different from that toward the willing and determined enemies of goodness and justice.

The God who condemned Amalek to utter extinction was the same God who tenderly sheltered the little bird of chapter 22. This same God appeared in the flesh, and in St. Luke 12 taught that the hand that upholds the little sparrow thrusts wicked men into hell.

There were three commands concerning vengeance on Amalek:

1. Remember what Amalek did to you by the way when you came out of Egypt (vs. 17).

2. When you become settled in Canaan, you

NOTES

shall blot out the remembrance of Amalek from under heaven (vs. 19).

3. You must not forget it.

There were two great sins of Amalek:

1. He cowardly attacked feeble, faint, and weary stragglers of Israel as they came out of Egypt (Ex. 17:8-16).

2. He did not fear God when he saw all the miracles He did for Israel in the wilderness (vs. 18).

Amalekites could not have been ignorant of God and His mighty acts and special blessings upon Israel, because of living in the same wilderness as a neighboring tribe. They hardened themselves, rejecting Jehovah and His dealings with His people, and became bitter enemies of both God and Israel. They provoked and invited this sentence of God upon themselves as predicted and commanded here.

This could be called a prophetical command. Amalek gave Israel trouble during the judges. God then commanded Saul to fulfill this prophecy and kill every Amalekite (I Sam. 14:48; 15:1-5). He completely broke the power of Amalek, but did not fully obey God in destroying all (I Sam. 15:10-35; 28:18). For this disobedience, Saul was rejected as king and destroyed (I Sam. 15:10-35; 28:18). Later, the remnant was destroyed by the Simeonites in the days of Hezekiah (I Chron. 4:39-43). It seems that Haman and his sons were the last of the Amalekites. They were destroyed in the time of Esther, and the prophecy was then literally and completely fulfilled.

In Bible typology Amalek was a type of the flesh. As Israel was commanded to destroy Amalek totally and completely, we as Christians are commanded by God to have total and complete victory over the flesh. As Israel could not defeat Amalek with her own power but had to have the power of God to accomplish this task, likewise, the Christian cannot defeat the flesh with the flesh. Only the Spirit of God can defeat the flesh (Rom. 8).

———■———

CHAPTER 26

This chapter constitutes a scene of joy and

victory as Israel obeys the Lord, rejoicing in the inheritance given them. It is a lesson for us today as well.

Verses 1 through 11 portray the offering of thanksgiving. This would signify a bountiful harvest and a thanksgiving offering unto the Lord as the Benefactor of Israel.

In the 5th verse the offerer was to say, *"A Syrian ready to perish was my father, and he went down into Egypt."* This is the only place where Jacob is called a Syrian. Abraham's relatives are called Syrians. They were not descendants of Aram, the son of Shem, but of Arphaxad, the son of Shem (Gen. 11:10-32). They were Syrians because of living in Syria or Padan-Aram (Gen. 28:2-7). The offerer was to confess that they had no personal merit; they were ready to perish; they were a member of a nation of slaves; that they had been redeemed by grace; and that they were now saved and happy in the land flowing with milk and honey.

The 11th verse states that the grace of God that was shown to this *"Syrian in Egypt"* was to be shown not only to his relatives and fellow countrymen, but to the Gentile stranger as well.

This passage is a proclamation of the carrying out of the Great Commission under the New Covenant. How can the modern Christian after having been given such Grace by God not show the same to the stranger? No wonder Paul said, *"I am a debtor."*

Back to the 8th verse, *"And the Lord brought us forth out of Egypt."* In this one verse the Lord gave five means of bringing Israel out of Egypt:

1. With a mighty hand (Hebrew *"yad chazakah"*), one that is strong to deal blows; irresistible in its operation; grasps enemies so that they cannot escape; and one that holds friends in such a powerful way that they cannot suffer harm.

2. With a stretched-out arm (Hebrew *"zeroa netuyah"*), indicating a series of mighty acts following one another in rapid succession.

3. With great terrors (Hebrew *"moraim gedolim"*), terror; dismay; consternation, caused by the ten plagues upon Egypt and acts of judgment on Israel in the wilderness.

4. With signs (Hebrew *"othoth"*), tokens of nearness and continual presence as manifested

NOTES

in the pillar of fire, cloud by day, the smoke and fire, lightnings, and other supernatural acts of God's power and glory.

5. With wonders (Hebrew *"mephethim"*), persuading by miraculous acts of power; miracles; something to marvel at; events that made one open the mouth and stand aghast; things hard to believe even though seen with the eyes.

Verses 12 through 15 give the law of special tithes for the Levites and the poor. This lovely scene of happiness and worship closes the teaching of the book. All is sunshine; the people are in possession of the goodly land by faith. They rejoice and feast therein with Jehovah, and their consciousness of salvation and security is based upon free grace and redeeming blood. They share their riches with the widows, the fatherless, the stranger, the poor, and the slaves. Every third year they give the special tithe of that year (vs. 12) to the needy within their gates. They did not rob God by withholding these gifts from the poor (vs. 13); they did not make an excuse of domestic affliction, or personal interest, and so withhold this bounty, thus they were in truth a holy people unto Jehovah their God (vs. 19).

Had Israel observed these commandments and these statutes, they would have been a nation of holy and happy worshipers. Israel would have been a Paradise of felicity, peace, and love.

CHAPTER 27

In verse 1 it says, *"Keep all the commandments."* These commands would make it easy for Israel to know and understand these commandments. Verses 1 through 8 would proclaim the manner in which God would write such.

The 2nd verse says, *"Set thee up great stones and plaster them with plaster."* It was a custom in Egypt and other lands to stucco over sandstone rocks and granite, then write in the plaster or paint the message to be preserved. Some such stones over 2000 years old are said to be in existence today.

Furthermore, Israel was commanded to

"Build an altar unto the Lord thy God in Mount Ebal" (vss. 4-5). Strangely enough, this altar was not to be on Mount Gerizim, which was the mount of blessings, but, rather, on Mount Ebal, which was the mount of cursing. Why? Men today are trying to build altars on the mount of blessing. To do so fully proclaims a lack of knowledge of the terrible lostness of mankind. The altar would represent Calvary. The primary purpose of Calvary was to pay the price owed by man regarding man's fall. It represented nothing but evil. Hence, the altar must be on the mount of evil (Ebal). On that altar of Calvary some 1600 years later, He who knew no sin would become sin (evil) that we might become the righteousness of God in Him.

Man loves to feel that he is now ready and, thereby, should ever be a recipient of God's blessings after being redeemed. However, man must know, even redeemed man, that God cannot bless man; he can only bless Christ in man.

Verse 5 says, *"Thou shalt not lift up any iron tool upon them."* This speaks of man's own self-righteous efforts to save himself. It goes all the way from Adam's fig leaves to Cain's offering of vegetables, to every false religion that has ever existed. Man is never satisfied with God's plan of redemption. He must pick up his "iron tool" which represents his own polluted self-righteousness and attempt to improve upon God's salvation. He always fails, as fail he must.

The altar of *"whole stones"* of verse 6, represents the finished work of Calvary. Man cannot improve on it, and, in fact, if man attempts to improve on it, he will be damned. The *"whole burnt offerings"* offered thereon represented the glorious Son of God Who would give His all for the salvation of mankind.

The *"peace offerings"* that were eaten there caused great rejoicing before the Lord of glory, and resulted from the terrible *"burnt offering"* representing the Lord Jesus Christ and our acceptance of Him. Peace cannot come unless we accept the Lord of glory and the price that He paid for the redemption of man.

Verses 12 and 13 tell us that six tribes were to go toward Gerizim and six tribes toward Ebal. All the people were to turn their faces toward Ebal, and as the priests and Levites pronounced the curses, they were to say

"amen." Then they were to all turn their faces toward Gerizim, and as the blessings were pronounced, they were to say *"amen."* After this, the stones were to be brought, the altar built, and the curses and blessings were to be written on the stones. Then sacrifices were offered on the stones.

It is noticeable that Moses assigned to the mount of blessing the children of Leah and Rachel except for Reuben and Zebulun, the eldest and youngest sons of Leah. These were assigned to the mount of cursing. The sons of the two handmaids and Zebulun were placed on the cursing side perhaps because he was the least of all the sons of Leah and Reuben due to his sin with his father's wife for which he had lost his birthright.

Verses 14 through 26 outline the 12 curses of disobedience on Mount Ebal. The Levites were to speak the curses with loud voices and in unison, and the people were to answer with a loud amen to each curse. In this manner, the people were to understand fully the commands of God and the curses promised if disobedience ensued.

CHAPTER 28

Verses 1 through 14 portray the 21 blessings of obedience as proclaimed on Mount Gerizim.

If these commands are not followed, verses 15 through 20 give 15 curses upon Israel and material prosperity. Verses 21 through 29 list some 30 curses of sickness, crop failure, war, captivity, business failure, and poverty.

By and large, the balance of the chapter through verse 68 proclaims more curses.

Such conditions, as well as the curses and blessings of God, are so plain that anyone can understand them and obey. Furthermore, it is made clear in Scripture that conditions must be met if blessings are to be received. Not only Israel but all others are required to live in continued obedience if blessings are experienced. It is plainly stated that if Israel failed of the grace of God through backsliding and rebellion, it was because they did not continue to do the will of God. *"That as the Lord rejoiced over you to do you good, and to multiply you (as long as you were in obedience); so the Lord will rejoice over you to destroy you, and to bring you to nought; and you shall be plucked from off the land whither thou goest to possess it. And the Lord shall scatter thee among all people, from the one end of the earth even to the other"* (vss. 63-68).

This has literally been fulfilled and is yet in fulfillment at the present time. Paul uses this example to warn Christians that if God did not spare Israel from cutting them off when they sinned, He would not spare others (Rom. 11:1-33). Thus, the truth is that only upon obedience will God bless any man, that only upon continued obedience will he continue to bless, and when the righteous turn from their righteousness and commit sin, they are cursed again of God (Ex. 32-33; Ezek. 18,33)

Having said all these curses would come upon Israel if they sinned, God was under obligation to bring them about for disobedience. His righteousness, justice, and truthfulness require this. There is no place under Law or Grace where a man can fail to obey and be blessed of God, for He has promised cursing for disobedience and blessing for obedience. His fulfillment of this has been demonstrated times without number among angels, demons, and men. The fact of this matter is that all persons need to learn to act accordingly, for there is no excuse for failure in man with the provision God has made for Him to remain in obedience (St. Matt. 6:24; Rom. 6:16-23; I Cor. 6:9-11).

The 53rd verse says, *"And thou shalt eat the fruit of thine own body."* This prediction of cannibalism in Israel is horrible to think about, and it shows to what extent they were brought down by God because of rebellion against Him and His covenant. This happened first in the days of Jehoram, son of Ahab (II Kings 6:24-31). The greatest wave of it was in the siege and destruction of Jerusalem by the Romans in A.D. 70. The prediction was, The woman among you who has been so delicate and refined that she would not venture to set her feet on the ground will become so vile and coarse that she will murder and eat her own husband, sons, daughters, and even her babies because of the siege (II Kings 6:29).

NOTES

During the siege of Jerusalem by Titus in A.D. 70, the Jews were crucified in such numbers before the walls that the Romans wanted more room for crosses. Multitudes in the city died of famine until the valleys outside were filled with them. Titus himself groaned and threw up his hands in horror and called God to witness that he was not responsible. No fewer than 600,000 who were thrown out the gates were counted by the Romans. Altogether, 1,100,000 Jews died; 97,000 were sold as slaves for trifling prices; 40,000 were freed because no one bought them; and 347,490 more, plus multitudes not counted, perished in many other ways. Hundreds of thousands were taken to Egypt in ships and offered for sale in the slave-market, but no man buying them, they were driven by the thousands into the desert where they miserably perished. The fulfillment of a prophecy 1600 years old is one of the many proofs that the Bible is supernatural.

Verse 63 says, *"So the Lord will rejoice over you to destroy you."* In two ways God said He would rejoice.

A. Rejoicing to do good to Israel when they were in obedience.

B. Rejoicing to destroy them when they were in stubborn and willful rebellion.

This latter rejoicing seems contrary to the true nature of God and His love and grace as stated in many passages, but when viewed in the light of all Scripture, it becomes understandable. We find a reason for His rejoicing in the destruction of the very people whom He had blessed by His grace. It was because of the hard-hearted, hard-headed, willful stubbornness and rebellion of Israel that God was forced to curse them and wash His hands of them for a time. In so doing, He was able to relieve Himself and give them up to their own ways. Not only Israel, but He was also forced to do this to the Gentile world as recorded in Romans 1:18-32. God reveals that He will take the same attitude toward all such rebels (Prov. 1:22-31). The reason plainly given in this passage is wholly just and righteous.

The Lord said, *"Ye shall be plucked from off the land"* (vs. 63). It is true that no man, demon, angel, or any other power can pluck a true believer from the hands of God - one who lives godly, hears the voice of the Lord and follows Him, but it is also true that if one does not live godly, that God Himself can do such plucking. Here He promises to do it. He will pluck up, cast away, and spew out of His mouth all backsliders and apostates who persist in sin and rebellion.

The Lord said that He would pluck Israel *"from off the land."* In what sense did God promise to pluck Israel? It was off the land, and it must be understood that this was to be the final judgment for their backslidings. The salvation of their souls was involved in this plucking up, for if they were not godly enough to remain in the land, they were not godly enough to be received in heaven. Thus, it did not concern their destruction as a nation only, but their being cut off from God also (Lev. 26:3-46). The sins for which God plucked up the nations of Canaan were eternal, death penalty sins - wickedness which caused the Gentiles to be damned eternally as well. Israel was, therefore, warned of the same temporal and eternal results if they committed the same sins (Lev. 18:27-30).

Verse 68 says, *"And the Lord shall bring thee into Egypt again with ships."* This was literally fulfilled with parts of Israel several times. As we have stated, they were sold as slaves in Egypt for trifling prices, and when there were no buyers, multiple thousands were marched into the desert where they died horribly among their enemies. No doubt the true meaning of bringing them into Egypt again is that the Lord would bring them in ships, as stated here, by way of Egypt through the Suez Canal in the regathering, never to be scattered again among the nations. Not only in this verse but in others, the bringing of Israel by ships and other means is predicted.

CHAPTER 29

Verse 1 says *"These are the words of the covenant."* This verse seem to belong particularly to the preceding chapter. In some copies of the Hebrew Bible it is considered as the 69th verse of chapter 28. It is a fitting summary for the previous part of the Palesti-

nian Covenant and a suitable introduction for what is to follow in the completion of this covenant.

This Palestinian Covenant was made in the plains of Moab about 39 years after the covenant at Sinai of Exodus 20-24. The words, *"beside the covenant which he made with them in Horeb,"* prove that the Palestinian Covenant was entirely different from the Mosaic made at Sinai, for the word "beside" could not mean an addition to the Mosaic Covenant.

Verse 2 says, *"You have seen all that the Lord did before your eyes in the land of Egypt unto Pharaoh."* The old generation was by now destroyed - all except Moses, Joshua, and Caleb (Num. 14:23-35), but many of the new generation were young at the time of the plagues in Egypt. At least, these great events were well known to all Israel.

The 5th verse says, *"Your clothes are not waxen old upon you, and the shoe is not waxen old upon thy foot."* Verses 5 and 6 mean that Israel had not been supplied by ordinary methods but by supernatural power which provided bread and drink in the wilderness experiences so that they might know the Lord.

The 9th verse says, *"That you may prosper in all that you do."* Material prosperity was promised for keeping the Palestinian Covenant and was also promised for keeping the Mosaic Covenant (Deut. 4:40).

The 10th verse says, *"You stand this day all of you before the Lord your God;"* The time of making the Palestinian Covenant seemed to be on the 120th birthday of Moses, which was also the day of his death. However, no doubt, the Lord had been dealing with Moses for quite some time concerning the particulars of this covenant.

The 15th verse says, *"But with him that standeth here with us this day before the Lord our God, and also with him that is not here with us this day."* This was a way of saying that He was making the Palestinian Covenant with all present and future generations; hence, it is an everlasting covenant.

The 18th verse says, *"Whose heart turneth away this day from the Lord our God."* This means any man, woman, family, or tribe who turned away from God in the heart to serve the idol gods of other nations was to suffer all the plagues of the Law. There were three things that God said He would curse:

1. The heart turning away from Him to serve other gods (vs. 18).

2. A root of bitterness bearing gall and wormwood (vs. 18).

3. Presumptuous sinning and defying God and His Word, and walking in the imagination of the heart in rebellion and sin (vs. 19).

The words *"a root that beareth gall and wormwood"* are the same as the root of bitterness defiling men (Heb. 12:15) and an evil heart of unbelief in turning away from the living God (Heb. 3:12). The word *"gall"* seems to be the poppy which has reference to opium and other narcotic sources. Christ, while on the Cross, was offered vinegar mixed with gall, which might have contained opium, but He refused to drink it (St. Matt. 27:34).

Verse 29 describes presumptuous sinning, the kind that despises the Word of God and puts Christ to open shame (Heb. 10:26-29).

Verse 20 says, *"His jealousy shall smoke against that man."* God's anger and jealousy will wax hot against the unrepentant backsliders in heart until they are destroyed by curses. From these passages we should understand God's unceasing anger against unrepentant sin. He said in the 20th verse, *"Shall blot out his name from under heaven."*

Verse 22 says, *"And the stranger that shall come from a far land, shall say, When they see the plagues of that land."* As described and predicted there, when the inhabitants sin, fertile lands became places of desolation because of being under God's curse. Strangers and travelers from afar have remarked or written about this concerning Israel down through the years.

This verse says, *"When they see the plagues of that land, and the sicknesses which the Lord hath laid upon it."* None can deny that God judges and cuts off backsliders in heart and conduct who have become apostates (Heb. 10:26-29). Both Palestine and Israel are outstanding examples of such judgment. Many centuries have witnessed God's judgments on both because of backslidings and rebellion.

Verse 23 says, *"And that the whole land thereof is brimstone, and salt, and burning, that it is not sown."* The long desolation of the land has been one of its most striking features

NOTES

up to recent times when God began to restore the people to the land and the land from its curse of many centuries. God not only promised the desolation because of sin, but He also predicted Israel's restoration to the land in the last days, and the land's fertility again. These things are now coming to pass before the eyes of all nations. The verse says as well, *"Like the overthrow of Sodom, and Gomorrah, Admah, and Zeboim, which the Lord overthrew in his anger."* The comparison here is not to show the method of destruction, but to assure judgment as the result of sin. God did not rain fire and brimstone upon the whole land of Palestine as upon the four cities named, but the land was desolate for many centuries as in their case. No less than 18 times the destruction of Sodom and Gomorrah is mentioned in Scripture, but only two times is that of Admah and Zeboim referred to (Hosea 11:8).

All four cities were destroyed because of sex perversion and other sins. Such practice, which is an abomination to Him, caused God to act in anger and wrath to rid the area of such corruption as an example to others (II Pet. 2:6). One of the great sins of America today is sexual perversion which includes lesbianism and homosexuality. This defiles the land and will cause the same anger and judgment of God now as it did then. America, Canada, and other "civilized" nations of the world are ripe for judgment. If He did it with His chosen people Israel, do we not think that He will do the same with us today?

The 24th verse says, *"What meaneth the heat of this great anger?"* The desolation of Palestine was to be so noticeable that any traveler could see the marks of God's wrath upon it. This happened exactly as God said it would.

The 25th verse says, *"Because they have forsaken the covenant of the Lord God of their fathers."* For Israel to forsake God and His covenant means that they once knew Him and obeyed the covenant and were in His grace and favor before such a time. This proves that grace and favor are no guarantee of obedience to God or of security in themselves. The only way to keep His grace in one's life is to remain in complete obedience, and if there is disobedience, to fall on one's face in humble contrition and repentance before God.

The words, *"rooted them out,"* of the 28th verse mean driven out of the land and disbursed among the nations. Sadly, this came to pass exactly as God said it would. The words, *"as it is this day,"* mean that God's anger will be no less hot in the future if Israel rebels.

The 29th verse concerning, *"the secret things belong unto the Lord our God,"* refers to the things that the Lord has not yet told us. However, God has given us all that we need to know concerning *"those things which are revealed."* We have been given enough light, in fact, an abundance of light that we may be able to follow the Lord according to *"the words of this law."*

CHAPTER 30

Verse 1 says, *"And it shall come to pass, when all these things are come upon thee."* This and the following verses are now beginning to be fulfilled after so many centuries.

Verse 2 says, *"And shall return unto the Lord thy God."* Israel has had a very checkered past but will have a glorious future.

Verse 3 says, *"And will return and gather thee from all of the nations."* This passage speaks of the return of the Lord Jesus Christ as is described in Revelation 19. Verses 2 and 3 speak of Israel turning to the Lord with whole heart and soul. Only a partial regathering of Israel has taken place in the recent past, and only a partial regathering will take place before the Second Coming of Christ. The final and complete regathering will be immediately after the Second Coming, when all will be gathered from every part of the earth (Isa. 11:10-12; St. Matt. 24:29-31).

The 5th verse says, *"And the Lord thy God will bring thee into the land which thy fathers possessed, and thou shalt possess it."* Whatever God promises, that He will do. The bringing back of Israel into the land has been in the face of insurmountable odds. The Arab world outnumbers Israel 40 to 1. Repeatedly, they have vowed to push Israel into the sea. Repeatedly, they have failed. Israel's existence is one of the greatest signs of the great promises of God

NOTES

being fulfilled. Israel in A.D. 70 was destroyed by the Romans and disbursed as slaves into basically every nation of that day on the face of the earth. They were scattered exactly as God said they would be. Repeated efforts to destroy this people have been made because of Satan's violent anger against them as God's chosen people and the promises made to them. Their survival has been a miracle. Their occupation of the land of Israel today against insurmountable odds is another miracle as well. The idea that Israel will give up the West Bank as a Palestinian State is highly unlikely. As well, America's treatment of Israel to bring about the great promises of God and the fulfillment of these promises will basically decide the future of this country. We are to never condone Israel's wrongdoing, but, at the same time, if America sets herself to block the fulfillment of God's promises, America will lose and not Israel. God will carry out His Word. If America participates in the carrying out of that Word, America will be blessed. If we seek to hinder the carrying out of God's Word, we will be cursed.

Verse 8 says, *"And thou shalt return and obey the voice of the Lord."* This is all God wanted of Israel, and that is all He wants of men today. The only difference is that we have the New Covenant now instead of the Old one, but we have many commandments to obey just as Israel had under the Old Covenant.

Verse 10 says, *"If thou shalt hearken."* These little "ifs" face us wherever we turn, and they must be reckoned with. If men obey, they are blessed, and if they disobey, they are cursed. This applies to all alike – those classed as saints or sinners.

The 11th verse says, *"It is not hidden from thee, neither is far off."* God's Word is plainly revealed and recorded in the most simple human language possible, so that none can rightfully claim that it is hard to understand because of its hidden meanings. The idea and the excuse of not reading the Bible because it is too hard to understand will not keep men from judgment.

The 14th verse says, *"That thou mayest do it."* There are 12 duties regarding the Word of God:

  1. Read publicly (Deut. 31:11-13).
  2. Read privately (Hab. 2:2; Rev. 1:2-3).

3. Study (II Tim. 2:15).

4. Expound (Neh. 8:8).

5. Search (St. John 5:39).

6. Meditate on day and night (Josh. 1:8).

7. Hear and practice (Rom. 2:13).

8. Desire (I Pet. 2:1-3).

9. Accept without change (Deut. 4:2; 12:32).

10. Preach (St. Mark 16:15).

11. Teach (Deut. 6:7; Rom. 1:16).

12. Believe (St. Mark 1:15).

Verse 19 says, *"Therefore choose life, that both thou and thy seed may live."* God advises and commands men to choose life by choosing His grace and means of entering into eternal life, thus cancelling death and the curses that cut off man from Him. Men can and must make the choice, for God does not force the will of anyone to serve Him, surrender to Him, or remain obedient to His will. All men are always, without exception, free to choose life or death, blessings or curses.

CHAPTER 31

The Law was represented by Moses. And due to the feebleness of man's moral nature, he was unable to bring the people into Canaan. Joshua, as typifying the living Saviour, now appears and is presented to the people as the great captain who would, without fail, bring them over Jordan. Joshua was a type of the Lord Jesus Christ, *"The law came by Moses, but grace and truth came by Jesus Christ."*

The 2nd verse says, *"I am an hundred and twenty years old this day."* Three things are stated in this passage. They are as follows:

1. I am 120 years old this day.

2. I can no more go out and come in.

This does not express physical infirmity or inability to perform his duties as leader of Israel, for it is clear from chapter 34:7 that *"his eye was not dim, nor his natural force abated."* The reason he could no more go out or come in was that on this day the Divine decree was that he should die. After this day he could no longer lead Israel or take them over Jordan.

3. The Lord said, *"You shall not go over*

NOTES

Jordan." This was the boundary of his life's journey, and it had now come to an end.

Verse 6 says, *"Be strong and of a good courage, fear not, nor be afraid of them."* Three commands (conquest instructions) were given to Israel:

1. To Israel – Be strong and of a good courage, fear not, nor be afraid of them.

2. To Joshua – Be strong and of a good courage.

3. Fear not, neither be dismayed.

As well, this is the command that the Lord gives every child of God.

The 9th verse says, *"And Moses wrote this law, and delivered it unto the priests the sons of Levi."* The sons of Levi, being the ministers of Israel, were the custodians of the written revelation of God, and they were to preserve and pass on the Word of God. The law was to be read during the Feast of Tabernacles every seventh year (vss. 9-13) so that they should perpetually remember that the land and all the bounties it produced for them belonged to Jehovah, and the Book was to be a witness that these riches would continue to be theirs if they were obedient. Sadly, it seems that this command was little heeded. There are really only four examples of this being carried out in the centuries that follow:

1. The first reading of the Law was during the conquest of Canaan (Josh. 8:35).

2. Jehoshaphat, approximately 600 years later, had the priests and Levites to teach the Law in all Israel (II Chron. 17:6-8).

3. Josiah, over 250 years after this, discovered the Law and had it read to all Israel (II Chron. 34:22-33).

4. The Law was again read approximately 300 years later (Neh. 8).

The 15th verse says, *"And the Lord appeared in the tabernacle in a pillar of a cloud."* This is the last time the Lord appeared to Israel to be recorded in the Pentateuch. This appearance was to give instructions to Joshua, the new leader of Israel and the successor of Moses. It is also the last time recorded that the pillar of cloud was seen in Israel. This is the only reference to the pillar in all of Deuteronomy.

Were this a history of human imagination, the inventor would never dream of closing the service of one great leader and beginning the exploits of another in such a cloud of gloom and despondency.

The 19th verse says, *"Now therefore write you this song for you, and teach it to the children of Israel."* Jehovah, foreknowing this apostasy, commanded Moses to write a song that was to be a witness to God against it. The words of the song occupy the next chapter.

Verse 29 says, *"And evil will befall you in the latter days."* This was a prophecy given by Moses that would befall Israel in the last days, and no doubt refers to the Great Tribulation they will yet go through – the time of trouble such as never was or ever will be again (St. Matt. 24:15-24). Through the great law-giver Moses, the Lord, in simple words, gave not only the present plan for Israel but their future as well.

CHAPTER 32

This is a glorious chapter portraying the song of Moses. The first reference of this song is found in verse 19 of chapter 31. The last reference is found in Revelation 15:3.

Five times in this song Jehovah is praised as the Rock (vss. 4, 15, 18, 30, 31). Verses 31 and 37, as well, refer to the false rocks of other nations.

This song beautifully portrays the future of Israel from Moses' day through endless eternity. We will briefly touch on these beautiful prophecies.

Four great facts are especially noticeable in this song.

1. That God in His secret councils, appointed Israel as the chief nation of the earth and the center of the earth as well and disposed all other nations in relation thereto (vs. 8).

2. That the Gentiles shall partake of the grace laid up for Israel (vss. 21, 43).

3. That ultimately all Israel shall be saved (vs. 43).

4. That all of these great truths are based upon and secured by the glory connected with the name of the Lord. Both Jew and Gentile would have long since perished, but God abides true to His nation and promises.

Verse 1 says, *"Give ear, oh ye heavens, and I will speak; and hear, oh earth, the words of my mouth."* Jesus Himself said, *"He that hath ears to hear, let him hear."* The command is given that all should hear what God has spoken. Therefore, it is incumbent upon us to make certain that every single individual on the face of the earth hear *"the words of God's mouth."* That is priority; everything else must take second, and third place. These were basically the last words of Jesus Christ in that which we call The Great Commission, *"Go ye into all the world and preach the gospel"* (St. Mark 16:15).

Verse 2 says, *"My doctrine shall drop as the rain."* The manner in which the Lord would give His revelation to us is in this 2nd verse. It is divided into four parts. Ultimately, it will include the whole of the Word of God.

1. As the rain. It shall come drop by drop, beginning slowly and increasing more and more until the whole revelation is complete (Isa. 29:9-11; II Tim. 3:16-17). When the final part was given to John on the Isle of Patmos in that which we know as the book of Revelation, the Word of God was then complete. It must not be added to or taken from.

2. As the dew. It shall descend gently, solidly, and mysteriously upon the heart and ear, moistening and bringing refreshment. How so much is the constant devotion to the Word of God like dew that settles upon the dryness of our soul.

3. As the small rain. It will be like sweeping showers accompanied by a strong gust of wind. Down through the centuries and periodically, the Word of God would sweep certain areas, bringing in Holy Ghost revival.

4. As the showers. It shall be like continual rain which is necessary for the planting and harvesting of the crops. Every move of God has always been accompanied by the anchor of the Word of God.

Someone has well said, "Much Bible, much freedom; little Bible, little freedom; no Bible, no freedom."

Verse 4 says, *"His work is perfect."* God never did create anything imperfect. All imperfection has come about through sin and rebellion by the choice and conduct of free moral agents (Rom. 5:12-21), *"For all his ways are judgment."* All of God's ways are just, right, decreed, and according to fixed laws and order. God is always justified, and man is always condemned.

Verse 8 says, *"When the most high divided to the nations their inheritance."* This means that God divided to the nations their inheritance and separated the sons of Adam and set the bounds of the people (Gen. 10:32). This makes the will of God plain as to segregation of the various nations; God, Himself, determined the boundaries for them. When Christ comes to reign, He will gather Israel from all lands and settle them in the Promised Land (Ezek. 37; St. Matt. 24:31). Others of distinct races will also be returned to the originally determined lands, no doubt. This in no way means that one race is superior to the other; neither does it mean that God is a respecter of persons, for He is not, *"He set the bounds of the people."* When God divided the nations their inheritance and set boundaries around their lands that they should not integrate and become a mixture of races, He reserved the Promised Land for Israel as His own portion where He would come and live in their midst forever. The land of promise in the millennial reign will be divided into 13 sections according to the number of the tribes (Ezek. 48). The original division of the earth was made with the three sons of Noah about 300 hundred years before Abraham.

Verses 7 through 14 celebrate God's goodness and bounty during the period of the Pentateuch, basically referring to Israel's present condition under God's guidance and tender love.

Verses 15 through 19 record Israel's evil response to God's goodness during the period of their kings.

Verse 20 contemplates the period between the captivity in Babylon and the coming of the Messiah.

Verse 21 relates to the period of the Acts of the Apostles.

Verses 22 to 33 relate to Israel's present dispersion.

Verses 34 to 43 to their sufferings under the future Antichrist and their final restoration.

The 15th verse says, *"But Jeshurun waxed fat, and kicked."* This is a symbolic name given by God to Israel, meaning the upright one. This makes it clear that God Himself recog-

NOTES

nized Israel as justified in His sight at first. Afterward, the nation forsook Him, rejected the Rock of their salvation, and provoked Him with their sinning to the point that He abhorred them. As we have stated, this period (vss. 15-19) portrays Israel under her kings and away from God.

Verse 20 says, *"I will see what their end shall be."* No statement in Scripture suggests that God knows every small detail of every act and thought of all free moral agents from all eternity past to all eternity future - even before they are in existence. Such is not necessary in order to understand the omniscience of God. God, being all-knowing, can know anything He so desires. However, many times in Scripture, we find Him seeing and knowing things when they happen, thus purposely limiting Himself in His dealings with His subjects in order that they may have free moral agency. As stated, verse 20 portrays Israel's terrible dispersion into Babylon and their continued backsliding until the First Advent of Christ. They were called, *"Children in whom is no faith."*

In verse 21 we see God's final dealings with Israel before their total destruction, *"I will provoke them to anger with a foolish nation."* This refers to God giving the Gospel through Peter, Paul, and others to the Gentile world.

Verse 21 was literally fulfilled in the book of Acts.

Verses 22 through 33 record the terrible anger of God against a nation that rejected Jesus Christ by hanging the Son the God on a cross, *"For a fire is kindled in mine anger, and shall burn unto the lowest hell."*

In the 24th verse He says, *"They shall be burnt with hunger, and devoured with burning heat, and with bitter destruction."* In A.D. 70, Titus completely destroyed Jerusalem. Over a million Jews died in this horror. From that day until 1948 they were basically in dispersion throughout the world. The horror of Hitler's holocaust where 6 million died in World War II is horribly fulfilled in the 25th verse, *"The sword without, and terror within."*

Verse 27 says, *"Were it not that I feared the wrath of the enemy."* At first glance this is a strange statement. Does it mean that God really fears the wrath of an enemy? No. The idea is that God feared that if He did not punish

Israel in such a supernatural way as to leave out all evidences of a human hand, His enemies would brag that it was by their own hand it was done and not by God's hand. Furthermore, God wanted Israel to know that it was His hand which was punishing them for their sins so they might repent and turn back to Him. The nations were to know that it was not their power or might that did it, even if at times they were used as the rod of chastening upon God's people.

Verse 35, *"To me belongeth vengeance and recompense,"* portrays the horror of the coming Antichrist. Jesus said He came in His Father's name, and Him they would not receive but "another" they shall receive. The "another" that Jesus was speaking of is the Antichrist (St. John 5:43).

Verse 41 portrays the coming of the Lord and the total defeat of the Antichrist with the salvation of Israel, *"If I whet my glittering sword, and mine hand take hold on judgment; I will render vengeance to mine enemies, and will reward them that hate me."*

The 42nd verse portrays the Battle of Armageddon, *"I will make mine arrows drunk with blood, and my sword shall devour flesh.*

Verse 43 says, *"Rejoice, oh ye nations, with his people: And will be merciful unto his land, and unto his people."* Hallelujah! Verse 43 portrays one of the greatest revivals in history, which proclaims Israel being restored. No wonder the Lord shouts, *"Rejoice!"*

Verse 46 says, *"Set your hearts unto all the words which I testify among you this day."*

The 47th verse says two things:

1. It is your life.

2. Through this thing you shall prolong your days in the land.

Jesus said, *"Man shall not live by bread alone but by every word that proceedeth out of the mouth of God."* His words are our life; His words give us continued victory.

CHAPTER 33

Chapter 33 portrays Moses' final address to the children of Israel. It begins with love. Verse

3 says, *"Yea, he loved the people."* By faith, He sees them as *"they sat down at thy feet."* Here is the manner in which God saw His people. He would love them as they sat at His feet. And then, beautifully, He would say, *"Everyone shall receive of thy words."* How wonderful it would have been had they done that. However, God is never defeated. In the millennial reign, this is exactly what will happen. He will love them, they will sit at His feet, and at long last they shall receive every one of His words.

Verse 6 says, *"Let Reuben live, and not die."* Here, we have the use of pleonasm or redundancy, where a statement made is immediately afterward put in another and sometimes opposite way to make it impossible for the sense to be missed - live, and not die. Such examples are often found in Scripture.

Verse 7 says, *"And this is the blessing of Judah."* If one will notice, Simeon is not mentioned in these blessings, the reason being that their inheritance was within the inheritance of Judah. Their inheritance was one, and their blessing would be one as well.

The 8th verse says, *"And of Levi."* And it says in the 9th verse, *"Neither did he acknowledge his brethren, nor knew his own children,"* referring, no doubt, to the High Priest and the Levites putting God first, even to the killing their own brethren who had sinned at the time of the golden calf (Ex. 32:26-28). For on that day the tribe of Levi won the priesthood.

Verse 12 says, *"And of Benjamin."* Paul was from the tribe of Benjamin and was, without doubt, its brightest light.

Verse 13 says, *"And of Joseph."* This would include Ephraim and Manasseh, Joseph's sons. Joseph was a type of Christ and could be said, *"blessed of the Lord."*

The 16th verse says, *"That was separated from his brethren."* This speaks of Joseph being sold into Egypt, but, as well, speaks of Christ being sold for 30 pieces of silver.

Verse 18 says, *"And of Zebulun"* and then, *"Issachar."* The word for them is *"rejoice."*

Verse 20 says, *"And of Gad."* Gad led in the victory with the other tribes of Israel in the conquest of the land and the settlement of Canaan. Gad could well be the first tribe to accept the Lord Jesus Christ at the Second Coming.

Verse 22 says, *"And of Dan."* Some have thought that possibly the Antichrist, who must be a Jew for Israel to accept him as the Messiah, could come from the tribe of Dan. However, at the Second Coming of Christ, *"he shall leap from Bashan,"* meaning he will not be slack in admitting his error and will speedily come to Christ.

Verse 23 says, *"And of Naphtali."* The word for him is, *"satisfied with favor and full with the blessing of the Lord."*

Verse 24 says, *"And of Asher."* He shall be *"blessed with children."*

Verses 25 through 29 proclaim Israel at peace in their land of promise in the days of the millennial reign with the Lord Jesus Christ as King of kings and Lord of lords, *"Happy art thou, oh Israel"* (vs. 29).

As noticed, Moses' great and glorious prophecies concerning the 12 tribes of Israel had to do by faith in that which was yet to come. It is still yet to come, but it shall come. When the Lord of glory breaks the skies asunder and comes back from heaven in His glorious power, then Israel will be gathered unto Him, and every iota of these prophecies will be fulfilled with each of these tribes totally and forever.

■

CHAPTER 34

Verse 1 says, *"And Moses went up from the plains of Moab unto the mountain of Nebo."*

There has been much controversy regarding the authorship of this last chapter of Deuteronomy, beginning with verse 5. However, it must be noted that this chapter is a part of the Pentateuch in all manuscripts. The only explanation is that Moses wrote by inspiration as the Lord gave him a blueprint for his own death and burial, or else Joshua wrote it. It is plainly stated that Joshua also wrote in the Book of the Law (Josh. 24:26). This we do know, whoever wrote it was inspired, and it is definitely a part of the book of Deuteronomy, and, thereby, of the Word of God.

Verse 4 says, *"And the Lord said unto him, this is the land."* And then says at the con-

clusion, *"But thou shalt not go over thither."* The Law, of which Moses was a type, could look at the land but could not possess it. Grace, of which Joshua was a type, could possess the land, *"The law came by Moses, but grace and truth by Jesus Christ."*

Verse 5 says, *"So Moses the servant of the Lord died there in the land of Moab, according to the word of the Lord."* So records the death of one of the greatest men of God that ever lived. He was born in Egypt with his parents as slaves; he was given his name by an Egyptian princess. Strangely enough, according to the hand of God, he was brought up in the palace of the Pharaoh, then the mightiest monarch on the face of the earth. He spent 40 years in Egypt being trained and educated to the highest degree. And then after committing manslaughter, ran for his life spending another 40 years on the backside of the desert close to Sinai. He spent the last 40 years of his life leading the children of Israel out of Egyptian bondage. Few, if any, have ever equalled the man Moses.

The 6th verse says, *"And he buried him in the valley in the land of Moab."* In other words, God Himself officiated at the funeral. And the latter portion of the 6th verse says, *"But no man knoweth of his sepulchre unto this day."* Man is so insensate and idolatrous that Israel would, without doubt, have given divine honors to the great dead leader who, while living, was treated with ingratitude and more than once set about to be murdered! Such is man, and such is his nature!

Verse 7 says, *"His eye was not dim, nor his natural force abated."* Moses did not die from disease, sickness, or old age. His strength remained unto the end. He died because God said it was time to go. He died on the first day of February, which was the day he was born 120 years earlier.

The 10th verse says, *"Whom the Lord knew face to face."* Few men, if any, have equalled Moses. The Holy Spirit here says, *"Not a prophet since in Israel like unto Moses."* In many respects he was greater than all others except the Lord Jesus Christ.

And so ends the Pentateuch – called the Five Books of Moses. Of all the writings of antiquity, the Pentateuch is the most remarkable. The very subjects it embraces makes it a necessity in the understanding of God's plan for man. It is the foundation of Divine revelation to man. Its explanation of the origin of all things, its code of laws, geography, chronology, history, and religion prove it to be a Divine work worthy of careful study and acceptance by the entirety of the human race.

Even though it is called the Five Books of Moses, in reality it should be called the Law of God, for a mere human could not have invented such a work.

There are several books or works that are called sacred or holy. They are as follows:

1. ZEND-AVESTA, by Zoroaster, about 1200 B.C., the sacred book of the Medes and Persians to revive the ancient Magain religion.

2. THE FOUR VEDAS, the four sacred books of the Hindus are the institutes of Menu: written by Menu, son of Brahma and containing the code of civil and religious laws of the Indians, written about 1100 B.C.

3. FIVE KINGS, the sacred book of the Chinese, written by Confucius about 1100 B.C.

4. THE PITIKES of the Buddhists, written by Gotama, founder of Buddhism about 600 B.C.

5. THE KORAN, written by Mohammed about A.D. 600.

6. THE EDDAS of Scandinavia, two religious codes containing mythology and traditions, written about A.D. 1100 or 1200.

7. THE BOOK OF MORMON, written in the 1800's by Joseph Smith.

All of these were written from about 500 to some 3500 years after Moses, and some are partly made up of quotations of the Old and New Testaments, the Talmud, which is a Jewish commentary of the Old Testament, and the Gospel of Barnabas. Others contain the best sayings of wise men within the race producing such a work, certain ethical, political, and moral aspirations of those people besides old traditions, mythological, and fantastic tales of gods, and their wars.

The sacred books of pagans reveal many erroneous and superstitious ideas which could only be the product of the human mind. Their sayings may have helped in the social life of some in the past; nevertheless, there is very little in them to elevate or inspire to righteous-

NOTES

ness and nothing to bring one a correct understanding of the true and living God. How different are the Pentateuch and the rest of the Bible which glow with truth like the sun compared to a candle!

In the Pentateuch God is supreme and the only King; the priest is His servant, even being prevented by the law from having earthly inheritance or secular power; the ruler of Israel is the vice-regent of God, obliged to rule according to His laws which are not to be changed, added to, or taken from. Despotism and priest-craft revealed in other so-called sacred writings would be impossible where the Laws of the Pentateuch are obeyed. Its rites and ceremonies are dignified, impressive, and free from the mysteries, divination, witchcraft, sorcery, enchantment, omens, and cruel, licentious practices which make pagan rites an abomination to God. The ceremonies of the Pentateuch point out the holiness of God, the sinfulness of man, the necessity of an atonement, and the moral state to which the Creator has promised to raise fallen man. The punishments of the five books called the Pentateuch are just, and the rewards are such as to inspire love of God and consecration to the highest good of all.

THE
BOOK OF JOSHUA

—■—

The Hebrew name *"Joshua"* is *"Jesus"* in the Greek. So, the Joshua that led the children of Israel into the Promised Land was a prefigurement of the Christ of glory Who leads the child of God into the spiritual Promised Land.

Many have thought that the land of promise was a type of heaven; it is not. It is a physical type of the spiritual inheritance given to us in this great Christian walk. There were Jebusites, Hivites, Canaanites, and others in the land of promise. These were enemies of God's people. There is not such in heaven.

—■—

CHAPTER 1

The Lord had promised this great land to the children of Israel; however, promise is one thing, possession is another. God said, *"I, even I, do give you the land."* Such was the promise, but the one condition of possession was the placing of the foot upon it (vs. 3). The children of Israel were delivered out of Egypt without any fight or war. God did it all. Likewise, redemption to the new-found Christian is all of God and none of him, with the exception of simply believing. All Israel had to do to be released from Egypt was to believe God. All the sinner has to do to be delivered from satanic bondage is to believe God. However, when it comes to possession of all this that God has promised us, this is another matter entirely. We have to fight for every foot of spiritual ground that we take, and Satan does not give ground easily. Why is it this way?

As God has designed redemption perfectly, He has also designed possession of the land

NOTES

perfectly. The allowing of great enemies to contest and hinder our progress builds spiritual character, faith, and maturity in the child of God. As we study this great book of Joshua, we are, in effect, studying our own Christian life. As the blueprint for victory was given by God to Joshua to "take the land," likewise, this is the same blueprint for victory in our own lives.

Moses, as representing the Law, could not bring Israel into the Promised Land. He must die, for he had made one failure under that Law and possession of Canaan by Law could only be by perfect obedience to it. Man, being a sinner, cannot give this perfect obedience. Joshua was a type of the risen Saviour and would bring Israel into the goodly land. Grace, operating in the power of the Holy Spirit, can bring men into the enjoyment of that which the Law, because of man's moral weakness on which it acts, can never be.

Moses was a servant in the wilderness; Joshua was a son in the land. The subject of Deuteronomy is the wilderness, that of Joshua is the land. Sadly, most Christian people are satisfied to be servants in the wilderness, for most of what we call church is sadly made up of that which is called law. It seems that few have the ambition to be sons in the land.

Joshua's success depended upon his obedience to his two companions - the eternal Word (vs. 5) and the written Word (vs. 8); of course, this speaks of Jesus and the Bible. Obedience to such companionship alone gives a victorious Christian experience.

When the question is asked, "What is the rule of faith?" For the Catholic Church, its answer would be, "The Church and its teaching." It would be the same for most Protestant churches. God's answer in this chapter and in all other chapters is "The Bible."

Verse 9 says, *"Have not I commanded thee? Be strong and of a good courage; be not afraid, neither be thou dismayed: For the Lord thy God is with thee withersoever thou goest."* This message was not to Joshua's ears only; in fact, it is for every single child of God who has ever lived. As one reads the instructions given to Joshua in the first nine verses, over and over again two things stand out, the Bible and faith; *"This book of the law shall not depart out of thy mouth"* (vs. 8) and *"Be not afraid."*

Verse 13 says, *"The Lord your God hath given you rest, and hath given you this land"*, and yet, they would have to take it all by war. It was a promise of faith. Their "rest" would only be disturbed if they endeavored to defeat the enemy with the flesh instead of the Spirit. Likewise, our "rest" in Christ is disturbed only whenever we attempt to overcome Satan with the flesh instead of with the Spirit.

Verse 16 proclaims obedience, *"All that thou commandest us we will do."* Too oftentimes the Church makes plans and then asks God to bless them. This is backwards. God will only bless what He has planned. He will not bless our plans. Frankly, God cannot bless fallen, weak, frail, sinful mortals. He can only bless the Lord Jesus Christ who is within us.

CHAPTER 2

This chapter portrays one of the greatest stories of salvation found in the entirety of the Word of God. It is the story of Rahab the harlot. Prayerfully, in this beautiful scenario we will not only see the vileness of man (and woman), but the grace of God as well.

Verse 1 says, *"And Joshua the son of Nun sent out of Shittim two men to spy secretly."* There was absolutely no military reason for Joshua sending these two men to spy out the land. Nothing was to be gained from this excursion militarily; therefore, the reason the Holy Spirit impressed this upon Joshua was spiritual. The reason was Rahab. God's grace will shine brightest among earth's most evil.

The entirety of this story is a beautiful type

of the two spies serving as the Word of God and the Holy Spirit. They came into Jericho which is a type of the world. They came for a special purpose and that was to rescue Rahab from the certain destruction that was to come. Rahab is a type of the Church. Men may blanch at that; however, if they do, then they do not understand what we really are - sinners saved by grace. Joshua was a type of the Lord Jesus Christ who would come and destroy that evil system, also the Second Coming of Christ to destroy earth's evil system.

In the literal story the spies may not have known Rahab's character, for the Hebrew text suggests that she was an innkeeper, while the Greek text of Hebrews 11:31 proves that she was a harlot.

This beautiful story of Rahab will conclude in the *"Rachab"* of the genealogy of Christ. What an honor! What a blessing! In another sense of the word the Church, the Body of Christ, will also be included in the genealogy of Christ as *"sons of God."*

Verse 10 says, *"For we have heard."* Rahab was a debauched member of a doomed race, yet grace saved her. She based her plea for salvation upon the fact that she was justly ordained by God to destruction. Many people refuse to bestir themselves in the matter of personal salvation because of the belief that if they are ordained to be saved, they will be saved, and if ordained to be lost, they will be lost. However, all sinners are justly ordained to be lost (Rom. 5:12); therefore, all sinners may be saved. Rahab prefaced her plea for salvation by declaring that she knew all were doomed to destruction, and because of this Divine judgment, she asked for a true token that would assure her of her safety in the day of wrath that was coming.

She was immediately provided with a way of salvation. It was a very simple way. The 18th verse says, *"Thou shalt bind this line of scarlet thread in the window."* A child could do that. Salvation today from the wrath to come is equally simple. Trusting in the Lord Jesus Christ and in His precious blood secures eternal salvation.

Rahab lost not a moment in making her calling and election sure.

The 21st verse says, *"And she bound the*

scarlet line in the window." When she did so, she was saved - that is, she was in safety, and assured of safety. Prior to binding the scarlet line in the window, she was ordained to destruction, but from the moment she trusted that "true token," she was ordained to salvation.

Rahab's assurance of salvation was not founded upon an inward experience but upon an outward experience - that is, the scarlet thread. In it was perfection, in herself imperfection. Looking upon that "true token" and believing the testimony respecting it, she was assured of deliverance in the day of doom that was coming. Thus, the outward token gave an inward peace. The believer in Jesus enjoys a similar peace. The preciousness of Christ's Blood and the testimony of Holy Scriptures concerning it is the outward token which brings assurance of salvation to the heart that trusts Christ.

It was vain for Rahab to seek for salvation upon the grounds of personal worthiness, for she had no personal worthiness. It is equally vain for the most moral to claim salvation on personal merit, for all have sinned, none are righteous, and all are under sentence of death (Rom. 5:12).

A faith that is born of God always evidences itself by seeking the salvation of others. The 13th verse says, *"And that you will save alive my father, and my mother, and my brethren, and my sisters, and all that they have, and deliver our lives from death,"* and they were all saved.

———◼———

CHAPTER 3

Verse 1 says *"and came to Jordan."* As the Red Sea miracle was a type of deliverance from Egypt, so will the Jordan opening be a type of deliverance from Egypt. Even though they were different generations, all had to come the same way. God has no grandchildren. Even though their fathers had experienced the tremendous miracle of the Red Sea, it would not count for this new generation. They must each have his own miracle experience of "born again."

NOTES

The second verse says, *"After three days, that the officers went through the host."* The three days prefigure Christ's death and resurrection. Jesus would be three days and nights in the heart of the earth. He would then rise from the dead and lead the Church to great victory.

Verse 3 says, *"When ye see the ark of the covenant of the Lord."* Israel was not to go after the great men of Israel, nor even the priests. They were to go after *"It,"* meaning the Ark. The Ark was a type of Christ, and, thereby, of grace. This generation who would go into the Promised Land was no more holy than their fathers who died in the wilderness. The difference was that those who died in the wilderness were a type of the Law which could never save, and now under Grace the responsibility, in essence, is no longer on the individual but on Christ (the Ark).

The 4th verse says, *"Yet there shall be a space between you and it, about two thousand cubits by measure:"* (about a mile). Consequently, there has always been and always will be a *"space"* between man and his Saviour. Despite the death-dealing teaching of false cults such as Mormonism or the New Age movement, man is not God and never shall be. Despite the great "born again" experience and the child of God by adoption becoming a "son of God," still, man is only adopted into the family of God and will always be a redeemed sinner, therefore, the "space."

"That you may know the way by which you must go." There was only one way across the Jordan river, which, incidentally, was normally only a few yards wide, but now, due to being at flood tide was over a mile wide. Jesus Christ is the way, the truth, and the life. There is no other way.

In verse 5 it says, *"Sanctify yourselves."* This passage is clear when we consider that to sanctify means to set apart. In this instance it meant that people were to sanctify themselves by washing their clothes and their bodies to be in readiness to experience the great power of God.

The 13th verse says, *"As soon as the soles of the feet of the priests that bear the ark of the Lord, the Lord of all the earth, shall rest in the waters of Jordan, that the waters of Jordan shall be cut off."* It should be instantly recognized that it was not the feet of the priests that caused the waters to *"stand upon an heap,"* but it was the Ark of God. As the Lord graciously allowed the great and glorious *"Ark of the Covenant"* to be carried by poor frail priests, likewise, the Lord has allowed poor frail man to preach His great and glorious Gospel of Jesus Christ (Eph. 4:11). However, we must always understand that the ones carrying are always imperfect as the Ark is always perfect. As well, the waters did not flee from the feet of the priests but from the Ark of the Covenant - the Lord Jesus Christ.

◼

CHAPTER 4

This chapter presents to the child of God two distinct memorials which are extremely important to every Christian.

Verse 1 says, *"That the Lord spake unto Joshua, saying,"* showing the extreme importance of that which is to be done which, as stated, is a valuable lesson to every child of God.

Verse 2 says, *"Take you twelve men out of the people."* This was a man for each tribe. The number 12 represents government. As well, it meant that every single person who passed across enjoyed the same type of salvation. None were saved more than others. Likewise, the "born again"experience for the most vile libertine is the same as the salvation experience for the good moral man. Both are horribly lost; both must have a glorious salvation. Consequently, the salvation is the same for both.

Verse 3 says, *"Take you hence out of the midst of Jordan, out of the place where the priests' feet stood firm, twelve stones."* These stones could well be called "victory stones." As the Ark had represented Christ, likewise, the stones would represent Christ. They would ultimately be taken to Gilgal and set up as a memorial.

The 6th verse says, *"That when your children ask their fathers in time to come, saying, What mean ye by these stones?"* Ever the same testimony must be of the salvation experience. As it was for the fathers, so for the children.

The message must not change. The stones represent the great power of God in delivering Israel from the wilderness as well as from Egypt. The great Rock, the Lord Jesus Christ, represents our salvation and must be told the same to the children as to the fathers. God help us when the children ask, "What means this?" that we will have instantly the miraculous story, "saved by grace."

The 7th verse says, *"Shall be for a memorial."* What is our memorial today? Too oftentimes it is the rank message of modernism which denies the mighty power of God, or the false cults that substitute "another Ark," or then, sadly, the Church that preaches "another gospel." The memorial must ever be "these stones."

The 9th verse says, *"And Joshua set up twelve stones in the midst of Jordan."* These 12 stones were totally different from the 12 that they had taken out of Jordan. These could be called "wilderness stones." They represent the terrible failure, sin, and defeat of the wilderness. In effect, Joshua was saying, "In the sea of God's forgetfulness." The Lord was telling Israel, "The wilderness is forgotten; the failures are buried. They will be covered by the Jordan not to be remembered anymore." They were to be placed *"where the feet of the priests which bare the Ark of the Covenant stood."* Every sin of the past is washed by the Blood of Jesus Christ. They are buried forever, not to be remembered against us anymore. And it says, *"And they are there unto this day."* Those stones representing the horrible wilderness failure were to be covered by the waters of God's grace. They were not to be seen anymore, nor were they to be remembered anymore. In the eyes of God they no longer existed. Sadly, too many Christians seem to delight in diving into the murky waters of life's Jordan, groping around on the bed of the sea of God's forgetfulness, and then when finding some stone, whether the correct one or not, delighting in bringing it to the surface and calling it to the attention of all concerned. How the anger of God would have burned red hot if the Israelites had attempted to retrieve these buried wilderness stones! How God's anger must burn red hot today when Christians attempt to retrieve, to remember, or to rehash that which God has forgotten! Likewise, when Satan comes to us attempting to bring his condemnation of our past failures, we must do as Paul said, *"Forgetting those things which are behind."* Hallelujah!

The 24th and closing verse of the chapter says, *"That all the people of the earth might know the hand of the Lord, that it is mighty."* Sadly, all the people of the earth do not know the hand of the Lord, that it is mighty. Hundreds of millions have never heard. He is mighty to save, but they do not know it. He is mighty to deliver, but they do not know it. God help us to take to a lost world the only message of redemption they will ever hear or know, the glorious message of the Lord Jesus Christ and His power to save.

CHAPTER 5

This chapter is a powerful portrayal of what God demands in order that we have victory. His demands will be totally opposite of that which the world demands.

Jericho was a fortress. It barred Israel's entrance into the Promised Land. Likewise, Satan has placed many fortresses at the entrance of the Promised Land to keep the child of God from inheriting that which God has promised him. As Jericho's conquest was impossible to Israel, at least as far as the flesh was concerned, likewise, our victory respecting the great fortresses that Satan has reared is impossible for us in the flesh as well. Let us see what the Lord required of Israel that day and what He requires of us today.

Verse 1 says, *"That their heart melted, neither was there spirit in them any more, because of the children of Israel."* The first verse of the 5th chapter speaks of all of the kings with their mighty fortresses who would oppose Israel. Their *"heart melted."* Satan would attempt to make us believe that our opposition is so formidable that it is hopeless. However, in spiritual reality the opposite is true. The Spirit of God had so worked on these enemies of Israel that they literally trembled in fear of the people of God. In spiritual reality Satan trembles in fear at the power of God

manifest in us. He doesn't want us to know it. He tries to hide it from us. He tries to make us believe that our opposition is so strong that we cannot hope to overcome. That is one of his chief tactics. But, in reality, he is already defeated, and his heart is trembling in fear. We should understand this; we should know this. We should shout the praises of God constantly. We should understand that instead of fear plaguing us, it is fear that plagues the enemy, *"their heart melted."* All of us want these great victories, and in this chapter we are given God's blueprint for victory. It is:

1. The death of self,
2. The testimony to the Blood and of the Lamb,
3. Feeding on the Word of God,
4. Subjection to Christ as Lord.

Let us first look at *"death to self."* Verse 2 says, *"Make thee sharp knives, and circumcise again the children of Israel the second time."* The battle with self is never ended once and for all. We would like for such to be, and, at times, we may foolishly think that it is. However, self keeps cropping up. It is a constant conflict between the flesh and the Spirit, hence, the words, *"the second time."* The death to self is illustrated in circumcision. This rite was a sign of "separation." Of course, the question is asked, "Separation from what?" It is separation from self. Most of the time when we think of separation, we are thinking of separation from the world. It certainly does include that. The world is an enemy to the child of God. However, our biggest enemy, of which circumcision is a type, is "self." What type of "self" are we speaking of? Strangely enough, the self part of man that must be separated by the Spirit of God (circumcised) is that which we would call "good." It is man's natural wisdom and goodness. It is most bitter for to a man to learn that all his goodness must be slain with the Sword of the Lord just as much as all his badness. But to the Christian this is most sweet, for it brings him into a resurrection life, and the power of that life takes all strength from Satan. Man, irregardless of his religion or his goodness, has no strength against Satan. Jericho's walls never fall before him! But if death to all that we think of as good, wise, and beautiful is suffered, it then becomes a shelter, for what can Satan do with a dead man? Paul wrote, *"We are the circumcision, and have no confidence in the flesh."*

The second principle of victory is the *"testimony to the blood of the Lamb."* Verse 10 says, *"And kept the passover."* Israel proclaimed her redemption out of Egypt and her position in the Land of Promise by keeping the Passover. We proclaim our redemption and dwelling because of the preciousness of the Blood of the Paschal Lamb. That is the reason that Paul with all of his education and worldly knowledge said, *"I determined to know nothing among you save Christ and Him crucified."* Why? Because the terrible bondages of humanity cannot be broken by the intellect, earthly wisdom, money, prestige, or education. It can only be broken by the power of the shed Blood of Jesus Christ. That was Israel's victory then; this is our victory now.

Third, we have *"feeding on the Word of God."* The 11th verse says, *"And they did eat of the old corn of the land."* This is the first time it is mentioned. Heretofore, Israel had feasted on manna which was angels' food. This suited the wilderness and its defective spiritual life. However, the *"old corn of the land,"* representing the powerful Word of God and the *"strong meat of the Word,"* is a necessity for the strength needed in spiritual conquests in the land of our inheritance. Sadly, the Bible is presently talked about, merchandised, spoken of, analyzed and dissected, but it is little read and meditated thereon. The present Church is almost a Bibleless family. Most of the preaching today is psychology or else a mixture of Bible and psychology. Some of it may be good, but it is not the Word of God. There is no other.

Fourth, we have *"subjection to Christ our Lord."* There must be a full surrender to Christ. The 13th verse says, *"There stood a man over against him with his sword drawn in his hand."*

The 14th verse says, *"As captain of the host of the Lord am I now come."* An absolute condition of victory is full and total surrender to the Lord Jesus Christ. He must be accepted as Captain, be permitted to plan, and be fully obeyed.

When Joshua understood Who this Man was, he fully surrendered his position of lead-

ership and his sword. In verse 13 He is called *"a man,"* and so He is. He is very God and very man, *"the man Christ Jesus."*

While in the wilderness Egypt reproached Israel with a taunt that Jehovah could not bring them into the Promised Land, and furthermore, all of Egypt that attaches itself to a servant of God is a reproach to Him. Joshua would yield total authority to the *"Captain"* as he *"fell on his face to the earth and did worship."* He would then ask the question, *"What saith my Lord unto his servant?"* The answer would be startling.

The Lord at the beginning of His command would not mention the conquest of Jericho, the great victories to be won, or all the great things He would do for Israel. He merely said, *"Loose thy shoe from off thy foot; for the place whereon thou standest is holy."* The child of God is so busy seeking great victory, riches, and power that he seldom seeks that which is the most important. The most important is that which is *"holy."* How many thousands of preachers are trying to defeat the evil one when they have never met the *"Captain"* or stood on that which is *"holy."* This is the secret of the Church; not the subjection of the Jerichos nor the defeat of the Amorites and the Canaanites, but that first we see Jesus and that which is holy. Then, and only then will the Jerichos fall and the Amorites and the Canaanites be defeated.

Verse 9 told us , *"This day have I rolled away the reproach of Egypt from off you,"* and this can only get done as we follow the *"Captain."* We cannot roll that reproach away from ourselves, only *"the Captain"* can.

CHAPTER 6

Now that the Lord has brought Joshua to the place of total surrender and obedience, He will give him instructions concerning Jericho. So oftentimes we get them backwards. We want the great victory pronouncement over Jericho without coming to the place of holiness. It does not work, and it cannot work. Now the Lord will give Joshua instructions.

The 2nd verse says, *"And the Lord said unto Joshua."* He tells him first that he will have victory over Jericho, *"I have given into thine hand Jericho."* So many Christians make their plans by attempting to get God to bless them. We have it backwards. God must make the plans, and then they will be blessed. Here, the Lord made the plans.

He then gives him instructions. To the natural mind they would be supercilious, *"Go round about the city once. Thus shalt thou do six days."*

If one will notice, in the 4th verse the number *"seven"* is used repeatedly. There are *"seven priests," "seven trumpets," "the seventh day,"* and then, *"seven times."* Why all of these sevens?

Everything in the Word of God is for an express purpose. Nothing is done for show or selfish occupation. All have a tremendous spiritual meaning.

In the Word of God the number *"seven"* denotes God's perfection, completion, totality, and all-in-all. Joshua is operating strictly in the spiritual sense. How often do we as Christians operate in the worldly sense? In other words, we borrow our ideas from the world, insert them into that which is called Christianity, and pass it off as the Word of God. God will have none of it. These are spiritual instructions of faith. The world, the natural mind, or Jericho will have absolutely no idea what they mean, as the natural mind cannot understand the things of the Spirit. Regrettably, most in the Church have no knowledge of the things of the Spirit; they only understand the things of the world.

The 8th verse says, *"And the ark of the covenant of the Lord followed them."* Why were the seven priests with the seven rams' horns placed before the Ark? Why not the Ark first?

The Lord has chosen that He work through men. That is His plan. If there are no men to work through, the work of God is not done. The Ark of God will only follow godly, consecrated, holy men - and here is where we make our mistake.

Men are not holy because of what they do. They are holy because of what Jesus has done. Some think because someone has failed they are, thereby, unholy. If they have repented,

there is no unholiness left. To be frank with you, there are no human beings who ever existed who have not failed. *"All have come short of the glory of God."* If lack of failure is a criteria for being used of God, then the Bible "greats" could never have been used. So, if you are allowing Satan (or men) to tell you that because you have failed you can never be used of God again, please remember this: The ones telling you this have failed over and over again and are now doing the service of Satan by mouthing their unbelief. The only failure that will prohibit an individual from marching around Jericho and ultimately blowing the victory note on the ram's horns and being followed by the Ark of the Lord is the failure of not repenting. And, regretfully, most of the Church is saddled with that failure.

God is not looking for perfect men. There aren't any. He is looking for those who will be *"poor and of a contrite spirit, and will tremble at His Word"* (Isaiah 66). This is God's method. God will follow the men who will obey Him. To be frank with you, He is looking for individuals who will admit their failures and repent before God, and then hear from heaven, pick up their rams' horn and march around the Jericho walls of their obstacles. The Ark of God will follow a man like that, and the walls will fall down flat. Hallelujah!

The 10th verse says two things, *"Ye shall not shout",* and *"Then shall ye shout."*

From the Word of God we are told there is a time to shout and a time not to shout. Why could they not shout at the beginning?

Millions today in Christendom are shouting with nothing to shout about. They have not heard from heaven. They have not seen the *"captain of the Lord of hosts."* They have not pulled off their shoes or stood on holy ground. Faith doesn't have to scream to make itself heard. So many trumpet the loudness of their profession to cover up the barrenness of their possession. Much of the shouting in modern day churches is superficial, hollow, and only on the surface. So, when should we shout?

The Scripture says, *"Then,"* which means after we have obeyed the Lord and done exactly what He has told us to do. We have appointed the seven priests with the seven trumpets. The Ark of God on the shoulders of the priests will follow the priests with the rams' horns, *"obedience is better than sacrifice."* Still, the shout must be by faith. They did not shout after the walls had fallen. They shouted before they fell. However, it must be remembered that their shout had nothing to do with the walls falling but simply was in obedience to God.

The 20th verse says, *"They took the city."* There is no record that one Israelite was lost. This is God's way. Sometimes we win great victories albeit with great loss. This is a sure sign that much flesh has been associated with what little of the Holy Spirit we have allowed to function; consequently, there is great loss. Here there is no loss at all, *"they took the city."* The reason that there was no loss is obvious. They followed the instructions of faith to the letter.

The 21st verse says, *"And they utterly destroyed all."* Every vestige of temper, jealously, ambition, pride, deceit, and envy must be *"utterly destroyed."* The problem of the Church is that we try to destroy the flesh with the flesh. We fail as ever we must. Flesh cannot destroy flesh. Sickness cannot heal sickness. Sin cannot save from sin. All of the rules of legalism in our churches cannot set one captive free. It can make evident more sin. But when the Spirit of God has His perfect and complete way, all is *"utterly destroyed."*

There is indication that Rahab was taken out immediately before the destruction of the city or else at the very outset because the 22nd verse says, *"But Joshua had said."* This implies past tense concerning the two men who had spied out the country. They were instructed to *"Go into the harlot's house, and bring out thence the woman, and all that she had."* The two men are types of the "Word of God and the Holy Spirit." Rahab the harlot is a type of the Church that is saved from the bondage of this world. As Joshua gave instructions for her and her's to be brought out, likewise, our heavenly Joshua, just before the Great Tribulation which will destroy this world's system or else at its outset, will bring out the Church and all that she has. Hallelujah!

Salvation by the scarlet line was not only simple; it was also sure. How many, if they had known, would have scoffed at Rahab for staking her life on this *"scarlet thread."* However, the scarlet thread, representing the precious Blood of Jesus Christ, was all that was needed. It is all that is needed today, as well. When the day of wrath came, the promise of safety prevailed.

The 26th verse says, *"Cursed be the man before the Lord, that riseth up and buildeth this city Jericho."* Why? Jericho was a type of the fortresses that Satan attempts to build within our lives. If we allow these fortresses (strongholds) of jealousy, envy, lust, greed, and pride to be rebuilt, we are cursed. Sin in the life of a Christian is just as deadly or even more so, than in the life of an unbeliever.

CHAPTER 7

Joshua 7 shows us the reason for failure in the life of the Christian – sin. As sin stopped the advance of God's people in the Land of Promise, so sin will stop the advance of God's people today. God's holiness cannot abide sin. Likewise, God's grace cannot refuse forgiveness to those who will truly repent. Sadly, there is very little evidence that Achan repented.

The 1st verse says, *"And the anger of the Lord was kindled."* Nothing angers God like sin; He cannot abide it, whether in the life of Moses or whether in the life of Achan. A hidden sin was the cause of Israel's defeat. In the life of victory God is the one and only strength of the Christian who has no other strength. But God cannot give that strength if sin be present. If He did, He would deny His own nature, which is holiness. When He acts in power in the midst of His people, He must act in harmony with His own nature; hence, He must judge sin in the camp of Israel with the same "fierce anger" with which He judged it in the city of Jericho. That judgment in both cases was death.

But if the discovery and judgment of sin is painful, and if there is faithfulness in dealing with it, then grace gives both blessing and victory, and the valley of Achor, which had been a valley of death, now becomes a door of hope (Hos. 2:5). Sin should be feared, but neither its bitterness nor its punishment should be dreaded, for it is at this point that God resumes His victory – giving fellowship with His child.

Verses 6 through 9 record the complaint of Joshua. Verse 9 says, *"For the Canaanites and all the inhabitants of the land shall hear of it."* Like Joshua, much of the church world constantly laments the problem. It is constantly said, "We need more education; money is the need; we need more organization"; however, these things never help. The problem is *"the accursed thing."*

The Lord said in the 11th verse, *"Israel hath sinned."* One sin brought all the nation to defeat and caused God to stop His blessing. One sin is what caused Adam and the whole race to be under the present curse (Gen. 2:19; Rom. 5:12-21). One sin brings the same result as committing all sins (James 2:9-10). Any one of the death penalty sins of St. Mark 7:19-21; Rom. 1:21-32; Gal. 5:19-21 will damn the soul of any person, regardless of his claims to salvation, for there is no respect of persons with God. Grace, love, mercy, and salvation from God do not license one to commit sin or free him from responsibility regarding the sin question. Sin has it's deadly effect upon all alike in every generation and every place among all races.

However, the moment the individual confesses his sin (I John 1:9) and humbly repents before God, the sin and the punishment for the sin is removed by the precious Blood of Jesus Christ.

The 21st verse says that Achan's sin was *"a goodly Babylonish garment, and two hundred shekels of silver, and a wedge of gold of fifty shekels weight."* Achan knew the command, *"And ye, in anywise keep yourselves from the accursed thing"* (Joshua 6:18). It seemed to be willful sin with no regard for the Word of God and was apparently accompanied by very little temptation. Babylon and money have a fateful attraction for the Christian. He finds these things among the unconverted around him, as they found them in Jericho, and his heart covets them. This explains the weakness of the modern Church today. These sins are enjoyed instead of being confessed and forsaken. God has therefore withdrawn His power, and there is universal weakness and defeat. Fellowship with God can only be enjoyed if resolute sepa-

NOTES

ration from all evil be observed. It seems that Achan's family joined with him in the stealing of these items and in their hiding of them. They would also join with him in the judgment.

Their sin, the 5th verse says, had caused the death of *"about thirty and six men."* The wages of sin is always death.

CHAPTER 8

Verse 1 says, *"I have given unto thy hand the king of Ai and his people, and his city, and his land."* Victories are easily won in the path of simplicity and faith, but if sin has been indulged, it causes considerable pain to win even small victories. Even though sin had by now been put away, still, much difficulty was engaged in to win the victory at Ai. None of this was seen in the capture of Jericho. This should be a glaring lesson for the entirety of the Church. God cannot abide sin. Sin makes easy matters very difficult.

The 20th verse says, speaking of the men of Ai, *"They had no power to flee this way or that way."* Now that sin had been properly removed, the power of God once again rested with His people and victory was theirs.

The 28th verse says, *"And Joshua burnt Ai and made it a heap forever."* Some time back in Israel, I took an experienced guide to show me the route of Joshua all the way from Gilgal, which was near the Jordan River close by Jericho, to Ai. Just as the Word of God says, no one knew exactly where it was. However, the location of the general vicinity could be pinpointed. The 28th verse says, *"Even a desolation unto this day,"* and so it is.

The 24th verse says, *"When Israel had made an end of slaying all the inhabitants of Ai,"* inferring that all had been put to the sword. Many, not knowing the Word of God or the disposition of the people in Canaan, may object. Possibly, the statement of an archaeologist some time back could well sum up the situation. He did not speak from a biblical or a spiritual stance but only from the evidence found. Basically, this is what he said:

"The God of the Old Testament Who

ordered the destruction of these people did future generations a tremendous service." And then he went on to say, *"The evil in which these people engaged themselves such as incest, bestiality, homosexuality, as well as wholesale human sacrifice to idols, so corrupted them that their destruction to protect other nations and future generations was demanded."*

Therefore, God gave instructions that they were all to be destroyed, men, women, and children. At times and in certain places even the animals were destroyed. However, at Ai the 27th verse says, *"Only the cattle and the spoil of that city Israel took for a prey unto themselves, according unto the Word of the Lord."*

Verses 30 through 35 portray the beautiful plan of salvation in the construction of the altar on Mount Ebal.

The 30th verse says, *"Then Joshua built an altar unto the Lord God of Israel in mount Ebal."*

The altar was a type of Calvary, typifying the Redeemer Who was yet to come. It was the secret of Israel's victory. The altar was built unto the Lord God of Israel; it was not built unto man. Why Ebal? There were two mountains in this valley, Mount Gerizim and Mount Ebal. Mount Gerizim had been labeled at God's direction by Moses as the mount of blessing, Mount Ebal as the mount of cursing. These two mountains situated basically in the center of Israel were to be a symbol forever of the blessings of God that would come upon His people for obedience, and the curse of God that would come for disobedience. Yet, Moses built his altar on Mount Ebal. Why? Most in the church world of today, especially the Charismatics, are building their churches, symbolically speaking, on Mount Gerizim. To the natural man who is not led by the Spirit, this certainly seems to be the logical choice. Everyone wants blessing. So we will build our altar on Mount Gerizim and obtain the blessing. However, that is not God's way.

As stated, Mount Ebal is the mount of cursing. The Lord had said, *"If you do not obey me, you will be cursed,"* and so Joshua built his altar on this mount. His doing so is where it ever should be built.

Mankind's problem is not a lack of blessing. Mankind's problem is that he is cursed. Since

the fall in the Garden of Eden, man has experienced the horrible curse of God. So, the curse is man's problem, not lack of blessing. When Joshua built his altar on Mount Ebal, he was, in effect, saying, "Man is lost; there is no way he can redeem himself. However, a Redeemer is coming Who will hang upon a tree and will take the curse of God upon Himself, thereby letting man go free." That is the reason Paul said, *"For I determined not to know any thing among you, save Jesus Christ, and him crucified."* Calvary is God's answer to man's sin. It is the only answer to man's sin.

The Church has tried to assuage man's fallen state with positive thinking, possibility thinking, psychoanalysis, and the health and wealth gospel. But all constitute an altar that is buit on Mount Gerizim and will never be accepted by God. Man's problem is not that he is slightly out of focus or that he needs a new automobile or a fatter paycheck. It is not that he needs to start thinking in a positive manner. Man's problem is sin, and the only cure for sin is the precious shed Blood of the Lord Jesus Christ, with man's acceptance of it as his redemption.

True blessings can only come if the curse of God is assuaged first. Admittedly, Mount Ebal and its altar is an ugly business. It is not palatable to the world at all, nor to the majority of the Church. No one wants to deal with a curse, only with a blessing. However, if that altar had not been built on Mount Ebal, there would never have been any blessing.

The 31st verse says, *"An altar of whole stones."* Why whole stones? The stones must be those designed by God and not man. Man has never been satisfied with the *"whole stones."* Calvary is not very pretty, so man has become very adept at fashioning stones of his own design. Admittedly, they are attractive, enticing, and beautiful according to appearance, but save no one. The 31st verse further adds, *"Over which no man hath lift up any iron."* Man must ever tamper with God's plan of salvation. It is never quite suitable enough. Therefore, he *"lifts up his iron."* He fashions the stone. He carves it into that which will be palatable to the ungodly and, thereby, acceptable. But once again, "It will set no captive free, nor mend a broken heart, nor recover sight for the blind, nor set at liberty one who is bruised."

The 31st verse says, *"They offered thereon burnt offerings unto the Lord, and sacrificed peace offerings."* The burnt offering was what was referred to as a *"whole burnt offering."* It meant that the entirety of the animal minus the skin was placed on the altar fires and totally consumed. It signifies two things:

1. That God would give His all for humanity in the sacrifice of His Son Jesus Christ

2. That to receive all that God would give, man must give his all as well.

The *"peace offerings"* signify the peace that comes only from God and will follow the sacrifice of the *"whole burnt offering."*

Most of the church world today knows little peace. The reason is that we have not given God our all. Too much is reserved for selfish pleasure. As well, it might be added that the altar fashioned by man would never be so crude as to engage in a bloody religion. Also, Jesus will not die on a man-made altar. The 32nd verse says, *"He wrote there upon the stones a copy of the law of Moses."* In these two verses we have the foundation of the work of God, Calvary, and the Word of God.

The 34th verse reads, *"He read all the words of the law, the blessings and the cursings."* Many love to hear the blessings read, but they will shun the church that reads the cursings. Blessing churches abound; they attract the multitudes because all want blessings. Few desire the churches that not only proclaim the blessings but the cursings as well.

There are myriad blessing churches; there are even a few cursing churches, however, both destroy. God demands that it be one – the *"blessings and cursings."*

The 35th verse says that Joshua read all the Word of God, and he didn't leave out any. What an indictment on most in the church world who pick and choose among the Word of God what they like and ignore what they dislike. But this passage says, *"There was not a word of all that Moses commanded, which Joshua read not before all the congregation of Israel."* The Word of God is the answer, but it must be all of the Word of God. It will meet the need of the men, the women, the little ones, and even the strangers. It holds the answer for all.

CHAPTER 9

As we have repeatedly said and will continue to say, the book of Joshua is a type of the Christian's spiritual experience in taking all that God has planned for him, in other words, the inheritance. If we will study, learn, and understand this book totally, we will understand the ways of the Holy Spirit and will, thereby, gain victory.

At Ai Israel trusted her own strength and did not pray, so was defeated. At Gibeon she trusted her own wisdom and did not pray, and again was defeated! Regrettably, the lesson taught and hopefully learned at Ai seemed to be forgotten almost immediately. Such is the natural heart!

This chapter seems to portend disaster, as under Law it must; however, Grace will turn it into something beautiful.

Verse 2 says, *"They gathered themselves together, to fight with Joshua and with Israel, with one accord."* Victories have been won, and Satan trembles with fear, so now the opposition will be more powerful. This is a perfect example of our spiritual warfare. If we rely totally upon the Lord Jesus Christ, certain victory is ours. Even though the *"gathering themselves together"* would seem to constitute overwhelming odds in their favor, still, it was no more difficult for the Lord Jesus Christ to defeat their confederation than it was for *few.*

The lesson that must be learned is this:

The powers of Satan are so formidable that we are hopeless to gain the victory if we attempt to do so by the flesh. Regrettably, almost all of the church world engages in spiritual warfare by the means of the flesh. We lose as lose we must. If the warfare is conducted God's way with Jesus Christ as its leader, then we win, as win we must.

The 14th verse speaks of the men of Gibeon who would deceive Joshua and Israel by subterfuge and would gain their desires. They did so because this verse says, *"And asked not counsel at the mouth of the Lord."* The judgment of God was upon the Gibeonites. Instructions were given that they were to be totally destroyed. The Gibeonites would profess to be from a far country and ask for clemency at the hand of Joshua. It would be granted; it would be a mistake. Satan, through the mouth of the Gibeonite, abundantly quoted the Bible to Joshua (vss. 6:9, 10, 24), just as afterwards he did to our heavenly Joshua, but the Lord defeated him with three verses out of the Law. Had Joshua so acted, he would have gotten the same victory.

Satan can only deceive Christians when they take management into their own hands instead of consulting the Lord. Communion with God gives a spiritual instinct which discerns an enemy and refuses to make him an ally.

Even though the Covenant by Joshua with the Gibeonites was made and was unlawful, still, the Lord did not punish them for making this Covenant. However, when Israel long afterward broke the Covenant, the Lord punished them for doing so (II Sam. 21:1-9). The Lord let Israel make this mistake without intervening, as He will oftentimes allow us to do.

The 21st verse says that the sentence was, *"Let them live; but let them be hewers of wood and drawers of water unto all the congregation."* This did not mean domestic slavery to Israelites but to *"the congregation."* This meant they were to hew wood for the sacrificial offerings for the brazen altar and to carry water for the brazen laver in which the priest would wash. These were to be their duties. The Law condemned them as the Law must, for it says in the 23rd verse, *"Now therefore you are cursed."* However, Grace, because of Calvary, brought them into glory and joy. The curse was turned into a blessing because of Calvary. They were ever so close to the Spirit and presence of God. As they hewed the wood and would bring it close to the brazen altar, they no doubt sensed the glorious presence of God constantly. As they drew the water and brought it close to the brazen laver, they were close to the glory of God. There is no greater place where anyone could be.

The picture of these Gibeonites is a perfect picture of humanity under the curse and, thereby, condemned. However, it is also a perfect picture of Calvary and the Word of God that sets the captive free. It seems these Gibeonites understood perfectly how the Lord had blessed them. They would become in Bible terminology *"the Nethinims."* This word means "given" – devoted to the sanctuary of Jehovah. They served in this capacity all through the judges, the kings, and the dispersion into Babylon. They were among the first to return with Ezra and Nehemiah, pledging themselves to keep the statutes given by God to Moses (Ezra 2:43-58; Neh. 7:60), and they are last seen in Nehemiah 3:26, 10:28, and 11:21 when they made their home outside the water-gate of Jerusalem. Why the water-gate? Because being near the water supply, they could more readily discharge the honorable bondage to which Joshua had condemned them of being drawers of water to the Temple of Jehovah. Thus, a curse pronounced by Law becomes, by Grace, a blessing. Hallelujah!

CHAPTER 10

Now we come to one of the greatest miracles ever recorded in the annals of human history. Satan would attempt to destroy the people of God. If Joshua had once depended upon the flesh in this episode as he did at Ai or with the Gibeonites, all would have been lost. But as he depended totally upon the Spirit, all was won.

Now the Gibeonites had been brought over to Israel's God. The former friends of the Gibeonites became very angry and sought to destroy all. The 4th verse says, *"Come up with me, and help me, that we may smite Gibeon: For it hath made peace with Joshua."* The moment the person comes to Jesus Christ, those who were formerly friends now become enemies. The 5th verse says, *"And made war against Gibeon."*

The 6th verse says, *"And the men of Gibeon sent unto Joshua."* This is the answer for the child of God, "Send unto our heavenly Joshua, the Lord Jesus Christ." The words are to the point, *"Come up to us quickly, and save us, and help us."* What a plea! What a petition! How so often all of us have uttered these words, "Come quickly, save us, and help us." Our heavenly Joshua never fails. He always comes to our aid.

Hallelujah!

The 8th verse says, *"And the Lord said unto Joshua, Fear them not: For I have delivered them into thine hand."* Were we withstanding such ourselves, we would be hopelessly defeated. But with our heavenly Joshua leading the charge, victory is certain. *"There shall not a man of them stand before thee."*

The 9th verse says that Joshua came immediately *"unto them suddenly, and went up from Gilgal all night."* When we call, He is there.

The 10th verse says, *"And the Lord discomfited them before Israel."* In the following verses we are given an incident of the great miracles that were performed.

The 11th verse says, *"That the Lord cast down great stones from heaven upon them."*

The 12th verse records Joshua saying, *"Sun, stand thou still upon Gibeon; and thou, Moon, in the valley of Ajalon."*

This great miracle has been confirmed by the state documents of Egypt, China, and Mexico which record this double-day. For such a delineation of the earth would keep those three countries in the sunlight. Lord Kingsborough in his history of the Mexicans, and the Chinese Philosopher Hauai-nan-tz quote these records.

The Word of God says this in the 14th verse, *"And there was no day like that before it or after it, that the Lord hearkened unto the voice of a man: For the Lord fought for Israel."* No devil or confederation of devils can overcome us if we will totally depend upon Jesus Christ. He will in this great time of distress *"hearken unto the voice of a man."*

After the tremendous victory had been won and the kings of these five cities had been brought before Joshua, *"He said unto the captains of the men of war which went with him, Come near, put your feet upon the necks of these kings."* The Bible says they did so.

And then the 25th verse says, *"For thus shall the Lord do to all your enemies against whom you fight."* There is but one way to deal with sin, and that is to place the triumphant foot of faith upon its neck and put it to death. It is impossible to improve sin, just as in the judgment of God it was impossible for Israel to improve these five kings. Man in his folly tries to improve what is opposed to and by God, but the failure of his efforts ever reveals his

NOTES

foolishness.

Over and over again in the balance of the 10th chapter, concerning victory at particular cities, the words will be used, *"He utterly destroyed them"* (vs. 28).

In the 30th verse it says, *"He let none remain in it."*

The 33rd verse says, *"Until he had left him none remaining."*

Verse 35 says, *"He utterly destroyed that day, according to all."*

Verse 37 says, *"He left none remaining."*

Over and over again throughout the chapter these words are used. To be sure, the Holy Spirit was not repetitive to fill up space. The lesson is very obvious.

Every vestige of envy, jealousy, pride, lust, immorality, uncontrollable temper, and self-will must be rooted out of the life of the child of God. There must be *"none remaining."* The Holy Spirit is insistent in this, *"none remaining."* That which remains is forever a snare to us. Ultimately, it will rise up and destroy us. There must be *"none remaining."*

There are those faint of heart who believe that it is impossible to overcome all the efforts of darkness. It is not impossible because the 42nd verse says, *"The Lord God of Israel fought for Israel."* We cannot hope to root out these enemies ourselves. Flesh cannot defeat flesh; sickness cannot heal sickness; man cannot cure man. The secret is found in the 43rd verse. *"And Joshua returned, and all Israel with him, unto the camp to Gilgal."* What is the secret?

Gilgal was the place of circumcision, which stood for separation. It meant victory over the flesh and over self-will. It must be completely understood that when all was destroyed in these cities, not only was all the bad destroyed, but all the good was destroyed as well.

Likewise, the Christian can easily destroy the evil but finds it very difficult to destroy the good. Our good works, man-made consecration, and extreme religiosity all may seem good, but they must be destroyed along with that which is evil, or else the evil will come back to haunt us, because man's self-will, which stems from the flesh, always leads to the works of the flesh, as is recorded in the book of Galatians.

CHAPTER 11

Chapter 11 is the continued saga of conquest. All the land must be eradicated of the enemy. All must be subdued, for this land is God's land. Likewise, since Jesus has come into the heart of the child of God, all of the enemy must be eradicated. Every semblance of that which is evil must be put away. Now the house will become a temple of the Holy Spirit (1 Cor. 3:16).

The conflict in the northern part of the holy land once again saw a confederation of the enemy against Joshua. The 4th verse says, *"Even as the sand that is upon the sea shore in multitude, with horses and chariots very many."* Satan's efforts against us are always accompanied by a multitude. He comes *"as a roaring lion."* If one does not depend totally upon the Lord Jesus Christ, our heavenly Joshua, then fear will overcome the individual.

But the 6th verse says, *"And the Lord said unto Joshua, Be not afraid because of them."* Over and over again the Lord keeps saying throughout the entirety of the Bible, *"fear not,"* or statements such as *"be not afraid of them."* Fear is, no doubt, one of the greatest weapons that Satan has and one of the Christian's greatest problems. We look at circumstances, and then we begin to fear. To be frank, fear is a spirit. Paul said, *"For God hath not given us the spirit of fear"* (II Tim. 1:7). Please allow me to speak more clearly: Every single Christian has been attacked numerous times by *"a spirit of fear."* This is far more than just a negative thought. It is actually a spirit of darkness sent by one of the *"principalities"* or *"powers,"* or one of the *"rulers of the darkness of this world,"* or maybe even by *"spiritual wickedness in high places"* (Eph. 6:12).

We have thought that a negative confession would occasion such. It certainly can play a part in it. However, most of the time the negative confession comes about because of the *"spirit of fear."* This is a spirit that can definitely be felt by the child of God. During this time, everything looks hopeless. The odds against us look absolutely overwhelming.

NOTES

Every problem seems to be bigger than life all because of a *"spirit of fear."* Our defense against this is as follows:

    a. The Word of God(St. John I),

    b. The whole armour of God (Eph. 6),

    c. The name of Jesus (St. Mark 16).

There are no other weapons. Actually, no other weapons are needed. So, the Lord will say to Joshua, *"Be not afraid."*

In the 10th verse we are told that *"Hazor beforetime was the head of all those kingdoms",* in other words the capital. However, Satan's capital must not be God's capital. Still, Gilgal, the place of circumcision and separation, must be God's capital concerning Israel at this particular time. Hazor was totally destroyed. Not a vestige of its former power remained to compete with Gilgal. The center and source of power must all be Divine. Therefore, the 11th verse says, *"And he burnt Hazor with fire."*

The 15th verse says, *"He left nothing undone of all that the Lord commanded Moses."* What a testimony! This is what the Holy Spirit is desiring within our lives. We must leave nothing undone that the Lord commands that we do, not only concerning our personal lives but His work as well. How many Christians today can say this which was said of Joshua? *"He left nothing undone."* God help us to do all that the Lord has told us to do.

The 19th verse says, *"There was not a city that made peace with the children of Israel."* In all the land of Canaan save the (Gibeonites), there was war. This is an ideal example of that which the child of God faces. Everything of the world must be defeated. We must not make peace with the enemy. There can be no compromise. To the degree that the world is left within our lives, we will face the same level of difficulty.

The 20th verse says, *"It was of the Lord to harden their hearts, that they should come against Israel in battle, that he might destroy them utterly."* There can never be an agreement made with the enemies of our soul. The Lord is totally opposed to these enemies (jealousy, envy, pride, greed); therefore, we must be opposed as well. This passage says, *"They might have no favor."*

The church world, by and large, refuses to

look at the enemies of God's people as God looks at them. The church world for the most part calls them "psychological maladjustments" or "the little child in us." Then psychology tries to ameliorate the problem by coming to terms with guilt, jealousy, and other problems. The Lord calls it sin and says, *"that He might destroy them utterly."* God's way is the only way. The world's way which has crept into the Church is not God's way and will find no victory.

The 21st verse says, *"And at that time came Joshua, and cut off the Anakims."* These *"Anakims"* were members of the giant races, descendants of the sons of God and the daughters of men. The fact that several places all over Canaan are mentioned here indicates that the giants were scattered far and wide instead of dwelling in only one part of the land (verse 21). The fact that Joshua utterly destroyed them and their cities and did not destroy all the cities of ordinary men (10:39) proves that the giants were dealt with much more severely than the others. Some of the giants were left only in Gaza, Gath, and Ashdod. One of the descendants of these giants, named Goliath, from the very area just mentioned will do battle with David about 450 years in the future.

CHAPTER 12

At first glance, this chapter seems to be uninteresting. However, to the Holy Spirit and to those who know and understand this great Christian life, this chapter is freighted with victory. The list of these kings and their cities defeated by the people of God represents a tremendous victory in the halls of heaven. They are typical of our victories in the Spirit.

Verse 1 says, *"Now these are the kings of the land, which the children of Israel smote."* And then it says, *"And possessed their land."* The inheritance that God has given us as Christians still must be taken. The only way we can possess it is to drive out the enemies (jealousy, envy, malice, pride, lust). It is a Promised Land; it is given to us by God. It is our inheritance, but at the same time, we have to take it by force

in faith. Whatever area of spiritual land that pride or jealousy or greed or self-will is occupying cannot be ours. The question must be asked, "How many of us have actually possessed all the land?"

The 8th verse says, *"In the mountains, and in the valleys, and in the plains, and in the springs, and in the wilderness, and in the south country."* There is no place that Satan does not desire to occupy and will, in fact, occupy if we allow him to. Actually, he wants more than just the mountains or just the plains. He wants it all. Yet, it has been given to us by God.

As we go down the long list of kings and cities that were defeated by Joshua and the people of Israel, beginning at verse 9, we must realize that each one of these places represents a definite victory by the power of the Holy Spirit.

For instance, in the 14th verse it says, *"The king of Hormah, one."* This place possibly means little to the unspiritual eye, but to those who know and understand what it represents, it symbolizes a great victory in our own lives. At this place Satan tried to stop us, but at this place the Lord gave us powerful victory.

There are 31 great victories recorded in this chapter, which also signifies 31 defeats for Satan. It is encouraging and touching to read of these 31 victories so definitely and individually recorded. There were not just 30 victories, but 31. Each victory was important in the eyes of God and precious to the heart of God, no matter how uninteresting and small they might appear to man. No victory over the enemy is small in God's mind. It should not be small in our minds either. Hallelujah!

CHAPTER 13

Verses 1 through 7 record the exact words of the Lord Jesus Christ. Verse 1 says, *"And the Lord said unto him."* Consequently, the words are extremely precious. As well, that which we glean should be powerful. We learn from this that God had a perfect plan for Israel as He has for us today. There was absolutely nothing uncertain in His arrangements, but, on the contrary, everything was orderly and well defined. As in the 12th chapter, great victories were recorded and itemized. Still, the Lord will gently remind them, *"There remaineth yet very much land to be possessed."*

Many times the flesh will become weary and stop short of God's best for our lives. That is the bane of Christendom. We never quite take all the land.

Verse 2 says, *"This is the land that yet remaineth."* The Holy Spirit has perfectly drawn out *"the borders."* That is what He intends for us to take. We have failed God and come short of total victory if we leave land unpossessed. How many enemies remain unsubdued in the hearts of Christians?

In the 13th verse the sad word, *"nevertheless,"* looms large. It is given to us by the Holy Spirit for our admonition. It says, *"The children of Israel expelled not the Geshurites, nor the Maachathites."* So, the Holy Spirit is telling us that pride and greed are allowed to remain. And sadder still, it says, *"But the Geshurites and the Maachathites dwell among the Israelites until this day."* The orders from the Lord had been explicit, *"expel all."* So, there was failure. How many Christians live with *"Geshurites"* and *"Macchathites"* all of their lives? They were born again many years ago. They became new creatures in Christ Jesus. They have won some victories, but still, the *"Geshurite"* remains (judging), or maybe it is the *"Macchathite"* (slander). The words scream out at us, *"until this day."* As you, the child of God, read these words, it is almost positive that each one of us can rejoice with Joshua regarding great victories like these recorded in chapter 12. It is also positive that most, if not all of us, will have to look with sadness at our heart and realize that some of these enemies of the Lord are with us *"until this day."* If the Holy Spirit said it here (and He did), then He is saying it to us as well.

—■—

CHAPTER 14

This is a victory chapter, and we should

NOTES

rejoice in it.

The 2nd verse says, *"By lot was their inheritance."* Eleazar, the High Priest, now acted with Joshua to divide the land by lot as instructed by Moses. The High Priest alone had the Urim and Thummim by which the lots could be cast. In other words the dividing of the land was not according to political stance, position, power, or prestige. The borders were designed by the Holy Spirit. Whatever the tribe of Ephraim received, it was designed by the Holy Spirit. That which Judah received was designed by the Holy Spirit. The tribes complained little about their inheritance.

There were really 13 tribes counting the tribe of Levi; however, they were not considered a tribe as far as inheritance of the land was concerned. The two sons of Joseph (Manasseh and Ephraim) took the part of their father. Therefore, regarding the sons of Jacob, Joseph his true son was not included, and instead, his two grandsons took the place of Joseph and of Levi. As far as the Levites were concerned, the Lord was their inheritance so that they could be ministers of the whole nation.

Sadly, little by little, the present-day church structure of denominations and denominationalism has gradually usurped authority over the Holy Spirit. God's biblical order of calling men and women to preach the Gospel and then designating where they should go to preach has been replaced by man, who, according to denominational politics, divides the land himself. However, it must be noted that whatever the Holy Spirit does, He will bless, but whatever man does, the Holy Spirit will not bless. So, by and large, we have an unblessed Church.

Beginning with the 6th verse to the conclusion of the chapter, we have the shining light of faith. It pertains to Caleb. Caleb was born in Egypt, but his faith would defeat the enemy totally and gain a place of such victory that the Holy Spirit would graphically record it.

His faith in the 11th verse says, *"As yet I am as strong this day as I was in the day that Moses sent me."* This is the boast of faith, and it must be noted that faith alone can boast.

This was not the idle boast of an old man who hates to see his strength fading away; it

NOTES

was truth, for afterward he expelled three great giants from his inheritance (Judg. 1:20). No doubt, Caleb lived to enjoy his possession many years. If he remained alive as long as Joshua, who was near the same age, he enjoyed it no less than 25 or 30 years.

Caleb's faith will claim the great mountains for a possession and not only expel the giants but even Arba, the greatest of the giants! Then this city of *"Kirjath-Arba,"* the city of the giants, will become *"Hebron,"* which speaks of fellowship.

Caleb's words in the 12th verse speak out to us even today, *"Now therefore give me this mountain."* Others may be satisfied but not Caleb. Faith is never satisfied. It must take all the land. It must expel all the giants. Its testimony forever will be, *"If the Lord will be with me, then I shall be able to drive them out, as the Lord said."*

The 13th verse says, *"And Joshua blessed him, and gave unto Caleb Hebron for an inheritance."* There were five reasons that Joshua could grant this request.

1. Because of the prophecy of verse 9, *"Surely the land whereon thy feet have trodden shall be thine inheritance, and thy children forever."*

2. Caleb's faithfulness (Num. 14:24).

3. Because of it being the request of a mighty man of faith in Israel, one of only two of the old generation that came out of Egypt (Num. 14:23-24).

4. The land requested was in the Judah portion of which Caleb was a member (I Chron. 4:1-15).

5. Because of the will of God by the Urim and Thummim (Ex. 28:30).

In other words, it was promised to him by the Word of the Lord. Therefore, every single child of God can have that which is promised to him in the Word of the God. He has promised every one of us victory if we will have faith and believe Him.

The key is in the 14th verse. It says, *"Because that he wholly followed the Lord God of Israel."* That was the key to victory in that day. It is the key to victory in our day.

CHAPTER 15

Verse 1 says, *"This then was the lot of the tribe of the children of Judah."* Judah was given the first inheritance. Why?

From the great tribe of Judah would come the Messiah. It had been prophesied by Jacob (Gen. 49:10).

As well, Judah would be the tribe that would hold the torch of faith higher for a longer period of time than any of the other tribes. Amazingly enough, in verse after verse we are given the exact instructions by the Holy Spirit. Nothing was left to chance.

Also, for each and every child of God the Lord has a distinct plan. Its borders in the spiritual sense are carefully defined. God help us to occupy and to carry out exactly what He has called us to do.

Once again, in verses 13-19 the Holy Spirit records the great faith of Caleb.

Verse 19 says, *"Give me a blessing,"* and then says *"Give me also springs of water."* The lady was Caleb's daughter, and her name was Achsah. The springs of water in the spiritual sense represent continued blessing. The land would continue to be fertile. It would continue to produce. It represented the flower of Caleb's faith.

Beginning with the 20th verse, city by city is outlined that was given unto Judah, but yet, the 63rd verse says:

"As for the Jebusites the inhabitants of Jerusalem, the children of Judah could not drive them out." The Jebusites were one of the most fierce tribes to occupy Canaan. They would occupy the city where the Lord would ultimately place His name. Satan would place his strongest forces there.

The area of the Christian's life in which the Lord has designed to touch in a greater way will be opposed by Satan stronger than any other part of the Christian experience. Sadly, it says, *"Judah could not drive them out."* Why? The answer could only be a lack of faith. So, the fierce Jebusites would *"dwell with the children of Judah at Jerusalem unto this day."* This was a glaring failure of faith on the part of Judah, for the Jebusites would be a thorn in Israel's flesh all the days of the judges on up until the time of David. David would be the first one to expel the Jebusites from the city where the Lord would place His name, Jerusalem.

As a child of God, the area in your life that Satan fights and hinders the most is the area where God wants to place His greatest glory. The Jebusite must go. He must not be allowed to stay. The reason for Satan's obstinacy is because of the plans that the Lord has for this area of your spiritual life.

CHAPTERS 16 & 17

We have put these two chapters together for a reason; Ephraim and Manasseh were the sons of Joseph. As stated, Judah's allotment was given first because it was from the tribe of Judah that the Messiah would come. Likewise, Joseph was a type of Christ; therefore, his sons would be next in line to receive their portion of the Promised Land.

The 1st verse says, *"And the lot of the children of Joseph fell,"* that is, came forth from the bag of the Urim and Thummim. Therefore, each particular place of each particular tribe was decided not by man but by the Holy Spirit. The first four verses will decide the borders of both Ephraim and Manasseh, being grouped together because they were sons of Joseph.

Verses 5 through 10 will decide the borders of Ephraim only.

Sadly, Ephraim failed in that which God demanded. The 10th verse says, *"And they drave not out the Canaanites that dwelt in Gezer."* The latter portion says, *"But the Canaanites dwell among the Ephraimites unto this day."* Ultimately, this thorn in Ephraim's side would result in exactly that which the Lord had said. The Canaanites would not gradually take on the ways of the Ephraimites, but the opposite would be true. Little by little, the Ephraimites, who were the people God, would take upon themselves the ways of the Canaanites which were the ways of the world.

The latter portion of the 10th verse says, *"And serve under tribute."* If we think we can

NOTES

gradually tame and convert Satan, we are sadly mistaken. Millions have tried; millions have failed. *"Under tribute"* is not enough; they must be driven out. Likewise, the child of God cannot come to terms with the envy, jealousy, pride, and lust that pervades his soul. Neither can it be made to serve Him; it must be rooted out.

Verses 1 through 11 of the 17th chapter give the borders of Manasseh. The 3rd verse says, *"But Zelophehad."* Even though this man sinned regarding the spying out of the land and rebelled against God, still, there is evidence that he repented because of his five daughters. They were women of faith as few women have been of faith. It says, *"Are the names of his daughters, Mahlah, and Noah, Hoglah, Milcah, and Tirzah."* Four times in the Word of God these daughters are named. So, the Holy Spirit must be attempting to draw our attention to something. In fact, He is, and that something is *"faith."* These daughters of Zelophehad had such faith that it caused God to literally rewrite the Bible. What a statement! But it is true. Zelophehad became famous because of the faith of his daughters.

Regrettably, verses 12-18 of the 17th chapter record the failure of Manasseh to drive out the enemy. The 12th verse says, *"Yet the children of Manasseh could not drive out the inhabitants of those cities."* Even though it is a negative, still, we are taught a valuable lesson regarding our own Christian experience.

Actually, this would be the story of most of the tribes. They would fail to drive out all the inhabitants of their inheritances, and this was the way that God said it would be, little by little, until they were able to possess the whole land (Ex. 23:29-33; Deut. 7:20-24).

In Christianity when a person comes to Christ, even though they are born again and, thereby, new creatures in Christ Jesus, still, there are many enemies of hindrance in their lives. At the moment of conversion, there is, of course, much victory, but then we begin to realize that all is not victory. Pride, jealousy, and lusts at times still remain. The battle begins. Slowly, these enemies are driven out or at least should be. However, this can be said. No Christian ever drives them all out immediately. Sadly, most of the Christians never drive them all out.

The 14th verse says, *"And the children of Joseph spake unto Joshua, saying, Why hast thou given me but one lot and one portion to inherit, seeing I am a great people."* As both Ephraim and Manasseh were quick to point out their own greatness, likewise, the child of God is quick to boast of his spiritual prowess when, in fact, there has been very little.

The 15th verse says, *"And Joshua answered them, If thou be a great people, then get thee up to the wood country and cut down for thyself there in the land of the Perizzites and of the giants."* Joshua's challenge to them was: *"If you are such a great people, then prove it by conquering more of the land."* He then told them, *"Destroy the giants."* Our heavenly Joshua, the Lord Jesus Christ, is demanding the same of us. Why do we boast of our great spiritual victories when powerful giants of the flesh still occupy our inheritance? The 16th verse tells of the children of Joseph complaining about the Canaanites saying, *"Have chariots of iron."*

The 18th verse speaks to this complaint by saying, *"Drive out the Canaanites, though they have iron chariots, and though they be strong."* The command could be given simply because they were not to do this great feat in their own strength. They were to do it by the power of God.

At times we may think the Lord is demanding too much of us when we consider the powerful opposition in our path. Yet, He can demand all He likes if, in effect, He is going to do it for us, which He does. In these passages you can see the gradual shift from the Spirit to the flesh by the sons of Joseph; hence, they are not able to drive out the enemy. Joshua is trying to pull them back to their rightful position in the power of God. Flesh causes us one series of defeats after another. Faith drives out the enemy and overcomes by the great power of God.

CHAPTER 18

The 18th chapter speaks of the Tabernacle

being set up at Shiloh, a survey of the unpossessed land, and the borders of Benjamin.

The 1st verse says, *"Assembled together at Shiloh, and set up the tabernacle of the congregation there."* No doubt, up to this time the Tabernacle had been set up at Gilgal. But now the center of worship was to come into the heart of Israel (with Shiloh at almost the center of the land). This was the same Tabernacle that Moses had made. It would remain here for almost 300 years. It would cease to be used when Solomon's Temple was built. The Tabernacle symbolized grace, whereas, the Temple would symbolize glory.

The 3rd verse says, *"How long are you slack to go to possess the land."* Why must the Holy Spirit ask us the same question over and over again?

The 16th verse says, *"The valley of the giants."* These giants were called by various names and were placed there by Satan to hinder the coming of the Messiah. They would attempt to corrupt the population by evil and subdue it by force. They were the results of the union of fallen angels and evil women. Without further explanation, their origin was totally of evil. They were of formidable power but were defeated by the people of God.

Likewise, there are *"giants"* in our own inheritance. Who are the giants in your life? They cannot be defeated by natural means. All the efforts of man fall down when attempting to assuage the terrible problems caused by envy, jealousy, pride, and greed. The changed heart is the only answer. Jesus Christ is that answer. He is not only the answer for the sinner, but He is the answer for the Christian, too. He and He alone can subdue these giants. Please remember, this is a battle to the death. No quarter is asked or given; you defeat the giant (in Jesus), or the giant defeats you.

This *"valley of the giants"* was in the inheritance of Benjamin. Saul, the first king of Israel, would be a product of Benjamin, and so would the beloved Paul of the book of Acts. Sadly, Saul would not defeat his giants, but Paul would. Yes, all have giants; all have to fight them. All either win or lose according to their dependence on Christ. No wonder Paul, of the tribe of Benjamin, of the valley of the giants, would say,

"It is not I, but Christ which liveth in me, and the life I now live in the flesh, I live by the faith of the son of God who loved me and gave himself for me." Hallelujah!

CHAPTER 19

In these final chapters of Joshua we see how the Lord in beautiful detail pointed out to the people all that belonged to them. It is very beautiful to learn how minutely, patiently, and repeatedly He described to His people the goodly land which He had given them. Notice how He divided it to them by families so that all would share alike, with no one family preferred over another.

Verse 1 says, *"And the second lot came forth to Simeon."* This was the second of the last seven lots and was by divine appointment, for Jacob had prophesied that Simeon and Levi would be divided in Jacob and scattered in Israel because they killed the men of Shechem (Gen. 34-49:7). This was literally fulfilled when Simeon was scattered in Judah and Levi was scattered in many parts of the other tribes. They had no inheritance – only cities to dwell in throughout the land. However, there is a beautiful story of grace that is attached to this passage as well. The latter portion of the 1st verse says, *"And their inheritance was within the inheritance of the children of Judah."*

As stated, Simeon was cursed. There was no way that this tribe could have an inheritance of their own. So, Judah shoved over and allowed Simeon to become a part of his inheritance. Likewise, Simeon is a type of poor, flawed, fallen man. We are cursed with no inheritance and, even worse, with a curse of God upon our heads. However, our heavenly Judah, the Lord Jesus Christ, has taken us (poor Simeonites) into His inheritance, and now, by grace, we enjoy the greatest inheritance of all.

For the 9th verse says, *"For the part of the children of Judah was too much for them: Therefore the children of Simeon had their inheritance within the inheritance of them."*

If one would study carefully the prophecies that Jacob gave in Genesis 49 concerning the

NOTES

various tribes and then the location and the borders given in these chapters, one would see what seems to be a slight discrepancy, but, actually, on further investigation the true meaning becomes clear.

For instance, in Genesis 49:13 and Deuteronomy 33:19, the prediction is that the portion of Zebulun is to be on the sea and a haven for ships. However, the inheritance given to Zebulun by Joshua at this particular time was not on the sea and was, thereby, no haven for ships. So, what we must understand is this: The prophecies that were given by Jacob pertain not only to the possession of the land in the days of Joshua but also to the great millennial reign which has not yet come. In the Millennium the allotment of land will be on a different principle. Each of the 12 great portions will run west from the Euphrates and the Persian Gulf to the Mediterranean, giving each tribe an outlet by water (Ezek. 48).

Verses 49-51 give us a beautiful example of great hunger for God. When all had been divided to the tribes, the 49th verse says, *"The children of Israel gave an inheritance to Joshua, the son of Nun among them."* It says this inheritance was given to him *"according to the word of the Lord."* This *"word of the Lord"* was given by the Urim and Thummim.

This should be the criteria for all that we receive from the Lord. Evidently, it seems that some did not believe that Joshua was to receive this inheritance, but when the Word of the Lord was sought, it was found that the promise was there.

Likewise, the devil by using Christians will try to tell the hungry heart that "it is not possible," or "the days of miracles are over," or "it is not for today." Who will you listen to, unbelieving men or the Word of God? Joshua paid no attention to what men said. His desires were according to what the Word of God said.

If the Word of God says you can have salvation (and it does), then regardless of what man says you can have it (Rom. 10:9-10). If the Word of God says you can have healing (and it does), then regardless of what man says you can have it (James 5:14). If the Word of God says you can be an overcomer (and it does), regardless of what man says you can have it (Rev. 2,3). If the Word of God says you can have the Baptism in the Holy Spirit with the evidence of speaking with other tongues (and it does), then regardless of what man says you can have it (Acts 2:4). The Word of God is the criteria. Let it be your standard.

The 50th verse says, *"Which he asked."* Jesus said to *"Ask"* and we would receive (Luke 11). Over and over again we are told to ask. James said, *"We have not because we ask not."* And then he went on to say that so often when we do ask, it is to *"consume it upon our lusts."*

Joshua asked for this added inheritance. If you want healing from the Lord, ask for it. If you want victory in certain areas of your life, ask for it. If you want the Baptism in the Holy Spirit, ask for it. If you don't get it the first time, keep asking. That is what Jesus said in the 11th chapter of Luke.

What did Joshua ask for? He asked for *"Timnath-serah."* The word "Timnath" means "the portion that remains." In other words, he did not believe the fallacious lie that once we get saved we have it all. (While it is certainly true that at salvation we are totally and completely saved, yet, we need to go on and receive the mighty Baptism in the Holy Spirit to give us power to do the works of Christ.) Joshua was asking for more; he wanted the portion that remains.

The word *"serah"* means "city of the sun." The old song says:

"Here the sun is always shining,
"Here the skies are always bright;
"Tis no place for gloomy Christians
    to abide,
"For my soul is filled with music,
"And my heart with pure delight,
"And I'm living on the hallelujah side."

Joshua didn't even ask for a city; he just asked for a place to build one. And the Bible said, *"He built the city, and dwelt therein."* This is a type of dwelling in the graciousness and glory of the Holy Spirit. It is the *"portion that remains"* for every child of God who will *"ask for it,"* take it, and *"build the city."*

The last verse of this chapter is especially important. Whenever the Holy Spirit repeats a statement, particular attention should be given to what is stated. So, here the fact is emphasized that God distributed the land to Israel; that He employed Eleazar, Joshua, and the

Heads of the Fathers as His agents; that the distribution was by lot(Urim and Thummim); that the lots were drawn at the door of the Tabernacle; and that all took place in Shiloh.

The ordered solemnity of these proceedings and the fact that God decided the portion for each tribe, effectually prevented any challenge as to the justness of the distribution. From this the lesson may be learned that they are happy and well provided for who allow God to choose for them.

CHAPTER 20

This chapter pertains to the cities of refuge. (Note: for further comments on this subject, see Numbers 35.)

Verse 2 says, *"Appoint out for your cities of refuge."* This provision by God portrayed God's mercy, compassion, and grace. It proclaims in beautiful material form how He goes to extremes to bring the sinner back home. The need for the cities of refuge would show man's cruelty; cruelty that was even attached to God's people. The fact of the cities of refuge would show that God is not man and is ever striving to bring the wayward home.

To the unspiritual eye, God's command in previous chapters to slay all (concerning the heathen) would seem somewhat contradictory considering the extra length that God would go regarding the salvation of His own. However, it must be remembered that the Canaanites, the Jebusites, and others had *"filled up"* their cup of iniquity. In their evil they had gone beyond redemption.

Regrettably, the Church is very quick to condemn, while the Lord is very quick to save.

Hebrews 6:18 sets forth Christ as the City of Refuge for sinners guilty of His Blood.

Verse 7 says, *"And they appointed."* This was done by the Urim and the Thummim. The six cities are listed in verses 7 and 8. They display by the meaning of their names the intention of God's direction for our lives. They are as follows:

1. Kedesh. The word means *"holiness."* By this we know that God's first demand is holi-

ness.

2. Shechem. This word means *"strength."* From this we see that our real strength lies in holiness.

3. Hebron. This means *"fellowship."* Now that we are in holiness and, thereby, receiving strength, there can be fellowship with God.

4. Bezer. The word means *"safety."* When there is fellowship with God, there is always safety.

5. Ramoth. This word means *"uplifting."* Now, in God's progression we can see the blessing as it starts to come.

6. Golan. The word means *"happiness."* If you will notice, God puts holiness first and happiness last. Man, sadly, reverses this, and there is little happiness.

The 6th verse says, *"Until the death of the High Priest,"* meaning that once the High Priest died the individual could then leave the city of refuge and go back to his home and his possessions. This is a picture of Israel in the last days restored to the Promised Land from which she, the slayer of the Messiah, has been exiled. This will not be totally fulfilled until the Coming of the Lord. He will appear as the dead yet living High Priest (*"I am He that liveth and was dead."*) at the occasion of that restoration. Then, all of the great promises that God made to the prophets of old will be fulfilled and realized. Sadly, God's will is seldom carried out. However, God's plan is always carried out. Ultimately, His plan for Israel will be carried forth to total victory.

CHAPTER 21

The detail given to Levi's inheritance in this chapter, even outlining their cities, is a beautiful picture of the Grace of God. (Actually, Levi had no inheritance as such, because the Lord was his inheritance.) What they were to receive would come out of the inheritance of all of the other tribes.

The tribe of Levi was broken down into three groups, *"the Kohathites, the Gershonites, and the Merarites."* They attended to the many duties of the Tabernacle. This is

their story.

Levi, along with Simeon (both Jacob's sons), had massacred the men of the small village of Shechem. They had taken vengeance because of their sister Dinah being raped. For this terrible crime they committed, God placed a curse upon both of them. The judgment was that they would be scattered in Israel. The judgment was carried out; however, God turned it into grace. They were made a kingdom of priests in the great land of Israel. They were given some 48 cities with pasture-lands. Three times in this chapter this gift is declared to have been according to the commandment of the Lord (vss. 2, 3, and 8).

The 6th verse says, *"which city is Hebron."* This was one of the six *"cities of refuge."* Actually, five of these *"cities of refuge"* would be listed in that which was given to Levi. The sixth, *"Bezer,"* was not listed. Quite possibly, the reason is found in the next chapter. Maybe it was because of the altar of man's rebellious imagination that was set up close to Bezer.

This chapter closes with the testimony that *"There failed not ought of any good thing which the Lord had spoken to Israel."* As well, nothing will fail that God has spoken to us.

CHAPTER 22

This 22nd chapter should be of great warning to every child of God. Verse 10 says, *"And the half tribe of Manasseh built there an altar by Jordan."* This altar was built close to Bezer, one of the cities of refuge. Yet, it seems that this *"City of Refuge"* was seldom, if ever, used because of this false altar that was built.

God had but one center of blessing, in type, and that would be Calvary. Any other altar, even an exact pattern, denied the Divine altar.

Man is forever attempting to imitate Christ's atoning work. Therefore, he adds other altars of spiritual blessing, which, in reality, attack God's only refuge for sinners.

The latter portion of the verse says, *"A great altar to see to."* How many *"great altars"* has man built or is building? They may look good and very similar to Calvary. Actually, the unspiritual eye cannot tell the difference, but the difference is great. God's altar, which is Calvary, will set men free. Man's *"great altar"* will set no one free.

Man is continually building altars which contain no bloody sacrifice. Man loves these types of altars. The altar outlined in this chapter contained no sacrifice. Calvary's altar is effective only because it contained the sacrifice, Who was Christ Jesus. The 23rd verse says, *"Or if to offer thereon burnt offering or meat offering,"* which they did not, neither could not.

The 27th verse says, *"But that it may be a witness between us."* God does not require that type of witness. Religious man's actions are always crowded with religious effort. It, thereby, seems like a good *"witness"* to the world. Unfortunately, the world, by and large, accepts this false witness, and so does most of the Church.

The 33rd verse says, *"And the thing pleased the children of Israel,"* but it does not say that it pleased God. Neither does it say that Joshua and the leaders of Israel sought counsel of the Lord concerning this matter. Israel forms her own positive conclusion because it *"looks so right."* Most of what today passes for Gospel pleases the Church, but it does not please God.

The 34th verse says, *"Call the altar Ed."* The word *"Ed"* means witness or testimony. Regrettably, most of the witness and testimony of the present-day Church is a barren, sacrificeless, sterile altar. It is an altar that receives very little criticism from the world. So much of the Church is *"well-pleased"* with it. But it must be remembered that it is an altar of man's making and, consequently, will not set one single, solitary soul free from the bondage of sin. Satan pays little mind to our building of altars; actually, he is the author of most altar building. It can look like Calvary; it can be pointed to with great delight. He finds no fault with that because he knows that it will set no captive free. Admittedly, the altar of Calvary is ugly. It is bloody and rejected by all of the world and almost all of the Church. But the altar called Calvary, of which there is no other because no other is needed, still sets men free!

NOTES

CHAPTER 23

Verse 1 says, *"After that the Lord had given rest unto Israel from all their enemies."* As we have stated several times, the book of Joshua is a blueprint outline for victory. In this book we have seen much war, as every Christian sees constant warfare with Satan. However, if we follow the Lord, there will come a time of *"rest"* from all our enemies. The *"rest"* that is being spoken of here can only come in Christ. As long as we're trying to defeat the enemy in our own strength, there will be no victory and there will be no "rest." But once Christ becomes predominant within our spiritual experience and He is doing the living in us, then we will have "rest." Joshua will give the criteria for continued victory and, thereby, continued "rest." It is as follows:

1. *"And to do all that is written in the book of the law of Moses,"* in other words, fidelity to the Bible. The Word of God is the criteria for every child of God. We must be very careful that we *"turn not aside there from to the right hand or to the left."* The bane of the Church today is turning either to the right or the left.

2. *"That you come not among these nations"* (vs. 7) means separation. Remember, it is not isolation but separation, *"Come ye out from among them and be ye separate saith the Lord."*

3. *"But cleave unto the Lord your God"* (vs. 8). This, of course, speaks of our love for God. We are to love Him as Jesus said, with all our *"heart, our mind, our soul, and our strength."* There you have the criteria: *"The Word of God, separation from the world, and love for God."* It has not changed; it is the same today.

If this is done, then, as the 10th verse says, *"One man of you shall chase a thousand."* There is no power like the child of God who is abiding by the Book, separating himself from the world, and loving the Lord with all of his heart.

Then we can expect *"Not one thing will fail of all the good things which the Lord your God spake concerning you."*

Then a warning is given, *"When you have transgressed the covenant of the Lord your God, you shall perish quickly from off the good land which he hath given unto you"* (vs. 16). Sadly, that is exactly what happened. Likewise, it will happen with any child of God who turns away from the Lord. In other words, we cannot have the Bible, separation, the love for God, and continued unrepentant transgressions at the same time; one or the other must go. God help us to choose that the transgressions go.

CHAPTER 24

This will be Joshua's final address to Israel. The 1st verse says, *"They presented themselves before God."* What a statement! What an awesome thought to *"present ourselves before God."* And yet, Christians in whom the Spirit of God constantly abides (I Cor. 3:15) are constantly *"presenting themselves before God."* Beginning with the 2nd verse, the address begins. It says, *"They served other gods."* This tells us that God did not choose Abraham because he was godly, good, or righteous. In fact, he was an idolater. It was Grace that looked at this idolater and saw something in his heart that would respond to God and, thereby, chose him. The sentence, *"They served other gods,"* could well apply to each and every one of us. Likewise, we have not been brought to Jesus because of our goodness but because of His Grace.

The word in the 3rd verse, *"And gave him Isaac,"* was the first tangible promise of the coming seed, the Lord Jesus Christ. It must be continually remembered that every single blessing that comes to the child of God is because of our heavenly Isaac, the Lord Jesus Christ. God does not and, in fact, cannot bless poor, fallen, sinful man. He can only bless Christ Who is in converted man.

The 6th verse will forever record God's great salvation plan, *"And I brought your fathers out of Egypt."* And then we are given the catalog of the great victories that came to Israel. Over and over again Satan will tell us there are no victories. However, we should ever

NOTES

point to the 11th verse where it names all the enemies of our soul, and then says, *"I delivered them into your hand."* Hallelujah! The song says:

"We've come this far by faith, leaning on the Lord."

"Trusting in His Holy Word, He's never failed me yet."

The 15th verse pictures man's free-moral agency, *"Choose you this day whom you will serve."* The doctrine of unconditional eternal security as taught by some is a fallacious doctrine, in other words, unscriptural. Our serving God is always by choice. We choose to get in, and if we so desire, we can choose to get out. However, I will say, as Joshua stated eternally, *"But as for me and my house, we will serve the Lord."*

The translation of the 19th verse makes it seem like God will not forgive sin, *"He will not forgive your transgressions nor your sins."* However, the actual meaning is that if we *"should forsake the Lord, to serve other gods"* (vs. 16), then He will not and, in fact, cannot continue to forgive our sins. The 19th verse says as well, *"He is a jealous God."* The Lord cannot abide us serving two masters. Continued idolatry cannot be continuously forgiven.

Sadly, Joshua knew that the people were idolators even then. The 23rd verse says, *"Now therefore put away, said he, the strange gods which are among you."* How strange it was for Israel to have these idols (albeit hidden) after they had seen God do such great and mighty things! How strange is it for us today to continue to have our idols, when *we* have seen God do such great things. An idol is any thing that takes the place of God.

Joshua was a prophet and knew that God was speaking these words through him. The 27th verse says, *"For it hath heard all the words of the Lord which He spake unto us."* Joshua was speaking not only of Israel but *"this stone."* Jesus, likewise, told the Pharisees that if the people stopped praising Him, the very stones would cry out. He could have had this moment in mind when He uttered those words.

The 30th verse says, *"And they buried him in the border of his inheritance in Timnath-serah."* As we have stated, the words *"Timnath--*

serah" mean the *"portion that remains."* They buried him in it because he had obtained it. God help us in this great and glorious day of grace to at least do as well. Tradition says that at the entrance of Joshua's tomb, the figure of the shining sun was carved into the solid rock, signifying the man who made the sun stand still.

The 31st verse says, *"And Israel served the Lord all the days of Joshua, and all the days of the elders that outlived Joshua, and which had known all the works of the Lord, that he had done for Israel."* Then Israel went into idolatry.

Every generation must have a move of God. No generation can live off the past experiences of the generation prior to them. Each must have their own Calvary, their own Resurrection, and their own Pentecost.

Verse 32 says, *"And the bones of Joseph, which the children of Israel brought out of Egypt, buried they in Shechem."* In the last chapter of Genesis (50:26), we have a record of the death of Joseph and his being in a coffin in Egypt. Here, in the last chapter of Joshua we have the final reference to Joseph being brought out of Egypt and buried in Shechem in the burying place of Abraham, Isaac, and Jacob. It was Joseph's inheritance; that is Ephraim's. Also, it signified Joseph's faith in God, which was the same as those who went before him. Even though Egypt beckoned so powerfully, still, thank God, Egypt never claimed them. Their heart and their faith was ever in Canaan.

NOTES

THE
BOOK OF JUDGES

—■—

The glory of the great victories of the book of Joshua stands as a beacon of light. Sadly, Judges is a book of defeat – defeat that resulted from unbelief and disobedience. Joshua is now dead, but God is not; hence, there is no reason for defeat.

—■—

CHAPTER 1

In the first 18 verses there is a beautiful proclamation of Judah's victories as given by God.

Verse 1 says, *"The children of Israel asked the Lord, saying, Who shall go up for us against the Canaanites first, to fight against them?"* This means they inquired by the Urim and Thummim. It was done so through the High Priest. Judges will start out with such victory and conclude with such ugly defeat. The reason for victory was obvious. They *"asked the Lord."*

Every child of God should ask the Lord concerning every move that is made. We should earnestly want, desire, and seek His counsel and guidance. The beloved John said that the Holy Spirit would *"lead us into all truth"* – if we would but ask.

Verse 2 proclaims, *"And the Lord said, Judah shall go up."* The Lord will always answer if we will always ask and believe.

The 3rd verse records a beautiful type of the Grace of God. It says, *"And Judah said unto Simeon his brother, Come up with me into my lot, that we may fight against the Canaanites."*

Simeon was Jacob's son; he would be the head of a great tribe, and, yet, Simeon had been

cursed by God because of the blood-letting at Shechem. The curse had been given in the form of a prophecy; it had been severe. Simeon, as well as Levi, would be scattered in Israel (Gen. 49:5-7). In other words, there would be no inheritance for them. However, whenever the land was parcelled out to the various tribes, as is recorded in the book of Joshua, Judah was given so much that he invited Simeon to come partake of his inheritance. This is a beautiful type of Christ's relationship with the sinner saved by Grace.

Simeon, a type of every poor, fallen, demented specimen of humanity, is invited by the Lord Jesus Christ, Who sprang from the tribe of Judah, to come up into His inheritance. The old song says:

"Hallelujah what a thought, Jesus full salvation brought,"

"Victory, yes victory."

"Let the powers of sin assail, heaven's grace shall never fail,"

"Victory, yes victory."

The 3rd verse says, *"And I likewise will go with thee into thy lot."* If we go with our heavenly Judah into His lot, then He will go with us into our lot. He will help us fight the Canaanites. He will guarantee us the victory. What a beautiful type. Simeon, who had nothing, now has everything. And so the Scripture says, *"So Simeon went with him."* God help us to go with *"Him,"* for *"He"* is our only hope.

Verse 6 says, *"And caught him, and cut off his thumbs and his great toes."* This was Adonibezek of the city of Bezek. God had given the command that he was to be killed, not tortured. When the Church leaves the ways of God, it always resorts to cruelty.

Verses 12 through 15 once again record the great feat of faith of Caleb's daughter and her husband. Caleb's faith passed down to his daughter and her husband. It must be ever remembered that this is the only thing that will go down to our children. Many Christians wonder why their children do not live for God. Quite possibly, it is because we pass down to them everything but faith. Faith in Jesus Christ will insure their salvation and, therefore, their victory. The *"springs of water"* of the 15th verse proclaim the eternal, continued blessing of faith. God will always honor it. Several times the Holy Spirit in the Bible will proclaim this great story of faith concerning Caleb and his family. It is done for a reason. The Lord wants to give us *"springs of living water,"* but it must come by faith. This is the type of *"water"* that Jesus was speaking of to the Samaritan woman at Jacob's well. *"If you drink of this water you will thirst again, but if you drink of the water that I shall give, it shall be in you a well of water springing up unto everlasting life"* (St. John 4).

The 19th verse gives the secret of victory and of defeat. It says, *"And the Lord was with Judah: and he drave out the inhabitants of the mountains."* There was nothing Judah could not do whenever he depended on the Lord. However, the latter portion of the verse says, *"But could not drive out the inhabitants of the valley, because they had chariots of iron."* Here is a glaring disposition of eyes that had been on the Lord but now are on *"chariots of iron."* How easy it is for us to take our eyes from the Lord and to begin to look at Satan's weapons. The God Who tore down the Jericho walls could easily destroy the chariots of iron, but Judah ceased to believe Him.

Verse 21 says, *"And the children of Benjamin did not drive out the Jebusites that inhabited Jerusalem."* Therefore it says, *"But the Jebusites dwell with the children of Benjamin in Jerusalem unto this day."* Jerusalem was to be the city where God would place His name, and Satan would contest it mightily. The Jebusites were some of the most fearsome and warlike people who faced Israel. Benjamin's faith failed; therefore, this thorn in Israel's side would remain there until David would dispossess them. If we allow any *"Jebusite"* to

remain in our spiritual inheritance, he will forever be a thorn in our flesh and a blight on our Christian experience. He must be rooted out.

Beautifully enough, in-between verses 19 and 21, which record terrible defeats, once again, the great faith of Caleb stands out. It says, *"He expelled thence the three sons of Anak."* These were giants, but Caleb's faith prevailed.

Over and over again the Holy Spirit records these words, *"Neither did Manasseh drive out the inhabitants"* (vs. 27).

"Neither did Ephraim drive out the Canaanites" (vs. 29). And so it's said of other tribes as well.

The 28th verse says, *"They put the Canaanites to tribute."* This was not the command of God. His command was extermination. There is no way that we can make sin work for us. Jealousy, envy, and pride cannot become friends and cannot serve us. We will destroy them, or they will ultimately destroy us, as these enemies ultimately destroyed Israel.

CHAPTER 2

The picture that this chapter portrays is of a people who have left their God. They have gone in their own directions with little thought as to the will of the Lord.

The 1st verse says, *"And an angel of the Lord came up from Gilgal to Bochim."* This is really the Lord Himself Who has come up to Bochim. Gilgal was Israel's first headquarters after crossing Jordan. It was also where Israel had experienced her first circumcision in the land and her first Passover.

The Tabernacle was now at Shiloh (Josh. 18:1). It would seem that the Lord would have been residing there between the Mercy Seat and the Cherubim. However, it is quite possible that God never intended for the Tabernacle to be moved to Shiloh, desiring that it remain at Gilgal. It seems that one of the few good things that happened there involved Hannah. She was praying that she might conceive, and that the

Lord would give her a baby boy. The Lord answered her prayer. She and her husband did conceive and the result was one of the greatest prophets who ever lived, Samuel. The Holy Spirit did not see fit to explain why the Lord was at Gilgal and not at Shiloh. This we do know; it was at Gilgal that the Lord was last seen (Josh. 5:13-15). It was at Gilgal that Israel received the power by which she overcame the Canaanite. The inward exercises of the heart, the putting to death of the members which are upon the earth, referring to true circumcision, has no outward glory. It is unimportant in the eyes of man, and it makes man little in his own eyes but fills the soul with power, making the presence of God real. Even then strength would not be shown at Gilgal – it would be shown at Jericho. However, the strength was obtained at Gilgal. This principle is the secret of overcoming.

But when Gilgal was forsaken, it was discovered that the Lord with His almighty power had been there and, seemingly, was still there. He comes up from Gilgal. The result of leaving Gilgal was to weep in the valley of Bochim. The tears were shed for lost blessings. Still, the people did not return to Gilgal. Praise and power at Gilgal were exchanged for weeping and weakness at Bochim. How much is this the picture of the modern Church. The 2nd verse will echo through the ages from the Lord, *"But ye have not obeyed my voice: why have ye done this?"*

The 4th verse records the response of so many people to the convicting power of the Holy Spirit, *"The people lifted up their voice, and wept."* Israel was under so much conviction that she would weep. However, she was not sorry enough for her backsliding to repent before God. Weeping that does not precede true biblical repentance only represents powerful Holy Ghost conviction. It does not represent the people acceding to that conviction.

At times Israel was penitent when God dealt with them, but at other times their hearts were hardened beyond any breaking. A general process of hardening continued in Israel from here to the time that there was no turning back, so God permitted them to go into captivity. This broke the people temporarily (Ezra 3:12; Neh. 8:9). Then Israel lapsed into hard-

NOTES

ness of heart again until, by the time the Messiah came, there was not the slightest indication of brokenness or willingness on the part of the people to do the will of God, apart from a few godly ones who wept much because of the impending destruction (St.Matt. 24:34-39; St.Luke 19:41). The leaders of Israel promoted a mob spirit against Christ and through hardness the nation was destroyed (Acts 7:51-52; 28:25-31).

Verses 6-10 send Israel back to the days of Joshua, *"And the people served the Lord all the days of Joshua, and all the days of the elders that outlived Joshua"* (verse 7). They are given here as an introduction to the long record of apostasies and judgments of Israel listed in the book of Judges. It is clear that as long as Israel served God, He caused them to prosper, but when they forsook Him, He no longer blessed them. Instead, He permitted defeat and servitude to their enemies, and various judgments to whip them into line again, seeking to save the nation from the sure destruction He had promised should they backslide and rebel against Him. The entirety of the book of Judges is a record of repeated sins, apostasy, judgment, and temporary repentance and consecration to God only during the lifetimes of particular leaders who God had raised up to deliver the people from their enemies. This program went on for over 400 years under the kings until the nation was destroyed and taken into captivity.

Verse 10 says, *"And there arose another generation after them, which knew not the Lord."* Each generation must have a move of God in their midst. They cannot spiritually survive on what happened to their fathers or their grandfathers. A denomination, no matter how spiritual and glorious its beginning, will wane, weaken, and spiritually die unless there is a Holy Ghost revival for each coming generation. Soon, without a move of God in its midst, a denomination, no matter how powerful its past, will lapse into religion, man-made rules and regulations, and eventually into apostasy. Each generation must have its move of God. As someone once said, "God has no grandchildren."

The Lord repeatedly told Israel that the heathen nations must be exterminated or else they would corrupt Israel. It came to pass exactly as the Lord said, for the 13th verse says, *"And they forsook the Lord, and served Baal and Ashtaroth."* Why? It would seem that Israel's major problem was a lack of spiritual leadership. When Joshua died and the elders who outlived him, it seems there was no one whose heart was such toward God that the hand of the Lord would be laid upon him. Consequently, without strong spiritual leadership the nation went into apostasy.

This is the same problem that plagues the Church today. There is little spiritually qualified leadership. The people have accepted, for their leaders, individuals who occupy man-made offices, in man-made denominations, elected on man-made ballots, to fill man-made positions. Consequently, they receive man-made leadership.

As well, over what is commonly referred to as "Christian television," most who call themselves leaders seem to be more concerned with how they look than what they say. Jeremiah said: *"The prophets prophesy falsely, and the priests bear rule by their means; and my people love to have it so"* (Jer. 5:31).

How could God's people who had known His mighty power, grace, and glory turn to serve such monstrosities as Baal and Ashtoreth?

The Christian without a continual flow of the Holy Spirit within his heart is never far from resorting to idol worship, either.

Baal was the male sun-god worshiped in western Asia among the heathen nations as their chief deity. His altars and sanctuaries were located on high places such as the summits of high mountains in order to get the first view of the rising sun and the last rays of the setting sun. The sun was believed to be the source and emblem of all life and the generative power of nature.

Ashtaroth is the plural and Ashtoreth the singular form of the name of the Canaanites' principle female deity. The feminine principle was supposed to be embodied in the moon to which the name "Ashtoreth" was given. The idol was a female with a crescent moon on her brow. It was set up in the temples and worshiped with the most revolting forms of immorality and sexual perversion. Under the

NOTES

guise of religion, all virtue and decency were surrendered.

The 14th verse says, *"And the anger of the Lord was hot against Israel."* God is just as incensed, or even more so, against evil in His own people than He is with the world's. He cannot abide sin in any shape, form, or fashion. If repentance is not engaged in, He will *"deliver them into the hands of spoilers."*

It must be clearly understood that everything that happens to a Christian is either caused by God or allowed by Him. No, God does not cause any sin, failure, disobedience, or rejection of Himself and His ways by His people. However, He does allow it. At the same time, He was the direct cause of the "spoilers" who came against Israel. It says, *"So that they could not any longer stand before their enemies."*

It should be well understood that Satan is ever anxious to destroy God's people. The only thing that holds him back is the power and presence of God within our lives. When sin drives out that presence, then the Lord many times allows the enemy to come in and cause us great problems.

The 15th verse says, *"Whithersoever they went out, the hand of the Lord was against them for evil."* This is a strange thing concerning God and His people. When Israel was obedient, no man could stand before them, but now when disobedient, they could not stand before any man. When Israel was obedient, the Lord prospered them and made them victorious wherever they went, but now the Lord cursed them wherever they went. The question must be asked, "Does God do the same today?" The answer is obvious, most definitely yes.

The greatest sign of God's love for His people, especially when they are in a rebellious state, is His chastisement of them.

A most horrifying sight is of those who claim to be Christians who have forsaken the ways of God, and, yet, there is no chastisement. It is a sign that they are no longer children but bastards (Heb. 12:8). Even though the judgment registered against Israel was terrible, still, the judgment itself was a sign that God loved them, was dealing with them, and was doing everything possible, even resorting to drastic means to bring them back to Himself.

The 16th verse says, *"Nevertheless the Lord raised up judges, which delivered them out of the hand of those that spoiled them."* The Hebrew word for judge means: one who sets right what has been set wrong. Strangely enough, these judges were all distinguished by some disability, as seen when each one's history is studied, and they will be found to illustrate the principle that God uses weak things to confound the mighty (I Cor. 1:27). With these judges God gave gracious revival, but after each revival the nation fell into deeper sin and bondage.

God raised up the judges because, *"His heart was grieved for the misery of Israel,"* and *"yet they would not hearken unto their judges"* but corrupted themselves more and more with their idols.

Some 16 judges appear in this book. Fifteen were chosen by God; one was a usurper.

The book of Joshua records the inheritance possessed: the book of Judges the inheritance despised. This book also contrasts the faithfulness of God and the faithlessness of Israel.

CHAPTER 3

Verse 1 says, *"Now these are the nations which the Lord left, to prove Israel by them."* By and large, the modern-day Church has been taught that any difficulty, hindrance, obstacle, or disturbance is a sign of a lack of faith. Perhaps this is the reason we have such puny Christians. This is Israel's third generation after coming out of Egypt. The generation under Moses was lost in the wilderness because of unbelief. The generation under Joshua who went into the Promised Land was mainly a victorious generation. This third generation will fail miserably. Can any move of God survive the second generation?

The first generation of the Early Church was victorious. The second generation was victorious as well; however, the third generation of what is referred to as the Early Church started the long decline into apostasy.

As we look at denominations today, most,

NOTES

spiritually speaking, are but a shell of what they once were. They began in the fire, but by the third generation they were already starting down the long road to apostasy. It seems that the brighter the flame at the beginning, the faster the decline when it does begin. For instance, the present day Pentecostal denominations, spiritually speaking, are a shadow of what they formerly were. They presently hold little resemblance to their beginnings.

When Peter in Acts 3 said to the lame man at the gate, *"Silver and gold have I none; but such as I have give I thee,"* he had the power of God to set this captive free. Someone once said that the Church no longer has to say, "Silver and gold have we none," but at the same time, neither can it say to the lame man at the gate, *"In the name of Jesus Christ of Nazareth rise up and walk."*

The Church is tempered by opposition. (By the amount of God that it has in it, by that same degree it will be opposed. Much God, much opposition. No God, no opposition.) The Lord allows "the Philistines, the Canaanites, and others" to put us to the proof that we may learn our own feebleness and God's ability to keep and bless us. It must always be remembered that prosperity without trial deadens the soul. There must be trial to hone faith, trust, and dependence on God.

The 4th verse says, *"And they were to prove Israel by them."* God can instantly take away every Philistine or Canaanite, but He allows these things to remain *"to prove the child of God by them."*

How so different the teaching of the Bible from the modern-day Church's. In the Bible, trials and tests were the keys to one's faith. Today, money and prosperity are the keys to one's faith.

Regrettably, the "proving of Israel" did not turn out well. The 6th verse says, *"And they took their daughters to be their wives, and gave their daughters to their sons, and served their gods."* In the 23rd chapter of Joshua we listed for you the three requirements of God. They are as follows:

1. The Word of God, the Bible, must be the criteria.

2. Separation from the world (not meaning

isolation).

3. To love the Lord with all one's heart.

All three of these requirements were forsaken by Israel. They turned their back on the Word of God, and they mingled with the world, for the 7th verse says, *"And forgat the Lord their God, and served Baalim and the groves."*

The 8th verse gives us an interesting statement. It says, *"He sold them."* The statement has reference to a transaction being completed. Even though the people to whom they were sold (Mesopotamians) had no idea of what God was doing, still, the Lord knew. In effect, He would sell them as slaves to these people. What would the Lord receive in return? Hopefully, He would receive a repentant people and that's exactly what happened, for the 9th verse says, *"And when the children of Israel cried unto the Lord, the Lord raised up a deliverer."* This deliverer was the first judge of Israel. His name was *"Othniel."* He was Caleb's nephew. The people under great bondage *"cried unto the Lord,"* which is exactly what the Lord desired. Sometimes, we Christians have to be placed under very trying circumstances before we will "cry unto the Lord."

The 10th verse says, *"And the Spirit of the Lord came upon him."* I want the reader to notice how the Lord was in charge of everything. The Lord used the Philistines and the Canaanites to *"prove"* His people (vss. 3-4). He used the Mesopotamians as His instrument of chastisement (verse 8). He used "Othniel" to deliver Israel unto their repentance (vss. 9-10). The *"Spirit of the Lord"* was the answer. It is the only answer. It is sad, but the majority of the Church knows absolutely nothing about *"the Spirit of the Lord."*

The 12th verse says, *"And the children of Israel did evil again in the sight of the Lord."* This will continue to be Israel's disposition, "doing evil" and being sold into the hands of the enemy; "crying to God," and the Lord raising up a deliverer for them. And then, sadly, the situation will be repeated over and over again.

All evil is forever *"in the sight of the Lord."* It is the Lord Who judges what is evil and what is not evil. Regrettably, today America and Canada, as well as the rest of the world, go about setting their own standards for what is right

and wrong, completely ignoring the Word of God. The Bible is the only criteria for what is right and wrong because the Bible is the Word of God. When it is abandoned, a nation is then left to drift aimlessly, as America drifts today.

Still, the sad disposition of Israel with their spiritual ups and downs is the plight of most of Christianity.

———■———

CHAPTER 4

Once again verse 2 uses the words, *"And the Lord sold them."* Their oppressor was one of the mightiest of all, "Sisera." It says in the 3rd verse, *"For he had nine hundred chariots of iron."* It also says, *"He mightily oppressed the children of Israel."* But then, exactly as the Holy Spirit is so prone to do, He will raise up an unlikely Saviour, for the 4th verse says, *"And Deborah."* Deborah, of course, was a woman and "a prophetess."

As we have stated, most, if not all the Judges had some type of disadvantage. Othniel was the son of a younger brother; Ehud was left-handed; Shamgar had but an ox-goad; Deborah was a woman; Gideon was the least in the poorest family in Manasseh; Jephthah was the son of a harlot, and Samson was a Nazarite.

All of Israel trembled before Sisera, but Deborah did not tremble. A woman's faith will win a great victory, and a woman's fidelity (Jael) will destroy a great tyrant.

First of all, the idea that God does not use women to preach the Gospel is foolishness. There are "prophets" as well as "prophetesses." Actually, the very first one to herald the great Gospel message of the Resurrection of Jesus Christ was a woman, Mary Magdalene. If the Scriptures are read apart from traditional teaching in some churches, no surprise will be felt at the calling and honors, as well as ministries given to women not only in the Old Testament but also in the New Testament. On this occasion Deborah would deliver Israel.

The 8th verse says, *"And Barak said unto her, If thou wilt go with me, then I will go."* Barak seemed to be a military leader of sorts. He obeyed Deborah's request, but his lack of faith to go alone robbed him of the honor of the victory. He seemed to want someone near to lean on. To one of such feeble faith, even the arm of a woman gives more confidence than the arm of God. God did not honor him with the victory because he did not honor God. Fear can never honor God. He cannot associate His glory with unbelief. Consequently, the faith and courage of Deborah and Jael stand in contrast to the unbelief and timidity of Barak. How many Christians today are given the glorious opportunity to wax bold and victorious for the Lord, but because of fear, they never quite rise to the occasion?

The 15th verse says, *"And the Lord discomfited Sisera."* The word "discomfited" implies supernatural intervention.

If you will notice, the Scripture will most of the time point out that it was the Lord Who performed the task. Yet, individuals of faith will be brought into it. They may perform the task, but at the same time, it is the Lord Who gives them the supernatural power to do so. As well, at other times the Lord, distinctly and apart from men and women of faith, will add to what is already being done. In this case it would say, *"They fought from heaven; the stars in their courses fought against Sisera"* (Judges 5:20). God is looking for faith. Talent, ability, expertise, knowledge, and wisdom may play some tiny part in the things that are done, but, by and large, it is the faith that God focuses on. We never honor God more than when we trust Him.

The 21st verse says, *"Then Jael Heber's wife took a nail of the tent . . . and smote the nail into his temples."* The Holy Spirit so honored Jael that He would refer to her as He only referred to the virgin Mary, *"Blessed above women"* (Judges 5:24). Mary was associated with the advent of Israel's redeemer; Jael was associated with the judgment of Israel's oppressor.

CHAPTER 5

Judges 5 is the proclamation of revival. Verse 1 says, *"Then sang Deborah and Barak."*

This is a praise to God for victory. Actually, there are some eight songs of praise recorded in Scripture. They are as follows:
1. Song of Moses (Ex. 15:1-19)
2. Song of Israel (Num. 21:17-18).
3. Song of Moses (Deut. 32:1-43)
4. Song of Deborah-Barak (Judg. 5:1-31)
5. Song of Hannah (I Sam. 2:1-10)
6. Song of David (II Sam. 22:1-51)
7. Song of the Redeemed (Rev. 5:8-10)
8. Song of Tribulation Saints (Rev. 15:3-4)

There are many other songs of praise listed in the book of Psalms; however, those listed above constitute other songs of praise.

There was an eightfold purpose to Deborah's song:
1. To thank God for the recent victory over the Canaanites and the deliverance of Israel from defeat and oppression for 20 years (5:1-8);
2. To celebrate the zeal and bravery of the rulers and people of certain tribes who had faith in God and had volunteered their services against a common foe (5:9-15; 18-19);
3. To censure the unbelief and lukewarmness of certain tribes who stayed at home, betraying the public cause of the people of God (5:15-17);
4. To honor God for His supernatural part in the uneven struggle between two earthly foes (5:20-22);
5. To curse those who refuse to take part in the spoil after victory was assured (5:23);
6. To bless the woman who was bold enough to slay Sisera (5:24-27);
7. To show the disappointment and anguish of the mother of Sisera (5:28-30);
8. To pronounce a blessing upon the people of God and a curse upon their enemies (5:31).

Verse 4 proclaims the hand of God in supernatural miracles by stating, *"The earth trembled, and the heavens dropped."*

Verse 6 shows the terrible condition to which Israel had sunk because of her spiritual declension. The land was full of anarchy and confusion, everywhere being infested with bandits. No public road was safe, and the people of the villages were forced to live in fortified places or in great numbers together to protect themselves from roving bands of wicked men. The 6th verse says, *"In the days of Jael, the highways were unoccupied, and the travellers walked through byways."* The enemy of our soul so desires to destroy our inheritance that we can take little advantage of the great blessings that God has afforded us. Of how many Christians can it be said that the highways of blessing are unoccupied, and the roads of victory untravelled?

The 8th verse tells us why, *"They chose new gods."* Regrettably, Israel chose gods that could not save them. They were overcome by their enemies, *"Then was war in the gates."* The 8th verse says, *"Was there a shield or spear seen among forty thousand in Israel?"* So, to face Sisera's 900 chariots of iron and his mighty army, God sent a rag-tag army of 10,000 without weapons. We might add that a woman was leading them. Israel had been reduced to this terrible state once again because, *"they chose new gods."*

Could it not be said today that the Church, as well, *"chose new gods"?* The god of modern-day Christianity (the Baptists, Methodists, Holiness, Pentecostals, and Charismatics) is for the most part the god of humanistic psychoanalysis-psychology. Psychology is the religion of secularism and humanism. It is atheistic at its core. Its apostles are Freud, Skinner, Maslow, Rogers, and a host of other similar ilk. The Church has bought it hook, line, and sinker. These individuals mentioned, who are mostly atheistic or at least humanistic, have replaced Matthew, Mark, Luke, and John. As Israel desperately needed a "Deborah" and a miracle from God, likewise, the Church needs the same.

The 13th verse records the great victory that God gave His people, *"the Lord made me have dominion over the mighty."*

Several of the tribes joined in the great battle, but some did not. Of the 10,000 men who fought against Sisera, most came from the tribes of Ephraim, Manasseh, Benjamin, Zebulun, Issachar, and Naphtali. Admittedly, some of these tribes only sent a few, but the rest of the tribes did not help at all. The Holy Spirit records some of the excuses. We would do well to fasten our attention on what the Holy Spirit says.

Reuben made great resolutions to help. The 15th verse uses the words, *"There were great thoughts of heart."* But because of *"divisions,"*

NOTES

(vs. 16) Reuben did nothing. Divisions are perhaps the greatest sin of the Church. How Satan must gloat over the splintered factions of various denominations and doctrinal beliefs. Paul would ask the question, *"Is Christ divided?"* Of course, the answer is no. But, sadly, the answer today is "Yes." If a local church is divided, it cannot do the work of God. One of the great problems of the Church at Corinth which occasioned Paul's words was division. False prophets had come in to cause these divisions. Consequently, the work of God halted for the time that these divisions lasted.

Verse 17 says that Gad, who came from Gilead, *"abode beyond Jordan."* They seemed to take the position, "out of sight, out of mind." Somehow they felt that Jordan was a barrier and, consequently, anything that happened on the other side of Jordan little affected them. By and large, the Church takes the same position today; "If it doesn't affect me I will not get involved." If the battle had been lost, Gad would have been very much involved.

Then the Scripture says, *"Why did Dan remain in ships?"* It was business as usual. Money took precedent over the work of God. Their interest was tied up in that which pertained to shekels. How much of the Church of today falls into this category as well? The Scripture says, *"Asher continued on the seashore, and abode in his breaches."* In other words, Asher was "up a creek." They were so spiritually disoriented and taken up with their little petty disturbances that they had no time for the great work of God. How so like the majority of the Church world today.

The 18th verse says, *"Zebulun and Naphtali were a people that jeoparded their lives."* Actually, these two tribes furnished the majority of the 10,000 men who fought the Canaanites. The other tribes provided only token numbers with Reuben, Gad, Dan, and Asher providing no one. How so like the Church regarding the great work of God in taking the Gospel of Jesus Christ to a lost world. Many do absolutely nothing toward the most important part of all, World Evangelism. Others give only a token amount, with a few doing all other giving.

The 21st verse says, *"The river of Kishon swept them away."* Some time ago I stood in the valley where this river of Kishon is. Actually, it is little more than a stream. There was a valley spread out on either side of this little trickle of water. In this valley Israel's 10,000 men without any weapons of war would be meat for Sisera's chariots. Incidentally, for these 10,000 men to face Sisera's 900 chariots of iron along with what was, no doubt, hundreds of thousands of his army, required tremendous faith, especially when we consider that the people of God were almost defenseless (vs. 8). This valley is perfect for the operation of chariots. Sisera could not lose, or so he thought. However, the 20th verse says, *"The stars in their courses fought against Sisera."* Mighty rains started to fall. The 4th verse says, *"And the heavens dropped, the clouds also dropped water,"* and that small river only a few feet across became a raging torrent. With a great rain this can happen in a few minutes time. It must have thrown his chariots around like fallen leaves. Hallelujah!

The 22nd verse says, *"The prancings of their mighty ones,"* signifying the arrogancy of Sisera and his military chieftains. However, their prancings were *"broken"* by the mighty power of Almighty God.

The 23rd verse records an indictment that should make the Church tremble. It says, *"Curse ye Meroz."* It must be remembered that these words were given to Deborah by the Holy Spirit, *"Said the angel of the Lord."* This would have been the One we now know as the Lord Jesus Christ. He then further says, *"Curse ye bitterly."* And then, *"Because they came not to the help of the Lord against the mighty."*

The Holy Spirit was careful to speak of the two tribes who provided the most of the soldiers. He was also careful to specify those who provided none. And then, *"Curse ye Meroz."* Who these individuals were we do not know. But this we do know; they had the opportunity to come *"to the help of the Lord,"* and they did not do it.

How many in the Church today not only fall into the position of the tribes who did not help because of difficulties in their own ranks, and are actually *"cursed by the angel of the Lord?"*

I think of the doors that the Holy Spirit has opened to take the Gospel to the world, especially to many who have never had the opportunity to hear even one time, and I feel so

NOTES

sad when only a few respond. Many are mired down like the tribes just mentioned, and many could help considering the opportunity given to them but blatantly refuse to do so. But the Lord said they were cursed then, and so are those today who do the same.

I wonder what His pronouncement would have been if some of the tribes of Israel had not only opposed Deborah and Barak but had joined Sisera as well?

CHAPTER 6

The closing prayer of Deborah is, *"So let all thine enemies perish, oh Lord."* This prayer would have been answered had Israel during their 40 years of rest after the great victory over Sisera allowed the Lord to reign supreme within their lives. But, regrettably, the 1st verse says, *"And the children of Israel did evil in the sight of the Lord."* If one looks at God's people in the book of Judges, then the book becomes laborious to read. However, if one will look instead at the Lord and His mercy and grace in this great book, then it takes on a totally different complexion. The 1st verse says, *"And the Lord delivered them into the hand of Midian seven years."* The Lord chastises those He loves. The Lord only resorts to these measures when all measures of mercy and grace have failed, but all is done in love with the express purpose of bringing His people back to Him. If one observes Christians who constantly live in a state of rebellion with no repentance and seemingly no chastisement, one must come to the conclusion that he is looking at bastards and not at children. The children of Israel were the Lord's children; therefore, He would chastise them to bring them back.

Midian was the son of Abraham by Keturah (Gen. 25:2-4). His descendants became bitter enemies of Israel in the days of Moses, who himself married a Midianite woman. The reason for such enmity is not stated. It appears from Numbers 31 that the Midianites were destroyed as a nation, but they multiplied again and became the leaders of this great multitude who came against Israel in the days of Gideon.

Generally, the greatest foe to the child of God is his own household.

Verse 2 records how that spiritual declension had brought Israel to a terrible low, *"Because of the Midianites the children of Israel made them the dens which are in the mountains, and caves, and strongholds."* Once again, Israel was a slave in her own inheritance. When one reads verse 2, one realizes that this is the exact position that Satan desires to bring every Christian.

The 3rd verse says, *"When Israel had sown."* This had to do with their crops. Then it says in the 4th verse, *"And destroyed the increase of the earth. . . .and left no sustenance for Israel, neither sheep, nor ox, or ass."* This is exactly Satan's method. He wants to destroy your increase until there is no sustenance left. How many Christians are already in that place and position?

The 5th verse gives us Satan's method, *"As grasshoppers for multitude."* And then it says, *"Without number."* Satan's methods vary little. He overwhelms us with the magnitude of the opposition brought against us. It is for but one purpose, *"And they entered into the land to destroy it."* Jesus used this term concerning Satan, *"To steal, to kill, and to destroy"* (St. John 10:10).

Verse 6 says, *"And Israel was greatly impoverished."* Impoverishment always follows sinful failure. Repentance is the only answer. The Scripture says, *"The children of Israel cried unto the Lord."* This was the purpose of the Lord delivering Israel into the hand of Midian. He wanted them to be brought to a place where they would *"cry unto the Lord."* So many of the things that we chafe at are actually meant for our blessing. The Lord squeezes us just enough so that we will cry out to Him, but even then our repentance too often is insincere and incomplete.

The 8th verse says, *"That the Lord sent a prophet unto the children of Israel."* This is the first occasion of the Scripture saying that the Lord had sent a prophet. Admittedly, others before this particular time were prophets, but this is the first occasion recorded. The sending of prophets by the Lord would include some of the greatest men of God who ever lived: Elijah, Elisha, Isaiah, Jeremiah, and Ezekiel. God

NOTES

would continue to send them until Israel would finally be destroyed because of rebellion.

In the 10th verse the prophet concluded his announcement by saying, *"But ye have not obeyed my voice."* These words constitute the "bottom line" for every problem we face. It is because *"We have not obeyed His voice."*

The angel of the Lord referred to in verse 11 is none other than the Lord Jesus Christ. He appeared unto Gideon.

In the 12th verse he is called by the Lord, *"thou mighty man of valor,"* and previously said, *"The Lord is with thee."* What a wonderful thing for the Lord to say about a man. The spiritual declension of Israel must have grieved Gideon's heart greatly for the Lord to have addressed him in this manner. I wonder what God would say of each of us? In the 13th verse Gideon would ask the question, *"Where be all his miracles which our fathers told us of?"* Gideon expressed the heart of so many Christians today who, having heard about the great things that God did in the past, long for Him to do so today. There was a reason for no miracles in Gideon's day, as there is a reason for no miracles (or precious few) in our day. The reason is sin.

In the 14th verse the Lord called Gideon *"mighty"* only because Gideon realized how weak he really was. The 15th verse says, *"I am the least in my father's house."* Humility is the demand of the Holy Spirit. Paul said, *"Most gladly, will I rather glory in my infirmities, that the power of Christ may rest upon me."* Such humility is in short supply today.

The 21st verse proclaims upon Gideon's request, *"And there arose up fire out of the rock."* Fire has always accompanied the mighty power of the Holy Spirit. When the Law was given on Mount Sinai, the mountain burned with fire. At specific times the fire fell on particular sacrifices offered by Israel. As Elijah prayed in the great contest between good and evil, the fire fell on Mount Carmel and consumed the sacrifice as well as the rocks, the water, and even the dust. On the Day of Pentecost the Holy Spirit would come upon redeemed mankind with tongues of fire upon their heads, for John had said that *"He shall baptize you with the Holy Ghost and with fire."* The fire of the Holy Spirit burns out the dross and purifies the content. The fire as expressed to Gideon was a sign God would purify Israel.

The appearance of the angel first caused fear, for the 23rd verse says, *"Fear not"* – and then brought peace, *"And called it Jehovah-Shalom,"* meaning *"The Lord of peace."* If we receive God's fire that burns the dross within our lives, then peace will always follow. I want you to notice the progression of the Holy Spirit.

First, by giving the sign of the fire, He tells Israel that He is going to cleanse the land.

And then in the 26th verse Gideon was instructed to *"Offer a burnt sacrifice with wood of the grove."* This took Israel to Calvary. Even though Israel would not have understood the word "Calvary," still, in symbolism, this is what it meant. The Lord is forever taking the Church back to Calvary.

The 30th verse shows us that despite Israel's crying unto the Lord (vs. 6), there was still no repentance, because the 30th verse says,

"Because he hath cast down the altar of Baal." The men of the city would try to kill Gideon because of this. Despite the prophet of God being sent and proclaiming God's message to them, they were still worshiping Baal. Men do not repent easily, and without proper leadership they will not repent at all. It must be understood that the altar of Baal had been erected at Gideon's father's house (vs. 25), *"Judgment must first begin at the house of God."* Gideon cannot hope to lead Israel into the destruction of their own idols until his is first destroyed. So, destroyed it is.

The 34th verse says, *"But the Spirit of the Lord came upon Gideon, and he blew a trumpet."*

The double test with the fleece in verses 36-40 teach us a great lesson. It teaches Gideon and us that God can withhold or grant blessings. If He so chooses, He can bless Gideon and no one else; likewise, He can bless everyone else but Gideon.

Whenever spiritual declension sets in on a denomination, one of the first signs is that the dew can come only on their fleece. Some churches think this, some preachers also; but God can put the dew, representing the Holy Spirit, on any fleece that He so desires. I am sure that Gideon got the message. The very

NOTES

moment a Christian, a church, or a denomination impugns the sovereignty of God, that is the moment God will take His dew from their fleece.

CHAPTER 7

This chapter is the story of great faith and great victory.

Verse 2 says, *"And the Lord said unto Gideon, the people that are with thee are too many for me."* The ever continuing thrust of the Church is for more and more numbers. While it is certainly true that numbers are important, still, large numbers portray no great spirituality to God. Actually, in this case they would portray the very opposite. God is not looking for mere numbers; He is looking for men and women who have faith. And irrespective of their small number, tremendous victories will be won.

The latter portion of the 2nd verse says, *"Mine own hand hath saved me."* Man has ever wanted to have a hand in his own salvation. Our *"own hand"* is probably the greatest hindrance to our spiritual victory. The old hymn says this:

"Nothing, either great or small,"
"Nothing, sinner, no,"
"Jesus did it, did it all,"
"Long, long ago!"

The 3rd verse says, *"Whosoever is fearful and afraid, let him return and depart."* As we look at this glorious story of Gideon, we are probably seeing close to the true percentage in the Church who really have faith. Out of 32,000, only some 301 (counting Gideon) had faith. That's about 1 percent of the total. It probably characterizes the modern-day Church. Out of this multitude fear was the greatest hindrance then, and fear is, no doubt, the greatest hindrance now. Fear always follows faithlessness. The first word that fallen man (Adam) uttered was, *"I was afraid."* Most everything that is done in the world is done from a basis of fear. That is sad but true. Wars begin because of fear. Most laws are made by Congress because of fear. Most church splits occur because of fear. Most preachers do the faithless things they do simply because of fear. I think one could say without any fear of contradiction that just about every action taken by religious denominations is taken from a platform of fear. Fear always says that man is in control and places God in a secondary position. Faith says that God is in control, and it makes little difference as to what man does.

The conclusion of the 3rd verse says, *"And there remained ten thousand."* These people could certainly be construed as godly, and yet the Lord will send 9,700 home. Why? The criteria would be how they drank the water.

The 6th verse says, *"And the number of them that lapped, putting their hand to their mouth, were three hundred men."* The other 9,700 bowed on their knees and drank the water directly from the brook. They were rejected. At least one of the reasons was that any true soldier would not take his eyes from the enemy even for a second. Those who bent over to drink for a short time would be blind to the enemy. Those who *"lapped"* were vigilant.

There are many Christians today who love the Lord with all of their heart, and, yet, Satan has maneuvered them into a position of trying to do something that God never called them to do. Satan has two major tactics with the child of God.

1. He destroys most of the Church with lukewarmness.

2. For those who are truly dedicated and consecrated to the Lord, he tries to destroy their effectiveness by sidetracking them into an effort in which God never called them, thereby, rendering them ineffective. God truly had called the 9,700 but not to be soldiers. As well, He has called every single Christian with a specific calling that is extremely important. And let us pray that God help us to not get out of our calling.

The 7th verse says, *"By the three hundred men that lapped will I save you."* He saw faith in their hearts. Oh, Lord, give us men and women of faith, for with them we can defeat the enemy! And then the Lord says, *"And let all the other people go every man unto his place."* Regrettably, too often these faithless men occupy positions of leadership in the Church. We should love and pray for them, but in places of responsibility give us men of faith.

The 9th verse says, *"That the Lord said unto me, Arise."* Fear always finds an excuse for not doing what God has said. Faith always says, *"Arise."*

The 12th verse says, *"Without number."* In other words, Satan's opposition was so overwhelming that it beggared description. If we are looking at the problem with fear, then, seemingly, the number continues to grow. If we are looking at it with faith, we cease to see the number, but we see God.

The 13th verse speaks of *"a dream."* It says, *"A cake of barley bread tumbled into the host of Midian."* The *"barley bread"* represents Gideon. Barley bread was the poorest of all bread. Yet, one cake of barley bread with God behind it could overturn the greatest tent in the camp of Midian. Hallelujah!

The *"three companies"* of the 16th verse speak of the Divine Trinity. With this power behind them and with faith in God, they could not fail. The *"trumpet"* was symbolic of the Word of God. That must be the proclamation of every preacher of the Gospel and the blowing of a certain sound. The *"empty pitchers"* speak of our lack of trust in the flesh. God cannot fill that which is already full of self-will, and what does God fill it with? The Scripture says, *"And lamps within the pitchers."* Jesus said, *"You are the light of the world."*

The 19th verse says, *"And brake the pitchers."* The story is always that the child of God must be broken before there can be any light given. Over and over again it would say that Jesus took the bread, blessed the bread, broke the bread, and then gave the bread. Being broken is not pleasant. But for the bread to be given and for the light to shine, the pitcher must be broken.

Then they were to realize that "the weapons of their warfare were not carnal, but mighty through God to the pulling down of strongholds." The 22nd verse says, *"And the Lord set every man's sword against his fellow."* The trumpets and the torches had but one purpose, and that was to announce the presence of God. The light of that Presence always puts the enemy to flight.

The 24th verse says, *"And Gideon sent messengers throughout all Mount Ephraim, saying, Come down against the Midianites."* Now that God had given great victory, there was time, place, and use for the many of Israel. Likewise, when the Lord opens the door to take the Gospel to hundreds of millions, there must be many who will step in the breach and help get the job done. Then the Lord gave great victory to this multitude who He at first had rejected. The 25th verse says, *"They took two princes of the Midianites."* They killed these princes and *"brought the heads of Orb and Zeeb to Gideon."* Their names meant *"raven and wolf,"* symbolic of demon powers that had attempted to destroy Israel. This is the posture that God wants Israel in. Instead of the raven and the wolf destroying Israel, Israel was to destroy the raven and the wolf. Every demon spirit must fall in the name of Jesus. These demon powers respond to no other. Whenever we go God's way and do God's bidding, even the lowliest Christian among us can come away with the trophies of the raven and the wolf in his hands, victorious in the mighty name of Jesus Christ.

—■—

CHAPTER 8

The 8th chapter records victory, inward strife, and idolatry. God has just given one of the greatest victories Israel has ever known. But now in the aftermath, whereas, the Spirit of the Lord had been followed totally at the outset, now the flesh will interrupt causing great difficulty. This is a perfect picture of the Church. Every once in a while we follow the Holy Spirit totally. Great victory is always the result. Most of the time the flesh intervenes causing terrible problems.

Verse 1 says, *"And they did chide with him sharply."* This speaks of the *"men of Ephraim."* Through Gideon's obedience to God, the Ephraimites joined in the victory and saw great results. However, instead of their being grateful for Gideon's leadership and the call of God on his life, instead, they *"did chide with him sharply."* The man of God will answer in humility and with wisdom. The men of Ephraim were taught with tenderness, whereas, the men of Succoth were taught with thorns. Grace dealt

NOTES

with Ephraim because Ephraim responded with grace. Succoth would not respond to grace; therefore, it had to be dealt with by righteousness. God help us to place ourselves in such a spiritual position that we, like Ephraim, will respond to grace. Otherwise, God will demand righteousness of us of which we are berift. The Church has never quite understood this. It loves to portray its righteousness which is always self-righteousness. God will have no part of it. He will only respond to the righteousness of Christ within our lives, which yields to grace.

Gideon's great faith would defeat the enemy, and, yet, others would enjoy the victory and the fruit. Gideon, as any true man of God, will find no fault with this. The man of faith is always satisfied with having done the work committed to him. He wants all to be likewise blessed. Now we will see how God deals with the sin of self-righteousness.

The 5th verse says, *"And he said unto the men of Succoth, Give I pray you, loaves of bread unto the people that follow me."* The people of Succoth would not give the bread; therefore, Gideon said, *"I will tear your flesh with the thorns of the wilderness and with briers."* The same God who extends grace will also respond with judgment to self-righteousness.

Regrettably, the 8th verse says, *"The men of Penuel answered him as the men of Succoth."* They too were met with the judgment of God and from Gideon. God looks very unkindly on that which will oppose His work.

The 16th verse says, *"He taught the men of Succoth."* How many times does God teach us with thorns and briers? But only if we refuse His Grace. Oh, that the Church could understand this.

Sadly, Satan is an angel of light and a minister of self-righteousness who knows how to set a snare for the feet of God's truest servants. This will be a religious snare as almost all snares are. He would take the gold of the Ishmaelites, who were part of the Midianites, and *"make an ephod thereof"* (vs. 27). And then the Scripture says, *"And all Israel went thither a-whoring after it."* The ephod was a beautiful garment worn by the high priest in which the Urim and the Thummim were kept. Somehow, in Gideon's thinking a golden ephod representing the wisdom and direction of the Holy Spirit would be most appropriate. This thing would *"become a snare unto Gideon, and to his house,"* as all religiosity is. Most of the *"whoring"* of the Church is after that which is religious. We make our denominations into golden ephods, or our church into a golden ephod, or our doctrine into a golden ephod, and they become snares. This thing became an idol, as so much in the Church today no longer constitutes true worship of God but is, in fact, an idol. God help us!

CHAPTER 9

The 9th chapter is a story of rebellion, which even characterizes the Church of the Living God. Abimelech is the culprit. He was the son of Gideon and a concubine who lived at Shechem (8:31). He aspired kingship after the death of Gideon and did rule three years after killing Gideon's 70 other sons, except Jotham (vss. 5-6). Working through his mother's people in Shechem and appealing to the city elders who naturally desired their city to become great, Abimelech sought to become king with Shechem as his capital. He was given money by the elders which enabled him to hire assassins to destroy the other sons of Gideon, giving him no rival from that source. He was then made king, although not approved or selected by the Living God.

The 4th verse says, *"Wherewith Abimelech hired vain and like persons which followed him."* This terrible apostasy followed Israel's great revival under Gideon. Gideon's calling was a work of the Spirit. Abimelech's calling was a work of the flesh. One brought life, the other death. In chapters 8 and 9 we have the picture of the spiritual Church and the carnal Church.

Verses 7-21 portray Jotham's allegory as both a parable and a prophecy. It was to have an immediate fulfillment, for the men of Shechem would elect the bramble to rule over them, and mutual destruction was the result.

However, the allegory will have a wider significance as well. In the Scriptures, Israel is

portrayed as a fig tree, an olive tree, and a vine. So, the bramble not only portrayed Israel's situation at the time in question, but it also is a forepicture of the Antichrist. In Israel's continued rebellion she will ultimately put her trust in the rule of the Antichrist with destruction as the result.

The 23rd verse says, *"Then God sent an evil spirit between Abimelech and the men of Shechem."* The idea of God using an evil spirit is foreign to most Christians. However, evil spirits not only do Satan's bidding, but they do God's bidding as well.

For instance, in I Kings 22, concerning the death of Ahab, the Lord used an evil spirit to bring all of this about (I Kings 22:19-23). The Scripture says in I Samuel that, *"The evil spirit from God came upon Saul"* (I Sam. 18:10).

So, I think it should be obvious that God does use evil spirits to help bring about His ultimate plan if the occasion so requires. Also, it should be noted that each occasion where it speaks of God ordering or sending an evil spirit, it is in a situation already fraught with evil. It must ever be known that God is in control of all things, both good and evil. According to Job 1, Satan's perimeters are drawn by God.

Verse 56 says, *"Thus God rendered the wickedness of Abimelech."* And then the 57th verse says, *"And all the evil of the men of Shechem did God render upon their heads."* The law of sowing and reaping is adhered to dogmatically in the government of God. Jesus once again spelled it out in no uncertain terms in St. Matthew 7:1-5.

We would do well to heed the admonition; what we sow, we reap.

CHAPTER 10

If one would count the number of years each Judge served, as well as the number of years of servitude to various heathen countries around about, one would come up with more than *"450 years until Samuel,"* as stated by Paul (Acts 13:20). However, the possibility definitely exists that some of the Judges overlapped and, as well, some of the servitudes.

The 10th chapter is a mixture of judgment and repentance. Actually, in this chapter one of the most clear-cut examples of repentance found in the entirety of the Word of God is given. We would do well to heed it.

The 6th verse says, *"And the children of Israel did evil again in the sight of the Lord."* This particular time appears to be the lowest point of debasement that they touched in this period of their history.

The Philistines on the west and the Ammonites on the east *"vexed and oppressed them."* They were pushed from two sides. The Bible says that Israel *"forsook the Lord, and served not him."* What a terrible indictment.

The 7th verse says, *"And the anger of the Lord was hot against Israel."* God's anger against sin is just as hot against His own children as it is the heathen. The child of God, despite the false doctrines that abound, must understand that God cannot condone sin in any form or capacity. Sin, in its truest form, is injury done to God, for sin is ultimately against God. And the Scripture says, *"He sold them into the hands of the Philistines, and into the hands of the children of Ammon."* As stated earlier, Israel was pushed from two sides for some 18 years.

The 7th verse once again uses the words, *"He sold them."* God's chastisement of His children denotes none other than His love. Every movement toward Israel, whether it was by mercy or judgment, was but for one purpose, and that was to bring Israel to God.

The 9th verse says, *"Israel was sore distressed."* Sin brings distress.

The repetition of the sin, the terrible bondage, and the slavery would be followed by these words. The 10th verse says, *"And the children of Israel cried unto the Lord."* This was the purpose of the judgment. God, at times, will sell us to the enemy, allowing us to be squeezed just enough so that we will *"cry unto the Lord."*

Verses 10-14 record an insincere repentance. It was a half-hearted confession by Israel, as it elicited no favorable response from God. It must ever be remembered that remorse is not repentance. Likewise, mental distress because of the painful results of sin is not repentance. There must be a sense of grief and

NOTES

dishonor occasioned to God and sorrow because He has been sinned against. That is repentance.

Beginning with the 15th verse, Israel will sincerely, contritely, and completely repent. Their repentance would basically be fivefold. This is a lesson that we should learn today. Here is what Israel said:

1. We have sinned (vs. 15). This is the first principle of true repentance. One must make confession or acknowledgement of his sins to be forgiven (I John 1:9). The person must say the same thing about himself that God says about him. He must repent not only of the bad but of the good as well. Sadly, this is what hinders most Christians. Some of us have become very adept at repenting of the bad; however, we find it very difficult, if not impossible to repent of the pharisaical good. True repentance demands that we repent not only of our bad but of our good also.

2. Do what you want with us. This is wholehearted surrender to the will of God and obedience to Him. This type of repentance makes no claim upon God. We acknowledge that we deserve terrible judgment. By rights, we should be condemned to hell. We parade no goodness before Him.

3. Deliver us only this day, we pray. There was a desperate earnestness for deliverance now, which is also necessary for full consecration. God cannot deliver us until we admit we cannot deliver ourselves. Man's constant fault is that he thinks he can set himself free. Remember, sin cannot deliver sin; sickness cannot heal sickness; bondage cannot deliver bondage; flesh cannot deliver flesh. There is only one Deliverer, and He is God.

4. They put away the strange gods from among them (vs. 16). This was proper and necessary restitution and manifested true repentance and sincerity. Israel abounded in strange gods. These gods were Baal and Ashtaroth. The strange gods did not pass away with Israel; they abound today in the Church as well. The "power of positive thinking gospel" is a strange god. The "possibility thinking gospel" is a strange god. The "health and wealth gospel" is a strange god. The "dominion teaching" is a strange god. The "psychological way" is a strange god. The list is almost endless. And

until we put away these strange gods, we cannot receive the mercy of God.

5. Serve the Lord. The acid test of any true repentance is actual consecration to God and dedication to truly serve Him.

One can make confession and a pretense of consecration with the mouth; he can pose as being truly penitent and desperate and carry out the acts of verse 15 without true repentance. However, one cannot do the two things of verse 16 without getting results from God. Putting into practice what we say is worth more than all burnt offerings, sacrifices, and superficial promises. To put away all gods and truly serve Jehovah is all that God has ever required of man. When anyone does this, he will be reconciled to God and have Him on his side in any problem.

Then the 16th verse says, *"And his soul was grieved for the misery of Israel."* God desires to send mercy when His people will only allow Him to do so.

Here is an extra note of interest concerning the "soul" of God. This is one of the many Scriptures that plainly says God has a soul. The soul of God, man, or any other being is the seat of the emotions, passions, appetites, desires, and feelings. That God has a soul, powers, and attributes just as do angels, demons, and men is very clearly revealed in Scripture.

——◼——

CHAPTER 11

The 11th chapter records the deliverance of Israel. The 1st verse says that God will use *"Jephthah."* It says he *"was a mighty man of valour."* But then it says, *"He was the son of an harlot."*

There is no way that Israel would accept this man, and the 2nd verse says, *"And they thrust out Jephthah."* They went on to say, *"Thou shalt not inherit in our father's house."* That which Israel refused to use, God would use. By and large, this is the story of the present-day Church. That which pleases man does not please God; that which pleases God does not please man. Why? The answer is simple. The flesh cannot please God; only faith can

please God. Ironically enough, Jephthah's birth was a work of the flesh; however, Jephthah's faith overcame that work of the flesh, as faith always will (Heb. 11:32). Now the Lord will right the wrong done by Israel to Jephthah by using Israel's enemies.

The 4th verse says, *"The children of Ammon made war against Israel."* God, all-knowing, is able to take events, place them in their proper position, and carry out His will.

Then the 5th verse says, *"The elders of Gilead went to fetch Jephthah."*

The 6th verse says, *"Come, and be our captain."* Why did they thrust him out to begin with? He was an embarrassment to them. Faith is always an embarrassment to the flesh. However, when the situation becomes critical, men of faith are eagerly sought after. Jephthah was a man of faith. It is sad when Israel would thrust out the only man of faith they had. They will now go to retrieve him.

The 7th verse says that Jephthah will say, *"Did not you hate me, and expel me out of my father's house?"* Once again we state, the flesh always hates faith. It will ever expel it. Why? As stated, faith is an embarrassment because faith always has to believe God despite the circumstances. The circumstance in this case was the ignominy of Jephthah's birth. Faith believes God despite the problems, despite the circumstances. When Nero put Paul in jail, Paul would not call himself a prisoner of Nero. Instead, faith said, *"I'm a prisoner of the Lord Jesus Christ."* Still, the flesh will always find itself ultimately *in distress.*

The 11th verse says, *"And the people made him head and captain over them."* They did so because the flesh cannot deliver the flesh; only faith can deliver from the flesh. So, they now make one born of a harlot as their captain. The Church, likewise, is so busy looking for the perfect person in the flesh it completely overlooks that which is of faith. The reason is simple. There is always something wrong with the man of faith, and the Church has no mind to see that there is something wrong with the flesh as well. But the flesh cannot see wrong in the flesh; it can only see wrong in faith. However, faith not only sees wrong in the flesh, but it sees its own wrong, admits it to God, and believes God anyway.

The 13th verse says that Ammon was demanding Israel's possession. Satan will always demand your possession. If he can stop you from occupying it, he will. If you occupy it, he will try to dislodge you. He will do so by denying the Bible if possible, and if not, by warring against you.

Jephthah's answer is, *"So whomsoever the Lord our God shall drive out from before us, them will we possess"* (vs. 24).

The 29th verse gives us the secret of victory in the Church, *"Then the Spirit of the Lord came upon Jephthah."* God's Spirit will only come upon a man of faith; it will not come upon the flesh. Self-righteous pride could never accept this. Jephthah is the son of a harlot, the result of a sinful act of his father, and, thereby, cursed. So, all good Israelites must reject him. However, faith overcomes sin, for only faith in the vicarious atoning work of the Lord Jesus Christ can overcome sin. The *"Spirit of the Lord"* did not come on the leaders of Israel; it did not come upon the High Priest; it did not come upon the Levites; it came upon Jephthah.

The 32nd verse says, *"And the Lord delivered them into his hands."* In the 15th verse of the 10th chapter Israel had cried to God for the Lord to deliver them. God would hear that cry and answer that petition. Jephthah would be the instrument the Lord would use to deliver Israel. Many people want deliverance but not God's way. If it can come through their denomination or their church with them setting the rules, then they will accept it. However, the reason that most people, even though they ask God for deliverance, never receive it is because they want to dictate the terms, and God will have none of it.

Incidentally, the vow that Jephthah foolishly made to the Lord concerning the offering up and sacrifice of the first thing that came out of his house did not mean the death or sacrifice of his daughter. It simply meant that she would remain a perpetual virgin, bringing no children into the world to continue the name and claim the inheritance.

Jephthah would be listed in faith's "Hall of Fame" of Hebrews 11. What an honor!

NOTES

CHAPTER 12

The 12th chapter is a sad picture of the Church in strife.

Verse 1 says, *"And the men of Ephraim gathered themselves together."* Regrettably, they gathered themselves together to destroy that which God had blessed. The flesh ever persecutes the Spirit. Why didn't they gather themselves together against Ammon when these heathen people threatened Israel? They were claiming that Jephthah did not give them an invitation to fight with him against Ammon. The 2nd verse declares that he did, *"And when I called you, you delivered me not out of their hands."*

Perhaps they were, as most Christians, so preoccupied with their own doings that they paid little attention to the call. How many Christians today are being called by God to help in World Evangelism; to help push back the darkness; to help bring in the harvest; but because of spiritual deafness they do not hear? Jesus said, *"If any man have ears to hear, let him hear."* Ephraim had no ears to hear. Sadly, most of Christendom has no ears to hear. Now, they will want to destroy the man that God has used to save them from Ammonnite oppression. Once again we say it, the flesh cannot abide the Spirit.

Now we have a civil war between brethren, for the 3rd verse says, *"Ye come up unto me this day, to fight against me."*

This is a sad picture of the Church. There are enemies galore to fight, but, instead, we fight each other.

The 6th verse says, *"And there fell at that time of the Ephraimites forty and two thousand."* How many casualties are there in the Church because of inner strife? How much of our energy do we spend in fighting among ourselves instead of against the enemy? Perhaps some of the old animosity against Jephthah remained in the heart of Ephraim. I think it is evident that they were little pleased with God's choice, as the Church is seldom pleased with God's choice.

Incidentally, the 42,000 given in the 6th

verse may have been 2,040 instead. The Hebrew lettering is very similar and could have been misinterpreted by a copiest. Again it could have been possible for Ephraim to have multiplied to such an extent that there could have been a loss of 42,000. It must be that any error in numbers would constitute a copiest error from the original or a copy of the original.

The 7th verse says, *"Then died Jephthah"* and *"was buried in one of the cities of Gilead,"* without giving any detail.

By contrast, *"Abdon"* of the 13th verse has great detail given concerning his burial (vs. 15). It seems that Jephthah, who risked his life, won a great victory and delivered Israel, but was buried in an unknown grave.

Abdon risked nothing that is recorded, and his grave is described with great minuteness. However, the Holy Spirit in Hebrews 11:32 places Jephthah's valorous name upon the golden tablets of faith and completely ignores Abdon. God never forgets those who trust and serve Him, however much they may be forgotten by man.

CHAPTER 13

Verse 1 says, *"Did evil again."* This repetition presents a sorry note concerning Israel, and, yet, I wonder if it's not characteristic of the majority of the Church. There are two major pictures presented to us in the book of Judges:

1. The compassion, grace, and mercy of the Lord in forgiving Israel over and over again, as well as coming to her rescue.

2. The terrible weakness of God's chosen people, which too much characterizes the majority of the Christian Church.

How many Christians is it said of them that they *"did evil again"* and that over and over? Verse 1 says, *"And the Lord delivered them into the hand of the Philistines forty years."* The Philistines now become prominent and continue to be so up to the time of David, when they are finally subdued.

The fact is that there are enemies within the Christian's heart, for the Philistine was an inward and not an outward foe. The inward

enemy can only be defeated by full consecration to God. Hence, the Lord called Samson to be a Nazarite.

Verse 2 says, *"And his wife was barren."* That which God will use to bring a deliverer will at the same time allow Satan much latitude to hinder. Consequently, he will make Manoah's wife barren, and the Lord will allow it. God allows Satan this type of latitude for two purposes:

1. To create in the heart and life of the party in question total trust and dependence on the Lord.

2. That the work be totally of the Spirit and none of the flesh.

Verse 3 says, *"And the angel of the Lord appeared unto the woman."* This was a preincarnate appearance of the Lord Jesus Christ. His message would be simple, *"Thou shalt conceive and bare a son."* The desperate need of the Church is to hear the voice of the Lord. There is nothing more powerful than a *"Thus saith the Lord."* Regrettably, the Church today constantly hears the racket of what proposes to be of God but seldom is. Mostly it is the voice of false doctrine, error, apostasy, and heresy.

Verses 4 and 5 proclaim that both mother and son would be Nazarites. The 5th verse says, *"For the child shall be a Nazarite unto God from the womb."* All Nazarites were to let their hair grow and to abstain from all fruit of the vine. These two verses have double meanings.

1. The 4th verse is a picture of what God demanded Israel bring, *"the Nazarite,"* the Lord Jesus Christ, into the world. Regrettably, Israel failed, but *"the Nazarite,"* the Lord Jesus Christ, did not fail.

2. The order of the Nazarite ordained by God demanded total consecration and was, in effect, a sign of weakness, as long hair meant weakness. So, the Lord would take Samson, place the Nazarite vow upon him, (denoting great weakness), and then put His Spirit upon Samson to make him the strongest man upon the face of the earth. This is a picture of what the Church should be. The Nazarite vow was threefold:

1. Do not touch a dead body; death is a portrayal of the Fall of man.

2. No alcoholic beverage of any nature.

3. Do not cut the hair; Samuel was a

Nazarite, as was John the Baptist.

The 8th verse says, *"Then Manoah entreated the Lord."* He said, *"Teach us what we will do."* This humble entreaty was responded to by God, as He always does. Men today are entreating everyone and everything except the Lord. Oh, if we would only ask Him to *"teach us what we shall do."*

Verse 9 says, *"And God hearkened to the voice of Manoah,"* as God always will do upon a humble request.

The 18th verse says, *"Why askest thou thus after my name, seeing it is "secret"?* The word, "secret," in the Hebrew means "wonderful." It not only means that He (the Lord Jesus Christ) is wonderful, but that He does wondrously as is recorded in verse 19.

The 20th verse says, *"The angel of the Lord ascended in the flame of the altar."* This pictures the Lord dying at Calvary, being resurrected, and ascending to heaven from the Mount of Olives.

The 24th verse says, *"And called His name Samson."* Also, *"the child grew, and the Lord blessed him."*

The 25th verse says, *"And the Spirit of the Lord began to move him."*

Both verses 24 and 25 are a portrayal of the Church. As Samson's birth was miraculous, so the birth of the Church was miraculous as well. The Church grew and the Lord blessed it. As well, *"the Spirit of the Lord"* moved on the Church *"at times."* Also, Samson's terrible spiritual declension portrays the Church exactly. And then, finally, Samson's victorious conclusion portrays the Church at the time of the Rapture as a *"glorious church."* Hallelujah!

CHAPTER 14

Verse 1 says, *"And Samson went down to Timnath."* It would be there he would see a daughter of the Philistines.

The depths of Satan may be recognized in his action toward Israel in connection with the Philistines. The other nations "mightily oppressed" Israel, but it is not stated that the Philistines did so. They simply "ruled" Israel,

NOTES

and so insensitive had Israel become to slavery that they accepted this yoke. This is the sad history of many Christians. Bondage to some inward form of evil is submitted to, its rule accepted, and spiritual insensitivity results.

The very purpose of Samson was separation. Regrettably, he does not follow, at least in the matter of morals, his Nazarite vow.

He says in the 2nd verse, *"Now therefore get her for me to wife."* Samson, as a type of the Church, "marries the world," which is far too prevalent today. For when we look at Samson, we see the Church. When we look at his failures, we look at the Church. When we look at the concluding victory, we also see the Church.

God will use Samson despite his marriage to the world, once again portraying two things:

1. God's mercy and grace to Samson (the Church).

2. God's eagerness to deliver Israel (the Church) and His anger at the Philistines (the world).

For the 4th verse says, *"But his father and his mother knew not that it was of the Lord."*

The above passage does not mean that God approved of or even condoned Samson's taking a wife of *"the uncircumcised Philistines."* But it does mean that Samson's failure did not abrogate God's judgment upon the Philistines. God would use a wayward Church (Samson) to *"seek occasion against the Philistines."* And the reason? *"The Philistines had dominion over Israel."* God desired to break that dominion. He was only partially able to do so because of Israel's failure.

The 5th verse says, *"Then went Samson down."* Even though the statement concerns a geographical sense, still, it could be a spiritual type as well. The *"young lion"* refers to Satan as *"a roaring lion."*

However, in the midst of Samson's spiritual declension and Satan's roaring against him, still, *"The Spirit of the Lord came mightily upon him."* Self-righteous Christians would take umbrage at such. Still, it must be remembered that God does not run His government on the principle of good and evil but according to the heart. The Scripture says, *"Man looks on the outward, but God looks on the heart."* Regrettably, the Church operates on the principle of good and evil. Too often it makes up its own rules as to what is good or evil. Does this mean that God condones evil? As Paul was fond of saying, *"God forbid."* However, if God operated on the principle of good and evil, then He would be able to use no one. The Psalmist would say, *"Lord, if thou mark iniquities, who can stand."* God looks at the heart of an individual and deals thusly with that individual regardless of the strength or the weakness. On this basis, *"The Spirit of the Lord came mightily upon him."* Sadly, a self-righteous church can never accept God's ways. That's the reason Jesus would say, *"The thieves and the harlots go into the kingdom of God before you,"* when speaking to the Pharisees. Did the Lord condone theft and harlotry? Once again as Paul said, *"God forbid."* However, the thief and the harlot knew what they were. The Pharisee would not admit what he was and would not repent or accept the Lord Jesus as his personal Saviour.

The words, *"And he had nothing in his hand,"* in the 6th verse concerning Samson's killing of the lion, speak that the *"weapons of our warfare are not carnal but mighty through God, to the pulling down of strongholds."*

The 8th verse says, *"A swarm of bees and honey in the carcass of the lion."* This speaks of the great victory that God intends for us to have over Satan, the roaring lion. That which seems to be our destruction, the Lord can turn into our blessing.

From verses 10 through 20, which concludes the chapter, we witness Samson's continued association with the world. As well, we see the Spirit of the Lord's continued association with Samson. No, it does not show God condoning sin. It does show God's compassion, mercy, and love.

As we read the story of Samson, how many of us look with pity upon God's champion, never seeming to realize that we are no different or perhaps even worse. Samson lost many battles; he also won many, but, in the final analysis, he won the war. Above all, he would be included in God's great "Hall of Fame" in Hebrews 11. What a compliment despite his failures! But still, this must be said about every Christian - despite our failures as well.

CHAPTER 15

Verses 1 through 6 portray the folly of Samson's direction. From these passages we learn some things about God's direction, His will, and His plan.

It must be ever understood that God uses all things, whether they be good or evil, to further His cause and His work.

God was neither the author of, nor did He condone Samson's courtship with the Philistines; therefore, Samson failed. However, the Lord would use this connection with the Philistines to His (the Lord's) advantage, while at the same time never condoning Samson's actions. If Samson had conducted himself correctly, God would have found another way to have destroyed the Philistines, with Samson being greatly blessed. As it was, Samson would fail God regarding his association with the heathen, and even though Samson would suffer great loss, still, God would further His own cause by using what was at hand to destroy the enemies of Israel.

Verse 8 says, *"And he smote them hip and thigh with a great slaughter."*

Verses 9 and 10 portray the efforts of Satan to destroy and the Church's response to it.

The 9th verse says, *"Then the Philistines went up, and pitched in Judah."* Israel had been reduced to the position of being servants to the Philistines. How many Christians suffer the same lot in their spiritual lives? They are, in fact, servants to sin. Instead of them ruling Satan, Satan rules them.

The 10th verse says, *"And the men of Judah said, Why are you come up against us?"* Israel, God's chosen, was not seeking victory, but rather accommodation. Israel wanted no problem or difficulty. They would not put up with anyone who was "rocking the boat." This was their glorious opportunity to help Samson regarding the Philistines and would have resulted in tremendous victory. However, Israel had long since succumbed to the domination of the Philistines. This is what the 11th verse says:

"Knowest thou not that the Philistines are

rulers over us?" They had long since accepted this place and position. How tragic! God's chosen people not only allowed the enemy to subdue them but rather seemed to enjoy it. They would tolerate no Nazarite seeking to free them from their enemies. Never mind that Samson had been appointed by God. Never mind that his birth was a miracle birth. Never mind that the Holy Spirit mightily came upon him. Israel at this time had no desire for God, no desire for His miracles, no desire for His appointed leadership, nor any desire to be free. How so characteristic of the present-day Church. Satan rules us, and we "love to have it so."

The 12th verse says, *"And they said unto him, We are come down to bind thee, that we may deliver thee into the hand of the Philistines."* What a tragedy! They were quite ready to hand Samson over to a cruel death in order to maintain their status quo. This condition of spiritual degradation marks the history of the Church. They want no part of Samson; they want no part of the plan of God. So, *"three thousand men of Judah"* will seek to deliver him to the Philistines.

What was Samson's opposition to them? There was no opposition at all. Facing them with meekness, he said to them in the 12th verse, *"Swear unto me, that you will not fall upon me yourselves."*

What irony! Samson is pleading with his own people not to kill him. Jesus would say to Israel, *"You have stoned the prophets, and killed them that I sent unto thee."* Regrettably, the Church has not changed today. It cannot accept a Samson, neither can it accept the will of God. If the deliverer will not come by the hand of their committees, they will not accept him. And it must be added: the deliverer who comes by their hand is no deliverer at all. What could the Church do if it joined with God in attempting to touch this world for Jesus Christ? But instead, to maintain its status quo, it will almost invariably oppose that which is called of God. How tragic! How sad!

It seems from the 13th verse that they gave him their promise, *"But surely we will not kill thee."* Why could they not have said, "We will help thee," or "We will fight the Philistines with thee?" But the best he could get out of

them was their promise not to kill him. Instead, they would bind him and deliver him to the Philistines. God help us! The scenario has changed little. However, let's see what God's response was.

The 14th verse says, *"The Philistines shouted against him: And the Spirit of the Lord came mightily upon him."* This was God's response to Judah's backsliding, *"And the cords that were upon his arms became as flax that was burned with fire, and his bands loosed from off his hands."* The Lord would show Israel what He thought of Israel's position. As well, it must be added that Samson did not use his God-given strength against his own people as wrong as they were; he used it against the enemies of the Lord. Hallelujah!

The 15th verse says, *"And slew a thousand men therewith."* What a victory! What rejoicing there must have been in heaven. However, God's chosen people, the men of Judah, had no part in this great victory. Actually, they attempted with all of their strength to hinder it. It seemed they would rather be ruled by the Philistines than to have Samson, called of God, to deliver them. Man, as well as the Church, has little desire to follow God. The opposition of the world is bitter to the Nazarite Christian, but the opposition of the Church is more bitter. "God's victories are usually won with despised instruments." The feeblest instrument is destruction to the enemy if God be behind it.

The 18th verse says that the great victory occasioned a great thirst, *"And he was sore athirst, and called on the Lord."* Now, as God had sent His Holy Spirit to move through Samson, wreaking great destruction on the Philistines, His power would lead Samson to the *"Living Water."* The miraculous thing about the power of God is that it desires to work in every facet of our lives. God can meet your need not only in the realm of victory over demon spirits, but in your finances, your marriage, your home, even for a weary man of God who must have a drink of water.

The 19th verse says, *"But God clave an hollow place that was in the jaw, and there came water there out."* The well that refreshed the fainting Samson was not found in the jawbone but in Lehi, the hollow place. It was a depression in the ground and was so named.

Samson would name the place *"Enhakkore."* It meant "the caller's fount." It implies that he called on God for water, and God supplied the need. God is our supply; there is no other. May we depend upon Him for everything.

CHAPTER 16

Verses 1 through 3 have been portrayed by some as a type of Christ. I realize that the self-righteous would blanch at such a statement, but, at the same time, we must realize that when Jesus came to this evil-ridden world, He Who knew no sin would, in fact, become sin that we might become the righteousness of God in Him. He descended to this earth, not to have guilty union with its fallen inhabitants but to redeem them, and at the dawning of the day He burst the bars of the tomb and ascended to the heavenly Hebron, thereby securing eternal life for the degraded sons of men.

The balance of this chapter records Satan's ever-present efforts to rob the child of God of his spiritual power. The enticements and allurements of the world are powerful seductions. The one desire by the enemy is to rob Samson of his spiritual power. The Church does not want it, and the world will seek to destroy it.

The 4th verse says, *"Whose name was Delilah."* This was Satan's greatest effort to date. It is very easy to condemn Samson because he was at fault. But at the same time, there is a side of this that most Christians do not consider.

Whenever one is called greatly by God as Samson was, then Satan is allowed great latitude to hinder that call. If we think that Samson was little more than a wayward "oaf" who had little spirituality, then we miss the point altogether. He was a man of God; he judged Israel 20 years; the Holy Spirit mightily used him; and, as well, and certainly not least, he was listed in God's great "Hall of Faith" in Hebrews 11. Years ago one preacher appropriately said these words:

1. When you hear something bad about a fellow Christian, remember that you are hear-

ing gossip and treat it as such.

2. Even if you feel that you know the facts, still, you have little knowledge of the powerful spiritual warfare involved.

3. If you had been placed in the same position, would you have done any better or even as well?

If we would but remember this simple admonition, our judgment of other Christians would be much less severe.

Samson was wrong, and he sinned for which he would pay a terrible price. But, yet, in all of Israel there was no one who had the faith of Samson. He alone would begin to deliver Israel. And once again before judgment is passed, remember:

There were but 16 individuals listed in God's "Hall of Faith" (Heb. 11); Samson was one of them. The Church may not have wanted him and had no desire for his presence, but God wanted him.

The 13th verse says, *"If thou weavest the seven locks of my head with the web."* At first Samson had mentioned his hands and then his feet, but now he mentions his hair. If one is on Satan's territory, ultimately one will divulge that which Satan desires. There is no human being who can defeat Satan on his own ground. The Holy Spirit always respected Samson's will, as the Holy Spirit respects our wills. Ultimately, sin is a choice. Many times the Holy Spirit came upon him so that great feats might be performed. However, the Holy Spirit did not now come upon him to stop the spiritual slide to destruction. The Holy Spirit will treat us accordingly.

The 17th verse says this, *"He told her all his heart, and said unto her, There hath not come a razor upon mine head; For I have been a Nazarite unto God from my mother's womb. If I be shaven then my strength shall go from me, and I shall become weak and become like any other man."* Samson would cast his pearls before swine. In turn, the swine would rend him. He would take the holiest of the holy into the most wicked of the wicked.

The 19th verse records the terrible moment, *"And she caused him to shave off the seven locks of his head."* Even though there is no scriptural assurance, still, the Lord could have told Samson to braid his hair in seven braids. Seven is God's perfect number. It denotes fulfillment, totality, and completion. Now the seven locks are gone. The Scripture said, *"His strength went from him."*

Obviously, the question should be asked, "Why did the Holy Spirit not leave him when the other acts of sin were committed, such as marrying a heathen woman or committing adultery with a harlot?" These things were terrible sins, but, yet, the Holy Spirit remained with him.

The answer is found in the mercy and grace of God. We may lament the fact that God showed Samson mercy and grace during these nearly 20 years of repeated offenses. However, instead of criticism, we should thank God for it, because God deals with us with compassion, love, grace, and understanding.

And, most of all, God looked at Samson's heart. That and that alone is really the secret. As we have stated previously in our commentary on these chapters, "God does not operate His work on the principle of good and evil; He operates it from the principle of the heart." Regrettably, the Church does the very opposite. It, in fact, does operate from the principle of good and evil. Sadly, little by little, the Church begins to make up its own rules. Certain sins are looked at as awful; certain sins are ignored. However, God looks at the heart. It must forever be understood that if God did operate His work from the principle of good and evil, none of us would be left. As the Psalmist said, *"Lord, if thou markest iniquities, who shall stand?"*

The 20th verse tells us this, *"And he wist not that the Lord was departed from him."* It seems that Samson, by and large, despite the ideas of some, had been faithful to his Nazarite vows. During all of this time, he had not touched a dead body, he had not drunk anything that pertained to the fruit of the vine, neither had he cut his hair. In other words, at least as far as the Nazarite vow was concerned, he had been faithful. There could be no sadder note for anyone than the words, *"The Lord was departed from him."*

The 21st verse says, *"And put out his eyes."* Sadly, Samson would lose his eyes, but, in reality, he would gain his sight. Spiritually speaking, he will now "see" better than ever before. It says, *"And bound him with fetters,"*

NOTES

and then, *"He did grind in the prison house."* Chastisement is designed by God for His children for one purpose and that is to redeem them. If one will notice, through the entirety of the Word of God the Lord may use the heathen, the ungodly, and the wicked as instruments of chastisement; however, He will never use His own people. The moment a Christian, a church, or a denomination think they can perform the chastisement themselves, they have just stepped into God's territory. He reserves this right for Himself. He has said, *"Touch not the Lord's anointed, and do my prophets no harm."*

Yes, it is perfectly scriptural for the Church to take corrective action against a member who refuses to repent regarding sin. Even then, they are merely to disassociate themselves regarding fellowship, and then their action ends (I Cor. 5). However, the moment there is repentance, they are to be welcomed back into the fellowship (II Cor. 2).

There are many Christians at this moment who have lost their "eyes," are "bound," and do "grind in the prison house." The measures are stern, but, prayerfully, it should cause them to be humbled before God and have their faith thereby return. The Holy Spirit is very careful to point this out.

The 22nd verse says, *"Howbeit the hair of his head began to grow again."* One wants to shout, "Hallelujah!" because, in effect, this is what it tells us.

Samson is crying out to his God, begging for forgiveness, and asking the Lord to restore him. The Holy Spirit will answer his prayer.

The 25th verse says, *"Call for Samson that he may make us sport."* The Hebrew word for *"sport"* seems to imply that Samson danced before the crowd, becoming the most humiliating of spectacles. Satan relishes this moment, not knowing that what looks like Samson's defeat is, in effect, Samson's victory. God will hear him as he prays. There can be no higher acclaim than that.

The 30th verse records his death as a great victory. His faith put him in God's "Hall of Faith."

The 31st verse says, *"Then his brethren and all the house of his father came down, and took him, and brought him up, and buried him.*

It is remarkable that they now come. Why did they not come previously? Why did they not help him fight against the powers of darkness? The casual, carnal reader of this portion of Judges may in skimming the surface see only the failure of Samson; however, the Holy Spirit, in fact, shows us the failure of Israel instead.

CHAPTER 17

Chapters 17-21 record the terrible spiritual declension of Israel through the 400 odd years of the Judges. In reading these chapters, one can well see the terrible superstitious state of a nation, a country, or a people who are without God. God is talked about but not served. Basically, man makes up his own religion as he goes, completely ignoring the true Word of God.

At this time in Israel's history, they had the five books of the Law written by Moses, as well as the book of Joshua. They ignored all. Chaos, murder, and rebellion were the results. Man's carnal ways always lead him to think he can reach God by his own efforts. He will try through money and false gods.

In the 3rd verse Micah's mother says, *"I had wholly dedicated the silver unto the Lord from my hand for my son, to make a graven image."* She will call Him *"Lord,"* meaning *"Covenant God."* But she will understand very little of what she says.

How many Christians at this time are taking their money and using it for what purports to be the work of God, but, in reality, will make nothing but a *"house of gods"*? In the 5th verse the Holy Spirit, by using the word *"gods,"* emphatically states that none of this was the work of the Lord but was from man's unregenerate heart. Sadly, most of the Church world is spending their money to make a *"house of gods."*

Then the Holy Spirit in verse 6 emphatically states, *"But every man did that which was right in his own eyes,"* meaning that it was not right in God's eyes.

The 10th verse says that Micah thinks that this meandering Levite can be his own per-

NOTES

sonal *"father and priest."* He would buy him for $60, a suit of clothes, and three meals a day. How many preachers in the world of Christendom are for sale? Preachers sell out for various reasons: some for guaranteed sustenance, as this Levite; some to deacon boards; some to their denominational hierarchy. Sadly, this chapter would characterize the majority of today's preachers. Their services are for sale to the highest bidder.

The 13th verse says, *"Now know I that the Lord will do me good, seeing I have a Levite to my priest."* What a shame God's true Tabernacle was ignored. His Word was ignored as well. When the Church deviates from the Word of God, superstition, foolishness, and absurdity become the rule.

It was not God's will that a priest function in any household. They were to function only at the Tabernacle. No house was to set up its own place of worship; that, as well, must be at the Tabernacle. However, the Word of God was completely ignored. Regrettably, Micah's "positive confession" will do him no good. The next chapter will relate how that his gods are stolen, and his place of "worship" desecrated. It must be plainly understood that evil begets evil. A little leaven will ultimately corrupt and rot the whole lump.

CHAPTER 18

The 1st verse says, *"The tribe of the Danites sought them an inheritance to dwell in."* It seems that either they had not occupied their rightful inheritance designed for them by the Holy Spirit, or that a portion of the Danites (some 600 men) went to the extreme northern part of Israel to establish a second area of occupation. They would build a city there which they called *"Dan"* - thus originating the expression, *"from Dan even to Beersheba."* Men are ever desirous, it seems, to leave that which God has appointed for them and to draw their own boundaries. They fail as fail they must. The only thing the Danites established in the northern part of Israel was a continued and greater idolatry.

The 4th verse says concerning their dealing with the priest at Micah's house, *"And hath hired me, and I am his priest."* How many preachers in one way or the other are *"hired"*? They thus become hirelings.

The 5th verse says, *"Ask counsel, we pray thee of God, that we may know whether our way which we go shall be prosperous."*

Most of the Christian world is asking counsel of that which purports to be of God, but, in reality, is not. They are asking counsel of the psychologists, psychiatrists, and therapists, worldly counselors who claim to be biblical but are not. However, we seldom seek counsel of God.

Men always love to have their self-made plans sanctioned by religion. It all seems so righteous, holy, and desirable. The world today is full of religion, but precious little of God. It is full of *"little gods,"* but experiences precious little of the God of glory. How many people today are asking God to prosper their unscriptural way? It must be understood that God cannot bless anything that is unscriptural.

The 6th verse says that the hired priest would give them the blessing they so desired, *"Go in peace: Before the Lord is your way wherein you go."* The action of the Danites in asking this Levite to divine for them shows how far the Word of God had already departed from them. They should have been shocked and grieved at the Levite assuming priestly functions. As well, they should have been indignant of the insistence of a house of idols in rivalry with the Tabernacle of Jehovah.

The 18th verse says, *"And these went into Micah's house, and fetched the carved image, the ephod, and the teraphim, and the molten image."*

It should be ever noticed that religion and violence go hand in hand. Religion is not of God and never has been. Actually, Satan is the author of religion. Religion simply refers to a false way of salvation, in other words, a way other than the true plan of salvation that comes from God alone. Mankind has religious affections; therefore, he must have religious objects, such as the *"graven image, the ephod, and the teraphim."* The situation has changed little. Much of the world of Christendom exercises its affections even in these enlightened

times on *"images, pictures, crosses, and symbols"* in what is popularly called *"worship."* Even though what I have just stated largely pertains to the Catholic church, still, the world of Protestantism is little different. It is not said that the majority of the Protestant denominations worship *"images and ephods;* however, their worship is, by and large, toward a denomination, a doctrine, a place, or even a preacher.

The 27th verse says of the city called *"Laish,"* that *"they smote them with the edge of the sword, and burnt the city with fire"* - and they did it all in the name of God. More blood has been spilled regarding religion than for any other reason in the history of mankind. Where religion rules, violence results.

The 29th verse says, *"And they called the name of the city Dan."* Changing the name of the city from Laish to Dan did not in any fashion make it a city of God. The heathen they replaced, in fact, were closer to God than these Danites. The heathen did not know better; the tribe of Dan did!

The 30th verse says, *"And the children of Dan set up the graven image: and Jonathan, the son of Gershom, the son of Manasseh."* Actually, Jonathan was the grandson of Moses. His contemporary in the high priesthood was Phinehas, the grandson of Aaron. Manasseh had no son called Gershom. Instead of the word *"Manasseh,"* the Hebrew word is *"Mosheh,"* Moses. It was altered to Manasseh in some copies, but all ancient authorities agree that it was a substitution for Moses to spare the reputation of the great law-giver and preserve the honor of his name and memory among Israel. In I Chronicles 24:20 Jonathan is called *"Sheubael,"* which means *"he returned to God."* It is supposed to be the name of Jonathan after his repentance, and it is used of him afterward.

The 31st verse tells us of these idols being set up all over the land *"all the time that the house of God was in Shiloh."* Why was this so? The answer is obvious. There was no power of God at Shiloh. The priests were corrupt. Therefore, the land was corrupt. The Tabernacle had been turned into little more than an idol itself; therefore, the rest of the land would be filled with idols as well.

As the Church goes, so goes the nation. If you have a declining, weak, vacillating Church (as we now have), you will have a declining, weak, vacillating nation. The strength of America is the Church (the Body of Christ). The strength of the Church is its devotion to the Word of God. Regrettably, there is little devotion and little strength - so goes the nation.

CHAPTER 19

The closing chapters of the book of Judges picture the moral darkness that settles down upon a nation or a church when the Bible is disregarded, and men follow the religious and social teachings of their own hearts.

The terrible message of the Levite was necessary to awaken the nation. So deep was the impure sleep to which Israel had fallen.

In this chapter we will see terrible depravity. Verse 1 says, *"A certain Levite sojourning on the side of Mount Ephraim who took to him a concubine."* Concubines were secondary wives and customary in those times. However, Jesus would say that Moses, because of the hardness of their hearts, suffered them to have more than one wife, but that in the beginning it was not so. The Levite, therefore, in having a secondary wife was allowed such action because of his hardened heart, but this was not the perfect plan of God. Men usually try to push away from God's direction as far as possible. Oh, how so much the heart of man would be blessed if he would strive constantly to get closer to God, instead of seeing how far away he can get and still be "in grace."

The 2nd verse says, *"And his concubine played the whore against him."* Sadly, all of Israel was "playing the whore" against God.

Verses 3-9 portray this *"certain Levite"* going to get his concubine to bring her home. If the people had been as zealous toward God as they were their "property," how much different the nation would have been.

Verses 10-20 tell us of his stay at Gibeah.

The 11th verse says, *"Let us turn in into this city of the Jebusites, and lodge in it."* At that time the Jebusites, who were supposed to have

been exterminated by the tribe of Judah, still occupied Jerusalem. So, from this we see another failure on Israel's part. However, the 12th verse says, *"We will pass over to Gibeah."* They would have been far better off to have stayed with the heathen Jebusites than the backslidden Benjamites, for the tribe of Benjamin occupied Gibeah.

There is nothing more cruel or ungodly than the people of the Lord who have lost their way, and Israel had lost her way.

Verses 22-25 concern the Sodomites of Gibeah. Now we see further spiritual declension. The area was so corrupt, being very similar to Sodom and Gomorrah, that the Sodomites would demand that this "certain Levite" be brought out to them. Be careful to remember these were God's chosen people.

It seems that the host of the house was so corrupt that he would give his daughter and the concubine to these Sodomites rather than the man. It seems the daughter was not given, but the concubine was. The words, *"So the man took his concubine, and brought her forth unto them,"* speak of violence. In other words, he took her by force and gave her to these jackals. The further away from God people get, the more cruel and unfeeling they become. Israel at this time still had a semblance of religion, but they did not have God. Religion is always heartless, cold, unfeeling, and cruel.

The woman would be returned dead the next morning.

CHAPTER 20

If the 20th chapter of Judges were studied carefully by all Christians, we would see ourselves as God sees us and would, consequently, be less judgmental in our attitude to others.

While it is certainly true that sin must be dealt with and put away, still, we must be very careful as to how this is done.

The request from Israel to the tribe of Benjamin was just and right. They said in the 13th verse, *"Deliver us the men, the children of Belial, which are in Gibeah, that we may put* them to death." The consequences were that the entire tribe of Benjamin would resist this demand.

At this time Israel should have asked the Lord what they should do. However, they made their own plans, "and went up to the house of God and asked counsel of God, and said, Which of us shall go up first to battle against the children of Benjamin?" They did not ask if they should go up or how they should proceed. They merely asked which tribe should go first. In other words they made their plans and then asked God to bless them. If they had allowed the Lord to make their plans, possibly the lives of some 60,000 men could have been spared (vs. 18). This verse also says, "And the Lord said, Judah shall go up first."

The men of Israel were shocked at what happened in Gibeah, as they certainly should have been. However, they were blind to the activities and power of evil in themselves. This is the reason Jesus carefully warned us not to judge (St. Matt. 7:1-5). The Lord would use this occasion not only to punish Benjamin but to punish the balance of Israel as well. The reason was that Israel was not conscious that they themselves were guilty of sins which cried out for Divine wrath.

Judah, along with the balance of the Israelites, would lose the battle that day and see some 22,000 of their men killed.

The 23rd verse says, "Israel went up and wept before the Lord until even, and asked counsel of the Lord, saying, Shall I go up again to battle against the children of Benjamin my brother?" Once again the Lord will say, "Go up against him."

Still, despite the terrible slaughter that Israel experienced, it seems they were yet lacking in the acknowledgement of their own sin. How hard it is for us to see ourselves. How quick we are to condemn others. Self-righteousness can always point out the flaws, faults, and foibles of everyone else. However, self-righteousness cannot see its own crime, its own sin, or its own folly. It, thereby, continues to point a finger of accusation at others. Once again, and to be sure, the tribe of Benjamin had sinned sorely. They should have been dealt with but only in God's way. Israel did three things wrong:

NOTES

1. They failed to acknowledge their own grievous culpability in sins that were equally as bad.

2. They took it upon themselves to be God's instrument of chastisement even though they were not worthy and, indeed, could never be. God would not tolerate it .

3. They failed to ask God's guidance and direction regarding what He wanted. They set out to do what they wanted and, thereby, met with disaster.

So, God would use the occasion to humble not only the tribe of Benjamin, but all of Israel as well.

The second battle will also end in disaster. The 25th verse says, "And destroyed down to the ground of the children of Israel again eighteen thousand men." Now there will be true repentance before God.

The 26th verse says, "And came unto the house of God and wept, and sat there before the Lord, and fasted that day until even, and offered burnt offerings before the Lord." Now they were recognizing their own sin as well as the sin of Benjamin. Now the Lord will deliver Benjamin into their hand.

The 35th verse says, "And the Lord smote Benjamin before Israel." That day Benjamin would lose 25,100 men. But notice, the passage says, "The Lord smote."

How much our self-righteous indignation flares up when we think of the foibles of others. How so quick we are to show how unrighteous the other person is and how righteous we are. And how so quick God will tolerate none of it. Sin must be dealt with but in God's way. He will not tolerate self-righteous action. Self-righteousness cost Israel about 40,000 men. These were husbands, brothers, sons, and fathers who would not go home to their families, simply because they were so quick to judge the hideous sins of others and too quick to hide their own. However, God sees all. Let us say it again, "God sees all."

CHAPTER 21

Israel at this stage was governed by error,

excitement, and personal zeal, but not by the Word of God.

The men of Jabesh-Gilead certainly deserved punishment, and had Israel sought the Lord earnestly, seeking His will regarding the matter, no doubt, this chapter would have been very different. However, when man takes matters into his own hands, judging from a position of self-righteousness, the end result will always be disaster.

The 4th verse says, *"And built there an altar, and offered burnt offerings and peace offerings."* The Scripture does not say if they were at Shiloh or not, or if they were, why they did not use the brazen altar that was already there. It could be that some of the enemies of Israel during some of the servitude in the period of the Judges destroyed the brazen altar and even other parts of the Tabernacle. The following facts seem to apply:

1. If the altar that was built were elsewhere from Shiloh, this would not have been according to the direction of God.

2. Or if the altar built was at Shiloh, it shows that Israel had been lax in obeying God regarding the daily sacrifices.

3. Despite the error, it seems that Israel at least was trying to find her way back to God - hence, the building of the altar.

The 19th verse says, *"Behold, there is a feast of the Lord in Shiloh yearly in a place which is on the north side of Bethel."* Further directions were then given. This shows a sad picture of the condition of the nation at this time. Although the Benjamites lived within a short distance of Shiloh where the Tabernacle was pitched, so complete was their neglect of it that the minute directions of verse 19 had to be given them to enable them to find it. Furthermore, the mention of only one yearly feast - God having commanded three - was an added proof of departure from the Word of God.

Verse 21 says, *"Come out to dance in dances."* This showed how heathen customs had invaded the house of God, for no such dancing was ordained in the book of Leviticus. However, today's present church activity has changed little. Amusement has replaced worship.

The lessons of this chapter and of the entire book, as well, are painful but needed. They

NOTES

teach that there never comes a point in the Christian life when prayer, watching, and the Bible may be laid aside. No position in Grace, no height of Christian experience, and no succession of spiritual victories can keep the soul from falling. Only daily fellowship with God, meditation upon and obedience to His Holy Word, and the ever present power of the indwelling Holy Spirit can preserve the Christian from spiritual declension.

It should be ever noted that a past experience of Divine blessing, no matter how rich and wonderful, is useless to the heart that is out of fellowship with God. The past is wonderful and provides a foundation; however, there must ever be a rich present.

There can never be a compromise with evil either in Egypt, the wilderness, or in our possession.

The Christian's wisdom is to seek refuge in *"death to self"* (Rom. 6); however, this refuge demands a "daily dying" and a spiritual reality.

THE
BOOK OF RUTH

■

The book of Ruth is a delight. It portrays beautifully the grace of God. Types and shadows abound. In this book we will see how God can take our wrong, place it into His right, and bring from it a great blessing – but only if we submit all to God in total contrition and humility.

■

CHAPTER 1

The book of Ruth belongs in the period of the Judges as verse 1 states. It also says, *"That there was a famine in the land."* Famines were used by God as a portrayal of His anger because of spiritual declension. This famine no doubt signified such. America's problems regarding the weather, unemployment, and the economy can be laid at the doorstep of spiritual declension. So it is with every nation. God controls all; we must never forget that. Verse 1 continues to say, *"Bethlehem-Judah."* Bethlehem means "house of bread." Ironically enough, there was poverty in the plenty. It says, *"Went to sojourn in the country of Moab."* This speaks of the family of Elimelech. This too was forbidden by God. Repentance is the only cure for spiritual declension, but how often do we compound our failure by adding to it? This family would suffer much because of this decision.

The 2nd verse says, *"And they came into the country of Moab, and continued there."* They, no doubt, intended on staying but a short time. However, their sojourn would last for some ten years.

Verses 3, 4, and 5 tell of the price they paid. Elimelech will die along with the two sons,

Mahlon and Chilion. Of this family only Naomi was left with her two daughters-in-law, "Orpah and Ruth."

Naomi is a picture of Israel in the last days under the "famine of the Antichrist," when they will flee to "Moab." In the Great Tribulation period Israel will lose much. However, she will come back home where she will be saved by Boaz, who is a type of Christ. Then Naomi (Israel) and her daughter-in-law Ruth, who is a Gentile and typifies the Church, will come in to the riches of their heavenly Boaz, the Lord Jesus Christ.

The 6th verse says, *"For she had heard in the country of Moab how that the Lord had visited his people in giving them bread."* The Jewish Targum says that an angel spoke to her and gave this information. At any rate she knows the famine is over. God help us that the Spirit of the Lord will move so mightily that it will be heard in foreign countries and all over the world, for that matter. *"The Lord has visited his people in giving them bread."* Praise the Lord! So, Naomi will go home.

The 11th verse says, *"Are there yet any more sons in my womb, that they may be your husbands?"* Jewish law stated that if the husband died then the wife was to marry his brother. If that was impossible as it was in this case, she was to marry the next of kin who was not already married. Hence, Naomi's words, *"no more sons in my womb."*

In the latter portion of the 13th verse, Naomi says, *"The hand of the Lord is gone out against me."* Naomi was prone to blame the Lord for her ill status. Likewise, most of us do the same thing. It's very difficult for Naomi or for us to recognize the fault as our own. If, in fact, the hand of the Lord is against us, it is because we have sinned. Still, if we return to Him as Naomi is returning to Bethlehem, we will find that "the Lord's face will shine on us once again."

The 14th verse says, *"But Ruth clave unto her."* The greatest invitation given to anyone was given to both Orpah and Ruth. Sadly, Orpah would go back to her idols. But Ruth, having caught a glimpse of the God of Israel, made her decision in the way of righteousness. She could never go back to the idols, the ungodliness, or the wickedness. She found a better way.

What could have been in the hearts of both of these women that one would say "no" to the Lord, while the other would say "yes." Both had the opportunity, but only one would accept. Her name is in history forever as the great-grandmother of David, and, ultimately, of the Son of David, the Messiah.

The consecration that Ruth makes is recorded in the 16th verse, and is, in fact, the consecration that every person must make in coming to the Lord Jesus Christ, *"For whither thou goest, I will go; and where thou lodgest, I will lodge: thy people shall be my people, and thy God my God: Where thou diest, will I die, and there will I be buried: the Lord do so to me and more also, if ought but death part thee and me"* (vss. 16-17).

In this consecration there is no looking back. The die is cast. She will forever turn her back upon the world of idolatry and rebellion against God. She will forever throw in her lot with those who worship the God of glory.

The 18th verse says, *"She was stedfastly minded."* Those who are, make it. Those who are not, don't make it.

The 19th verse says, *"Is this Naomi?"* Ruth was with Naomi, and she was a Moabitess cursed by God because of the rebellion of her people. It was a disgrace for Naomi to have Ruth with her. So the question, *"Is this Naomi?"* is more an exclamation than a question. To have a Moabite who was cursed by God with her was unthinkable. However, the faith of this little Moabitess will reach out beyond the curse of God and bring down grace. God will always reward faith with grace.

Once again the 21st verse says, *"And the Almighty hath afflicted me."* Naomi blames

God, as we blame God. In reality, the problem is ours and ours alone. Whatever is wrong, it's our fault, not God's fault. This must ever be remembered, "It's not God's fault." It may be the devil's fault; it may be someone else's fault; or it may be mine alone or a combination of all three, but it's never God's. This must be forever settled. *"Let God be true, and every man a liar."*

The 22nd verse explicitly states by the Holy Spirit, *"So Naomi returned, and Ruth the Moabitess."* The Holy Spirit wants us to know who Ruth is, that we may know what Ruth becomes. He is at the same time telling us that as He changed Ruth's life, He can change our lives as well.

This verse also says, *"In the beginning of barley harvest."* This was Passover time. In effect, the Holy Spirit is saying, "When I see the Blood I will pass over you." There is no sin the Blood cannot cover. There is no life the cleansing of the Blood cannot change. It will change Ruth; it can change us.

CHAPTER 2

The 1st verse says, *"And his name was Boaz."* It also says he was *"a mighty man of wealth."* Boaz is a type of Christ, with Ruth, being a Gentile, as a type of the Church. The terrible losses in the land of Moab portray the dispersion and, thereby, judgment of Israel.

The 2nd verse says, *"Let me now go to the field, and glean ears of corn."* The welfare system of Israel in that day, which was given by God in the Law of Moses, stated that the poor during the harvest could go into the fields and glean the leavings. In this law the reapers were instructed to not glean the corners of the fields and leave a little something along the way. Furthermore, this shows that Ruth, even though a very lovely young lady, did not feel she was too good to stoop to the lowest social level in order that she and her mother-in-law might have food to eat. God can use no other kind. What a lesson we can learn from this. The old adage that says, "God helps those who help themselves," is not bad advice. In this we learn two things about Ruth:

1. Her willingness to work, even at the lowest task.

2. Her humility.

No wonder this young lady will be placed in the lineage of Christ in spite of her being a Gentile.

Verse 3 says, *"And her hap was to light on a part of the field belonging to Boaz."* The way the Holy Spirit had these words constructed tells us that He was guiding Ruth constantly. She may have thought that she chose a field by chance; however, it was no chance at all. The Lord will be involved in every aspect of our lives if we will only give Him an opportunity to do so.

The 4th verse says, *"And, behold, Boaz."* This man was extremely wealthy. He was of the tribe of Judah and in the direct line of the Messiah. He is mentioned 19 times in the book of Ruth. The greeting was, *"The Lord be with you."* And they answered him, *"The Lord bless thee."* This was the daily greeting of godly men and their servants in Israel. The master would say, "The Lord be with you," and the servants would answer, "The Lord bless you." It was equal to the master asking for the presence of God with the workers, and for their divine protection and preservation as they labored. It was the same when the servants expressed a desire for the master to be blessed of God that he might enjoy the increase of the field and have wisdom regarding how to use it for God's glory. If such mutual love and respect were shared alike by employer and employees in all lands, it would be as near the days of heaven on earth as possible.

The 15th verse says, *"Whose damsel is this?"* This question even though asked casually by Boaz would be answered by the Holy Spirit. Ruth would be the great-grandmother of David, and, thereby, of the Son of David.

The 6th verse says, *"It is the Moabitish damsel."* To those around her, Ruth was reduced to the level of gleaning as she was poverty stricken. Also she was a Moabitess with all its resultant connotations. However, heaven would answer the question in a much different way.

The 10th verse says, *"Then she fell on her face, and bowed herself to the ground."* This denotes her humility. The great compliment of

NOTES

humility is enjoyed by so few of the majority of Christendom, and, yet, it is possibly the greatest grace that God could ever bestow upon anyone. The only personal thing that Jesus ever said about Himself was, *"I am meek and lowly in heart."* Then Ruth would say, *"I am a stranger."* She was a stranger to the commonwealth of Israel, an alien to the promises of God. However, great grace would change her from a stranger to a child.

The 11th verse says, *"And Boaz answered and said unto her, It hath fully been shewed me."* Boaz made it clear that he had already been informed of her consecration as a proselyte to the Hebrew faith, and of her decision to leave her own people, her native land and its gods to live with people who were strangers to her. He then pronounced a blessing from the God of Israel upon her. The Hebrew Targum adds to this answer of Boaz to Ruth, *"It has been certainly told me by the word of the wise, that what the Lord hath decreed* (Deut. 23:3). *And it hath surely said to me by prophecy, that kings and prophets shall proceed from thee because of the good which thou hast done."*

The 12th verse says, *"Under whose wings thou art come to trust."* What a beautiful way of proclaiming the salvation of Ruth.

The 16th verse proclaims the cry of every child of God to the Heavenly Father, *"And let fall also some of the handfuls of purpose."*

The 20th verse says, *"The man is near of kin unto us, one of our next kinsmen."* Naomi was speaking of the law of the kinsmen redeemer. It meant to buy back a relative's property and marry his widow. When a Hebrew was forced to sell his inheritance because of poverty, the nearest relative was to redeem it for him (Lev. 25:25). If one acted as a kinsmen redeemer for one who had died without a son, he was obliged to marry the widow. Should he refuse to take possession of the property, he was not under obligation to marry the widow. Boaz had no right to redeem the property until the nearest kinsmen refused, which he did.

The 23rd verse says, *"The end of barley harvest and of wheat harvest."* The harvests were the most important time of the year in Israel. Events were reckoned from harvest times. The three great yearly gatherings of Israel took place at the time of the three harvest seasons (Ex. 23:16; 34:21-22).

1. The feasts of Passover, First-fruits, and Unleavened Bread were held every April in connection with the barley harvest.

2. The feast of Pentecost was held seven weeks later at the time of the wheat harvest. (These two harvests were the times of Ruth.)

3. The feast of Tabernacles was held at the end of the year at the time of the fruit harvest. The feast of Trumpets and the Day of Atonement preceded that of Tabernacles, and Israel would gather and remain at all three, which were held in October.

CHAPTER 3

This chapter is rich in its application and glorious in its study.

Verses 1-4 portray to us the entirety of the plan of God for our lives. It is as follows:

1. *"Shall I not seek rest for thee, that it may be well with thee?"* (vs. 1). In this instance Naomi is a type of the Holy Spirit. He seeks our rest that it may be well with us. In other words, the Holy Spirit has only good for us and nothing bad. He is the One Who draws us to Christ; He introduces us to the Lamb of God; He teaches us; He leads us; He guides us. His business is to ever lead us to Christ. Hallelujah!

2. *"Wash thyself"* (vs. 3). This speaks of the salvation experience, with the word *"wash"* being an apt description. The pollution, wickedness, filth, and stench of sin must be washed away. Literally, at salvation and, spiritually speaking, we are washed.

3. *"Anoint thee."* This speaks of the mighty Baptism in the Holy Spirit, hence, the anointing. Whenever the sinner comes to Jesus and is washed by the blood of the Lamb, then God anoints that person for special service. Every single Christian has a work to do for God. This is an anointing of power (Acts 1:8) that we may do the works of Christ.

4. *"Put thy raiment upon thee."* After salvation, the entire complexity of our life totally changes. Now, we put on the garment of praise. It is not only an inward change, but it is an outward change as well. No, it has nothing to

do with material externals. It is the change effected by the power of the Holy Spirit working within our hearts and lives. It speaks of an inward change that produces itself outwardly. The vile temper is changed to meekness; hate is changed to love. The outward garments include the shoes (spiritually speaking) which also mean a change of direction.

5. *"And get thee down to the floor."* This speaks of humility. Beautifully, the Holy Spirit brings us to the salvation experience. Regretfully, many stop right there. However, some go on to the Baptism in the Holy Spirit. As well, some experience a tremendous change within their lives, as all could experience if they would allow the Holy Spirit to have His total way. But only precious few arrive at the place of humility. Pride is the source of all sin; it is the opposite of humility. It is the hardest sin to strangle within our lives. The literal meaning of the word "humility" is "a river that runs low." Conversely, a river that runs high and fast destroys everything in its path, which is characteristic of pride.

The "river that runs low" provides life-giving nourishment and refreshment but destroys no one. Such is the child of God who has arrived at this place.

The 5th verse says, *"All that thou sayest unto me I will do."* Oh, if every child of God would only say this to the Holy Spirit. If one will notice the progression of the book of Ruth that person will see the gifts being supplied by Boaz to Ruth. For a time she was satisfied with these gifts, but the sweeter and deeper joy of union with Boaz himself was suggested to her by Naomi. This marks an important stage in Christian development. At first, the forgiveness that Christ gives, together with His other gifts, satisfies the heart, but later a deeper desire is awakened to be occupied with the Giver rather than with His gifts. The soul hungers for the closest intimacy with Jesus Christ.

The 8th verse says, *"And, behold, a woman lay at his feet."* The boldness of faith and love is very precious to the Lord Jesus Christ. He commands *"boldness"* in drawing near to Him (Heb. 4:16). To be timid, therefore, is to be disobedient, and it grieves His heart. Ruth's boldness in drawing nigh to Boaz made her all the more precious in his eyes.

The 10th verse says, *"Blessed be thou of the Lord, my daughter."* God loves faith.

The 11th verse says, *"I will do to thee all that thou requirest."* The Lord will not respond to wishful thinking, mere desire, or sometimes even need, but He will respond to faith.

The 12th verse says, *"Howbeit there is a kinsmen nearer than I."* The kinsman nearer to Ruth was the one referred to in 4:1 as *"Ho, such a one."* This individual represented the Law. In effect, it had first claim on the Lord Jesus Christ. However, it refused its right of redemption. It refused because the Law could never save. Only Boaz, our heavenly redeemer, could save.

CHAPTER 4

With this chapter we will pick up the last verse of the 3rd chapter. The 18th verse says, *"Then said she,* [the Holy Spirit] *Sit still, my daughter."* Herein lies the principle of salvation by faith. The 2nd chapter of Galatians contrasts two principles for the obtaining of life and righteousness:

1. Works of law – which pertain to religious ceremonies, personal moral efforts, and works of the flesh. It can never save.

2. Salvation by faith, depending on no works, but totally upon Christ – "sitting still."

The Holy Spirit teaches us that nothing can be had upon the first principle, but everything upon the second. So, Ruth would *"sit still,"* wholly trusting Boaz, and, as a result, obtain her heart's desire.

The 4th verse says, *"If thou wilt redeem it."* Sadly, the Law could never redeem. It was not actually created by God to redeem. It, in fact, was ordained by God that sin would appear to be sin, in other words to show the horror of sin. There was no redeeming virtue in the Law. "Ho, such a one" represents the Law.

The latter part of the 4th verse says, *"I will redeem it."* Man has ever felt that his own works, merit, and personal efforts could redeem himself. It fails as fail it must.

The 5th verse says, *"To raise up the name of*

the dead upon his inheritance." This speaks of those who are *"dead in sin"* being raised to the *"newness of life."*

The 6th verse says, *"And the kinsman said, I cannot redeem it for myself."* All who would try to earn their salvation by their good works, church membership, water baptism, the Lord's Supper, favorite doctrines, ad infinitum, must be warned that they as well will have to say, *"I cannot redeem it for myself."*

The 8th verse says, *"Therefore the kinsman said unto Boaz, Buy it for thee."* Our salvation was not purchased by such corruptible things as silver and gold, but by the precious Blood of Jesus. Truly, the Lord Jesus Christ did "buy it for us."

The 9th verse says, *"Ye are witnesses this day,"* as Boaz stated that all who observed these proceedings were witnesses, likewise, there are many witnesses to the great sacrifice of Calvary and the price paid for our souls by the Lord Jesus Christ. The Blood is a witness; the Word of God is a witness; our changed lives are a witness.

The 11th verse says, *"We are witnesses."* Let the unbeliever know and understand that at the judgment bar of God, all the witnesses who once before witnessed for him, now witness against Him.

The 11th verse continues, *"And be famous in Bethlehem."* Verses 11 and 12 are more of a prophecy than a statement. Bethlehem will ever be famous for us today, and, in fact, always will be. The reason being that the Son of David, the great descendant of Ruth, would be born in Bethlehem some 1200 years later. How beautifully and wondrously this prophecy has come to pass.

The 13th verse says, *"And she bare a son."* I wonder what her thoughts were when she looked at her son? Did she realize the tremendous consequences of it all? Probably not! And neither do we.

The 14th verse says, *"That his name may be famous in Israel."* This refers to Boaz, but even more so to our heavenly Boaz.

Christ is famous in Israel and the world. His fame in Israel will not blossom until the beginning of the millennial reign. Then this prophecy will be fulfilled in its glorious totality.

The 15th verse says, *"And he shall be unto*

thee a restorer of thy life." After the Great Tribulation which portrays Israel's great sorrow, Israel will be restored to life by her heavenly Boaz. He will *"nourish"* her, as he has nourished the Gentile Church. Truly, Boaz nourished Naomi in her old age, which is, as well, a type of Israel. He also married Ruth who is a type of the Church.

The 17th verse says, *"There is a son born to Naomi,"* simply meaning that he was born to Naomi through Boaz and Ruth who were fulfilling the Law by raising up seed for the dead (Ruth's dead husband) and keeping his name alive. Their seed was reckoned or counted to take the place of the dead to carry on his place in Israel (Deut. 25:5-10). This "Son" Who would be born of Israel (Naomi) will one day rule the world. His name ultimately would be "the Lord Jesus Christ," the Son of David, the Son of Abraham.

NOTES

THE
BOOK OF I SAMUEL

—■—

The book of I Samuel will record great defeats as well as great victories. It will record Israel's insistence at having her way rather than God's way, bringing great sorrow. It will, as well, record God bringing His plan into focus regardless of Israel's self-will.

Actually, as one reads this history of Israel consisting of the two books of Samuel and the two books of Kings, one will notice some slight differences in the two books of I and II Chronicles that gives Israel's history. The difference that is recorded is of vast significance to the child of God. For instance, II Samuel will record David's great failure with Bathsheba and her husband Uriah. This terrible failure, however, will be totally omitted in I Chronicles. Why? The answer is that the Holy Spirit in I and II Samuel and I and II Kings allows us to see the kingdom and the work of God as man sees it. I and II Chronicles is as the Holy Spirit sees it. No, David's great sin with Bathsheba was not ignored by God; quite the contrary was the case. However, when God forgives, the slate is wiped clean and the justification process is brought into force, treating the sin as though it never happened.

—■—

CHAPTER 1

The 1st chapter of I Samuel is a delight. It should increase faith in the heart of the reader.

The 1st verse says, *"Now there was a certain man of Ra-ma-tha-im-zo-phim, of mount Ephraim, and his name was Elkanah."*

The 2nd verse says, *"He had two wives."* Polygamy was a failure that seemed to be toler-

ated by God, at least in the Old Testament. In the garden of Eden the Lord gave Adam one wife, Eve. It would seem if He desired or intended that man have more, provision would have been made at that time. It wasn't made; therefore, one wife for one husband seemed to be the plan of God. This we do know, multiple wives generally caused great sorrow and difficulty. It says, *"The name of the one was Hannah."* This great lady of faith is the subject of this chapter. Few equal her in history. She will have the honor and the pleasure of introducing the coming Messiah under a name that he had not heretofore been known, *"His anointed,"* and to be the first woman to do so.

The 3rd verse says, *"And the two sons of Eli, Hophni and Phinehas, the priests of the Lord, were there."* This will set the stage for the corruption of Israel during the time of Hannah. These priests were wicked. Even though it does not seem that Eli the great high priest involved himself in their wickedness, still, he allowed his sons to conduct themselves as they chose. The 3rd verse as well says, *"To sacrifice unto the Lord of hosts."* This meant that Elkanah offered peace offerings to Jehovah, pouring out the blood at the foot of the altar, burning the fat with fire, leaving the breast and the right shoulder for the priest, and taking the rest for himself and his family to eat during the feast. Of the families' part each one received a portion, but Hannah was given a double portion. The Levites, the poor, the widows, and orphans were permitted to eat of this kind of offering also (Deut. 16:11).

The 5th verse says, *"But the Lord had shut up her womb."* There are many such statements in the Bible, especially in the Old Testament, proclaiming the Lord doing such and such things. Some would deny that the Lord had done this, claiming that He would not do so to anyone. However, that is incorrect. The Lord did exactly as the Scripture said He did. Why?

1. The Lord is omniscient (all-knowing) and omnipotent (all-powerful) and omnipresent (everywhere), meaning that He is in total control of everything. The Lord controls this planet and all its inhabitants; He controls all of the spirit world and its inhabitants, both good and evil. Satan can only do to a follower of the Lord what the Lord allows him to do. In other words, Satan is on a tether. So, in effect, everything that happens to a believer is either caused by the Lord or allowed by the Lord. No, the Lord does not cause anyone to sin, but He does allow anyone to sin who desires to do so. They will have to suffer the consequences, but God will allow them free will.

2. Whenever a great work is to be accomplished, the Lord allows or causes very severe things to happen to the individual involved to test one's faith. Great faith must be tested greatly.

3. God allows or causes such, in order that the individual may learn total dependence on Jehovah.

4. As well, there must be no effort of the flesh that succeeds; therefore, God makes it impossible (whatever the test) in order that the Holy Spirit may be the Author of the victory.

5. That which comes to every child of God, especially to those who are greatly called of God, comes in the manner of a test. God tests; Satan tempts. The difference is that temptation by Satan is to get us to do wrong. The test given by God is to get us to do right.

Verse 6 says, *"And her adversary also provoked her sore, for to make her fret."* The Lord allowed this adversary who was Peninnah, Elkanah's second wife, to do these things in order that Hannah might learn patience, compassion, and faith in God while not condoning Peninnah's wrong.

The 7th verse says, *"And as he did so year by year."* This test of faith went on for at least several years. Hannah's womb was barren, and, yet, she wanted a child so very much and a son at that. Her adversary would provoke her because she had no children. The implication

was that she told Hannah *"the Lord had shut up her womb"* because of sin, disobedience, or the curse of God that was upon her. The only thing that would sustain Hannah was her faith. It is not too difficult for faith to be sustained over a short period of time but under these circumstances and for testing year after year, most would fail. Therefore, Hannah's great faith is a tremendous source of encouragement for us all.

The 10th verse says, *"And she was in bitterness of soul, and prayed unto the Lord, and wept sore."* Never has there been any more earnestness in prayer than what is recorded here. This should encourage every person who has sought the Lord a long time for a particular thing and still has not received it. The Lord allowed all the hindrances and placed within her heart an overwhelming desire for that which was impossible in the flesh to conceive, namely, a son. The type of intercession and travail that is recorded here is seldom known or heard of in the modern-day Church. Hannah would not quit; she would not give up; she intended to stay the course until she received what God desired for her to receive.

The 11th verse says, *"And she vowed a vow."* The vow was that she would give the child to the Lord, and that he would be a Nazarite from her womb, *"no razor come upon his head."* Why it took several years for this prayer to be answered is not known. Perhaps, the consecration she makes as recorded in the 11th verse throws some light on the subject. Possibly, she did not want to give this child unto the Lord, at least in this fashion. But now, finally, she agrees to do so.

The 13th verse says, *"Now Hannah, she spake in her heart; only her lips moved, but her voice was not heard."* This type of prayer was spoken before the Tabernacle at Shiloh. It shows us that true prayer comes from the heart. It has little, if anything, to do with the volume of our profession. It is the heart that counts. The 14th verse is a sad indictment of that which was evidently taking place about the Tabernacle constantly. Eli says unto her, *"Put away thine wine from thee."* He thought due to her weeping and sore travail that she was drunk. Evidently he had seen much of such behaviour around the Tabernacle.

The 15th verse says that Hannah would answer thusly, *"But have poured out my soul before the Lord."* Most prayers are never answered simply because they do not reach the degree of travail or faith of Hannah.

The 17th verse says, *"And the God of Israel grant thee thy petition."* Whatever spiritual condition that Eli was in, still, God used him to give Hannah this great word of prophecy. Her prayer had been heard after all these years.

The 18th verse proclaims Hannah's faith. Even though there is no physical evidence of God answering this prayer, still, *"the woman went her way, and did eat, and her countenance was no more sad."* God had spoken to her soul; it would be done.

The 19th verse says, *"And they rose up in the morning early, and worshipped before the Lord."* This was before returning to Ramah, their home. How sweet this worship must have been. How many years had she left this place heavy of heart with her prayer unanswered? But now as she worships, her faith at long last is being rewarded. For this great 19th verse says, *"And the Lord remembered her."*

The 20th verse says, *"She bare a son, and called his name Samuel."* The name means, "ask him of the Lord."

The 22nd verse says that she will keep her vow before God and give up Samuel when he is weaned, *"I will not go up until the child be weaned."*

When he was weaned (vs. 24) which was between 3 and 5 years old, she would bring with her for sacrifice a bullock for a whole burnt offering, *"flour"* for a meal (thanksgiving) offering, and *"a bottle of wine"* which would be poured out at least in part before the Lord.

The 28th verse says, *"Therefore also I have lent him to the Lord."* The Lord had given Samuel to her, in turn, she would give Samuel back to the Lord forever. The latter portion of the verse says, *"And he worshipped the Lord there."* It would seem from 2:11 that the child Samuel was old enough to minister to the Lord at the direction of Eli, so he was old enough to worship the Lord as well. The pronoun "he" however, according to some versions is "they," referring to the parents, Samuel, and others if they were present at this great consecration.

NOTES

CHAPTER 2

The second chapter begins with the words, *"And Hannah prayed."* The following through verse 10 records Hannah's prayer or song. The Chaldee reads, *"And Hannah prayed in the spirit of prophecy."* This expresses the true nature of the song of prayer. It is poetic and prophetic and takes its place along with the songs of Moses, Miriam, Deborah, David, Elizabeth, Mary, and others - Psalmists and prophets whose inspired utterances have been recorded in the Bible. A particular characteristic of all these songs is that they sprang forth from the individual with reference to things of a personal nature, then widen to include the nature and acts of God, and the glories of the coming kingdom of the Messiah and of God among men in all eternity, making reference to things of the future.

The 2nd verse says, *"There is none holy as the Lord."* All of man's personal holiness is rejected by God. The only holiness that God recognizes in the heart of the individual is that which is imputed unto him by the Lord. In other words, imputed holiness. Man is not worthy of this holiness and, indeed, never could be. Therefore, it is given freely to us by God upon the acceptance of His Son and our Saviour the Lord Jesus Christ.

The 3rd verse says, *"Talk no more so exceeding proudly."* We are told here that God resists pride and arrogancy. It further says, *"The Lord is a God of knowledge."* God knows what is in our hearts, whether it is pride and arrogance or humility. It says as well, *"And by him actions are weighed."* It's not what man thinks that counts. It's what God knows that counts.

Verse 4 says, *"The bows of the mighty men are broken."* We are being told here by the Holy Spirit that man's strength, ability, and personal prowess do not count with God. And then it says, *"And they that stumbled are girded with strength."* This means that those who do not depend on their own strength, their good works, their church membership, or anything else man has, but, instead, depend totally on the Lord are *"girded with strength."*

The 5th verse says, *"So that the barren hath born seven,"* referring to Hannah who was ultimately given seven children. She had three sons and two daughters after Samuel, so the barren did bring forth. The seventh is not mentioned so it could be that she had a seventh child who did not live (vs. 21).

Verses 6-8 refer to the total authority and control of the Lord. The great problem of the Church is that it too often borrows from the world, attempts to incorporate worldly thought into the Church and then attempts to make it work. It never does. The Lord is dependent on no one. We as children of God should not be, either. If we look at all to man, we will receive the help that man can give, which is precious little. If we look to God, we receive the help that God can give, which is unending.

The 8th verse says, *"And to make them inherit the throne of glory."* This speaks of God taking the poorest of the poor from the dust, placing within them His salvation, and causing them to inherit the throne of glory. This speaks of salvation when man is raised out of dust to the glory of God.

This tremendous statement in verses 6, 7, and 8 is capped by the words, *"for the pillars of the earth are the Lord's, and he hath set the world upon them."* This means that everything hangs upon God and God alone. This is a fact of Divine government which is distasteful to man.

The 9th verse says, *"He will keep the feet of his saints,"* implying that the Lord is the only One Who can. And then it says, *"For by strength shall no man prevail."* Man's personal strength, which constitutes the flesh, is his greatest adversary. Too often the Church depends upon its own strength. The child of God follows suit. However, irrespective as to how educated, consecrated, dedicated, rich, or talented we may be, by trusting in these we shall fail.

The 10th verse extols the coming Messiah. When Hannah used the word "king," this was the second prophecy of God's king, the Messiah. Balaam was the first prophet to call Him king (Num. 24:7). This was sóme 40 to 60 years before Israel had kings.

And then she said, *"And exalt the horn of his*

anointed." This is the first reference to the Messiah where this term, "his anointed" is used. So, Hannah was the first one to use this term, making it even more special because she was a woman. From this point on others take up the theme of God's Anointed One - the Messiah (Psa. 22; 45:7; Isa. 61:1; Dan. 9:25-26).

So ends the song of Hannah which should be read together with the song of Mary (Luke 1:46). The theme of both is one and the same, Christ, His glory as king and priest: and God's action in government in raising up the meek and casting down the proud.

The 12th verse says, *"Now the sons of Eli were sons of Belial; they knew not the Lord."* The great Tabernacle of God, the center of Israel's worship, where God was to dwell between the Mercy Seat and the Cherubim, had now sunk to the level of total spiritual declension.

The 17th verse says, *"For men abhorred the offering of the Lord"* because of the terrible sins of Eli's priestly sons. The duty of Hophni and Phinehas as commanded by God in Leviticus was:

1. To burn the fat of the peace offering upon the altar.

2. To accept the breast and shoulder as their portion.

3. To eat them sodden, that is boiled.

4. The remainder of the animal was to be partaken of by the worshiper.

5. These men little adhered to the command of God. They took what they wanted by force, causing those who brought their sacrifices to abhor such.

The further away from God that the Church gets, drawing closer to man's ways, likewise, the more cruel and vicious the Church becomes. The people then become mere pawns, being "used" to hold up a religious structure. The further away from God that a denomination gets, the more demands are placed upon its preachers and people - demands that are always unscriptural.

Verse 18 says, *"But Samuel ministered before the Lord, being a child, being girded with a linen ephod."* The ephod that he had was not the same as the ephod of the high priest but a linen robe of the ordinary priest and Levites. Still, there were many irregularities in the

Tabernacle program. First of all, no child was supposed to minister to the Lord in the Tabernacle. Even though the Lord would not hold this against Samuel, He would hold it against Eli, who was responsible.

Verses 22-26 speak of Israel's continued spiritual declension, especially concerning the sons of Eli. Verse 22 says, *"They lay with the women that assembled at the door of the tabernacle of the congregation."* Why did God not slay these two priests as he slew Nadab and Abihu? The answer is because He was then dwelling in power in the camp, but in Eli's day He had withdrawn Himself because of Israel's apostasy. An electric wire will kill if it is charged but will offer no harm if not charged.

The Church today asks for revival, as it should. However, Holy Ghost revival will not only bring great life, but it will bring great death as well. The closer to the Lord the Church comes, the more quickly its sins are judged. The reason these priests could sin with impunity was because God had vacated the premises.

The 27th verse shows the great mercy and compassion of God, *"And there came a man of God unto Eli."* The message of this man of God would be one of judgment upon Israel, Eli, and his sons.

Verse 35 says, *"And I will raise me up a faithful priest."* This speaks of the coming Messiah Who will rule in the millennial reign, and also the priests who will serve under Him, the "anointed forever."

CHAPTER 3

Even though the 3rd chapter begins in a foreboding manner, still, it presents a highlight in that God will now begin to speak to Israel. Despite the sin, iniquity, and failure, Israel's glory days are about to begin. It must be ever remembered that these days begin only with God speaking. If God is silent, there may be much religious activity in the Church, but, still, there is nothing accomplished. If God speaks, there may be much failure, but, still, great things will be accomplished.

NOTES

The 1st verse says, *"And the child Samuel ministered unto the Lord before Eli."* Eli seemed to place his sons as more precious to him than the Law of God. Still, it seems that in some respects his heart cried out to Jehovah. The Scripture says, *"And the word of the Lord was precious in those days; there was no open vision."* This means that revelations, prophecies, visions, and contact with Jehovah was scarce and, therefore, valuable. There was no prophet with whom the revelations and secrets were known to dwell and to whom anyone could go for help in time of need and public crises. Regrettably, nothing better can be said of the modern Church at this time. The word *"precious"* means *"scarce."* There are hundreds of thousands of churches in America, Canada, and other parts of the world, but there is precious little true Word of God being preached in these churches. Psychology is preached; theory is preached; philosophy is preached; and the latest fad that can be found in the majority of Christian bookstores - but precious little of the Word of God.

The first three verses picture the moral condition of the nation. Night reigned; the lamp of God was going out in the Temple; the high priest's eyes had grown dim so that he could not clearly see. Both he and Samuel were asleep.

Verse 3 says, *"And ere the lamp of God went out in the temple of the Lord."* The *"lamp of God"* was the golden candlestick that sat immediately to the left as the priest entered the Tabernacle. It gave light for the table of shewbread and the altar of worship. The lamps were to be served each morning and evening with fresh oil being supplied. There seemed to be little concern, and the lamps were going out.

How many pulpits today would fall under that condemnation, *"the lamp of God went out."* Today, the lamp of God is the Bible. If it is not preached and proclaimed, there is no light. Let it be stated once again, "The Bible is the only light in the world. There is no other light."

The 4th verse says, *"That the Lord called Samuel."* At this dark moment in Israel's history God chose to reveal Himself, not to some influential personage, but to a little boy.

The 7th verse says, *"Now Samuel did not yet know the Lord."* This is speaking of the first revelation of God given to Samuel. He, being a child, was not acquainted with the way that God spoke and revealed Himself.

For the Church to survive, the Lord must speak. For the preacher to have the anointing to proclaim, the Lord must speak.

The 10th verse says, *"And the Lord came, and stood, and called as at other times, Samuel, Samuel."* This was the very same one who said, *"Martha, Martha"* and *"Simon, Simon."* There is nothing greater that can happen to a nation, a church, a preacher, or a child of God than to hear the voice of God. True, the Lord spoke to Samuel in an audible voice. However, the Lord speaks to the child of God constantly by the power of the Holy Spirit. Actually, when the sinner is convicted by the Holy Spirit in order that they may give their heart and life to the Lord Jesus Christ, this is the Lord "speaking" to that person. Without this they could not be saved. Likewise, the child of God ideally should walk so close to the Lord that the Lord will speak to that person, constantly giving guidance, direction, and instruction. If he doesn't speak to the person, it is because there is no place in his heart for the Holy Spirit. If He is there, He will speak.

This is the greatest thing that could happen to Israel. Even though at the outset God's voice was little understood, still, He was speaking. May God speak to the preachers, the churches, and to our nation.

Verses 11-14 proclaim the message that God gave. It would be a message of judgment. Still, better to receive a message of judgment from God than no message at all. Because with every message of judgment that God gives, there is also a call to repentance. Sadly, too often the message of judgment is not heeded. It would not be heeded here either. The message was fourfold:

1. I will do a new thing in Israel, at which all ears will tingle.

2. In that day I will perform against Eli all things which I have spoken concerning his house.

3. When I begin, I will also make an end.

4. The house of Eli shall not be purged of their iniquity with sacrifice and offering forever.

NOTES

The 15th verse says, *"And opened the doors of the house of the Lord."* This reveals one of the duties in the ministry of Samuel. He was a doorkeeper in the house of the Lord.

The 18th verse says, *"It is the Lord: let him do what seemeth him good."* Eli was godly enough personally to acknowledge the message of God and submit to His judgment pronounced upon his house. He knew Jehovah would do nothing but what was right, even in judgment. This afforded him time to prepare to meet God and set his house in order. Genuine repentance and turning to righteousness on the part of Eli and his sons would have averted this judgment. Regrettably, there was no repentance.

The 19th verse is astounding in its complexion. It says, *"The Lord was with him, and did let none of his words fall to the ground."* Prophecies in this day and age are given galore with very few coming to pass. Many call themselves prophets without God calling them to be prophets. Still, God is continuing to set in the Church apostles, prophets, evangelists, pastors, and teachers. The words, *"let none of his words fall to the ground,"* mean that Samuel spoke only as God inspired him, so that every prediction was literally fulfilled. He also gave only sound and Divine counsel to Israel, so that all his counsels were received as coming from the Lord.

The 21st verse says, *"For the Lord revealed himself to Samuel in Shiloh by the word of the Lord."* This expression simply means, "by the Spirit of prophecy" as in Revelation 19:10.

CHAPTER 4

This chapter, much like the 3rd, is foreboding, but it will usher in the fulfillment of the prophecies given to Samuel.

The word of the Lord was revealed unto Samuel and, thereby, to Israel. It would arouse the hostility of Satan, for the 1st verse says, *"Now Israel went out against the Philistines to battle."* Whenever God reveals Himself, the hostility of the enemy is aroused. Directly, God revealed Himself in Shiloh; the Philistine revealed himself in Aphek.

The Scripture says, *"Beside Ebenezer."* It was not named this until some 20 years later (7:12). This was to be a day of defeat, but, yet, faith would look forward to a future day of victory. The word "Ebenezer" means "stone of help," which refers to the Lord Jesus Christ. This should be a comfort for every child of God that today's defeat can become tomorrow's victory.

The 2nd verse says, *"Israel was smitten before the Philistines."* It says they lost 4,000 men. Every defeat and every victory, are allowed by God for specific purposes. Greater defeats were coming. They could have been avoided if Israel at this time would have repented.

The 3rd verse says, *"Let us fetch the ark of the covenant of the Lord out of Shiloh unto us."*

If Israel had fallen on their faces before God in weeping and contrition, repenting of their sins before the door of the Tabernacle, the future could have been different. Instead, they would use the Ark as a magic symbol, thinking, somehow, it would atone for their evil and guarantee the presence and blessing of God. How so much today does the Church follow suit. We think that all of our "religious activity" will atone for our sins and backslidings. The Ark itself was not the glory. It only represented the glory. The Ark could do nothing. It was the God Who dwelt between the Mercy Seat and the Cherubim Who did it all. The Church has much symbolism, but that's all it is, symbolism. If God is not there, no victory will accrue. It must be clearly understood that nothing can take the place of broken, contrite, and humble repentance before God. Regrettably, like Israel, the Church will do almost anything except repent.

The 4th verse says, *"And the two sons of Eli, Hophni and Phinehas, were there with the ark of the covenant of God."* Being near the Ark did not make them holy. Actually, it would only bring death. These two individuals would intrude into the Holy of holies where only the high priest should go once a year, and then not without blood. They would come filled with sin and without blood. As a result, they would die. The only way we can approach the living God is

by blood, the Blood of Jesus Christ. The Church seems to have arrived at a place of such spiritual declension that it thinks it little needs the Blood of Jesus Christ. In place of the Blood, it has substituted constitutions and by-laws, rules and regulations, psychological counseling, ad nauseam. It is only the Blood of Jesus that can take away sin.

The 5th verse says, *"All Israel shouted with a great shout."* So is our activity. Religious business abounds. Too often we shout, when, in reality, our shouts are empty and hollow. Too many try to cover up the bareness of their possession by the loudness of their profession.

The 7th verse says, *"And the Philistines were afraid, for they said, God is come into the camp."* How wonderful it would have been if God had come into the camp. How many of our churches shout when there is nothing to shout about? It's easy to learn the rhetoric, enjoy the symbolism, and to have the "noise of the shout" as the 6th verse says. But that's all it is too many times, "noise."

For this terrible sin, Israel would experience an even greater defeat. The 10th verse says, *"And there was a very great slaughter;"* The message was taken to Eli and, thereby, to Israel. It was in three parts.

1. *"Israel is fled before the Philistines"* (vs. 17) - 30,000 men are dead.

2. Your two sons, Hophni and Phineas are dead.

3. The Ark of God is taken.

The message would kill Eli as well. No doubt he was stunned at the loss of his sons and some 30,000 men of Israel (34,000 total). However, the loss of the Ark of God was the greatest loss of all. The 18th verse says, *"His neck brake, and he died."* It says, *"And he had judged Israel forty years."* His time was filled with spiritual declension and wickedness. How much different it could have been if he had followed the Lord.

His daughter-in-law seemed to understand the plight of Israel more than all. She died at the birth of her child, naming him "Ichabod," (vss. 19-22) with the word meaning *"the glory is departed from Israel."* There could be no worse message. The glory of God was the strength of Israel. Now, the glory was gone. The glory of God, as well, is the strength of the

Church, not our beautiful buildings, nor our educational institutions, nor our expensive appointments, but the glory of God. The chapter would close with the words, *"for the ark of God is taken."*

This was the first time the Ark was captured in over 500 years, and, in fact, the only time it was ever captured (note the results). The Ark remained in the Temple of Solomon until the Babylonian captivity, at which time Jeremiah is supposed to have taken it and hidden it in a cave. There it was supposed to remain, it is said, until the coming of the Messiah.

We never read of the worship of God at Shiloh after this. The Ark was actually never brought back to Shiloh and the Tabernacle. It remained in Kirjath-jearim nearly 70 years. (The 20 years mentioned in 7:1-2 is only for a specific period.)

The Ark was mentioned once again in the record of Saul's reign (I Sam. 14-18). In David's reign it was brought to Jerusalem from Gibeah. The Tabernacle was also in Jerusalem at that time (II Sam. 7:2; 11:11). The Ark was taken with David in his flight from Absalom and then brought again to Jerusalem (II Sam. 15:24-29). Solomon brought it into the Temple after its completion. When Nebuchadnezzar took Jerusalem some 500 years after the time of David, there is no mention of the Ark of God being taken with the other utensils to Babylon. As stated, tradition says that Jeremiah hid the Ark in a cave.

Some modern claims have been made that the Ark has been found in a cave under Jerusalem but has been sealed off by the Arabs and is unapproachable by the Jews. One or two have said that they actually saw it before the opening was sealed over. No validity can be given to this claim.

---■---

CHAPTER 5

The Ark of God would not be a blessing to unrepentant Israel, but it would be a curse to the mocking Philistines. We will learn from this chapter that God rules all.

The 1st verse says, *"And the Philistines took*

the ark of God." Knowing nothing about the ways of God, they would automatically think that Israel was defeated because their god Dagon was more powerful than Israel's God, Who was represented by the Ark. Unregenerate men make stupid judgments regarding God. Paul would say that *"the natural heart understandeth not the things of the Lord, for they are spiritually discerned."*

The 3rd verse says, *"Dagon was fallen upon his face to the earth."* At Ashdod, one of the five main cities of Philistia, there was a temple of Dagon, the national god whose shape was like that of a man at the upper part and that of a fish at the lower part. Here is where they brought the Ark and set it by Dagon and where God began to perform miracles of judgment upon the Philistines.

This was God's way of telling the Philistines that *"every knee shall bow, and every tongue shall confess."* It must be clearly understood that there is one God. All these others that call themselves gods, in effect, are no gods at all. They were actually representatives of demon spirits.

At first, the statue of Dagon fell to the earth. However, the 4th verse says, *"And the head of Dagon and both the palms of this hands were cut off upon the threshold."*

Little by little the Lord inflicted punishment with an attempt, as well, to get the Philistines to repent. The 6th verse says, *"But the hand of the Lord was heavy upon them of Ashdod, and he destroyed them."*

At first He would tell them their god was no God at all by the statue falling to the earth. Then by the severing of the head and the hands, He would tell the Philistines that their god had no power against Him. Now the pressure will increase by tumors appearing on their bodies.

The 7th verse gives their answer. Instead of repenting and begging God to forgive them, thereby, accepting the God of Israel, instead, they say, *"The ark of the God of Israel shall not abide with us."* It is amazing how many people and even some Christians think they can run from God. Their response is, "Get rid of God." Entire churches and, actually, entire denominations have done the same thing. The Lord being present always upsets men's plans. He does things not printed in the bulletin. His intention is to get us to repent. Sadly, most reject that offer and, instead, send Him away as did the Philistines.

The 11th verse says that even after seeing the great power of God, the Philistines would not repent. They continued to say, *"Send away the ark of the God of Israel."*

Some 1100 years later Jesus would visit the district of Gadara, which was across the sea of Galilee. He would cast some 2,000 demons (and possibly many more) out of the one referred to as the maniac of Gadara. This man would experience a tremendous miracle, being restored to his right mind. And, yet, the people of the district, when coming to observe the one who Jesus had miraculously restored, would place more value on the hogs than they did on the message of Christ. They would implore the Lord of glory to leave their area.

When America was fighting for its independence from the British, the little island country of Haiti was blooming with prosperity. It is said that leaders in Haiti at that time would promise their island kingdom, then so prosperous, to be given to Satan if he would only allow them their independence from the French. We should note the contrast.

America asked God to help her receive independence from the British. Haiti asked Satan. Now, some 200 years later as one looks at Haiti, the horror of that decision made some 200 years ago is obvious.

As well, America is saying today that we have no time for God. It is not so much the "separation of church and state." It is, rather, "the separation of God and state."

Paul says in the first chapter of Romans, *"And as they did not like to retain God in their knowledge."* He goes on to say that God would turn them over to a reprobate mind. America has made it plain and clear from judgments rendered by the Supreme Court down to the lowest level that we "do not like to retain God in our knowledge." Therefore, America is swiftly becoming a reprobate nation.

The 11th verse says as well, *"The hand of God was very heavy there."* With glaring opportunity for repentance spurned, there is nothing left but "the heavy hand of God."

At this juncture in their history the Philistines would lose the glorious opportunity of

accepting the Lord of glory as their Saviour. Instead, they would continue to opt for their idol gods. They would ultimately be totally destroyed.

CHAPTER 6

"In the country of the Philistines seven months." During the seven months that the Ark of the Lord was in Philistia and especially with God's great display of power, the Philistines had a golden opportunity to repent and serve the God of Israel. Despite seeing the great power of God during the seven long months, there was no repentance, only the hurried desire to get rid of the "Ark of the Lord." Amazing is the ability of man to resist and reject God. The deep ignorance and incurable rebellion of man's heart appear throughout this episode. When God evidenced His mighty power before the Philistines, they were convinced but not converted. Men proudly declare that they will become Christians if convinced by evidence. They deceive themselves. They are by nature Philistines, and Philistines they will remain in spite of the most overwhelming proof of God's Being and power.

The 4th verse says, *"What shall be the trespass offering which we shall return to him?"* They would make for Him *"five golden emerods, and five golden mice."* The reason for giving golden emerods and mice was because both had been a part of the plague upon them - the emerods marred their bodies and the mice marred their land. In both the Septuagint and the Vulgate we have information that the country swarmed with mice during this plague of emerods upon the people.

The Lord, of course, would not accept their golden trinkets. We smile, but I wonder if we are any different today. We try to give God our talent, education, ability, money, and beautiful buildings. He will accept none of it. He will only accept His Son Jesus Christ and the Blood that was shed at Calvary's Cross.

The 6th verse portrays the religious knowledge of the Philistines. Their advice was carefully presented, *"Wherefore then do ye harden your hearts, as the Egyptians and Pharaoh hardened their hearts?"* It is amazing how much they knew, and, still, they would continue to resist. Their entire effort was to escape judgment, not to repent.

The 7th verse says, *"Now therefore make a new cart."* On this cart they would place the Ark of the Covenant. This was contrary to the Law of God, because the Ark was to be borne by priests who were consecrated and otherwise qualified to do so. Being ignorant of the Word of God, they would escape the judgment of this act. However, David's *"new cart"* would produce sad results.

The 19th verse says, *"And he smote the men of Bethshemesh, because they had looked into the ark of the Lord."* First of all the people of Israel, except for the soldiers in the previous battle lost, had never seen the Ark of God. As well, they had not been taught the proper respect and reverence for this which was the holiest of God. Their curiosity was little different than the Philistines. The Scripture says, *"Even he smote of the people fifty thousand and threescore and ten men."* There is some question here regarding this number, simply because of the smallness of the population in this area and the similarity of Hebrew letters which could have caused a copyist mistake. The Septuagint reads, "He smote among them 70 men, including 50 of the men's thousand." Even 70 slain in such a small place would be a great slaughter. At any rate men died because of their casual curiosity.

The 21st verse says, *"Come ye down, and fetch it up to you."* The Philistines, like the inhabitants of Beth-shemesh, would desire that someone else come and get the Ark.

Multiple thousands of churches have requested the same. They would rather have man's ways, man's rules and regulations, man's constitutions and by-laws. When the cover is pulled off and we are put to the test, the Church, as Beth-shemesh, little wants the Lord. If God is there, the spectacle of His blessing and judgment are side by side. The Church has repeatedly through the ages tried to have only one aspect of God, namely the blessing. That is not possible. There is a *mountain of blessing* and a *mountain of cursing.* There is redemption, and there is judg-

NOTES

ment. Consequently, there is heaven, and there is hell. The God of blessing only does not exist. If, in fact, He did exist, He would not be worth serving. Moses said, *"I set before you the way of life and the way of death."*

CHAPTER 7

This chapter portrays a great revival under the preaching of Samuel. From this move of God, we will in the modern-day Church learn some things that we desperately need to know as well.

The 1st verse says, *"And brought it into the house of Abinadab."* This is speaking of the Ark of God. There is much evidence that it was neglected and not at all respected. Kirjath-jearim was about eight miles northeast of Beth-shemesh. It would remain in this location for approximately 20 years (vs. 2), in which time Israel was more or less under the yoke of the Philistines. It seems it would remain there during the 40 year reign of Saul. David would reign approximately ten years (7 years in Judah and three years over the whole of Israel) before the Ark would be brought to Jerusalem. This is a total of approximately 70 years. Furthermore, when the Ark was finally found by David, it seems that it had been discarded and was standing alone out in a field next to the woods. The Psalm of David says, *"Lo, we heard of it at Ephratah: we found it in the fields of the wood"* (Psa. 132:6). What a tragedy! Yet, I wonder if the glory of God has not been abandoned in the modern Church even more so than it was with Israel.

The 2nd verse says, *"The time was long."* The time is always long when we are out of the will of God. This was not the place for the Ark of God. Its place was in the Tabernacle. The 2nd verse says as well, *"All the house of Israel lamented after the Lord."* Too often men want God, but they want Him on their terms. To this wish He will not respond.

Verse 3 gives us the tremendous recipe for Holy Ghost revival. It says, *"Samuel spake."* Samuel preached, as is obvious. Today, more than ever, we need preachers. We have talk show hosts, seminars, symposiums, musicals, concerts, and dramas, but, God, give us somebody who will preach! The following is his message:

1. *"If you do return unto the Lord with all your hearts."* God deals with the heart; He does not deal with the intellect. He would not stoop to that level. Men at times make a show of returning to the Lord with outward externals. The only kind of return that God will recognize is that which is from the heart. The very word "return" speaks of repentance, with the word meaning to "do an about-face." This is the desperate need of the Church.

2. *"Put away the strange gods and Ashtaroth from among you."* The Church today looks with amusement at the Israel of old and their "strange gods." Do we fare any better? Today, the strange gods of false doctrine, error, self-esteem, psychology, health and wealth, and dominion teaching are rife. These are strange gods. Over television a short time ago one of the espousers of one of these doctrines said, "Jesus died on Calvary to glorify His self-esteem." This is blasphemy pure and simple, and, yet, Pentecostal preachers were seated with this man nodding their head in the affirmative. How the mighty have fallen!

3. *"Prepare your hearts unto the Lord."* As Israel of old was encouraged to prepare their hearts unto the Lord, so, we should earnestly do the same. How can one do that? The answer is simple, prayer and the Word of God. Prayer meetings where the heart is bared before God and where the Lord is encouraged to cleanse away the spiritual debris is the greatest preparation ever. The Word of God should be earnestly solicited. It and it alone holds the answer to man's dilemma. Sadly, modernists in all ranks of the Church are claiming that man is facing problems today that others at different times did not have to face. Consequently, they say that the Bible is ill prepared to address itself to these difficulties. Hence, both the Bible and psychology are needed, they say. This is heresy to say the least and will address itself in the next part of Samuel's message.

4. *"Serve him only."* This is a strange term, but it means Israel served the Lord as well as Baal, Ashtaroth, and others. This is exactly the mode of present-day religion. We will serve the

NOTES

Lord and psychology; the Lord and the virgin Mary; the Lord and a particular denomination.

If we serve Him, the Scripture plainly says, *"He will deliver you."* Deliverance is man's need, not counseling. Satan is trying to destroy the human family. He, by and large, holds humanity in his clutches. All the counseling, therapy, and psychoanalysis in the world cannot set the captive free. Only the power of God can deliver. Jesus said, *"The Spirit of the Lord is upon Me to preach deliverance to the captives."* Hallelujah!

The 4th verse declares that Israel *"did put away Baalim and Ashtaroth, and served the Lord only."* The Lord help us to put away our modern Baals.

The 6th verse portrays a strange thing. It says, *"And drew water, and poured it out before the Lord, and fasted on that day."* What was the significance of this? Samuel was saying to the Lord, in effect, "We are as weak as water." Actually, there is nothing anymore weaker than water that has been poured out. This is the place where man must come to before God can finally begin to perform a work within his life. Israel says, *"We have sinned against the Lord."* How so hard it is to admit this. Even above that, how so hard it is to get the Church to admit that. Jesus was able to get the thieves and harlots to admit it. He was never able to get the religious leaders of Israel to admit it.

The 7th verse says, *"And when the Philistines heard."* Holy Ghost revival will always inspire Satanic opposition. Most churches experience no opposition from the evil one simply because there is no move of God in their midst. Satan would throw his best at Israel. It says, *"the lords of the Philistines went up against Israel."* Satan's chief demons were instructed to stop this move of God. The 7th verse says, *"They were afraid of the Philistines."* Israel had been under Philistia rule for over 20 years. They were by and large unarmed. Still, they had one weapon. *"Cease not to cry unto the Lord our God for us"* was their appeal to Samuel. When we get in trouble, how so often we cry unto everyone except the One Who can really save us, "the Lord our God."

The Philistines were an ominous looking crowd. Their soldiers were dressed in the finest of armor. They had on their heads giant plumes that protruded from the top of their helmets, making them look even bigger than life. In other words, they were fiercesome. Satan comes against us *"as a roaring lion."* Still, he is no match for the Lord of glory.

The 9th verse says, *"And Samuel took a sucking lamb."* This little baby lamb was a type of Jesus Christ dying in His weakness, and, thereby, saving us in His strength. In other words, His weakness was His strength. Paul said the same thing in II Corinthians 12: *"When I'm weak I am strong."* This little lamb was offered as a *"burnt offering wholly unto the Lord."* The answer was the Blood of the Lord Jesus Christ in type. The Bible says, *"The Lord heard him."* One wants to shout, Hallelujah!

At the very time the sacrifice was being offered, typifying the price that Jesus Christ would pay at Calvary some 1100 years in the future, the 10th verse says, *"The Philistines drew near to battle against Israel."* The Scripture says, *"But the Lord thundered."* Whatever this thunder was it *"discomfited them."* Heretofore, the Philistines had seen Israel's weak defense of symbolism. Now they were seeing the Lord of glory. Regrettably, the world has seen little of the God of glory at this particular time. It has seemingly seen little more than all the cathedrals, symbolism, statues, relics, buildings, and poor fallen men. It has seen little of the Lord. When it does, it will never forget it.

The 12th verse says, *"Then Samuel took a stone."* The stone was a type of Christ. Jesus said, *"Upon this rock I'll build my church."* Paul said, *"That Rock was Christ."* Israel's defense was Christ. Our defense is Christ. Jesus must be the centerpiece of our salvation or we have no salvation at all. The water poured out was a type of Christ; the sucking lamb was a type of Christ; the whole burnt offering was a type of Christ; the stone was a type of Christ, *"and called the name of it Ebenezer"* meaning, *"the Lord helped us."* The Lord desires to help us but only on His terms.

The 13th verse says, *"All the days of Samuel."* God would not work through the priesthood; He would not work through other mighty men in Israel; He would work through Samuel. And it says, *"The Philistines were sub-*

dued." The Church does not need more beautiful buildings. It needs men of God.

The 14th verse says, *"Were restored to Israel."* The Lord wants to give back all that Satan has stolen. And then, *"There was peace."*

CHAPTER 8

Someone has said that God has no grandchildren; true. A father cannot transmit faith to his sons, nor can he make prophets out of them. Regrettably, Samuel's sons were no better as judges than Eli's sons were as priests.

Samuel was probably about 20 years old when Eli died. At that time he began his judgeship. At this particular time he must have been about 60 years old - when he started making his sons judges in Israel. He continued to judge and exercise the office of the prophet during most of Saul's reign. He is supposed to have died about two years before the death of Saul (25:1), which would have made him near 100 years old at death.

The 5th verse says, *"Now make us a king to judge us like all the nations."* Israel's sin was twofold:

1. They wanted their own ways instead of God's ways.

2. Their desire for a king to be like other nations was a work of the flesh and not of the Spirit. It would, thereby, bring untold sorrow.

A king whom they could see, although he would be only a feeble, foolish, and dying man, was preferred to an unseen Almighty king, Wise and Eternal.

The nation wished to be like the surrounding nations, forgetting that their glory and happiness consisted in being unlike these nations.

Multitudes of professing Christians today are in the same condition of spiritual feebleness. They want the Lord but at the same time want to be like the world.

The 6th verse says, *"But the thing displeased Samuel."* The request for a king was evil in Samuel's eyes because of the rebellion and impatience of the people in not waiting for the king whom God had promised (Gen. 17:7,

16; Num. 24:17; Deut. 17:14-20).

The 7th verse says, *"For they have not rejected thee, but they have rejected me."* Oftentimes, when we think we have rejected only a man and for reasons we think are valid, in reality, we have rejected God. This is a sobering thought that we should deeply contemplate. Here, a nation would reject God's way and bring upon themselves terrible difficulties. For the reign of Saul, the king demanded by the people, would be little more than a reign of dissension, foolishness, rejection of God, and division. Without fear of contradiction one can say that this is the bane of the modern Church and the modern Christian. Too often we reject the work of the Spirit, demanding the work of the flesh, bringing destruction upon ourselves.

The 9th verse says, *"Now therefore hearken unto their voice: howbeit yet protest solemnly unto them."* God in His tender love would plainly tell them of the treatment they would receive from the king of their own choice. Six times the fact is repeated: *"He will take."* Oftentimes, through a work of the flesh, we can bring things into existence which are contrary to God's will. No matter the face that we put upon it, it will only bring troubles and difficulties. How often and how lovingly God by His Holy Spirit, through His Word, and through His servants, warns His children of the bitter consequences to follow if, in self-will, they pursue a desired path. As with Israel, God permits self-will to have its own way. How much better it would have been if Israel had placed themselves and their difficulties in God's hands and asked Him to plan for them.

The 19th verse says, *"Nevertheless the people refused to obey the voice of Samuel; and they said, "Nay."* Too often our response to God is "No" rather than "Yes."

Just as impoverishment and servitude resulted as predicted by Samuel from Israel's self-willed establishment of a human government, so spiritual poverty and loss of liberty follow in the Christian life when there is subjection to the commandments and doctrines of men instead of to the authority of the Word of God.

NOTES

CHAPTER 9

In referring back to the previous chapter and setting the stage for the 9th chapter, Israel would grow weary of Samuel because he was flawed. He allowed his sons to take bribes and to pervert judgment. As stated, he was flawed. Regrettably, all of God's men are flawed. There has never been one who wasn't. In a great test of faith, Abraham would go down into Egypt and lie about his wife. This was a far more grievous sin than one would suspect. It was designed by Satan to hinder the "seed," the Lord Jesus Christ. Isaac, likewise, would be flawed, attempting to bless Esau when God had told him at the birth of the boys that Jacob should be blessed. Jacob would stumble for so many, many years in such a flawed state before finally becoming "Israel." Oh, that David would not have had the blot of Bathsheba and Uriah in his life, but he did. So, due to these flaws, the Church, by and large, does not want or desire God's men. It would rather resort to a committee, a symposium, an organizational chart, in other words, a work of the flesh. Saul would be a work of the flesh. His 40 year reign would bring nothing but sorrow.

The 2nd verse says, *"He was higher than any of the people."* He probably stood about seven feet tall. He looked like a king, and, so, the people would gladly accept him.

For a moment let us look at the contrast to the Apostle Paul. Both men had the same name; both were members of the same tribe; but the one exhibits the power of the "flesh," the other the power of the "Spirit." As to physical strength, and a personal attractive appearance, Saul of Tarsus was wholly unlike King Saul, for Paul's "bodily presence" was weak (II Cor. 10:10). However, King Saul "was a work of the flesh" and would bring only destruction. Paul of the New Testament was "a work of the Spirit" and would bring only life.

Beauty and height of stature distinguished the son of Kish, but his life illustrated the fruitless effort of the "old man" to live as the "new man" (Rom. 7).

His reign is a demonstration of how "the

flesh," the natural will of man, no matter how cultivated and religious, is wholly a stranger to the springs and energies of the spiritual life. The "flesh" can never do anything right. It is either too courageous or too cowardly, too forward or too backward, too weak or too strong, too wise or too foolish.

The 3rd verse says, *"And the asses of Kish Saul's father were lost."* David would "keep" his father's sheep. Saul would "lose" his father's donkeys. The 6th verse says, *"And he said unto him, Behold now, there is in this city a man of God."* The greatest thing that can happen to any city is for a "man of God" to reside there. And, yet, the world has absolutely no idea what is in its midst, if, in fact, it be so blessed to have such.

The 15th verse says, *"Now the Lord had told Samuel in his ear a day before Saul came, saying."* Even though Israel was doing wrong and their choice would be disastrous, still, the Lord would do all within His power to give them a man.

The 16th verse says, *"To-morrow about this time I will send thee a man out of the land of Benjamin."* Most probably it was God's choice for David to be the first king of Israel. Satan, of course, would attempt to stop this by a work of the flesh, for Saul would attempt to kill David many times. The flesh will always try to kill the Spirit.

Strangely enough, the entire Gospel message is pictured beautifully from verses 3 through 27. It is as follows:

1. The wanderer vainly seeks a lost possession (vss. 3 and 4). Man on this journey of life is seeking something he has lost, but he's not quite sure as to what it really is. It is actually the seeking of lost innocence.

2. Man is totally ignorant of the Saviour. Saul was totally ignorant of the man of God, Samuel (vs. 6). The servant told Saul of this "man of God." We must be Christ's servants and tell the lost about Jesus.

3. Man tries to purchase redemption when he does hear of it. Saul would try to purchase Samuel's favor (vss. 7 and 8). Sinners conceive that it is possible to purchase salvation by religious emotions and efforts - which are absolutely valueless.

4. The Lord depends on us, His body, to

show the unbelievers the way. There were *"young maidens"* who would show Saul where Samuel was (vs. 11).

5. Jesus is always looking for the sinner, as verses 14 through 19 show us how accessible Christ is and that He is always on the watch for those who are coming to Him. Samuel was watching for Saul, as Jesus at Sychar's well was watching for the wayward woman.

6. To the believing sinner Jesus will give fellowship for which the heart craves, also He will give instruction and guidance and satisfy the hunger of the heart. Samuel tells Saul all of these things (vs. 19).

7. To receive all of this, God requires humility. Saul would evidence such as, *"the smallest of the tribes of Israel"* (vs. 21). His life would have been far different if he had remained in this posture of humility.

8. The Lord will honor those who come to Him. Likewise, Samuel would honor Saul by having him *"sit in the chiefest place among them that were bidden"* (vs. 22). This is a beautiful picture of the Lord taking a beggar and making him a king.

9. And last of all, the Lord will show the seeking sinner the *"word of God"* which explains the mysteries of life (vs. 27). As well, Samuel would show Saul the *"word of God."* The Bible holds the answer to man's every dilemma. All other is false and deviate. The Word of God is *"a lamp unto our feet."* Now, we have a road-map for this journey of life.

CHAPTER 10

The 1st verse says, *"Then Samuel took a vial of oil, and poured it upon his head."* This was the inaugural of Saul, the first king of Israel. It was the people's choice and not God's. Hence, it would be a work of the flesh and, thereby, bring great sorrow to Israel. As well, this work of the flesh would do all within its power to hinder the coming work of the Spirit who would be David, God's choice regarding Israel's first king. Despite objections Israel would demand her way. God would acquiesce to their desire. They wanted Saul, so Saul they would have.

Samuel would take a vial of oil which denoted the anointing of the Holy Spirit and anoint Saul. All the outward trappings of God's help were there. However, that which was outward could not change that which was inward - an evil heart of unbelief. That which is not God's will can easily be outwardly anointed by men, and often is. Still, it is not God's choice and will bear no good fruit. With the exception of Samuel in this position, I think that one could say without fear of contradiction that every single man who is anointed by man, like Saul, is a work of the flesh, which characterizes almost all of the modern-day Church. That which man anoints, God will not. Sadly, that which God anoints, man will not.

Still, God would give Saul three signs that would symbolically portray to him what God expected and how spiritual victory could come to Saul. Sadly, Saul was so spiritually dull that he little understood the pictures God painted for him. The three signs are as follows:

1. *"Then thou shalt find two men by Rachel's sepulchre."* Rachel was the first sign to Saul. Jacob loved Rachel greatly, as God loved Saul. But, still, Rachel was barren as Saul was barren. Part of her problem was her hatred of Leah (Gen. 29:31). Then Rachel would resort to superstition (mandrakes-Gen. 30:14). Saul will ultimately resort to witchcraft, as well. Thankfully, Rachel would find her way with God. Saul would not. If Saul had greatly considered this "sign" and its meaning, maybe his future would have been different.

2. *"And there shall meet thee three men going up to God to Bethel."* These three men would be carrying lambs, bread, and wine. They were ordinary men, not of the rich class of Israel. The common people would hear Jesus gladly. As well, Saul was being told by the Lord, "You are to take special care of these; do not oppress them."

3. *"After that thou shalt come to the hill of God, where is the garrison of the Philistines."* Wherever there is a *"hill of God,"* Satan will attempt to establish a *"garrison of the Philistines."* The Lord was telling Saul that Israel must be delivered from the Philistines.

The 6th verse says, *"And shalt be turned into another man."* This would be done by *"the Spirit of the Lord."* God would do all that He

could to help Saul be the man that he should be.

The 9th verse says as well, *"God gave him another heart."* God can give certain things, but He will not force anyone to live right.

In the 11th verse they ask, *"Is Saul also among the prophets?"* This shows that Saul had been anything but among the prophets in times past. Actually, he lived only a few short miles from the home of Samuel, and, yet, he had no knowledge of this great prophet. In effect, the Lord was telling Saul that he must change the company he had kept in the past.

In verse 19 we're told the chilling warning of Samuel was given to Israel once again, *"And ye have this day rejected your God."* In all of this we see the tender hand of the Lord repeatedly warning the people and then trying to help Saul, but it would prove to be to no avail.

The 22nd verse says, *"Behold, he hath hid himself among the stuff."* This speaks of Saul's beginning humility. If he had remained in this posture, the Lord would have helped him, blessed him, and used him. But sadly, he became the opposite of this beginning.

The 23rd verse says, *"He was higher than any of the people from his shoulders and upward."* To the people Saul looked like a king. They would make the mistake that so many make. Man judges almost entirely from outward observance. God looks at the heart. Outwardly Saul measured up. Inwardly he would be the opposite.

The 26th verse says, *"A band of men, whose hearts God had touched."* The Lord gave to Saul the proper individuals to help him get started in the kingdom. There was no excuse for Saul's future actions or his conduct. Neither is there any excuse for ours.

CHAPTER 11

The 1st verse says, *"Then Nahash the Ammonite came up and encamped against Jabesh-Gilead."* This chapter will reveal a great victory, with Saul following the Lord. The victories would have continued if Saul had continued to follow the Lord.

"Nahash" was the head of the Ammonites, bitter enemies of Israel. This chapter portrays a perfect picture of Satan's attempt to dominate God's people. It also portrays God's picture of victory.

The word "Nahash" means "bright shining serpent." This is a perfect picture of Satan. The word "Jabesh-Gilead" means "hill of witnessing." Satan will encamp against us to destroy our "witness." The Israelites desired to "make a covenant" with Nahash. They even offered to serve him. However, his terms were high, as Satan's terms always are. Regrettably, the Church ever tries to make accommodations with Satan, even offering to serve him if he will not greatly oppose.

Verse 2 proclaims the condition of the covenant, *"That I may thrust out all your right eyes."* Why this? The answer is simple. When the soldier held up his shield to ward off the enemy, the tip of the shield covered his left eye, with his right eye looking out over the shield to fight the approaching adversary. With the "right eye" thrust out, Israel in effect would be blind. The reason most Christians do not oppose Satan is because they are blind. They have already made a covenant with him by allowing him to thrust out their "right eye." They cannot now see to fight, therefore, they are of no difficulty to the evil one. Millions of Christians are constantly saying, "I cannot see what's wrong with . . . ." No, they cannot see because they are blind.

Thankfully, Israel does not give in to these demands. The 3rd verse says they would ask for "seven days respite." Nahash would hold them in such contempt that he would accede to their request. I wonder if Satan looks at the modern-day Church, and, likewise, holds it in contempt?

Verse 6 says, *"And the Spirit of God came upon Saul when he heard those tidings."* This is the answer and the only answer to Nahash the *"bright shining serpent."* The Spirit of God must move. We cannot fight Satan in our own strength; we can only overcome him by the Spirit of God. The 6th verse says as well, *"And his anger was kindled greatly."* There is a place for righteous indignation. Jesus was angry at the deplorable state of the Temple, "His house." It is time that the Church becomes angry at

NOTES

what Satan has reduced us to. It is time that the individual Christian, likewise, becomes angry at the demands placed upon him by Satan.

The 7th verse says, *"He took a yoke of oxen and hewed them in pieces."* He would tell Israel that if they did not help Him, all that they had would be hewed to pieces by the Ammonites as the oxen were. We will have victory over Satan, or Satan will have victory over us. The symbol that Saul sent to the whole of Israel was, no doubt, generated by the Spirit of God. It would serve to awaken Israel admirably. The 7th verse would say as well, *"And they came out with one consent."* If the Church can get over its divisions, there is little limit as to what it can do.

The 11th verse says, *"That Saul put the people in three companies."* Those three companies are, "the Name of Jesus, the Blood of the Lamb, and the Word of God." With this, they *"slew the Ammonites until the heat of the day."* Hallelujah!

The 15th verse says, *"And all the people went to Gilgal."* Gilgal means, "the reproach has rolled away." It was also the place of circumcision, hence, separation. It was appropriate for the kingdom of Israel to be started and accepted by all Israel at Gilgal, for this was their first place of entrance into Canaan (Josh. 5:2-10). Circumcision, in effect, meant "death to self." It represented the "good" side of man that must be repented of. We have little difficulty of repenting of the bad things. We have much difficulty repenting of the good things. However, it is mostly the "good" things that are killing us. If Saul had taken a lesson from the place called "Gilgal," his victories could have continued. But "self" would be Saul's greatest enemy, as "self" is our greatest enemy. The "good" of our "self" comes from the good side of the "Tree of the Knowledge of Good and Evil." Because it is "good," it deceives us. However, it must be repented of and forsaken as well as the "bad." The pseudo gospel of "self-esteem" is no panacea for mankind's greatest problem. Actually, it exacerbates the difficulty, rather than alleviates it.

CHAPTER 12

The 1st verse says, *"And Samuel said unto all Israel, Behold I have hearkened unto your voice."* Their voice had demanded a king. God's voice had spoken the very opposite. God would tell Samuel, "Give them what they want." However, it would bring leanness of soul.

The 2nd verse says, *"My sons are with you,"* which speaks of Samuel rectifying the failure he had made regarding the appointing of his unregenerate sons as judges over Israel. They had taken bribes and perverted judgment. Eli did not correct his sons, Samuel did.

The 5th verse ties in with verse 2, *"He is witness."* How much better off we would be if we understood that at all times, *"He is witness."* Sadly, too often we conduct ourselves as though God does not see.

Verse 6 says, *"It is the Lord that advanced Moses and Aaron."* Regrettably, the Church seldom seems to understand this. Through religious politics, religious leaders attempt to advance individuals of their own making. However, if the Lord does not advance the subject, there is, in reality, no advancement. As well, we should only desire the advancement that God gives. It is seldom that religious leaders advance anyone except to make that person beholden to them.

Too many students attend Bible colleges with the idea that their denomination will "furnish them with a place to preach." To attend such an institution is to trust in man for advancement instead of God. This is totally contrary to the Word of God and to the ministry. The God-called preacher of the Gospel is to trust God for advancement and God alone. While it is true that men help and are sometimes used by God, still, the total trust must be in God and not man.

The 17th verse says, *"That your wickedness is great, which you have done in the sight of the Lord, in asking you a king."*

The 18th verse adds, *"So Samuel called unto the Lord; and the Lord sent thunder and rain that day."* This was called *"a great thing"* (vss. 16-17), because rain in the time of harvest

was so exceptional that it would be taken as a Divine act of judgment. Why did God show this type of disapproval?

He wanted them to know that as the storm destroyed their crops that were ready to be harvested (at least in the immediate locality), likewise, their present direction would bring blight instead of blessing.

The 20th verse says, *"Fear not, you have done all this wickedness: yet turn not aside from following the Lord, but serve the Lord with all your heart."* A terrible sin had been committed that would lead in the wrong direction, thereby, bringing great difficulties. However, Israel was encouraged to continue serving the Lord. Satan takes advantage of our failure by telling us, "It is no use." God forbid that there be any type of failure. However, if so, the answer is not in discontinuing our serving the Lord, but, rather, in throwing ourselves at His feet, asking forgiveness, and continuing to serve Him *"with all your heart."*

As the 21st verse says, the temptation is to *"go after vain things, which cannot profit nor deliver."* Whether we succeed or fail, God is the answer. Whether there is victory or defeat, God is still the answer. Everything else is "vain." It has no answer.

And then we have the great promise in the 22nd verse, *"For the Lord will not forsake his people."* What a glorious statement! If we will come to Him despite the failure, He will not turn us away. The only way that God will reject a person is for that person to reject the Lord and to continue unrepentant in that rejection. If we will come to Him, no matter how much a failure, He will not forsake us.

Even though Israel had sinned greatly in demanding a king, still, Samuel said, *"God forbid that I should sin against the Lord in ceasing to pray for you"* (vs. 23). I wonder how many Christians sin daily by not praying for those whom they need to pray for.

CHAPTER 13

This chapter will account for a great victory in war but great sin on the part of Saul. The victory will be won by the faith of Jonathan, not of Saul.

The 1st verse that says, *"Saul reigned one year,"* seems to speak of Saul reigning in spiritual victory for this particular time. However, in his second year he started to lose his way with God.

The 3rd verse then says, *"And Jonathan smote the garrison of the Philistines."* This was the first act in the war for independence from Philistia and was probably the first feat at arms. Jonathan, a man of faith, would do it and not Saul, his father.

The 5th verse says, *"And the Philistines gathered themselves together to fight with Israel."* Whenever faith acts, Satan opposes; and, hence, the Philistines are found quickly encamped at Michmash. Satan, who knows and dreads the power of faith, brought up his agents as the sand which is on the seashore in multitude.

Saul represents Christendom as officially the visible kingdom of God upon earth but corrupted and enslaved; yet, within this broken kingdom it is still possible for faith to win her victories as Jonathan won this.

That which seeks its strength in the wisdom and energy of man can never go beyond the source from which it springs. But that which energized the heart of Jonathan was the Divine gift of faith, and because Divine, it was victorious over the world in spite of the universal ruin which met Jonathan's eye on every side. That which is born of God overcomes the world (I John 5:4).

Verse 6 says, *"Then the people did hide themselves."* Unbelief always exaggerates a problem; faith minimizes it, at least faith in God. The Church today, spiritually speaking, basically hides itself in "caves, thickets, rocks, and in high places, and in pits." We should be touching the world with the great and glorious Gospel of Jesus Christ, but, instead, we are *"distressed."*

The 9th verse says, *"And Saul said, bring hither a burnt offering to me, and peace offerings and he offered the burnt offering."* At this juncture Saul would intrude into the priests' office. Only faith can wait on God. Self-will can never wait; it must always "do something." The flesh must always trust its own energy. It sur-

mises that because it is a religious "burnt offering," that it will be sanctioned by God. The Church today, spiritually speaking, offers burnt offerings galore. However, they are offerings that God will not accept. We are seeing here, with the very first king of Israel, man placing himself in charge of God's work on earth. It has not ceased from that day until this. The Pope claims he is the vicar of God on earth. The protestant world claims its denominational heads are the vicars of God on earth. Preachers claim they are the vicars of God on earth.

However, the 13th verse says, *"Thou hast done foolishly."* God's Divine order must never be circumvented. His Divine order is always faith that is based on His Word and never in rules and regulations.

The cry of God will always be for *"a man after his own heart"* (vs. 14). How difficult it is to find such. We have men after their own hearts; after other mens' hearts, after the heart of their denominations; but seldom after God's own heart.

The 15th verse says that Israel had *"about six hundred men"* to face 30,000 chariots and 6000 horsemen, and innumerable soldiers on foot. Against this host was only one man and God; that man was Jonathan.

Israel had been so denuded by the Philistines that the 19th verse says, *"There was no smith found throughout all the land of Israel."* The blacksmith was the one who helped make weapons. It would be the same in a spiritual sense as the prayer warriors in our Churches. How well would Satan have succeeded if it could be said, "There was no intercessor found throughout all the Church." The intercessor before God is the one who forges the spiritual weapon, *"For the weapons of our warfare are not carnal, but mighty through God."* I wonder if the condition of the Church today is any different than the Israel of this particular time. For the 22nd verse says, *"That there was neither sword nor spear found in the hand of any of the people."*

Actually, there were two weapons in all of Israel, and they were *"with Saul and with Jonathan."* Saul's weapon was useless because it was held in the hand of unbelief. Jonathan's weapon, which was faith, would totally defeat the Philistines.

CHAPTER 14

Now faith moves Jonathan, and Jonathan moves by faith. The 1st verse says, *"Come, let us go over to the Philistines' garrison."* Faith will ever move toward the enemy. Jonathan would be that man of faith. Whenever faith is found, God displays His strength. Thus, the ugliness of unbelief in Saul is contrasted with the beauty of faith in action in Jonathan.

Jonathan represents faith that will "go." However, the 2nd verse says, *"And Saul tarried."* Unbelief never goes anywhere. He would remain with his 600 men while Jonathan went with only his armor-bearer. Faith does not ask permission, *"But he told not his father."* It just does what needs to be done.

Neither does it advertise itself, for the 3rd verse says, *"And the people knew not that Jonathan was gone."*

Faith never lessens nor creates difficulties. Her path is open, very narrow, and made difficult by sharp rocks on either hand. *"A sharp rock on the one side, and a sharp rock on the other side"* (vs. 4).

The 6th verse says, *"It may be that the Lord will work for us, for there is no restraint to the Lord to save by many or by few."* Faith's fair flower looks never so fair as when blooming in such a rocky and savage defile, beset with enemies, such as pictured here. Jonathan did not think of himself, and his words to his armor-bearer do not express doubt as to God's ability to overcome them but assurance.

It is quite true that Israel at this time was a moral ruin, but faith nullifies circumstances and builds upon Divine promises. This characterizes faith. Though broken and sinful, yet God was with and for His people, and not with or for the uncircumcised Philistines.

When men look to God, they understand that God is not restrained by many or by few. He is not dependent on numbers or on anyone or anything. The Church seems to think that the more bloated its rolls are, the stronger it is. God is not looking for numbers, riches, educa-

NOTES

tion, wealth, power, talent, or ability. God is looking for faith.

The 7th verse says, *"And his armourbearer said unto him, Do all that is in thine heart: Turn thee; Behold I am with thee according to thy heart."* The greatest asset a man of God can have is for individuals to follow him in his faith. As well, it must be said, "Woe be unto the individual who follows a man in his unbelief." One man of the caliber of this unnamed armorbearer is worth all of Saul's 600 men, and more. *"If any two of you shall agree as touching . . . ."*

The 10th verse says, *"But if they say thus come up unto us; then we will go up."* Faith is not presumption, and, in fact, is never presumptuous. Most of that today which is called faith is, in fact, presumption. It presumes upon that which God has not said and does not intend. True faith never creates difficulties, nor leaps from the pinnacle of the Temple expecting God to bear the consequences. Thus, there was no boasting in Jonathan, as it is in presumption. There was only expectation from God. He went forth to witness for God in the very stronghold of the enemy. If they bid him come up, they will foolishly open the path into their very fortress.

The 12th verse says that the Philistines answered, *"Come up to us, and we will shew you a thing."* Satan always boasts; he is as a roaring lion. However, he is only as a lion, not actually a lion. And hear the cry of faith, *"For the Lord hath delivered them into the hand of Israel."* Notice, Jonathan did not say that the Lord had delivered them into his hand, but *"into the hand of Israel."* He was to be nothing - the God of Israel was to be everything.

The 14th verse says, *"Was about twenty men,"* speaking of those who Jonathan and his armor-bearer killed. God will not begin to move until faith begins to act.

For the 15th verse says, *"And there was trembling in the host, in the field, and among all the people."* The Bible adds, *"The earth quaked."*

The 16th verse says, *"And they went on beating down one another."* Faith's great passion is always that God should manifest Himself. A supernatural terror seized the Philistines, for it was manifest that God and not Jonathan was the Author of these manifestations.

The question could well be asked, "Why couldn't God send the earthquake without having Jonathan exercise his faith?" This is the order in which God has chosen to work. God can do anything; however, He has chosen to operate through faith that characterizes His people. He will not work otherwise. If there had not been a Jonathan to exercise faith, the Philistines that day would not have been defeated. God must have men and women of faith. The greatest honor a man can bring God is to simply believe Him.

At the very moment that God is giving a tremendous victory to Israel with the Philistines being defeated, the flesh in the person of Saul is trying to find out what's going on. The 17th verse says, *"Number now, and see who is gone from us."* Unbelief will tremble in fear, not knowing what to do, thinking that imminent defeat is at hand when faith has already won the victory.

The flesh will cry out, "Bring hither the Ark of God," when it actually means to bring the "ephod of God." The flesh is ever so religious, but it has no faith.

In Jonathan is seen the quietness and confidence of the "new man," but in Saul the fussiness, excitement, folly, and impotence of the "old man." Unbelief never knows what to do, but it can furnish itself with the accessories of religious ceremony. It can build an altar (vs. 35), call for the Ark (vs. 18), and lean upon the priestly member of a condemned house (vs. 19), but it never knows what to do. It is all excitement, activity, and emotion, but no faith. Unbelief, however good its intentions in trying to help the work of faith, can do nothing but spoil it. It makes man seem very great and God very small. In this section of the chapter the words "I" and "me" and "my" fill Saul's mouth. Contrast this with Jonathan's language in the first part of this chapter.

The 20th verse says, *"And they came to the battle."* Finally, Saul joins the fray.

Then the 21st verse says, *"Moreover the Hebrews that were with the Philistines before that time."* In this great revival the children of God who had lost their way completely going out into the world, now come back to the Lord

as a result of Jonathan's faith.

Now the "flesh" continues to hinder the Spirit of God. For the 24th verse says, *"And the men of Israel were distressed that day."* The flesh must do something, so Saul will forbid the people to eat any food. Carnal zeal hinders or limits victory, and when man intrudes himself into the work of God - bringing his own strength into it - he stops it. His foolish command to put to death those who failed to obey his laws only made more visible the disobedience of his own heart to obey God's Laws.

The 26th verse says, *"Behold, the honey dropped."* In the path of faith there is honey; in the path of unbelief there is hunger. For the 31st verse says, *"And the people were very faint."* God furnishes ample refreshment upon the heavenly way so that there is *"a stream of honey"* and upon the very battlefield at that. The corrupt Christian Church is a sad illustration today of the same intrusion of man's will into God's kingdom. But there are those today who, like happy Jonathan, live and fight with God, and whose faith in Him leads them so far ahead on the celestial road that they neither hear nor heed the senseless laws which poor men holding man-made offices in Christendom make. For the 45th verse says, *"Shall Jonathan die, who hath wrought this great salvation in Israel?"* Religious man, always in the flesh, loves to make his rules and regulations and kill those who disobey them. The answer of the Holy Spirit is, *"God forbid."*

So long as Jonathan by faith took the lead, everything prospered, but when Saul, that is, unbelief, put himself at the head, the effect was to lose the full fruit of the victory. For the 46th verse says, *"Then Saul went up from following the Philistines."*

Except in verse 21, the Holy Spirit gives the heavenly name of "Israelite" even to the most timid of those who accompanied Saul and Jonathan in the battle, but in verse 21 refuses it to those who lived at peace with the Philistines, calling them "Hebrews."

Still, despite acute failure the 47th verse says, *"So Saul took the kingdom over Israel, and fought against all his enemies on every side."* The following verses account for his victories. Even now, God would accept him and bless him greatly if only he would turn with his "whole heart" to the Lord.

The 52nd verse says, *"And there was sore war against the Philistines all the days of Saul."* If the Philistines plague us *"all our days,"* it must tell us that flesh is attempting to thwart the Philistine instead of the Holy Spirit. If we walk after the flesh, we die. If we follow after the Spirit, we live. Ultimately, Saul would die at the hand of the Philistines. Ultimately, David would live at the hands of the Holy Spirit.

CHAPTER 15

This chapter will highlight the war with Amalek. Saul was here commissioned to destroy the Amalekite nation for their sins against Israel when coming out of Egypt (Ex. 17:8-16; Num. 24:20).

The 2nd verse says, *"Thus saith the Lord of hosts, I remember that which Amalek did to Israel."* The Scripture says, *"And every transgression and disobedience received a just recompense of reward"* (Heb. 2:2). God forgets nothing, good or bad. This should be a solemn warning for all. Someone has said, "The mills of God grind slowly, but they grind exceedingly fine," meaning that nothing is missed. The only place for fault and failure is under the Blood of Jesus. Otherwise, we will answer for it. Now, some 500 years have passed with God giving Amalek ample time for repentance, but Amalek did not repent. If every person in the world understood this correctly, there would probably be less ill treatment of others.

The 3rd verse says, *"Now go and smite Amalek, and utterly destroy all that they have, and spare them not."* Amalek in Bible typology is a "type of the flesh." The flesh pertains to the "Adamic nature" or "the sin nature." It characterizes man's own efforts to save himself, whether by good works, money, education, or religion. It is the bane of the child of God. It is the source of the Christian's greatest conflict. Paul says, *"So then they that are in the flesh cannot please God"* (Rom. 8:8). He continues, *"For if you live after the flesh, you shall die"* (Rom. 8:13). Most of that in the world today which purports to be the work of God is actu-

ally works of the flesh. Saul was a work of the flesh, simply because he was the choice of the people and not of God. David was a work of the Spirit because he was the choice of God. That which is of the Spirit emanates totally from God. That which is of the flesh emanates totally from man.

Amalek was a descendant of Esau and was a type of the flesh. God loved Jacob and hated Esau. Why? Both men were equally bad with no personal merit, which would, in fact, characterize the whole of humanity. So why did God choose Jacob and not Esau? God chose Jacob, not because he was good, for he wasn't; He chose him because there was something in his heart that reached out toward God. From his heart Jacob desired the things of the Spirit. From Esau's heart Esau desired the things of the flesh. So, both would be Bible types - Jacob of the Spirit and Esau of the flesh. Consequently, that which came from Esau, who was Amalek, would be a type of the flesh. God demands that we destroy such. The Christian will find this is the most difficult conflict that he will face - a conflict basically that never ends. The command of God was that they "destroy all" - and that's where the rub comes in.

Verse 7 says, *"And Saul smote the Amalekites."*

However, the 9th verse says, *"But Saul and the people spared Agag, and the best of the sheep."*

This has always been the problem of Christians. We desire to destroy "everything that is vile and refuse"; however, it is very difficult for us to destroy "the best." We can certainly see the need for destroying the "vile," but we cannot see the need for destroying the "best." What do we mean by the "best?" Whenever Cain brought his vegetables to offer a sacrifice to the Lord, they were the product of his own hands and, also, his very best. He could not understand why God would not accept them. Did that mean there was something wrong with vegetables? No! It just simply meant that it was not what God would accept. He would only accept the slain Lamb, which represented Christ. Consequently, man tries to give God his church membership, his religious activity, his good works, his good deeds, and God will not accept them. As far as offering these things to God to atone for our sins and to make us "good" in God's sight, all of this must be destroyed. It does not necessarily mean that these things should be discontinued. In fact, they may be very good in their place and very desirable. Still, these things, as good as they might be, don't buy us favor with God. God operates totally on the basis of faith, and that means faith totally in Christ and what He did at Calvary and the Resurrection. Everything else, as Paul said, must be counted as "dung."

So, what Saul did those long years ago is still being done today in almost every Christian life in one way or the other.

This is no doubt man's greatest sin. For the 11th verse says, *"It repenteth me that I have set up Saul to be king."* These were the words of God, and it simply means that God had changed His purpose or plan concerning Saul. Had he been obedient, then his kingdom would have been established (13:13), but because he had been disobedient, his kingdom would not continue with him.

In the 13th verse Saul would say, *"I have performed the commandment of the Lord."* Much of Christendom today will say the same thing. And, yet, in the 14th verse Samuel says, *What meaneth then this bleating of the sheep in mine ears?"* We are very quick to inform the Lord that we have carried out His will, even in spite of our actions being covered with religious activity all the time, the flesh is "bleating" in God's ears.

In modern Christian vernacular, the child of God is very pleased with himself that he has destroyed the vile, such as adultery, swearing, stealing, dirty jokes, or fornication. However, it is very difficult for the modern Christian (or those in any age for that matter) to see that he must destroy the "good" as well.

Verse 22 says, *"Behold, to obey is better than sacrifice."* Obedience is more important than all forms of religion - sacrifices, offerings, rituals, ceremonies. It is the chief end of all true salvation, and rebellion and stubbornness are manifestations of failure in conforming to truth. In other words, it is much better to obey the Lord in the first place than to disobey and then to have to ask for forgiveness, trusting in the sacrifice of Calvary. True, the Lord will

forgive if we sincerely confess and ask His forgiveness; however, it is better not to perform the deed of unbelief in the first place.

Verse 23 says, *"For rebellion is as the sin of witchcraft, and stubbornness is as iniquity and idolatry."* What does this mean? The tap root of all failure is "rebellion." It is the cause of every broken home, wasted life, and warped mind - rebellion against God and His Word. "Witchcraft" is man's efforts to manipulate the spirit world. All witchcraft is of Satan. So, when an individual rebels against God, they are in effect saying, "I can handle the world of demon spirits without any help from God."

Likewise, "stubbornness" is as "iniquity" (willful sin). To equate "stubbornness" with "idolatry" is not clear to the carnal mind. However, refusing to obey God out of "stubbornness," in effect, makes an idol of oneself. In other words, "I know more than God knows." So, one becomes his own god.

Verse 24 records an incomplete repentance. Saul says, *"I have sinned."* This type of repentance God will not hear nor accept. Sadly, it is the blight of the majority of the Church, as well.

The 28th verse records the intent of God's direction, *"The Lord hath rent the kingdom of Israel from thee this day, and hath given it to a neighbor of thine, that is better than thou."* Even though David was not mentioned, David is the one that the Holy Spirit is speaking of. Saul would continue to serve for a particular period of time as King of Israel; however, in God's mind the change had begun in the spirit realm at that moment.

Verse 29 says, *"And also the Strength of Israel will not lie nor repent: For he is not a man, that he should repent."* This was quoted by Samuel from the account of Balaam as given in Numbers 23:19. The Divine title, *"the Strength of Israel"* is used here for the very first time in Scripture.

The 30th verse says, *"Yet honour me now, I pray thee, before the elders of my people."* Saul was more concerned about how he looked in regards to the people than with God. So it is with the majority of that which is called the Church.

Verses 32 through 35 tell us what God expects us to do with the flesh. Verse 32 says,

"And Agag came unto him delicately." Because of this posture of "goodness," it is very difficult for us to take the necessary steps regarding what must be done with this side of the flesh. It is very difficult to realize that our good works, good intentions, good deeds, church membership, religious activity, and even our consecrated prayer life purchases no merit with God. Please allow me to say it again in this chapter, "It does not necessarily mean that these things should be discontinued; actually, most of them should be continued. But we must ever know that these things buy us no favor with God."

The 33rd verse says, *"And Samuel hewed Agag in pieces before the Lord in Gilgal."* Most of the Church will not do this, and most who do it are criticized severely by the others in the Church. We love our "Agags." The idea of hewing them in pieces is very distasteful. We are proud of our Baptist heritage, Pentecostal heritage, Holiness heritage, and so forth; however, all must be "hewed in pieces."

■

CHAPTER 16

This chapter starts off with Samuel in a depressed state. However, this will prove to be one of the greatest moments in the entirety of the Word of God.

The 1st verse shows us what we see and, conversely, what God sees, *"How long wilt thou mourn for Saul?"*

Samuel was in a dejected, discouraged condition. As far as he was concerned, there was little future for Israel. Saul had lost his way with God. There seemed to be no light at the end of this tunnel. As well, many today "mourn" for the Church. Still, what does the Word of God say? *"Tis a glorious church."* Sadly, the Church "mourns" when it should be shouting, and shouts when it should be "mourning." At this stage Samuel should have been shouting, but, instead, he was "mourning."

"Seeing I have rejected him." God had tried to make this "work of the flesh" acceptable, but Saul would not cooperate; therefore, God

NOTES

"rejected him." Israel would continue to look to Saul as their king long after God had rejected him. Much of the time this is the case. The Church accepts what God has rejected, and God rejects what the Church has accepted.

"Fill thine horn with oil and go." The *"oil"* is a type of the Holy Spirit. It signifies that these men are to rule by the guidance, leading, and the direction of the Holy Spirit. If there is to be any spiritual success, every apostle, prophet, evangelist, pastor, and teacher must be "anointed by the Holy Spirit." This time the "anointing" will be on a work of the Spirit and not a work of the flesh.

The Lord further says, *"I have provided me a king among his sons."* Samuel was "mourning"; God was "providing." Instead of Israel folding, Israel was really about to begin. Instead of the sun setting, the sun was now rising. The world, and even God's chosen one, Samuel, may look at the present-day Church and see nothing but spiritual declension. But one can feel sure that God has provided.

The 2nd verse says, *"If Saul hear it, he will kill me."* The "flesh" always tries to kill the Spirit. The two cannot abide. This work of the flesh demanded by Israel will hinder, and quite possibly delay the work of the Spirit. How so much the Church deprives itself because it follows the ways of man and not of the Lord. It is said, "The very work of the flesh that causes us so much difficulty and problem, is, in fact, created by our own design."

The 3rd verse says, *"And thou shalt anoint unto me him whom I name unto thee."* Why didn't the Lord tell Samuel exactly who to anoint at the outset? Why did He keep Samuel in suspense? By and large, this is God's way. He wants us to learn trust and dependence in Him. He very seldom tells us more than a step at a time.

In the 5th verse Samuel says, *"Come with me to the sacrifice."* The tremendous lesson given to us in this passage is one that every child of God should eagerly learn. God was about to anoint David as the king of Israel, and, in fact, he would be the greatest king who ever lived. David's name would be the very first human name in the New Testament and the very last human name in the New Testament. And, yet, David would undergo tremendous tribulation, tests, difficulties, and heartache. Today, by and large, the clarion call in the Church is "come with me to riches, and fame, and popularity, and health and wealth." However, those calls are not from the Lord. The Lord always says, *"Come with me to the sacrifice."* The first message that was given to the Apostle Paul after his conversion was *"tell Paul what things he must suffer for My name's sake."* The Scripture says that *"Jesus learned obedience by the things He suffered."* The Church has repeatedly tried to find a way around the suffering and the tribulation. If we are to be what God wants us to be, there is no way around it. The sacrifice that Christ made at Calvary must be entered into by every child of God. Why?

While it is true that salvation comes instantly upon the expression of our faith in Christ, still, so much "self" remains in all of us that the only way it can be successfully eradicated is by "sacrifice." Paul asked the Lord that the thorn may be removed. The answer would be, *"My grace is sufficient for thee."* Paul needed the thorn (sacrifice). We need it, as well.

The 6th verse says, *"Surely the Lord's anointed is before him."* The subject was "Eliab." This was David's brother. Samuel would have chosen him instantly. He looked the part of the king. So Samuel would say, *"Surely."*

It is impossible for man, even though so godly, to choose the one who God will use. Entire denominations try it. Entire denominations fail, as fail they must. That which looks so good to man looks as nothing to God. Why?

The 7th verse says, *"For the Lord seeth not as man seeth."* It is so easy for us to *"look on his countenance,"* or *"on the height of his stature."* The Church is so easily fooled because too often it does not see as God sees, for the Scripture says this, *"For man looketh on the outward appearance, but the Lord looketh on the heart."*

In this passage we find the strategy of God. As I have stated previously in this volume, "God does not perform His work on the basis of good and evil." And why not? The answer is simple; if He did so, none of us would ever be used by God simply because the evil is paramount - and even in the best of us. So the Lord performs His

NOTES

work according to *"the heart."*

If the Lord carried out His work on the basis of good and evil, Abraham would have never made it, neither would have Isaac or Jacob. The great statement, *"the God of Abraham, and of Isaac, and of Jacob,"* would never have been made simply because they did not measure up, and, in fact, none ever have, and none ever will. So, the Lord looks on the heart of the person, regarding His use of that person.

The 10th verse says that the refusal was complete regarding all of Jesse's sons who were present, for Samuel says, *"The Lord hath not chosen these."* Sadly, the Church would have probably chosen all of them.

The 11th verse says, *"There remaineth yet the youngest, and behold, he keepeth the sheep."* Jesse did not even think David worthy enough to introduce to Samuel. That which man would not choose, God would because He looked on the heart.

The 12th verse says, *"And the Lord said, Arise, anoint Him: for this is he."* Now, for the first time in Israel's history regarding a king, this is a work of the Spirit and not of the flesh.

The 13th verse says, *"The Spirit of the Lord came upon David from that day forward."* If one will notice, the *"Spirit of the Lord"* was linked with David from that very moment. This is the second time the name "David" is used in Scripture. It will no doubt be the most illuminating name other than the Lord Jesus Christ Himself given in the entirety of the Word. However, it must ever be remembered that God did not choose David because of any great moral quality in him. He chose him because of a cry for God from David's heart, despite the lack of moral virtue. David was probably about 15 years old at this time.

God would not immediately set David upon the throne as He had done in the case of Saul. He had to be tested first, humbled, and made to feel his dependence on God and the sufficiency of God to uphold him and maintain him. Hence, at the very outset of his life regarding his call, he is brought face to face with Satan (vs. 23). So it was with the Blessed One of whom David is a type. His public life began with an encounter with Satan. It was thus, and by His subsequent sufferings, that David was molded and trained to be the channel through which the Psalms were given to the world.

The 14th verse troubles some Christians for it says, *"But the Spirit of the Lord departed from Saul, and an evil spirit from the Lord troubled him."* The Spirit of the Lord did not arbitrarily depart from Saul, but did so because Saul no longer wanted God. The "Spirit" will not stay where He is not wanted. Instead, an evil spirit was allowed by God to go to Saul and trouble him. Evil spirits would plague every child of God constantly, but the Lord will not allow this to happen, but this He does allow, He gives us the proper spiritual armaments for total and complete victory. But we must always remember, it's either "the Holy Spirit or an evil spirit."

Verses 14-23 do not follow the previous part of the chapter in chronological order. Actually, these latter passages come in between 19:9, 10 to show the contrast between the two spirits of Saul and David and the success of one and failure of the other.

In regard to this evil spirit that came to Saul, the 23rd verse says, *"that David took an harp, and played with his hands."* Whenever David, who no doubt was anointed by the Holy Spirit, would begin to play his harp, the *"evil spirit departed from him (Saul)."*

Music is one of the most powerful factors in the world, whether used by Satan or God. Millions of young people have been led to a life of immorality, drugs, alcohol, and demon possession because of ungodly modern rock music. It was designed by Satan for the purpose of bringing evil spirits upon young people, which would lead them into these devious practices, which in turn would destroy them. It has succeeded greatly.

In the Church Satan has basically designed the same avenue of approach by what is commonly referred to as "Contemporary Christian Music" or "Christian Rock Music." It is argued that these types of music are used to pull young people from the world to the Lord. Only a carnal mind would suggest such foolishness. God does not use the devil to convict people of their sins. The Holy Spirit does that. The ways of the world and of Satan can never be used to perform the work of God. The Holy Spirit will have none of it.

In fact, sacred music is not designed by God

NOTES

for the world. It is designed for the child of God to worship the Lord. While it is certainly true at times that sacred music anointed by the Holy Spirit will touch the hearts and lives of the unbeliever, thereby, bringing them to the Lord Jesus Christ, still, its major function is a vehicle of worship by the child of God.

Music (of whatever style) as designed by God comes in three parts, "harmony, melody, and rhythm." If any of these three parts are tampered with, worship is stopped altogether, and for a reason. If the "harmony" or the "melody" are confused or perverted, no worship of God is possible, simply because the musical structure as designed by God has been abrogated. Likewise, the "rhythm" can be perverted so as to appeal only to the flesh and not the spirit. In this case worship may be continued, but it basically appeals only to the emotion and not to the spirit. The spirit of man is the part of man that worships God. Jesus said, *"True worshippers shall worship the Father in spirit and in truth."* The word "spirit" refers to the seat of worship, with music being one of the greatest vehicles of worship given by God. Contemporary Christian Music, which means music that is similar or even identical to its counterpart in the worship of Satan, which is rock-n-roll, in fact, cannot be used to worship God. It is impossible to worship God with this type of music because the basic structure ordained by God of "harmony, melody, and rhythm" has been perverted. Individuals may respond by the clapping of hands or with bodily rhythm, but it will not be worship of God.

In fact, all true worship of God concerning music was basically originated by the Holy Spirit through David. Every choir, soloist, or the use of musical instruments in our churches had its beginnings with David who was called *"the sweet singer of Israel."* David originated, under the guidance of the Holy Spirit, the great choirs that worshiped God on the Temple site even before the building of this great structure.

Most of the Psalms, which was the earth's first song book, were written by David.

Actually, most of the worship of God regarding music as we know it today had its origination with David as the Holy Spirit used him.

So when we read the 23rd verse of this chapter, we are actually reading the very first mention of God's use of music for worship, for refreshing, and for healing. In fact, music is one of the greatest healing agents on the face of the earth, and it is derived from the 23rd verse, *"So Saul was refreshed, and was well."*

CHAPTER 17

This is one of the greatest chapters of victory found in the entirety of the Word of God. In it is the pattern for our own victory, because the Goliaths in the spiritual sense who hinder our Christian progress, are no less real than the Goliath that David faced so long ago. As David won the victory, we can win the victory, too. And all because our heavenly David defeated Satan, the greatest Goliath of them all, some 2000 years ago.

Verse 1 says, *"Now the Philistines gathered together their armies to battle."* This is a picture of Satan working through the flesh to hinder the child of God. The spiritual conflict is no less severe than the physical conflict of this chapter.

The 4th verse says, *"And there went out a champion out of the camp of the Philistines, named Goliath."* How many Goliaths in the spiritual sense have we faced? How many have we defeated?

The number "6" is stamped upon Goliath (vss. 4-7). He was 6 cubits high and he had 6 pieces of armor. The number "6" was stamped upon Nebuchadnezzar's golden image, and it will identify the future Antichrist; the number of whose name will be 666 (Rev. 13:18).

The apt description of Goliath given in verses 4-7 is a portrayal of what we face in the spiritual. The demon powers of darkness who oppose the child of God come no less equipped.

The 8th verse says, *"Choose you a man for you, and let him come down to me."* Satan knows in the natural he cannot be defeated, but he reckons without a man of faith. David would be a man of faith.

The 11th verse says, *"They were dismayed, and greatly afraid."* God does not give us the

NOTES

spirit of fear, as Paul said to Timothy. The abundance of fear is because of the lack of love. For John said, *"Perfect love casteth out fear."*

The 15th verse says, *"But David went and returned from Saul."* Evidently, David had gone several times to the *"valley of Elah"* carrying foodstuff to his brothers. So, this particular occasion when he would face Goliath was not the only time he had been to the battlefront. However, this was the first time that he had been there when the Philistine giant presented himself.

The 26th verse portrays David saying, *"For who is this uncircumcised Philistine, that he should defy the armies of the living God?"* Only faith could ask this type of question. All of Israel was trembling at the presence of Goliath. But David trembled not and why? The Spirit of the Lord was upon him. Still, when faith steps out, the Church will always criticize.

The 28th verse says, *"And Eliab's anger was kindled against David."* David was sent by his father to his brothers to bless them and do them good, but, like Joseph's brothers when he was sent to bless them, he met with envy and hatred. Thus it was with God's beloved Son. His brothers, Mary's sons, did not believe on him (St. John 7:5), and with her sought to lay hold upon Him as being beside Himself (Mark 3:32); also His Jewish brethren nailed Him to the Tree. Regrettably, the greatest opposition will not come from the enemy but from our own "brethren."

The 33rd verse says, *"Thou art not able to go against this Philistine."* Saul would say these words because unbelief always says, *"Thou art not able."* Faith, as Caleb, always says, *"We are able to go up at once and possess the land."* The 36th verse states, *"Thy servant slew both the lion and the bear:"* The reason we have trouble with "Goliath" is because we have not yet slain the *"lion and the bear."* David knew his faith could take the giant because his faith had already taken the *"lion and the bear."*

In the 37th verse he says, *"He will deliver me out of the hand of this Philistine."* God is the only One Who can deliver us out of the hand of Satan. No man can. The Church today has, by and large, given itself over to the psychologists, the therapists, and the counselors. We refuse to admit that our need is "deliverance." The Christian Church is so confused that when it thinks of the word "deliverance," it automatically thinks of demon possession. True, those who are demon possessed need deliverance. However, the child of God who is facing an acute attack by a Goliath of hell needs deliverance from this enemy as well (II Cor. 1). However, it takes faith to be delivered. The Church today has little faith in God. It has more faith in man. Consequently, there are precious few deliverances.

The 38th verse says, *"And Saul armed David with his armour."* The "flesh" will ever try to hinder faith by clothing it with unbelief. *"Saul's armour"* will defeat no Philistines. It will destroy no Goliath, and, yet, the Church keeps trying to wear it. Take it off and put on the whole armor of God.

David would be detained a moment by unbelief but would soon gather his spiritual perspective and allow faith to proceed. For the 39th verse says, *"I cannot go with these: for I have not proved them. And David put them off him."* Thank God, he would never *"prove them."* Sadly, millions of Christians are trying to "prove them." They ever meet with failure as ever they must.

The 40th verse says, *"And he took his staff in his hand."* The *"staff"* is a type of the Word of God. He did not want *"Saul's armour"* for it was the ways of the world, but he did want *"his staff"* for it was the Word of God. The Word of God holds the answer for man's dilemma. And it should be said, "only the Word of God holds the answer."

"And chose him five smooth stones." The *"five smooth stones"* that David chose to go in his sling could well have been the five names of the "one" smooth stone Who would destroy Goliath. Isaiah gives us those names. *"His name shall be called Wonderful, Counsellor, The Mighty God, The Everlasting Father, The Prince of Peace."* The Scripture says, *"out of the brook."* The brook was a type of the Holy Spirit. So, the Holy Spirit would glorify Jesus Christ. *"And put them in a shepherd's bag."* The shepherd's bag represents the gifts of the Spirit of which we are given the manifestation thereof. And then it adds, *"The sling was in his hand."* The *"sling"* represents David's faith, *"and he drew near to the Philistine."* Faith

NOTES

always draws near to its problem. Unbelief runs away, as Israel had been doing, and faith draws near, as David did.

The 42nd verse says, *"He disdained him."* This speaks of Goliath ridiculing David. The tactic of Satan is to ridicule faith. Regrettably, it works on many Christians, for they turn and run.

The 45th verse states, *"But I come to thee in the name of the Lord of hosts."* Satan's weaponry no matter how lethal or powerful is no match whatsoever for *"the name of the Lord of hosts."* When will we realize this? Instead, we try to fight Satan's "sword" with our "sword" of the world. Our "shield" is too often not of faith but the same as the world. It must be clearly understood that "flesh cannot defeat flesh; sin cannot save from sin; sickness cannot heal sickness; man cannot deliver man; a worldly spirit cannot defeat Satan's spirits.

However, the moment we take *"the name"* with us, devils are cast out, the sick are healed, and the power of darkness is broken. What is that name? That name is "Jesus" - and "there is none other name under heaven whereby man can be saved."

The 46th verse says, *"This day."* How long will we face Goliath with the armament of this world? How long will we continue to carry the load? The Holy Spirit says, *"This day will the Lord deliver thee into mine hand."*

The 47th verse plainly says, *"That the Lord saveth not with sword and spear: for the battle is the Lord's."* The sooner we learn that the *"battle is the Lord's"* and not ours, the sooner we will win the victory.

The 49th verse adds, *"And took thence a stone, and slang it, and smote the Philistine in his forehead."* Faith will take the *"name"* and *"sling it."* And then, *"He fell upon his face to the earth."* Satan will not fall until we hit him with *"the name."*

The 50th verse emphasizes once again the point that we cannot do it with "the ways of the world," *"but there was no sword in the hand of David."* We must do it with the "ways of God."

The 51st verse says, *"And when the Philistines saw their champion was dead, they fled."* If we resist the devil in the scriptural manner, he will flee.

The 52nd verse says, *"And the men of Israel*

and of Judah arose, and shouted." It is time for camp meeting. The Church ought to "shout" because Goliath has been defeated.

The 54th verse says, "And David took the head of the Philistine, and brought it to Jerusalem." Two thousand years ago our heavenly David walked out of the tomb with the head of Satan in His hand. And because He lives, I shall live also.

The 55th verse asks, "Whose son is this youth?" Saul asked this question of David because unbelief never recognizes faith. Faith can easily recognize unbelief, but unbelief can never recognize faith.

The 58th verse says, "And Saul said to him, Whose son art thou?" One day, Israel who has been of the flesh for so very long, will ask Jesus Who He is. The Son of David will then say, "I am the son of God born in Bethlehem."

CHAPTER 18

The 1st verse says, "The soul of Jonathan was knit with the soul of David." Jonathan was Saul's son. He seemed to be the only member of this family who had a heart toward God. He recognized the touch of God in David's life. He also recognized the evil in his father's life. He would never forsake his father, but he would choose David over Saul. Not many people have this type of consecration to the Lord. However, this is what Jesus demanded when He said, "He that loveth father or mother more than me cannot be My disciple" (Matt. 10:37). Regrettably, not many have this type of consecration.

The 3rd verse says, "Then Jonathan and David made a covenant." This covenant will be detailed in the 4th verse. It basically means this:

Whatever belonged to Jonathan, now belonged to David. (He, in effect, was giving him the kingdom, especially because he knew that God had called him for such.) Whatever belonged to David, now belonged to Jonathan, as well. They would go so far as to lay down their lives for each other if necessary. It would also extend to their children; hence, this is the reason that David would bring Mephibosheth

NOTES

into the palace and give him place and position (II Sam. 9).

The covenant that is spoken of is basically a type of the great Covenant that is made between the Lord Jesus Christ and the repentant heart. What a blessing!

The 5th verse states, "And behaved himself wisely." The Holy Spirit will bear this out concerning David several times. Then the Scripture says, "And Saul set him over the men of war." It is not clear if this means that David was set over the entire army, which is doubtful, or whether he was set over a particular group of exceptionally heroic individuals. Probably, the latter is correct.

The events that transpire in the balance of the chapter actually portray Saul's downfall and eventual death.

The 6th verse says, "When David was returned from the slaughter of the Philistines." David was probably about 17 or 18 years old at this time. He was so powerful because of the Spirit of the Lord Who was with him. If allowed to continue, he, no doubt, would have completely destroyed the Philistines from out of Israel, which would have gained victory over Saul's greatest enemy, for the Philistines would eventually kill Saul.

The 7th verse says, "Saul hath slain his thousands, and David his ten thousands." Saul, on the edge of total spiritual oblivion, now allows jealousy to totally captivate him. He cannot bear having David praised more highly than himself.

The 8th verse adds, "And Saul was very wroth." The downward side to total spiritual wreckage and the ultimate loss of his soul is now fully in motion. It will not be reversed. At any time if Saul had totally repented from his heart, God would have heard him and helped him. But this was not to be. This chapter characterizes the lives of so many Christians. So many are like Saul, and so few are like David.

The Church should ever remember that the anointing of the Holy Spirit is what it must follow. No, it should not condone the wrongs of David, but, likewise, never should it forsake him.

The 10th verse says, "And it came to pass on the morrow, that the evil spirit from God came *upon Saul."* In other words, the Lord allowed an evil spirit to come upon Saul. God is over all, and nothing can move, function, or operate without God's specific approval. So, due to Saul's evil heart and his rejection of God and all that God was doing, God allowed evil spirits to plague Saul. The Scripture states, *He prophesied."* However, it must be understood that he did not prophesy by the Spirit of God. He did so by demon spirits. There are actually seven examples in Scripture of demon spirits or even Satan himself prophesying. They are as follows:

1. Satan, through the serpent, predicting eternal life and divine likeness for man should he eat of the tree of knowledge of good and evil (Gen. 3:4-5).

2. Saul prophesying here (vs. 10).

3. The familiar spirit imitating Samuel and predicting the death of Saul and his sons (I Sam. 28:7-25).

4. Lying prophets of Ahab (I Kings 22:6-28).

5. False prophets of Jeremiah (Jer. 23:15-19, 32; 27:9-11; 28:1-17).

6. False prophets of Ezekiel (Ezek. 13).

7. False prophets of latter days (St. Matt. 24:1-14; II Thess. 2:8-12; I Tim. 4; II Peter 2; Rev. 13:11-18).

Sadly, much of that which goes under the heading of "prophecy" in the modern Church is not from God. In most cases it is out of one's own mind. In other cases it is from evil spirits. However, this in no way should negate the value of the gift of prophecy as one of the nine gifts of the Spirit. The very reason there are so many imitations and counterfeits is because there is a real and genuine gift. Every Christian should seek the Lord, that, if it be God's will, they would be given the real and genuine gift of prophecy.

The 11th verse says, *"And Saul cast the javelin; for he said, I will smite David."* The flesh must ever persecute the Spirit. Of course, the inquisitive heart asks, "Why did God not take Saul out at the beginning? Why would God allow Saul to remain a thorn in David's side causing him untold difficulty?"

It must ever be remembered that God uses all things to His advantage and to His glory. He is God, and, therefore, omniscient, (all-knowing), omnipotent (all-powerful), and omni-

NOTES

present (everywhere). God can use all things to His glory, even those which are in opposition to Him.

The Lord would not immediately take Saul out for the same reason that He does not take out all who are wicked. There is a continuous effort by the Holy Spirit to get the people to repent. Some few do.

Also, the Lord will use those like Saul to cause David to rely totally on the Lord and to learn trust and dependence on God. We wonder at times why the Lord does not move all the obstacles and difficulties in our path. He leaves them there because we need them to be there. They cause us to pray and to learn total dependence on the Lord. As Saul was David's thorn in the flesh, likewise, Paul had a thorn in the flesh. He would repeatedly ask the Lord to remove it. The Lord would tell him, *"My grace is sufficient for thee."*

So, if Saul had repented and lived for God as he should have, the Lord would have used that for His glory even in a greater way. But still, despite Saul's wickedness, the Lord used that also to teach David dependence and trust.

The 12th verse says, *"And Saul was afraid of David, because the Lord was with him."* The flesh is always afraid of the Spirit and, thereby, seeks to destroy it. Sadly, there is a great "fear" in the Church of any who are genuinely called of God.

So the 13th verse says, *"Saul removed him from him."* This was the biggest mistake that Saul ever made. Even though the Spirit of the Lord had left Saul, still, the Lord had placed in Saul's path the very one who the Spirit of God was with. What a blessing he could have been to Saul. However, the flesh must ever remove the Spirit. Even though it brings great blessing, still, it cannot abide the constant presence of the Lord.

The 14th verse says, *"And David behaved himself wisely in all his ways; and the Lord was with him."* What does this mean? Among other things it means that David did not allow himself to hate Saul. Even though he was reduced in rank as is obvious in the 13th verse, still, he would seek to serve Saul to the very best of his ability. No greater statement could be made about anyone than, *"and the Lord was with him."*

Verses 17 through 30 proclaim a plot designed by Satan and used by Saul to hurt David severely or even get him killed. This is the way it went.

The 21st verse says, *"And Saul said, I will give him her, that she may be a snare to him."* He was speaking of his daughter, Michal. For her hand, he would condemn the lives of 100 Philistines.

The 25th verse states, *"But Saul thought to make David fall by the hand of the Philistines."* However, the 27th verse continues, *"Wherefore David arose and went, he and his men, and slew of the Philistines two hundred men."* Some may blanch at the killing of so many individuals. However, the following must be understood:

1. These tribes in the confines of Israel, including the Philistines, were evil beyond compare. One archaeologist has stated, "The God Who gave the instructions that these people should be exterminated did future generations an untold service."

2. They were sworn enemies of Israel and the God of Israel to the extent that they would either subjugate Israel or destroy Israel.

3. God had given instructions that these people were to be totally and completely exterminated for their evil.

4. So the curse of death that Saul placed upon David was turned into a blessing. David's great feat of military prowess against the Philistines and his resultant victory only made him more famous in Israel. If Saul had read his Bible, he would have known from the Word of God that such would not work against God's people. For Baalim had prophesied some 500 years before, *"Surely there is no enchantment against Jacob, neither is there any divination against Israel"* (Num. 23:23). What God has blessed cannot be cursed.

CHAPTER 19

This chapter portrays Saul sinking even further into the morass of spiritual wreckage. It also portrays the last effort by God to bring this man to his senses, an effort that Saul

rejected.

The 1st verse says, *"And Saul spake to Jonathan his son, and to all his servants, that they should kill David."* As we have repeatedly said, the "flesh" must always persecute the "Spirit." This is a spiritual war that began at the very outset (Cain and Abel) and will not cease until the trump of God sounds. In this one Scripture we are given a portrayal of the opposition that Satan uses against the work of God.

No doubt, the Philistines strongly desired to kill David. However, Saul desired to do so even more. Consequently, the individual who is anointed by God will face far worse opposition from that which is called the "Church" than it does from the world.

However, the 2nd verse says, *"But Jonathan Saul's son delighted much in David."* At this time David was probably about 20 years old, with Jonathan being about 40. The love of Jonathan was like that of a father and son, or as true brothers in the same nation - not the low, depraved, unnatural homosexual and demonized love which some have sought to attach to this story. Theirs was a genuine affection which was pure and normal, as it should be with all men.

The 4th verse states, *"And Jonathan spake good of David unto Saul his father."* It took much courage for Jonathan to speak favorably of David. It shows the true righteousness of God that dwelt within him. Regrettably, most Christians will do whatever "Saul" wants. Why?

Sadly, most serve a doctrine, a particular church, a denomination, or a religious hierarchy; therefore, they do what is demanded of them. However, thank God for the "Jonathans" who say, as is recorded in verse 5, *"Wherefore then wilt thou sin against innocent blood?"*

The 7th verse says, *"And Jonathan brought David to Saul, and he was in his presence, as in times past."* For David even to come back into the presence of Saul required tremendous courage on his part. Only days earlier Saul had tried to kill him. Sadly, Saul had not changed. So, the situation really would not change. That which is called of God, despite its efforts, cannot long abide in the presence of "Saul," which is a type of man-made religious hierarchy. It is an impossible combination.

Verse 8 through 10 record a tremendous victory by David against the Philistines. The 8th verse says, *"And slew them with a great slaughter."*

The Holy Spirit from the Lord was upon David. And the 9th verse says, *"And the evil spirit from the Lord was upon Saul."* Saul is now given over to a reprobate mind. This is the seventh mention of the evil spirit from God coming upon Saul.

The 10th verse states that, *"Saul sought to smite David even to the wall with the javelin."* This is the last time that David will appear in Saul's presence in this fashion. Previously, the healing music of his harp, anointed by the Holy Spirit, would soothe Saul, but no longer. Still, the Holy Spirit will make one more effort to bring Saul back.

So, the 18th verse says, *"David fled, and escaped, and came to Samuel to Ramah."*

The 20th verse says, *"And when they saw the company of the prophets prophesying."* These prophecies were from God and not an evil spirit, for the Scripture says, *"The Spirit of God was upon the messengers of Saul, and they also prophesied.*

The 23rd verse records the last attempt by God to salvage Saul. It says, *"And the Spirit of God was upon him also, and he went on, and prophesied."* As well, this prophecy was from the *"Spirit of God"* and not evil spirits.

When the 24th verse uses the words *"And lay down naked all that day and all that night,"* it does not mean that Saul stripped off all of his clothing. It means that he stripped off his armor and kingly robes. In other words, he was "naked" of these items but not naked as we think of nakedness.

This was God's last attempt to bring Saul back to the right way. After this, Saul would go even deeper into spiritual oblivion.

CHAPTER 20

The 1st verse says, *"And David fled."* As the highest leadership (Saul) of Israel rejected David with a part of that leadership (Jonathan) accepting him, this portrays the highest of

NOTES

Israel rejecting the Lord Jesus Christ, with part of its leadership accepting Him. However, as Jonathan, the small part of the leadership who accepted Christ (Joseph of Arimathaea and Nicodemus), had very little influence on the decision of the hierarchy. In this instance David was and is a type of the true King of Israel, now rejected and hated by the world. But just as the kingdom came ultimately to David, and just as he gave high positions in that kingdom to those who had loved him when an outcast, so will Christ the Lord ultimately receive the dominion of the earth, and He will appoint to great honor those who now love and follow Him.

The 2nd verse proclaims Jonathan saying, *"Behold, my father will do nothing either great or small, but that he will shew it me."* Jonathan, who still had hopes that his father would come to his senses, is a picture of those in the institutionalized Church who are torn between David, God's anointed, and Saul, man's anointed. As Jonathan was dearly beloved of the Lord, so are these individuals, whoever they may be. Still, as Jonathan died trying to defend Saul, likewise, they will die trying to defend man's anointed.

At this time David is an outcast, with his future clouded. Still, if Jonathan had thrown in his lot conclusively with David, he, no doubt, would have been mightily used of God in coming years. Jonathan, one of Israel's brightest lights and one of God's choicest, would die defending his father against the Philistines in a lost cause.

There are three portrayals at this time in Israel's history that are pregnant with meaning. They are as follows:

1. Saul, who is a type of the man-centered apostate Church.

2. Jonathan, who represents the godly people who are ensconced in the apostate Church (a remnant) and are torn between Saul (man's choice) and David (God's choice).

3. David, who represents God's anointed, is not only opposed by the world but also to an even greater degree by the apostate Church.

The 33rd verse says, *"And Saul cast a javelin at him to smite him."* The Jonathans of this world should clearly realize that the moment they lean toward "God's anointed," David, that

Saul (the apostate Church) will attempt to kill them. They keep thinking they can bring the two together, or that Saul (the apostate Church) will finally begin to go God's way. Finally, it must be realized that as there was no redemption for Saul because of an apostate heart, there is no redemption for the apostate Church. Paul wrote Timothy, *"And they shall turn away their ears from the truth, and shall be turned unto fables"* (II Tim. 4:4).

The 34th verse says, *"For he was grieved for David, because his father had done him shame."* The "grieving" for the state of Israel's spiritual welfare was normal and right under such circumstances. However, he would have been far better off to have thrown in his lot with David, rather than to have stayed with his wayward father. He would not lose his soul for such action, but he would lose his effectiveness for God.

How many millions of godly people sit in an apostate church that has long since lost its way with God with no evidence whatsoever of returning to God's ways and thinking somehow that they can effect a change. Instead, the situation in a spiritual sense grows progressively worse.

The 42nd verse says, *"And Jonathan said to David, Go in peace."* The latter part of the verse says, *"And Jonathan went into the city."* Where was David going? From henceforth he would be hunted like an animal. Saul would repeatedly try to kill him. Basically, only those who were in distress or "wanted" themselves, would follow David. So, it was much easier for Jonathan to *"go into the city."*

Multiple millions of Christians down through the ages have had to make these decisions. Whom do I follow? It is so easy to continue to follow a denomination simply because of tradition and past ties. It is never easy to follow God's anointed because of the circumstances. Still, this must ever be remembered:

If the child of God follows Saul, he will lose all of his spiritual effectiveness and could lose his soul. If he wants to be effective for God and wants his life to count for the Lord Jesus Christ, he must follow the man with the anointing, David. Yes, it will demand a faith walk. From all outward observances, it will not be enticing. All that David can promise is hard-

ship and difficulty. He will be an outcast in his own country, but all of these things must be forgotten. Only one thing is of paramount importance, and that is the call of God and the anointing of the Holy Spirit. David was called and anointed by God; Saul wasn't. That is enough. There need not be, and, indeed, must not be any other reason. We follow the call and the anointing of the Holy Spirit.

CHAPTER 21

This chapter will show the foibles of David. What will be read in the following passages is one of the reasons that the Church has great difficulty in following a man, even though anointed. Men, being human, are altogether flawed. There are no exceptions. So, it's much "safer" to follow an institution than it is a man. Still, there are several things that should be noted concerning this situation.

1. Institutions are man-made, mainly unscriptural, and, therefore, unblessed by God. Still, being glutted with religious machinery, they give the appearance of much religious activity, thereby, deceiving most of the Church world.

2. Everything that is done by God is done through a man, even though flawed. Even in denominations, no work for God is carried out by the machinery of the denomination. Anything that is done for God is done by an individual who is touched and anointed by the Holy Spirit, even though in that denomination. So, everything that is done on this planet for the Lord Jesus Christ is, without exception, done through individuals anointed by the Holy Spirit. Most of the time the individual is greatly opposed by the organized structure, as David was opposed by Saul.

Verse 1 says, *"Why art thou alone, and no man with thee?"* David was alone, at least as far as any other government officials were concerned. However, the 4th verse says that some *"young men"* were with him. Little by little a goodly number of Israel's distressed and harried would come to David. But now as he begins his wanderings, his chances of survival look very slim. He will have almost no help at this stage.

When one embarks upon the path of faith, one must embark alone. To be sure, it is a lonely path, but this is the way that God has designed it. Gradually, others will gravitate to this pathway, but at the beginning it is a lone decision.

In the 2nd verse David says, *"The king hath commanded me a business."* The statement is untrue. In effect, David lied. It will not be his last mistake. Many individuals have the erroneous conception that if God calls an individual, especially with the magnitude of David's call, then the individual must be nearly perfect. No, quite the contrary. With every call of God of this magnitude will, as well, also come tremendous opposition. Not only will the opposition come from Saul, but from demon powers of darkness who will, no doubt, do all within hell's power to hinder David in this faith walk. At times through fear he will succumb and commit a wrongdoing. No, when this happens God does not throw David overboard, neither will He do so to anyone who is touched by the Holy Spirit. God will work with a person, strengthening him to overcome the weaknesses that are in every single Christian's life, even in those who are greatly called of God. The Holy Spirit through Paul says that the *"calling and the gifts are without repentance."* God doesn't change His mind, and the individual cannot change his mind. True, the one who is called may turn his back on God and refuse to do the work of God, which, no doubt, at times happens. But as far as God is concerned, the call is still there and always will be there.

So, David will lie to Ahimelech, the priest, which, in effect, would occasion his death, and every priest who was there. In the eyes of God, David would not be responsible for these deaths; Saul would. However, David's lie will at least play a part in the death of a great many innocent people.

David had no weapons, so he sought them, and the 9th verse says, *"And the priest said, The sword of Goliath the Philistine, whom thou slewest in the valley of Elah, behold, it is here."* The sword of Goliath did not save the giant, neither could it save David.

The 10th verse states, *"And David arose and*

NOTES

fled that day for fear of Saul." It is so easy to fault David for his actions at this stage. However, would we have done any better? That's the great question. It's not only that we would not have done any better, we probably would not have done nearly so well. The following statement is printed elsewhere in this volume, but it is important enough to be repeated.

1. When we hear something derogatory about a child of God, we should remember that what we're hearing is gossip and should treat it as such.

2. Even though, in fact, we may know the details, still, we have little understanding of the actual spiritual conflict involved and should be very careful what we say.

3. As stated, if we were placed in the same position, would we do any better, or even as well?

The things that David did as outlined in this chapter and in other chapters are wrong and cannot be glazed over or ignored. However, we make a gargantuan mistake if we think, placed in the same position, we would have done better. The 10th verse continues to say, *"And went to Achish the king of Gath."* Achish was a Philistine. In effect, David was going over to the enemies of God. So much of the wrongdoing that comes by the child of God is caused by fear. David had been anointed to be the king of Israel. True faith would have known that God would not allow anything to happen to him until the plan of God was finished and complete. However, the squeeze that God would allow upon David would show the imperfections in David's faith.

When God calls an individual for such a notable service as He called David, the call is not given because of the maturity of faith or consecration resident within that individual. In fact, the great necessities such as faith, consecration, maturity, and dedication are only there in minute quantities. David would have to grow into the greatness of faith and consecration. He could only do so by being put to the test. He would fail the test, as fail he must. But through the failure and, in fact, many other failures, gradually, his love for God would increase along with his faith and consecration.

Previously we saw what faith did when it

took the giant's head in its hands and walked away with it. Now we see what fear does. The 13th verse says, *"And scrabbled* (dribbled) *on the doors of the gate, and let his spittle fall down upon his beard."* This is God's man in an extremely humiliating position of feigning madness (insanity) to escape the Philistine.

Why does God, Who can do anything, and Who is all-powerful, allow His children, and especially one who He has called like David to be placed in such circumstances?

The answer, although not at all times so obvious, is relatively simple, especially with someone like David. God allows it for David and all like him, to learn trust and dependence. There is no other way to do it.

Regrettably, the institutionalized Church, at this stage in David's life, would have felt that he was an embarrassment, even ignoring all the victories that had gone before. Dismissal would, no doubt, have been the ruling of the moment. In fact, David had done wrong, and as well, he would have broken several of the man-made rules and regulations. So, the institutionalized Church would have washed their hands of him. However, God did not.

———◼———

CHAPTER 22

The 1st verse says, *"David therefore departed thence and escaped to the cave Adullam."* This cave was a large one near the city of Adullam in Judah, which was about 12 miles southwest of Bethlehem and about 20 or more miles from Nob, a place about 2 miles north of Jerusalem. This would be David's headquarters. David would compose Psalm 57 on this occasion. Actually, many of the Psalms that were composed by David, and, we might add, inspired by the Holy Spirit, were written during times of great distress.

Going back to the 21st chapter when David appeared before Achish, the king of Gath (a Philistine), and even though David seems out of the will of God and operating in fear, he composed Psalm 56 at this particular time.

Along with his brethren and all his father's house the second verse says, *"And every one*

that was in distress, and every one that was in debt, and every one that was discontented, gathered themselves unto him." There were about *"four hundred men."*

In this physical scene we can catch the spiritual sense of the true Church of God. Israel and the Church were very similar regarding spiritual position.

Israel the nation was regarded as "God's chosen." But still, only a small remnant in Israel proper were actually true servants of God. The prophets over and over again would speak of national Israel as a *"harlot nation"* (Hosea 1:2). They would also at times speak of the "remnant" who were really the true Israel, who lived for God. In Jesus' day the nation as a whole had apostatized along with its religious leadership. However, in the midst of this apostasy there was a remnant who loved the Lord and followed the Lord Jesus Christ.

Likewise, the Church as a whole has apostatized. Regrettably, the situation will not get better but worse. However, in this apostatized Church there is a "remnant" who loves the Lord Jesus Christ and actually constitutes the "true Body of Christ."

So David's position in the *"cave Adullam"* is a type of the small remnant who truly are called of God and live for God. This is the position today in Christendom. The outward form of a testimony for God exists, but its living reality is only found among those who know, love, and serve their rejected Lord. Such persons are despised by the great and proud and, as well, by much of the religious hierarchy. However, the Lord calls them "the excellent in the earth," and He says that in them is all His delight (Psa. 16:3).

The 3rd verse says, *"Till I know what God will do for me."* Even though David had been anointed by Samuel as the future king of Israel, and the Holy Spirit had come upon him from that very moment, still, due to circumstances, he did not exactly know what the Lord would do with him. Faith is an unworldly virtue. It very seldom explains more than a step at a time. To fully realize its benefits and to gather all it guarantees, one must learn trust and dependence. David and those who were with him had to enter the "Bible college of faith."

From these words we know that David was

seeking the Lord incessantly as to direction, "Lord what do you want me to do?"

The answer comes in the 5th verse, *"And the prophet Gad said unto David. Abide not in the hold; depart, and get thee into the land of Judah."* To the earnest seeking heart, God will always give purpose and direction. If we seem to have no direction, we should abide where we are until the Lord says "move." Unbelief always hurries and scurries. Faith does not move until God says "move."

The awful results in verses 6 through 19 say, *"And Nob, the city of the priests, smote he with the edge of the sword."* Saul would kill all the priests with the exception of "Abiathar" who *"escaped, and fled after David"* (vs. 20). Saul would kill some 85 men of God as well as women and children.

Incidentally, Abiathar was of the line of priests of Eli. He had a son who was also joint priest with Zadok for a while (I Chron. 18:16; 24:6). Solomon deposed Ahimelech because he espoused his brother's cause to become king, and Zadok became sole high priest (I Kings 1:7-42). Thus, the prophecy to Eli of the cutting off of his house as priest was finally fulfilled (I Sam. 2:31), for Abiathar was the last of his line to be high-priest. Eli and Abiathar were of the house of Ithamar, and Zadok was of the house of Eleazar. By this act of Saul, he caused the transfer of the Urim and Thummim to David, and, as stated, the prophecy to Eli of the cutting-off of his house was fulfilled.

Saul is the epitome of religion. It is a cruel, bloodthirsty business. Regrettably, most of what is referred to as "Christianity" is actually religion and has no relationship to Christianity. Christianity is really not religion. Actually, it is a relationship with a person, and that person is Christ. Religion is made up of rules, regulations, laws, stipulations, and ceremonies. It has no relationship to Christ. It may speak of Him and talk of Him, but it looks for its salvation in its ritualistic ceremonies, as well as its rules and regulations.

It must be clearly noted that David declared no war against Saul. He did not use the anointing that the Holy Spirit gave him to hurt Saul in any manner. He would, rather, despite Saul's evil intentions against him, continue to love Saul with all his heart.

NOTES

The 23rd verse says, *"Abide thou with me, fear not."* These were the words spoken to "Abiathar," the high-priest of Israel. To Abiathar at this moment, it may not have seemed like much future awaited him. He along with David would be hunted and threatened. However, when he threw in his lot with David, this would be the greatest move he ever made. Likewise, those who are in *"distress," "in debt,"* and *"discontented"* will find that when they side with the Lord's anointed that despite the difficulties, from thereon they will be marked for greatness.

CHAPTER 23

This chapter is freighted with the leading of the Holy Spirit. It will show David's faith, as well as the depravity of the men of Keilah.

The 1st verse states, *"They robbed the threshingfloors."* The Philistines, as well as others, were very adept at robbing the increase, just as Satan robs the increase of our spiritual lives, if we allow him to do so.

The 2nd verse says, *"Therefore David inquired of the Lord."* The Lord told him to go *"smite these Philistines."* He told him to *"save Keilah."* He will do so but will receive no thanks for his efforts. Regrettably, most of the Church would rather be ruled by the Philistines than to be saved by David.

The 3rd verse relates to us that *"David's men"* did not necessarily show David's faith regarding this excursion. This is normal. When God speaks, He only speaks to the leader. David shows patience with their lack of faith. For the 4th verse says, *"Then David inquired of the Lord yet again."* This time, it seems, his men shared his faith.

More than likely David's means of communicating with the Lord was by the "Urim and Thummim."

As we have stated elsewhere in this volume, what the "Urim and Thummim" were, no one exactly knows. It is known that whatever they were, they were kept in some type of pocket or container in the back of the "ephod." This was a vest-like garment worn by the great high priest. The word "Urim" means "lights," with the word "Thummim" meaning "perfection." It seems that questions were asked, and when the lot was drawn from the "Ephod," it would give a "yes" or "no" answer.

The 5th verse says, *"And fought with the Philistines."* The record is clear that David never fought Saul. However, Saul, no doubt, loudly trumpeted his contention that David fought him incessantly, but it was not so.

Even though the true minister of the Gospel must diligently *"Contend for the faith once delivered unto the saints,"* his fight must never become personal regarding individuals in the apostate Church. The moment one uses the anointing to fight against some denomination, church, or alleged Christian body, the anointing of the Holy Spirit will be lost. Satan has been very successful in steering many God-called ministers into personal and private fights. David's objective was always the Philistine. Our objective must be the foes of darkness.

Verses 10 through 12 record the perfidy of the men of Keilah. In the 11th verse David asks the Lord, *"Will the men of Keilah deliver me up into his hand?"* He was speaking of the hand of Saul.

The 12th verse says, *"And the Lord said, They will deliver thee up."* It is difficult to imagine the attitude and wickedness of these men of Keilah who had been delivered by David from the Philistines, but to gain fame and fortune would deliver David over to Saul. David ventured his life to save the men of Keilah, and they, with base ingratitude, promptly prepared to betray him.

Thus, it was with Him of whom David was a type. The Lord Jesus Christ came to redeem Israel and to save the Gentile, and they joined together to crucify Him. Such is fallen man!

The 14th verse states, *"And Saul sought him every day, but God delivered him not into his hand."* David's way may have seemed precarious, and to the natural eye it was. However, Saul's way was impossible. What God has placed His anointing upon, men, despite their eagerness and efforts, cannot overcome.

The 16th verse says, *"And Jonathan Saul's son arose, and went to David into the wood, and strengthened his hand in God."*

In the 17th verse we realize that Jonathan was well aware of all that God had called David to do. For he says, *"And thou shalt be king over Israel."* Still, Jonathan, for whatever reason, would not throw in his lot totally with David.

The 18th verse says, *"And David abode in the wood, and Jonathan went to his house."* Jonathan would in no way help his father Saul in his attempts to kill David, but, at the same time, he never fully threw in his lot with David, either. If he had broken with Saul completely, joining David in his test of faith and not return to his house, quite possibly that which he said, *"And I shall be next unto thee,"* would have been realized. He did not do that, and he was never heard from again in the Holy Scriptures until he appears slain by the Philistines on Mount Gilboa.

Not at all taking away from Jonathan's fidelity, still, so many Christians face the same choice that Jonathan faced. They cannot quite bring themselves to make the break and join David completely, and will, thereby, live in a state of spiritual limbo, accomplishing little for the Lord. How many today is the Lord calling to, saying, *"Come out from among them and be ye separate"?* How many are obeying?

True, Saul could promise wealth and position to his followers, while David could only offer hunger and hardship. The children of faith are, as a rule, poor and few in number; the children of rebellion are oftentimes many and rich. David would have neither home nor refuge, but he had the Word of God, the call of God, and communion with God. This was his portion in exile and the portion of all who followed him. Saul, though king of Israel, had neither the Word of God, the call of God, nor communion with God. Many will trade the Word, the call, and the communion for wealth, power, and position. It is a sorry trade.

Verses 19 through 26 record Satan, through Saul, hemming David in, so it seemed impossible to escape. The 26th verse says, *"For Saul and his men compassed David and his men around about to take them."*

Sometimes God in His wisdom does not deliver His servant until all appears lost, and faith seems a deception. David was apparently overcome, with escape impossible. But at the very last moment he was delivered. For the 27th verse says, *"But there came a messenger unto Saul, saying, Haste thee, and come; for the Philistines have invaded the land."* This was Divine intervention to protect David when Saul was about to overtake him. Faith may come at the last minute, but it is never late. Great faith must be tested greatly, and so it was. God delights in the impossible. Actually, He only works when it is impossible.

————■————

CHAPTER 24

In this chapter we will see two great truths that are brought out to us by the Holy Spirit. They are as follows:

1. The great lengths that Saul would go to in order to kill David. Saul is a type of apostate religion that must, or at least attempt to kill that which is called of God, of which David is a type.

2. The great reluctance that David will have to harm Saul. This portrays the true child of God who will not take matters into his own hands but will place all in the hands of the Lord.

The 2nd verse says, *"And went to seek David and his men upon the rocks of the wild goats."* Saul takes 3000 chosen men of Israel into an almost inaccessible area, attempting to kill David. Saul's enemy was not David; it was the Philistines. But, yet, most of his energy is spent trying to kill God's anointed.

Why would he do such a thing? He would do so because he knew that God had called David and anointed him to be the king of Israel. The apostate Church is little concerned about the call of God. Its main concern is power. It will cling to that at any cost, even to the killing of God's anointed. This battle has raged from the very beginning. The first murder was a "religious" murder. Cain killed Abel because God accepted Abel's sacrifice and refused Cain's. Joseph's greatest enemies were his brethren. The greatest hindrance to the Apostle Paul in taking the Gospel of Jesus Christ to a lost world was not Rome but Jerusalem.

The 4th verse says, *"Behold the day of*

NOTES

which the Lord said unto thee, Behold, I will deliver thine enemy into thine hand." Saul had gone into a large cave in which he would ultimately lie down for an hour or so of sleep. As he lay down, he, no doubt, threw his kingly robe over his feet. David and several of his men were at the side of the cave and could have easily killed Saul. The Jewish rabbins explain that Saul did not expect anyone to be in the cave because of a spider's web over its mouth. Seeing this, they say he became careless and did not examine the place before resting.

The supposed promise of verse 4 had never been given by God. Such is man! Promises that are given he lightly esteems, and Promises that are not given he invents and believes. The child of God must be careful that he does not read into the Word of God what is not there. As well, he should not fail to claim all the Promises of God. David does not take the opportunity to kill Saul, but he cuts off a portion of his robe.

The 5th verse says, *"That David's heart smote him, because he had cut off Saul's skirt."* The carnal mind immediately takes advantage of this opportunity. However, the spiritual mind knows that this is not God's way.

The 6th verse says, *"The Lord forbid that I should do this thing unto my master, the Lord's anointed."* This does not mean that Saul was anointed by the Holy Spirit, for he was not. It means that he had been "anointed" to be king of Israel. Even though Saul was man's choice, still, God had played a part in allowing this man to be king of Israel. By no stretch of the imagination could Saul be called "God's anointed" according to the power of the Holy Spirit. But still, David goes to extra lengths to make certain that he does not lay his hand on that which is God's sole responsibility.

The reader should notice the difference in the two spirits. Saul would go to any length to kill David, irrespective that he is without doubt, "God's anointed." David, on the other hand, takes great precaution that he does not touch that which is the sole responsibility of the Lord, even though greatly corrupt. This is a perfect picture of the apostate Church that will go to any length to preserve its power. As well, it should be a perfect picture of the true Church of Jesus Christ, that will go to any length not to intrude into the sole domain of the Lord. However, this in no way prevents the true child of God from "contending for the faith once delivered unto the saints." For instance, Paul would never oppose Jerusalem, but he would go to any length to "defend the faith." Martin Luther would not oppose Rome, as such, but would even at the risk of his own life proclaim "justification by faith." Likewise, David would never forfeit the call of God on his life to be the king of Israel, despite the fact that Saul was king and his family by all natural rights should continue. However, David would allow the Lord to do this in His own time.

The 7th verse says, *"And suffered them not to rise against Saul."* So, even though given the opportunity, David does not take matters into his own hands and kill Saul.

The 20th verse records Saul's reasons, *"thou shalt surely be king, and that the kingdom of Israel shall be established in thine hand."* Saul knew this but would go to any length to circumvent such. However, he was signing his own death warrant. He was fighting against God, a battle, regardless of his resources, he could not hope to win. A battle, it might also be added, despite David's circumstances, that David could not lose.

CHAPTER 25

The 1st verse says, *"And Samuel died."* Samuel died at a ripe old age and all Israel mourned for him as they did for Moses, Joshua, and other great, recognized leaders. It is supposed that he died about two years before Saul did when he was around 98 years of age. The 1st verse says as well, *"And David arose, and went down to the wilderness of Paran."* Whether David went to the funeral of Samuel is not known, but to him it was clear that with Samuel's death came the removal of the last restraining power in Saul's life; so he departed further from Saul. He went down to the wilderness of Paran, which was south of Judea, and into the country of the Amalekites in the Negeb, a triangular shaped region from Beersheba on the north to the gulf of Aqaba in the south and Egypt on the west.

There are three great figures in this chapter. They are Samuel, David, and Abigail. They typify the Law, Christ, and the true Israel. The Scripture says that the Law and the Prophets were until John; then the King appeared, but in rejection and hatred, yet, loving hearts joined Him, shared His exile and sufferings, animated by the knowledge that those who suffered with him should reign with Him (II Tim. 2:12).

Accordingly Samuel disappears, as the Law would disappear when Christ came. Now Abigail appears, who is the true Israel. She will by faith accept the true King, the Lord Jesus Christ, and reject Saul, who at this stage is a type of the Law. Abigail would leave her wealthy home to be an outcast and a wanderer with David.

The 10th verse speaks of Nabal, as he asks, *"Who is David?"* There are three things about Nabal that should be noted:

1. He was very great in wealth. The 2nd verse says, *"very great."*

2. The 3rd verse says, *"But the man was churlish and evil in his doings."* He was *"of the house of Caleb"* but not of the spirit and faith of Caleb.

3. He was opposed to God's choice, *"and who is the son of Jesse?"* (vs. 10). Nabal will not survive the ordeal.

David asks for help from this man, needing food and provision. He was not asking for charity for the 16th verse says, *"They were a wall unto us both by night and day."* In other words, David's men, encamped close by Nabal's possessions, were a blessing instead of a hindrance. As Nabal did not know, understand, nor even care for these things, likewise, the world in general does not realize or recognize the "salt of the earth" that is in its midst. Every city is greatly blessed concerning the number of true Christians who are in its confines. Likewise, every nation that is blessed owes that blessing to the children of God in its midst. Still, as Nabal, it little recognizes such or even cares. Actually, if given opportunity much of the time the world will oppose the child of God, as Nabal opposed David.

The 13th verse gives us an idea of David's personality for it says, *"And David said unto his men, Gird ye on every man his sword."* David was the called of God for that particular time, being probably closer to God than any other human being alive on the face of the earth. Yet, we will see how imperfect David was. No man is perfect even though he is a type of Christ. David takes matters into his own hands. Yet, God would intervene and deliver him from this snare. Abigail is the instrument of that deliverance.

Not only is Abigail beautiful in person, but she is even more beautiful in character. Her faith and her intelligence are admirable. She judges both Nabal and Saul as God judged them. She recognizes in David his title as king despite his personal imperfection. She also recognizes his valour in fighting God's battles, and where others only see a rebel, she sees a redeemer. All this is not merely just the intelligence of the head; it is accompanied by the affection of the heart (vss. 23-31).

The 38th verse says, *"That the Lord smote Nabal, that he died."* Why would God smite Nabal and not smite Saul? The answer is simple but not very desirable. David needed Saul. In other words, Saul was a necessity. Saul kept David on his face before God. Saul's very presence of anger and murder necessitated David constantly seeking the Lord for guidance, strength, and help. So, God would allow Saul to remain. Oftentimes, we try to rid ourselves of an enemy, when, in reality, God wants it to remain in order to keep us on our face before the Lord. As He will eventually remove Saul, He will eventually remove the difficulty that plagues us. Still, in the meantime, it may seem to be extremely harmful to us, but, in reality it forces us to our knees, which is a great blessing.

The human consecration is always flawed. David would walk by faith regarding the harming of Saul, which he would not do, still, he would succumb to selfish desire when it came to Nabal. This is the story of even the strongest child of God. David's greatest problem really was not Saul; it was self. Unrighteous self would be smothered regarding Saul. Regrettably, it would be loosed regarding Nabal and spared only because of God's intervention. We think the Sauls and the Nabals of our lives are our real enemies. They really aren't. It is always self.

NOTES

CHAPTER 26

Verse 1 says, *"And the Ziphites came unto Saul to Gibeah, saying, Doth not David hide himself in the hill of Hachilah?"* This is the third time that David would be betrayed by his own countrymen - actually twice by these Ziphites. These individuals sought to curry favor with Saul by betraying David. One must remember that even though totally corrupt, this was what might be referred to as the "Church" of its day. In present-day religious circles, which have very little, if any, spiritual strength, and have what is basically political or civil government, modern-day "Ziphites" will play the political game even at the expense of their own souls to curry favor with the religious hierarchy.

The 2nd verse says, *"To seek David in the wilderness of Ziph."* In this chapter we see a portrayal of the unregenerate religious man, totally controlled by the Adamic or sin nature. We also witness the regenerate God-called man, even though still retaining the sin nature, nevertheless, not being controlled by it. It would seem from the 24th chapter and according to the great display of love that David showed toward Saul, that this man would have ceased his relentless quest to kill "God's anointed." However, we see that "the natural man" totally controlled by the "sin nature" is the helpless but willing tool of evil. We also see that the "spiritual man" never accustoms himself to evil, even though at times failing. Saul illustrates the first example, David, the second. Saul knew that David was God's chosen king, and that he would certainly reign, and, yet, he again and again sought to destroy him. Such is the power of evil! Satan is also the helpless but willing agent of sin; this fact respecting man's fallen nature, proves the absolute necessity of a new moral creation.

David illustrates the truth that the "spiritual nature" can never accustom itself to evil. Man's sinful, unregenerate, wicked nature accustoms itself to evil after a little time even ceasing to be shocked by its manifestations.

Between the spiritual and the natural

nature there is in this world "a great space," just as is described in verse 13, *"a great space being between them."* These "two natures" are eternally separated. It is impossible to cultivate the one so that it will develop into the other. Many have believed this to be possible. It is known as the doctrine of "moral evolution." Even though man has tried to bridge this gap with education, money, culture, prestige, great religious activity, and many other things, still, there is a great gulf fixed between these two natures which makes a transition from the one to the other impossible, hence, the necessity of being *"created anew in Christ Jesus"* (Eph. 2:10).

Every single individual in the world, both believer and unbeliever, has an "Adamic" or "sin nature." The unbeliever is totally controlled by the "sin nature," as Saul, while the believer, as symbolized by David, although still retaining the sin nature, will not be controlled at all by it. The unbeliever is controlled by evil; in other words, the sin nature controls the individual. He may have some choice as to what type of sin he would commit but no choice as to committing the sin. With the believer, even though retaining the sin nature, Jesus Christ rules and reigns in the heart and life. Sadly, even in the life of the believer as we have viewed David from time to time, there will be failures. However, the believer can never accustom himself to that failure or practice the same.

John writes, *"If we say that we have no sin (sin nature) we deceive ourselves, and the truth is not in us"* (I John 1:8).

Someone has described the sin nature in the life of the unbeliever as a roaring conflagration that will ultimately destroy all. It has also been described in the life of the believer, who is ruled by Christ, as remaining but smothered. However, if the child of God allows "self" to rule even for a short period of time, this smothered "sin nature" will once again roar into life. This is what Paul was speaking of in Romans 7:15. He also says in the Epistle to the Galatians that if we *"walk in the Spirit, we will not fulfill the lust of the flesh (sin nature)"* (Gal. 5:16).

Many have taught sanctification as a definite work of Grace that eliminates and eradicates the "sin nature." However, this is not

NOTES

scriptural. At this present time the child of God is sanctified and justified, but he is not yet glorified. Paul writes, *"For the earnest expectation of the creature waiteth for the manifestation of the sons of God"* (Rom. 8:19).

He also says, *"Waiting for the adoption, to wit, the redemption of our body"* (Rom. 8:23). Then the "sin nature" will be forever eradicated.

In the 8th verse Abishai says to David, *"God hath delivered thine enemy into thine hand this day."* Even though the advice given brought God into its quest, still, it was not godly. The advice and counsel of our brethren should be eagerly sought after. However, it is often flawed as Abishai's counsel to David. So, the man of God must ever seek to hear from heaven, and, as God gave direction to David, He will give direction to us.

For the 9th verse says, *"Destroy him not."* It would seem so natural to the carnal mind, even though a follower of God's anointed, for one to take advantage of this opportunity. However, God's ways are not man's ways. In retrospect, if David had killed Saul, it would have been a black stain on David's life that would have sullied the title, *"a man after God's own heart."* In David's actions regarding Saul, we see *"God's own heart."* God is ever seeking the sinner; He is ever showing mercy; He is ever extending grace. God's hand ever calls, *"Come unto me."* So, as we view David's actions regarding Saul, we are viewing the actions of Christ toward even the vilest of sinners who seek to destroy God's work.

The 10th verse gives the will of the Lord, *"The Lord shall smite him."* Whenever religious man usurps Christ's position as "head of the Church," he eagerly will kill God's anointed, thinking he is doing God a service. However, when the Spirit of Christ reigns, the headship of Christ is never abrogated.

The 12th verse says, *"Because a deep sleep from the Lord was fallen upon them."* The Lord would supernaturally protect David. However, had David taken matters into his own hands as was suggested by his associate, quite possibly this protection by the Lord would not have been forthcoming. We can only expect God's best if we go entirely God's way.

The 19th verse says, *"Go, serve other gods."*

This was the greatest sin of all against David and his men - driving them away from the worship of the true God and virtually telling them to go serve other gods. How so similar to modern-day institutionalized religion, *"We will shun you and ban you from our Churches if you do not do exactly as we say, no matter how unscriptural."*

———◼———

CHAPTER 27

We attempted to portray in chapter 26 how the "sin nature" still resides in the heart and life of the believer, even though not controlling him. Still, it will be the occasion of failure, as is recorded in this chapter; failure, we might add, that will always exact a high price.

Verse 1 says, *"And David said in his heart."* David now resorts to fear instead of faith. As the pressure intensifies, it becomes increasingly more difficult to keep one's eye on nothing but the Promises of God. Fear crowds from every side, so he says, *"I shall now perish."* This was not faith talking but fear. He also says, *"I should speedily escape into the land of the Philistines."* In this he would be disobeying the Divine command to dwell in the land of Judah (I Sam. 22:5).

It should always be remembered that there is no half-way house between fellowship with God and fellowship with the Philistine. If the Philistine is made a refuge, then David must dwell in the midst of them and declare himself ready to fight with them against the people of God. God, in His love and pity for His servant (as us), overrules all for David's safety, but, at the same time sorely chastising him (I Sam. 30).

There is a possibility that David's action in joining Achish delayed his possession of the Kingdom.

In actual Christian life, as in the Scriptures, despondency and unbelief always seem to quickly follow great crises of faith. It was so with Elijah (I Kings 19), as with David and Peter, and others. It would seem as if an unusual effort of faith exhausted the heart, which is the vessel of that faith, with the result

NOTES

being that fear and weakness occur. However, it must be quickly added that no such failure or fault was ever seen in the Man, Jesus Christ.

The 5th verse says, *"Let them give me a place."* Heretofore, David has asked the Lord; now he is asking a Philistine king. The only thing he will receive from this man is that which is thought to benefit the Philistines, not David.

The 6th verse says, *"Then Achish gave him Ziklag."* Ziklag was a border town between Judah and the Philistines. Satan loves for the child of God to dwell as close to the world as possible. Of course, the argument could be readily made that with constant threats on David's life, he had little choice. This is human reasoning, and it is never God's way.

The 7th verse states, *"David dwelt in the country of the Philistines a full year and four months."* One might as well say that David was some 16 months out of the will of God. With every Christian there are always great difficulties and circumstances that seem to give us license to do that which is not the perfect will of God. However, the direction is always wrong. Despite Saul's constant threat, David's place was in Judah, not Philistia. Likewise, the place of the child of God is in the center of God's will, not the periphery.

Verses 8 through 12 record the result of this disobedience. The 8th verse says, *"And David and his men went up, and invaded."*

The 9th verse adds, *"And left neither man nor woman alive."* Here was a man who would not harm Saul when given the opportunity, yet, would ruthlessly kill hundreds or even thousands of men and women among the heathen. While it is true God had given directions that these individuals (Geshurites, Gezrites, and Amalekites) were to be destroyed, He did not thus intend in this fashion. No doubt, David justified his actions, as we justify our actions in wrongdoing. Still, this does not make it right. These 16 months were a black time in David's life. It was not a time of faith and trust in God; it was a time of fear.

CHAPTER 28

This chapter records the story of failure, both on the part of David and Saul. The Holy Spirit will graphically record the happenings.

Verse 1 says, *"That the Philistines gathered their armies together for warfare, to fight with Israel."* These are Israel's greatest enemies. They are also the enemies of God. These are the people who David has so long defeated, and now he has joined them. There is no excuse on David's part. When a Christian seeks the protection and patronage of a man of the world, he must place himself and his spiritual gifts at the disposition of his protector. This is a sad and degrading bondage. This was David's unworthy and God-dishonoring relation with Achish. In such circumstances Satan does not fail to provide earthly honors, and, accordingly, Achish made David captain of this bodyguard. *"Therefore will I make thee keeper of mine head for ever"* (vs. 2). Immediately in verse 3 the Holy Spirit records, *"Now Samuel was dead."* The spiritual tide of Israel had never been worse. David was God's only light, and now it dims low.

The 5th verse states of Saul, *"He was afraid, and his heart greatly trembled."* The mercy and grace of God had been extended to Saul for some 40 years. He had spurned each Gospel call.

The 6th verse says, *"And when Saul enquired of the Lord, the Lord answered him not."* However, it must be quickly added that Saul did not inquire of the Lord in humble contrition and repentance. To have truly repented, he would have made things right with David. That he did not do. We can only expect an answer from the Lord when we ask on God's terms. Regrettably, most do not desire to do that. If Saul had speedily sent for David, earnestly seeking his forgiveness which David would have readily granted, and then confessed his rebellion to God, pleading for mercy, these last chapters of Saul's life would have been written differently. The Lord is full of compassion and mercy. He will forgive and pardon, if we will but come before Him in humility and contrition.

The 7th verse says, *"Seek me a woman that hath a familiar spirit."* We blanch at such conduct; however, the majority of the inhabitants of the world are seeking information from "familiar spirits."

The 11th verse says, *"Bring me up Samuel."* He would not listen to Samuel when the great prophet was alive, so why should he seek his counsel now?

There is much controversy by Bible scholars as to whether Samuel actually came up, or whether it was a demon spirit impersonating Samuel. Either could have been possible. However, this truth should be made known:

Saul received absolutely no help whatsoever from trying to communicate with the dead, likewise, all others seeking such will receive the same - nothing.

Sadly, the majority of the world through horoscopes, psychic readings, fortune-telling, and psychologists endeavors to receive instruction, guidance, counsel or leading. All of these and many more that have not been named have demon spirits as the underlying factors. Demon spirits are always the underlying agents in all false doctrine, error, or direction that leads one astray from the Word of God. The Word of God forbids any trafficking with demon spirits, either directly or indirectly. Thankfully, a few in the world seek the counsel of the Word of God, which is the only truth. *All* else is false.

CHAPTER 29

Bible scholars have long since argued what David's intentions were regarding this 29th chapter. We can only form conclusions according to that which the Holy Spirit gives us. This was not a high point of David's life to date. Actually, it would be the lowest and most wretched to this moment. It would seem that he would profess himself ready and eager to fight against God's beloved people and to help Satan destroy them! He told many lies to Achish, the king of the Philistines, but the lie of this chapter was the crowning lie to date. He professed devotion to the Philistine monarch, while no doubt rejoicing secretly at escaping from so dreadful a position. For the 6th verse says, *"The lords favour thee not."* All of this shows how deeply a child of God can fall when he leans upon the hand of man and not upon the hand of God.

Back in the 5th verse, the Philistines asked the question, *"Is not this David?"* There are basically two lessons from this chapter that we need to learn. They are as follows:

1. The path of faith is not always an easy way. At times it is very tiring to our nature. There is an ever-present temptation to seek ease from the thorns through which that path sometimes leads. The persecution of professors of redemption oftentimes has the effect of throwing the servant of God into the arms of the enemies of God, just as Saul's hatred drove David to the Philistines. Still, this does not make it right. Actually, it only happens when the Christian follows his own will and thinks by doing so to avoid the very difficulties which, had he walked with God, would have become channels of teaching and refreshment to his soul. The more glorious a work there is for faith, the more sure is nature to become weary if faith grows feeble. How dreadful it would have been for David had he actually fought against the Israel of God and sought to slay the king whose life he had twice so touchingly saved!

2. The weaknesses of God's chosen! It should always be remembered that failure, despite the grace of God, always and without exception, carries with it its own punishment - even more in the life of one who has been grandly touched by the Holy Spirit. Too often Christendom reads only perfection into the life of God's champions; however, they do so by ignoring the Word of God. The individual is never called by God because he meets God's requirements. Actually, he never does. Always, he is woefully unprepared, immature, and lacking in proper faith. It is the work of the Holy Spirit, among other things, to bring David and others like him to the place of maturity that God desires. It does not come easy. A great call always demands a great test. Sooner or later there will be failure; it is inevitable. It may not be known all the time to the general Christian public, but God knows. It is a part of the growing process. Regretfully, oftentimes

one learns more from the failures than one does from the victories. The reasons should be obvious. At times, faith shines brighter during failure than victory, the reason being the pressure applied. Faith will either rise to the occasion or else quit. True men of God may fail, but they do not quit.

It is very easy for the passing glance to be critical of David. The fact is, he was wrong and terribly so. However, it must forever be remembered that what God demanded of David, at least at that time, was demanded of no other human being on the face of the earth. God uses failures to teach. Regrettably, fellow Christians many times use failures to destroy.

CHAPTER 30

There is no way that any person can see entirely into the spirit world. However, there are some things as followers of the Lord that we do know. They are as follows:

1. Satan at all times would attempt to destroy the child of God but is held back by the Lord. In other words, the child of God enjoys the total protection of the Lord Jesus Christ against the wiles of Satan. It is pictured graphically in the first chapter of Job as a hedge. Occasionally, the Lord will allow this hedge to be removed, at least to a certain degree.

2. If we stray from the Lord, as David had strayed by going into the land of the Philistines for some 16 months, this seems to allow Satan some leeway in causing us great difficulties. Because David strayed from the will of the Lord, God would allow the Amalekites to smite Ziklag.

For the 1st verse says, *". . . and smitten Ziklag, and burned it with fire."* The invaders killed no one but, rather, carried them away to be used or sold as slaves. It seems that this was allowed by the Lord because of David's spiritual declension regarding his sojourn with God's enemies, the Philistines.

This bitter trial brings David back to the Lord and affects a true restoration of his soul. Suffering and loss accompany departure from the Lord, and there must be chastisement in

NOTES

order for communion to be restored. Chastising is grievous, but it yields the peaceable fruit of righteousness (Heb. 12:11).

Concerning this terrible loss, the 6th verse says, *"And David was greatly distressed."* This, no doubt, was the low-water mark in David's life as he stood looking at the ashes of Ziklag, knowing that his family, as well as the families of all his men, had been taken captive. Great was the distress of his soul. Many people have to be brought to a "burnt Ziklag" before finally making things right with the Lord. Even though it would look grievous, still, all of this was allowed by the Lord because He loved David. As well, the Lord allows certain distressful things to happen to us because He loves us. He wants us once again to throw ourselves at His feet, admitting our wrongdoing, and to make things right with Him.

The 6th verse also says, *"For the people spake of stoning him."* They blamed him, and, in reality, it was his fault, but he was still God's anointed, and their only hope of recovering what they had lost. How so often we try to "stone" that which alone can help us. Condemnation heaped upon the propagator of fault is never the answer, but how often we as Christians seem to enjoy condemning or "stoning" the one we see who is to blame. It must ever be recognized that *all* the chastisement tendered toward a child of God is to be done by the Lord exclusively and never by a fellow Christian. Why?

In this situation all were guilty. Yes, David was the leader, but at the same time, his men did not have to follow him. They had done so of their own choice. So, his failure to trust God in the matter of the Philistines was their failure as well. Even if the failure was not theirs, no man is worthy to stone another. About 1000 years later Jesus would say, *"He that is without sin among you let him cast the first stone."*

This 6th verse is freighted with spiritual direction for it says, *"But David encouraged himself in the Lord his God."* What David did is the answer to every situation, and, yet, we so seldom travel that direction. We attempt to encourage ourselves too often in what will not profit. David went to the One Who could really help him, and that was the Lord. The moment David did this, communion was restored; res-

toration was complete.

The 7th verse says, *"Bring me hither the ephod."* The ephod would have the Urim and the Thummim. In the 27th chapter when David went over to the Philistines, there is no record that he "inquired" of the Lord. But now victory has been restored. David is once again seeking counsel from the One Who can really help him.

The 8th verse says, *"And he answered him."* What a beautiful statement given by the Holy Spirit. How do we know that spiritual victory was won and communion restored? We know that because now God is answering David's prayers. Spiritual victory must be ours before material, financial, or physical victory can come. Now, David has the spiritual victory. The Holy Spirit says, *"Pursue."* So, David begins with the total assurance that God is with him.

The 11th verse says, *"And they found an Egyptian in the field."* Now David is a type of Christ. The "Egyptian" is a type of the poor lost sinner far from God. He was *"brought to David,"* as you and I one day were brought to our Heavenly David. In turn David *"gave him bread, and drink."* Jesus, likewise, gave us Heavenly provision which satisfied the longings of our soul.

The 12th verse says, *"His spirit came again to him."* There is no life except in Christ. Now the Egyptian follows David. Formerly he had been a child of Ham, the slave of an Amalekite and an enemy to David. This is a true picture of the sinner, by nature a child of wrath (Eph. 2:3); by practice a slave to "the flesh"; by action an enemy to Christ; and by condition lost, sick and dying. David's servants, filled with David's spirit, found the Egyptian and brought him to David and laid him at his feet. Happy place! He there found bread, water, and figs, and two clusters of raisins; which represented life, strength, health, and joy - the new wine of the new kingdom.

The 18th verse says, *"And David recovered all."* What a statement! Satan, as well as many Christians, will attempt to make the child of God believe that it is not possible to "recover all." But the Scripture says differently. Actually, the Holy Spirit records it twice, for the 19th verse says as well, *"David recovered all."*

"Oh happy day! Oh happy day! When Jesus

took my sins away." It is possible through Christ to recover what Satan has stolen, and we in our foolishness have squandered. Actually, the very emphasis of God's great plan of redemption is that man may recover what he has lost. This is a perfect picture of wayward humanity that lost its way with God and began to follow the "Philistine" but, finally, even in the midst of chastisement and great loss, finds its way back to the feet of the world's Redeemer. There and only there can it recover all. The balance of this chapter portrays two tremendous blessings. They are as follows:

1. The 24th verse states, *"So shall his part be that tarrieth by the stuff: they shall part alike."* David, with some 600 men, goes to recover their great loss; however, some 200, according to the 21st verse, become so faint they are not able to join the battle. David demands that those who tarried behind *"by the stuff"* share alike with those who won the great victory. Paul in Romans 10 basically says the same thing, *"The sender would be just as important as the sent."*

2. Great blessings came from David to be given to all of Israel. For the 26th verse says, *"He sent of the spoil unto the elders of Judah."* There is no blessing that comes from man's choice, which had been Saul. There was great blessing that would come from God's choice, which was David. As well, David sent "presents" to his "friends" who had helped him when he was fleeing from Saul. The leadership of Israel demanded that no help be given unto David. So, those who helped David during these years of crisis did so at their own risk. Now, there would begin a blessing to these individuals that would never stop. Whenever we help those who God has called, even to a "cup of water," God will take notice, and we can be sure that blessing will be forthcoming.

CHAPTER 31

The battle that is recorded in chapter 31 would take the life of Saul, Jonathan, and Saul's other sons but should have never been fought.

The 1st verse opens with the words, *"Now*

NOTES

the Philistines fought against Israel." If Saul had yielded totally to the Lord, the Philistines would have long since been defeated. Saul did not yield to the Lord, consequently, the Philistines would not be defeated. So much in the world depends upon the spiritual condition of the Church. How many Philistines are left fighting us when, if our consecration had been complete, they would long since have ceased to be?

The 3rd verse says, *"And the battle went sore against Saul."* There was no other way it could go. Samuel was dead; David had been spurned by Saul who had attempted to kill him. As well, Saul had resorted to demon spirits. The battle could go no other way.

The 4th verse says that Saul committed suicide, *"Therefore Saul took a sword, and fell upon it."* The horror of total despair records every moment of this scene. How different it could have been. There was a time the Spirit of God came upon Saul, but now the Philistines came upon him instead.

The 7th verse says concerning cities in Israel, *"And the Philistines came and dwelt in them."* Saul was never able to dislodge them so, ultimately, they would dislodge Saul and occupy that which belonged to the people of God. So it is with Satan. Israel had demanded a king. Their choice was of the *"flesh"* and not of the *"Spirit."* Therefore, there would be little victory. Finally, David, God's choice, will occupy the throne (after some period of time), the Philistines will be dislodged, and Israel will be well on her way to becoming the mightiest nation on the face of the earth. She will extend her boundaries to that promised by the Lord, which was to the river of Egypt and the Gulf of Akabah, and then north to the Euphrates, taking in all of Philistia, Amalek, Edom, Moab, Syria, and other countries - but only when God's way was enjoined.

The 9th verse says concerning Israel's defeat and the death of Saul, *"To publish it in the house of their idols, and among the people."* In their minds their god had defeated the God of Israel.

America and Canada, failing to realize that God is the source of their blessings, are gradually coming to the place that they do not like to *"retain God in their knowledge."* Recent

Supreme Court decisions have borne this out. Therefore, the only alternative is a reprobate mind (Romans 1). America and Canada are facing that which Israel faced with the death of Saul unless there is Holy Ghost revival.

In the public school system of America, as well as in other areas of public means, Mohammed, Buddha, Confucius, or any other "false deity" can be extolled, but not Jesus Christ.

God help us that the final chapter of our two nations does not conclude as the final chapter of I Samuel.

NOTES

THE
BOOK OF II SAMUEL

—■—

There is no break between the two books of Samuel. They were one in the Hebrew text, being first divided by the Septuagint translators about 285 B.C. They have been continued as two books in every version since, but in our study we shall proceed with II Samuel without a break. The same thing happened to the book of Kings and that of Chronicles - each was originally one book, then divided into two. Ezra and Nehemiah also were one book at first, and then made into two.

We will now begin the story of David's reign over Israel which lasted for some 40 years. It will continue through all of II Samuel and into chapters 1 and 2 of I Kings and chapters 11-29 of I Chronicles.

—■—

CHAPTER 1

Verse 1 says, *"When David was returned."* The Holy Spirit in bringing out this word had far more in mind than the return to Ziklag from the *"slaughter of the Amalekites."* David had, as well, returned from some 16 months of disobedience to God. What a glorious moment when the child of God realizes his fault and his failure and then "returns to total dependence on God."

In this book of II Samuel we will study victories in the Spirit as few men have ever known. We will also, sadly and regrettably, study defeats such as few men have ever known.

Quite possibly, David was honored by the Lord as no human being has ever been honored. The Messiah, the Son of the living God, would be called, *"the son of David."* David's name would be the first human name in the New Testament (Matt. 1:1) and the last human name in the New Testament (Rev. 22:16).

No doubt, the reason for such tribulation allowed by God was because of the high place and position that God would give to him. Many want the "place and position" without the tribulation. It is not to be.

A life of conflict is bitter to the flesh but enriching to the spirit. Nature wearies of it, but a life of prosperity is full of snares to the soul.

As long as David acted in the simplicity of faith, his conduct was beautified. Faith made him simple and satisfied, whether as a shepherd boy or a king; whether loved by Saul or hated by him; whether victorious in secret or in public. Faith elevated and dignified him, and enabled him to endure courageously the hardships against which nature can only murmur and grow impatient. Faith enabled him to look above and beyond circumstances and people, to see and trust the Great Shepherd upon whose all-sufficiency he rested. Faith was the most precious gift he had; faith is the most precious gift we have. Faith made David willing to be a slave on earth because He whom he loved was in heaven, and he would one day awake in His likeness!

However, at times our weakened human nature grows weary of the conflict and rebels at circumstances. Self-will then leads into positions where God cannot be glorified. David would face this oftentimes. His life was not perfect.

As we began this chapter David had just recently returned to the life of faith. He had fallen from his lofty estate and had dishonored among the Philistines the Master whom he loved! But, Hallelujah, where sin abounded grace did much more abound, and, therefore, it was in this sad period of his life that he was chastened and then enthroned.

The reader should take note of this. The most saddened spiritual despondency to date would be immediately followed by the greatest victory.

The 8th verse says, *"I am an Amalekite."* This man gave David news of the death of Saul, even lying to David by claiming to have killed the king of Israel. It is interesting to note that the crown, which Saul had forfeited by failure to obey God regarding the Amalekites, was taken off by an Amalekite.

The 15th verse says that David did to this man what Saul had failed to do, *"And he smote him that he died."* As we have stated previously, "Amalek" is a type of the flesh. We will either kill it, or it will kill us. As well, it must ever be remembered that we cannot kill the "Amalekite" in our own strength. Flesh cannot overcome flesh. The Holy Spirit through us must slay "Amalek."

Verses 17 through 27 record *"this lamentation."* This is really a martial ode, and one of the first and finest odes in the Old Testament. David's own sufferings are forgotten, while his fervent love and deep grief for his king and his best friend, Jonathan, are expressed. There is no bitter or revengeful word or exultation over the death of his greatest enemy, Saul. The song is about the mighty warrior, the anointed of the Lord, the delight of his people, and the father of his beloved friend. The title of the ode in Hebrew is "Kesheth, the bow."

Only a divine love could cause David to speak thusly about the man who had made at least 21 attempts to kill him. This is pure, Christ-like love that God wants to give to every one of His people. This is one of the reasons that David was called *"a man after God's own heart."*

CHAPTER 2

The 1st verse says, *"David inquired of the Lord."* There is a marked spiritual turn in David's life from Ziklag on. The Ziklags are

terrible to the flesh and invigorating to the spirit. The Church by its "confession" principle has repeatedly tried to eliminate the "Ziklags" from our experience. The Church has failed, as fail it must, because its "confession" is not the will of God. At times, and sadly so, a "Ziklag" is needed. Now the Lord will tell him to leave this burned out area and go *"unto Hebron."* This would become his capital for 7½ years, and then Jerusalem would become the capital of united Israel. The Church is ever so slow to recognize that which God has long since ordained. The 4th verse says, *"And the men of Judah came, and there they anointed David king over the house of Judah."* So begins the golden age of Israel, and yet for 7½ years only a small part of the Church will accept God's anointed.

Verses 5 through 7 portray David making a gentle appeal to others of Israel to join him. However, at this time the flesh in so much of Israel remains dominant.

Verses 8 through 11 pictures *"the house of Saul"* and *"the house of David."* They stand in opposition one to the other. The one pictures the life as governed by Self; the other, the life as governed by God. The latter life alone secures victory.

How so often the Church follows the path of *"Abner the son of Ner."* Abner makes Saul's son, *"Ishbosheth",* king. The 9th verse says, *"Over all Israel."* Abner's action was that of "the natural man." He knew that David was God's elect king, yet, in self-will and ambition he set up his king. This was rebellion against God. David's move was spiritual, directed and designed by God. Abner's move was religious and, thereby, political, designed by man. The Church too often follows the latter.

The Holy Spirit in the 10th verse says, *"But the house of Judah followed David."* How much the Church misses because it follows Abner instead of David!

Verses 12 through 24 portray Abner attacking God's king and kingdom. Active opposition to Christ and His Kingdom quickly follows upon the establishment of a rival kingdom in the heart. The flesh is never satisfied to seek only its own; it must also destroy the things of "the Spirit."

The 17th verse tells us that the true men of

God who were *"servants of David"* would defeat Abner.

The balance of the chapter shows further conflict involved. The sharp swords that destroyed the young men of Israel should have been used against the Philistines. The 31st verse says, *"So that three hundred and three-score men died."* The destructive energy which rival groups within the Church employ against each other would accomplish great things if used against the common evil instead of each other. But, sadly, most of the energy of the Church is spent fighting not Satan but one another.

The 32nd verse closes with the words, *"And they came to Hebron at break of day."* The sun was now beginning to rise for Israel. The long night of spiritual declension was over. There would be other hardships and difficulties. However, the sun was not setting; it was rising. Hallelujah!

———■———

CHAPTER 3

This chapter will not pose victory for David. In the previous chapter we saw David inquiring of the Lord. In chapter 3 there seemed to be no inquiring of the Lord, and there seemed to be terrible mistakes made.

The blight of the Church is its political maneuvering. The shock to the Body of Christ would be acute if it knew how little was taken to the Lord in prayer. So much is like this chapter, only political maneuvering.

The 1st verse says, *"Now there was long war."* Actually this war lasted approximately 7½ years. It was between *"the house of David"* and *"the house of Saul."* It was the flesh persecuting him who was born after the Spirit (Gal. 4:29). A carnal nature is the enemy of the spiritual, but victory is assured to the latter. This 1st verse portrays the progress of the child of God. The "walking after the flesh", which is "the house of Saul", should become less and less while the "walking after the Spirit", which is "the house of David", should become more and more.

As well, David is a type of Christ, but while

recognizing that all types are imperfect, he portrays the coming kingdom age when the Lord will rule in personal glory. There is scriptural evidence from the prophets that Christ will establish His millennial reign in detail after His appearance and not by one overwhelming and universal action.

In this chapter, regrettably, we see David leaving the victorious path of faith and fellowship with God to walk the crooked and dark ways of man. There is no record that David even once asked counsel of God; on the contrary, he accepts the counsel of man and plans and schemes for himself.

Verses 2 through 5 proclaim his polygamy. The world would applaud these politics of making alliances with heathen princes and others, and marriages which would later bear bitter fruit in their offspring, such as Amnon, Absalom, and Adonijah.

The flesh has its champion as the 6th verse proclaims, *"That Abner made himself strong for the house of Saul."* Now the "flesh" attempts to join hands with the "Spirit." It is a political move and not a spiritual one. The 10th verse says of Abner, *"And to set up the throne of David over Israel and over Judah, from Dan even to Beersheba."*

The 12th verse proclaims this "political move."

The 13th verse also proclaims that David does not seek the face of God but readily says, *"I will make a league with thee."* How long does it take us to learn that no "league" can ever be made between the flesh and the Spirit? One is carnal and of the world and, thereby, of Satan. The other is spiritual and of heaven and, thereby, of God. There is no record that David ever once inquired of the Lord for direction in any of these matters.

Now we see a clash between Joab and Abner. Both are evil. Joab was clever, ambitious, blood-thirsty, and heartless. He was an ungodly man who deemed it politically proper to effect a zeal for God. The Church is filled with these types. They are close to the anointing but never of it.

It seems that Abner may have been morally superior to Joab, but he was a rebel to his God. He had no real heart for David as God's king, but was moved to help him because he saw the crown had shifted.

David was king of Judah and on the verge of becoming king of all Israel through God. Yet, he had now entered into the political fray, and, therefore, had no direction from God regarding Joab's murder of Abner. He tried to satisfy his conscience with a religious panoply of *"weeping"* (vs. 32) and *"fasting"* (vs. 35). He loudly denounced the murderer, but yet did nothing about it, and gave a state funeral for the murdered.

In verse 39 he says, *"And I am this day weak, though anointed king."* Had he at this period walked with God, he would not have had to make the sad and bitter confession of his weakness.

CHAPTER 4

When we look at the 4th chapter realizing that these are God's chosen people, the picture presented is not one that gladdens the heart. We find the worst of evil ensconced therein, and, as well, we find God's chosen anointed seems to walk alternately in the flesh and in the Spirit. How so similar to the modern-day Church.

Capsuled in this, as it is related in the 4th verse, it says, *"That he fell, and became lame. And his name was Mephibosheth."* And yet, the lameness of this little 5 year old boy will turn into one of the greatest blessings he ever had. Ultimately, because of a covenant that David had made with his father Jonathan, Mephibosheth will one day be brought into the palace. God keeps His promises.

Speaking of Saul's son, "Ishbosheth," who now ruled Israel and for selfish desires had ignored God's choice of David as king, would now pay the supreme penalty. The 6th verse says, *"And they smote him."* When will men learn that they cannot win out over God? Irrespective of the seeming weakness of God's position and the seeming strength of man's position, God's position will ultimately triumph.

David executed the two men who committed this murder, for the 12th verse says,

"And they slew them." Still, the previous chapter tells us that he took no action whatsoever regarding the murder of Abner by Joab. Why?

God's men do not always do everything right, but we can be assured that God's men always pay the penalty for doing wrong. Joab would be a thorn in David's side for the entirety of his reign.

CHAPTER 5

The 1st verse says, *"Then came all the tribes of Israel to David."* The child of God is quick to follow his own whim, and slow to follow the will of God. Finally, after so much bloodshed, the will of God begins to be carried out in Israel. It was easy to get Saul, man's choice, on the throne; however, it was difficult to get David, God's choice, on the throne.

Verse 2 proclaims the wickedness of the elders of Israel when they said, *"And the Lord said to thee, thou shalt feed my people Israel."* They knew it all the time and yet waited 7½ years to carry out the will of God. Someone aptly said that man's problem is not that he doesn't know the will of God, but that he doesn't do the will of God.

The 3rd verse says, *"And they anointed David king over Israel."* This was his third anointing; first by Samuel when he was but a boy, second, when he was anointed to be king over Judah, and now over the entirety of Israel.

The 4th verse says, *"David was thirty years old when he began to reign."* Jesus was 30 years old when He began His public ministry. As well, He reigned over the powers of darkness, albeit not over Israel. One day soon He will reign not only over the powers of darkness, but over Israel as well.

The 6th verse proclaims David made Jerusalem his capital. It was at this time inhabited by the "Jebusites." They had controlled it ever since the conquest of Canaan except for a short time when it was in the hands of Judah (Josh. 10:1-5).

There is a tremendous spiritual analogy evident in these verses. Israel, the land of promise, was a physical type of the spiritual

Promised Land that we have in Christ. As Satan erected a stronghold in the middle of Israel that was ever a thorn in Israel's side, likewise, he endeavors to erect a stronghold in our spiritual lives. The first thing that David would do would be to defeat the Jebusites. This was priority. Likewise, the tearing down of every satanic stronghold in our lives must be priority as well.

The 6th verse says the Jebusites taunted David saying, *"Except thou take away the blind and the lame, thou shalt not come in hither."* In effect, they were saying their stronghold was so powerful that the *"blind and lame"* could defeat David. As well, Satan will taunt the child of God, making him believe that he (Satan) is invincible. There was little reason to think otherwise, simply because this Jebusite stronghold had been there for hundreds of years. Too sadly, strongholds have been in the lives of Christians far too long. Therefore, they taunt the child of God.

The 7th verse says, *"Nevertheless David took the stronghold of Zion."* It seems that the 76th Psalm may have been written to glorify God and to commemorate this great victory. He says in the 5th verse, *"The mighty men of Jebus could not find their hands."* Irrespective of the strength of Satan, if we will root out the stronghold of the enemy within our lives, the Lord will give us whatever power is needed to overcome the enemy.

The 8th verse says, *"And the lame and the blind, that are hated of David's soul."* In the spiritual sense David was saying that he "hated" anything that would cause Israel to be spiritually *"lame"* or *"blind."* He says, *"The blind and the lame shall not come into the house."*

The 9th verse says, *"So David dwelt in the fort."* The Lord wants to take that which has once been the stronghold of Satan and make it the stronghold of victory. Moses was a hot-tempered fanatic, but God made him the meekest man on the face of the earth. Saul was a man of hate, but he became Paul the man of love. That which has been our weakness, God desires it to become our strength.

The 10th verse says, *"And David went on, and grew great."* He did so for two reasons:

1. He would root Satan's strongholds out of Israel.

NOTES

2. *"And the Lord God of host was with him."*

Referring back to Saul, this Jebusite stronghold was situated in Jerusalem through the entirety of Saul's reign. Saul never was able to defeat the Jebusites. As he was never able to defeat that which was within, ultimately, that which was without (the Philistines) destroyed him. We must first defeat the enemies that are within our own hearts, such as pride, jealousy, envy, or malice. Until this was done, the great outward victories that David soon began to experience could not be won. Likewise, it is so in our lives as well.

The 11th verse says, *"And Hiram King of Tyre sent messengers to David."* Hiram brought gifts to David, as the Gentile world will bring gifts to Christ when He begins to rule in the Kingdom Age. Hallelujah!

Verses 13 through 16 once again refer to David's polygamy, which was later proved not the will of God. However, grace in the midst of the failure will shine. For in the 14th verse the two names, *"Nathan"* and *"Solomon,"* are given unto us. The Davidic line all the way to Christ will follow through Solomon. As well, the kingly line through Mary will come through Nathan.

The 17th verse says, *"But when the Philistines heard that they had anointed David king over Israel."* Satan is little concerned until he hears of the "anointing." Nothing will break his yoke except the "anointing." Of this you can be sure, Satan little "hears" that which much of the religious world makes great ado about. However, he "hears" very well whenever the Holy Spirit begins to "anoint." Satan will always "seek David" to destroy him because of the anointing. Someone once asked the great preacher, E. M. Bounds, if Satan greatly opposed every Christian. His answer was simple and to the point, "Satan little bothers with most Christians because they are of little bother to him. However, those that are mightily anointed will feel the full brunt of his attack."

The 18th verse says, *"In the valley of Rephaim."* This word, "Rephaim," means "giants." So, Satan throws his biggest and his best at us. That presents no problem whatsoever if we are opposing him in the Spirit of the Lord. However, if our opposition to him is according to "self" or "the flesh," then we will have real problems. Sadly, most Christians, even the best, will at times oppose the enemy "in the flesh" while thinking we are opposing him "in the Spirit."

The 19th verse says, *"And David inquired of the Lord."* The criteria is that we seek the face of God regarding every step we take. Regrettably, the Church, at this time in history, rarely inquires of the Lord at all. Most of the time inquiry is of other men, such as psychologists or counselors. It should ever be understood that if we seek the face of men, irrespective of their education or stature, we will get the help that only men can give, which is none at all. Conversely, if we seek the face of God, we will receive the help that God can give, which is omnipotent. Yes, we should seek counsel from godly men, but at the same time, the Word is the criteria, and we should ever seek the face of God.

The 19th verse as well says, *"Go up."* This was God's command; therefore, victory was certain.

The 20th verse says, *"And David smote them there."* If the Lord is directing the battle, this will always be the outcome. David says, *"The Lord hath broken forth upon mine enemies."* That is the answer for the entirety of the Church - and the only answer.

However, the 22nd verse says, *"And the Philistines came up yet again."* Satan will always be back. The battle is unceasing. The Scripture says, *"And spread themselves in the valley of Rephaim."* David had just won a great victory. So the temptation would be to do the same thing now as was done before.

There are precious few Christians who *"inquire of the Lord."* And then the few who do seldom do so as minutely as David.

The 23rd verse says, *"And when David inquired of the Lord, he said, Thou shalt not go up."* Previously, the Lord had said *"Go up."* Now He says, *"Thou shalt not go up."* So often we judge these conflicts as purely physical, financial, or material. In reality, they are *all* spiritual. Therefore, we must seek the Lord about every move that is made. It would have been so easy for David to have charged in exactly as he had done before. However, had he done so, the battle would have been lost. New

directions are now given by the Lord.

The 24th verse says, *"When thou hearest the sound of a going in the tops of the mulberry trees."* For the Scripture says, *"For then shall the Lord go out before thee, to smite the host of the Philistines."*

In this passage we are given by the Holy Spirit a step-by-step approach to victory.

The 25th verse says, *"And David did so, as the Lord had commanded him."* There was a great victory.

This sound was one of a going, meaning the sound of a mighty army on the march, which struck terror to the Philistines and caused them to be confused and panic-stricken. It is said that the sound was the noise of horses' hoofs. The Philistines would have reasoned that some other mighty army was appearing suddenly behind them to help David. This was God's way of bringing the victory. How easy are His ways; how difficult are our ways.

CHAPTER 6

This chapter is freighted with failure and victory. A tremendous and valuable lesson will be forthcoming as the child of God digests the lessons taught.

Verse 1 says, *"Again, David gathered together all the chosen men of Israel."* I Chronicles 13:1 says that *"David consulted with every leader."* Before fighting the Philistine, David will *"inquire of the Lord."* Before performing the work of God, David will not inquire of the Lord. Why? The same question could be asked pertaining to almost all of what is called "the Church." David would consult with his leaders, not with God. If the Church has a crowning sin, this is it. Everything the child of God does is important, consequently, everything must be taken to the Lord, especially that which pertains directly to the work of God.

So, David and the *"leaders of Israel"* make their plans without God, which, in effect, will glorify man instead of God. Regrettably, we try to fight Satan in the flesh, and we always lose. Sadly, we try to please God in the flesh, and we always lose as well.

For a long time (approximately 70 years), the Ark of God had been without a home. Actually, it had been at the *"house of Abinadab."* There is some indication according to the Psalms that it was little attended, possibly even sitting out in a field (Psa. 132:6). It says, *"We found it in the fields of the wood."* If this is to be taken literally, it would seem that the Ark had weeds growing up around it, with little concern or regard for its protection. Regrettably, the Spirit of God is treated thusly in most of our churches. In our hearts and lives it seems the same is true as well. Even though David would do wrong, still, he was attempting to bring the Ark of God to its rightful place. Most of the Church world today has little concern for the Spirit of God. It seems at the outset that David, as well as the leaders of Israel, didn't even really know where the Ark was. It had been separated from the Tabernacle, which was now at Gibeon, for many years. It was placed in the *"house of Abinadab"* when it was brought from the land of the Philistines (I Sam. 7:1). This was approximately 20 years before Saul was made king. It remained there all during his reign which was 40 years, as well as through David's reign of Judah which was seven years. This particular time is thought to have been approximately three years after David was anointed king over both Israel and Judah. This would make approximately 70 years total. Think of it! The *"Ark of God,"* which was the most sacred vessel in all of Israel, the place where God dwelt between the Mercy Seat and the Cherubim, was actually relegated to a place of obscurity and neglect. But how so much does this picture God in America and Canada? He is by and large ignored.

The 3rd verse says that the counsel of the *"leaders of Israel"* would borrow the Philistine manner and *"set the ark of God upon a new cart."* The Law of Moses said that the priests should carry the Ark upon their shoulders. But now it is on a *"new cart."* There is always an abundance of *"new carts."* To name a few at this present time would include: Name It and Claim It, Dominion Teaching, Denominationalism, Psychology, Imagery, Unconditional Eternal Security, Sinless Perfection, Ultimate Reconciliation, Baptismal Regeneration, Sal-

NOTES

vation by Works, Church Membership Salvation, Liberty as an Occasion to the Flesh, Seventh Day Worship, and others. As is obvious concerning *"new carts,"* the list is endless.

The 5th verse tells us of great religious activity, *"And David and all the house of Israel played before the Lord."* *"New carts"* are always accompanied by great religious activity. However, all of this is a work of the flesh.

Had David inquired of the Lord and consulted the Bible (Num. 4:15), success and not disaster would have resulted. But he consulted man (I Chron. 13), imitated the Philistine, and organized a great public function in which David and his plans largely obscured God and His glory, consequently, the day ended in anger and fear. All this was the planning of the "flesh."

What man has set up, he feels himself bound to sustain. But the God of Israel needed not, as the gods of the nations, a human hand to uphold Him. It must be learned that God will judge the "flesh" in an Israelite as in a Philistine - and even more so, we might add. The living God is a consuming fire to the actions of the carnal nature, whether inside or outside the family of God.

The 6th verse says, *"And when they came to Nathan's threshing floor."* There will always be a *"threshing floor."* The Scripture then says, *"Uzzah put forth his hand to the Ark of God."*

Then the 7th verse states, *"And the anger of the Lord was kindled against Uzzah."*

We may look at this and tremble in fear, thinking within our heart how glad we are that God does not conduct Himself thusly today. Oh, but He does. Millions are "dying" spiritually. The *"anger of God"* is no less *"kindled"* today than it was then. Most churches, sadly, are breeding grounds of death instead of life. Most pulpits are "death" instead of life.

The 8th verse says that David *"was displeased,"* and the 9th verse continues, *"David was afraid."* Displeased or not, God would not change His Word even for the one who was *"after his own heart."* So David asked, *"How shall the ark of the Lord come to me?"* This should be the cry of every child of God. Our only salvation is *"the ark,"* or what it represents. Despite the tragedy of the day, David knew that his salvation lay within the *"ark of the Lord."*

Some Christians say, "We need revival." However, it must be known that if revival comes, not only will life come, but also death. All of that which is carnal and *"of the flesh"* must die. Revival will bring "fear." Men do not properly fear God. The closer we get to Him, the more demonstration of His power we see that brings both death and life and, thereby, fear - albeit a healthy fear.

The 10th verse says, *"Carried it aside into the house of Obed-edom."* There is some indication that this man was a Gentile, *"the Gittite."* If so, he was a convert to Israel's Lord, and the Scripture says, *"The Lord blessed Obed-edom, and all his household."* There is every indication that this man inquired as to how the Ark of the Lord should be attended. If so, he would have first of all put the Ark in a correct place somewhere in his house. He would not have been able to do all that the Holy Spirit demanded. For instance, when the Ark was to be moved, first of all the *"covering veil"* was to be placed over it (Num. 4). This was the veil on which were inscribed cherubims that hung between the Holy Place and the Most Holy Place. On that was to be placed a *"covering of badgers' skins."* And then over that, *"A cloth wholly of blue."* He would not have had the *"covering veil"* nor the *"badgers' skins,"* but he would probably have had a *"cloth of blue."* If so, he would have placed it over the Ark according to the Word of the Lord.

This one thing we do know, when it says, *"The Lord blessed,"* it means exactly what it says. It further says in the 12th verse, *"And all that pertaineth unto him."* All because *"of the Ark of God!"* This is the source of blessing; there is no other. If we go according to God's way, we not only live, but are greatly blessed.

Now David knew that God was not angry with him without cause. So, according to the Word of the Lord, he corrects the situation and brings up the Ark of God *"with gladness."*

The 13th verse says that sacrifices were offered every *"six paces."* This means about every 18 feet. I realize this might sound like extravagance; however, when we speak of Calvary, of which the sacrifices represented, there can be no extravagance.

The 14th verse says, *"And David danced."*

Now, it is not mere religious ceremony, but it is *"in the Spirit"*, because it says *"before the Lord."* Religious ceremony producing religious activity has no spiritual merit whatsoever. However, activity produced by the *"Spirit"* is the blessing of the Church. It also says, *"David was girded with a linen ephod."* There is some dissension as to exactly what the Hebrew means. There are two schools of thought:

A. A priestly garment of which David had no right to wear, which the Lord evidently overlooked.

B. A garment that was actually worn by little children, which more than likely was the garment that David actually wore.

The 15th verse says, *"With shouting, and with the sound of the trumpet."* We are looking at Holy Ghost revival. This is the strength of Israel, not its mighty army, not its wealth, but *"the ark of the Lord."*

The 16th verse tells us that the *"flesh"* can never approve of the things of *"the Spirit."* For speaking of David's wife who was called *"Saul's daughter"* it says, *"She despised him in her heart."* The *"flesh"* will always *"despise the Spirit."*

Verses 17 through 19 give us in type the Lord's Supper, for the 19th verse says, *"A cake of bread"*, and *"a piece of flesh,"* and *"a flagon of wine."* This speaks of Jesus as the Bread of Life, giving His perfect body for our salvation and through which comes the joy of the Lord - the wine.

Verses 20 through 23 record the opposition within the *"house of God."* All that happened in the realm of the Holy Spirit was repulsive to *"the daughter of Saul."* Likewise, the moving of the Holy Spirit is always repulsive to those in the Church, in which there seems to be an abundance of *"the flesh."*

The 23rd verse says of this *"daughter of Saul"* that she *"had no child unto the day of her death."* Actually, she would have five stepsons from her other husband and his wife (21:8) but none of her own. She would be barren. The *"flesh"* is always barren. Only *"the Spirit"* can give life.

CHAPTER 7

This chapter is basically a prophecy that pertains to Israel of David's time, but more than all pertains to the coming Kingdom Age with Jesus Christ as Ruler and Lord.

The 1st verse says, *"And it came to pass, when the king sat in his house."* This pictures the Lord Jesus Christ in a posture of absolute Lordship. The great plan of redemption has been won at Calvary. He is now *"sat down at the right hand of the Father."* At the Second Coming and in a beautiful rebuilt Jerusalem, He will as King, *"sat in his house."*

The Scripture as well says, *"The Lord hath given him rest round about from all his enemies."* This has three meanings:

1. The Lord had given David glorious victory and rest over all the enemies, such as the Hittites, Jebusites, and Canaanites.

2. In a spiritual sense the Lord not only desires but demands that we as well have *"rest"* from *"all our enemies."* If we follow Him conclusively, this He will do for us.

3. It pertains to the Lord Jesus Christ, at the Second Coming, Who will rule and reign from Jerusalem over the entirety of planet Earth.

The 2nd verse says that David now speaks of *"an house of cedar."* He is talking about building a *"house of God."*

The 3rd verse portrays the entrance of *"Nathan."* The prophet, thinking in very temporal and present terms, says to David, *"Go, do."* As usual, man's thoughts are far beneath those of God's.

The 4th verse says, *"That the word of the Lord came unto Nathan, saying."* What will now be revealed is so absolutely mind-boggling that David can hardly grasp it. The Lord says three things to David:

1. Through the 17th verse, the Lord tells David the house to be built will be a House far greater than any which David could imagine. He, in effect, says, *"Thine house and thy kingdom shall be established forever"* (vs. 16). The Lord always does far more than what we could ever begin to think.

2. *"I took thee from the sheepcote"* (vs. 8). Now, He tells David admittance into that House will be by the way of humility and the shed Blood, *"the sheep."* He also tells David the House to be built will be different from what he thought. In the one House his heart was inflated with the wonderful things he proposed to do for God, but in the other House his heart was amazed at the wonderful things God proposed to do for him. For in this the Lord would reveal to him the coming of the Messiah. The House would not be for God; it would be for man.

3. The House will be eternal, for verse 16 says, *"Thy throne shall be established forever."* Three things are said in this passage:

A. *"Thine house."*

B. *"Thy kingdom."*

C. *"Thy throne."*

All of this pertains not only to Solomon who will build the Temple, but more than all, to the Lord Jesus Christ, David's Son.

The 17th verse says that this striking vision *"did Nathan speak unto David."*

The 19th verse reveals that David understood the revelation, *"And is this the manner of man, Oh Lord God?"* This refers to the promise that the Seed of the woman shall bruise the serpent's head (Gen. 3:15); that is, from David's line the Messiah would come to be the eternal King of the earth. David now knows that through him the Messiah will come.

His answer to that in the 20th verse was, *"And what can David say more unto thee?"* What could anyone say to such a startling revelation?

Now in humble contrition, as the 27th verse records, David says, *"Hast revealed to thy servant, saying, I will build thee an house."* How small David must have felt when thinking of building the Lord a house. Instead, the Lord says, *"I will build you a house."* Every person who has ever named the name of Jesus Christ has entered *"into this House."*

"Oh happy day, oh happy day,"

"When Jesus washed my sins away."

In the 29th verse David says, *"Let the house of thy servant be blessed forever."* The House must be blessed forever and ever, simply because this House is *"the Lord Jesus Christ."*

CHAPTER 8

Verse 1 says, *"And after this it came to pass, that David smote the Philistines."* The 1st verse of chapter 7 says that David had *"rest from all his enemies."* No, there is no contradiction. The answer is this: These enemies were subdued enough so they would not cause Israel problems. However, they had not been defeated. Now, they will be defeated. Too oftentimes in the lives of Christians we arrive at what may be called a spiritual stalemate with jealousy, envy, and pride. However, these sins are not completely defeated within our lives, inasmuch as Christ having complete control. The Holy Spirit desires that we *"smite them."* It says, *"David took Methegammah."* This means the reigning mother city, meaning Gath and all her towns, the head city of the Philistines from which they held sway over Israel. While it is true that in our spiritual lives we have defeated many of the lesser demons, still, we must defeat the *"powers and principalities."*

The 2nd verse proclaims how the Holy Spirit *"measured them with a line"* and then, *"casting them down to the ground."* What a refreshing thought that the Holy Spirit is measuring our enemies for defeat, instead of the enemy measuring us for defeat. Hallelujah!

The 3rd verse portrays David extending the kingdom to its furtherest outreach, *"at the River Euphrates."* Thus, for the first time Israel extended her possessions to the River Euphrates, the eastern border of the Promised Land. It was promised in Genesis 15:18-21; I Chronicles 18:3. The Word of God has promised us complete victory. Have we taken all the land, or is there some that is still occupied by the enemy?

Verses 4 through 8 portray the great spoils of the victory. The Holy Spirit has so much for us if we will only allow Him to defeat the enemy.

The 6th verse says, *"And the Lord preserved David whithersoever he went."* David did not do it, so could take no credit for it.

The 11th verse says, *"Which also King David did dedicate unto the Lord."* This seems to be

but a footnote in a long list of glorious victories. However, it portrays to us David's continued dedication. Most of us never subdue the enemy in order for great victory to be ours. The few of us who do are often turned by the prosperity that comes. This 11th verse should be a passage of consecration to us.

The 13th verse says, *"And David gat him a name."* Concerning the Son of David, it says, *"In my name you shall cast out devils ."*

The 15th verse proclaims David organizing a reputable government. It says, *"Judgment and justice unto all his people."* This is the type of government, whether it be civil or spiritual, that God demands.

Verses 16 through 18 portray David promoting certain individuals to glory who had suffered with him in his rejection. Likewise, one day those of us who have suffered with Christ in His rejection will be promoted with Him in His glory. Hallelujah!

CHAPTER 9

This chapter portrays one of the most beautiful examples of grace found in the entirety of the Word of God. It portrays David as a type of the Lord of glory, with Jonathan as a type of Christ. Mephibosheth is a type of the poor wayward sinner, lost without God, deformed and crippled.

Verse 1 says, *"That I may shew him kindness for Jonathan's sake."* This verse proclaims the great truth that God pardons and blesses sinners *"for Christ's sake"* (Eph. 4:3). There is no merit in any of us that would warrant the "kindness" of God, but all is done for us because of Christ. David is actually referring back to the happenings of I Samuel 18 where he made a covenant with Jonathan. The covenant pertains to the great price that Jesus paid at Calvary.

The 1st verse shows David seeking Mephibosheth. Ever is the Lord seeking the sinner.

The 2nd verse says, *"A servant whose name was Ziba."* Ziba here portrays a type of the Holy Spirit. He will lead David to Mephibosheth.

The 3rd verse says, *"Lame on his feet."* This is an apt description of the lost souls who do not know the Lord Jesus Christ. Truly they are "lame on their feet." They do not walk properly. This young man's name was *"Mephibosheth."* He was born of the rebellious and doomed *"house of Saul."* His name signifies, "out of my mouth proceeds reproach."

The 4th verse says, *"In Lodebar."* This word means "no pasture" or "desert place." As well, there is absolutely no spiritual food in the world. The soul can find absolutely no sustenance in this "desert place."

The 5th verse says, *"Then king David sent, and fetched him."* What a beautiful statement. He was a rebel by nature, a sinner by practice, morally deformed, self-convicted, and far from God. Yet, David *"for Jonathan's sake"* sought him and found him, pardoned him and enriched him, and gave him a place among his sons. Then he brought him into his banqueting house, and his banner over him was love.

Mephibosheth's response to this grace was that he came, he believed, he accepted, and he loved. There was only one real condition imposed by David and that was he surrender unreservedly to David, which he did. The moment the sinner surrenders to the Saviour, instantly there is a consciousness of forgiveness, life, and glory.

The 6th verse says, *"He fell on his face and did reverence."*

He as well said in the 8th verse, *"A dead dog as I am."* He did what is so hard for most people to do, and that is to admit that they are spiritually crippled, deformed, and unable to save themselves. In other words, *"a dead dog."* However, that simple task is far too hard for most. Their pride will not allow them to do it, and, consequently, their pride will keep them from the riches of God's grace.

The 9th verse begins with the tremendous glory and blessing that David would give to Mephibosheth, and, likewise, that the Lord gives unto us. They are as follows:

1. *"I have given unto thy master's son all that pertained to Saul and to all his house"* (vs. 9). One of the great works of art in all of history is the painting, "Paradise Lost, and Paradise Regained." David restored to Mephibosheth all that had been lost. Likewise, with the great

born-again experience the Lord Jesus Christ restores to us that which was lost at the fall.

2. *"And thou shalt bring in the fruits"* (vs. 10). At Lodebar, which is the desert place, there are no fruits because the ground is barren. Now, since coming to Jesus there are *"fruits."*

3. *"Thy master's son shall eat bread always at my table"* (vs. 10). This speaks of fellowship, fellowship in the palace, and most of all with David. So now that we've come to Jesus, we have fellowship with the King of kings and the Lord of lords.

Now with the three great blessings given to us, we have first of all "restoration," then "productivity" (fruit bearing) and "fellowship."

The Holy Spirit reminds us that of all these blessings none were merited by Mephibosheth, for the 13th verse says, *"And was lame on both his feet."* It should quickly be added that the tables of those days were totally unlike the tables of today. Their tables were basically flat on the floor with the individual seated on the floor, reclining somewhat on his side, with his feet protruding out the back. So, the lame feet were obviously visible, signifying that all was of grace.

CHAPTER 10

The 2nd verse says, *"Then said David, I will shew kindness unto Hanun the son of Nahash."* Remarkably enough, the 1st verse of chapter 9 starts out with the words, *"That I may shew him kindness."* So there is a vast similarity in David's dealings, not only with Mephibosheth but also with the heathen king, *"Hanun."* However, the response was totally different. Mephibosheth would respond with reverence and with humility. Hanun will respond with insult and threat. Mephibosheth will accept David's grace and be honored. Hanun will despise it and be judged. It is folly to reject the grace, and madness to resist the power of God's chosen king.

The 4th verse portrays the indignity and insult heaped upon David's servants, *"And shaved off the one half of their beards."* Regrettably, the majority of the world treats the kindness of God with utter contempt. Why?

There is a hostility in the hearts of men toward God. This shows in man's rejection of God. God's "chosen" would take the Son of God and put Him on a cross. Likewise, the prophets were stoned, and today the rejection of God by the general population as well as the leadership of the various nations of the world is almost total.

However, it must ever be understood that as judgment was forthcoming by David, likewise, judgment will be forthcoming by God upon a world that has forgotten Him days without number. The 18th verse says, *"And David slew the men of seven hundred chariots of the Syrians, and forty thousand horsemen, and smote Shobach the captain of their host."*

At Calvary the Lord Jesus Christ defeated Satan as well as every minion of darkness. Still, at the Battle of Armageddon the Lord Jesus Christ will take vengeance, like David, against the forces of the Antichrist.

The 19th verse says, *"They made peace with Israel, and served them."* Likewise, during the great millennial reign of Christ there will be peace, and every nation in the world will serve the Lord Jesus Christ.

So, in this chapter we have a kaleidoscopic account of God's kindness to this world and the sending of His Son Jesus Christ to save humanity; of the world's rejection of God's kindness; of not only rejection but outright hostility; and the victory of the Lord Jesus Christ at the Battle of Armageddon; as well as the rule and the reign of Christ in the great Kingdom Age to come.

CHAPTER 11

This chapter portrays what is at least one of the saddest accounts concerning failure found in the entirety of the Word of God. The sin could not have been blacker or the crime more hideous. David, the man after God's own heart, would murder one of his choice servants in cold blood and then take his wife. However, out of this horror will come the great attributes of God that will be a signal portrayal of the Grace of God.

NOTES

This chapter testifies to the inspiration of the Bible, for only the Holy Spirit could record so faithfully such infamy and horror. It gives us a true insight into man's nature as sinful and fallen, and it teaches the reader the humbling lesson that such is the nature he possesses. Also, if Divine restraints are withheld and temptations sufficiently attractive and skillfully proffered, there is no depth of evil and shame and falsehood to which he will not fall. There are many questions that we would like answers to from this scenario. They are as follows:

1. How could a man *"after God's own heart"* do such a thing?

2. How could one who had the energy of faith to destroy a Goliath, as well as a lion and a bear, fail to destroy this ungodly impulse within his life?

3. How could the man who took the *"Jebusite fortress"* fail to destroy the inner fortress of Satan within his own life?

4. How could the man who wrote nearly half the Psalms sink to this level?

5. How could the man who instituted the great choirs of Israel, consequently perfecting the worship of God that basically characterizes every true Church of Jesus Christ, succumb to this evil?

6. How could the man through whose loins would come the ultimate honor of all, *"the son of David,"* fail in such a manner?

The answers are found even at the beginning of this ignoble chapter.

The 1st verse says, *"And it came to pass, after the year was expired, at the time when kings go forth to battle, that David sent Joab."*

Satan's method of downfall was perfected in the Garden of Eden. He has not changed it since. He has not needed to, for it works well. This is what Satan did in the Garden of Eden:

A. *"Ye shall be as gods"* (Gen. 3:5). This constitutes the *"pride of life."*

B. *"And when the woman saw"* (Gen. 3:6). This is the *"lust of the eyes."*

C. *"She took of the fruit thereof and did eat"* (Gen. 3:6). This is the *"lust of the flesh."*

So, the scenario of Satan is honed in the Garden of Eden, *"the pride of life, the lust of the eyes, the lust of the flesh."*

Here is what makes this scenario so deadly:

Once the person has committed the sin of *"the pride of life,"* he is basically helpless against the *"lust of the eyes, and the lust of flesh."* In other words, Satan can put anything in front of the eyes that he desires, and the individual is, by and large, helpless to refuse it.

Many ask the question as we have already asked repeatedly, "How could David have done such a thing?" This same question could be asked of every Christian who has ever lived, "How could they do such a thing?" The answer is relatively simple. The following is what happened to David, and the following is basically what happens to us as well:

1. *"At the times when kings go forth to battle, that David sent Joab"* (vs. 1). David was anointed by God in many capacities; however, at least one of his greatest anointings of the Lord was to do battle against the enemy. However, at this time it certainly seems that possibly David had become lifted up in himself, and instead of going forth to battle as he was accustomed to do, he sent Joab. The city was *"Rabbah"* (present day Ammon, Jordan). David, with his anointing, could have taken the city in days. It would take Joab many months. The Holy Spirit said, *"It was the time when kings go forth to battle,"* but David did not go.

He now crossed the line, perhaps without even knowing it. Pride is such a deceitful thing. It is the foundation of all sin, with pride being the cause of Lucifer's downfall (Ezek. 28:17). After the sin of *"the pride of life"* is committed, Satan can now propose the sin of *"the lust of the eyes."* David will be helpless to resist. Did David realize he was doing wrong? Certainly he did. Did he try to stop himself? More than likely he did. However, down the slippery slope, he is no longer master of his own fate. When one commits the sin of *"the pride of life,"* he has in some fashion become lifted up in himself and is no longer depending on the Lord for strength, help, and guidance. Therefore, he becomes a pawn in Satan's hands. The next step was inevitable.

2. *"And from the roof he saw a woman washing herself."* (vs. 2).

This is the *"lust of the the eyes."* Multiple millions of Christians commit this sin without ever going to the following and final step, but only because opportunity does not present

itself. This is what Jesus was speaking of when He said, *"If you look after a woman to lust after her, you have committed adultery already in your heart."* The sin was committed, even though the opportunity to carry it out was lacking. David would not lack the opportunity.

3. *"And David sent messengers, and took her"* (vs. 4). This is the *"lust of the flesh."*

The 5th verse says, *"I am with child."* These are the words of "Bathsheba." Had David immediately said he sinned against God, Uriah, and Bathsheba, then cast himself with anguish of heart upon God, the Lord would have made a way of escape and forgiveness consistent with Himself and morally instructive to David. But David dares not. Instead, David tries to cover his sin. It should be ever understood that there is no covering of sin except for the precious Blood of Jesus Christ. Also, that cannot be afforded unless one humbly and truly repents before God.

The scenario from verses 6 through 13 unfolds as subterfuge, lying, and chicanery are all used by David to carry out the plan of deception on Uriah. David's plans will fail.

Verse 15 records, *"And he wrote in the letter, saying, Set ye Uriah at the forefront of the hottest battle."* Uriah was one of David's mighty men (23:39). To make him the bearer of the letter arranging for his murder was a depth of infamy which is appalling. How could the man who wrote the 23rd Psalm do this?

Sin never betters itself. The slide is always downward. Irrespective of how holy man has been or how educated he might be, sin is a force and power that only can be dealt with by the precious Blood of Jesus Christ. It is so powerful that even though God could speak worlds into existence, still, He could not speak sin out of existence. He would have to die on a cruel Cross, offering up the perfect sacrifice to pay in full sin's demands. One at this stage not only sees the horror of David's sins, but if one reads the record aright, he also sees the horror of his own sins. Only the Holy Spirit could so faithfully record the evil as much as he would record the glory.

The 21st verse records, *"Thy servant Uriah the Hittite is dead also."* These words made heaven weep; they also nailed Jesus Christ to a bloody Cross. Uriah died serving his king, never knowing that his king had made his wife pregnant, and had, in fact, ordered his own death, but God knew.

In the 25th verse, with callousness, David says, *"Thus shalt thou say unto Joab, let not this thing displease thee."* Sin destroys the tenderness of the heart; it makes one cold, hard, and calloused. Uriah is just another statistic, *"For the sword devoureth one as well as another."* Still, even though it did not displease Joab, in the 27th verse it says, *"But the thing that David had done displeased the Lord."* The record reveals that God will show no more favor to *"His anointed"* than He will to the most ungodly.

———■———

CHAPTER 12

Verse 1 says *"And the Lord sent Nathan unto David."* On Nathan's last visit to David as recorded in chapter 7, the prophet had brought the greatest message that could ever be brought to a mere mortal. He said to David that through his lineage would come the Messiah, the King of kings (II Sam. 7:18-19). Now, God by the same prophet sends the worst message that a man could ever hear. Beautifully and strangely enough because of the grace of God, the second message of doom because of David's great sin does not nullify the great message of honor and redemption that had been given at the beginning. This is something that the Church cannot quite understand because it fails to understand the Grace of God.

Nathan delivers the message that the Lord told him to deliver. The 5th verse records that David, at least at the beginning, little understood the message. He said, *"The man that hath done this thing shall surely die:"*

The 7th verse records Nathan saying to David, *"Thou art the man."* This should be a tremendous lesson to every child of God. How so quickly we pass judgment on others, never realizing that, in fact, we are passing judgment on ourselves. That's the reason that Jesus said, *"Judge not"* (Matt. 7:1).

David committed this grievous sin because the 9th verse records, *"Wherefore hast thou*

NOTES

despised the commandment of the Lord, to do evil in his sight?" The "despising the commandment of the Lord" was because of the sin of "the pride of life." The judgment will be threefold:

1. *"Now therefore the sword shall never depart from thine house"* (vs. 10).

2. *"I will take thy wives before thine eyes, and give them unto thy neighbour"* (vs. 11).

3. *"For thou didst it secretly: but I will do this thing before all Israel, and before the sun"* (vs. 12).

All of this came to pass exactly as God said. God is no respecter of persons regarding blessing, neither is He a respecter of persons regarding judgment.

The 13th verse records true repentance, for David said, *"I have sinned against the Lord."* David had a true knowledge of God, and, therefore, when charged with his sin his first thought was not the punishment that would surely follow, but the injury done to God. It must ever be understood that ultimately all sin is directed at God. Sin is an insult to God; a slap in His face; a denial of His rulership; a threat against His kingdom. God's response to true repentance was the same as it always has been, *"The Lord also hath put away thy sin; thou shalt not die."* Perhaps, David had never heard greater words. The frown of God cannot be abided; His smile is ever sought.

The 14th verse records the damage done to God's work on this earth. *"Thou hast given great occasion to the enemies of the Lord to blaspheme."* Therefore a further judgment was added. *"The child also that is born unto thee shall surely die."* It came under the heading of the third judgment.

The 15th verse says, *"And Nathan departed unto his house,"* with heavy heart, no doubt. The prophet had gladly obeyed the Lord in bringing the first message of coming glory and greatness to David. However, the task of this visit weighed heavy indeed, for the Scripture says, *"And the Lord struck the child."*

The 16th verse says, *"David therefore besought God for the child."*

The 22nd verse says, *"For I said, Who can tell whether God will be gracious to me, that the child may live?"* The one who wrote the 23rd Psalm knew of the grace and mercy of the

Lord - perhaps as no other man ever knew it. But, yet, grace and mercy would know best that the child die. The stigma that the innocent child would bear as a result of David and its mother's sin would be a load that God did not deem desirable. It must ever be understood what God does is from a heart of love, set in a foundation of grace and mercy. So, His kindness to David would not be in allowing the child to live, but by allowing it to die.

In the 23rd verse David uttered the words of the Resurrection, *"I shall go to him, but he shall not return to me."* Every single parent who has ever lived, who has trusted Jesus Christ as Saviour, upon the death of a tiny loved one can say the same identical thing because of the price paid at Calvary and the Resurrection.

Verse 24 proclaims that, *"Where sin abounded, grace did much more abound."* For it says, *"And she bare a son, and he called his name Solomon: and the Lord loved him."* Sadly, the majority of the Church world, not understanding the love and the grace of God, would curse the fruit of this union called *"Solomon."* But the Scripture says, *"The Lord loved him."*

Now *"Nathan the prophet"* brings another message from the Lord, a message of love and grace that, no doubt, spoke peace, communion, and restored relationship to David and Bathsheba. The Lord said through Nathan, *"And he called his name Jedidiah, because of the Lord."* It means "beloved of the Lord." The comfort that David and Bathsheba took from this could only be understood in the light of the words of the old song:

"Oh the joys of sins forgiven,
"Oh the bliss the blood-washed know,
"Oh the peace that's sent from heaven,
"Where the healing waters flow."

And, yet, even though this terrible sin was washed, cleansed, forgiven, and put away, still the reminder would ever be present, for the 29th verse says, *"And David gathered all the people together, and went to Rabbah, and fought against it, and took it."* As David came close to take the surrender of the king of Rabbah, his eyes, no doubt, looked at the place by the wall where Uriah had died. In David's heart he, no doubt, said of Uriah as he said of the child who died, *"I shall go to him, but he shall*

NOTES

not return to me."

CHAPTER 13

This chapter begins with *"Absalom,"* as if the Holy Spirit is warning us that the coming rebellion led by Absalom begins here. Absalom was the third son of David by his wife, Maacah, a foreign woman and princess of Geshur. He was perfect in body, handsome, charming, eloquent, and dignified, but traitorous, murderous, merciless, godless, and self-conceited. He murdered his brother, betrayed his father, and died in vanity, seeking a kingdom he was in no way qualified to rule. Until his death, he portrayed the *"Absalom spirit"* that is so prevalent in the Church world. The *"Absalom spirit"* is the spirit that attempts to usurp authority over God's anointed, God's way, and God's plan. It is very religious and, at the same time, very satanic. It is perhaps the most destructive spirit found in the work of God.

This chapter is filled with hate, murder, rape, and deceit - all within David's house. At this time David was 53 years old, Amnon 22, Absalom 20, Tamar 15, and Solomon 2. Amnon was probably regarded by Absalom and the people as the Crown Prince - in other words, the heir to the throne. We learn several things in this chapter:

1. That had David obeyed the Word of God and married but one wife chosen for him by God, he would have escaped the bitter sorrows that flow from polygamy.

2. That even though David was a man after God's own heart (yes, even after the terrible sin with Bathsheba and the murdering of Uriah), still, it did not transfer to his children. With the exception of Solomon and possibly Nathan, the fruit was bitter indeed. Somehow, David did not obey the Word and raise these sons as he should have, because Solomon would write years later, *"Train up a child in the way he should go: And when he is old, he will not depart from it"* (Prov. 22:6). Maybe Solomon had all of these things in mind when he wrote those words.

3. Irrespective of how godly David was (and

he was godly), this godliness and touch of God within David's life could not be transferred to his sons or to anyone else. Someone has stated that "God has no grandchildren." Every individual, even those with godly parents, must have their own experience with God. God's touch is not transferable.

4. Even in the family of God there are really very precious few who have a distinct touch of God in their lives. Very few fall into the category of David. Most, sadly, fall into the category of Absalom, Amnon, and Adonijah. We must remember that Israel was the "Church" of its day.

5. About two years after the prophecy had been given to David by *"Nathan the prophet,"* the judgments that had been pronounced began to come to pass. They continued for seven years. Could David have done anything to have avoided these judgments coming to pass? No, there was nothing that David could do. His only recourse was to seek the face of God continually, which he no doubt did, and ask the Lord to give him wisdom and guidance in dealing with each situation as it arose. In this we learn that events transpire within our lives and our ministries which have a lot to do with our actions. If David had not committed this terrible sin with Bathsheba, no doubt his sons would have been no less ungodly, but at the same time the Lord would have guided events that would have held back the rape of Tamar, the murder by Absalom of Amnon, and the eventual rebellion of Absalom himself. God is in control of everything, but at the same time, godly or ungodly actions on our part determine oftentimes God's actions toward us. This is a sobering thought, but one that we should well contemplate.

6. We learn from this chapter, as well as the entirety of the Word of God, that the Lord works not from "what might have been" but from "what is." Most Christians unscripturally function from a "what if" posture or a "what might have been if only" posture. Those that do so seldom do anything for God. The simple reason is in their thinking that whatever should have been, now due to failure or whatever, can no longer be. This reasoning takes the past, present, and future out of God's hands and places it in man's hands. If the child of

God, regardless of circumstances, places every failure, every sin, or every situation at the foot of the Cross, and walks in humility, contrition, and brokenness before God, the Lord is able to take "what is," irrespective of what it might be, and turn it into a blessing. God's very business is turning curses into blessings. It may not be done overnight, but if we will trust Him, it will be done.

The unfortunate thing is that most Christians make up their own rules, consequently ignoring the Word of God.

CHAPTER 14

In this chapter we see the plotting, scheming, and ungodly plans of men. However, there is not one instance recorded where David cries out to God for leadership and guidance. How refreshing are the words in David's younger years, *"And David inquired of the Lord."* How sad there is only silence regarding counsel from God.

Now, David is safe and secure on his throne with all enemies defeated. Sometimes this is the most dangerous place to be, for David's greatest enemy now is "self." Someone has aptly said that when Jesus died on Calvary, He did so not only to save us from sin, but from self as well.

The actors in this portrayal who begin the greatest rebellion ever (Absalom) have much worldly wisdom, but no godly wisdom. They are as follows:

1. *"Joab."* Joab was close to the anointing but knew nothing of the anointing. Despite all of his military conquests which were derived not from Joab's skill but from David's anointing, he would never really understand the source of his victories or the reason for Israel's blessings. He was never listed as one of David's mighty men. He seemed to be bereft of spiritual knowledge. He was a schemer and an opportunist. The 21st verse says that David acquiesced to Joab's will and did not seek the will of God.

2. *"A wise woman."* This woman was a pawn, an actor, in this great drama that would

result in such great hurt to Israel and to the work of God. How so often does the Church bring in its *"wise people,"* consisting of psychologists, counselors, and others who are *"wise"* in the ways of the world but not at all in the ways of God. David partially acceded to her request concerning Absalom. Again, he did not inquire of the Lord.

3. *"Absalom."* The 24th verse says he returned from exile to Israel but *"saw not the king's face"* - hence, the seed of rebellion is born.

When dependence upon God and subjection to His Word cease to govern one's life, then it is easy for the wisdom of this world to entangle the heart. All this teaches a lesson which man is so slow to learn, that a Christian embitters his days by acting independently of God. Amid all the movements of this chapter was God inquired of? He does not once appear.

David was at this time about 56 years old, Absalom 24, and Solomon 6.

Regrettably, the political maneuverings so amazingly correspond with the political maneuverings of the Church. How little we ask the Lord and how little help that we receive. The Holy Spirit is rarely the guide and inspiration of the modern-day Church. Instead, the psychologist has become the guru of advice and counsel. Actually, in the major Christian denominations if the Lord is inquired of and God's Word adhered to, disfellowship is often the result. Sadly, in most Christian circles if an individual in times of trouble inquires of the Lord and adheres to God's Word, the individual is given no credibility, with sarcasm being the general response. However, it is better to have the sarcasm of man and the smile of God, than to have the smile of man and the anger of God. God expects His people to consult Him for counsel, advice, and instruction. As well, that which is given by the Holy Spirit will always coincide with the Word of God.

CHAPTER 15

Verse 1 says, *"Absalom prepared him chariots and horses, and fifty men to run*

before him." Carnal men and even the Church are easily swayed with pomp, pride, and ceremony. Absalom appealed to the carnal and not the spiritual. At this time there seemed to be such little spiritual strength in Israel that they readily fell for the carnal. Regrettably, the Church is little different today.

Absalom easily deceived the people by a profession of devotion to them (vs. 4) and as easily deceived his father by a profession of devotion to God (vss. 7 and 8).

Because man has fallen from God's moral image, therefore he can readily deceive and be deceived (II Tim. 3:13).

The web of deceit is so easily woven the 4th verse says, *"Oh that I were made judge in the land."* And then the 5th verse, *"And took him, and kissed him."*

The latter portion of the 6th verse says, *"So Absalom stole the hearts of the men of Israel."* The surprise was not that Absalom would do such a thing. The surprise was that Israel was so spiritually weak that they fell for this.

The reason they were so easily swayed is because Israel had judged David not according to the Word of God but according to outward appearances. He had committed terrible sin with Bathsheba and, of course, by now the knowledge that he had affected the murder of Uriah was known throughout the nation. The Psalmist said that David became the song of the drunkards. In Israel's eyes they were justified in their decision. However, any decision that is the opposite of the Word of God can only bring ruin and wreckage.

The "Absalom spirit" now seeks to usurp authority over God. It will fail, but the damage will be great. The "Absalom spirit" is rampant in the work of God today. This spirit is comprised of any effort made by anyone to anoint themselves in the place of that which God has anointed. Most church fights start because of an "Absalom spirit." The "Absalom spirit" is replete in most religious denominations because political maneuvering is the norm. Therefore, the "Absalom spirit" rules.

The 9th verse says, *"And the king said unto him, Go in peace."* If David had inquired of the Lord, he would not be in this precarious position. Actually, there will be no "peace." Rather, it will be "war."

Incidentally, the *"forty years"* of verse 7 refers to 40 years since David's anointing (I Sam. 16). David was anointed to be king of Israel when he was about 16 years old. So it would have been about 40 years after this time, which means that David now was about 56 years old.

The die is now cast for the rebellion to succeed. In the eyes of most it could not fail. He had stolen the hearts of the men of Israel, and, as well, he had according to verse 12 the advice, support, and counsel of *"Ahithophel the Gilonite."* This man had been David's counsellor. He was one of the most brilliant in Israel, for the Holy Spirit said it *"was as if a man had enquired at the oracle of God"* (16:23). Also, he was the father of one of David's heroes. Absalom and Ahithophel, no doubt, had been in contact before regarding this very rebellion. In fact, Ahithophel may have instigated it, having longed for some way to take vengeance on David for sinning with his granddaughter and murdering her husband, for Bathsheba was Ahithophel's granddaughter. Still, the wisest men in the world with the wisest counsel and even with the mightest army could not defeat that which God had ordained.

The 21st verse says, *"Surely in what place my lord the king shall be, whether in death or life, even there also will thy servant be."* The loyalty of Ittai the Philistine, and the royal body-guard of 600 Philistines which he commanded, here stand in contrast with the disloyalty of Absalom and the men of Israel. They illustrate the present loyalty of the Gentile nations to the Son of David, when rejected by His own nation and people.

In verses 24-31 David's actions portray his ever Christ-likeness in times of crises. Knowing the judgment of God that had been pronounced against him and not knowing the plan of God regarding his continued position, he would do the following things, recognizing that he merited only wrath.

1. *"Carry back the ark of God into the city"* (vs. 25). This was Israel's holiest vessel. God dwelt between the Mercy Seat and the Cherubim. David felt he was not worthy to have this holy symbol in his presence. In other words, he was saying, "I do not take God for granted." What a lesson for us today.

NOTES

2. *"Let him do to me as seemeth good unto him"* (vs. 26). Completely, David puts himself into the hands of God. He does not justify himself but places himself instead totally at God's mercy.

3. *"And wept as he went up, and had his head covered, and he went barefoot."* If there was ever a picture of repentance and humility before God, this was it. It is this that God demands of us as well.

The 31st verse proclaims David's prayer, *"O Lord, I pray thee, turn the counsel of Ahithophel into foolishness."* Now, when it's almost too late, David asks counsel of God.

And, yet, in verse 34 he turns around and attempts to answer his own prayer concerning *"Hushai."* He says, *"Then mayest thou for me defeat the counsel of Ahithophel."*

David now prays, but it seems he is not yet ready to trust. Man's poor confused heart is always ready in times of stress and danger "to do something." And, generally, that "something" is evil or foolish. We are ever trying to "help God." Through the mercy of God, David's "helping the Lord" seems to have been overlooked and blessed by God. How so graceful and merciful the Lord is to us, at times overruling our mistakes and failures due to our lack of trust. How kind He is to us when we deserve the opposite.

The hearts of Israel judged Absalom to be more morally qualified to rule Israel than David because of David's great sin. However, they judged wrongly. God had put away David's sin, but the tragedy was that Israel had not. Therefore, in their spiritual ignorance they took upon themselves a tyrant and threw out the man of God. As well, God overruled even the wicked intentions of unforgiving Israel.

CHAPTER 16

This chapter is freighted with deceit, lying, cursing, and ungodly counsel which would, nevertheless, fulfill the prophecy of the Lord.

Verses 1 through 4 reveal Mephibosheth's servant lying and scheming to effect a gain of property. At this time of all times, every man in

Israel should have been crying to God for help. However, some would take advantage of the crises as opportunity for personal gain. No wonder it is said, "The love of money is the root of all evil." I am afraid that "Ziba" is too much akin to so many in the modern-day Church.

Verses 5 through 14 record a disciple of Satan, *"whose name was Shimei."* The 5th verse says, *"And cursed still as he came."*

The 7th verse says that he called David *"thou bloody man, and thou man of Belial"* (Satan). Shimei's denunciation of David as the murderer of Saul was unjust, but David could not resent it because he was the murderer of Uriah.

David had a far greater grasp of the malignity of his sin than most. The hurt of the Church is that it does not understand the gravity of all sin, not just some sins. Abishai said in the 9th verse, *"Let me go over, I pray thee, and take off his head."* But David refused to listen to any offer that would cause such bloodshed. He suffered this as part of the chastening of God for his sin with Bathsheba. His answer to Abishai expressed a deep and humble resignation to the course of providence. Insults such as this are very difficult to endure but not for David, as he fully recognized himself as under the Divine hand of chastening for his sin. For the balance of his life, he was mindful of this cursing by Shimei, but he was determined never to avenge it in his lifetime. He left the matter to the wisdom of Solomon, it being one of the last things he mentioned in his dying hour (I Kings 2:8-11).

Verses 15 through 23 record the degradation of David's wives in the sight of all Israel, fulfilling the prophecy of Nathan, and doubtless feelings of revenge against David for his treatment of Bathsheba. Ahithophel gives this counsel, and the Holy Spirit says in the 23rd verse, *"And the counsel of Ahithophel, which he counselled in those days, was as if a man had enquired at the oracle of God."* It is so sad that this man, who had been so instrumental in Israel's prosperity and was so anointed of God regarding wisdom from heaven, that his last counsel was given in an attempt to destroy God's anointing in Israel. Evidently, due to Bathsheba, Ahithophel's granddaughter, he was not able to forgive David. Consequently, his gift was used to overthrow *"the sweet singer*

NOTES

of Israel." Bitterness, anger, and desire for revenge cost him his life and his soul. The lesson should not be lost upon us. Men may vacillate and even fall, but the call of God upon a man's life never changes. It is without repentance. David repented, but Ahithophel did not accept his repentance. The terrible judgment that awaited Ahithophel awaits all who will not accept God's ways. The mills of God may grind exceedingly slow, but they will grind exceedingly fine. God help us to learn from this lesson.

David was relegated to a place of humiliation that few men have known. He accepted it patiently as the chastening of the Lord. David allowed this chastening, designed by the Holy Spirit, to draw him into a closer fellowship with the Lord. His heart was taught that his sorrows, the fruit of his sins, were occasions of spiritual enrichment to him. It was when burdened with these sorrows and conscious of their justice and, yet, at the same time in a heart truly and eternally bound to God, the Holy Spirit inspired David to write the great 51st Psalm. These are confessions of sin and integrity which Christ will cause repentant Israel in the latter day to utter, and which He in sympathy with them will utter with them and for them.

Thus, at this terrible time David became a type of the Messiah, suffering with His people, confessing their sins as His own, and baring his breast to the sword of Jehovah (Zech. 13:7) as if He were the guilty one.

In all this there is a great encouragement for the child of God in circumstances where faith might fail and the heart be discouraged. This chapter is a valuable testimony that God does not cast off His people when they sin against Him; that He forgives them when they confess their faults; that He overrules all to enrich their knowledge of Himself; and that He furnishes them with expressions and sentiments proper to restoration of the soul.

CHAPTER 17

Verses 1 through 4 record the plotting of

NOTES

Ahithophel, David's advisor, with Absalom, and as the 4th verse says, *"All the elders of Israel"* plotted to murder David. For the 2nd verse says, *"And I will smite the king only."* All of these men had received nothing from David but good. How true it is that the heart is desperately wicked (Jer. 17:9). Every blessing that Israel presently had, which were many, had come through the anointing of the Holy Spirit upon David. And now they tried to murder him. The "Absalom spirit" is set along side the "Spirit of God" in the Church. It opposes greatly the "Spirit of God." If one will look at the history of the work of God throughout the Bible as well as Church history, one will see that the "Absalom spirit", by and large, reigns supreme. Seldom is the "Spirit of God" given preeminence.

This chapter is a striking fore-picture of Israel's rejection of the Son of David. At that time, as well, the "Absalom spirit" occupied the spiritual throne of Israel. Consequently, it would kill the Lord of glory, and as Ahithophel would betray David and then hang himself, so would Judas do.

The number of soldiers who had thrown in their lot with Ahithophel must have been many for him to be able to *"choose out twelve thousand men"* (vs. 1) to *"pursue after David."* His advice to Absalom was that David hurriedly be smitten while *"weary and weak",* before he could gather an army. However, verses 5 through 13 portray the counsel of *"Hushai",* which was the opposite of *"Ahithophel's."* Hushai's counsel, which was wrong, appealed to the vainglorious pride of Absalom and, instead, was heeded. He counseled Absalom to wait and gather a large army, then lead it himself. He should then kill his father to prove his prowess as a military commander.

All of Israel knew of David's ability as a military commander. Actually, he was mightily anointed of God to defeat Israel's enemies. So, Hushai pointed out that if Absalom could personally kill him in battle, this would indeed prove his greatness. It appealed to the evil, wicked vanity of Absalom. Therefore, he rejected Ahithophel's advice and accepted Hushai's. For the 14th verse says, *"For the Lord had appointed to defeat the good counsel of Ahithophel, to the intent that the Lord might bring evil upon Absalom."*

Men who make their plans without God, regardless of the advantages they seem to have, make their plans in vain.

In the 17th verse the Scripture says, *"And a wench went and told them."* The Hebrew word for "wench" is "Shiphchah." It means "handmaid" and would have been far better to have been translated in that manner. In the 17th verse we see the "handmaid" named along with the mighty king of Israel, *"king David",* and all by the Holy Spirit. This is an encouraging instance of how useful the most insignificant person can be to the Lord of glory in the interests of His Kingdom. So, the Lord used two young men by the names of *"Jonathan and Ahimaaz",* as well as a "handmaid" and *"the woman"* (vs. 19) to get the message to David that he must quickly pass over the Jordan River in order to escape Absalom.

The 24th verse says, *"Then David came to Mahanaim."* The word means "two camps." It was on the east side of Jordan. It was named by Jacob of old when he came out of Syria at the behest of the Lord on his way back to "the promised land." He was met by two camps of angels, hence the name (Gen. 32:1-2). Here Jacob was met by his brother Esau with some 400 men, which caused Jacob to fear for his life. It was here that he wrestled with the angel, and his name was changed from "Jacob", the deceiver, to "Israel," prince with God. One must wonder if David went here intentionally. Did he have Jacob in mind at this time of great distress when he *"came to Mahanaim?"* This we do know, it was at this time he wrote the 42nd and 43rd Psalms. The modern day church, little understanding the grace of God, has great difficulty understanding how God could use David to write these great Psalms after the terrible sin with Bathsheba and Uriah. Failure to understand such is a failure to understand God's great redemption plan, which includes mercy and forgiveness upon proper scriptural repentance. And we might quickly add, of which every single Christian on the face of the earth must lean upon from time to time. For the Scripture says, *"All have sinned, and come short of the glory of God"* (Rom. 3:23). And *"If we say we have no sin, we deceive ourselves, and the truth is not in us"* (I

John 1:8). However, this in no way gives license to sin, but simply means that despite the holiest attributes, failure is ever present in one form or the other in the child of God. The Christian is ever in need of the cleansing agency of the precious Blood of Jesus Christ.

The 23rd verse says concerning Ahithophel, *"And hanged himself, and died."* So died the man who would not forgive David and had fomented a rebellion to dethrone "God's anointed." The child of God must ever understand that he is obligated to forgive those whom God forgives. To do less is to set oneself on the road to disaster.

The 25th verse says, *"And Absalom made Amasa captain of the host instead of Joab."* It is ironic that both Joab and Amasa were David's nephews. Joab at this time remained loyal, Amasa joined the rebellion.

All who joined the rebellion would rue this day, but not because of David. If men could only understand that they must follow "God's anointed" rather than the "Absalom spirit." Admittedly, sometimes it takes great faith to do so, especially when we realize that God rests His Spirit in "earthen vessels." Regrettably, not all men have faith.

Verses 27 through 29 tell us of the help that the Holy Spirit garnered for David. Three men brought these gifts, *"Shobi", "Machir",* and *"Barzillai."* At a time like this for anyone to say, "I love you", is a blessing that can only be understood if one has walked where David walked. The Holy Spirit was so gracious as to record the kindness of these men. He will likewise record for eternity the kindness of all those who will stand by "God's anointed."

CHAPTER 18

The 1st verse says, *"And David numbered the people that were with him."* Josephus said that he had 4,000 men. He divided his army into 3 groups:

1. One-third under Joab.
2. One-third under Abishai.
3. One-third under Ittai.

Ittai was a Philistine who had accepted

David's God. These are his words, *"Surely in what place my lord the king shall be, whether in death or life, even there also will thy servant be"* (II Sam. 15:21). (This confession of faith was somewhat like another Gentile, Ruth the Moabitess.) He, as the other two, was no doubt a powerful military leader. With only 4,000 soldiers facing an army of possibly well over 100,000 men, David had to have supernatural help.

For the 7th verse says, *"A great slaughter that day of twenty thousand men"* - and this is speaking of the army of Israel. It doesn't say how many men David's army lost, if any. Oftentimes, when the Spirit of God moved mightily regarding the army of the Lord, not a single man would be lost, but there would be a tremendous loss on the opposing side.

Verses 9 through 18 portray the death of this rebel against his father and against the plan of God. The 9th verse says, *"His head caught hold of the oak."* Josephus writes that Absalom was entangled by his long hair in the boughs of the tree. His death must, therefore, have been one of prolonged agony until terminated by the lances of his former friend Joab and his young men. The latter portion of the verse says, *"And the mule that was under him went away"* - the mule rode on. It is ironical that this dumb beast, when given the opportunity to leave, did so immediately. There is a slight similarity here to the situation of Balaam.

The 14th verse says, *"And he took three darts in his hand, and thrust them through the heart of Absalom."*

The 15th verse says some *"ten young men"* continued to hack at his body after he had expired.

The 16th verse says that Joab in order to stop the slaughter *"blew the trumpet, and the people returned from pursuing after Israel."*

The *"pillar"* of verse 18 and the *"heap of stones"* of verse 17 mark the aim and the end of ambition. The pillar was surmounted by *"a hand"* (Heb.), indicative of victory, but the grave was heaped with stones, expressing infamy. Such must ever be the inglorious end of all who rebel against God's elect King, Jesus Christ - for He is exactly the One Whom Absalom rebelled against. What was the difference in David's and Absalom's sin?

Of course, all sin is heinous in the eyes of

God and is actually directed against Him. The following is the basic difference:

1. David's sin was a sin of passion, with the murder of Uriah an effort to cover up the sin. Absalom's sin had as its fountain the sin of Satan himself in his rebellion against God. In other words, Absalom entered into Satan's rebellion. It was a far more heinous sin than his father David's. However, most of the church world does not see it that way, but actually would join Absalom because outwardly it looks so right.

2. David's sin was not joined by anyone else, whereas Absalom's sin was joined by the majority of Israel. In other words, they became associates with his sin, which, in fact, threatened the very foundation of Israel's existence.

3. David repented immediately when his sin was found out because he was a man of God. There is no record that Absalom ever really knew God, and, therefore, there was no repentance.

Verses 19 through 32 proclaim the message that was delivered to David from the battlefield. The 19th verse says, *"Then said Ahimaaz the son of Zadok, Let me now run and bear the king tidings."* The problem was Ahimaaz wanted to *"run"* but actually had no message to deliver. There are very many voices in the world that claim to speak for God, but as the 22nd verse says, *"Wherefore wilt thou run, my son, seeing that thou hast no tidings ready?"* However, the 21st verse says, *"Then said Joab to Cushi, Go tell the king what thou hast seen."* Actually, *"Cushi"* was not able to run as fast as *"Ahimaaz"*; however, he had a message to deliver when he got there. The important thing is not the "running" but the "message." The 29th verse says concerning Ahimaaz, *"I saw a great tumult, but I knew not what it was."* Multiple tens of thousands of preachers have seen some *"great tumult",* but they *"knew not what it was,"* and, consequently, have nothing to say.

The 32nd verse says that *"Cushi"* could not run as fast as his counterpart, but he did have a message to deliver when he finally arrived. God give us preachers who have been touched by the Lord and have something to say.

The 33rd verse says of David, *"O my son Absalom, my son, my son Absalom! would God*

I had died for thee." David's bitter grief was, no doubt, deepened by the consciousness that his own sin had perhaps contributed in some way toward Absalom's rebellion and death. As well, the pain and the hurt was deepened by the realization that there was no hope in such a death. He knew that Absalom died lost.

CHAPTER 19

Verse 1 says, *"The king weepeth and mourneth for Absalom."* No doubt, David's actions before his army that had fought so valiantly to defend the kingdom against the rebellion of Absalom were little understood by the people. Most of his loyal followers looked at the situation as that of a father who was grief-stricken over his son. However, most did not understand the tremendous spiritual implications. Absalom died lost, and this was the reason for David's great grief.

The 2nd verse says, *"And the victory that day was turned into mourning unto all the people."* The *"mourning"* was far more justified than the people even realized. Israel was in a terrible state. The reasons were:

1. The far greater majority of Israel had joined in the rebellion with Absalom, thereby, rebelling against David who was God's anointed.

2. The 9th verse says, *"And all the people were at strife throughout all the tribes of Israel."*

3. Due to David's great sin, the people had lost confidence in the king. If they had faced the situation according to the Word of God and understood and accepted David's repentance, the confidence would not have been lost. Nevertheless, like so many do, everything *but* the Word of God is adhered to.

It must ever be stated that the Word of God is the criteria for any and all situations. What man says or thinks is of little import if it does not agree with the Word of God. The state of Israel as presented here is a perfect picture of the Church in most times of crises. Man's opinions and viewpoints are adhered to with the Word of God little consulted. There is no record that David or Israel *"inquired of the Lord"*, therefore, the *"strife"* of the 9th verse.

The 11th verse says, *"Speak unto the elders of Judah."* It seems these individuals were undecided about whether to bring David back, and if they were a part of the *"elders of Israel"*, (17:4) one could well understand why. Hours before they had been a part of the rebellion of Absalom.

As we have previously stated, Israel at this time was a powerful nation, actually one of the most powerful in the world of that day. The people had been blessed greatly because of David being king. Nevertheless, then, as now, "the Church" allows its own prejudices and personal feelings to enter into any and all situations, most of the time ignoring the Word of God.

The 13th verse implies that Joab had become so insolent that David attempted to set him aside. It seems clear that Joab had little affection for David, and at heart was a rebel. I think this fact was manifested by Solomon, who executed a righteous judgment upon him.

The 13th verse says, *"If thou be not captain of the host before me continually in the room of Joab."* David was speaking of *"Amasa,"* who was his nephew. Nevertheless, this seemed to be a very unwise move, particularly considering that just hours before Amasa had been the military leader of Absalom's rebellion against David.

The striking portrayal is that it seems David little consulted the Lord during this most crucial time. The judgments and decision that he made were political and not spiritual.

Verses 15 through 23 record David returning to Jerusalem. He was met by *"Shimei,"* the man who cursed David when he fled from Absalom (16:5-13). He had a thousand Benjamites with him to welcome David back and ask pardon for cursing him. The 1000 were perhaps a show to emphasize that he was a man of influence, and many would become David's enemies if he did not forgive.

The 23rd verse says concerning Shimei, *"Thou shalt not die."* Whether this decision was in keeping with the Holy Spirit or not cannot be known. Perhaps, the reason David did not execute judgment upon the man at this time was the very reason he did not do so some

NOTES

days before. He felt, no doubt, that due to his own sin against Uriah, that he could little execute judgment upon Shimei. Nevertheless, one of the last requests that David made when dying was to ask Solomon to deal with Shimei as he saw fit when he turned the kingdom over to him (I Kings 2:8-9, 36-46).

Even though in the 20th verse Shimei says, *"For thy servant doth know that I have sinned,"* he in no way truly repented from the heart. His statement was a matter of expediency. This proved to be so when he rebelled against Solomon and paid with his life.

Verses 9 through 14 record David's political judgments, as verses 15 through 23 record Shimei's deceit. However, verses 24-30 record Mephibosheth's faithfulness.

In the 29th verse David says to Mephibosheth, *"Thou and Ziba divide the land."* Inasmuch as *"Ziba"* had deceived David at the outset concerning Mephibosheth (16:4), it would seem once again that David's judgment was incorrect regarding giving even a small portion of the estate to Ziba, much less half of it. Nevertheless, the moral of this passage is the godliness of Mephibosheth. Israel had little regard for the anointed leadership of David who had brought such blessing. Unthankfulness characterized their actions. However, Mephibosheth, in the midst of a sea of ingratitude, is a shining light of Christ-likeness. Mephibosheth said that he had little interest in the land, money, or property. His only concern was "David." How many Christians today are serving the Lord because of what is "in it for them," and how many are serving Him because they truly "love Him?"

Verses 31 through 40 portray *"Barzillai the Gileadite."* The 32nd verse says, *"Even fourscore years old"* - 80 years old. In the evening tide of his life the Holy Spirit portrays him standing by the side of God's anointed, irrespective of the conduct of the majority of Israel. This man knew the Word of God. He did not deter from the righteous path. What a glorious way to go out.

Verses 41 through 43 record the division between Judah and Benjamin on the one side and the 10 tribes on the other. Little by little it crystalized and became even wider with each new crises. About 50 years from this time they were definitely divided into two kingdoms (I Kings 12).

CHAPTER 20

Verse 1 says, *"We have no part in David."* Upon the rebellion of Absalom, several things stand out sharply. They are as follows:

1. David's terrible sin of adultery with Bathsheba and the horrible murder of her husband Uriah was partially the cause of the dissension, strife, and continued rebellion in Israel. No doubt, the weight and responsibility of this weighed heavily upon David. Due to David's walking very close to God, he felt this responsibility and blame most keenly .

2. The spiritual shallowness of Israel at this time of crisis rises to the surface. Most will pursue after their own designs and desires, completely ignoring the Word of God. They will forget that David is the vessel who God has used to bring great blessing to Israel and to their households. Likewise, that which God has forgiven they have refused to forgive. If the Word of God had been followed, they would have forgiven David readily, albeit with great sorrow. As well, they would have recognized that due to David's repentance, God had not lifted His anointing, and, thereby, would brook no usurpation of David's position and authority. Had they followed the Word of God, many lives in Israel would have been saved, and much hurt and pain would have been avoided.

3. At times like these, individuals such as *"Sheba",* whom the Bible calls *"a man of Belial"* (Satan), will take advantage of the opportunity to further their own designs and aims. Sadly, in every church there are people "of Belial." They are in the Church but not of the Church. Sheba, as well, had the "Absalom spirit" and wanted "no part" of the ways of God.

The 2nd verse says this second revolt under Sheba was widespread, for the Scripture says, *"So every man of Israel went up from after David, and followed Sheba."* It then says, *"The men of Judah clave unto their king."* So, more and more the rift between Israel and Judah will widen. David has put out one fire, but now

another one breaks out.

Verses 4 and 5 proclaim David's intention of replacing Joab with *"Amasa"* as the military leader of Israel. However, Amasa's lack of energy showed either incapacity or disloyalty, for the Scripture says, *"He tarried longer than the set time."*

The following verses illustrate the craftiness of Joab. The 10th verse says concerning Amasa and his death at the hand of Joab, *"So he smote him therewith in the fifth rib."* And then it says, *"He died."* So, by force Joab once again maintains the leadership of the army of the people of God.

The 11th verse says, *"And he that is for David, let him go after Joab."* Nevertheless, it must be understood that Joab's occupation of this position is not because of fidelity to the Lord or His anointed but because of place and position. How many today are in the Church, fulfilling particular duties not because of love for God, but because of position, money, popularity, or self-will.

The following passages record the death of Sheba and the putting down of the rebellion.

In some small measure the *"wise woman"* of verse 16 is a type of the Holy Spirit. She directs in a manner in which action should be done without further bloodshed. If we would only seek, solicit, and plead the help of the Holy Spirit in all of our actions, how so much better would our direction be. But, instead, so oftentimes we resort to everything other than the *"wise woman."*

Verses 23 through 26 record by the Holy Spirit the restoration of David's kingdom, but at great cost. All that had gone on before was the efforts of Satan. The ordered structure under David was now recorded, despite the ungodliness of some of its participants such as Joab, as God's will. How so much better off Israel would have been had they adhered to that in the beginning.

The 26th verse says, *"About David."* Israel would have inserted "Absalom" or even "Sheba." Man, and even the Church, so seldom desires God's ways.

CHAPTER 21

This is a remarkable chapter, and, prayerfully, the Lord will help us to divulge the great spiritual truths contained therein.

First of all, some have said or conjectured that this experience of chapter 21 took place early in David's reign; however, there is no proof of such. The word "then" in the 1st verse should settle the question regarding the time as being after the preceding events of Absalom's rebellion.

Concerning a "famine" that had gripped Israel for some three years, the 1st verse says, *"David inquired of the Lord, and the Lord answered."* Certain things are said to us in this 1st verse:

1. Famines were generally a sign from God of His disapproval concerning Israel's spiritual declension. It must ever be understood that God takes a direct hand in all events pertaining to His people. He will bless consecration and dedication. Likewise, He will send judgment on spiritual wickedness and declension.

2. David finally asked the Lord as to the cause of the famine. Israel had, no doubt, suffered greatly in these three years. Perhaps much of the suffering could have been avoided had David gone to the Lord much earlier. Why do we take things to the Lord only after they reach the crisis stage?

3. The Scripture says concerning Saul, *"Because he slew the Gibeonites."* Nearly 500 years before, Joshua had made a covenant with the Gibeonites, promising to protect them (Josh. 9). Saul had broken that covenant and killed some of the Gibeonites. This chapter will portray to us the fact that God keeps His promises. Joshua had made a covenant with these people, and God expected that covenant to be kept.

The 3rd verse records, *"Wherefore David said unto the Gibeonites, What shall I do for you?"* The Lord had told David the reason for the famine, but there is no record that He had told David what to do about it. David should not have asked the Gibeonites; he should have asked the Lord as to how the anger of God

NOTES

could be appeased.

According to verses 7 through 9, David acceded to the demand of the Gibeonites, and took seven relatives of Saul and hung them. However, the 7th verse says that, *"The king spared Mephibosheth, the son of Jonathan."* However, another "Mephibosheth" of verse 8 who was the son of "Rizpah" was chosen for execution. The 9th verse says, *"They hanged them in the hill before the Lord."* Once again, David did not inquire of the Word of the Lord. For the Law of Moses plainly says, *"Neither shall the children be put to death for the fathers: Every man shall be put to death for his own sin"* (Deut. 24:16). So, David's taking these relatives of Saul and executing them for Saul's sin was ungodly and unscriptural. When we deviate from the Word of God, terrible injustice is always done.

The 10th verse records that the act of "Rizpah" brings David to his senses. Her two sons were hanged with the other five. She took a sackcloth and spread it upon a rock in order that she could keep watch over the bodies of her sons for a time of about five months. She maintained vigil in the open field on that shadeless rock, exposed to heat by day and coldness by night, from the day of their execution in April until the fall rains.

The 14th verse says, *"And after that God was entreated for the land."* It does seem that whatever David did regarding the reburial of the bones of Saul and Jonathan along with the seven men who had been hung had something to do with God being *"entreated for the land."* Exactly what it was, we do not know. The Scripture is silent; therefore, we have to be as well.

In the 12th verse the Holy Spirit, referring back to the death of Saul, mentions the fact that *"The Philistines had slain Saul in Gilboa."* Then the Holy Spirit records in the 15th verse, *"Moreover the Philistines had yet war again with Israel."* It then says that David *"fought against the Philistines."*

In this narrative one can see that if Satan had managed to destroy Saul by the hand of the Philistines (allowed by God), likewise, Satan would attempt to see David destroyed by the Philistines. Saul was about 60 years old when he was killed by the Philistines. David was about 60 years old at the time of this war, as well. The 15th verse says, *"And David waxed faint."*

However, it should be quickly added that David *"waxed faint"* because he was fighting the Philistines who were the enemies of the Lord. The only ones who never wax faint are those who never fight. The Church is full of them. Nevertheless, the few who dare fight the Philistines will find themselves sooner or later having *"waxed faint."* Regrettably, the Church does not look too favorably upon those who *"wax faint."* Regrettably, the Church as a whole does not fight many Philistines either.

The 16th verse says, *"And Ish-bi-be-nob."* This was the *"son of the giant"* who the Scripture said was *"thought to have slain David."* There is a tremendous scriptural lesson here.

First of all, the word *"Ish"* in the Hebrew means *"a man"* The entirety of the name means *"a man who dwells on the mountain."* *"Man"* is always the greatest enemy of the child of God. He had a *"new sword"* which was not the Word of God.

It should be quickly added that he did not dare try to kill David before his *"waxing faint."* However, he took advantage of David's weakened condition. Today, Ish-bi-be-nob has joined the Church. It is the age-old struggle of the flesh and the Spirit. Too many in the Church today have the "Ish-bi-be-nob" spirit.

But the 17th verse says, *"But Abishai the son of Zeruiah succoured him."* Which are you, "an Ish-bi-be-nob" or an Abishai?" One would try to kill David; the other would *"succour him."*

I can see Abishai now in the middle of the conflict as he sees David fall. First of all, he will run and help him up. Paul says as much in Galatians 6:1. If somehow you can see "Abishai" as he struggles to pick David up, you can see what Christianity is all about. He helped David, first of all, and then he *"smote the Philistine and killed him."* Thank God for the "Abishais."

The latter portion of the 17th verse says, *"That thou quench not the light of Israel."* How could they call David the light of Israel, especially after the episode with Bathsheba and Uriah? They called him *"the light of Israel"* because he was *"the light of Israel."* It shows that God not only forgives sin, but He forgets sin. The child of God should do the same. The

22nd verse says, *"And fell by the hand of David, and by the hand of his servants."* What a glorious statement. And, yet, the great feats of courage evidenced by David's servants were only because of David's anointing.

CHAPTER 22

This chapter provides us with beautiful spiritual insight that should give us a greater understanding of God and His dealings with man. Some of the things that we learn from this Psalm (song) are as follows:

1. This Song or Psalm is virtually identical to the 18th Psalm, but with some minor exceptions.

2. This Psalm was given by the Holy Spirit to David near the end of his life and reign. For the 1st verse says, *"In the day that the Lord had delivered him out of the hand of all his enemies, and out of the hand of Saul."*

3. This Psalm has two persons as its intended subject, David and the Messiah, the Lord Jesus Christ. However, the greater meaning is by far referring to the Lord Jesus Christ. It points prophetically to the Messiah, Who, in His sufferings and the glories that are to follow will fulfill and satisfy the language of these utterances.

4. David spoke these words by inspiration, because the 1st verse says, *"And David spake unto the Lord the words of this song."* Inspiration is the special influence of the Holy Spirit upon the minds of individuals which qualifies them to make a divine record of the infallible Will and Word of God to men.

5. The Holy Spirit placed this Psalm at the conclusion of the historical narrative of David to portray the difference of fallibility, which was David, and infallibility, which was the Holy Spirit upon David. Self-righteousness can never understand the Grace of God. It can only see David's terrible sins and faults. It can never see the repentant heart or the Blood of Jesus Christ that cleanses from all sin.

6. In this Psalm and concerning the description given, we learn of the tremendous struggle between good and evil. Words as given

in the 2nd verse such as, *"The Lord is my rock, and my fortress, and my deliverer,"* speak of tremendous need for such against the powers of darkness (demon spirits). The 3rd verse says, *"Thou savest me from violence."* Paul mentions to Timothy about *"warring a good warfare."* The 5th verse speaks of *"waves of death."* This refers to the constant brushes with death that David had as Satan repeatedly tried to kill him. The 7th verse proclaims, *"In my distress I called upon the Lord."* The Lord is the only answer, and David says, *"And my cry did enter into his ears."* Many other verses speak of the mighty power of God made evident through mighty deliverances.

When the words of this Psalm are studied carefully, then we begin to understand the tremendous forces of opposition that were brought against David, as well as against every child of God who attempts to carry out the call of God on his life. Many false doctrines have attempted to take the tribulation out of Christianity. However, it must always be remembered that this conflict is of eternal consequence. The stakes are high and, likewise, the contest bitter, but victory is assured to all of those who can say, *"He is the tower of salvation for his king: And sheweth mercy to his anointed"* (vs. 51).

CHAPTER 23

The first verse says, *"Now these be the last words of David,"* and, hence, they are very important. We know what the heart of David was by these "last words." First of all he spoke concerning himself, *"the anointed."* In chapter after chapter concerning David I have used the word "anointed." The Church needs to understand that in all of David's difficulties and problems, which included the cold-blooded murder of one of his mighty men, Uriah, that the anointing of the Holy Spirit never left him because of his truly repentant heart. All sin with God is horrible. However, sin falls into two categories, "pride and passion." In Proverbs 6 the Holy Spirit lists seven things that God hates. Pride leads the list with all falling into

NOTES

this category and none falling into the category of "passion." The Church little concerns itself with the sins of "pride" which God hates, and, by and large, directs its attention to the sins of "passion." To be sure, all sin, including "pride and passion", is abominable to God. As well, every human being who has ever lived, including the Bible greats, has failed in one or both categories. There are no exceptions except Christ.

David then used the words, *"the God of Jacob."* This means the God Who met Jacob when he had nothing and deserved nothing, and Who promised him all things - the God of all grace. In effect, David put himself in the same category as this poor scheming Jacob who was ultimately changed by God.

He then used the words, *"the sweet psalmist of Israel",* meaning that God had given him so many of the Psalms (songs).

The 2nd verse says, *"The Spirit of the Lord spake by me",* meaning that the mouth was David's, but the words were the Lord's.

The 4th verse says, *"And he shall be as the light of the morning."* Now David speaks of the coming Messiah. Of Him the Holy Spirit uses the words, *"the light of the morning",* and *"the sun riseth",* and *"a morning without clouds."* He then speaks of Him as *"tender grass after rain."*

In the fifth verse he says, *"Although my house be not so with God,"* meaning that neither he nor any member of his family fulfilled or, in fact, could fulfill the promises of this prophecy, but he rejoices in the knowledge that, in keeping with the terms of the Everlasting Covenant, ordered in all things and sure, made with him, there would be born into his family the great King described in these last words.

Verses 6 and 7 adequately describe the thorny path that the child of God must travel by stating, *"But the man that shall touch them must be fenced with iron."* He says, *"They cannot be taken with hands"* (vs. 6). In other words, there is no way that man with his limited power can overcome the powers of darkness. He can only win the victory by being *"fenced with iron"* and having the *"staff of a spear"* - in other words, the *"whole armour of God"* (Eph. 6).

Now the 8th verse catalogs *"the names of the mighty men whom David had."* It must be understood that they were *"mighty"* because of being with David. Likewise, this chapter catalogs the *"mighty men"* in Christ who, down through the ages, have helped Christ bring in the kingdom of God. They were given titles such as *"the Tachmonite",* as well the rightful name, *"Adino."* He killed *"eight hundred"* of the enemy *"at one time."*

The 9th verse says, *"Eleazar"* and then his title, *"the Ahohite."* The 10th verse says, *"He smote the Philistines until his hand was weary, and his hand clave unto the sword."* May we as ministers of the Gospel hold the sword of the Spirit, which is the Word of God, with such a grip that the hand and the sword will become one. Only then will *"the Lord wrought a great victory."*

Verses 11 and 12 speak of *"Shammah"* who defended a small piece of ground. This tells us that not one single part of our Christian life must be given to the enemy. Hallelujah!

Verses 13 through 17 speak of three of these mighty men who went to David in the *"cave of Adullam."* This was *"the harvest time."* They had turned their back upon the riches and prosperity of the world to join David in exile. As well, so must we as children of God turn our backs upon all that pertains to this world that we may stand beside Christ. They were so close to David that they heard his sigh regarding the desire for a *"drink of the water of the well of Bethlehem."* God help us to be so close to the heart of Christ that we can hear His sigh regarding the great needs in Africa, China, or the far flung nations of this world and bring Him souls from these regions that have been touched with the "water of life."

The 16th verse says that David did not drink the water but, instead, *"poured it out unto the Lord."* We really cannot find our lives until we, in effect, pour them out before the Lord. If we keep our lives, we lose them. If we lose our lives, we find true life.

The 18th verse says that Joab was only mentioned as the brother of *"Abishai,"* not as one of David's mighty men.

The 20th verse speaks of *"Benaiah"* slaying *"two lionlike men of Moab."* These were the heroes of Moab and thus of Satan. They were defeated by *"Benaiah."* Likewise, irrespective of the power of the demon forces sent against us, in the name of Jesus Christ we can and must defeat them. Benaiah also tracked down a lion in the snow and killed him, as well. We, likewise, must track down every sin in our life and smite it.

The 21st verse records the *"Egyptian",* who is a type of the world, with a *"spear in his hand"* designed to destroy us. But *"Benaiah"* did *"pluck the spear out of the Egyptian's hand, and slew him with his own spear."* Spiritually speaking, it must be remembered that the battle is to the death, the death of us or the powers of darkness. God help us to destroy the *"Egyptians",* who typify the world within our lives.

Verses 24 through 39 record 31 other mighty men. All of these typify that records are kept in the portals of glory concerning the acts of faith of every child of God. What does the record show concerning you and me?

CHAPTER 24

This chapter is freighted with the stubborn rebellion of man and the Church, and contains God's only remedy for this terrible plague.

Verse 1 says, *"And again the anger of the Lord was kindled against Israel."* The word *"again"* signifies that the Lord had been angry with Israel many times before. I am positive that the *"anger of the Lord"* has been kindled against all of us many times because of our stubbornness, disobedience, and rebellion. Every child of God should ask himself the question, "Is what I'm doing pleasing or displeasing to the Lord?" Either God's frown or His shining face is upon us. Which is it?

The Scripture says, *"He moved David against them to say, Go, number Israel and Judah."* I Chronicles 21 says that Satan was the instigator of this. No, there is no contradiction. The Holy Spirit designed it this way in both books (the Lord in II Samuel and Satan in I Chronicles) for a specific reason. Against a child of God Satan can do nothing unless the Lord allows him latitude. So, whether it says

"Satan or God" concerning a child of God, the Lord is the instigator. The Scripture is basically silent as to what aroused the anger of the Lord. However, this we do know, whatever course it took, it was sin. There is some indication that David desired to expand his borders beyond the original design of the Lord. Also, there is some slight indication that Israel was resorting to idol worship.

The 3rd verse records Joab's reply to the king's request, *"But why doth my lord the king delight in this thing?"* It is easy to detect the "flesh" in another, and so Joab, a man of the world, readily recognized the folly of David. David's action ministered only to his self-importance, for he said in verse 2, *"That I may know."* Also, the Law of Moses demanded that a *"half-shekel"* of silver be given to the Tabernacle for every person numbered (Exodus 30:11-16). There is no record that David did this. His failure to do so was a denial of the great truth that no man, woman, or child, whether moral or immoral, can be a member of God's family apart from redemption by the precious Blood of Christ. This redemption money was the foundation upon which the Tabernacle stood. Fellowship with God is based alone upon a similar foundation.

It took nearly ten months for this command to be obeyed regarding the numbering of Israel, and the 10th verse says, *"And David's heart smote him after that he had numbered the people."* It should be quickly stated that David's heart did not smite him until the sin was accomplished. Sin when accomplished occasions disgust; it is the pursuit of it which has such a hateful attraction for the heart. When the sin is committed, Satan no longer cares to hide its ugliness. So now *"David's heart"* smites him. One of the chief ministries of the Holy Spirit is to smite with conviction. Regrettably, in today's modern church circles Holy Ghost conviction is as scarce as the proverbial hen's teeth. Actually, in most of Christendom it is denied. Nevertheless, the great office work of the Holy Spirit to smite with conviction is several fold in its application:

1. The Holy Spirit only smites those who belong to Him. Consequently, if an individual can sin with impunity without the "smiting" of

NOTES

the Holy Spirit, this is the greatest sign of all that the individual is not a child of God.

2. This is a part of the office work of the Holy Spirit that leads us away from the "sin nature" that still abides in the life of the child of God.

3. This is a part of the "reproving" or "convicting" of the world of *"sin, and of righteousness, and of judgment"* (St. John 16:8). In this world the Holy Spirit is the only One Who sets the standards for sin, righteousness, and for judgment. All other standards are false.

4. As well, this is a part of the office work of the Holy Spirit to *"guide you into all truth"* (St. John 16:13). There is no truth but God's truth, and Jesus Christ is truth.

David then says, *"I have sinned greatly in that I have done."* David always acknowledged his wrongdoing and humbled himself, and made restitution as far as possible regarding failure. He confessed his sin and prayed to be cleansed from the iniquity and foolishness, for he said, *"For I have done very foolishly."* Sin makes fools of men, even the most brilliant of men. There is no wisdom in sin; there is no light in sin; there is only stupidity, foolishness, and absurdity.

The 11th verse proclaims the fact that *"the word of the Lord came unto the prophet Gad."* The great need of America, Canada, and the world is for the *"word of the Lord"* to come to men of God. Even if it is a word of judgment, it is far better than no word at all, simply because with every word of judgment, God always brings a word of mercy and of grace.

The 12th verse records the divine retribution, *"Thus saith the Lord, I offer thee three things."* David could choose one of the three: *"Seven years of famine, to flee three months before thine enemies, or three days' pestilence in thy land."* Some may argue that in this day of grace sin has no penalty. While it is certainly true that grace upon proper repentance and the forsaking of sin will cover, wash, and cleanse from all iniquity, still, there is always a penalty for sin. The hurt, loss, pain, suffering, humiliation, and disgrace cannot be escaped. Neither should it be escaped in order that men may ever know the terrible poison and evil sin has caused. Every heartache and pain in this world can be summed up in one word. That word is "sin."

The 14th verse records David saying, *"I am in a great strait."* Sin does this. It backs people against the wall. It puts them in a narrow confine. It reduces their mobility. Every way of escape seems to be blocked. Then David expresses his desire to *"fall into the hand of the Lord",* and says, *"Let me not fall into the hand of man."* As David knew from experience, man has precious little mercy, and religious man has no mercy at all.

The 15th verse records the *"pestilence"* that fell upon Israel in some three days' time, resulting in the death of *"seventy thousand men."* What these individuals did, no one knows. However, knowing the mercy and the grace of God, they at least must have been guilty of idolatry for the Lord to take such drastic action.

The 16th verse suggests that even Jerusalem was about to be destroyed, but the Scripture says, *"The Lord repented him of the evil."* In other words, God willed a change of action. The Scripture says, *"And the angel of the Lord was by the threshingplace of Araunah the Jebusite."* This place will figure very prominently in the future of Israel, because it will be the place where the Lord will direct that the Temple under Solomon would be built. So, God turned a terrible judgment into a beautiful testimony of grace. The lesson once again becomes clear, that if we place everything in the hand of the Lord, humbling ourselves before Him and fully confessing our wrongdoing, that the Lord will turn judgment into grace and, thereby, into blessing. However, it must be understood that this in no way negates the penalty for sin.

The 18th verse says that David did *"rear an altar."* The judgment along with the altar prefigures Christ as the sin-offering, which He should accomplish at Jerusalem. David, as a type of Christ, foreshadows this, for no priest is mentioned. The altar is a type of Calvary.

The 24th verse proclaims Araunah, the Jebusite, offering to give the oxen for the "burnt sacrifice" without cost, for David says in the 24th verse, *"Neither will I offer burnt offerings unto the Lord of that which doth cost me nothing."* The sin of the Church is that it is forever attempting to offer God that which

costs nothing. There is always a price tag.

The 25th verse says, *"And David built there an altar unto the Lord, and offered burnt offerings and peace offerings."* Even though it is not mentioned in this chapter, I Chronicles 21 records the fire from heaven falling to consume the sacrifice, which is a type of the judgment on Christ instead of us.

The concluding portion says, *"So the Lord was intreated for the land, and the plague was stayed from Israel."* There is a *"plague"* called sin that is destroying this world and causing multiple hundreds of millions to be eternally lost. There is only one cure for that plague, and that is the precious, atoning, vicarious offering of the Blood of the Lord Jesus Christ, and our acceptance of Him. All the churches in the world will not stay the "plague." All the good works, good intentions, money, prestige, or education will not stop this plague of sin. Only the precious Blood of Jesus Christ can. God will be satisfied with nothing else.

THE
BOOK OF I KINGS

—■—

I Kings and II Kings were originally one book and were divided into two books or scrolls by the Septuagint translators in the Third Century B.C. The books are named for their contents – the history of the kings of Israel and Judah from Solomon to the Babylonian captivity, a period of somewhat over 400 years.

They begin with a record concerning King David and end with one regarding the king of Babylon. They open with an account of the building of the Temple and close with its destruction. It opens with the Temple built and closes with the Temple burnt. It commences with deliverance from the Philistines and ends with captivity to the Chaldeans.

They begin with the story of David's first successor and end with the last one released from captivity. The characters of all the kings of Israel and Judah are tested by the standard of David, not David's moral conduct, but his fidelity to the Law, which was held up before all his successors as a standard to be aimed at. For great as were his sins and his crimes – and they were neither excused nor covered up by God. He was and is for all time a remarkable and an earnest lover of Divine Truth. His fame as the sweet Psalmist of Israel will live forever.

—■—

CHAPTER 1

Verse 1 opens with the words *"Now king David."* The first king of Israel, Saul, is not once mentioned in I Kings and II Kings. It is as if he never existed because Saul was the people's choice, while David was God's choice.

The 5th verse says, *"Then Adonijah the son*

of Haggith exalted himself, saying, I will be king." Adonijah, Joab, and Abiathar set up their kingdom in opposition to God's elect king. God had no place in their hearts, and, so, Solomon did not suit them either. God's choice never does suit man.

This unholy triumvirate is a type of that which controls so much of the Church world today.

1. Adonijah: This man represents the world of religion that has no regard for the call of God or the will of God but by religious politics will seek to gain fortune and position in the Church. Most of the so-called "spiritual leadership" in the modern Church is made up of such.

2. Joab: This man, as well, cares nothing for the will of God or the call of God but will constantly test the way the religious wind is blowing, in order that he may throw in his lot with it and, thereby, feather his own nest. The Church world is full of these religious opportunists.

3. Abiathar: This man occupied the high priesthood of Israel jointly with Zadok. He, as well, is an opportunist. He will see the crowning of Adonijah as an opportunity to secure the priesthood for himself alone. As well, he will have no regard for the will of God or the call of God. The modern Church is full of these "religious leaders."

The Bible student would do himself well to study carefully the ungodly intentions of this triumvirate, for it pictures the modern-day Church world. In this chapter we will see this effort of Satan derailed, with God's man being placed on the throne. However, the far greater majority of times in the Bible and throughout Church history there has been no David to carry out the will of God. Instead, "Adonijah, Joab, and Abiathar" gain the ascendancy. It is no less true today.

The 12th verse implies that had this trio gained their advantage, Solomon and all who pertained to him would have been killed, for the Scripture says, *"That thou mayest save thine own life and the life of thy son Solomon."* Not only will this religious effort attempt to place the "will of man" on the throne instead of the "will of God," but, as well, must kill that which is appointed of God. It must ever be understood that this effort by Satan which is so prominent in the Church world is never satisfied with just gaining religious ascendancy. It must kill that which pertains to the Lord. This raging conflict did not begin with I Kings; it started at the dawn of time. Cain's sacrifice was rejected by the Lord while Abel's was accepted. Therefore, Cain must kill Abel. The flesh must kill the spirit. The "will of man" must kill the "will of God." Too often it succeeds.

The 39th verse says, *"And Zadok the priest took an horn of oil out of the tabernacle, and anointed Solomon."* This was God's choice. How do we know? We know because of what the Lord said as recorded in II Samuel 12, *"And he called his name Jedidiah, because of the Lord"* (II Sam. 12:24-25).

Concerning Adonijah, the 51st verse says, *"For, lo, he hath caught hold on the horns of the altar."* The rite of asylum in sacred places was common to all nations, and though not formerly declared in the Mosaic Law, it was clearly recognized as is evident in Exodus 21:14, where it is directed to be refused under certain circumstances. It would seem from the text and from 2:28 that if an accused person could take hold of the horns of the altar, he was safe unless his crime was of a horrible nature. The cities of refuge were appointed for the same purpose (Num. 35:15-32).

The 52nd verse proclaims the mercy of Solomon granted to Adonijah, *"If he will shew himself a worthy man, there shall not an hair of him fall to the earth."* However, future chapters will show that he was not a *"worthy man."*

NOTES

CHAPTER 2

The 1st verse says, *"Now the days of David drew nigh that he should die."* How long David lived after making Solomon king is not stated, but at the time he drew near death, he gave a final charge to the new king. The charge was fivefold:

1. *"Shew yourself a man"* (vs. 2).

2. *"Keep the charge of the Lord your God"* (vs. 3).

3. *You know what Joab did to me. You are to use your wisdom regarding this situation* (vss. 5-6).

4. *Because of the kindness that "Barzillai the Gileadite" showed to me, allow his sons to eat at your table, for they came to me when I fled from Absalom your brother* (vs 7).

5. *You must deal with Shimei who cursed me with a grievous curse in the day when I fled from Absalom. Now therefore, hold him not guiltless. As well, use your wisdom regarding this situation* (vss. 8-9).

The deathbed charge of David to Solomon was, therefore, altogether admirable. It was not that of a revengeful private person, but it was the judicial act of a chief magistrate conscious of his responsibility when handing over his office to his successor.

However, David prefaced his instructions to Solomon by pointing out that success lay only in close adherence and full subjection to the written Word of God, *"To walk in His ways, to keep His statutes, and His commandments, and His judgments"* (vs. 3).

Of these individuals of rebellion, which, of course, did not include *"Barzillai"* David knew that their traitorous hearts would continue to overthrow God's choice of king, who was Solomon. The Holy Spirit, no doubt, guided David in his instructions given to Solomon.

The 10th verse says, *"So David slept with his fathers."* And so died one of the greatest men of God who ever lived. He wrote about half of the Psalms. In some ways he filled the offices of prophet, priest, and king. He was a type of Christ, and his successor would ultimately be called "the son of David," and then "King of kings and Lord of lords." Despite the sins, faults, and failures, his heart was ever after God. His name was the first human name in the New Testament (Matt. 1:1) and the last human name in the New Testament (Rev. 22:16). During the great Kingdom Age to come under the Lord Jesus Christ, he will once again rule Israel in all of her glory, fulfilling the great prophecies that were given to him by Nathan the prophet.

The 11th verse says that he *"reigned over Israel forty years,"* with the first seven years of that reign being only over Judah. His reign in the Millennium will be 1,000 years, and then forever and ever.

The 12th verse says concerning Solomon, *"His kingdom was established greatly."* As David is a type of Christ who brought salvation to Israel and the world, likewise, Solomon is a type of Christ who will reign over an established kingdom with all enemies defeated, in what is known as the "Kingdom Age" or the "Millennial Reign."

Referring back to the sons of *"Barzillai the Gileadite,"* there were honors reserved which pointed to the assured positions of glory which those will have in Christ's coming kingdom who now share with Him in being despised and rejected of men.

However, it must ever be remembered that David and Solomon were but types, and poor, frail, human types at that, which ultimately always fail. Nevertheless, the One they pointed to, the Lord Jesus Christ, has never failed, and in fact, will never fail.

Solomon was perhaps about 20 years of age when he took the throne. As the Lord Jesus Christ will rid the earth of enemies at the beginning of the great Millennial Reign, likewise, Solomon would put down all usurpation by pretenders to the throne.

The 27th verse says, *"So Solomon thrust out Abiathar from being priest unto the Lord."* This removal of Abiathar from the priesthood was a definite fulfillment of the cutting off of the house of Eli. Here we have the fulfillment of God's rejection of the house of Ithamar (I Chron. 24:3) to which Eli belonged, and the reestablishment of the high priesthood in the line of Eleazar.

The 46th verse proclaims the approval by

NOTES

the Holy Spirit of Solomon's actions regarding *"Joab, Abiathar, and Shimei,"* for it says, *"And the kingdom was established in the hand of Solomon."*

CHAPTER 3

The 1st verse as recorded by the Holy Spirit gives us a clue to the cause of Solomon's fall in later years, for it says, *"And Solomon made affinity with Pharaoh king of Egypt, and took Pharaoh's daughter, and brought her into the city of David."* The word *"affinity"* means relationship by marriage. This was done, no doubt, for political reasons in order to strengthen his kingdom and on the same grounds he had an alliance with the king of Tyre. These were his most powerful neighbors at this time. In so doing however, Solomon broke the Law of God which forbade making alliances and intermarrying with foreign nations lest they should lead the hearts of Israel away from Jehovah to other gods (Ex. 34:16; Deut. 7:3-4). We do not find the Lord rebuking him in this chapter, even though the Holy Spirit did record the event. Nevertheless, it was unlawful. We find it referred to elsewhere as his folly (11:1-9).

The 2nd verse says, *"Only the people sacrificed in high places."* This seems to be a statement of regret rather than censure. It introduces a contrast by the writer meaning to say that there was one exception to the flourishing condition of the nation – the people sacrificed in high places. The Law of God did not necessarily condemn a high place, but the wrong use of one for idolatry. All high places used for idolatry were to be destroyed (Deut. 12:2). Actually, Israel was not to offer sacrifices except at the door of the Tabernacle (Lev. 17:3-5). These high places, although now used for the worship of God, would later lead to idolatry.

At this time the Brazen Altar was at Gibeon, where the Tabernacle was as well. The Ark was in the city of David. The Brazen Altar was visible; the Ark was hidden. The Brazen Altar pictures Christ lifted up from the earth in suffering, rejection, and death; the Ark shows

Christ hidden in the heavenlies awaiting the time of His manifestation in glory. In the sad days of the Judges and of Saul, the Tabernacle was forsaken, and the Ark, disrupted from the Brazen Altar, was cast aside. All would not be united until the building of the Temple.

The 4th verse says, *"And the king went to Gibeon to sacrifice there."* Gibeon was about four miles from Jerusalem. The Tabernacle Moses made was located here at this time (II Chron. 1:3-4). There was another Tabernacle in Jerusalem (3:15) which housed the Ark of the Covenant. So, verses 2 and 4 suggest that there were, contrary to the Law, divided places of worship in Israel.

In this we learn of the frailty of the human family and of the grace of God. The Holy Spirit is ever seeking to lead the individual into that which is totally God's way. God starts with no perfect people and seldom concludes with such. He looks for a yielding, obedient heart.

The 5th verse says, *"In Gibeon the Lord appeared to Solomon in a dream by night."* In this dream the Lord says, *Ask what I shall give thee."* It is plainly implied that the request would be granted. Those who express the desire to have God say to them what He did to Solomon should realize that He does – and even more. It should be understood that the promises are for our particular needs, which would not fully be Solomon's. They are as follows:

1. Ask, seek, and knock (Matt. 7:7).
2. Nothing shall be impossible unto you (Matt. 17:20).
3. All things, whatsoever you shall ask in prayer, believing, you shall receive (Matt. 21:21-22).
4. All things are possible to him that believeth (Mark 9:23; 11:22-24).
5. Ask what you will, and it shall be done unto you (John 15:7).

The 7th verse denotes that which is required by God of all who would receive from Him, *"and I am but a little child."* This denotes humility.

The 9th verse records by the Holy Spirit Solomon's request, *"Give therefore thy servant an understanding heart to judge thy people."* There are many who claim that Solomon should have asked for other things such as love,

NOTES

or holiness. While this certainly may be true, still, the 10th verse says, *"And the speech pleased the Lord that Solomon had asked this thing."* Therefore, if it pleases God, it should please us. There are 12 things recorded in the Bible that are said to be pleasing to God. They are as follows:

1. That Israel was blessed (Num. 24:1).
2. Israel was His people (I Sam. 12:22).
3. Solomon's prayer (I Kings 3:10).
4. Bruising of the Messiah (Isa. 53:10).
5. Messiah's life and mission (Matt. 3:17).
6. Saving of souls by preaching (I Cor. 1:21).
7. Setting members in the Church (I Cor. 12:18).
8. Resurrection of dead bodies (I Cor. 15:38).
9. Separation of Paul (Gal. 1:15).
10. All fulness dwelling in Christ (Col. 1:19).
11. Enoch's life and faith (Heb. 11:5).
12. Sacrifices of praise (Heb. 13:16).

In the 12th verse the Lord tells Solomon that no other mortal before him or after him would be given such wisdom of God, *"So that there was none like thee before thee, neither after thee shall any arise like unto thee."* He was a type of Christ.

The 14th verse gives Solomon an added promise, *"As thy father David did walk, then I will lengthen thy days."* Solomon did not do this and died at about 60 years of age. He could have lived many more years through obedience.

The 15th verse says after the dream was given to Solomon, *"And he came to Jerusalem, and stood before the ark of the covenant of the Lord, and offered up burnt offerings, and offered peace offerings."* This proves that the Tabernacle where the Ark was kept was not in Gibeon but in Jerusalem. It seems that Moses' Tabernacle was at Gibeon with another Tabernacle, perhaps made by David in Jerusalem. It seems that *"burnt offerings"* and *"peace offerings"* were offered before the Ark. If this were so, then there must have been two Brazen Altars, with one being in Gibeon and the other in Jerusalem. If this was so, then it was not according to the commandment of the Lord. It would not be rectified until some years later when the Temple would be completed.

Verses 16-28 prove God's gift of wisdom to

Solomon, and that it pertained to every walk of life. For the 28th verse says, *"For they saw that the wisdom of God was in him, to do judgment."*

With this wisdom that God gave him, Israel would become the most powerful nation on the face of the earth of that day. And it should quickly be stated that it was not by the means of military might, but by wisdom alone.

—■—

CHAPTER 4

Verse 1 says, *"So King Solomon was king over all Israel."* Verses 2-19 give his principle officers. It seems their appointment was made according to Solomon's great wisdom which, in effect, was an appointment by the Holy Spirit. Had the "work of the flesh" of chapter 2 prevailed concerning "Adonijah" and "Joab" with "Abiathar," tyrants would now have ruled Israel, making life utterly miserable for the whole kingdom. Most, if not all the nations of the world are ruled by those who have little or no knowledge of God. Consequently, in many countries demon spirits actually rule, with the result being misery, starvation, tyranny, death and destruction.

Verse 20 says, *"Eating and drinking, and making merry."* All of this resulted from the one fact that Solomon, God's choice, was king. The destruction of the rebels and the enthronement of God's elect prince originated this universal contentment and prosperity. It is a forepicture of the happy day that awaits the earth when the rebels who now govern it and fill it with misery will be overthrown, and the Prince of Peace, the greater than Solomon (Matt. 12:42) will take unto Himself His great power and reign gloriously before His ancient people, Israel.

The present miseries that oppress the nations which they vainly try to remove by repeated efforts will have an end whenever the Messiah returns and takes the government of this world into His mighty hands.

The 24th verse says, *"For he had dominion over all the region."* In that glorious day Jesus Christ will have *"dominion"* over the entirety of

the earth. Tyrants, rebels, and despots will have no place in this coming grand and glorious kingdom. Consequently, as the Scripture says, *"And he had peace on all sides around about him."* Men today vainly look for peace. They created the "League of Nations" which failed to stop World War II, and now the "United Nations" which will fail to stop the coming Battle of Armageddon. However, when the "Prince of Peace" comes back, there will be "peace," but only when He returns.

Then as the 25th verse says, *"Judah and Israel dwelt safely."* What a glorious time when there will be no war, no privation, no want, and no misery. The Scripture further says, *"Every man under his vine and under his fig tree,"* denoting total and complete security and safety.

The 27th verse says, *"They lacked nothing."* Much of the world at this time goes to bed hungry. Every day hundreds or even thousands succumb to what is referred to as the "silent death." They simply fall down through weakness and starvation and are unable to arise, especially the children. This happens despite the fact that great portions of the world are glutted with food. However, let it ever be said that according to the Word of God, when Jesus Christ returns, of every nation and every person on the face of the earth, it will be said *"They lacked nothing."*

The 29th verse says, *"And God gave Solomon wisdom and understanding exceeding much, and largeness of heart."* Once again we proclaim that the *"greater than Solomon is coming."*

The 31st verse states, *"For he was wiser than all men."* If this was said of Solomon, and it was, how much more will it be said of the Lord Jesus Christ.

Verses 32 and 33 proclaim that his wisdom would cover every avenue and facet of life.

The 34th verse proclaims the mighty power of Israel under the reign of Solomon. This power would not be as the result of mighty armies or navies, but, instead, would be the only kingdom on the face of the earth that was ever built by wisdom, for it says, *"And there came of all people to hear the wisdom of Solomon, from all kings of the earth, which had heard of his wisdom."* Not only was Israel greatly blessed, but every nation that took advantage of Solomon's wisdom was blessed as well. The great questions were brought to Solomon, and the answers were forthcoming, resulting in tremendous prosperity for all.

In the days of the Kingdom Age when Jesus Christ rules and reigns in Jerusalem, *"All kings of the earth"* will come to Him. Hallelujah!

CHAPTER 5

This chapter begins with the preparations of Solomon to construct the Temple – no doubt, the grandest building ever constructed by man. The entirety of its design down to the most minute detail had already been given to David by the Holy Spirit.

The 1st verse says, *"For Hiram was ever a lover of David."* There was never a record of any type of conflict between Lebanon and Israel during the time of David and Solomon. The Hebrews were always at peace with the Phoenicians. As well, they would now share in the great blessing of God that would come upon Israel. *"Hiram"* is a type of the Gentile kings, presidents, and world leaders during the time of the Kingdom Age who will ever be "lovers of the Lord Jesus Christ."

The 4th verse says, *"But now the Lord my God hath given me rest on every side."* What a beautiful statement! Paul writes, *"For we know that the whole creation groaneth and travaileth in pain together until now"* (Rom. 8:22). Since the Garden of Eden, planet Earth has suffered and labored under the curse of sin. Satan has ruled as a "prince of the powers of the air." The results have been chaos, murder, hate, pain, starvation, and war. When Jesus comes back there will be *"rest on every side."* As well, there will be *"neither adversary nor evil occurrent."* Sickness, suffering, starvation, and want will no longer be.

The 5th verse says *"To build an house unto the name of the Lord my God."* The building of the Temple as God's dwelling place and throne, was an earnest of the fulfillment of the promise yet to be realized of the establishment of Jehovah's house and government in the millen-

nial earth.

Thus the Temple with its many chambers could possibly be viewed as a type of the Father's house with its many mansions (St. John 14:1).

This house that would be built would depend upon the faithfulness and obedience of Solomon, which was temporal. However in the Kingdom Age to come the faithfulness and obedience will depend upon the "Divine Solomon," because obedience is assured, the fellowship is, therefore, perpetual.

The 6th verse says, *"Hew me cedar trees out of Lebanon."* Cedar was used in some parts of the house, which in turn was overlaid with gold. The cedar still grows in Lebanon on parts of the mountains, but it is not so plentiful as in ancient times. The Tyrians made masts for their ships from it (Ezek. 27:5). It seems that the Assyrians and other people also cut down many of these trees to take to their own countries, which added to the scarcity as time went on. The Hebrew word for "Cedar" appears to be used not only for the cedar, but, also for other timber trees such as the fir and juniper.

The *"Hiram"* of Solomon's time was not the Hiram of David's day but, rather, his son. Meander of Ephesus who wrote a history of Tyre in Greek about 300 B.C. mentioned this Hiram as the son of the Hiram also called "Abibaal," king of Tyre and said that he ascended the throne when he was 19 years old, and that he reigned 34 years, dying at the age of 53. He was succeeded by his son, Beleazar. This history speaks at length on the dealings of Hiram with Solomon.

The 12th verse says *"And there was peace between Hiram and Solomon: and they two made a league together."* This league was broken many years later by Tyre, and for this the people were judged (Amos 1:9).

Verses 13-18 proclaim that 183,300 laborers and overseers worked on the Temple. Considering the tremendous number of men and the length of time it took to build the Temple (7 years), along with the costly materials, one can understand the reason for the price tag – in today's inflated dollar approximately 2 trillion dollars.

The 17th verse says, *"They brought great stones."* Some of these stones were extra large and heavy. The largest said to be found in modern Jerusalem thus far is 38 feet, 9 inches long and weighs a little bit over 100 tons. It is, no doubt, one of the many stones hewn out of the mountains in the days of Solomon. The marks of Phoenician masons are still on some stones. They were fully cut on the mountains to exact size so that no chiseling or hammering took place when they were set together. The same was true of the wooden beams, so that the use of no tool was heard in the construction (I Kings 6:7).

CHAPTER 6

Verse 1 says, *"And it came to pass in the four hundred and eightieth year."* This verse illustrates the promise that God not only forgives but also forgets sin, for the years of Israel's bondage to the nations are omitted. The lesson, at the same time, is taught that years or days spent in bondage to the world are forever lost. Thus, what appears a chronological error in the text, is found to be a designed message of comfort and warning.

As stated, the 480 years given in the text was not the whole time or the period between the Exodus and the fourth year of Solomon's reign. It really refers to the 480th year of the security of Israel as a nation. It does not include the 40 years of Sinai and the wandering in the wilderness, the period of the conquest of Canaan, and division of the land (about ten years), or the three years of confusion under Abimelech and the 111 years of servitude during the judges. The entire period from the Exodus to the fourth year of Solomon was 645 years. However, there is a possibility that some of the periods designated in the book of Judges overlapped with other periods which would have shortened the entirety of the time by a number of years. But there is no way this can be determined.

The 2nd verses gives the "length" and the "breadth," as well as the "height" of the Temple. It is given in cubits. Also, there is some dissension regarding the actual size of the cubit. Some have judged it to be 25 inches and

NOTES

others 18 inches. We will use 18 inches to the cubit for our measurement. This would have made the building 90 feet long, 30 feet wide, and 45 feet high. The building certainly was not large.

However, as the 5th verse describes, there were "chambers" or rooms built around the sides and the rear of the Temple, which would have broadened its shape according to its height. Only when we consider the manner in which the building was constructed and the materials used can we understand the reason for the tremendous cost (approximately $2 trillion in 1993 currency).

The 7th verse says, *"So that there was neither hammer nor ax nor any tool of iron heard in the house while it was in building."* This means that all the stones and timbers were cut to exact size, being fully prepared for their places before being brought to the Temple site. These were so perfect that it was not necessary to use a hammer, ax, or any other such tool during the entire construction work. This is one of the reasons for the great cost of the building. The purpose was that it was to be the dwelling place for the thrice-holy God.

Verses 11-14 record the Davidic Covenant confirmed in Solomon (II Sam. 7:17). The 13th verse says, *"And I will dwell among the children of Israel, and will not forsake my people Israel."* This was a conditional prophecy based upon obedience. Then, when obedience was rendered, the Lord promised to perform His Word which He had spoken to both David and Solomon concerning the continuation of the kingdom and God dwelling in the midst of His people. The prophecy never was completely fulfilled, for Solomon rebelled and Israel sinned until God could not bless them further or dwell in their midst.

God laid down the conditions on which He would dwell among Israel and not forsake them, and the fact that He ceased to dwell with them and forsook them is proof that they did not continue meeting the conditions. As recorded in the 12th verse, these are to *"walk in my statutes, and execute my judgments, and keep all my commandments to walk in them."*

God would have proved Himself untrue before all people if He had continued His grace with them when they sinned and refused to repent. So it is today. If a believer sins, God is obligated to impute it to him. There is no place in Christ or out of Christ where one is not held responsible and where he does not incur the death penalty for breaking the New Covenant laws when sin is committed. Sin must be repented of and forsaken for God's grace to continue. Israel's problem was that she would not repent nor forsake her sin.

Just as God promised not to forsake Israel as long as they lived true to Him, so He also promised to forsake them when they sinned and refused to repent, regardless of past grace and blessings.

The 21st verse says, *"So Solomon overlaid the house within with pure gold."* The cedar of the walls of the holy and most holy places were carved with knops and flowers. The boards fully covered the inside so that no stone of the walls was seen, and they were covered with pure gold. The Altar was also covered with gold, as well as the petition between the holy and most holy places. Again, this is one of the reasons as to the great cost of the house.

Verse 20 tells us that the "Oracle" or the "Holy of Holies" was "twenty cubits" wide (30 feet), with the same in length and height. This was the same width of the house as well (30 feet). We also see in II Chronicles 4, that the Great Brazen Altar was also 20 cubits square (30 feet). The reason was that atonement and glory are one. Atonement is the theology of heaven, and the entrance to God's home is as wide as the home itself. What a thrilling revelation. In other words, Calvary is just as large as the house of God.

Verses 23-28 describe the "Oracle" or the "Holy of Holies."

Verse 23 says, *"Two cherubims of olive tree, each ten cubits high"* (15 feet high). Each set of wings was five cubits long (seven and a half feet). One pair of wings touched the wall at the rear, with the other set of wings touching each other in the middle. The entire span of both Cherubim was 30 feet, in other words covering the entirety of the "Holy of Holies." The 28th verse says, *"And he overlaid the cherubims with gold."*

The Cherubim symbolized judgment. Their wings met over the blood-sprinkled Mercy Seat and reached to either extremity of

the most Holy Place. God's judgments have Calvary for their center and are as wide as His Home.

Beneath the huge Cherubim whose wings stretched from wall to wall was placed the Ark of the Covenant with the Mercy Seat. The smaller Cherubim that Moses had made were attached to the Mercy Seat and made of the same mass of gold. The smaller Cherubim looked downward upon the sprinkled blood; the huge Cherubim made of olive-wood and covered with gold looked outward. Whereas, Moses' Tabernacle in the wilderness before the erection of the Temple was a type of Calvary and redemption, Solomon's Temple was a type of the Kingdom Age and of righteousness. God's perfect judgments will, in the Millennium, be enabled to look out from Calvary upon a kingdom wherein shall dwell righteousness. This is not now possible for righteousness retreated to heaven when Christ went to the Father (St. John 16:10).

The Cherubim which were overlaid with pure gold for righteousness characterizes judgment when the kingdoms of this world will become the kingdoms of Jehovah and of His Christ.

Thus, the dwelling place of God was resplendent with gold, which expressed deity and Divine righteousness.

Verses 29 and 30 speak of "Cherubims" which represent God's judgments and His holiness. The "palm trees" and "open flowers" represent a perfect environment. "Gold" represents deity. It is "within and without," meaning all of God.

Verses 31-35 portray the "doors of the Holy of holies." The 31st verse says, *"He made doors of olive tree."*

There is no veil mentioned in the Temple as in the Tabernacle because the figure here is not that of access to God but of dwelling with God. There are folding doors which open. Millennial fellowship will be real but partial. Full fellowship with God will only be enjoyed in the New Heavens and the New Earth.

The two folding doors between the porch and the most holy places, with the post and lentels, took up one-fourth of the wall. These doors symbolize the perfection and the acceptance of Christ as the new and living way to

God. He is the door through which if any man enter in, he shall be saved – saved because of the gratified eye and heart of God which rest with complacency upon the door, not upon the one who enters.

The doors were beautified with chased work and gold of Cherubim, palm trees, and opened flowers. Such is, was, and ever will be Jesus the Lamb of God, the Son of God.

The 36th verse speaks of the "inner court." The inner court is spoken of here with the outer court mentioned in II Chronicles 4:9. The inner court was perhaps the same as the higher court of Jeremiah 36:10, being raised above the outer one by a few steps. It seems the inner court surrounded the Temple building and was perhaps double the size of the Temple all the way around. The outside width of the Temple counting the outside rooms was about 40 cubits – about 60 feet. The inner court would have been approximately 160 feet from the Temple itself on all sides. There may have been more space in front to make room for the Brazen Altar and sacrifices. The outer court was evidently much larger, measuring perhaps 350 to some 500 feet.

The 38th verse says, *"So was he seven years in building it."*

CHAPTER 7

Verse 1 says *"But Solomon was building his own house thirteen years."* How many men he used as workers on his house is not stated, but it is significant that the Holy Spirit records the time it took Solomon to build his own house in comparison to God's house. These buildings were quite larger than the Temple. They, no doubt, housed the government ministries of Israel. Both, the building of the Temple which took seven years and the building of the government houses which took some thirteen years, were, no doubt, types of that which will be done in the Millennial Reign. In Solomon's kingdom the Temple was first built as, no doubt, in the coming Kingdom Age the Temple will be the first major structure to be built, rightly so, because the worship of God is the

NOTES

singular most important thing there is. Ezekiel chapters 40-48 describe the building of the millennial Temple. It, no doubt, took longer to build the government buildings under Solomon than it did the Temple simply because Israel's great expenditure of energy was spent foremost on the Temple. As well, it will, no doubt, take much longer in the Millennial Reign to finish the great government buildings that will be needed, than it will to construct the Temple. And as previously stated, this is simply because the worship of God is by far more important, with the greater energy spent on the Temple.

Verses 1-12 record the fact that Solomon used the same kind of stone, wood, and other materials in the building of the government structures as he did the Temple. These buildings were as beautiful and magnificent as the Temple as well. The Holy Spirit, no doubt, recorded the beauty of these government structures to insinuate the fact that government in the Kingdom Age will be beautiful for the first time in history. Isaiah writes, *"The government shall be upon His shoulders"* (Isa. 9:6-7).

Verses 13-22 strangely and beautifully portray the work of the Holy Spirit within our hearts and lives.

The 13th verse says, *"And fetched Hiram out of Tyre."* Incidentally, even though this man bore the same name, this Hiram was not the king of Tyre. He was a metal worker and had charge of all the castings of pillars, brazen sea, and many other things used in the Temple furnishings.

In this instance he was a type of the Holy Spirit, for the 14th verse says, *"a worker in brass"* (copper). Copper (brass) is a type of humanity. It can be shined to a high gloss, but at the same time it can tarnish very easily. The Scripture says of him, as the Holy Spirit, *"He was filled with wisdom, and understanding, and cunning to work all works in brass (copper)."* It is the work of the Holy Spirit to take our lives, which are rough, crude, and spoiled, and make of them that which our heavenly Solomon desires. For the 14th verse continues to say, *"and wrought all his work."* The Holy Spirit is making of the child of God what the Lord Jesus Christ wants, not what we want.

The 15th verse portrays the making of the Christian, for the Scripture says, *"For he cast two pillars of brass."* These pillars are types of the child of God. Jesus states in the book of Revelation, *"Him that overcometh will I make a pillar in the temple of my God"* (Rev. 3:12). As the Temple was a type of Christ and the pillars a type of the child of God, no doubt, Jesus had these pillars in mind when He made the statement concerning the overcoming Christian. The Scripture says, *"Eighteen cubits high apiece."* Using 18 inches to the cubit this would mean that the pillars were 27 feet high and 18 feet around. If one adds the *"chapiters"* of the 16th verse and the *"lily work"* of the 19th verse, then the pillars stood about 40 feet high. They weighed about 20 tons each and were made of brass.

In I Chronicles 18:8 it says concerning David's conquest of Zobah, *"Brought David very much brass, wherewith Solomon made the brazen sea, and the pillars, and the vessels of brass."* This is the battle as is recorded in II Samuel 8 where it says, *"David smote also Hadadezer, the son of Rehob, king of Zobah"* (vs. 3). The name *"Hadadezer"* means "my mighty demon helper." David's going to this farthest border to establish Israel's dominion as was promised by God would defeat this mighty king and, consequently, bring back *"very much brass."*

This is a type of the salvation experience of the child of God. One day our heavenly David invaded our domain where we had been held captive by demon powers. The Lord Jesus Christ defeated these powers of darkness and brought us from darkness to light.

When David took all of this gold, silver, and brass (with brass being a type of humanity), he brought all of it back to Jerusalem. No doubt, among the brass there were brass candelabra, brass doorstops, brass doorknobs, brass altar rails, etc. They were all brought back to Jerusalem and placed in storage to await the construction of the Temple.

As we have stated, all of these brass fixtures are a type of the child of God who has been delivered from heathenistic bondage and brought into the house of the Lord.

Whenever we first came to Jesus, we, no doubt, thought that due to our "great worth"

NOTES

the Lord would use us mightily and immediately. But, instead, as all of these brass fixtures were brought to Jerusalem and placed in a warehouse, you and I, at times to our chagrin, seemingly, are placed on a shelf. Some of us have been so beautiful and useful in the world, that surely the Lord can use us mightily now that we are in His kingdom. Strangely enough all the pieces of brass were placed together. Likewise, the Baptist candelabra is placed with a Charismatic doorstop. The Pentecostal doorknob is placed with the Holiness altar rail. We find to our amazement that as far as the Lord is concerned there is no difference in us. Little do we realize that we have to lose all former identity, no matter the talents, personality, ability, or energy that we had in the service of *"Hadadezer."* All of this must be eliminated and melted down as the 15th verse says, *"For he cast two pillars of brass."* It is the doctrine of "death and resurrection." It took only a short period of time to get Moses out of Egypt, but it took some 40 years to get Egypt out of Moses. He had to be taken to the "backside of the desert." It was the doctrine of "death and resurrection." We must die to all the former energy, efforts, and ability. We must be resurrected in His likeness and His likeness alone. Many Christians have the mistaken idea that very talented, unique individuals can be greatly used of the Lord because of their great talent and ability. Quite the contrary! All of the earthly, carnal talent, and ability must die, and we must be resurrected in the likeness of Christ.

The 46th verse says, *"In the plain of Jordan did the king cast them, in the clay ground."*

The "casting" of the child of God in this dying experience is not at all pleasant. As someone has said, "It is not pleasant to die, or even to see someone die." But to be used by Christ as He desires to use us, all former identity of the flesh and the carnal attitude must be erased.

No doubt, when the wagons come to transport all of the brass fixtures to the *"clay ground of Succoth,"* it must have, "spiritually speaking," created bewilderment. The Baptist candelabra says to the Holiness altar rail, "What are they doing to us now?" What they're doing to us is this:

All of that which we have been so proud of,

so taken with, and so excited about, must lose its identity. At *"Succoth"* and *"Zarthan"* great furnaces were built with great castings for the molten metal to be poured therein for the great pillars to be built.

How many Christians never make it to the furnace where their personal ambition, carnality, and self-righteousness can be melted down so that self (it is construed as too painful), therefore, may shrink back from such? However, for us to become what God wants us to become, this process must take place.

As all the different brass fixtures carrying identity of the past life are thrown into the furnace, little by little, as the heat increases we see the various pieces begin to melt. Little by little the brass doorknob that once may have graced a heathen door, or the brass candelabra that gave light to a heathen room, or the brass altar rail that guarded a heathenistic idol, gradually loses its identity. The heat is intensified until the shape is lost and finally all of it begins to melt and flow together making one pillar. The Church is one body, not many.

Then the molten metal was poured into the casting in the clay ground of *"Succoth."* It is a process that every child of God must go through, if he is to be used by the Lord Jesus Christ. And then when casting is complete, no longer is the identity of the former and past life recognizable. Now all have been heated to such an extent in the furnace of affliction, that they form the part of one pillar, and, in fact, become "one." Jesus said, *"I will make of you a pillar in the temple of My God."* Hallelujah! Still, the process is not yet finished.

On top of the giant pillar there is a *"chapiter."* This consists of *"chain work"* (vs. 17), meaning that we are tied irrevocably to the Lord Jesus Christ. Paul uses the term *"a prisoner of Jesus Christ"* (Phil. 1:1).

The 18th verse says regarding the chapiters, *"To cover the chapiters that were upon the top, with pomegrantes."* This denotes the "Fruit of the Spirit."

The 19th verse proclaims that the *"top of the pillars were of lily work."* The *"lily"* has to do with the purity of the Lord Jesus Christ that now becomes ours.

The 21st verse says, *"And called the name thereof Jachin."* The name means "He (God)

NOTES

will establish." The second one was called "Boaz," which means "in Him (God) is strength." So, in effect, this is telling us that God is the only One Who can establish us in Him, and that it is only through His strength that we can be what He wants us to be.

Still, the two giant pillars that sat immediately in front of the Temple actually held up nothing. They were strictly for ornamentation. Likewise, God doesn't have to have us to establish His Kingdom. We are not really needed in His great Temple. However, He has given us a beautiful and prominent place in the immediate front of His Temple, which pertains to His great work. We serve no great purpose except ornamentation.

It is said that after Solomon's Temple was completed, and the two beautiful giant pillars that shone brightly were set up in front of the Temple, travelers coming from distant countries would time their arrival so they might spend the night outside the city of Jerusalem.

The Temple faced the east and the rising sun. It is said that the travelers would arise early to watch the sun break above Mount Olivet and cast its rays upon those two giant brass pillars. As the sun rose in intensity, with the rays striking the huge brass pillars, it would seem as if the whole of the Temple and even Jerusalem would become alive with light.

Likewise, as the Son of righteousness arises with healing in His wings, with His light reflecting off of us, the beauty is beyond compare, with the illumination touching the whole of mankind. We must ever remember that we within ourselves are not that light; we are merely a reflection of the light of the Son of righteousness.

The 23rd verse says, *"And he made a molten sea."* This great Brazen Laver was about 15 feet across. Its height was about 7½ feet. It was about 45 feet *"round about."* It stood upon 12 brazen oxen cast of brass. Three looked in each of the four directions with their hinder parts inward and under the Brazen Laver which was a handbreadth, or about 4 inches thick, with the brim made like that of a cup with flowers of lilies. The entirety of the huge apparatus weighed 25 to 30 tons. It would have held well over 15,000 gallons of water and with the water would have weighed over 100 tons. There were

10 small lavers that were supposed to contain roughly 300 gallons of water each, with these lavers weighing about two tons each. Jewish writers say that the water was changed daily, so as to always be pure for use in the ceremonial worship.

At the front of the Tabernacle in the wilderness there was but one laver; in the Temple of Solomon there were 11. These magnificent vessels of polished brass, highly ornamented, foreshadowed the purity, the glory, the grace, the sufficiency, the perfection, and the power of the government which Immanuel will establish in the future millennial earth. It will be a powerful government, hence, the "oxen," and a pure government, hence, the *"flowers of lilies"* (vs. 26).

In this chapter the Holy Spirit designedly omits any mention of the great Brazen Altar, for here attention is drawn to the King Himself, and not to the subject of access to Him!

Verses 48-51 portray the *"altar of gold"* which was the Altar of Worship that sat immediately in front of the Holiest of Holies. And the *"table of gold,"* of which actually 10 were made, with 5 placed on one side of the holy place and 5 on the other.

Likewise, the 49th verse says, *"The candlesticks of pure gold"* and that 5 were on one side and 5 on the other. These would be intermingled with the Tables of Shewbread on both sides of the "holy place." Attention is drawn by the Spirit to these holy vessels made of *"gold"* which portray the deity of Christ. While it is true that God became man and dwelt with us, still, He never ceased to be God or deity.

CHAPTER 8

The 8th chapter portrays the dedication of the Temple and also prefigures the origination of worship in the Kingdom Age. Approximately a year would lapse between the completion of the Temple and its dedication. This great event would occur in the Year of Jubilee during the Feast of Tabernacles, and in connection with the Great Day of Atonement. The Feast of Trumpets, which was a type in Jewish history of

the Rapture of the Church, would be extended to last for some seven days. This would be followed by the Great Day of Atonement, which prefigures the cleansing of Israel at the beginning of the Kingdom Age. Then following the Great Day of Atonement was the "Feast of Tabernacles," which within itself symbolizes the Kingdom Age. These three great Jewish feast days have not yet been fulfilled in type. They will be fulfilled when the great millennial Temple is built as is recorded in Ezekiel chapters 40-48, of which Solomon's Temple was a type. All of this took place in the month of October.

The 1st verse says, *"That they might bring up the ark of the covenant of the Lord out of the city of David."* For many years (over 100) the Ark of the Covenant and the Tabernacle had been separated. The Tabernacle was now at Gibeon with the other of its holy vessels, while the *"ark of the covenant"* was in Jerusalem.

The 3rd verse says, *"And the priests took up the ark."* The priests alone were set apart to carry the Ark. Solomon did not make the mistake David had made by seeking to bring it to Jerusalem on a cart instead of being carried by the priests, as God commanded (Deut. 10:8).

As well the 4th verse says, *"And all the holy vessels that were in the tabernacle,"* which was brought from Gibeon.

The 5th verse proclaims that despite the gold and the glamour of the great Temple that had just been completed and was ready for dedication, still, Calvary was the foundation for everything, as the 5th verse says, *"Sacrificing sheep and oxen, that could not be told nor numbered for multitude."*

It seems that of all the holy vessels made by Moses that the *"ark of the covenant"* was the only vessel used in the new Temple. The other vessels such as the Brazen Altar, and the Table of Shewbread were, no doubt, placed in the treasury of the Lord.

The 6th verse states that the *"ark of the covenant"* was taken *"to the most holy place, even under the wings of the cherubims."* These were the two huge Cherubims that were made of olive wood and overlaid with gold, whose wing span spread from one wall to the other wall. The two wings covering the Ark were the inner wings of the Cherubim that touched each other in the center of the room. Each

Cherubim had two sets of wings, with the outside wings reaching to the back wall, and the front set of wings reaching forward touching the wings of the opposing Cherubim. The wing spread of each was about 15 feet. The wings were probably about 10 feet above the Ark which, no doubt, rested on a table which sat on the floor.

The 8th verse says, *"And they drew out the staves."* The staves were partially taken out of the rings of the Ark by which it was carried, so that the ends could be seen from the holy place but not from the porch outside the holy place. In this way the Ark never needed to be handled, as the staves could be easily put back into the rings without even touching the Ark. It seems that it was unlawful to take them wholly out of the rings. Pulling the staves out so the ends could be seen, indicated the Ark had found its resting place in the Temple and was not to be borne anymore. It had a permanent house, not a tent as before.

The 9th verse says, *"There was nothing in the ark save the two tables of stone."* At this time there was nothing in the Ark but the Ten Commandments. In Hebrews 9:4 Paul mentioned the golden pot of Manna and Aaron's rod. He was speaking of the Ark while in the Tabernacle instead of the Temple. It is not known when these two things were removed. It was either by the Philistines when they had the Ark, or when the events of I Samuel 5 and 6 took place. At any rate we do know that whatever happened, God did not allow the *"two tables of stone"* containing the Ten Commandments to be taken. There was a reason for that.

"Aaron's rod" and the *"pot of manna"* were types of Christ, which in type would not be necessary with the advent of Christ Himself. However, the *"Ten Commandments"* were a type of the Word of God which endures forever. For the Law of God was hidden in the Messiah's heart (Psa. 119:11) as it was hidden in the ark. The Law will be the basis and rule of righteousness which will govern the Millennium in the Kingdom Age.

The 9th verse further says, *"When the Lord made a covenant with the children of Israel, when they came out of the land of Egypt."* Ever would the Lord remind Israel of her deliverance from Egypt, as we are ever reminded of

our great and glorious salvation. When the disciples came back after a preaching tour rejoicing that demons had been subject to them in the name of Jesus, they were told by the Lord to rejoice rather because their names were written down in heaven.

The 10th verse says, *"That the cloud filled the house of the Lord."* The Lord did not reside in the Temple even when it was finished. He resided between the Mercy Seat and the Cherubim of the *"ark of the covenant."* When it was moved from its former resting place in Jerusalem to the Holy of Holies in the Temple, then *"the cloud filled the house."* It must be ever understood that the *"house"* is nothing without the *"cloud."* As the song says, "Anywhere is home if Christ my Lord is there."

The 11th verse says, *"So that the priests could not stand to minister because of the cloud."* It simply means that the power of God was so strong that the knees of the priests buckled. The Church little knows the power of God, having substituted in its place the false glory and false worship that characterizes so much of that which pertains to the Lord. It says, *"For the glory of the Lord had filled the house of the Lord."* This is the secret of the Church; it is the secret of the child of God. Without this, the Church is nothing more than a human institution; with this, the Church is a living organism.

Verses 12-21 record Solomon's message to the people. The 16th verse says, *"But I chose David to be over my people Israel."* Satan would fight this choice as he ever fights all of God's choices. Regrettably, too much of the Church world joins in with Satan in opposing that which God chooses.

Solomon's dedicatorial prayer reveals much concerning his knowledge of the Lord and His work.

The 22nd verse says, *"And Solomon stood before the altar of the Lord."* This was the Brazen Altar of sacrifice in the court outside the Temple. He stretched out his hands toward heaven, and before he began praying, he knelt before the Lord (vs. 54). Solomon correctly began his petition at Calvary of which the *"altar of the Lord"* was a type. Every petition to the Lord must come via Calvary. All of our worship must go through Calvary. All of our position in Christ must be at Calvary. Too oftentimes the Church has built its temples and costly edifices but has allowed itself to be spiritually hypnotized by the grandeur of its earthly possessions while forgetting Calvary. Paul would forever say, *"I determined to know nothing among you save Christ and Him crucified."* Why? The answer is simple:

Deliverance comes through Calvary and Calvary alone; likewise, the blessings come through Calvary and Calvary alone; outside of Calvary, representing the shed Blood, God could not, and, in fact, would not even look at us.

Solomon based his petition on the principle that man is a flawed, sinful, stained individual, for he says in the 46th verse, *"If they sin against thee (for there is no man that sinneth not)."* The question is not, "if man sins." The question is, "when man sins." In all of his great petition he appeals for mercy and grace upon the basis of proper repentance toward God, for the 47th verse states, *"We have sinned, and have done perversely, we have committed wickedness."*

He then says in the 48th verse, *"And so return unto thee with all their heart, and with all their soul."* This, and this alone, is true repentance.

The implication in the 49th verse is, *"Then hear thou their prayer and their supplication in heaven thy dwelling place, and maintain their cause."*

The 50th verse shouts "forgiveness" and "compassion," which are the hallmarks of the great Grace of God.

The 62nd verse says, *"Offered sacrifice before the Lord."* The 63rd verse says *"peace offerings"* with the 64th verse talking about *"burnt offerings"* and *"meat (food) offerings,"* as well as the *"fat of the peace offerings."* Even though the huge Brazen Altar, which was some 30 feet wide, was being used to its fullest extent, still, so many thousands of animals were being offered that this area was too small. Consequently, the middle of the court – the whole area where the Brazen Altar was, became one large place of sacrifice in order to offer so many thousands of animals.

Once again typifying the great Kingdom Age the 66th verse says, *"And went unto their*

NOTES

tents joyful and glad of heart for all the goodness that the Lord had done for David his servant, and for Israel his people." The world has never seen the like of such again and will not see it again until the Lord Jesus Christ Himself comes back, of which this glorious moment is a type.

CHAPTER 9

The 9th chapter portrays these words concerning the Lord's response to Solomon's prayer. The 2nd verse says, *"That the Lord appeared to Solomon the second time."* This was after some 20 years of building the Temple, his own palace, and government structures. Of course, any appearance of the Lord is of eternal consequence. This particular appearance promised great blessing but also gave great warning.

The 3rd verse says, *"I have heard thy prayer and thy supplication."* In effect, He was telling Solomon that He had accepted his prayer and petition.

The 4th verse states, *"And if thou wilt walk before me, as David thy father walked."* David was ever used as the example. Self-righteousness would have great difficulty in accepting David as such, especially considering his great failures. However, only Phariseeism or self-righteousness would have such difficulty. Those who truly know themselves and truly know God and His grace have no difficulty whatsoever. The hardest thing for self-righteous man to accept is the Word of Christ where He states, *"There is none good but one, that is, God."* (St. Matt. 19:17). God's conditions for blessings are as follows:

1. "Integrity of heart."

2. "To do according to all that I have commanded thee."

3. "Keep My statutes and My judgments."

The blessing as given in verse 5 is as follows, *"Then I will establish the throne of thy kingdom upon Israel for ever."* In other words, Israel would be the premier nation of the world then and forever. Nevertheless, this committal to Solomon and Israel was conditional upon obedience. Tragically, the condition was violated, and, as a consequence, the government of the earth was taken out of the hands of Israel and placed in the hands of Nebuchadnezzar and the Gentiles, by whom Jehovah's Throne and House were cast down by God's just decree. However, let it quickly be said, that when the greater than Solomon comes, that Throne will be reestablished, and His Kingdom shall have no end.

The path of safety pointed out by God to Solomon was obedience and attachment to the Bible (vs. 4). But Solomon, instead of obeying the Word of God occupied himself and his people with the construction of great buildings and the building of a kingdom. Had he instead multiplied copies of the Scriptures and filled Israel with them, how much better off he would have been. Still, the modern Church follows in his footsteps. We think somehow that bigness, money, power, prestige, and worldly favor construe the blessings of God, when, in reality, most of the time it leads us away from the blessings of God.

In the 8th verse the Lord tells Solomon that it doesn't matter how "big" or how "high" this house is, the Lord will pull it down. And when the world asks "Why?" the 9th verse records the answer, *"Because they forsook the Lord their God."*

If America and Canada, or any nation in the world for that matter, loses their way, the reason always is, *"Because they forsook the Lord their God."* As well, it can be said of any individual. We would do well to heed those words and say them over and over.

Verses 11-24 record the energy and activity of Israel. Someone said of the great Methodist church:

"At the turn of the century (1900) the Methodist church was the most powerful move of God in America. We had the choice of building massive buildings (churches) and universities, or taking the Gospel of Jesus Christ to the world." They went on to say, "We opted for the building of structures and the Methodist church died."

No doubt, the same could be said of every other church.

At the conclusion of this litany two things are said:

NOTES

Verse 24 says, *"But Pharaoh's daughter came up out of the city of David unto her house which Solomon had built for her."*

Verse 26-28 speak of an abundance of gold being *"brought to king Solomon."*

In the middle of all of this the 25th verse says, *"And three times in a year did Solomon offer burnt offerings and peace offerings upon the altar which he built unto the Lord."* These three annual feasts of which all the males of Israel were commanded to attend were, "the Passover, Pentecost, and Tabernacles." The point is this:

The carrying on of great religious activity in the midst of great disobedience soothes the conscience, and for a period of time masks the spiritual deterioration. Even then the deterioration was taking place. Solomon was trafficking with Egypt, multiplying wives, multiplying horses, and amassing great amounts of gold. All was forbidden by the Law of God (Deut. 17:16-17). If he had multiplied the Word of God instead, how different things would have been.

CHAPTER 10

Much of this chapter portrays the coming Kingdom Age, giving us an idea as to how the Lord Jesus Christ will rule the world during this particular time. Still, the latter part of the chapter portrays the tragic downward slide of Solomon.

Verse 1 says, *"And when the queen of Sheba heard of the fame of Solomon."* This queen portrays the heads of state from every country in the world in the coming Kingdom Age that will *"hear of the fame"* of the Lord Jesus Christ. Isaiah says that His name would be called *"Wonderful, Counselor, Mighty God, Everlasting Father, and Prince of Peace."* Verse 1 says, *"She came to prove him with hard questions."* This is a forepicture of the nations of the world that will be coming to the feet of Jesus Christ with their questions concerning "spiritual matters, agriculture, industry, science, medicine, and other things." The Lord Jesus Christ will give these ambassadors the answers to their hardest of questions, consequently, insuring their prosperity.

The 3rd verse says, *"And Solomon told her all her questions."* At that time the Lord Jesus Christ will give the answers that the world has long sought after. He will, no doubt, point them first of all to His own redeeming grace, for He says, *"Seek ye first the kingdom of God, and His righteousness, and all these things shall be added unto you."* Governmental leaders, ambassadors, scientists, and men of learning, will ask Him questions that men have pondered over from the beginning of time. The *"greater than Solomon"* will "tell them all," giving the answer to every question. Men of medicine will seek the cure for any and all diseases. Most probably the Lord will tell them what plant or tree that will contain the cure. (Rev. 22:2) Others will come from desert countries asking how they can make the desert fertile again. The answers will be instant (Isaiah 35:1). Captains of industry will seek to learn how to turn a war economy into a peace economy. The answer will go forth (Isa. 2:4). The environmentalists will want to know how to clean up the environment from the pollution that now ravages the earth. The answer will not only be given, but portrayed as well (Isa. 30:26). Medical scientists will want to know how to restore sight to the blind and hearing to the deaf, as well as mobility to the paralyzed and speech to the dumb. The King of kings will instantly provide the answers (Isa. 35:3-6). Men that deal in agriculture will ask how the water problem can be solved. The answer will be forthcoming (Isa. 35:7). Actually, there will not be a single question asked concerning the betterment of planet Earth and mankind that will not be answered completely by the Lord Jesus Christ, for Scripture says, *"There was not any thing hid from the king, which he told her not."*

The 4th verse says, *"And when the queen of Sheba had seen all Solomon's wisdom, and the house that he had built."* The glory of the Lord Jesus Christ is going to be so resplendent that the leaders of nations will be as the queen of Sheba, *"There was no more spirit in her"* (vs. 5). For the first time in human history man is going to see what this planet could be like with Satan locked away, and the Lord Jesus Christ reigning as King of kings and Lord of lords.

The 6th verse proclaims, *"It was a true report."* The ambassadors and state leaders will go back to their respective countries with their message being announced over every television and radio station. As well, the newspapers and magazines will proclaim that everything that the prophets had said, and everything that they had heard was *"a true report."* They will also say *"the half was not told."* They will say *"Thy wisdom and prosperity exceedeth the fame which I heard"* (vs. 7).

Verse 8 proclaims the state of all who follow the Lord Jesus Christ, *"Happy are thy men."* The reason is that the Lord will *"do judgment and justice"* (vs.9).

The 13th verse proclaims, *"And king Solomon gave unto the queen of Sheba all her desire."* As well the *"greater than Solomon"* in the great Kingdom Age to come will show the nations of the world how to have spiritual and material prosperity. Man's every righteous *"desire"* shall be realized. Consequently, *"all the earth sought to Solomon, to hear his wisdom"* (vs. 24). It might be quickly added that if this happened in Solomon's day, how much more will it happen when *"a greater than Solomon"* is here.

Sadly, the balance of this chapter along with the 11th chapter proclaims the beginning of Solomon's spiritual declension.

The 27th verse records his multiplying silver and gold with the 28th verse portraying his multiplying of horses. This was in violation of the Law of God in Deuteronomy 17:16-17. All types ultimately break down as Solomon broke down. But, thankfully, the Anti-type, the Lord Jesus Christ, will suffer no spiritual declension and, thereby, no resultant destruction.

CHAPTER 11

The 1st verse starts with the words, *"But King Solomon loved many strange women."* Then the latter portion of the 3rd verse says, *"And his wives turned away his heart."* At this time Israel was the most powerful nation on the face of the earth. As well, Solomon was the wisest man who had ever lived, with his wisdom being given to him by God. Also, the Lord had appeared unto Solomon twice. So, why would he do this thing? As to the "why" of a person's heart, we cannot tell. Jeremiah says, *"The heart is deceitful above all things, and desperately wicked: Who can know it?"* However, this we do know:

1. Past blessings from God, such as the appearances of the Lord to Solomon, even though of tremendous import at that particular time, will not suffice for today's journey. There must ever be fresh revelations. Evidently, due to Solomon's backsliding and his lack of desire toward God in later years, there were no fresh revelations.

2. The great gift of wisdom that God had given to Solomon, even though continuing to abide even in Solomon's great transgressions, could not stave the terrible spiritual declension. Only a constant day-by-day walk of holiness and humility before the Lord will guarantee one's spiritual progress. Many today try to function with "gifts" which were once truly given and in some cases truly remain but in no way will take the place of righteousness.

3. As well, it seems that the humility which once characterized Solomon (I Kings 3:7) is now no longer present. He seems to be lifted up in pride. If one would study the sin problem of every Christian, one would probably find that all follow the same course. The sin of the *"pride of life"* is at first committed. Once this sin is committed, humility no longer characterizes the saint of God. They become lifted up in themselves, trusting their own power and strength. At that time, the individual becomes a perfect target for the *"lust of the eye"* of which Satan can choose according to his own desire. The individual at this stage pretty much becomes helpless. The last and final step is the *"lust of the flesh."* Ultimately, it will bring death.

This prescription was followed in the Garden of Eden (Gen. 3:5-6) by Satan, and has varied little, if at all, since.

Verse 4 tells in what way his wives *"turned away his heart."* It was *"after other gods."* God hates all sin, especially idolatry. This same verse says that the heart of David was *"perfect with the Lord his God."* Self-righteousness could never understand this statement,

NOTES

especially in view of the fact of the horrid sin of David with Bathsheba and then the murder of her husband, Uriah. David failed in many other areas as well. However, in one way or the other, the same could be said of every single Christian. All have failed miserably. Whether known or unknown in the eyes of man, still, it is known in the eyes of God. And yet, God would call this man, as well as others, "perfect." How could such be?

The answer is *"justification."* With the sin truly repented of, God counts it as if it had never been. So, the Lord could say of David, *"perfect,"* despite the terrible sins mentioned, for the simple reason they had been truly repented of, washed, and cleansed. Justification demands that God looks at such as though it never happened. The same could have been said of Solomon had he truly repented. The Scripture is silent regarding even the last days of Solomon pertaining to his relationship with God.

The 7th verse says, *"Then did Solomon build an high place for Chemosh."* Other false deities are named as well, and it says, *"In the hill that is before Jerusalem."* This was Mount Olivet.

On Mount Zion the Temple of God stood with the many sacrifices being offered daily. God dwelt between the Mercy Seat and the Cherubim in the Holy of Holies. Yet immediately in front of the "Temple of the Lord" were the temples of the false gods of abomination. The 8th verse says, *"which burnt incense and sacrificed unto their gods."* At the same time these *"strange wives"* were offering up incense and sacrifices to their gods, incense was being offered up in the Holy Place to the God of glory. How could Solomon with his vaunted wisdom given by God allow such a thing to be done? The answer of the 3rd verse keeps coming back, *"And his wives turned away his heart."*

Sadly, this characterizes the majority of the Church world today, and even our personal lives. We speak of God and in some measure serve God, but, at the same time allow idols to reign supreme. Jesus will not share the throne of the heart with that which is evil for very long. One or the other, sooner or later, must go. Ultimately, the Lord would leave Israel. He began that leaving here at this point.

The 9th verse says, *"And the Lord was angry with Solomon."* There is a special Hebrew verb used in the Bible for *"to be angry."* It is only used of Divine anger. It occurs 14 times. Here and in five other passages a form of the verb is used expressing the forcing of oneself to be angry with a person who is loved. The Lord loved Solomon and did not desire to be angry with him. However, God is angry with any and all, if sin is present.

The 11th verse says that the Lord said this to Solomon, *"I will surely rend the kingdom from thee, and will give it to thy servant."* Probably the prophet, *"Ahijah,"* delivered this message to Solomon. At this stage and with this message, Solomon could have repented and turned away this pronouncement. He did not.

The 13th verse more specifically states what the Lord would do, *"But will give one tribe to thy son for David my servant's sake."* This one tribe would be *"Judah."* However, it seems that Benjamin and Simeon, who had their inheritance within the inheritance of Judah, as well as Levi, would remain with the *"one tribe"* of Judah.

The 14th verse says, *"And the Lord stirred up an adversary unto Solomon, Hadad the Edomite."* This word is recorded in verse 23 as well concerning *"another adversary Rezon."* The words, *"stirred up,"* speak of the Lord having total control over all. *"Hadad"* and *"Rezon"* were adversaries to Solomon all along. However, because the Lord allowed this to be, there was nothing they could do about it.

This shows that our obedience to the Lord holds back the satanic adversaries that would cause us much difficulty. As well, it shows that disobedience to the Lord *"stirs up"* adversaries who are allowed to cause us much difficulty. Still, all adversaries against the child of God are not necessarily caused by disobedience. The adversaries stirred up against the Apostle Paul were not caused by Paul's disobedience but were rather allowed by the Lord to perfect humility, dependence on the Lord, and spiritual growth in Paul's life. The same can happen to us as well.

The 26th verse says, *"And Jeroboam the son of Nebat, even he lifted up his hand against the king."* So, we have external adversaries as well as internal adversaries. Jeroboam was an Isra-

NOTES

elite from the tribe of *"Ephraim."* The 28th verse says, *"Was a mighty man of valour."* Solomon would seek to bless him and *"make him ruler over all the charge of the house of Joseph"* (the tribe of Ephraim). His appointment to be Chief of the House of Joseph doubtless gave birth to the ambition to be Chief of the whole nation, and Ahijah's prophecy would confirm it.

Solomon and Jeroboam both illustrate the evil and unbelief of man's heart. Jeroboam would not wait for God to give him the kingdom but tried to get it by his own efforts. So fallen is man's nature that he will use Divine promises and the daily gifts of God's love for the accomplishment and gratification of his own unholy desires, and degrade the very gifts and promises of God to the service of the *"flesh."*

The 38th verse records God's outstretched hand to Jeroboam by saying, *"And it shall be, if thou wilt hearken to all that I command thee, and will walk in my ways, that I will be with thee."* However, Jeroboam had no heart after God.

Solomon, upon hearing the message of the prophet Ahijah to Jeroboam, would not yield in humility to the Lord. But instead, the 40th verse says, *"Solomon sought therefore to kill Jeroboam"* because God had chosen him; thus, he manifested the murderous hatred of the natural heart against God and His plan.

The 40th verse contains the last statement made about Solomon by the Holy Spirit personally. The next statement concerning Solomon will be made regarding his death.

Of course, the question is asked about the man who was wiser than any man who ever lived, and yet not wise enough to live for God. Did he make this right with God at the very last? The Scripture does not say, but there is some small evidence that he may have.

For instance, I and II Kings record the state of nations, kings, and men, as seen by man. I and II Chronicles record the state of nations, kings, and men, as seen by God. In I Chronicles 20 the time period is given that David was tempted and committed sin with Bathsheba. However, it is passed over completely by the writer of the Chronicles. Because God had forgiven and cleansed David, this was how He saw the situation. Therefore, it was not mentioned.

(In II Samuel 11 it would be mentioned in detail.) In II Chronicles 1-9 the history of Solomon is given. The terrible spiritual declension concerning these heathen wives who *"turned away his heart from God"* is not mentioned. There is some evidence here that Solomon at the very last repented, and, therefore, God washed the stain of the terrible rebellion and idolatry away. One would certainly hope that the writer of Proverbs, Ecclesiastes, and the Song of Solomon certainly did this, at least at the very end.

CHAPTER 12

Chapter 12 records the split of Judah and Israel. Through the years Israel will go under several names, Samaria, Israel, Ephraim.

The 1st verse says, *"And Rehoboam went to Shechem."* The first step taken by Rehoboam was a judicious one. He, no doubt, sought to cement the dissatisfied Ephraimites to himself by being crowned king in their chief city. This should have caused them to submit to the tribe of Judah, as this was a great honor given them. Shechem lay on the flank of Mount Gerizim, directly opposite Mount Ebal, the mounts of curses and blessings (Deut. 11:29; 27:1-8). It was a national sanctuary (Josh. 24:1), and the site of Abraham's first altar (Gen. 12:6). Isaac and Jacob had both lived here. Joseph was buried here; Jacob's well was also located here as well (St. John 4:5).

Because of the unrest, Rehoboam's motives, no doubt, were political. Sadly, the majority of the motives of the Church are too often political. Jerusalem was the city where God had chosen to place His name. It was where the Temple was constructed, and that by the command of the Lord. Jerusalem was the spiritual center of Israel. This should have been the place to crown Rehoboam king. However, there was precious little spirituality about Rehoboam, so he would choose "Shechem."

While Rehoboam was trying to appease the northern kingdom of Israel, they were sending to Egypt to bring in "Jeroboam" who was in exile, for fear of Solomon.

NOTES

A delegation from Israel with Jeroboam will then go to the new king of Israel, "Rehoboam." They will ask for certain promises. The 6th verse says, *"And King Rehoboam consulted with the old men,"* and they gave him their advice.

The 8th verse then says, *"He consulted with the young men,"* and they gave him their advice. Nowhere is it said that he consulted with God. The Church's greatest problem is that it too oftentimes consults with men, completely ignoring God. While it is certainly true that we should seek the counsel of those who are experienced in the Word, nevertheless, our chief counsel must be the Holy Spirit. He will always abide by the Book. Most of the time, even in the Church, men will not abide by the Bible.

Rehoboam will listen to "men" and the worst of the lot at that. He permitted the youth of the kingdom to cause him to make one of the greatest mistakes a ruler ever made. Through this one choice and wrong decision, many wars were fought and hundreds of thousands of lives were lost. Much bitterness, hatred, jealousy, idolatry, and numerous other sins also resulted. There seems to be no end to the harm done to God's cause in Israel by this one man's folly because he did not consult the Lord.

The 16th verse proclaims that Israel will say upon Rehoboam's decision, *"What portion have we in David?"* Not only were they politically renouncing Judah (David), but more than that, they were renouncing the Temple, the worshiping of God, the sacrifices, and the Law of Moses.

Now the Church is split exactly as Satan desires. Satan divides and conquers. These two factions pretty well describe every denominational split (or church split) that has ever happened. One side will not want the Lord at all saying, "What portion have we in David?" And the other side will pay lip service to the ways of God but will mostly "consult with men." Thank God for the few who will hold "to David." This rebellion of Israel would last for some 260 years until they were finally taken captive into Assyria.

The 16th verse further says, *"So Israel departed unto their tents."* This was the beginning of 260 years of division and strife between the two nations of Israel. Wars, bloodshed, and intrigue became the program of a once united and godly people. God's plan for a united nation being a blessing to all other nations of the earth has now come to a definite standstill and both kingdoms face ruin and dispersion among the Gentiles. Now they would not only have to defend themselves against the heathen, but much of their energy would be spent in fighting each other. How this so characterizes the Church. The 20th verse concerning Jeroboam says, *"And made him king over all Israel."* Therefore, Rehoboam's foray into Shechem for political expediency and his *"consulting with men"* did him little good. His kingdom is torn in two.

The 21st verse proclaims his energy regarding combat with Israel. He will fight to retain his kingdom. Once again, he does not ask the Lord.

However, through the prophecy of *"Shemaiah the man of God,"* he was told, *"Ye shall not go up, nor fight against your brethren the children of Israel"* (vs. 24). To Rehoboam's credit, he would heed the Word of the Lord. Three times in this one sentence the Word of the Lord will be referred to showing its great significance.

1. *"Thus saith the Lord."*

2. *"They hearkened therefore to the word of the Lord."*

3. *"According to the word of the Lord."*

The Holy Spirit is telling us that if *"the word of the Lord"* was adhered to all along, Israel would not have come to this sad state. That is true of all of us.

Now Israel will begin to depart further and further from the Lord, for the 25th verse says, *"Then Jeroboam built Shechem in Mount Ephraim."* Now Jerusalem, which the Lord had chosen, was no longer the capital of Israel; Shechem was. (Jerusalem was still the capital of Judah.)

The 28th verse says, *"Where upon the king (Jeroboam) took counsel, and made two calves of gold."* He announced to Israel, *"Behold thy gods, O Israel, which brought thee up out of the land of Egypt."* The great redemption given to Israel by God concerning their deliverance from Egypt was now attributed to a *"golden calf."* I wonder if we're doing any different

today in the modern Church when we attribute the help that God gives us to humanistic psychology?

The 30th verse says, *"And this thing became a sin."* The expression concerning Jeroboam, *"made Israel to sin,"* is used 23 times.

The 33rd verse says concerning the false religion that Jeroboam had made, *"which he had devised of his own heart."* This is where all false religions come from, and, no doubt, Satan had placed it into his heart, for he is the spirit that works in all sons of disobedience (St. John 8:44; Eph. 2:1-3; I John 3:8).

The slightest spiritual declension will cause one to turn from God to heathenistic idols. The situation has changed little today. While it is true that the Church no longer makes *"golden calves,"* still, we make idols in our hearts. Therefore, the ugly picture that is drawn for us in these respective chapters by the Holy Spirit is too often a picture of our own hearts.

CHAPTER 13

Israel, the northern kingdom, is very comfortable with her new religion – "the two calves of gold." Jeroboam, arrayed as king and priest, stands by his altar offering incense to "god." The entire court assists, together with a vast multitude of worshipers. Nothing is lacking to win the admiration of the religious world, but suddenly something happens.

Verse 1 says, *"And behold, there came a man of God out of Judah by the word of the Lord unto Bethel."*

First of all, there are precious few who can be called *"of God."* They are the strength of the Church, the nation, and the world. Sadly, they are in short supply. He is sent by *"the Word of the Lord."*

Verse 2 says, *"He cried against the altar in the Word of the Lord."* This altar was a *"bastard altar,"* designed by man, which called golden calves God. There was only one Altar in all of Israel that God would recognize, and that was in Jerusalem. The Altar that was in Jerusalem at the Temple was designed by the Holy Spirit, which portrayed Calvary, yet to come. This *"altar"* of Jeroboam's would deliver no one. It is representative of the multitudinous altars of this world and devised by the hand of man, with many of them in Christendom. It must be remembered that Israel was *"God's chosen people."* Now the Church is split with one side, *"Judah,"* somewhat worshiping God in a tepid fashion, with the other side, *"Israel,"* worshiping *"golden calves."* It is not unlike the Church today, for false altars abound.

The prophet addresses his message from the Lord toward the altar saying, *"Behold, a child shall be born unto the house of David, Josiah by name."* This message from the Lord proclaimed tremendous future portend. It is as follows:

1. If Israel persisted in these *"altars"* of a false way of salvation, it would ultimately destroy the land – which it did.

2. Even at this late date, if Israel would repent, God would restore His salvation to His people (vs. 6).

That as *"Josiah"* would some 348 years later destroy this altar, likewise, all false religion in Israel would ultimately be destroyed by *"a child that shall be born unto the house of David,"* with the name of the Lord Jesus Christ.

This prophecy has not yet been completely fulfilled, but it will be when Jesus Christ comes back in the midst of the Battle of Armageddon and completely and eternally destroys this *"altar."*

The 4th verse proclaims Jeroboam's anger at the prophet by saying, *"Lay hold on him."* Man has ever tried to stop the Word of God. He will listen to every false message that is given by every heathen priest with no reaction, but the moment the *"Word of the Lord"* is pronounced, he will resort even to violence to stop it.

For instance: Islam is perhaps the most violent religion on the face of the earth, advocating the progress of the Moslem faith by the sword. It is today responsible for much of the terrorist activity in the world. And, yet, the American press has nothing negative to say about this *"false altar."* It reserves all its wrath against Christianity.

The Scripture says, *"His hand, which he put forth against him, dried up."* The extended *"dried up"* hand of Jeroboam is a picture of that which will happen to the Antichrist during the Battle of Armageddon. The *"man of sin"* will put forth his hand against the Lord Jesus Christ. It will *"dry up."*

According to the 5th verse, as the *"altar also was rent, and the ashes poured out"* at this time, the same will happen with all false altars when Jesus Christ comes back.

The 6th verse says concerning the petition of Jeroboam, *"Entreat now the face of the Lord thy God, and pray for me, that my hand may be restored me again."* The prophet prayed and the *"king's hand was restored him."*

Despite the fact that one of the most striking displays of power is recorded, still, Jeroboam did not repent. It is amazing at man's ability to see and sense the power of God in operation and still rebel. Miracles, as wonderful as they are, do not bring people to Jesus. It is the convicting power of the Holy Spirit upon a weeping heart that does so. Regrettably, the Pentecostal and Charismatic Church too often seeks after "signs," when all the time God is attempting to reach our hearts. God is a worker of miracles today, but He desires to show the Church His "ways" more than His "acts." Regrettably, the Church seeks His "acts," rather than His "ways." Sadly, there is little repentance. (Psa. 103:7)

The ungodly king will seek an accommodation with the prophet, *"Come home with me, and refresh thyself, and I will give thee a reward"* (vs. 7). This is the greatest danger that the Church faces. It is very difficult for it to turn down the *"reward."* The modern Church so seeks after the accommodations of the world, its plaudits, approval, and reward, that it will compromise its message, substitute its altar, and seek "unity" at any price.

The prophet of God will now say "no," but, regrettably, will later say "yes."

The 10th verse says, *"So he went another way."* To deviate at all from the path that God has laid out through His Word is to invite disaster. The prophet was only a few miles from Judah. If he had gone as he came, which was, no doubt, by the command of the Lord, he would not have suffered the fate that awaited him. But he *"went another way."* How so many begin aright but then soon find *"another way."*

The 11th verse says, *"Now there dwelt an old prophet in Bethel."* This prophet had long since turned his back on God. Why didn't God use *"the old prophet"* to speak to Jeroboam? He, no doubt, lived within walking distance of the *"altar."* The word *"old"* signifies that the man had once known the Lord, but now had compromised his ministry and his message.

The 18th verse says he will lie to "the man of God" and say, *"An angel spake unto me by the Word of the Lord, saying."* Paul may have had these words in mind when he said, *"But though we or an angel from heaven, preach any other gospel unto you than that which we have preached unto you, let him be accursed"* (Gal. 1:8).

The 19th verse says, *"So he went back with him,"* which was direct disobedience to the Word of God. It would cost him his life. As well, it will cost the life of the Church. The two greatest dangers of the Church are (a) "the Jeroboams," who represent the world and its ways, and (b) "the old prophets," who represent the apostate Church.

Sadly, the true Church of Jesus Christ too often succumbs to one or the other.

The old prophet whose duty it was to have testified against the evil around him bore with it, and, by his silence, sanctioned it; therefore, he was very anxious that the "man of God" should approve his unfaithfulness by association with it. Consequently, the "man of God" was ensnared.

There are great principles that stand out in this sad commentary. They are as follows:

1. It is the duty of the man of God to proclaim the Word of the Lord.

2. The man of God is to be separated from evil and to accredit his testimony against it.

3. The man of God is commanded by the Lord to warn men of the wrath to come.

There are, however, *"old prophets"* who live in guilty fellowship with the world, and these are ever anxious to get faithful servants of the Word of God to sanction their unfaithfulness by compromising intimacy with them.

Strangely enough, the Lord will use the *"old prophet"* to cry out *"against the man of God,"* and to deliver a message of judgment against him. He would disobey God by listening to this man, and, in turn, God would have

this man pronounce his doom. Many blanch at the fierceness of the Lord in bringing about the demise of the *"man of God."* However, the sin of compromising the Word is far worse than sins of passion. God's pronouncement of judgment upon a wayward Israel was now compromised by the *"man of God"* associating with its backslidden *"old prophet."* In God's eyes the compromise of the *"old prophet"* was as bad as Jeroboam's two golden calves.

The *"lion"* of verse 24 *"slew him"* and never touched the mule or ate the corpse. The lion was sent by God. The *"old prophet"* would request, *"bury me in the sepulchre wherein the man of God is buried"* (vs 31). He had no problem being with him in death, but he would not stand with him in life.

The 33rd verse says, *"After this thing Jeroboam would turn not from his evil way."* All that God had done did not deter him. Man has a marvelous ability to resist the Holy Spirit.

At the Great White Throne Judgment when men stand before God, they will not be able to say that God did not extend mercy to them. However, many will be able to say that the Church showed them no mercy because it sent no one to tell them of Jesus.

CHAPTER 14

The 1st verse says, *"At that time Abijah the son of Jeroboam fell sick."* This sickness and eventual death would be the Lord's doing. He had tried to reach Jeroboam by miracles, but to no avail. He will now try to reach him through the death of his son. Still, Jeroboam would rebel.

In verses 1-4 one can see the depths of sin to which Jeroboam had taken Israel. He had no confidence in these *"golden calves,"* which had taken Israel to the depths. The *"calves"* were merely political expediency to keep Israel from going to Jerusalem to worship God. He knew that Jehovah controlled all. Still, he would not serve Him.

The 5th verse says, *"And the Lord said unto A-hi-jah."* This man was the prophet who had been sent by God to Jeroboam, who told him of the kingdom. Few men have been dealt with by the Lord such as Jeroboam. It is almost as if the Lord is pleading with him to repent.

Even the *"heavy tidings"* of verse 6 was the hand of God. He would try to bring Jeroboam to his senses, as he has tried to bring multiple hundreds of millions to their senses but, tragically, to no avail.

The 7th verse says, *"Go, tell Jeroboam, thus saith the Lord God of Israel."* It doesn't matter if it is a king or a dying son; the Lord's plan will ultimately be realized. When will men ever see this?

The 8th verse proclaims this statement concerning David, *"Who kept my commandments, and who followed me with all his heart, to do that only which was right in mine eyes."* A self-righteous Church world can never understand this, especially considering Bathsheba and Uriah. Nevertheless, the answer is simple. David repented. All sin repented of and, consequently, washed by the Blood of Jesus Christ is not only forgiven by God, but forgotten. It is called *"justification."* It then stands in the eyes of God as though it never happened. Those who try to earn their salvation by works, rules, or regulations cannot abide this. Those who receive and accept their salvation at the hand of a loving God because they have admitted their sin and thrown themselves on the love of God and accepted His mercy, understand perfectly.

The 9th verse uses a peculiar term, *"And hast cast me behind thy back."* It would seem from this statement that Jeroboam had once known the Lord in a very real way. He had received prophecies, and then was promised a sure house and a kingdom if he would obey. This one passage alone, along with all the many others in the Word of God, dispute the fallacious doctrine of *"unconditional security."*

The 12th verse says, *"The child shall die."* The word *"child"* in the Hebrew has reference to one who could even be in his late teens. There are few men whom God dealt with as He dealt with Jeroboam. If the death of a son (or daughter) has no effect on a parent regarding their relationship with God, then there is very little else that God can do.

The 13th verse says, *"And all Israel shall mourn for him."* Evidently, Abijah had some qualities in him toward God that endeared him

to the whole of Israel. The Scripture says, *"Because in him there is found some good thing toward the Lord God of Israel in the house of Jeroboam."* So, God would take the young man, as a flower would be plucked from a garbage dump.

The 14th verse says, *"The Lord shall raise him up a king over Israel who shall cut off the house of Jeroboam that day."* This was fulfilled some 20 years later when Baasha destroyed all of Jeroboam's seed (15:27-31). This prophecy in no way meant that Baasha would be godly; in fact, he was evil. It does show that God rules in the affairs of men, setting up one and pulling down another.

The 15th verse says, *"For the Lord shall smite Israel."* He even said what He would do with them, *"And shall scatter them beyond the river,"* meaning the River Euphrates, when Israel would be taken captive by the Assyrians. This happened about 250 years after the prophecy was given. It would be done because of the great sins of Israel, *"provoking the Lord to anger."*

The cause for the anger is expressed in the 16th verse, *"Who did sin, and who made Israel to sin."* This is speaking of the leadership of Jeroboam who instigated and fomented this terrible apostasy that was the ruin of Israel. It must ever be remembered that these people were *"God's chosen people."* However, God cannot abide sin in even those who are His *"chosen."*

The 22nd verse now refers to the southern kingdom of Judah, for it says, *"And Judah did evil in the sight of the Lord."* So, we have both Israel and Judah going into deep apostasy.

Among the many sins that Judah committed, the 24th verse spells out, *"And there were also sodomites in the land."* Sodomites are homosexuals who commit the sin of Sodom (Gen. 17). Here, it refers to male prostitutes dedicated to idolatry involving this sin (II Kings 23:7). Such was forbidden by the Law of God (Deut. 23:17-18). Sodomites were connected with the Asherah. Originally, this idol was worshiped as a symbol of the Tree of Life, but later perverted to mean the origin of life and pictured with the male organs of procreation (Ezek. 16:17). Such symbols became the objects of worship carried on with all forms of

NOTES

impurity, perversion, and licentiousness by crowds of devotees involved in demonized and obscene orgies. The worship centered in the Canaanite nations and then spread into others. Relics of it are found among all heathen peoples. The first mention of the idol in the Bible stamps it as a special object of God's hatred. It was at this idol that God revealed His name as *"Jealous"* (Ex. 34:14).

The implication in the 24th verse is that if the sin of *"sodomy"* continued, that the Lord would cast out *"the children of Israel"* from the land exactly as He had cast out the *"nations"* that previously occupied this land.

The sin of *"sodomy"* is fastly becoming America's and Canada's greatest sin. Now we have homosexual marriages with the courts sanctioning adoption of children into this ungodly union. America is very close to legislation that will give sodomites *"equal rights,"* meaning that no place of business can refuse to hire a sodomite because of their so-called sexual preference. This would go for the Armed Forces as well. The "sodomite" lobby in Washington is powerful. Its goal is that laws be passed forcing even Churches to show no discrimination toward *"sodomites."* Canada (it is said) now has laws on the books that forbid any negative mention of homosexuality over radio or television stations.

If the twin nations of the United States and Canada lose their way (and they *are* losing their way), the sin of *"sodomy"* will have a great deal to do with it. God hates all sin, but especially the sin of *"sodomy."*

Can the *"sodomite"* be saved? Certainly, they can! When Jesus Christ died on Calvary, He died that *"Whosoever will may come,"* and that includes the homosexual. However, it must ever be remembered that the *"sodomite"* is not saved *in* his sin, but *from* his sin. This sin is the same as all other sin. The drunkard who comes to Jesus is saved *from* his sin, and not in his sin. In other words, the drunkenness must cease. The same would go for stealing, lying, cheating, or profanity. God does not save *in* sin; He saves *from* sin.

Verse 25 says, *"That Shishak king of Egypt came up against Jerusalem."* Shishak was founder of the 22nd Egyptian Dynasty. He invaded Judah, took Jerusalem, and carried away all the treasures of the king's house, and the shields of gold which Solomon had made. This was allowed by God because Judah had transgressed against Him (II Chron. 12:2). Shishak had an army of 1200 chariots, 60,000 horsemen, and innumerable foot-soldiers of Egyptians, Lubims, and Sukkiims, and Ethiopians (II Chron. 12:3). Judah humbled themselves, and God spared them total destruction (II Chron. 12:4-12).

The 26th verse says, *"And he took away all the shields of gold which Solomon had made."* It seems these *"shields of gold"* were used by *"The guard, which kept the door of the king's house"* (vs. 27). This verse says, *"And King Rehoboam made in their stead brasen (copper) shields."* This *"guard"* had to do with the *"treasures"* of the house of the Lord. How many shields there were is not stated here.

The *"shields of gold"* in some ways represent God's blessing upon Israel. The *"shields of brass"* in some ways represent the sorry state to which Israel now found herself in. Just a short time before, she was the most powerful nation on the face of the earth. And now because of her transgression against God, the Lord allows the *"king of Egypt"* to do damage to Israel.

Spiritually speaking, how many of our shields today in the modern Church are *"shields of brass"* rather than *"shields of gold?"* The *"gold"* was a type of God's deity, meaning that the Lord was Israel's leader, chief, and captain. The *"brass"* represents humanity, which meant that Judah was now, by and large, man-led instead of God-led. I'm afraid this holds true for the modern-day Church as well.

CHAPTER 15

Verse 1 says, *"reigned Abijam over Judah."*

The 2nd verse then says *"And his mother's name was Maachah, the daughter of Abishalom."* We must understand that in the Old Testament the terms *"daughter"* or *"granddaughter"* are identical. In other words, the Bible does not distinguish between the two. It seems that his mother was the daughter of the son-in-law of Absalom. The Holy Spirit brought this out that we may understand the statement, *"And he walked in all the sins of his father"* (vs. 3). The *"Absalom spirit"* had its deadly effect on all whom it touched.

As well, the 3rd verse speaks of *"the heart of David his father"* as *"perfect."* David was selected by the Holy Spirit as ever the example of righteousness for all of Israel's kings. It would be very difficult for the self-righteous to understand or even accept this. How could it be so, especially when we realize the terrible sin that David committed with Bathsheba and the murdering of her husband Uriah? The Holy Spirit tells us how!

Men look on the outward, but God looks on the *"heart."* David's *"heart"* was ever toward God. He would sin greatly, but he would repent greatly. His repentance according to justification would blot the sin out as though it had never been committed. And so it is with all who throw themselves on the mercy of God, truly repenting in humble, broken contrition. Repentance is an ugly business; therefore, the Church does not delight in it at all. Most religious leaders cannot repent because of their man-made *"position."* Others that desperately need to repent (most) dare not do so because of the actions that a self-righteous Church would carry out against them. The message of the Old Testament prophets was *"repent."* The message of John the Baptist was *"repent."* The message of the Lord Jesus Christ was *"repent."* The message of Paul, Peter, and the rest of the apostles, likewise, was *"repent."* It is the message of the Word of God, but it is not the message of the modern day Church.

The 4th verse says, *"for David's sake"* that the blessings of the Lord would be given to Judah and Jerusalem. Likewise, *"for Jesus sake,"* we who deserve nothing are given everything.

The 5th verse as well extolls the example of David and then at the last mentions, *"save only in the matter of Uriah the Hittite."* This should ever be a proclamation, and from the Holy Spirit at that, that if the sinning Christian will throw himself at the foot of the cross, the Lord can wipe the slate clean. To the modern Church David would have been forever finished. He would not have been allowed behind a pulpit. He would have been shunned and rejected.

NOTES

However, the Holy Spirit uses this terminology concerning David:

"His heart was perfect with the Lord his God" (vs. 3). The 4th verse says, *"for David's sake."* The 5th verse says, *"Because David did that which was right in the eyes of the Lord."* It must ever be said that it is not so very important regarding the *"eyes of man"* but only the *"eyes of the Lord."* If all men smiled and God frowns, the smile of man will serve little. If all men frown and God smiles, then all the frowns will not hinder.

The 6th verse says, *"And there was war."* It speaks of the conflict between Rehoboam and Jeroboam, which is symbolic of so much of what has plagued the Church down through the centuries. The Church should be trying to win the world for Jesus Christ. Instead, much of its energy is squandered away in division and infighting.

The 9th verse says, *"Reigned Asa over Judah."* In the 10th verse it says, *"His mother's name."* It was actually his grandmother. In the Hebrew there is no word for grandmother or grandfather.

In the 11th verse there is a pleasant change. The Scripture says, *"And Asa did that which was right in the eyes of the Lord, as did David his father."* Concerning the kings of Judah and Israel, when one reads the word *"evil"* beside their name, there is a sick feeling. At the same time when one reads the words, *"that which was right"* (righteous), there is a feeling of elation. Whenever we read that which the Holy Spirit has written about these particular individuals, we must as well understand that one or the other is written beside our name. Once again the 11th verse uses the words *"in the eyes of the Lord."* This is the only thing that really matters. Too many are concerned about the *"eyes of man"* and not about *"the eyes of the Lord."*

The 12th verse says, *"And he took away the sodomites out of the land."* The Scriptures do not say what he did with them, but the Holy Spirit draws our attention to this as well as the *"removal of all the idols"* and signifies that this was *"right in the eyes of the Lord."* The 14th verse says, *"But the high places were not removed."* This was brought out by the Holy Spirit for a reason. The *"high places"* were generally locations where altars to Jehovah were built and proper sacrifices offered. However, most of them were soon turned into idolatry where every act imaginable was practiced. We are given very little information, and it seems that the Holy Spirit absolved Asa for responsibility, for the Scripture says, *"Nevertheless Asa's heart was perfect with the Lord all his days."* Once again it calls attention to Asa's *"heart"* and not all of his actions because some of his actions *"all his days"* were not perfect toward God.

The 18th verse directs attention to one of the wrongs committed by Asa, for it says, *"And king Asa sent them to Benhadad,"* who was the *"king of Syria."* Asa's calling of Benhadad to his aid was condemned by the prophet, Hanani (II Chron. 17:7). An alliance had been made between Benhadad's father (vs. 19), and Abijam which helped the latter get victory over Jeroboam (II Chron. 13:17-20). This alliance had been brought to an end by Baasha, the successor of Benhadad. It was only natural that Asa should endeavor to break up this league and secure the Syrian troops for himself. The Israelites had begun to call in foreign help against each other when Jeroboam called for the aid of Shishak, king of Egypt. They continued such a program until both kingdoms were taken into captivity and both were destroyed as nations.

The 23rd verse also records another of Asa's failures, but only alludes to it here, with much more detail given in II Chronicles 16. The 23rd verse says, *"Nevertheless in the time of his old age he was diseased in his feet."* The writer of Chronicles mentions that Asa at this time did not seek the Lord, but turned to the physicians – and he died. No, by this action he did not lose his soul, but he did shorten his life.

The 27th verse says, *"Baasha smote him at Gibbethon, which belonged to the Philistines."*

Two solemn facts appear in Nadab's reign. The first: that the predicted wrath of God surely comes to pass; the second: that the judgment often falls at a time when circumstances deny its probability. The affairs of the kingdom are so prosperous that the king is enabled to carry the war into the Philistine country and besiege one of their great cities. In the midst of this prosperity, Divine judgment

strikes him, and he and the entire royal family perish. Had Nadab attacked idolatry instead of attacking the Philistines, how different would have been his conclusion! He knew well the doom pronounced against him by Ahijah the Shilonite, but his doing evil in the sight of the Lord and his walking in the way of his father show that he did not believe in the threatened wrath of God.

It pictures multitudes today who, though they continually hear of the wrath that is coming, yet cover their sins, and persistently pursue their worldly concern. Like Nadab they will be suddenly cut off without remedy, and, like him, they will involve others in the same destruction.

The 29th verse says, *"And it came to pass, when he reigned, that he smote all the house of Jeroboam."* Baasha, by destroying Jeroboam's house, fulfilled I Kings 14. God's prophecies always come to pass.

CHAPTER 16

Verse 1 says, *"Then the word of the Lord came to Jehu the son of Hanani against Baasha, saying,"* The prophet Jehu is called by God to deliver a message against Baasha, the King of Israel. The message was not to him, but rather *"against"* him. Because of *"the Word of the Lord,"* Baasha or Israel would be without excuse.

The 2nd verse says of the Lord, *"Forasmuch as I exalted thee out of the dust."* Baasha was the second man whom God exalted thus far over the ten tribes. In other words, Baasha was placed there by the Lord. The first one, Jeroboam, was cut off completely because of his sins. Baasha, who started the dynasty, was raised up to destroy Jeroboam's house, but he also went into the same sins Jeroboam was responsible for. Now God predicted his house would be totally cut off. Baasha fulfilled the prophecy of the destruction of all belonging to Jeroboam, but the 7th verse which says, *"And because he killed him,"* seems to mean that Baasha executed the judgment with personal and cruel delight; therefore, God smote his family. Later on in the Bible this same principle reappears. The Babylonians were judged by God because they also mercilessly executed His wrath upon Israel. Christian people should never indulge in personal satisfaction on witnessing or hearing of Divine chastisement upon others.

The 5th verse says of Baasha (and of others) concerning his might, *"Are they not written in the book of the Chronicles of the kings of Israel?"* That book is now lost to sacred history. Why? Because there is no profit to be had from the doings of the workers of iniquity.

God would not only execute special judgment upon Baasha because of his terrible sin of *"provoking the Lord God of Israel to anger with their vanities"* (vs. 13), but also on Baasha's son, *"Elah,"* as well as *"Zimri"* and *"Omri."* These four kings leave one sad record upon the page of sacred history – that they did evil.

According to the 26th verse and many others, *"For he walked in all the way of Jeroboam the son of Nebat,"* it seems this man Jeroboam was the epitome of evil, because all evil was judged against his evil. His wickedness was not a wickedness of passion, but of design; therefore, it was more evil.

The 28th verse introduces the most wicked king of all, *"And Ahab his son reigned in his stead."* The 30th verse says, *"And Ahab the son of Omri did evil in the sight of the Lord above all that were before him."* Ahab committed all the sins of those who were before him, but added to that sin in the 31st verse, *"He took to wife Jezebel the daughter of Ethbaal king of Zidonians."* Jezebel would introduce Baal worship in Israel in a manner that it had not known previously – a sin that God hated supremely.

The Holy Spirit takes the occasion in verse 34 to introduce the fulfilling of the prophecy given to *"Joshua the son of Nun."* For it says, *"In his days did Heil the Bethelite build Jericho."* Ignoring or despising the Bible, he moves against the prediction of Joshua, given 500 years ago, and rebuilds the walls which the judgment of God had thrown down. Upon laying the foundations his eldest son is smitten with death. It, as well, seems that he may have lost two other sons as the walls rose higher. His youngest son descended into the grave on the completion of the work. Ahab should have

NOTES

learned from this how vain, and how deadly is the result of opposing God. Elijah, as well, should have learned how impotent his punishment to turn away man from his purpose, not because of impotency in the punishment, but because of the incurable rebellion of man's will. He should have learned that grace alone can break down the natural heart. He should have interceded for Israel and not *"against"* Israel. Romans 11:2 interprets his ministry and furnishes its keynote. Even though he was one of the greatest prophets who ever lived, still, his efforts to force Israel by *"law"* instead of *"grace,"* were unbiblical and, thereby, of no profit. Regrettably, too many in the Church today attempt to carry on the same program of law vs. grace, with the same results – none. The following chapter will provide direction.

CHAPTER 17

The 1st verse says, *"And Elijah the Tishbite."* His name means *"God is Jehovah."* He is mentioned some 68 times in the Old Testament and some 30 times in the New Testament (called Elias). Elijah is considered one of the greatest of the prophets. He is not called a writing prophet because of not leaving any book like the ones from Isaiah to Malachi, but he did write four verses (II Chron. 21:12-15). No prophet has been more vividly described, and none has been counterfeited as he has been. Many in all ages have claimed to be Elijah, the reason being that he is clearly predicted to come back to the earth to help restore Israel just before the second advent of Christ (Mal. 4:5-6; Rev. 11:3-12). Elijah is also revealed as one of the two anointed men who now stand before the God of the whole earth, symbolized by two olive trees and two candlesticks (Zech. 14:11-14; Rev. 11:3-12). He is the only prophet who people try to identify with John the Baptist, and the only one who John the Baptist imitated in spirit, power, and ministry (Matt. 11:14; Mark. 9:12-13).

Almost nothing is known about Elijah except that he came from *"Gilead."* He simply burst on the scene as a flaming meteor.

He said to Ahab, *"There shall not be dew nor rain these years, but according to my word."* It seems from the text that God gave Elijah the power to do what he desired. In other words, He gave him liberty of action. And so he resolved by suffering to force the nation back to the Law. Only in glory (Luke 9:31), did he learn that grace in atonement can accomplish this. It would seem that throughout Elijah's ministry God would make successive efforts to teach him this great truth. However, at the beginning of his ministry he would resort to Law, saying, *"There shall not be dew nor rain these years, but according to my word."* The 2nd verse says that now, *"the word of the Lord came unto him, saying."* This Word tells him, *"Hide thyself by the brook Cherith."* The word *"Cherith"* means *"separation."* So, the Holy Spirit at the outset of Elijah's ministry will *"hide"* him for a period of time – possibly several months. This place of solitude, privacy, and communion with God, is in some measure needed by every minister of the Gospel. Elijah would learn the great miracles of God, *"I have commanded the ravens to feed thee there,"* as well as other valuable lessons.

Incidentally, many Christians are like *"the ravens."* They may think of themselves as having little ability, no talent, and of little worthwhile use. However, without *"the ravens"* Elijah would have starved to death. God used the ravens, and He can use you as well.

The 7th verse says, *"After a while, that the brook dried up."* Two lessons are learned from this:

1. Whenever God gets ready for us to move, *"the brook will dry up."*

2. The mighty prophet in his determination to force Israel back to Jehovah is compelled to watch the brook daily for many days as it becomes more and more shallow. Eventually, it drys up, thus impressing upon him the terrible suffering of the unhappy people of Israel. Thus was he designed to feel the misery that reigned in Israel.

The 8th verse again proclaims, *"The word of the Lord came unto him, saying."* It tells him, *"Arise, get thee to Zarephath"* (vs. 9). This was a Gentile city in *"Zidon."* So, now he is forced to go to a Gentile city, which, no doubt, he had no desire to do, where God had

"commanded a widow woman there to sustain thee." Strangely enough the *"widow woman"* God had commanded was so poor that she was on the verge of dying from starvation – and yet, this is the one that God chose to use.

How so very much we as Christians limit God – and most of the time we limit Him because of *"religion."* Elijah's *"religion"* would not have allowed him to have been fed by a *"raven"* which was an unclean bird. And now he must go to *"Zidon"* which is a Gentile city, and as well forbidden. In all of this the Lord would attempt to teach Elijah a lesson. It would not be easily learned.

According to the 18th verse the woman is laboring under condemnation. She feels that her great distress is not only from the famine but because of her sin; therefore, she says, *"That we may eat it and die."*

So many people think of God in entirely wrong terms. They think He is a God of condemnation. Yes, God hates sin, but He loves the sinner more than He hates the sin. Therefore, Jesus said, *"For God sent not His Son into the world to condemn the world; but that the world through Him might be saved"* (St. John 3:17).

God will give this woman a miracle, but He will require faith of her as well. The 11th verse says of Elijah, *"Bring me, I pray thee, a morsel of bread in thine hand."*

The 12th verse proclaims the woman relating her condition being reduced to *"an handful of meal, and a little oil."* She said, *"That we may eat it, and die."* It seems that she, even though a Gentile, at least in some way knew God, for the 12th verse also says, *"As the Lord thy God liveth."* Maybe she had previously cried to Israel's God for help, and this was God's way of answering her prayer. He would send to her one of the mightiest prophets who ever lived. God will always respond to the seeking, crying heart.

The 13th verse says that *"Elijah said unto her, Fear not."* Over 300 times in the Word of God the Lord sends this message to a hurting, seeking soul, *"Fear not."* That message through the Lord Jesus Christ and by the power of the Holy Spirit is still being sent today. He is still saying, *"Fear not."* Hallelujah!

Now the Lord will require faith of her, for

Elijah says, *"But make me thereof a little cake first."* To do this the woman would have to use all of her meager sustenance. However, despite the difficulty, this Gentile woman had faith in God. She would obey the prophet.

How many Christians in dire circumstances are moved upon by the Lord to first give to Him. It takes faith to do it, but it will truly bring a bountiful harvest. This was God's promise:

The 14th verse says, *"For thus saith the Lord God of Israel. The barrel of meal shall not waste, neither shall the cruse of oil fail."* The time was specified *"until the day that the Lord sendeth rain upon the earth."*

The 15th verse says, *"And she went and did according to the saying of Elijah."* This was a test of her faith. If she believed that Elijah was God's man and that God had actually spoken these words, she would act upon it and tremendous would be the results. It is the same today. It has not changed. Faith always demands action. It is never passive. Oftentimes, it goes against reason. It is generally a question of one believing the Word of God.

The 16th verse says, *"And the barrel of meal wasted not, neither did the cruse of oil fail."* And then it says, *"According to the word of the Lord, which he spake by Elijah."* The Scripture says that God upholds His Word even above His Name.

The 18th verse calls to mind her guilt and condemnation, for it says, *"Art thou come unto me to call my sin to remembrance, and to slay my son?"* So many people in the world think of God as One who kills instead of giving life. True, God is a God of judgment, but only after all longsuffering, compassion, and mercy have failed. Once again the Lord, through the death of this boy and despite the woman's sin, shows grace and raises the son to life. This was another lesson to Elijah, teaching him that grace, not judgment, wins the sinner to God.

The statement of verse 24, *"And that the word of the Lord in thy mouth is truth,"* is a statement of faith far greater than the present miracle. This Gentile woman is exclaiming the fact that Israel's God is now her God. From the scriptural hint given here and there (verses 9, 18, and 24), it seems that she had been searching for truth for quite some time. If, in fact, she

NOTES

had previously sought the Lord before the coming of Elijah, He had answered her prayer in a remarkable way. Some 900 years later the Lord Jesus Christ referred back to this moment, showing us that the path of God is through faith. It is never through religion, works, posture or position. It is through faith.

CHAPTER 18

The 1st verse says, *"And it came to pass after many days."* This concerns the drought that has now lasted into its third year. The Lord says to Elijah, *"Go, shew thyself unto Ahab; and I will send rain upon the earth."* The ground was cracked, barren, and dry. It was the same way spiritually. As well there is a spiritual drought that has characterized so many lives. In Israel there was very little left that was green. Because of lack of rain everything had died. In many Christian lives, churches, and even entire denominations one will look in vain for spiritual growth or life. It is barren. The word *"many days"* sobs with a Divine anguish. What untold suffering lies under that little word! How it seems to throb with pity!

The 2nd verse says *"And there was a sore famine in Samaria."* As well, there is a *"sore famine"* in America, Canada, and even in most of the world for the Word of God.

Sometime back the question was asked of an educator how long it would take to rewrite a Bible college curriculum. The answer was: *"From six months to a year."* Then the question was asked, *"Why not use the curriculum already written, called the Bible?"* That's what was done in this particular Bible college, but, sadly, that is generally not the case. There is truly a *"sore famine"* of the Word of God. Preachers preach psychology from behind their pulpits, or the latest fads. At a gathering of N.R.B. (National Religious Broadcasters) some time back the statement was made, *"Hellfire preaching is out; from now on it will be psychologists and counseling."* Sadly, they were right. However, these things mentioned are not the Word of God. They will set no captive free. They will heal no broken heart.

They will not set at liberty them that are bruised. Only the Word of God can do that.

Verses 3-6 proclaim the efforts by Ahab to find water. He went to great trouble and expense. One hour of repentance before God could have long since solved the problem. Israel is now in her third year of drought. It could have ended long before with proper repentance. Tragically, most individuals would rather proceed in their own rebellion than to humble themselves before God.

He called his governor who was Obadiah. In the 3rd verse the Holy Spirit quickly points out, *"Now Obadiah feared the Lord greatly."* Even under the very nose of Ahab, the Lord had an individual who had not bowed the knee to Baal.

He was placed there by the Holy Spirit, no doubt, and according to the 4th verse to save the prophets of Israel because the Scripture says, *"That Obadiah took an hundred prophets, and hid them by fifty in a cave, and fed them with bread and water."* Ahab and Jezebel had sworn death to every prophet of God. However, Ahab's bread fed these prophets.

As Obadiah looked for water at the behest of Ahab, the 7th verse says, *"Behold Elijah met him."* The 8th verse states that Elijah said to him, *"Tell thy Lord, Behold, Elijah is here."* (In the Hebrew it merely says *"Behold, Elijah."*) The Holy Spirit has told Elijah that it's time to bring this famine to a close. As stated in the previous chapter, it seems that God had given Elijah latitude regarding direction. Elijah chose judgment instead of grace. Now the Holy Spirit in evidencing grace will portray Himself mightily.

The 10th verse proclaims that Ahab had searched nations and kingdoms trying to find Elijah, when all of the time he had been at the brook Cherith and at the widow's house of Zarephath. The 10th verse says, *"to seek thee."* Why? He knew that Elijah had stopped the rain. He also knew that Elijah was the only one through whom God would work to bring back the rain.

Upon the meeting of righteousness with evil, the 17th verse proclaims the words of Ahab, *"Art thou he that troubleth Israel?"* Men ever seek to blame others for their own sin.

The 18th verse quickly proclaims Elijah's

NOTES

answer, *"But thou, and thy father's house."* And then he says, *"And thou hast followed Baalim."* Elijah delivered the Word of the Lord even at the risk of his own life. He did not await an answer from Ahab. But the 19th verse says that he said, *"Now therefore send, and gather to me all Israel unto mount Carmel."* Ahab obeys because, as stated, the nation is destitute. It will be a time of one of the greatest miracles ever recorded in human history.

The 20th verse records Ahab obeying Elijah regarding the prophets of Baal, *"And gathered the prophets together unto mount Carmel."* There were *"four hundred and fifty"* of them. There were also 400 prophets of the groves. This pertained to the Asherah. The worship of Asherah was so obscene and wicked that it would be improper to describe its filth of obscenity. It is not clear whether both sets of prophets came or not (850 total), but it seems that only the prophets of Baal were summoned to the meeting at Carmel. Baal was the god of fire. Elijah's challenge would make the issue decisive, for he says in the 24th verse, *"And the God that answereth by fire, let him be God."*

In the 21st verse the challenge was given, *"How long halt ye between two opinions?"* The multiple tens of thousands at Carmel were given the option to follow the one who answered by fire.

The 24th verse says, *"And all the people answered and said, It is well spoken."*

Verses 25-29 record the efforts of the prophets of Baal to bring fire from heaven. It was quite common for these evil prophets to hide an individual in their huge altar to begin fire in order that it might come out of the various vents, thereby, deceiving the people. Tradition says that these 450 prophets of Baal attempted the same, but that the man they hid in their altar suffocated. They then went into a frenzy cutting themselves until the 28th verse says, *"The blood gushed out upon them."* The 29th verse as well says, *"There was neither voice, nor any to answer, nor any that regarded."* The world today considers itself too cultured, educated, and enlightened to indulge in such foolishness. However, false gods continue to abound. Religious superstition plagues the whole of humanity. At this moment hundreds of millions light candles to

Buddha while leaving their offerings. But as the Scripture says, *"There is no answer."* Nearly a billion each day will prostrate themselves some five times to the one they called Allah. It is the religion of Islam. But *"There is no answer,"* because Jesus said, *"No man cometh to the Father but by Me."* Entire nations of the world are gripped in demonic Spiritism, with candles being lit for departed loved ones and prayers made to demon spirits. *"There is no answer."* Much of the world believes in reincarnation, with India steeped in its demonic Hinduism, believing that their loved ones have been reincarnated in the form of animals or people. The Scripture continues to say, *"There is no answer."* Multiple hundreds of millions in Catholicism worship the Virgin Mary, offering prayers to her and other dead saints. The Scripture screams, *"There is no answer."*

Sadly, large segments of what is referred to as Christianity seeks to unify itself with the Catholic church, even looking to the Pope in some manner of supremacy, while the Catholic church seeks unity with varied religions of the world. The Holy Spirit through the Apostle Paul still cries, *"Come out from among them and be ye separate saith the Lord"* (II Cor. 6:17).

The following verses proclaim the need of the modern Church. It proclaims the answer to its *"famine"* and *"spiritual drought."* That which Elijah did so many years ago is the crying need of this hour.

The 30th verse says, *"And Elijah said unto all the people, Come near unto me."* God give us God-called prophets, with a message burning in their hearts, who cannot be bought with money and will not compromise their convictions or their message but will say to a lost and dying humanity, *"Come near unto me."* The Scripture says, *"And he repaired the altar of the Lord that was broken down."*

The *"altar"* is a type of Calvary. There were many altars in Israel but no *"altar"* called Calvary. It was *"broken down."* Is it any different in the Church today? Most of the preachers behind Christian pulpits no longer even believe in the Blood of Jesus Christ. They do not even believe that He was and is the Son of God. He is called a *"good man"* but somewhat deluded and deceived. It is strange to understand how that a man can be *"good"* and a liar at the same time.

No, Jesus Christ was and is the Son of the living God. They dish up a mild pablum called psychology, positive-thinking, possibility-thinking, and a host of other religious band-aids with which they attempt to cover the terrible cancer called sin. The only answer to the ills of mankind is *"the altar" (Calvary).* There is no other panacea; there is no other solution. Satan responds to no humanistic theology. He laughs at man's pitiful efforts to deliver himself. Only Calvary can set men free. That's the reason the Apostle Paul cried, *"For I determined not to know anything among you, save Jesus Christ and Him crucified."* (I Cor. 2:2). The preachers need to repair the *"altar"* that is *"broken down."* Until the Church does this, it is at best a bloated, fat, unhealthy, stumbling giant that cannot see its way in a darkened world.

The 31st verse says, *"And Elijah took twelve stones, according to the number of the tribes of the sons of Jacob."* These "twelve" stones will represent two things:

1. The 12 tribes of Israel. Elijah remembers that Jehovah had said to broken Jacob, *"Israel shall be thy name,"* and in the energy of this faith he constructs the Altar with 12 stones.

2. Twelve in the Bible refers to government; God's government. There were "twelve" tribes of Israel; there were "twelve" apostles; the new Jerusalem will be "12,000" furlongs in length, breadth, and in height. There will be "twelve" gates in the wall with the names of the "twelve" tribes of the children of Israel inscribed upon them; the wall of the city will have "twelve" foundations, with the names of the "twelve" apostles of the Lamb inscribed on them as well. The "twelve" foundations will be garnished with "twelve" different precious stones; the "twelve" gates will be made of "twelve" pearls; there will be "twelve" great broadways going out from the "twelve" gates of the city. There will be "twelve" great rivers flowing down the midst of the "twelve" great broadways going through the "twelve" gates into all parts of the earth on both sides of the "twelve" great rivers flowing for some "12,000" furlongs. Through the "twelve" great broadways there will be rows of trees of life, bearing "twelve" manner of fruits.

So I think it is obvious and plain that when

Elijah took the *"twelve stones"* it was under the guidance of the Holy Spirit representing God's great government. Still, it must ever be said that this is God's government and not man's. Regrettably, the Church has, by and large, ignored God's government and instituted into its place man's government. One preacher a short time ago looked at a book containing the constitution and by-laws of his denomination. He remarked to someone standing nearby, *"It is bigger than the Bible."* Men love their own laws; they have little regard for God's laws. So, when Elijah took the *"twelve stones"* he was, in effect, saying, *"It is not thus saith man, but thus saith the Lord."* Most of that which passes for Church government is, *"Thus saith man."*

The 32nd verse proclaims that God's government will always *"build an altar in the name of the Lord."* In other words, God's government will always point to Calvary.

The 32nd verse says as well, *"And he made a trench about the altar."* This speaks of separation. God's people have always been a separate people. Still, it must be quickly noted that it is separation and not isolation. We are in the world but never of the world. Israel was commanded to be separate from the other nations. Likewise, the Church is commanded to *"come out from among them and be ye separate, saith the Lord"* (II Cor. 6:17). The Church is in the world, but the world had better not be in the Church. However, it should be ever noted that the world cannot be kept out of the Church with man's rules and by-laws. Law has never saved anyone. Calvary is the answer to the world. Therefore, Calvary is the answer to the Church. When men are pulled to the Cross they will automatically be separate from the world.

Someone has said, *"The Cross separates man from the world, and the Baptism in the Holy Spirit separates man from a cold, dead, formal religion."* The *"trench"* was there then; the *"trench"* is there now. It is of the Holy Spirit, and woe be unto any man or woman who attempts to fill it up with anything except the *"water of the Word."*

The 33rd verse says, *"And he put the wood in order."* The *"wood"* typifies the cross of Calvary. The verse also says, *"Cut the bullock in pieces."* The *"bullock"* represents the Lord

NOTES

Jesus Christ. The *"pieces"* represent two things. They are as follows:

1. Sin is an insidious horror that involves itself to the very depths of our being. It is not merely an external situation. In other words, the sin problem cannot be assuaged by a better environment, a new location, or a change of geography. Neither can it be assuaged by education, culture, or refinement. Neither can it be soothed, counseled, or made none effective by the rudiments of humanistic psychology. While it definitely affects the external even more so, it rots the internal. Sin is a problem of the heart which affects the totality of one's being.

2. The *"pieces"* represents the terrible price that Jesus Christ paid at Calvary for man's redemption. The lictor's lash will cut His back to pieces, but it will take more than that to redeem mankind. His beard will be plucked from His cheeks, but it will take more than that as well. It will take His heart, burst and broken, draining of blood from the multitudinous wounds, to cleanse the black heart of evil mankind.

"Laid him on the wood" speaks of the *"bullock."* This, of course, typifies Christ being nailed to the Cross. Also, *"Fill four barrels with water"* speaks of the Word of God. Paul used the term, *"the washing of water by the Word"* (Eph. 5:26). The term *"pour it on the burnt sacrifice, and on the wood,"* means that everything Jesus did at Calvary was all according to the Word of God. It was done three times, *"Did it the third time,"* signifying the office work of *"the Father, the Son, and the Holy Ghost."*

The 35th verse says, *"And he filled the trench also with water."* The *"trench,"* which speaks of separation, can only be filled with *"water"* which typifies the Word of God. Anytime the Church tries to institute a type of separation according to its own rules and regulations, it will cause disruption in the Body, and will be disobedience to God. Unfortunately, man loves to make his own rules and dig his own *"trench,"* filling it with that of his own substance. It must be filled with the *"water"* of the Word and that alone.

After Elijah's prayer the 38th verse declares, *"Then the fire of the Lord fell, and consumed the burnt sacrifice,"* also consuming the *"wood,"* the *"stones,"* the *"dust,"* and licking up the *"water."*

The *"fire of the Lord"* was a type of God's judgment upon sin. The *"fire"* should have fallen on Israel, the prophets of Baal, and even Elijah, but, instead, it fell on the *"bullock,"* which is a type of Christ. Likewise, Jesus Christ would die on Calvary, taking the punishment that rightfully belonged to you and me in order that we might be saved.

Some blanch at Elijah's being included in the judgment, but only if they lack understanding in the Word of God. There is no human being who has ever lived that is worthy within his own right to escape the judgment of God. The Scripture says, *"All have sinned."* Even the best of us (whomever that may be) cannot qualify for the Grace of God. The moment we think we do, we are automatically disqualified. Actually, the qualification for God's Grace is that we are disqualified and willing to admit it.

Elijah admits as much in his prayer in the 36th verse when he says, *"And that I have done all these things at thy word."* Everyone of us deserve judgment – even the child of God. We escape that judgment by admitting that we deserve it, and accepting our substitute Who took the judgment in our place, the Lord Jesus Christ.

Concerning the 450 prophets of Baal, the 40th verse says, *"Elijah brought them down to the brook Kishon, and slew them there."* This is the only answer for false doctrine. The efforts being made by the Church for unity at any cost is contrary to the Word of God, to say the least. Elijah could come to no accommodations with the prophets of Baal. Neither can the true preacher of the Gospel come to accommodations with that which is obviously false.

The 41st verse heralds a coming revival for it says, *"For there is a sound of abundance of rain."* Whenever the Word of God is adhered to, with Calvary once again becoming the center point of all that is done, then the spiritual drought will end, and there will be an *"abundance of rain."*

The 42nd verse portrays the humility that must characterize the man of God in order to receive from heaven what is so desperately needed. It says, *"Cast himself down upon the*

earth, and put his face between his knees." Those words are the answer to every pulpit, every church, every home, and every problem that plagues our lives. Why is it so hard for us to do this? Why do we seek everyone's opinion, and not God's knowledge? And if we do seek His face, too often it is with a haughty attitude, denying all humility. God will accept nothing such as this. The church desperately needs revival. The 42nd verse tells us how to have it.

The 43rd verse portrays faith. It says, *"Go again seven times."* About the greatest admittance of the Church is the admittance of the servant when he states, *"There is nothing."* We have been so compromised in our faith, being led to believe that if we snap our fingers, God is to do it immediately. If it's not done, we quit, being taught that it's not *"faith"* to continue. That is unbiblical. No, it doesn't take the Lord long to do anything, but it does take a while for us to be brought to the place and position desired by the Holy Spirit. Elijah was one of the greatest men of God who ever lived, but the Lord would teach even Elijah something in this episode. He would be taught a valuable lesson on the Grace of God. It is sad, but the Church knows so little about the Grace of God. *"Seven times"* speaks of God's fulfillment and completion. It speaks of a perfect work, a work that He desires to do within our lives.

The 44th verse tells us what is coming, *"There ariseth a little cloud out of the sea, like a man's hand."* It must ever be said that what looks like only a *"little cloud"* to the unbeliever, the doubter, and the skeptic is, in fact, that which with faith can mean a coming deluge.

For the 45th verse says, *"The heaven was black with clouds and wind."* The *"little cloud"* that, no doubt, was scoffed at, had now grown to cover the entirety of the heavens. And the Scripture says, *"And there was a great rain."* Hallelujah! There is no church in the world that is more backslidden, or in a state of spiritual declension, such as Israel of old, and yet God sent *"a great rain"* of Holy Ghost revival. If we will meet the conditions that Elijah met, the *"rain"* of the glory and the power of God will come.

The 46th verse proclaims a tremendous miracle. The Scripture says, *"And the hand of the Lord was on Elijah."* This expression always refers to the power of the Lord being made evident in a miraculous way. This display of God's power was probably the greatest lesson that Elijah would learn in the entirety of this episode. It would be a lesson of humility designed by the Holy Spirit. The Scripture says, *"And he girded up his loins, and ran before Ahab to the entrance of Jezreel."* It was only the compelling Grace of the Lord Jesus that could constrain a prophet of judgment and fire to be concerned about the physical needs of a blood-stained idolater like Ahab and then to attend him as a slave, for it was the duty of a slave to run before his master's chariot. How amazing is the love of God! Therefore, God's noblest servant is compelled to attend him as a slave. How so much the Lord Jesus Christ would teach His disciples and us as well that the minister is to be the *"servant of all."*

To man's judgment the first picture of the fire falling from heaven concerning Elijah is the grandest; the second, with prayer being made for the rain is somewhat less impressive; and the third, with Elijah running before the chariot is abject. However, to the spiritual eye it is the reverse!

The first picture presents the trimphant prophet standing beside his blazing altar; the second pictures him on the lonely mountain-top bowed in expectant prayer; the third depicts him as a slave splashing through the mud of the highway before the chariot of Ahab. To the spiritual mind this is the noblest picture of the three, for it portrays and illustrates the great grace of Him Who came to minister and to give His life for the most violent of His enemies (Luke 22:50-51).

CHAPTER 19

The Bible student would do well to carefully study this 19th chapter. By and large, it shows the wasted efforts of one of the greatest prophets who ever lived, Elijah. By and large, it also portrays the wasted efforts of so many Christians – all because we do not know God as we ought to know Him, and neither do we know ourselves as we should.

NOTES

Ahab portrayed to Jezebel, no doubt, in living color, *"all that Elijah had done."* Then the 2nd verse says, *"Then Jezebel sent a messenger unto Elijah."* The message contained a threat of death within the next 24 hours.

It should have been obvious to Elijah that Jezebel's threat was empty. As well, it should be noted to the child of God that immediately after a great victory, Satan often attacks with great success. Elijah has just witnessed and been the instrument of some of the greatest miracles ever given to a man. However, the faith of yesterday does not seem to suffice for the need of today. The child of God must ever have a continued deposit of the touch of God, even on a daily basis. For a reason that will become all too obvious, Elijah allows fear to take the place of faith. Almost the entirety of this chapter will portray the operation of fear. How different it will be compared to the preceding chapter.

First of all, if Jezebel was so sure of her position, why did she not send soldiers to kill Elijah instead of a messenger with a threat? She did not do so because she feared for the life of the soldiers and even herself. As the fear of Elijah was totally unfounded, so is the fear of the child of God unfounded.

Satan is the one who really operates in fear. He covers it by bluster and blow. Too often he succeeds. Elijah, by faith, has just killed 450 prophets of Baal, and, now, he is fearful of one woman. Satan's threats come in every direction. Too often we believe his lies instead of the truth of the Word of God.

The 3rd verse says, *"And when he saw that, he arose, and went for his life."* Now, Elijah, who was one of the mightiest prophets who ever lived, is operating from fear. Fear always leads one away from the will of God. Faith always leads one toward the will of God, but now fear is in control. He went to Beersheba, and the Scripture says, *"And left his servant there."* Fear always seeks isolation. He was now in such a spiritual state of fear that he didn't even want his servant to see his condition. Millions of Christians have come to this place – perhaps every Christian at one time or the other. As to the why of his state and the cause of the fear, it will become more readily obvious.

The 4th verse says, *"But he himself went a day's journey into the wilderness."* There is some minute indication that Elijah knew where he was going, which will become more clear. It will be a futile trip because God does not work backwards; He works forward. The *"wilderness"* would be somewhat a type of his own spiritual position – and that immediately after some of the greatest miracles that any man had ever seen. It must be understood that God did not tell Elijah to come to Beersheba, the wilderness, or even *"unto Horeb the mount of God."* This was Elijah's trip and not God's. Too many trips that the Christian takes are on his own and not according to the leading of the Holy Spirit – and yet, the Heavenly Father continues to watch over us as tenderly as He did the great prophet.

He sat down under a *"juniper tree"* and *"requested for himself that he might die."* This is a sad statement for the mightiest man of God on the face of the earth. Strangely enough, God did not permit him to die even until now. Elijah is now over 3500 years old and still alive in his mortal body, having been translated that he should not see death until the future tribulation, when he will die as one of the two witnesses (Zech. 4:11-14; Rev. 11:3-12). Thank the Lord that God does not answer all our prayers. Fear leads one to this state, and at the same time we all at one time or the other have faced the same hopelessness and helplessness, but God does not desert us. His tender care of the faithless prophet is just as touching now as during the times of great victories. The Church would do well to emulate its Heavenly Father in such circumstances. Regrettably, the Church for the most part operates from political expediency instead of the Word of God. Elijah states, *"It is enough."* In other words, *"I cannot go any further."* Every child of God, sooner or later, has faced this; therefore, the Holy Spirit, while not bringing about this episode in Elijah's life, still would use this circumstance to teach every Christian that even the greatest can succumb to fear. Many great men and women of God have faced this moment. Moses did, and so did David. Jeremiah did as well, and so did most of the great prophets and patriarchs.

The 5th verse records the following, *"An angel touched him, and said unto him, Arise and eat."* No doubt, this angel had followed him all the way from Mount Carmel. He tend-

NOTES

erly watches over the great prophet. But even the *"angel's touch"* did not bring him to his spiritual senses.

The 7th verse records, *"The angel of the Lord came again the second time and touched him."* Still, this mighty experience did not stop Elijah from his journey of fear. It must ever be understood that experiences, as wonderful as they are, and as much as we all desire them, cannot take the place of faith. We only come back to the path of obedience and righteousness when we come back to the path of faith. The angel says to him, *"Because the journey is too great for thee"* – and yet, it was a journey that was not ordained of God. Incidentally, it would be a round-trip journey of approximately 500 miles – all of it out of the will of God, and, yet, in this wayward journey the Lord would never leave Elijah's side. How many wayward trips have all of us taken? And, yet, the Lord never leaves us or forsakes us. The Christian should understand that every journey of fear is too great for us. The reason is that our energy is from the flesh and not the Spirit. Still, the Lord will help the great prophet even in his disobedience, as He oftentimes helps us even in our disobedience.

The 8th verse proclaims a supernatural strength that came to him as a result of the gift of the angel, *"And went in the strength of that meat forty days and forty nights unto Horeb the mount of God."* Horeb was about 180 miles from where he had sat under *"a juniper tree."* Why Horeb?

Even though it cannot be proven, there is a possibility that the cave in which Elijah arrived at was the *"clift of the rock"* in which Moses had stood while the Lord passed by (Ex. 33:22). So oftentimes fear will take the child of God back to a place of experience, either of his or of others. This type of journey will seldom help, because the place that the individual must go has nothing to do with geography, but a person. And that person is the Lord Jesus Christ. Fear can only take us to what once was, but no longer is. Only faith can take us to God.

The 9th verse says, *"And he came thither unto a cave, and lodged there."* Too many Christians are still in *"a cave."* But even there, *"the word of the Lord came to him."* The Holy Spirit is careful to document the exact terminology. It is called *"the word of the Lord."* The Bible is the answer for the child of God. It holds the solution to every single problem that we may have in our person or our plans. The Lord says to him, *"What doest thou here Elijah?"* This question could well be asked at one time or the other of every child of God. This is a question which should have brought Elijah to repentance and sorrow because faithlessness is sin (Rom. 14:23). Most of the Church operates in faithlessness but never one time thinks of repenting of such.

At once Elijah begins to speak well of himself and ill of the nation. He should have set himself aside and interceded for, and not against, Israel as Romans 11 teaches. He was angry because the people would not listen to him and turn to Jehovah.

The angry prophet, crouching with embittered heart in the cavern, pictured the nation. The *"flesh"* in him was just as hateful as the *"flesh"* in them. He is invited to come forth and meet God. As Israel refused, Elijah likewise refuses. He must therefore be compelled to come forth.

The 11th and 12th verses proclaim a *"great and strong wind that rent the mountains, and break in pieces the rocks before the Lord,"* and *"an earthquake"* as well as *"a fire."* It says that the *"Lord was not in the wind, earthquake, or fire."* The Church too often follows *"wind, earthquakes, and fire,"* which typify signs and wonders.

Then the 12th verse says, *"A still small voice."* The meaning is clear.

The child of God must live so close to the Lord that he can hear that *"still small voice."* Most of us are too far away to hear it. We are so taken up with the din, racket, and clamor of religion that even if God speaks, we cannot hear Him. Too many times we are fooled by the *"wind, earthquake, and fire,"* because our carnal attention is directed to these. One has to live very close to God in order to hear the *"still small voice."* Had Elijah's heart not been occupied with self, he would have learned that tempests, earthquakes, and fire cannot accomplish what the gentle voice of love can. He should have recognized that there was little difference between his heart and that of the nation, and that as force failed to make him

NOTES

leave his cave, so it failed and must fail to compel men to leave their sins.

It is very difficult for the self-righteous Christian to equate Elijah with sinful, evil Israel. But as stated, *"self"* is just as hateful and sinful in one as the other.

And once again the 13th verse says, *"What doest thou here, Elijah?"* He repeats his angry and foolish words and intercedes against Israel. Had he loved sinners as his Lord did, how different would have been his action and language!

The Lord basically ignores Elijah's answer both times.

The 15th verse says, *"And the Lord said unto him, Go, return on thy way to the wilderness of Damascus."* The path of faith must retrace its steps back to the place we were in when fear compelled us to do otherwise. It will be a long journey for Elijah (nearly 300 miles) as it is a long journey for every Christian. The Lord will demand three things of him:

1. *"Anoint Hazael to be king over Syria."*

2. *"And Jehu the son of Nimshi shalt thou anoint to be king over Israel."*

3. *"And Elisha the son of Shaphat of Abelmeholah shalt thou anoint to be prophet in thy room"* (verse 16).

These passages denote to us the fact that God ruled even in the heathen nations (Syria) that surrounded Israel. In other words, every single thing that had to do with *"his chosen people,"* even though they at this time were in a backslidden condition, was controlled by God. As well, the Lord controls events that surround every child of God.

The 18th verse proclaims that the Lord gently rebuked Elijah at his statement, *"Even I only, am left."* The Lord told him, *"Yet I have left me seven thousand in Israel, all the knees which have not bowed unto Baal."*

If you will notice in the 14th verse, Elijah's preoccupation with *"self"* was the cause of his fear and is the cause of our fear as well. He said, *"I have been,"* and then *"and I."* And then, *"Even I only."* And last of all he would say, *"My life."*

The 19th verse says, *"So he departed thence, and found Elisha the son of Shaphat, who was plowing."* Not far off was a large divinity school in which a body of students was being prepared for the prophetic office. Upon none of these did Elijah cast his mantle, but, guided by the Holy Spirit, he cast it upon a plowboy. How different are God's thoughts from man's! He chooses *"Amos,"* who was a gatherer of sycamore fruit, or *"Paul,"* who was not one of the 12, or *"Moody,"* who was uneducated, and through men like these He rebukes, and refreshes the *"official ministry."*

———■———

CHAPTER 20

The entirety of the 20th chapter pertains to God's efforts at bringing Israel back to a place of repentance. He will give them great victories over the Syrians, victories that could be constituted as none other than miracles. And, yet, Ahab would not turn away from his wickedness, and Israel would not repent.

Verses 1-12 pertain to the threat that *"Benhadad the king of Syria"* made against Israel. There were 32 kings in an alliance with Benhadad, along with all their horses and chariots.

The 3rd verse proclaims of Benhadad, *"Thy silver and thy gold is mine."* The lesson we learn from this is as follows:

1. Israel was backslidden and was being led by an ungodly king, but, still, they were *"God's property."*

2. The silver and the gold, as well as the remainder of the prosperity of Israel, had been given to them by God. So, when Benhadad made his boast, in reality, it was not against Israel but against God.

3. At times God would allow heathen nations to chastise His people. However, almost always they would go too far in this chastisement, and then would suffer judgment themselves at the hands of God. Still, at this time God would not desire Syria's victory over Israel. Therefore, there was no way that Syria could succeed in this endeavor.

4. That which the Holy Spirit is attempting to bring to our attention is the fact that God's property is protected by God. To lay hands for harm on that which belongs to God is a serious matter indeed – even though the spiritual con-

NOTES

dition of Israel was actually little better than that of Syria.

The 13th verse says, *"And, behold, there came a prophet unto Ahab."* The message was one of victory for Israel, even though Israel's army was pitifully small and was outnumbered most probably even 20 or 30 times. This should portray to us the fact that God is not limited or helped by numbers.

The Church at this time has run aground on three things, (a) education, (b) money, (c) numbers. Yes, all three are important, but none of the three carry any spiritual power. The Church, by and large, spends its energy attempting to obtain the three things mentioned, when, in reality, it should be spending its energy seeking the face of God and attempting to draw closer to the Lord Jesus Christ.

Even this great victory, which was promised and given by God, would mark no repentance on the part of Israel and Ahab.

Still, the 22nd verse says, *"And the prophet came to the king of Israel."* Satan, through *"the king of Syria,"* at the beginning of the following year would once again attack Israel.

The 23rd verse proclaims the worship of heathen gods by the Syrians. Every heathen country attributed their military and economic success to their particular *"god."* They had reasoned, *"Their gods are gods of the hills."* So, now they would fight in the valley and, supposedly, their god would be stronger than Israel's God.

The spiritual situation has changed little from that day until this. The whole world has just witnessed the demise of atheistic communism. They had proclaimed *"no God,"* and God called them *"a fool"* (Psa. 14:1).

Look at the part of the world that is ruled by satanic Hinduism. It is steeped in ignorance, superstition, and poverty. The same can be said for Buddhism.

Most of Africa is ruled by witchcraft, Islam, Catholicism, and Christianity. (No, Catholicism is not Christianity; it is a mixture of witchcraft, other religions, and some Christianity thrown in.) Despite the boasts of Christendom concerning the evangelization of Africa, still, only a small part of the continent of Africa can accurately be said to be Christian. Africa suffers accordingly.

The world of Islam controls nearly 1 billion human beings. It substitutes the Koran for the Bible. It is a false book with a false message, as its prophet Mohammed was a false prophet. Islam is the author of most of the terrorism in the world today. Its prosperity, by and large, comes from American money for Islamic oil. It is advancing at a fearful rate, evangelizing the world by force and by money. The religion of Islam could well have a great part to play in the coming great Tribulation Period and the rise of the Antichrist.

Most of Central and South America is ruled by superstitious Catholicism, and, thereby, worships a god that does not exist, namely the Virgin Mary. Christianity definitely is making some inroads into Latin America but still has much ground to cover.

The point is this. The God of the Bible is the bringer of all blessing and salvation. There is no other. Sadly, most of the world worships demon spirits in one form or the other. Correspondingly, most of the world is steeped in superstition, heathenism, abject poverty, and slavery. America and Canada, along with England and certain other countries, have experienced many blessings because of biblical Christianity. Regrettably, these nations little recognize or understand the source of their blessing. They attribute such to their educational processes, secular humanism, or to their own prideful self. True biblical Christianity in many nations of the world has never been weaker; consequently, the fountain of light that has been provided to a lost world is dimmer today than ever before. England at this time is boasting of a spiritual renaissance. And what do they call a *"spiritual renaissance?"* The Anglican priests in the Church of England are using the Koran at least once a month in their services. How the mighty have fallen. America is little, if any better. In the public school systems of America and other public institutions, God or the Lord Jesus Christ cannot be mentioned under the guise of the separation of Church and State. We are fast becoming a secular, humanist, atheistic nation. We are forgetting the fact that there is no light but the light of the Gospel. There is no true education but the education of the Word of God. There is no blessing apart from God.

Sadly, America and Canada, as well as the other nations of the world that espouse Christianity, are little better, if any at all, than the Israel of Ahab's day. God is still helping us, but how long will He do so with our present spiritual state?

After Israel's second defeat of Syria, the 34th verse says, *"So he made a covenant with him, and sent him away."* This speaks of the covenant between Ahab and Benhadad. God was very displeased with this, for the 42nd verse says, *"Thus saith the Lord, because thou hast let go out of thy hand a man whom I appointed to utter destruction."* This *"covenant"* that Ahab made with Syria was not for his good but for his destruction.

Regrettably, Christianity today has as its watchword, *"unity,"* which is the same as *"covenant."* As Ahab compromised the will and the Word of God, likewise, the *"unity"* procession of modern Christianity compromises the Word of God.

CHAPTER 21

Strangely enough, Ahab was a great king, at least as far as his public works and palaces testify. He was a gifted and able prince and far surpassed other kings of Israel in the energy, culture, and splendor of his reign. But, yet, the Word of God says that he was wicked beyond compare.

The 1st verse says, *"That Naboth the Jezreelite had a vineyard."* The entirety of this chapter concerns this vineyard. The Scripture says it was *"hard by the palace of Ahab king of Samaria."* Naboth's vineyard is a type of the spiritual inheritance that every child of God has. As his vineyard bordered Ahab's palace, so our spiritual inheritance (vineyard) borders the world. The same pressure that was applied by Ahab against Naboth to sell his vineyard will be applied to us by the forces of darkness to compromise our convictions. As this battle was to the death, so will the battle that we fight be unto the death. We have but one of two choices:

1. We can refuse Satan any part in that which God has given us.

2. We can sell out to Ahab – the world.

The first one will bring physical death but spiritual life. The second one will bring physical life but spiritual death.

The 2nd verse says of Ahab as he speaks to Naboth, *"Give me thy vineyard, that I may have it for a garden of herbs."* Ahab's offer will be in two directions. First, *"a better vineyard"* or *"the worth of it in money."* Satan professes to have better vineyards. He lies. If He has better vineyards, why does he want yours? The temptation to sell out for personal gain is powerful. Many are yielding to it. But Simon Peter writes, *"Our redemption was not purchased by such corruptible things as silver and gold, but by the precious blood of Jesus."* (I Pet. 1:18-19). So, money cannot buy this vineyard.

The 3rd verse says of Naboth to Ahab, *"The Lord forbid it me, that I should give the inheritance of my fathers unto thee."* As Naboth's vineyard was given unto him by the Lord of glory, likewise, our vineyard of salvation is given to us by the Lord of glory.

Actually, the Law of Moses forbade the sale of ancestral rights except in extreme destitution, and even then the property would always return to the original owners in the year of release (Lev. 25:23-25; Num. 36:7). In those days, such inheritances from forefathers which had been passed on for many generations in the same family were considered priceless, and to part with such was almost like parting with life itself because, first of all, it was given by God and held very dear associations connected with it concerning one's ancestors.

Our answer must be the same as Naboth's, *"The Lord forbid it me."* Satan will ever try to take our *"vineyard."* He must be repulsed even unto the death.

The 10th verse says concerning Naboth, *"Stone him, that he may die."* So, Naboth paid with his life for his refusal to give or to sell his vineyard to Ahab. Are we willing to lay down our lives for that which God has given unto us? Esau sold his for a bowl of soup. Cain sold his for the price of a lamb. Jesus said, *"Unless you lose your life you cannot save it"* (St. Matt. 10:39). So, Naboth would die, stoned to death, but at the same time he would live forever.

The 16th verse says concerning Naboth's vineyard that Ahab rose up *"to take possession*

of it."

Then the 17th verse proclaims that *"The word of the Lord came to Elijah the Tishbite, saying."* The *"Word"* will be severe. In effect, it says, *"What you sow you will reap."* It should ever be understood that this is an unbreakable law with God. The only thing that can abate the stern judgment is repentance. The Lord Jesus Himself taught, *"And with what measure you mete, it shall be measured to you again"* (St. Matt. 7:2). The pronouncement of doom would be on both Ahab and Jezebel.

For the 25th verse states, *"But there was none like unto Ahab, which did sell himself to work wickedness in the sight of the Lord, whom Jezebel his wife stirred up."* Ahab was the most wicked king of Israel thus far. The wickedness of the kings was increasing in spite of the judgments of God. It is said of Jeroboam, the first king of the ten tribes, that he turned not from his evil and that he laid the foundation of sin for all his people (I Kings 13:33-34). It was said of Nadab, Baasha, and Elah, the 2nd, 3rd, and 4th kings of the ten tribes, that they walked in the way of Jeroboam and of Omri. It is said that he did worse than all the kings before him. And now, of Ahab it is stated that there was none like him this far. This program of ever-increasing wickedness continued until the whole nation had to be destroyed.

The thoughts of man's heart toward God are thoughts of unbelief, rebellion, and hatred, while the thoughts of God's heart toward man are thoughts of pity and love.

This chapter opens with Ahab refusing to listen to God's loving voice which had spoken to him so plainly in the remarkable victory given to him over the Syrians, but willingly listening to Jezebel's cruel voice prompting him to, perhaps, commit the blackest of his black crimes.

What Ahab had (Benhadad of the last chapter) he let go, and what he had not (the vineyard) he covets. Such is the heart of the unspiritual man.

And, yet, the 27th verse says, *"And it came to pass, when Ahab heard those words, that he rent his clothes, and put sackcloth upon his flesh, and fasted, and lay in sackcloth, and went softly."*

Ahab's humility and repentance was evidently sincere – at least for a time. God would not have spoken to a halfhearted repentance. It was evidently genuine, at least for a while, for God sent Elijah back to the king commending him and predicting mercy in his days.

In this scenario one can easily see that which God asks for and actually demands – humility. Repentance is seldom engaged in by the Church, simply because it is an ugly business. One has to admit wrongdoing. It seems that only the most destitute can do so. Of the myriad of man-made offices so predominate in the Church, one almost never hears of repentance from those who occupy these man-made positions. Why? First of all and for the most part, the positions mentioned, of whatever capacity, are man-made and, thereby, unscriptural. To play the political game in order to occupy one of these offices almost invariably precludes any type of humility. With some few exceptions only those who would desire such positions, do so because of pride. Consequently, pride does not lend itself toward repentance.

Actually, at this particular time repentance is such a rarity in the Church, that the Church really does not even know what to do with one who repents. Due to a plethora of man-made rules, repentance toward God is not even recognized, only repentance toward man. God will not accept repentance toward man simply because it is God Who has been offended. There is not a single Christian denomination in the world today (that I'm aware of) that will accept repentance toward God. Every single one that I'm aware of completely ignores the Word of God and makes up their own rules, which, by and large, deny repentance. Repentance is always toward God and never toward man. While it certainly may be true that repentance toward God may include the asking of forgiveness of man, still, all sin is in its conception directed toward God.

If one will notice, Ahab, who was one of the most wicked men alive, repented instantly, and God forgave instantly. Repentance is admitting the wrong, condemning oneself, and totally justifying God. It is completely turning around from the erroneous direction that one has been traveling. So, Ahab, at least for a short period of time, turned away from the devilish

NOTES

path that he had previously been traveling.

CHAPTER 22

The 1st verse says, *"And they continued three years without war between Syria and Israel."* This was because of the two great defeats that Syria had suffered at the hands of Israel and because of Ahab's repentance. But now, Ahab resorts to his old ways. Prosperity is often more dangerous to the Christian life than adversity. Outwardly, all was prosperous with Ahab – he had an ivory palace – but the secret of the Lord was with Elijah, and he knew the doom that was coming upon all this glory.

There was also an outward reformation. The prophets of Baal do not appear in this chapter, but, on the contrary, 400 professed prophets of Jehovah do.

The 2nd verse says that Jehoshaphat was asked to join and even sanction this religious effort, and the Bible says that he *"came down to the king of Isreal."* He did not only go down topographically but spiritually as well. It was the beginning of an alliance that caused Jehoshaphat and his ancestors many problems.

How so much better if Ahab had gone *"up"* to Jerusalem, admitted his terrible sin, and sacrificed at the great Altar before the Temple, and pleaded with God to have mercy upon his soul. That is the only alliance God will honor. This alliance that Jehoshaphat participated in was condemned by God from the beginning.

The 4th verse says concerning Jehoshaphat's participation, *"I am as thou art."* He publicly made such a statement but, in reality, Jehoshaphat was totally unlike Ahab.

In our failure we so often ask God to place His blessings upon such. So, Jehoshaphat says, *"Inquire, I pray thee, at the word of the Lord today."*

And then the 6th verse says, *"Then the king of Israel gathered the prophets together about four hundred men."* These prophets claimed to be of the Lord but were not. They characterize the myriad of those who call themselves prophets in Christendom today. There were precious few true prophets of God then; there are precious few true prophets of God now.

The falsity of these prophets was evident to Jehoshaphat, for he asks in the 7th verse, *"Is there not here a prophet of the Lord besides?"* The tragedy is that the Church today hardly knows the difference in the prophets who prophesy out of their own mind and those who speak, *"Thus saith the Lord."*

The 8th verse says concerning the request for a true prophet, *"There is yet one man, Micaiah the son of Imlah."* Elijah was alive at this time and had already given several messages to Ahab but was ignored or elsewhere. Admittedly, God does not have many, but He does have some few, *"yet one man."* Ahab says of him, *"But I hate him."* The prophet's job is a thankless task. He is seldom sent to bring good news but mostly bad. By and large, he is hated by not only the world, but a carnal church as well. Ahab says of him, *"For he doth not prophecy good concerning me, but evil."* There was no good that Micaiah could prophesy of Ahab.

Verses 10-14 proclaim a religious spectacle, in that *"all the prophets prophesied before them."* They even used the word (vs. 11), *"Thus saith the Lord."* But, in reality, the Lord had not said anything – at least not yet. Their messages were all positive, *"Go up and prosper,"* and *"The Lord shall deliver."* America, Canada, and the rest of the world are getting far too many messages like these. The major words in Christendom today are *"prosper"* and *"success."* These messages, as delivered then by false prophets, are delivered today by false prophets. The words should be *"repentance"* and *"repentance."*

The 13th verse says that as the prophet Micaiah came forth, that the threat was given, *"Let thy word, I pray thee, be like the word of one of them, and speak that which is good."*

The 14th verse says his answer was, *"As the Lord liveth, what the Lord saith unto me, that will I speak."* God, give us men that money cannot buy, who will not compromise their message, who will hear only what *"Thus saith the Lord,"* and be not fearful of delivering that Word to a lost and dying world.

As Micaiah stands before Ahab and Jehoshaphat and the 400 prophets of Baal, the 17th verse says, *"He said, I saw all Israel scat-*

NOTES

tered upon the hills." He also predicted the death of Ahab, *"As sheep that have not a shepherd."*

Verses 19-23 give us a portrayal of the spirit world seldom seen in the Bible.

The 19th verse says that the prophet Micaiah stated, *"I saw the Lord sitting on his throne."* He then told of *"the host of heaven standing by him."*

The 20th verse proclaims that the Lord asked a question, *"Who shall persuade Ahab?"*

Then strangely enough, the 21st verse says, *"And there came forth a spirit, and stood before the Lord, and said, I will persuade him."* This *"spirit"* was a *"lying spirit in the mouth of all his prophets"* (vs 22). The Lord gave him permission to do so. We learn several things from these passages:

1. According to this passage and Job 1, spirits of darkness, as well as Satan, have access at times to the throne of God.

2. This *"lying spirit"* would inspire these false prophets to prophesy the evil that was desired.

All of this reveals that God and His heavenly host, including demons on certain occasions, have conferences concerning the affairs of men on earth. This one had to do with only one part of the earth, one people on the earth, and one king in particular. He was in rebellion against God and in league with idol gods, and listening to their prophets instead of true prophets of Jehovah. So God permitted him to be deceived instead of saving him from such deception.

There was very little that could be done with such a stubborn man – one consecrated to demon worship and demon prophets. Micaiah had been sent to Ahab, but he would not receive Jehovah's instructions. In this case, II Thessalonians 2:8-12 is clearly illustrated. Because he and his associates had no love for the truth that they might be saved, *"God sent them a strong delusion, that they should believe a lie, that they might be damned who believed not the truth, but had pleasure in unrighteousness."*

The idea is that God permitted such deception to take the place of the rejected truth. If men will not have the truth, they will automatically have a substitute that will be more in harmony with their wicked ways for the time being.

Ahab would not have the truth and would not listen to Jehovah, but he would have lies and listen to his false prophets.

This passage simply gives an insight into the spirit realm showing that behind all human acts there are good and bad spirits seeking to carry out the respected wills of their masters. The Lord protects as long as He can, and when there is nothing else He can do to turn men from their wicked ways, error, and harm, He then permits demon spirits to deceive and cause them to go further astray – and in this case even unto death.

This indicates that many spirits in heaven have the right of hearing matters important enough to be discussed. Even demon spirits have access to some conferences (Job 1:6; 2:1; Rev. 12:9-12).

It is clear that all things here were on a volunteer basis. The Lord first inquired for someone willing to persuade Ahab. The talks were on a voluntary basis also. When an evil spirit volunteered, the Lord inquired as to how he would persuade Ahab and was told that he would be a lying spirit in the mouths of Ahab's prophets. Then the Lord gave permission.

Upon Micaiah's prophecy to Ahab, a prophecy that he did not desire to hear, Zedekiah, who seemed to be the leader of the 400 false prophets, *"smote Micaiah on the cheek"* (vs. 24).

The 27th verse says that Ahab demanded that they *"put Micaiah in the prison, and feed him with bread of affliction and with water of affliction, until I come in peace."*

The 28th verse proclaims Micaiah saying, *"If thou return at all in peace, the Lord hath not spoken by me."*

The 29th verse says, *"So the king of Israel and Jehoshaphat the king of Judah went up to Ramoth-Gilead."* This alliance with Ahab revealed a secret root of spiritual weakness in Jehoshaphat's heart, the fruit of which was disastrous to his children. Jehoshaphat did not help Ahab to return to truth, but Ahab helped Jehoshaphat to be unfaithful to Jehovah.

The bravery of Micaiah condemns the cowardice of Jehoshaphat. At this instance, Micaiah is the king and Jehoshaphat the slave. Jehoshaphat should have stepped down from

his throne, thrown his mantle around the courageous prophet, and valiantly taken his stand at his side.

There is no one more cowardly and contemptible than a Christan who walks with the religious world. Micaiah is led away to prison and to torture, and Jehoshaphat raises neither hand nor voice on his behalf.

Two royal fools at once meet in these verses. Jehoshaphat was a fool to go into battle at Ahab's suggestion in his royal robes, or at all for that matter. Ahab was a greater fool to propose to escape the Divine doom pronounced upon him by going into battle without his royal robes. God is not mocked; the arrow of death, winged by wrath both just and holy, pierces him. His dead body is brought to Samaria, his chariot is washed at a loathsome pool where harlots were accustomed to wash themselves, and dogs licked up his blood. Such was the sordid and horrible end of Ahab! For the 37th verse says, *"So the king died."* Contrast his end with that of his great enemy, Elijah: The one mounts up to heaven in his chariot; the other goes down to death from his chariot.

God loved Ahab and sought to save him again and again, but all in vain.

Jehoshaphat's reign in this book is disposed of in 10 verses, but 102 verses are devoted to it in II Chronicles. The meaning is this:

To the unspiritual eye, Jehoshaphat would have been uninteresting beside the glitter of Ahab. But to the spiritual eye, which is given in II Chronicles, Ahab is of no interest at all, with Jehoshaphat demanding God's attention.

The 43rd verse says of Jehoshaphat, *"Doing that which was right in the eyes of the Lord."* The Holy Spirit will be careful to delineate this direction of Jehoshaphat, but, at the same time, will use the word, *"nevertheless,"* to denote the *"high places that were not taken away."* These were places where *"the people offered and burnt incense."* There was to be only one place of sacrifice, and that was to be at the Temple in Jerusalem. So, it seems that the Holy Spirit was displeased with Jehoshaphat's actions in not taking away the high places. Evidently there were some reasons that Jehoshaphat would not do this; thereby, the Holy Spirit absolved him of much of the blame.

The 46th verse, however, says, *"And the remnant of the Sodomites, which remained in the days of his father Asa, he took out of the land."* There seems to be only a few *"Sodomites"* left; however, the Holy Spirit is quick to proclaim the fact that Jehoshaphat removed even these few. Too often the child of God is willing to allow *"the remnant"* of evil to remain. The Holy Spirit demands that everything that is evil be *"taken out."*

The 48th and 49th verses proclaim Jehoshaphat's alliance with Ahab's son, *"Ahaziah."* They had plans to go in union to *"Ophir for gold."* However, these ships were destroyed by a storm before they were used. They were broken by God because Jehoshaphat made a covenant with Ahaziah, Ahab's son. He would not permit Ahaziah to join him after that.

The 51st verse declares that Ahaziah began to reign over Israel in *"the seventeenth year of Jehoshaphat king of Judah."* The 17th year of Jehoshaphat was eight years before his death. Thus, it was in these eight years that Ahaziah and Jehoshaphat were in league to build a navy together. It was destroyed, and after that Jehoshaphat would not continue the agreement.

It seems that Jehoshaphat had a penchant to form some type of alliance with his evil, ungodly, northern neighbor, Israel. He failed at this time and again. And yet, the Scripture says, *"He turned not aside from it, doing that which was right in the eyes of the Lord."* How are the two reconciled?

None of these statements concerning kings or individuals *"doing right in the eyes of the Lord"* mean perfection on the part of the individual involved. There has never been a perfect man, only the Lord Jesus Christ.

What it does mean was that Jehoshaphat, despite his failures, had a heart that was toward God, desiring to do the will of the Lord. It would also seem that he was quick to repent, once understanding his wrong direction. For the 49th verse says concerning a continued alliance with *"Ahaziah," "But Jehoshaphat would not."*

Man looks on the outward appearance, but the Holy Spirit is especially careful to not only denote the spiritual strength but the spiritual

NOTES

weakness as well. At this point we must be quick to add, *"God looks on the heart."*

THE
BOOK OF II KINGS

CHAPTER 1

Verse 1 says, *"Then Moab rebelled against Israel after the death of Ahab."* The word *"then"* indicates the book is a continuation of I Kings. The two books were one up to the time of the Septuagint translators in the 3rd Century B.C. It was then that the book of Kings was divided into two sections.

Moab had been subdued by David (II Sam. 8:2; 23:20), and after the division of the kingdom, it passed to the ten-tribe kingdom. Moabites were greatly oppressed by Omri and Ahab, and on the death of the latter, Mesha, king of Moab, rebelled and gained independence. The Moabite stone discovered in 1868 at Dibon in Moab is revealing. The writing is in ancient Hebrew characters down to the time of 140 B.C. when it was replaced by modern square characters in use today.

According to the stone, Mesha, son of Chemosh-Meleck, king of Moab of Dibon, saw his desire upon his enemies after Omri, and Ahab had oppressed them for many days. It tells of his victories at Ataroth, Kerioth, Nebo, Jahaz, and other places. It gives all credit to Chemosh, national god of Moab for past defeats and slavery to Israel, because he was angry, and it gives the god credit for victories won after this.

Verse 2 tells of *"Ahaziah"* the son of Ahab, king of Israel, who *"was sick."* It also says that he *"sent messengers, and said unto them, Go inquire of Baal-zebub the god of Ekron whether I shall recover of this disease."*

The 3rd verse says, *"But the angel of the*

NOTES

Lord said to Elijah." The question was to be addressed to Ahaziah, *"Is it not because there is not a God in Israel that ye go to inquire of Baal-zebub?"*

The Jews changed the name to *"Beel-zebub,"* lord of the dung hill (Matt. 12:24). This god is the prince of idols and idolatry, the worst and chief of all wickedness.

Ahaziah therefore cast away the last remnant of faith in the salvation afforded by the Lord and believed in by the Patriarchs of Israel, and consulted a foreign oracle as if the voice of God were silent in his own country.

By and large, the sin of the modern Church is little different from the sin of Ahaziah. Having opted for the humanistic, even atheistic fallacy of psychology, it has, by and large, forsaken the God of the Bible. It has tried to cover its sin by labeling its foray into modernism with the term *"Christian psychology."* However, such does not exist. Psychology is not a true science; its various methods of treatment are worthy of a Roman circus. It has its roots in atheism, evolution, and humanism. It is the total opposite of the Bible. *"Christian psychology,"* so-called, is no different whatsoever from any other type of psychology. The name *"Christian"* is given to it only to fool a gullible Christian public who has, as well, by and large, forsaken the Bible. Christians are thereby lulled into spiritual sleep, thinking that *"Christian psychology"* offers a body of learning that is different from secular psychology. It does not.

In the Church this farce goes under the guise of *"all truth is God's truth."* The meaning is that *"if it is truth it must come from God."* However, let it be ever stated that truth is not a philosophy, it is a person, and that person is the

NOTES

Lord Jesus Christ. The Scriptures tell us that *"Jesus is truth, the Holy Spirit is truth, and the Word is truth"* (St. John 14:6; 17:17; I John 5:6). The Word of God claims to hold the answer to all of man's spiritual problems. Simon Peter said this: *"According as his divine power hath given unto us all things that pertain unto life and godliness, through the knowledge of him that hath called us to glory and virtue"* (II Pet. 1:3).

Many *"Christian psychologists"* are claiming that humanity is now facing spiritual problems and difficulties that the Bible does not address itself to. That is a lie and blasphemy as well.

For a Christian who professes to serve God and claims that the Lord Jesus Christ is the Saviour of mankind to resort to a psychologist is the same as Ahaziah appealing to Baal-zebub, for demon spirits are the instigators of both.

The Word of God and prayer are almost foreign entities in much of the modern Church. It little believes that God delivers and sets the captive free.

The denominational world by denying the power of God opted for humanistic psychology years ago. The Pentecostal and Charismatic world has followed suit.

The 4th verse says, *"Now therefore thus saith the Lord."* The answer will be given concerning Baal-zebub and all other gods, including psychology, *"But shalt surely die."* Sadly, spiritual death reigns in the modern Church just as surely as it reigned in ancient Israel.

Verses 9 through 16 portray to the seeking reader that which God demands of those who would come to Him. Too many approach God with the same arrogant demands as the first two captains who were sent after Elijah. Each had 50 soldiers with him. The Scripture says in the 12th verse, *"And the fire of God came down from heaven, and consumed him and his fifty."* With the advent of the modern faith movement, much of the Church has lost its fear of God. Because of this erroneous teaching, many look at God as a glorified bellhop ready to do our bidding at the snap of our fingers. As death reigned then for these arrogant acts, spiritual death reigns now as well.

The 13th verse proclaims, *"And the third captain of fifty went up, and came and fell on his knees before Elijah."* The Church has, by and large, forgotten the broken, humble contrition of a seeking soul crying to God for mercy and help.

As well, the *"little god"* syndrome of the modern Charismatic movement has no scriptural validity, and, in fact, is instigated by the same demon spirits that would promote Baal-zebub, for all false doctrine is instigated and inspired by demon spirits.

The 15th verse proclaims these words, *"And the angel of the Lord said unto Elijah."* He once again proclaimed to Ahaziah, *"Is it not because there is no God in Israel to inquire of his Word?"* (vs. 16). God give us modern-day Elijahs who will stand up to the Satan-inspired false doctrines that plague the modern Church and will proclaim, *"Thus saith the Lord."* The cry today in the Church is *"unity,"* which means to embrace all. The *"unity"* message is false doctrine as well, inspired by demon spirits. There is one criteria and only one, *"To the law and to the testimony: if they speak not according to this Word, it is because there is no light in them"* (Isa. 8:20).

CHAPTER 2

Elisha, since called of God, had now been with Elijah for approximately 10 years. What a training ground this provided, and it was orchestrated by the Holy Spirit.

The method of training provided by the Holy Spirit, which is little adhered to in the world of theological education, is the method here provided regarding Elisha and Elijah. The Holy Spirit desired that Elisha catch Elijah's spirit. He wanted Elisha to learn by first-hand observation His methods in the life of Elijah. Consequently, the mighty moving and power of the Holy Spirit that functioned in Elijah would now function in Elisha. This is God's way. As stated, it is rarely practiced in theological education.

The main purpose of theological study is to learn the Bible and to "catch the spirit" of someone who God has laid His hand on. Anything else regarding the work of God is of little consequence. Too often students attend Bible colleges, sitting under teachers who have precious little of the call of God within their lives. Worse still, there is no one, most often, at these particular schools who has been touched mightily by the Holy Spirit so that the student might catch the vision, the flame, and the spirit of the person in question. This is God's way in both the Old and New Testaments.

Jesus gathered around Him 12 disciples as well as the 70. They learned not only what He taught them, but what He gave to them through His spirit as well.

In the Early Church, the Apostle Paul gathered individuals around him who would catch his spirit. They then went out and built churches and touched the hearts and lives of multitudes.

I again want to emphasize that this is God's method. It will work. Actually, it is the only thing that will work.

Verse 1 says, *"And it came to pass, when the Lord would take up Elijah into heaven by a whirlwind."* By revelation it seems that it was known that the Lord would take Elijah, and that by one of the most grandiose methods in the history of man. The Scripture says, *"That Elijah went with Elisha from Gilgal."* (This was not the Gilgal close to Jericho that contained Joshua's headquarters when Israel came into the Promise Land, but another Gilgal that was close to Shiloh in Samaria.)

In verses 2 - 6 we see what it takes for a person to have the power of God within his life.

The second verse says that Elisha told Elijah to *"tarry here,"* that *"as the Lord liveth and as thy soul liveth, I will not leave thee."* The most important thing in Elisha's life was sticking close to Elijah. This is where the anointing resided. Therefore, this is where Elisha wanted to be. As well, he knew that this day Elijah would be translated. And there was a request burning in his heart, instigated by the Holy Spirit, that he would ask of Elijah. Therefore, he will not leave Elijah's side.

Today, millions ask the question, "what church should I attend?" Or "what preacher should I listen to?" Or, "what denomination should I belong to?" The answer is simple. Follow that which is anointed by the Holy

NOTES

Spirit. This is where the LIFE of the spirit resides, and yet precious few seem to desire this place. But this is exactly the place where Elisha wanted to be. The latter part of the sixth verse says, *"And they two went on."*

There have never been many who will pay the price for the miracle working power of God. Verses 7 and 8 delineate this sad truth. For verse 7 says concerning some 50 men of the sons of the prophets that *"they stood to view afar off."* Why were they not with Elijah and Elisha? They were not with these two because as future verses proclaim, *"They were unbelievers."*

In this scenario it is possible to see the complexion of the modern Church. Only a precious few desire to be where the anointing is. The majority *"view afar off."*

The eighth verse proclaims Elijah dividing the waters of Jordan, as it says he *"smote the waters,"* and then *"they were divided hither and thither."* However, the Scripture says that *"they two went over on dry ground,"* speaking of Elijah and Elisha. Why did not the *"50 men of the sons of the prophets"* follow as well? As stated, they were unbelievers, as is most of the Church.

The ninth verse proclaims Elijah requesting of Elisha, *"Ask what I shall do for thee, before I be taken away from thee?"* What a question! That question is asked of the whole Church. The answer in the last few years has been very revealing: money, fame, prestige, influence, recognition, approval, dominion, and more. Precious few have answered as Elisha. *"Let a double portion of thy spirit be upon me."* Actually, Elisha was asking for the portion of the firstborn. Elijah responded, *"Thou hast asked a hard thing."* The word *"hard"* means, *"thou hast made a great claim."* It expresses the greatness of the appetite of the heart of Elisha for spiritual power. In other words, Elijah's response, *"a hard thing,"* was in actuality an approval of Elisha's request. He would then continue this spirit that Elisha had been functioning in from the very beginning, *"if thou see me,"* speaking of his coming translation. Elisha's faith that had remained so very close thus far would have little difficulty in the remainder of the distance.

The 11th verse says, *"As they still went on,*

and talked." What was the gist of the conversation? The some ten years of instruction were now at an end. Elijah was ready to go; Elisha was ready to carry on. And then the Scripture says, *"Behold,"* or *"Suddenly."* And then it states, *"A chariot of fire, and horses of fire."* This quote "fire" was the fire of the Holy Spirit. It covered the chariot and the horses (yes, there are spirit horses in heaven). The Scripture says, *"And parted them both asunder,"* but not in a negative sort of way. The Scripture reads, *"Elijah went up by a whirlwind into heaven."* And the 12th verse blessedly states, *"And Elisha saw it."* Hallelujah! So now he would receive the double portion. His answer was, *"My father, my father, the chariot of Israel, and the horsemen thereof."* What did he mean by this statement?

He meant that this had been the strength of Israel - not its mighty army, not its splendor, but in this prophet, Elijah. Likewise, the light of any nation is the Gospel that it preaches, and the one who preaches it. Actually, this same word would be said of Elisha shortly before he died.

By faith Elisha knew that the request had been granted because *"he took hold of his own clothes, and rent them in two pieces,"* meaning he was no longer the learner but the prophet.

For the 13th verse says, *"He took up also the mantle of Elijah that fell from him."* This quote, *"mantle,"* was a sort of cape that went around Elijah's shoulders and now was on Elisha's. The burden of the Church is that if there is one who wears the mantle, too often there is no one to pass it on to. Yes, there are many "prophets," but very few Elishas.

The unbelief of *"fifty men of the sons of the prophets"* becomes very obvious as verses 16 through 18 proclaim the unbelief as to Elijah's destination. They had been witnesses of Elijah's translation and, as well, the first miracle of Elisha. They even testified that the Spirit of Elijah now rested upon Elisha, but they did not believe that he had been translated, even though they had seen it with their own eyes. The 17th verse states, *"They sought three days, but found him not."* This kind which makes up the vast majority of the modern Church affects the Kingdom of God none at all. They drive back no darkness; they bring no light. They

open no Jordans, even though they decorate its banks. Much of their energy is spent in trying to disprove the miracles of God. It is amazing that the far greater majority of the Church is only involved in religion and not in God at all. Therefore, they really do not know Him, only a little about Him.

Verses 19 through 22 record the great Gospel plan of salvation.

Verse 19 proclaims the men of Jericho saying to Elisha, *"The situation of this city is pleasant, as my lord seeth: but the water is naught, and the ground barren."* Jericho is the city of the curse, and by God at that, simply because of its heathen worship in the days of Joshua. As well, the world is cursed because of its sin. In fact, it could be, as Jericho, a pleasant place. But instead the water is poisoned and the ground barren.

The 20th verse proclaims Elisha saying, *"Bring me a new cruse."* This is symbolic of the sinless body of the Lord Jesus Christ. The "salt" in it - a type of the incorruptible Word of God that in its plenitude dwelt in Him, was the vehicle of this great healing power.

The 21st verse says he should *"cast the salt in there,"* speaking of the poisoned spring of waters. The only answer for a sin-cursed world and its poisoned springs is the Word of God. There is no other answer. That's the reason it is imperative that this great and glorious Gospel of Jesus Christ be taken to the whole world. There is no other answer. The Word of God is not one answer; it is the only answer. And to that the Bible says, *"Thus saith the Lord."* And then He states, *"I have healed these waters."* He alone can heal the broken heart; can set the captive free; can recover sight to the blind; can set at liberty them that are bruised; can preach the acceptable year of the Lord. Only Jesus! *"There shall not be from thence any more death or barren land."* There's a spring bubbling out of the ground in Jericho not far from the old ruins that is said to be this very spring. The waters are still pure, clean, and sweet. There is no more *"death or barren land."* As well, during the days of the Millennial Reign after Jesus comes back, there will be *"no more death or barren land"* on the entirety of planet Earth. However, the answer is Jesus, and Jesus, and Jesus - the only answer for a hurting world. One can put Mohammed in these waters and there will be no healing, or Karl Marx, or Buddha, or Sigmund Freud, or any other man who has ever lived for that matter - only Jesus.

The 23rd verse says, *"There came forth little children out of the city, and mocked him."* The words, *"little children"* are probably an unfortunate translation. The Hebrew word is *"na'ar."* The same word was used of Isaac when he was 28 years old, and of Joseph when he was 39 years old. So these individuals were infidel young men of Bethel who were worshipers of the golden calf instead of Jehovah. The words *"bald head"* do not necessarily mean that Elisha had no hair; it could have signified a worthless fellow. At any rate, it was a term of contempt. Here it was equal to blasphemy of God, for these individuals were mocking Elisha as a prophet of Jehovah, in contemptuous allusion to the translation of Elijah, which they no doubt denied and made fun of. The idea seems to be: *"go up* (be translated) *like Elijah, you worthless fellow!"*

Whenever the 24th verse says, *"and cursed them in the name of the Lord,"* it had nothing to do with profanity, but was a proclamation of their lost condition. Then it says, *"two she bears out of the wood, and tare forty and two children of them."*

Verses 19 through 25 portray both sides of the Spirit of God. Those who will go to Him for help, asking for relief from their difficult problems, will experience the *"healing of the Lord."*

Likewise those who mock and ridicule the Lord will suffer righteous judgment. Every human being should heed these two examples, for they portray God exactly as He is.

CHAPTER 3

The 1st verse says, *"Now Jehoram the son of Ahab began to reign over Israel in Samaria."*

The 2nd verse says, *"And he wrought evil in the sight of the Lord."* However, the Holy Spirit said that his evil was not as pronounced as his father Ahab or his mother Jezebel, for the Holy Spirit pointed out, *"for he put away the image of Baal that his father had made."* But then in

NOTES

the 3rd verse the Holy Spirit says, *"Nevertheless he cleaved unto the sins of Jeroboam."* *"Sin"* principally means the substitution of a god other than the Lord Jesus, and *"holiness"* means fidelity to that God and Saviour. Any sin that a person may commit, be it a *"sin of passion"* or a *"sin of pride,"* is the substitution of another god in the place of the Lord Jesus Christ. As Christians, we fail to equate our sin with the idol worship of Israel, such as Baal or Chemosh. We picture in our minds Israel of old kneeling down to these heathenistic idols, and congratulate ourselves on our great consecration, in that we are far more spiritually enlightened. However, any sin, be it pride, lust, jealousy, or lying, is the substitution of another god in the place of the Lord Jesus Christ. Our *"sin"* is just as hideous in the eyes of God as the sins of Israel of old. John said, *"Little children, keep yourselves from idols"* (I John 5:21).

The incurable insubjection of the natural will, even in a Christian, to the Word of the Lord is seen in Jehoshaphat. In spite of two severe lessons from God, he, for the third time, unites with the religious world in a *"laudable"* enterprise.

1. He joined Ahab to recover Ramoth, nearly losing his life, and was sharply rebuked by the prophet Jehu.

2. He united with Ahab's son Ahaziah in ship building, but his ships were broken.

3. Now he unites with Jehoram, Ahaziah's brother, in making war upon their neighbors, with the result that once again he nearly loses his life.

So the 7th verse says that Jehoram requested of Jehoshaphat his help against the king of Moab. Jehoshaphat agreed by saying, *"I am as thou art, my people as thy people."* An old sin is an easy sin. As with every Christian it is easier for Satan to maneuver us down a path well traveled.

The 9th verse proclaims the difficulties of their *"seven days journey,"* for the Scripture says there was no water for the host.

The 10th verse proclaims that Jehoram, even though an idol worshipper, blamed *"the Lord"* for their predicament.

The 11th verse proclaims Jehoshaphat's reliance upon the Lord for he said, *"Is there*

NOTES

not here a prophet of the Lord?" The answer was forthcoming, *"Here is Elisha, the son of Shaphat."* And then a strange statement of identification was made about Elisha. It says, *"which poured water on the hands of Elijah."* To pour water on the hands of anyone is the action of a servant. Public and brilliant ministries must be preceded by humble and hidden ones. This is God's method of teaching disciples. He desires ones who He will use mightily in the future to pour water on the hands of those who are being mightily used at the present. If they cannot function in this realm of servant-ministry, then they will not be fit for use at a later time.

Elisha, in no uncertain terms, told Jehoram to *"get thee to the prophets of thy father, and to the prophets of thy mother"* (verse 13).

In the 14th verse Elisha further said, *"Were it not that I regard the presence of Jehoshaphat king of Judah, I would not look toward thee, nor see thee."* There is no way that a church, a denomination, a fellowship, a city, or a country can understand how blessed it is if God's anointed is in their midst. Only because of Jehoshaphat would God move. So, in effect, Jehoram and the king of Edom owed their lives to Jehoshaphat. Denominations or fellowships owe their blessing to men of God who are among them, and not to a man-made hierarchy. Entire nations owe their blessing to men of God in their midst, of whom they have little or no knowledge at all. Even for ten righteous God would have spared Sodom and Gomorrah. How much does He withhold judgment from people, cities, and even nations because of the child of God in their midst?

The 15th verse proclaims the anointing, *"but now bring me a minstrel."* Most probably these were musicians who came, sang and played the Psalms. When this happened, the Scripture says, *"The hand of the Lord came upon him"* - meaning Elisha. Likewise, when David played, the evil spirits that troubled Saul would depart from him. Why? Because of the anointing of the Holy Spirit on David and upon the musicians mentioned in this passage. There are seven major religions in the world of which Christianity is one (Christianity is really not a religion, but a relationship with a person,

Christ Jesus.) Of these seven major religions there is only one that has a song book, and that is Christianity. The others have nothing to sing about. The worship of the Lord in singing and music elicits joy, praise, and spiritual wellbeing. The first thing that goes when a church or a people lose their way is the song. The first thing that comes when people start to draw closer to God is the song.

In the dryness of this wilderness the Lord says, *"Make this valley full of ditches."* Faith obeys, even though this was the dry season when rain was unlikely. However, *"with God, all things are possible."* No matter how sinful or wicked the situation, no matter how dry the spiritual desert, faith, despite the scoffing, will *"make the valley full of ditches."* They will preach the Word of God, and the Word will not return void. It will accomplish its intended purpose. Just because there is no water in the ditch, yet, do not sell it short.

For the 17th verse says, *"Thus saith the Lord."* He then proclaimed, *"You will not see wind, nor shall you see rain,"* and then the pronouncement was made, *"Yet that valley shall be filled with water that you may drink."* Most of the time the Church cannot believe what it cannot see. The writer of Hebrews said that faith is the *"evidence of things not seen."*

The announcement must have had a startling effect from the statement made in the 18th verse, *"and this is but a light thing in the sight of the Lord."* Unbelief always looks at the circumstances; faith looks to God. Not only would there be plenty of water, but *"He will deliver the Moabites also into your hand."*

The 20th verse says, *"Behold, there came water by the way of Edom."* Where did the water come from? Maybe there was a flash flood in the mountains that brought the water down to Edom. But however it came, the Scripture says, *"The country was filled with water."*

The water was not from their general locality because the 22nd verse says, *"And the sun shone upon the water."* With the sun shining upon the water the Moabites would *"see the water as red as blood."*

They would think that Israel was smitten, and, consequently, would cry, *"To the spoil."* Likewise, when Satan saw the ground at the foot of Calvary red with blood, he thought surely that heaven was totally defeated; instead it was Satan's defeat.

Likewise, as the 24th verse says, *"The Israelites rose up and smote the Moabites."* Every victory is won by the Blood of Jesus Christ. The Cross is the answer to man's ills. There is no other. Sadly, the Church little believes anymore in the effectiveness of the Blood of Jesus Christ.

In desperation the king of Moab took *"his eldest son"* to *"offer him for a burnt offering upon the wall."* Religion is a horrid business; it demands the physical and spiritual death of its victims, while Christianity demands death to the carnal man that the spiritual man may reign. Upon the offering up of the eldest son of the king of Moab to the *"fire-god,"* terror strikes these superstitious Israelites - and they hastened back to their own land.

This chapter is somewhat strange, and the reason is because God has no part in idolatrous Israel. He only comes to their rescue because of Jehoshaphat, even though Jehoshaphat is out of the will of God at the time. In this we see the greatness of God's mercy and compassion - even when we are out of His will and wrongly directed.

—■—

CHAPTER 4

The Word of God is full of pictures, types, allegories, and symbols of God's great plan and design for the human race. God, being omniscient (all-knowing) and omnipotent (all-powerful), is able to weave His plan into circumstances, happenings, prophets, people, and nations. Consequently, Moses' ministry was a type of the Law. Joshua's ministry was a type of Grace. As well, Elijah's ministry was a type of the Law, with Elisha's ministry being a type of Grace. The sufficiency of grace in relation to man's folly and need appears in the miracles of Elisha. He is a saviour to Israel and a healer to the Gentiles.

In the previous chapter living water is abundantly given to the three kings who are about to perish. This same grace now grants an overflowing provision of wealth to the

NOTES

impoverished widow. The succeeding miracles strikingly prove that *"grace upon grace"* is the measure that hastens to the help of needy and sinful men. These miracles characterize Elisha's ministry. The thirsty are refreshed; the poor and needy provided for; the childless made the joyful mother of children; the dead raised to life; the broken-hearted bound up; the hungry healed and fed; the lepers cleansed; and victory given over all the power of the enemy. Such is Christ to broken humanity.

Verse 1 says, *"Thy servant my husband is dead."* There is some intimation that this woman's husband, one of the sons of the prophets, was known to Elisha. In these passages we will see a striking miracle that is brought about. However, the question must be asked, *"If God would do such a thing as multiply the oil, why did not he heal this woman's husband?"* Christians have pondered these questions from the very beginning. The answers are probably as varied as the people involved. God performs miracles in response to faith and His will. Faith will never override the will of God. Was it the will of God for this man to die at this time? We have to conclude that it was. And, yet, the will of God is never arbitrary. It is much of the time based on variables, in other words, the faith, consecration, and purpose of the individual involved. Sometimes it is obvious, and sometimes as in Job's case it is not obvious.

The woman says, *"And the creditor is come to take unto him my two sons to be bondmen."*

Many a Christian is like this widow. There is depression, poverty, and bondage in the life, instead of joy, wealth, and liberty. Even though the death of this man may have been the will of God (according to circumstances), still, the plight of this home was not God's will. It is God's will that we be in health and prosper, even as our soul doth prosper (III John 2).

Satan never ceases in his efforts to deprive the child of God of his rightful inheritance in Christ Jesus.

In response to her request, Elisha asks her this question, *"Tell me, what hast thou in the house?"* (vs. 2). The question in being broadened can apply to us as well. It is as follows:

1. What we have in the house, which is the temple of the Holy Spirit, may be detrimental

to our walk with God and, thereby, hinders that which we can receive from God. Jesus would cleanse the Temple. Perhaps our Temple needs cleansing as well.

2. And, yet, what we have in the house as a child of God is the Holy Spirit. It is represented by the *"pot of oil."* Sadly, most Christians are using everything except the Holy Spirit - the pot of oil. The pot of oil, so lightly regarded by human wisdom or overlooked totally, as the rock in the case of Israel (Num. 20:8), responds at once when appealed to, and the house is filled with the *"life more abundant."*

The 3rd verse says, *"Even empty vessels; borrow not a few."* God can only fill that which is empty. Regrettably, most of Christendom is *"full"* but not with the Spirit of God. They are *"full"* of man's ingenuity, human wisdom, carnality, and the machinery of modern religion. Those are a lot of the things *"in the house"* that we need to clean out in order that we may be filled.

The Church is ever satisfied to subsist on meager spiritual rations, when, if we would provide more empty vessels, God would fill them up - *"borrow not a few."*

The 4th verse says, *"Shut the door upon thee and upon thy sons."* This speaks of faith. They would, no doubt, begin to praise God for that which the prophet had told them. The empty vessels littered the room. They began to praise God. Then the 5th verse says, *"She poured out."* It must ever be understood that the Holy Spirit is inexhaustible. As long as there are *"empty vessels,"* it will continue to *"pour out."* I repeat again, "The Church must empty itself of all that which is not of the Word in order that the Holy Spirit may fill us."

The 6th verse says as soon as *"there was not a vessel more, the oil stayed."*

The 7th verse says that the Holy Spirit would *"pay the debt, and live thou and thy children of the rest."* *Life* for the child of God is the *"Holy Spirit"* and nothing else. Ezekiel said, *"Every thing shall live whither the river (Holy Spirit) cometh"* (Ezek. 47:9).

Verses 8 through 37 as well proclaim another great miracle and much instruction.

The 8th verse says, *"Where was a great woman."* This woman was wealthy, yet she did not allow her riches to lift her up in pride as

happens to so many, but rather it drew her closer to God.

The 10th verse says that she would *"make a little chamber"* (a room) for Elisha that he might use as often as he desired.

The 13th verse proclaims Elisha saying, *"Thou hast been careful for us with all this care; what is to be done for thee?"* In this passage we are plainly told that God honors and rewards, even greatly so, every good thing done for Him. The Word of God is replete with these many promises. How so few Christians take full advantage of it. This woman's kindness would reap her tremendous benefits. How much more could we be blessed if we did more for God? What a question! *"What is to be done for thee?"*

The 14th verse says, *"And Gehazi answered, Verily she hath no child, and her husband is old."*

The 16th verse implies that the answer is instant, *"About this season according to the time of life, thou shalt embrace a son."* When God gives, He gives that which is impossible to be obtained from any other source. He gives us what we cannot give ourselves, and what others cannot give to us. His gifts are always miraculous. So, He would give the woman and her husband a child.

Satan always attempts to destroy that which God has given. It takes faith not only to obtain from God what we desire but to keep that which God has given us. Sometimes it takes more faith to keep it than to receive it.

The child had a sun stroke, and the 20th verse says, *"and then died."*

When the 8th verse uses the term, *"a great woman,"* it not only was speaking of her wealth but, no doubt, of her great faith. For the 21st verse says, *"And laid him on the bed of the man of God."* Her faith was saying, *"God gave him to me, and Satan cannot take him from me."* Her response of faith was tremendous.

As she goes to Mount Carmel to Elisha, he sees her *"afar off"* and sends Gehazi to meet her, asking the question, *"Is it well?"* - and even of the child. Her answer is the answer of faith, *"It is well."* Circumstances said that her child was then dead; faith said, *"It is well."* Everything the eye could see and the hand could touch pointed toward death, but faith continued to say, *"It is well."* When will the Church realize this great truth.

We are too quick to praise the devil with our complaints, our murmurings and our faithlessness. This woman's answer praised God. It is not easy to stare death in the face or to look at wreckage, and in the face of circumstances say, *"It is well."*

The 27th verse not only shows her earnest entreatment, but, as well, her humility. *"When she came to the man of God to the hill, she caught him by the feet."* Gehazi, who represents religion, *"thrusts her away,"* as religion must. But Elisha, who represents grace, says, *"Let her alone."* Oh, that somehow we could turn from Gehazi to Elisha!

Elisha then tells Gehazi to go ahead and *"lay my staff upon the face of the child"* (vs. 29). However, the seeking soul says, *"I will not leave thee"* (vs. 30). So Elisha must follow her.

The 31st verse says that, *"Gehazi passed on before them, and laid the staff upon the face of the child."* The prophet of God will teach her that a dead staff laid upon a dead face cannot give life. Religious ceremonies however scriptural are paralyzed in the presence of death. Religion has never set anyone free; ceremony has never set anyone free. We must ever understand that the Church has no saving power. All saving power comes through Jesus Christ directly to the person in need.

The 34th verse proclaims the love and the grace represented in Elisha. In effect, his life will become the life of the child. The Church desires to win the world without dirtying its hands. It cannot be done. Our *"mouth must be upon his mouth,"* and our *"eyes upon his eyes,"* and our *"hands upon his hands."* Jesus did not save mankind by passing a decree; He saved man by becoming one with man. The Church can only give the salvation that God has afforded by becoming one with man as well.

The 35th verse says, *"The child opened his eyes."*

The 38th verse records the *"dearth (famine) in the land."* Elisha offered God's provision and said, *"Set on the great pot,"* for surely, the Gospel occupies a great container.

However, one man was not satisfied with that which the Lord had provided, so the 39th verse says that he went out into the *"field to gather herbs."* And the herbs were from a *"wild vine."* He came with a *"lap full"* and *"shred them into the pot of pottage."* These "herbs of the wild vine" represents all false doctrine.

The 40th verse proclaims that as they began to eat someone cried, *"Oh thou man of God, there is death in the pot."* The herbs were poison - all false doctrine brings death. Sadly, much doctrine is unscriptural.

This is so representative of the table that was richly spread in the Garden of Eden, but, dissatisfied with its abundance, man added to it, and thus brought death upon himself and upon his children. Men are ever trying to add to the Word of God; it will only bring death. When will the Church realize this?

In the 41st verse Elisha says, *"Then bring meal."* The meal is a type of the Word of God. The only answer for the *"death in the pot"* is the *"Word of God."* When will we quit trying to take away or add to the Word of God? Every time it brings "death."

Dying men in their despair turn to God for salvation, and once more Divine grace responds to their need.

Jesus, the Bread of Life, came down from heaven, descended into death; by the sacrifice of Himself He destroyed death, and in His death sinners find life.

Elisha commands, *"Pour out for the people, that they may eat."* These poisoned and dying men in order to be saved had only to believe Elisha's testimony that there was life in the pottage, and take and eat. So, death-doomed men believing God's testimony that whosoever believeth upon His beloved Son shall never die, accept that testimony, trust Christ, and find life in Him.

The 42nd verse, as well, proclaims another miracle. It says, *"Brought the man of God bread of the firstfruits, twenty loaves of barley."* These 20 loaves of barley and *"full ears of corn"* represent *"the Word of God and the Lord Jesus Christ."* It is said, *"Give unto the people, that they may eat."*

The servant is astonished and says, *"What, should I sit this before an hundred men?"*

Men judge Jesus Christ the same as the prophet's servant judged the barley cakes. They do not believe that He can satisfy the hunger of their hearts. They think it is impossible to satisfy their hunger with what He is and provides. However, all that the world offers can never satisfy man's hunger. Jesus alone can satisfy and give even more. For the 43rd verse says, *"For thus saith the Lord, they shall eat, and shall leave thereof."*

So, there was plenty, and there was even some left. And the 44th verse says, *"According to the Word of the Lord."*

The world looks at Jesus Christ, thinks of Him as a peasant or a prophet at best. Therefore, they refuse to accept Him, never realizing that He is the Son of God Who alone can satisfy the hunger of the human heart. As someone has said, "The soul of man is so big that only God can fill it up."

CHAPTER 5

This chapter is without a doubt one of the most beautiful chapters of grace and salvation found in the entirety of the Word of God. It will tell us the following:

1. What man is.
2. Who God is.
3. How to reach God.

The 1st verse says, *"Now Naaman, captain of the host of the king of Syria."* This man at this particular time was probably the most powerful military captain in the world. The Scripture also says he was *"a great man"* and *"honourable,"* and *"a mighty man in valour."* But then it says, *"He was a leper."*

Leprosy in the Old Testament was a type of the spiritual condition of unregenerate man. Leprosy would gradually eat away the vitals, ultimately resulting in death; there was no cure for it. Likewise, sin will eat away the vitals resulting in spiritual death. There is no earthly cure for sin, as well.

Most of the world would think of Naaman's greatness, his honor, and his valour, and would surmise that this would bring salvation. It did not then; it does not now. The Holy Spirit is telling us that irrespective of man's achievements, wealth, power, and position, still, he is an unregenerate, loathsome sinner, on his way to eternal darkness, and none of these great

NOTES

things will save him, for he is *"a leper."* This was Naaman's condition; it is likewise the condition of the world today.

Verse 2 says, *"Brought away captive out of the land of Israel a little maid."* This *"little maid"* will figure prominently in history. The Holy Spirit does not even give her name, however, her testimony will affect nations. How so much this should give encouragement to every single child of God. Satan is very adept at telling individuals that their life is of no consequence regarding the work of God. However, this girl even though a slave, would affect millions in a positive way by her testimony. Her tremendous accomplishment was that she was simply faithful.

It would have been very easy for her to have been bitter, morose, and angry toward God for Him allowing her to be taken captive away from her land and family, and made a slave in Syria. But she exhibited none of these evil traits. She retained her testimony. About the things she did not understand, she left in the hands of God.

When the time was right, the Holy Spirit gave her the opportunity of a lifetime. The 3rd verse says that she testified to Naaman's wife concerning his leprosy, *"Would God my Lord were with the prophet that is in Samaria! For he would recover him of his leprosy."* What a testimony this girl had. The whole of Israel had little faith in God, but this girl retained her testimony despite the circumstances. As well, millions were saying, "God does not perform miracles today, nor does He heal today." But this *"little maid"* retained her faith in God. Hallelujah!

The 5th verse proclaims Naaman doing what men ever attempt to do – pay God for what He does. So he would take with him *"ten talents of silver, and six thousand pieces of gold, and more."* It was equal to approximately three million dollars. Nevertheless, the Scripture says, *"Come, buy wine and milk without money and without price"* (Isaiah 55:1).

Verses 6 and 7 proclaim the protocol regarding the king of Israel used by Naaman. Concerning the healing of Naaman's leprosy, the king of Israel says, *"Am I God?"*

Some part of the Christian world in its *"kingdom now"* teaching is attempting to convert the world by means that are not scriptural. Their claim is that Christianity will gradually take over the world, bringing in good government, and then welcome Jesus Christ back. The Word of God teaches the very opposite. Paul said, *"In the last days perilous times shall come"* (II Tim. 3:1). The world is not going to get better; it is going to get worse. It will culminate not in governments of the world becoming Christian, but, rather, in the governments of the world joining in with the Antichrist. Society cannot be saved, for society is doomed. Actually, we are not told to save society, but to save men out of society. It is the business of the Church to proclaim the Gospel of Jesus Christ to lost humanity (St. Mark 16:15). This world will only be changed when Jesus Christ Himself comes back. One cannot have a kingdom without a King, and that King is Jesus (Rev. 19).

So, the idea that God works from nation to nation by appointed government leaders, symbolizing some type of *"pseudo Christian kingdom age philosophy"* is fallacious indeed. There is nothing in the Word of God that even remotely hints at such. God calls men to preach the Gospel. That and that alone is His method of evangelization.

Verses 7 and 8 proclaim the two directions, side by side, flowing the opposite of each other. The present day *"kingdom now"* teaching is ensconced in the 7th verse. As the king of Israel proclaimed his inability to *"recover a man of his leprosy,"* likewise, the *"kingdom now"* teaching will recover no one from their sin.

However, the 8th verse proclaims the very opposite. It portrays a God-called prophet by the name of Elisha, and, in effect, he says, *"Bring him to me,"* and *"He shall know that there is a prophet in Israel."* Hallelujah!

The 9th verse proclaims Naaman coming to the house of Elisha; it says, *"and stood at the door."* The Lord will know exactly how to appeal to this man. He will touch him in the area of his greatest sin – pride.

Elisha did not even come out to meet him, but, instead, *"sent a messenger unto him, saying, Go and wash in Jordan seven times, and thy flesh shall come again to thee, and thou shall be clean."*

The 11th verse proclaims the fury of

NOTES

Naaman, for it says he *"was wroth."* Naaman was a powerful man and warranted more than this curt dismissal. Entire nations trembled at his presence. He was the mightiest military chieftain on the face of the earth. Who does this Elisha think he is?

All of this is pride which is the crowning sin of the human race. It is the reason that most never receive from God. Every individual must come to the Lord the same way, the great, the rich, the poor, the small – they are all the same to the Lord, poor, wretched lepers. Still, man does not see himself in this capacity. Irrespective of how loathsome he may be, he still sees himself as mostly good, when, in reality, there is no good present. Regardless of man's financial or political position, in the eyes of God he is a loathsome sinner, with no capabilities of saving himself. It is very difficult for man to see himself in this condition. That's the reason that Naaman was *"wroth."* That's the reason the Pharisees killed Christ. They could not see themselves as defiled, wretched, and in desperate need of a Saviour. Surely their good works were sufficient. The modern Church is no better; its crowning need is repentance – not so much for its evil works, but for its good works, which, in reality, are not so good after all.

The 12th verse proclaims Naaman's answer, *"Are not Abana and Pharpar, rivers of Damascus, better than all the waters of Israel?"* True, the two rivers mentioned by Naaman were two of the most beautiful, clear, and clean streams in the world. The waters were crystal clear, whereas Jordan was basically muddy. So, the exclamation of Naaman is the same the world over.

The Jordan river was a type of Calvary. Modern man, as well as ancient man, has ever wondered at its veracity. Surely, man's rivers are of much greater quality. Education, wealth, culture, refinement – all are better than the muddy waters of Jordan. The world has always stumbled over Calvary. The reasons are obvious. The world refuses to admit its evil, claiming that there is only a slight maladjustment which can be easily rectified by the waters of *"Abana and Pharpar."* Nevertheless, man's problem is not maladjustment; man's problem is that he is a leper – and there is no cure for leprosy. So Naaman *"went away in a rage."* Man has ever raged at God's solution, because man's problem is pride.

The 13th verse says, *"And his servants came near, and spake unto him."* Thank God for the servants. The man, even though a heathen, was a great preacher. He said, *"If the prophet had bid thee to do some great thing."* Men are ever asking "what can I do to earn my salvation?" Most of the world is trying to buy its salvation by its good works. All will fail for two reasons:

1. The price is more than man can ever hope to pay.

2. It has already been paid by the precious Blood of Christ. So, the proclamation is *"Wash, and be clean."*

The Scripture is very brief, but oh so explicit. It says, *"Then went he down, and dipped himself seven times in Jordan."* Not two times or even six times, but *"seven times."* Why seven? There was nothing magic about the number, only that it denoted God's total and complete redemption. In other words, a *"finished work."* Salvation makes a man whole. It addresses itself to every need of the human heart. Nothing is left undone. It satisfies. The Scripture denotes his complete healing, *"His flesh came again like unto the flesh of a little child, and he was clean."* How many tens of millions have dipped in the waters of Calvary and have seen all of their sins washed away? Man is spiritually dirty. This *"dirt" cannot be cleansed by the "soap"* of this world, but only by the precious Blood of Jesus Christ.

Naaman now retraces his steps, going from Jordan back to Elisha's house in Samaria. The 15th verse says, *"And he returned to the man of God."* However, there is a vast difference in Naaman at this time. The pride is gone. The leprosy is gone. The scene must have been quite impressive, for it says, *"All his company."* No doubt, there were many soldiers with Naaman, even powerful government officials from Syria. And now they say, *"Behold, now I know that there is no God in all the earth, but in Israel."* Hallelujah! In the 4th chapter of Luke the Lord Jesus Christ will Himself refer to this moment. There were many lepers in Israel at this time. Why were they not healed? They were not healed because they would not believe God. They would not come to the prophet Elisha. Naaman came, and with much

difficulty, believed and received. You can come as well!

The 15th verse as well proclaims Naaman endeavoring to give an offering to Elisha. But the 16th verse proclaims Elisha's answer, *"I will receive none."* Why?

There is even some evidence that Elisha did receive offerings at other times. So, why not this time?

This entire episode was a picture portrayed by God of His grace. One cannot buy grace. Money or good works is not the coin of this realm. If Elisha had taken money, it would instantly have nullified the work of grace. It would have made a mockery of the Blood of Jesus Christ.

The 17th verse proclaims Naaman making a strange request, *"I pray thee, be given to thy servant two mules' burden of earth."* His reason for this was two-fold:

1. He knew the Lord of Israel was truly God and not these heathen idols. Therefore, he wanted a part of Israel with him in Syria.

2. He desired to offer *"burnt offerings"* to the Lord of Israel and felt that the soil of Syria was improper. Inasmuch as Israel was *"God's land,"* Naaman was far more theologically sound than we might at first realize.

At any rate, Elisha approved of his request and said, *"Go in peace."*

Verses 20 through 27 proclaim the efforts of Gehazi to change the great plan of salvation from *"the grace of God,"* to *"salvation by works."* It was met with severe and stern judgment, for Naaman's leprosy will now cleave to Gehazi. Was God cruel in doing this? No, God would have been cruel in not doing it.

Elisha says in the 27th verse, *"The leprosy therefore of Naaman shall cleave unto thee."*

By and large, the Church of today has turned the Grace of God into *"salvation by works."* It places the constitution and bylaws of various denominations on a par with or even superior to the Word of God. Whenever men leave the Word of God, regardless of their religiosity and good works, they have then nullified the Grace of God, and have as Paul wrote, *"fallen from grace"* (Gal. 5:4).

Gehazi's sin and his incurring of Naaman's leprosy is a type of man voiding the grace of God by "works salvation." His acceptance of money was, in effect, saying that salvation could be purchased. Likewise, any preacher, church, denomination, or individual who will add any stipulation to the Word of God or take away from it, has, in effect, *"fallen from grace."* Therefore, sadly, the majority of the Church world bases its salvation at least in part on *"works,"* and is, thereby, *"fallen from grace."*

———————— ■ ————————

CHAPTER 6

Verse 1 says, *"And the sons of the prophets said unto Elisha."* It seems here that Elisha had some connection with the *"sons of the prophets"* (school of the prophets). Their unbelief of chapter 2 seems to at least have given way to some faith. Prayerfully, their association with Elisha had done much to direct them toward the Lord. It is interesting that the Holy Spirit refers to them as *"sons of the prophets."* One can only be a prophet, an apostle, an evangelist, a pastor, or teacher if they are called by the Holy Spirit as such. If, in fact, the calling is there, then immeasurable benefit is awarded if they can associate with an Elisha. However, there is little record that God used these individuals in much capacity. They proposed larger quarters for their school.

The 2nd verse proclaims Elisha's answer, *"Go ye."* One requested of Elisha that he *"go with thy servants,"* and he answered, *"I will go."* Of all the things they studied in this *"school of the prophets,"* their association with Elisha was by far their greatest instruction. The following proclaims the reason why.

In their preparation of the building of the school, the 5th verse says, *"The axe head fell into the water,"* and then the man cries, *"Alas, master! for it was borrowed."*

To modern society, the axe head seems an insignificant matter. In that day it represented a sizeable investment, and, thereby, a heavy loss.

The 6th verse proclaims Elisha asking, *"Where fell it?"* Then it says, *"He cut down a stick, and cast in thither."* The *"stick"* no matter how crude, was symbolic of the Cross of Jesus Christ. For when he did this, the Scrip-

NOTES

ture says, *"And the iron did swim."* What lessons do we learn from this?

1. The most important lesson is the power of Calvary. Every single blessing received by the child of God comes through Calvary. Healing comes through Calvary; miracles come through Calvary; direction and leading of the Holy Spirit come through Calvary. Without Calvary there would be no miracles, no healing, and no redemption. So, the *"stick"* as crude as it is, represents the Cross being applied to the problem. The modern Church has, by and large, set the Cross aside. Sadly, this applies to the Pentecostals and the Charismatics as well. Of course, there are exceptions, but precious few. The modern Church member rarely takes his problems to the Cross; he takes them to the psychologist, the counselor, or the therapist whose body of learning is basically from humanistic and even atheistic sources. Yes, the *"stick"* is crude. Paul said to the Jews it was a *"stumbling block,"* and unto the Greeks *"foolishness."* But then he said, *"But unto them which are called, both Jews and Greeks, Christ the power of God, and the wisdom of God"* (I Cor. 1:23-24). About the only thing that one can say for the *"stick"* is, *"it works."* And it might be quickly added, *"nothing else does."*

2. It was important that the students not only study about the power of God, but that they see the power of God demonstrated. This lesson was a thousand times more lasting than any other. In this episode the Holy Spirit is *"teaching"* them His way. Now, their learning would not all be in the head, but some would be in the heart.

The student who *"put out his hand, and took it,"* referring to the axe head that did swim, would never forget this powerful demonstration of the Holy Spirit. Now, the Lord was no longer philosophical, He was personal. How so much this is needed in our present "Bible colleges." It is sad, but one educator said recently, "At most Bible colleges you can get a degree in most anything except Bible."

The 8th verse says, *"Then the king of Syria warred against Israel."* This was some time, even possibly some years, after the healing of Naaman.

Despite Israel's spiritual degeneracy, the Lord helped them through Elisha. For the 9th verse says, *"And the man of God sent unto the king of Israel."* He disclosed the king of Syria's plans three or more times.

The king thought he had a traitor in his midst, but the 12th verse says, *"None, my lord, oh king: but Elisha, the prophet that is in Israel, telleth the king of Israel the words that thou speakest in thy bedchamber."* Evidently, Elisha made no secret of the instructions that he was giving to the king of Israel concerning the king of Syria. It seems from this that the king of Syria should have been convicted in his heart for his misdeeds, but he was not. It is amazing at man's ability to resist God. In his stupidity, he sends his army to take Elisha.

The 15th verse says, *"Behold, an host compassed the city both with horses and chariots."* It is ironic that an entire army was sent to take just one man - and failed. Elisha's servant asks, *"Alas, my master! How shall we do?"*

What has happened and will follow is a tremendous lesson for the child of God.

First of all, the Holy Spirit is telling us not to be daunted by that which appears on the surface. If the Christian walks in the *"flesh,"* he will allow this *"host"* of opposition to stagger him. However, if he walks in the *"Spirit,"* he will understand what is really going on. The trouble with the world, and most Christians, is that they know what is happening, but they don't know what's going on.

The 16th verse proclaims what was *"going on."* Elisha said, *"Fear not."* Over 300 times in the Word of God the Holy Spirit tells us, *"Fear not."* Fear, John wrote, is caused by a *"lack of love."* For he said, *"Perfect love casteth out fear"* (I John 4:18). If we truly love the Lord with an unflawed love, we will know that our Heavenly Father will not allow anything to happen to us but that which is good for us. Admittedly, it may not seem good at the present time but will prove so in the future.

And then Elisha answers, *"For they that be with us are more than they that be with them."* What a statement! In the Spirit Elisha could see this; however, his servant could not. So in the 17th verse it says, *"Elisha prayed, and said, Lord, I pray thee, open his eyes, that he may see."* What he saw was *"the mountain was full of horses and chariots of fire round about Elisha."* Hallelujah!

The Holy Spirit allowed this to happen that you and I may understand by faith that we are surrounded by such, even though not seen by the natural eye. What an encouragement!

Of course the question begs to be asked that if this is true with every child of God (and it is), then how could anything bad ever happen to any Christian?

At times Christians walk in faithlessness or even sin and disobedience. If such happens (and often it does), God will then allow certain adversaries to come through these *"surrounding chariots"* (I Kings 11:23). It will be God's chastisement, never in a punitive sense (destructive), but in a corrective and redemptive sense.

The army of Syria little knew what they were up against. All they saw was one prophet and his servant. Little did they realize they were facing *"horses and chariots of fire round about Elisha."* The 18th verse says, *"Elisha prayed unto the Lord, and said, Smite this people, I pray thee, with blindness."* According to Elisha's prayer, they were smitten.

The Bible student lacking in spiritual maturity may blanch somewhat at the Lord smiting them *"with blindness."* Nevertheless, it must be clearly understood that the same Gospel that softens, also hardens. As well, that which opens blinded eyes, can close open eyes. The Gospel always has a powerful effect on anyone, whether it be positive or negative. The effect is according to the response of the individual. But, still, a great work of grace would be afforded to this army.

The 19th verse proclaims Elisha saying to the blind Syrian army, *"I will bring you to the man, whom you seek."* No, it was not a lie. Their intention was to stop Elisha because he was hindering them from getting to the king of Israel. The king of Israel was the one who they were really seeking.

The 20th verse proclaims Elisha praying for the healing of this army, and they were healed.

The 22nd verse pictures a great work of grace. The king of Israel would kill them. However, Elisha proclaims the love of God to them. The 22nd verse says that he said, *"Set bread and water before them, that they may eat and drink and go to their master."*

Then the 23rd verse says, *"So the bands of Syria came no more into the land of Israel.*

This is a beautiful portrayal of the great work of grace. This is God's method. However, if men spurn His grace, He will ultimately deal with them in judgment - Divine retribution.

The 24th verse says, *"That Benhadad king of Syria gathered all his host, and went up, and besieged Samaria."* No, there is no contradiction between verses 23 and verses 24. The 23rd verse is speaking of military escapades regarding *"the king of Syria"* of verse 8. Between verses 23 and 24 several years pass, and there is a new regime in Syria. This would never have happened had Ahab put Benhadad to death when he was in his power. The sufferings recorded in this passage would have been avoided. This siege and its horrors fulfilled the prophecy then made to Ahab by the rebuking prophet (I Kings 20:31-34).

The 25th verse records *"a great famine in Samaria"* as a result of the Syrian army besieging the city.

The siege had become so severe that the people of Israel, God's chosen people, had resorted to cannibalism. Verse 29 says, *"So we boiled my son and did eat him."* Moses had predicted that this would happen if the people turned their back upon God (Deut. 28:53-57). So now, in all of its attendant horror, it is happening.

The 31st verse proclaims Jehoram, the king of Israel, blaming Elisha for Israel's predicament. He wanted to kill Elisha, so he said, *"If the head of Elisha the son of Shaphat shall stand on him this day."* The king could have solved the entire problem with proper repentance; instead, he blamed the man of God. Men seldom, for all their difficulties, put the blame where it rightfully belongs, on themselves.

Verses 32 and 33 proclaim the Spirit of God informing Elisha of the king's threat. Not long before, the Syrian king had tried to take Elisha, and now the king of Israel endeavors to do the same. Both will fail.

At times the Lord protects His prophets with great intervention and power. At other times He allows them to be killed (Matt. 23:37).

NOTES

CHAPTER 7

This chapter provides much instruction regarding the circumstances of even the most afflicted child of God.

The 1st verse says, *"Then Elisha said, Hear ye the word of the Lord: Thus saith the Lord, tomorrow about this time shall a measure of fine flour be sold for a shekel."* How amazing is the grace that, in response to the murderous unbelief of the king's heart and the scornful unbelief of the courtier's, promised such an abundance of food, and so soon that it was to be had almost for nothing. A righteous judgment, however, forbids its enjoyment to the unbelieving captain.

It is strange considering the woeful condition of Samaria with the people even resorting to cannibalism that verse 2 declares one of the government officials upon hearing the words of Elisha exclaimed, *"Behold, if the Lord would make windows in heaven, might this thing be?"* Elisha said to him, *"Thou shalt see it with thine eyes, but thou shalt not eat thereof."* The reward of unbelief would be death, as the reward of unbelief is always death.

Verse 3 says, *"And there were four leprous men at the entering in of the gate."* Leprosy in the Old Testament was a type of sin. It's horrid desperation was such that in the eyes of Israel, a leper was hopeless. How many Christians find themselves in such a perilous condition, a condition, we might add, so disastrous that there is no help from any quarter except God. Nevertheless, no condition is such that God cannot change it. And now they utter the great positive question of faith, *"Why sit we here until we die?"* In these very words you can feel faith. How many Christians have given up? How many have quit? Faith demands action. So, these four lepers act. Faith in God is the most powerful commodity on the face of the earth or in heaven, for that matter. God wants His people to seek His will and to believe Him. The greatest single thing that a Christian can do is to believe God.

So, the lepers go into the camp of the Syrians and the 5th verse says, *"Behold, there was no man there."* Why?

Verse 6 says, *"For the Lord had made the host of the Syrians to hear a noise of chariots."* The Syrians thought some powerful army from a hired nation was coming upon them and fled. How easy it is for the Lord to do anything. How so important it is for the Christian not to limit God, and, sadly, how so much we do limit Him. The following verses proclaim an abundance that the lepers found.

The 9th verse says, *"This day is a day of good tidings."* The sun had set the day before on a day of disaster for Samaria, but the sun would now rise on one of the greatest days of blessing in her history. Faith in God would do this thing.

In type, Samaria is a picture of the world with its hunger, starvation, pain, and agony. The lepers, as pitiful as they were, are a type of preachers of the Gospel of good news. The abundance that they found is a type of the Gospel of Jesus Christ that can satisfy the hunger and the craving of a starving world.

The lepers, in effect, said, "We must not hold our peace." Tragically, too many preachers are holding their peace when they ought to be shouting it from the housetops. How could four lepers deliver Israel? How can a few poor preachers deliver a starving dying world? Really, the lepers or the preachers within themselves cannot. However, the abundance of that which God has provided can. We must not hold our peace; we must herald this "good news" far and wide.

Verses 17 through 20 record the death of the man who in verse 2 had scoffed at Elisha's pronouncement. The 20th verse says, *"For the people trode upon him in the gate, and he died."* God hates unbelief just as much as He loves faith.

CHAPTER 8

As the 7th chapter expressed a time of tremendous blessing, the 8th chapter expresses a time of tremendous judgment. The 1st verse says, *"For the Lord hath called for a famine, and it shall also come upon the land seven*

years." This famine was to last twice as long as the one in the days of Elijah. The woman whose son Elisha had restored to life was told to go elsewhere to *"sojourn."* Because of this woman's faithfulness, we can see the continual hand of the Lord in His protection of her. Famines in the Old Testament were called by God because of a nation's great sin. Rain would be withheld; other disasters would plague the land, all resulting in famine because of sin. When this happened, the famine would come upon the just and the unjust.

I believe that one can say with certainty that due to the fall of man as is outlined at the beginning of Genesis, and Satan's becoming the prince of the powers of the air and the god of this world, natural disasters are mostly his handiwork. The storm that came up, as recorded in Matthew 8 when Jesus was asleep in the boat, certainly was not caused by God. It was caused by Satan. Yet, some so-called natural disasters are ordained by the Lord because of great sin on the part of the people. The 3rd verse jumps ahead seven years to the end of the famine and speaks of the Shunammite woman coming back from the land of the Philistines to Israel. There is a connection with this and the following verse.

Verse 4 speaks of Gehazi talking to the king of Israel who had said, *"Tell me, I pray thee, all the great things that Elisha hath done."* Yet, all of these great things had not served the purpose to cause this king or Israel to repent. The king desired to hear the story of miracles, but nothing must be said of righteousness, temperance, or judgment to come. Chapter 5 records Gehazi being stricken with leprosy. So, the account of the healing of Naaman may not have been given in chronological order. In other words, it is possible that it happened after this incident. If that is incorrect, then possibly Gehazi was healed. However, there is no scriptural record of such.

Verse 5 records Gehazi's telling the story of the Shunammite woman's son being raised from the dead. As he is relating this experience, the woman in question comes into the palace. And Gehazi says, *"Oh king, this is the woman."* She is there to request of the king that something be done to restore her land and property that was taken from her when she had fled the famine some seven years earlier.

The 6th verse proclaims the king saying, *"Restore all that was hers."* The Holy Spirit went to great lengths in relating this for the expressed purpose of showing God's watchful care over this woman. The Lord had her come to the palace at exactly the same time that Gehazi was telling her own story. For the good deed she had done to the Lord's prophet in building him an apartment onto her house some ten years earlier, the Lord would continue to bless her. Our gifts to Him are so fleeting. His blessing to us is everlasting.

The balance of this chapter shows God's dealing with nations that did not particularly belong to Him. Yet, they bordered Israel, and, therefore, God designed direction. Anyone who comes in contact with God's children enters at least in some measure into God's dealings with them. The working of God with His children is so powerful that it affects all whom they come in contact with. As to how it affects them, this is dependent upon their actions toward the Christian.

So the 7th verse says, *"And Elisha came to Damascus."*

The king of Syria, Benhadad, was sick. So the 8th verse says, *"The king said unto Hazael, Take a present in thine hand, and go, meet the man of God, and inquire of the Lord by him, saying, Shall I recover of this disease?"* It's amazing how much faith that a wicked king like Benhadad would have in Elisha, and in the Lord as well, and still not repent of his wrongdoing.

So the 9th verse says that Hazael took quite a present, *"forty camels' burden."* Whether Elisha received or accepted this gift is not known.

The 10th verse proclaims God's message in a twofold manner:

A. He could recover, but he won't.

B. Because Hazael will kill him. (This is the same Hazael who, some 20 years earlier the Lord had told Elijah would be king over Syria (I Kings 19:18.)

The 15th verse says that Hazael murdered Benhadad and says as well, *"And Hazael reigned in his stead."* God, by foreknowledge some 20 years earlier, informed Elijah that Hazael would be king. Of course, the Lord had nothing

NOTES

to do with Hazael's actions, but for His own reasons would allow Benhadad's death.

The 11th verse says, *"And the man of God wept,* meaning Elisha, because of *"the evil that thou wilt do unto the children of Israel* (vs. 12).

Because of Israel's great sin, the Lord allowed depraved Hazael to become king. This should inform us that our consecration to God, or our rebellion against God, determine many things that will happen to us.

Verses 16-19 proclaim the results of Jehoshaphat's sin in his constant union with Ahab and his family.

The 18th verse says of *"Jehoram the son of Jehoshaphat,"* that *"he walked in the way of the kings of Israel, as did the house of Ahab: For the daughter of Ahab was his wife."* And then the Holy Spirit says, *"He did evil in the sight of the Lord."*

Jehoram's great evil demanded punishment, but the 19th verse says, *"Yet the Lord would not destroy Judah for David his servant's sake."* And then it says, *"He promised him to give him alway a light and to his children."* The light here refers to a king and a kingdom according to the Davidic Covenant of II Samuel 7. A natural consequence of Jehoram's apostasy would have been the destruction of the house of David and the starting of another dynasty, as in the case of Jeroboam (I Kings 14:10), but the promises to David prevented this, and Jehoram was punished in other ways.

One of those punishments is recorded in verses 20-22, *"In his days Edom revolted from under the hand of Judah."* The 22nd verse says, *"Libnah revolted at the same time."*

Verses 25-29 record the continued evil of Ahaziah the 6th king of Judah. The 27th verse says, *"And he walked in the way of the house of Ahab."* And then the Holy Spirit proclaims, *"For he was the son-in-law of the house of Ahab."* Jehoshaphat's sin of *"unity"* would take its deadly toll for years to come.

One German saint was asked the question as he lay on his deathbed, "What do you think you have learned in living for God?" The answer was instant, "I have learned how horrible that sin is."

CHAPTER 9

Verse 1 says, *"And Elisha the prophet called one of the children of the prophets, and said . . ."* The judgment of the house of Ahab now commences. Jehu is the Divine instrument chosen to execute that judgment. He illustrates how zealous an unconverted man can be for God when it suits his personal interests and ambitions to attack national evils. What he did on behalf of righteousness he did well and with energy. But his zeal was carnal; he utterly destroyed Baal but permitted the golden calves to exist. This fact alone shows that his heart was a stranger to Divine faith. He was an instrument of God's wrath, carrying out God's will at least in the destruction of Ahab and his family. But he never had a personal knowledge of God. So now the second part of Elijah's prophecy those years earlier concerning the anointing of Jehu as king over Israel comes to pass (I Kings 19:16).

The 3rd verse says, *"Then take the box of oil, and pour it on his head, and say, Thus saith the Lord, I have anointed thee king over Israel."* Ordinarily they would laugh at *"the young man the prophet"* (verse 4), but personal interest causes Jehu to instantly accept. He has a room full of witnesses to verify his claim. The message was three-fold.

1. *"Thus saith the Lord God of Israel, I have anointed thee king over the people of the Lord, even over Israel."* They were called *"the people of the Lord"* even though they were in deep sin. This did not mean they were saved, only that God was still dealing with them, attempting to bring them to a place of repentance (verse 6).

2. *"And thou shalt smite the house of Ahab thy master"* (verse 7). He meant "the whole house of Ahab." He would cast the dead body of the king upon the very piece of ground which the vineyard of Naboth formerly occupied, thereby attesting the fulfillment of the prophecy (verse 24-26).

3. *"And the dogs shall eat Jezebel in the portion of Jezreel"* (verse 10).

The word *"whoredoms"* in verse 22 means *"idolatries"*, and is to be so understood

NOTES

throughout the books of the Old Testament except where the context clearly states otherwise. Nevertheless, much of the idol worship included whoredoms, fornication, and immorality of every evil nature.

The 36th verse proclaims the fulfillment of the awful prophecy by *"Elijah the Tishbite, saying, In the portion of Jezreel shall dogs eat the flesh of Jezebel."* Jezebel is thrown down; the horses are splashed with her blood; the dogs turned from the skull and hands and feet that had designed and executed such abominations, and no tomb but infamy perpetuates her memory.

Of all the so-called holy books in the world, the Bible is the only one that contains prophecy. Actually, a little over a third of the Bible is prophecy, with about a third being history, and about a third being instruction. There are simple laws that one should follow on interpretation of prophecy. Assuming that God is desirous of speaking to man in mysteries, many believe erroneously that prophecy cannot be understood before it is fulfilled, and, furthermore, that it is given in lofty figures of speech with so many illusions to manners, customs, times, and places unknown to the average reader that it cannot be understood without special help. The regrettable thing is that along with this concept of prophecy, some add further complications by overlooking simple facts which, if taken literally as written, would make a clear understanding possible.

There are 10 rules that one should follow in order to understand prophecy:

1. Forget the idea that God seeks to bewilder man or hide from him the very revelation He wished to give him, or that He desires to make it mysterious.

2. Give the same meaning to the words of prophecy that you give to the words of history - the same meaning to those in the Bible that you give to words used by men otherwise. The belief that the language of the Bible has a different and mystical meaning and cannot be understood in a literal sense is wrong.

3. Do not change the literal meaning of prophecy or any other Scripture to a spiritual or symbolic meaning, such as making the earthquake of the sixth seal (Rev. 6:12-17) to be the breaking up of society, the darkening of the

planets (Rev. 8:12) to be spiritual darkness, or the creatures out of the pit (Rev. 9) to be false religions.

4. Do not seek to find hidden meanings in the words of Scripture, such as making the USA in JerUSAlem represent the United States.

5. Believe that prophecy can be understood as it is without any changes or additions, and recognize it simply as a record beforehand of what is to happen sometime after its utterance. Actually, prophecy is history in advance and should be understood as a future, historical record.

6. Forget the idea that prophecy must be fulfilled before it can be understood. All true prophecy is as clear before its predictions take place as after their fulfillment.

7. Do not interpret God's own interpretation of any symbol or prophecy, or change His meaning from that which is plainly and obviously clear.

8. Give only one meaning to a passage, the plain literal meaning, unless it is made clear that a double meaning should be understood. There are two main laws regarding prophecy: *"The law of double reference,"* and *"The law of prophetic perspective."* The latter allows the giving of future events as if they were continuous and successive, when there may be thousands of years between them. This must be taken into consideration in such passages as Isaiah 61:1-3, quoted in Luke 4:17-20. Christ repeated only the portion of that prophecy which was fulfilled in His day.

9. Recognize a prophet primarily as a preacher of righteousness, for this is the key to the interpretation of many prophecies. He was not only a fore-teller, but a forth-teller - a speaker for God to rebuke, instruct, and correct.

10. One main thing to be aware of in all prophecy is the history of the writer, his times, and the circumstances under which he spoke or wrote, the purpose of his predictions, the people to whom he wrote, and the subject of his message. With these in mind and a knowledge of the manners, customs, idioms, and expressions of the age and people he was associated with, there should be no misunderstanding about anything a prophet has written.

NOTES

CHAPTER 10

Verse 1 says, *"And Ahab had seventy sons in Samaria."* By the large number of sons that Ahab had, which would have included grandsons and great-grandsons as well, Ahab showed he was doing all within his power to continue his dynasty (the word *"sons"* includes grandsons and great-grandsons, inasmuch as there is no Hebrew word for these designations). Jezreel, the scene of the cruel murder of Naboth and his sons, becomes the theater of the just wrath of God upon the murderers. Here may be learned something of how God regards sin and judges it, and if in longsuffering grace he delays the judgment, this longsuffering heightens the terror of the Divine anger. In harmony with this, how appalling is the expression in the Book of Revelation, *"the wrath of the Lamb"* - not the wrath of the lion, but *"the wrath of the Lamb."*

The 16th verse proclaims the determination of Jehu, for it says, *"And see my zeal for the Lord."* Man can be very zealous for God as Jehu was and yet not know Him, but this zeal only goes as far as it suits personal interests or religious and political pursuits. The zeal of such persons only lasts so long as it suits their purposes.

The 28th verse proclaims, *"Thus Jehu destroyed Baal out of Israel."*

The 29th verse says concerning the sins of Jeroboam, *"Jehu departed not from among them, to wit, the golden calves."*

The 30th verse proclaims the Lord rewarding Jehu for *"executing that which is right in mine eyes."* The reward that the Lord promised him was in the permitting of his children to continue as rulers in Israel to the fourth generation. These four generations were:

1. Jehoahaz (13:1-9)
2. Joash (13:10-25; 14-16)
3. Jeroboam II (14:16-29)
4. Zechariah (14:28-29; 15:8-12)

The 31st verse says sadly of Jehu, *"Took no heed to walk in the law of the Lord God of Israel with all his heart."* At this stage the Lord began to cut off Israel and would finish it as is recorded in chapter 17. For the 32nd verse says, *"In those days the Lord began to cut Israel short."*

What a golden opportunity Jehu had to incur the blessings of God, but he had no real love for the Lord. Everything he did only suited himself. How many politicians in America today only pay lip-service to God or even in some small measure to His Word, but their heart is far from Him? Sadly, almost the entirety of business, professional, and government structure in America falls into this category. Is it possible that at this time God is beginning to cut America and Canada short?

CHAPTER 11

Once more, we see the terrible effects of Jehoshaphat's sin in attempting to align himself with idolatrous Israel.

The 1st verse says, *"And when Athaliah the mother of Ahaziah saw that her son was dead, she arose and destroyed all the seed royal."*

This woman, *"Athaliah,"* was the only ruling queen of both Judah and Israel. She was the granddaughter of Omri (II Chron. 22:2), and the daughter of Ahab and Jezebel. The marriage between Jehoram, king of Judah, and Athaliah, daughter of Jezebel, was part of Satan's grand design to introduce idolatry into Judah so that Athaliah might do for Judah what Jezebel did for Israel.

Jehoshaphat began his reign by strengthening himself against Israel (II Chron. 17:1), but he married his son to the idolatrous daughter of Israel's worst rulers, Ahab and Jezebel. The leaven worked morally and politically and was used by Satan in an effort to destroy the *"Seed of the woman,"* the Messiah, whom he was determined to prevent from coming into the world.

Jehoram, king of Judah, began this destruction by killing all his brethren (II Chron. 21:4). The Arabians came and destroyed all his sons except for the youngest, Azariah (II Chron. 22:1). Then Athaliah killed all the sons of Ahaziah on his death, or thought she did, but the infant Joash was rescued, being the

NOTES

only one left in the line of the coming Messiah.

Jehosheba, wife of Jehoiada, the high priest, was sister to the late king, and, thereby, aunt to the infant Joash. She must have been a woman of nerve and ability.

Verse 2 says, *"Took Joash the son of Ahaziah, and stole him from among the king's sons which were slain."* It was a courageous act on her part to enter such a slaughterhouse. It may be assumed that she did so to look with grief and horror upon her murdered nephews and cousins. The infant Joash lay among them apparently dead. She found him, however, still living, stole him and hid him.

Joash was hidden for nearly seven years, while the faithfulness of Jehovah's word hung upon the Divine preservation of the child's life.

Athaliah was one of the most evil women who ever lived. Imagine a woman killing her grandchildren and other close relatives as Athaliah did to further her political ambitions.

Verse 4 says, *"And the seventh year Jehoiada sent and fetched the rulers."* Jehoiada, the high priest, now saw his opportunity to overthrow this evil queen. So the 12th verse says, *"He brought forth the king's son, and put the crown upon him, and gave him the testimony."* (The testimony was a copy of the Law of Moses by which he should govern and mete out justice to the people.)

The facts related in this chapter illustrate past, present, and future prophecy. A false religious power (Athaliah) obtains the mastery; the true king is slain; his child is raised up from among the dead, then hidden for nearly seven years in the Temple of God. In the seventh year he comes forth; takes to himself his kingdom; the usurper is slain, peace reigns; and all the people rejoice.

This is Messianic history and promise. By wicked men Christ was crucified and slain; God raised Him from the dead; He is now hidden in heaven, the true Temple of God. In the morning of the seventh year, that is, the Millennium, He will appear and take unto Himself His great power which has already been given to Him but not yet exercised. He will then ascend the throne of Jehovah at Jerusalem and reign before his ancients gloriously, having cast out of His kingdom all things that cause stumbling and them that work iniquity.

The 3rd verse speaks of Athaliah reigning *"six years."* As the number of man is six, this number of years pictures what the apostle calls *"man's day,"* as contrasted with *"the day of the Lord."* As stated, the number 6 in the Bible is associated with man. Man was created on the 6th day; Goliath had 6 pieces of armour; 6 instruments formed Nebuchadnezar's band; and the name of Antichrist will be a computation of three sixes.

Verses 13-16 record the slaying of Athaliah, for the 16th verse says, *"And there was she slain."* Regarding spiritual matters in the life of the Christian, all that is foreign to the will of God in one's life must be slain. It must clearly be understood that the Christian cannot come to terms with sin, failure, or rebellion in any fashion.

The slaying of sin, however, cannot be brought about in the life of the Christian by personal effort, ambition, or consecration. It can only be brought about as we allow the Lord Jesus Christ to live within us to overcome this hard taskmaster. If sin in any form is allowed to remain, it will spread and destroy. It must be slain by the Lord Jesus Christ.

As well, verses 17-21 record the cleansing of the Land, for the 18th verse says, *"Went into the house of Baal, and break it down."* The major problem of the child of God, as with Israel, is idol worship. Paul says, *"My dearly beloved, flee from idols"* (I Cor. 10:14). John writes, *"Children, keep yourselves from idols"* (I John. 5:21). All sin is, in effect, idol worship. Any sin that the Christian may commit, in effect, becomes an idol in the place of the Lord Jesus Christ. For every sin there is a demon spirit instituting and promoting such. When we commit the sin, whatever it may be, in effect, that sin (demon spirit) takes the place of the Lord Jesus Christ within our lives, and, thereby, becomes our god. That's the reason that both Paul and John spoke of the horror of idol worship. How many Christians have a *"Baal"* in their lives?

Verses 17-21 proclaim revival. What is revival? Revival is not people being saved, as wonderful as that is. Neither is it believers going down the streets in demonstrations beating big drums, calling attention to their cause. But revival, rather, is Christians going back to

Calvary and allowing the Holy Spirit to *"clean out"* of their hearts and lives all jealousy, envy, malice, pride, lust, and others. In other words, idols.

The 20th verse says, *"And all the people of the land rejoiced."* Revival always brings rejoicing, not only in our own hearts and in the Church, but also in heaven. Too oftentimes the rejoicing of the present-day child of God rings empty. There can be no rejoicing as long as there are *"Baals"* in our lives. Instead, there should be weeping and repentance until our lives are cleaned up.

In this chapter Jehoiada is a type of the Holy Spirit. He fearlessly and faithfully pursues the righteous course until the will of God is carried out. Allow your *"Jehoiada"* to have His way within your heart and life. He will clean out the Temple, the city, and the land.

Contrasted with the 10th chapter, the 11th chapter proclaims Holy Ghost revival. The 10th chapter proclaims man's efforts at revival. It is superficial only. Jehu, a type of man, had no heart for God, so there could be no real revival. Jehoiada, a type of the Holy Spirit, is the only one who can truly bring Holy Ghost revival. Man's efforts at revival only serve the purpose of covering up the barrenness of their possession. The churches are full of such. Their machinery grinds unceasingly. When it ends, there is nothing to show for it.

However, when the Holy Spirit is allowed to have His way, He brings us back to Calvary, cleans up the spiritual debris within our lives, and restores us to spiritual health in the Father. God help us, for we need a Holy Ghost revival!

CHAPTER 12

The 2nd verse says, *"And Jehoash (Joash) did that which was right in the sight of the Lord all his days wherein Jehoiada the priest instructed him."* This means all the days of Jehoiada only, while he was alive to keep him from doing wrong, for when Jehoiada died at the age of 130 years, Joash (Jehoash) did evil in God's sight and brought judgment upon his people as well as himself. For this, God permitted a small band of Syrians to conquer a large army of Judah (II Chron. 24:14-27).

In likening Jehoiada to the Holy Spirit, one could say that as long as the Holy Spirit is there to lead, guide, and teach, then spiritual righteousness will be paramount. However, when the Holy Spirit is no longer there, or else ignored, spiritual declension sets in. By and large, Joash characterizes the modern day Church. It began by depending on the Holy Spirit, and then drifted away from the Spirit of God, going into deep sin.

Verse 3 says, *"But the high places were not taken away."*

This is repeated six times in the history of the kings. The term *"high places"* is found some 77 times; its first use being in connection with the worship of Baal (Num. 22:41). Israel was commanded by God to destroy all such places (Num. 33:52; Deut. 33:29). They are first mentioned in Israel in the reign of Solomon (I Kings 3:2-4), who built a large one himself (I Kings 11:7).

From Solomon's time forward they were numerous and continued throughout the time of most of the kings of Israel and Judah. They were removed in the reign of Hezekiah, 16th king of Judah, when all the groves were burned, the images broken, and the brazen serpent that Moses made was destroyed. They were built again by Manasseh, son of Hezekiah, and again destroyed by Josiah.

Why Jehoiada was not able to persuade Joash to destroy the high places is not known. Perhaps he tried and Joash refused. This type of worship was not normally idolatrous worship, but it was forbidden by God for many reasons; one, no doubt, was that it militated against the unity of the nation in that it favored a relapse to idolatry.

But most of all, there was to be one center of worship for Israel, as there is but one place of worship for the Christian, that is Calvary.

Verses 4-16 proclaim the repairing of the Temple. From the completion of the Temple in the 11th year of Solomon to the 23rd year of Joash was 153 years. By this time, no doubt, the wooden part of the building needed to be replaced. This time period would affect some of the stone work, also.

It seems that the money collected for the repair of the house of God was used by the priests for their own personal expenses. Without a doubt, the priests of the Lord for the past six years had been woefully neglected, despite their needs being many.

The 4th verse seems to imply that the priests were little considered, with all the funds being designated toward repair.

The 9th verse seems to imply that this problem had been solved. The various monies that came in for the normal carrying on of the priestly duties seemingly would continue to go to the priest, with a special *"chest"* being provided for money to be inserted for the Temple repairs.

CHAPTER 13

Verse 1 says, *"Jehoahaz the son of Jehu began to reign over Israel."*

Verse 2 records, *"And he did that which was evil in the sight of the Lord."*

Verse 3, *"And the anger of the Lord was kindled against Israel."*

These three verses describe very well the plight of man. Wherever he is, by and large, he *"does evil."* Consequently, the anger of the Lord is kindled. Out of all of God's creation, which consists of myriad of universes, it seems that only planet Earth is in a state of rebellion - hence, the anger of God. However, God's love is greater than His anger. In any number of ways He could have poured out judgment upon this planet, but, instead, He poured it out on His only Son, the Lord Jesus Christ. Such is God's love.

Verse 4 says, *"And Jehoahaz besought the Lord, and the Lord hearkened unto him."* It is remarkable how Jehovah was merciful and blessed His people whenever it was at all possible, sometimes helping evil kings in times of desperate need even though afterward they would not do right. Because it says, *"He saw the oppression of Israel."* Israel's sin had allowed the *"king of Syria to oppress them."* How much *"oppression"* do we encounter because of our sin? This one thing is clear.

Irrespective of what we have done or how bleak the situation, the only answer is, *"and Jehoahaz besought the Lord."*

This was about the only reason some of the kings of Israel sought God. Such was the history of Israel, more or less, from the very beginning. During a period of 450 years, God delivered them from servitude under nations around about. They would serve other gods and go into the greatest of sins until Jehovah would permit them to be defeated. Then in their distress they would call upon Him for mercy and deliverance, and He would raise up a deliverer to set them free again (Judges 6:1).

At times, they would serve God all the days of the deliverer, but when he died they would go into sin, be brought down as before, and call upon the Lord for help.

When wicked, evil Manasseh was in captivity and affliction, he prayed and God restored him (II Chron. 33:11-13). And so it was with several other kings who were in desperate trouble. There is no other refuge but God. There is no other anchor for the soul but the Lord.

For the 5th verse says, *"And the Lord gave Israel a Saviour."* The gift of Jehovah and the principle which turned away wrath and provided a Saviour was not the existence of any moral worthiness in Israel, for she had none, but the unconditional covenant made with Abraham, as stated in verse 23. In effect, it was *"for Abraham's sake,"* and then at times *"for David's sake,"* and then *"for Jonathan's sake.* All illustrate the principle of Ephesians 4:32, *"for Christ's sake."* This great principle of salvation gives all the glory to the Saviour and none to the person saved.

The 6th verse says, *"Nevertheless they departed not from the sins of the house of Jeroboam."* The fidelity with which the ten tribes clung to the worship of the golden calf, rebukes and instructs the Christian. It rebukes for, alas, how defective is the loyalty of even the most saintly person to Christ?

Over and over again, the gist of the test makes it clear that Jehovah Elohim is not a Divinity invented by the Israelites, as some think, for if that had been so, then they would have served him faithfully. But the fact that they were continually forsaking Him and turn-

NOTES

ing to idols, and that there was perpetual contention between them and God proves the testimony of the Bible that the God of Israel is God over all, blessed forever.

The 14th verse says, *"Now Elisha was fallen sick of his sickness whereof he died."* Elisha's ministry lasted for about 66 years. The first 20 years appeared to have been active years, closing with the anointing of Hazael. Then follows a long silence of about 45 years, and he now once more appears, very sick and dying. Some very dedicated Christians believe that true servants of God are never afflicted with sickness, nor can be because all sickness comes from the Devil. While it is certainly true that all sickness comes from the Devil as a result of the fall of man, still, due to the fact that we do not as of yet have glorified bodies, true servants of God and even mighty prophets such as Elisha ultimately fall sick and die of sickness.

Nevertheless, Elisha's sickness did not show a lack of faith on his part, just as sickness does not necessarily show a lack of faith on the part of modern prophets.

Elisha performed more miracles than any prophet in the Old Testament, so why could he not believe God for his own healing at the last?

Many men misunderstand the anointing of God upon one such as Elisha. The prophet did not use the anointing; the anointing used the prophet. Men today make the mistake of trying to use God, instead of God using them. That is basically the mistake of the modern Charismatic movement.

Even in the midst of Elisha's sickness, he predicted great coming victories for Israel.

"Joash the king of Israel came down upon him, and wept over his face." It is amazing how that Joash, as well as previous kings of Israel, knew of the worth of Elisha, but still would not serve Elisha's God. Men love their sins!

And then he said, *"Oh my father, my father, the chariot of Israel, and the horsemen thereof."* Joash realized two things:

1. That the strength of Israel was not its army or its natural resources, but, in reality, was wrapped up in this frail prophet. Likewise, the strength of America, or any other country in the world for that matter, is the child of God who truly knows Jesus Christ. Sadly, in many countries of the world, there are hardly any

Christians at all.

2. By using the phrase he used as given above, it is possible that Joash thought Elisha might be translated as Elijah was. How wonderful it is for one to live so close to God that even the unsaved, such as Joash, would feel that translation was eminent.

Concerning the coming conflict with Syria, Elisha says, *"Take bow and arrows."* The Holy Spirit through Elisha was letting Joash know that the differences with Syria would not be reconciled; there would be war.

In the 16th verse he says to the king of Israel, *"Put thine hand upon the bow."* By this, Elisha was telling Joash that he would be the one who would lead the conflict against Syria. And then the 16th verse says, *"And Elisha put his hands upon the king's hands."* What a beautiful picture it must have been for the ancient and knarled hands of the aged prophet to be placed on the hands of the king of Israel. He places his hands upon the king's hands to make it clear that the victory would be wholly of grace and from God, and that it would be absolutely certain.

The faith, however, in the heart of the king, divided as it was between Jehovah and the golden calf, was necessarily feeble and moved the grief and indignation of the mighty heart of Elisha who loved the people and thirsted for their complete deliverance.

The 17th verse says, *"And he said, Open the window eastward."* This direction was for two reasons:

1. The window opened eastward signifies the direction of Syria.

2. The direction, *"eastward,"* signifies a beginning for Israel if they will only heed the voice of the Lord. In effect, Elisha was telling Joash, that if he would believe the Lord and walk softly before the God of Israel, that Israel's future was not ending, but beginning, hence, the direction of the rising sun.

The 18th verse proclaims Elisha's command to *"Take the arrows, and smite upon the ground."* The Scripture says, *"He smote thrice, and stayed."* This portrays his faithlessness. While it was true that his belief in Elisha was strong, still, if the king was to be a part of the miracle in respect to his faith, then his extreme, acute spiritual weakness is obvious.

The 19th verse states, *"And the man of God was wroth with him."* The major problem of man is never believing God for too much, but in not believing for enough. God must grow exasperated, even wrathful at our faithlessness.

The 20th verse says, *"And Elisha died, and they buried him."* Thus died one of the greatest men of God who ever lived. One day every child of God who has ever lived will ultimately have the pleasure in the portals of glory of discussing these events contained in the Word of God with this great prophet.

His great faith records one more miracle. The 21st verse says, *"And touched the bones of Elisha, he revived, and stood upon his feet."* This miracle of Elisha's bones was the 32nd and final miracle of his great experience with God. The miracles of his ministry numbered twice as many as Elijah's, and some were twice as great. What a story this soldier had in being killed in this conflict, with his body cast into *"the sepulchre of Elisha,"* and then touching the bones of Elisha where the power of God raised the man from the dead. Hallelujah!

Verses 22-25 record the fulfillment of Elisha's last prophecy. The 23rd verse says, *"And would not destroy them, neither cast he them from his presence as yet."* Despite Israel's sin, the Lord would be *"gracious"* and *"have compassion,"* and even *"respect"* because of *"his covenant with Abraham, Isaac, and Jacob."* However, the words *"as yet"* are given by the Holy Spirit denoting the fact that even though mercy was extended, if repentance was not forthcoming, which it would not be, they would be cast out of His presence, as they eventually were.

CHAPTER 14

Verse 1 says, *"Reigned Amaziah the son of Joash king of Judah."* This was the fourth good king in Judah, but with reservations.

The Holy Spirit in verse 3 says, *"And he did that which was right in the sight of the Lord."* But then the Holy Spirit goes on to say, *"Yet not like David his father: He did according to all things as Joash his father did."* That is, he began well and ended badly. In effect, the Holy Spirit is saying, "He did right, but not like David." Thus we have constant reminders of David as the ideal in these books of Kings and Chronicles, the standard by which all others are mentioned in God's sight.

When God uses David as an example, it is not as a man who thinks first of all of David's sins and failures. God thinks of his true nature, faithful heart, and zeal for Jehovah in living free from idolatry and the gross wickedness of so many of the rulers in those days. David was a man after God's heart who loved Jehovah, considered Him, and obeyed Him when corrected.

The 4th verse says, "Howbeit the high places were not taken away." Over and over again in the text the Holy Spirit points this out. Jerusalem and the Temple site were the only places where the people were to offer sacrifice and burn incense. Even though they did burn sacrifice and incense to the Lord in the high places, still, the Lord was displeased.

In the 6th verse the Holy Spirit is careful to bring out, "That the children of the murderers he slew not: according unto that which is written in the book of the law of Moses." This was at the beginning of Amaziah's reign, and it seems that he was doing all within his power to obey the Word of God. Had he continued thusly, great victory would have been his and Judah's.

The 7th verse proclaims his great victory in taking the almost impregnable Petra, called Sela. The 7th verse says, "And called the name of it Joktheel unto this day." This name means "subdued by God." Thus he honored God Who gave him the victory.

Now begins his downfall. He declared war upon the northern kingdom of Israel and was not in the will of God in doing this. Jehoash, the king of Israel, spoke to him as is recorded in the 10th verse, "And thine heart hath lifted thee up." Evidently, Amaziah's victory in Edom caused him to become exalted and lifted up in pride.

The 11th verse records, "But Amaziah would not hear." How many Christians have been given a "correct word" that was sent to them by the Lord, irrespective of the vehicle, but "would not hear."

The 12th verse records the conclusion, "And Judah was put to the worse before Israel."

NOTES

Jehoash will "break down the wall of Jerusalem, and take all the gold and silver, found in the house of the Lord" (vss. 13-14).

Because of Amaziah's pride, Judah lost the war, the protection of the wall of Jerusalem, all the public silver and gold, all the vessels of the Temple, and all the treasures of the king's house, and was completely humiliated before her enemies. It took years to recover what was lost in a few hours of time, all through pride and selfishness. Pride is the biggest contender that the child of God must deal with constantly.

Due to Amaziah's foolishness, the 19th verse says, "Now they made a conspiracy against him in Jerusalem." It says, "And slew him there." He was one of the 12 kings of Israel and Judah who was assassinated.

The 21st verse says, "And all the people of Judah took Azariah, which was sixteen years old, and made him king." This man was also known as Uzziah.

The 22nd verse says, "After that the king slept with his fathers." It was in the year that he died that Isaiah had the great vision where he saw the Lord, which began his great prophecies. Isaiah would continue his prophecies through four kings, Uzziah, Jotham, Ahaz, and Hezekiah.

The 23rd verse records the ascension to the throne of Jeroboam II. He "reigned forty and one years." And the 24th verse says, "Did that which was evil in the sight of the Lord." He will be compared to his namesake, "Jeroboam the son of Nebat, who made Israel to sin."

Verses 25-27 record the blessings of God upon his very prosperous reign despite the "evil" that he did "in the sight of the Lord." The 25th verse says that he won great military victories "according to the word of the Lord God of Israel, which he spake by the hand of his servant Jonah, the son of Amittai, the prophet." This "Jonah" was the author of the book of Jonah, who was commanded by God to go preach in the city of Ninevah.

The prosperous reign of Jeroboam II seemingly conflicts with the fact that he worshiped the golden calf. However, verses 25-28 reveal the profound depths of love and grace in the heart of God toward His erring children. Guilty and rebellious as they were, He promised them a Saviour by the word of the prophet

Jonah, *"For he saw the affliction of Israel that it was very bitter"* (vs. 26). Israel at this time was in such a state that the Scripture says, *"For there was not any shut up, nor any left, nor any helper for Israel."* So, He would *"save them by the hand of Jeroboam the son of Joash."*

The 28th verse says, *"He recovered Damascus, and Hamath."* These two cities were both in the kingdom of David and Solomon. However, Damascus was lost again soon to Rezin (16:5-18).

Over and over again in these passages concerning the kings of Israel and Judah, the Holy Spirit points out to us the reason for their blessings, which was the Grace of God, and the reason for their failure, which was sin. We would do very well to heed this.

CHAPTER 15

How refreshing it is for the Holy Spirit to say, *"And he did that which was right in the sight of the Lord,"* (vs. 3). And, yet, the word "perfect" can be used of no one, except that which is seen through the precious Blood of Jesus Christ. For the Scripture says, *"All have sinned."* The 3rd verse tells us how he sinned, *"According to all that his father Amaziah had done."* As his father Amaziah started well and ended poorly, so did Azariah. He finished as a leper because of sin.

Once again (vs. 4) the Holy Spirit speaks of the *"high places."* He is displeased with this. From this we should learn how it grieves the Holy Spirit to have any abiding sin within our lives. Please understand that it is the intention of the Holy Spirit to warn us by repetition of our own shortcomings.

Verse 5 says, *"And the Lord smote the king, so that he was a leper unto the day of his death."* II Chronicles 26:16-21 gives the reason - pride. It was the same problem that affected his father, *"Amaziah."*

The Holy Spirit, by the account of these occurrences, seems to be relating to us that sin confessed and forsaken is not only washed clean, but its effects are destroyed as well. Conversely, sin that is not dealt with but lasts

until the moment of death seems to carry with it evil effects, even though the individual may experience a death-bed repentance.

The death of this royal leper taught Isaiah that he was a moral leper and needed Divine cleansing (Isa. 6).

At this period the prophets Hosea, Joel, Amos, Micah, Isaiah, and Jonah exercised their ministry. Their prophecies should be studied in connection with the history of these kings. They foretold the doom of both the northern and southern kingdoms. Actually, in ministry, Hosea followed Elisha.

Verses 8 and 9 tell of the ascending of Zechariah to the throne of Israel. The 9th verse once again says, *"And he did that which was evil in the sight of the Lord."* It once again mentions, *"the sins of Jeroboam the son of Behat, who made Israel to sin."* Some 21 times the Holy Spirit solemnly records this terrible fact. It should be clearly understood that the only cleansing of sin is by the precious Blood of Jesus Christ. Otherwise, the terrible effects of sin actually continue on forever. This is the basic reason Paul recorded in Romans that the *"whole creation groaneth and travaileth in pain together until now"* (Rom. 8:22). Likewise, *"Righteousness exalteth a nation"* (Prov. 14:34), and, thereby, will last forever. The Lord can cancel out the effects of sin through the precious Blood of Jesus Christ. However, Satan cannot cancel out the effects of righteousness.

The 12th verse records the prophecy that had been given to Jehu saying, *"Thy son shall sit on the throne of Israel unto the fourth generation. And so it came to pass."* This prophecy was fulfilled in the death of Zechariah.

Verse 16 records the terrible sins of Menahem. It says, *"And all the women therein that were with child he ripped up."* One can see the depravity of such a nature regarding the type of sin that is committed.

The 19th verse says, *"And Pul the king of Assyria came against the land."* It is not coincidence that the first distinct mention of Assyria in Scripture as an aggressive power immediately follows the account of the terrible sin of Menahem, even to the murdering of thousands of women and little children. By this time Assyria had been rising to a great power for nearly a century and had reached far beyond the River Euphrates, even to Egypt. From here on the history of the two kingdoms of Israel is linked with that of Assyria and Babylon.

Verse 29 says, *"And carried them captive to Assyria."* This was the first carrying away of the Israelites into captivity. It continued until the ten-tribe kingdom was destroyed (Ch. 17). Then the Assyrians took some people captive from Judah in the days of Manasseh (II Chron. 33:11-13). Later, in the days of Jehoiakin and Zedekiah the whole of Judah was taken to Babylon. (By this time the Assyrians had been defeated by the Babylonians.)

The 37th verse says, *"In those days the Lord began to send against Judah, Rezin the king of Syria."* Because Jotham walked righteously before the Lord, the Lord held off the coming fury that would burst forth under sinful Ahaz. It is interesting to note the terminology in that the Lord was the author of what Syria did. No, Syria had no knowledge of such. Nevertheless, the Lord due to Judah's unrighteousness would stir up Syria against Judah. Our obedience brings blessing from God. Our sin brings chastisement from God in the form of judgment, in order that we may repent. Some few do repent. Regrettably, most never do.

CHAPTER 16

Verse 1 says, *"Ahaz the son of Jotham king of Judah began to reign."* Ahaz was the worst of all the kings of Judah; he imitated the worst of the kings of the ten tribes - Ahab and Ahaziah, by establishing Baal worship again in Judah when it had been rooted out of the ten tribes by Jehu (10:19-31) and out of Judah by Jehoiada (11:17-21). Ahaz even made his sons to pass through the fire according to all the abominations of the heathen and burned incense in the high places, on the hills, and under every green tree.

In all that the Holy Spirit says about King Ahaz in the books of Kings, Chronicles, and Isaiah, there is a throbbing of anguish which the reader can feel, and also a note of indignation, as, for example, in the words, *"this is that*

King Ahaz" (II Chron. 28:22). His full name, as it appears in the Assyrian state records, was Jehoahaz, which means *"the possession of Jehovah,"* but the Spirit of God strikes the Jehovah syllable out of his name and invariably calls him *"Ahaz,"* which means *"possession."* Such was his life, for he was led, influenced, and possessed by anyone or anything except God.

The 3rd verse which says, *"And made his son to pass through the fire,"* refers to the heathen idol, *"Moloch,"* the god of fire. A fire would be built in its bulbous belly until its outstretched arms became red-hot. Little children, as sacrifices to this demonic image, would be tied to its outstretched arms and burned alive by the thousands. The horror of his sin knows no bounds.

The 5th verse says concerning *"Rezen king of Syria and Pekah son of Remaliah king of Israel came up to Jerusalem to war."* It then says, *"Besieged Ahaz, but could not overcome him."* No doubt, Ahaz was lifted up in pride because of his successful defense against the kings of Syria and Israel. However, his victory had nothing to do with his ability or righteousness but, instead, was because of the promise that the Lord had made to the house of David.

The 7th verse records these words, *"Ahaz sent messengers to Tiglath-pileser king of Assyria."* He sought a confederation with this king. The Lord through Isaiah earnestly counseled him not to invite the king of Assyria to help him against the confederate kings of Israel and Damascus. He, however, followed his own counsel with success, but the ultimate result was ruin.

His history illustrates how disastrous it is to the spiritual profit of a man when his own plans succeed.

The 10th verse says, *"And saw an altar that was at Damascus."* He set up this heathen altar and was helped by *"Urijah the priest"* (vs. 11).

The 14th verse says, *"And he brought also the brazen altar, which was before the Lord."* The latter portion of the verse says he *"put it on the north side of the altar"* (heathen altar). The 14th verse is the bane of the modern Church. The Lord's altar (brazen altar) has not been completely discarded; instead, we have added a *"heathen altar"* to the *"Lord's altar."*

In the 15th verse King Ahaz commands that all the sacrifices be offered upon the *"great altar"* with the *"brazen altar"* given consideration as to what use to make of it. The Church at this point in time is basically in this same place. For the most part, it has not completely discarded the *"brazen altar"* (Calvary), but neither does it use it anymore. Instead, it uses the *"heathen altar"* of *"possibility thinking, self-esteem, psychology, or dominion teaching."*

The 17th verse says, *"And King Ahaz cut off the borders of the bases, and removed the laver."* He actually removed the brazen oxen from the beneath the great laver, as well as the borders of the bases of the smaller lavers. He put the great laver on stones and gave all this to the king of Assyria.

The *"laver"* is a type of the Word of God. Even though it remained, the oxen which had been designed by the Holy Spirit were given away. The *"oxen"* represented the power and assurance of the Word of God. Basically, Ahaz was saying that he had no more confidence in the Word of God. The Church today is saying the same thing. The Bible has not been completely thrown away; it has just been discarded to the place of "no confidence." The Church as a whole has turned to psychology. It little believes anymore that Jesus delivers or that Jesus sets the captive free. The degradation of the laver in verse 17 illustrates the hostility of man's heart to the great Bible doctrine of *"Jesus Christ and Him crucified"* as the only answer for man's sin.

CHAPTER 17

Verse 1 records the ascension to the throne of *"Hosea."* The 2nd verse says, *"And he did that which was evil in the sight of the Lord."* But then adds, *"But not as the kings of Israel that were before him."* Nevertheless, judgment was due, for God had been longsuffering in His dealings with the ten tribes for some 260 years. Not one king of the 19 had been godly. It seems that when national sins reach a certain height, after scores of admonitions and judgment with no repentance forthcoming, total destruction

NOTES

and abandonment of the nation is the only thing left. In such cases, forces have been set in motion that only genuine forsaking of sin can stop. Even then, if God does not see fit to work a miracle in a nation's behalf, the judgment will still come.

The 5th verse speaks of the *"king of Assyria that went up to Samaria, and besieged it three years."* Now the judgment begins. The ten tribes of the Northern kingdom will be carried *"away into Assyria"* (vs. 6).

The 12th verse gives the reason, *"for they served idols."*

Time and again *"the Lord testified against Israel, and against Judah, by all the prophets"* (vs. 13).

But yet, the 14th verse says, *"Not withstanding they would not hear, but hardened their necks."*

And then it says in verse 18, *"Therefore the Lord was very angry with Israel, and removed him out of his sight: There was none left but the tribe of Judah only."*

Verses 19 and 20 record as well that *"Judah kept not the commandments of the Lord their God, but walked in the statutes of Israel which they made."* And then the 20th verse says, *"And the Lord rejected all the seed of Israel."* The word *"all"* refers to Judah as well, who would go into captivity about 133 years later.

God had to reject Judah (at a later time) because of their sins, for He is no respecter of persons. The judgment upon Judah was delayed because eight of the kings out of 20 were somewhat godly, and they brought periods of revival which turned the people back to Jehovah for a time.

After the captivity of the ten tribes as recorded here, Judah went deeper into sin and finally had to be destroyed and taken into captivity as well. This made the whole 13 tribes in captivity to Babylon, for in the meantime Babylon overthrew the Assyrian empire and now ruled all the countries where the 13 tribes were scattered.

When Cyrus gave commandment for all Israelites or Jews to go back to their own land and rebuild the city of Jerusalem and their Temple after he had overthrown Babylon, it opened the door for all the 13 tribes to become united again as one nation. At the first advent of Christ they were all one nation and back in the land.

Verse 24 gives us the beginning of the New Testament Samaritans, *"And placed them in the cities of Samaria instead of the children of Israel."* These individuals subsequently intermixed with the Jews who returned from captivity, hence, this culminated in a mixed breed. The Jews in Jesus' day would basically have nothing to do with them.

There are five cities mentioned in the 24th verse. Each of these cities had their own particular idol god that they took with them to Samaria. These gods are as follows:

Nergal: This god was the patron of hunting, and was supposed to represent the deified hero and hunter, Nimrod. His symbol was a man-lion.

Ashima: This was the god of Hamath, a deity worshiped under the figure of a goat without wool.

Nibhaz: He was the god of the Avites. This idol was in the form of a man with the head of a dog.

Tartak: This god was in the form of an ass.

Adrammelech: This god was identical with Molech. Human sacrifices were offered to it.

Samaria, with an outward worship of Jehovah, was devoted to these five idols or *"husbands."* This is one of the reasons that the Lord said to the Samaritan woman in John 4, that *"you worship you know not what."* Her actual, personal conduct illustrated the nation, for Jesus said to her: *"Thou hast had five husbands, and he whom thou now hast is not thy husband"* (the God of our father Jacob, whom the nation professed to worship). He then presents Himself to her heart as the true husband (no doubt, as well, she had had five literal husbands).

Verse 25 says, *"That they feared not the Lord: Therefore the Lord sent lions among them, which slew some of them."* The expulsion of the Israelites from God's pleasant land and the introduction of lions into it by God shows that both the people and the land belonged to Him. Because the people were His people, therefore, He carried them away. Because the land was His land, therefore, He brought the lions in. The Holy Spirit states that the lions were instruments of God's discipline

and teaching.

Verse 33 says of the Samaritans, *"They feared the Lord, and served their own gods."* The people of Samaria worshiped all these gods in their own way, in all high places, and in their own cities. They feared Jehovah but served other gods; that is, they were afraid of Him but not enough to serve Him or keep His laws. Nevertheless, little by little they began to forsake their idol gods and draw closer to Jehovah. In 409 B.C. they erected a temple to Jehovah on Mount Gerizim. They laid aside their idols, accepted the Pentateuch as their religious textbook, and began to observe the whole Law. The Jews did not take advantage of this desire on the part of the Samaritans for Jehovah but always remained segregated from them because of their mixed nationality. Nevertheless, Jesus ministered to them extensively during His three and one-half years of public ministry.

CHAPTER 18

Verse 1 says, *"That Hezekiah the son of Ahaz king of Judah began to reign."* So begins the reign of one of Judah's godliest kings. And yet from the ascension of Hezekiah to the captivity, the Assyrians and the Babylonians overshadow the house of David and call forth those exercises of heart which are painful to the flesh but profitable to the Spirit. These enemies (Assyrians) appeared because of Israel's unfaithfulness. So it is in the Christian life. Fidelity to the Lord and to His precious Book saves the Christian from those trials which a lack of fidelity surely brings, and, yet, the pitying love and wisdom of God may use these very griefs as instruments of spiritual enrichment to those who, like Hezekiah and Josiah, really love Him, even though that love is imperfect.

Hezekiah began his reign as a vassal of the king of Assyria by whom he was placed upon the throne during the lifetime of his father Ahaz.

Verse 3 records the godliness of this king, *"And he did that which was right in the sight of the Lord, according to all that David his father*

NOTES

did." Once again David is used as the example. Few would come up to this example as Hezekiah did.

The 4th verse records the revival under Hezekiah: *"He removed the high places, and break the images, and cut down the groves."* Over and over again in previous chapters the Holy Spirit records that Israel yet sacrificed in the high places. But now, refreshingly, it records the very opposite. And then it says, *"And break in pieces the brazen serpent that Moses had made."* The brazen serpent was over 900 years old by this time. It had become an object of worship. The Scripture says that Hezekiah *"called it Nehushtan"* with contempt. The word means *"a bit of copper."* Originally, it was set up by God as a symbol of the coming redemption of Calvary. But so prone is the heart to idolatry, that the Holy Spirit here records the action of Hezekiah with approval. As well, the true man of God today will condemn the Paschal Supper of the Catholic church because it has become an idolatrous sacrament.

The Holy Spirit in verses 5 and 6 records these statements about Hezekiah:

1. He trusted in the Lord God of Israel.
2. There was none like him.
3. He cleaved to the Lord.
4. He kept His commandments.

And now the Holy Spirit records what the Lord did for him:

1. The Lord was with him.
2. He prospered wherever he went.
3. He broke the yoke of Assyria.
4. He conquered the Philistines.

The 8th verse says, *"From the tower of the watchman to the fenced city."* The watchman's tower is placed in desolate districts; the fenced city is a populous center. The expression, therefore, means that Hezekiah smote the Philistines throughout the entirety of Judah.

This victory over the Philistine, who was an internal enemy, and the later victory over the Assyrian, who was an external enemy, illustrates the fact that victory over both inward and outward temptation is promised to the overcomer.

Verses 9-12 repeat the information already given in the previous chapter. It is, no doubt, introduced designedly by the Holy Spirit as a solemn reminder to the house of David and to Christian people of today that God has the same controversy with evil and will judge it with a like judgment, whether it be practiced by the followers of David or of Jeroboam.

The 13th verse proclaims the Assyrian invasion of Judah. This was eight years after the captivity of the ten tribes. If Hezekiah had yielded, no doubt, Sennacherib would have taken the whole kingdom of Judah into captivity. But God gave them victory over the Assyrians because of Hezekiah's trust in Him. It was not until some 125 years later that the Babylonians took the Jews captive.

Sennacherib now has all of Judah with the exception of Jerusalem. The 15th verse says, *"Hezekiah gave him all the silver that was found in the house of the Lord, and in the treasures of the king's house."* The 16th verse says as well, *"At that time did Hezekiah cut off the gold from the doors of the temple of the Lord."* And then it says, *"And gave it to the king of Assyria."* The repetition of Hezekiah's name in the 16th verse after being given in the 15th verse emphasizes a lesson. The very Hezekiah who overlaid the pillars of the Temple of Jehovah with gold was the very same Hezekiah who cut off the gold and sent it to the Assyrian king as tribute. Unbelief is costly, and compromise seldom delivers. Had Hezekiah at this time trusted fully, he would not have suffered this abuse to the Temple of the Lord.

Irrespective of Hezekiah's efforts of compromise, the 17th verse says that *"the king of Assyria sent a great host against Jerusalem."*

It appears from the monuments that Sennacherib, content with his tribute and captives, went back to Nineveh. Hezekiah, left to himself, repented of his submission and commenced negotiations with Egypt (vss. 21-24), which implied treason against the king of Assyria.

Then Sennacherib led another expedition into Palestine, following the regular coast route into Philistia. He planned to conquer Egypt, leaving Jerusalem alone for the time being. While he was besieging Lachish on his way to meet the Egyptians, he decided to try out the Jews by sending an army to fight against Jerusalem.

The 33rd verse says of the boasts of the

Assyrians, *"Hath any of the gods of the nations delivered at all his land out of the hand of the king of Assyria?"* The Assyrian monuments give evidence of a custom which illustrates the haughty language of this text. It was their practice to take the idols of the various nations to Assyria where they were assigned a place among the captive gods. Here, they were boasting that their god was more powerful than all others, so it was vain to expect Jehovah to rescue them, especially since He did not rescue their brethren in Samaria.

They, as countless others, would rue the day that they compared their gods to Jehovah!

CHAPTER 19

Regarding the boast of Rabshakeh, the field general of the Assyrian army, that he would destroy Jerusalem, the 1st verse says, *"When king Hezekiah heard it, that he rent his clothes, and covered himself with sackcloth, and went into the house of the Lord."*

Hezekiah's actions portray humility and total dependence upon God. The words *"rent his clothes"* refer to a total lack of dependence on his own ability, or in Israel's strength. The word *"sackcloth"* refers to his humbling himself in the sight of God. The *"house of the Lord"* refers to the Holy of Holies, where God dwelt between the Mercy Seat and the Cherubim. The only help for Judah was God. Likewise, the only help for us today is God. But how so far removed are we from total dependence on Him. As well, our petition must be clothed in humility, or God will not heed.

The 2nd verse says, *"To Isaiah the prophet the son of Amoz."* This is the first mention of the prophet in the Bible. Hezekiah was the fourth king in whose reign he had prophesied (Isa. 1:1). The passages in the book of Isaiah which refer to these events are 10:5-19; 14:24-27; 22:1-25; 36:1-37. Hezekiah would, as well, seek the help of Isaiah, the prophet.

The 3rd verse says, *"For the children are come to the birth, and there is not strength to bring forth."* This passage can be interpreted thusly.

NOTES

There comes a time for men, churches, and even nations to fulfill the plan of God for their lives and destinies. The *"strength"* that is referred to here does not speak of personal or national strength. It has to do with God's strength. Hezekiah knew that Judah had sinned, and that maybe Assyria's invasion was chastisement from God. Therefore, he could not claim righteousness on the part of Judah regarding his petition to the Lord. He could only cry for mercy.

Likewise, at this present time in history God is ready to bring in the harvest. However, the Church has *"not strength to bring forth."*

Therefore, the only hope for the Church is the same hope that Hezekiah had of throwing ourselves on the mercy of God, that is in humility, brokenness, and with a crushed spirit, depending not at all upon ourselves but totally upon Him. If we will do so, God will hear us as He heard Hezekiah so long ago.

The 6th verse records God's answer, *"Thus saith the Lord, be not afraid of the words which thou hast heard"* - referring to the king of Assyria.

And then in the 7th verse the Lord says, *"And I will cause him to fall by the sword in his own land."*

Verses 8-13 record once again Assyria boasting against Jerusalem and the God of Jerusalem.

Faith is ever tested. Satan does not fold just because God has given us His Word of strength. He will do all within his power to make the child of God doubt. He says in the 10th verse, *"Let not thy God in whom thou trustest deceive thee."* Satan used Rabshakeh to send a letter to Hezekiah to produce fear.

The 14th verse says, *"And Hezekiah received the letter of the hand of the messengers, and read it."* Hezekiah's faith did not wane. The Scripture says he *"spread it before the Lord."* Verses 15-19 record his prayer.

First of all, he gave allegiance to God as the ruler *"of all the kingdoms of the earth."* Consequently, God could do with them as He liked.

The 16th verse says he petitioned the Lord to *"hear the words of Sennacherib,"* which had been sent by Rabshakeh, with all of this *"to reproach the living God."* And the 19th verse says he petitioned the Lord, *"save thou us out of his hand."*

Once again the Lord speaks through Isaiah, for the 20th verse says, *"Then Isaiah the son of Amoz sent to Hezekiah, saying, Thus saith the Lord God of Israel."* The Lord responded by saying, *"I am God and there is no other."* He says several things:

1. *"I have heard."*

2. *"And laughed thee to scorn."*

3. *"Whom hast thou reproached and blasphemed?"*

4. *"Even against the Holy one of Israel."*

5. *"Therefore I will put My hook in thy nose, and My bridle in thy lips."*

6. *"The zeal of the Lord of Hosts shall do this."*

7. *"And shall not come into this city, saith the Lord."*

This entire episode lasted for some two years with the children of Israel not planting crops because of the feared invasion. However, the 29th verse says, *"And in the third year sow ye, and reap."*

The sign given to show that God would do this was that Israel would be free from any siege and could roam the fields to gather such food as grew of itself for the rest of this particular year and the next. After that, they would sow and reap again in a normal way.

This happened as predicted, and it was not until about 125 years later that they were destroyed as a nation and taken into captivity.

In the 28th verse where the Lord says, *"Put My hook in thy nose, and My bridle in thy lips,"* sculptures show that the kings of Assyria and Babylon were in the habit of actually putting a ring or fishhook through the flesh of their more distinguished prisoners, then attaching a throng or rope and leading them about as with a bridle. In Assyria the ring or hook was passed through the lower lip, while in Babylon it was through the membrane of the nose. Thus God threatens Sennacherib with the punishment he had inflicted on others many times. God did not do this literally, so it expresses figuratively the complete defeat and humiliation of Sennacherib whenever he would be judged by Him.

The 34th verse says, *"For I will defend this city, to save it, for mine own sake, and for my*

servant David's sake." It was not because of any moral beauty in Hezekiah that God delivered Jerusalem, but for his Own sake and for David's sake - true David, the Lord Jesus Christ.

Verse 35 records one of the greatest miracles of the Old Testament, *"The angel of the Lord went out, and smote in the camp of the Assyrians an hundred four-score and five thousand."* How this was done the Scripture does not say. The only answer is, *"They were all dead corpses"* (dead bodies). How simple it was for the Lord.

Concerning *"Sennacherib king of Assyria,"* it says in the 37th verse, *"His sons smote him with the sword."* Ancient history records that Sennacherib bequeathed his throne to his youngest son, Esarhaddon, and in order to gain the favor of his god, promised to sacrifice the two elder sons to that divinity. These sons, doubtless prompted by fear on the one hand and by jealousy on the other, murdered their father in December of that year, but six months later were obliged to flee into Armenia to escape the vengeance of Esarhaddon.

In recent times we have seen the mightiest nation of atheism on the face of the earth, the Soviet Union, literally come to pieces before the eyes of the whole world. Basically, their communistic, atheistic leaders made the same boast in the face of God as Sennacherib. Their end was basically the same as Sennacherib's. God is not to be mocked. The mills of God grind exceedingly small (slowly), but they grind exceedingly fine (they miss nothing).

CHAPTER 20

Verse 1 says, *"In those days was Hezekiah sick unto death."* This was in about the 14th year of his reign, which would have made Hezekiah about 39 years old. These events would have transpired some time in the two-year period of the invasion of Judah by the Assyrians and immediately preceding the miraculous deliverance of the 19th chapter. In this passage the reason is not given for Hezekiah's sickness; however, II Chronicles 32, in effect, says that Hezekiah due to the blessings of God had become lifted up in pride. It seems that the people of Judah and Jerusalem had likewise gone into sin. Therefore, the Assyrian invasion and Hezekiah's sickness with threatened death was the judgment of God upon Hezekiah, Judah, and Jerusalem because of their sin. Hezekiah had begun his reign with one of the greatest spiritual reforms ever. Consequently, God blessed him abundantly, and then the blessing turned his head. It is very difficult for most people to receive the blessings of God without thinking that they had something to do with it. Almost invariably, they start to imagine themselves as someone great, a sin that God cannot tolerate. This is one of the primary reasons that God had to allow the thorn to remain in Paul's life as a constant reminder of his frail, flawed humanity and the necessity of a constant dependence upon the Lord (II Cor. 12). This is the reason that Solomon, in effect, said, *"Give me neither poverty nor riches"* (Prov. 30:8).

The Prophet Isaiah was sent unto Hezekiah with the message, *"Thus saith the Lord, Set thine house in order; for thou shalt die, and not live."* Hezekiah's pride must have been acute. God had to use drastic measures to bring him to his spiritual senses. God is all-knowing; therefore, He knew what Hezekiah would do upon this announcement. Of the sins that the Bible says that God hates, pride leads the list (Prov. 6:16-17). There is every evidence that pride is the foundation sin of the universe. Pride seems to have been the sin that caused Lucifer's downfall (Isa. 14; Ezek. 28). Likewise, it was the sin that caused the fall of man in the Garden of Eden. The bait that Satan used was pride, for the Scripture says concerning Adam and Eve, *"And you shall be as gods"* (Gen. 3:5). Justification by *"works"* generates religious pride, which characterizes much of what is called "the Church." Justification by "faith" generates humility because it places total dependence on God and none on fallen self.

The command by God, *"Set thine house in order,"* refers to his spiritual house. It is a statement that every single human being on the face of the earth would do well to heed. The sadness is that most houses are not in order.

The 2nd verse records Hezekiah's repentance and the humbling of himself. It says,

NOTES

"Then he turned his face to the wall." The statement, *"face to the wall,"* means that Hezekiah saw himself as undone, helpless, and totally dependent on the mercy of God. It also means that he turned his face away from all the riches, glory, and grandeur of Judah and Jerusalem. This is the only kind of prayer that God will honor. Perhaps, the Holy Spirit had Hezekiah in mind when he made this statement through Isaiah, *"But to this man will I look, even to him that is poor and of a contrite spirit, and trembleth at my word"* (Isa. 66:2).

It seems from Hezekiah's short prayer (vs. 3) that it was the opposite of humility. However, in effect, Hezekiah was telling the Lord that he had tried to keep the Law of God to the very best of his ability, *"I have walked before thee in truth and with a perfect heart."* And yet, the latter portion of the 3rd verse which says, *"And Hezekiah wept sore,"* refers to the fact that Hezekiah now understood that his diligent effort to keep the Law of God, as noble as it was, gained him no merit with God. Instead, he had allowed the *"justification by faith"* to be turned into *"justification by works."* Therefore, pride had generated within his heart and life, so he wept.

The answer from the Lord was immediate, for before Isaiah had *"gone out into the middle court, that the word of the Lord came to him, saying"* (vs. 4). God will always respond to a broken heart.

The Word in the 5th verse was, *"I will heal thee."* He further states, *"And I will add unto thy days fifteen years."* He then says, *"I will deliver thee and this city out of the hand of the king of Assyria."* God can turn things around immediately if He so desires upon our proper confession and repentance of sin. The watchword of the Church once was, "You need Jesus." Now, sadly, the watch-word of the Church is "You need counseling." How so regrettably sad. Hezekiah could have been counseled forever, and there would have been no help from that source. However, Hezekiah went to the Lord, and God turned an extremely ugly situation around. He is no respecter of persons. If He did it for Hezekiah, He will do it for me and for you. Hezekiah was one of the few men in history who would know basically the exact day on which he would die - 15 years later.

NOTES

The 5th verse says of the Lord, *"I will heal thee."* And then the 7th verse says, *"Take a lump of figs and lay it on the boil."* The critic may argue that if God healed him, why was the lump of figs needed as a poultice? Did God need the figs to complete the healing? Definitely not! Everything that God does is to generate faith in the heart and the life of the individual in question. God does nothing to cater to the pride of our heart, only to the faith. So, he told Isaiah to tell the attendants to use *"a lump of figs."* As well, proper faith will always generate humility and obedience. What difference does it make if God heals instantly or uses a doctor, medicine, or other means to bring about His desired effect. God's purposes are far greater than ours. Most of the time we can only see the desired healing; God sees spiritual growth, as well, and will function accordingly.

The 8th verse records Hezekiah asking Isaiah, *"What shall be the sign that the Lord will heal me, and that I shall go up into the house of the Lord the third day?"* This which Hezekiah asked and the Lord would do had a special significance concerning the coming of the Messiah. There is even a possibility, due to the prophecies of Isaiah (Isa. 53), that Hezekiah thought the Messiah would come at this particular time (during Hezekiah's reign). The healing of Hezekiah and his going into the *"House of the Lord on the third day"* referred to the Resurrection of the Lord on the third day - some 700 years in the future.

The 10th verse says, *"But let the shadow return backward ten degrees,"* referring to the sun dial. This would be a notable miracle and would make a *"long day."* This *"long day"* would be equalled out somewhat by the *"short day"* when Jesus died on Calvary (Matt. 27:45).

The event of the *"long day"* was, of course, known over the world of that day. The following report was given in one of the archaeological discoveries.

"In the affair of the Scientific Inquirers, who were sent from Babel, to inquire about the remarkable event which has happened on earth, this sign and remarkable event refers to the going back of the shadow on the sun dial, which was so remarkable that even the Chaldean astronomers came to inquire about the God who could turn the sun backward. Fur-

thermore, Greek historians informed Alexander the Great that it was one of the great wonders recorded in their scientific books. This shows that the happening was not merely the moving of a shadow, but the going backward of the sun. The matter was known in various lands, and the Chaldeans came to inquire about it when they learned that it was caused by Israel's God."

For the Bible says in the 12th verse, *"At that time Berodach-Baladan, the son of Baladan, king of Babylon, sent letters and a present unto Hezekiah."* He did this by the hand of emissaries sent from Babylon. At this time Babylon and Ninevah were two great city-states competing for supremacy in Assyria. Actually, at this time Babylon was not nearly the power that Ninevah was. So, the prophecy that Isaiah would shortly give concerning the coming supremacy of Babylon would certainly not seem practical at this particular time. But as are all prophecies given by the Lord, they always come to pass exactly as stated.

Secular history relates that at this moment in history, the king of Babylon was seeking allies to strengthen him against the king of Assyria; hence, this was one of his reasons for his embassage to Hezekiah. It seems that Hezekiah agreed to help and to form a treaty, because the 13th verse says, *"And Hezekiah hearkened unto them."* Hezekiah's object in showing them the house of his armour and the house of his treasures was to convince the ambassadors of the power of Judah.

Isaiah asked Hezekiah, *"What have they seen in thine house?"* (vs. 15). Hezekiah answered, *"All the things that are in mine house have they seen."* It seems that the humbling process of Hezekiah took place over a period of time, as it generally does with all of us. He did not show the ambassadors from Babylon the things of God, but, rather, the riches of Judah. He will be rebuked for it. Actually, much of what is shown to these Babylonian emissaries will be given to the king of Assyria instead (18:13-16). And, yet, the prophecy given by Isaiah in the 17th verse, *"Shall be carried into Babylon: nothing shall be left, saith the Lord,"* refers to Judah who would completely lose her way with God and be taken in chains to Babylon. It would be fulfilled about 125 years later.

The 20th verse says, *"He made a pool and a conduit, and brought water into the city."* The conduit is still there today. It was a long underground engineering feed, running from Gihon down to the pool of Siloam.

CHAPTER 21

Verse 1 says, *"Manasseh was twelve years old when he began to reign, and he reigned fifty and five years in Jerusalem."* As Hezekiah was at least one of the godliest kings of Judah, his son Manasseh was the most ungodly - and then strangely enough he would reign the longest, 55 years. When he took the throne of Judah, the kingdom was at its most richest and powerful, except possibly when Rehoboam, Solomon's son, became king many years earlier. He in no way, at least at the beginning, recognized the blessings of God upon Judah. But, instead, as the 2nd verse says, *"He did that which was evil in the sight of the Lord, after the abominations of the heathen."*

Verses 3-9 record the type of evil that he engaged in. The 3rd verse says, *"Baal,"* the fire-god, that is, the sun, moon and stars, was adored as the originator of life; and then it says, *"a grove."* This was the *"Asherah,"* the phallus, which was bowed down to as the author of life. This was most degrading, and it was what the king placed in the Temple of God (vs. 7). In this verse the words, *"a graven image of the grove,"* means a carved Asherah. It was removed by Josiah (ch. 23:6). The word, "phallus," is a Greek word, and means the male organ of procreation. It was held to symbolize the giver of life. It was made of wood, stone, or metal, and was generally a tree trimmed into a shape of the male organ, and intended to recall the Tree of Life which had once stood in the Garden of Eden. It was the most debased of all forms of idolatry. It is, without doubt, to this that Ezekiel in chapter 8 refers when describing with indignation the abominable idolatry practiced in the very Temple of God at Jerusalem. Ezekiel exclaims in verse 17, *"They put the branch to the nose,"* not their nose, but *"the*

NOTES

nose," that is *"God's face."* In other words, they thrust the Asherah, that is, the phallus, into the very face of God Himself Who dwelt between the Mercy Seat and the Cherubim. This they did by publicly placing it in the Temple. The Holy Spirit, when recording in verses 2-7 the abominations of Manasseh, reserves this abomination to the end, being the climax. It is popularly termed "phallic worship."

The 8th verse proclaims the Lord desiring to do great things for Israel *"only if they will observe to do according to all that I have commanded them."*

But the 9th verse says, *"They hearkened not."*

This is why these predictions are to have a future fulfillment. Israel never obeyed all that was commanded them; instead, they always went into sin. Therefore, God could not bless them with an eternal temple and city, or give them a permanent land to dwell in. When the Messiah comes and Israel is brought to repentance and converted, these prophecies will be literally fulfilled.

The 9th verse also says, *"Manasseh seduced them."* This is not said of any other king of Judah. He not only sinned himself but spent time and effort to seduce others to join him in his sinning.

The 10th verse records the efforts by the Lord to warn Manasseh by sending *"his servants the prophets."*

The 13th verse proclaims that the judgment would be severe, *"And I will wipe Jerusalem as a man wipeth a dish, wiping it, and turning it upside down.*

The 16th verse says, *"Moreover Manasseh shed innocent blood very much."* It is held by many that he even killed Isaiah the prophet. Josephus says that he did not even spare the prophets.

The 6th verse records the words, *"And he made his son pass through the fire,"* which may have had to do with the *"innocent blood,"* referring to the offering of babies and little children to these horrifying heathen gods.

The captivity and restoration of Manasseh are recorded in the book of II Chronicles. It says this:

"And when he was in affliction, he besought the Lord his God, and humbled himself greatly

before the God of his fathers" (II Chron. 33:12).

It seems that Manasseh tried to undo all the terrible evil he had done. At any rate, God accepted his repentance and restored him to the throne.

The restoration of Manasseh to his throne two years before his death was thought by some to be improbable, owing to the historic character of the kings of Assyria. Recent excavations, however, reveal that at this very time the princes of Tyre and Egypt were restored to their governments by the Assyrian monarch and loaded with many gifts. Clemency to Manasseh, even according to the historical data, is exactly as the Bible says.

The 19th verse tells of the succession to the throne of Manasseh's son, Amon. According to the 20th verse, he did *"evil in the sight of the Lord, as his father Manasseh did."*

Even though Manasseh's repentance and conversion greatly affected him and Judah, still, it had no affect for the good upon his son Amon, for the 22nd verse says, *"He forsook the Lord God of his fathers, and walked not in the way of the Lord."*

The 24th verse says that he was assassinated, *"and the people of the land made Josiah his son king in his stead."*

Despite great spiritual reforms under Hezekiah and then under his great-grandson Josiah, still, Judah would, by and large, continue to go ever downward until the Holy Spirit said, *"There was no remedy"* (II Chron. 36:16).

CHAPTER 22

Verse 1 says, *"Josiah was eight years old when he began to reign."* Josiah was the second youngest king to begin his reign, with Joash being the youngest at 7 years old when he began to reign. Manasseh, Josiah's grandfather, was brought up under godly Hezekiah, his father. Sadly, Manasseh became the worst king of all, but repented at the end. Josiah, the grandson of Manasseh, was brought up under his wicked father Amon, but became one of the most godly kings.

In the 2nd verse the Holy Spirit uses a

beautiful term, of which it was said of no other, *"And turned not aside to the right hand or to the left."* He was predicted by name more than 300 years before his birth (I Kings 13:2). In noting the comments made by the Holy Spirit concerning these particular kings, it should give us pause regarding the comments that He makes of us.

The 3rd verse says, *"And it came to pass in the eighteenth year of King Josiah."*

The Prophet Jeremiah stood in the same relation to Josiah as Isaiah was to Hezekiah. There is a possibility that Josiah and Jeremiah were boys together, and that Jeremiah helped in the conversion of Josiah. His conversion took place when he was 16 years old (eight years into his reign). Jeremiah was called to be a prophet in the 13th year of Josiah's reign (Jer. 1:2), and when Josiah was 21 years old.

Through neglect the Temple of the Lord was in a state of disrepair, so the 5th verse says, *"To repair the breaches of the house."*

In the 8th verse there is recorded a notable find, *"I have found the book of the law in the house of the Lord."* The repair of the Temple led to the discovery of the original Pentateuch, which had been written by the hand of Moses and laid up by the side of the Ark. It probably was hidden there during the reigns of Manasseh and Amon because of their wickedness in turning against Jehovah. It had been written by Moses from the mouth of God more than 800 years before Josiah was born.

The 11th verse says, *"When the king had heard the words of the book of the law, that he rent his clothes."*

It is easy for a man to know whether he has spiritual life or not if, when reading the Bible, he is neither comforted nor terrified. Then it is evident that his soul is dead. Josiah was truly born from above, for he trembled exceedingly when hearing words written by God those many years before.

The 13th verse says, *"Go ye inquire of the Lord for me."*

So, according to the 14th verse, the highest officers in the land were sent unto a woman preacher, *"Went unto Huldah, the prophetess."* Why were they not commanded to go to the great men preachers, Jeremiah and Zephaniah, who were at this time attached to the court? No doubt, the Holy Spirit, for whatever reason, moved upon him to go to Huldah. There are other women preachers mentioned in the Bible as well: Miriam, Deborah, Noadiah, Isaiah's wife, Anna, and Phillip's daughters, together with the many women preachers forever famed in the letters of the Apostle Paul.

The word *"college"* in the 14th verse has no reference to an institution of academic learning. Rather, it refers to a certain district of the city.

The 16th verse proclaims Huldah the prophetess predicting the coming *"evil upon this place."* But concerning Josiah, the 19th verse says, *"And thou hast humbled thyself before the Lord."* Consequently, as the 20th verse says, *"Thou shalt be gathered into thy grave in peace."* The word *"peace"* refers to Josiah not seeing the terrible evil that God would bring upon Judah because of her iniquity. Actually, Josiah would die at 39 years of age in battle against Egypt. His death would be a result of his self-will. He would not lose his soul, but he would lose his reign.

CHAPTER 23

Josiah instituted one of the greatest spiritual reforms ever known to Judah. Still, according to Jeremiah, even at the time that Josiah was destroying idolatry, the nation was secretly planning its restoration, which was quickly affected after Josiah's death. But, still, Josiah did all that he could do to bring the people back to the Bible.

The 2nd verse says, *"And all the people, both small and great: and he read in their ears all the words of the book of the covenant which was found in the house of the Lord."* The book that was spoken of is the Pentateuch (Genesis, Exodus, Leviticus, Numbers, and Deuteronomy.) The Holy Spirit is careful to delineate that Josiah addressed seven different groups of people *"elders, men of Judah, the inhabitants of Jerusalem, the priests, the prophets, and all the people, the small and the great,"* in other words, everyone. This shows us that the

NOTES

Word of God is for everyone and not just for a privileged class as the Catholic church has tried to say for many centuries. Sadly, even in the Protestant world the Bible is basically an unread book. The people too often, little knowing the Word of God, accept whatever is told them from behind the pulpit. As well, too often the Bible in the modern pulpit is basically used as window dressing. Instead, the latest psychological fad is preached as Gospel, when, in reality, it is no Gospel at all.

The 3rd verse records the beginning of the reform according to the Word of God and the covenant made before the Lord. The covenant consists of the following:

1. *"To keep his commandments and his testimonies and his statutes."*

2. *"With all their heart and with all their soul."*

3. *"To perform the words in this covenant that were written in this book."*

The thousands that were, no doubt, there ratified the covenant.

Next, they destroyed Baal worship and the Baal priests. Concerning all the vessels and things that were made for Baal, the 4th verse says, *"He burned them without Jerusalem in the fields of Kidron, and carried the ashes of them unto Bethel."* The ashes that were carried to Bethel to defile the altar of Jeroboam was predicted in I Kings 13:2, where even the name of Josiah was mentioned 322 years before he was born and 348 years before the prediction was fulfilled.

The 5th verse says, *"And he put down the idolatrous priests."* These were black-robed instead of white-robed as God's priests. They were not the *"kohen"* appointed by God, but *"kemarim"* appointed by man. Each separate idol had its own priest, so there were many orders of priests in Israel: those who burned incense in the high places ordained by the kings of Israel from the lowest of the people; those who burned incense to Baal; and those who burned it to the sun, moon, planets, and all the hosts of heaven.

The words in the 5th verse, *"To the planets,"* refer to the 12 signs of the zodiac.

The 6th verse says, *"And he brought out the grove from the house of the Lord."* Here is a clear reference proving that the words *"grove"* and *"groves,"* which were used with idolatry so many times, do not indicate a group of growing trees. Such could not be in the Temple building. They refer to *"Asherahs"* or *"gods"* made of trunks of trees fashioned like the male sex organ. The idea that such abomination was in the very house of God where the Lord dwelt between the Mercy Seat and the Cherubim is unthinkable. This shows how far down Israel had sunk.

The latter portion of the 6th verse shows with what indignation Josiah destroyed this abominable idol. The Scripture says, *"And stamped it small to powder, and cast the powder thereof upon the graves of the children of the people."*

The 7th verse says, *"And he break down the houses of the sodomites."* The sin of homosexuality, which God condemned more than any other sexual sin, was practiced here in the Temple. Besides these, they had many women prostitutes consecrated to idols to attract men. The *"women"* mentioned in verse 7 were harlots in the worship of the Asherah. One of their duties was the weaving of coverings for these Asherah, and they seemed to have been in various colors.

The 8th verse says, *"And defiled the high places."* These *"high places"* were throughout the entire kingdom, both North and South. Although God alone was worshiped on most of them, still, the Law commanded that incense and sacrifice be confined to the one altar at Jerusalem. As well, the child of God has one altar, which is Calvary. The priests who officiated in these *"high places"* were allowed to come to the Temple at Jerusalem and to officiate in some limited manner, but not at the Altar of Jehovah.

The 10th verse says, *"And he defiled Topheth."* The word *"Topheth"* is derived from *"toph,"* which means *"a drum."* Because of the cries of the children being burned in the fire of Molech, the drums and noisy worship would drown out such cries so the worship could be tolerated.

A fire would be ignited in the belly of this idol, and little boys and girls were tied to its outstretched arms. As the arms grew red hot because of the fire, these idol priests would beat these drums to drown out the screams of

the dying children. This is so horrible that it defies description.

The 11th verse says, *"He took away the horses that the kings of Judah had given to the sun."* The custom of dedicating a chariot and horses to the sun was a Persian practice. When he made sacrifices, the king of Persia offered a white horse to the sun. They mounted their horses early in the morning and rode to the rising orb of the sun as if to salute it, then offered the horses in sacrifice. Manasseh heard of this custom and imitated it to some extent, maybe not actually slaying the horses, but dedicating them to the sun. The idea came from regarding the sun as a charioteer who drove his horses daily across the sky.

The 13th verse says, *"The mount of corruption."* This was the Mount of Olives and was so-called because of the idolatries connected with it. Here, Solomon had promoted the idol worship of his wives, part of which is mentioned: Ashtoreth, Chemosh, Milcom, abominations of Zidon, Moab, and Ammon. Josiah defiled these idols and their places of worship on the Mount of Olives by breaking down their images and Asherahs, *"And filled their places with the bones of men."*

Verses 21-23 record the greatest Passover ever conducted at Jerusalem.

The 22nd verse says, *"Surely there was not holden such a passover from the days of the judges."* After destroying all the idolatrous places in Jerusalem, Samaria, Bethel, and other cities throughout the realm and completely ridding the country of all idol worship, Josiah now commanded the people who were left to keep the Passover and observe all the Law. No such Passover had been held in Israel from the days of the judges and kings up to this time. This was also said of the one Hezekiah held, which was true up to that time, but this one exceeded it.

Hezekiah's Passover was held just before the captivity of the Northern kingdom; Josiah's immediately preceded that of the Southern kingdom being led into captivity.

Concerning Josiah, the 25th verse says, *"And like unto him was there no king before him, that turned to the Lord with all his heart, and with all his soul, and with all his might, according to the law of Moses; neither after him arose there any like him."*

However, in the 26th verse, the Lord says, *"Notwithstanding the Lord turned not from the fierceness of his great wrath."* Regardless of the reformation of Josiah, Jehovah did not see fit to turn away all His wrath, for He knew the change would last only during the days of Josiah, and that Judah would follow the old pattern of most of the previous kings of Israel and Judah by continuing to sin. He had already determined the destruction of Judah because of the long record of sin and rebellion. However, if He had seen a deep-rooted reformation, something of a permanent nature, there is no doubt that He would have changed His plans of destruction. He even said that He would bless the very small remnant left after the destruction of Judah if they would only stay in the land and obey Him. So He surely would have done as much for the whole nation if the change in Josiah's day had continued.

The 29th verse records the death of Josiah. He was killed by *"Pharoah-Nechoh king of Egypt."* It says, *"And king Josiah went against him."* Why Josiah went against him is not known. It could have been because the Egyptian armies were going through Judah.

Josiah perished on the famous field of battle where Barak defeated Sisera. Had he been as subject to the Word of God in his later years as in his former, he would not have thus fallen by the sword.

Still, the Holy Spirit said such glorious things of him as had not been said of any other king.

The 30th verse says that, *"The people of the land took Jehoahaz the son of Josiah, and anointed him, and made him king in his father's stead."*

The three months' reign of Jehoahaz is briefly dismissed by the Holy Spirit with the statement that *"He did evil in the sight of the Lord,"* and as predicted by Jeremiah, he was carried captive into Egypt and died there.

CHAPTER 24

Verse 1 says, *"In his days Nebuchadnezzar king of Babylon came up, and Jehoiakim became his servant three years."*

There were two kings who reigned eleven years each - Jehoiakim and Zedekiah; and two who reigned three months each - Jehoahaz and Jehoiachin, all after the good reign of Josiah. The time was drawing near when the kingdom of Judah would pay for its sins, going into captivity like the ten tribes about 111 years before.

In the book of Daniel God reveals the great fact that He took the government of the world out of Israel's hand and placed it in the hand of Nebuchadnezzar to whom it was said: *"Thou art this head of gold."*

It was God's will that unrepentant Judah be punished for her many sins and that Nebuchadnezzar would be the chastening rod. So, consequently, when the 1st verse says concerning Jehoiakim that he *"rebelled against him,"* this was very displeasing to the Lord.

Therefore, in the 2nd verse it says, *"And the Lord sent against him bands of Chaldees, Syrians, Moabites, and Ammonites to begin destroying Judah, as He had predicted by the prophets."* Then came Nebuchadnezzar whom He had predicted by name as being the one to destroy Judah and Jerusalem. God commanded the destruction of Judah, and their removal out of the land for the sins of the kings and the people.

In this narrative because of sin, God is not blessing His chosen people but is actually working against them. God cannot abide sin or the refusal to repent on the part of anyone.

The 3rd verse says, *"To remove them out of his sight."*

The 4th verse which makes the statement, *"Which the Lord would not pardon,"* does not refer to Manasseh not being forgiven by the Lord when he did truly repent, but it does refer to Judah who kept going back into the most hideous of sins.

The 6th verse says concerning Jehoiakim, *"slept with his fathers."* This speaks of his death. It says nothing about him being buried because he was not buried. His body was left in the open field and treated like a beast.

Verse 7 speaks of the ascension of the mighty Babylonian Empire, for it says, *"And the king of Egypt came not again any more out of his land,"* meaning that Babylon had conquered Egypt.

The Lord favored the rise of the Babylonians over the Egyptians after considering the fact that His own people Israel had turned their backs upon their Creator.

Civilization from this point would gradually begin to go westward. Egypt's demise would continue. Babylon would grow powerful and strong, and then in the last days of Daniel the golden kingdom would be defeated by the Medes and the Persians.

Then God would speed up the process with an entirely new way of thinking with the rise of the Grecian Empire under Alexander the Great. Democracy now, at least after a fashion, would make its debut. Then the mighty Roman Empire would come into play, ruling the world more or less for 1,000 years. It was during this time, as Daniel had prophesied, that the Messiah would come.

The Gospel of the New Testament, beginning at Jerusalem, would ultimately shift to Antioch, and then under the Apostle Paul would gradually push westward to England, and then finally to America and the rest of the world.

About 100 years after the advent of the Early Church, the Church would gradually begin to apostatize, ultimately going into what would be known as the Catholic church, with its "justification by works." The battle would rage all the way up through the Dark Ages until the time of the Reformation, with its battle cry, "The just shall live by faith."

Then civilization was pushed forward again at the turn of the 19th century, with the outpouring of the Holy Spirit. With this outpouring came an enlightenment of intelligence. It seems that the nations of the world that embraced the Holy Spirit, even in a limited way, were blessed by God in the realm of advancement and achievement. Consequently, almost all of the inventions that have taken place in any and every field since the turn of the

NOTES

century, have come about through nations that have at least in some small way, embraced the outpouring of the Holy Spirit.

Now with great technological advancement, the evangelization of every nation that the Holy Spirit has promoted since the very beginning, is within the grasp of the Body of Christ.

The 10th verse says, *"At that time"* (in the reign of Jehoiachin), *"the servants of Nebuchadnezzar king of Babylon came up against Jerusalem, and the city was besieged."*

The 14th verse says, *"And he carried away all Jerusalem, and all the princes, and all the mighty men of valour."*

In this first deportation were carried away Mordecai, Ezekiel, Daniel, and Nehemiah.

The 18th verse says, *"Zedekiah was twenty and one years old when he began to reign."*

The 20th verse says, *"That Zedekiah rebelled against the king of Babylon."* The first part of the verse says, *"For through the anger of the Lord,"* meaning that God permitted Zedekiah to rebel, for it was determined that Judah should be destroyed at this time and go into captivity because of repeated sinning.

This was to be the last rebellion of Judah, for Nebuchadnezzar was determined to take all the Jews captive except for a few of the poorest people in the land. He intended to destroy the nation and make it ineffective as a military power, so that he would have no more trouble from this source.

CHAPTER 25

The 1st verse says concerning Nebuchadnezzar that *"came he, and all his hosts, against Jerusalem, and pitched against it."* The exact day of this siege was revealed to Ezekiel in a vision in far away Babylon (Ezek. 24:1).

The 3rd verse says, *"The famine prevailed in the city."* This had been prophesied by Moses and others if, in fact, Israel would turn her back upon God, which she did.

Concerning the king, the 7th verse says, *"And put out the eyes of Zedekiah, and bound him with fetters of brass, and carried him to*

Babylon." The wrath of God fell as predicted by Jeremiah, and Judah was carried into captivity with the last king dying a blinded prisoner in Babylon.

The prophets, Jeremiah and Ezekiel, predicted that he should see the king of Babylon but not the city of Babylon, and, yet, he would die there. So it came to pass. He saw the king of Babylon at Riblah where his eyes were put out. He was then carried to Babylon, and being blind, he could not see. Then he died there.

The 13th verse says, *"And the pillars of brass that were in the house of the Lord."* These giant copper pillars represent the people of God. There were two of them. They set at the immediate front of the Temple.

The Lord Jesus Christ some 600 years later said, *"Him that overcometh will I make a pillar in the temple of my God."* The children of Israel did not overcome; therefore, they could not be pillars in the Temple of God. So, they were taken away. The term concerning the pillars, *"break in pieces,"* aptly describes the children of Israel who were literally broken in pieces.

Verses 13-17 have little interest for the unspiritual mind, but to the heart who knows God, how full of agony they appear! These precious vessels and all this gathered wealth designed by God Himself to express the millennial glories of Christ as King and Priest were broken, dishonored, and carried to Babylon. This was a sad result of the unbelief of the elect nation to whom God had entrusted such glories!

The latter portion of the 21st verse says, *"So Judah was carried away out of their land."* This completed the judgment of God upon Judah, the people He had sought to bless for centuries and could not because of their sins and stubbornness. He tried redeeming them again 70 years later but had to permit their total destruction again as a nation in A.D. 70 because of their rejection of Christ (Luke 21:20-24).

After the fall of Jerusalem and the appointment of Gedaliah as governor, many went into Egypt in defiance of God and His prophets (Jer. 42-43). The 26th verse says, *"Arose, and came to Egypt."* Jeremiah told them that Egypt would also be given to Nebuchadnezzar and they, therefore, would still be in his dominion (Jer. 44:29-30).

NOTES

Jehoiachin, who had been taken captive into Babylon sometime earlier, was held some 37 years in Babylon. He was liberated by Evil-Merodach in the first year of his reign. Merodach exalted Jehoiachin higher than any other of the captive kings in Babylon, even permitting him to eat at his own table until his death.

Thus, Jehovah's throne at Jerusalem was cast down, and man's throne at Babylon was set up, and, strangely, God recognized it and committed to it the government of the world. With it commences the *"times of the Gentiles,"* which are to continue up to, and close with the reign of the last great king of Babylon, the Antichrist.

The display of love, patience, and pity of God to unbelieving and rebellious Israel up to the very capture of the city is most impressive. Over and over again through the prophets Jeremiah and Ezekiel, the Lord appealed to the people to repent, but, sadly, they would not.

THE
BOOK OF I CHRONICLES

The name *"Chronicles"* is from the Hebrew, *"Dibrei hayyamim,"* which means, *"words of the days,"* or in modern language, *"the diary."* But how intensely interesting - a diary kept by God!

The two books, like I and II Kings, were only one originally. The division was the work of the Septuagint translators and was adopted by Jerome, then by various branches of the western Church.

The two books of Chronicles are not new history; they cover many things written before. They belong to quite another part of the Old Testament because they do not follow in sequence after the books of Kings. They are, according to the Jewish Canon, the conclusion of the Old Testament, and the genealogies here lead to those of the New Testament. They begin with the first Adam and end looking forward to the second Adam (Christ). They deal primarily with the kingdom of Judah, because Christ was to be the successor of David on an eternal throne. As compared with I and II Kings which give the history from the human standpoint, the two books of Chronicles give the history from the divine standpoint.

The former records are as man ruled history; the latter are as God overruled it. Only four verses are devoted to Hezekiah's reformation in II Kings; whereas, three whole chapters are given to it in Chronicles. The books of Chronicles give God's standpoint, pointing to the moral side and giving reasons for both judgments and mercies.

The books of Kings are chronological in order; whereas, in Chronicles chronology is sometimes ignored in order to bring out causes or consequences for the purpose of comparison and contrast between records.

NOTES

In Kings we have the complete history of both houses of Israel, while in Chronicles we have only that which pertains to the house of David and of Judah as being founded on the covenant God made with David of the tribe of Judah found in II Samuel 7 and I Chronicles 17. The Chronicles are entirely independent of the books of Samuel and Kings and the differences between them are designed to be so. Many critics create their own difficulties by first assuming that all the books should be alike, which they are not, so they conclude that there are many discrepancies and corruptions in the text, when actually the writings are full of divine instruction containing editions for our learning.

CHAPTER 1

Verse 1 says, *"Adam."* The writer of Chronicles began abruptly with *"Adam,"* supposing that his readers would understand from the first book of the Bible about the origin of Adam, the first man from whom all other men have their beings (Gen. 1:26-31; 2:7).

Verse 4 says, *"Noah."* There are ten generations from Adam to Noah or from Adam to the flood. The balance of the 4th verse says, *"Shem, Ham, and Japheth."* From these three came all the descendants of planet Earth.

Verse 5 gives the *"sons of Japheth."* The descendants of Japheth overran Europe, England, and, eventually, the United States.

The 8th verse says, *"the sons of Ham."* The descendants of Ham first went into the Middle East, where they were exterminated or driven

417

out by the *"sons of Shem"* and eventually populated Africa.

The 17th verse says, *"The sons of Shem,"* who overran the Middle East.

The 19th verse gives us an interesting comment by the Holy Spirit. It says, *"Because in his days the earth was divided."* Today, there is mounting evidence that our continents were one time joined together. It is said that the continents could be fitted together like a jigsaw puzzle; the east coastline of South America matches the west-coastline of Africa, with the rounded corner of Brazil fitting into the Gulf of Guinea. The facing coasts of the United States and Europe can be fitted together as well.

At last, scientists are waking up to a fact which the Bible recorded as truth about 4000 years ago (Gen. 10:25). It was in the days of *"Peleg"* that God divided the earth after the confusion of tongues and the scattering of the people abroad over the face of the earth from Babel (Gen. 11:7-9).

Without this truth, we have no explanation for the presence of the American Indians and inhabitants of numerous islands before the discoveries made by explorers from the Old World.

The 28th verse says, *"The sons of Abraham, Isaac, and Ishmael."* The first ten generations, as stated, went from Adam to Noah. As well, there were ten generations from Noah to Abraham, or a period of nearly 2100 years from Adam to the 75th year of Abraham (Gen. 12:4).

Isaac, though younger than Ishmael, is placed first as the legitimate heir since Sarah was the only true wife of Abraham. But in the genealogy the sons of Ishmael and of Abraham's second wife are put first, so that the true line of the Messiah might be dealt with more fully, for that is the real purpose of all the genealogies.

Ishmael, Abraham's son through Hagar, had 12 sons like Jacob had. They were also the heads of 12 tribes, making 24 tribes who descended from Abraham through two of his sons.

The 12 tribes that came from Hagar settled in the countries of Arabia. They were the fulfillment of a prediction made by God of Ishmael, a prediction of 12 princes who would multiply exceedingly (Gen. 17:20; 25:12-18).

In verse 34 it says, *"The sons of Isaac; Esau and Israel (Jacob)."* Now, the author comes back to Isaac and his seed, Esau and Jacob, and follows the main purpose of his writing, dealing briefly with the seed of Esau first before going into the more lengthy genealogies of the seed of Jacob of Israel. After this He writes 12 chapters recording the genealogies of Jacob's sons to the time of Saul and David.

The 35th verse says, *"The sons of Esau, Eliphaz. . . ."* This was the Eliphaz of the book of Job who was a Temanite (Job 2:11; 4:1).

The 36th verse says, *". . .and Amalek."* This man, a descendant of Esau, was noted for his opposition to Israel. The Amalekites were the first to attack the nation while coming out of Egypt. For this God swore that they would have war from generation to generation and ultimately be destroyed. This was true, and they were finally destroyed by Saul - all but a few. One of the reasons Saul was cut off was that he spared some of the Amalekites (I Sam. 15). They were a symbol of the flesh ever at war with the Spirit.

CHAPTER 2

Verses 1 and 2 list the 12 sons of Jacob (Israel). These sons are not listed in rank of birth. The six sons of Leah are given first, then the four sons of Rachel and her maid with Joseph and Benjamin, the sons of Rachel, between the two sons of her maid. After that came the two sons of Leah's maid. To speculate why they are listed in this order is useless, for there are no less than 24 combinations of such names.

Verse 3 says, *"The sons of Judah."* After listing the 12 sons of Jacob, the writer takes up the sons and descendants of Judah, the fourth son of Jacob and Leah. The reason for dealing with Judah first was that he was to be the chief and ruling tribe of the 12, and the Messiah was to come through him (Gen. 49:8-12).

The 3rd verse also says, *"And Er, the first-born of Judah, was evil in the sight of the Lord; and he slew him."* The evil thing that caused the Lord to slay Er was not recorded either in

Genesis 38 or elsewhere in Scripture. All we know is that it was something God hated so much that He slew him. It could have been the same sin for which God killed Onan as in Genesis 38:8-10 - that of refusing to have off-spring. This sin (Onanism) was the first sin that caused God to take human life, unless the sin of Er was something different. God commanded man to multiply and replenish the earth with his own kind, and a sin of this nature was against bringing into existence one in God's own image and likeness.

The 5th verse says, *"The sons of Pharez."* The line of the Messiah came through Pharez of these twins (Ruth 4:18; Luke 3:23-38). The kingly line also came through him (Matt. 1:1-17).

The 15th verse says, *"David the seventh."* Actually, we know that Jesse, David's father, begat eight sons (I Sam. 16:6-11; 17:12-14). Here, only seven are numbered and named. David was the youngest (I Sam. 16:11), so the eighth may have died while young and without offspring. While it was proper to mention eight sons in the history, it was unnecessary to do so in the genealogy.

The 16th verse says, *"Abishai, and Joab, and Asahel."* These three nephews of David played important roles in David's kingdom, especially Joab who was captain of the host until the death of David.

The 55th verse says, *". . . which dwelt at Jabez,"* of which more will be said momentarily. This is a city that was supposed to have been founded by Jabez of 4:9-10.

As well, the 55th verse says, *". . . are the Kenites that came of Hemath, the father of the house of Rechab."* The Kenites were the descendants of Jethro, father-in-law of Moses (Judg. 1:16; 4:11-17). It is unusual that they should be alluded to as the descendants of Judah. This was because they were attached to the tribe of Judah in their inheritance and had become intermixed with them for so many centuries.

CHAPTER 3

Chapter 3 principally concerns itself with

NOTES

David. Verse 1 says, *"Now these were the sons of David which were born unto him in Hebron."*

Verse 5 adds, *"And these were born unto him in Jerusalem."*

The six mentioned in verses 1-4 were born to him in Hebron while he reigned there for seven years and six months. The others of verses 5-8 were born in Jerusalem when he reigned over the United Kingdom of Israel for 33 years. David reigned first over Judah and then over all of Israel. This was the first division of the Kingdom of Israel, the second and final division being after the death of Solomon when ten tribes were given to Jeroboam. Rehoboam kept Judah, Benjamin, Levi, and many people from the other ten tribes who filtered down to Judah.

Verse 5 also mentions *"Nathan."* He was the son through whom the Messiah actually came. This was Mary's family line (Luke 3:23-38). Joseph was of the kingly line through *"Solomon,"* also found in the 5th verse.

The 10th verse says, *"And Solomon's son was Rehoboam."* There were 21 royal descendants of David through Solomon who occupied the throne of Judah. They are as follows:

Rehoboam, Abijam, Asa, Jehoshaphat, Joram, Ahaziah, Joash, Amaziah, Azariah, Jotham, Ahaz, Hezekiah, Manasseh, Amon, Josiah, Johanan, Jehoahaz, Jedekiah, Jehoiakim, Jeconiah, and Zedekiah.

The wicked queen *"Athaliah,"* who reigned six years in Judah, is not listed here in the royal genealogy. She reigned between Ahaziah and Joash. As well, *"Johanan"* was really not a king, and nothing else is known about him.

The 17th verse says, *"And the sons of Jeconiah."* (He was also called *"Jehoiachin"* or *"Coniah."*)

Though Jehoiachin had eight sons, not one of them or any descendant of any one of them could ever sit on the throne of David and rule in Jerusalem over Israel, for God had cursed him and his seed forever, cutting them off from kingship.

The next king of Judah was not of his seed; he was an uncle.

The Eternal King of Judah was to be the Messiah, Who was not to come of the kingly line, yet had to obtain the throne rites through the kingly line to fulfill the Davidic Covenant regarding an eternal king of David's seed.

This was completely met in Mary, the virgin mother of the Messiah, who came through Nathan, the son of David, who was not the kingly line, and in Joseph who was the legal heir to the throne through Solomon, the son of David. When Joseph (whose genealogy is in Matthew 1:1-17) married Mary (whose genealogy is in Luke 3:23-38), it caused Jesus to be counted the firstborn of the family of Joseph and Mary, and, therefore, the legal heir to the throne of David. And, yet, he did not come through Jehoiachin (Coniah) so that the curse of Jeremiah 22:4-30 was literally fulfilled.

CHAPTER 4

The 1st verse says, *"The sons of Judah."*

After giving us a long list of descendants of Judah in chapters two and three from Judah to Jeconiah, the last king of Judah of David's line, the writer begins again with descendants of Judah and traces them through Hur, Shobal, Ashur, Chelub, Kenaz, Caleb, and Shelah. In this chapter there are three interesting observations.

Verses 9 and 10 give this little refreshing note on *"Jabez."* Verse 9 says, *"And Jabez was more honourable than his brethren."* The Holy Spirit began this notation concerning this man by making the statement just mentioned. The reason was the trust in God and hunger for God that Jabez had.

The Scripture says, *"And his mother called his name Jabez."* In Hebrew culture the mother, with some few exceptions, always named the child. In that culture the name was very important. If the Holy Spirit did not impress upon her the name that was to be given, as He sometimes did, she would name the child according to what she wanted him to be or because of something that had happened in the family that was either a blessing or a curse (especially the boys). This lady in naming her little boy *"Jabez"* which means *"he makes sorrow,"* either did not want him, or else felt she could not properly care for him. Therefore, the child by being given this name would

always be reminded of the negative circumstances of his birth. This severe hindrance could have turned him toward bitterness, which would have destroyed him, or toward God. Jabez allowed it to turn him toward God. Every difficulty in the life of any person who knows the Lord, irrespective of its severity, can be turned into a blessing. God specializes in turning the curse into a blessing. Regrettably, too many individuals grow embittered, blaming others and even God for their circumstances. Thusly, their circumstances only grow worse. There is another way, and the 10th verse tells us what it is:

"And Jabez called on the God of Israel." This is man's answer for any and all problems. There is no other. Regrettably, the Church turns to humanistic psychology, the latest fad, or even to the New Age movement. The answer, and, in fact, the only answer, is that of which Jabez availed himself. He made five requests:

1. Bless me indeed.
2. Enlarge my coast.
3. Let your hand be with me.
4. Keep me from evil.
5. Keep me from grief.

God heard Jabez, and we have all the right in the world to believe that He will also hear all others who pray likewise from the heart, for He is no respecter of persons (Rom. 2:11). (There is some indication that the city Jabez in Judah was named after him in 2:55).

The second incident of blessing in this chapter is found in the 18th verse, *"The daughter of Pharaoh, which Mered took."* This passage makes this woman immortal! She was an Egyptian and the daughter of Pharaoh as well. She converts, joins the people of God, and receives a new name, Bithiah, which means *"the daughter of Jehovah!"*

The proud daughter of the Egyptian monarch degrades herself (in Egypt's eyes) by becoming the wife of a Hebrew slave. No doubt, her name was, therefore, with ignominy, erased from the royal genealogy of Egypt, but— what eternal glory – engraved among the daughters of the royal family of heaven!

The third beautiful incident is found in verses 21-23. It says, *"The sons of Shelah the son of Judah,"* and then it says in the 23rd verse, *"These were the potters,"* and *"There they dwelt with the king for his work."*

Verses 22 and 23 may be thus read: *"Jokim and Saraph, who married in Moab, returned to Bethlehem."* (These records are ancient). These were the potters who dwelt among plants and hedges with the king for his work. Like Ruth and Naomi (Ruth 1:19), they returned from Moab to Bethlehem and were employed on the royal estate in a very humble position. But the Holy Spirit seems to add with exquisite grace that the work, though lowly, was work *"for the king,"* and they dwelt there *"with the king!"* No doubt, the king dwelt in the palace and they in a cottage down by the plants and hedges, but it is recorded of them that *"they dwelt with the king!"* Such is grace that today points to some hidden ministries that were afar off and ennobles them by recording that *"they dwell with the king for his work."* Excavations at around the turn of the century at this pottery site have revealed vessels bearing the names of the potters as given in these verses.

All three of these beautiful incidents regard individuals of low estate, (or else would be rendered such as in the daughter of Pharaoh), thus signifying by the Holy Spirit that *"not many mighty, not many noble are called."* What a blessing to so many of us who fall into these categories of the *"lowly."*

The 40th verse says, *"For they of Ham had dwelt there of old."* This tells us that the descendants of Ham (Noah's son) possessed these parts in ancient times. When and by whom they were driven out is not fully known. We know that from then to the conquest of Canaan by Israel the giants ruled that section and might have driven out the sons of Ham. The reason the Simeonites conquered it was to possess the pastureland.

CHAPTER 5

The 1st verse says, *"Now the sons of Reuben the firstborn of Israel"* (Jacob). Reuben, being the firstborn, should have had the birthright, but he forfeited it due to sin on his part. Therefore, the Scripture says, *"And the genealogy is*

NOTES

not to be reckoned after the birthright." Reuben was the first son of Jacob and Leah. He was unstable and did not possess the traits of priest, prophet, or king. That is why his genealogy was not given first. In his place Judah inherited the kingly rites (Gen. 49:10), and Joseph inherited the other blessings of the birthright.

For verse 2 says, *"For Judah prevailed above his brethren, and of him came the chief ruler; but the birthright was Joseph's."* There are about ten verses devoted to the record of the sons of Reuben compared to about a hundred for Judah.

The genealogy carrying the history all the way from Jacob to the captivity speaks of a special victory that was won during the days of Saul, the first king of Israel. It speaks of the sons of Reuben making war with particular heathen tribes in Israel. The 20th verse says, *And they were helped against them,"* and then it gives the reason why by saying, *"For they cried to God in the battle, and he was intreated of them; because they put their trust in him."* Even though Reuben so many years before had sinned and forfeited the birthright, still God would not deny Reuben the privilege of repentance (which he did) or many of the privileges that went with the honor of being a son of Jacob, such as his name being forever inscribed on one of the 12 gates of the New Jerusalem (Rev. 21:12). As well, God would bless his descendants as is here recorded. Through both Moses and Ezekiel, the Lord would inform Israel and all of mankind that each person would be responsible for his own sin and not the sins of others (Ezek. 18:1-4).

The 22nd verse says, *"For there fell down many slain, because the war was of God."* God's plan was for several things to be brought about regarding His people Israel. It would include the defeat of certain heathen tribes. All God required of His people was faith. Sadly, in the later portion of this chapter even that is lacking.

Verses 25 and 26 speaks of idolatry and the first captivity of Israel to Assyria.

Verse 25 says, *"And they transgressed against the God of their fathers."* In other words, they went into idolatry.

The 26th verse says, *"And the God of Israel*

stirred up the spirit of Pul king of Assyria, and the spirit of Tilgath-pilneser king of Assyria." Even though these two heathen kings of Assyria thought the idea was theirs regarding the invasion of Israel, still, behind the scenes God was pulling the strings and setting the stage. In other words, this heathen nation *"Assyria"* was God's rod of chastisement.

I think it can scripturally be said that God continues with the same methods today (Heb. 12:5-11). The methods that God may choose to use will vary.

CHAPTER 6

The 1st verse says, *"The sons of Levi; Gershom, Kohath, and Merari."* These were three branches of the Levites who were responsible for various services to the Tabernacle and then to the Temple. The 48th verse says, *"Their brethren also the Levites were appointed unto all manner of service of the tabernacle of the house of God."* Of the tribe of Levi there were basically five great areas of duty:

1. The Gershonites (Num. 3:21-4:27) - a particular described work in the Tabernacle and then later in the Temple.

2. The Kohathites (Num. 3:27-4:37) - a particular described work in the Tabernacle and later in the Temple.

3. The Merarites (Num. 3:17-4:45) - a particular described work in the Tabernacle and later in the Temple.

4. Choir leaders in the house of the Lord - *"Heman the Kohathite,"* *"Asaph the Gershonite,"* and *"Ethan the Merarite."* The 31st verse says, *"And these are they whom David set over the service of song in the house of the Lord, after that the ark had rest."* The great part that music plays in worship, by and large, had its beginning with David and the choirs.

For the 32nd verse says, *"And they ministered before the dwelling place of the tabernacle of the congregation with singing, until Solomon had built the house of the Lord in Jerusalem."* It is said that each day the various choirs under the three lead singers gathered at the Temple site and ministered in worship and

NOTES

singing. Some even said that this was done each day at the rising of the sun. This greeted Jerusalem at the beginning of each new day with worship and praise unto the Lord. Hallelujah! (Incidentally, Heman was Samuel's grandson - verse 33.)

5. The Priest. Verse 49 says, *"But Aaron and his sons offered upon the altar of the burnt offering, and the altar of incense, and were appointed for all the work of the place most holy."* Only the priests were allowed to do this work, not the kings nor prophets unless they were of the tribe of Levi. Kings were never of this tribe, but sometimes a prophet would also be a Levite. All of the Levites whether priests, or choir directors came from one of the branches of *"Gershon, Kohath, and Merari."* The term *"Levite,"* referring to the descendants of Levi, is found 293 times in the Bible.

CHAPTER 7

Chapter 7 denotes the generations or the genealogy of the tribes of *"Issachar, Benjamin, Naphtali, Manasseh, Ephraim, and Asher."* It should be understood that only partial genealogies of most of the tribes of Israel are given. The tribe of Dan is not mentioned in these genealogies. The reason why is not known. Some have suggested that Dan went into idol worship, therefore was omitted here as well as in Revelation chapter 7. However, all of the tribes went into idol worship. As well, it has been suggested that Dan may possibly be the tribe from which the Antichrist will come. Genesis 49:17 does lend some credence to this theory. One thing is certain: The Holy Spirit left out Dan for a purpose and a reason. It definitely was not an oversight.

Concerning the tribes, several times the Word of God says, *"They were valiant men of might in their generation"* (Verse 2). And then in the 7th verse it says, *"Mighty men of valour."*

Actually, this term will be used concerning several of the tribes. The might and glory of Israel when they were actually serving God, is almost beyond our comprehension. During the latter half of David's reign and the entirety of Solomon's reign, Israel was the mightiest nation on the earth of that day. The degree of intelligence possessed by these people so far eclipsed any other people or nation in the world that there was no comparison. No wonder when the Queen of Sheba saw the glory of Israel that the Scripture says, *"There was no more spirit left in her"* (I Kings 10:5). And then she said that what she had heard was not exaggeration, *"It was a true report"* (I Kings 10:6). Israel only lost her way whenever she turned her back on God.

The Apostle Paul would ask the question, *"What advantage then hath the Jew?"* (Rom. 3:1). And then he would answer, *"Much every way"* (Rom. 3:2).

One day the glory of Israel will be reestablished. Paul, in effect, says, *"If, in consequence of their rebellion, the riches of God's grace have come to the Gentile world, how much more will the world be blessed when Israel comes to her fullness of blessing again"* (Rom. 11:12).

The 15th verse says concerning the sons of Manasseh, *"And the name of the second was Zelophehad: and Zelophehad had daughters."* Once again this man is mentioned, with his fame being derived from the faith of his daughters (Num. 26:33). God always honors faith. Tragically, doubt never dies unless washed by the Blood of Jesus, and, gloriously, faith never dies but extends its influence forever.

CHAPTER 8

This chapter gives the generations or the genealogy of the tribe of Benjamin from the birth of the youngest son of Jacob to the captivity. The writer gives a long list of the sons of Benjamin leading up to the family of Saul, which is given in some 40 verses. The date of the writing was after the captivity into Babylon. This shows that Benjamin and the other tribes were restored after the Babylonian captivity.

After the death of Solomon and with the advent of his son Rehoboam to the throne, Israel split into the northern and southern

kingdoms. Supposedly, 11 of the 12 tribes went into the northern kingdom which was called by a variety of names, *"Israel, Samaria, and Ephraim,"* with the southern kingdom containing only Judah. However, there is much evidence that Benjamin remained true and loyal to Judah. For the 28th verse says concerning many of the chief men of the tribe of Benjamin, *"these dwelt in Jerusalem."* This proves that Benjamin adhered to the worship of the true God and remained loyal to Judah. As well, it seems that Simeon, whose inheritance was within the inheritance of Judah, may have remained loyal also.

From the tribe of Benjamin would come the first king of Israel, *"Saul."* As well, from the tribe of Benjamin would come Saul's namesake, *"Saul"* (Paul) of the New Testament, one of the greatest men of God who ever lived.

It is ironic that Saul, the first king of Israel, was thought to have brought fame and glory to the tribe of Benjamin, but, instead, brought disgrace. Yet, Saul of Tarsus (Paul), who was thought to have brought only disgrace to the tribe of Benjamin, instead, brought the tribe everlasting glory. They will recognize such when Israel is once again restored in the great Millennial Reign. That which man chooses has no merit with God. That which God chooses, sadly, has no merit with man.

CHAPTER 9

The 1st verse says, *"So all Israel were reckoned by genealogies."* And then it says, *"Behold, they were written in the book of the kings of Israel and Judah."* This is a book which we do not have now but which no doubt contained a complete record of the genealogies of Israel. From this the author of Chronicles took only a part to serve his purpose of identifying certain key men in the history of the nation by giving their background so that something could be known of the coming Messiah's ancestors.

During the time of Christ, the genealogy of every tribe and also of every family in Israel was kept in the Temple. This was very important for several reasons.

First of all, each family of Israel could trace their ancestry all the way back to Abraham.

Second, each family could know to which tribe they belonged.

Third, each family could know the portion of the land that had been allotted to their tribe during the days of Joshua, and even the part that belonged to their immediate family. (However, during the time of Christ, many of the inheritances had been lost due to Roman occupation.)

Fourth, Israel could know the kingly line as well as the lineage of the high priest. (At the time of Christ, Israel had not had a king for nearly 600 years. However, if the kingly line had continued unbroken, Joseph, Jesus' foster father, would have been king of Israel. As well, the lineage of the Aaronic priesthood had long since been broken because of sin and the Roman occupation. At this time, the office of the high priest was bought and sold as a political office.)

Fifth and most important of all, Israel knew that the Messiah was to come through the tribe of Judah (Gen. 49:10), and that if the kingly line of David from the tribe of Judah had continued, Jesus would now be the king of Israel. There was no excuse for Israel not to know His identity. Along with His miracles and His anointing that was greater than any other, they could easily have gone to the genealogical records at the Temple in Jerusalem and verified His genealogical claim. The claim was irrefutable.

The 2nd verse says, *"The Nethinims."* Some think these were the descendants of the Gibeonites who deceived Joshua at the beginning of the occupation of Canaan, and who were made *"hewers of wood and drawers of water unto all the congregation"* (Josh. 9:21). If this in fact is correct, Grace would have taken a people who were doomed to die by the curse of God and would have granted them life everlasting. Their sentence as servants would have given them access to the brazen altar (wood for the altar) and the brazen laver (water for the laver), and, thereby, closeness to the presence of God. How so like the poor sinner who is doomed to die, but Grace reverses the sentence and brings us into the very presence of God.

Hallelujah!

The 3rd verse says, *"And in Jerusalem dwelt of the children of Judah, and of the children of Benjamin, and of the children of Ephraim, and Manasseh."* The children of the two tribes of Ephraim and Manasseh were representative of the ten tribes, for the northern ten-tribe kingdom was often called Ephraim. This proves that many of the whole 13 tribes of Israel returned to make the new nation after the Babylonian captivity, not just Judah and Benjamin.

It also proves that Israelites from the other tribes besides Judah and Benjamin were included in the people known as Jews.

The 22nd verse has an interesting observation. It says, *"Whom David and Samuel the seer did ordain in their set office."* Here we have proof that Samuel and David counseled together and received revelations of the coming Temple worship. Such things were thus planned during the lifetime of Saul when David was driven from Saul's court as a fugitive and an outlaw.

The 33rd verse says, *"And these are the singers."* And then it says, *"For they were employed in that work day and night."* This refers to the rebuilding of the Temple and Jerusalem after the captivity in Babylon. It seems that great efforts were being made to carry on the worship of God as it had been instituted by David about 500 years before.

CHAPTER 10

Verse 1 says, *"And the men of Israel fled from before the Philistines, and fell down slain in mount Gilboa."* The Holy Spirit in the last 10 verses of the 9th chapter recites the pedigree of King Saul, and then in chapter 10 repeats the circumstances of that monarch's death and thus presents an introduction to the kingdom of David. This is an exceedingly sad chapter.

It is evident over and over again that when the Lord was with Israel, they won their battles. When He did not help Israel, they lost their battles. Israel's strength was God; Israel's power was God; Israel's glory was God. The only thing that could separate Israel from God was

NOTES

sin. The same holds true for us today.

"Mount Gilboa" is situated at the northwestern end of the valley of Megiddo. One can stand on a hill near by Nazareth, which is situated across the valley of Megiddo on the eastern side, and easily see *"Mount Gilboa."* It was here where Saul and his sons died.

In I Samuel the *"fact"* of the wrath of God on Saul is recorded. In I Chronicles the *"reason"* for God's wrath is recorded. This is an illustration of the characteristic difference between the book of Kings and the book of Chronicles.

The 2nd verse says, *"And the Philistines slew Jonathan, and Abinadab, and Malchishua, the sons of Saul."* These were the ones who accompanied him into the battle. There were other sons who stayed at home and did not die. The Holy Spirit places Jonathan's name first. How different it could have been for Jonathan had he forsaken his father's court and thrown in completely with David. He loved and stood up for David, but he never joined him in exile. It ultimately cost him his life. There is some reason to believe that Jonathan had seriously considered throwing in his lot completely with David, for he said, *"And thou shalt be king over Israel, and I shall be next unto thee"* (I Sam. 23:17).

However, the Holy Spirit then says, *"And David abode in the wood, and Jonathan went to his house"* (I Sam. 23:18). Even though the Holy Spirit gave very little enlightenment upon the subject, still, it seems from what was said that the Spirit of God dealt with Jonathan concerning a total alignment with David.

The 4th verse records the ignoble end of the first king of Israel because of sin. The Holy Spirit says, *"So Saul took a sword, and fell upon it."* In other words, he committed suicide. He started so well and concluded so poorly. At any time along the way he could have turned to God, and the Lord would have shown grace and mercy. He failed to defeat the enemy within, which was self-will, jealousy, and pride, therefore, the enemy without, *"the Philistines,"* ultimately defeated him.

The 7th verse says concerning the Israelites who lived in that part of Israel, *"They forsook their cities, and fled: and the Philistines came and dwelt in them."* How many cities were forsaken is not stated, but it appears that all of them on the west of Jordan and in this particular battle section became Philistine cities for a time, 10 or 12 years, perhaps. When David became king over all Israel, these cities were recovered and the kingdom of Israel for the first time became truly great. It extended to the river of Egypt and the gulf of Akabah, north to the Euphrates, taking in all of Philistia, Amalek, Edom, Moab, Syria, and other countries. Of course, it was Satan's strong desire that the Philistines dwell in that which belonged to God's people Israel. Likewise, it is Satan's desire that the enemy take that which God has promised to us as our rightful possession. Therefore, the battle ever rages with Satan trying to mar our inheritance.

The 8th verse says, *"When the Philistines came to strip the slain, that they found Saul and his sons fallen in mount Gilboa."* The evidence is obvious that Satan wants the last drop of blood. There can be no compromise with the evil one. We destroy him or he destroys us.

The 9th verse says, *"They took his head."* It was customary to take the heads of conquered kings and make sport with them in the houses of the gods and in the cities of their own people. Victories were great times of celebration.

Taking *"his head"* is something additional to I Samuel 31:9-10, and *"his body,"* as referred to there, is something additional to this passage. This shows that I and II Chronicles were not copies made by men of I and II Samuel and I and II Kings, but that the two accounts given in Samuel, Kings, and Chronicles were written by the Spirit of God. The different information given in both accounts shows an independent composition by an infallible Author.

The 12th verse says, *"And buried their bones under the oak in Jabesh."* I Samuel 31:12 says they burned them first and then buried them. They did the burning at night and then buried the bones under a tree. The city of *"Jabesh"* was where Saul had won his first military victory. The name *"Jabesh"* means *"hill of witnessing."* There he had fought *"Nahash the Ammonite"* (I Sam. 11) whose name means *"bright shining serpent."* So, Saul defeated the *"bright shining serpent"* at first but was defeated by the *"bright shining serpent" at the last.

I Samuel 31 records the fact of Saul's death. I Chronicles 10 records the reason. Men could see the outward historic event, but only the Spirit of God could reveal the cause of the event. The 13th verse says, *"So Saul died for his transgression which he committed against the Lord."* There were two reasons:

1. *"Even against the word of the Lord, which he kept not."*

2. *"And also for asking counsel of one that had a familiar spirit, and to inquire of it."*

Some may possibly read the words in I Samuel, *"And when Saul inquired of the Lord, the Lord answered him not, neither by dreams, nor by Urim, nor by prophets"* (I Sam. 28:6), and think there is a contradiction with I Chronicles 10:14. It should be noted that Hebrew scholars point out that the verb *"to inquire"* used in I Samuel is a different verb from that used in I Chronicles where it says, *"And inquired not of the Lord"* (Verse 14). The verb recorded in I Samuel records an outward and formal action; the other, referred to in I Chronicles, records an inward and deep emotion. Had Saul inquired of the Lord with the same intense earnestness with which he inquired of the witch, how prompt and gracious would have been the response!

The 14th verse as well says, *"Therefore he slew him, and turned the kingdom unto David the son of Jesse."* Even though in the past David had many opportunities to kill Saul, he would not do it. Even though when encouraged to by his men, he left it in the hands of the Lord. So, how much more gracious it reads concerning the death of Saul, *"Therefore He (God) slew him,"* instead of David. David's reasoning was correct, even though Saul was not God's will as the first king of Israel; still, after the people demanded a king, the Lord chose Saul on their behalf. Even though Saul repeatedly tried to kill David and brought much hardship upon *"God's anointed,"* still, David always respected him because God had selected him. Therefore, he left matters in the hands of the Lord. What a lesson we should learn from this.

NOTES

CHAPTER 11

Verse 1 says, *"Then all Israel gathered themselves to David."* It seems the people finally began to realize that David was God's man for the kingdom. By this time he had reigned over Judah in Hebron for seven and a half years. There were three reasons they gave as to why they should make David king:

1. He was their own, *"Thy bone and thy flesh."*

2. He was a great general, *"He that leddest out and broughtest in Israel."*

3. He was called by God, *"And the Lord thy God said unto thee, thou shalt feed My people Israel, and thou shall be ruler over My people Israel"* (Verse 2).

It is noticeable that they put God and His Word last just as men do today. These reasons, confessed by themselves, should have brought them to David's side long before, but, as a rule, men will not do what they know to be their duty until self-interest impels them.

Thus, David, the commanding figure of the first book of Chronicles, is introduced. He is a type of his greater Son, Jesus. Characteristically, the first event of the book is the deliverance of Jerusalem from the Jebusites and David's ascension to the throne of Jehovah on Zion. Such will be the action of Israel's great King in a future happy day.

So the 3rd verse says, *"And they anointed David king over Israel, according to the word of the Lord by Samuel."* Consequently, there are three things concerning David in this chapter:

1. His coronation (verse 3).

2. His new capital (verses 4-9).

3. His captains (verses 10-47).

The 4th verse says, *"And David and all Israel went to Jerusalem, which is Jebus; where the Jebusites were."*

David and his men, being led by the will of God, moved the capital of all Israel to Jerusalem. God had chosen Jerusalem as an eternal city in His plan, so now He led them there according to His will in the fulfillment of this plan. Jerusalem had long been a stronghold of the Jebusites who had controlled it ever since the conquest of Canaan, except for a short time when it was in the hands of Judah (Josh. 10:1-5). (It is said that Jerusalem is the "navel of the world" because it sits in the exact center of the planet.) It was said that the Jebusites were so strong that even mighty Egypt would not come against them.

Saul during his 40 year reign did not defeat the Jebusites. Actually, there is no record that he even attacked them.

As a type, the Jebusites symbolize a stronghold that Satan erects within our hearts and lives. Saul never did defeat the Jebusites who were within; consequently, the Philistines who were without eventually defeated him. Likewise, if we do not defeat the strongholds that are within our lives, those without will ultimately overcome us.

So, the very first thing that David did after becoming king was to defeat the Jebusites.

And yet the 5th verse says, *"And the inhabitants of Jebus said to David, thou shalt not come hither."* Satan will ever taunt us, declaring that since he has inhabited this stronghold for so long, he cannot be dislodged now. (II Sam. 5:7 calls it a *"stronghold."*)

But then the 5th verse continues to say, *"Nevertheless David took the castle of Zion, which is the City of David."* In other words, the Lord helped David take this stronghold of Satan that stood as a thorn in Israel's side and make it His capital city, *"the City of David."* Likewise, the Lord desires to take the area within our lives that has caused us so much difficulty, and make it our strength. Only the Lord can do so.

Man has ever tried to succeed in changing himself by his own efforts, education, personal strength, and ability. He has never been able to do so. Only the Lord Jesus Christ can change a person for the better.

The 6th verse says, *"And David said, Whosoever smiteth the Jebusites first shall be chief and captain."* The verse goes on to say, *"So Joab the son of Zeruiah went up first, and was chief."*

David was a type of Christ, but all types will fail. David, instead of personally capturing the city, offers to make chief and captain whoever does so, and this action fastens Joab, who at heart was a traitor, as a thorn in his side. David

NOTES

was mightily anointed by God for many things. The chief of which seemed to be military conquest. He should have been his own military chief and captain.

There is some evidence in this account of the taking of Jerusalem that concerns Uriah the Hittite. The mighty men who are listed in the remainder of this chapter at least in part owed the sight of their domicile to their prowess in the taking of the city of Jebus. Possibly, Uriah the Hittite did a great service for the king in helping to take this city, because it seems from II Samuel 11 that his house was next to David's. Those who gave the greatest account of themselves in this conflict were allowed to live closest to the king.

The *"City of David"* was called *"Zion"* (verse 5). The word is found 152 times in Scripture and only in the Old Testament (It is called Sion in the New Testament). This stronghold was one of the five heights on which Jerusalem was built - Akra, Bezetha, Moriah, Ophel, and Zion. Some consider Ophel and Zion to be the same. Zion and the City of David are the same. The word came to be used of Jerusalem and all Israel in general. The Church and Christians are never called Zion.

The 9th verse says, *"So David waxed greater and greater: for the Lord of Hosts was with him."* The victories were all tied to the Lord.

The 10th verse speaks of the *"mighty men whom David had, who strengthened themselves with him in the kingdom."*

There are 52 mighty men who are listed in this chapter. This is at the beginning of David's reign. At the conclusion of his reign and just before he died, only 37 mighty men are listed (II Sam. 23:8-39). Evidently, some 15 of them died or proved unfaithful during the reign and were, therefore, not counted with the 37 at the close of David's rule.

Among these 52 mighty men, Joab is not listed.

It should be understood that the *"might"* of these *"mighty men"* did not come from their own prowess but, instead, from David's anointing.

Also, it must ever be understood that God places His anointing only upon a man or a woman. He does not anoint denominations, church officials (just because they are church officials), committees, boards, or groups.

The Bible method is for God to anoint a man (or a woman), and for other individuals to gather around that person and draw from that anointing. This was so with Abraham, with Moses, with Joshua, with the Apostle Paul, and above all with the Lord Jesus Christ. Instead, the Church has substituted denominations, committees, or positions. There is no anointing in these.

Some of the deeds of these mighty men are listed. The first one is *"Jashobeam"* (verse 11). It says that he *"lifted up his spear against three hundred slain by him at one time."* II Samuel 23:8 reads 800 men. No, there is no contradiction. If the two accounts give two different numbers one of two things has happened:

1. The incident in question is not the same as the one given in the first account.

2. Some of the old manuscripts became marred through use, and copyists were, thereby, faced with difficulty. The fault is not with the original as inspired by God. All mistakes are from copyists or marred manuscripts and not from God's giving contradictory statements in the inspired records.

Verses 13 and 14 speak of a *"parcel of ground full of barley."* It says that *"Eleazar"* and *"David"* faced the Philistines *"and delivered it, and slew the Philistines."*

Barley being the least of all the grains, many, perhaps, would have thought it not worthy to defend. However, God desires that Satan be rooted out of every part of our inheritance, no matter how seemingly insignificant.

Verses 15 through 19 record the *"three captains"* who *"break through the host of the Philistines, and drew water out of the well of Bethlehem."* It then says that David *"poured it out to the Lord."* This speaks of the Lord Jesus Christ Who in the *"name of the Father, and of the Son, and of the Holy Ghost"* would *"break through the host of the Philistines"* (Satan) and then *"draw water"* out of the well of salvation. The *"water"* would be representative of His own life that would be *"poured out to the Lord."*

The 19th verse says, *"For with the jeopardy of their lives they brought it."* Jesus not only jeopardized His life but actually gave it.

The 20th verse says, *"And Abishai the*

brother of Joab." His accomplishment is that of killing 300 enemy soldiers in one battle. He was not among the first three of the mighty men but was the head of the second three; therefore, he was the fourth of the mighty men. Shammah, the third of the first three is not mentioned here but is listed in II Samuel 23:11-17. The reason for this is not known. He is mentioned in verse 27 but, perhaps, had not attained to the first three at this early part of David's reign and became numbered with them later as recorded in II Samuel 23:11-17. This list was made at the end of David's rule.

The 22nd verse says, *"Benaiah."* The Holy Spirit saw fit to list three mighty feats of bravery.

1. He slew two lion-like men of Moab.

2. He slew a lion in the midst of a pit in the time of snow.

3. He slew an Egyptian who had a spear in his hand. The Egyptian was 7 feet 6 inches tall with a spear like a weaver's beam. He went to him with a staff, plucked the spear out of his hand, and slew the man with his spear. The two *"lion-like men of Moab"* means they were mighty heroes of Moab.

The 25th verse says, *"And David set him over his guard."* There is a great spiritual meaning here.

Demon spirits of which the defeated represents will attempt to destroy the child of God. We must *"guard"* ourselves from their encroachment as *"Benaiah"* did.

The 41st verse says, *"Uriah the Hittite."* Likewise, Uriah was listed in II Samuel 23, although dead. An exception in listing him even though dead, perhaps, was because of the connection with David as the husband of the woman with whom he sinned.

CHAPTER 12

This is a glorious chapter as Israel finally begins to do God's will. The chapter begins in David's darkest days. It closes with unimaginable victory.

The first verse says, *"Now these are they that came to David to Ziklag."*

Ziklag was David's last encampment as an exile from Saul before becoming king of Judah. It had been a place of great defeat with the Amalekites smiting Ziklag and burning it with fire while David and his men were away. All of their families were taken captive. So it was a time of great distress (1 Sam. 30:6). But, as well, the Lord gave David a great victory here because he defeated the Amalekites and recovered all, plus much spoil.

It is easy to see that despite the discouragement of the hour while David was at Ziklag, the Spirit of God began to move upon individuals all over the land of Israel that they might come to David. As stated, it was God's time. The 1st verse also says, *"Mighty men, helpers of the war."*

The Church must ever understand that we are in a war and will be so until the return of the Lord Jesus Christ. Consequently, we need *"helpers of the war."* This war is against the powers of darkness, for *"We wrestle not against flesh and blood, but against principalities, against powers, against the rulers of the darkness of this world, against spiritual wickedness in high places"* (Eph. 6:12).

Unfortunately, in the last few years great segments of the body of Christ have utilized their spiritual energy to obtain wealth instead of the main purpose of driving back the darkness and overcoming the powers of Satan.

There are some things that should be said about these *"mighty men"* who came to David as *"helpers of the war."*

1. The mighty men who had shared his rejection now would share his glory, and both their names and deeds are entered upon the imperishable tablets of his kingdom as an encouragement for all those who now suffer with Christ but shall presently reign with Him (II Tim. 2:12).

2. These men became mighty because of their companionship with David. Some of them had been with Saul, but they did not become mighty men until they left Saul and joined David. Companionship with David made heroes of men who had been formerly ordinary. History abounds with instances of timid women and nerveless men performing the noblest of deeds because of companionship with the Lord Jesus Christ.

NOTES

3. With David, these individuals became overcomers. As long as they were servants of Saul, they were overcome by the Philistines. But from the day they became the servants of David, they overcame the Philistines because their master overcame them. So it is today; those who trust in the power of man's religion (Saul) are overcome by inward passions (the Philistines), but those who submit to God's salvation (David) prove that He can subdue all these appetites to Himself.

4. Their leader *"David"* had slain *"the Philistine"* (Goliath) and, thereby, assured the victory over all Philistines. Likewise, the Lord Jesus Christ defeated *"the Philistine"* (Satan) and assured us victory over all Philistines. When God acts in power, He gives strength to the weak and turns them into an army of warriors. Whenever God has raised up a mighty man, in a very short time mighty men show themselves on all sides. For he with whom God is attracts those in whose hearts the Spirit is speaking, and presently there is a great host like the host of God!

It must be remembered that when these came to David at Ziklag, he was a fugitive. Likewise, when they came to David a little later at Hebron, he was still not accepted as the king over all of Israel. It will never be popular to follow God's anointed. If it is popular, it is not of God.

The second verse says of those who came to David, *"Even of Saul's brethren of Benjamin."* Even though these were Benjamites and, consequently, from Saul's tribe, still they knew the anointing of God rested on David and not on Saul. How much faith did it take for these men to forsake Saul and come to David? How much faith does it take today for men to forsake man's religion and come to David, even though he is a fugitive, but has the anointing of the Holy Spirit.

Verses 8 through 15 speak of the *"Gadites who separated themselves unto David."* It says they were *"fit for the battle,"* and, likewise, they came *"into the hold to the wilderness."* When they came to David there was no assurance of glory, but they made a decision that they would *"separate themselves unto Him."* There has to be a separation from man's way to God's way. There would be hindrances to stop them, such as Jordan *"when it had overflown all his banks"* (verse 15). The reason was because these Gadites' *"faces were like the faces of lions, and were as swift as the roes upon the mountains."* This is the criteria for those who would follow Jesus Christ.

Verses 16 through 18 record other Benjamites who joined David at Ziklag. It seems that David was not certain of their loyalty so he asks the question, *"If you be come peaceably?"* Then the 18th verse says, *"Then the Spirit came upon Amasai."* This refers to the Spirit of God Who was not only upon Amasai but inspired him to bring his men to join David. He says, *"Thine are we, David, and on thy side."* This must ever be the statement of any child of God concerning the Lord Jesus Christ. As Amasai burned his bridges behind him, consequently, we as children of the living God must do the same in our service for Jesus Christ. Amasai was not looking back. We must not look back either. The reason he had come to David was because *"thy God helpeth thee."*

Verses 19 through 29 record the men from *"Manasseh."* The 19th verse says, *"And there fell some of Manasseh to David."* This implies that some would not come. They would continue to follow that which was not of God. But, thank the Lord, *"some"* came to David. The Scripture says they were all *"mighty men of valour."*

Then during the seven and a half years when David was king over Judah with his capital at Hebron, the 22nd verse says, *"For at that time day by day there came to David to help him, until it was a great host like the host of God."* Even though David was the anointed of God, still, he needed this *"great host."* The Holy Spirit was quick to say that it was *"like the host of God."* What could the *"great host"* called the Church do if it were *"the host of God?"* Too often it is the *"host of man"* instead of *"the host of God."*

The 23rd verse says that this host *"was ready armed to the war."* They were not coming to be armed, they were *"ready armed."* So many today in Christendom are not armed, and, therefore, are of no consequence to the work of God. God give us a host like the host of God who is *"ready armed to the war."*

They were there for one purpose and that was

"to turn the kingdom of Saul to him, (David) *according to the word of the Lord."* They knew their mission. They were called of God. So many in the Church today do not know their mission. Our business is to take this *"kingdom of Saul"* (the world) and turn it over to our heavenly David because it is *"according to the word of the Lord."* Nothing else counts. Sadly, the Church spends most of its energy on prestige and position. It little carries out that which is *"the word of the Lord,"* namely, the taking of the Gospel of Jesus Christ to a lost world.

The 31st verse says of Manasseh, *"which were expressed by name, to come and make David king."* These individuals were not ashamed of their mission. They wanted all to know their purpose. It was *"to make David king."* God give us Christians who are not ashamed of the fact. They have but one purpose and mission in life, and that is to make Jesus king.

The 32nd verse says concerning the *"children of Issachar"* that they were *"men that had understanding of the times, to know what Israel ought to do."* If we follow the Holy Spirit like they did, we will have understanding of the times. *Only* those who follow the Lord will *"know what the Church ought to do."*

It says of *"Zebulun"* in verse 33 that they were *"expert in war,"* then *"with all instruments of war,"* and then, *"fifty thousand."*

How is it that only 6,800 of Judah came (verse 24) and 50,000 of the tribe of Zebulun came? The numbers denote accuracy and fidelity to present-day spiritual facts. Although David himself was of the tribe of Judah, still, Judah would little respond. Benjamin, Simeon, and Levi were associated with Judah as well, and the record will show small response. Likewise, these were the tribes that crucified the Son of David, the Lord Jesus Christ.

The latter portion of the 33rd verse says, *"Which could keep rank: they were not of double heart."* What a statement! Too many Christians cannot keep rank simply because their heart is divided between the world and the Lord Jesus Christ, or else between denominational religion and the Lord Jesus Christ. No matter the danger in battle, these men from Zebulun would keep rank. How many Christians today can *"keep rank"*? The *"double* heart" is the bane of all of Christendom. The heart is divided between Christ and other pursuits. Too often the Church is deceived because it equates a denomination or fidelity to that denomination as fidelity to Christ. It is not. The two cannot be joined. As someone has said, "Make a list of your priorities." And then he said, "There had better be only one name on that list, Jesus."

Verses 38 through 40 record the great *"joy in Israel."* Now that the Spirit of God is in command and Israel is at long last obeying God's command *"to make David king,"* there will be the following:

1. Fellowship: Union with the Lord always denotes glorious fellowship, for whenever we are of *"one heart,"* there will be glorious fellowship.

2. Plenty: There is never lack when the Spirit of the Lord has His way. The word that is used concerning this *"plenty"* is *"abundantly."*

3. Joy: The joy of the Lord will always follow *"fellowship"* and *"plenty."*

It should be noted that in the entirety of this chapter, the seven and a half year reign in Hebron over Judah is not referred to once. It was God's will for David to be king over all of Israel, not just Judah. Likewise, the Lord must be king over all of our lives, not just part of them.

CHAPTER 13

Even though this chapter begins with the spiritual greatness of Israel, still, it begins with sadness. The 1st verse says, *"And David consulted with the captains of thousands and hundreds, and with every leader."* However, it doesn't say that David consulted with God. How so often we assume that we know what God wants, when, in reality, we don't. The modern Church is so quick to seek the advice of frail humans, and this statement in no way is meant to demean the counsel of godly brethren. Still, there are two things that must always be done concerning the work of God:

1. We always must go to God first, seeking His counsel and His direction.

NOTES

2. Whatever counsel or advice that we receive from men, even though they may be ever so godly, must coincide perfectly with the Word of God. If it doesn't, it must be rejected out of hand.

David's failure to consult with the Lord is amazing, especially when we consider that David's strength was in being led by the Holy Spirit. Also, if the student will observe carefully David's life, he will easily notice how the Holy Spirit observed David's seeking the will of God regarding direction. It should also be noted how carefully the Holy Spirit portrays David's actions when he did not inquire of the Lord. Every time this happened David brought upon himself great difficulties. This time would be no exception. What a lesson this should be for us today.

The plans are great. There are great festivities. The action is noble. For the 3rd verse says, *"And let us bring again the ark of our God to us."* Men think because their plans are noble and their motivations correct that God will bless their efforts without fail. Nevertheless, He is sorely displeased when we attempt to do "good things our way." God has no interest in man's ways. Our ways, regardless of our great show of religion, are not God's ways. Perhaps, the boldest task of the Holy Spirit in our lives is to bring us from our own ways to God's ways. Unfortunately, God's ways cannot be learned easily nor quickly. Perhaps, as David, we spend a lifetime learning this great truth. What lessons we could learn from the Word of God if we would only heed such lessons. They are there for our admonition. Paul writes, *"Now all these things happened unto them for ensamples: and they are written for our admonition, upon whom the ends of the world are come"* (1 Cor. 10:11). But, still, as David, we seem to have to learn the hard way.

The latter portion of the 3rd verse says, *"For we enquired not at it in the days of Saul."* It is ironic that the entire motive for the bringing up of the Ark was to *"inquire of it,"* yet, David did not inquire of the Lord concerning this all important task.

The 5th verse says, *"So David gathered all Israel together."* Their purpose was to *"bring the ark of God from Kirjath-Jearim."* How many times does the Church with great fanfare rush forward to carry out its bold plans when, in reality, those plans will not bring life but death. Great religious activity never denotes great spiritual depth. Nevertheless, the clatter of religious machinery, combined with the noise of great religious profession, completely fools most people.

The 7th verse says, *"And they carried the ark of God in a new cart."* Why not? It seemed the proper thing to do. The Philistines had sent the Ark of God back to Israel in this manner (1 Sam. 6:7). There is even a slim possibility that it could have even been the same *"new cart."* The modern Church is full of *"new carts,"* or "the ways of the world." It must be clearly noted that any and everything instituted by man is always and without exception a *"new cart."* It is doomed to failure. All directions for all things are laid down in the Word of God (II Pet. 1:3). Any deviation will always bring death. Most of the so-called Gospel of today is, in fact, a *"new cart."* It may sound good to the natural mind and look good to the unspiritual eye, but it will set no captive free nor heal any broken heart. It is not the Gospel of Jesus Christ; it is a *"new cart."*

The Holy Spirit is quick to point out that *"Uzza and Ahio drave the cart."* The Ark of God, according to the Word of God was supposed to be carried by the priests (Ex. 37:5; Num. 4:15; Deut. 10:8; Josh. 3:8-14). So, with all the information and instruction given, there was no excuse.

The 8th verse records the great religious activity, *"And David and all Israel played before God with all their might, and with singing, and with harps."* How much does this characterize our modern-day Church? It is all very religious, but very wrong. It is all very loud, but lost. It is all with great activity, but not by the Holy Spirit.

Verse 9 says, *"And when they came unto the threshingfloor of Chidon"* (this is the same as *"Nachon"* in II Sam. 6:6). The threshingfloor was very near Jerusalem, so it would seem that the day that had begun so well would end accordingly. Nevertheless, there is always *"a threshingfloor."* The threshingfloor was where the grain was separated from the husks. On this memorable day the spiritual grain would be separated from the husk as well (Matt.

NOTES

3:11-12).

The next few verses may seem to be cruelty on the part of God. However, once we see the reasons for the action, we will know that God was not cruel at all. "One of the worst things that can happen to a child of God is for his man-made plans to succeed."

The 9th verse says, *"Uzza put forth his hand to hold the Ark; for the oxen stumbled."* The action of Uzza, that would have been applauded by a carnal Church, but which brought death instead, was for several reasons:

1. Uzza was attempting to associate himself with things of which he had no calling.

2. Uzza and his carnality had absolutely no idea as to the great power of God manifested in this vessel. He little knew that God resided between the Mercy Seat and the Cherubim.

3. He had little concern regarding the handling of *"sacred things."* How many Uzzas do we have in the modern Church today?

4. It seems that Uzza had been appointed to this task by David or else by others of high rank; therefore, he thought this absolved him of all responsibility. Likewise, multiple millions are fed error by apostate preachers and priests, thinking this absolves them of all responsibility. In fact, it absolves them of no responsibility at all. If the preacher or the priest preaches an erroneous doctrine, the preacher and the priest will surely answer to God. However, the hearer of the apostate religion will, likewise, be held responsible according to the Word of God. We can never shift responsibility to someone else. Standing before God one day and saying, *"They said,"* will not waive the penalty of the broken law. And, yet, hundreds of millions are like Uzza, totally oblivious to their instant danger and destruction because of dependence upon the word of false teachers.

The 10th verse says, *"And the anger of the Lord was kindled against Uzza, and he smote him."* The latter part of the verse says, *"And there he died before God"* - in other words, in the face of God for his sin of *"putting his hand to the ark."*

To the unspiritual eye, the Lord's actions seem to be cruel. Nevertheless, upon proper investigation, our surprise is not that God did this thing, but that He did not do it years before.

It seems with some investigation that the Ark of God had not been in use for about 70 years. The Tabernacle was now at Gibeon; however, the Ark of the Covenant was not in its *"Holy of Holies."* The Scripture says that approximately 70 years before, it was placed in the *"house of Abinadab"* when it was brought from the land of the Philistines (1 Sam. 7:1). This was approximately 20 years before Saul was made king. Why Samuel at this time did not take the Ark to Shiloh where the Tabernacle was then located is not known. Possibly he did, but the Scripture seems to indicate otherwise. It seems to have remained in the *"house of Abinadab"* for the 20 years before Saul was made king and during his reign of some 40 years, as well as through David's reign over Judah, which was some seven years. After David was made king over both Judah and Israel, it was three years before he would attempt to bring the Ark into Jerusalem. This was approximately 70 years.

There is some indication, according to the Psalms, that it was neglected, possibly even sitting out in a field (Psa. 132:6). It says, *"We found it in the fields of the wood."* If this is to be taken literally, it seems that the Ark, which was the most sacred vessel in the Tabernacle and actually where God dwelt between its Mercy Seat and the Cherubim, was ignored, probably with weeds growing up around it. Sadly, the Spirit of God is treated thusly in most churches. If this is what happened, the fact that God didn't strike someone dead at the *"house of Abinadab"* long before now is a further testimony of the patience and love of God.

We little understand the true spiritual picture if we think the same is not happening today. Most churches are full of death, with people dying by the millions because of a lack of fidelity to the Word of God. Every Christian should take spiritual inventory regarding the church they attend. Most churches are promoters of the *"new cart,"* and, therefore, have no life, but only bring death.

The 11th verse says, *"And David was displeased."*

And then the 12th verse says, *"And David was afraid."* His displeasure was turned into acute fear. He realized how close he had come

NOTES

to death on this day. Sadly, most of the Church today is only *"displeased."* There is very little *"fear of God"* left. It is bad enough to do wrong as David did. It is even worse still to not tremble at our wrongdoing. But, with impunity, millions think nothing of placing their calloused spiritual hands on the Ark of God. Nevertheless, it must be remembered that it brought death then, and it will bring death now.

David's heart sobbed, *"How shall I bring the ark of God home to me?"*

The Church today claims to desire revival. I am not sure if it knows what it's asking for. True spiritual revival not only brings life, glory, and salvation, but it also brings destruction, sorrow, and death. Acts 5 is a perfect example of this. Holy Ghost revival exposes sin as well as error and all false teaching. Holy Ghost revival always brings men back to the Bible, for straying from the Bible is always the cause of our difficulty in the first place.

The 13th verse says, *"So David brought not the ark home to himself to the City of David."* David now realizes that this manifestation of God's glory is better left elsewhere until he can set his spiritual house in order.

Scripture says, *"But carried it aside into the house of Obed-edom the Gittite."* This particular verse is a perfect example of what has happened to Israel, and, thereby, the Word of God being brought to the Gentiles. There is some evidence that Obed-edom was a Gentile who had converted to the God of Abraham, Isaac, and Jacob. It seems he was formerly a Philistine. Israel would ultimately reject the "Ark of God," and it would be given to the Gentiles. The Church at this time is the result of the Ark going to the *"house of Obed-edom,"* which is a symbol of the Gentile Church.

The 14th verse says, *"And the Lord blessed the house of Obed-edom, and all that he had."* (Oh happy day, oh happy day, when Jesus washed my sins away!) Likewise, the Lord has blessed the Gentile Church because it has opened its arms to the Gospel of Jesus Christ. Noah had prophesied these very words so many long years before, *"God shall enlarge Japheth (the Gentiles) and He shall dwell in the tents of Shem"* (the Jews) (Gen. 27). (It is possible that Obed-edom was not Gentile, but that the name *"the Gittite"* in 13:13 only means he or his family once lived in Philistia. He functioned with the Levites as a Levite, but he also could have been a proselyte.)

CHAPTER 14

Verse 1 says, *"Now Hiram king of Tyre sent messengers to David, and timber of cedars."*

The 2nd verse says, *"And David perceived the Lord had confirmed him king over Israel, for his kingdom was lifted up on high."* The first two verses picture the coming day when Christ, the Shepherd of His people, shall be confirmed by God the Father as King over Israel, and when the Gentile princes, here represented by Hiram, shall bring their offerings to His feet.

David perceived that the Lord had established his kingdom because of this fact, but more so that Israel was the flock of God. Grace had elected that flock and had chosen David as its shepherd.

Even though David was a type of Christ, still, all types break down, for the 3rd verse says, *"And David took more wives at Jerusalem."* Even though it was tolerated by God, still, such was not His will.

But where sin abounds, grace much more abounds. Therefore, grace changed David's failure concerning the "wives", for among the other children would come forth Nathan and Solomon. The 4th verse shows both *"Nathan and Solomon"* entitled to the throne. As well, this verse establishes their connection with Christ, for Nathan was the progenitor of Mary, and Solomon of Joseph.

Now that the Lord had moved in lifting up David's kingdom on high, the 8th verse says, *"And when the Philistines heard that David was anointed king over all Israel."* Satan is little concerned about our ability, money, education, or prestige. He is concerned about *"the anointing."* The Church never seems to learn this. It, by and large, encourages all things which God ignores and too often opposes that which God honors, *"the anointing."*

Likewise, Satan is little bothered by our

beautiful buildings, educational institutions, degrees conferred upon our ministers, pride, place, and position. But, he is greatly stirred up over *"the anointing."*

The 8th verse as well says, *"Went up to seek David."* The word *"seek"* means *"to kill him."* Prior to this, Saul had *"sought"* him with murderous purpose. Satan will do anything and go to any length to *"seek"* the one who is anointed in order to kill him (or her). Sadly, the Church too oftentimes aids and abets Satan in his *"seeking."*

The 8th verse also says, *"And David heard of it, and went out against them."* Some Christians erroneously think that if God is in it, there will be no opposition. However, the very opposite is true. The more the Holy Spirit is present, the more that Satan opposes. Those whom Satan opposes little means there is little fear from that quarter. The modern Church, by and large, lauds those who are only opposed a little or none at all. Sadly, it too oftentimes sides with the evil one in his opposition to *"the anointed."*

The 9th verse says, *"And the Philistines came and spread themselves in the valley of Rephaim."* The word *"Rephaim"* means *"giants."* So David faced the Philistines in the *"valley of the giants."* Against the anointed, Satan sends his most powerful force. Paul wrote, *"We wrestle not against flesh and blood, but against principalities, against powers, against the rulers of the darkness of this world, against spiritual wickedness in high places"* (Eph. 6:12). It must be clearly understood that the *"flesh"* cannot overcome these *"giants."* They can be overcome only by *"the Spirit of God."* The Philistines dwelt in the land. They illustrate the energies of sin that dwell in the Christian (Rom. 7:17). Whenever Christ is enthroned as king over the whole life, these energies gather themselves together to oppose Him in the believer's heart where Divine faith and a child-like obedience have the upper hand. There must be complete victory over them.

The 10th verse says, *"And David enquired of God."* The directions that God gives for victory are beautiful lessons to the Christian. David sought careful direction from the Lord (perhaps he had learned his lesson well concerning a lack of inquiry regarding the bringing up of the Ark). He would take nothing for granted. Consequently, he would experience victory, *"And the Lord said unto him, Go up."*

The 11th verse proclaims a great victory. *"Then David said, God hath broken in upon mine enemies."* The Scripture says, *"They called the name of that place Baalperazim."* It means *"the Lord of breaking through."* The prefix on the place was called *"Baal"* which speaks of heathen gods. So, in effect, David is saying, *"The Lord has broken through and defeated these idol gods."* How many idol gods are in our lives? They are *"our enemies."* David's description is entertaining *"like the breaking forth of waters."* The *"waters"* which typify the Spirit of God and the Word of God would sweep away these idol gods that threatened destruction for Israel. We must ever learn that the stranglehold that Satan has in our lives can only be *"broken"* by the *"waters"* of the Holy Spirit and the *"Word of God sweeping these things away."* They cannot be destroyed by human ingenuity!

The 12th verse says the Philistines abandoned their gods. They were of no consequence in the face of the God of Israel. Likewise, the little gods that threaten our Christian experience can be easily swept away by the Word of God and the Spirit of God. The Scripture says, *"They were burned with fire."*

This typifies that which John the Baptist said at the first advent of Christ, *"He shall baptize you with the Holy Ghost, and with fire: whose fan is in his hand, and he will throughly purge his floor, and gather His wheat in the garner; but he will burn up the chaff with unquenchable fire"* (St. Matt. 3:11-12).

The 13th verse says, *"And the Philistines yet again spread themselves abroad in the valley."* Our mistake is large if we think Satan will not come again. He probes for an opportunity. Just because there has been great victory does not mean that he will not come *"yet again."* The victory of the first day and the methods which grace counseled for the winning of it are not to be rested upon in order to secure victory for the next day. Upon the first day the Divine command was, *"Go up!"*

However, the 14th verse says, *"Therefore David enquired again of God."* Now the same

NOTES

voice says, *"Go not up."* Had David thought it unnecessary to pray previous to the second battle, he would, no doubt, have been defeated. He learned that God cannot give victories to the "flesh." Flesh must be humbled and made dead. So David is commanded to run away from the Philistines, which was very humbling to so brave a warrior who then learns to hide, wait, and listen for the power and leading of the Holy Spirit.

No two victories are alike; hence, there must be definite exercises of heart and prayer if the Philistine is to be defeated, not only the first time, but the second time as well. *"Trust and obey"* is that which the Lord demands.

The 15th verse says, *"When thou shalt hear a sound of going in the tops of the mulberry trees."* David was to listen for this *"certain sound."* Luke writes that on the day of Pentecost, *"And suddenly there came a sound from heaven as of a rushing mighty wind"* (Acts 2:2). As this *"sound"* portended the coming of the Holy Spirit on the day of Pentecost, likewise, this *"sound"* that David heard was the coming of the same Holy Spirit.

The 16th verse says, *"David therefore did as God commanded him."* The instructions would make sense to no one except the one who was accustomed to following the Holy Spirit. God's ways are not our ways; neither are they intended to be. God is not attempting to become more acclimated to us. He is attempting to make us more acclimated to Him.

There was irony in the great victory that God gave David. The defeat of the great host of the Philistines began at *"Gibeon."* This was the very home of Saul whom they had defeated. Now, by the power of God they were run out of *"Gibeon even to Gazer."* They were allowed no place in Israel as Satan should be allowed no place in our lives. If we will believe God, the very place that has been our defeat (Gibeon) will now be the place of our victory.

The 17th verse records *"the fame of David which went out into all the lands."* Great victories on the part of the child of God will bring the *"fame of Jesus Christ into all the lands."*

As well, *"the fear of him upon all nations"* can only be brought about by great victories in the lives of God's children.

CHAPTER 15

The 1st verse says, *"And David made him houses in the City of David, and prepared a place for the Ark of God, and pitched for it a tent."* The Holy Spirit is careful to point out that David made for himself *"houses,"* but for the Ark of God he *"pitched for it a tent."* Why he did not bring the Tabernacle from Gibeon, which contained the Brazen Altar, the Brazen Laver and others is not known. Perhaps the Lord desired that this experience be a type of the coming Kingdom Age.

The action here is the setting up of the Throne of Jehovah, that is, the Ark, in Zion. David is the central figure. The High Priest is not seen. David, as king and priest - like unto Melchizedek distributing bread and wine - appears in connection with the Throne, and blesses the people. Grace is the foundation upon which all is here established.

The Tabernacle and the Brazen Altar are at a distance in Gibeon. They represent the First Covenant (now passed away), and the Holy Spirit carries David and Israel forward into the liberty of the New Covenant. The whole scene is prophetic of the day when the Son of David will establish His Throne in Zion and reign gloriously thereon as King and Priest before His ancients.

There will be in that day the remembrance of the One Great Sacrifice once accomplished at Calvary, just as upon this day the Blood once sprinkled upon the Mercy Seat of the Ark was the memorial of the atonement consummated at the Brazen Altar.

Calvary will not be repeated in the day when Israel's King appears in Zion, but its remembrance as being the foundation of all blessing will be very prominent.

So is it in this chapter. The Brazen Altar and the Tabernacle are at Gibeon; the Ark is not brought there by David, but, instead, to Zion.

Thus, prophetically, the placing of the Ark in Zion and not at Gibeon was a setting aside of the First Covenant and a setting up of the Second.

Verse 2 says, *"Then David said, None ought*

to carry the Ark of God but the Levites." David searched the Scriptures and learned there how the Ark should be carried (Num. 4:15).

The great processional that will go into Jerusalem with the Ark of God in its midst will be designed by the Holy Spirit. David seemingly wrote Psalm 68 to commemorate this great event. There were 862 priests and Levites plus others consecrated to bear the Ark and to offer sacrifices.

The 12th verse proclaims that no mistake as before would be made this time. For David says, *"Sanctify yourselves."* This simply means to be *"set apart for holy use."* No man can cleanse himself from sin; therefore, that is not the meaning in this passage.

The 13th verse speaks of David admitting his sin of some three months earlier, *"For that we sought him not after the due order."* He was speaking of the manner in which the Ark of God was to be transported.

The 15th verse says, *"Bare the Ark of God upon their shoulders with the staves thereon, as Moses commanded according to the Word of the Lord."* This speaks of the Levites and is, thereby, God's way. That God would ordain His Mighty Glory to be transported on the shoulders of frail priests must ever be understood that it was not because of any merit or personal holiness on the part of the priests, but on the part of God. Likewise, God anoints those He calls to take His great and glorious Gospel. However, the call is not because that the Lord saw any merit in the ones who are called, but only because of the Grace of God.

Now David appoints singers and musicians to praise God before the Ark. The 16th verse says, *"By lifting up the voice with joy."* This time it will not be an empty profession. The joy will be real because they abide by the Word of God.

There will be three special choirs that will lead the procession. The first choir will be led by *"the Levites"* of whom the leaders are *"Heman"* (Samuel's grandson), *"Asaph,"* and *"Ethan"* (verse 17). It should be noticed that *"Obed-edom"* is with the Ark. Actually, the 24th verse says that *"Obed-edom and Jehiah were doorkeepers for the Ark."* Some three months earlier David had left the Ark at the house of *"Obed-edom."* He had been so blessed by God that when David came to remove the Ark from his house, he resolved to go with it and remain forever. He had tasted of the Glory of God; nothing else would ever satisfy. So many today have such little interest in the things of God, and because they have little tasted of the Glory of God. Once we have seen, felt, witnessed, and experienced His great *"glory,"* nothing else will ever satisfy again. Jesus said, *"If you drink of this water you'll thirst again, but if you drink of the water that I shall give, you shall never thirst"* (St. John 4).

As the first choir was made up of *"the Levites,"* the second choir was made up of *"the Alamoth"* who were the maiden singers (verse 20).

The third choir was made up of the *"men singers"* (verse 21).

All three choirs are referred to in Psalms 68:25. The mens' choir seemingly went before the musicians who were following the maidens playing timbrels among or in-between the men singers and the musicians. What a glorious day this was!

The 26th verse says, *"That they offered seven bullocks and seven rams."* The proper meat and drink offerings were made with each sacrifice as commanded in Numbers 15. This was done according to the instructions of the Holy Spirit. The sacrifices represented Calvary for two reasons:

1. The great joy they had was all because of the price that Jesus Christ would pay at Calvary's Cross. Likewise, the "joys of sins forgiven" and the "bliss the Bloodwashed know," are all because of the price paid at Calvary.

2. The *"Ark of God,"* representing the *"glory of God,"* could in no way rest within their midst except for Calvary. The song says:

"Oh, the grace that drew salvation's plan,
"Oh, the love that brought it down to man,
"Oh, the mighty gulf our God did span,
at Calvary."

The 27th verse says, *"And David was clothed with a robe of fine linen."* This represents the *"righteousness of the saints,"* and, once again, a righteousness that did not come from the merit of David, but from the merit of the slain Lamb - hence, the sacrifices.

The Scripture as well says, *"David also had upon him an Ephod of linen."* This was the

NOTES

garment for priests and Levites, not kings, but since he was a type of Christ who was to be a priest - King (Zech. 6:12-13), David was allowed by God to use it on this occasion as a type.

The 28th verse says, *"With shouting."* This time they had something to shout about. All of our shouting, no matter how loud, will never atone for our deviation from the Word of God. However, *"shouting"* because of obeying the Word of God, is a shout of victory.

The 29th verse says, *"Michal the daughter of Saul looking out at a window saw King David dancing and playing: and she despised him in her heart."* The *"flesh"* can never understand the things of the *"Spirit."* Actually, the *"flesh"* despises all that which is of the *"Spirit."* II Samuel 6:20-23 states that *"She was childless to the day of her death."* Likewise, if the Church disobeys the Word of God, there will be no joy, and, likewise, the Church will be barren.

CHAPTER 16

Now, and finally according to God's way, the 1st verse says, *"They brought the ark of God, and set it in the midst of the tent that David had pitched for it."* The latter part of the verse says, *"They offered burnt sacrifices and peace offerings before God."* It seems these offerings were offered at Gibeon (verse 39); however, the term *"before God"* could mean, *"before the Lord that dwelt between the Mercy Seat and the Cherubim."* If that is the case, it could mean that the sacrifices were offered very near the *"Ark of the Covenant"* in Jerusalem, but most probably the sacrifices were offered at Gibeon.

The 3rd verse says, *"Both man and woman, to every one a loaf of bread, and a good piece of flesh, and a flagon of wine."* It is very difficult to explain to the reader the significance of this moment in Israel's history. The *"Ark of God"* was symbolic of all of Israel's power, strength, and glory. With the *"Ark,"* she was the most powerful nation on earth. Without the *"Ark,"* she was nothing. David understood this. Sadly, most of the kings who were to come did not understand it. Likewise, the presence of God in our churches is the only thing of any value. Buildings, money, denominationalism, or religiosity cannot set one captive free. Only the power of God can do such. His power resides in His presence. The death knell has sounded in the Church, when it can continue to operate without the presence of God. Most churches are little more than a business. There is no presence of God, and, in fact, never has been. Then the Holy Spirit dwelt between the Mercy Seat and the Cherubim. Now He dwells within our hearts (1 Cor. 3:16).

In a symbolic sense of the word, the people were partaking of that which we refer to as *"the Lord's Supper."* This gesture by David toward the people of Israel was, no doubt, instituted by the Holy Spirit. It denoted fellowship, joy, and communion. There is nothing greater than the presence of God filling our hearts and our lives.

The 4th verse says, *"And he appointed certain of the Levites to minister before the ark of the Lord."*

The 6th verse says, *"continually before the ark of the covenant of God."* This means both morning and evening and at the time of the morning and evening sacrifices. Once again, whether they were actually offering sacrifices there or at Gibeon where the Tabernacle was located is not readily known. At any rate, the choirs would worship the Lord each day at 9 a.m. (the time of the morning sacrifice), and 3 p.m. (the time of the evening sacrifice), by singing the Psalms. This would be done each day with the exception of the Sabbath, which was a day of rest. As these choirs were quite large and there were many musicians, this must have made a glorious *"joyful sound"* each day in Jerusalem.

The 7th verse records these words, *"Then on that day David delivered first this psalm to thank the Lord into the hand of Asaph and his brethren."* The Psalms (songs) was earth's first songbook. David wrote at least half of those that are recorded and possibly others that do not bear his name. At the last Passover with Christ, Mark said, *"And when they had sung an hymn* (Psalm), *they went out unto the Mount of Olives"* (St. Mark 14:26). Some parts of the following Psalm are incorporated into Psalm 105. There are five basic things said in verses 8 through 13:

NOTES

1. *"Give thanks."*
2. *"Sing unto Him."*
3. *"Glory ye in His holy name."*
4. *"Seek the Lord."*
5. *"Remember His marvelous works."*

In this arrangement which was given by the Holy Spirit, we have a compendium of what the Lord wants from us regarding worship. So oftentimes our worship is not scriptural. It must ever be remembered, if, in fact, it is not scriptural, the Lord will not accept it.

Probably the entire message of this beautiful Psalm given by David to Asaph is stated in the 25th verse, *"For great is the Lord, and greatly to be praised."*

Going back to the 11th verse the words, *"His strength,"* should read, *"The Ark of His strength,"* for it is there that the seeker gets strength.

As the 31st verse says, *"And let men say among the nations, The Lord reigneth,"* meaning, that one day in the coming Kingdom Age the whole world will say, *"The Lord reigneth."*

In the 37th verse, once again the Holy Spirit reminds us, *"to minister before the Ark continually, as every day's work required."* The great celebration of worship was not to be discontinued after the installment of the Ark. It was to be *"continually."* Too often those who name the name of Christ worship the Lord only on selected days or times. The Holy Spirit is saying, *"Everyday, continually."*

The 38th verse says, *"And Obed-edom."* This man in who's house the Ark of God had been left by David for some three months, would forsake all that he had in order to be near the *"Ark."* He would be associated with the singers and musicians. The Holy Spirit would be so pleased with his actions, dedication, and service, that He would mention his name some 20 times throughout the Word of God and always in a positive way. What an honor!

CHAPTER 17

Everything pertaining to the Temple speaks of the Kingdom Age (that is to come), portraying God's glory. The Tabernacle portrays God's grace; the Temple portrays God's glory. Therefore, the Tabernacle at this particular time would be separated from the Ark of the Covenant, with the Tabernacle residing at Gibeon and the Ark residing in Jerusalem.

The 1st verse says, *"As David sat in his house."* This speaks of the Lord Jesus Christ residing in Jerusalem in the glories of the Kingdom Age. All enemies are defeated. David desires to build a house for the Lord. This pictures the beginning of the Kingdom Age when the Lord Jesus Christ as a *"greater than Solomon"* will begin to build His *"House."* When this glorious day comes, the redeemed sons of Jacob will sing aloud unto God and, invited by them, the ransomed nations will join in the mighty anthem. Unitedly, they will sing, *"His mercy endureth forever."* In that day, Christ will appear as the true Ark of the Covenant upon Mount Zion. The song, therefore, of Chapter 16 contains every subject which the presence of Christ in Zion would give occasion to celebrate, prior to the full display of His glory as the *"Greater than Solomon."*

Both David and Solomon were types of Christ. David, subduing all his enemies, casting the Jebusite out of Zion, and setting up there the throne of Jehovah, is a type of the Messiah. Messiah is stated in Exodus 15 to be Jehovah, the Man of war. In Revelation 19 it states that He makes war righteously. As the great Captain of the Host, He will overcome all His enemies, establish His throne in Zion, redeem Israel, and make the Gentiles subject to His sceptre. Having accomplished all this, He will then, as the Divine Solomon, display the glory of His Millennial Reign. The building of the Temple was designed to symbolize that glory.

The Tabernacle, given to Moses in the wilderness, foretold His first advent in humility; the Temple of Solomon foretold His second Advent in power and great glory.

Hence, David could not build that Temple, for he typifies Messiah as a Man of war, destroying his enemies and setting up his Throne.

Solomon, typifying Christ as the Prince of Peace, builds the glorious palace of Jehovah, and in doing so gives a forepicture of the time when the kingdoms of this world shall become

NOTES

the kingdom of our Lord and of His Christ, the Son of David, Who shall reign forever and ever.

Verse 2 says, *"Then Nathan said unto David, Do all that is in thine heart; for God is with thee."* Too often we assume that we know what God wants and desires, when actually we don't. Every time our decision is made without the Lord's direction, we fail.

Second, that which God desires to do is always so far greater than we could ever begin to think or imagine. David had a present Temple in mind. God had an eternal Temple in mind.

Consequently, the 3rd verse says, *"That the Word of God came to Nathan, saying, Go and tell David My servant, Thus saith the Lord, Thou shalt not build Me an house to dwell in."* The Lord will thusly address David because He has far more in mind than David does.

The 7th verse records the price of admission into this house. It is trust in the *"slain Lamb"* (the sheep), by the root of humility. *"I took thee from the sheepcote, even from following the sheep, that thou shouldest be ruler over my people Israel."*

The 9th verse proclaims God's unconditional covenant with Israel, *"And they shall dwell in their place, and shall be moved no more."* However, it must be quickly stated that this *"Davidic Covenant"* is unconditional only in the sense that God will bring the promises to pass irrespective. The only thing that is unconditional is the Covenant itself. Whoever enters into this Covenant is conditional upon faith and obedience to God. The whole Gospel program of requirements is that of obedience and living soberly, righteously, and godly in this present world (2 Cor. 5:17-18).

At the Second Coming of Christ, Israel, after the horrid Battle of Armageddon, will through much suffering be brought to the Lord Jesus Christ. At that time she will accept Him as her King and her Saviour. She will then dwell in the land *"and shall be moved no more."*

In the 10th verse the Lord further opens the door, showing David His intentions. *"Moreover I will subdue all thine enemies. Furthermore, I tell thee that the Lord will build thee an house."* In a sense, partially, this has been fulfilled. God did subdue all the earthly enemies of David in his day, but the more complete fulfillment of enemies being put down still awaits fulfillment under the Messiah (Isa. 9:6-7).

The promise to David to *"build thee an house"* has also been only partially fulfilled. God did build David a house, but his sons went into sin and lost the throne as well as the land. The final and complete fulfillment with an eternal King to reign on an eternal throne in particular will be fulfilled in the Messiah in the Kingdom Age.

The 11th verse proclaims the glory of that promise. *"I will raise up thy seed after thee, which shall be of thy sons; and I will establish his kingdom."* This has a double application, with Solomon being spoken of in the immediate present, but far more so in the Lord Jesus Christ as the *"Son of David."*

The 12th verse says, *"He shall build me an house, and I will establish his throne forever."* Once again, this speaks of Solomon, and it will be totally fulfilled in the Kingdom Age. But, more perfectly, it speaks of the Lord Jesus Christ Who is the *"Greater than Solomon."*

The balance of the chapter portrays David's understanding of this great promise and Covenant. Now, understanding what the Lord's intentions are, David is overwhelmed. The 1st verse says, *"He sat in his house."* The 16th verse says, *"He sat before the Lord."* There was a touch of pride in the 1st verse. There is nothing but humility in the 16th verse, and after he understands the far reaching, even eternal plans of Jehovah, His exclaimed answer is, *"Who am I, oh Lord God, and what is mine house, that Thou has brought me hitherto?"* In this is the coming incarnation, God becoming a man. David now knows fully and beyond the shadow of a doubt that the Lord Jesus Christ will come through his lineage. No wonder he says, *"Who am I, oh Lord God?"*

In the 17th verse he mentions the *"small thing."* He is, in effect, saying, *"That which I desire to do is insignificant in comparison to that which you will do."* Even though it is not recorded in this chapter, still in II Samuel 7:19, David says, *"And is this the manner of man, oh Lord God?"* This refers to the promise that the Seed of the woman shall bruise the serpent's head (Gen. 3:15); that is, from David's line the

Messiah will come, bringing eternal salvation and reigning as the eternal King of the earth. When he uses the words, *"A man of high degree,"* he is saying, in effect, *"I am a man of low degree, but yet through the One who is to come and in my lineage, He will make me a man of high degree."*

In the 18th verse he further says, *"For Thou knowest Thy servant,"* meaning that David in no way could merit this great and high honor as no child of God can merit the high honor of salvation freely given by the Lord Jesus Christ.

The 19th verse says, *"Hast thou done all this greatness, in making known all these great things?"* Once again, David exclaims the Glory of God which is so much greater than what he at first thought. As well, the Lord reveals Himself to David regarding the eternal glory.

The 20th verse heralds David's praises to God as he begins to grasp the glory of that of which the Lord has spoken, *"Oh, Lord, there is none like thee."*

The 21st verse records God's promise made to Abraham, *"And what one nation in the earth is like Thy people Israel?"* Israel is God's time clock. Also, let it quickly be said that the Gentile Church is not Israel. We can only claim to be *"Spiritual Israel."* The geography called the *"land of Israel"* is extremely important in the eyes of God. He even calls it *"My land."* Likewise, the *"people of Israel"* are greatly important in the eyes of God, with promises having been made to Abraham, Isaac, and Jacob. These promises concerning these people will be kept.

In 1948 they began to filter back into the land. They have continued to grow stronger from that day until this. All of this is in fulfillment of Bible prophecy. Regrettably, they will accept the Antichrist as the Messiah, and then with rude awakening realize that they have been deceived. During the Battle of Armageddon it will look like Satan's efforts at final extermination will ultimately succeed. And then according to Revelation 19, the Lord Jesus Christ will come back. Israel will then accept Him as the Messiah and serve Him gloriously forever.

The conclusion of the 21st verse says, *"whom Thou hast redeemed out of Egypt,"* once again stating that Israel's salvation is identical with the salvation of the Gentiles, and that by the *"slain Lamb."*

The 25th verse says, *"Thy servant hath found in his heart to pray before Thee."* When prayers are found in the heart, they are the result of gratitude or the overflow of some desperate need.

The 26th verse says, *"And now, Lord, Thou art God, and hast promised."* God keeps His promises!

The 27th verse speaks of blessing. *"For Thou hast blessed, oh Lord, and it shall be blessed forever."* What God has blessed Satan cannot curse.

CHAPTER 18

This chapter is freighted with victory and the reasons why such victory is afforded. With Christ as a type of the Ark being now enthroned in Zion the center of the Kingdom, David soon enjoys complete victories over all enemies, both at home and foreign. The Philistines, internal enemies, are first bridled, and then the external foes are brought into subjection.

This illustrates the moral fact, always true, that when Christ is set upon the throne of the heart, victory over both inward and outward enemies is assured. But the inward is always first conquered as in the case of David and the Philistines in this chapter. For verse 1 says, *"That David smote the Philistines."*

And then verse 2 and following says, *"He smote Moab, and Hadarezer king of Zobah (verse 3), and the Syrians."*

The 6th verse as well as the 13th verse says, *"Thus the Lord preserved David withersoever he went."* Whenever the Holy Spirit repeats a statement, He is drawing significant attention to the moment. Many Christians will have victories over one or even a few areas in their life or at a particular time in their Christian experience. However, few, as David, subdue all enemies. It is the will of God and even the insistence of the Lord that we subdue not just some of our spiritual enemies, but all. The Holy Spirit will not be satisfied till such is done. Sadly, with most it is never done.

NOTES

The 11th verse says, *"Them also king David dedicated unto the Lord."* This speaks of all the gold and silver, etc. David reserved none for himself. He would give it completely to the Lord. No doubt, much of the gold and silver that was taken in these expeditions would be later used in the construction of the Temple. How so hard it is for Christians to be blessed. The blessing is intended to be given to others, but so oftentimes we selfishly reserve it for ourselves. David, instead, *"dedicated it unto the Lord."*

The 14th verse says, *"So David reigned over all Israel."* This means that no enemy occupied any part of the land. How many of us can say that we *"reign over all the possession that God has given us?"*

CHAPTER 19

This chapter is a perfect example of God's love for this world and His efforts to save mankind. It is also a picture of man's rejection of the love, graciousness, and kindness of the Lord of glory. It also pictures Armageddon and the efforts to destroy our *"heavenly David."* It, as well, portrays the total victory brought about in the Battle of Armageddon by our Lord and Saviour Jesus Christ and the subjugation of all of God's enemies.

Verse 2 says, *"And David said, I will show kindness unto Hanun the son of Nahash."* These individuals were heathens and, thereby, aliens to the commonwealth of Israel and strangers to the Promise. Their right and just desert was Judgment. This, as well, typifies the whole of the human race. Actually, the name *"Nahash"* means *"bright shining serpent"* – Satan. Mankind is filled with Satan and can, thereby, lay no claim on the grace and glory of God through its own merit. The extended hand to the sons of Satan which characterizes the entirety of the human race is only because of the *"kindness"* of our heavenly David.

The 2nd verse further says, *"David sent messengers to comfort him."* Likewise, our heavenly David is constantly sending *"messengers,"* preachers of the Gospel, with the good news of the glorious Gospel of Jesus Christ which alone can bring *"comfort."*

The 2nd verse continues to say, *"So the servants of David came into the land of the children of Ammon."* As well, we are to take the Gospel to the whole world. God's priority is the propagation of His message. Everything else that the Church does must lead to the proclamation of the Gospel - the Great Commission.

The 4th verse says, *"Wherefore Hanun took David's servants . . ."* They were shamefully treated, as Paul was shamefully treated, and as the apostles as well, as most every one of God's servants who have attempted to take this Gospel of Jesus Christ to a lost world. The manner in which they were treated was designed especially to humiliate them. Likewise, the world will greatly humiliate anyone who attempts to bring the great and glorious Gospel of Jesus Christ to the hardened heart. Jesus would say of this world system, *"If it loved Me, it will love you."* It did not love Him, so it will not love us. By and large, there will be total rejection of the *"comfort"* of the great message of Redemption. But yet, some few will accept.

The 7th verse proclaims the efforts of the enemy to destroy David and Israel, *"So they hired thirty and two thousand chariots."* This speaks in prophetic tone of the Antichrist who will attempt to once and for all overthrow Christ and to destroy Israel. However, let the allied hosts be ever so strong, yet they can not overcome the Divine energy which offered Grace, and that, being rejected, decrees Judgment.

As the 18th verse says, *"But the Syrians fled before Israel."* So will the armies of the Antichrist flee before our heavenly David.

The 19th verse says, *"They made peace with David, and became his servant."* Likewise, at the conclusion of the great Battle of Armageddon with Jesus Christ reigning as the Lord of heaven and earth, the world will make peace with our heavenly David, and, in effect, will become His servant.

CHAPTER 20

Verse 1 says, *"But David tarried at Jerusalem."* This chapter coincides with II Samuel 11, but with a glaring difference. David's sin with Bathsheba and the sin concerning her husband are totally omitted. Why?

1. As we have stated at the beginning of the Commentary on I Chronicles, the two books of Chronicles give the history from the Divine standpoint. The books of I and II Samuel and I and II Kings give these accounts from the human standpoint. There is a tremendously valuable lesson here to be learned. God does not see things as man sees them and vice versa. Consequently, one of the great works in the heart and life of the believer by the Holy Spirit is to help us to *"see"* as God sees. This spiritual place and position is not easily arrived at. There must be a complete submissiveness to the Will of God, and the Will of God will always adhere totally to the Word of God.

2. When a Christian is forgiven, God, true to His promise, forgets the sin and omits it from the later books of His remembrance. This is called *"justification by faith."* Sanctification *"makes"* one not guilty; whereas, Justification *"declares"* one not guilty. So, in effect, by the lack of any mention of David's sin, the Lord has declared him not guilty of such. How can this be?

It can be such with David as with every single believer who has ever lived, because God has placed the penalty of the broken Law on His Son, Jesus Christ. Jesus Christ at Calvary took upon Himself the penalty, which was death, of every person who has ever lived. Likewise, the price to be paid for the penalty was death. He offered up the perfect sacrifice at Calvary, which was His sinless body. Therefore, He satisfied all claims that Satan had against the human race. And now, *"Whosoever believes in Him, shall not perish, but have everlasting life"* (St. John 3:16). Before Calvary, men were saved by looking forward to it. After Calvary, men are saved by looking backward to it.

So, when David repented (the 51st Psalm), the Lord washed him, cleansed him, forgave him, and redeemed him. The sin was not only put away, but David was exonerated as if he never committed the sin. Hallelujah!

That is the reason the Holy Spirit could come to this particular time frame concerning David's history and never even mention the terrible sin with Bathsheba and to Uriah. The sin was gone. Likewise, for every single child of God who has ever lived, every sin they have ever committed before conversion or after if properly confessed and put away is totally forgotten by God after conversion. The Church should do the same, but, regrettably, it little does so. That's the reason Paul said to the Church at Corinth concerning someone who had sinned and had repented, *"For to this end also did I write, that I might know the proof of you, whether you be obedient in all things"* (II Cor. 2:9). Paul wanted to make certain that the Church had forgiven this individual. It is ironic after the individual sinned and before repentance, the person was on trial (I Cor. 5). Now, after the person's repentance, the Church is on trial.

The 1st verse says as well, *"And Joab smote Rabbah, and destroyed it"* (present day Ammon, Jordan).

The 2nd verse says, *"And David took the crown of their king from off his head."* A great victory had been won. This is a picture of our spiritual life in Christ Jesus. Satan endeavors to reign as king in some part of our spiritual inheritance. The Holy Spirit demands that we destroy Satan's kingdom and take the crown from his head – and in every part of our life.

The 2nd verse as well says, *"And it was set upon David's head."* Revelation 1:6 says, *"And hath made us kings and priests unto God."* The Lord demands that we be king over all the possession that He has forgiven us, and that Satan have no place in it. Concerning any part of our spiritual possession, does the crown sit on Satan's head for some part of it or on our heads?

Concerning those David took captive the 3rd verse says, *"And cut them with saws."* The Hebrew word is *"sur"* and does not necessarily mean literally to cut with something material. The better translation most probably would have been to *"put them"* or *"appoint them"* to particular tasks.

NOTES

Verses 4 through 8 record the last mention of giants, with the first mention being in Genesis 6:4. In this last account of the giants, which are mentioned in I Samuel 17, II Samuel 21, and I Chronicles 20, some five are spoken of. They are as follows:

1. Goliath – He was most probably the oldest of the giants and was killed by David (I Sam. 17).

2. Sippai – (verse 4). Called Saph (II Sam. 21:18).

3. Lahmi – Brother of Goliath (verse 5; II Sam. 21:19).

4. The giant with six fingers and six toes on each hand and foot (verse 6:8: II Sam. 21:20-22).

5. Ish-bi-be-nob (II Sam. 21:16-17).

ʹ It seems these five giants were brothers (II Sam. 21:19-22). These were the last of the mighty races of giants who were the offspring of fallen angels and women in Satan's efforts to do away with the pure Adamic race, so that the Seed of the woman (the Lord Jesus Christ) might not come into the world to redeem Adam's race (Gen. 6:4).

They also represent hindrances in our particular Christian lives that seek to usurp authority over God's rule. Every satanic *"giant"* in our lives must be destroyed. They cannot be reasoned with, nor can we come to terms with such. There is no room for compromise. The *"flesh"* must die. The *"Spirit"* must reign supreme. Paul writes, *"Let not sin (a giant) therefore reign in your mortal body"* (Rom. 6:12). As there were giants in Israel (the God given possession), likewise, there are giants in every Christian's life. As the giants were destroyed by David and his mighty men, likewise, the giants can only be destroyed by our *"Heavenly David,"* Who is the Lord Jesus Christ. Within our own strength and power we cannot destroy these giants, but through Christ, all can and will be destroyed.

━━■━━

CHAPTER 21

As the last chapter was of victory, this chapter is of defeat, and yet tells of a great coming victory. *"For where sin did abound, grace did much more abound"* (Rom.5:20).

Verse 1 says, *"And Satan stood up against Israel, and provoked David to number Israel."* II Samuel 24:1 says, *"God moved David"* to do such. Is there a contradiction? No, we learn from these passages that Satan can do nothing against a child of God but that God allows it. God permits Satan a limited power as His agent for bringing merited Judgment among men.

The 2nd verse says of the command of David, *"Go number Israel."* And then he says, *"That I may know it."*

When Satan fails to break down a servant of God by one plan, he tries another and generally succeeds. As a rule, his first plan is violent; his second plan is usually subtle. He lays a semi-religious trap for the Christian's foot, and thus causes him to fall. So it was here with David! What the Philistines, the Ammonites, and the Syrians failed to affect, this mental weapon of subtle temptation accomplished.

What could be more laudable than to verify the truthfulness of the promise made to Abraham that his children should exceed the stars in multitude! However, to seek to carnally verify a Divine promise brings deadness to the soul! And such a desire leads not *to* the Bible, but *from* the Bible.

There is no evidence that David referred to Exodus 30:12 which demands, *"When thou takest the sum of the children of Israel after their number, then shall they give every man a ransom for his soul unto the Lord."* If this was not done, the Scripture plainly says there would be a *"plague among them"* (Ex. 30:12).

Had David obeyed the Word of God, the foundation of the Temple, which was shortly to be built, would have been laid as that of the Tabernacle was with the redemption money of the thousands of Israel, instead of the blood of the 70,000 who perished.

After a victory there is always a secret temptation in the heart of a Christian to search for a personal and carnal cause. How guilty we all are. A preacher is tempted to think that the conversions reported during his ministry resulted from the clearness, the force, or the eloquence of his preaching. Thus it was with David.

Conqueror over all his enemies, he wishes

to find out for himself the strength of the weapon, his standing army, which was his glory and with which he gained his victories. So he takes his eye off the strength of God from Whom alone the victories came. This sin, and it is a great one, brings famine, defeat, and death to the soul.

The 3rd verse proclaims Joab saying, *"Why doth my Lord require this thing?"* And then Joab says, *"Why will he be a cause of trespass to Israel?"* Joab was a man of the world. He had not the spiritual insight of David. And yet, at times such will have a better spiritual insight than a self-willed Christian.

After the census was taken, the 7th verse says, *"And God was displeased with this thing."* And then it says, *"Therefore He smote Israel."* God can tolerate sin no more in His most chosen, David, than He can in the most vile sinner. Sin is reckoned with by God irrespective of whose life it resides within.

Verse 8 declares David saying unto the Lord, *"I have sinned greatly."* David repented of his sin prior to God's visit to him. He confessed he had sinned greatly against God. His admission that he had sinned, and that he had sinned greatly, and that he had sinned against God, all reveal a heart that really knew God and loved Him. He says to the Lord, *"Do away the iniquity of thy servant; for I have done very foolishly."* Sin always make fools of men irrespective of whom they may be. It would make a fool of God's chosen, David.

The 9th verse says, *"And the Lord God spake unto Gad, David's seer, saying."*

For the Christian who would foolishly think they can sin with impudence, merely asking God's forgiveness with no aftermath is foolish indeed. Sin carries its own punishment. In one way or the other, it will always reap death. However, it must always be understood that God will administer the punishment in the believer's life, and not his fellow Christian. And why?

Wicked men chastising wicked men will not be tolerated by God. Even if God uses a man as His instrument of punishment, it will always be an unwitting man – in other words, the man will not know that he is being used by God as an instrument of punishment. Christians who would desire punishment upon other Christians for sins imagined or real are only asking for punishment upon themselves. No Christian is worthy to punish another Christian, for that prerogative belongs to God.

The 13th verse proclaims David's consternation regarding God's punishment for his sin. He says, *"I am in a great strait."* Sin puts men in *"a great strait."* David's answer concerning his punishment should be a warning and a lesson for all. He says, *"Let me fall now into the hand of the Lord; for very great are his mercies; but let me not fall into the hand of man."* Regrettably, the hand of man, even in the Church, is always extra heavy. That's the reason Paul said in Galatians 6:1 that only those who are *"spiritual"* should participate in the restoration process. Regrettably, there are precious few who fall into the category of *"spiritual."* David had been in the hand of man before, namely Saul. So, he throws himself on the Mercy of God.

The 14th verse says, *"So the Lord sent pestilence upon Israel."* What type of pestilence it was, the Scripture does not really say. However, this should be a lesson for us to remember. In Exodus 30:12 the Lord said there would be a *"plague among them"* if the *"half shekel"* was not paid as ransom money for each person. It should be understood here that God means what He says. It says, *"There fell of Israel seventy thousand men."* This is some 20,000 more than the American forces lost in Vietnam in some ten years of fighting.

What had these individuals done that merited such punishment? The Bible is silent regarding the implication of their sin, but of this we can be sure. For this 70,000 men to be selected in Israel was a sure indication that God alone designated the punishment and the individuals.

The question begs to be asked that if God blotted out David's terrible sin with Bathsheba and to Uriah, recording it in II Samuel 11 but not recording it in I Chronicles 20, why was this sin of II Samuel 24 not treated thusly in I Chronicles 21 (the sin of numbering the people)? Does God treat all sin alike? Could this sin of numbering the people even have been worse than David's sin with Bathsheba and to Uriah? And if so, doesn't God treat all sin just alike according to the precious Blood of Jesus?

NOTES

There are two types of sin. They are:

1. Sins of passion (Gal. 5:19-21) of which David sinned with Bathsheba and to Uriah. These sins are so bad that Paul wrote, *"That they which do such things shall not inherit the kingdom of God,"* meaning to continue in these types of sins.

2. The sin of pride. This sin is just as deadly as the sins of the flesh but far more subtle. The sin of pride is the foundation sin of the universe. It is what caused Satan's fall (Isa. 14 - Ezek. 28), and man's fall in the Garden of Eden (Gen. 3). The sin of pride is the sin of *"playing god."* Satan said, *"And you shall be as gods"* (Gen. 3:5). This sin is subtle because it is deceptive. This is actually the sin that nailed Christ to the Cross. It was not the thieves, harlots, or publicans who killed Christ. It was the Church leaders (Pharisees) of the day. The *"sin of pride"* actually says in its spirit, *"I know more than God knows and can guide my destiny far better."* That's the reason the sin of the modern-day Church of the *"psychological way"* is so deadly. In effect it is saying, *"We know more about the human need than God knows, and we can cure man of his psychological maladjustments."* It is fairly simple to get someone to confess and repent of the *"sin of passion."* It is almost impossible to get someone to confess and repent of the *"sin of pride."* This is the sin that characterizes religion. It is the most deadly sin of all. Of the sins that God hates, *"pride"* leads the list (Prov. 6:16).

The *"sins of passion"* pretty well incorporate themselves according to individuals. The *"sin of pride"* incorporates itself in an entire house, a church, or the entirety of a religious denomination. Even though all sin is directed against God, still, the *"sin of pride"* spreads like a cancer to cover an entire people. There is evidence that David repented (I Chron. 21:8). There is no evidence that the *"seventy thousand men"* repented.

In David's sin with Bathsheba and to Uriah, only two people, David and Bathsheba were involved. They repented, and, therefore, the sin was blotted out. With this sin of numbering the people, great segments of the nation were involved. David repented; the others didn't. Therefore, even though David was forgiven and cleansed, still, the sin, because it was national, remained.

The 15th verse records the awful spectacle of the *"angel"* standing *"over Jerusalem to destroy it."* The Scripture says, *"He repented,"* speaking of God and regarding the destruction that He was about to carry out on Jerusalem. The word *"repent"* regarding the Lord does not mean that God did something wrong. It simply means that He *"turned around,"* stopping the process He was about to carry out. The Scripture says, *"I am the Lord, I change not"* (Mal. 3:6). No, God never changes; however, His direction may vary according to the obedience or rebellion of man.

The 15th verse also says, *"The angel of the Lord stood by the threshingfloor of Ornan (Araunah) the Jebusite."* John the Baptist said that the Lord Jesus Christ, through the power of the Holy Spirit, would take us to the threshingfloor in order to separate the wheat from the chaff (Matt. 3:12).

The sin of *"numbering the people"* which constituted great pride was at least one of, if not the greatest sin, that Israel ever committed. This is the only sin that records an angel *"having a sword in his hand stretched out over Jerusalem."*

As stated, all sin is horrible and directed against God; however, some sins are worse than others. Jesus said concerning the Pharisees, *"Therefore he,* [the Pharisees] *that delivered me unto thee hath the greater sin"* (St. John 19:11). Their sin was the sin of pride, and, as well, some 35 years later this *"angel"* would completely destroy Jerusalem with 1,100,000 Jews being slaughtered. He would do the same thing in Jeremiah's and Ezekiel's day, when Jerusalem was destroyed (Ezek. 9).

The 16th verse says as well, *"Then David and the elders of Israel, who were clothed in sackcloth, fell upon their faces."* This denotes humility and repentance. God has promised to look with favor at such (Isa. 66:2).

David, in the 17th verse, is crying to God, for mercy on the part of the people saying, *"O Lord God, be on me, and on my father's house; but not on thy people, that they should be plagued."* David now becomes a type of Christ making intercession for the people. The Lord heeded it, and Jerusalem was spared. How often does the Lord cry to the Father on our

NOTES

behalf?

The 18th verse records, *"The angel of the Lord commanded Gad to say to David, that David should go up, and set up an altar unto the Lord in the threshingfloor."*

We should, with great crushing of spirit, understand the implication of this passage. The threshingfloor, which denotes the separation (with violence) of the grain from the chaff, would completely destroy us were it not for the *"altar."* Even as believers, still, our grain is sheathed in husks or chaff. In other words, the Holy Spirit has been able to do a work that should bring forth fruit, but the *"flesh"* is still so predominant that the grain is totally covered by the chaff (flesh). The separation of it is a painful and even violent process which would kill us were it not for the Cross. So, the precious shed Blood of Christ that washes the sinner clean must be built on the *"threshingfloor."*

David's folly gives Divine Grace the opportunity of fixing the spot where sin was to be atoned for and fellowship with God restored and maintained. The picture is striking: the wrath of God about to fall on the city, the guilty king confessing his sin, the spotless Sacrifice slain, and the Judgment of God vindicated and honored.

This Grace is the more apparent and all-embracing when it is noticed that the ground upon which this most satisfactory Sacrifice was offered up belonged to a Gentile, Araunah, the Jebusite.

Araunah, the Jebusite, offers to give David his threshingfloor for the construction of the Altar without price.

But the 24th verse says of David, *"But I will verily buy it for the full price."* Sin can never be atoned for without the *"full price"* of the Blood of Calvary. The problems with the Church are bloodless altars and a crossless salvation. Such does not exist. Man cannot be redeemed by half measures. It has to be the *"full price"* – the precious shed Blood of the Lord Jesus Christ.

The 26th verse says, *"And David built there an altar unto the Lord, and offered burnt offerings and peace offerings, and called upon the Lord."* David here is a striking type of Christ accepting that while David was personally guilty, Christ the true King and High Prince of

Israel, was sinless. Here David takes all the sin upon himself, offers the sacrifice, intercedes for the people, satisfies Divine justice, and restores peace with God. Sovereign Grace shines in every action of this scene. No priest is seen other than David. David could not go to the Tabernacle at Gibeon, for that represents the Law, and there was no salvation for him there. If he and the balance of Israel are to be delivered from the avenging sword of the angel, God Himself must provide a salvation upon another principle, that is, salvation by Grace; and this is what is seen at the threshingfloor of the Jebusite.

The 26th verse says as well, *"And He answered him from heaven by fire upon the altar of burnt offering."* What a sight that must have been. The lamb is laid on the hastily built Altar. It is the exact spot where the future Temple will be built. The heavens then split open with a lightning bolt of Judgment fire striking the Altar and the Sacrifice. This is a picture of God's Judgment on sin. A Judgement, we may quickly add, that should have fallen on David and on us for that matter, but, instead, fell on Christ.

Then and only then, the 27th verse says concerning the angel, *"And he put up his sword again unto the sheath thereof."* The only thing that stands in-between Judgment of the entirety of this planet is the Cross of Christ. The only thing that keeps entire nations from being wiped off the face of the earth, or any human being for that matter, is the Cross of Christ. God could either smite the planet or smite the Cross. Thank God, He smote His Son upon the Cross.

The sight of this terrible sin (Jerusalem) would now become the sight of Grace and Mercy. Grace if allowed will always wash away sin and point to a greater victory.

Verses 28 and 29 proclaim to us that the Lord told David that this site would now become the site of the Temple that is to soon be constructed.

The 28th verse says, *"Then he sacrificed there."*

The *"fear"* of verse 30, *"for he was afraid because of the sword of the angel of the Lord,"* is because the Tabernacle represents the Law. God gave the Law and commanded man to keep

it, but gave no power to do so. Therefore, it produced a *"fear."* The Temple, albeit continuing to be a type of the Law, would even more so be a type of Grace.

It is interesting that the Temple site belonged to a Gentile, and, as well, many of the men employed in the building of the Temple under Solomon were Gentiles. This accords with the Lord's declaration that the House was to be a House of Prayer for all nations, and it will be in coming millennial days.

CHAPTER 22

Verse 1 says, *"Then David said, This is the house of the Lord God."* In other words, *"This is where the House of the Lord will be built."* And then he states, *"And this is the altar of the burnt offering for Israel,"* in other words, where God smote the Sacrifice by sending fire from heaven, and, thereby, denoting the Temple site.

This one verse of Scripture (I Chron. 22:1) is the cause of much conflict in the Middle East and more particularly in Jerusalem. This is the site where Solomon, David's son, did build the great Temple. As of now, the Moslem world controls this site, and, yet, in the very near future Israel must rebuild her Temple on this site. It is the flash point of the world. At the time of this writing, the Moslem world has appropriated some $20 million to refurbish the roof on the present *"Dome of the Rock."* They fully have no intention of giving up this site, claiming it as the third most holy site in the world of Islam. Islam claims that Ishmael was the promised seed instead of Isaac. They believe in God but claim that Mohammed is His prophet. They also believe that Jesus Christ was a great prophet, but not the Son of God. They believe the only way to the Father (Allah) is through Mohammed. Christianity and the Bible teach that the only way to the Father is through Jesus Christ.

The Hebrew scholars in Jerusalem in the archaeological excavations have hoped that the Temple site would be other than the rock where Abraham is supposed to have offered Isaac and where the present Dome now sits. More than likely, they will find that this site is the correct site. In some way the Dome of the Rock will have to be moved in order for the new Jewish Temple to be built. How it will be done, especially at this time, no one knows, but it will be done. Daniel said the Sacrifice would begin again with the Antichrist causing the Sacrifice and oblation to cease. The Temple will have to be rebuilt for the Sacrifices to begin and then to be stopped by the Antichrist (Dan. 9:27).

David's heart until the day of his death would be for the preparation of the Temple construction. For the 2nd verse says, *"And David commanded."*

Then the 3rd verse says, *"And David prepared."* Here we have the beginning of gathering the materials for the Temple – not counted in the seven and one-half years of the actual construction by Solomon.

Then the 5th verse proclaims, *"And David said."* The words that he uses are those which the Lord has given unto him by revelation, *"The house that is to be builded for the Lord must be exceeding magnifical, of fame and of glory throughout all countries."* And then it says, *"So David prepared abundantly before his death."* This *"House"* was to be *"in type,"* the Millennial glory of the Messiah, just as the Tabernacle had set forth His mediatorial glory.

The 6th verse says, *"Then he called for Solomon his son."*

In the 9th verse he proclaims that Solomon was named before he was born, *"For his name shall be Solomon, and I will give peace and quietness unto Israel in his days."* Solomon was one of seven men in the Bible named before birth.

Verses 8-10 repeat what has already been pointed out that David typifies Christ as a man of war, destroying his enemies, and Solomon, as Christ, the Prince of Peace, reigning over a kingdom freed from these enemies.

There was one condition to all the glory that would characterize Israel, *"Thou takest heed to fulfill the statutes and judgments which the Lord charged Moses with concerning Israel."* (vs. 13). Adherence to the Word of God was the criteria then; adherence to the Word of God is the criteria now.

The 14th verse says concerning David,

"Now, behold in my trouble I have prepared for the House of the Lord." These words confirm what so often appears in the character of David, that all through his stormy life of warfare, his heart was true to one great purpose, the establishment of the House of God and the Peace of God in the midst of the People of God.

The secret of David's great victories, despite his great defeats, is found in the 19th verse, *"Now set your heart and your soul to seek the Lord your God."* This is basically the same word that Christ gave in Matthew 6:33, *"But seek ye first the kingdom of God and His righteousness; and all these things shall be added unto you."* When one does this with all the heart and soul, all other things will work out for his good. He can build temples, work miracles, and perform innumerable and impossible feats through just such a program as this.

CHAPTER 23

Verse 1 says, *"So when David was old and full of days, he made Solomon his son king over Israel."* Both David and Solomon were types of Christ. As previously stated, David was a type of Christ, defeating all his enemies and putting down Satan and all the menions of darkness. Solomon is a type of Christ, resting in splendor and Glory, victorious and triumphant over all enemies, reigning in the coming Kingdom Age such as the world has never known.

The enthronement of Solomon during the lifetime of David is twice recorded by the Holy Spirit by design. This section is, therefore, introduced by the union of David and Solomon as King and Priest. David orders everything as though he were the High Priest. So it will be by-and-by. The Great King and Priest, Christ Jesus, will, as David and Solomon in unison, build the Temple of Jehovah, and will not only bear the Glory of it, but be the Glory of it.

Verse 2 says, *"And he gathered together all the princes of Israel, with the priests and the Levites."* This is a foretype of the glorious day when the Lord Jesus Christ will reign supreme in Jerusalem and will, as outlined by Ezekiel chapters 40-48, gather the worship classes (priests and Levites) together to establish the worship of God in Israel, and for the entire world for that matter. So, what we are seeing portrayed here is a shadow of the greater fulfillment that is yet to come at the outset of the Kingdom Age.

Verse 3 says, *"Now the Levites were numbered from the age of thirty years and upward."* This was changed to 25 years in Numbers 8:24 and to 20 years by David in verse 27. The reason for the lowering of the age was because of the need for greater numbers to service the Temple in the great Work for God.

Verse 5 says, *"Moreover four thousand were porters; and four thousand praised the Lord with the instruments which I had made, said David, to praise therewith."* It is interesting to note that the workers and the worshipers are equal in number. This principle should be true of every church and of every believer. It is not always so. Many are willing to worship, but not to work, and many to work, but not to worship.

Sadly, most churches do not work or worship, and then if there is activity, it is mostly centered in *"work"* with very little worship. We are shown here the high priority that the Holy Spirit places on worship. If the Holy Spirit designated such, and He did, then it is incumbent upon us to realize the significance of what He is telling us. If there is an imbalance, the Work of God will greatly suffer. Sadly, most churches put little emphasis on worship. Most do not even know what Spirit-inspired worship really is. Jesus said to the woman at the well, *"God is a Spirit: and they that worship Him must worship Him in Spirit and truth"* (St. John 4:24). He had just told the woman, *"Ye worship ye know not what"* (vs. 22). This statement could apply to most of that which calls itself *"Christian."*

Some years back, a man made the statement, *"I am the worship leader in my church."* When asked what he did, his answer was this, *"Sometimes I bring in folk singers dressed in the type of costumes that go with their particular folk songs."* And then he said, *"After a wedding, I take the 'holy water' and sprinkle it on the people in the Sunday morning service."*

The foolishness that characterizes such is what passes for *"worship"* in most churches. No wonder Jesus said, *"You know not what you worship."* Any worship of God must be by the power and leading of the Holy Spirit which will always be according to the Word of God.

Worship is not limited exclusively to choirs, singers, and musical instruments, but these do play a great part in worship of God.

The Holy Spirit, through David, originated worship even as we know it today. It began with him, even as a boy tending the sheep, strumming his harp, and singing praises unto the Lord. The Holy Spirit has directed it thusly that a choir will gather at the morning sacrifice (9 a.m.) and at the evening sacrifice (3 p.m.) *"to thank and praise the Lord"* (vs 30). What praise and glory this must have been in Jerusalem in those days! Once again, this is a foreshadow of that which is to come under the Lord Jesus Christ during the Kingdom Age.

The 5th verse seems to imply that the 4000 worshiped with the instruments of music, *"which I made."* This does not mean that he made 4000 different types of instruments, but, no doubt, David, under the guidance of the Holy Spirit, did design several different types. They were used *"to praise therewith."*

Music is one of the most powerful moving forces known to man; therefore, Satan has used it greatly to *"steal, kill, and destroy"* (St. John 10:10). However, music and singing were designed by God, and for the expressed purpose of worshiping the Lord (Job 38:7).

The 6th verse proclaims the three sons of Levi, *"Gershon, Kohath, and Merari."* All of the many thousands of Levites who served in the work of God came under one of these three designations.

The 25th verse says, *"That they may dwell in Jerusalem forever."* This was God's original intention, but because of sin they were driven from Jerusalm and all the Holy Land. But in the future, they will be restored and fulfill God's purpose to the letter (Isa. 11:1-12).

CHAPTER 24

Verse 1 says, *"Now these are the divisions of the sons of Aaron."* The Temple was not yet built, and, in fact, would not be built until

NOTES

constructed by Solomon. However, every part about it was already in David's heart, designed there by the Holy Spirit. All of its activities concerning the Levites and the Priests were given to David by the Holy Spirit, even down to the most minute detail. Nothing was left to chance or to guess.

These *"divisions"* or *"orders"* were designed by the Holy Spirit concerning the services of the Priests. Aaron, Moses' brother, was the very first High Priest. He had four sons, *"Nadab, Abihu, Eleazar, and Ithamar."*

The 2nd verse says, *"But Nadab and Abihu died before their father and had no children."* Actually, they were stricken dead by God with fire from the Holy of Holies because of offering *"strange fire"* before the Lord (Lev. 10). Therefore, all of the order of Priests would derive from the two remaining sons, *"Eleazar, and Ithamar."* The reason they were so very important is because they were types of Christ. *"Eleazar"* had 16 sons, with *"Ithamar"* having 8 sons, for a total of 24. Therefore, all the order or divisions of Priests would come from these original 24 sons, constituting 24 different orders. In other words, the names of these sons were given in verses 7 through 18. Naturally, they had lived some 500 years before. However, the order of Priests would retain these respective names.

The 7th verse says, *"Now the first lot came forth Jehoiarib, the second to Jedaiah."* So, the first order of the Priests (consisting of many priests) would have been the *"Jehoiarib order or division."* The second, third, and so forth, would have been after their own respective names given in these passages. These 24 chief men who went by the respective name given were governors of the House of the Lord in their own turn, one week at a time. Each priest would serve from Sabbath to Sabbath. Zacharias (Luke 1:5), the father of John the Baptist, belonged to the eighth course, which is the course of Abijah (vs. 10). It is interesting to learn from Luke 1:5 how the Divine Son of David, through all the changes of Israel's history, watched over and maintained these courses of the Priests.

If every Christian was as skillful in the Word of righteousness as they should be, they would never find these lists of names dull but, on the contrary, full of spiritual wealth. The Holy Spirit wrote these lists and, in so doing, designed the profit of God's people.

The 5th verse says, *"Thus were they divided by lot."* This refers to the Urim and Thummim. Absolutely nothing about the Temple, its furnishings, fixtures, design, the order of the Priests as well as the Levites was left to chance. Everything was ordered, guided, and directed by the Holy Spirit. It might also be quickly added that it was placed in the heart of David and made ready for Solomon that when the Temple would be constructed, every single thing concerning its order, its worship, and its purpose would have been previously prepared.

Verses 20 through 31 also give the order or courses of the Levites. They were 24 courses as well. Whereas the Priests had to do with the Sacrifices (the Priests were also Levites), the balance of the Levites had to do with the worship, which concerned the music and singing, and so on.

———■———

CHAPTER 25

Verse 1 says, *"Moreover David and the captains of the host separated to the service of the sons of Asaph, and of Hemen, and of Jeduthun, who should prophesy with harps, with psalteries, and with cymbals."* We are now told of the division of the 4000 singers into 24 courses or weekly periods by lot (the Urim and Thummim). There was no such provision for song and worship in the Tabernacle in the wilderness as in the Temple of Solomon, and this was because the former spoke of a provided Redemption, but the latter of an accomplished Salvation. The reader should well note the volume of praise that was to fill the Temple area and all of Jerusalem. It was symbolic of that which will fill not only the Temple area and Jerusalem during the Kingdom Age, but the entirety of the earth. For Isaiah said, *"For the earth shall be full of the knowledge of the Lord, as the waters cover the sea"* (Isa. 11:9). As well, in our present-day churches, volumes of praise should fill the sanctuary constantly. And inasmuch as we are now the Temple of the Holy

Spirit (I Cor. 3:16), a volume of praise to the Lord should fill our hearts constantly. Surely, by now the Bible student has learned the premium that God places on praise. Jesus came from the Tribe of Judah, which means *"praise."*

The overseership of this service seemed to be divided under the following:

1. The sons of Asaph (vs. 2).
2. The sons of Jeduthun (vs. 2).
3. The sons of Heman (vs. 4-7).

They were given charge of the great choirs and the musicians with a strange term being attached to such, *"Who should prophesy with harps, with psalteries, and with cymbals."* The *"psalms of the Lord"* (vs. 7) were basically the same as that which would be given in I Corinthians 14:3 which speak to men to edification, exhortation, and comfort. This was accomplished by the singing and the music and is, as well, accomplished thusly today. In other words, when anyone sings *"the songs of the Lord,"* which will always glorify God, they are, in effect, *"prophesying."* We would do well to note that the Holy Spirit uses the word *"prophesy."* For such to be, the *"flesh"* must have no place, only the *"Spirit."* Sadly, too much of that which passes for Christian music emphasizes the *"flesh"* instead of the *"Spirit."*

Music has three characteristics:

1. Melody.
2. Harmony.
3. Rhythm.

All three coordinate with each other to produce the worship that the Holy Spirit intends. So-called Contemporary Christian Music destroys the harmony and the melody. Consequently, it neither produces nor elicits praise and worship. Efforts to worship thusly are fruitless.

Likewise, rhythm is legitimate and scriptural providing measures of accompaniment according to the cymbals, etc. – unless it is rhythm for the sake of rhythm, thereby, catering to the flesh. Then it becomes spiritually illegitimate.

These 4000 singers would have been divided into 24 choirs with a little bit over 150 members to the choir except, no doubt, for special occasions, when several of the choirs or even all of the singers would have joined together. They each served at their appointed

NOTES

times.

According to verse 7, they were helped by the 288 skilled musicians and skilled singers, who, as well, performed in particular orders. It says, *"That were instructed in the songs of the Lord."* What a beautiful statement. These *"songs of the Lord"* made up at this particular time at least part of the Psalms as we now know them.

The Holy Spirit takes special note, as the 4th verse says, *"of Heman and his fourteen sons."* In the Hebrew it seems that the names of his sons form a sentence, and this sentence glorifies God for *"lifting up the horn."* The Holy Spirit specifically says, *"And God gave to Heman fourteen sons and three daughters,"* meaning that these were especially used in the service of the Lord. How blessed Heman was!

These choirs, we are told, were very lively in their worship, hence, the different types of percussion instruments used.

Tradition says that at times the choirs would be divided into two sections, with the men on one side and the ladies on the other. A phrase or a stanza would be sung by one group and then answered by the other. Thus, the Temple was to be filled with song. As well, praise will characterize the great Kingdom Age to come. So, today, an accomplished salvation fills the believer's mouth with singing and with praise.

———◼———

CHAPTER 26

The 1st verse says, *"Concerning the divisions of the porters."* There were 4000 porters (23:5). They were Levites as well. They were divided into 24 courses by lot (the Urim and the Thummim) and were ruled by 93 chiefs. They were porters (workers) of the Temple service. Just as worship at the Throne was the subject of the prior chapter, so service at the gate is the theme of this chapter. Grace is its opening note. For the 1st verse also says, *"Of the Korhites was Meshelemiah the son of Kore, of the sons of Asaph."* These were the sons (or descendants) of Korah who had led the rebellion against Moses over 500 years before

(Num. 16). Where sin abounds, Grace will much more abound. The sons of Korah are first chosen as door-keepers, their duty being to prevent the presumption of which their father was guilty. Such are the ways of God! The sinful sons of a rebellious father are set on high by Him, and heavenly things are committed to their hands. Such is Grace.

Verse 4 also records a beautiful work of Grace. It says, *"Moreover the sons of Obed-edom."*

He had eight sons, and the 5th verse says, *"For God blessed him."*

The 6th verse mentions his first son, *"Shemaiah,"* speaking of the sons who were born to him, and says, *"For they were mighty men of valour."*

Then the 8th verse uses the words, *"Able men for strength."* And then it says, *"were threescore and two [62] of Obed-edom."*

Loyalty to truth enriches the heart; Obed-edom illustrates this. The 13th verse says that "the small as the great" had their place in the work of God. This teaches the lesson that every Christian, no matter how young or lowly, is responsible to guard every truth of the Gospel.

There were gates to be kept and treasures to be guarded. Only *"valiant men"* (vs. 7) and *"discreet counselors"* could effectually undertake such service. Spiritual courage and wisdom are needed in order to contend earnestly for the faith which was once delivered to the saints.

It is remarkable that the Holy Spirit will mention Obed-edom's name some 20 times throughout the Word of God. After the Ark of the Covenant was left at his house (I Chron. 13:13), Obed-edom was never the same again. David was about ten years into his 40-year reign (seven years Judah, with three years over all of Israel) when the Ark was brought into Jerusalem. Whether Obed-edom lived the entirety of the remainder of the 30 years of David's reign is not known. However, this we do know: When he experienced the glory of God with the Ark being in his house for some three months, he never wanted to leave it. Wherever the Ark was, that was where Obed-edom wanted to be. No doubt, oftentimes, he would relate the experience and exclaim with miraculous awe how he had been so near the Ark.

NOTES

The love for God that Obed-edom had, which is verified by the Holy Spirit, is the same love that God demands of us today. As He blessed Obed-edom, He will bless us as well, providing our love is as Obed-edom's.

When the day came that he left this pale of life and was ushered into Abraham's bosom, this is probably what happened:

When Jesus died on Calvary's Cross and then went down into Paradise and *"led captivity captive"* (Eph. 4:8), no doubt, when Obed-edom first laid his eyes on the King of kings and Lord of lords as Jesus walked into the place we now know as Paradise, he, no doubt, exclaimed, *"This is the one Who I saw, and this is the presence that I felt,"* for the Ark of the Covenant was a type of the Lord Jesus Christ.

This chapter proves how real to David's heart was the House of Glory that was to be built. The 13th verse says, *"For every gate,"* as for the northward, southward, westward, and eastward, every avenue was guarded and every causeway and gate effectually protected.

Such should be the fidelity of every child of God today to every department of revealed truth respecting the Person, Work, and Glory of the Lord Jesus Christ, of whom this Temple was but a symbol.

The 27th verse says, *"out of the spoils won in battles did they dedicate to maintain the House of the Lord."* This passage recalls the oft forgotten lesson, that the Spiritual Temple of Jehovah must be built up with *"spoils won in battle."* There must be labor in prayer, battling with wicked spirits in heavenly places, and sharp encounters with the devil and his human servants if spoil, that is, souls, are to be won to Jesus Christ.

These doorkeepers were to exclude evil, and treasurekeepers were to guard the Spiritual Wealth. This implies warfare. Paul told Timothy to *"war a good warfare."* He was a doorkeeper and a treasurekeeper (I Tim. 1:3; 4:20).

Verses 29 through 32 refer to civil appointments of officers and judges over government business. This refers to business outside the Temple worship and services.

1700 officers and judges were appointed on the west side of Jordan to take care of the business of the King, and 2700 on the east side.

The 31st verse says they were *"mighty men of valour."* The appointment of these officers by David in unison with his appointment of the Priests shows how fully the Holy Spirit carried him forward unto the day when Christ, as David and Solomon, and as King and Priest, will make all sacred and civil nominations in His Kingdom. As well, it shows that God honors and rewards proper business activity as a dedication to His service. It is to be carried on with the same consecration and dedication to God, even as the Temple worship and service. We must conduct ourselves thusly today.

CHAPTER 27

Verses 1 through 15 pertain to David's standing army which numbered 288,000. These were divided into 12 monthly courses of 24,000 each. In other words, all 288,000 were not on duty at all times. Only 24,000 in their respective month would stand duty, with the others going about their business in their homes, etc. Counting all of the officers, leaders, and personal guard, the total number would have been approximately 300,000. Of course, during times of emergency larger numbers than that could easily be marshaled.

It is interesting to note the exact manner in which the Holy Spirit appointed the army, as well as the exact manner in which it would stand guard.

If one will carefully notice, the Holy Spirit appointed the affairs of the nation of Israel in all capacities, which would have included the worship, with all the Temple duties, the civil government, as well as the military appointments. Nothing was left to chance; nothing was left to the wisdom or the ability of man. All was designated by the Holy Spirit.

Likewise, the Holy Spirit desires to guide every facet of our being, be it physical, domestical, financial, or spiritual. In other words, the Holy Spirit desires control in every single facet of our lives. However, control will never be taken, but must be given.

If the Holy Spirit has His perfect way, prosperity is guaranteed. Nevertheless, the pros-

perity will be God's prosperity and not man's.

Verses 23 and 24 portray the displeasure of God when man attempts to take matters into his own hands. The 23rd verse says, *"But David took not the number of them from twenty years old and under: Because the Lord had said he would increase Israel like the stars of the heavens."*

No census was taken of any in the tribes under the age of 20, for by this time the new age limit for entering some service was in force (I Chron. 23:27). This numbering was the same as the satanic-inspired count of chapter 21 for which God sent a plague which killed 70,000 men in Jerusalem alone. God promised that Israel would be as the sand, dust, and stars – innumerable, and somehow, it stirred His wrath for David to undertake any counting of the people, whether in doubt of the promise being fulfilled or in plans for future conquest.

Verses 33 and 34 mention both *"Ahithophel and Joab."* This illustrates the sad truth that it is possible to have a very high official position in the spiritual household of the King of kings, and, yet, at heart be a rebel to the Lord Jesus Christ!

CHAPTER 28

The 1st verse says, *"And David assembled."* This was David's last assembly for Israel.

The 2nd verse says, *"Then David the King stood up on his feet, and said, Hear me, my brethren, and my people."* This address will show that David in his dying hour was more concerned with the House of God than with anything else in his Kingdom. This shows where his heart, attention, and devotion were. It was not on money, riches, fame, power, or glory; it was on the Lord. All the battles, privation, want, and tribulation had been for this time. The House of God would be built. And, yet, as the Lord had already told David, David was not really building the Lord a house, the Lord was building David a house. Hallelujah!

As David calls all the many thousands of Israel together, he will encourage them to be a part of this great work that God will perform.

He will invite and even urge everyone, young and old, rich and poor, to take a share in the setting up of this House of Glory. It was true that their gifts were poor indeed compared with his, but they were precious to him and to God. Such is the Grace of the Lord of glory!

He could build His spiritual Temple without human assistance, but in His wonderful Grace He invites men to become fellow-labourers with Himself, and in the coming days of His Kingdom, He will acknowledge the efforts of such fellow-labourers as though they had done great things.

In David's last address, *"the Lord"* is the keynote. David made nothing of himself – all was God and the Divine election.

The king will point to his election and to his rejection with equal subjection of heart. He first speaks of his rejection in being forbidden to build the Temple, *"But God said unto me, thou shalt not build an house for my name, because thou hast been a man of war, and hast shed blood"* (vs. 3). He then humbly recalls his election as king of Israel. For the 4th verse states, *"Howbeit the Lord God of Israel chose me before all the house of my father to be king over Israel forever."* To David's disciplined heart, the one Divine action was as much to be accepted and admired as the other. Praise the Lord!

Verses 5 and 6 portray God's choice for the erection of the Temple. Verse 5 says, *"He hath chosen Solomon my son to sit upon the throne of the kingdom of the Lord over Israel."*

And then verse 6 says, *"And he said unto me, Solomon thy son, he shall build my house and my courts."*

Solomon, for a time, was a child of God. He loved the Lord and walked in all His Statutes (I Kings 3:3), and the Lord loved him (II Sam. 12:24). In later life though Solomon grew cold toward Jehovah and loved many strange women who turned his heart away from God (I Kings 11:1-8). The Lord then became angry with Solomon and turned against him in his backslidings (I Kings 11:9-40). The Lord took his kingdom from him and finally destroyed it because of sin. The Kingdom will be renewed again when Israel comes to repentance (Zech. 12:10). Under the Messiah, this Kingdom shall continue eternally.

NOTES

Whether Solomon came back to the Lord in his closing days of life is not known. However, there is some small scriptural evidence that he did.

The instructions that the Holy Spirit, through David, gives to Solomon, are for us today as well.

The 9th verse says, *"And serve him with a perfect heart and with a willing mind."* Actually, this is the only thing that any individual can give to God, *"An obedient heart and a willing mind."* The Lord has to furnish all else.

The 9th verse continues to say, *"For the Lord searcheth all hearts, and understandeth all the imaginations of the thought."*

The Lord does not operate His Kingdom on the principle of good and evil for the simple reason that there are no *"good"* individuals. Jesus Himself said, *"There is none good but God."* He rather operates it on the principle of the willing (obedient) or rebellious heart. In other words, *"man looketh on the outward appearance, but God looks on the heart"* (I Sam. 16:7).

The 9th verse continues, *"If thou seek him, he will be found of thee; but if thou forsake him, he will cast thee off forever."* This is one of the greatest promises found in the entirety of the Word of God. Irrespective of the disposition of the individual involved, if the person seeks the Lord with all his heart, the Lord will be found. What a consolation! As well, irrespective of whom we may be, if we turn our back on the Lord, He will turn His back on us. Every human being would do well to carefully heed the 9th verse of this striking chapter.

The 11th verse says, *"Then David gave to Solomon his son the pattern."*

And then the 12th verse says, *"And the pattern of all that he had by the Spirit."*

The closing verses of this chapter are most important, not only because they declare that the Temple of Solomon was wholly planned by God and an absolutely full pattern of it and its vessels given to David – nothing was left to his or to Solomon's imagination – but it throws a great light upon the mode of inspiration. This appears in verses 12 and 19. Here, David says that this Divine pattern was communicated to him by his being compelled by the Hand, or the Spirit of Jehovah, to record it all in writing.

The verse, therefore, pictures David drawing the pattern of every portion of the Temple, great or small, and of every article of its varied ministry, and writing notes explanatory of the drawings, and divining the woods and metals to be used, and the weight of the several metals, and he is seen to do this all when under the inspiration of the Holy Spirit. As well, from this explanation we are given a view as to how the Bible in its entirety was written.

Nothing was left to Solomon's or David's genius or taste. All was *"by the Spirit"*; all was Divine!

CHAPTER 29

As David's final address continues, the second verse says, *"Now I have prepared with all my might for the house of my God."* David's preparation was never for himself, but for God. And then the Lord abundantly blesses David – a blessing so abundant that it defies description. This is basically what Jesus said, *"Seek ye first the kingdom of God, and His righteousness, and all these other things shall be added unto you."*

Someone has said, *"Make your list of things of importance"* and then he adds, *"Make sure there's only one name on that list, Jesus."*

The secret of David's preparation is in the third verse, *"Moreover, because I have set my affection to the house of my God."* This is where David's love was. The Lord said, *"Love not the world, neither the things that are in the world."* What we love is what we prepare for.

The third verse as well says, *"which I have given to the house of my God."* In today's inflationary dollar, David would have personally given over $10 billion for the construction of the Temple (the cost of the Temple would be over $1 trillion in 1993 currency).

The fifth verse proclaims David asking this question, *"And who then is willing to consecrate his service this day unto the Lord?"* What a question!

Several things must be noted about this question:

1. Our service to God is always on a volun-

NOTES

tary basis.

2. God accepts the consecration of all, both small and great.

3. This question is a test of faith because God is the One Who gave it to us in the first place.

4. As God has freely given to us, will we freely give to Him?

The sixth verse says concerning the leaders of Israel, *"offered willingly."* Their total gifts came somewhat to approximately $15 billion.

The ninth verse says, *"Then the people rejoiced."* This tremendous offering given by a willing heart to the Lord elicits tremendous joy, for the Holy Spirit says, *"Because with perfect heart they offered willingly to the Lord."* The word *"perfect heart"* specifies that their motivation was not one of greed. Too often the Christian gives in order to receive. This is not really giving. It is more of an investment or even a gamble. God will have none of it. The Apostle Paul in his tremendous treatment of the Grace of giving in II Corinthians chapters 7 and 8 extols the abundance of God's blessings that come to the liberal giver. However, he says that our giving is *"to prove the sincerity of our love"* (II Cor. 8:8). God will accept giving on no other basis.

Now, the unselfish giving of the people will be anchored in Calvary. For the 21st verse says, *"And they sacrificed sacrifices unto the Lord, and offered burnt offerings unto the Lord."* It seems that the sacrifices may have been offered on the threshingfloor of Araunah, the Jebusite, where the Temple would be built. All is ever anchored in Calvary. All the gold and silver given on this memorable occasion could not purchase the redemption of even one soul. This could only be brought about by the precious shed Blood of the Lord Jesus Christ. The giving of the people pointed toward Calvary; the Temple site pointed toward Calvary; the construction of the Temple itself would point toward Calvary. The 21st verse says as well, *"A thousand bullocks, a thousand rams, and a thousand lambs."* The entirety of the Temple site must have been saturated with blood. To the unspiritual eye this would have been a gruesome and unacceptable site. To those who knew their Lord and His Love for lost mankind, it would speak of Redemption so glorious that it would beggar description.

Whenever our worship is anchored in Calvary as the 22nd verse says, there will always be *"great gladness."*

The 22nd verse as well says, *"And they made Solomon the son of David king the second time."* This has reference to the first anointing as is outlined in I Kings 1. However, this anointing is before the entirety of Israel. This double consecration was necessary because he was Divinely designed to be a type of the Greater than Solomon. Two key-words unlock the significance of these two crownings. The key-words are *"the altar of burnt-offering"* (chapter 22:1), and the *"throne of Jehovah"* (chapter 29:23). The first symbolizes Grace; the second, Glory. The first is connected with Calvary; the second, with the New Jerusalem. The setting up of the Altar of burnt-offering on the threshingfloor of Araunah, the Jebusite, was followed by the first coronation of Solomon. The completion of the material for the Temple occasioned the second crowning. So with Christ, Sacrificed upon Calvary, He is crowned in the heavens; His spiritual Temple completed, He will ascend the Throne of Jehovah at Jerusalem in the crowning day that will mark the beginning of the Kingdom Age.

Concerning David, the 28th verse says, *"And he died in a good old age, full of days, riches, and honor: and Solomon his son reigned in his stead."* David lived about 25,568 days, which was nothing compared to what God's plan was when man was created. God intended he should live eternal days and never grow old, but sin caused man to come short of the glory of God (Rom. 3:23).

So concluded the life of one of the greatest men of God who ever lived. David wrote over half the Psalms. He was given the plans for the Temple which would be the greatest building ever constructed by the hand of man. Above all he would be the ancestor of the Incarnation, of whom the Son of David would be named. His name is the first human name in the New Testament (Matt. 1:1). It is, as well, the last human name in the New Testament (Rev. 22:16).

When one realizes that the glory, splendor, and honor we witness at the close of David's life which began as a shepherd boy tending his

NOTES

father's sheep, we are humbled. As his life closes, perhaps one of the verses of John Newton's great song, "Amazing Grace," would be fitting.

"Through many dangers, toils, and snares,
"I have already come,
"But Grace has led me safe thus far,
"And Grace will lead me on."

THE
BOOK OF II CHRONICLES

NOTES

CHAPTER 1

This chapter is glorious, and yet at the same time sad, because Solomon will take the reigns of control out of the hands of the Holy Spirit and place them into his own hands. The opening verses present Solomon as a Christ confessor; the closing verses decry him as a horsedealer! This sad fall resulted from not reading and obeying the Bible. It forbade him to go down to Egypt for horses (Deut. 17:16). The Bible is always necessary to holiness. Solomon's wisdom did not save him from Egypt's horses, nor from Egypt's idols! Disobedience to the Word of the Lord sets the feet on a downward and slippery path; first the horses, and then the idols! Union with the world in commerce quickly leads to social intercourse and ends in idolatry (I John 5:21).

Verse 1 says, *"And Solomon the son of David was strengthened in his kingdom, and the Lord his God was with him, and magnified him exceedingly."* For a time Solomon would magnify the Lord, and then would close his life by magnifying himself. He was the third king of Israel. He began reigning 81 years after the kingdom was established.

He was the first of David's descendants to reign in unbroken succession for the next 513 years. From the end of that time until today, the Israelites have not had a kingdom, and they will not have one until the Messiah comes to reign. He will rebuild the Tabernacle of David and reestablish the Kingdom to sit on the Throne of David forever (Isa. 9:6-7; Zech. 14:5-9; Rev. 20:1-10). Christ was the last Son of

David in the Bible genealogies, and He will be the next King on the Throne of David (Luke 3:23-38).

Solomon was *"magnified exceedingly"* because *"God was with him."* Nothing greater could be said of a man than the statement, *"God is with him."*

The first act of Solomon is to confess without shame to the whole world that he and all Israel owed everything to the Blood of the Lamb. He sought to set out something of the infinite preciousness of the Blood by offering 1,000 burnt-offerings upon the Brazen Altar made by Bezaleel nearly 600 years before. But 10,000 times 10,000 offerings could never worthily exhibit the preciousness of that Blood! It was, however, a glorious testimony on the part of Solomon at the commencement of his reign. How glorious it would have been had Solomon maintained this testimony without fault to the close of his reign!

The 3rd verse says, *"For there was the tabernacle of the congregation of God, which Moses the servant of the Lord had made in the wilderness."*

The *"tabernacle"* was a type of the wilderness struggle. Even though the struggle was long and hard, still, the Tabernacle remained. Likewise, the Lord Jesus Christ, of which the Tabernacle is a type, will *"never leave us or forsake us."*

The *"ark of God"* of verse 4 that was *"in a tent in Jerusalem"* is a type of the *"land possessed."* It represents the Throne of God and victory in the inheritance.

The *"Temple"* represents the glorious Kingdom Age to come. Therefore, all three that are mentioned in chapters 1 and 2 portray the Christian life.

God would honor Solomon's allegiance to the *"Blood of the Lamb."* For the 7th verse says, *"In that night did God appear unto Solomon, and said unto him, Ask what I shall give thee."* This appearance was in a dream, but it was just as real as if God had appeared to him in actual visible form.

The Lord told Solomon to ask what he wanted, and it is plainly implied that the request would be granted. Those who express the desire to have God say to them what He did to Solomon should realize that He does (and even more). The following will make such clear:

1. Ask and you shall receive (Matt. 7:7).

2. Nothing shall be impossible unto you (Matt. 17:20).

3. All things, whatsoever you shall ask in prayer, believing, you shall receive (Matt. 21:21-22).

4. All things are possible to him that believeth (Mark 9:23) – plus many more that we cannot name for lack of room.

Solomon's request is given in the 10th verse, *"Give me now wisdom and knowledge, that I may go out and come in before this people."*

This request of Solomon set the pattern for all who desire to please God and be blessed by Him. It was wisdom and understanding in the science of government to judge Israel in true justice. He desired gifts that would best qualify him for his work and calling in life. Too often men pray for gifts which, they think, will make them great in the eyes of others. They want to imitate the greatness of some other man, and, actually, they are not called or qualified for that particular work. Consequently, their motive is one of selfishness and self-gratification.

The 11th verse says, *"And God said to Solomon."* In I Kings 3:10 the Holy Spirit says, *"The speech pleased the Lord that Solomon had asked this thing."* Many regarding Solomon's request have demeaned his choice, claiming he could have asked better. However, if the Holy Spirit said that God was pleased with it, and He did, surely, it should be good enough for us.

The 12th verse records God's pleasure by saying, *"Wisdom and knowledge is granted unto thee."* The Lord would also add of that

which Solomon did not ask, *"Riches, wealth, and honour."* He then says, *"Such as none of the kings have had that have been before thee, neither shall there any after thee have the like."* As David, Solomon was a type of Christ; therefore, at least in part, the reason that this was given to Solomon was because of the One who he would represent, namely the Lord Jesus Christ. David was a type of Christ in securing victory; hence the many wars and bloodshed. Solomon was a type of Christ reigning supreme in Jerusalem in the Kingdom Age that is yet to come, hence the splendor, glory, and riches.

Verse 16 says, *"And Solomon had horses brought out of Egypt."* How sad is the descent from verse 13 to verse 14. The words in verse 16, *"and linen yarn,"* should read from the Hebrew, *"in droves."* Actually, it seems that Solomon became a wholesale horsedealer! His Egyptian agents bought the horses in droves, forwarded them to Jerusalem, and the king resold them to the neighboring kings at a profit. It would appear incredible that a king of such amazing wealth would stoop to such traffic. However, it does not appear incredible to those who have been taught by the Spirit, through the Scriptures, something of the ignoble follies of the human heart, even in positions of great splendor.

CHAPTER 2

The 1st verse says, *"And Solomon determined to build an house for the name of the Lord, and an house for his kingdom."* The wording of this passage proclaims to us that Solomon's determination was even more than the prompting to do so by his father David. The Holy Spirit is, in fact, now helping him.

Verse 2 proclaims 153,600 men, all foreigners, as workers preparing the timbers and the stones for the Temple. These men were Gentiles, actually prisoners of war, justly condemned to hard labor for life. David could easily have put these men to death, as he might justly have done. For when they were captured, they had been attempting to kill David, destroy

Israel, and the God of Israel. So, David's allowing these people to remain alive was an act of mercy on his part.

Any one of these individuals could have subscribed to the God of Abraham, Isaac, and Jacob by submitting to the Law of Moses and to circumcision. They would have become free men. Possibly some of them did this.

When Solomon made them fellow-workers with himself in the building of the Temple, this forms together a picture of Christ Who saves men and makes them captives, allowing them to be fellow-laborers in the building of His great spiritual Temple. What an honor to be able to work for the Lord in the construction of this holy edifice in any capacity.

The 3rd verse says, *"And Solomon sent to Huram the king of Tyre."* He writes this man (called Hiram in I Kings 5) a beautiful letter that portrays the glory of Christ.

This is not the Hiram of David's day, but the son of the Hiram of II Samuel 5:11. Meander of Ephesus, who wrote a history of Tyre in Greek about 300 B.C., mentioned him as the son of Abibeal, King of Tyre, and said that he ascended the throne when he was 19 years old, that he reigned 34 years, and died at the age of 53, being succeeded by his son, Baleazar. This history speaks at length on the dealings of Hiram with Solomon.

Solomon goes into spiritual detail in his letter to Hiram.

The 4th verse proclaims first of all that he said, *"Behold, I build an house to the name of the Lord my God."* At the outset, Solomon proclaims to Hiram that this grand building is not to glorify Solomon, but *"the Lord my God."*

And then he says, *"To burn before him sweet incense, and for the continual shewbread, and for the burnt offerings morning and evening."* The mention of these three particulars portrays Christ. The *"sweet incense"* speaks of His glorious presence. The *"continual shewbread"* speaks of His continual life, for Jesus is the *"bread of life."* The *"burnt offerings"* speak of His glorious sacrifice of Calvary that would forever atone for the sins of man in their redemption.

The 5th verse proclaims His greatness, for it says, *"For great is our God above all gods."*

NOTES

The testimony of Solomon to the greatness of God above the heathen entities of surrounding nations is a witness to his boldness of testimony. He did not flinch from proclaiming the greatness of God over the insignificance of the god of Tyre.

The 6th verse is quick to proclaim that Solomon knows this house cannot even think of containing God. For it says, *"But who is able to build him an house, seeing the heaven of heavens cannot contain him?"* This refers back to the time that David desired to build a house for the Lord (I Chron. 17), and the Lord, in effect, telling David, *"I do not want nor need your house, and furthermore, I will build you a house."* (I Chron. 17:10). The major problem of the Church is that it tries to build the Lord a house, when in fact He will have none of it. He doesn't need a house. We are the ones who need the house, and that house is Jesus.

The 6th verse continues to exclaim the words of Solomon, *"Who am I then?"* If Solomon had maintained this humility, what a glorious example he would have been.

Verses 7-10 list that which Solomon desires to help in the construction of *"this house."* It is remarkable in Solomon's letter that nearly two-thirds of his letter extolls the God of Glory, with only about one-third of it itemizing his request.

Actually, the Millennial Temple yet to be built, will be the eternal capital of God among men, and the place where the Trinity will be seen. Visibly and bodily they will carry on their program of dwelling among men and ruling the universe.

The 11th verse proclaims these words, *"Then Huram (Hiram) the king of Tyre answered in writing."*

The 12th verse has this heathen king proclaiming the greatness of the Lord by saying, *"Blessed be the Lord God of Israel, that made heaven and earth."* This heathen had more spiritual sense than the majority of Christianized America and Canada, claiming evolution as the maker of such.

In effect, Hiram states that he is honored to have a part in this *"House of God"* that is to be built. Hiram and the kingdom of Tyre will, no doubt, be greatly blessed because of their participation in this great work for God.

CHAPTER 3

Verse 1 says, *"Then Solomon began to build the house of the Lord at Jerusalem in mount Moriah, where the Lord appeared unto David his father, in the place that David had prepared in the threshingfloor of Ornan (Araunah) the Jebusite."* This is the first mention of Mount Moriah since Genesis 22:2. It is never mentioned after this. Moriah was the place where Abraham offered up Isaac and where David saw the destroying angel - where he was commanded to build an altar to atone for the sin of numbering Israel (II Sam. 24:17-25).

The Temple of Solomon was a forepicture of the millennial glory of Christ as Melchizedek, while the Tabernacle in the Wilderness set out His Grace as a Saviour.

Nothing was left to the imagination of Moses in the building of the Tabernacle or of Solomon in the building of the Temple. Grace was expressed by the Tabernacle; Glory by the Temple. As silver is resplendent of grace; therefore, it was prominent in the Tabernacle. Gold speaks of deity and glory, hence, was prominent in the Temple. The Tabernacle spoke of access to God; the Temple, of fellowship with God.

The first building (the Tabernacle) pictures Christ in His First Advent; the later building, the Temple, pictures Christ in His Second Advent. The first building has sand for a floor; the second, gold. The first is a tent; the second, a Temple. But whether a tent or Temple, the materials, the vessels, and all the gathered wealth of each are precious and utter His praise.

Both the Tabernacle and the Temple speak of fellowship with God which can only come through the Atonement of Christ.

Both Solomon and the Temple picture Christ's glorious Kingdom over the earth. Solomon in His glory, riches, and wisdom sets out the person of Christ. The Temple symbolizes the nature of Christ - gold prefiguring His deity, cedar His humanity, but all has Grace in Atonement as its foundation, for this building of glory was built upon the threshingfloor of

NOTES

Araunah, the Jebusite.

At the present (1993), *"Mount Moriah"* is the flash point of the world. It is now occupied by one of the holy sites of Islam called the Dome of the Rock. Bible prophecy says the Jews will rebuild their Temple (Matt. 24:15). Due to this passage (and others), the Temple has to be built in this exact spot. Therefore, the Dome of the Rock must be moved. How this will be brought about at this time is not known. Nevertheless, Bible prophecy says it will be brought about; therefore, it will.

The building was not large. The 3rd verse says, *"The length by cubits after the first measure was three-score cubits (90 feet), and the breadth 20 cubits (30 feet, using 18 inches to the cubit)."* Considering that it was all handmade with copious amounts of gold, silver, and precious stones, this accounts for its tremendous cost.

The 4th verse says, *"The height was an hundred and twenty."* This is definitely a copyist error in one of the old manuscripts. This would make the Temple 180 feet high - twice as high as it was long. In I Kings 6:2 it states that the height was 30 cubits, or 45 feet high, counting 18 inches to the cubit. This would be normal for the highest part of the Temple and for the three stories of chambers (I Kings 6:8).

The 6th verse says, *"And he garnished the house with precious stones for beauty."* This explains what was done with the many precious stones and gems of various colors which David had gathered to beautify the Temple (I Chron. 29:2). This must have been a beautiful sight to behold. The *"precious stones"* speak of the redeemed. *"And they shall be mine, saith the Lord of hosts, in that day when I make up my jewels."* (Mal. 3:17).

The 7th verse says, *"And graved Cherubims on the walls."* The *"Cherubim"* speak of God's Holiness. The *"palm trees"* speak of a perfect climate. The *"chains"* speak of the never-ceasing link of the child of God to the Lord Jesus Christ.

The 8th verse says, *"And he made the most holy house."* This means the most holy place, the smallest of the two main rooms of the Temple where the Ark of the Covenant was placed. It was 20 cubits, or 30 feet square and overlaid with pure gold (I Kings 6:20). The Scripture says the amount of gold was *"six hundred talents."* In today's inflated dollar (1993), that would account for nearly one and three-quarter billion dollars - and that was the cost of only the gold in this one room.

The flooring, the ceiling, the walls, the ornamentation, the costly stones, the precious woods, the gold, the brass, the carved Cherubim, the veils, the two pillars and all the vessels of the house, together with its golden doors, and the dedicated treasures - all picture the Glories, the Perfections, the Graces, the Ministries, the Activities, and the Offices of Christ in His Second Advent and Millennial Reign.

Upon entering either chamber of the Sanctuary (the Holy Place or the Most Holy Place), nothing was seen above, beneath, or on either side but the purest gold wrought by Divine inspiration into exquisite ornamentation - palm trees and wreathen work and Cherubim.

The 9th verse says, *"And the weight of the nails was fifty shekels of gold."* This means each nail in 1993 currency costs nearly $50,000. It is so beautiful as to how the Grace of the Holy Spirit drew attention to the nails used in the construction of this great Temple. He does not overlook such small and simple things when detailing all these dazzling splendors. He alone saw them, for they were hidden, but they held all together and are remembered and named by God.

Were a golden lampstand to speak slightingly of the little golden nail, as some great preachers are sometimes tempted so to treat a Junior Sunday School teacher, the nail could reply that it was also formed of pure gold and had an indispensable office in the structure of this great House of God.

Verse 10 says, *"And in the most holy house he made two cherubims of image work, and overlaid them with gold."* These two Cherubim were very large, their wings reaching across the width of the most Holy Place - 30 feet. Each wing was five cubits or seven and one-half feet long. The outer ones touched the wall of the house while the inner ones touched each other. Thus, the two Cherubim with their four wings outstretched took up the whole width of the room. These were completely covered with

NOTES

gold, and they stood on their feet, which were like those of a calf (Ezek. 1:7).

The latter portion of the 13th verse says, *"And their faces were inward."*

There is some indication that the word *"inward"* in the Hebrew, as it is used in verse 13, means *"toward the house,"* in other words, outward.

In Moses' Tabernacle, the Cherubim looked down upon the blood-sprinkled Mercy Seat, for only there could their eyes rest with satisfaction all around, being under the reign of sin and death. But here the new Cherubim looked *"outward"* upon a kingdom governed in righteousness by the King of Righteousness.

There is no way that the mind of man can grasp what the Holy of Holies must have looked like with these huge Cherubim with their outstretched wings covering the entirety of the room. Even though this was only symbolic of the real which is in heaven, still, it must have been an awesome sight. How wonderful will it be when at long last we stand before the Throne of God and hear the Cherubim and the Seraphim (Isa. 6:1-8) cry *"Holy, Holy, Holy, Lord God almighty, which was, and is, and is to come"* (Rev. 4:8).

The Cherubim in Moses' Tabernacle looked down on the Mercy Seat and the shed blood, because the work was not yet finished. Now, the Cherubim look outward upon a finished work of the Grace and Glory of God. Hallelujah!

Verse 14 says, *"And he made the vail of blue, and purple, and crimson, and fine linen, and wrought cherubims thereon."* The Veil of the Temple is here described as being like that in the Tabernacle of Moses. It is not mentioned in I Kings at all. In I Kings 6:31 the Holy Spirit records the fact that there were doors made of olive wood between the Most Holy Place and the Holy Place. It does not mention the Veil. In this passage it mentions *"the veil"* but does not mention the doors. Quite possibly, the Veil hung immediately behind the doors. Therefore, when the doors were opened, the Veil would remain, continuing to hide the Holy of Holies from the inquisitive stare.

The *"blue"* stands for the origin of our salvation in Christ, which came from heaven. The *"purple"* stands for His position as King. The *"crimson* stands for His precious shed

Blood. The *"fine linen"* stands for his perfect righteousness. The *"Cherubims"* stand for His holiness - all pointed to Christ.

Verses 15-17 point to the two front pillars. For detailed notes on these pillars and their meaning, please refer to I Kings 7.

CHAPTER 4

Even though detailed accounts are given of these holy vessels in I Kings 7, still, possibly an added blessing will be forthcoming with a further account.

Verse 1 says, *"Moreover he made an altar of brass (copper), twenty cubits the length thereof, and twenty cubits the breadth thereof, and ten cubits the height thereof."* This meant that the Altar was 30 feet square and 15 feet high (using 18 inches to the cubit). Also, the Brazen Altar was the same dimension as the Most Holy Place regarding length and breadth. The Altar portrayed God's judgment on sin. The Holy of Holies portrayed His Mercy and Grace. Therefore, God's Mercy and Grace is as large as His Judgment. In other words, as much as God hates sin, He loves the sinner more.

The 2nd verse says, *"Also he made a molten sea of ten cubits from brim to brim."* The molten sea was cast in a foundry like the pillars of verses 15 and 16. It was 15 feet from brim to brim; 7½ feet high, and 45 feet all the way around.

There were rows of knobs around the rim of the bowl (I Kings 7:24). It stood upon 12 oxen cast out of brass; three looked in each of the four directions with their hinder parts inward and under the Brazen Laver which was a handbreadth, or about four inches thick; the brim was made like that of a cup with flowers and lilies (vss. 2-5).

The molten sea was an immense vase of solid brass weighing 15 to 20 tons. Having its 7 ½ foot depth filled would have taken approximately 25,000 gallons of water. Completely filled, it would have weighed about 75 tons.

The ten small lavers were supposed to contain about 300 gallons of water each, which

NOTES

make each one weigh about two tons. Jewish writers say that the water was changed daily so as to be always fresh and pure for use in the ceremonial worship.

Verse 3 says, *"And under it was the similitude of oxen."* Here we have a supplementary idea of that of I Kings 7:24, where knops or knobs only are mentioned. This explains that they were in the shape of oxen - ten such knobs to each cubit or 18 inches. In fact, there were two rows of such cast all the way around the molten sea (vs. 3) which sat upon the hinder parts of the 12 great brazen oxen made with extra strong legs to carry the weight of the 75 ton laver and water.

Verse 5 says concerning the amount of water it would hold, *"And held three thousand baths."* I Kings 7:26 says, *"two thousand baths."* There is no contradiction. The 3,000 baths were the maximum amount of water that the molten sea would hold, 2,000 baths being the amount it generally held. 2,000 were about 16,750 gallons, a *"bath"* being 67 pints. The 3,000 bath capacity would be 25,125 gallons.

The 6th verse says, *"He made also ten lavers, and put five on the right hand, and five on the left, to wash in them."* The ten lavers were much smaller than the molten sea. These were for the washing of sacrifices.

The Brazen Laver was a type of the Word of God. As the priest would look into the water, he would see his reflection as in a mirror; likewise, when we read and study the Word of God, we see our reflection in the Word proclaiming to us what we are. The *"oxen"* stand for the indestructibility, power, and strength of the Word of God.

Verse 7 says, *"And he made ten candlesticks of gold according to their form."* Ten golden candlesticks were made for the Temple, compared to one for the Tabernacle of Moses. Five were placed on one side of the Holy Place and five on the other.

Verse 8 says, *"He made also ten tables."* These tables were either the Tables of Shewbread, or else were tables for the lamps to be set on (more probably they were tables of shewbread). Both the Candlesticks and the Tables of Shewbread were representative of Christ. Jesus is the *"Bread of Life"* and the *"Light of the World."* The Tabernacle, which represented the Grace of God, only had one golden Lampstand and one Table of Shewbread. The Temple, representing the greater Glory of God in the great Kingdom Age, will have ten times as much as the Tabernacle, representing the fact that the Glory, Illumination, and Majesty of Christ will be ten times greater in the coming Kingdom Age.

The 11th verse says, *"And Huram (Hiram) made the pots, and the shovels, and the basons."* Hiram is symbolic of the Holy Spirit and His development of every part of the work and ministry of every child of God. Some of us are *"pots,"* some are *"shovels,"* and some are *"basons,"* but all are developed by the Holy Spirit; therefore, all are equally needed.

The 11th verse further says, *"And Huram finished the work that he was to make for king Solomon for the house of God."* This typifies the Holy Spirit finishing the work regarding the Church. This He shall do and shall present us faultless before the Throne of God (Jude 24).

Verses 12 through 16 portray all the vessels made by Hiram, typifying the Holy Spirit. All have their place in the Temple, as every Christian has his place in the great work of God. Brass (copper), of which these vessels were made, is a type of humanity. With suitable polishing, they shine brightly; however, they tarnish easily.

The 17th verse says, *"In the plain of Jordan did the king cast them, in the clay ground between Succoth and Ze-red-a-thah."* This represents death and burial, in other words, death and resurrection. There must be death to self. That which seems so beautiful to the unspiritual eye is, in fact, so ugly to the eye of the Lord. Former identity must be lost; truly, the Holy Spirit is making a *"new creature."* Spiritually speaking, we must die (to self) and must be buried (clay ground). Then when we are brought out of the mold or casting, we are in the image of the Heavenly, whether it be a *"base"* or a *"pot"* or a *"fleshhook,"* or even one of the great *"pillars."* The process of being brought from where we once were to where He desires us is a painful process. The spiritual journey that seems to be so short is nevertheless divided by a great chasm. Only the concentrated, patient, graceful work of the Holy Spirit can ultimately make us what He

NOTES

wants us to be. This we cannot do for ourselves, irrespective of how hard we try. He alone can make us into a holy *"pot"* or *"base"* or *"pillar."*

The 19th verse says, *"The golden altar also."* No doubt, this refers to the Holy Altar of Incense that sat in the Holy Place immediately in front of the Most Holy Place. Even though ten Lavers, and ten Candlesticks, and ten Tables were made, still, it seems only one *"golden altar"* was made. It seems that all of the vessels and their utensils on the outside were made of brass (copper), as all the vessels that were inside the Temple were made of gold.

The 22nd verse says, *"And the doors of the house of the temple, were of gold."* These doors are representative of Jesus Christ. He said, *"I am the door."* He is very man and very God, hence, *"gold."* There is no way into this *"house of God"* except through the Lord Jesus Christ.

CHAPTER 5

"Thus all the work that Solomon made for the house of the Lord was finished." Solomon was seven years in building the Temple (I Kings 6:38). Now it was time for this magnificent structure to be dedicated. However, its magnificence was little added to by the gold, silver, and precious stones. Its magnificence was the *"glory of the Lord"* (vs. 14).

The 2nd verse says, *"Then Solomon assembled the elders of Israel."* The 3rd verse says, *"In the feast which was in the seventh month."* This was the Feast of Tabernacles in October (Lev. 23:33). The first step in this dedication would be *"to bring up the ark of the covenant of the Lord out of the city of David, which is Zion."* The magnificence and glory of the Temple was not gold, silver, and precious stones (as stated), but rather was the Glory of God who resided between the Mercy Seat and the Cherubim. Without this, the Temple was just another costly building. When will the Church realize that its glory is not buildings, education, place, position, or earthly power, but, instead, the Glory of God.

The 4th verse says, *"And the Levites took up the ark."* The Priests were also Levites, and they were the only ones who could carry the Ark. Levites who were not priests were as unfit to carry it as ordinary laymen. It was the Priests who brought the Ark into the Temple (I Kings 8:3).

Verse 5 says, *"And all the holy vessels."* This speaks of the vessels such as the Golden Lampstand, Table of Shewbread, and Altar of Worship that were in Moses' Tabernacle, which was then at Gibeon. It, as well, no doubt referred to the Brazen Altar and the Brazen Laver. (The Ark of the Covenant had been kept in a separate tent in Jerusalem.) All of these *"holy vessels"* were by now a little over 600 years old. They, no doubt, were put *"among the treasures of the House of God"* in a separate chamber.

At the beginning of these proceedings, the 6th verse says, *"Sacrificed sheep and oxen, which could not be told nor numbered for multitude."* All the gold and precious stones in this magnificent Temple could not redeem one precious soul; only the Blood of Jesus could. Consequently, the thousands of animals that were slaughtered which, no doubt, soaked the ground with blood, was an eternal type of the great price that would be paid at Calvary's Cross. The song says:

"What can take away my sins, nothing but the blood of Jesus.

"What can make me whole again, nothing but the blood of Jesus."

Likewise, the glory of God that would be manifested could only do so because precious Blood had been shed. God's holiness is of such magnitude that man could never even begin to approach Him except through the Blood.

The 7th verse says, *"And the priests brought in the ark of the covenant of the Lord unto his place, to the oracle of the house, into the most holy place, even under the wings of the cherubims."* The Ark was placed in the middle of the Most Holy Place between the two Cherubims and under their wings. There was sufficient room even for the staves. These were partially taken out of the rings of the Ark by which it was carried, so that the ends could be seen from the Holy Place but not from the porch outside (I Kings 8:8). In this way the Ark never needed to be handled, as the staves could be easily put back into the rings without anyone's hands ever touching the Ark.

NOTES

It seems that it was unlawful to take the staves wholly out of the rings. Pulling them out so the ends could be seen indicated the Ark had found its resting place in the Temple and was not to be borne anymore. It had a permanent house, not a tent as before.

Verse 9 says, *"And they drew out the staves of the ark."* And then it says, *"And there it is unto this day."* This proves that this section of II Chronicles was written before the destruction of the Temple.

Verse 10 says, *"There was nothing in the ark save two tables which Moses put therein at Horeb."* At this time there was nothing in the Ark but the Ten Commandments. When in Hebrews 9:4 Paul mentioned the golden pot of Manna and Aaron's Rod, he was speaking of the Ark while in the Tabernacle instead of the Temple. It is not known when these two things were removed. It could have been when the Philistines had the Ark, or when many men were killed for looking into it, as in I Samuel 5-6.

We know that the original stones on which the Ten Commandments were written were in existence at this time.

The 11th verse says, *"And it came to pass, when the priests were come out of the holy place."* When the Priests had taken the Ark into the Temple into the Most Holy Place and had finished arranging the furniture and had left never to enter this place again except for the visit of the High Priest once a year, the Glory of God filled the Temple so that the Priests could not minister because of it.

This Glory was a symbol of the Divine presence of God, which had been promised before the Ark was begun (Ex. 29:43) and had filled the Tabernacle as soon as it was completed (Ex. 40:34), and had been seen on the journeys of the children of Israel (Ex. 13:21-22; 14:24; Num. 14:14).

The words, *"and did not wait by course,"* meant that the courses appointed by David had not begun (I Chron. 24).

The 12th verse proclaims the beginning of the worship. Many were there *"arrayed in white linen."* And, as well, *"an hundred and twenty priests sounding with trumpets."* What a sight this must have been!

The 13th verse says that whatever Psalm they used, this phrase was predominate, *"And praised the Lord, saying, For he is good; for his mercy endureth for ever."* How glorious that the Holy Spirit in the midst of the grandeur of this dedication points out *"His mercy."* And then it says, *"Then the house was filled with a cloud, even the house of the Lord."*

The 14th verse states, *"So that the priests could not stand to minister by reason of the cloud: for the glory of the Lord had filled the house of God."* Most people do not understand the power of God. Most churches have no idea as to what the power of God is. When one understands that the power of the Lord was so present that as the Priests went about their duties, their knees would buckle under them, and they would fall to the floor. This is what our churches desperately need. This will bring conviction of sin as nothing else will. This is what the preacher needs; this is what every Christian needs.

Paul says that we are now the Temple of God (I Cor. 3:16), and that the Spirit of God dwelleth in us. This house (Temple) was arranged totally by the Holy Spirit and, thereby, perfect, consequently, with the Spirit of God moving mightily. Is our *"house"* arranged by the Holy Spirit? Is He allowed to have His perfect way within our lives? If He is, then *"the glory of the Lord will fill this House of God, as well."*

CHAPTER 6

The entirety of this chapter is broken into two parts:

1. The sermon of Solomon – vss. 1-11.
2. The prayer of Solomon – vss. 14-42.

It begins thusly:

"Then said Solomon, the Lord hath said that he would dwell in the thick darkness." Where God ever said this is not recorded. Solomon may have taken the idea from the fact of God's appearance in darkness at Sinai (Ex. 20:21).

The New Testament says that God dwells in a light no man can approach unto, and no man has seen nor can see; that is, no man has ever seen nor can see God in all His Glory (I Tim. 6:16).

Verse 2 says, *"But I have built an house of habitation for thee."* Here, Solomon told God that he had built Him a house to dwell in, a settled place so that He would not be in a tent to be moved from place to place. He offered it to Jehovah as a dwelling place forever.

After saying this to the Lord, the king turned to the congregation and blessed them as they stood (vs.3).

The 5th verse says, *"Neither chose I any man to be a ruler over my people Israel."* For about 500 years God had not chosen any particular place among Israel where a house should be built for Himself, nor had He chosen any man to be a permanent ruler over Israel.

Now, He made it clear that He had chosen Jerusalem as the place of His headquarters on earth, and David as the one through whom all the future kings of Israel should come (II Sam. 7; I Chron. 17). The idea of a house for God originated with David, but God told him he could not build the Temple because of his being a man of blood and war; his son would be permitted to do so. Here, the record shows that Solomon had completed the work and was now preaching the dedicatory sermon and praying the dedicatory prayer.

This makes it clear that God did not choose Saul as He chose David. In Saul's case, God merely overruled the choice of the people who were determined to have a king so as to be like the other nations. The choice of a king then was not from God, for He protested their choice (I Sam. 8:5-22). He simply allowed what was best for the moment in view of the people's demands (I Sam. 9-10).

The 8th verse says, *"Thou didst well in that it was in thine heart."* This was speaking of David. And yet would, in effect, say to him that He (God) really did not need a house, but, instead, would build David (and all mankind) a house (I Chron. 17).

Concerning Solomon, the 12th verse says, *"And he stood before the altar of the Lord in the presence of all the congregation of Israel, and spread forth his hands."* This was the large Brazen Altar in the outer court. The congregation evidently stood all about the court and on the outside of the Temple grounds as far as the eye could see. Solomon stood before this Altar in prayer and stretched his hands out toward heaven, but before he prayed, he knelt before the Lord (I Kings 8:34).

In the dedication prayer, beginning with the 14th verse, he says concerning the Lord, *"which keepest covenant, and shewest mercy unto thy servants, that walk before thee with all their hearts."* No man will ever be able to say in all eternity that God has not kept His part of every contract with men or fulfilled every promise to them. He also has fulfilled and always will fulfill His obligations to humanity, for the promises of God are Yea, and Amen (II Cor. 1:20).

In the 18th verse Solomon asks a question in his prayer, *"But will God in very deed dwell with men on the earth?"* This question can be answered in the affirmative. God will indeed dwell on the earth, in person, and in visible form in all eternity, as He now dwells in heaven (Isa. 66:22-24; Tit. 2:13; Rev. 31:1-27; 22:4-5).

Solomon also says, *"Behold, heaven and the heaven of heavens cannot contain thee; how much less this house which I have built!"* Solomon understands the Glory of God, hence, the idea that the Lord would dwell in this particular house. Yes, He would dwell there, but, at the same time, be everywhere else as well. God is omniscient, *"all-knowing,"* and omnipotent, *"all-powerful,"* and omnipresent, *"everywhere."*

The 19th verse says, *"Have respect therefore to the prayer of thy servant, and to his supplication."* Prayer includes every thought and word from the heart that is Godward. If ever there was a prayer going direct to God, this one was.

The 24th verse says, *"And if thy people Israel be put to the worse before the enemy."* In the Holy Spirit during prayer, Solomon seems to sense the future of Israel prophetically. Consequently, the many prophetical events mentioned in these verses could not have been guesswork on the part of Solomon. Israel experienced every one of them in due time, so, technically, the predicting of them would be considered prophecy.

However, we probably should not list them as definite prophecy inasmuch as the statements are general and were made in connection with conditions of answered prayer.

Had Solomon been guessing, he most

likely would have made more favorable statements, for everything at this time pointed to a long and happy period under the blessing of God.

He also says in the 24th verse, *"Because they have sinned against thee."* This is the only reason Israel was ever defeated, either before or after Solomon's time. Sin is to blame for all the troubles and curses among men. In verses 24 and 25 we see the remedy for sin as well as the result.

The 26th verse says, *"When the heaven is shut up, and there is no rain, because they have sinned against thee."* No rain was recognized as a curse from God. In the Millennium, withholding the rain will be a means of forcing recognition of the Messiah and fulfillment of all laws (Zech. 14:16-21).

He says, *"Yet if they pray toward this place, and confess thy name, and turn from their sin, when thou dost afflict them."* Praying toward this Temple, this city, and this land is referred to eight times in this prayer. It was done so because at that particular time that is where God dwelt. Today, in this great dispensation of Grace, it doesn't really matter which direction a person faces while praying, the reason being that the Lord, through the power of the Holy Spirit, now lives in the heart of born-again man (I Cor. 3:16) and not in some particular temple or building. While it was true at that particular time that the Temple was the *"House of God"* because the Lord dwelt there, individuals would pray toward Jerusalem, but not anymore.

In the 27th verse he says, *"And send rain upon thy land, which thou hast given unto thy people for an inheritance."* The land between the River Euphrates and the Mediterranean, and from the Red Sea on the south to Hamath on the north is the only land promised in all Scripture for all the tribes of Israel. Theories teaching that America and England are new promised lands for Israel are in error; there is no hint of such in Scripture.

In the 32nd verse, Solomon says, *"Moreover concerning the stranger."* Solomon, in his wisdom, did not forget the Gentiles whom God had in mind to bless from the very beginning of His calling of Abraham, Isaac, and Jacob. All nations were to be blessed through Israel and their seed.

As well, this would imply the preaching of the Gospel, for how could individuals come to the God of Israel if they did not hear? (Rom. 10:9-17; I Cor. 1:18-24).

As well, Solomon says, *"Come and pray in this house."* In the Millennium and the New Earth, all nations will go to Jerusalem to pray and to worship. However, all people will continue to pray and worship exactly as they do now as well (Isa. 2:2-4; Zech. 8:23).

In the 33rd verse Solomon says, *"That all people of the earth may know thy name, and fear thee, as doth thy people Israel."* It is true that at that time David had brought Israel, as a whole, to a place of respect for God so that they feared Him. This wonderful state continued through most of the days of Solomon, but after him, Israel went into many sins and had to be destroyed as a nation twice (II Kings 24-25). In the Millennium, when Christ reigns visibly on earth, Israel will fear and know God again (Zech. 8:23; 14:16-21).

In the 35th verse he says, *"And maintain their cause."* God does maintain the cause of His people as long as they live right, but when sin is committed, He, Himself, becomes their Judge and metes out the penalty for sin. Twice here, Solomon prayed for God to maintain the cause of Israel.

In the 40th verse Solomon says, *"Let thine ears be attent unto the prayer that is made in this place."* This means all prayer said in this place and is so worded in I Kings 8:52. In this Solomon had a better understanding of the possibilities of the Gospel than many today who reject the Bible doctrine of Christians having prayers answered through faith. He prayed that this would be the experience of both Israel and the Gentiles. Thus, it should be with Christians as well, for great are the many promises of God given to us, and all are always and without exception, *"Yea and Amen to those who believe"* (II Cor. 1:20; I Pet. 1:1-9).

In the 41st verse he says, *"Thou, and the ark of thy strength: let thy priests, O Lord God, be clothed with salvation, and let thy saints rejoice in goodness."* The word *"saints"* in the Hebrew reads, *"men of grace,"* that is, those who are subjects of the Grace of God. This plainly shows that men in Old Testament times were under Grace as well as they are in New Testament times. It is true that the fullness of Grace came by Jesus Christ, but men had Grace before He came as proved by the spiritual experiences of individuals in the Old Testament. Actually, everyone has been saved by Grace, for there is no other way that an individual can be saved (Eph. 2:8).

In the 42nd verse he says, *"O Lord God, turn not away the face of thine anointed: remember the mercies of David thy servant."* God's anointed is the Messiah. Every blessing that we receive comes through the Lord Jesus Christ. Actually, God cannot bless sinful fallen man; He can only bless His Son, Jesus Christ. So, when Christ lives within us, then the blessing comes. Without Christ there is no blessing.

CHAPTER 7

II Chronicles 7:1 says, *"Now when Solomon had made an end of praying, the fire came down from heaven, and consumed the burnt offering and the sacrifices; and the glory of the Lord filled the house."*

This is additional to I Kings 8:63-64, and again shows the Divine acceptance of sacrifices until the Messiah should come to offer Himself as the one great, eternal sacrifice for all men. The fire of God from heaven has fallen several times on such occasions (Gen. 4:4; 15:17; Lev. 9:24; I Kings 18:38).

The scene of this chapter is one of grandeur and awe. The king, with uplifted hands, kneeling in royal robes upon the brazen platform; the vast multitude prostrate upon the ground; the fire from heaven consuming the sacrifice upon the Brazen Altar; and the Cloud of the Glory of Jehovah filling the House of Jehovah - all formed a scene of mysterious splendor such as the world has never witnessed.

The fact that this was the only Temple in the whole world in which the one true God was worshiped adds to the moral grandeur of the scene.

The spiritual knowledge that Solomon possessed, and the visible fire that burned upon the Altar, came from heaven; both originated there; both were Divine. Man could not have created that miraculous fire, nor that equally miraculous knowledge. The fact of the existence of God was attested by the fire. No other nation possessed this knowledge of God, nor could any nation by reason or culture obtain such knowledge. It could only be had by revelation. Thus, both the fire and the teaching of the prayer came from heaven.

The *"burnt offering"* on the Altar signifies that God gives His all in the person of Jesus Christ. The fire upon that sacrifice signifies the judgment of God that should have come upon us, but, instead, would fall upon the perfect offering for sin, the Christ of Calvary.

The *"glory of the Lord"* can only come through Calvary. In too many churches Calvary has been relegated to second or even third place or completely ignored altogether. Let it be ever understood that God's glory cannot rest upon anything except the precious shed Blood of Jesus Christ. If we want the *"glory of the Lord to fill the house,"* we must place the preeminence on Calvary. Paul said, *"Glory in the cross."* He also said, *"I determined to know nothing among you save Christ and him crucified."*

The 2nd verse says, *"And the priests could not enter into the house of the Lord."* As the Priests could not enter the House of the Lord because of the *"glory of the Lord,"* likewise, Satan, sin, and shame cannot enter the house if the *"glory of the Lord fills the house."*

Verse 3 says, *"And when all the children of Israel saw how the fire came down."* The Church must see the *"fire come down."* John said, *"He shall baptize you with the Holy Ghost and with fire."* On the Day of Pentecost the *"fire came down."* It is still here. If we want it enough, it will burn brightly again (St. Luke 11:13). In the praise and worship of Israel the Holy Spirit brought the words to their hearts that He had given to David, *"For he is good; for his mercy endureth forever."*

The 5th verse says, speaking of the number of sacrifices, *"twenty and two thousand oxen and an hundred and twenty thousand sheep:"* The brook Kidron that ran between the Mt. of Olives and the Temple site, ran red with blood, showing Israel that her great blessing was built on the foundation of the shed Blood of Christ.

Even though the number of sacrifices offered was staggering, still, it could not even begin to portray Calvary. The blood of bulls and goats can never take away sin, nevertheless, they point to the Lamb of God that will take away all sin.

The 7th verse says, *"Burnt offerings, and the fat of the peace offerings."* The *"burnt offerings"* signify that God has given His all, and thereby, expects Israel's all. The *"fat"* signifies that the prosperity of Israel does not come from her genius or her intellect, but from the sacrifice of Christ at Calvary. The *"peace offerings"* symbolize the peace of God that comes when the proper sacrifice is made. There is no *"peace"* but that which comes through Calvary.

Verses 8 and 9 signify that Solomon kept the Feast of Dedication of the Temple for seven days and also the Feast of Tabernacles for an additional seven days, making altogether 14 days of feasting at this time.

The 10th verse proclaims that the people were sent away to their homes, *"glad and merry in heart for the goodness that the Lord had shewed unto David, and to Solomon, and to Israel his people."* They had feasted on the abundant food of the sacrifices that portrayed Christ. Jesus would say, *"Unless you eat my flesh and drink my blood."* He was not speaking of literal flesh of which this was a type, but of His Word (St. John 6:53-63). This speaks of Jesus, the coming Lord and Master of one's life. A mental acceptance of what the Lord did at Calvary is not enough; there must be a partaking of Christ.

Obeying the Word of God and partaking of Christ always produces gladness and joy. Notice, it says, *"in heart."* This is not mere happiness but, rather, joy. Happiness has to do with externals, events, happenings, and feelings. The joy of the Lord, which can only be given by the Lord, comes from within and is not shaken by events, happenings, or feelings. There is no such thing as a true joy of the heart among those who are not partakers of Christ. Joy, this beautiful fruit of the Spirit, is peculiar only to the child of God. Money cannot buy it; place and position has no affect upon it; it is given solely as we partake of Christ.

Verse 11 says, *"Thus Solomon finished the house of the Lord."* True, however, the Lord had not finished the house that He was to build for the human family, namely Jesus Christ. The 12th verse says, *"And the Lord appeared to Solomon by night."* If one compares I Kings 7:37 and 9:1 with II Chronicles 7:1 and 8:1, it appears that some 13 years intervened between Solomon's prayer and its full answer. The fire from heaven was an immediate answer, and this later answer is a comforting instance of how God does not forget prayer. One of the great fundamentals of Faith is its *"persistence until the answer comes."* The Master outlined this in the parable of the three loaves in St. Luke 11. Faithlessness may have interest, but only for a short time. True faith stays the course. It keeps believing even though the thing is not yet done, but, in fact, counts it as done until it is actually done.

The Lord says, *"And have chosen this place to myself for an house of sacrifice."* In effect, the Church is, as well, an house of sacrifice, namely Calvary. And yet, in recent years we have tried to make the Church something else. The modern Church has tried to make itself a house of blessing without the house of sacrifice. It cannot be done. There is no blessing of God on anything except *"the sacrifice."* Calvary must ever be the foundation of the Gospel. It must be thusly proclaimed constantly. Sadly, too many preachers are silent regarding Calvary. They claim to believe it while promoting other avenues as the panacea for man's ills. Be it ever remembered that the Church is *"an house of sacrifice."*

The 13th verse says, *"If I shut up heaven and there be no rain."* The Lord then mentions *"the devourer"* and *"pestilence."* This answer from the Lord pertains not only to ancient Israel, but to us today as well. It was directed to the following:

1. Solomon.
2. Israel.
3. The present-day Church.

There is a note of sadness and Divine anxiety in the Lord's answer, for but a day or two (so to speak) afterwards, Solomon prostrated himself before idols and became a wicked old man! It may not be unreasonable to believe that this interval of some 13 years was permitted as a test, and that God in His love, in order to save the King from his impending fall, then

NOTES

appeared to him by night with His message of assurance and warning.

Two humbling facts appear in this history: First, man cannot of himself learn to know God - God must reveal Himself to him; Second, unless restrained by Grace, man turns away from this glorious revelation and becomes a worshiper of devils.

Verse 14 says, *"If my people, which are called by my name."* This passage contains one of the greatest promises ever given by God to man. It is so very simple in its direction and application. For anyone who is in trouble for any reason, this passage applies to you. Here are the conditions:

1. Humble yourselves.
2. Pray, and seek my face.
3. Turn from your wicked ways.

Sadly, the Church has, by and large, forsaken God's way for man's way. It will profess to believe what is said, but, in fact, will opt for other prescriptions. The following is what God said He will do if we do what He said to do.

1. Then will I hear from heaven.
2. And will forgive your sin.
3. And will heal your land.

What a glorious promise, but, regrettably, so few Christians take advantage of it. Millions engage themselves in an endless cacophony of counseling or group therapy, with the latter being little better than witchcraft. God's prescription is true; it works, but is so seldom recommended by the modern pulpit.

The 15th verse says, *"Now mine eyes shall be open, and mine ears attent unto the prayer that is made in this place."* Under the old economy of God, prayer was always directed toward the Temple, irrespective of where in the world the believer was because God dwelt in this place between the Mercy Seat and the Cherubim. Now, under the new Covenant, God no longer dwells in a *"temple made with hands,"* but in the Temple of our hearts (I Cor. 3:16). Consequently, the child of God can pray anywhere at any time, directing his prayer to God the Father in the name of Jesus (St. John 16:23). As well, God's *"eyes"* will be open and His *"ears"* attent to the type of prayer that is spoken of in the 14th verse. It must be from a platform of humility; it must be the seeking of His face; it must be with the heart's total intent to turn from wicked ways. Then the need will be met with the power of God being given to the seeker.

The 16th verse says, *"For now have I chosen and sanctified this house."* The word *"sanctify"* means to be *"set apart."* It does not really mean cleansing from sin, although this will be accomplished in the process. The *"setting apart"* does not do the cleansing. One can sanctify himself or set himself apart to God all the days of his life, but if he does not have faith in the Blood of Christ to cleanse from all sin, the cleansing will never take place. New Testament sanctification means *"made not guilty."* As the believer trusts Christ and the cleansing of the shed Blood of Calvary, the Lord makes the person not guilty, setting him apart for sacred service and use (I Cor. 6:11). This passage tells us first of all that we are *"washed,"* which means to be cleansed by the Blood. And then second, we are *"sanctified"* which makes one not guilty, and, in effect, sets the person apart for God's use only. Then, the child of God is *"justified,"* which means *"declared not guilty."* All of this is done *"in the name of the Lord Jesus, and by the Spirit of our God."*

As then, the Lord sanctified the house that Solomon had built; now He sanctifies our house, in effect, our body, which is the Temple of the Holy Spirit (I Cor. 3:16).

The 18th verse proclaiming the Davidic Covenant, says, *"According as I have covenanted with David thy father,"* is unconditional, for it contemplates Christ.

The 19th verse says, *"But if ye turn away, and forsake my statutes and my commandments."* Verses 19 through 22 portray the Solomonic Covenant, which is conditional.

The 22nd verse, in effect, says if Solomon or his sons forsake the Lord, the Lord will forsake them.

These two covenants basically proclaim the correct scriptural teaching on predestination. It is predestined that God will have a Church (the Davidic Covenant). This will be, and man's acceptance, rejection, failure, or otherwise, does not alter the fact. However, who will be in this Church (the Solomonic Covenant) will depend on obedience - vss. 19 through 22.

NOTES

CHAPTER 8

Verse 1 says, *"And it came to pass at the end of twenty years."*

This chapter in small measure pictures the peace and plenty which will characterize the Millennial earth. Fenced cities are built to protect the land, and store cities furnished to provide food for its people.

At the same time, the former enemies of Israel are made subject, and the King of Tyre as representative of the Gentiles contributes to the Glory of the Kingdom. All this was an earnest of the dominion promised to Israel and will surely yet be given to them.

The 6th verse says, *"And all that Solomon desired to build in Jerusalem, and in Lebanon, and throughout all the land of his dominion."* So much of the world as designed by man has specialized in destruction instead of construction. However, during the Kingdom Age when Jesus will reign supreme from Jerusalem over the entirety of the earth, there will be no destruction except that which is evil. Rather, there will be construction. For the first time, the world will see what the earth could really be like under God's government instead of man's flawed and faulty government.

Back to verse 3, it says, *"And Solomon went to Hamath-zobah, and prevailed against it."* In the entirety of Solomon's reign this was the only war that Solomon fought. This typifies the scarcity of such in the coming Kingdom Age. As the nations of the world of Solomon's day realized the futility of trying to oppose such a powerful kingdom as Israel, likewise, the world during the days of the Kingdom Age when Jesus reigns supreme will realize the futility of attempting to oppose His Almighty Power. As well, Satan at that time along with his host of demon spirits will be locked away.

The 8th verse proclaims the Gentiles paying tribute to Solomon and to Israel, *"Them did Solomon make to pay tribute until this day."* Likewise, in the coming Kingdom Age the Gentile world will pay tribute to the Lord of Glory. But, yet, it will not be in the form of ruinous taxation. As the various tribes listed in verse 7, *"Hittites, Amorites, etc.,"* paid tribute, still, they were allowed to live in peace in the most glorious economy and kingdom on the face of the earth. They were furnished safety, protection, and prosperity. It will be the same even on a far greater basis in the coming Kingdom Age.

Verse 9 proclaims the *"children of Israel"* who were made *"chief of his captains, and captains of his chariots and horsemen."* This typifies Israel and the Blood-washed saints of God in the Kingdom Age. Israel, during the Kingdom Age under David, who is under Christ, will finally carry out the plan of God designed for her (Jer. 30:8-9). During this time the saints of God (all who have ever lived) will have glorified bodies. It will be a time of unprecedented peace and prosperity.

The 11th verse says, *"And Solomon brought up the daughter of Pharaoh out of the city of David."* Solomon had been living in the city of David during the time that the Temple and his own palace were being built. He did not consider her fit to be around the holy places where the Ark of Jehovah had come.

With such a Gentile wife, Solomon was starting out the wrong way, and he did not learn the lesson he should have learned, for he later loved many foreign women who turned his heart away from God (I Kings 11:1-9). Solomon, like all other types, was a broken figure of Him Who is to come. Nevertheless, the antitype, Who is Christ, will be perfect.

Verses 12 and 13 record Solomon's faithfulness in worship. It says, *"Then Solomon offered burnt offerings unto the Lord on the altar of the Lord."* Then, after the Temple was completed and after he had brought his wife out of the city of David so that the sacred and holy places might not be defiled anymore, he offered burnt-offerings before the Lord upon the Brazen Altar, even a certain number of daily offerings according to the commandment of Moses. This refers to the morning and evening Sacrifices, the additional offerings on the Sabbaths, and the special ones at new moons and the solemn feasts.

The 13th verse says, *"Three times in the year."* The solemn feasts are here explained to be the *"Feast of Unleavened Bread"* (in April), the *"Feast of Pentecost"* 50 days later, and the

"Feast of Tabernacles" (in October). All the males of Israel were supposed to gather three times a year on these special feasts (Ex. 23:14; Deut. 16:16).

The 14th verse says, *"And he appointed, according to the order of David."* This was the appointment of the 24 courses of the priests in their services (I Chron. 24), the 24 courses of the Levites to sing and play music (I Chron. 25), and the 24 courses of the porters (I Chron. 26). All this had been revealed to David by the Holy Spirit, and now at last it was being obeyed as he had left instructions. For it said, *"For so had David the man of God commanded."*

The 15th verse says, *"And they departed not from the commandment of the king."* Sadly, there is too much departure at this present time from the *"commandment of the king."* However, during the days of the coming Millennial Reign, there will be no departing from the *"commandment of the king."*

The 16th verse says, *"So the house of the Lord was perfected."* This is the desire and the work of the Holy Spirit that He may *"perfect the house of the Lord,"* the house now being our bodies which are Temples of the Holy Spirit. This "house of the Lord" that Solomon built was now perfected. How many of us can say that, *"our house of the Lord"* is perfected? How much work yet needs to be done? If we will ask the Lord, He will tell us.

CHAPTER 9

Verse 1 says, *"And when the Queen of Sheba heard of the fame of Solomon."* Solomon was a type of Christ, albeit an imperfect type as all types are. Jesus would say of Himself, *"a greater than Solomon."* How the Queen of Sheba heard of the fame of Solomon, no one knows, but she did hear. As well, the whole world must hear of the fame of the Lord Jesus Christ. It is incumbent upon us, the Church, to take this great and glorious Gospel to the whole world. They must hear! Of all of God's work, this is priority. And, yet, so little attention is given to World Evangelism. The world of Islam, which has no message to tell, spends approximately

100 times more to propagate the false gospel of Islam than we do in Christianity. Why are we so lax in carrying out Christ's last command? (Mark 16:15).

The 1st verse says, *"She came."* The Glory of the Lord having now risen upon Israel, the kings of the Gentiles come to that light bringing their riches with them and find there a glory and a wisdom such as the world had never seen. None of these monarchs are mentioned particularly except the Queen of Sheba, the Holy Spirit reserving that dignity for a woman. She is further honored by the Lord Himself in Matthew 12:42 where he predicts her reappearance in the Resurrection.

This queen hears of the fame of Solomon. At first she does not believe the report, but after a little while, moved by its repetition, she determines to put the matter to the test. She undertakes a long, fatiguing, and expensive journey; she finds that the report is true, but that the half had not been told her. The effect is the destruction of all her self-complacency, and that the surpassing glory of Solomon and his court makes her and her court of no value. She gives gifts to Solomon - gifts which could be measured. Solomon gives her gifts - gifts which could not be measured, and she returned to her land having learned of the one and only true God.

How much nobler this African queen was than are the men of today! Like her, they hear the fame of the *"greater than Solomon,"* and, like her, they do not believe the report. But, unlike her, they do not bestir themselves to test what they have heard. If they did so bestir themselves, they would find that all that is said about the love and saving power of the Lord Jesus Christ is true, and they too would exclaim that the half had not been told!

The Scripture said, *"She came to prove Solomon with hard questions."* What did these questions consist of? The *"hard questions,"* no doubt, pertained to the great questions of life, *"Is there life after death?"* and *"Is man more than an animal?"* and so forth.

The 2nd verse says, *"And Solomon told her all her questions."* Only the *"greater than Solomon"* holds the answers to life's perplexing questions. There are no other answers or solutions. Jesus Christ is the Word (St. John 1), and

the Word has the answer to every single problem of life that man may have. So, sadly, the modern Church is, by and large, replacing the Word of God with other sources. Jeremiah said, *"For my people have committed two evils; they have forsaken me the fountain of living waters, and hewed them out cisterns, broken cisterns, that can hold no water"* (Jer. 2:13).

The 2nd verse as well says, *"And there was nothing hid from Solomon which he told her not."* If the honest heart will earnestly seek, that which it desires will be revealed by the Lord Jesus Christ.

The 3rd verse says, *"And when the queen of Sheba had seen."* She saw the glory of God.

The Tabernacle that God gave to Moses is a beautiful example of this. When the Queen of Sheba heard of the fame of Solomon, she did not believe it. Consequently, when one looks at the exterior of the Tabernacle, there is nothing enticing about it. Actually, its exterior was rough, brownish, unspectacular badger skins. Nevertheless, if one walked inside the Tabernacle, their eyes would meet with a splendor that defies description. Most all was gold, typifying the deity of Christ.

As the 1st verse says, until one *"communes"* with Christ, they can never know the glory and the splendor of all that Christ is and has. For anyone who cares to investigate, Christ is waiting. The results will be as it was with the Queen of Sheba, for the Scripture says, *"There was no more spirit in her."* No wonder Simon Peter would call this great salvation, *"Joy unspeakable and full of glory"* (I Pet. 1:8).

The 5th verse proclaims of the Queen of Sheba concerning Solomon, *"It was a true report."* Everything the Word of God says about the Lord Jesus Christ is *"a true report."* Is this great and glorious salvation real? Yes, *"it is a true report."* Does it change men's lives? Yes, *"it is a true report."* Does it truly bring abiding peace? Yes, *"it is a true report."* Are we, in fact, given eternal life? Yes, *"it is a true report."*

The 6th verse says, *"Howbeit I believed not their words, until I came, and mine eyes had seen it."* The Lord Jesus Christ invites inspection. His appeal to the hungry heart is, *"Come unto me, all ye that labour and are heavy laden, and I will give you rest."* For all that come, they will say, *"For thou exceedest the fame that I* heard." In other words, as the 6th verse says, *"The one half of the greatness of thy wisdom was not told me."*

And then she says in the 7th verse concerning the subjects of Solomon, *"Happy are thy men, and happy are these thy servants."* The only true happiness in the world is that which has been provided by the *"greater than Solomon."* It is a happiness that is based on the fruit of the Spirit, joy.

No wonder she then says, *"Blessed be the Lord thy God."* The Queen of Sheba now worships and praises the Lord. As well, anyone who feasts upon the *"greater than Solomon,"* will likewise praise the Lord. People who call themselves Christians of which praise is foreign actually do not know the Lord. Churches that claim to worship Him and never praise Him, and, in fact, are shamed by praise, really do not know Him. To know Him is to truly worship and praise Him.

The 9th verse says, *"And she gave the king an hundred and twenty talents of gold."* As stated, what she gave Him could be measured. What He gave her could not be measured. Yet, when a person partakes of Christ, knowing of the great salvation that has been afforded, his first reaction is that this great message must be taken to others. Therefore, as the Queen of Sheba gave, likewise, the Blood-washed child of God will give.

If one will notice, the 9th verse says, *"She gave,"* and the 12th verse says, *"And King Solomon gave."* What did he give? The Scripture is plain, *"All her desire, whatsoever she asked."* And, yet, our *"greater than Solomon"* admonishes us to ask of Him accordingly and He will give (St. Luke 11).

The 13th verse says, *"Six hundred and three score and six talents of gold."* This is 666 talents of gold. Solomon, as well, had six steps to his throne (vs. 18). This stamps imperfection upon all his glory, for *"six"* is the number of man and comes just short of *"seven"* which is the number of perfection. Man was created on the sixth day. Goliath and Nebuchadnezzar's great images present this number, and finally it reappears in the Antichrist. Only the *"greater than Solomon"* Who is *"very man"* and *"very God"* can be *"seven."* Despite all the glory given to Solomon, still, he was but a man, hence, the

number *"six."* Perfection will come only when Jesus Christ rules and reigns.

The 20th verse says, *"And all the drinking vessels of king Solomon were of gold."* And then it says, *"None were of silver; it was not any thing accounted of in the days of Solomon."* What a statement! This portrays the great prosperity that will characterize this planet when Jesus Christ comes back. Much of the world goes to bed hungry each night. Every day hundreds or even thousands of little children fall down too weak to rise from hunger. It is called the *"silent death."* And this, despite the fact that planet Earth even now in its cursed state has the capacity to feed 100 billion people. When He comes back, there will be no more *"silent death."*

The 22nd verse says, "And King Solomon passed all the kings of the earth in riches and wisdom." Likewise, Jesus Christ, when reigning from Jerusalem in the days of the coming Kingdom Age, will be the wisest King Who has ever lived, and, thereby, brings riches and prosperity to the entirety of the planet.

The 31st verse says, *"And Solomon slept with his fathers, and he was buried in the city of David his father."* The fact that God did not record the great sins of Solomon in his latter years is some indication that Solomon asked for and received mercy, forgiveness, and Grace. If so, these sins would have been washed away and, thereby, unrecorded. This is about the only indication that we have that Solomon may have made things right with God before he died.

CHAPTER 10

The 1st verse says, *"And Rehoboam went to Shechem: for to Shechem were all Israel come to make him king."* Jerusalem was where the Lord had placed His name, and, yet, for political purposes and without consulting the Lord Rehoboam will go to Shechem. So much of what is today called *"Christianity"* is operated upon the rudiment of political expediency and not according to *"thus saith the Lord."* The Church, sadly, is even more political than civil government. As Rehoboam's efforts were not of God, likewise, the political nature of the Church is not of God either.

The 2nd verse says, *"That Jeroboam returned out of Egypt."* It is instructive to point out the dissatisfaction of the nation with the glorious reign of Solomon with all of its prosperity, and, yet, much of Israel would elect Solomon's enemy Jeroboam as king. This is a perfect picture of Revelation 20. There it is foretold that although Christ will maintain an absolutely perfect and prosperous government over the entirety of the earth for 1,000 years, yet the world will be dissatisfied with that reign of glory and righteousness and will call back Satan from exile as Israel called back Jeroboam, and for a short time enthrone him as prince over the earth. Shechem was the national sanctuary and capital before the Divine selection of Jerusalem (Josh. 24:1). It was the site of Abraham's first altar and was Jacob's first home. Here, Joseph was buried, and here the tribes met. Shechem now would become the capital of the northern kingdom, Israel. However, Shechem was not the place that God had chosen to put His name; Jerusalem was that place.

Concerning the demands of Israel, the 6th verse says, *"And king Rehoboam took counsel with the old men."* It then says in the 8th verse that he *"took counsel with the young men"* as well. However, there is no place that it says that he took counsel with God. There seems to be little desire here for the will of God. All is political expediency. Likewise, the Church is in constant counsel with various of its segments, but there is precious little of *"Thus saith the Lord."* Likewise, millions of Christians seek counsel with counselors, doctors, and psychologists, but precious few seek counsel with God. The demand made by Israel would not be heeded by the king, for the 15th verse says, *"So the king hearkened not unto the people: for the cause was of God."*

The fulfillment of the prediction of Ahijah affords an instance similar to many others in the Scriptures of prophecies being accomplished by the operation of human passions and seemingly, in the natural course of events. Men think they are obeying their own wills and carrying out their own plans unconscious that

the matter is of God and permitted and overruled by Him for the performance of His Word. In the 16th verse Israel says, *"What portion have we in David?"* This was the beginning of 260 years of division and strife between the two nations of Israel. Wars, bloodshed, and intrigue became the program of a once united and godly people. God's plan for a united nation being a blessing to all other nations of the earth had now come to a definite standstill, and both kingdoms faced ruin and dispersion among the Gentiles. Little did these rebels realize what their departure to their tents meant for the future when the Scripture said, *"So all Israel went to their tents."* When people rebel against God, they seldom think of the results, but only of the present.

The 17th verse says, *"But as for the children of Israel that dwelt in the cities of Judah, Rehoboam reigned over them."* The northern kingdom under Jeroboam would be called by several names; Israel, Samaria, and Ephraim. Some ten tribes would be loyal to the northern confederacy. The southern confederacy, called Judah, would have some three tribes that would remain loyal to it; Judah, Benjamin, and Levi. Shechem would be the capital of the northern confederacy (Samaria) with Jerusalem being the capital of the southern confederacy.

The 19th verse says, *"And Israel rebelled against the house of David unto this day."* When they asked the question as is given in verse 16, *"What portion have we in David?"* They were, in effect, saying that they no longer desired to worship the God of Abraham, Isaac, and Jacob. Their rebellion was not really against Rehoboam or Jerusalem, but, in fact, was against God. The Scripture says that *"rebellion is as the sin of witchcraft."* It replaces the God of heaven with the god of devils.

CHAPTER 11

Verse 1 says, *"That he might bring the kingdom again to Rehoboam."* Once again, Rehoboam did this thing without consulting the Lord. However, the Lord would nevertheless consult him.

The 2nd verse says, *"But the word of the Lord came to Shemaiah the man of God, saying, Thus saith the Lord, Ye shall not go up, nor fight against your brethren"* (vs. 4). As God would not force Israel to serve Him; likewise, He will not force men to serve Him today. Salvation can never be by force; it must always be from a *"willing heart."* The great blight of the Church has always been the contention that ever seems to rage within its own ranks. All of the 12 tribes, regardless of their spiritual declension, were called *"God's people."* In other words, they were the *"Church"* of their day. Now they are split and divided and would have slaughtered each other except for the intervention of God. Sadly, the Church fights much more within its own ranks than it does against the powers of darkness. The picture that is presented here is, sadly, a picture of the modern Church. Most in the Israel of yesteryear little sought the will of God. Most in the Church of today little seek the Word of God.

The 4th verse continues to say, *"For this thing is done of me."* God will not force their unity, as He will not force our unity; so He will let them have their way of division. To Judah's credit, they *"obeyed the words of the Lord and returned from going against Jeroboam."* As the result, hundreds of thousands of lives were, no doubt, saved.

In the 5th verse it says, *"For defense in Judah."* Rehoboam would attempt to strengthen Judah. Egypt was his enemy on one side, as Israel was his enemy on the other. His true defense was in God, but he little knew it.

After the division of Israel, the history of the northern kingdom in II Chronicles is no longer continued as it was in I Kings. The kings of the tribes of the northern confederacy are mentioned only when necessary in recording the history of the House of David and Judah.

The 13th verse says, *"And the priest and the Levites that were in all Israel resorted to him out of all their coasts."* All worship of God had been discontinued in the northern confederacy; consequently, many Priests and Levites moved to Jerusalem.

For the 14th verse says, *"For the Levites left their suburbs and their possession, and came*

to Judah and Jerusalem." Living for God means forsaking all. It would seem farfetched to the carnal mind for individuals to leave their home, friends, and even family to go where God is moving. Nevertheless, this has characterized true followers of the Lord from the very beginning. People who attend a church only for the reason that it is *"close to their home,"* have little knowledge of the Lord in their hearts. They are seeking convenience and not consecration. Conversely, there are some few who will drive any distance or even pull up roots and relocate where the Spirit of God is moving.

They will do so because as the 15th verse says, *"And he (Jeroboam) ordained him priests for the high places, and for the devils."* Because of devil worship, the northern confederacy would be destroyed as a nation about 749 B.C. (II Sam. 17). One hundred and thirty-three years later (616 B.C.) Judah was also destroyed for her sins (I Kings 24-25). Seventy years later (546 B.C.) the godly of all the 13 tribes returned to make a nation again and were all recognized as the Jews of Israel in the days of Jesus Christ.

The 17th verse says, *"For three years they walked in the way of David and Solomon."* This, of course, was speaking of the southern kingdom of Judah and Rehoboam - but for only three years. It is amazing as to how the Holy Spirit delineated the time down to almost the day. After this time, Rehoboam and Judah went into sin. God permitted Egypt to conquer them and take all their treasures away (12:2-12). If he had continued in the godly way, no kingdom or combination of kingdoms could have overcome him.

CHAPTER 12

Verse 1 says, *"And it came to pass, when Rehoboam had established the kingdom, and had strengthened himself, he forsook the law of the Lord, and all Israel with him."* Prosperity sometimes is not a blessing. Too much of the time when believers are blessed, they do exactly as Rehoboam did, they forsake *"the law of the*

NOTES

Lord." Few can remain humble in times of prosperity. Most become prideful and lifted up within themselves. Rehoboam was not the exception. Sadly, he is the rule.

The 2nd verse says, *"And it came to pass, that in the fifth year of king Rehoboam Shishak king of Egypt came up against Jerusalem."* Less than five years after the death of Solomon, the whole United Kingdom of Israel was divided into two kingdoms, the northern confederacy, having gone into apostasy, and now the southern confederacy of Judah having experienced both apostasy and military defeat by a foreign king who even robbed the treasuries of Judah and disgraced the whole nation - this after only three years of righteousness.

Thus through sin, such a wonderful kingdom that had ruled many kings and countries from the Euphrates to Egypt and whose king had all the other kings coming to him to hear his wisdom and present him with gifts was now in complete humiliation before these same kings and countries.

The Holy Spirit is very explicit; He says, *"Because they had transgressed against the Lord."*

The 4th verse says of Shishak, *"And he took."* Shishak was founder of the 22nd Egyptian Dynasty. He was powerful but in no way could he have taken the cities of Judah unless Judah had *"transgressed against the Lord."* The Lord was Judah's power and strength. There was only one condition for them to retain His power and strength, and that was to keep His commandments and his statutes. As long as they did that, no nation in the world could defeat them. However, when they *"forsook the law of the Lord,"* defeat was inevitable.

The 5th verse proclaims the Lord in His mercy giving Judah warning. It says, *"Then came Shemaiah the prophet to Rehoboam."* The Lord speaks to them, *"You have forsaken me, and therefore have I also left you in the hand of Shishak."* No warning could be more clearer than this. If we follow the Lord, we receive His blessing. If we forsake the Lord, He allows enemies to intrude upon us. Our blessings are tied totally to Him.

The 6th verse says concerning *"the princes of Israel,"* and *"the king."* It says, *"They humbled themselves."* Once again we see the wonderful mercy of God manifested at the least degree of repentance and self-humbling. Their repentance was not very deep; nevertheless, the Lord would honor it. In effect, this is what they said, *"The Lord is righteous,"* meaning that He was justified in what He had done, and that they deserved it.

In the 7th verse the Scripture says, *"But I will grant them some deliverance."* Notice the words, *"some deliverance."* They would not have a complete deliverance, only *"some deliverance."* Their repentance was partial; therefore, their deliverance was partial.

The lesson would continue because the 8th verse says, *"Nevertheless they shall be his servants; that they may know my service, and the service of the kingdoms of the countries."* This meant that Judah may learn to obey and know the difference between serving God and serving ungodly nations. Also, that they may know that serving God and serving man are far different.

So, the 9th verse proclaims that God allowed Shishak to *"carry away all the shields of gold which Solomon had made."*

The 10th verse then says, *"Instead of which king Rehoboam made shields of brass."* The shields of gold borne by the king's bodyguard when the monarch went up to the House of the Lord were carried into Egypt. They were replaced by brazen shields. The world robs the Church of Divine realities in public worship, and the Church tries to hide the loss by substituting imitations. How many Churches today have *"shields of brass"* instead of *"shields of gold?"* The *"shields of gold"* represents deity. They are symbolic of God's glory, protection, and power. Now these *"shields of brass"* (copper) are symbolic of man and man's ways. The Church world has substituted virtually all of its *"shields of gold"* for *"shields of brass."*

The 12th verse refers back to the 6th verse. It says, *"When he humbled himself, the wrath of the Lord turned from him."* Humility is the only coin that will spend in God's economy. The Lord says in Isaiah, *"To this man will I look, even to him that is poor and of a contrite spirit, and trembleth at my word"* (Isa. 66:2).

The 14th verse proclaims that he did not

receive a full deliverance because there was no full repentance. It says, *"And he did evil, because he prepared not his heart to seek the Lord."* What an indictment! If he had prepared his heart to seek God, then he would have become established in grace and in faith sufficiently to stay true to God.

CHAPTER 13

The 1st verse says, *"Now in the eighteenth year of king Jeroboam began Abijah to reign over Judah."* Abijah began to reign in the 18th year of Jeroboam, four years before Jeroboam died (I Kings 14:20). The wars that have continued off and on during the reigns of Rehoboam and Jeroboam now continue when Abijah was made king, but God gave him a great victory from which Jeroboam never did fully recover. It is very interesting that the Holy Spirit changed His name from Abijam, which means *"the tumult of the sea,"* to Abijah, which means *"Jehovah is my father."* It says in I Kings 15 that he *"walked in all the sins of his father."* Those sins are not mentioned here in II Chronicles, giving some hint that he may have repented.

In the 2nd verse the Holy Spirit is careful to say, *"His mother's name also was Michaiah,"* which means *"who is like Jehovah."* It was changed from Maachah, which means *"oppression."* I Kings 15:13 says that she had been an idol-worshiper. Perhaps she repented as well. The 2nd verse also says, *"And there was war between Abijah and Jeroboam."* Once again we see the people of God fighting each other, and all because of sin.

Verse 3 says, *"And Abijah set the battle in array with an army of valiant men of war, even four hundred thousand chosen men."* A few years before this, Rehoboam could muster only 180,000 chosen men (11:1), indicating that many thousands of the northern confederacy had come down to become a part of the kingdom of Judah, which is called *"all Israel"* (12:1). In this battle Jeroboam will have 800,000 chosen men. Note the steady increase of Judah and the steady decrease of the northern king-

NOTES

dom, called Israel. When the nation first divided, Rehoboam could only muster 180,000; 18 years later Abijah could muster 400,000. Six years afterward, Asa had 580,000 (14:8); 32 years after that, Jehoshaphat had 1,160,000 beside those in the fenced cities throughout all Judah (17:14-19). This increase of Judah was caused mainly by a constant immigration from Israel to Judah.

Verses 4-12 record the statement made by Abijah to Jeroboam concerning the battle. He says in verse 4, *"Hear me, thou Jeroboam, and all Israel."* The statement that he makes proclaims a tremendous knowledge of the Word of God. He calls attention to the Lord making David king over Israel, and in the 5th verse says, *"Even to him and to his sons by a covenant of salt."* This is mentioned two other times in the Word of God (Lev. 2:13; Num. 18:19). This covenant became a symbol of incorruptibility of God's Covenant, and the perpetuity of man's obligation to Him. The term *"a covenant of salt"* referred to the solemnizing of any inviolable covenant. In other words, Abijah is telling Jeroboam that he is attempting to destroy what God has ordained. It is so sad, but most of the Church world in modern times (and perhaps for all time), has constantly attempted, as Jeroboam, to destroy the true work of God. It desires to substitute its own ways for God's ways. The reason for the division in Israel, the constant strife, and the spiritual poverty was because of a neglect of the Word of God. It is the same today.

The 8th verse reminds Jeroboam of his worship of the *"golden calves,"* which in some measure was the same as the religion of Egypt.

The 9th verse says that Jeroboam had substituted his own priesthood for God's Priesthood.

In the 10th verse Abijah proclaims of Judah, *"But as for us, the Lord is our God and we have not forsaken him."*

The 11th verse proclaims his extensive knowledge of the ways of God and the Law of Moses. It indicates as well that Judah, at least at this time, was attempting to follow the ways of God. For he says, *"For we keep the charge of the Lord our God."*

The 12th verse proclaims him saying, *"And, behold, God himself is with us for our cap-*

tain." In fact, God was with him, and his sure word may have been a sign of his repentance. He makes one more plea to the northern kingdom, Israel, *"O children of Israel, fight not against the Lord God of your fathers; for ye shall not prosper."* Irrespective of the seeming odds, no man, country, power, or kingdom can prosper fighting against God.

Jeroboam, because of having twice as many soldiers as Abijah, thinks his victory is certain. He ignores Abijah's message, for the 13th verse says, *"But Jeroboam caused an ambushment to come about behind them."* In other words, the army of Judah was surrounded.

However, the 14th verse says, *"And they (Judah) cried unto the Lord, and the priests sounded with the trumpets."* Man's only hope is to *"cry unto the Lord;"* nevertheless, so few do. It seems that even the Church would rather resort to anything other than the Lord. However, there is no help other than the Lord.

The 15th verse says, *"Then the men of Judah gave a shout."* Their *"shout"* was a *"shout of faith."* Abijah's words were not empty rhetoric; they were depending on God. And the Scripture says, *"That God smote Jeroboam and all Israel before Abijah and Judah."* The Holy Spirit is careful to denote the cause of the victory as being God. In the natural there is no way that Abijah's 400,000 men could even hope to defeat Jeroboam's 800,000 men, especially when the 3rd verse says concerning Jeroboam's army that they were *"mighty men of valour."* But God fought for Judah.

The 16th verse says, *"And God delivered them into their hand."*

The 17th verse says, *"So there fell down slain of Israel 500,000 chosen men."* Jeroboam's *"mighty men of valour"* are now stricken down. In this one battle Israel lost more men than America lost in the entirety of World War II.

Some would think God cruel for engaging in such carnage; however, even this act of judgment shows the mercy of God. Israel's decision to forsake the God of Abraham, Isaac, and Jacob and to resort to idol-worship was their decision. In fact, they had set themselves against God. Not only were they resorting to idol-worship and, thereby, forsaking God, but, as well, they would destroy Judah, Jerusalem,

and all that pertained to God. God did not resort to this measure until there was no other choice.

Some may feel the number of slain to be an exaggeration; however, the method of battle in those days was far different than now. Much of the effort in modern conflict is to destroy equipment; then it was to destroy men. Hand-to-hand combat can produce many casualties, which should be obvious.

The 18th verse specifically states, *"And the children of Judah prevailed, because they relied upon the Lord God of their fathers."* God was the reason for their victory; God is the reason for our victory.

The 20th verse says concerning Jeroboam, *"And the Lord struck him, and he died."* The meaning is simple. God terminated his life because he had set himself to do evil.

Contrary to verse 20, the 21st verse says, *"But Abijah waxed mighty,"* giving some slight indication that maybe Abijah repented of his following the sins of his father, Rehoboam.

CHAPTER 14

Verse 1 says, *"And Asa his son reigned in his stead."* Abijah is now dead, and Asa is on the throne. The Scripture uses the term, *"In his days the land was quiet ten years."* There was ten years without war; ten years of peace and prosperity, and the reason was:

Verse 2 says, *"And Asa did that which was good and right in the eyes of the Lord his God."* Notice the terminology, *"In the eyes of the Lord his God."* Too many attempt to do that which is right in the eyes of others. Asa wanted to do that which was *"right in the eyes of the Lord his God."*

Consequently, the 3rd verse says, *"He took away the altars of the strange gods."* Evidently, Judah under Abijah had been involved at least to some degree in idol-worship. Hence, the statement made about Abijah in I Kings 15.

The 4th verse signals the beginning of a revival in Judah, for it says, *"And commanded Judah to seek the Lord God of their fathers, and to do the law and the commandment."* Asa points Judah to the Bible. How so badly we need preachers today who will point the people to the Bible. But too oftentimes the people are being pointed in every direction except the Bible.

The 5th verse says concerning the blessing of God, *"And the kingdom was quiet before him."* The lesson should be plain to every Christian that sin opens the door for strife, opposition, destruction, and all manner of turbulence, while seeking the ways of God and following the Word of God insures serenity, rest, and peace. No, it does not mean such in perpetuity, because Satan will surely oppose the child of God. But it does mean peace and then victory when Satan does oppose.

The 6th verse again says, *"For the land had rest, and he had no war in those years; because the Lord had given him rest."* How beautiful is this statement! How so few enjoy such! Jesus Himself would say, *"Come unto me, all ye that labour and are heavy laden, and I will give you rest."* The Lord of Glory is the only One Who can.

So, the 7th verse once again brings out by the hand of the Holy Spirit, *"Because we have sought the Lord our God, we have sought him, and he hath given us rest on every side."* Five times in these seven verses the Holy Spirit alludes to this great blessing *"of rest"* (vss. 1, 5, 6, 7). The 7th verse says as well, *"So they built and prospered."*

The Holy Spirit in the 8th verse alludes to the fact of the power of Judah. They had 580,000 *"mighty men of valour."*

The 9th verse records the efforts of Satan to destroy the blessing that God had given unto Judah, for it says concerning the Ethiopians, *"a thousand thousand, and three hundred chariots."* This was one million men who came against Judah. Satan will always come *"as a roaring lion."*

The 11th verse and following prove that even though Asa had a mighty army, still, he did not rely on such, but on God. For it says, *"And Asa cried unto the Lord his God."* How complimentary of this man that he did not rely upon his strength, his power, or his prosperity, but, rather, he relied on the Lord. Too often blessing and prosperity, even though from God, turn the hearts and the heads of men away

NOTES

from God, but Asa seems, at least at this time, to have trusted solely in the Lord. For this is what he said:

"Lord, it is nothing with thee to help, whether with many, or with them that have no power." Ethiopia's one million men had no affect on God whatsoever. Asa is saying that God could use many or a few; numbers mean nothing to Him; obstacles mean nothing to Him. Asa says, *"For we rest on thee, and in thy name we go against this multitude."* This is the secret of victory for every child of God. The authority of the believer is the privilege of using the mighty *"name of Jesus."* Jesus said, *"In my name shall they cast out devils; they shall speak with new tongues; they shall take up (in the Greek, put away) serpents; and if they drink any deadly thing, it shall not hurt them; they shall lay hands on the sick, and they shall recover"* (Mark 16:17-18).

The Church, by and large, runs aground on three things:

1. People.
2. Money.
3. Education.

None of these three are wrong within themselves. However, if we compromise our convictions in order that more people may join our cause, we have just lost our way with God. As well, if we get our eyes on money, we have just lost the power. Certainly, God places no premium on ignorance, but man's education never equips him for the work of God.

God has given His Church three mighty weapons that are sure to bring victory. They are as follows:

1. Faith in God.
2. The Word of God.
3. The Name of Jesus.

When we use the above, it will be said of us as it was said of Asa, *"Let no man prevail against thee."*

Then the 12th verse says, *"So the Lord smote the Ethiopians before Asa, and before Judah; and the Ethiopians fled."* Satan will not flee before people, money, or education. He will flee before *"faith in God, the mighty Name of Jesus, and the Word of God."*

The 13th verse records the fact that Satan was so defeated that *"They could not recover themselves."* And then it says, *"For they were destroyed before the Lord, and before His hosts."*

The 14th verse says, *"For the fear of the Lord came upon them."* Whenever God is on our side, the *"fear of the Lord"* will come upon our enemies, and the reward will be great, for the Scripture says, *"For there was exceeding much spoil in them."* God would reward the faith of His people as God always rewards the faith of His people.

The 15th verse says, *"And returned to Jerusalem,"* but with great joy.

CHAPTER 15

Verse 1 says, *"And the Spirit of God came upon Azariah the son of Obed."* This is the only place that the prophet Azariah is mentioned. The message given to Azariah for Asa was one of promise, tinted with warning. At the close of Asa's life, he would in some measure depart from the Word of God.

This is what the Lord said unto him, and it is found in verse 2, *"The Lord is with you, while ye be with him; And if ye seek him, he will be found of you; but if ye forsake him, he will forsake you."* In this passage are three eternal and unchangeable facts:

1. The Lord is with you while you are with Him.

2. If you seek Him, He will be found of you.

3. If you forsake Him, He will forsake you.

These eternal facts are true of an individual or a nation, Jews or Gentiles, people under Law or under Grace, and in one age as well as another. Whoever seeks God with a whole heart finds Him, and as long as he remains in that relationship with Him, God will not forsake him.

There is no such thing as God being with those who do not remain with Him; neither is there such a thing as man forsaking God and God not forsaking man. It has been demonstrated that God has forsaken angels as well as men when they have forsaken Him, many of them being eternally doomed.

The beginning of the 2nd verse records the admonition of the Lord, *"Hear ye me."* We

NOTES

would do well to do so.

The 3rd verse says, *"Now for a long season Israel hath been without the true God."* This *"long season"* was, no doubt, referring to the last years of Solomon, the 14 years of Rehoboam's reign (11:17; 12:1), and the three years of Abijah's reign (I Kings 15:1-4). This would have been true many times during the period of the Judges as well.

Nevertheless, in the 4th verse the Lord gives a great promise, *"But when they in their trouble did turn unto the Lord God of Israel, and sought him, he was found of them."* One has to shout, *"Hallelujah!"* The promise is clear; God will not forsake those who turn to Him and seek Him. The Scripture is emphatic, *"He was found of them."*

Verses 5 and 6 make it clear that spiritual declension happened to Israel many times, and that they had to seek the Lord in great distress. In *"those times"* there was *"no peace"* and there were *"great vexations."* Then it says in the 6th verse, *"For God did vex them with all adversity."* Even though they were His chosen people, called of Him and loved of Him, still, in times of spiritual declension God would *"vex them with all adversity."* This should be a warning to every Christian. God desires to bless us, but if we desire to oppose Him, He will, instead, *"vex us."*

The 7th verse proclaims Asa being encouraged. It says, *"Be ye strong therefore, and let not your hands be weak."* God told Moses to *"be strong."* He as well told Joshua to *"be strong."* The forces of darkness are relentless. Satan is ever vigilant to hinder the child of God. Therefore, the admonishment by the Holy Spirit is *"Be strong."*

Through the prophet the Lord has just told of judgment that would come if Israel sinned. He now says the opposite, *"Your work shall be rewarded."*

To Asa's credit, he heeded the words of the prophet, and according to the 8th verse, *"He took courage."* He did two things:

1. He put away the abominable idols out of all the land of Judah and Benjamin.

2. He renewed the Altar of the Lord that was before the porch of the Lord.

This is the key to victory in any life. We turn our back on the sin business and come back to

Calvary. Hallelujah!

The great revival that broke out in Judah spread to the northern kingdom of Israel, for the 9th verse says, *"For they fell to him out of Israel in abundance, when they saw that the Lord his God was with him."*

God help us that men can see *"the anointing of the Holy Spirit"* in our lives, and the *"fruit of the Spirit"* in our Christian growth.

The 11th verse says, *"That they offered to the Lord in sacrifice, seven hundred oxen and seven thousand sheep."* According to Numbers 31:25-54, the Lord's portion was to be one animal out of every 500 from the half that belonged to the men of war, and one out of every 50 of the other half of the spoils that belonged to the congregation. On this basis (11 animals for the Lord out of every 1,000 taken), the total spoil must have numbered approximately 63,000 oxen and 636,000 sheep. When the 14th verse of the last chapter said *"exceeding much spoil,"* it meant exactly that.

The 12th verse proclaims Judah entering into a *"covenant to seek the Lord God of their fathers with all their heart and with all their soul."*

As well, it seems in the 13th verse that they *"put to death"* any man or woman that did not *"seek the Lord God of Israel."* This is a law of the people and not of God. Anything that pertains to God always has to be of a willing heart. Salvation is never by force or threat. The Scripture says, *"Whosoever will."*

Nevertheless, at the same time, it seems that God honored their effort because as the 15th verse says, *"He was found of them."* And then as an added blessing, it says, *"The Lord gave them rest round about."*

The 16th verse says, *"Concerning Maachah the mother of Asa the king, he removed her from being queen."* As the Hebrew language has no word for grandmother or grandfather, this woman was probably his *"grandmother."* She was a worshiper of the Asherah." This was a wooden stump that was carved in the likeness of the male organ.

The 17th verse says, *"But the high places were not taken away out of Israel."* Whether this meant Judah or the northern confederacy is not clear, but more than likely it referred to Judah. The *"high places,"* at least in this

NOTES

instance, would have been used to sacrifice to Jehovah, but still, it was not in keeping with the commandment of God that the sacrifices be offered only at the Temple at Jerusalem. Consequently, the Holy Spirit says this for a reason.

When it uses the words, *"nevertheless the heart of Asa was perfect in all his days,"* it does not mean *"sinless perfection,"* but that his heart was perfect as far as idolatry was concerned.

The 19th verse says, *"And there was no more war unto the five and thirtieth year of the reign of Asa."* Asa had peace the first ten years of his reign (14:1). Then came the Ethiopian invasion of Judah (14:9-15). After that, there was peace for 25 years (15:19); then came war with Baasha, king of the northern confederacy of Israel (16:1-6). Because he trusted in Syria at that time instead of God, wars were pronounced upon him for the rest of his reign - six more years (16:9).

CHAPTER 16

Verse 1 says, *"And the six and thirtieth year of the reign of Asa, Baasha king of Israel came up against Judah, and built Ramah, to the intent that he might let none go out or come in to Asa."* No doubt, tens of thousands of people from the northern kingdom of Israel, due to the worship of golden calves, were coming down to Judah that they might worship God at the Temple. Baasha, king of Israel, was attempting to stop this flight by building this border city of Ramah.

Conversely, worshipers of the true God do not have to be banned from going elsewhere. One of Satan's greatest ploys is to place the true worship of God *"off limits"* and to threaten by force anyone who would attempt to do so. One of the chief ploys of the apostate Church is to threaten with excommunication anyone who would go to certain places to worship the Lord. I want to repeat it again:

If it is of God, the people do not have to be threatened.

During the last year of Jesus' public ministry, anyone who followed Him was threatened with excommunication from the synagogue. Likewise, for centuries the Catholic Church would excommunicate anyone who attended any type of protestant Church. Denominations are fond of banning certain churches, ministries, or preachers and threatening any adherent with excommunication if they attend their services. Any time religious leaders do such, it is a sure sign that they are not following the Lord. As the people of Israel would do well to rebel against Baasha and his golden calf-worship; likewise, every Christian should hear the voice of the Shepherd (Jesus) and follow Him (St. John 10:4-5).

What Baasha did against Judah was an act of war. The 2nd verse says, *"Then Asa brought out silver and gold out of the treasures of the house of the Lord and of the king's house, and sent to Benhadad king of Syria."* Asa had had many years of peace. Regrettably, in these last years he seemingly lost his way with God. Rather than trust God to help him regarding Baasha, he hired the King of Syria. Asa's plan would succeed militarily but fail spiritually. Consequently, the victorious Asa of chapter 14 becomes the defeated Asa of chapter 16. It seems that spiritual victories teach the natural heart nothing. New victories cannot be won by the remembrance of old faith; there must be a fresh exercise of faith in every crisis.

As stated, Asa was successful. However, the success of self-made plans is a disaster. Asa's scheme in bribing the Syrian king to falsehood and treachery succeeded for the moment, but the real result was that he lost the opportunity of destroying both Baasha and Benhadad.

As a result of this faithless act, the 7th verse says, *"And at that time Hanani the seer came to Asa king of Judah."* The message to Asa is twofold:

1. *"Because thou hast relied on the king of Syria."*

2. *"And not relied on the Lord thy God."*

The Lord further says, *"Therefore is the host of the king of Syria escaped out of thine hand."* Judah's enemy was ever Syria. It seems that it was in the plan of God for Judah to defeat Syria in the very near future. This plan would be thwarted because of Asa's faithlessness.

Is it possible that God makes plans for us

NOTES

which speak of great victory, and we forfeit those plans by our faithlessness? Rather than trusting Him, we trust man.

The 8th verse proclaims the prophet reminding Asa of the great victory that the Lord helped him to win over *"the Ethiopians."*

A tremendous promise is given in verse 9. It says, *"For the eyes of the Lord run to and fro throughout the whole earth, to shew himself strong in the behalf of them whose heart is perfect toward him."* If God is doing the same today, and He is, my prayer would be thusly:

"Oh God, help me that my heart would be perfect toward thee, that your eyes may rest upon me to shew yourself strong on my behalf."

The Lord further says, *"Herein thou hast done foolishly: therefore from henceforth thou shalt have wars."* Asa would have someone else (Syria) to fight his war. God was sorely displeased because it showed lack of trust in Jehovah. Now, the very opposite of what Asa wanted would come upon him, constant war.

Proper repentance could have turned the situation, but Asa did the opposite. The 10th verse says, *"Then Asa was wroth with the seer, and put him in a prison house."* This is the same Asa who instituted the great revival of chapter 15. As well, the Scripture says, *"Asa oppressed some of the people the same time."* What exactly he did, the Holy Spirit does not say.

The Holy Spirit in the 11th verse records an interesting statement, *"And, behold, the acts of Asa, first and last."* The statement, *"first and last,"* signifies that there was a difference in Asa in his last years.

As a result of his faithlessness concerning the northern kingdom of Israel, he would have wars. As the result of his treatment of the prophet and the people, the 12th verse says, *"And Asa in the thirty and ninth year of his reign was diseased in his feet."* God permitted this disease as the result of Asa's actions. I wonder today how many Christians have diseases because of similar actions.

The 12th verse continues to say, *"Yet in his disease he sought not to the Lord, but to the physicians."* This statement tells us that if Asa had sought the Lord, God would have forgiven him and healed him. The *"physicians"* who are spoken of here could have been Egyptian physicians who were in high repute at foreign courts in ancient times, and who pretended to expel diseases by charms, incantations, and mystic arts.

The 13th verse shows us God's thoughts concerning such, for it says, *"And Asa slept with his fathers, and died."* Whether he repented at the very last is not known. If he did not, he died eternally lost.

CHAPTER 17

Now *"Jehoshaphat"* reigns as the king of Judah. He is a godly man, yet with one glaring weakness; forming alliances with heathenistic Israel. Nevertheless, this chapter is all sweetness and light. The 1st verse says, *"And strengthened himself against Israel."* Strangely enough, he would fortify himself greatly in a military sense against Israel, but, yet, he will compromise his spiritual stand by forming an alliance with the same people.

Many church denominations *"strengthen themselves against evil"* in their early days. However, when God begins to bless, and they are no longer poverty-stricken and weak, then, sadly, too many compromise their convictions by their alliance with the world. Alliance with the world prevents victory over the world.

In these beginning years of Jehoshaphat's reign, the 3rd verse says, *"And the Lord was with Jehoshaphat."* What a beautiful statement! Men always prosper when God is with them, and God is always with them if they will walk in the first ways of David. What are these *"first ways?"* This is an unusual expression referring to the ways of David in the early part of his life and reign before he committed sin with Bathsheba and had Uriah killed, and sought to number the people (II Sam. 11-12:24). This is what the Holy Spirit said about Jehoshaphat:

1. *"He walked in the first ways of his father David."*

2. *"And sought not unto Baalim."*

3. *"But sought to the Lord God of his father."*

4. *"And walked in his commandments, not after the doings of Israel."*

Because he did these things, the 5th verse says, *"Therefore the Lord stablished the kingdom in his hand."*

The 6th verse says, *"And his heart was lifted up (encouraged) in the ways of the Lord."* And then it says, *"Moreover he took away the high places and groves out of Judah."* As explained, the people were not sacrificing to idols at these *"high places and groves,"* but were sacrificing to Jehovah. Yet, this was against the Law of God inasmuch as they were supposed to sacrifice in Jerusalem. Almost invariably, the sacrifices to Jehovah would eventually degenerate into sacrifices to idols.

Jehoshaphat commanded these *"high places and groves"* to be taken away, but the people did not do their part in obeying him (I Kings 22:43).

The 7th verse proclaims Jehoshaphat doing something that had never been done before. It says, *"To teach in the cities of Judah."*

The 9th verse says, *"And they taught in Judah, and had the book of the law of the Lord with them, and went about throughout all the cities of Judah, and taught the people."* This was the first great teaching mission instituted by any king of Israel. The Law of Moses was taken from city to city and taught to the people. All questions about the Law were no doubt answered during the teaching sessions. (The *"law of the Lord"* was the Pentateuch - Genesis, Exodus, Leviticus, Numbers, and Deuteronomy.) Fidelity to the Word of God is the key to all blessing from God. Regrettably, even in the Church, the Bible is generally an unread book. Too often with many Christians it is a mere decoration that sits on the coffee table. The Christian should meditate on the Word of God day and night. We should read it incessantly. But, instead, and too often, newspapers, periodicals, and magazines, take precedent over the Word of God.

The 10th verse shows that God was immensely pleased with Jehoshaphat's teaching program, for it says, *"And the fear of the Lord fell upon all the kingdoms of the lands that were round about Judah."* The lesson is made clear over and over again that if we serve the Lord with humility, He will bless us immeasurably.

He will work for us; He will fight for us. It says, *"So that they made no war against Jehoshaphat."* God can stop the people from making war or He can cause them to make war. It depends on our faith and our consecration.

The 11th verse proclaims that which God intends for every Christian. It says, *"Also, some of the Philistines brought Jehoshaphat presents."* Then it says, *"The Arabians brought him flocks."* How sad it is when we read conversely that these same nations would take by force, that which belonged to the people of God, but here they are bringing to Jehoshaphat *"presents"* and *"silver."*

The 12th verse says, *"And Jehoshaphat waxed great exceedingly."* His *"greatness"* was all the blessings of God. Can we expect the same today? Yes, we can, but only if we adhere to the *"ways of the Lord."*

CHAPTER 18

As the previous chapter proclaimed blessing, this chapter proclaims compromise.

Verse 1 says, *"Now Jehoshaphat had riches and honour in abundance, and joined affinity with Ahab."* Riches and honor are more dangerous to the spiritual life than contempt and poverty. It is much better for the Christian if most are cursing him instead of praising him. Probably the greatest danger to the Church is *"joining affinity with the world."* This leaven that Satan introduced into Judah would ultimately drench Jerusalem with blood. Satan would set two traps for Jehoshaphat. They are as follows:

1. *"And Ahab killed sheep and oxen for him (Jehoshaphat) in abundance."* In this verse Satan will *"feast"* Jehoshaphat. In verse 31 he will try to *"kill"* Jehoshaphat. This was the first trap.

2. Jehoshaphat marries his son Jehoram to Athaliah, the daughter of Ahab (21:6). The world would, no doubt, call this a brilliant match, but, ultimately, it would bring great shedding of blood to Jerusalem. This was the second trap.

Verse 2 says, *"He went down to Ahab."*

Truly, he *"went down"* spiritually. When the Christian *"goes down"* to the world, he is received with great hospitality, but immediately is made a tool of the world. The 2nd verse continues to say, *"And persuaded him to go up to him to Ramoth-gilead"* - hence, a tool.

The 3rd verse says, *"And Ahab king of Israel said unto Jehoshaphat king of Judah, Wilt thou go with me to Ramoth-gilead?"* Jehoshaphat answers falsely by saying, *"I am as thou art, and my people as thy people."* Jehoshaphat was led by God, as Ahab was led by Satan. The people of Judah were worshipers of the true God, with the people of Israel worshiping Baal. There was no similarity between the two. Jehoshaphat sins grievously in his *"affinity."* This is, by and large, the sin of the Church despite the fact that the Holy Spirit through Paul said, *"Come out from among them and be ye separate, saith the Lord."*

The 4th verse portrays Jehoshaphat saying to Ahab, *"Inquire, I pray thee, at the word of the Lord today."* If Jehoshaphat had inquired of the Lord previously, he would not even be here with Ahab.

The 5th verse proclaims the prophesying of *"four hundred prophets."* They prophesied what the king wanted to hear by saying, *"Go up; for God will deliver it into the king's hand."* Likewise, the Church today abounds with *"prophets."* They prophesy continuously, but they prophesy out of their own minds, because precious few are actually from the Lord.

At least Jehoshaphat knew that their prophecies did not ring true, for he said in the 6th verse, *"Is there not here a prophet of the Lord?"*

The 7th verse says concerning the reply of Ahab, *"There is yet one man, by whom we may inquire of the Lord: but I hate him."* Sadly, the ratio of 400-1 would pretty well hold true today. Prophets abound on every corner, but precious few are actually from the Lord. Of this you can be sure, the few that are from the Lord are "hated."

The 8th verse says, *"Fetch quickly Micaiah the son of Imla."* Micaiah was God's prophet, and more than likely was in prison.

The 9th verse proclaims Jehoshaphat and Ahab both *"on his throne, clothed in their robes."* The false prophets led by *"Zedekiah"* continue to prophesy their prosperity. Jehoshaphat is in a sorry state.

The 12th verse proclaims the demand of the messenger to Micaiah, *"And speak thou good."* The times have changed; the demand has not. The apostate Church is still saying, *"Speak thou good."* As Israel of old could not tolerate the truth, the modern Church cannot tolerate the truth, either.

The 13th verse records Micaiah's answer, *"As the Lord liveth, even what my God saith, that will I speak."* There aren't many prophets of Micaiah's stature. His determination to speak only what *"Thus saith the Lord"* would earn him continued imprisonment, the bread and water of affliction, and without Jehoshaphat lifting a hand to help him (vs. 26).

Verses 16 through 22 give us a vivid account of the court of heaven. Seldom are we given such insight. This is what the prophet Micaiah said:

"I did see all Israel scattered upon the mountains, as sheep that have no shepherd" (vs. 16). God's message to Ahab through Micaiah was a message of love. He plainly told this bloodstained idolater that if he went up to the battle, he would surely perish. Ahab closed his ears to the gracious message and thought to outwit God by disguising himself, but he perished.

Verses 18-22 will show us how the Lord carried out Ahab's death. The 18th verse gives us a picture of the Throne of the Lord. It says, *"I saw the Lord sitting upon his throne, and all the host of heaven standing on his right hand and on his left."*

The 19th verse records the question of the Lord, *"And the Lord said, Who shall entice Ahab king of Israel?"* If Ahab had repented, this scene would not have taken place. But despite the warning of the Lord, he will carry out his own self-will. It will be to his doom.

In answer to the Lord's question, the 20th verse says, *"Then there came out a spirit, and stood before the Lord, and said, I will entice him."*

The 21st verse tells us the manner of that enticement, *"I will go out, and be a lying spirit in the mouth of all his prophets."*

This reveals that God and His heavenly host, including demons on certain occasions,

NOTES

have conferences concerning the affairs of men on earth. Such is plainly taught in Job 1-2; Daniel 4; and Revelation 12. This one had to do with only one part of the earth, one people on the earth, and one king in particular. He was in rebellion against God, in league with idol gods, and listening to their prophets instead of the true prophets of Jehovah, so God permitted him to be deceived instead of saving him from such deception.

There was very little that could be done with such a stubborn man - one consecrated to demon worship and demon prophets. Micaiah had been sent to Ahab, but he would not receive Jehovah's instructions. In this case, II Thessalonians 2:8-12 is clearly illustrated because he and his associates had no love for the truth that they might be saved, so God sent them a strong delusion that they should believe a lie: that they might be damned who believe not the truth, but had pleasure in unrighteousness.

The idea is that God permitted such deception to take the place of the truth rejected. If men will not have the truth, they will automatically have a substitute that will be more in harmony with their wicked ways for the time being. Ahab would not have truth and would not listen to Jehovah, but he would have lies and listen to the prophets of Baal. This passage, giving an insight into the spirit-realm, shows that behind all human acts there are good and bad spirits seeking to carry out the respective wills of their masters. The Lord protects as long as the individual follows the Lord. However, when the individual follows after his own ways, then God allows such to be led into error and harm. He then permits demon spirits to deceive and cause them to go further astray.

As well, we should realize that God controls not only the heavenly host, but also the world of darkness. Satan can only do what God allows him to do.

The 23rd verse says, *"Then Zedekiah the son of Chenaanah came near, and smote Micaiah upon the cheek."* Jehoshaphat saw this, and, yet, did not lift his hand to help the prophet of God. Judah would pay dearly for Jehoshaphat's sin.

Before Micaiah was led away to prison, he

NOTES

CHAPTER 19

turned to all the people who were present who had heard God's pronouncement and said, *"Hearken, all ye people."* Sadly, they did not hearken, and Ahab was killed.

How stupid men are! The 29th verse says, *"And the king of Israel said unto Jehoshaphat, I will disguise myself."* If men spend as much time trying to please God as they do trying to out-wit God, how much better off they would be.

In this chapter we are allowed to see into three courts:

1. The court of Ahab (vs. 9).
2. The court of heaven (vss. 18-22).
3. The court of Syria (vs. 30).

One court would reject God; the other court (Syria) had no knowledge of God, and God's court would decide all. Likewise, the courts of the world make their decisions, little realizing that it is the *"court of heaven"* that really makes the decisions.

Satan will attempt to kill Jehoshaphat; he will nearly succeed. Even though Jehoshaphat had greatly failed the Lord, still, as the 31st verse proclaims, *"But Jehoshaphat cried out, and the Lord helped him: and God moved them to depart from him."* Only by the direct intervention of God was Jehoshaphat spared. The mercy of God shines so brightly here. How many times has each of us failed the Lord, and, yet, the Lord comes to our rescue despite our failure? What a great God we serve!

Despite all Ahab's ploys, the 33rd verse proclaims God's ways, for it says, *"And a certain man drew a bow at venture, and smote the king of Israel between the joints of the harness."* Even though the Syrians did not know who Ahab was, still, an arrow shot at random found its target. The Word of God always comes to pass.

The 34th verse says, *"And about the time of the sun going down he died."* The sun went *"down"* for Ahab in more ways than one. He not only lost his life, but his soul - despite the fact that God had attempted to show him mercy and grace. His death is a portrayal of rebellion - a rebellion that characterizes most of the human race. How many today are headed toward their doom, spurning the love, grace, and mercy of God along with repeated warning? Their *"sun is going down."*

This chapter proclaims rebuke and repentance. The 1st verse says, *"And Jehoshaphat the king of Judah returned to his house in peace to Jerusalem"* - but only because the Lord was merciful to him. The last verse of the previous chapter spoke of Ahab dying. The 1st verse of this chapter speaks of Jehoshaphat *"in peace."* The two kings are perfect examples of rebellion against God which brings death and serving God which brings life, despite Jehoshaphat's unfaithfulness.

The 2nd verse proclaims that the Lord would send a prophet to meet Jehoshaphat. It says, *"And Jehu the son of Hanani the seer went out to meet him, and said to King Jehoshaphat."* Part of the message would be negative. It is as follows:

1. *"Why do you help the ungodly?"*
2. *"Why do you love them that hate the Lord?"*
3. *"Therefore is wrath upon thee from before the Lord."*

However, the 3rd verse records a positive side to the message from the Lord. It is as follows:

1. *"Nevertheless there are good things found in thee."*
2. *"Thou hast taken away the groves out of the land."*
3. *"Thou hast prepared thine heart to seek God."*

The Scripture does not actually say that Jehoshaphat repented, but there is evidence that he did. For the 4th verse says, *"And Jehoshaphat dwelt at Jerusalem: And he went out again through the people from Beersheba to Mount Ephraim."* The word *"again"* proves this to be the second revival of teaching the Law of Moses in bringing the people back to God. So, this is evidence that Jehoshaphat heeded, at least at this time, the words of the Lord from the prophet.

Verses 5-11 record his efforts to bring justice to Judah, even down to the poorest of the poor. The 5th verse says, *"And he set judges in the land throughout all the fenced cities of*

Judah, city by city." He charged these judges to judge in justice for God, and not for man; to judge in the fear of God, and to take heed not to sin by having respect of persons or taking bribes. In Jerusalem he set the priests and Levites and chief of the fathers of Israel to judge and even take care of the cases appealed to the higher court. He charged these also to judge in the fear of God, faithfully with a perfect heart.

CHAPTER 20

The 1st verse says concerning the *"children of Moab"* and the *"children of Ammon"* that they *"came against Jehoshaphat to battle."* The Lord allowed this invasion to take place for one of two reasons:

1. Because of Jehoshaphat's alliance with Ahab, which greatly displeased the Lord.

2. At times the Lord will allow attacks by the enemy, not because it is a punishment for failure, but in order that we may deepen our fidelity to the Word and depend on Him. It would be somewhat like Paul's *"thorn in the flesh."*

The 2nd verse proclaims that the effort by Judah's enemies was more than a skirmish; it was a concentrated effort by the powers of darkness to destroy Judah. It says, *"There cometh a great multitude against thee."* Satan's attacks are always subtle, powerful, and overwhelming. Within the natural it is impossible to defeat him. Consequently, there must be explicit trust in God or else there will be defeat. Too oftentimes the Christian opposes Satan *"in the flesh,"* instead of *"in the Spirit."* I think it can be safely said that every Christian has done this at one time or the other. If we deviate from the Word of God in any fashion, we lose. If we adhere totally to the Word of God, we win. What Jehoshaphat did is a beautiful example for us. If we will do as he did, victory will be ours as well.

In the 3rd verse it says, *"And Jehoshaphat feared."* This is not the type of fear that Paul spoke of in II Timothy 1, *"the spirit of fear,"* but was, rather, the type of fear that every Christian at times has, and, in fact, should have (II Cor. 7:5). He allowed this fear to drive him to the

NOTES

Lord, for it says, *"And set himself to seek the Lord, and proclaimed a fast throughout all Judah."*

That is the first requirement for the child of God. Regrettably, far too many Christians set themselves to seek the advice of men, namely counselors, and psychologists, among others. There is no help from these sources.

The 4th verse proclaims the second thing that Jehoshaphat did. Whereas, he *"set himself"* in verse 3, now he calls all of Judah together to *"ask help of the Lord."* It says, *"Even out of all the cities of Judah they came to seek the Lord."* In times of crisis we need the help of other Christians to pray with us. Whenever two Christians gather together to seek the face of the Lord, the power not only doubles, but it increases tenfold or more. Consequently, whenever many Christians gather together, the power is not increased according to the number there, but multiplies manifold. The modern Church has, by and large, forgotten the secret of consecrated prayer.

Verses 5-13 record Jehoshaphat's prayer to the Lord. It is an excellent example for us to follow. The only difference in his prayer then and our prayer now is that we pray to the *"Lord God"* in the name *"Jesus Christ"* (St. John 16:23). Otherwise, the prayer was identical to that which we should pray. It was a prayer of faith.

The 6th verse begins with Jehoshaphat proclaiming God as Ruler *"over all the kingdoms of the heathen."* In other words, even though heathen powers did not serve God, still, they could not do anything except that which the Lord allowed them to do. Especially, when they would come against God's people, their victory or defeat would depend upon the faith and the humility of those who name the name of the Lord. He further adds, *"So that none is able to withstand thee."* Satan's power at times is mighty. However, God's power is Almighty.

The 7th verse proclaims this Word, *"Art not thou our God?"* He was their God, and they were His children. Now, Satan is attempting to take the possession and inheritance that was given by the Lord. He further says, *"And gavest it to the seed of Abraham thy friend forever."* The word *"forever"* signifies the fact that our inheritance is never to be taken from us by the powers of darkness. God intends for us to keep it forever.

The 8th verse says, *"And have built thee a sanctuary."* It is God's desire that we build Him a sanctuary in the form of the *"Temple of the Holy Spirit,"* which is our body. The Temple (or Sanctuary) in those days was a building made with hands. Now, it is our physical body in which the Holy Spirit dwells (I Cor. 3:16).

In the 9th verse Jehoshaphat goes back to the prayer of Solomon (II Chron. 6:28). He is saying that irrespective of the cause of the problem, be it *"sword"* or *"judgment"* or *"pestilence"* or *"famine,"* that if we *"cry unto thee in our affliction, then thou wilt hear and help."* That is the promise of God, and it is a promise that He will keep, but only if we go His way. I am not remiss in my statement if I say that virtually all of the Church has abandoned *"God's way,"* and has, rather, accepted *"man's way."* David said, *"Give us help from trouble: For vain is the help of man"* (Psa. 60:11). One of the problems with the modern Church is that we have been wrongly taught by the *"faith message"* that we are to ask God to do something, and if we have faith, He will do it immediately - or at least very soon. This teaching is error. God, at times, does answer speedily, but, at times, we have to *"wait"* on Him. This situation recorded in this chapter probably took place over a period of several weeks, or even months. Nevertheless, whatever time we would have to wait on the Lord before the answer comes can only be for our benefit. David said, *"Wait, I say, on the Lord"* (Psa. 27:14).

In the 12th verse Jehoshaphat says four things:

1. *"Wilt thou not judge them?"*

2. *"For we have no might against this great company that cometh against us."*

3. *"Neither know we what to do."*

4. *"But our eyes are upon thee."*

So many times we do not know what to do, but He does know what to do. The question must be asked:

"To whom or to what do we have our eyes on?"

Our faith must be that if we approach God according to His Word, with our eyes upon Him, that He will answer. The answer may come soon or it may be long, but it will come.

The 14th verse says, *"Then upon Jahaziel came the Spirit of the Lord in the midst of the congregation."*

The 15th verse proclaims the answer of the Lord:

1. *"Be not afraid nor dismayed by reason of this great multitude."*

2. *"For the battle is not yours, but God's."*

3. *"You shall not need to fight in this battle"* (verse 17).

4. *"Stand ye still, and see the salvation of the Lord with you."*

Notice God's answer. First, He says, *"Be not afraid."* The anxiety that Jehoshaphat previously had is now ended. As well, how so often we forget that the battle is not ours, but God's. If we within ourselves fight Satan, we will lose every time. Actually, the only fight we are supposed to engage in is the *"good fight of faith"* (I Tim. 6:12).

Most Christians lose their fight, not because of insincerity, a lack of integrity, or lack of effort. They lose because they do not fight God's way. If we engage Satan in any manner except the *"scriptural manner,"* defeat will be ours. If we are scriptural in our *"battle,"* victory will be ours - in other words, let the Lord do it. The words *"stand ye still,"* means no dependance on *"the flesh"* but all on *"the Spirit."*

After this great answer from the Lord, the 18th verse declares that Jehoshaphat and all of Judah *"fell before the Lord, worshipping the Lord."*

Verses 20 and 21 proclaim that which God told Jehoshaphat to do concerning the deployment of the army. To the natural mind it was foolishness; to the spiritual mind it was victory.

The 21st verse says, *"He appointed singers unto the Lord, and that should praise the beauty of holiness, as they went out before the army."* They were to say, *"Praise the Lord: For his mercy endureth forever."* This shows us that *"holiness and praise"* are our strength, and not the might and power of man. How so little the Church understands this. They did deploy *"the army,"* but actually it would do very little except gather the spoil. Their victory was *"holiness and praise."* As well, it is our victory today.

The 22nd verse says, *"And when they began to sing and to praise, the Lord sent ambushments against the children of Ammon, Moab, and Mt. Seir."* And it says, *"They were smitten."*

The ambushments that were set by the Lord were not of the Israelites, so must have been angelic hosts. The Targum interprets this as angels. Evidently, the angels of God appeared suddenly, and the children of Ammon and Moab became so confused that they began to destroy the Edomites; then, after destroying them, they were so confused that they began destroying one another.

This is the same miraculous happening that will take place at the Battle of Armageddon where, without a doubt, angels will be present (Zech. 14:12-14).

By the time Israel's army arrived, there was no need to fight as God had told them, and all they did was to gather the spoil, which amounted to an abundance of riches, precious jewels and other things. They gathered the spoil for three days and had more than they could carry.

The 27th verse says, *"Then they returned."* And then it says, *"with joy."* The Scripture then says, *"For the Lord had made them to rejoice over their enemies."* One of two things happens with every child of God; either we rejoice in our victory over the enemy, or he rejoices in his victory over us.

The 29th verse says, *"And the fear of God was on all the kingdoms of those countries."* Such a miraculous defeat of the Moabites, Ammonites, and Edomites was soon known by all nations round about.

Not in all the history of the world up to this time had there been such a defeat of an earthly army by God and His angels. There had been a great destruction of Pharaoh and his host in the Red Sea, but not by actual liers-in-wait as on this occasion. After this, there was a great defeat caused by one angel who killed 185,000 men of war in one night during the days of Hezekiah (Isa. 37:36-38). The only other happening like this will be at Armageddon (Zech. 14:12-15; Rev. 19:11-21).

The 30th verse says concerning Jehoshaphat and Judah, *"For his God gave him rest round about."* Only God can give *"rest."*

The 33rd verse speaks of failure, but not on

the part of Jehoshaphat. He had given orders that the *"high places"* were to be taken away. But the Scripture says, *"Howbeit the high places were not taken away: for as yet the people had not prepared their hearts unto the God of their fathers."* Even after these great victories, still, the peoples' hearts were not after God. What a tragedy!

Once again Jehoshaphat will succumb to his old sin. It says, *"And after this did Jehoshaphat king of Judah join himself with Ahaziah king of Israel, who did very wickedly."*

Concerning this alliance, the 37th verse says, *"Because thou hast joined thyself with Ahaziah, the Lord hath broken thy works and the ships were broken, that they were not able to go to Tarshish."*

Jehoshaphat died at 60 years old. Quite possibly his early death was because of this failure.

When the 32nd verse says, *"And departed not from it, doing that which was right in the sight of the Lord,"* it is speaking of idol-worship. Jehoshaphat, despite his sin regarding alliances with the northern kingdom of Israel, never succumbed in any manner to idol-worship.

CHAPTER 21

The 2nd verse says, *"Jehoshaphat king of Israel."* No, this was not an error in transcription. It does show that God recognized the faithful remnant of Judah as His entire people. As well today, and under the New Covenant, the Holy Spirit through Paul calls the Church, *"a spiritual Israel"* (Rom. 2:28-29).

Jehoshaphat is now dead. He was one of the godliest kings that Judah had. His son Jehoram, his *"firstborn,"* now takes the throne. He was one of the most evil kings that Judah had. The implication in the 3rd verse is that quite possibly Jehoshaphat did not have the mind of God regarding the selection of Jehoram. It says this, *"But the kingdom gave he to Jehoram; because he was the firstborn."* Most of the time this law of the firstborn held true even in the throne rights, but not always.

God overruled in some cases because the first-born was not the suitable one for a position. He certainly was not the suitable one here.

The 4th verse says, *"He strengthened himself, and slew all his brethren with the sword, and divers also of the princes of Israel."* He strengthened himself by murder and ruthlessness instead of doing it the way his godly father had done by the blessing of God. Such so-called strengthening was really weakening himself and diminishing the blessing of God upon his kingdom, for he did not prosper for such crimes. He only caused God to turn against him, and this led to revolt and wars which could have been completely avoided by righteousness and the protection of God.

Verse 2 says that he had six brothers. He killed all of these.

Now we are able to see the leaven that was in the life of Jehoshaphat concerning his alliance with Ahab. For it says, *"And he walked in the way of the kings of Israel, like as did the house of Ahab: for he had the daughter of Ahab to wife: and he wrought that which was evil in the eyes of the Lord"* (verse 6).

Despite this glut of evil, the 7th verse says, *"Howbeit the Lord would not destroy the house of David, because of the covenant that he had made with David."*

The 10th verse proclaims that the *"Edomites revolted,"* as well as *"Libnah."* And then it says, *"Because he had forsaken the Lord God of his fathers."* Over and over again we will see blessing coming because of adherence to the Word of God. And, as well, we will see judgment because of failure to adhere to the Word of God.

The 11th verse proclaims his further apostasy. It says, *"And caused the inhabitants of Jerusalem to commit fornication, and compelled Judah thereto."* Jehoshaphat had given the orders that these *"high places"* were to be removed. Jehoram acted the opposite. This was mostly the worship of the *"Asherah."* It was the male sex organ that was carved out of a tree trunk, that would stand from 10 - 20 feet high. This, as the god of fertility, would be worshiped with all type of sexual sins being practiced. The worship of the Asherah was little different than most modern movies. The direction would be slightly different, with the end results being

NOTES

the same.

The 12th verse says, *"And there came a writing to him from Elijah the prophet."* Elijah would soon be translated; however, by prophecy the Lord had given Elijah a word for this moment. He had written it down, and it would now be given to Jehoram, king of Judah.

The prophecy was to the point; it stated that because Jehoram had not walked in the ways of his father Jehoshaphat, but, instead, had followed the kings of Israel, therefore, the following would happen:

1. *"Behold, with a great plague will the Lord smite thy people."*

2. *"And thou shalt have great sickness by disease of thy bowels, until thy bowels fall out by reason of the sickness day by day."*

At this stage, Jehoram could have repented and quite possibly avoided this terrible judgment. He did not repent, and the judgment was not avoided.

The 16th verse says, *"Moreover the Lord stirred up against Jehoram the spirit of the Philistines, and of the Arabians, that were near the Ethiopians."* The Philistines and Arabians were tributary under Jehoshaphat (17:11). Through sin, Jehoram lost these people, as well as Edom and Libnah. They were the ones God used to fulfill the prophecy of verse 14. They broke into Jerusalem taking all the treasures in the king's house and all his wives and sons, so that the royal line of David was cut off except for one son, the youngest. Verse 17 says, *"Save Jehoahaz, the youngest of his sons."* This was the first of two times in this period that the royal line was cut off except for one boy (22:10).

Verse 18 records Elijah's prophecy being fulfilled, *"And after all this the Lord smote him in his bowels with an incurable disease."*

The 20th verse says, *"He died, and departed without being desired,"* that is, unregretted. How many because of sin depart without being desired?

◼

CHAPTER 22

Verse 1 says, *"And the inhabitants of Jerusalem made Ahaziah his youngest son king in his stead."* This king had three names: *"Ahaziah, Azariah, and Jehoahaz."* All have the same meaning in Hebrew, *"Jehovah taketh hold."* However, Jehovah had no opportunity to take hold in the life of this wicked king.

The leaven that was in the life of Jehoshaphat concerning his alliance with Ahab will now continue its rot. For the 2nd verse says, *"His mother's name also was Athaliah the daughter of Omri."* She was actually the granddaughter of Omri, but daughter of Ahab and Jezebel (the Hebrew language had no designation such as *"granddaughter or grandson, or the like").*

The 3rd verse says, *"He also walked in the ways of the house of Ahab: For his mother was his counselor to do wickedly."* He followed his wicked father, Jehoram, who had walked in all the wicked ways of Ahab and Jezebel, his mother being his counselor in wickedness. She was the daughter of Ahab and Jezebel and just as wicked. She even killed all her grandsons except one and seized the throne of Judah which she kept for six years.

The 7th verse says concerning Ahaziah's death, *"And the destruction of Ahaziah was of God by coming to Joram."* God determined the destruction of Ahaziah because of his sins. It was brought about by Jehu whom the Lord caused to be king of the ten tribes. He killed both Jehoram (Joram), king of the ten tribes, and Ahaziah of Judah.

The 9th verse says because of sin, *"So the house of Ahaziah had no power to keep still the kingdom."*

The 10th verse says, continuing the rot of the leaven, *"But when Athaliah the mother of Ahaziah saw that her son was dead, she arose and destroyed all the seed royal of the house of Judah."* She destroyed all except Joash, one little boy who they hid in the Temple so that the royal line of David might be continued to fulfill the Davidic Covenant which promised a king on the throne of Judah as long as they had a kingdom with any possibility of righteousness. This was Satan's third attempt to destroy the royal line of David, so that God's Word could not be fulfilled.

The 11th verse says, *"But Jehoshabeath, the daughter of the king, took Joash the son of Ahaziah, and stole him from among the king's*

sons that were slain." Evidently, this bloody queen thought she had killed them all, not realizing that the infant was not dead. From this bloodstained room the daughter of Jehoram (Jehoshaphat's son) stole away baby Joash. She *"hid him from Athaliah, so that she slew him not."*

The 12th verse says that he was *"hid in the house of God six years: and Athaliah reigned over the land."* At this time, the Temple was not in use. The people were worshiping idols on the mountaintops and other places. So, the *"House of God"* was the logical place for him to be hidden.

CHAPTER 23

Verse 1 says, *"And in the seventh year Jehoiada strengthened himself."* The *"seventh year"* refers to the length of time between Ahaziah's assassination through the reign of the wicked queen Athaliah. Joash was now seven years old. Jehoiada was the Great High Priest of Judah, but since there was no worship of Jehovah in the Temple, he had no work and no authority in apostate Judah. He now took Joash, the rightful heir to the throne of David and the kingdom of Judah, and made him king, bringing about a new revival of worship of the Lord. He strengthened himself by doing the following:

1. Making a league with captains of hundreds of soldiers (vs. 1).

2. Gathering the Levites (vs. 2).

3. Gathering the chief of the fathers of Israel.

4. Making a covenant between the king (Joash) and the congregation through the elders (vs. 3).

It is obvious from what was done that Judah was greatly sick of this bloody queen, Athaliah. As well, and no doubt, Jehoiada was strengthened by the Lord.

The 3rd verse says, *"And all the congregation made a covenant with the king in the house of God."* This is speaking of Joash.

At the appointed time, the 11th verse says, *"They brought out the king's son (Joash), and put upon him the crown, and gave him the testimony* (the Law of Moses), *and made him king."*

By now the news of the crowning of the new king, Joash, spread like wildfire through Jerusalem. Wicked Queen Athaliah *"heard the noise,"* and the 12th verse says, *"She came to the people into the house of the Lord."* Then the *"captains"* took her outside of the Temple and the 15th verse says, *"They slew her there."*

The 16th verse says, *"And Jehoiada made a covenant."* That covenant was that *"They should be the Lord's people."* Then they all went to the house of Baal, broke it down, broke the altars and images, and slew the priests of Baal.

After that, Jehoiada restored the offices of the House of the Lord according to the Law of Moses, and the 24 courses ordained by David.

The porters were then set at the various gates to see that no unclean thing should enter into the Temple courts and grounds. Finally, the king was brought down from the House of the Lord to his own house before all Israel.

The 21st verse says, *"And all the people of the land rejoiced: and the city was quiet, after that they had slain Athaliah with the sword."* Now, the light of God would burn once again in the city in which He had chosen to place His name, and with the people that He had chosen to be His people.

CHAPTER 24

The 1st verse says, *"Joash was seven years old when he began to reign."* Joash was the youngest king to reign in all Israel, and the fifth king to reign for 40 years. He is called *"Jehoash"* in II Kings 12:2.

The 2nd verse gives us an interesting insight. It says, *"And Joash did that which was right in the sight of the Lord all the days of Jehoiada the priest."* Whenever Jehoiada died, Joash went into deep apostasy and sin. There is every indication that he died lost. Under the tutelage of godly Jehoiada, he had an excellent beginning. For the 4th verse says, *"That Joash was minded to repair the house of the Lord."*

The half-shekel (for each person) redemption money was levied against all the people of Judah.

The 6th verse calls it, *"The collection, according to the commandment of Moses the servant of the Lord."* This redemption money (Ex. 30:13-16) was to be used for the repair work.

For the 7th verse says, *"For the sons of Athaliah, that wicked woman, had broken up the house of God."* If one will notice, there were precious few times that God allowed outsiders to damage the *"house of the Lord."* Most of the damage came from wicked kings, and in this case, a wicked queen. Likewise, most of the damage done to the work of God today is little done by the world, but, instead, by false doctrine in an apostate Church.

The 14th verse says, *"And they offered burnt offerings in the house of the Lord continually all the days of Jehoiada."* Once again the sacrifices were established. However, when Jehoiada would die, this too would stop.

Verse 15 says, *"But Jehoiada waxed old, and was full of days when he died; an hundred and thirty years old."* Jehoiada was born in Solomon's reign. He therefore lived through six reigns.

The 16th verse says, *"And they buried him in the city of David among the kings, because he had done good in Israel, both toward God, and toward his house."* What a testimony given by the Holy Spirit to the faithfulness of Jehoiada.

The 17th verse says, *"Now after the death of Jehoiada came the princes of Judah."* And it says, *"Then the king hearkened unto them."* At the commencement of his reign, Joash leaned on Jehoiada who was a godly man. Afterwards, he leaned on the princes of Judah who were wicked men. To lean on men, whether they be good or wicked, is disastrous. Had the king leaned *"only upon God,"* how different would have been his history.

The 18th verse sadly records the backsliding of Judah. It says, *"They left the house of the Lord God of their fathers, and served groves and idols."* It was the princes of Judah this time that led the king into sin and apostasy. Usually the king led the princes and the people astray, but not here. They too worshiped the

"Asherah."

The 18th verse says, *"And wrath came upon Judah and Jerusalem for this their trespass."* God cannot abide sin, even in His chosen people. He is angry with the wicked every day.

The Holy Spirit faithfully records in the 19th verse, *"Yet he sent prophets to them, to bring them again unto the Lord, and they testified against them: but they would not give ear."* What an indictment! It is bad enough to die lost having never heard. The horror of dying lost after having heard is beyond comprehension. The word, *"testified,"* can be translated *"protestantes."* This is the first instance of the word *"protestant"* being used in history. It comes from two words: *"pro"* - for, and *"testans,"* which means witnessings. It means a witnessing for God and his truth, not merely against evil. Here, God sent prophets who protested the backsliding of Judah and declared the truth of God, but they would not hear.

Concerning the prophets sent to Judah, the 20th verse says, *"And the spirit of God came upon Zechariah the son of Jehoiada the priest."* He said, *"Thus saith God, because you have forsaken the Lord he hath also forsaken you."* The Zechariah who was stoned here was not the prophet who wrote the book of Zechariah, for he did not live until after the Babylonian captivities (Zech. 1:1). This prophet was a son of Jehoiada and lived at least 150-170 years before the captivities. Both men were stoned, one in the court of the Temple, and the other between the Temple and the altar (St. Matt. 23:35).

There could be no more awful pronouncement than the words, *"God hath forsaken you."*

The 21st verse says, *"And they conspired against him, and stoned him."* The Scripture further says that they stoned him *"at the commandment of the king."* He slew the son of his friend and benefactor, Jehoiada.

The 22nd verse says, *"Thus Joash the king remembered not the kindness which Jehoiada his father had done to him, but slew his son."*

Because of Joash's sin, the 23rd verse says, *"That the host of Syria came up against him."*

The 24th verse proclaims that the army of the Syrians was but *"a small company of men"* and it says, *"The Lord delivered a very great host into their hand, because they had for-*

saken the Lord God of their fathers."

The 25th verse says that besides the invasion of Syria in the last months of his life, *"They left him in great diseases."* And then, *"His own servants slew him on his bed, and he died."* They buried Jehoiada among the kings, but when Joash died, it said, *"They buried him not in the sepulchers of the kings."* How obvious it is that the blessings of God come upon righteousness. As well, how obvious it is that the judgment of God comes upon unrighteousness.

CHAPTER 25

Joash is now dead so Amaziah his son will take the throne. The 2nd verse says of him, *"And he did that which was right in the sight of the Lord, but not with a perfect heart."*

According to the 4th verse, at least at the beginning of his reign he seems to have tried to follow the Bible. For it says, *"But did as it is written in the law in the book of Moses."* This was not a copy of the book, but the book itself. It was a *"written"* book; its content was the Law; and, lastly, God was the author of that Law. The book was, therefore, inspired.

Now a series of spiritual failures begins on Amaziah's part. They are as follows:

1. *"Moreover Amaziah gathered Judah together."* This speaks of a preparation for war against Edom. There is no evidence that he sought the Lord concerning this military move.

2. *"He hired also an hundred thousand mighty men of valour out of Israel."* This was displeasing to the Lord. For God would send to him *"a man of God"* (verse 7) and say, *"Let not the army of Israel go with thee; for the Lord is not with Israel."* The 8th verse seems to say that if Judah persisted in taking the army of Israel with her that *"God shall make thee fall before the enemy."*

The 9th verse proclaims that Amaziah was much more concerned about the money lost than obeying God. Sadly, this is the concern of most people, even Christians. We seem to forget that *"the Lord is able to give thee much more than this"* (verse 9).

3. The 12th verse says, *"And cast them down from the top of the rock, that they all were broken to pieces."* It seems that he ruthlessly executed 10,000 people.

4. *"That he brought the gods of the children of Seir, and set them up to be his gods, and bowed down himself before them, and burned incense unto them."* How stupid! The Lord will send a prophet and say to him, *"Why hast thou sought after the gods of the people, which could not deliver their own people out of thine hand"* (verse 15)? The king threatens to kill the prophet.

One should notice that God, before judgment, will make every attempt to turn the individual around. Most of the time it is to no avail.

5. The 17th verse says concerning a proposed invasion of the northern kingdom of Israel by Amaziah that he *"took advice."* However, this counsel was not of God. Millions today take advice, but virtually all of it is from man, with almost none from God. Amaziah will declare war on Israel, *"Let us see one another in the face."* This was but another step down in his long slide to spiritual oblivion.

The king of Israel, Joash, attempts to dissuade Amaziah. He is not successful. For the 20th verse says, *"But Amaziah would not hear; for it came of God that he might deliver them into the hand of their enemies."* He would do this *"because they sought after the gods of Edom."* So often this was the reason for judgment upon both Israel and Judah; it caused more judgment than any other sin. Idolatry finally led to the destruction of the nation.

The 22nd verse says concerning the war, *"And Judah was put to the worse before Israel."* God was now opposed to Judah. There was no way they could win.

The 27th verse says, *"Now after the time that Amaziah did turn away from following the Lord."* The Holy Spirit will pinpoint the exact *"time"* that this happened. Now he is at the mercy of Satan. It says, *"And slew him there."*

The 28th verse says concerning his burial place, *"in the city of Judah."* When the king turned away from the Lord, the Holy Spirit declined to call his burial place by the lofty titles of *"The city of David"* or *"Jerusalem,"* but,

NOTES

instead, called it *"The city of Judah."* It seems that idol-worship and pride was the cause of Amaziah's fall. To be sure, idol-worship and pride are the cause of the fall of any Christian.

CHAPTER 26

The 1st verse says, *"Then all the people of Judah took Uzziah, who was sixteen years old, and made him king."* Uzziah is named Azariah in II Kings. He was four years old at the time of his father's murder. He was 16 years of age when crowned. The 4th verse says, *"And he did that which was right in the sight of the Lord, according to all that his father Amaziah did."* This is the fifth king (besides David) of Israel's 42 kings (both Judah and Israel) who did that which was right in the sight of the Jehovah. And, yet, this statement was qualified, being linked to *"his father Amaziah."*

Verse 5 says, *"And he sought God in the days of Zechariah, who had understanding in the visions of God."* This was not the *"Zechariah,"* the son of Jehoadah, who lived some years prior, because he was murdered by Joash, Uzziah's grandfather. Neither was it the Zechariah who wrote the book of Zechariah. All we know about this Zechariah is what is said here. It seems that Uzziah leaned on him. It is dangerous to lean even on a good man. The 5th verse says as well, *"And as long as he sought the Lord, God made him to prosper."* What a statement! The words, *"sought the Lord,"* mean not only to desire to do what God desires, but to seek His face incessantly. This is the secret of spiritual, domestic, financial, and mental victory.

The 7th verse says, *"And God helped him."* Then it speaks of various enemies who would come against Israel.

The 15th verse says, *"And he made in Jerusalem engines, invented by cunning men."* These *"engines"* were called by the Romans, *"balista."* They could throw stones, weighing some 300 pounds a quarter of a mile. Pliny states that the *"balista"* was a Syrian invention. That statement has a curious relation to this verse. The passage also states, *"For he was marvelously helped, till he was strong,"* meaning that God prospered him so greatly that people marveled. However, when he became strong he entered into the zone of extreme danger.

Because the 16th verse says, *"But when he was strong, his heart was lifted up to his destruction."* Paul wrote, *"When we are weak, then are we strong"* (II Cor. 12). Strong Christians are in very great danger. It is better to be persecuted and criticized by the Church than to be praised and lauded. The first drives us to our knees, with the latter lifting us up in pride. The verse also says, *"He transgressed against the Lord."*

His transgression was far more serious than we realize. He attempted *"to burn incense upon the altar of incense."* In God's economy of *"the law,"* the priest stood as a type of Christ as a mediator between God and man. In effect, Uzziah, like Cain, claimed the right to personally worship God without the intervention of an ongoing Saviour.

The Lord smote him. For it says in the 19th verse, *"The leprosy even rose up in his forehead before the priests in the house of the Lord, from beside the incense altar."* On the forehead of the High Priest were the words *"Holiness to the Lord"* (Christ). On the forehead of Uzziah was *"sinfulness"* (leprosy).

The 21st verse says, *"For he was cut off from the house of the Lord."* Possibly he repented, but there is no evidence that he did. The last thing the Holy Spirit said about him was, *"He is a leper."*

CHAPTER 27

Verse 1 says, *"Jotham was twenty and five years old when he began to reign."* He was 20 when he became co-regent with his father.

The 2nd verse says, *"And he did that which was right in the sight of the Lord, according to all that his father Uzziah did."* This was the sixth king (besides David) of Israel's 42 kings who did right in the sight of God (both Judah and Israel). The verse also says, *"Howbeit he entered not into the temple of the Lord."* This

probably means that, terrified by the fate of his father, he did not attend the Temple services. If this be so, then Uzziah, Jotham, and Ahaz illustrate how incurably diseased is the natural heart. The first king boldly intrudes into the Temple, the second timidly stands away from it, and the third shuts it up!

The latter portion of the 2nd verse says, *"And the people did yet corruptly."*

Four times in verses 3 and 4 it says, *"He built,"* and then lists what he built. If Jotham, instead of building fortified cities, castles, and towers in the mountains and in the forests, had broken down the high places at which the people did corruptly, quite possibly, it would have brought revival to Judah. Regrettably, there has never been a perfect man. All, even when diligently trying to follow the Lord, are freighted with failure. It is the Grace of God that gives us the victory, not our perfection.

The 5th verse says, *"He fought also with the king of the Ammonites, and prevailed against them."*

The 6th verse proclaims the Holy Spirit saying, *"So Jotham became mighty, because he prepared his ways before the Lord his God."* What a beautiful statement!

CHAPTER 28

Verse 1 says, *"Ahaz was twenty years old when he began to reign."* Ahaz was one of the most ungodly kings who ever ruled over Judah. The Holy Spirit says of him, *"But he did not that which was right in the sight of the Lord, like David his father."* Ahaz's father, Jotham, was godly. Likewise, Hezekiah, Ahaz's son would be godly, but Ahaz would be ungodly. The following is a list of his sins:

1. *"For he walked in the ways of the kings of Israel"* (vs. 2).

2. *"And made also molten images of Baalim"* (vs. 2).

3. *"He burnt incense in the valley of the son of Hinnom"* (vs. 3).

4. *"Burnt his children in the fire* (to Moloch)*"* (human sacrifice - vs. 3).

5. *"He sacrificed also and burnt incense in*

the high places, on the hills, and under every green tree" (vs.4).

For these sins the 5th verse says, *"Wherefore the Lord his God delivered him into the hand of the king of Syria; and they smote him."* It also says, *"He was also delivered into the hand of the king of Israel, who smote him with a great slaughter"* - *"slew in Judah and hundred and twenty thousand in one day, which were all valiant men;"* (vs. 6). All of this was *"because they had forsaken the Lord God of their fathers."*

Verses 7 and 8 record that Israel *"carried away captive of their brethren two hundred thousand."* Over and over again the Word of God is replete with examples of kings who did right and were blessed, and then kings who did wrong and were judged. Paul would say that all of this is *"for our examples"* (I Cor. 10:11).

Verse 9 says, *"But a prophet of the Lord was there, whose name was Oded."* This prophet in Israel (Samaria) would have a stern rebuke for Israel because of taking some 200,000 women, sons, and daughters captive. He said, *"Because the Lord God of your fathers was wroth with Judah, He hath delivered them into your hand, and you have slain them in a rage that reacheth up unto heaven."*

The 10th verse says that the prophet Oded reminds Israel, *"But are there not with you, even with you, sins against the Lord your God?"*

The 11th verse proclaims the demand by God that the captives from Judah be released, for the prophet says, *"For the fierce wrath of the Lord is upon you."*

An important principle appears in verses 5-15. When executing God's judgment upon transgressors or delivering His messages of wrath to sinners, there must be no jubilation on the part of the messenger, nor excess of temper in the instrument. If called by God to such a service, the person or persons employed should be filled with self-judgment, humility, and compassion.

To Israel's credit, and for one of a few times, they would heed the prophet of God. For the 15th verse says concerning the captives that they *"clothed all,"* and *"shod them,"* and *"gave them to eat,"* and *"anointed them."* They even gently *"carried all the feeble"* back to Jericho,

NOTES

which was among their own people.

After all the problems of being defeated by both Syria and Israel, still, Ahaz will not seek the face of the Lord but, instead, will *"send unto the kings of Assyria to help him"* (verse 16).

The 17th verse proclaims that now the *"Edomites had come and smitten Judah, and carried away captives. The Philistines also had invaded the cities of the low country"* (verse 18).

The 19th verse once again gives the reasons for Judah's ill-treatment. It says, *"For the Lord brought Judah low because of Ahaz king of Israel,"* for it says, *"He made Judah naked, and transgressed sore against the Lord."* The word *"naked"* has to do with being *"naked to the judgment of God"* - and because of sin. The judgment that the Lord brings is always redemptive in its application. In other words, it is intended to bring the person or the nation to repentance. In this case it would not.

Back at the 16th verse it said that Ahaz asked for help from the king of Assyria. The 20th verse says, *"And Tilgath-pilneser king of Assyria came unto him, and distressed him, but strengthened him not."* Ahaz would have to take treasures out of the Temple and other places to pay the Assyrians in order that they might lift the hand of oppression. Still, the Scripture says, *"He helped him not."*

The Psalmist said that we should trust the Lord because *"vain is the help of man"* (Psa. 108:12). Men never seem to learn. Ahaz would rather lean on the arm of a charlatan than on the arm of God.

The 22nd verse sadly says, *"And in the time of his distress did he trespass yet more against the Lord."* God's efforts to bring him to his spiritual senses by bringing judgment upon him had the opposite effect. Trouble in this case only hardened Ahaz and made him more wicked then before. The Holy Spirit would say, *"This is that king Ahaz."* There are three especially branded transgressors in the Word of God. They are:

1. Cain (Gen. 4:15).
2. Dathan (Num. 26:9).
3. Ahaz (vss. 22-25).

The 23rd verse records Ahaz concerning the gods of Syria saying, *"Therefore will I sacrifice to them, that they may help me."* When we read the account of Ahaz, his plight because of his rebellion seems to be so clear, and, yet, most of the world and even the Church seek help from that other than God. And as the Holy Spirit said of him, He says of all others as well, *"But they were the ruin of him, and of all Israel."*

The 24th verse says he *"shut up the doors of the house of the Lord."* Today, tragically, the Church is shutting the covers of the Bible, the only revealed body of truth in the world. Most preaching and teaching of that which professes to be the Word of God is, rather, psychology. It is subtle in its application, but oh, so deadly. Psychology places the emphasis on the person or the problem instead of Christ. There is no profit in the victim or the symptom. There is only profit in the Victor, who is Christ.

The 25th verse says, *"And provoked to anger the Lord God of his fathers."* Anything that departs from the Bible, be it the obvious evil of Ahaz or the subtle solution of psychology, angers the Lord of glory.

It is with great relief in the 27th verse that the Holy Spirit closes out the sordid history of Ahaz by saying, *"And Hezekiah his son reigned in his stead."*

—■—

CHAPTER 29

Concerning Hezekiah the Holy Spirit says in the 2nd verse, *"And he did that which was right in the sight of the Lord, according to all that David his father had done."* David was always used as the yardstick or the example. A self-righteous Church will have great difficulty in understanding this, especially concerning David's failures. Nevertheless, David's heart that was ever after God would see the great Grace of God that would cover every sin and every failure. David's greatness certainly was not in his failures; however, it definitely was in his heart that ever reached out toward the Lord.

Hezekiah was 25 years old when he began to reign, and the 3rd verse says, *"He in the first year of his reign, in the first month."* It was if though the Holy Spirit were urging Hezekiah on. He must reverse the terrible evil and wick-

NOTES

edness instituted by his father, Ahaz. So, he began immediately. The following is a list of some 25 things that Hezekiah did:

1. The first month of his reign he opened the doors of the Temple which had been shut by his father (28:24).

2. Brought in the Priests and Levites and charged them to sanctify themselves and the Temple (29:4-11).

3. Confessed and acknowledged the sins of his father for which judgment had come upon Judah (29:6-9).

4. Made a new covenant with God to turn away His wrath (29:10).

5. Charged the Priests and Levites to start and continue the worship of Jehovah in the Temple (29:11).

6. Gathered the rulers of Judah together and went up to the Temple to sacrifice (29:15).

7. Set the Levites in the Temple to play instruments and sing as David had commanded (29:25-30).

8. Encouraged and commanded sacrifices from the congregation, and there were so many that there were not enough Priests to do the work (29:31-36).

9. Invited people from the ten tribes to keep the Passover in Jerusalem (30:1-14).

10. Held a Passover such as had not been held for many years (30:15-17).

11. Interceded for the people to receive healing (30:18-20).

12. Used the Passover Feast as an occasion to teach the people (30:12-22).

13. Extended the feast seven more days (30:23-27).

14. Destroyed all idolatry (31:1).

15. Restored the 24 courses of the Priests (31:2).

16. Restored daily sacrifices (31:3).

17. Restored support of ministers by tithes from the people (31:4-10).

18. Restored storehouses for the abundance of tithes brought in (31:11-15).

19. Regulated tithe distribution to all males of the Levites (31:16-19).

20. Did the right and truthful things in all parts of the Law (31:20-21).

21. Prepared to defend Jerusalem (32:1-6).

22. Encouraged Judah to trust God (32:7-8).

23. Prayed in the time of danger (32:20).

24. Humbled himself in judgment (32:26).

25. Made many public improvements (32:27-30).

Verse 5 says regarding Hezekiah to the Levites, *"Sanctify now yourselves."* The word *"sanctify"* or *"sanctification"* simply means in this case to *"set apart for the exclusive use of God."* They were ordered as well to *"sanctify the house of the Lord God of your fathers."* By doing that, they would *"carry forth the filthiness out of the holy place."* That, as well, is what He demands that we do in our own lives. In other words, *"clean up."* Every Christian should heed these words. What are we doing that is not pleasing to the Lord? What about the places we go, the things we read, the company we keep? We must *"carry the filthiness out of the holy place,"* and in the spiritual, that means our lives – our hearts.

Verse 6 says, *"And turned their backs."* This aptly describes our conduct toward God. We cannot look Him in the face, consequently, we turn our backs and begin to walk in another direction. Only repentance, which means a *"turning around,"* can correct the situation.

The 7th verse tells us what happened:

1. *"Shut up the doors of the porch."* This would be the same today as the Bible no longer being preached from behind the pulpit. Something else has been substituted in its place. We have *"shut up the Word of God."*

2. *"Put out the lamps."* This spoke of the Golden Lampstand that sat in the Holy Place. Its light was a type of the *"light of the world,"* Who was the Lord Jesus Christ. Its oil is a type of the Holy Spirit. When the Bible is not preached and the Holy Spirit is not replenished, then the lamps go out. This characterizes too many lives.

3. *"And have not burned incense."* This speaks of the Altar of Incense, which is a type of intercession made for us by Christ. Coals of fire were to be taken from the Brazen Altar, placed on the Altar of Incense with the pure frankincense and the other ingredients poured on it. As the incense would hit the coals of fire, it would fill the Holy Place with fragrance. This was the intercession for the people; it was no longer being offered. Most modern-day churches have no connection with Calvary,

and, consequently, provide no intercession for the people. The *"Altar of Incense"* had to do with prayer and with worship. Any prayer and worship that's not *"in Spirit and in Truth"* is not recognized by God. Tragically, that would affect most churches.

4. Nor *"offered burnt offerings."* These were the five Levitical sacrifices that spoke of the one sacrifice of Christ at Calvary - which is the bedrock of all Christianity. As the sacrifices had been stopped, likewise, Calvary is little preached in most of our churches. There are basically four classes of churches in Christendom. They are as follows:

A. The modernist churches who do not believe the Bible, nor that Jesus is the Son of God, or that Calvary effected anything.

B. Churches that claim to believe in the atoning work of Calvary, but completely ignore it.

C. Churches that claim to preach Calvary, but, instead, preach psychology, or a prosperity gospel, or something else.

D. Churches that preach *"Jesus Christ and Him crucified"* as the foundation of all faith. These, sadly, are few and far between.

The 8th verse proclaims that as a result of Israel's backsliding, *"He hath delivered them to trouble, to astonishment, and to hissing, as you see with your eyes."* This was the result of Israel's backsliding; it is the result of the modern Church's backsliding.

When Hezekiah instituted these reforms and cried to God for revival, Judah was in a terrible state. Likewise, the present Church is in a terrible state. It may even be that the modern Church is in worse shape than the Judah of old. At least Judah knew the difference in right and wrong. The modern Church has little understanding anymore as to what is right or what is wrong. He says, *"Now it is in mine heart to make a covenant with the Lord God of Israel, that his fierce wrath may turn away from us."* Every move of God must begin in the *"heart."* It cannot begin in committees, denominations, political elections, or more rules and regulations. It had to begin with the *"heart."*

The 12th verse says, *"Then the Levites arose."* The names of these 14 Levites have no interest for the historians of this world, but such an interest for the Holy Spirit that they are here all set out, and they have been read already by hundreds of millions of people for nearly 2800 years. Thank God, *"the Levites"* heard the word of Hezekiah and proceeded to carry out that which would lead to a revival in Judah.

The 16th verse says, *"And the priests went into the inner part of the house of the Lord, to cleanse it."* This is where revival must begin, in the *"inner part,"* which means *"the heart."* Due to neglect and no worship of God, all activity had ceased. As well, much debris had been thrown all over the Holy Place and the Most Holy Place. The Scripture says they *"brought out all the uncleanness."* This constitutes true revival. Revival that only addresses itself to the outward is no revival at all. It must begin with the *"inner heart,"* which can only be done by the Holy Spirit.

The 18th verse says, *"We have cleansed."* This is always the first requirement of the Holy Spirit. Things must be cleaned up. This will be the first sign of revival.

The 22nd verse says they instituted the precious Blood of Calvary, *"Likewise, when they had killed the rams, they sprinkled the blood upon the altar."* This was the first time in years this had been done. Now, that which typed the great price that Christ would pay at Calvary was once again instituted. True revival will always lead the Church back to Calvary - every time to Calvary.

The 24th verse says, *"To make an atonement for all Israel."* The song says:

"What can take away my sins, nothing but the Blood of Jesus."

"What can make me whole again, nothing but the Blood of Jesus."

When Calvary was reinstituted, the 27th verse says, *"The song of the Lord began also with the trumpets, and with the instruments ordained by David king of Israel."* Now there is rejoicing. The first thing that leaves when the Spirit of God leaves, is the singing and the music. The first thing that comes back when the Spirit of God returns is the singing and the music (worship).

Then the 28th verse says, *"And all the congregation worshipped."* Under Hezekiah, we are seeing true Holy Ghost revival.

The 30th verse says, *"To sing praise unto the Lord with the words of David, and Asaph the seer."* In other words, they began to sing the Psalms, *"And they sang praises with gladness."*

The 36th verse says, *"For the thing was done suddenly."* When God begins to move, things are always done suddenly. Let's look at the order once again:

1. They cleaned up the House of the Lord (vs 16).

2. They reinstituted Calvary as the foundation of all their worship (vs.22).

3. They began to rejoice (vs 27).

4. True worship followed (vs. 28).

CHAPTER 30

Verse 1 says concerning Hezekiah's invitation to the whole of *"Israel and Judah"* regarding the Passover, *"That they should come to the house of the Lord at Jerusalem, to keep the passover unto the Lord God of Israel."* The Passover had not been kept for *"a long time"* (vs.5). The invitation would go out from Dan to Beersheba. The Passover is a type of Calvary, for the Lord had said to Moses, *"And when I see the blood, I will pass over you"* (Ex. 12:13). The only thing that stands between the fierce anger of God and the people is *"the Blood of Jesus Christ."* Self-righteousness tends to think that surely God looks at all of our good works; He doesn't. He looks only at the precious shed Blood of Jesus Christ. If the Church does not preach and proclaim the Blood, it preaches nothing that is of any value to its adherents. The Passover is a type of Calvary. All of God's dealing with Israel were hinged to *"the Passover."* The feast days, sacrifices, and rituals of all of Israel, has as its foundation, *"the Passover."* Likewise, everything in the Church must be tied to Calvary. Calvary must be the foundation. Our worship must spring from Calvary. Our prosperity must come from Calvary. Our preaching must be Calvary-centered. No wonder Paul would say, *"I determined to know nothing among you save Christ and him crucified."* How many churches have Calvary as their foundation? Precious few.

The 8th verse says, *"That the fierceness of his wrath may turn away from you."* The only thing that assuages the anger of God is Calvary. *"His wrath"* will either be turned toward the unrepentant Christian or Calvary. Sin must be paid for. If we accept the price that He paid at Calvary, then His wrath has already been expended toward His Son, the Lord Jesus Christ. If we do not accept the price that was paid at Calvary, then His wrath is turned toward us.

The 9th verse, in effect, says no matter what the sin, if we will believe in the precious shed Blood of Jesus Christ that *"The Lord your God is gracious and merciful, and will not turn away his face from you, if you return unto him."* However, let it be ever understood that the only prayer God will answer is the prayer that is anchored in the price of Calvary.

The 10th verse proclaims that Hezekiah sends messengers to every city, town, and village in both Israel and Judah, asking them to come to *"the Passover,"* *"But they* [Israel] *laughed them to scorn and mocked them."* Such is the attitude of much of the Church today. *"Laughter, scorn, and mockery"* meet that which anchors itself in Calvary. The watchword of the Church today is *"psychology."* The queen of the sciences in the major universities of the nation was once theology. Now, it is psychology. Because of this reproach, too many preachers have ceased to preach *"Jesus Christ and Him crucified."*

However, as the 11th verse says, *"Nevertheless divers of Asher and Manasseh and of Zebulun humbled themselves, and came to Jerusalem."* What a beautiful statement! Many will laugh and mock, but many, as well, will accept and receive.

The 12th verse proclaims that the moment the pure Gospel of Jesus Christ is preached, that despite the laughter and the mockery, still, *"The hand of God was to give them one heart to do the commandment."* God will honor His Word; some will believe!

Verses 18-20 proclaim that many *"Had not properly cleansed themselves"* regarding the Passover, but *"yet did they eat the passover otherwise than it was written"* As well, most who come to Calvary sadly do not properly

come, but still the Lord accepts all. It says, *"Hezekiah prayed for them, saying, The good Lord pardon every one."*

The 20th verse says, *"And the Lord hearkened to Hezekiah, and healed the people."* There is no *"healing"* other than Calvary. All other cisterns are broken and *"can hold no water"* (Jer. 2).

The 24th verse says, *"A thousand bullocks"* and *"seven thousand sheep,"* along with another *"thousand bullocks,"* and another *"ten thousand sheep."* The conduits carrying the blood from the Temple Mount would have caused the Brook Kidron that ran between the Temple Mount and Olivet, to run red with blood. This is obnoxious and repulsive to the unspiritual eye, but to those who know their God, Calvary is the greatest sight this side of heaven.

The 26th verse says, *"So there was great joy in Jerusalem."* Calvary alone brings *"great joy."* Nothing else will.

The 27th verse says, *"And their prayer came up to this holy dwelling place, even unto heaven."* Allow us to state it again, *"The only prayer that God will hear is that which is anchored in Calvary's Cross."*

CHAPTER 31

Verse 1 says, *"Until they had utterly destroyed them all."* After the Temple was cleansed, and the priests and the people had been sanctified and had held the 14 day Feast of the Passover and Unleavened Bread, the rest of the reformation program was set in order.

Leaving the joyous feast at Jerusalem, the people went out to the cities of Judah and broke the images in pieces, cut down the groves (the Asherahs - male reproductive organ fashioned out of a tree trunk, etc.), and utterly destroyed them all. Then the people returned to their own homes. Under the leading and guidance of the Holy Spirit the people determined to destroy idol-worship in Judah.

The modern Church little thinks in our cultured age that there is any danger from idol-worship. However, the Holy Spirit through

John said, *"Little children, keep yourselves from idols."* This was said because as idol-worship was the problem in Hezekiah's day and the problem in John's day, it is the problem today as well. Anything that is placed ahead of the Lord Jesus Christ, be it money, fame, education, hobbies, religious denominations, or anything else, becomes an idol. Consequently, for many Christians money is the idol, or even a particular religious denomination. They need to be destroyed until Jesus Christ is all in all.

Verse 2 says, *"And Hezekiah appointed the courses of the priests and the Levites after their courses."* This was thought of as so much foolishness by Ahaz, likewise, the carnal mind sees no profit in such, but the spiritual mind understands its value. If we ignore the Bible, we lose our love for God. If we love the Bible, we will love God. Hezekiah loved the Bible, so he would obey the Bible.

The 24 courses of the Priests and Levites in the Temple sacrifices and music were commanded to be continued again by Hezekiah. For some time these services had been discontinued. Now they were reinstated during the reign of good Hezekiah and discontinued again in the reign of his son.

The 5th verse says, *"And the tithe of all things brought they in abundantly."* Whenever the Church is on fire for God, money is given liberally to the work of God. Whenever the Church loses its way, there is very little giving. To have to beg for money to take the Gospel of Jesus Christ to a lost world is a foreign thing to an on-fire Church.

The 10th verse proclaims that as revival broke out across the land, the giving was so abundant that the Priests said, *"We have had enough to eat, and have left plenty."* This will always be the case when people believe God and begin to give from their increase. When this happens, it is as the Priests said, *"For the Lord hath blessed his people."*

The 11th verse proclaims that the Lord blessed so much that they had to *"prepare chambers in the house of the Lord"* to contain all the blessings.

The 21st verse says of Hezekiah, *"He did it with all his heart, and prospered."* Hallelujah!

CHAPTER 32

Verse 1 says, *"After these things, and the establishment thereof, Sennacherib king of Assyria came, and entered into Judah."* *"After these things"* means after the great revival under Hezekiah, the king of Assyria made war on Judah. He had already taken the ten tribes into captivity, and now his heart was lifted up to take Judah also. In this he overstepped himself, for he had been commissioned by the Lord to destroy the ten-tribe kingdom only. God defeated his purpose and delivered Hezekiah after testing his faith and permitting Judah to be tested.

Verse 3 says concerning Hezekiah's defense, *"To stop the waters of the fountains which were without the city."* Hezekiah stopped the fountain which is now known as the *"Virgin's Fount"* (the upper Gihon) on the east of Ophel. Through the conduit he made (II Kings 20:20), the water from this fount was brought down to the lower Gihon (Pool of Siloam). Now the upper Gihon was simply covered over and hidden from the enemy on the outside, making the water supply of Jerusalem safe by means of the two Gihons. Isaiah speaks of the waters of Shiloah that flow softly from their hidden fount beneath Ophel (Isa. 8:6). He also refers to these works of Hezekiah in Isaiah 22:8-11. In Psalms 46:4, this river that makes glad is contrasted with the raging waters of Assyria.

In the 7th verse concerning Sennacherib Hezekiah says, *"For there be more with us than be with him."* Great faith in a great God would come against a great enemy and win a great victory. As ever, faith is the ingredient.

The 8th verse says, *"With him is an arm of flesh: but with us is the Lord our God to help us, and to fight our battles."* Our problem is that too often we attempt to defeat the flesh with the flesh. It cannot be done. Our strength must be *"the Lord our God."*

The 9th verse says, *"After this did Sennacherib king of Assyria send his servants to Jerusalem."* According to II Kings 18:14-16, this was after Hezekiah had already lost all the defense cities of Judah outside of Jerusalem and had confessed his offense against the king of Assyria and given him money and gold and silver. The Assyrian king, not being satisfied with this, replied that he wanted to take all the people captive. Thinking he had Judah to the point of absolute surrender, he sent servants to Jerusalem to announce the terms.

Hezekiah was wrong to have submitted to Sennacherib. As well, Satan desires to take all that we have. There is no way we can come to terms with the evil one. He will not be satisfied with taking just a few cities in Judah; he wants Jerusalem as well to make all the people captive.

Faithfulness to the Word of God is sometimes rewarded with outward prosperity, but always meets with Satanic hostility. Christian people, therefore, should not think it a strange experience if, when seeking to fully follow the Lord, they are suddenly confronted with sharp trials. If, like Hezekiah, they lean only upon God for deliverance, they will find as he did that the angel of Jehovah is *"mighty to save."*

The 12th verse says concerning Sennacherib's emissaries, *"Hath not the same Hezekiah taken away his high places and his altars?"* They then say, *"Ye shall worship before one altar, and burn incense upon it."* Verse 12 illustrates that wherever there is obedience to the teaching of the Bible, it will be misinterpreted by people of the world. The written Word commanded there should be only one Altar in Israel; man approves of many.

In the 13th verse Sennacherib's emissaries ask, *"Know ye not what I and my fathers have done unto all the people of other lands?"* The Assyrian monuments give evidence of a custom which illustrates the haughty language here. It was their practice to bring the idols of the various nations to Assyria where they were assigned a place among the captive gods. This passage shows them boasting that their god was more powerful than all others, so it was vain to expect Jehovah to rescue the people, especially since He did not rescue their brethren in Samaria (II Kings 17).

The 16th verse says, *"And his servants spake yet more against the Lord God, and against his servant Hezekiah."* The Holy Spirit here shows us that the Lord is just as displeased with His servants being spoken against as *"Himself."*

This is no doubt one of the reasons Jehovah manifested His power over that of the Assyrians. He wanted to prove to them, as well as to men in all ages, that He was and still is the only true and living eternal God. Here, His power was challenged, and He was insulted by such talk and so was His king over Judah. It was, therefore, time for Him to show Himself strong in behalf of those who trusted in Him.

To do this, Jehovah sent only one of the innumerable angels on Israel's side, and he slew 185,000 men in one night. As expressed in verse 21, he cut off the mighty men of valour, the leaders, and captains of the army of Assyria (II Kings 19:35; Isa. 37:36-38).

The question then was: *"If the gods of Assyria could not prevail over one angel, how could they prevail over Jehovah and innumerable angels?"*

The 17th verse says, *"He wrote also letters to rail on the Lord God of Israel."*

When this was done, the 20th verse says, *"Hezekiah the king, and the prophet Isaiah the son of Amoz, prayed and cried to heaven."* Too many in the modern Church no longer cry to God, but, instead, they resort to psychology which has as its source the same as witchcraft - Satan.

In the Holy Spirit's beautiful and simple way, the 21st verse says, *"And the Lord sent an angel."* He would meet their insults with sarcasm; consequently, *"The king of Assyria returned with shame of face to his own land."* There his own sons *"slew him."*

The 22nd verse says, *"Thus the Lord saved Hezekiah and the inhabitants of Jerusalem."* And then it says, *"And guided them on every side."* What a beautiful statement! The Holy Spirit will lead and guide us into all truth.

As a result of this tremendous miracle, the 23rd verse says, *"He was magnified in the sight of all nations from thenceforth."* In other words, Judah became at least one of the most powerful nations on the face of the earth all because of Hezekiah's faith, and the blessings of God.

Before the great victory given to Hezekiah, the 24th verse says, *"In those days Hezekiah was sick to the death."* It seems this sickness came upon him because of pride, because the

25th verse says, *"But Hezekiah rendered not again according to the benefit done to him; for his heart was lifted up."* Someone has said that *"praise and prosperity are the greatest obstacles for a Christian to overcome."* Hezekiah did not overcome it, but, rather, succumbed to it.

However, the 26th verse says, *"Notwithstanding Hezekiah humbled himself for the pride of his heart."* Pride is the foundational sin of the human race. It is what caused the fall of Adam and Eve in the Garden of Eden (Gen. 3). It is the crowning sin of the Church as well. Thankfully, he would repent so that *"the wrath of the Lord came not upon them in the days of Hezekiah."*

The 31st verse says concerning Hezekiah's healing, *"Howbeit in the business of the ambassadors of the princes of Babylon, who sent unto him to inquire of the wonder that was done in the land."* The Fenton translation reads: *"In the affair of the Scientific Inquirers, who were sent from Babel, to inquire about the remarkable event which happened on earth."* This sign and remarkable event refers to the going back of the shadow on the sun dial, which was so remarkable that even the Chaldean astronomers came to inquire about the God Who could turn the sun backward. Furthermore, Greek historians informed Alexander the Great that it was one of the great wonders recorded in their scientific books. This shows that the happening was not merely the moving of a shadow, but the going backward of the earth in its rotation. The matter was known in various lands, and the Chaldeans came to inquire about it when they learned that it was caused by Israel's God.

Instead of Hezekiah showing *"these ambassadors"* the God of Israel, he, rather, showed them his riches and prosperity. For the Scripture says, *"God left him, to try him, that he might know all that was in his heart."* Man, even the most dedicated and consecrated Christian, will invariably turn aside if *"God leaves us"* even for a moment.

Had he kept close to Jehovah, he would have spoken to the ambassadors of His unsearchable riches, and not of his own poor treasures of silver and gold.

The 33rd verse says, *"And they buried him in the chiefest of the sepulchres of the sons of David."* This was not said of any man before or after this. It must have meant that he was buried next to David's tomb. Despite Hezekiah's failures, he was one of the godliest kings who ever reigned over Judah.

NOTES

CHAPTER 33

Verse 1 says concerning Manasseh, *"And he reigned fifty and five years in Jerusalem."* Manasseh, one of the most wicked of all the 42 kings of Israel (Israel and Judah), reigned longer than any other - 55 years. It can be explained only by the mercy of God. Manasseh did not repent and serve God faithfully until after his captivity to Babylon. How many years he was wicked is not known. There is this difference between him and Saul, Solomon, Uzziah, and others - he began his reign as a wicked king but ended it as a good one; they began as good kings and ended their rule as bad ones.

To the natural mind it would seem strange that Hezekiah, who was a blessing to his people, only reigned 29 years, but Manasseh, who was a malediction to his people, reigned 55 years. And, yet, the reasons are obvious. Why the Lord took Hezekiah when he was only 54 years old, we can only surmise. Quite possibly, the Lord looked down and saw that Hezekiah would lose his way if allowed to live longer. Manasseh lived until he was 67 years old. It is obvious that the Lord let him live so long because, looking into the future, He saw that Manasseh would humble himself and repent, thereby coming back to God. Everything that God does is an act of mercy. Even His judgment is redemptive, if only the individual or the nation will allow it to be so.

Manasseh started out so evil, being the most evil of all the kings of Judah. The 2nd verse says, *"But did that which was evil in the sight of the Lord, like unto the abominations of the heathen."*

The Holy Spirit then says, *"Whom the Lord had cast out before the children of Israel."* This was said for a purpose. Not too many years from then Judah would be cast out as well.

Verses 3-10 record his terrible acts. They are as follows:

1. *"For he built again the high places which Hezekiah his father had broken down, and he reared up altars for Baalim, and made groves, and worshipped all the host of heaven, and served them"* (vs. 3). Consequently, Judah became a nation of idol worshipers. They worshiped *"Baal"* and the *"groves,"* which consisted of the male reproductive organ that was fashioned out of a tree trunk, and the stars of the heavens.

2. *"And he built altars in the house of the Lord."* He took away all the holy utensils, and even the Ark of the Covenant, and set up altars to Baal (vs. 4).

3. *"And he built altars for all the host of heaven in the two courts of the house of the Lord"* (vs. 5). This means that he worshiped the sun, moon, stars, and planets of the heavens. These *"altars"* took the place of the great Brazen Altar built by Solomon and the great Brazen Laver.

4. *"And he caused his children to pass through the fire in the valley of the son of Hinnom."* This pertains to the awful horror of the worship of the god *"Moloch."* This thing was made somewhat like a modern Buddha which sat on the ground with its arms outstretched. A fire would be built in its bulbous belly. Eventually, the entirety of this metal monster would grow red-hot. Before the fire was built, little children would be tied to the arms. And then gradually as the metal arms grew red-hot, the priests would beat their drums to drown out the screams of the dying children.

5. *"Also he observed times, and used enchantments, and used witchcraft, and dealt with a familiar spirit, and with wizards"* (vs.6). Under the wicked reign of Manasseh, the entire nation of Judah was led by demon spirits. Regrettably, much of the world today is led by demon spirits.

6. *"And he set a carved image, the idol which he had made, in the house of God."* This was probably the *"Asherah,"* which, as stated, was made out of a tree trunk. The height varied anywhere from 3 feet to 20 feet tall. Most probably this terrible idol was set up in the Holy of Holies in the place of the *"Ark of the*

NOTES

Covenant."

The 9th verse says that Manasseh *"did worse than the heathen, whom the Lord had destroyed before the children of Israel."*

And still the 10th verse proclaims the mercy and the Grace of God, for it says, *"And the Lord spake unto Manasseh, and to his people: but they would not hearken."*

The 11th verse says, *"Wherefore the Lord brought upon them the captains of the host of the king of Assyria, which took Manasseh among the thorns, and bound him with fetters, and carried him to Babylon."* This was an act of mercy with God as He attempted to bring Manasseh to his senses. It accomplished its purpose.

For the 12th verse says, *"And when he was in affliction, he besought the Lord his God, and humbled himself greatly before the God of his fathers."* This is why the Lord allowed Manasseh to rule as long as he did. As well, this was why the Lord allowed him to be taken captive to Babylon. It had the desired effect upon Manasseh. Time and time again the Lord chastises His children by attempting to bring them to a place of repentance.

Despite all of his sin and iniquity, the Holy Spirit says that Manasseh *"prayed unto Him"* (the Lord, vs. 13). The Bible says the Lord *"heard his supplication, and brought him again to Jerusalem into his kingdom."* There could be no more beautiful illustration of the mercy and the Grace of God than that which was extended to Manasseh. If the Lord would do that to this king who wrought more evil in Judah than any other king before him, He will do it for anyone else. There are only two requirements:

1. To humble oneself.
2. To pray unto God.

Then the 13th verse further says, *"Then Manasseh knew that the Lord he was God."*

The following verse now states the things that Manasseh tried to do to correct the wickedness and the evil he had brought into Judah. The 14th verse says, *"Now after this he built a wall."* This simply means he repaired the wall and *"raised it up to a very great height."* This was the wall that enclosed Jerusalem.

The 15th verse says, *"And he took away the strange gods, and the idol out of the house of* the Lord, and all the altars that he had built in the mount of the house of the Lord, and in Jerusalem, and cast them out of the city." This within itself would show that his repentance was true.

The 16th verse says, "And he repaired the altar of the Lord, and sacrificed thereon peace offerings and thank offerings." Once again the sacrifices are re-instituted at the Temple in Jerusalem.

Now, Manasseh will die after ruling some 55 years. And the 21st verse says that "Amon," his son, will reign in his place. The 22nd verse says, "But he did that which was evil in the sight of the Lord."

The 23rd verse says, "And humbled not himself before the Lord as Manasseh his father." That which God demanded, he would not do. But the Scripture says, "Amon trespassed more and more."

The 24th verse records his end. It says, "And his servants conspired against him, and slew him in his own house." Despite the example of his father, he still would not humble himself before God. True and sad is the story of much of the human race. So few will humble themselves and repent as Manasseh did.

CHAPTER 34

The 1st verse says, "Josiah was eight years old when he began to reign." His father Amon was ungodly. Josiah will be one of the most godly - and, yet, Judah's sun is beginning to set.

The Holy Spirit says of Josiah concerning his consecration, "And he walked in the ways of David his father, and declined neither to the right hand, nor to the left." What a beautiful statement!

Verse 3 tells of his conversion. It says, "For in the eighth year of his reign, while he was yet young, he began to seek after the God of David his father." This means that Josiah was 16 years old when he gave his heart to God. When he was 20 years old, he began "to purge Judah and Jerusalem from the high places, and the groves, and the carved images, and the molten images." During the four years from Josiah's

conversion to the time that he began to "purge Judah and Jerusalem," the Holy Spirit, no doubt, dealt with him greatly and inspired him to carry forth this great work.

The 5th verse says, "And he burnt the bones of the priests upon their altars." This, of course, was speaking of the ungodly priests who had burned incense on the altar at Bethel. Some 348 years before, the prophet who was called "a man of God," that came out of Judah to Bethel, "cried against the altar." He prophesied at that time that a "child shall be born unto the house of David, Josiah by name." In other words, he called Josiah's name 320 years before Josiah was born (I Kings 13:2).

The 8th verse says, "Now in the eighteenth year of his reign." This was five or six years after Jeremiah began to prophesy (Jer. 2:2). The great prophet was therefore present at the time of these reformations and the great Passover Feast of these chapters. Josiah was now 26 years old, and the Scripture says he sent men to "repair the house of the Lord his God."

The 12th verse says, "All that could skill of instruments of music." It seems from this that the Levites played instruments and sang praises unto the Lord while the work on the Temple was being done. Actually, they had the general oversight of all the work and were the scribes, officers, porters, gatekeepers, and treasurers of the Temple.

And then something happened that was to be the greatest thing yet under Josiah. The 14th verse says, "The priests found a book of the law of the Lord given to Moses." This was, no doubt, the original book of the Pentateuch - the one actually written by Moses (II Kings 22:8). It could have been hidden during the reign of Manasseh or Amon, or even some other wicked king before them. When the book was taken to the king and read before him, he rent his clothes as a sign of utter despair. It must not be supposed that there was no other copy of the Law of Moses up to this time, for many copies are frequently referred to in the historical books of Israel before this, but it is important, in view of present-day criticism, to note that this book found among the many records in the Temple was the one written by Moses. The Hebrew should have been translated literally here thus: "The actual engraving of the law of *the Ever-living in the hand of Moses."*

The 18th verse says concerning the Law of God, *"And Shaphan read it before the king."*

The 19th verse says, *"And it came to pass, when the king had heard the words of the law, that he rent his clothes."* Learning from it how defective the reformation was, he proceeded to a thorough one. A cleansing of the heart and life under the searchlight of the Word of God differs vastly from a reformation initiated by the feeble light of conscience or by tradition. But loyalty to conscience led by the Lord leads to the discovery of the Word of God.

The Bible will always point people to the Lord, for the 21st verse says of Josiah, *"Go, inquire of the Lord for me."* The *"words of the book"* convicted Josiah.

The 22nd verse says that they went to *"Huldah the prophetess."* The king commanded his servant to inquire of the Lord concerning all the curses pronounced in the Law of Moses. He recognized that Israel had been breaking the Law and that God had already sent wrath upon them for their sins. The record about curses in Leviticus 26 and Deuteronomy 27-28 was sufficiently clear to convict of sin.

The word *"college"* found in the 22nd verse is probably a poor translation. It means the *"second rank of buildings joining the palace."*

The 23rd verse says, *"And she answered them, thus saith the Lord God of Israel."*

The Holy Spirit alludes to the Law that has been broken, but then says in the 27th verse concerning Josiah, *"Because thine heart was tender, and thou didst humble thyself before God, when thou heardest his words against this place."*

It seems from the pronouncement by the Holy Spirit against Judah, that Josiah's reform merely delayed the coming judgment. It did not halt it. He tells Josiah, *"Neither shall thine eye see all the evil that I will bring upon this place"* (vs. 28).

Josiah shared the Word of God with all *"the elders of Judah and Jerusalem"* (vs. 29).

The 31st verse proclaims him, *"making a covenant before the Lord, to walk after the Lord, and to keep his commandments."*

The 32nd verse says he not only did this, but *"caused all that were present in Jerusalem*

and Benjamin to stand to it."

Concerning this Great Reformation based on the Word of God, the 33rd verse says, *"And all his days they departed not from following the Lord, the God of their fathers."*

Every true revival is based on the Word of God. The Bible is the only revealed Truth on the face of the earth. It is *"the Word of God."*

When one considers all the religious books such as the *"Koran"* and the *"Book of Mormon,"* plus the various other religious works that have come and gone down through the centuries and compares them with the Bible, then the utter falsity of these other books pale them into insignificance.

As well, when one realizes that the Word of God is the only body of revealed Truth on the face of the earth, then we should devote our time, our attention, and even our very lives to understanding its contents. It is the only *"light"* in the world.

Joshua was the first of the great men of God in the Bible who actually had a portion of the written Word of God (the Pentateuch written by Moses). He was told, *"This book of the law shall not depart out of thy mouth; but thou shalt meditate therein day and night, that thou mayest observe to do according to all that is written therein: For then thou shalt make thy way prosperous, and then thou shalt have good success"* (Josh. 1:8).

There is not a spiritual problem that is not addressed in the Word of God. There is not a difficulty for which it does not have a solution. There is not a question that it cannot answer; there is not a life that the God of its pages cannot change; there is not a broken heart that its Words cannot mend; there is not a darkness that its light cannot dispel; not a sin that the Blood of its pages cannot wash away.

Truly, *"Thy word is a lamp unto my feet, and a light unto my path"* (Psa. 119:105).

CHAPTER 35

Verse 1 says, *"Moreover Josiah kept a passover unto the Lord in Jerusalem."* Three verses in Kings are given to Josiah's Passover - here

19 verses are given.

As we have previously stated, the *"Passover"* was the foundation of all Israel's worship and God's dealings with His people. It represents Israel's deliverance out of Egypt by the slain lamb and the shedding of innocent blood. Likewise, the entirety of the foundation of Christendom is founded on Calvary of which the Passover is a type, *"When I see the blood, I will pass over you"* (Ex. 12:13).

Verse 3 makes it clear that the *"Ark of the Covenant"* had been taken out of the Holy of Holies, for the Scripture says, *"Put the holy ark in the house which Solomon the son of David king of Israel did build."* Quite possibly, Josiah's wicked father Amon had it removed.

The question should be asked as to why God did not strike dead the wicked individuals who would have with impunity gone into the Holy of Holies and removed the Ark as He did Uzza when he *"put forth his hand to hold the ark."* (I Chron. 13:9-10). Even though the Scripture is silent on the subject, quite possibly the Lord did strike them dead, but at a different time and in a different way. God seldom works the same way twice. However, the following should be noted:

The Jews in Jesus' day handled Him roughly, Him of whom the Ark was a type. They were not immediately stricken by God, but about A.D. 70 when Titus, the Roman general, invaded Jerusalem, some 1,100,000 died. Let no man think that if God does not move instantly as He did in the case of Uzza that He will not move at all. Someone has said:

"The mills of God grind slowly, but they grind exceedingly fine." - In other words, they miss nothing.

The 12th verse says, *"To offer unto the Lord, as it is written in the book of Moses."* Thus, with joy the Holy Spirit describes how closely Josiah kept to the written Word of God in the observance of this Passover. Josiah was referring to the Pentateuch which consists of Genesis, Exodus, Leviticus, Numbers, and Deuteronomy.

Verse 6 records that Josiah believed that Moses wrote the Pentateuch, and verse 12 shows his acquaintanceship with the book of Exodus - especially chapter 12.

The 15th verse proclaims that as the sacri-

fices were offered, this was ever accompanied by music, singing, and worship, for the Scripture says, *"And the singers the sons of Asaph were in their place according to the commandment of David."* When Calvary is held up as the foundation of the faith, it always elicits joy.

As well, the Scripture says, *"The porters waited at every gate; they might not depart from their service."* These were the gatekeepers who made certain that the Law of the Lord was adhered to regarding the sacrifices. The process and the manner in which all were done as well shows Josiah's adherence to the Word of God.

The 18th verse says, *"And there was no passover like to that kept in Israel from the days of Samuel the prophet."* This was also said of Hezekiah's observance of the Passover. The statement was true in both cases, for Hezekiah kept a Passover such as had never been kept up to his day (30:26), and here Josiah kept one that was greater than Hezekiah's.

The 19th verse says, *"In the eighteenth year of the reign of Josiah was this passover kept."* This was five or six years after Jeremiah began his ministry. There is a possibility that Jeremiah was Josiah's father-in-law.

The 20th verse says, *"After all this, when Josiah had prepared the temple, Necho king of Egypt came up to fight against Char-che-mish by Euphrates."* The Scripture then says, *"And Josiah went out against him."*

This heathen monarch, according to the 21st verse, sent *"ambassadors to him."* He attempted to dissuade Josiah from opposing, even saying, *"For God commanded me to make haste."* Necho then made the statement, *"Forbear thee from meddling with God, who is with me, that he destroy thee not."* This is quite a statement coming from a heathen, but, yet, the Holy Spirit would ultimately say that he was right.

Pharaoh-Necho was founder of the 25th Dynasty during the reign of Manasseh, King of Judah. He came up against Car-che-mish, the fortress of Chemosh on the River Euphrates, and Josiah went out to meet him in war.

The 22nd verse says, *"Nevertheless Josiah would not turn his face from him, but disguised himself, that he might fight with him."* The Holy Spirit says that the *"words of Necho were from the mouth of God."*

Some 13 years after Josiah had restored the Temple worship, he foolishly lost his life at Megiddo, the scene of Barak's triumph. Those who, like Josiah, are famed for loyalty to the Bible, need prayerfully to cultivate the habit of daily believing dependence upon God - the life of faith - for so deceptive is the heart that it will pride itself upon subjection to the Scriptures, and, because of that pride, refuse to accept a message from God because a heathen is the messenger.

The *"flesh"* in Josiah was hated by God just as much as the *"flesh"* in Ahab. Both thought to disguise themselves to make void the Word of God. Likewise, the *"flesh"* in the Apostle Paul when he was coming down from the third heaven was exactly the same as when he was going up to Damascus to torture and murder the disciples of the Lord Jesus Christ, hence, the necessity for the *"thorn."* All pride is sin. Religious pride is the worst sin of all.

The 23rd verse says concerning the king, *"And the archers shot at king Josiah."* The 24th verse says, *"And he died."* No, he did not lose his soul, but he did lose his life.

The 25th verse says, *"And Jeremiah lamented for Josiah."* This does not refer to the book of Lamentations in our Bible, but to other records of Lamentations concerning Josiah about 35 years before this subject of the book of Lamentations written by Jeremiah.

In the 26th verse the Holy Spirit refers to the *"acts of Josiah"* by saying, *"His goodness, according to that which was written in the law of the Lord."* This means that his goodness was in harmony with obedience to the Law of the Lord as written in the Law of Moses. The acts of Josiah were written in the Law of the Lord.

CHAPTER 36

Chronicles is the last book in the Hebrew Bible; therefore, this is the last chapter. This fact adds solemnly to the words in verse 16 that, *"There was no remedy."*

The 1st verse says, *"Then the people of the land took Jehoahaz the son of Josiah, and made*

him king." This man reigned only three months, and this was the shortest of any reign in Judah, though not as short as that of two kings in the ten-tribe kingdom of Israel. Zimri reigned only seven days (I Kings 16:16) and Shallum only one month (II Kings 15:13). Jehoahaz was a wicked king or he would not have been destroyed. In II Kings 23:32 we read that he did that which was evil in the sight of God.

Now that Josiah had opposed him and had been killed in the process, the 3rd verse says, *"The king of Egypt put him down at Jerusalem, and condemned the land in an hundred talents of silver and a talent of gold."* Now Judah will become a vassal state of Egypt.

Necho, the king of Egypt, would in turn make Jehoiakim king over Judah. The 5th verse says, *"He did that which was evil in the sight of the Lord his God."* The words, *"his God,"* mean that God fervently dealt with him to bring him to the true way. Nevertheless, despite the heavy dealings by the Holy Spirit, Jehoiakim continued to *"do evil."* The words, *"in the sight of the Lord . . ."* mean *"in his face."*

Egypt began to wane in power upon the advent and rise of mighty Babylon, for the 6th verse says, *"Against him* (Jehoiakim) *came up Neb-u-chad-nez-zar king of Babylon, and bound him in fetters, to carry him to Babylon."*

The 7th verse also says that *"Neb-u-chad-nez-zar also carried of the vessels of the house of the Lord to Babylon, and put them in his temple at Babylon."* These holy vessels could have consisted of the *"Table of Shewbread,"* and the *"Golden Lampstand,"* and the *"Altar of Worship,"* and even possibly the *"Brazen Altar,"* and the *"Brazen Laver."* These articles were put in the Temple of the god Bel (a derivative of Baal). The various heathenistic gods of countries defeated by Babylon were placed in the temple of Bel as a sign of the superiority of Bel. There were no idol gods at the Temple in Jerusalem when Nebuchadnezzar sacked the House of God. So he took *"the vessels."* With all the major *"vessels"* taken, no doubt, the smaller vessels such as cups, were taken also. Years later, Belshazzar would *"drink wine"* in these holy vessels. The handwriting on the wall would pronounce his death hours later.

There were actually three deportations to Babylon. They are as follows:

1. The one under Jehoiakim. During this deportation, Daniel and the three Hebrew children were taken to Babylon, with an indefinite number of others (II Kings 24:14; Dan. 1:1-3).

2. The one under Jehoiachin. In this, Mordecai and Esther, as well as Ezekiel, were taken to Babylon (II Kings 24:10-16).

3. The one under Zedekiah. With this last deportation, Jerusalem, as well as the Temple, was completely destroyed, and the 70 years of predicted Babylonian captivity began (Jer. 25:9-12; Dan. 9:2).

(Concerning the holy vessels mentioned in verse 7, there is no record of the *"Ark of the Covenant"* being taken. Tradition says that Jeremiah hid it in a cave.)

The 9th verse says, *"Jehoiachin was eight year old when he began to reign."* The *"eight"* should be *"eighteen,"* as in II Kings 24:8, the error was made, no doubt, by a copyist. Such a mistake was easy to make in transcribing numeral letters of the Hebrew text. Jehoiachin had to be more than eight years old, for three months later when taken to Babylon he had several wives (II Kings 24:15). He had seed also (Jer. 22:28), and this would require him to be more than eight years of age. The Scripture says, *"He did that which was evil in the sight of the Lord."*

The 10th verse says, *"And brought him to Babylon, with the godly vessels of the house of the Lord."* Quite possibly, there were more *"vessels"* that still remained at the Temple which had not been taken in the first deportation, or maybe new ones had been made to take the place of the original ones taken.

Concerning the next king, *"Zedekiah,"* the Holy Spirit says, *"And he did that which was evil in the sight of the Lord his God."* It further says, *"And humbled not himself before Jeremiah the prophet speaking from the mouth of the Lord"* (vs. 12). It also says, *"And hardened his heart from turning unto the Lord God of Israel"* (vs. 13). Zedekiah is mentioned 48 times in the book of Jeremiah. He had ample opportunity to turn to God and to obey Him, but he *"hardened his heart."* It is terrible to sin in any case, but it is more terrible than all to sin against light.

NOTES

Verses 15 and 16 once again record by the Holy Spirit the effort of the Lord to turn Judah around. The Scripture says, *"And the Lord God of their father sent to them by his messengers."* There was no excuse that they did not know; they had been repeatedly told, but the 16th verse says, *"But they mocked the messengers of God, and despised his words, and misused his prophets, until the wrath of the Lord arose against his people, till there was no remedy."* It is one thing for man to say, *"till there was no remedy";* it is another thing quite entirely for the Lord to say, *"till there was no remedy."*

The 15th verse says, *"Because he had compassion on his people."* The 17th verse says, *"And he had no compassion."* His compassion can be exhausted.

The 19th verse says concerning the one building on the face of the earth that was inhabited by God, *"And they (the Babylonians) burnt the house of God."* In effect, God was saying that Judah was no longer His people. Now they belonged to the Babylonian king, for the 17th verse says, *"He gave them all into his hand."* No longer do they belong to God, but they belong to Babylon. In the Garden of Eden, Adam and Eve made a choice and, in effect, said, *"We no longer belong to God but to Satan."* Consequently, rivers of blood have run through the human family from that day until this. It will not be corrected until Jesus Christ comes back (Rev. 19).

The 21st verse gives an interesting aside, *"Until the land had enjoyed her sabbaths: for as long as she lay desolate she kept sabbath, to fulfill threescore and ten years."* The Law of Moses had demanded that every seventh year that the entirety of the land (Israel) should rest. It was called *"a sabbath of rest unto the land."* On the seventh year He said, *"Thou shalt neither sow thy field, nor prune thy vineyard"* (Lev. 25:3-4). For some 490 years, Israel had ignored this Law of God. Consequently, Israel *"owed"* the Lord 70 years of sabbaths. Her deportation to Babylon would be for 70 years, thereby guaranteeing that the land would lay fallow and would *"enjoy her sabbaths."* God says what He means and means what He says.

The 22nd verse speaks concerning the conclusion of that 70-year period, *"The Lord stirred up the spirit of Cyrus king of Persia."* He made a proclamation throughout all his kingdom, putting it in writing, saying that the God of heaven had charged him to build Him a house in Jerusalem, which was in Judah. He also gave freedom to all of Israel, so that any who chose to do so could return to the homeland (King Cyrus was Esther's son).

He says in the 23rd verse, *"And He* (God) *hath charged me to build Him an house in Jerusalem."* This concerned the rebuilding of the Temple under Ezra.

As previously stated, the book of II Chronicles is the last one in the Hebrew Bible. The last words are very impressive, *"The Lord his God be with him, and let him go up."*

Hallelujah!

NOTES